EQ

EQ

Encyclopaedia of the Qurʾān

VOLUME FIVE

Si–Z

Jane Dammen McAuliffe, *General Editor*

Brill, Leiden–Boston

2006

Koninklijke Brill NV incorporates the imprints Brill Academic Publishers, Martinus Nijhoff Publishers and VSP.

ISBN 90 04 12356 3

Printed in The Netherlands on acid-free paper.

ABBREVIATIONS

AI = *Annales islamologiques*
AIUON = *Annali dell' Istituto Universitario Orientale di Napoli*
AO = *Acta orientalia*
AO-H = *Acta orientalia (Academiae Scientiarum Hungaricae)*
Arabica = *Arabica. Revue d'études arabes*
ARW = *Archiv für Religionswissenschaft*
AUU = *Acta Universitatis Upsaliensis*
BASOR = *Bulletin of the American Schools of Oriental Research*
BEO = *Bulletin d'études orientales de l'Institut Français de Damas*
BGA = *Bibliotheca geographorum arabicorum*
BIFAO = *Bulletin de l'Institut Français d'Archéologie Orientale du Caire*
BO = *Bibliotheca orientalis*
BSA = *Budapest studies in Arabic*
BSOAS = *Bulletin of the School of Oriental and African Studies*
Der Islam = *Der Islam. Zeitschrift für Geschichte und Kultur des islamischen Orients*
EI[1] = *Encyclopaedia of Islam*, 1st ed., Leiden 1913-38
EI[2] = *Encyclopaedia of Islam*, new ed., Leiden 1954-2002
ER = *Encyclopedia of religion*, ed. M. Eliade, New York 1986
ERE = *Encyclopaedia of religion and ethics*
GMS = *Gibb memorial series*
HO = *Handbuch der Orientalistik*
IA = *Islâm ansiklopedisi*
IBLA = *Revue de l'Institut des Belles Lettres Arabes, Tunis*
IC = *Islamic culture*
IJMES = *International journal of Middle East studies*
IOS = *Israel oriental studies*
IQ = *The Islamic quarterly*
Iran = *Iran. Journal of the British Institute of Persian Studies*
JA = *Journal asiatique*
JAL = *Journal of Arabic literature*
JAOS = *Journal of the American Oriental Society*
JE = *Jewish encyclopaedia*
JESHO = *Journal of the economic and social history of the Orient*
JIS = *Journal of Islamic studies*
JNES = *Journal of Near Eastern studies*
JRAS = *Journal of the Royal Asiatic Society*
JSAI = *Jerusalem studies in Arabic and Islam*
JSS = *Journal of Semitic studies*
MFOB = *Mélanges de la Faculté Orientale de l'Université St. Joseph de Beyrouth*
MIDEO = *Mélanges de l'Institut Dominicain d'études orientales du Caire*
MO = *Le monde oriental*
MSOS = *Mitteilungen des Seminars für orientalische Sprachen, westasiatische Studien*
Muséon = *Le Muséon. Revue des études orientales*
MW = *The Muslim world*
OC = *Oriens christianus*

OLZ = *Orientalistische Literaturzeitung*
Orientalia = *Orientalia. Commentarii periodici Pontificii Instituti Biblici*
Qanṭara = *al-Qanṭara. Revista de estudios arabes*
QSA = *Quaderni de studi arabi*
RCEA = *Répertoire chronologique d'épigraphie arabe*
REI = *Revue des études islamiques*
REJ = *Revue des études juives*
REMMM = *Revue du monde musulman et de la Méditerranée*
RHR = *Revue de l'histoire des religions*
RIMA = *Revue de l'Institut des Manuscrits Arabes*
RMM = *Revue du monde musulman*
RO = *Rocznik Orientalistyczny*
ROC = *Revue de l'orient chrétien*
RSO = *Rivista degli studi orientali*
SIr = *Studia iranica*
SI = *Studia islamica*
WI = *Die Welt des Islams*
WKAS = *Wörterbuch der klassischen arabischen Sprache*
WO = *Welt des Orients*
WZKM = *Wiener Zeitschrift für die Kunde des Morgenlandes*
ZAL = *Zeitschrift für arabische Linguistik*
ZDMG = *Zeitschrift der Deutschen Morgenländischen Gesellschaft*
ZGAIW = *Zeitschrift für Geschichte der arabisch-islamischen Wissenschaften*
ZS = *Zeitschrift für Semitistik*

AUTHORS OF ARTICLES

VOLUME V

Binyamin Abrahamov, Bar-Ilan University
Camilla P. Adang, Tel-Aviv University
Scott C. Alexander, Catholic Theological Union, Chicago
Mohammed Arkoun, Sorbonne University
Ali S.A. Asani, Harvard University
Margot Badran, Northwestern University
Daniel Beaumont, University of Rochester
James A. Bellamy, University of Michigan
Sheila Blair, Boston College
Hartmut Bobzin, University of Erlangen
Michael Bonner, University of Michigan
Gerhard Böwering, Yale University
Paolo Luigi Branca, Catholic University, Milan
William M. Brinner, University of California, Berkeley
Jonathan E. Brockopp, Pennsylvania State University
David B. Burrell, University of Notre Dame
Amila Buturovic, York University, Canada
Jacqueline Chabbi, University of Paris
Masudul Alam Choudhury, Sultan Qaboos University, Oman
Frederick S. Colby, Miami University, Oxford, OH
Michael A. Cook, Princeton University
Patricia Crone, Institute for Advanced Study, Princeton
Stefania Cunial, Ca' Foscari University, Venice
Stephan Dähne, Orient-Institut der Deutschen Morgenländischen Gesellschaft, Beirut
Maria Massi Dakake, George Mason University
Natana J. De Long-Bas, Boston College
Pieternella van Doorn-Harder, Valparaiso University
Dale F. Eickelman, Dartmouth College
Herbert Eisenstein, University of Vienna
Salwa M.S. El-Awa, University of Birmingham
Jamal Elias, Amherst College
Amira El-Zein, Tufts University
R. Michael Feener, The University of California, Riverside
Reuven Firestone, Hebrew Union College, Los Angeles
Ersilia Francesca, Università degli Studi di Napoli "L'Orientale"
Yohanan Friedmann, Hebrew University, Jerusalem
Dmitry V. Frolov, Moscow University
Avner Giladi, University of Haifa

Claude Gilliot, University of Aix-en-Provence
Joseph Ginat, University of Oklahoma
Valerie Gonzalez, Dartmouth College
Matthew S. Gordon, Miami University, Oxford, OH
Sebastian Günther, University of Toronto
Rosalind W. Gwynne, University of Tennessee
Shahla Haeri, Boston University
Gerald R. Hawting, University of London
Paul L. Heck, Georgetown University
Margaretha T. Heemskerk, Radboud University, Nijmegen
Marcia Hermansen, Loyola University, Chicago
Thomas Emil Homerin, University of Rochester
Robert Kevin Jaques, Indiana University
Anthony Hearle Johns, Australian National University
David Johnston, Yale University
Gautier H.A. Juynboll, Leiden, The Netherlands
Ahmet T. Karamustafa, Washington University, St. Louis
Bustami Mohamed Khir, University of Birmingham
Alexander D. Knysh, University of Michigan
Kathryn Kueny, Fordham University
Scott Kugle, University of Leiden
Paul Kunitzsch, University of Munich
Ella Landau-Tasseron, Hebrew University, Jerusalem
Joseph Lowry, University of Pennsylvania
David Marshall, Lambeth Palace, London
Ingrid Mattson, Hartford Seminary
Mustansir Mir, Youngstown State University
Robert G. Morrison, Whitman College
Harald Motzki, Radboud University, Nijmegen
Tilman Nagel, University of Göttingen
John A. Nawas, Catholic University Leuven
Angelika Neuwirth, Free University, Berlin
Ute Pietruschka, Philipps University, Marburg
Matthias Radscheit, Bonn, Germany
Bernd R. Radtke, University of Utrecht
Wim Raven, University of Frankfurt
Bassel A. Reyahi, Toronto, Canada
Gabriel Said Reynolds, University of Notre Dame
Andrew Rippin, University of Victoria
Christian Julien Robin, Centre National de la Recherche Scientifique, Aix-en-Provence
Chase F. Robinson, University of Oxford
Ruth Roded, Hebrew University, Jerusalem
Uri Rubin, Tel-Aviv University
Michael Schub, Trinity College, Hartford, CN
Michael A. Sells, Haverford College
Irfan Shahid, Georgetown University
Mona Siddiqui, Glasgow University
Kemal Silay, Indiana University
Priscilla P. Soucek, New York University
Devin J. Stewart, Emory University
Barbara Stowasser, Georgetown University
David Thomas, University of Birmingham
Heidi Toelle, Sorbonne University
Shawkat M. Toorawa, Cornell University
Roberto Tottoli, Università degli Studi di Napoli "L'Orientale"
Kees Wagtendonk, University of Amsterdam (emeritus)
David Waines, Lancaster University
Lutz Wiederhold, University Halle-Wittenberg
Muhammad Qasim Zaman, Brown University

SHORT TITLES

Abbott, *Studies II*
N. Abbott, *Studies in Arabic literary papyri. II. Qur'ānic commentary and tradition,* Chicago 1967

ʿAbd al-Bāqī
Muḥammad Fu'ād ʿAbd al-Bāqī, *al-Muʿjam al-mufahras li-alfāẓ al-Qur'ān al-karīm,* Cairo 1945

ʿAbd al-Jabbār, *Mutashābih*
ʿAbd al-Jabbār b. Aḥmad al-Asadābādī al-Qāḍī al-Hamadhānī, *Mutashābih al-Qur'ān,* ed. ʿAdnān M. Zarzūr, 2 vols., Cairo 1969

ʿAbd al-Jabbār, *Tanzīh*
ʿAbd al-Jabbār b. Aḥmad al-Asadābādī al-Qāḍī al-Hamadhānī, *Tanzīh al-Qur'ān ʿan al-maṭāʿin,* Beirut 1966

ʿAbd al-Raḥmān, *ʿAṣrī*
ʿĀ'isha ʿAbd al-Raḥmān, *al-Qur'ān wa-l-tafsīr al-ʿaṣrī,* Cairo 1970

ʿAbd al-Raḥmān, *Tafsīr*
ʿĀ'isha ʿAbd al-Raḥmān, *al-Tafsīr al-bayānī lil-Qur'ān al-karīm,* 3rd ed., Cairo 1968

ʿAbd al-Razzāq, *Muṣannaf*
ʿAbd al-Razzāq b. Hammām al-Ṣanʿānī, *al-Muṣannaf,* ed. Ḥabīb al-Raḥmān al-Aʿẓamī, 11 vols., Beirut 1390/1970; 2nd ed. Johannesburg 1983; ed. Muḥammad Sālim Samāra, 4 vols. (with indices of ḥadīth), Beirut 1408/1988

ʿAbd al-Razzāq, *Tafsīr*
ʿAbd al-Razzāq b. Hammām al-Ṣanʿānī, *al-Tafsīr,* ed. Muṣṭafā Muslim Muḥammad, 3 vols. in 4, Riyadh 1410/1989; ed. ʿAbd al-Muʿṭī Amīn Qalʿajī, 2 vols., Beirut 1411/1991; ed. Maḥmūd Muḥammad ʿAbduh, 3 vols., Beirut 1419/1999

Abū Dāwūd
Abū Dāwūd Sulaymān b. al-Ashʿath al-Sijistānī, *Sunan,* ed. Muḥammad Muḥyī l-Dīn ʿAbd al-Ḥamīd, 4 vols., Cairo 1339/1920; ed. Kamāl Yūsuf al-Ḥūt, 2 vols., Beirut 1988

Abū l-Futūḥ Rāzī, *Rawḥ*
Abū l-Futūḥ Ḥusayn b. ʿAlī Rāzī, *Rawḥ al-jinān wa-rūḥ al-janān,* 12 vols., Tehran 1282-7/1962-5; 5 vols., Qumm n.d.

Abū Ḥayyān, *Baḥr*
Abū Ḥayyān al-Gharnāṭī, *Tafsīr al-baḥr al-muḥīṭ,* 8 vols., Cairo 1328-9/1911; repr. Beirut 1983; ed. ʿĀdil Aḥmad ʿAbd al-Mawjūd and ʿAlī Muḥammad Muʿawwaḍ, 8 vols., Beirut 1993

Abū l-Layth al-Samarqandī, *Tafsīr*
Abū l-Layth Naṣr b. Muḥammad b. Aḥmad al-Samarqandī, *Baḥr al-ʿulūm,* ed. ʿAbd al-Raḥīm Aḥmad al-Zaqqa, 3 vols., Baghdad 1985-6; ed. ʿAlī Muḥammad Muʿawwaḍ et al., 3 vols., Beirut 1413/1993

Abū Shāma, *Murshid*
ʿAbd al-Raḥmān b. Ismāʿīl Abū Shāma, *Kitāb al-Murshid al-wajīz ilā ʿulūm tataʿallaq bi-l-kitāb al-ʿazīz,* ed. Ṭayyar Altikulaç, Istanbul 1968

Abū ʿUbayd, *Faḍāʾil*
Abū ʿUbayd al-Qāsim b. Sallām, *Faḍāʾil al-Qurʾān,* ed. Wahbī Sulaymān Khāwajī, Beirut 1411/1991

Abū ʿUbayd, *Gharīb*
Abū ʿUbayd al-Qāsim b. Sallām, *Gharīb al-ḥadīth,* ed. Muḥammad ʿAbd al-Muʿīd Khān, 4 vols., Hyderabad 1384-7/1964-7; 2 vols., Beirut 1406/1986; ed. Ḥusayn Muḥammad M. Sharaf et al., 4 vols., Cairo 1404-15/1984-94; ed. Masʿūd Ḥijāzī et al., Cairo 1419/1999

Abū ʿUbayd, *Nāsikh*
Abū ʿUbayd al-Qāsim b. Sallām, *Kitāb al-Nāsikh wa-l-mansūkh,* ed. J. Burton, Cambridge 1987

Abū ʿUbayda, *Majāz*
Abū ʿUbayda Maʿmar b. al-Muthannā al-Taymī, *Majāz al-Qurʾān,* ed. F. Sezgin, 2 vols., Cairo 1954-62

Akhfash, *Maʿānī*
Abū l-Ḥasan Saʿīd b. Masʿada al-Akhfash al-Awsaṭ, *Maʿānī l-Qurʾān,* ed. Fāʾiz Fāris al-Ḥamad, 2nd ed., 2 vols., Kuwait 1981; ed. ʿAbd al-Amīr Muḥammad Amīn al-Ward, Beirut 1405/1985; ed. Hudā Maḥmūd Qurrāʿa, Cairo 1990

Allard, *Analyse*
M. Allard, *Analyse conceptuelle du Coran sur cartes perforées,* Paris 1963

Ālūsī, *Rūḥ*
Maḥmūd b. ʿAbdallāh al-Ālūsī, *Rūḥ al-maʿānī fī tafsīr al-Qurʾān al-ʿaẓīm wa-l-sabʿ al-mathānī,* 30 vols. in 15, Cairo 1345/1926; repr. Beirut n.d.

ʿĀmilī, *Aʿyān*
Muḥsin al-Amīn al-ʿĀmilī, *Aʿyān al-shīʿa,* 56 parts, Damascus 1935-63; 11 vols., Beirut 1986

Anbārī, *Bayān*
Abū l-Barakāt ʿAbd al-Raḥmān b. Muḥammad b. al-Anbārī, *al-Bayān fī gharīb iʿrāb al-Qurʾān,* ed. Ṭāhā ʿAbd al-Ḥamīd and Muṣṭafā al-Saqqā, 2 vols., Cairo 1969-70

Anbārī, *Nuzha*
Abū l-Barakāt ʿAbd al-Raḥmān b. Muḥammad al-Anbārī, *Nuzhat al-alibbāʾ fī ṭabaqāt al-udabāʾ,* Cairo 1294; Stockholm 1963; ed. Ibrāhīm al-Sāmarrāʾī, Baghdad 1970

Arberry
A.J. Arberry, *The Koran interpreted,* London 1955

Arkoun, *Lectures*
M. Arkoun, *Lectures du Coran,* Paris 1982

ʿAyyāshī, *Tafsīr*
Muḥammad b. Masʿūd al-ʿAyyāshī, *Tafsīr,* 2 vols., Tehran 1380/1961

Baghawī, *Maʿālim*
al-Ḥusayn b. Masʿūd al-Shāfiʿī al-Baghawī, *Tafsīr al-Baghawī al-musammā bi-Maʿālim al-tanzīl,* ed. Khālid ʿAbd al-Raḥmān al-ʿAkk and Marwān Sawār, 4 vols., Beirut 1983

Baghdādī, *Farq*
Abū Manṣūr ʿAbd al-Qāhir b. Tāhir al-Baghdādī, *al-Farq bayna l-firāq,* ed. Muḥammad Badr, Cairo 1328/1910; ed. Muḥammad Muḥyī l-Dīn ʿAbd al-Ḥamīd, Cairo n.d.

Baghdādī, *Taʾrīkh Baghdād*
Abū Bakr Aḥmad b. ʿAlī al-Khaṭīb al-Baghdādī, *Taʾrīkh Baghdād,* 14 vols., Cairo 1349/1931

Baḥrānī, *Burhān*
Hāshim b. Sulaymān al-Baḥrānī, *Kitāb al-Burhān fī tafsīr al-Qurʾān,* ed. Maḥmūd b. Jaʿfar al-Mūsawī al-Zarandī et al., 4 vols., Tehran 1375/1995; repr. Beirut 1403/1983

Baljon, *Modern*
I.M.S. Baljon, *Modern Muslim Koran interpretation (1880-1960),* Leiden 1961, 1968

Bāqillānī, *Iʿjāz*
al-Qāḍī Abū Bakr Muḥammad b. al-Ṭayyib al-Bāqillānī, *Iʿjāz al-Qurʾān,* ed. al-Sayyid Aḥmad Ṣaqr, Cairo 1954

Bāqillānī, *Intiṣār*
al-Qāḍī Abū Bakr Muḥammad b. al-Ṭayyib al-Bāqillānī, *Nukat al-intiṣār li-naql al-Qurʾān,* ed. Muḥammad Zaghlūl Salām, Alexandria 1971

Bayḍāwī, *Anwār*
ʿAbdallāh b. ʿUmar al-Bayḍāwī, *Anwār al-tanzīl wa-asrār al-taʾwīl,* ed. H.O. Fleischer, 2 vols., Leipzig 1846; Beirut 1988

Beeston, *CHAL*
A.F.L. Beeston et al., eds., *The Cambridge history of Arabic literature,* 4 vols. to date, Cambridge 1983-

Bell, *Commentary*
R. Bell, *A commentary on the Qurʾān,* ed. C.E. Bosworth and M.E.J. Richardson, 2 vols., Manchester 1991

Bell, *Qurʾān*
R. Bell, *The Qurʾān. Translated, with a critical re-arrangement of the sūras,* 2 vols., Edinburgh 1939; repr. 1960

Beltz, *Mythen*
W. Beltz, *Die Mythen des Koran. Der Schlüssel zum Islam,* Düsseldorf 1980

Bergsträsser, *Verneinungs*
G. Bergsträsser, *Verneinungs- und Fragepartikeln und Verwandtes im Ḳurʾān,* Leipzig 1914

Biqāʿī, *Naẓm*
Burhān al-Dīn Ibrāhīm b. ʿUmar al-Biqāʿī, *Naẓm al-durar fī tanāsub al-āyāt wa-l-suwar,* 22 vols., Hyderabad 1969-84; repr. Cairo 1992

Birkeland, *Lord*
H. Birkeland, *The Lord guideth. Studies on primitive Islam,* Oslo 1956

Birkeland, *Opposition*
H. Birkeland, *Old Muslim opposition against interpretation of the Koran,* Oslo 1955

Blachère
R. Blachère, *Le Coran. Traduit de l'arabe,* Paris 1966

Blachère, *Introduction*
R. Blachère, *Introduction au Coran,* Paris 1947

Bobzin, *Koran*
H. Bobzin, *Der Koran. Eine Einführung,* Munich 1999

Bobzin, *Reformation*
H. Bobzin, *Der Koran im Zeitalter der Reformation. Studien zur Frühgeschichte der Arabistik und Islamkunde in Europa,* Beirut/Stuttgart 1995

Bouman, *Conflit*
J. Bouman, *Le conflit autour du Coran et la solution d'al-Bāqillānī,* Amsterdam 1959

Bouman, *Gott und Mensch*
J. Bouman, *Gott und Mensch im Koran. Eine Strukturform religiöser Anthropologie anhand des Beispiels Allāh und Muḥammad,* Darmstadt 1977

Böwering, *Mystical*
G. Böwering, *The mystical vision of existence in classical Islam. The qurʾānic hermeneutics of the Ṣūfī Sahl at-Tustarī (d. 283/896),* Berlin 1980

Brockelmann, *GAL*
C. Brockelmann, *Geschichte der arabischen Litteratur,* 2nd ed., 2 vols. and 3 vols. suppl., Leiden 1943-9; with new introduction, Leiden 1996

Buhl, *Das Leben*
F. Buhl, *Das Leben Muhammeds,* trans. H.H. Schaeder, Leipzig 1930; 1931 (3rd ed.)

Bukhārī, *Ṣaḥīḥ*
Abū ʿAbdallāh Muḥammad b. Ismāʿīl al-Bukhārī, *Kitāb al-Jāmiʿ al-ṣaḥīḥ,* ed. L. Krehl and T.W. Juynboll, 4 vols., Leiden 1862-1908; 9 vols., Cairo 1958

Burton, *Collection*
J. Burton, *The collection of the Qurʾān,* Cambridge 1977

Chabbi, *Seigneur*
J. Chabbi, *Le seigneur des tribus. L'islam de Mahomet,* Paris 1997

Creswell, *EMA*
K.A.C. Creswell, *Early Muslim architecture,* 2 vols., Oxford 1932-40; 2nd ed., London 1969

Dāmaghānī, *Wujūh*
al-Ḥusayn b. Muḥammad al-Dāmaghānī, *al-Wujūh wa-l-naẓāʾir li-alfāẓ Kitāb Allāh al-ʿazīz,* ed. Muḥammad Ḥasan Abū l-ʿAẓm al-Zafītī, 2 vols., Cairo 1412-16/

1992-5; ed. ʿAbd al-ʿAzīz Sayyid al-Ahl (as *Qāmūs al-Qurʾān*), Beirut 1970
Damīrī, *Ḥayāt*
Muḥammad b. Mūsā al-Damīrī, *Ḥayāt al-ḥayawān al-kubrā*, 2 vols., Cairo 1956
Dānī, *Muqniʿ*
Abū ʿAmr ʿUthmān b. Saʿīd al-Dānī, *al-Muqniʿ fī rasm maṣāḥif al-amṣār maʿa Kitāb al-Naqṭ = Orthographie und Punktierung des Koran*, ed. O. Pretzl, Leipzig/Istanbul 1932; ed. Muḥammad al-Ṣadīq Qamḥawī, Cairo n.d.
Dānī, *Naqṭ*
Abū ʿAmr ʿUthmān b. Saʿīd al-Dānī, *al-Muḥkam fī naqṭ al-maṣāḥif*, ed. ʿIzzat Ḥasan, Damascus 1379/1960
Dānī, *Taysīr*
Abū ʿAmr ʿUthmān b. Saʿīd al-Dānī, *Kitāb al-Taysīr fī l-qirāʾāt al-sabʿ = Das Lehrbuch der sieben Koranlesungen*, ed. O. Pretzl, Leipzig/Istanbul 1930
Dāraquṭnī, *Muʾtalif*
Abū l-Ḥasan ʿAlī b. ʿUmar al-Dāraquṭnī, *al-Muʾtalif wa-l-mukhtalif*, ed. Muwaffaq b. ʿAbdallāh b. ʿAbd al-Qādir, 5 vols., Beirut 1986
Dārimī, *Sunan*
ʿAbdallāh b. ʿAbd al-Rāḥmān al-Dārimī, *Sunan*, Cairo 1966
Darwaza, *Tafsīr*
Muḥammad ʿIzzat Darwaza, *al-Tafsir al-ḥadīth*, 12 vols., Cairo 1381-3/1962-4
Dāwūdī, *Ṭabaqāt*
Muḥammad b. ʿAlī al-Dāwūdī, *Ṭabaqāt al-mufassirīn*, ed. ʿAlī Muḥammad ʿUmar, 2 vols., Beirut 1983
Dhahabī, *Mufassirūn*
Muḥammad Ḥusayn al-Dhahabī, *al-Tafsīr wa-l-mufassirūn*, 2 vols., Cairo 1976
Dhahabī, *Qurrāʾ*
Shams al-Dīn Muḥammad b. Aḥmad al-Dhahabī, *Maʿrifat al-qurrāʾ al-kibār ʿalā l-ṭabaqāt wa-l-aʿṣār*, ed. Sayyid Jad al-Ḥaqq, n.p. 1969
Dhahabī, *Siyar*
Shams al-Dīn Muḥammad b. Aḥmad al-Dhahabī, *Siyar aʿlām al-nubalāʾ*, ed. Shuʿayb al-Arnaʾūṭ et al., 25 vols., Beirut 1981-8
Dhahabī, *Tadhkira*
Shams al-Dīn Muḥammad b. Aḥmad al-Dhahabī, *Tadhkirat al-ḥuffāẓ*, 4 vols., Hyderabad 1375/1955
Dhahabī, *Taʾrīkh*
Shams al-Dīn Muḥammad b. Aḥmad al-Dhahabī, *Taʾrīkh al-Islām*, ed. ʿUmar ʿAbd al-Salām Tadmurī, 52 vols. to date, Beirut 1989-; 4 vols. (years 601-640), ed. Bashshār ʿAwwād Maʿrūf et al., Beirut 1408/1988
van Ess, *TG*
J. van Ess, *Theologie und Gesellschaft im 2. und 3. Jahrhundert Hidschra. Eine Geschichte des religiösen Denkens im frühen Islam*, 6 vols., Berlin/New York 1991-7
Fārisī, *Ḥujja*
Abū ʿAlī al-Ḥasan b. ʿAlī al-Fārisī, *al-Ḥujja lil-qurrāʾ al-sabʿa*, ed. Badr al-Dīn al-Qahwajī et al., 6 vols., Damascus 1984-92
Farrāʾ, *Maʿānī*
Abū Zakariyyāʾ Yaḥyā b. Ziyād al-Farrāʾ, *Maʿānī l-Qurʾān*, ed. Aḥmad Yūsuf Najātī and Muḥammad ʿAlī l-Najjār, 3 vols., Cairo 1955-72
Fīrūzābādī, *Baṣāʾir*
Majd al-Dīn Muḥammad b. Yaʿqūb al-Fīrūzābādī *Baṣāʾir dhawī l-tamyīz fī laṭāʾif al-kitāb al-ʿazīz*, ed. Muḥammad ʿAlī l-Najjār, 6 vols., Cairo 1964-73; repr. Beirut n.d.
GAP
W. Fischer and H. Gätje, eds., *Grundriss der arabischen Philologie*, 3 vols., Wiesbaden 1982-92
Gardet and Anawati, *Introduction*
L. Gardet and M.M. Anawati, *Introduction à la théologie musulmane*, Paris 1948, 3rd ed., 1981
Gilliot, *Elt*
C. Gilliot, *Exégèse, langue, et théologie en Islam. L'exégèse coranique de Ṭabarī (m. 310/923)*, Paris 1990

Gimaret, *Jubbāʾī*
D. Gimaret, *Une lecture muʿtazilite du Coran. Le tafsīr d'Abū ʿAlī al-Djubbāʾī (m. 303/915) partiellement reconstitué à partir de ses citateurs,* Louvain/Paris 1994

Goldziher, *GS*
I. Goldziher, *Gesammelte Schriften,* ed. J. Desomogyi, 6 vols., Hildesheim 1967-73

Goldziher, *MS*
I. Goldziher, *Muhammedanische Studien,* 2 vols., Halle 1888-90;
trans., C.R. Barber and S.M. Stern, *Muslim studies,* London 1967-72

Goldziher, *Richtungen*
I. Goldziher, *Die Richtungen der islamischen Koranauslegung,* Leiden 1920; repr. 1970

Graham, *Beyond*
W.A. Graham, *Beyond the written word. Oral aspects of scripture in the history of religion,* Cambridge and New York 1989

Grimme, *Mohammed, I-II*
H. Grimme, *Mohammed. I, Das Leben nach den Quellen. II, Einleitung in den Koran. System der koranischen Theologie,* Münster 1892-5

Grünbaum, *Beiträge*
M. Grünbaum, *Neue Beiträge zur semitischen Sagenkunde,* Leiden 1893

Ḥājjī Khalīfa, *Kashf*
Muṣṭafā ʿAbdallāh Ḥājjī Khalīfa, *Kashf al-ẓunūn,* ed. and trans. G. Flügel, 7 vols., Leipzig 1835-58; ed. Şerefettin Yaltkaya and Kilisli Rifat Bilge, 2 vols., Istanbul 1941-3; repr. Beirut 1992-3

Hawting, *Idolatry*
G.R. Hawting, *The idea of idolatry and the emergence of Islam. From polemic to history,* Cambridge 1999

Hawting and Shareef, *Approaches*
G.R. Hawting and A.A. Shareef (eds.), *Approaches to the Qurʾān,* London 1993

Ḥawwā, *Tafsīr*
Saʿīd Ḥawwā, *al-Asās fī l-tafsīr,* 11 vols., Cairo 1405/1985

Horovitz, *KU*
J. Horovitz, *Koranische Untersuchungen,* Berlin/Leipzig 1926

Hūd b. Muḥakkam, *Tafsīr*
Hūd b. Muḥakkam/Muḥkim al-Huwwārī, *Tafsīr,* ed. Balḥājj Saʿīd Sharīfī, 4 vols., Beirut 1990

Ibn ʿAbbās, *Gharīb*
ʿAbdallāh b. ʿAbbās (attributed to), *Gharīb al-Qurʾān,* ed. Muḥammad ʿAbd al-Raḥīm, Beirut 1993

Ibn Abī l-Iṣbaʿ, *Badīʿ*
Ibn Abī l-Iṣbaʿ al-Miṣrī, *Badīʿ al-Qurʾān,* ed. Ḥifnī Muḥammad Sharaf, Cairo n.d.

Ibn Abī Uṣaybiʿa, *ʿUyūn*
Aḥmad b. al-Qāsim b. Abī Uṣaybiʿa, *ʿUyūn al-anbāʾ fī ṭabaqāt al-aṭibbāʾ,* ed. A. Müller, 2 vols., Cairo 1299/1882; 3 vols., Beirut 1957

Ibn al-Anbārī, *Īḍāḥ*
Abū Bakr Muḥammad b. al-Qāsim b. al-Anbārī, *Īḍāḥ al-waqf wa-l-ibtidāʾ fī Kitāb Allāh,* ed. Muḥyī l-Dīn ʿAbd al-Raḥmān Ramaḍān, 2 vols., Damascus 1391/1971

Ibn al-ʿArabī, *Aḥkām*
Muḥammad b. ʿAbdallāh Abū Bakr b. al-ʿArabī, *Aḥkām al-Qurʾān,* 2nd ed., Cairo 1392/1972

Ibn al-ʿArabī, *Tafsīr*
Muḥammad b. ʿAbdallāh Abū Bakr b. al-ʿArabī, *Tafsīr al-Qurʾān,* 2 vols., Beirut 1968 (see Qāshānī)

Ibn ʿAsākir, *Taʾrīkh*
ʿAlī b. al-Ḥasan b. ʿAsākir, *Taʾrīkh madīnat Dimashq,* abridged ed. ʿAbd al-Qādir Bardān and Aḥmad ʿUbayd, 7 vols., Damascus 1329-51/1911-31; facsimile ed., 19 vols., Amman n.d.; 29 vols., Damascus 1404-8/1984-8; ed. Muḥyī l-Dīn ʿUmar b. Gharāma al-ʿAmrāwī, 80 vols., Beirut 1995-2000

Ibn ʿĀshūr, *Tafsīr*
Muḥammad al-Ṭāhir b. ʿĀshūr, *al-Tafsīr al-taḥrīrī wa-l-tanwīrī,* 30 vols., Tunis 1984

Ibn ʿAskar, *Takmīl*
Muḥammad b. ʿAlī al-Ghassānī b. ʿAskar, *al-Takmīl wa-l-itmām li-Kitāb al-Taʿrīf wa-l-iʿlām,* ed. Ḥasan Ismāʿīl Marwa, Beirut/Damascus 1418/1997 (see Suhaylī)

Ibn al-Athīr, *Kāmil*
ʿIzz al-Dīn ʿAlī b. al-Athīr, *al-Kāmil fī l-taʾrīkh,* ed. C.J. Tornberg, 14 vols., Leiden 1851-76; corrected repr. 13 vols., Beirut 1385-7/1965-7
Ibn al-Athīr, *Nihāya*
Majd al-Dīn al-Mubārak b. al-Athīr, *al-Nihāya fī gharīb al-ḥadīth wa-l-athar,* ed. Ṭāhir Aḥmad al-Zāwī and Maḥmūd al-Ṭanāḥī, 5 vols., Cairo 1963-6
Ibn ʿAṭiyya, *Muḥarrar*
Abū Muḥammad ʿAbd al-Ḥaqq b. Ghālib b. ʿAṭiyya al-Gharnāṭī, *al-Muḥarrar al-wajīz,* ed. ʿAbd al-Salām ʿAbd al-Shāfī Muḥammad, 5 vols., Beirut 1413/1993
Ibn Ḍurays, *Faḍāʾil*
Muḥammad b. Ayyūb b. Ḍurays, *Faḍāʾil al-Qurʾān,* ed. Ghazwa Budayr, Damascus 1988
Ibn Ḥajar, *Tahdhīb*
Ibn Ḥajar al-ʿAsqalānī, *Tahdhīb al-tahdhīb,* 12 vols., Hyderabad 1325-7/1907-9; Beirut 1968
Ibn Ḥanbal, *Musnad*
Aḥmad b. Ḥanbal, *Musnad,* ed. Muḥammad al-Zuhrī al-Ghamrāwī, 6 vols., Cairo 1313/1895; repr. Beirut 1978; ed. Aḥmad Muḥammad Shākir et al., 20 vols., Cairo 1416/1995
Ibn Ḥazm, *Milal*
ʿAlī b. Aḥmad b. Saʿīd b. Ḥazm, *al-Fiṣal fī l-milal wa-l-ahwāʾ wa-l-niḥal,* ed. Muḥammad Ibrāhīm Naṣr and ʿAbd al-Raḥmān ʿUmayra, 5 vols., Beirut 1995
Ibn al-ʿImād, *Shadharāt*
ʿAbd al-Ḥayy b. Aḥmad b. al-ʿImād, *Shadharāt al-dhahab fī akhbār man dhahab,* 8 vols., Cairo 1350-1/1931-2; repr. Beirut n.d.
Ibn Isḥāq, *Sīra*
Muḥammad b. Isḥāq, *Sīrat rasūl Allāh* (recension of ʿAbd al-Malik b. Hishām), ed. F. Wüstenfeld, Göttingen 1858-60; repr. Beirut n.d.; ed. Muṣṭafā al-Ṣaqqā et al., 4 vols. in 2, 2nd ed., Cairo 1955
Ibn Isḥāq-Guillaume
Muḥammad b. Isḥāq, *The life of Muhammad. A translation of Ibn Isḥāq's* Sīrat rasūl Allāh, trans. A. Guillaume, Oxford 1955; repr. Karachi 1967
Ibn al-Jawzī, *Funūn*
Abū l-Faraj ʿAbd al-Raḥmān b. ʿAlī b. al-Jawzī, *Funūn al-afnān fī ʿajāʾib ʿulūm al-Qurʾān,* ed. Rashīd ʿAbd al-Raḥmān al-ʿUbaydī, Baghdad 1408/1988
Ibn al-Jawzī, *Muntaẓam*
Abū l-Faraj ʿAbd al-Raḥmān b. ʿAlī b. al-Jawzī, *al-Muntaẓam fī taʾrīkh al-mulūk wa-l-umam,* ed. Muḥammad and Muṣṭafā ʿAbd al-Qādir ʿAṭā, 19 vols., Beirut 1412/1922; ed. Suhayl Zakkār, 11 vols. in 13, Beirut 1995-6
Ibn al-Jawzī, *Nuzha*
Abū l-Faraj ʿAbd al-Raḥmān b. ʿAlī b. al-Jawzī, *Nuzhat al-aʿyun al-nawāẓir fī ʿilm al-wujūh wa-l-naẓāʾir,* ed. Muḥammad ʿAbd al-Karīm Kāẓim al-Rāḍī, Beirut 1404/1984
Ibn al-Jawzī, *Zād*
Abū l-Faraj ʿAbd al-Raḥmān b. ʿAlī b. al-Jawzī, *Zād al-masīr fī ʿilm al-tafsīr,* intr. Muḥammad Zuhayr al-Shāwīsh, 9 vols., Damascus 1384-5/1964-5; annot. Aḥmad Shams al-Dīn, 8 vols., Beirut 1414/1994
Ibn al-Jazarī, *Ghāya*
Shams al-Dīn Abū l-Khayr Muḥammad b. Muḥammad b. al-Jazarī, *Ghāyat al-nihāya fī ṭabaqāt al-qurrāʾ = Das biographische Lexikon der Koranleser,* 3 vols. in 2, ed. G. Bergsträsser and O. Pretzl, Leipzig/Cairo 1933-5
Ibn al-Jazarī, *Munjid*
Shams al-Dīn Abū l-Khayr Muḥammad b. Muḥammad b. al-Jazarī, *Munjid al-muqriʾīn wa-murshid al-ṭālibīn,* ed. Muḥammad Ḥabīb Allāh al-Shanqīṭī et al., Cairo 1350/1931; Beirut 1980
Ibn al-Jazarī, *Nashr*
Shams al-Dīn Abū l-Khayr Muḥammad b. Muḥammad b. al-Jazarī, *Kitāb al-Nashr fī l-qirāʾāt al-ʿashr,* ed. ʿAlī Muḥammad al-Ḍabbāʿ, 2 vols., Cairo 1940; repr. Beirut n.d.
Ibn Jinnī, *Muḥtasab*
Abū l-Fatḥ ʿUthmān b. Jinnī, *al-Muḥtasab fī*

tabyīn wujūh shawādhdh al-qirāʾāt wa-l-īḍāḥ ʿanhā, 2 vols., ed. ʿAlī al-Najdī Nāṣif et al., Cairo 1386-9/1966-9; repr. 1994

Ibn Kathīr, *Bidāya*
ʿImād al-Dīn Ismāʿīl b. ʿUmar b. Kathīr, *al-Bidāya wa-l-nihāya,* 14 vols., Beirut/Riyadh 1966; repr. Beirut 1988

Ibn Kathīr, *Faḍāʾil*
ʿImād al-Dīn Ismāʿīl b. ʿUmar b. Kathīr, *Faḍāʾil al-Qurʾān,* Beirut 1979

Ibn Kathīr, *Tafsīr*
ʿImād al-Dīn Ismāʿīl b. ʿUmar b. Kathīr, *Tafsīr al-Qurʾān al-ʿaẓīm,* ed. ʿAbd al-ʿAzīz Ghunaym et al., 8 vols., Cairo 1390/1971; 4 vols., Cairo n.d.; repr. Beirut 1980

Ibn Khālawayh, *Ḥujja*
Abū ʿAbdallāh al-Ḥusayn b. Aḥmad b. Khālawayh, *al-Ḥujja fī l-qirāʾāt al-sabʿ,* ed. ʿAbd al-ʿĀl Salīm Mukarram, Beirut 1971

Ibn Khālawayh, *Iʿrāb*
Abū ʿAbdallāh al-Ḥusayn b. Aḥmad b. Khālawayh, *Iʿrāb thalāthīn sūra min al-Qurʾān al-karīm,* Baghdad 1967

Ibn Khālawayh, *Iʿrāb al-qirāʾāt*
Abū ʿAbdallāh al-Ḥusayn b. Aḥmad b. Khālawayh, *Iʿrāb al-qirāʾāt al-sabʿ wa-ʿilaluhā,* ed. ʿAbd al-Raḥmān b. Sulaymān al-ʿUthaymīn, 2 vols., Cairo 1413/1992

Ibn Khaldūn, *ʿIbar*
ʿAbd al-Raḥmān b. Khaldūn, *Kitāb al-ʿIbar,* ed. Naṣr al-Ḥūrīnī, 7 vols., Būlāq 1284/1867

Ibn Khaldūn-Rosenthal
ʿAbd al-Raḥmān b. Khaldūn, *The Muqaddimah,* trans. F. Rosenthal, 3 vols., New York 1958; 2nd rev. ed., Princeton 1967

Ibn Khallikān, *Wafayāt*
Shams al-Dīn b. Khallikān, *Wafayāt al-aʿyān wa-anbāʾ abnāʾ al-zamān,* ed. F. Wüstenfeld, 4 vols., Göttingen 1835-50; ed. Iḥsān ʿAbbās, 8 vols., Beirut 1968-72; trans. M. de Slane, *Ibn Khallikān's biographical dictionary,* 4 vols., Paris 1842-71; repr. New York 1961

Ibn Māja
Muḥammad b. Yazīd b. Māja, *Sunan,* ed. Muḥammad Fuʾād ʿAbd al-Bāqī, 2 vols., Cairo 1952-3

Ibn Mujāhid, *Sabʿa*
Abū Bakr Aḥmad b. Mūsā b. Mujāhid, *Kitāb al-Sabʿa fī l-qirāʾāt,* ed. Shawqī Ḍayf, Cairo 1979

Ibn al-Nadīm, *Fihrist*
Muḥammad b. Isḥāq b. al-Nadīm, *Kitāb al-Fihrist,* ed. G. Flügel, 2 vols., Leipzig 1871-2; ed. Riḍā Tajaddud, Tehran 1971; 2nd ed., Beirut 1988

Ibn al-Nadīm-Dodge
Muḥammad b. Isḥāq b. al-Nadīm, *The Fihrist of al-Nadīm,* trans. B. Dodge, 2 vols., New York/London 1970

Ibn al-Naqīb, *Muqaddima*
Abū ʿAbdallāh Muḥammad b. Sulaymān al-Naqīb, *Muqaddimat al-tafsīr fī ʿulūm al-bayān wa-l-maʿānī wa-l-badīʿ wa-iʿjāz al-Qurʾān,* ed. Zakariyyāʾ Saʿīd ʿAlī, Cairo 1415/1995

Ibn Qayyim al-Jawziyya, *Tibyān*
Muḥammad b. Abī Bakr b. Qayyim al-Jawziyya, *al-Tibyān fī aqsām al-Qurʾān,* Beirut 1982

Ibn al-Qifṭī, *Ḥukamāʾ*
Abū l-Ḥasan ʿAlī b. Yūsuf b. al-Qifṭī, *Taʾrīkh al-ḥukamāʾ,* ed. J. Lippert, Leipzig 1903; repr. Baghdad 1967

Ibn Qutayba, *Gharīb*
Abū Muḥammad ʿAbdallāh b. Muslim al-Dīnawarī b. Qutayba, *Tafsīr gharīb al-Qurʾān,* ed. al-Sayyid Aḥmad Ṣaqr, Cairo 1958; Beirut 1978

Ibn Qutayba, *al-Shiʿr*
Abū Muḥammad ʿAbdallāh b. Muslim al-Dīnawarī b. Qutayba, *Kitāb al-Shiʿr wa-l-shuʿarāʾ,* ed. M.J. de Goeje, Leiden 1900

Ibn Qutayba, *Taʾwīl*
Abū Muḥammad ʿAbdallāh b. Muslim al-Dīnawarī b. Qutayba, *Taʾwīl mushkil al-Qurʾān,* ed. al-Sayyid Aḥmad Ṣaqr, Cairo 1954; Cairo 1973; Medina 1981

Ibn Qutayba-Lecomte
G. Lecomte, *Le traité des divergences du hadīt d'Ibn Qutayba,* Damascus 1962

Ibn Sa'd, *Ṭabaqāt*
Muḥammad b. Sa'd, *al-Ṭabaqāt al-kubrā*, ed. H. Sachau et al., 9 vols., Leiden 1905-40; ed. Iḥsān 'Abbās, 9 vols., Beirut 1957-8
Ibn Taymiyya, *Daqā'iq*
Taqī l-Dīn Aḥmad b. 'Abd al-Ḥalīm b. Taymiyya, *Daqā'iq al-tafsīr. al-Jāmi' li-tafsīr al-Imām Ibn Taymiyya*, ed. Muḥammad al-Sayyid al-Julaynid, 6 vols. in 3, Jedda/Beirut/Damascus 1986
Ibn Taymiyya, *Muqaddima*
Taqī l-Dīn Aḥmad b. 'Abd al-Ḥalīm b. Taymiyya, *Muqaddima fī uṣūl al-tafsīr*, Beirut 1392/1972; Riyadh 1382/1962
Ibn Wahb, *al-Jāmi'*
'Abdallāh b. Wahb, *al-Ǧāmi'. Die Koranswissenschaften*, ed. M. Muranyi, Wiesbaden 1992
Ibyārī, *Mawsū'a*
Ibrāhīm al-Ibyārī and 'Abd al-Ṣabūr Marzūq, *al-Mawsū'a al-qur'āniyya*, 6 vols., Cairo 1388/1969; 11 vols., Cairo 1405/1984
Ihsanoglu, *Translations*
E. İhsanoğlu (ed.), *World bibliography of translations of the meanings of the holy Qur'ān. Printed translations 1515-1980*, Istanbul 1406/1986
Iṣfahānī, *Aghānī*
Abū l-Faraj al-Iṣfahānī, *Kitāb al-Aghānī*, 21 vols. in 7, Cairo 1323/1905; 25 vols., Beirut 1955-62
Iṣfahānī, *Muqaddima*
Abū l-Ḥasan al-'Āmilī al-Iṣfahānī, *Muqaddimat tafsīr mir'āt al-anwār wa-mishkāt al-asrār*, ed. Maḥmūd b. Ja'far al-Mūsawī al-Zarandī, Tehran 1374/1954
Iṣlāḥī, *Tadabbur*
Amīn Aḥsan Iṣlāḥī, *Tadabbur-i Qur'ān*, 8 vols., Lahore 1967-80
'Iyāḍ b. Mūsā, *Shifā'*
al-Qāḍī Abū l-Faḍl 'Iyāḍ b. Mūsā, *al-Shifā' bi-ta'rīf ḥuqūq al-muṣṭafā*, 2 vols. in 1, Damascus 1978; ed. Muḥammad Amīn Qarah 'Alī et al., Amman 1407/1986
Izutsu, *Concepts*
Toshihiko Izutsu, *Ethico-religious concepts in the Qur'ān*, Montreal 1966
Izutsu, *God*
Toshihiko Izutsu, *God and man in the Koran*, New York 1964; repr. 1980
Jāḥiẓ, *Bayān*
'Amr b. Baḥr al-Jāḥiẓ, *al-Bayān wa-l-tabyīn*, ed. 'Abd al-Salām Muḥammad Hārūn, 4 vols., Cairo 1948-50; repr. Beirut n.d.
Jalālayn
Jalāl al-Dīn Muḥammad b. Aḥmad al-Maḥallī and Jalāl al-Dīn al-Suyūṭī, *Tafsīr al-Jalālayn*, Damascus 1385/1965
Jansen, *Egypt*
J.J.G. Jansen, *The interpretation of the Koran in modern Egypt*, Leiden 1974, 1980
Jaṣṣāṣ, *Aḥkām*
Abū Bakr Aḥmad b. 'Abdallāh al-Jaṣṣāṣ al-Rāzī, *Aḥkām al-Qur'ān*, 3 vols., Istanbul 1335-8/1916-19
Jawālīqī, *Mu'arrab*
Abū Manṣūr Mawhūb b. Aḥmad al-Jawālīqī, *al-Mu'arrab min al-kalām al-'ajamī 'alā ḥurūf al-mu'jam*, ed. Aḥmad Muḥammad Shākir, Cairo 1361/1942
Jeffery, *For. vocab.*
A. Jeffery, *Foreign vocabulary of the Qur'ān*, Baroda 1938
Jeffery, *Materials*
A. Jeffery, *Materials for the history of the text of the Qur'ān. The Kitāb al-Maṣāḥif of Ibn Abī Dāwūd together with a collection of the variant readings from the codices of Ibn Mas'ūd, etc.*, Leiden 1937
Jeffery, *Muqaddimas*
A. Jeffery, *Two muqaddimas to the Qur'ānic sciences. The muqaddima to the* Kitab al-Mabani *and the muqaddima of Ibn 'Atiyya to his* Tafsir, Cairo 1954
Jurjānī, *Asrār*
'Abd al-Qāhir al-Jurjānī, *Asrār al-balāgha*, ed. H. Ritter, Istanbul 1954
Jurjānī, *Dalā'il*
'Abd al-Qāhir al-Jurjānī, *Dalā'il i'jāz al-*

Qur'ān, Cairo 1372; ed. Maḥmūd Muḥammad Shākir, Cairo 1404/1984

Justi, *Namenbuch*
F. Justi, *Iranisches Namenbuch*, Marburg 1895

Kaḥḥāla, *Muʿjam*
ʿUmar Riḍā Kaḥḥāla, *Muʿjam al-muʾallifīn*, 15 vols. in 8, Beirut n.d.; Damascus 1957-61

Kaḥḥāla, *Nisāʾ*
ʿUmar Riḍā Kaḥḥāla, *Aʿlām al-nisāʾ fī ʿālamay al-ʿArab wa-l-Islām*, 5 vols., Damascus 1379/1959

Kāshānī, *Minhaj*
Mullā Fatḥ Allāh Kāshānī, *Minhaj al-ṣādiqīn fī ilzām al-mukhālifīn*, 10 vols., Tehran 1347[solar]/1969

Kāshānī, *Ṣāfī*
Mullā Muḥsin Fayd Kāshānī, *al-Ṣāfī fī tafsīr kalām Allāh al-wāfī*, ed. Ḥusayn al-Aʿlamī, 5 vols., Beirut 1399/1979

Khāzin, *Lubāb*
ʿAlāʾ al-Dīn al-Khāzin, *Lubāb al-taʾwīl fī maʿānī l-tanzīl*, Cairo 1381/1961

Khwānsārī, *Rawdāt*
Muḥammad Bāqir al-Mūsawī al-Khwānsārī, *Rawdāt al-jannāt*, ed. Asad Allāh Ismāʿīlīyān, 8 vols., Tehran 1392/1972

Kisāʾī, *Mutashābih*
ʿAlī b. Ḥamza al-Kisāʾī, *Kitāb Mutashābih al-Qurʾān*, ed. Ṣabīḥ al-Tamīmī, Tripoli 1994

Kisāʾī, *Qiṣaṣ*
Muḥammad b. ʿAbdallāh al-Kisāʾī, *Vita prophetarum auctore Muḥammed ben ʿAbdallāh al-Kisāʾī*, ed. I. Eisenberg, 2 vols., Leiden 1922-3

Kulaynī, *Kāfī*
Abū Jaʿfar Muḥammad b. Yaʿqūb al-Kulaynī, *Rawḍat al-kāfī*, ed. ʿAlī Akbar al-Ghifārī, Najaf 1395/1966; repr. Beirut n.d.

Kutubī, *Fawāt*
Ibn Shākir al-Kutubī, *Fawāt al-wafayāt*, 2 vols., Cairo 1299/1882; ed. Iḥsān ʿAbbās, 5 vols., Beirut 1973-4

Lane
E.W. Lane, *An Arabic-English lexicon*, 1 vol. in 8 parts., London 1863-93; New York 1955-6; repr. 2 vols., Cambridge 1984

Lecker, *Muslims*
M. Lecker, *Muslims, Jews and pagans. Studies on early Islamic Medina*, Leiden 1995

Le Strange, *Lands*
G. Le Strange, *The lands of the eastern caliphate*, 2nd ed., Cambridge 1930

Lisān al-ʿArab
Muḥammad b. al-Mukarram b. Manẓūr, *Lisān al-ʿArab*, 15 vols., Beirut 1955-6; ed. ʿAlī Shīrī, 18 vols., Beirut 1988

Lüling, *Ur-Qurʾān*
G. Lüling, *Über den Ur-Qurʾān. Ansätze zur Rekonstruktion der vorislamisch-christlichen Strophenlieder im Qurʾān*, Erlangen 1972; 2nd ed. 1993

Makkī, *Ibāna*
Makkī b. Abī Ṭālib al-Qaysī, *Kitāb al-Ibāna ʿan maʿānī l-qirāʾāt*, ed. Muḥyī l-Dīn Ramaḍān, Damascus 1979

Makkī, *Kashf*
Makkī b. Abī Ṭālib al-Qaysī, *al-Kashf ʿan wujūh al-qirāʾāt al-sabʿ wa-ʿilalihā wa-ḥujajihā*, ed. Muḥyī l-Dīn Ramaḍān, 2 vols., Damascus 1974

Makkī, *Mushkil*
Makkī b. Abī Ṭālib al-Qaysī, *Mushkil iʿrāb al-Qurʾān*, ed. Yāsīn M. al-Sawwās, Damascus 1974

Mālik, *Muwaṭṭaʾ*
Mālik b. Anas, *al-Muwaṭṭaʾ*, ed. Muḥammad Fuʾād ʿAbd al-Bāqī, Cairo 1952-3; Beirut 1985; ed. ʿAbd al-Majīd Turkī, Beirut 1994

Masʿūdī, *Murūj*
Abū ʿAlī b. al-Ḥusayn al-Masʿūdī, *Murūj al-dhahab*, ed. C. Barbier de Meynard and Pavet de Courteille, 9 vols., Paris 1861-77; ed. and trans. Ch. Pellat, *Les prairies d'or*, 7 vols. text (1966-79) and 5 vols. translation, Paris-Beirut 1962-97; ed. Qāsim al-Shamāʿī al-Rifāʿī, 4 vols., Beirut 1989

Māturīdī, *Taʾwīlāt*
Abū Manṣūr Muḥammad b. Muḥammad al-Māturīdī, *Taʾwīlāt ahl al-sunna,* ed. Ibrāhīm and al-Sayyid ʿAwadayn, Cairo 1391/1971; ed. Jāsim Muḥammad al-Jubūrī, Baghdad 1404/1983

Māwardī, *Nukat*
ʿAlī b. Muḥammad al-Māwardī, *al-Nukat wa-l-ʿuyūn fī l-tafsīr,* ed. al-Sayyid b. ʿAbd al-Maqṣūd b. ʿAbd al-Raḥīm, 6 vols., Beirut 1412/1992

McAuliffe, *Qurʾānic*
J.D. McAuliffe, *Qurʾānic Christians. An analysis of classical and modern exegesis,* Cambridge 1991

Mir, *Dictionary*
M. Mir, *Dictionary of Qurʾānic terms and concepts,* New York 1987

Mir, *Verbal*
M. Mir, *Verbal idioms of the Qurʾān,* Ann Arbor, MI 1989

Mufaḍḍaliyyāt
al-Mufaḍḍal b. Muḥammad al-Ḍabbī, *al-Mufaḍḍaliyyāt,* ed. Aḥmad Muḥammad Shākir and ʿAbd al-Salām Muḥammad Hārūn, Cairo 1942

Muir, *Mahomet*
W. Muir, *The life of Mahomet. With introductory chapters on the original sources of the biography of Mahomet, I-IV,* London 1858-61

Mujāhid, *Tafsīr*
Abū l-Ḥajjāj Mujāhid b. Jabr, *al-Tafsīr,* ed. ʿAbd al-Raḥmān b. Ṭāhir b. Muḥammad al-Suwartī, Qatar 1976; ed. Muḥammad ʿAbd al-Salām Abū l-Nīl, Cairo 1989

Mukarram, *Muʿjam al-qirāʾāt*
ʿAbd al-Āl Salīm Mukarram, *Muʿjam al-qirāʾāt al-qurʾāniyya,* 8 vols. to date, Kuwait 1982-

Muqātil, *Ashbāh*
Abū l-Ḥasan Muqātil b. Sulaymān al-Balkhī, *al-Ashbāh wa-l-naẓāʾir fī l-Qurʾān al-karīm,* ed. ʿAbdallāh Maḥmūd Shiḥāta, Cairo 1975

Muqātil, *Khams miʾa*
Abū l-Ḥasan Muqātil b. Sulaymān al-Balkhī, *Tafsīr al-khams miʾat āya min al-Qurʾān,* ed. I. Goldfeld, Shfaram 1980

Muqātil, *Tafsīr*
Abū l-Ḥasan Muqātil b. Sulaymān al-Balkhī, *al-Tafsīr,* ed. ʿAbdallāh Maḥmūd Shiḥāta, 5 vols., Cairo 1980-7

Muslim, *Ṣaḥīḥ*
Muslim b. al-Ḥajjāj, *Ṣaḥīḥ,* ed. Muḥammad Fuʾād ʿAbd al-Bāqī, 5 vols., Cairo 1955-6

Nāfiʿ, *Masāʾil*
Masāʾil al-Imām ʿan asʾilat Nāfiʿ b. al-Azraq wa-ajwibat ʿAbd Allāh b. ʿAbbas, ed. ʿAbd al-Raḥmān ʿUmayra, Cairo 1413/1994

Nagel, *Einschübe*
T. Nagel, *Medinensische Einschübe in mekkanischen Suren,* Göttingen 1995

Nagel, *Koran*
T. Nagel, *Der Koran. Einführung-Texte-Erläuterungen,* Munich 1983

Naḥḥās, *Iʿrāb*
Abū Jaʿfar Aḥmad b. Muḥammad al-Naḥḥās, *Iʿrāb al-Qurʾān,* ed. Zuhayr Ghāzī Zāhid, 2nd ed., 5 vols., Beirut 1985, 1988

Nasafī, *Tafsīr*
ʿAbdallāh b. Aḥmad b. Maḥmūd al-Nasafī, *Madārik al-tanzīl wa-ḥaqāʾiq al-taʾwīl,* ed. Zakariyyāʾ ʿUmayrāt, 2 vols. Beirut 1415/1995

Nasāʾī, *Faḍāʾil*
Aḥmad b. Shuʿayb al-Nasāʾī, *Faḍāʾil al-Qurʾān,* ed. Samīr al-Khūlī, Beirut 1985

Nasāʾī, *Sunan*
Aḥmad b. Shuʿayb al-Nasāʾī, *al-Sunan al-kubrā,* ed. ʿAbd al-Ghaffār Sulaymān al-Bundārī and al-Sayyid Kisrawī Ḥasan, 6 vols., Beirut 1411/1991

Nawawī, *Sharḥ*
Abū Zakariyyāʾ Yaḥyā b. Sharaf al-Nawawī, *Sharḥ Ṣaḥīḥ Muslim,* 18 vols. in 9, Cairo 1349/1929-30; ed. Khalīl Muḥammad Shīḥā, 19 vols. in 10, Beirut 1995

Neuwirth, *Studien*
A. Neuwirth, *Studien zur Komposition der mekkanischen Suren,* Berlin 1981

Nīsābūrī, *Tafsīr*
Niẓām al-Dīn al-Ḥasan b. Muḥammad b.

al-Ḥusayn al-Qummī al-Nīsābūrī al-Aʿraj, *Tafsīr gharāʾib al-Qurʾān wa-raghāʾib al-furqān,* on the margin of Ṭabarī, *Jāmiʿ al-bayān,* 30 vols., Cairo 1323-9/1905-11; repr. Beirut 1392/1972; ed. Ibrāhīm ʿAṭwa ʿAwaḍ, 13 vols., Cairo 1962-4

Nöldeke, *GQ*
T. Nöldeke, *Geschichte des Qorāns,* new edition by F. Schwally, G. Bergsträsser and O. Pretzl, 3 vols., Leipzig 1909-38

Nwyia, *Exégèse*
P. Nwyia, *Exégèse coranique et langage mystique. Nouvel essai sur le lexique technique des mystiques musulmans,* Beirut 1970

Paret, *Kommentar*
R. Paret, *Der Koran. Kommentar und Konkordanz,* Stuttgart 1971; 1977; Kohlhammer 1980

Paret, *Koran*
R. Paret, *Der Koran. Übersetzung,* Stuttgart 1962

Paret (ed.), *Koran*
R. Paret (ed.) *Der Koran,* Darmstadt 1975

Penrice, *Dictionary*
J. Penrice, *A dictionary and glossary of the Koran,* London 1873; repr. 1971

Pickthall, *Koran*
M.M. Pickthall, *The meaning of the glorious Koran,* London 1930; New York 1976

Qāshānī, *Taʾwīl*
ʿAbd al-Razzāq al-Qāshānī, *Taʾwīl al-Qurʾān,* 2 vols., Beirut 1968 (see Ibn al-ʿArabī)

Qāsimī, *Tafsīr*
Muḥammad Jamāl al-Dīn al-Qāsimī, *Maḥāsin al-taʾwīl,* 18 vols., Cairo 1957-70

Qasṭallānī, *Laṭāʾif*
Aḥmad b. Muḥammad b. Abī Bakr al-Qasṭallānī, *Laṭāʾif al-ishārāt li-funūn al-qirāʾāt,* ed. ʿĀmir al-Sayyid ʿUthmān and ʿAbd al-Ṣabūr Shāhīn, Cairo 1972

Qasṭallānī, *Mawāhib*
Aḥmad b. Muḥammad b. Abī Bakr al-Qasṭallānī, *al-Mawāhib al-laduniyya bi-l-minaḥ al-muḥammadiyya,* ed. Ṣāliḥ Aḥmad al-Shāmī, 4 vols., Beirut/Damascus/Amman 1412/1991

Qummī, *Tafsīr*
Abū l-Ḥasan ʿAlī b. Ibrāhīm al-Qummī, *Tafsīr,* ed. Ṭayyib al-Mūsāwī al-Jazāʾirī, 2 vols., Najaf 1387/1967; Beirut 1991

Qurṭubī, *Jāmiʿ*
Abū ʿAbdallāh Muḥammad b. Aḥmad al-Qurṭubī, *al-Jāmiʿ li-aḥkām al-Qurʾān,* ed. Aḥmad ʿAbd al-ʿAlīm al-Bardūnī et al., 20 vols., Cairo 1952-67; Beirut 1965-7

Qushayrī, *Laṭāʾif*
Abū l-Qāsim ʿAbd al-Karīm b. Hawāzin al-Qushayrī, *Laṭāʾif al-ishārāt,* ed. Ibrāḥim Basyūnī, 6 vols., Cairo 1968-71

Quṭb, *Ẓilāl*
Sayyid Quṭb Ibrāhīm Ḥusayn Shādhilī, *Fī ẓilāl al-Qurʾān,* 6 vols., Beirut 1393-4/1973-4; rev. 11th ed., Cairo 1993

al-Rāghib al-Iṣfahānī, *Mufradāt*
Abū l-Qāsim al-Ḥusayn al-Rāghib al-Iṣfahānī, *Muʿjam mufradāt alfāẓ al-Qurʾān,* Beirut 1392/1972

Rashīd Riḍā, *Manār*
Muḥammad Rashīd Riḍā and Muḥammad ʿAbduh, *Tafsīr al-Qurʾān al-ḥakīm al-shahīr bi-Tafsīr al-Manār,* 12 vols., Beirut n.d.

Rāzī, *Tafsīr*
Fakhr al-Dīn al-Rāzī, *al-Tafsīr al-kabīr (Mafātīḥ al-ghayb),* ed. Muḥammad Muḥyī l-Dīn ʿAbd al-Ḥamīd, 32 vols. in 16, Cairo 1352/1933; Tehran n.d.; Beirut 1981

Rippin, *Approaches*
Andrew Rippin (ed.), *Approaches to the history of the interpretation of the Qurʾān,* Oxford 1988

Rummānī et al., *Rasāʾil*
ʿAlī b. ʿĪsā al-Rummānī, Ḥamd b. Muḥammad al-Khaṭṭābī and ʿAbd al-Qāhir al-Jurjānī, *Thalāth rasāʾil fī iʿjāz al-Qurʾān,* ed. Muḥammad Khalaf Allāh Aḥmad and Muḥammad Zaghlūl Sallām, Cairo 1976

Rūzbihān al-Baqlī, *ʿArāʾis*
Rūzbihān b. Abī Naṣr al-Baqlī, *ʿArāʾis al-bayān fī ḥaqāʾiq al-Qurʾān,* 2 vols., Cawnpore 1301/1884

Ṣābūnī, *Tafsīr*
Muḥammad ʿAlī Ṣābūnī, *Ṣafwat al-tafāsīr. Tafsīr lil-Qurʾān al-karīm,* 3 vols., Beirut 1981
Ṣafadī, *Wāfī*
Khalīl b. Aybak al-Ṣafadī, *al-Wāfī bi-l-wafayāt. Das biographische Lexikon des Ṣalāḥaddīn Ḫalīl ibn Aibak aṣ-Ṣafadī,* ed. H. Ritter et al., 24 vols. to date, Wiesbaden-Beirut-Damascus 1962-
Sakhāwī, *Jamāl*
ʿAlam al-Dīn ʿAlī b. Muḥammad al-Sakhāwi, *Jamāl al-qurrāʾ wa-kamāl al-iqrāʾ,* ed. ʿAlī Ḥusayn al-Bawwāb, 2 vols., Mecca 1408/1987
Ṣaliḥī, *Subul*
Shams al-Dīn Muḥammad b. Yūsuf al-Ṣāliḥī, *Subul al-hudā wa-l-rashād,* ed. ʿĀdil Aḥmad ʿAbd al-Mawjūd and ʿAlī Muḥammad Muʿawwaḍ, 12 vols., Beirut 1414/1993
Samʿānī, *Ansāb*
ʿAbd al-Karīm b. Muḥammad al-Samʿānī, *Kitāb al-Ansāb,* facsimile ed., D.S. Margoliouth, Leiden 1912; ed. Muḥammad ʿAbd al-Muʿīd Khān et al., 13 vols., Hyderabad 1382-1402/1962-82
Schawāhid-Indices
A. Fischer and E. Bräunlich (eds.), *Indices der Reimwörter und der Dichter der in den arabischen Schawāhid-Kommentaren und in verwandten Werken erläuterten Belegverse,* Leipzig 1934-45
Schwarzbaum, *Legends*
H. Schwarzbaum, *Biblical and extra-biblical legends in Islamic folk-literature,* Wallford-Hessen 1982
Sezgin, *GAS*
F. Sezgin, *Geschichte des arabischen Schrifttums,* 9 vols., Leiden 1967-84
Shāfiʿī, *Aḥkām*
Muḥammad b. Idrīs al-Shāfiʿī, *Aḥkām al-Qurʾān,* 2 vols. in 1, Beirut 1980
Shāfiʿī, *Mufassirān*
Muḥammad Shāfiʿī, *Mufassirān-i shīʿah,* Shiraz 1349[solar]/1970
Shahrastānī, *Milal*
Abū l-Fatḥ Muḥammad al-Shahrastānī, *al-Milal wa-l-niḥal,* ed. W. Cureton, 2 vols., London 1846; ed. Muḥammad Fatḥ Allāh Badrān, 2 vols., Cairo 1947-55; ed. Fahmī Muḥammad, Beirut 1992
Shawkānī, *Tafsīr*
Abū ʿAbdallāh Muḥammad b. ʿAlī al-Shawkānī, *Fatḥ al-qadīr al-jāmiʿ bayna fannay l-riwāya wa-l-dirāya fī ʿilm al-tafsīr,* 5 vols., Cairo 1349/1930; repr. Beirut 1973
Sibṭ Ibn al-Jawzī, *Mirʾāt*
Shams al-Dīn Abū l-Muẓaffar Yūsuf b. Qizoğlu Sibṭ Ibn al-Jawzī, *Mirʾāt al-zamān fī taʾrīkh al-aʿyān,* ed. Iḥsān ʿAbbās, Beirut 1405/1985
Speyer, *Erzählungen*
Heinrich Speyer, *Die biblischen Erzählungen im Qoran,* Gräfenhainich 1931; repr. Hildesheim 1961
Sprenger, *Mohammad*
A. Sprenger, *Das Leben und die Lehre des Mohammad,* 3 vols., 2nd ed., Berlin 1869
Storey, *PL*
C.A. Storey, *Persian literature. A bio-bibliographical survey,* 2 vols. in 5, London 1927
Sufyān al-Thawrī, *Tafsīr*
Abū ʿAbdallāh Sufyān al-Thawrī, *al-Tafsīr,* ed. Imtiyāz ʿAlī ʿArshī, Beirut 1403/1983
Suhaylī, *Taʿrīf*
Abū l-Qāsim ʿAbd al-Raḥmān b. ʿAbdallāh al-Suhaylī, *al-Taʿrīf wa-l-iʿlām fī mā ubhima fī l-Qurʾān min al-asmāʾ wa-l-aʿlām,* ed. ʿAbdallāh Muḥammad ʿAlī al-Naqrāṭ, Tripoli 1401/1992
Sulamī, *Ziyādāt*
Abū ʿAbd al-Raḥmān Muḥammad b. al-Ḥusayn al-Sulamī, *Ziyādāt ḥaqāʾiq al-tafsīr,* ed. G. Böwering, Beirut 1995
Suyūṭī, *Durr*
Jalāl al-Dīn al-Suyūṭī, *al-Durr al-manthūr fī l-tafsīr bi-l-maʾthūr,* 6 vols., Beirut 1990
Suyūṭī, *Ḥuffāẓ*
Jalāl al-Dīn al-Suyūṭī, *Ṭabaqāt al-ḥuffāẓ,* ed. ʿAlī Muḥammad ʿUmar, Cairo 1973

Suyūṭī, *Itqān*
Jalāl al-Dīn al-Suyūṭī, *al-Itqān fī ʿulūm al-Qurʾān,* ed. Muḥammad Abū l-Faḍl Ibrāhīm, 4 vols. in 2, Cairo 1967

Suyūṭī, *Khaṣāʾiṣ*
Jalāl al-Dīn al-Suyūṭī, *al-Khaṣāʾiṣ al-kubrā,* Hyderabad 1320/1902; repr. Beirut n.d.

Suyūṭī, *Mufḥamāt*
Jalāl al-Dīn al-Suyūṭī, *al-Mufḥamāt al-aqrān fī mubhamāt al-Qurʾān,* ed. Muṣṭafā Dīb al-Bughā, Damascus and Beirut 1403/1982

Suyūṭī, *Muhadhdhab*
Jalāl al-Dīn al-Suyūṭī, *al-Muhadhdhab fī mā waqaʿa fī l-Qurʾān min al-muʿarrab,* ed. al-Tihāmī al-Rājī al-Hāshimī, Rabat n.d.; in *Rasāʾil fī l-fiqh wa-l-lugha,* ed. ʿAbdallāh al-Jubūrī, Beirut 1982, pp. 179-235

Suyūṭī, *Ṭabaqāt*
Jalāl al-Dīn al-Suyūṭī, *Ṭabaqāt al-mufassirīn,* ed. ʿAlī Muḥammad ʿUmar, Cairo 1976

Suyūṭī, *Taḥbīr*
Jalāl al-Dīn al-Suyūṭī, *al-Taḥbīr fī ʿilm al-tafsīr,* ed. Fatḥī ʿAbd al-Qādir Farīd, Cairo 1406/1986

Suyūṭī, *Tanāsuq*
Jalāl al-Dīn al-Suyūṭī, *Tanāsuq al-durar fī tanāsub al-suwar,* ed. ʿAbd al-Qādir Aḥmad ʿAṭā, Beirut 1406/1986

Ṭabarānī, *Awsaṭ*
Abū l-Qāsim Sulaymān b. Aḥmad al-Ṭabarānī, *al-Muʿjam al-awsaṭ,* ed. Ṭāriq b. ʿAwaḍ Allāh b. Muḥammad and ʿAbd al-Muḥsin Ibrāhīm al-Ḥusaynī, 10 vols., Cairo 1415/1995

Ṭabarānī, *Kabīr*
Abū l-Qāsim Sulaymān b. Aḥmad al-Ṭabarānī, *al-Muʿjam al-kabīr,* ed. Ḥamdī ʿAbd al-Majīd al-Salafī, vols. i-xii, xvii-xx and xxii-xxv, Baghdad 1398-1404/1977-83; Mosul 1401/1983

Ṭabarī, *Tafsīr*
Abū Jaʿfar Muḥammad b. Jarīr al-Ṭabarī, *Jāmiʿ al-bayān ʿan taʾwīl āy al-Qurʾān* [up to Q 14:27], ed. Maḥmūd Muḥammad Shākir and Aḥmad Muḥammad Shākir, 16 vols., Cairo 1954-68; 2nd ed. for some vols., Cairo 1969; ed. Aḥmad Saʿīd ʿAlī et al., 30 vols., Cairo 1373-77/1954-7; repr. Beirut 1984

Ṭabarī, *Taʾrīkh*
Abū Jaʿfar Muḥammad b. Jarīr al-Ṭabarī, *Taʾrīkh al-rusul wa-l-mulūk,* ed. M.J. de Goeje et al., 15 vols., Leiden 1879-1901; ed. Muḥammad Abū l-Faḍl Ibrāhīm, 10 vols., Cairo 1960-9

Ṭabarsī, *Majmaʿ*
Abū ʿAlī l-Faḍl b. al-Ḥasan al-Ṭabarsī, *Majmaʿ al-bayān fī tafsīr al-Qurʾān,* intr. Muḥsin al-Amīn al-Ḥusaynī al-ʿĀmilī, 30 vols. in 6, Beirut 1380/1961

Ṭabāṭabāʾī, *Mīzān*
Muḥammad Ḥusayn Ṭabāṭabāʾī, *al-Mīzān fī tafsīr al-Qurʾān,* 20 vols., Beirut 1393-4/1973-4; vol. xxi, Beirut 1985

Tāj al-ʿarūs
Muḥibb al-Dīn al-Sayyid Muḥammad Murtaḍā al-Zabīdī, *Sharḥ al-qāmūs al-musammā Tāj al-ʿarūs min jawāhir al-Qāmūs,* 10 vols., Cairo 1306-7/1889; ed. ʿAbd al-Sattār Aḥmad Faraj et al., 40 vols., Kuwait 1965-2001

Thaʿālibī, *Iʿjāz*
ʿAbd al-Malik b. Muḥammad al-Thaʿālibī, *al-Iʿjāz wa-l-ījāz,* ed. Iskandar Āṣāt, Constantinople 1897; Beirut 1983

Thaʿālibī, *Iqtibās*
ʿAbd al-Malik b. Muḥammad al-Thaʿālibī, *al-Iqtibās min al-Qurʾān al-karīm,* ed. Ibtisām Marhūn al-Ṣaffār and Mujāhid Muṣṭafā Bahjat, 2 vols. in 1, Cairo 1412/1992

Thaʿālibī, *Yatīma*
ʿAbd al-Malik b. Muḥammad al-Thaʿālibī, *Yatīmāt al-dahr fī maḥāsin ahl al-ʿaṣr,* 4 vols., Damascus 1304/1886-7; ed. Muḥammad Muḥyī l-Dīn ʿAbd al-Ḥamīd, 4 vols., Cairo 1375-7/1956-8

Thaʿlabī, *Qiṣaṣ*
Aḥmad b. Muḥammad b. Ibrāhīm al-Thaʿlabī, *Qiṣaṣ al-anbiyāʾ al-musammā bi-ʿArāʾis al-majālis,* Cairo 1322; repr. Beirut 1980

Thaʿlabī-Goldfeld
I. Goldfeld, *Qurʾānic commentary in the eastern Islamic tradition of the first four centuries of the hijra. An annotated edition of the preface to al-Thaʿlabī's "Kitāb al-Kashf wa-l-bayān ʿan Tafsīr al-Qurʾān,"* Acre 1984

Tirmidhī, *Ṣaḥīḥ*
Abū ʿĪsā Muḥammad b. ʿĪsā al-Tirmidhī, *al-Jāmiʿ al-ṣaḥīḥ*, ed. Aḥmad Muḥammad Shākir et al., 5 vols., Cairo 1937-65

Ṭūsī, *Fihrist*
Muḥammad b. al-Ḥasan al-Ṭūsī, *al-Fihrist*, Najaf 1356/1937; Beirut 1983

Ṭūsī, *Tibyān*
Muḥammad b. al-Ḥasan al-Ṭūsī, *al-Tibyān fī tafsīr al-Qurʾān*, intr. Āghā Buzurk al-Ṭihrānī, 10 vols., Najaf 1376-83/1957-63

Tustarī, *Tafsīr*
Sahl b. ʿAbdallāh al-Tustarī, *Tafsīr al-Qurʾān al-ʿaẓīm*, Cairo 1329/1911

ʿUkbarī, *Tibyān*
Abū l-Baqāʾ ʿAbdallāh b. al-Ḥusayn al-ʿUkbarī, *al-Tibyān fī iʿrāb al-Qurʾān*, ed. ʿAlī Muḥammad al-Bajāwī, 2 vols., Cairo 1396/1976

Wagtendonk, *Fasting*
K. Wagtendonk, *Fasting in the Koran*, Leiden 1968

Wāḥidī, *Asbāb*
Abū l-Ḥasan ʿAlī b. Aḥmad al-Nīsābūrī al-Wāḥidī, *Asbāb al-nuzūl*, Cairo 1968

Wāḥidī, *Wasīṭ*
Abū l-Ḥasan ʿAlī b. Aḥmad al-Nīsābūrī al-Wāḥidī, *al-Wasīṭ fī tafsīr al-Qurʾān*, ed. ʿĀdil Aḥmad ʿAbd al-Mawjūd et al., 4 vols., Beirut 1415/1994

Wansbrough, *QS*
J. Wansbrough, *Quranic studies. Sources and methods of scriptural interpretation*, Oxford 1977

Wāqidī, *Maghāzī*
Muḥammad b. ʿUmar al-Wāqidī, *Kitāb al-Maghāzī*, ed. M. Jones, 3 vols., London 1966

Watt-Bell, *Introduction*
W.M. Watt, *Bell's introduction to the Qurʾān*, Edinburgh 1970, 1991

Wensinck, *Concordance*
A.J. Wensinck et al., *Concordance et indices de la tradition musulmane*, 8 vols., Leiden 1936-79; repr. 8 vols. in 4, 1992

Wensinck, *Handbook*
A.J. Wensinck, *A handbook of early Muhammadan tradition*, Leiden 1927

Wild, *Text*
S. Wild (ed.), *The Qurʾān as text*, Leiden 1996

Yaḥyā b. Sallām, *Tafsīr*
Yaḥyā b. Sallām al-Baṣrī, *al-Taṣārīf. Tafsīr al-Qurʾān mimmā shtabahat asmāʾuhu wa-taṣarrafat maʿānīhi*, ed. Hind Shalabī, Tunis 1979

Yaʿqūbī, *Buldān*
Aḥmad b. Abī Yaʿqūb b. Wāḍiḥ al-Yaʿqūbī, *Kitāb al-Buldān*, ed. M.J. de Goeje, Leiden 1892, 1967

Yaʿqūbī, *Taʾrīkh*
Aḥmad b. Abī Yaʿqūb b. Wāḍiḥ al-Yaʿqūbī, *Ibn Wādhih qui dicitur al-Jaʿqubi historiae*, ed. M.T. Houtsma, 2 vols., Leiden 1883; repr. 1969

Yāqūt, *Buldān*
Yāqūt b. ʿAbdallāh al-Ḥamawī, *Muʿjam al-buldān*, ed. F. Wüstenfeld, 6 vols., Leipzig 1863-6; 5 vols., Beirut 1374-6/1955-7; ed. Farīd ʿAbd al-ʿAzīz al-Jundī, 7 vols., Beirut 1990

Yāqūt, *Irshād*
Yāqūt b. ʿAbdallāh al-Ḥamawī, *Irshād al-arīb ilā maʿrifat al-adīb. Muʿjam al-udabāʾ*, ed. D.S. Margoliouth, 7 vols., London and Leiden 1923-6; ed. Iḥsān ʿAbbās, 7 vols., Beirut 1993

Zajjāj, *Maʿānī*
Abū Isḥāq Ibrāhīm b. Muḥammad b. al-Sarī l-Zajjāj, *Maʿānī l-Qurʾān wa-iʿrābuhu*, ed. ʿAbd al-Jalīl ʿAbduh Shalabī, 5 vols., Beirut 1408/1988

Zamakhsharī, *Asās*
Maḥmūd b. ʿUmar al-Zamakhsharī, *Asās al-balāgha*, Beirut 1979

Zamakhsharī, *Kashshāf*
Maḥmūd b. ʿUmar al-Zamakhsharī, *al-*

Kashshāf ʿan ḥaqāʾiq ghawāmiḍ al-tanzīl wa-ʿuyūn al-aqāwīl fī wujūh al-taʾwīl, 4 vols., Beirut 1366/1947; ed. Muḥammad ʿAbd al-Salām Shāhīn, 4 vols., Beirut 1995

Zambaur, *Manuel*
E. de Zambaur, *Manuel de généalogie et de chronologie pour l'histoire de l'Islam*, Hanover 1927; repr. Bad Pyrmont 1955

Zarkashī, *Burhān*
Badr al-Dīn al-Zarkashī, *al-Burhān fī ʿulūm al-Qurʾān*, ed. Muḥammad Abū l-Faḍl Ibrāhīm, 4 vols., Cairo 1957; Beirut 1972; ed. Yūsuf ʿAbd al-Raḥmān al-Marʿashlī et al., 4 vols., Beirut 1994

Zayd b. ʿAlī, *Musnad*
Zayd b. ʿAlī Zayn al-ʿĀbidīn, *Musnad*, ed. Bakr b. Muḥammad ʿĀshūr, 1328/1910; Beirut 1983

Ziriklī, *Aʿlām*
Khayr al-Dīn al-Ziriklī, *al-Aʿlām. Qāmūs tarājim li-ashhar al-rijāl wa-l-nisāʾ min al-ʿArab wa-l-mustaʿribīn wa-l-mustashriqīn*, 10 vols., Damascus 1373-8/1954-9; 8 vols., Beirut 1979

Zubaydī, *Ṭabaqāt*
Abū Bakr Muḥammad b. al-Ḥasan al-Zubaydī, *Ṭabaqāt al-naḥwiyyīn wa-l-lughawiyyīn*, ed. Muḥammad Abū l-Faḍl Ibrāhīm, Cairo 1373/1954

Zubayrī, *Nasab*
Muṣʿab al-Zubayrī, *Nasab Quraysh*, ed. E. Lévi-Provençal, Cairo 1953

Zurqānī, *Sharḥ*
Muḥammad b. ʿAbd al-Bāqī al-Miṣrī al-Mālik, *Sharḥ al-mawāhib al-laduniyya*, ed. Muḥammad ʿAbd al-ʿAzīz al-Khālidī, 12 vols., Beirut 1417/1996

S

[continued]

Sickness see illness and health

Ṣiffīn, Battle of

Battle which took place during the first civil war between the fourth caliph (q.v.), ʿAlī b. Abī Ṭālib (q.v.), and Muʿāwiya b. Abī Sufyān, governor of Syria, in Ṣafar 37/July 657. Muʿāwiya, facing removal from his post by ʿAlī, decided to revive the cause of a recently defeated coalition of Medinan religious elite who had demanded that ʿAlī punish the assassins of his caliphal predecessor, ʿUthmān b. ʿAffān (see ʿuthmān). ʿAlī refused to do so, given his ambivalence about ʿUthmān's assassination (Ṭabarī, *Taʾrīkh,* i, 3275-8; Balādhurī, *Ansāb,* ii, 194-7; Minqarī, *Waqʿa,* 31-3, 58, 82; see politics and the qurʾān; shīʿa). The sources say that after a series of letters exchanged between the two leaders, the battle between ʿAlī's predominantly Iraqi army and Muʿāwiya's largely Syrian supporters was joined on Ṣafar 8/July 26 at Ṣiffīn, located near al-Raqqa along the Euphrates river in northern Iraq (q.v.). The battle lasted, by various accounts, two or three days, by the end of which ʿAlī had gained the advantage. To avert probable defeat, Muʿāwiya, following the advice of ʿAmr b. al-ʿĀṣ, ordered his troops to bear aloft copies of the Qurʾān (or a copy of the Qurʾān) on the ends of their spears — imitating a precedent set by ʿAlī at the earlier Battle of the Camel (Balādhurī, *Ansāb,* ii, 170-1; Ibn Aʿtham, *Futūḥ,* ii, 315) — and calling for arbitration (q.v.) on the basis of the scripture (Minqarī, *Waqʿa,* 476-82; Ṭabarī, *Taʾrīkh,* i, 3329-30 [trans. 79-80]; Balādhurī, *Ansāb,* ii, 226-7).

ʿAlī, initially reluctant to submit to arbitration, eventually agreed under pressure from some of his supporters, including the Iraqi Qurʾān readers (*qurrāʾ;* Minqarī, *Waqʿa,* 489-92; Ṭabarī, *Taʾrīkh,* i, 3330 [trans. 79]; see reciters of the qurʾān). The more reliable of the two versions of the arbitration agreement found in the early sources stipulated that an arbitrator be nominated from each side and that the two meet on neutral territory to resolve the dispute on the basis of the Qurʾān and, should no clear directive be found in the scripture, on the "just, unifying and not divisive sunna" (q.v.; Minqarī, *Waqʿa,* 510; Balādhurī, *Ansāb,* ii, 226, 230; Ṭabarī, *Taʾrīkh,* i, 3336 [trans. 85-6]). Muʿāwiya named ʿAmr b. al-ʿĀṣ as his representative. ʿAlī sought to name one of his equally trusted men but was pressured by influential members of his camp to name

Abū Mūsā l-Ashʿarī, a well-respected but neutral figure (Balādhurī, *Ansāb,* ii, 230; Ṭabarī, *Taʾrīkh,* i, 3333-4 [trans. 82-3]). The arbitrators seem to have met on two occasions — at Dūmat al-Jandal in Shawwāl-Dhū l-Qaʿda 37/April 658 and later at Adhruḥ in Shaʿbān 38/January 659. While the sources sometimes conflate these two meetings and their outcomes, it seems that at the first meeting, the arbitrators agreed that ʿUthmān had been killed unjustly. ʿAmr connected this judgment to Q 17:33: "Whosever is slain unjustly, we have given authority (q.v.) to his heir," and argued for Muʿāwiya's right to the caliphate as the kinsman of ʿUthmān (see MURDER; CORRUPTION; KINSHIP). Abū Mūsā rejected ʿAmr's interpretation and the arbitration was considered a failure by ʿAlī (Minqarī, *Waqʿa,* 541; Masʿūdī, *Murūj/Prairies d'or,* § 1705-8, iii, 145-8 [Fr. trans. 668-71]; Ibn al-Athīr, *Kāmil,* iii, 331). The second meeting at Adhruḥ, apparently not endorsed by ʿAlī, ended with a ruse whereby Abū Mūsā was tricked into deposing ʿAlī, leaving Muʿāwiya as caliph by default (Minqarī, *Waqʿa,* 544-6; Ṭabarī, *Taʾrīkh,* i, 3341-3 [trans. 90-2]). Although the results of this meeting were not widely recognized outside of Syria, ʿAlī faced growing opposition among his supporters over the terms of the arbitration and its outcome. Many dissenters — including some *qurrāʾ* who initially favored arbitration but reversed their opinion upon learning of its terms — had seceded from ʿAlī's camp even prior to the meeting of the arbitrators, claiming that "judgment belongs to God alone" *(lā ḥukma illā lillāhi),* a slogan that echoes the qurʾānic statement *ini l-ḥukmu illā lillāhi* (Q 6:57; 12:40, 67). They also demanded that ʿAlī repent of his submission to a process that placed men in judgment over the Qurʾān (see LAW AND THE QURʾĀN). Many of these secessionists, later referred to as "Khārijīs" (q.v.), permanently broke with ʿAlī after the failure of the arbitration and suffered a devastating military defeat at his hands some months later.

Maria Massi Dakake

Bibliography
Primary: al-Balādhurī, Aḥmad b. Yaḥyā, *Ansāb al-ashrāf,* ed. M. al-Firdaws al-ʿAẓm, 15 vols., Damascus 1996-; Ibn Abī l-Ḥadīd, *Sharḥ Nahj al-balāgha,* ed. M. Abū l-Faḍl Ibrāhīm, 20 vols., Cairo 1959-64; Ibn Aʿtham al-Kūfī, *Kitāb al-Futūḥ,* 7 vols., Hyderabad 1968; Ibn al-Athīr, *Kāmil,* 12 vols., Beirut 1979; Ibn Kathīr, *Bidāya,* ed. ʿA.M. Muʿawwaḍ and ʿĀ.A. ʿAbd al-Mawjūd, 8 vols., Beirut 1994; Khalīfa b. Khayyāṭ, *Taʾrīkh,* ed. A.D. al-ʿUmarī, Najaf 1967; Masʿūdī, *Murūj,* 7 vols., Beirut 1966-79; Fr. trans. Ch. Pellat, *Les prairies d'or,* 5 vols., 1962-97; al-Minqarī, Naṣr b. Muzāḥim, *Waqʿat Ṣiffīn,* ed. ʿA. Hārūn, Cairo 1962; Ṭabarī, *Taʾrīkh,* ed. de Goeje; id., *The history of al-Ṭabarī.* xvii. *The first civil war,* trans. G.R Hawting, Albany 1996; Yaʿqūbī, *Taʾrīkh,* ed. ʿA. Muhannā, 2 vols., Beirut 1993.
Secondary: M. Hinds, The Siffin arbitration agreement, in *JSS* 17 (1972), 93-129; W. Madelung, *Succession to Muḥammad. A study of the early caliphate,* Cambridge 1997; C. Petersen, *ʿAlī and Muʿāwiya in early Arabic traditions,* Copenhagen 1964.

Sight

see VISION AND BLINDNESS; SEEING AND HEARING

Signs

Indications or portents, foreshadowing or confirming something. The concept of sign, one of the most commonly exhibited concepts in the Qurʾān, is expressed mainly by the word *āya* (pl. *āyāt*) in almost four hundred instances and by the word *bayyina* (pl. *bayyināt*) in approximately sixty cases. Several other words also convey the principal idea or some nuances of *āya,* for example: lesson (*ʿibra,* Q 12:111), pattern (*uswa,* Q 60:4), fact, story, discourse (*ḥadīth,*

Q 45:6), example (*mathal,* Q 43:57; see PARABLE), proof (q.v.; *burhān,* Q 4:174), proof (*sulṭān,* Q 30:35), signs (*shaʿāʾir,* Q 22:36), signs (*āthār,* Q 30:50; see GENERATIONS; AIR AND WIND; GEOGRAPHY), sign (*dalīl,* Q 25:45).

The word *āya* (sign) has no root in Arabic and is very probably a loan-word from Syriac or Aramaic (*āthā;* see FOREIGN VOCABULARY) where it indicates not only the ideas of sign and miracle (see MIRACLES; MARVELS), as in biblical and rabbinic Hebrew *(ōth),* but also the notions of argument and proof. (Arab philologists who have tried to find a stem and a form of this word have arrived at different solutions; either the word is derived from *a-w-y* or from *a-y-y* and its form is either *faʿala* or *faʿla* or *fāʿila;* cf. *Lisān al-ʿArab;* see GRAMMAR AND THE QURʾĀN.) The word occurs in pre-Islamic poetry (see POETRY AND POETS) in the meaning of a sign or token and in this meaning it also appears in the Qurʾān (Q 26:128, "as a sign for passers by"). In the Qurʾān, *āya* also often denotes argument and proof. These shades of meaning can be explained in the light of the polemical character of parts of the Qurʾān which are influenced by Muḥammad's struggles with the unbelievers, the Jews and the Christians (see POLEMIC AND POLEMICAL LANGUAGE; BELIEF AND UNBELIEF; JEWS AND JUDAISM; CHRISTIANS AND CHRISTIANITY).

Expressions of signs

The scripture attests to the numerous and diverse signs which exist in the earth (q.v.) and in humankind: "In the earth are signs for those having sure faith (q.v.), and in yourselves; what, do you not see?" (Q 51:20-1; see SEEING AND HEARING; VISION AND BLINDNESS). These signs are so obvious that one cannot ignore them. Being produced by God (Q 6:109; 7:203; 29:50) and only with his permission (Q 13:38; 40:78), such signs can be detected in all spheres of life. Both animate and inanimate objects provide signs (Fakhr al-Dīn al-Rāzī [d. 606/1210] makes a distinction between signs in man, *dalāʾil al-anfus,* and signs in the world, *dalāʾil al-āfāq;* Rāzī, *Tafsīr,* xxv, 111), as in "O my people, this is the she-camel of God, to be a sign for you" (Q 11:64; see CAMEL; ṢĀLIḤ) and "And it is God who sends down out of heaven water (q.v.), and therewith revives the earth after it is dead. Surely in that is a sign for a people who listen" (Q 16:65; cf. 30:24; see HEAVEN AND SKY; HEARING AND DEAFNESS). God's providential design is demonstrated through his acts in nature and in human beings (see NATURE AS SIGNS; GRACE; BLESSING). A typical sign-passage is Q 13:2-3:

> God is he who raised up the heavens without pillars you can see, then he sat himself upon the throne (see THRONE OF GOD); he subjected the sun (q.v.) and the moon (q.v.), each one running to a term stated. He directs the affair; he distinguishes the signs; haply you will have faith in the encounter with your lord (q.v.). It is he who stretched out the earth and set therein firm mountains and rivers, and of every fruit he placed there two kinds, covering the day with the night (see DAY AND NIGHT). Surely in that are signs for a people who reflect (see REFLECTION AND DELIBERATION; AGRICULTURE AND VEGETATION).

Sustenance (q.v.) and dress are given to humankind by God as a sign of his providence:

> Children of Adam! We have sent down on you a garment to cover your shameful parts (see CLOTHING; MODESTY; NUDITY), and adornment *(rīsh);* and the garment of godfearing — that is better; that is one of

God's signs; haply they will remember (Q 7:26; see REMEMBRANCE).

Have they not seen that God spreads out the provision to whom he wills or is sparing [with it]? Surely in that are signs for a people who believe (Q 30:37).

To these signs are added the variety of human languages (see LANGUAGE) and colors (q.v.) and their differentiated activities by night and day (Q 30:22-3). God also intervenes in historical events by punishing wicked peoples; this intervention serves as a sign for those who fear the punishment of the last day (Q 11:102-3; see LAST JUDGMENT; HISTORY AND THE QURʾĀN; CHASTISEMENT AND PUNISHMENT; PUNISHMENT STORIES; REWARD AND PUNISHMENT). In like manner God prevents the enemies [of Muslims] from injuring them (Q 48:20) and he causes some people, especially prophets, to overcome others to prevent their corrupting of the earth (Q 2:251-2; see PROPHETS AND PROPHETHOOD; CORRUPTION). According to the context of Q 3:58, what has happened to the prophets are signs. Mary (q.v.), Jesus' (q.v.) mother, became a sign because of her chastity (q.v.) which caused God to breathe into her something of his spirit (q.v.; Q 21:91).

Functions of signs

Having examined some of the objects which serve as signs, this discussion can turn to the functions of *āyāt*. Most of the signs in scripture have the purpose of calling on humankind to thank God (e.g. Q 16:14; 30:46; 36:73; see GRATITUDE AND INGRATITUDE) and to worship (q.v.) him (cf. Q 10:3). Considering the frequent occurrence of words denoting signs in the Qurʾān (see, for example, the beginning of Q 45 in which the word *āyāt* occurs in almost every verse), it is possible to state that Muḥammad regarded signs as the best means to call people to believe in God and his messenger (q.v.), a means preferable to frightening them with the horrors of the day of judgment. *Āyāt* are miracles done by God for the sake of people. Signs in "ask the Children of Israel (q.v.) how many a clear sign we gave," (Q 2:211) are interpreted to mean the splitting of the Red Sea, and the bringing down of the manna and the quail (see ANIMAL LIFE). The aim of these miracles was to compel the Children of Israel to believe in God, but they refused to believe. Those who deny God's miracles are doomed to suffer God's severe punishment (Q 3:11; 4:56). Miracles also aim at causing people to believe in prophets (Q 58:5); Moses (q.v.) tried to persuade Pharaoh (q.v.) that he had been sent by God (Q 7:103-6). Muhammad's prophecy is not proved directly by *āyāt;* rather it is proved through legitimating his message by *āyāt*. When the message is demonstrated to be genuine, the messenger is a true prophet. Through the use of analogy the Qurʾān attempts to convince people to believe in certain tenets of Islam, such as the resurrection (q.v.). According to Q 2:259, a man passed near a ruined town and asked how shall God give its dead people life. To show this man his power, God put him to death and revived him after one hundred years. The aim of this personal miracle is to show God's ability to resurrect the dead (Ibn Kathīr, *Tafsīr,* i, 558). The miracle here serves as proof based on analogy: just as God put this man to death and then restored him to life, so can he put all people to death and then revive them on the day of judgment (see DEATH AND THE DEAD). Resurrection is also demonstrated through God's creation (q.v.) of the world. If God's ability to create extends to such an enormous act, the more so his ability to revive the dead: "Have they not seen that God who created the heavens and earth, not being wearied by creating them (see

SABBATH), is able to give life to the dead?" (Q 46:33; cf. 75:38-40). Another proof is learned from the rain sent by God. Just as the rain revives the earth, causing plants to sprout, so can God restore the dead to life (cf. Q 35:9).

From the contents and context of Q 3:13 it is obvious that an *āya* is also a lesson *(ʿibra):* There has already been a sign for you in the two companies that met [at the battle of Badr (q.v.)], one company fighting for the sake of God and another unbelieving; [the unbelievers] saw [the Muslims] twice the like of them, as the eye sees, but God supports with his help whom he will. Surely, in that is a lesson for the wise (see WISDOM; IGNORANCE; TEACHING).

The lesson God conveys here is that he can make a few people overcome many. Again God's power and his help for man are proven (see VICTORY; POWER AND IMPOTENCE; TRUST AND PATIENCE). Whereas in Q 2:259, mentioned above, the analogy is to be learned by stages, here the conclusion from the story is directly inferred. That God punishes evil people is a widespread idea throughout the Qurʾān (see GOOD AND EVIL). Sometimes the Qurʾān points out that whoever fears the punishment of the last judgment should take a lesson from God's previous punishments:

Such is the punishment [literally "seizing," *akhdh*] of your lord, when he punishes [the evildoers of] the cities; surely his punishment is painful, terrible. Surely in that is a sign for him who fears the chastisement of the world to come… (Q 11:102-3; see also Q 15:77; 25:37; 26:103, 121, 139, 158, 174, 190; 27:52; 29:35; 34:19).

The lesson to be learned is not only from God's punishment but also from his reward to the righteous: God saved Noah (q.v.) as he did the people and animals that were in Noah's ark (q.v.; e.g. Q 29:15; 54:15). The history of a family such as Joseph (q.v.) and his brothers serves, too, as a lesson (Q 12:7; see also BROTHER AND BROTHERHOOD; BENJAMIN). A lesson can also be learned from a parable (Q 2:266). Sometimes a sign serves as a trial (q.v.) for a people, whether they will believe or not (Q 44:33). Another aim of the signs is to show that God acts for the benefit of humans in many spheres of life such as sustenance or transportation (Q 16:5-18; see VEHICLES). Finally, a sign may function as a metaphor (q.v.), its explanation being given by exegetes (see EXEGESIS OF THE QURʾĀN: CLASSICAL AND MEDIEVAL); good and bad land are similes for the believer and the unbeliever respectively (*Jalālayn,* ad Q 7:58; cf. 10:24).

Reactions to signs

Reactions to signs, proofs and miracles differ — some people believe in them (Q 6:54, 99) while others do not, or they display a negative attitude toward them. Some people are obstinately reluctant to draw conclusions from God's acts aiming at the preservation of the world: "We set up the heaven as a roof well-protected; yet still from our signs they are turning away" (Q 21:32; cf. 6:157; 15:81; 36:46). Refusing to recognize God's signs is regarded by the Qurʾān as the gravest wrongdoing: "And who does greater evil than he who, being reminded of the signs of his lord, turns away from them…" (Q 18:57; 32:22). These rejecters consider signs to be witchcraft: "Yet if they see a sign they turn away, and they say: 'A continuous sorcery'" (Q 54:2; cf. 27:13; 46:7; see MAGIC). In addition, Muḥammad suffered from the mockery (q.v.) of his opponents (see OPPOSITION TO MUḤAMMAD): "Say: 'What, then were you mocking God, and his signs, and his messenger'?" (Q 9:65; cf. 18:56,

106; 30:10; 45:9, 35). The most common example of such negative reactions is that of evildoers who disbelieve in God's signs: "We have sent down to you clear signs, and only the evildoers disbelieve in them" (Q 2:99). Other evildoers (see EVIL DEEDS) are identified with those who killed prophets (Q 3:21; see MURDER; BLOODSHED). In the qur'ānic view, the refusal to recognize God's signs is connected to rejection of his messengers who point to those signs (see SIN, MAJOR AND MINOR; ETHICS AND THE QUR'ĀN). Whoever questions God's existence and power is an evildoer, and vice versa, those who fear (q.v.) God and give alms believe in God's signs (Q 7:156; cf. Birkeland, Interpretation, 13-29; see ALMSGIVING; PIETY). The verb *kadhdhaba* (he accused someone of lying, or discovered someone to be lying, or regarded something as a lie, or denied something; see LIE) is used to indicate another kind of reaction to the signs considered by the Qur'ān as the gravest act (Q 6:21). "(Their way is) like the way of Pharaoh's folk and those before them; they denied the signs..." (Q 8:54; see also Q 5:10, 86, where in both verses *kadhdhaba* comes along with *kafara,* he disbelieved; cf. Q 6:21, 39, 150; 10:95; 7:176-7, 182; 20:56). In Q 6:33 it is emphasized that Muḥammad's opponents, the unbelievers, did not accuse him of lying but they denied *(jaḥada)* God's signs. The verb *jaḥada* and its equivalents, *ankara* and *ẓalama,* appear several times in the qur'ānic text as expressions of the reaction to God's signs (Q 7:9; 11:59; 29:49; 31:32; 40:63, 81; 41:15; 46:26). In two verses the verb *istakbara* (he became haughty) occurs with the verb *kadhdhaba,* as in "Those who regard our signs as lies and display haughtiness (see ARROGANCE; PRIDE) toward them shall be the inhabitants of the fire (q.v.; see also HELL AND HELLFIRE) forever" (Q 7:36 and Q 7:40), and without *kadhdhaba* in other verses (Q 7:133; 10:75; 45:31). In one place the unbelievers' arrogance and mockery are depicted as a deception (Q 10:75). Another kind of negative reaction to the signs is disputation *(jidāl)* which is associated with unbelief: "None but the unbelievers dispute concerning the signs of God..." (Q 40:4; see DEBATE AND DISPUTATION). But the unbelievers have no proof to support their dispute which derives from their arrogance (cf. Q 40:35, 56). In several verses the opponents' disputation is expressed through mockery; they accuse Muḥammad of telling ancient stories (Q 6:25; 8:31; 68:15; 83:13). Twice, the unbelievers are regarded as heedless of the signs (Q 7:136; 10:7). They also defame the signs (Q 41:40) and oppose them (Q 74:16). In sum, the unbelievers express their reaction to God's signs in several ways — denial, mockery, contestation, opposition and heedlessness. As a text characterized, *inter alia,* by polemics, the Qur'ān frequently refers to its opponents, and naturally emphasizes their negative attitude toward the signs.

Signs as linguistic communication

The word *āya,* apart from connoting nonlinguistic communication between God and man (Cf. Izutsu, *God,* 133), also contains the additional meanings of a basic unit or a passage of revelation, namely, linguistic communication (see REVELATION AND INSPIRATION; VERSES). In the Qur'ān itself there is no indication as to the length of these units or passages. Q 2:106 reads: "And for whatever unit of revelation (or passage, *āya*) we abrogate or cast into oblivion, we bring a better or the like of it..." (cf. Q 16:101; 24:1; see ABROGATION). Also when the Qur'ān states that "Those are *āyāt* of the wise scripture" (Q 10:1; 12:1; 13:1, in several beginnings of sūras [q.v.] which constitute a fixed formula), it seems to point to a basic unit of revelation or to passages, although the meaning of signs cannot be ruled out altogether. *Āyāt* are mentioned in the context of interpretation *(taʾwīl),* a fact that alludes to linguistic communication (Q 3:7). Similarly, it is more probable that *āyāt* mean units of revelation when appearing with the verb *talā* (he recited): "The People of the Book (q.v.) are not all alike. [Among them is] a righteous community who recite God's *āyāt* in the hours of the night..." (Q 3:113, and Q 19:73; 33:34; see VIGILS; RECITATION OF THE QURʾĀN). According to some interpreters of the Qurʾān, the plural word *āyāt* also means the Qurʾān itself (e.g. *Jalālayn,* ad Q 27:81; 29:23, 49; 31:7; 34:43). It is, however, possible to conclude from the context of some verses that *āyāt* are identified with the scripture, as in "Our lord, send among them a messenger, one of them, who shall recite to them your signs, and teach them the book (q.v.) and the wisdom..." (Q 2:129; cf. 2:151; 10:15). According to Q 3:2-4, not only is the Qurʾān designated as *āyāt* but also the Hebrew Bible and the New Testament (see TORAH; GOSPELS).

A further extension of the meaning of *āya,* one with legal connotations, is certainly discernible from Q 2:231:

When you divorce women, and they have reached their term, then retain them honorably or set them free honorably; do not retain them by force, to transgress [this law]; whoever does that has wronged himself. Take not God's laws *(āyāt)* in mockery... (see MARRIAGE AND DIVORCE; BOUNDARIES AND PRECEPTS; LAW AND THE QURʾĀN).

The word *āyāt* also occurs in the context of God's giving ordinances (Q 2:187, 221; 24:58, 61). And there is another stylistic phenomenon which proves the notion that *āyāt* may also be used as a term for laws. The formula "in such a manner God makes clear to you his *āyāt* (signs)" is found both after a sentence which speaks about God's graces, namely, his help for and saving of the believers (Q 3:103), and after a sentence which talks about the expiation of oaths (q.v.; Q 5:89; see also BREAKING TRUSTS AND CONTRACTS; CONTRACTS AND ALLIANCES). Just as in the former example *āyāt* seems to mean signs, so in the latter *āyāt* seems to mean laws. Our suggestion is that the above-mentioned formula refers to the sentences which precede it. To sum up, *āyāt* has the following basic meanings: signs, miracles, proofs, basic units or passages of revelations, the Qurʾān and other holy books, and laws.

Structure of sign-passages

Most sign-passages (i.e. groups of sign-verses) are characterized by introductory as well as concluding formulas (see FORM AND STRUCTURE OF THE QURʾĀN). The introductory phrase presents God's acts and the concluding sentence emphasizes the fact that these acts are signs for people who reflect, or understand. Q 13:2-3 reads:

God is he who raised up the heavens without pillars you can see, then he sat himself upon the throne. He subjected the sun and the moon, each running to a term stated. He directs the world (literally: the affair) [and] he makes the signs clear so that you will be certain of the encounter with your lord. It is he who stretched out the earth and set therein firm mountains and rivers, and of every fruit he placed there two kinds, and covered the day with the night. Surely in that are signs for a people who reflect.

In some sign-passages the first words are: "And of his signs..." (Q 30:20). There are, however, sign-passages in which the word "signs" is absent (Q 6:141; 13:12-15; 16:3-8, 80; 30:48-51; 32:4-9). On the whole, the sign-passages have no uniform internal order, except that there might be a special division and a hierarchy of the signs in some places, as indicated by exegetes (see below *Later development*).

Most of the verbs connected with signs indicate the mode of their arrival to humankind: "to bring," *atā bi, ātā, jāʾa bi* (cf. Q 2:106, 211; 43:47), "to bring down or to reveal," *nazzala, anzala* (e.g. Q 6:37; 10:20), "to come," *atā* (e.g. Q 6:158), and "to send," *baʿatha bi, arsala bi* (e.g. Q 10:75; 11:96). Some verbs *(bayyana, ṣarrafa, faṣṣala)* indicate that the signs are explained or made clear (Q 5:75; 6:46; 7:174; 9:11), and some others (e.g. *dhakkara, qaṣṣa)* indicate that the signs are mentioned, told and recited (Q 6:130; 8:31; 10:71; see NARRATIVES). In the light of the polemical character of many parts of the Qurʾān, it seems that these verbs are intended to deliver the message that God's signs not only exist but are brought down to people, they are transmitted by recounting or recitation and, beyond that, they are made clear in order to convince humans of God's power and providence, so that they will worship him. Without the Prophet's explanation, signs remain a "means of non-linguistic communication" (Izutsu, *God,* 133-9), which humanity is obliged to decipher. In addition, there is the phenomenon that some signs are depicted as clear signs (*āyāt bayyināt,* Q 2:99; 3:97; 17:101). We do not know the difference between *āya* and *bayyina* (as a noun), the latter literally meaning "clear sign." In Q 20:133 and Q 7:73, the identification of *āya* with *bayyina* is transparent, and in other places *bayyina* applies to the same sign which is expressed elsewhere by *āya* (Q 7:105). *Āyāt bayyināt,* however, seem never to be applied to natural wonders, rather only to historical or supernatural signs (Rahman, *Major themes,* 72).

Later development

The natural phenomena that appear in the Qurʾān serve Muslim scholars as corroboration for the argument from design. The teleological argument is used to prove the existence of God, his unity, wisdom, and rule of the world through the wonderful design observed in the world (see SOVEREIGNTY; KINGS AND RULERS; GOD AND HIS ATTRIBUTES). Although this argument is found in Greek philosophy (Socrates, Aristotle, the Stoics) and in Christian thought (Augustine [d. 430], Boethius [d. 524] and, in the Muslim era, John of Damascus [d. ca. 143/750], Theodore Abū Qurra [d. ca. 210/825] and ʿAmmār al-Baṣrī [d. ca. 210/825], who very probably influenced Muslim theologians; on the early interactions between Christian and Muslim theologians, see e.g. Griffith, Faith and reason), one cannot ignore the numerous examples of the argument in the Qurʾān (cf. Gwynne, *Logic*), which certainly induced Muslim theologians to employ it. It seems that Muʿtazilī theologians first used the argument from design (Hishām al-Fuwaṭī [d. ca. 229/844], al-Naẓẓām [d. bef. 232/847], al-Jāḥiẓ [d. 255/869]; see MUʿTAZILĪS). This argument then passed to other theologians, whether they belonged to mainstream Muslims, such as al-Muḥāsibī (d. 243/857), to Ashʿarī theologians like al-Ashʿarī (d. 324/935), al-Bāqillānī (d. 403/1013) and al-Ghazālī (d. 505/1111), or to sectarians, such as the Zaydī Imām al-Qāsim b. Ibrāhīm (d. 246/860; see HERESY). Even the Aristotelian philosopher Ibn Rushd (d. 595/1198) states that he prefers arguments for God's existence that appear in the Qurʾān to speculative arguments (see THEOLOGY AND THE QURʾĀN). His form of the teleological argumentation (see COSMOLOGY), the argument from God's providence, which shows that the design of the world aims to benefit people, is one that is much cited in the Qurʾān.

The exegetes of the Qurʾān naturally placed much importance on God's signs and the conclusions derived from them concerning God's power and his rule of the world (Ṭabarī, *Tafsīr,* ad Q 30:24; Ibn Kathīr, *Tafsīr,* ad Q 30:21). Generally, however, al-Ṭabarī (d. 310/923), Ibn Kathīr (d. 774/1373) and other traditionalist exegetes did not investigate sign-passages as a whole, nor did they analyze the inter-connections between signs. Such examinations were carried out by rationalist exegetes such as Fakhr al-Dīn al-Rāzī (d. 606/1210), who divides sign-passages according to their functions, the connections between them, and their hierarchical structure (Rāzī, *Tafsīr,* ad Q 30:22-7). Q 30:22-5 reads:

> And of his signs is the creation of the heavens and earth and the variety of your languages and colors... and of his signs is your slumbering by night, and your seeking by day after his bounty... and of his signs he shows you lightning (see WEATHER), for fear and hope, and that he sends down out of heaven water and he revives the earth with it after it is dead... and of his signs is that the heaven and earth stand [firm] by his command...

Al-Rāzī divides these signs into necessary accidents *(aʿrāḍ lāzima),* namely, accidents which are part of the essence of a thing, and those which are transitory *(aʿrāḍ mufāriqa),* some departing quickly, such as redness of the face as a result of shame, and others slowly, such as youth (cf. Jurjānī, *Taʿrīfāt,* 153-4; see YOUTH AND OLD AGE). First the Qurʾān points out two examples of necessary accidents (the various languages and colors of people), and then two examples of *aʿrāḍ mufāriqa* (sleep at night and the search for means of subsistence during the day; see PAIRS AND PAIRING). God makes the *aʿrāḍ mufāriqa* of the last two verses which deal with heaven and earth come before their *aʿrāḍ lāzima,* for heaven and earth are stable and changes are more marvelous in them than in humankind. Thus, al-Rāzī organizes signs according to their characteristics. Q 30:8 reads: "Have they not reflected on themselves? God did not create the heavens and the earth and what is between them save with the truth...." Al-Rāzī notices that in this verse signs in people *(dalāʾil al-anfus)* precede signs in the heavens and earth *(dalāʾil al-āfāq),* whereas in Q 41:53, "We shall show them our signs in the horizons *(al-āfāq)* and in themselves...," signs in the heavens and earth take precedence. The solution to this contradiction lies in the distinction between the agents of the verbs mentioned in these verses: when the agent is human, the signs stated are easy to perceive, for they are in humans themselves and people cannot ignore them, while the signs which God mentions about the world are more difficult to perceive, for they are remote from humanity. What God mentions last is understood by people first because they progress in knowing God's signs in stages (Rāzī, *Tafsīr,* xxv, 99, ad Q 30:8). Such sophisticated interpretation occurs neither in classical nor in modern exegesis (see EXEGESIS OF THE QURʾĀN: EARLY MODERN AND CONTEMPORARY; PHILOSOPHY AND THE QURʾĀN). Scientific exegesis, which searches for elements and terminology of science in the Qurʾān, does appear in classical texts, but is not as widespread as it has become in the modern era (Jansen, *Interpretation,* 36-8; see SCIENCE AND THE QURʾĀN).

Modern exegetes tend to deal not only with separate words in a verse or with a complete verse but also with whole sign-passages, paraphrasing their ideas and drawing conclusions from them. Q 10:5-6 reads:

It is he who made the sun a radiance, and the moon a light (q.v.), and determined it by stations, that you might know the number of the years and the reckoning. God created that only with the truth, explaining the signs to a people who know. In the alteration of night and day, and what God has created in the heavens and the earth, surely, there are signs for godfearing people.

Muḥammad Rashīd Riḍā (d. 1935), whose interpretation of the Qurʾān follows the teachings of his master, the great Muslim reformist Muḥammad ʿAbduh (d. 1905), states that these two verses direct the Muslim to God's cosmological signs which prove his power to revive the dead and to reward man (cf. Darwaza, *Tafsīr,* vi, 287). According to Rashīd Riḍā, these signs also show God's wisdom and the regular design in creation, and, characteristically of modern exegesis, he points out that they stimulate man to study astronomy, a science which the ancestors favored because of the guidance of the Qurʾān (see PLANETS AND STARS). Furthermore, study of the cosmological signs proves that Islam is a religion based on knowledge (see KNOWLEDGE AND LEARNING) and science *(dīn ʿilmī),* not on blindly following authority (q.v.; *taqlīd*). The scientific discoveries of the secrets of light in this generation prove God's sagacity (Rashīd Riḍā, *Manār,* xi, 301-5). In ʿAbduh's work, the jinn (q.v.) are identified with microbes (Jansen, *Interpretation,* 43). Extensive scientific exegesis *(tafsīr ʿilmī)* is found in Muḥammad Farīd Wajdī's (d. 1940) *al-Muṣḥaf al-mufassar,* "The Qurʾān Interpreted" (Jansen, *Interpretation,* 46-7). A typical modern discussion of sign-passages is found in Sayyid Quṭb's (d. 1966) interpretation of the beginning of Q 30 (vv. 1-32). In his view, sign-passages do not stand apart; there is a close connection between what happens to humans and the natural phenomena, and this is expressed through the notion that God is the source of all things (Quṭb, *Ẓilāl,* vi, 436). The function of the signs is to prompt humans to believe in God (ibid., 448-9). Whoever makes such signs, Quṭb emphatically states, is the same one who sends messengers to humankind, restores people to life, and so on (ibid., 463), as in the second part of the sūra (vv. 33-60).

The notion that all future scientific discoveries are mentioned in the Qurʾān, whether directly or indirectly, is a common modern notion. Muṣṭafā Kamāl Maḥmūd (b. 1921), an Egyptian physician, writer and a qurʾānic exegete, is very fond of scientific exegesis. He finds allusions to recent scientific discoveries in the qurʾānic description of creation (Maḥmūd, *Muḥāwala,* ed. 1970, 51, 60-4; cf. Rippin, *Muslims,* 95-7). He partially accepts Darwin's theory of evolution, claiming that God is responsible for the evolution of the species in stages (Maḥmūd, *Muḥāwala,* ed. 1970, 59-60; ed. 1999, 67-8). Among the various natural phenomena which support the scientific knowledge found in the Qurʾān, he points to the state of the embryo (Q 39:6; Maḥmūd, *Muḥāwala,* ed. 1970, 65-8; see BIOLOGY AS THE CREATION AND STAGES OF LIFE). Some modern exegetes regard the scientific contents of the Qurʾān as proof of the veracity of Muḥammad's prophecy and consequently the truthfulness of the qurʾānic ideas. According to these scholars, the scientific elements attest to a miracle that is even greater than the miracle of the literary supremacy of the Qurʾān (see INIMITABILITY; LANGUAGE AND STYLE OF THE QURʾĀN). The scientific interpretation, however, has not gone unchallenged. Muslim scholars themselves have charged the adherents of scientific exegesis with failing to pay proper attention to the context of the verses discussed, to philological considerations and to the fact that the Qurʾān was addressed to Arabs (q.v.), speaking in their language and informing only of the sciences known in the Prophet's era (see OCCASIONS OF REVELATION; SĪRA AND THE QURʾĀN; PRE-ISLAMIC ARABIA AND THE QURʾĀN). Moreover, they insist that the Qurʾān presents an ethical and religious message (see VIRTUES AND VICES, COMMANDING AND FORBIDDING; ESCHATOLOGY) and that a limited text cannot contain the ever-changing views of scientists in the nineteenth and twentieth centuries (Hussein, Commentaire; Jansen, *Interpretation,* 47-54).

Binyamin Abrahamov

Bibliography
Primary: M.ʿI. Darwaza, *al-Tafsīr al-ḥadīth,* 12 vols., Cairo 1381-3/1962-4; Ibn Kathīr, *Tafsīr,* 7 vols., Beirut 1385/1966, repr. Beirut 1389/1970; al-Jurjānī, ʿAlī b. Muḥammad, *Kitāb al-Taʿrīfāt,* ed. G. Flügel, Leipzig 1847, repr. Beirut 1978; *Lisān al-ʿArab,* 15 vols., Beirut 1955-6; ed. ʿAlī Shīrī, 18 vols., Beirut 1988; Quṭb, *Ẓilāl;* Rashīd Riḍā, *Manār;* Rāzī, *Tafsīr,* 16 vols., Beirut n.d.; Suyūṭī, *Itqān;* Ṭabarī, *Tafsīr,* 12 vols., Cairo 1323-9/1905-11, repr. Beirut 1986-7; Ṭanṭāwī Jawharī, *al-Jawāhir fī tafsīr al-Qurʾān al-mushtamil ʿalā ʿajāʾib badāʾiʿ al-mukawwanāt wa-gharāʾib al-āyāt al-bāhirāt,* 26 vols., Cairo 1350/1930.
Secondary: B. Abrahamov (ed.), *al-Qāsim b. Ibrāhīm on the proof of God's existence, Kitāb al-dalīl al-kabīr,* Leiden 1990; ʿAbd al-Bāqī; A.J. Arberry, *The Koran interpreted,* Oxford 1983; H. Birkeland, The interpretation of surah 107, in *SI* 9 (1958), 13-29; W.A. Graham, "The winds to herald his mercy" and other "signs for those of certain faith," in S.H. Lee, W. Proudfoot and A. Blackwell (eds.), *Faithful imagining. Essays in honor of R.R. Niebuhr,* Atlanta 1995, 19-38; S. Griffith, Faith and reason in Christian Kalām. Theodore Abū Qurrah on discerning the true religion, in S.Kh. Samir and J.S. Nielsen (eds.), *Christian Arabic apologetics during the Abbasid period (750-1258),* Leiden 1994, 1-43; K. Hussein, Le commentaire "scientifique" du Coran. Une innovation absurde, in *MIDEO* 16 (1983), 293-300; Izutsu, *God;* J.J.G. Jansen, *The interpretation of the Qurʾān in modern Egypt,* Leiden 1974; Jeffery, *For. vocab.*; M.K. Maḥmūd, *al-Qurʾān muḥāwala li-fahm ʿaṣrī,* Beirut 1970, Cairo 1999 (rev. ed.); Neuwirth, *Studien;* M.M. Pickthall, *The meaning of the glorious Koran,* New York 1953; M. Radscheit, "Iʿǧāz al-Qurʾān" im Koran, in Wild, *Text,* 113-23; F. Rahman, *Major themes of the Qurʾān,* Chicago 1980; A. Rippin, *Muslims. Their religious beliefs and practices.* ii. *The contemporary period,* London 1993; A. Schimmel, *Deciphering the signs of God. A phenomenological approach to Islam,* Albany 1994; Watt-Bell, *Introduction.*

Sijjīn

see BOOK; HEAVENLY BOOK; ANGEL

Silk

Lustrous fiber produced by insect larvae frequently used in fine materials. The terms *ḥarīr* and *sundus,* "silk," are attested five times in the Qurʾān (Q 22:23, 35:33, 76:12, and 18:31 and 44:53, respectively). These terms appear exclusively in passages dedicated to the description of paradise that, with the fire of the hell promised to the unbelievers, draws a central binary theme in the qurʾānic discourse focused on an eschatological perspective (see PARADISE; HELL AND HELLFIRE; ESCHATOLOGY). Therefore, the luxury of silk constitutes one of the paradigmatic elements of Islamic heavenly ontology (Q 55 and Q 56 provide the most detailed developments on the theme paradise/hell; see PAIRS AND PAIRING). Depictions of the qurʾānic paradise (also called *al-khuld* or *dār al-salām*) rest upon three major categories that reflect the traditional conception of the ideal life-style in Arab society. The first category is obviously the heavenly landscape comprising bucolic gardens (see GARDEN), live springs of pure water (q.v.), rivers of milk (q.v.), honey (q.v.) and wine (q.v.; see also INTOXICANTS; SPRINGS AND FOUNTAINS), and trees producing the most delightful fruits (see AGRICULTURE AND VEGETATION; TREE(S)). The second concerns creatures of two kinds, symbols of beauty and sensual happiness, namely immortal male youngsters and virgins with large eyes *(ḥūrun ʿīnun)* that will accompany and serve the rewarded in the afterlife (e.g. Q 55:72; 56:17, 22; 76:19; see REWARD AND PUNISHMENT; HOURIS). The third category, to which belongs the mention of silk, consists of an array of precious items, accessories and furniture that embellish the heavenly scenery as the most comfortable and beautifully equipped, something humans would dream of enjoying. Two main materials, textile and metalwork, contribute to idyllic images of the paradise that allow an easier comprehension of the ineffable concepts of eternity (q.v.) and life after death (see RESURRECTION; DEATH AND THE DEAD). Clearly referring to the cultural context of the qurʾānic revelation, a recurrent image presents the rewarded as garbed in silk or other fine fabrics and wearing valuable jewels (Q 22:23; see METALS AND MINERALS; PRE-ISLAMIC ARABIA AND THE QURʾĀN). This image appears in radical contrast to that of the ordinary life in this world whose practical necessities require wearing utilitarian clothes made of rough material, as indicated in Q 16:80: "He has given you the skins of beasts for tents, that you may find them light when you shift your quarters, or when you halt; and from their wool and soft fur and hair has he supplied you with furniture and goods for temporary use" (see equally Q 16:81; see HIDES AND FLEECE).

A range of other heavenly works of textile, supposing both an artistic *savoir-faire* and a high material value, complete the rather realistic picture of a wealthy home (see HOUSE, DOMESTIC AND DIVINE). These include cushions carefully disposed upon ordered sets of beds, spread carpets and rugs (Q 88:13-6), some of them displaying rich adornment on the edges (Q 55:54). Occasionally, the Qurʾān describes these accessories as green in color (Q 55:76; see COLORS), adding another degree of heavenly attribute. In addition to costly furnishing and clothing, the righteous will eat and drink delicious food and beverages in silver and gold dishes and cups (Q 43:71; 76:15-16, 21; see CUPS AND VESSELS; FOOD AND DRINK; GOLD). Q 18:31 delivers a kind of representative summary of the whole topic: "Decked shall they be therein with bracelets of gold, and green robes of silk and rich brocade shall they wear, reclining therein on thrones." As a result, in addition to its marvelous and supra-natural aspect, the qurʾānic paradise offers all the advantages of sensible beauty and pleasure, even luxury. Its aesthetic strongly evokes earthly enjoyments. Therefore, the question of interpretation of this eschatological theme raised many discussions among the exegetes, theologians, philosophers and mystics (see EXEGESIS OF THE QURʾĀN: CLASSICAL AND MEDIEVAL; ṢŪFISM AND THE QURʾĀN; PHILOSOPHY AND THE QURʾĀN; Sourdel and Sourdel, *Dictionnaire*, 656-7 [Paradis]). Whereas the traditionists accepted the literal qurʾānic description of paradise, in accordance with the manifest meaning of the text, the Muʿtazilīs (q.v.) did not accept certain aspects of it that challenge reason (see INTELLECT). The latter interpreted these passages at a second level of meaning, attributing to them a second signification (see POLYSEMY). Similarly, the philosophers understood the promised delights as a metaphorical or allegorical proposition, fully comprehensible only by the wise and knowledgeable (see METAPHOR; LITERARY STRUCTURES OF THE QURʾĀN) while maintaining that the colorful qurʾānic narrative is intended chiefly for the common people. The Ashʿarīs stand between these two opposing trends, arguing that the heavenly enjoyments belong to another order, although these enjoyments do display features that are analogous to earthly ones. The Ṣūfīs also found in these verses allegorical signification but without rejecting the literal meaning; they consider the Qurʾān a cognitive construction with multiple layers. Some other theologians, like al-Ghazālī (d. 505/1111), proposed an alternative to these various ideas, asserting that the believer himself should interpret the nature of the ultimate reward according to his own intellectual faculties and spiritual qualities.

Silk became an important part of Islamic culture that developed both the arts of textile fabrication and the economy linked to them. The social and political context of Islam in the middle ages, with sumptuous courts flourishing in the great cities of the Muslim empire and a wide network of trade roads stretching from the Atlantic ocean to India, central and eastern Asia, fostered the manufacture and sale of precious objects in general, and silk items in particular (Sourdel and Sourdel, *Dictionnaire*, 535-7 [Marchandes, activités]). The ancient trans-Asian trading corridor, known as "the silk road," which was revived in the seventh/thirteenth century under the Mongol empire, stimulated the trade of this fine material through commercial centers populated by Muslim merchants who were spread across the whole landmass. Silk was used to make lavish court robes in officially controlled workshops designated by the Persian noun *ṭirāz*, located in palaces (Sourdel and Sourdel, *Dictionnaire*, 806, Ṭirāz). These luxurious garments were distributed as honorary gifts during princely ceremonies. Silk was also, as it still is, a component of particularly fine carpets and rugs of the Islamic world (see MATERIAL CULTURE AND THE QURʾĀN).

V. Gonzalez

Bibliography
Primary: Bukhārī, *Ṣaḥīḥ;* al-Ghazālī, Abū Ḥāmid Muḥammad b. Muḥammad, *al-Munqidh min al-ḍalāl*, Damascus 1956; Ibn al-ʿArabī, *Tafsīr*, 2 vols., Beirut 1978; Ibn al-Jawzī, *Funūn;* Ṭabarī, *Tafsīr*.
Secondary: E. Ashtor, *Levant trade in the later middle ages*, Princeton 1983; Böwering, *Mystical;* K.A.C. Creswell, *A bibliography of the architecture, arts and crafts of Islam to 1st Jan 1960*, Cairo 1961, and suppl.; Gardet and Anawati, *Introduction;* Gimaret, *Jubbāʾī;* G.E. von Grunebaum, *Themes in medieval Arabic literature*, London 1981; M. Lombard, *Les textiles dans le monde musulman*, Paris/The Hague 1978; Mir, *Dictionary;* Nwyia, *Exégèse;* D.S. Richards (ed.), *Islam and the trade of Asia*, Oxford 1970; S. Quṭb, *al-Taṣwīr al-fannī fī l-Qurʾān*, Cairo 1989; ʿA. Shalaq, *al-ʿAql fī l-turāth al-jamālī ʿinda l-aʿrāb*, Beirut 1985 (esp. "al-Jamāl wa-l-ḥusn fī l-Qurʾān" and "al-Jamāl fī l-ḥadīth al-nabawī"); D. Sourdel and J. Sourdel, *Dictionnaire historique de l'Islam*, Paris 1996.

Silliness see MOCKERY; LAUGHTER

Silver see GOLD; METALS AND MINERALS

Simile

The comparison of two things, made explicit — and distinguished from metaphor (q.v.) — by the use of "like" or "as." "Zayd fought like a lion" is a simile. In Arabic rhetoric (see ARABIC LANGUAGE; RHETORIC AND THE QURʾĀN; LITERARY STRUCTURES OF THE QURʾĀN), "simile" or *tashbīh* has the same general sense, and the same general distinction is made between simile and metaphor *(istiʿāra)*. The "like" or "as" in the simile is usually made with the particle *ka*, though a locution using the noun *mathal* may substitute. Early works on rhetoric placed great emphasis on simile; al-Marzubānī (d. 384/994) in *al-Muwashsha* made simile one of the "four pillars of poetry" (see van Gelder, *Tashbīh;* see POETRY AND POETS). Not surprisingly, proponents of the doctrine of the inimitability (q.v.) of the Qurʾān, like al-Rummānī (d. 384/994) and al-Bāqillānī (d. 403/1013), listed its excellent similes among the rhetorical qualities that make it inimitable. Al-Bāqillānī (*Iʿjāz*, 263-8) compared them favorably with the outstanding similes found in poets like Imruʾ al-Qays and Bashshār b. Burd. From a rhetorical standpoint, the interest in qurʾānic simile culminates in the work of Ibn Nāqiyā (d. 485/1092) entitled *al-Jumān fī tashbīhāt al-Qurʾān*.

Although similes are common in the Qurʾān, the word *tashbīh* is not found there. The term *mathal*, however, sometimes clearly means "simile." At the same time, it must be said that *mathal* is also used to mean short narrative passages that we would be more likely to call "parables," and it seems no clear distinction is made between these two forms by the Qurʾān, nor, for that matter, by some of the rhetoricians (see PARABLE). They are taken to be the same sort of rhetorical device, *mathal*. Perhaps that word is best rendered by the similarly comprehensive term "analogy." Two passages show this. In Q 56:22-3 the plural form, *amthāl*, introduces a simile: "The houris (q.v.) whose eyes are like hidden pearls" *(wa-ḥūrun ʿīnun ka-amthāli l-luʾluʾi l-maknūni)*, whereas Q 18:32-45, which is also termed a *mathal*, clearly exceeds the bounds of what is usually called simile: "Coin for them an analogy *(wa-ḍrib lahum mathalan)* of two men, unto one of whom we had assigned two gardens of grapes and we had surrounded both with date-palms and put between them tillage (see GARDEN; DATE PALM; AGRICULTURE AND VEGETATION).…" It goes on to relate a parable about two farmers, one pious, the other disdainful and proud; as one would expect, the former is rewarded and the latter punished (see REWARD AND PUNISHMENT; PRIDE; INSOLENCE AND OBSTINACY; PIETY).

Uses and examples

In the Qurʾān the simile is often made simply with *ka:* Q 7:179 "Those are like cattle" *(ūlāʾika ka-l-anʿām)* but quite commonly a qurʾānic simile is made with a characteristic pleonasm, *ka-mathal*. As Ibn Nāqiyā shows through numerous examples, qurʾānic similes make use of the same imagery found in Arabic poetry, both pre-Islamic and later (see SYMBOLIC IMAGERY). The first simile (Q 2:17), using the pleonasm *ka-mathal*, compares the hypocrites (q.v.; *al-munāfiqūn;* see HYPOCRITES AND HYPOCRISY) to someone who blunders in the dark (see DARKNESS) after having briefly enjoyed the light (q.v.) of a fire (q.v.): "Their likeness is the likeness of one who lit a fire *(mathaluhum ka-mathali lladhī istawqada nāran)*, and when it illuminated his surroundings, God took away their fire and left them in darkness. They do not see (see VISION AND BLINDNESS)." This simile is soon followed by another: "Or like the rain clouds in the sky with darkness and thunder and lightning in it (see WEATHER), they put their fingers in their ears against the thunderbolts" (Q 2:19; see HEARING AND DEAFNESS; SEEING AND HEARING).

Aspects of God's creation (q.v.) provoke a number of similes. Q 36:39, "And for the moon (q.v.) we have devised stations until it returns like an old, withered palm stalk," i.e. curved and small; Q 55:14, "He created man from clay (q.v.) like crockery"; Q 55:24, "His are ships (q.v.) that sail on the sea like mountains." Heaven and hell (see HELL AND HELLFIRE) are the subject of colorful similes. The houris of paradise (q.v.), for example, are described thus: "And with them are ones who lower their eyes, pure as the hidden eggs [of ostriches]" (Q 37:48-9). Likewise, the painful features of hell are also described through similes. The liquid given to the damned is like molten lead (see FOOD AND DRINK; HOT AND

COLD): Q 18:29 "And if they call for help, they will be given water like molten lead scalding their faces, an evil drink."

A fairly limited number of peoples, places and events probably account for most of the similes in the Qurʾān. Recourse to simile is especially frequent in the case of various "enemies (q.v.) of God" *(aʿdāʾ Allāh),* most prominently the unbelievers *(al-kāfirūn;* see BELIEF AND UNBELIEF; GRATITUDE AND INGRATITUDE), the polytheists *(al-mushrikūn;* see POLYTHEISM AND ATHEISM) and the aforementioned hypocrites. Q 7:176 compares an unbeliever to a dog (q.v.): "He is like the dog, if you chase him away, he pants, and if you leave him alone, he pants." Two memorable similes compare the futile acts of unbelievers to ashes (q.v.) and to a mirage (see also TRANSITORINESS). Q 14:18: "Those who disbelieve in their lord (q.v.), their deeds are like ashes which the winds blow on a stormy day" (see GOOD DEEDS; EVIL DEEDS). And Q 24:39: "Those who disbelieve, their deeds are like a mirage in a desert. Someone thirsty reckons it to be water (q.v.) until he reaches it and finds nothing in it."

Q 13:14 tells us that the polytheist who prays to idols (see IDOLS AND IMAGES) is "like a man who stretches his hands to water for the water to come to it, but the water does not come." Q 29:41 compares the refuge the polytheist seeks in his idols to a spider (q.v.) web: "Those who take other protectors besides God (see CLIENTS AND CLIENTAGE; PROTECTION) are like the spider who takes a house — truly the spider's house is the flimsiest of houses!" Q 63:4 compares the hypocrites to blocks of wood: "And when you see them, their persons please you, and if they speak you listen to what they say. [Yet] they are like blocks of wood propped against each other."

Two particular events, judgment day (see LAST JUDGMENT) and the destruction of wicked peoples (see PUNISHMENT STORIES; CHASTISEMENT AND PUNISHMENT), are frequent subjects of similes, e.g. the annihilation of the people of ʿĀd (q.v.) in Q 54:19-20: "We sent upon them a roaring wind (see AIR AND WIND) on a day of unrelenting calamity which snatched them away as though they were the trunks of uprooted palm trees." Q 69:7 says that the same people after their destruction seemed "as though they were the hollow trunks of palm trees." Q 55:37 describes the appearance of the sky on judgment day (see APOCALYPSE): "And when the skies are split open, they will be red like stained leather." Q 70:8-9 has: "A day when the sky will be like molten brass and the mountains will be like tufts of wool." Q 101:4 describes the commotion of the resurrected people (see RESURRECTION) thus: "... a day when the people will be like moths scattered about."

In sum, similes vary greatly in tone, some are majestic, some homespun — as Q 2:26 says, "God does not disdain to make a similitude of a gnat" *(inna llāha lā yastaḥyi an yaḍriba mathalan mā baʿūḍatan).* Sometimes a sardonic tone is struck (see LANGUAGE AND STYLE OF THE QURʾĀN). A memorable simile in Q 62:5 concerns Jews (see JEWS AND JUDAISM) and the Torah (q.v.): "The likeness of those who were given the Torah to carry and then ignored it is that of a donkey carrying books *(asfār).*"

In addition to their illustrative, semantic role, similes often seem to have a rhetorical, emphatic role in the organization of qurʾānic discourse. Similes not infrequently open or close a subsection of a sūra (q.v.; see also FORM AND STRUCTURE OF THE QURʾĀN). For example, the rather ordinary simile in Q 11:24 which compares believers and unbelievers to the seeing and the blind, respectively, is followed immediately by stories of the prophets (see PROPHETS

AND PROPHETHOOD) Noah (q.v.), Hūd (q.v.) and Ṣāliḥ (q.v.), and the "vanished peoples" to whom they were sent — the heedless people whom God destroyed. Similarly, the famous or infamous comparison of Torah-bearers just cited, Q 62:5, introduces a discussion of the Jews. The similes in Q 54:20, 57:20, 69:7 and 105:5 offer tart summations of the preceding passages.

The Qurʾān, in its characteristically self-conscious way, tells us that the simile is one of God's favored rhetorical devices for educating people (see KNOWLEDGE AND LEARNING; TEACHING; INTELLECT): *wa-la-qad ṣarrafnā fī hādhā l-qurʾāni lil-nāsi min kulli mathalin,* "We have put in this Qurʾān every sort of similitude for people" (Q 18:54) and *wa-la-qad ḍarabnā lil-nāsi fī hādhā l-qurʾāni min kulli mathalin laʿallahum yatadhakkarūna,* "We have coined for people in this Qurʾān every kind of similitude. Perhaps they will take heed" (Q 39:27; see WARNING). Indeed, the Qurʾān even goes so far as to use simile to comment on simile/analogy itself. Interestingly enough, the chief characteristic of good rhetoric is stability, that of bad rhetoric instability:

> Have you not seen how God has made an analogy? A good word is like a good tree (see TREES). Its roots are firm and its branches are in heaven. It gives its fruit in every season with its lord's permission. God coins similes for people that they may reflect. The analogy of a bad word is with a bad tree, uprooted from the earth, possessing no stability (Q 14:24-6).

Commentators on simile

Commentators devote considerable attention to these and other similes (see EXEGESIS OF THE QURʾĀN: CLASSICAL AND MEDIEVAL). Often their concern is simply to elucidate the obscurity of the simile. For example, in Q 2:17 it is the free mixture of singular and plural pronouns referring to the same party; while in Q 2:19 the entire basis of the simile seems at first confused since, as one reads, it becomes apparent that the hypocrites are not being compared to the rain clouds, despite *ka-ṣayyib,* but rather to people frightened by a thunderstorm.

As might be expected, commentators, depending on their outlook and interests, offer a wide range of interpretations of such similes. To take the example of Q 14:24-6 cited above, al-Ṭabarī (d. 310/923) says, "Interpreters differ on the meaning of 'a good word' *(kalima ṭayyiba).* Some of them say it is the faith (q.v.) of the believer" (*Tafsīr,* xiii, 135; see also SPEECH; WORD OF GOD). He goes on to say that some specifically equate it with the *shahādat lā illāha illā llāh,* it being firm *(thābit),* meaning the *shahāda* is firmly fixed in the heart of the believer (see WITNESS TO FAITH). A very early exegete, Mujāhid (d. 104/722), tells us that the good tree is a date palm. Others say a good word means the believer himself who is on earth (q.v.) and who works and speaks on earth and so his deeds and his speech reach heaven while he is still on earth. Yet others say the tree in this simile is a tree in heaven but al-Ṭabarī considers it more likely to be a date palm.

Al-Zamakhsharī (d. 538/1144), a Muʿtazilī (see MUʿTAZILA), tells us that "good word" means the word *tawḥīd,* the oneness and unity of God (see GOD AND HIS ATTRIBUTES). Al-Rāzī (d. 606/1210), who rejects the necessity of the tree being a date palm, devotes four and a half pages to explicating the "tree" and its four attributes, its goodness, its firm roots, its lofty branches, and its constant supply of fruit.

On the other hand, we learn from the Shīʿī commentary of al-Kāshī (d. ca. 910/

1505) that the imām (q.v.) Jaʿfar al-Ṣādiq (d. 148/765) said of the good tree: "The Messenger of God is its root, the Prince of the Believers (ʿAlī) is its trunk, the imāms among the descendants of both are its branches, the knowledge of the imāms constitutes its fruit" (Gätje, *Qurʾān,* 243). Not surprisingly, al-Kāshī tells us that the bad tree is the Umayyads (see SHĪʿISM AND THE QURʾĀN; POLITICS AND THE QURʾĀN; ʿALĪ B. ABĪ ṬĀLIB).

Two other similes also address the topic of figurative language in the Qurʾān. The first is Q 2:26, mentioned above, "Verily, God does not disdain to make an analogy with a gnat..." This al-Rāzī tells us is meant as a rebuke to the unbelievers who had falsely claimed that mention of such humble creatures as the bee, the fly, the spider and the ant was unworthy of divine discourse (see ANIMAL LIFE). Wrong, al-Rāzī says, because God has created both great and humble things,

> and the little weighs upon him no less than the big, and the great is no more difficult for him than the small... and it is perfectly apposite to mention flies when God wishes to show how ugly is the polytheists' worship of idols... or to make an analogy with a spider web in order to show how trifling and flimsy their religion is (Rāzī, *Tafsīr,* ii, 134-5).

The other simile, in Q 13:17, is yet more complicated since it encloses one simile within another:

> He sent down water from the sky and the river beds *(awdiya)* flowed with it. But the flood carried away the scum floating on its surface — and like it is the scum which comes from that which they heat with fire seeking to make jewelry and tools — likewise, God shows what is true and what is false. The scum is cast away with distaste, while what benefits people remains on this earth.

Al-Ṭabarī writes that this is an analogy that God makes with truth (q.v.) and falsehood (see ASTRAY; IGNORANCE; LIE), with faith (q.v.) and unbelief. God is saying that the similarity of the truth in its permanence and of error (q.v.) in its evanescence is like the water which God sends down from the sky to the earth. The *wādīs* flow with it, the large ones with large quantities and the small ones with small quantities. The flood carries a swelling scum or foam, and this is one of two analogies pertaining to truth and falsehood. The truth is like the water (q.v.) which remains and which God has sent, while the foam which is of no benefit is falsehood. The other analogy — "and like it is the scum which comes from that which they heat with fire seeking to make jewelry and tools" — is the analogy of truth and falsehood with gold (q.v.) and silver and brass and lead and iron (see METALS AND MINERALS) from which people obtain benefits (see GRACE; BLESSING), while falsehood is like the scum which goes away without being of any benefit while the pure gold and silver remain. Likewise, God compares faith and unbelief, the futility of unbelief and the failure of the unbeliever being a punishment, while faith is that with lasting benefit (Ṭabarī, *Tafsīr,* xiii, 90). Al-Rāzī sharpens the analogy making the rain the Qurʾān and the *wādīs* the hearts of believers (see HEART), which according to their capacities contain more or less of the truth, while the foam and scum that are carried away and vanish are the doubts and obscurities (see UNCERTAINTY) that will vanish in the hereafter when only the truth will remain (Rāzī, *Tafsīr,* xix, 34-5; see also PAIRS AND PAIRING).

Probably the most well-known qurʾānic simile, and also one of the most commented on, is the so-called Light Verse (Q 24:35). This verse begins with a metaphor, "God is the light (q.v.) of heaven (see HEAVENS AND SKY; PLANETS AND STARS) and earth," but then quickly switches to simile,

the likeness of his light is like a niche which holds a lamp (q.v.). The lamp is in a glass which shines like a pearl-like star. It is kindled from a blessed tree, an olive neither of the east nor the west whose oil would almost glow forth itself though no fire touched it. Light upon light. God guides to his light whom he wills. God makes analogies for people. God knows all things.

Al-Ṭabarī, al-Zamakhsharī and al-Rāzī devote considerable space to mapping out the various parts of this elaborate simile, and al-Ghazālī (d. 505/1111) writes an entire book about it, *Mishkāt al-anwār,* drawing an analogy between the five elements of the simile: the niche, the glass, the lamp, the tree and the oil, and the senses, the imagination, the intellect, language, and prophecy. (For more on these interpretations, see METAPHOR.)

Similes, with the uncertainties of interpretation, could also be the topics of theological debate (see THEOLOGY AND THE QURʾĀN). One such exchange took place between the governor of Baghdād and Ibn Ḥanbal (d. 241/855) during the inquisition (q.v.; *miḥna*) on the issue of the createdness of the Qurʾān (q.v.):

Governor: Does not God say, 'We have made it an Arabic (see ARABIC LANGUAGE) Qurʾān' (Q 43:3). How could it be made without being *created?*
Ibn Ḥanbal: But God says, 'and He *made* them like green blades devoured...' (Q 105:5; see GRASSES). Does that mean He *created* them [like green blades devoured]? (Cook, *Koran,* 110).

More broadly, it can be said that just as there are theological dimensions to metaphor — whence the hasty insistence of commentators to assure us that "God is the light" must be understood as meaning "He is the possessor of light" (Zamakhsharī, *Kashshāf,* ad Q 24:35) — even so the simile has theological dimensions. For the notion of similitude in relation to God must also be placed in the context of the Qurʾān's insistence on the absolute oneness and uniqueness of God and the impossibility of likening anyone or anything to him (see ANTHROPOMORPHISM). Thus, Q 42:11, *laysa ka-mithlihi shayʾ*, "There is nothing like him." In this context, it can be seen that similitude is a definitive notion in the qurʾānic universe; similitude is a common quality of God's creation but since similarity requires at least two objects, similitude is a quality that is found *only* in his creation. This is reflected in theological debate about anthropomorphism in which the opposed terms *tashbīh/tanzīh* are employed. In such debates *tashbīh* is the negative term which denotes anthropomorphism.

Daniel Beaumont

Bibliography
Primary: Bāqillānī, *Iʿjāz;* al-Ghazālī, Abū Ḥāmid Muḥammad b. Muḥammad, *Mishkāt al-anwār,* Cairo 1964; trans. W.H.T. Gairdner, *al-Ghazzali's* Mishkāt al-Anwār, Lahore 1952; Ibn Nāqiyā, Abū l-Qāsim ʿAbd al-Bāqī b. Muḥammad, *al-Jumān fī l-tashbīhāt al-Qurʾān,* Alexandria 1974; Rāzī, *Tafsīr,* Beirut 1981; Ṭabarī, *Tafsīr,* Cairo 1987; Zamakhsharī, *Kashshāf,* Beirut 1995.
Secondary: M. Cook, *The Koran. A very short introduction,* Oxford 2000; H. Gätje, *The Qurʾān and its exegesis,* trans. A.T. Welch, London 1976; G.J.H. van Gelder, Tashbīh (a), in *EI²*, x, 341; Pickthall, *Koran.*

Similitude see PARABLE

Sin, Major and Minor

Greater and lesser transgressions of the law of God. The Qurʾān promises that God will forgive minor sins if human beings abstain from the major ones (Q 4:31; 53:31-2; see FORGIVENESS). The most common characterization of "major" sins in exegesis and theology is *kabāʾir* (sing. *kabīra;* literally the "big ones"), a term that occurs in this sense in the Qurʾān (cf. Q 4:31; 42:37; 53:32). A common theological characterization of "minor" sins is *ṣaghāʾir* (sing. *ṣaghīra,* as in Q 18:49; see THEOLOGY AND THE QURʾĀN; EXEGESIS OF THE QURʾĀN: CLASSICAL AND MEDIEVAL). All deeds, major and minor, are recorded, and their register *(kitāb)* is to be given to each individual on the day of judgment (see LAST JUDGMENT; HEAVENLY BOOK; GOOD DEEDS; EVIL DEEDS), much to the consternation of the sinners (*mujrimīn,* Q 18:49; cf. 54:52-3; see REWARD AND PUNISHMENT).

Terms designating "sin" in the Qurʾān's vocabulary include: *dhanb* (pl. *dhunūb;* e.g. Q 3:11, 16, 193; 8:54; 12:29; 67:11); *fāḥisha* (and other terms from the same Arabic root, i.e. *f-ḥ-sh;* e.g. Q 2:169; 4:22; 12:24; 17:32; 27:54); *ḥaraj* (e.g. Q 9:91; 48:17); *ithm* (e.g. Q 2:173, 181-2, 219; 4:20, 48, 50, 112; 33:58; 42:37; 49:12); *junāḥ* (Q 2:198, 235; 4:102; 33:51); *jurm* (in the form of various derivatives from the root *j-r-m;* e.g. Q 6:147; 7:40; 9:66; 10:17; 11:35; 18:49; 45:31; 83:29); *khaṭīʾa* (and terms derived from the same root, *kh-ṭ-ʾ;* Q 2:81; 4:112; 12:97; 17:31; 69:9; 71:25); *lamam* (Q 53:32); *maʿṣiya* (pl. *maʿāṣī;* cf. Q 58:8-9); and *sayyiʾa* (pl. *sayyiʾāt;* Q 3:193; 4:31; 7:153; 29:7). Whether a particular term denotes a major or a minor sin is often not clear from the Qurʾān itself and the same term might be used to denote major or minor sins. Thus the term *sayyiʾa* occurs in Q 4:31 in the sense of a minor infraction (also in Q 3:193) but elsewhere (as in Q 7:153; 35:43) it refers to evil deeds of a graver kind (cf. Dāmaghānī, *Wujūh,* i, 423f., s.v. *al-sayyiʾāt;* also Zamakhsharī, *Kashshāf,* i, 159, ad Q 2:81, where *sayyiʾa* is glossed as *kabīra min al-kabāʾir*). Many commentators do, however, consider terms like *dhanb* and *ithm* (as well as *maʿṣiya,* a common gloss for *ithm:* cf. Ṭabarī, *Tafsīr,* v, 476, ad Q 7:33) to refer to major sins and understand *lamam, sayyiʾa* and *khaṭīʾa* to mean minor sins. Irrespective of the actual terms used, few commentators deny that there is in fact a distinction to be made between major and minor sins (cf. Haytamī, *Zawājir,* i, 11f.); precisely which sins belong in what category is, however, a matter of great uncertainty.

Definitions

Ibn ʿAbbās (d. ca. 68/687), a major early authority in exegetical matters, is reported to have defined the *kabīra* as "every sin that God has stamped with fire (q.v.), [his] displeasure, [his] curse (q.v.), or with [the threat of his] punishment" (Ṭabarī, *Tafsīr,* iv, 44, ad Q 4:31 [no. 9213]). More vaguely, yet in underscoring the sense of sin as transgression, he held "everything in which God is disobeyed [to be] a major sin" (ibid., no. 9211; see DISOBEDIENCE). Other early definitions related major sins not just to acts for which God has promised hell (see HELL AND HELLFIRE) but also those for which the *ḥudūd,* or the legal punishments explicitly prescribed by the Qurʾān and the sunna (q.v.), are to be executed (cf. ibid., no. 9219; see CHASTISEMENT AND PUNISHMENT; LAW AND THE QURʾĀN). Such views were elaborated on and systematized in works specifically devoted to cataloguing major sins. Shams al-Dīn al-Dhahabī (d. 748/1348), the author of one such book, defines major sins as anything "in regard to which there is a *ḥadd* in this world, such as murder (q.v.), adultery, and theft (q.v.); or about which there is a threat of [God's] anger (q.v.) and punishment in the hereafter; as well as anything whose perpetrator has been cursed by our Prophet" (Dhahabī, *Kabāʾir,* 6; see ADULTERY AND FORNICATION; BLOODSHED). Ibn Ḥajar al-Haytamī (d. 974/1567), whose dissatisfaction with al-Dhahabī's book led him to write what became one of the most influential works on the subject, gives a broad sampling of both overlapping and alternative views on how to define major sins. Inter alia, the *kabāʾir* are sins that have been expressly forbidden (q.v.) in the Qurʾān and the sunna or accompanied with dire warnings in these foundational texts; acts that entail the *ḥadd*-penalties; sins that result in a loss of one's legal and public standing *(ʿadāla),* since they suggest a lack of concern with conformity to religious norms; and, indeed, sins that become "major" precisely because they are committed without a sense of fear (q.v.) or remorse (Haytamī, *Zawājir,* i, 12-17; ii, 425-7; see REPENTANCE AND PENANCE).

Others saw aspects of greater or lesser gravity as inhering in almost all sins. According to al-Ḥalīmī (d. 403/1012), a minor sin can become a major sin because of the context *(qarīna)* in which it is committed just as a major sin can, in turn, become abominable *(fāḥisha)* by the circumstances attending upon it. Thus, unlawful homicide is a major sin, but to murder a relative (see KINSHIP; FAMILY), for instance, or to do so in the sacred precincts (q.v.; of Mecca [q.v.] and Medina [q.v.]) make it the more abominable because it is not just the sanctity of the victim's life but also other sacred boundaries that have been violated (see SACRED AND PROFANE). To steal some paltry object would be a minor sin, not subject to the legal penalty; but this becomes a major sin when the victim of such theft is so poor as not to be able to dispense even with such an object (Ḥalīmī, *Minhāj,* i, 396-400; paraphrased in Ibn Ḥajar, *Fatḥ,* xii, 227f.; see POVERTY AND THE POOR). Al-Ḥalīmī thought that the only sin that does not admit of degrees of gravity is *kufr* — disbelief in God (see BELIEF AND UNBELIEF; GRATITUDE AND INGRATITUDE) — though Ibn Ḥajar al-ʿAsqalānī (d. 852/1449; *Fatḥ,* xii, 227) suggests in his rejoinder that this cardinal sin, too, can be classified according to its degrees of abomination.

In the end, as al-Haytamī and others recognized, the various definitions of major sin are mere "approximations" to the idea, which itself remains elusive. So, too, therefore, does the question of the *number* of sins that might be thought of as "major" — with estimates often ranging from four to seven hundred (Haytamī, *Zawājir,* i, 18). Al-Dhahabī's work on the subject gives brief accounts of seventy major sins; al-Haytamī describes no less than 476 major sins, which he proceeds to divide between the "interior" and the "exterior." Even as they acknowledged the distinction between major and minor sins, the primary interest of those concerned with such matters has tended to be with the major sins, usually leaving the minor ones as the subject of dire warnings about taking them lightly. (Some, like Ibn Nujaym [d. 970/1563], did however concern themselves explicitly with listing both major and minor sins.)

Sins in the Qurʾān's enumeration

Without providing any clear ranking of sins, the Qurʾān does not leave any doubt about what it considers to be the worst of them: the associating of anything or anyone with God (*shirk;* see POLYTHEISM AND ATHEISM), a "great sin" *(ithm ʿaẓīm)* that God will not forgive though he might forgive everything else (Q 4:48). Q 17:23-38, in cataloguing a number of God's commands, mentions several acts that are to be avoided for "their sinfulness *(sayyi'uhu)* is abhorrent to your lord" (q.v.; Q 17:38). In addition to *shirk*, some of the sins that are mentioned as such or are easily derivable from this list include: insolence towards one's parents (q.v.; see also INSOLENCE AND OBSTINACY); wastefulness as well as miserliness; the killing of one's children (q.v.) for fear of impoverishment (a reference to a pre-Islamic Arabian practice characterized here as a "great wrong" *[khiṭ'an kabīra]*: Q 17:31; see INFANTICIDE); wrongful murder of other sorts; fornication (described here as "an abomination and an evil way" *[fāḥisha wa-sā'a sabīlan]*: Q 17:32); usurping the property (q.v.) of orphans (q.v.); dishonesty in business transactions (see ECONOMICS; TRADE AND COMMERCE); saying things of which one has no knowledge (see IGNORANCE; KNOWLEDGE AND LEARNING); and haughtiness (see PRIDE; ARROGANCE). (Also cf. Izutsu, *Concepts*, 228; for shorter lists, see, inter alia: Q 6:151-2; 25:67-8, 72. Some early exegetes also held that what the Qur'ān regards as major sins are to be located in the various prohibitions mentioned in the first thirty verses of Q 4; cf. Ṭabarī, *Tafsīr*, iv, 39-40 [ad Q 4:31]; see LAWFUL AND UNLAWFUL.) A fuller, though by no means exhaustive sampling of qur'ānic sins would include — besides the *ḥadd*-penalties (for drinking, adultery and fornication, false accusation of adultery and fornication, theft, and brigandage; see INTOXICANTS; WINE) and besides chronic neglect of the fundamental ritual obligations (see PRAYER; WITNESS TO FAITH; PILGRIMAGE; ALMSGIVING; RAMAḌĀN; FASTING; RITUAL AND THE QUR'ĀN) — such diverse items as slander (Q 24:11; 33:58), undue suspicion (q.v.; *ẓann*) and backbiting (Q 49:11-12; also see GOSSIP); lying (*qawl al-zūr*, Q 22:30; see LIE) and concealing legal testimony (Q 2:283; see WITNESSING AND TESTIFYING); practicing usury (q.v.; Q 2:275-6, 278-9; 3:130-1); homosexuality (q.v.; cf. Q 26:165 f.; 21:74); "hurting" God, his Prophet, or other believers (Q 33:57-8); and other individual and collective transgressions against the "limits" established by God. (For various qur'ānic terms evoking the idea of transgression, cf. Izutsu, *Concepts*, 164-77 and passim, esp. 172 f.; also see BOUNDARIES AND PRECEPTS.) In general, as the foregoing samples indicate, the interest of the Qur'ān is not with providing any detailed, let alone systematic, catalog of sins, but rather with affirming what Izutsu *(Concepts)* has called a "basic moral dichotomy" between belief and unbelief, virtue and vice, the good and the bad (see GOOD AND EVIL; VIRTUES AND VICES, COMMANDING AND FORBIDDING).

Lists of major sins are more readily accessible in ḥadīth (see ḤADĪTH AND THE QUR'ĀN), though there continues to be considerable uncertainty on precisely which, or how many, fall into that category. A tradition reported on the authority of the Prophet's Companion Abū Hurayra lists the following seven as major sins: associating anyone with God; sorcery (see MAGIC); unlawful homicide; usurping the property of the orphan; usury; fleeing from the battlefield (see EXPEDITIONS AND BATTLES; HYPOCRITES AND HYPOCRISY; FIGHTING); and slandering believing women (Bukhārī, *Ṣaḥīḥ*, *K. al-Waṣāyā*, no. 23; ibid., *K. al-Ḥudūd*, no. 44; Muslim, *Ṣaḥīḥ*, *K. al-Īmān*, no. 145; Abū Dāwūd, *Sunan*, *K. al-Waṣāyā*, no. 2874; Haytamī, *Zawājir*, i, 18). Again, other lists are much more expansive and Ibn ʿAbbās is often quoted as saying that the major sins are "closer to 700 than they are to seven, except that no sin is 'major' when forgiveness is sought for it, that is when one undertakes proper repentance *(tawba)*, just as no sin is 'minor' if one persists in it" (Ṭabarī, *Tafsīr*, iv, 44, ad Q 4:31 [no. 9208]).

Sin, repentance, and forgiveness

Islam, like Judaism, has no concept of an "original sin" (see FALL OF MAN). Every soul (q.v.) bears its own burden (Q 6:164; 17:15; 29:12; see INTERCESSION), though God does not overburden anyone (Q 2:286). Sins also have evil consequences during one's present life, so that whatever harm one is afflicted by is "what your hands have earned" (Q 42:30; also cf. Izutsu, *Concepts*, 227, on the dual meaning of the word *sayyi'a* as both "misfortune" and "evil deed," which may perhaps be taken to evoke the idea of misfortune as being at least partly a result of evil deeds). The punishment visited by God upon particular communities is likewise the result of their sinfulness (cf. Q 17:16-17; 22:45, 48; see PUNISHMENT STORIES). Conversely, sins are removed through good deeds (Q 11:114) and, in any case, God forgives a great deal (Q 42:30). Indeed, were God to hold people to account for all that they do, no living being would remain on the face of the earth (Q 35:45; see MERCY).

While responsibility for one's actions lies with the individual, the question whether these actions necessarily determine one's fate in the hereafter was much debated among the Muslim theologians (see FREEDOM AND PREDESTINATION). The Qur'ān suggests both that each individual will be judged according to his or her own conduct (cf. Q 2:286) and that the decision to punish or pardon people for their sins rests ultimately, and solely, with God (Q 2:284). All humans being prone to sin (cf. Q 12:53), the pious are much given to seeking God's forgiveness (cf. Q 3:193-5; see PIETY). Indeed, this is a major trait that distinguishes them from the sinners and the unbelievers, who are not only unmindful of the consequences of their actions but also too arrogant to repent for them. The prophets (see PROPHETS AND PROPHETHOOD) not only seek forgiveness for their own sins (see below), but also for those of others (cf. Q 47:19); and, according to the traditional Sunnī view, they will intercede on behalf of their followers on the day of judgment (cf. Elder, *Commentary*, 112-14).

Q 39:53 holds out God's promise to forgive *all* sins *(al-dhunūb)* and therefore instructs those who have exceeded the bounds *(asrafū ʿalā anfusihim)* not to despair of God's mercy. Yet Q 4:48 states that "God will not forgive the associating of anyone with him, but he might forgive anything less than that for whomsoever he wills." The exegetes tried to resolve the discrepancy between the two verses in different ways. Some held that Q 39:53 sought to reassure those who had committed major sins, and who feared their damnation on account of them even if they were to convert to Islam or, in case of Muslim sinners, even if they were to repent of their major sins. On this view, even the major sins were not "deadly" as long as they were followed by repentance; and this was true even of *shirk*, the gravest of sins (cf. Ṭabarī, *Tafsīr*, xi, 14-17, ad Q 39:53). A different view saw Q 4:48 as not abrogating but delimiting the purport of Q 39:53: while God might forgive any sin he wishes to, he would not forgive *shirk* unless one has repented of it (Ṭabarī, *Tafsīr*, xi, 17 [no. 30, 188]; also cf. Haytamī, *Zawājir*, i, 62f.).

God's forgiveness had not always come without a heavy, this-worldly, penalty, however. Those among the Children of Israel (q.v.) who had been guilty of worshipping the calf had to pay dearly for this sin: as described by the Qur'ān, the price of repentance in this instance was death for the guilty (Q 2:54; and cf. al-Ṭabarī's commentary on this verse, *Tafsīr*, i, 325-8; see CALF OF GOLD). Repentance for the sin of *shirk* does not carry such penalties for the Qur'ān's own addressees (cf. Haytamī, *Zawājir*, ii, 190). In the case of sins that are also crimes, however, such as stealing, adultery, or murder, the exegetes and jurists generally held that repentance ought to accompany but does not, by itself, suffice to absolve one of the sin in question (but cf. Q 28:15-17, where Moses [q.v.] seeks the forgiveness of God for a homicide and is forgiven). While all sin involves transgressing limits laid down by God, the jurists made a distinction between the violation of "the rights of God" and that of "the rights of human beings" (cf. Johansen, *Contingency*, 212-18). The rights of God, to be upheld by the ruler or his representatives, involve the *ḥadd*-penalties (see KINGS AND RULERS; POLITICS AND THE QURʾĀN). On the other hand, infraction of the rights of human beings, a category that also included homicide, was negotiable in the sense that the wronged party might decide to forgo punishment or opt for monetary compensation rather than for physical retaliation (q.v.). Absolution from the sin of violating the rights of human beings required not just the seeking of forgiveness from God but also the legal punishment entailed by the crime in question or forgiveness from the wronged party (cf. Ṭabarī's discussion of Q 5:45 in *Tafsīr*, iv, 598-604). Juristic classifications of the rights of God and of human beings, or what these categories entailed, are not to be found in the Qurʾān, though the combination of the moral and the legal norms that is characteristic of Islamic law is itself firmly grounded in it (see ETHICS AND THE QURʾĀN).

Theological discourses on the grave sinner

If God might forgive all major sins — even, as many commentators saw it, the most heinous sin of *shirk* — if one repented of them, does it follow that one who did not so repent was doomed to damnation? And what was the status of the person committing major sins, the grave sinner, in relation to the community of Muslims of which he professed to be a member? These questions, which lie at the heart of the early development of Islamic theology, arose when many first generation Muslims strongly disapproved of the conduct of ʿUthmān b. ʿAffān (r. 23-35/644-56), Muḥammad's third successor as caliph (q.v.), accused him of remaining unrepentant after committing major sins, and murdered him (see ʿUTHMĀN). The Khārijīs (q.v.), who may well be regarded as Islam's first "sect," insisted that ʿUthmān's murder was justified; so, too, was that of ʿUthmān's successor, ʿAlī b. Abī Ṭālib (q.v.; r. 35-40/656-61), who had himself become a grave sinner by agreeing to negotiate with other grave sinners (see ARBITRATION; ṢIFFĪN) and it was a Khārijī who assassinated ʿAlī in 40/661. In general, the Khārijīs believed that anyone who committed a major sin but failed to repent was consigned to eternal damnation and that, in his present life, he also ceased to be a member of the community of Muslims. Despite this uncompromising position, the Khārijīs soon came to have their own extremists as well as their moderates; and while the extremist groups held that the grave sinner — which effectively meant anyone who disagreed with their principles — might legitimately be killed, the more moderate Khārijīs, the Ibāḍiyya, allowed mutual coexistence with other Muslims even as they denied the status of believers to them (Ashʿarī, *Maqālāt*, 104f.). Given that the Khārijīs were typically a minority, the latter stance was a matter not just of toleration but also of self-preservation; and it is no surprise that only those who espoused it have survived to the present day.

In opposition to the Khārijīs of various stripes, the Murjiʾīs insisted that major sins did not make one an unbeliever and that the grave sinner continued to be a member of the community of Muslims. But they suspended judgment on whether either

ʿUthmān or ʿAlī, or any other of Muḥammad's Companions involved in the first *fitna* — which is the conventional designation for the chaotic events between the murder of ʿUthmān in 35/656 and that of ʿAlī in 40/661 — had committed major sins. As Crone and Zimmermann (*Epistle*, 221-3) have shown, the Murjiʾīs of the first century of Islam held that the grave sinner was indeed damned forever; it was just that, in the cases of ʿUthmān, ʿAlī, as well as of others embroiled in the *fitna*, they simply did not know who had committed major sins and therefore thought it best to suspend judgment on the matter. It was later second/eighth century Murjiʾīs, such as Abū Ḥanīfa (d. 150/767), the eponymous founder of the Ḥanafī school of Sunnī law, who came to hold the view that the fate even of the grave sinner was to be determined by God on the day of judgment and the question was best deferred until then (ibid., 223). This attitude, towards the participants in the first *fitna* and towards the status of the grave sinner in general, eventually came to be adopted by the Sunnīs, with the significant difference, however, that judgment on questions of sin and guilt was now also deferred because, by the middle of the third/ninth century, the definition of a Sunnī "orthodoxy" had come to be predicated on reverence for the Companions of the Prophet (q.v.) as a whole, irrespective of the particular, and mutually antagonistic, positions they might have held towards one another (cf. ibid., 229).

Like the Murjiʾīs, the Muʿtazilī theologians, who came to prominence from the middle of the second/eighth century, did not banish the grave sinner from the community. But, unlike the Murjiʾīs, and also unlike those who later emerged as the Sunnīs, the Muʿtazilīs (see MUʿTAZILA) assigned an "intermediate state" to the grave sinner so that he was neither a believer nor an unbeliever but a "transgressor" *(fāsiq)*, though, as such, still a member of the Muslim community. Unlike the later Murjiʾīs, the Muʿtazilīs mostly thought that such transgressors were doomed to eternal damnation (cf. the creed of the famous Muʿtazilī Qurʾān-commentator, al-Zamakhsharī, in Schmidtke, *Muʿtazilite creed*, 76). As for minor sins, the Muʿtazilīs espoused the view that such sins would be weighed against one's good deeds and cancelled out through them *(taḥābut)* as long, of course, as the good deeds outweighed the sins (cf. Schmidtke, *Theology*, 227f.). Shīʿī theology was strongly influenced by the Muʿtazila; but unlike the latter and in accord with the Sunnīs, Shīʿī theologians did not believe in the eternal damnation of the Muslim grave sinner (for the developed Sunnī position on the matter, cf. Elder, *Commentary*, 114f.; see SHĪʿISM AND THE QURʾĀN; SHĪʿA).

Sin, error, and infallibility

Sin involves an element of intentionality as well as of knowledge that the act in question entails disapproval or punishment and that it is forbidden. (On the question of sinful acts committed in ignorance, see Q 4:17; 6:54, and the discussion of these verses in the major commentaries.) This marks off sin from "error" *(khaṭāʾ)*, a term whose primary connotation is legal rather than ethical (cf. Schacht, Khaṭaʾ; for other connotations of "error," elucidated with reference to the qurʾānic term *ḍalāl*, see ERROR; ASTRAY). Thus, while intentional homicide is a crime as well as a major sin (cf. Q 4:93, and Ṭabarī, *Tafsīr*, iv, 220-3, for a discussion of whether God would forgive the premeditated murder of a believer despite the murderer's repentance), the same is not true of unintentional homicide; the latter does, however, require the payment of compensation for that act (Q 4:92; see BLOOD MONEY). Accounts describing the altercations between the caliph ʿUthmān and those who eventually murdered him have the latter demand that the caliph submit himself to retaliation by those he had wronged, with ʿUthmān responding that the caliph *(imām)* commits errors just as he does what is right and that no retaliation is required for his errors (Ṭabarī, *Taʾrīkh*, i, 2995f.; and cf. ibid., 3043). Many early jurists believed, for their part, that even when the effort to arrive at a legal ruling on the basis of systematic reflection on the foundational texts *(ijtihād)* led to different and thus possibly erroneous results, the effort itself deserved a reward from God; and since a jurist made that effort, he was "right" even when he seemed to have missed the mark (cf. Schacht, Khaṭāʾ; van Ess, *TG*, ii, 161-4). An error was thus not a sin as long as one did not persist in it after having become aware of it.

What sort of an error or even a sin might be imputed to a prophet was a contested issue from Islam's first centuries (see IMPECCABILITY). The Qurʾān recognizes prophets as sinning (as in the case of Adam; cf. Q 20:121; see ADAM AND EVE) or coming close to it (as Joseph [q.v.] did; cf. Q 12:24); as seeking, or being asked to seek, forgiveness for their sins (Q 7:22-3; 11:47; 47:19); and as being forgiven by God for their sins (e.g. Q 2:35-7; 28:15-16; 48:2). In an episode during Muḥammad's early prophetic career in Mecca, Satan is said to have interpolated into Muḥammad's revelation verses that spoke approvingly of the intercession of certain Meccan deities (see Ṭabarī, *Taʾrīkh*, i, 1191-6; see SATANIC VERSES; DEVIL; REVELATION AND INSPIRATION). These verses (which immediately followed Q 53:20) were "abrogated" once Muḥammad was informed that their source was Satan rather than God (cf. Q 22:52; see ABROGATION). This incident raised troubling questions for many Muslims, in particular about the integrity of the Qurʾān (see INIMITABILITY; CREATEDNESS OF THE QURʾĀN) and about Muḥammad's vulnerability to error and sin. The historicity of the episode concerning the Satanic verses was thus denied by many, a view that went hand in hand with the articulation of the doctrine of the infallibility of the Prophet in Islam's first centuries. Yet, while most Muslims today concur in denying this episode, many prominent scholars of the earlier centuries, including al-Ṭabarī (d. 310/923), the Muʿtazilī exegete al-Zamakhsharī (d. 538/1144; cf. *Kashshāf*, iii, 161f., commenting on Q 22:52) and the Ḥanbalī jurist Ibn Taymiyya (d. 728/1328), accepted its historicity. For Ibn Taymiyya, a prophet is infallible not in the sense of being immune to error or sin but only in being secure from persistence in it. On this view, the episode of the Satanic verses poses no problem in that Muḥammad promptly sought God's forgiveness for his error — which, to Ibn Taymiyya, is what it was, rather than a sin — and the matter was clarified by a subsequent revelation (see Ahmed, Ibn Taymiyyah).

That a prophet might commit a *major* sin was not a possibility to be countenanced, however, by Ibn Taymiyya or by anyone else (Ahmed, Ibn Taymiyyah, 86 and passim). Minor sins were another matter, though as al-Zamakhsharī said, in commenting on Q 93:7, prophets both before and after the beginning of their prophetic career were immune not only from the major sins but also from "disgraceful minor sins" *(al-ṣaghāʾir al-shāʾina*, as in *Kashshāf*, iv, 756; he does not, however, give any examples of such minor sins). The Shīʿa agreed with others in insisting on the immunity (q.v.) of the prophets from sin and error, but they extended such immunity to their imāms (see IMĀM) as well. An early Shīʿī theologian, Hishām b. al-Ḥakam (d. 179/795-6), had argued for the immunity of the imāms from sin and error, but not of the prophets, on the grounds that while a prophet can be corrected through divine intervention, an imām had no such channel available and hence needed the immunity in question. But this doctrine never caught on in standard formulations of Shīʿī theology (see Bar-Asher, *Scripture*, 159-79; on Hishām's position, Ashʿarī, *Maqālāt*, 48).

Modern discourses

With unprecedented modern efforts towards the codification of the *sharīʿa*, certain contemporary Muslim scholars have visualized legislation not only in areas traditionally left to the discretion of rulers and judges but also to regulate matters previously thought of only as sinful behavior rather than as legal infractions. The Egyptian religious scholar Yūsuf al-Qaraḍāwī (b. 1926), one of the most influential of the contemporary *ʿulamāʾ*, has argued, for instance, that considerations of "public interest" require that states legislate punishments for usurious transactions, the usurpation of the orphan's property, the non-performance of the ritual obligations, the harassment of women and other evils. "There are hundreds of sins, forms of opposition [to the divine law], and wrongs that the *sharīʿa* has forbidden, or has commanded doing the opposite of, but it has not established a specific penalty for them. And so," he says, "they need legislation" (*Siyāsa*, 95-6; quotation from 96). While many earlier definitions of sin, especially of major sin, had included under that rubric both moral transgressions and crimes for which the foundational texts had prescribed specific punishments *(ḥudūd)*, the distinction between sin and crime or between moral and legal norms was not thereby effaced (cf. Johansen, *Contingency*, 71 and passim). This is not to say, of course, that sin had previously been only a "private" matter. Indeed, Muslim scholars have long recognized the obligation of "forbidding wrong" even when the offense affects no one but the actor him- or herself; and the activities of vigilantes who felt obligated to intervene even in privately committed wrongs are extensively reported in the historical sources. Yet, Muslim scholars often also disapproved of such vigilantism, just as they sought to protect an individual's privacy even when doing so meant that many wrongs would go unpunished (on all this, see Cook, *Commanding right*). A proposal such as al-Qaraḍāwī's would deal with the problem of vigilantism but only at the expense of privacy; and in combating sin, it ends up legitimizing the intrusive powers of the state, an outcome about which not only medieval scholars but also many modern *ʿulamāʾ* have had grave misgivings (see OPPRESSION).

In seeking to reinterpret Islam's foundational texts and its institutions in ways that would make them more compatible with what are perceived to be the demands of the modern world, other, "modernist," readings of the Qurʾān often lay a new stress on individual moral responsibility (q.v.) and a this-worldly orientation (see WORLD); and conceptions of sin and related ideas have been interpreted accordingly. The influential Pakistani modernist Fazlur Rahman (d. 1988) sees the qurʾānic notion of *taqwā* as guiding individuals through the tensions and the extremes to which they, as human beings, are inherently susceptible; and sin, wrong, or evil signifies precisely the failure to successfully navigate one's course through these tensions (cf. Rahman, *Major themes*, 27 and passim). Rahman sees the qurʾānic concept of sin — though he seems to prefer the term "evil" to "sin" — primarily in terms of its deleterious effects on human welfare in the present world and, more specifically, with reference to what it contributes to the failure of human moral endeavors. To him, the Qurʾān's overall "attitude is quite optimistic with regard to the sequel of human endeavor." Yet, this optimism is predicated on, and illustrative of, the Qur'ān's "action orientation and practicality." Within the framework of that orientation, smaller failings are remediable, and this — in his telling rendition of Q 4:31 — is the point of God's forgiveness of minor sins: "If you avoid the major evils that have been prohibited to you, we shall obliterate *[the effects of]* occasional and small lapses" (ibid., 30; brackets in the original, emphasis added). By the same token, *individual* failings are more likely to be forgiven by God than are failures in a people's "collective performance"; the latter are much more grave, even irremediable, in their effect (ibid., 52, and 37-64, passim; see OPPRESSED ON EARTH, THE).

For all their severe disagreements with the modernists, "Islamists" (or "fundamentalists") are often no less concerned, in seeking the public implementation of Islamic norms, with demonstrating the Qur'ān's "action orientation and practicality." Thus, in a passage like Q 17:23-38, where one might previously have seen a catalog of some of the major sins to be avoided (cf. Izutsu, *Concepts*, 229), the influential Pakistani Islamist Sayyid Abū l-Aʿlā Mawdūdī (d. 1399/1979) finds the "manifesto of the Prophet's mission..., making the intellectual, moral, cultural, economic and legal bases of the Islamic society and state of the future known to the world" (Mawdūdī, *Understanding*, v, 34; also cf. id., *Islamic law*, 202-13). The first of these "bases" is, of course, the injunction not to worship (q.v.) anyone but God, which is not simply a matter of avoiding *shirk* but of "recogniz[ing] and submit[ting] to his sovereignty (q.v.) to the exclusion of any other sovereignty" (Mawdūdī, *Understanding*, v, 35, commenting on Q 17:23). According to the Egyptian Islamist Sayyid Quṭb (d. 1966), himself much influenced by Mawdūdī, whether a society bases itself on a recognition of this divine sovereignty determines its overall orientation, viz., whether it is a properly Islamic society rather than one living in pagan ignorance (*jāhiliyya;* see e.g. Quṭb, *Ẓilāl*, iii, 1217 and 1229-34, discussing Q 6:151-3; see AGE OF IGNORANCE). Unlike many a medieval commentator, detailed catalogs or relative rankings of major and minor sins are matters far less pressing than are the implications of this overarching orientation.

Muhammad Qasim Zaman

Bibliography

Primary: Abū Dāwūd, *Sunan;* al-Ashʿarī, Abū l-Ḥasan ʿAlī b. Ismāʿīl, *Maqālāt al-islāmiyyīn*, ed. H. Ritter, Wiesbaden 1980; Bukhārī, *Ṣaḥīḥ;* P. Crone and F. Zimmermann, *The epistle of Sālim ibn Dhakwān*, Oxford 2001; Dāmaghānī, *Wujūh*, ed. Zafītī; Dhahabī, Shams al-Dīn Muḥammad b. Aḥmad, *al-Kabāʾir*, Cairo 1980; E.E. Elder, *A commentary on the creed of Islam. Saʿd al-Dīn al-Taftāzānī on the creed of Najm al-Dīn al-Nasafī*, New York 1950; al-Ghazālī, Abū Ḥāmid Muḥammad, *Iḥyāʾ ʿulūm al-dīn*, ed. A. al-Khālidī, 5 vols., Beirut 1998; al-Ḥalīmī, Abū ʿAbdallāh al-Ḥusayn b. al-Ḥasan, *al-Minhāj fī shuʿab al-īmān*, ed. Ḥ.M. Fawda, Damascus 1979; Ibn Ḥajar al-ʿAsqalānī, *Fatḥ al-bārī*, 15 vols., Riyadh 2000; Ibn Ḥajar al-Haytamī, *al-Zawājir ʿan iqtirāf al-kabāʾir*, ed. Kh.M. Shīḥā and M. Kh. Ḥalabī, 2 vols., Beirut 1998; Ibn Nujaym, Zayn al-Dīn b. Ibrāhīm, *Sharḥ Risālat al-ṣaghāʾir wa-l-kabāʾir*, ed. Kh. al-Mays, Beirut 1981; Ibn Taymiyya, Risāla fī l-tawba, in M.R. Slim (ed.), *Jāmiʿ al-rasāʾil li-Ibn Taymiyya*, 1 vol., Cairo 1969, i, 217-79; Abū l-Aʿlā Mawdūdī, *The Islamic law and constitution*, trans. K. Ahmad, Lahore 1960; id., *Towards understanding the Qurʾān*, trans. Z.I. Ansari, 7 vols. to date, Leicester 1988-2000; Quṭb, *Ẓilāl;* Rāzī, *Tafsīr*, 17 vols., Beirut 2000; S. Schmidtke, *A Muʿtazilite creed of az-Zamakhsharī (d. 538/1144)*, Stuttgart 1997; Ṭabarī, *Tafsīr*, 13 vols., Beirut 1999; id., *Taʾrīkh*, ed. de Goeje; Wensinck, *Concordance*, s.vv. *ʾ-th-m, ʿ-ṣ-y, dh-n-b, f-ḥ-sh, k-b-r, kh-ṭ-a;* Zamakhsharī, *Kashshāf*.

Secondary: S. Ahmed, Ibn Taymiyyah and the Satanic verses, in *SI* 87 (1998), 67-124; M.M. Bar-Asher, *Scripture and exegesis in early Imāmī Shiism*, Leiden 1999; M. Cook, *Commanding right and forbidding wrong in Islamic thought*, Cambridge 2000;

van Ess, *TG;* W.R.W. Gardner, *The qurʾanic doctrine of sin,* Madras 1914; Izutsu, *Concepts;* B. Johansen, *Contingency in a sacred law. Legal and ethical norms in the Muslim fiqh,* Leiden 1999; W. Madelung, Early Sunnī doctrine concerning faith as reflected in the *Kitāb al-Īmān* of Abū ʿUbayd al-Qāsim b. Sallām (d. 224/839), in *SI* 32 (1970), 233-54; Y. al-Qaraḍāwī, *al-Siyāsa al-sharʿiyya fī ḍawʾ nuṣūṣ al-sharīʿa wa-maqāṣidihā,* Beirut 2000; F. Rahman, *Major themes of the Qurʾān,* Minneapolis 1980; J. Schacht, Khaṭāʾ, in *EI²*, iv, 1100-2; S. Schmidtke, *The theology of ʿAllāma al-Ḥillī (d. 726/1325),* Berlin 1991; R. Stehly, Un problème de la théologie islamique. La définition des fautes graves *(kabāʾir),* in *REI* 65/2 (1977), 165-81; A.J. Wensinck, *The Muslim creed,* Cambridge 1932; id./L. Gardet, Khaṭīʾa, in *EI²*, iv, 1106-9.

Sinai

The triangularly shaped peninsula that witnessed the wanderings of the Israelites after their flight from Egypt on the way to their promised land in Canaan, under the leadership of Moses (q.v.); the scene of the latter's miracles (q.v.) and, above all, the region where the Decalogue was given and God's covenant (q.v.) with Israel (q.v.) concluded. All of these matters are recorded in many of the sūras (q.v.) of the Qurʾān, with variations from the biblical accounts (see NARRATIVES; CHILDREN OF ISRAEL).

The term Sinai appears twice in the Qurʾān, in Q 23:20 as *saynāʾ* and in Q 95:2 as *sīnīn,* possibly a dittograph of the letter *sīn,* more assonant with *zaytūn* than *sīn* (cf. *il yāsīn,* Q 37:130). In both cases, the word is preceded by the term *ṭūr,* "mountain," the compound referring to one spot in the peninsula, namely, Mount Sinai.

The peninsula was especially important in Moses' career, more important than Egypt (q.v.) or Canaan, since it witnessed the birth of Mosaic Judaism (see JEWS AND JUDAISM), when the law and the covenant were given to Israel through him at Mount Sinai. Consequently, in the Qurʾān, it is of great significance, derived from the importance of Moses as the most frequently mentioned biblical figure in the qurʾānic text (157 times, as opposed to 25 for Jesus [q.v.]) and from the image of the prophet Muḥammad himself. For Moses was a model for the latter — as a legislator, as a prophet of action who led his people and, above all, as one to whom God foretold the prophethood of Muḥammad in Q 7:157 (see PROPHETS AND PROPHETHOOD), which the exegetes related to Deuteronomy 18:15.

In the vast peninsula, the holiest *locus sanctus* was Mount Sinai, which, as just mentioned, witnessed the giving of the law and the covenant. It occurs seven times without the addition of Sinai, simply as *al-ṭūr,* "the mountain" (cf. *Exod* 19:2, 3; 24:4, etc.), the Arabic definite article giving *al-ṭūr* the uniqueness it has given to other terms, such as *al-bayt,* "the Kaʿba" (see KAʿBA; HOUSE, DOMESTIC AND DIVINE), *al-rasūl,* "the prophet, Muḥammad" (see MESSENGER), and *al-madīna,* Yathrib, the Prophet's city (see MEDINA). Of the many references to *al-ṭūr,* the most important are two. One occurs in Q 95:2, where the phrase *ṭūr sīnīn* appears as part of a tripartite asseveration involving Palestine, Mount Sinai and Mecca (q.v.). In that sūra, God honors Mount Sinai by including it as an element in the asseveration and, what is more, by allying Mount Sinai as the scene of the Decalogue, to Palestine as the holy land. In this sūra, the concept of holiness is expressed territorially by reference to three *loca sancta,* and the tripartite oath (see OATHS) reflects the qurʾānic perception of the essential identity of the three Abrahamic religions (see ABRAHAM). The other important reference is in Q 52, which opens with an oath by *al-ṭūr,* followed by five other elements included in the oath, the first four of which, the book (q.v.), the parchment, the house and the roof, have a natural affinity with *al-ṭūr,* when they are conceived as elements in the monastery/

fortress of Mount Sinai, rebuilt by the emperor Justinian in the sixth century C.E.; otherwise the four elements are incongruous with, and incomprehensible as a sequence to the first element in the oath — *al-ṭūr*. The monastery became a very popular pilgrimage destination, visited by Christians, including Christian Arabs, who lived so close to it (see CHRISTIANS AND CHRISTIANITY). This, together with some specific topographical references to *al-ṭūr* in the Qurʾān, such as the right side of it as in Q 19:52 and Q 20:80 (see LEFT HAND AND RIGHT HAND), suggest that the Arabs (q.v.) of Muḥammad's time, whom the Qurʾān addressed, were familiar with Mount Sinai, possibly including Muḥammad himself, who, fifteen years before his call, had led caravans to such termini of the spice route as Gaza and Elat, from where routes led to Mount Sinai (see CARAVAN). Two verses in Q 28 (Q 28:44, 46), in which the Qurʾān says that Muḥammad was not at Mount Sinai when Moses was there, are tantalizing in this context. A covenant alleged to have been issued by the Prophet to the monks of Mount Sinai has been haunted by the ghosts of authenticity.

Irfan Shahīd

Bibliography
ʿA.S. ʿAṭiyya, *The Arabic manuscripts of Mount Sinai*, Baltimore, MD 1955, xviii, xxix, 25, 26; C. Bailey, Sīnāʾ, in *EI²*, ix, 625; P. Figueras, Pilgrims to Sinai in the Byzantine Negev, in *Jahrbuch für Antike und Christentum, Ergänzungsband* 20 (1995), 756-62, esp. 756-8; P.-L. Gatier, Les traditions et l'histoire du Sinaï du IVe au VIIe siècle, in *L'Arabie préislamique et son environnment historique et culturel. Actes du Colloque de Strasbourg, 24-27 Juin, 1987*, Leiden 1989, 499-523; J.J. Hobbs, *Mount Sinai*, Austin, TX 1995; Horovitz, *KU*, 123-5; Jeffery, *For. vocab.*, 184-5 (with bibliography); P. Maiberger, *Topographische und historische Untersuchungen zum Sinaiproblem. Worauf beruht die Identifizierung des Ǧabal Mūsā mit dem Sinai?* Freiburg 1984.

Sincerity see VIRTUES AND VICES, COMMANDING AND FORBIDDING

Sīnīn see SINAI

Sīra and the Qurʾān

Sīra is a branch of Arabic literature that is devoted to the earliest salvation history of Islam and focuses on God's actions towards his prophet Muḥammad and through him, i.e. the revelation of the Qurʾān and the foundation of an Islamic community. The term *sīra* can also connote a work belonging to that literature.

Sīra is the noun of kind *(fiʿla)* of the Arabic verb *sāra*, "to go," "to travel," etc., indicating the manner of doing what is expressed by the verb (see ARABIC LANGUAGE; GRAMMAR AND THE QURʾĀN). Hence it originally means "way of going," but the most frequent meaning is "way of acting, conduct, way of life" (see also TRADITION AND CUSTOM). In the Qurʾān the word *sīra* occurs only in Q 20:21, where it means "way of acting," or "condition" and has nothing to do with the literature under discussion. The word also came to mean "the life and times of...," "vita," "biography." In the second/eighth century it was applied to the history of various Persian kings, and also to the lives and times of some Umayyad caliphs (see CALIPH).

In present day Muslim usage, the *sīra* par excellence is that of the Prophet: *sīrat rasūl Allāh* or *al-sīra al-nabawiyya*, which is often rendered as "the biography of the Prophet." But this designation is imprecise. The life and times of Muḥammad (q.v.) are pivotal in the *sīra*, but it also contains reports and narrations about the ancient history of Arabia (see PRE-ISLAMIC ARABIA AND THE QURʾĀN), the earlier prophets (see PROPHETS AND PROPHETHOOD;

MESSENGER), the Companions (see COMPANIONS OF THE PROPHET) and the first caliphs, whose *sunna* (q.v.) was relevant for the Islamic community. Furthermore it deals with qurʾānic exegesis (see EXEGESIS OF THE QURʾĀN: CLASSICAL AND MEDIEVAL) and the occasions and ways of qurʾānic revelation (see REVELATION AND INSPIRATION; OCCASIONS OF REVELATION); and it preserves letters, speeches, documents, genealogies, lists of names, and poetry (see POETRY AND POETS; RHETORIC AND THE QURʾĀN).

Sīra *or* maghāzī

In the first centuries of Islam, most collections of *sīra* texts were formulated with the name of *maghāzī*, "expeditions" (see EXPEDITIONS AND BATTLES), although they also contained texts on non-military matters. Whatever their name, the collections consist of the same kind of greatly heterogeneous, rather fragmentary material that belong to different genres (Hinds, Maghāzī; id., 'Maghāzī' and 'sīra'; Jarrar, *Prophetenbiographie*, 1-59; Schöller, *Exegetisches Denken*, 37-49).

The earliest sources

Sīra works have been written throughout the centuries, and one may even count modern biographies of the Prophet among them. Since the *sīra* is a whole branch of literature, there is no point in studying only the one book by Ibn Isḥāq (d. 150/767) in the edition of Ibn Hishām (d. ca. 213/828) that became famous. Here follows a survey of the earliest sources, which have the greatest relevance to our subject. About half of them can be studied in translations (see TOOLS FOR THE STUDY OF THE QURʾĀN). For the later *sīra* works see Kister, Sīrah, 366-7; Schöller, *Exegetisches Denken*, 64-70.

Qiṣṣa

The first to occupy themselves intensely with the Qurʾān, the Prophet and early Islamic knowledge in general were the storytellers or preachers named *qāṣṣ* (pl. *quṣṣāṣ;* see Pellat, Ḳāṣṣ; Duri, *Rise*, index s.v. *qiṣaṣ;* Norris, Elements; see TEACHING AND PREACHING THE QURʾĀN). They commenced their activities in private gatherings and sometimes in the mosque (q.v.). In the Umayyad period they obtained official permission to address the faithful in the mosques. In their sermons they would encourage soldiers and curse the enemies of Islam (see PATH OR WAY; FIGHTING; JIHĀD), but also explain the Qurʾān, depict hell (see HELL AND HELLFIRE) and paradise (q.v.) and recount the life of the Prophet and the lives of his predecessors.

Their stories (*qiṣṣa*, pl. *qiṣaṣ*) were both edifying and entertaining and did not eschew flights of fancy. When expanding on the qurʾānic stories about earlier prophets they often drew upon Jewish and Christian narratives, both biblical and non-biblical (see Vajda, Isrāʾīliyyāt; see JEWS AND JUDAISM; CHRISTIANS AND CHRISTIANITY; SCRIPTURE AND THE QURʾĀN). What had already begun in the Qurʾān was continued in these stories: Muḥammad is positioned as the last prophet in a succession of earlier prophets, while the latter, for their part, are given characteristics of Muḥammad (see NARRATIVES).

After the Umayyad period, the storytellers were banned from the mosque again and again. Their reputation deteriorated and they ended on the streets, always popular with the public, but frowned upon by the religious establishment. Their inclination to exaggerate and fantasize irritated pious believers and ḥadīth scholars (see ḤADĪTH AND THE QURʾĀN), and the extra-Islamic material they divulged was increasingly deemed unacceptable (see TRADITIONAL DISCIPLINES OF QURʾĀNIC STUDY).

For the *sīra*, the early activities of storytellers are of great importance. Since they were not writers, and since they lost their good reputation quite early, hardly any of their narratives have been collected in books under their names. But in some form or other their stories seeped into *sīra* and *tafsīr* works, in spite of frequent attempts of the compilers to dissociate themselves from them.

One often recognizes a storyteller's contribution by its style. The story of the Prophet's bargaining with God in heaven about the number of obligatory prayers (e.g. Ibn Isḥāq, *Sīra*, 271; Ibn Isḥāq-Guillaume, 186-7; see PRAYER; ASCENSION), which has clear biblical precedents, has all the characteristics of an orally performed story (see ORALITY). Also the Prophet's world-renouncing address at the graveyard of Medina (q.v.) shortly before his death (Ibn Isḥāq, *Sīra*, 1000; Ibn Isḥāq-Guillaume, 678) has the pietistic ring of a *qiṣṣa*, although it is recorded with a chain of transmitters or *isnād* (other examples in Duri, *Rise*, 113; see ASCETICISM; PIETY; ABSTINENCE).

Wahb b. Munabbih

One storyteller who is relatively well documented is the Yemenite Wahb b. Munabbih (ca. 34-110/654-728; see Wahb, *Papyrus;* Khoury, Wahb; id., Les sources, 23-7; Duri, *Rise*, 122-35), who was well-versed in the biblical and pre-Islamic heritage and familiar with stories about the Prophet. Several books were ascribed to him. Whatever form they may have had, there was one about the creation (q.v.) and the early prophets and another about the pre-Islamic history of Yemen (q.v.). In these fields, Wahb was considered an authority and quoted extensively by *sīra* authors like Ibn Isḥāq, Ibn Hishām, al-Ṭabarī (d. 310/923) and others, but his texts about the expeditions and battles of the Prophet they did not find reliable enough to quote. Long *sīra* quotations from Wahb b. Munabbih can, however, be found with the Ṣūfī author Abū Nuʿaym al-Iṣfahānī (336-430/948-1038; *Ḥilyat al-Awliyāʾ*, iv, 72-81; see ṢŪFISM AND THE QURʾĀN).

Two larger pieces ascribed to Wahb have been preserved in a third/ninth century papyrus. One is a part of the story of David (q.v.); the other is a *sīra* text that covers some events concerning the Prophet's meeting with envoys from Medina at ʿAqaba, his emigration (q.v.) and a military expedition by ʿAlī (see ʿALĪ B. ABĪ ṬĀLIB). The narrative is lengthy, abounds in poetry and contains miracle stories (see MARVELS; MIRACLES; e.g. the Prophet healing with "the breath of God"; Wahb, *Papyrus*, 142; see ILLNESS AND HEALTH; MEDICINE AND THE QURʾĀN). In its present shape, the text may not contain Wahb's own wordings; the same applies to the quotations in Abū Nuʿaym; yet both clusters do exude the *qiṣṣa* atmosphere and reveal a pre-"scholarly" stage of *sīra* activity.

ʿUrwa b. al-Zubayr

ʿUrwa b. al-Zubayr (ca. 23-93/643-712; Schoeler, ʿUrwa; id., *Character*, 28-32; Stülpnagel, *ʿUrwa;* Sezgin, *GAS*, i, 278-9; Duri, *Rise*, 76-95; Görke, Ḥudaybiya; Horovitz, Biographies, 548-52), a traditionist and historian from Medina, belonged to the establishment of early Islam. The Umayyad caliph ʿAbd al-Malik (r. 65-85/685-705) and his successor al-Walīd (r. 86-96/705-15) wrote to ʿUrwa for information about certain events that happened during and after the time of the Prophet. ʿUrwa's answers form a first attempt at historiography. These letters, however, are without the edifying and entertaining character of *qiṣaṣ*. Taking into account that ʿAbd al-Malik did not appreciate the then current *maghāzī*-stories (Schoeler, *Character,* 47; Jarrar, *Prophetenbiographie,* 20-3), ʿUrwa perhaps deliberately composed his letters as no-nonsense, memorizable summaries, meant to lay down in writing the politically correct versions of important events (see also POLITICS AND THE QURʾĀN). Yet, he must have drawn upon longer narratives.

The letters are scattered over various sources (on these and on the German and Italian translations see Schoeler, ʿUrwa; for Eng. trans. see Ṭabarī, *Taʾrīkh,* index, and Rubin, *Eye,* 157-61). They can be recognized by an introduction of the kind: "ʿAbd al-Malik asked about [...] and ʿUrwa wrote back [...]," although this formula is sometimes lacking. There is a fair chance that the letters indeed go back to ʿUrwa, although his wording may have suffered in the course of transmission. ʿUrwa did *not* write a book; the work published under the title *Kitāb Maghāzī rasūl Allāh* is a later concoction.

Mūsā b. ʿUqba

Mūsā b. ʿUqba al-Asadī (ca. 55-141/675-758; Sezgin, *GAS,* i, 286-7; Schoeler, Mūsā; Schacht, On Mūsā; Horovitz, Biographies, 164-7) was a Medinan scholar and historian, who collected and disseminated material on the Prophet's life, but also on the pre-Islamic period and the first caliphs. Being a client of the Zubayr family (see TRIBES AND CLANS; CLIENTS AND CLIENTAGE; ARABS) and a pupil of al-Zuhrī, he was in an excellent position to do so. His *Kitāb al-Maghāzī,* i.e. his notebook to be copied by pupils, is not extant. A selection of nineteen ḥadīths has, however, been preserved in a Berlin manuscript. G. Schoeler defends Mūsā against J. Schacht, who maintained that these texts were not really transmitted by him. He demonstrates that Mūsā's source indications (mostly al-Zuhrī) are not fictitious, and in one case even proves the authenticity of al-Zuhrī's source, who is no other than ʿUrwa b. al-Zubayr. His argument rests on the analysis of more Mūsā quotations and parallel texts than Schacht had at his disposal, and on using the common-link method (see Juynboll, Ḥadīth, 378-81).

A current scholarly desideratum is the collection and study of all Mūsā quotations that are scattered over various sources (some references in Sezgin, *GAS,* i, 287). Pending that, we have only an impression of Mūsā's activities and interests. In none of his texts seen by the present author does he refer to the Qurʾān. He does not shun *qiṣṣa* or miracle stories but has also a clear interest in chronology.

al-Zuhrī

One of the central figures of the *sīra* literature was Muḥammad b. Muslim b. Shihāb al-Zuhrī (d. 124/742; Lecker, al-Zuhrī; Horovitz, Biographies, 33-50; Schoeler, *Character,* 32-7, 47-8; Duri, *Rise,* 27-9, 113-17), a collector of both ḥadīth and stories, who was also interested in genealogy and the early caliphs. He was the most important pupil of ʿUrwa b. al-Zubayr. His works may have been no more than note books for private use and reading sessions for civil servants and pupils, but he did lend the beginning of a structure to the *sīra.* His narratives are often lengthy and have the form of ḥadīth, i.e. they have chains of transmission.

Al-Zuhrī was consulted and patronized by the Umayyad court, which implied that he should not write favorably about ʿAlī (see SHĪʿA; SHĪʿISM AND THE QURʾĀN). Allegedly he was asked by an Umayyad governor to compose a book on genealogy and a second one on *maghāzī.* The order for the first work was soon cancelled but he was to continue on the second one. Whether he really wrote it is unknown (Schoeler, *Charakter*, 47; Jarrar, *Prophetenbiographie*, 23-32). Maʿmar b. Rāshid (see below) offers a more or less uniform block of texts from al-Zuhrī's collection. His traces are found in all later *sīra* compilations.

Ibn Isḥāq and his editors

Muḥammad b. Isḥāq (Medina; ca. 85-150/704-67 [Baghdād]) is the most important author of *sīra* literature (Schoeler, *Charakter*, 37-51; Newby, *Making*, 1-31; Duri, *Rise*, 32-7; Jones, Ibn Isḥāḳ). He seems to have specialized early in narrations and history. His main teacher was al-Zuhrī, and several relatives of ʿUrwa b. al-Zubayr were informants of his. Not all scholars in Medina appreciated Ibn Isḥāq's work. By his time, narratives were generally losing ground to legal ḥadīth with fully-fledged chains of transmission (see LAW AND THE QURʾĀN; ABROGATION). He therefore left his native town and settled in Iraq (q.v.), where he found a more appreciative audience. Caliph al-Manṣūr (r. 136-58/754-75) asked him to write an all-encompassing history book, from the creation of Adam (see ADAM AND EVE) to the present day. The material on the Prophet that Ibn Isḥāq had previously collected and dictated to his pupils, was integrated into this book and given a central position. His magnum opus consisted of three volumes. The first one, *al-Mubtadaʾ* ("In the beginning") dealt with the creation of the world, the early prophets from Adam to Jesus (q.v.), and the Arabs in pre-Islamic times. In the second part, *al-Baʿth* ("The mission"), the life of the Prophet was depicted until his emigration to Medina. In part three, *al-Maghāzī* ("Expeditions and battles"), Muḥammad's activities in Medina were described. A fourth volume was added about his successors, the caliphs. Ibn Isḥāq did not merely collect materials, like his predecessors; he composed a work with a structure, sometimes chronological, sometimes arranged by subject matter.

Apparently there was only one copy of his work, and it was held in the court library in Baghdād. Ibn Isḥāq continued "publishing" from it by dictating parts to his pupils, who wrote them down verbatim. Large parts of the book, especially of the first three parts, have been handed down to us in the dictations and extracts of his pupils, and in the works of later compilers who edited these.

Three of Ibn Isḥāq's editors are worth mentioning here. The most widely known is ʿAbd al-Malik b. Hishām (d. ca. 215/830 in Egypt; see Watt, Ibn Hishām; Schoeler, *Charakter*, 50-3), whose selection from Ibn Isḥāq's work was the first *sīra* text to be transmitted in a fixed form (Arabic text: Ibn Isḥāq, *Sīra*, ed. Wüstenfeld; trans. Ibn Isḥāq-Guillaume, which displays *in margine* the page numbers of the Wüstenfeld edition). By editing only part of the original work Ibn Hishām narrowed the perspective down to the Prophet and ancient Arabia: he deals with the Kaʿba (q.v.) and the Christians and Jews on the peninsula, but not the earlier prophets. He explains difficult words and expressions in notes of his own, adds narratives, poetry and genealogical data. Ibn Hishām made judgments about the theological "purity" in the texts he selected and left out passages that he found offensive.

Al-Ṭabarī (d. 310/923; see Bosworth, al-Ṭabarī) transmits in his *Taʾrīkh* considerable parts of Ibn Isḥāq's work. For the *Kitāb al-Mubtadaʾ*, al-Ṭabarī is even our main source (Ṭabarī, *Taʾrīkh*, i, 9-872, fragments; trans. vols. i-iv, index; the stories of the prophets also in Newby, *Making*). The part on Muḥammad, in a version related to that of Ibn Hishām, but shorter, is scattered over Ṭabarī, *Taʾrīkh*, i, 1073-1837.

Two striking stories that Ibn Hishām had not included are those about Muḥammad's intended suicide (Ṭabarī, *Ta᾿rīkh,* i, 1147) and the "satanic verses" (q.v.; ibid., i, 1192-6). The *Ta᾿rīkh* is conceived as a universal history; Muḥammad is once again the central part between the earliest history (here including the kings of Persia) and the later periods of the caliphs. Much of Ibn Isḥāq's *sīra* material is also found in al-Ṭabarī's *Tafsīr,* but there it has to be laboriously gleaned from his exegesis of individual qur᾿ānic verses (some references in Newby, *Making*).

The least known edition of a part of Ibn Isḥāq's work is that by Aḥmad b. ʿAbd al-Jabbār al-ʿUṭāridī (177-272/794-886; Sezgin, GAS, i, 146). It is based on the transmission of Ibn Isḥāq's pupil Yūnus b. Bukayr (d. 199/815; Sezgin, GAS, i, 289). The extant text, which covers roughly one fifth of Ibn Hishām's recension, was not printed until 1976, and there is no translation yet. On the whole, al-ʿUṭāridī has some Ibn Isḥāq material that Ibn Hishām would have frowned upon. Moreover, he includes texts that do not go back to Ibn Isḥāq at all (Ibn Isḥāq-ʿUṭāridī; Muranyi, Riwāya; description of contents in Guillaume, *New light;* translated fragments in Rubin, *Eye,* index s.v. Yūnus b. Bukayr, and in Schoeler, *Character,* index s.v. Yūnus and al-ʿUṭāridī).

Maʿmar b. Rāshid

A medium sized, as yet untranslated *maghāzī* collection by the Yemenite Maʿmar b. Rāshid (96-154/714-70) is preserved in ʿAbd al-Razzāq, *Muṣannaf,* v, 9718-84 (Horovitz, Biographies, 167-9; Sezgin, GAS, i, 290-1; Schoeler, *Character,* 40). His work is important, since it gives an insight into the collection of al-Zuhrī, his primary source. Maʿmar offers no continuing story. His texts about important events are arranged more or less chronologically and following these are texts about the private life of the Prophet. His material included stories about the ancient prophets, which are quoted in al-Ṭabarī (*Ta᾿rīkh,* i, Index). Quotations from him can also be found in al-Wāqidī (d. 207/822) and Ibn Saʿd (d. 230/845).

al-Wāqidī

Muḥammad b. ʿUmar al-Wāqidī (130-207/747-822; see Leder, al-Wāḳidī; Duri, *Rise,* 37-9; Schoeler, *Charakter,* 137-41) was a fully-fledged historian. Due to his favorable position at the ʿAbbāsid court, he had the best possible library at his disposal; moreover he owned many books himself. He also did research by visiting the sites of battles and interviewing the descendants of the combatants. His only extant work, *al-Maghāzī,* of which we have a German translation, is an indispensable source on the expeditions and battles of the Prophet and displays a great interest in chronology (see HISTORY AND THE QURĀN). Other *sīra* texts by al-Wāqidī, e.g. a book on the death of the Prophet, have reached us in quotations in the works of his secretary Ibn Saʿd.

Typically, al-Wāqidī not only copied his sources, but also re-shaped and combined various traditions under collective chains of transmission. The question of whether he plagiarized Ibn Isḥāq remains controversial.

Ibn Saʿd

Ibn Saʿd Muḥammad b. Saʿd (168-230/784-845) wrote *Akhbār al-nabī,* the life and times of the Prophet, which is the first extant full biography of the Prophet after Ibn Isḥāq and of which an English translation is available (Fück, Ibn Saʿd; Duri, *Rise,* 39-40; Horovitz, Biographies, 521-6). A later editor integrated it into Ibn Saʿd's *Kitāb al-Ṭabaqāt al-kabīr,* a work on the Companions of the Prophet and successive generations of ḥadīth transmitters, of which it became the first part. Having been the secretary of al-Wāqidī, Ibn Saʿd heavily depends on the latter's works and is an important source for al-Wāqidī's lost works. In the *Akhbār,* the pre-Islamic section is limited to some of the early prophets and the ancestry of Muḥammad. The Meccan period is presented chronologically, interrupted only by a survey of the signs of prophethood. The chronological account of the Medinan period is interspersed with thematically arranged collections of traditions on various specialized subjects. These have proper chains of transmission, whereas the longer narratives often have collective *isnād*s. For the part on the expeditions and battles, one might prefer al-Wāqidī's *Maghāzī,* of which Ibn Saʿd offers only an abridged version, although he also included some material from elsewhere. The *Akhbār al-nabī* ends with detailed sections on the Prophet's final illness, death and burial, his heritage, and elegies on him (see also NAMES OF THE PROPHET). Here he draws upon al-Wāqidī's lost book on the death of the Prophet, but once more he enriches the section with many traditions, all with *isnād*s. For the lives of the Companions who play a part in the *sīra,* Ibn Saʿd's *Ṭabaqāt* proper is of key importance.

Ḥadīth collections

Several ḥadīth collections have a *maghāzī* section, e.g. those of Ibn Abī Shayba (*Muṣannaf,* xiv, 283-601) and al-Bukhārī's (d. 256/870) *Ṣaḥīḥ, Maghāzī.* Above we have made special mention of Maʿmar's collection, since that is presented as a distinct block with a certain degree of composition, which is not the case elsewhere. Otherwise, *sīra* fragments are found throughout the ḥadīth collections. Many narratives that would have had a defective chain of transmission or none at all in early *sīra* compilations were preserved as acceptable by being admitted into the "canonical" ḥadīth collections. Ḥadīth, however, often does not want to narrate, but focuses on what is lawful and ethical (see LAWFUL AND UNLAWFUL; ETHICS AND THE QURʾĀN). This may lead to a re- or decontextualization of *sīra* elements in ḥadīth. It is interesting to see, for instance, how the Prophet's use of a toothpick on his deathbed (Ibn Isḥāq, *Sīra,* 1011; Ibn Isḥāq-Guillaume, 682) turned from a minor narrative detail into an example for daily life in ḥadīth (Bukhārī, *Ṣaḥīḥ, Maghāzī,* 83; *Jumʿa,* 9 and see Wensinck, *Concordance,* s.v. siwāk).

Sīra *and scripture*

The Qurʾān is neither the only, nor the oldest text that had an impact on the *sīra.* In the first place, there was a heritage of ancient Arabic narrative literature, the "days of the Arabs" (*ayyām al-ʿarab;* see Mittwoch, Ayyām; Duri, *Rise,* 16-20 and index), which were stories about battles and fights interspersed with poetry (see FIGHTING; DAYS OF GOD). They served as models for accounts of military expeditions in the *sīra.* Large parts of the *sīra* originated in reaction to the Bible, the apocrypha and exegetical traditions of both Jews and Christians, as well as Christian saints' legends (for the latter, see e.g. Newby, Example). The authority of the new Prophet over the earlier prophets had to be established, and the superiority of the Qurʾān to the scriptures of others had to be demonstrated (see POLEMIC AND POLEMICAL LANGUAGE).

U. Rubin has pointed out that the Bible and the literature around it were the first scriptural influence in more *sīra* passages than had been realized before. He demonstrated by various examples how biblical references, which occur at an early stage of a text, were later removed or replaced by qurʾānic ones, since the *sīra* compilers or authors were increasingly embarrassed by the original background of their material (Rubin, *Eye;* see also Vajda, Isrāʾīliyyāt, and below under "Qur'ānization"). It is not always easy to recognize the traces of these forms of literature, since later *sīra* authors tried to erase them. Textual parallels, however remote, are rare; it is mostly the subject matter or the pattern of a narrative that can be recognized as Jewish or Christian in origin. For a better understanding of the intertextuality in the *sīra,* it is therefore necessary to study it in the context of all relevant previous literature, not only in connection with the Qur'ān.

The Qur'ān is part of the subject matter of the *sīra,* but it has also various other relations with it. Since the *sīra* is fragmentary and consists of many genres, every genre must be studied to ascertain how it reacts to qur'ānic scripture. But first the various Qur'ān-related activities in *sīra* texts must be described.

Certain *sīra* texts originate from an exegetical impulse. They elaborate on qur'ānic passages by commenting, expanding, or historicizing them through episodes of the life of the Prophet and his entourage. Other texts originated in a non-scriptural impulse, and qur'ānic words or passages were added to them secondarily (qur'ānization). This was done for a diversity of reasons: to edify; to create an elevated atmosphere; to lend weight to a statement or argument; or to replace other "scripture" or poetry that an earlier stage of the text had contained. A great many texts, however, are so complex that it is difficult to decide which impulse was predominant.

Commenting on the Qur'ān

In its narrative parts, the *sīra* is to a large extent qur'ānic exegesis *(tafsīr).* Ibn Isḥāq's method does not differ much from that of his contemporary, the qur'ānic exegete Muqātil b. Sulaymān (d. 150/767; Wansbrough, *QS,* 122-7). When we focus on the details, various methods of exegesis can be discerned. Several of them are manifest in two single passages: the commentary on Q 108 (Ibn Isḥāq, *Sīra,* 261-2; Ibn Isḥāq-Guillaume, 180-1, 725) and on Q 93 (Ibn Isḥāq, *Sīra,* 156-7; Ibn Isḥāq-Guillaume, 713-14).

Lexical explanation of one rare, difficult or ambiguous word. This is not typical of *sīra* texts, but it does occur, notably with Ibn Hishām, and a few times with Ibn Isḥāq (see DIFFICULT PASSAGES; AMBIGUOUS). A single word may be explained: a) by a single synonym. *Al-kawthar* (Q 108:1) is "great" (see SPRINGS AND FOUNTAINS; WATER OF PARADISE); *sajā* in Q 93:2 means "to be quiet"; b) by a number of words. Ibn Hishām explains the word *nādī* in Q 96:17, "let him then call his *nādī,*" as: "the meeting place in which people gather together and settle their affairs" (Ibn Isḥāq, *Sīra,* 200; Ibn Isḥāq-Guillaume, 720); c) with the help of other qur'ānic verses where the word occurs. Ibn Hishām continues by referring to *nādī* in Q 29:29 and to the synonym *nadī* in Q 19:73; d) with the help of a quotation from early poetry where the same word is used. At Q 93:2: "By the night (see DAY AND NIGHT) when it is quiet *(sajā),*" Ibn Hishām mentions a synonym for *sajā,* but he adds: "[The poet] Umayya b. Abī al-Ṣalt says: '[...] and *the night was quiet* in blackest gloom.' "

Paraphrase, explaining a sentence or passage by rewriting it in other words. Unknown words are replaced by well-known ones; the meaning of ambiguous words is fixed by the use of unambiguous words. "Your lord (q.v.) has neither forsaken you nor loathes you" (Q 93:3), is paraphrased: "meaning that he has not left you and abandoned you, nor hated you after having loved you." With the words "after having loved you," the paraphrase slips into another exegetical mode: expansion.

Specifying what is vague, with the help of external information and/or the free flow of thought. Al-Ṭabarī (*Taʾrīkh,* i, 1142) explains "on the day of the *furqān,* on the day when the two armies met" (Q 8:41; see CRITERION) as: "the battle of the Prophet with the polytheists (see POLYTHEISM AND ATHEISM; OPPOSITION TO MUḤAMMAD) at Badr (q.v.), which took place on the morning of the seventeenth of Ramaḍān (q.v.)."

Ibn Isḥāq quotes a ḥadīth according to which *kawthar* is "a river as broad as from Ṣanʿāʾ to Ayla. Its water pots are in number as the stars of heaven (see PLANETS AND STARS; HEAVEN AND SKY). Birds go down to it with necks like camels […]." In an ascension story (Ṭabarī, *Taʾrīkh,* i, 1158), *kawthar* is described as "a river [in paradise] whiter than milk (q.v.) and sweeter than honey (q.v.), with pearly domes on either side of it."

Identifying the anonymous. Who was the man with the horns whose story is told in Q 18:83-98? Ibn Isḥāq heard from a Persian source that he was an Egyptian of Greek extraction, whose name he mentions. But he also quotes a ḥadīth, according to which he was an angel. Ibn Hishām knows another name: it was Alexander (q.v.), who built Alexandria (Ibn Isḥāq, *Sīra,* 197; Ibn Isḥāq-Guillaume, 139, 719). This is an example of the unbridled imagination of the storytellers, who left no bit of the Qurʾān unexplained. The *sīra* has yet another purpose, to identify persons who are referred to in the scripture. It aims to link qurʾānic passages to situations and to record the history of early Islam, on which see below.

Narrative expansion

A short example of narrative expansion is found below, under "Linking scripture to situations" with the case of Jadd b. Qays. Two incomprehensible words in the scripture are explained by building a few sentences around them. A story can also be built around the framework of a qurʾānic passage. Maʿmar's narrative (ʿAbd al-Razzāq, *Muṣannaf,* 389-90 [no. 9743]) about the Qurayshite plot to kill the Prophet on the eve of his *hijra* is an expansion of Q 8:30: "[Remember] when the unbelievers plotted against you, to confine you, kill you or expel you. They plotted, but God plotted also, and God is the best of plotters." In the narration, the Qurayshites (see QURAYSH) gather in their council chamber, assisted by Satan in disguise. They discuss these three possible ways of dealing with Muḥammad, expelling, confining or killing him, and accept the third proposal. (To create greater suspense, the order was slightly changed.) God's counterplot consists in warning the Prophet, who can escape unseen, while ʿAlī is to sleep in the Prophet's bed, so that the Qurayshites would find only him. The whole story follows the structure of the qurʾānic verse; only the satanic motif is foreign to it.

With Ibn Isḥāq, whose work shows a well-balanced composition, *sīra* narratives that are linked to a qurʾānic passage can be much longer, and the verses need not even to be quoted. The story of the Prophet's ascension (Ibn Isḥāq, *Sīra,* 263-72; Ibn Isḥāq-Guillaume, 181-7) is preceded and followed by mentions of enemies who mocked the Prophet and of how they were punished (see MOCKERY; CHASTISEMENT AND PUNISHMENT). After the ascension story, Ibn Isḥāq continues with Gabriel (q.v.) arriving to punish the men. Apparently Ibn Isḥāq had a qurʾānic passage in mind: "And they say: '[…] we will not believe you until you […] ascend to heaven. Yet, we will not believe in your ascension, until you send down to us a book we can read'" (Q 17:90-3). Ibn Isḥāq here wants to apply the qurʾānic motif that unbelievers ask for signs (q.v.), and when these are given to them, still do not believe (see REFLECTION AND DELIBERATION; PROVOCATION).

Qur'ānization

While a *sīra* narrative may start from a qur'ānic word or pericope that is explained or expanded, the opposite can be found as well: a narrative starts from an extra-qur'ānic impulse, as e.g. the desire to tell a certain story, and is then enriched with scriptural material. This can be called "qur'ānization."

A simple form of it may be called decorative qur'ānization: the use of qur'ānic wordings to elevate the style register and to create a pious atmosphere. When Ibn Isḥāq once wanted to say "as a bringer of good tidings to all mankind" (Ibn Isḥāq, *Sīra,* 150; Ibn Isḥāq-Guillaume, 104), he did not use his own words, but preferred the syntactically unusual wordings of Q 34:28. When 'Ā'isha, in the "account of the lie" (q.v.; see also Spellberg, 'Ā'isha, 56-8), tried to build courage within herself, she borrowed the words that Jacob (q.v.) had used in his distress according to Q 12:18 (Ibn Isḥāq, *Sīra,* 735; Ibn Isḥāq-Guillaume, 496). The narrator put qur'ānic words in her mouth to show what a pious woman she was.

Not just one sentence, but the story as a whole is elevated when a narrative element is added that is built around a qur'ānic phrase, irrespective of its meaning in the original context. In the ascension story, the Prophet comments on the immense numbers of angels in heaven with the words of Q 74:31: "And none knows the armies of God but he" (Ibn Isḥāq, *Sīra,* 268; Ibn Isḥāq-Guillaume, 185; see TROOPS; RANKS AND ORDERS). In the verse itself, this phrase refers to the guardians of hell. When during the Prophet's visit to heaven the number of obligatory prayers is reduced, he is notified in qur'ānic wording: "The word is not changed with me" (Q 50:29; 'Abd al-Razzāq, *Muṣannaf,* 9719), which originally referred to the day of judgment (see LAST JUDGMENT).

But qur'ānization can take on much wider dimensions. Above, we have introduced Ma'mar's Qur'ān-based version of the story about the plot to kill the Prophet. In Ibn Isḥāq (*Sīra,* 323-6; Ibn Isḥāq-Guillaume, 221-3), that story is much longer. A narrator decided to add the qur'ānic motif of the Prophet being called a poet. The suggestion that comes up among the plotters is to confine him and to subject him to the same fate that befell the poets Zuhayr and Nābigha and others. Hereby Q 52:30 is put to use: "Or they say: 'A poet for whom we await an uncertain fate.'" The verse itself does not occur in the narrative, but the linking words are obvious: "poet(s)" and "await" *(tarabbaṣa).* For those who had not recognized it yet, Ibn Isḥāq quotes the verse in full after his narrative, as one of the verses "that God revealed about that day." Whereas the story as a whole is Qur'ān-based, this part is qur'ānized.

In that same story yet another type of qur'ānization can be seen. Wahb's version has an additional motif: God impairs the sight (see VISION AND BLINDNESS) of those who lie in wait to kill the Prophet. Miraculously, they cannot see how he walks past them and do not even notice him strewing dust onto their heads. This is illustrated by a piece of poetry attributed to 'Alī (Wahb, *Papyrus,* 140-4). The partial blindness fits well into the story and anticipates the same motif that occurs somewhat later in the story of the Prophet's emigration (cf. Rubin, *Hijra,* 60-1). Ibn Isḥāq (*Sīra,* 326; Ibn Isḥāq-Guillaume, 222), however, instead of quoting poetry, tells us that the Prophet recited Q 36:1-9 at the occasion. The choice of these verses is a bit awkward, for only Q 36:9 fits the situation: "And we covered them and they could not see." If Wahb indeed represents an older text stage, this is a case of the phenomenon that Rubin pointed out: in time, qurʾānic elements tend to replace other types of literature, since poetry or biblical texts were increasingly deemed unfit to occur in *sīra* texts (Rubin, *Eye*, 33-5, 227). Large-scale qurʾānization takes place in the reports on the battles of the Prophet; see below under "*Maghāzī*."

Linking scripture to situations

A typical objective of *sīra* is to establish a link between a qurʾānic passage (mostly a verse) and a moment in the life of the Prophet. Within the plot of a narrative, a qurʾānic verse may serve as the impulse for a subsequent action. A verse with an imperative almost cries out for a story about how the command was executed. When the verse, "and warn your closest clan members" (Q 26:214) was revealed, the Prophet warned his nephew ʿAlī and his other relatives (Ṭabarī, *Taʾrīkh*, i, 1171-4). After the revelation of, "Speak of the kindness of your lord" (Q 93:11), the Prophet began to speak secretly about God's kindness to everyone he could trust (Ibn Isḥāq, *Sīra*, 157; Ibn Isḥāq-Guillaume, 112).

But in most cases the order is the other way round: something happens, and then a qurʾānic verse is revealed. These kinds of texts are known as "occasions of revelation" (see Rippin, Occasions; Rubin, *Eye*, 226-33; Schöller, *Exegetisches Denken*, 128-33). A complete "occasion" report is characterized by the following features (not necessarily in this order): a reference to some event or situation, mostly in combination with the name(s) of one or more persons, a place, and/or an indication of time; some qurʾānic words which anticipate the qurʾānic passage that is about to be revealed; a formula like: "(Then) God revealed about …" or: "This verse was revealed about […]," and finally the quoting of the revealed passage itself.

A perfect, but late example is presented in Rippin, Occasions, 570. An example from the *sīra*, with a somewhat different structure, is: "Some mockers said to the Prophet: 'Muḥammad, if an angel had been sent to you […].' Then God revealed concerning these words of theirs: "They say: 'Why has not an angel been sent down to him?'" (Q 6:8; Ibn Isḥāq, *Sīra*, 262; Ibn Isḥāq-Guillaume, 181).

Complete "occasion"-stories are amply represented in *sīra* texts. The *sīra*, however, also contains many of them in less complete or preliminary stages. Some examples are: "Then revelations stopped for a time, so that the Prophet was distressed and grieved (see JOY AND MISERY). Then Gabriel brought him Q 93 […]" (Ibn Isḥāq, *Sīra*, 156; Ibn Isḥāq-Guillaume, 111). Ibn Isḥāq (*Sīra*, 171; Ibn Isḥāq-Guillaume, 121-2) relates about a person who had called the Prophet a sorcerer (see MAGIC), and then says: "About him Q 74:11-22 was revealed." But he does not say that it was revealed at that occasion, and as regards contents, there is no connection between the qurʾānic passage and the story. An enemy makes some insulting proposals to the Prophet. Then the latter recites Q 41:1-5, and the man leaves him in peace. This is not formally an occasion; it sounds as if the Prophet knew these verses already and recited them from memory (Ibn Isḥāq, *Sīra*, 186; Ibn Isḥāq-Guillaume, 132-3).

Sīra texts seemingly avoid the pretension of knowing God's reasons for his revelations. The Qurʾān exegete Muqātil b. Sulaymān (*Tafsīr* i, 458, ad Q 5:11) says in all innocence: "This verse was revealed *because* […] *(li-anna)*," but the *sīra* confines itself to *fī*, "concerning"; although the suggestion of causality is always there.

Scholarly opinion differs about the role of the "occasions" in the *sīra*. Lammens seems to consider the whole *sīra* a compilation of "occasions," with the exception of "a vague oral tradition" or "a primitive core" (Lammens, Koran and tradition, 170, 171). To Rubin, the *sīra* contains no occasions: "... none of the Qurʾānic verses which appear in the biography of Muḥammad can be regarded as the primary source of the story" (Rubin, *Eye*, 227). Both points of view are extremes, but there are enough cases where the exegetical impulse is obvious and where no qurʾānization can be discovered.

In certain texts, the aspect of "identifying the anonymous" seems to prevail. When the Qurʾān alludes to an unknown speaker or sinner (see SIN, MAJOR AND MINOR), the occasion-report knows who this person is. When a narrator says: "This verse was revealed concerning so-and-so," the intention may be to enhance or undermine the reputation of that person; see below under "Merits of the Companions."

An "occasion" with a multiple and complicated intention is related in connection with the expedition to Tabūk (see EXPEDITIONS AND BATTLES). While preparing for it, the Prophet asks Jadd b. Qays whether he wants to fight the Byzantines (q.v.). Jadd answers: "Will you *allow me* to stay behind *and not tempt me,* for everyone knows that I am strongly addicted to women and I am afraid that if I see the Byzantine women I shall not be able to control myself." About him the verse came down: "Among them there is one who says: 'Allow me and do not tempt me' ..." (Q 9:49; Ibn Isḥāq, *Sīra,* 894; Ibn Isḥāq-Guillaume, 602-3). This verse existed before the story. It raised three questions: Who was the "one who says"? The exegete names him. What do his words "allow me" and "do not tempt me" mean? It is explained by means of the rather strained narrative expansion, in which the very qurʾānic words are put into Jadd's mouth. In what situation did Jadd use these words? Within the report, the connection with the Tabūk expedition is created only by the mention of the Byzantine women. Outside the narrative it is corroborated by its place in the larger context of that expedition. The exegetical activities apparently were carried out only after the assignment of Q 9 to that expedition, which in itself is a case of qurʾānization. Apart from exegesis and qurʾānization, the "occasions" serve to "historicize" the Qurʾān (see Rippin, Occasions, 572) and to establish its chronology (see Böwering, Chronology). This was important for the study of law (see Burton, Abrogation), but several *sīra* compilers, who show no interest in law, deal with chronology simply out of historiographical interest.

The genres within the sīra

Now we will address the various genres within the *sīra* literature, and the degree of their scripturality. There are many places where one is tempted to consider qurʾānic exegesis as a genre, as well. Since the exegetical intention, however, pervades the whole *sīra,* it seemed preferable to treat it in the broader framework above.

Prophetic legend

Under this heading we group the texts about prophets and prophecy that aim at elaborating Muḥammad's prophetic features (Andræ, *Person Muhammeds,* ch. 1; Newby, *Making,* 1-32). The positioning of Muḥammad as the last and the best among the prophets that had already been established in the Qurʾān was completed in the *sīra*. Characteristics of the ancient prophets were ascribed to Muḥammad and vice versa. The impulse may have been the need for qurʾānic exegesis, but the elaborations in *qiṣṣa* and *sīra* are often of biblical or post-biblical inspiration and therefore scriptural in the wider sense. Many stories about the earlier prophets were collected in Ibn Isḥāq's *Kitāb al-Mubtadaʾ,* now partially preserved in al-Ṭabarī, *Taʾrīkh,* i, 86-795 (trans. also in Newby, *Making*).

A number of examples may illustrate how extant literary topics were remodeled to fit Muḥammad. The annunciation by Jesus (q.v.) of a comforter, or the Holy Spirit (q.v.; John 15:26) was applied to Muḥammad in the *sīra* (Ibn Isḥāq, *Sīra,* 150; Ibn Isḥāq-Guillaume, 104). Muḥammad's mother received an annunciation during her pregnancy not unlike the mother of Jesus (Luke 1:26-38; Ibn Isḥāq, *Sīra,* 102; Ibn Isḥāq-Guillaume, 69). These are only small-scale examples, but the annunciation is a major motif in the *sīra,* which has recently been studied by Rubin (*Eye,* 21-43). Jews and Christians are said to have known of the birth of Muḥammad in advance. They were supposed to have read in their scriptures about the coming of Muḥammad and his characteristics, so that they could recognize him as a child. The biblical texts that Jews and Christians had applied to the coming of the Messiah, or the Holy Spirit respectively, were now reinterpreted to make them refer to Muḥammad (Ibn Saʿd, *Ṭabaqāt* I, ii, 87-9; trans. i, 421-6).

When Muḥammad was with his wet-nurse, he grew up uncommonly fast (Ibn Isḥāq, *Sīra,* 105; Ibn Isḥāq-Guillaume, 71), and he was not the only prophet who did so. The Gospels of the Infancy abound in examples of Jesus' precocity.

The topic of Muḥammad's ascension (Ibn Isḥāq, *Sīra,* 263-71; Ibn Isḥāq-Guillaume, 181-7) may have been inspired by Q 17:90-3 (see Sells, Ascension, 177), but the story itself stands in a long tradition of Persian, Jewish and Christian accounts. Certain details in it are reminiscent of specific texts: e.g. the description of punishments in hell (Ibn Isḥāq, *Sīra,* 269; Ibn Isḥāq-Guillaume, 185-6; see HELL AND HELLFIRE) has parallels in the *Apocalypsis Pauli* and the Persian text *Ardā Wirāz Nāmag.*

The initial refusal of Muḥammad to recite (see RECITATION OF THE QURʾĀN) when Gabriel brought him the revelation on mount Ḥirāʾ (*mā aqraʾu;* Ibn Isḥāq, *Sīra,* 152; Ibn Isḥāq-Guillaume, 106 has a mistaken translation) has precedents in the excuses of several other prophets (cf. Exodus 3:11-4:13; Jeremiah 1:6; Jonah 1:2-3 and Q 37:140).

The *sīra* sometimes recapitulates prophetic characteristics in general statements, most of which are rooted in biblical or qurʾānic scripture. E.g. the saying "There is no prophet but has shepherded a flock" (Ibn Isḥāq, *Sīra,* 106; Ibn Isḥāq-Guillaume, 72) holds true of the qurʾānic Moses (q.v.; Q 28:22-8) and of the patriarchs as well as Moses, David (q.v.) in the Bible and, metaphorically, of Jesus, "the good shepherd" (John 10:11, 14).

The dictum "A prophet does not die without being given the choice" (Ibn Isḥāq, *Sīra,* 1008; Ibn Isḥāq-Guillaume, 680), however, applies only to Muḥammad. Several prophets had not died in the normal way. Idrīs (q.v.) was raised to a high place (Q 19:57). In the Bible it was Enoch, Moses and Elijah (q.v.) who were "raised." Jesus was resurrected and then raised into heaven (see RESURRECTION). Since Q 3:144 mentions the possibility of the Prophet's death, Islamic legend had to go its own way on this point. Muḥammad was given the choice between remaining alive or joining the highest companions (*al-rafīq al-aʿlā;* cf. Q 4:69) in paradise (Ibn Isḥāq, *Sīra,* 1000, 1011; Ibn Isḥāq-Guillaume, 678, 682). Yet, an attempt was made to make his death resemble the forty-day absence of Moses on Mount Sinai (q.v.; Ibn Isḥāq, *Sīra,* 1012; Ibn Isḥāq-Guillaume, 682).

In the Qur᾿ān, miracles (q.v.) play a part in the stories of most prophets, but to Muḥammad they are given only sparsely. The miracles that are alluded to in the Qur᾿ān, as, for example, the intervention of angels in the battles of Badr (q.v.) and Ḥunayn (q.v.), are elaborated in the *sīra*. In addition to that, *sīra* texts have few inhibitions about making more miracles happen to or through the Prophet (Andræ, *Person Muhammeds*, 46-68), such as stones and trees talking to him, trees changing places, the multiplication of water and food, healings, the discovery of poisoned food, and even an unexpected win in a wrestling match (Ibn Isḥāq, *Sīra*, 258; Ibn Isḥāq-Guillaume, 178). Ibn Saʿd (*Ṭabaqāt* I, i, 96-135; trans. i, 170-219) collected these "signs of prophecy" in a separate chapter; also al-Bukhārī has a small collection (*Ṣaḥīḥ*, *Manāqib*, 25). Later on, they developed into a literary genre in its own right (*dalāʾil al-nubuwwa*; cf. Kister, Sīrah, 355).

Maghāzī

As we have said at the start, the word *maghāzī* could be applied to the *sīra* literature as a whole. Here we will deal with *maghāzī* in the narrower sense: stories about the raids, military campaigns and battles organized or attended by the Prophet (see Faizer, Expeditions, and its bibliography; M. Hinds, Maghāzī; Duri, *Rise*, index s.v. *maghāzī*; Jones, Maghāzī). They may vary from the assassination of a single person through small raids to campaigns of considerable dimensions. The main sources are Ibn Isḥāq and al-Wāqidī. Both tried to establish a chronology, as Mūsā b. ʿUqba apparently also intended to do, but no reliable chronological table can be verified (Schöller, *Exegetisches Denken*, 215-29; Jones, Chronology). A convenient survey of all the battle accounts and their sources in English is found in Watt, *Medina* (esp. 339-43).

Maghāzī stories originally had nothing to do with the Qur᾿ān. They were a continuation of the pre-Islamic tales of tribal battles (*ayyām al-ʿarab*). In the (theoretical) original *maghāzī* stories, prose was mixed with poetry; they contained names of participants and heroes, names of places and a description of the action, sometimes with its occasion and consequences (see GEOGRAPHY AND THE QUR᾿ĀN). But such stories that are free of ideology do not exist in the *sīra*.

The story of Hamza's expedition to the coast, with its exchange of poetry as the main part (Ibn Isḥāq, *Sīra*, 419-21; Ibn Isḥāq-Guillaume, 283-5), has an ancient structure, but the poetry has already been touched by qur᾿ānic vocabulary. In the small report on the so-called "barley meal raid" the poetry comes after the story (Ibn Isḥāq, *Sīra*, 543-4; Ibn Isḥāq-Guillaume, 361-2; Ṭabarī, *Taʾrīkh*, i, 1365). Both sources have different poems; apparently they were felt to be interchangeable. Al-Wāqidī (*Maghāzī*, 181-2) has only two lines, from the same poem as in Ibn Isḥāq. The later the source, the less poetry it contains.
At the end of another expedition story, a qur᾿ānic verse is quoted that was associated with it secondarily. The story takes the shape of an "occasion of revelation." Then follows the poetry that was composed about that expedition (Ibn Isḥāq, *Sīra*, 642-8; Ibn Isḥāq-Guillaume, 429-33).

This pattern is followed in the larger reports as well. The account of the battle of Badr (q.v.; Ibn Isḥāq, *Sīra*, 427-539; Ibn Isḥāq-Guillaume, 289-360) is a mix of all sorts of sources, but is essentially a narrative on a battle. It has some poetry and was apparently already interspersed early with a few qur᾿ānic elements: God's promise, the help of fighting angels, the enemy being supported by Satan (see DEVIL; ENEMIES; PARTIES AND FACTIONS). Then follow several bundles of texts. One is the collected poetry on the subject, which one can imagine had been integrated into the narrative itself at an earlier stage. Furthermore, there are lists of participants and of the fallen.

Almost immediately after the account proper follows a Qurʾān-centered collection, in which large passages from Q 8 are applied to this battle. In them, the story of Badr is re-told in the light of the Qurʾān. The parts of Q 8, which were chosen more or less arbitrarily, are applied verse by verse to the details of the battle (Wansbrough, *Sectarian milieu,* 25-31). This is a case of qurʾānization. In al-Wāqidī (*Maghāzī,* 19-128) these qurʾānic passages are integrated into the battle story itself, although a separate part on Q 8 is also maintained, rather redundantly; perhaps only because it was there (al-Wāqidī, *Maghāzī,* 131-8; Wansbrough, *Sectarian milieu,* 25-31). This pattern is followed in several larger *maghāzī* stories: Uḥud, the battle of the trench (see PEOPLE OF THE DITCH; UKHDŪD), Qurayẓa (q.v.), Naḍīr (q.v.). Each of them has received "its" sūra. But it also happens that the qurʾānic passage is the origin of the very story, as is the case in Ibn Isḥāq's report on the expedition against the Jewish tribe Qaynuqāʿ (q.v.; Q 5:51-8; see Schöller, *Exegetisches Denken,* 232).

Even within the *maghāzī* genre there may be an impact of the Bible. Von Mžik pointed to parallels between the biblical story of Gideon (Judges 7:2-22; cf. Q 2:249) and certain elements in the Badr story. Both recount a victory of a host of some 300 men facing fearful odds. In both cases God offers help, and the defeat of the enemy is predicted by a dream of someone in the enemy camp (Ibn Isḥāq, *Sīra,* 428-9, 506, 516; Ibn Isḥāq-Guillaume, 290-1, 336, 340; Jones, Dream).

Last, but not least, the various *maghāzī* texts may influence each other. Schöller (*Exegetisches Denken,* 241-9) shows that al-Wāqidī's version of the Qaynuqāʿ story borrowed elements from reports about the expulsion of other Jewish tribes.

Poetry

One genre in the *sīra* that has no connection with the Qurʾān is poetry (Horovitz, Einlagen; Kister, Sīrah, 357-61; Wansbrough, *Milieu,* 32-9). Of old, storytellers had combined prose with poetry in their stories, and the *sīra* narrators continued this tradition. The poetry has functions similar to those of speeches (see DIALOGUE): it captivates the audience by switching to another mode, underlining a point or emphasizing a dramatic moment. In *sīra* narratives too, battling or dying heroes are given their chance to improvise poetry, be it self-praise, vituperation or a rhyming creed, and relatives declaim elegies for those who fell. Such poems often have little merit and are ascribed to unlikely poets. Even more than the narrative parts of the *sīra,* they were severely criticized (ʿArafat, Early critics).

Often enough, the pieces of poetry are not "insertions" that could be cut out without damaging the story or the report, but indispensable constituents of it (Wansbrough, *Sectarian milieu,* 38-9; an extreme case: Ibn Isḥāq, *Sīra,* 144-9; Ibn Isḥāq-Guillaume, 100-3). Poetry was not unproblematic to early Muslims, since the Qurʾān takes a hard line on it (Q 26:224-6; 52:29-30). The story of the Prophet's approval of a long poem by the newly converted Kaʿb b. Zuhayr (Ibn Isḥāq, *Sīra,* 887-92; Ibn Isḥāq-Guillaume, 597-601; Zwettler, The poet) was one of the means to legitimize poetry that fulfilled the Islamic condition of not provoking intertribal hostility.

The *sīra* pays much attention to the verse of Ḥassān b. Thābit (d. ca. 50/669; see ʿArafat, Ḥassān), the "court poet" and elegist of the Prophet (Ibn Isḥāq, *Sīra,* 1022-6 and index; Ibn Isḥāq-Guillaume, 689-90, 795-8 and index). Much of the verse ascribed to him is considered spurious today.

The qurʾānic verdict on poetry, as well as the increasing authority of the Qurʾān in general, resulted in a decreasing use of poetry and an increasing application of qurʾānic material in *sīra* texts through the years (cf. Rubin, *Eye,* 227, 121). As we saw, Ibn Isḥāq placed all the relevant poetry after the accounts of the larger battles. Maybe the reconstitution and qurʾānization (on which see above) of these long narratives had already taken place in his sources and made it impossible to keep the verses in their original places, or he himself felt it proper to give this poetry a less prominent place. For a case of poetry being replaced by qurʾānic text in a later version of a narrative, see above under "Qurʾānization"; about the use of pre-Islamic poetry in the Qurʾān exegesis see above under "Commenting on the Qurʾān."

Addresses

Sīra texts contain speeches and sermons by the Prophet at solemn occasions, e.g. his first sermons in Medina (Ibn Isḥāq, *Sīra,* 340-1; Ibn Isḥāq-Guillaume, 230-1), his speech at the door of the Kaʿba after the conquest of Mecca (q.v.; Ibn Isḥāq, *Sīra,* 821; Ibn Isḥāq-Guillaume, 553; see CONQUESTS) and during the Farewell Pilgrimage (q.v.; Ibn Isḥāq, *Sīra,* 968-9; Ibn Isḥāq-Guillaume, 650-1). They are a mix of *qiṣṣa*-style piety and regulations, enriched with some qurʾānic allusions or quotations. Some speeches by other persons have been written down: one by the Prophet's uncle ʿAbbās at the ʿAqaba meeting (Ibn Isḥāq, *Sīra,* 296; Ibn Isḥāq-Guillaume, 203) and one of Jaʿfar b. Abī Ṭālib at the court of the Negus (Ibn Isḥāq, *Sīra,* 968-9; Ibn Isḥāq-Guillaume, 650-1; see ABYSSINIA). Speeches have a similar function as poetry, or in some cases as documents: they catch the attention and emphasize the importance of what is brought forward (Wansbrough, *Sectarian milieu,* 38).

Written documents

In this context "written documents" means texts that present themselves as such. The question of whether they are fictitious or not need not bother us. In *sīra* collections, various types of documents are found:

Treaties. The "Document *(kitāb)* of Medina" (Ibn Isḥāq, *Sīra,* 341-4; Ibn Isḥāq-Guillaume, 231-3), is an agreement between "Muḥammad the Prophet" and "the believers and Muslims of Quraysh (q.v.) and Yathrib [= Medina (q.v.)] and those who follow them, join them, and strive alongside them," including Jewish groups. The "Document," whose textual unity remains controversial, is generally considered to be very old. It contains no allusions to the Qurʾān and has a matter-of-fact attitude towards the Jewish tribes of Medina, which are included in the community *(umma),* whereas the mainstream *sīra* stories are hostile to the Jews and full of intertextuality. The names of the three Jewish tribes (Naḍīr, Qurayẓa, Qaynuqāʿ), which through the *sīra* have become widely known in the Islamic tradition, do not appear in the Document (Humphreys, *Islamic history,* 92-8, with bibliography; Rubin, Constitution). The text of the Ḥudaybiya (q.v.) treaty is given in full (Ibn Isḥāq, *Sīra,* 747-8; Ibn Isḥāq-Guillaume, 504-5). Treaties with tribes (see TRIBES AND CLANS; APOSTASY) are often embodied in letters.

Correspondence of the Prophet with governors, Arabian tribes, foreign rulers and others (Ibn Abī Shayba, *Muṣannaf,* xiv, 336-46, nos. 18,475-86; Ibn Saʿd, *Ṭabaqāt* I, ii, 15-38;

trans. i, 304-45; spread all over Ibn Isḥāq, al-Ṭabarī and al-Wāqidī; Hamidullah, *Documents;* Sperber, Schreiben Muḥammads). Most of this correspondence contains no allusions to the Qurʾān; notable exceptions are the letters to the rulers of Persia and Ethiopia (Ṭabarī, *Taʾrīkh,* i, 1569-71), and the false prophet Musaylima (q.v.). Letters with qurʾānic content are unlikely to be old (see also ORALITY AND WRITING IN ARABIA).

Lists. Sīra texts contain lists. Most of them enumerate names of persons, e.g. the oldest converts to Islam; the participants in battles; those who were killed in action (on both sides); the emigrants to Ethiopia and to Medina (see EMIGRANTS AND HELPERS), as well as those who returned from exile in Ethiopia or who died in that country; the participants in certain negotiations (see CONTRACTS AND ALLIANCES; BREAKING TRUSTS AND CONTRACTS); the members of certain tribes who came to the Prophet; those who received part of the booty (q.v.). Such lists may have been copied from government registers, where they originally had the practical function of establishing the rank of a person or his descendants with the "Islamic elite," and the size of the state income that could be claimed (see Duri, Dīwān; Puin, *Dīwān*). Their purpose in the *sīra* is related to that of the genre of "Merits" (on which see below), i.e. to enhance the reputation of the Companions mentioned therein. Purely historiographical are surveys of the Prophet's military actions (Ibn Isḥāq, *Sīra,* 972-3; Ibn Isḥāq-Guillaume, 659-60; also Ibn Saʿd, *Ṭabaqāt* II, i, 1-2; trans. ii, 2). The greatest list makers were al-Wāqidī and Ibn Saʿd. The latter went to great lengths: he listed even the camels and goats of the Prophet (Ibn Saʿd, *Ṭabaqāt* I, ii, 176-9; trans. i, 584-90; see CAMEL; HIDES AND FLEECE; ANIMAL LIFE).

Most lists in the *sīra* are by their nature not scriptural. But there are exceptions: the enumeration of twelve leaders of the Helpers is linked to the twelve disciples of Jesus (Ibn Isḥāq, *Sīra,* 299; Ibn Isḥāq-Guillaume, 204; see APOSTLE). The description of the route taken by Muḥammad in his emigration to Medina, a trajectory unspectacular in itself (Ibn Isḥāq, *Sīra,* 332-3; Ibn Isḥāq-Guillaume, 226-7), may be inspired by the biblical list of stopping places during Israel's (q.v.) exodus (Numbers 33; see also CHILDREN OF ISRAEL).

Genealogy

In the tribally organized Arabian society, genealogy had always stood in the center of historiographical interest, with all the fictionality it inevitably involved (Rosenthal, Nasab; id., *Historiography,* 95-100; Duri, *Rise,* 41-2, 50-4; Kister, Sīrah, 361-2; Noth/Conrad, *Historical tradition,* 37-8). The aspiration was to establish one's filiation from the noblest Arabian forebears possible, ideally from the legendary Maʿadd (see PRE-ISLAMIC ARABIA AND THE QURʾĀN).

Sīra authors continued this activity. Their first aim was to establish the purity of Muḥammad's pedigree and the nobility of his ancestors. Ibn Isḥāq's genealogy of the Prophet in the male line (Ibn Isḥāq, *Sīra,* 3; Ibn Isḥāq-Guillaume, 3) goes further back than Maʿadd. About half of the fifty names are Arabic, but beyond Maʿadd the names are biblical (cf. Genesis 5 and 11:10-32; Ṭabarī, *Taʾrīkh,* i, 1113-23). They link the Prophet to some of the key figures of Islamic salvation (q.v.) history: Ishmael (q.v.), Abraham (q.v.), Noah (q.v.) and Adam (see ADAM AND EVE), thus elaborating the qurʾānic motif of Muḥammad being the last in a succession of prophets. Ibn Isḥāq's genealogy is reminiscent of that of

"Jesus Christ, the son of David, the son of Abraham" at the beginning of the New Testament (42 names in the reversed order; Matthew 1:1-17).

A list of the ancient prophets from Adam to Muḥammad, with their respective pedigrees (Ibn Saʿd, *Ṭabaqāt* I, i, 26-7; trans. i, 48-9), functions as a kind of spiritual genealogy of the latter. It establishes a relation without claiming physical filiation.

There are endless genealogies of the early prophets, notably in al-Ṭabarī's *Taʾrīkh* and Ibn Saʿd's *Ṭabaqāt*, that are not linked to Muḥammad. These are obviously biblically inspired. On the other hand, several ḥadīth criticize the mentioning of biblical names in the Prophet's genealogy ("genealogists are liars"), arguing that the Qurʾān leaves his oldest forebears unnamed; others replace them with purely Arabic names (Ibn Saʿd, *Ṭabaqāt* I, i, 27-9; trans. i, 49-52). There are non-scriptural genealogies of Muḥammad's father and mother. Many traditions establish the pedigree of the female ancestors of the Prophet in the maternal line (Ibn Saʿd, *Ṭabaqāt* I, i, 30-6; trans. i, 54-63; see PATRIARCHY; GENDER). All of them are purely Arabian. There are more than one hundred "mothers," well distributed over all tribes. Apparently the objective was to demonstrate how firmly connected with all Arabian tribes the Prophet was, and to counter-balance the large impact of non-Arabic traditions.

The numerous genealogies of Companions of the Prophet that found their way into *sīra* texts are also non-scriptural, including those of the Prophet's wives (see WIVES OF THE PROPHET). They intend to show the nobility of these persons and their closeness to the Prophet, and serve similar purposes as the "Merits" texts.

The merits of the Companions

The *sīra* is not only interested in the Prophet, but also in his Companions who constituted the first Islamic community (see Muranyi, *Prophetengenossen;* id., Ṣaḥāba). Apart from being an archive of genealogies and lists of these Companions' names, it also contains many narratives about their deeds. By such stories people wanted to keep the past alive, as they had always done. Later generations tried to put their forebears in a favorable light, to recount their deeds that were approved or praised by the Prophet, and to emphasize their merits *(faḍāʾil, manāqib)* for nascent Islam, if need be by contrasting them to the demerits *(mathālib)* of others. There was also a practical reason to do so. A Companion's position in a list of beneficiaries of donations (see above under "Written documents") was corroborated by reports about him. Moreover, before the sunna of the Prophet became predominant in Islamic law, the scholars were just as interested in the "way of acting" (*sīra* or *sunna*) of the earliest caliphs and other prestigious Companions as a means of establishing the right behavior. Hence several *sīra* works also dealt with the period after the death of the Prophet.

A specific type of text on merits that features in the *sīra* is that of the *awāʾil,* which record by whom something was done for the first time (see Rosenthal, Awāʾil; Ibn Abī Shayba, *Muṣannaf,* xiv, 68-147). The first male who believed in the Prophet was ʿAlī (Ibn Isḥāq, *Sīra,* 158-61; Ibn Isḥāq-Guillaume, 114-15). ʿAbdallāh b. Masʿūd was the first after the Prophet to recite the Qurʾān openly in Mecca (Ibn Isḥāq, *Sīra,* 202; Ibn Isḥāq-Guillaume, 141); the first to hold Friday prayers in Medina was Muṣʿab b. ʿUmayr (Mūsā b. ʿUqba, Fragm. 2; see FRIDAY PRAYER). It may have come naturally for the community to have more regard for the earliest Muslims than for later converts. The first emigrants from Mecca and the first helpers in Medina, as groups, enjoy a special esteem as well.

The functioning of the "merits" genre as an instrument of public opinion may be demonstrated by the example of one Companion. Saʿd b. Abī Waqqāṣ (d. after 40/660; see Hawting, Saʿd) was one of the first Muslims. He led several military expeditions, took part in all major battles and was to become a successful general. But when he commanded the army that defeated the Persians at Qādisiyya (ca. 14/635), he did not attend the battle in person — allegedly for health reasons. Some authors criticize him for this absence. In a *sīra* narrative this criticism is apparently given more weight by projecting it back into the lifetime of the Prophet. It says that Saʿd for some trivial reason failed to take part in a raid on which the Prophet had sent him (Ibn Isḥāq, *Sīra*, 424; Ibn Isḥāq-Guillaume, 287; Ṭabarī, *Taʾrīkh*, i, 1274, 1277; cf. Watt, *Medina*, 6). In contrast, other texts state emphatically that Saʿd was the first to shed blood (Ibn Isḥāq, *Sīra*, 166; Ibn Isḥāq-Guillaume, 118) and the first to shoot an arrow for the cause of Islam (Ibn Isḥāq, *Sīra*, 416; Ibn Isḥāq-Guillaume, 281; Wāqidī, *Maghāzī*, 10; Ṭabarī, *Taʾrīkh*, i, 1267). Are these mere praises of Saʿd or attempts to wipe away the blot on his reputation? At any rate, the example shows how a Companion could be given positive or negative "press" in *sīra* texts.

The attitudes towards the most prominent Companions, the first caliphs, strongly diverge in the *sīra*. Both their adherents and adversaries tried to make their points in the various narratives, e.g. in those about the death-bed of the Prophet, where the matter of his succession was an issue. A special case is ʿAbbās b. ʿAbd al-Muṭṭalib (see Watt, ʿAbbās). He was Muḥammad's uncle, but not a "Companion," since he never became a Muslim. To the ʿAbbāsid rulers he was a prestigious forebear. Hence we see that Ibn Isḥāq, who worked for the ʿAbbāsid court, has favorable accounts of him (Ibn Isḥāq, *Sīra*, 296, 1007; Ibn Isḥāq-Guillaume, 203, 680), whereas Wahb b. Munabbih is negative about him (Wahb, *Papyrus*, 126). Mūsā b. ʿUqba (Fragm. no. 6) attempts to establish his kinship with the Helpers of Medina.

Merits have their counterparts in demerits *(mathālib)*. These are not always presented as subtly as in the case of Saʿd. In the story about the Muslim emigrants to Ethiopia and the visit paid to the Negus by pagan Meccans (Ibn Isḥāq, *Sīra*, 217-22; Ibn Isḥāq-Guillaume, 150-3; Raven, Negus, 200-1), the good characters are early Muslims with impeccable records, whereas the villains were known as late and possibly opportunistic converts.

There is little qurʾānic material in the "merits," apart from some mentions of privileged groups of Companions in Q 9:100; 56:10-11; 59:9-10, but there are many qurʾānic verses about the hypocrites, who are also an extensive topic in the *sīra* (see HYPOCRITES AND HYPOCRISY). There is no biblical background, unless one thinks of vague thematic parallels, e.g. that of ʿUmar, a harsh enemy of Islam, turning into its most ardent defender (Ibn Isḥāq, *Sīra*, 224-7; Ibn Isḥāq-Guillaume, 155-7), as Paul had been for nascent Christianity (Acts 9:1-29).

The deeds of the Companions also found their way into ḥadīth collections in chapters entitled *faḍāʾil* or *manāqib al-aṣḥāb* and, from Ibn Saʿd's *Ṭabaqāt* onwards, in works especially dedicated to them (see Kern, Companions, primary bibliography).

Apart from showing an interest in individuals, the *sīra* also preserves pieces of tribal history, such as reports on delegations of tribes to the Prophet and their treaties with him, or on conflicts between tribes. Also the rivalry between the Emigrants and Helpers finds its expression in the *sīra*.

Sīra *and historiography*

Can *sīra* texts be useful sources for a reliable biography of Muḥammad, or for the historiography of early Islam? The question has occupied Orientalists for a century and a half (Jeffery, Quest; Peters, Quest; Ibn Warraq, *Quest;* Rodinson, Survey; Watt, Reliability; Schoeler, *Charakter,* 9-24; Schöller, *Exegetisches Denken,* 1-5, 106-14; Motzki, *Biography,* xi-xv). Ernest Renan (1823-1893) was full of confidence: whereas the origins of other religions are lost in mystery and dreams, Islam, as he wrote in 1851, "was born in the full light of history; its roots are on the surface. The life of its founder is as well known to us as that of any sixteenth-century reformer" (quoted in Ibn Warraq, *Quest,* 129; French original in Gilliot, Muḥammad, 4). It set the tune for the rest of the nineteenth century: whereas Orientalists and Christian theologians deconstructed the Bible and left little of the life of Jesus and the founding myths of Christianity, they were quite naive towards the sources on early Islam. The German Julius Wellhausen (1844-1918) is another example of this type of Orientalist. He hypercritically dissected the Hebrew Bible, but was rather uncritical when it came to accepting Islamic tradition. These old-style Orientalists left no room for a divine inspiration of the Qurʾān or for miracles, and since Ignaz Goldziher (1850-1921) they had a keen eye for political or doctrinal tendencies in the sources. But when texts contradicted each other, they eliminated the less likely ones and assumed that there was enough left to reconstruct the historical past "as it had really been."

This was strongly doubted by Caetani, who edited a synopsis (*Annali;* 1905-07) of all early sources known at the time, which was preceded by a critical introduction. Henri Lammens (1862-1937) was equally skeptical. He considered the whole *sīra* dependent on the Qurʾān and therefore historically unreliable. The period after the First World War in Europe was not favorable for critical *sīra* studies (see POST-ENLIGHTENMENT ACADEMIC STUDY OF THE QURʾĀN). The wave of skepticism seemed over and the quest for "what had really happened" was resumed. Scholarly biographies of Muḥammad were written, the apogee of which was the monumental work by Watt, which appeared in the fifties *(Mecca; Medina)*.

The belief in the usefulness of *sīra* texts for historiography was shaken in the seventies by a new wave of criticism and skepticism. Wansbrough dated the Qurʾān much later than did all others, and applied "source criticism" to the *sīra,* as it had been done with the Bible, analyzing the various literary genres and which purposes they served. Crone and Cook, in their controversial *Hagarism* (1977) continued this literary approach. Moreover they displayed a fundamental mistrust of Islamic tradition and brought forward the hitherto neglected extra-Islamic sources — a line of research further pursued by Hoyland in *Seeing Islam* — and had a keen eye for the material, economic and geographical realities of the Arabian lands (see TRADE AND COMMERCE; ECONOMICS; CARAVAN). In her *Meccan trade* (1987), Crone reduced the legendary Meccan trade republic, and thereby the rise of Islam, to realistic proportions.

A lasting outcome of modern research has been the awareness of many *sīra* genres as literature. *Sīra* narratives are neither police records nor eyewitness reports, nor transcripts of things said, but are structured along the lines of sometimes long established literary patterns. They belong to certain genres and, as all literature, display a good deal of intertextuality. In general one might say: the more intertextuality an account reveals, the less likely a source it is for historiography (see HISTORY AND THE QURʾĀN; LITERATURE AND THE QURʾĀN). A text that originated on the base of a biblical or qurʾānic text or along the pattern of a saint's legend can be used for the history of ideas in their time of origin, but not for that of the events that are represented. Equally unusable are texts that want to preach or to glorify. Some of the genres (documents, genealogy, "merits") present themselves as historical sources, but even they are of limited use for historiography in the modern sense. The *sīra* as a whole is a vehicle of salvation (q.v.) history rather than scientific history.

A post-skeptical attitude, no longer keen on deconstruction, is found with Rubin, in whose book "the effort to isolate the 'historical' from the 'fictional' in the early Islamic texts is given up entirely" (Rubin, *Eye,* 3) and with Schöller, to whom any historical information that might be found in the *sīra* would be "a by-product, in a way, within the complex process that resulted in the formation of the prophetic biography" (*Exegetisches Denken,* 36). A certain nostalgia for "a true historical biography of the Prophet" can be heard in Schoeler, *Charakter,* and in Motzki (*Biography,* 233), which does not keep them from applying fully up-to-date research methods. Peters shows himself well aware of the nature of the sources and at the same time gropes his way towards a biography (Peters, *Origins*). To non-Muslims the idea that little might be known about Muḥammad may be slightly disturbing, but not more than that. To Muslims, the problem has a different dimension. Of old, the *sīra* had less prestige than ḥadīth, yet undermining the historicity of the *sīra* may well be felt as an attack on the religion itself. It would be most important to take note of what present-day Muslims have brought forward on the subject, but unfortunately a survey or study of modern Muslim attitudes towards *sīra* criticism is still lacking.

Wim Raven

Bibliography
(see also the bibliographies of the articles EXPEDITIONS AND BATTLES; MUḤAMMAD)
Primary: Abū Nuʿaym al-Iṣfahānī, *Ḥilyat al-awliyāʾ wa-ṭabaqāt al-aṣfiyāʾ,* 10 vols., Cairo 1932-8; Bukhārī, *Ṣaḥīḥ;* Ibn Abī Shayba, *al-Kitāb al-Muṣannaf fī l-aḥādīth wa-l-āthār,* ed. ʿAbd al-Khāliq al-Afghānī, 15 vols., Hyderabad/Bombay 1399-1403/1979-83; Ibn Isḥāq, *Sīra,* ed. Wüstenfeld; Ibn Isḥāq-Guillaume; Ibn Isḥāq-ʿUṭāridī, *Sīrat Ibn Isḥāq al-mussammā bi-Kitāb al-Mubtadaʾ wa-l-mabʿath wa-l-maghāzī,* ed. M. Ḥamīd Allāh, Rabat 1976, repr. Konya 1401/1981 (another ed.: Ibn Isḥāq, *Kitāb al-Siyar wa-l-maghāzī,* ed. S. Zakkār, Beirut 1389/1978); Ibn Saʿd, *Ṭabaqāt,* ed. Sachau; Eng. trans. of the *sīra* part: *Ibn Saʿd's Kitab al-Tabaqat al-kabīr,* trans. S. Moinul Haq and H.K. Ghazanfar, Karachi, vol. 1, 1967, vol. 2, 1972 (Pakistan Historical Society Publication Nos. 46, 59); Maʿmar b. Rāshid, *[Kitāb al-Maghāzī],* in ʿAbd al-Razzāq, *Muṣannaf,* nos. 9718-84; Mūsā b. ʿUqba, *Aḥādīth muntakhaba min Maghāzī —,* ed. M.Ḥ. Salmān, Beirut 1991; id., *al-Maghāzī,* ed. M. Bāqashīsh Abū Mālik, Agadir 1994; *Mūsā b. ʿUqba:* E. Sachau, Das Berliner Fragment des Mûsâ Ibn ʿUḳba. Ein Beitrag zur Kenntniss der ältesten arabischen Geschichtsliteratur, in *Sitzungsberichte der Königlich Preussischen Akademie der Wissenschaften* (1904), 445-70 (text, German trans. and comm.; Eng. trans. in Ibn Isḥāq-Guillaume, xliii-vii); Ṭabarī, *Tafsīr;* id., *Taʾrīkh;* Eng. trans E. Yarshater (ed.), *The history of al-Ṭabarī. An annotated translation,* 39 vols., Albany 1985-1999; ʿUrwa b. al-Zubayr, *Maghāzī rasūl Allāh, bi-riwāyat Abī l-Aswad ʿanhu,* ed. M.M. al-Aʿẓamī, Riyadh 1981 (this is *not* a book by ʿUrwa); Wahb b. Munabbih: R.G. Khoury, *Der Heidelberger Papyrus PSR Heid Arab 23. 1. Leben und Werk des Dichters. 2. Faksimiletafeln,* Wiesbaden 1972 (ed., Ger. trans. and study); Wāqidī, *Kitāb al-Maghāzī,* ed. M. Jones, 3 vols., London 1965-6 (abr. Ger. trans. J. Wellhausen, *Muhammed in Medina. Das ist Vakidi's Kitab alMaghazi in verkürzter deutscher Wiedergabe,* Berlin 1882); al-Zuhrī, Muḥammad b. Muslim,

al-Maghāzī al-nabawiyya, ed. and intro. S. Zakkār, Damascus 1980 (this is *not* by al-Zuhrī, but roughly identical with Maʿmar b. Rāshid's *Maghāzī*).
Secondary: T. Andræ, *Die person Muhammeds in lehre und glaube seiner gemeinde,* Stockholm 1918; W. ʿArafat, An aspect of the forger's art in early Islamic poetry, in BSOAS 28 (1965), 477-82; id., Early critics of the authenticity of the poetry in the *sîra,* in BSOAS 21 (1958), 453-63; id., Ḥassān ibn Thābit, in EI², iii, 271-3; C.H. Becker, Prinzipielles zu Lammens' Sīrastudien, in *Der Islam* 4 (1913), 263-9 (Eng. trans. as "Matters of fundamental importance for research into the life of Muhammad," in Ibn Warraq, *The quest for the historical Muhammad,* Amherst, NY 2000, 330-6); C. E. Bosworth, al-Ṭabarī, in EI², x, 11-15; G. Böwering, Chronology and the Qurʾān, in EQ, i, 316-35; J. Burton, Abrogation, in EQ, i, 11-19; L. Caetani, *Annali dell' Islam* [i-ii], Milan 1905-7; P. Crone, *Meccan trade and the rise of Islam,* Princeton 1987; id. and M. Cook, *Hagarism. The making of the Islamic world,* Cambridge 1977; A.A. Duri, Dīwān i, in EI², ii, 323-7; id., *The rise of historical writing among the Arabs,* ed. and trans. L.I. Conrad, intro. F.M. Donner, Princeton 1983 (= updated trans. of *Baḥth fī nashʾat ʿilm al-taʾrīkh ʿinda l-ʿarab,* Beirut 1960); S. El Calamawy, Narrative elements in the *ḥadīth* literature, in Beeston, CHAL, i, 308-16; T. Fahd (ed.), *La vie du prophète Mahomet. Colloque de Strasbourg (octobre 1980),* Paris 1983; R. Faizer, Expeditions and battles, in EQ, ii, 143-53; J.W. Fück, Ibn Saʿd, in EI², iii, 922-3; Cl. Gilliot, Exegesis of the Qurʾān: Classical and medieval, in EQ, ii, 99-124; id., *Muḥammad,* le Coran et les 'contraintes de l'histoire,' in Wild, *Text,* 3-26; Goldziher, MS; A. Görke, The historical tradition about al-Ḥudaybiya. A study of ʿUrwa b. al-Zubayr's account, in H. Motzki (ed.), *The biography of Muḥammad. The issue of the sources,* Leiden 2000, 240-75; A. Guillaume, *New light on the life of Muhammad,* Manchester n.d. (*JSS* Monograph no. 1); M. Hamidullah, *Documents sur la diplomatie musulmane à l'époque du Prophète et des khalifes orthodoxes,* Paris 1935; id., *Textes arabes,* Cairo 1941 (reprinted as: *Majmūʿat al-wathāʾiq al-siyāsiyya fī l-ʿahd al-nabawī wa-l-khilāfa l-rāshida,* Cairo n. d.); G. Hawting, Saʿd b. Abī Waḳḳāṣ, in EI², viii, 696-7; M. Hinds, al-Maghāzī, in EI², v, 1161-4; id., 'Maghāzī' and 'Sīra' in early Islamic scholarship, in T. Fahd (ed.), *La vie du prophète Mahomet. Colloque de Strasbourg (octobre 1980),* Paris 1983, 57-66; J. Horovitz, The earliest biographies of the Prophet and their authors, in IC 1 (1927), 535-59; 2 (1928), 22-50, 164-82, 495-526; repr. ed. L.I. Conrad, *The earliest biographies of the prophet and their authors,* Princeton 2002; id., KU; id., Die poetischen Einlagen der Sīra, in *Islamica* 2 (1926), 308-12; R.G. Hoyland, *Seeing Islam as others saw it. A survey and evaluation of Christian, Jewish and Zoroastrian writings on early Islam,* Princeton 1997; R.S. Humphreys, *Islamic history. A framework for inquiry,* rev. ed., London 1991; Ibn Warraq, *The quest for the historical Muhammad,* Amherst, NY 2000; M. Jarrar, *Die Prophetenbiographie im islamischen Spanien. Ein Beitrag zur Überlieferungs- und Redaktionsgeschichte,* Frankfurt-am-Main 1989; A. Jeffery, The quest of the historical Mohammed, in MW 16 (1926), 327-48 (repr. in Ibn Warraq, *The quest for the historical Muhammad,* Amherst, NY 2000, 339-57); J.M.B. Jones, The chronology of the Maghāzī. A textual survey, in BSOAS 19 (1957), 245-80; id., Ibn Isḥāḳ, in EI², iii, 810-11; id., Ibn Isḥāq and al-Wāqidī. The dream of ʿĀtika and the raid to Nakhla in relation to the charge of plagiarism, in BSOAS 22 (1959), 41-51; id., The maghāzī literature, in Beeston, CHAL, i, 344-51; G.H.A. Juynboll, Ḥadīth and the Qurʾān, in EQ, ii, 376-97; L. Kern, Companions of the Prophet, in EQ, i, 386-90; R.G. Khoury, Les sources islamiques de la 'sîra' avant Ibn Hishâm (m. 213/834) et leur valeur historique, in T. Fahd (ed.), *La vie du prophète Mahomet. Colloque de Strasbourg (octobre 1980),* Paris 1983, 7-29; id., Wahb b. Munabbih, in EI², xi, 34-6; M.J. Kister, The *sīrah* literature, in Beeston, CHAL, i, 352-67; H. Lammens, L'âge de Mahomet et la chronologie de la Sîra, in JA [2nd ser.] 17 (1911), 209-50 (trans. as 'The age of Muhammad and the chronology of the sira,' in Ibn Warraq, *The quest for the historical Muhammad,* Amherst, NY 2000, 188-217); id., Caractéristique de Mahomet d'après le Qoran, in *Recherches de science religieuse* 20 (1930), 416-38; id., *Fāṭima et les filles de Mahomet. Notes critiques pour l'étude de la Sīra,* Rome 1912 (trans. as 'Fatima and the daughters of Muhammad,' in Ibn Warraq, *The quest for the historical Muhammad,* Amherst, NY 2000, 218-329); id., Qoran et Tradition. Comment fut composée la vie de Mahomet, in *Recherches de science religieuse* 1 (1910), 26-51 (trans. as 'The Koran and tradition. How the life of Muhammad was composed,' in Ibn Warraq, *The quest for the historical Muhammad,* Amherst, NY 2000, 169-87); M. Lecker, al-Zuhrī, Ibn Shihāb, in EI², xi, 565-6; S. Leder, al-Wāḳidī, in EI², xi, 101-3; E. Mittwoch, Ayyām al-ʿarab, in EI², i, 793-4; H. Motzki (ed.), *The biography of Muḥammad. The issue of the sources,* Leiden 2000; id., The murder of Ibn Abī l-Ḥuqayq. On the origin and reliability of some maghāzī-reports, in id. (ed.), *The biography of Muḥammad. The issue of the sources,* Leiden 2000, 170-239; M. Muranyi, Ibn Isḥāq's

Kitāb al-Maġāzī in der riwāya von Yūnus b. Bukair. Bemerkungen zur frühen Überlieferungsgeschichte, in *JSAI* 14 (1991), 214-75; id., *Die Prophetengenossen in der frühislamischen Geschichte,* PhD diss., Bonn 1973; id., Ṣaḥāba, in *EI²*, viii, 827-9; H. von Mžik, Die Gideon-Saul-Legende und die Überlieferung der Schlacht bei Badr. Ein Beitrag zur ältesten Geschichte des Islām, in *WZKM* 29 (1915), 371-83; G.D. Newby, An example of Coptic literary influence on Ibn Isḥāq's *Sīrah,* in *JNES* 31 (1972), 22-8; id., *The making of the last prophet. A reconstruction of the earliest biography of Muhammad,* Columbia, SC 1989; H.T. Norris, *Qiṣaṣ* elements in the Qur'ān, in Beeston, *CHAL,* i, 246-59; A. Noth and L.I. Conrad, *The early Arabic historical tradition. A source-critical study,* Princeton 1994; Ch. Pellat, Ḳāṣṣ, in *EI²*, iv, 733-5; F.E. Peters, *Muhammad and the origins of Islam,* New York 1994; id., The quest of the historical Muhammad, in *IJMES* 23 (1991), 291-315; rev. version in id., *Muhammad and the origins of Islam,* New York 1994, 257-68; G.-R. Puin, *Der Dīwān von ʿUmar ibn al-Ḫaṭṭāb,* PhD diss., Bonn 1970; W. Raven, Sīra, in *EI²*, ix, 660-3; id., Some early Islamic texts on the negus of Abyssinia, in *JSS* 33 (1988), 197-218; A. Rippin, The function of *asbāb al-nuzūl* in qur'ānic exegesis, in *BSOAS* 51 (1988), 1-20; repr. in Ibn Warraq, *The quest for the historical Muhammad,* Amherst, NY 2000, 392-419; id., Occasions of revelation, in *EQ,* iii, 569-73; M. Rodinson, A critical survey of modern studies on Muhammad, in M. Swartz, *Studies on Islam,* New York 1981, 23-85; F. Rosenthal, Awā'il, in *EI²*, i, 758-9; id., *A history of Muslim historiography,* Leiden 1968²; id., Nasab, in *EI²*, vii, 967-8; U. Rubin, The 'Constitution of Medina'. Some notes, in *SI* 62 (1985), 5-23; id., *The eye of the beholder. The life of Muḥammad as viewed by the early Muslims. A textual analysis,* Princeton 1995; id. (ed.), *The life of Muhammad,* Aldershot 1998 (a collection of articles); id., The life of Muḥammad and the Qur'ān. The case of Muḥammad's hijra, in *JSAI* 28 (2003), 40-64; id., Muḥammad, in *EQ,* iii, 440-58; J. Schacht, On Mūsa ibn ʿUqba's Kitāb al-Maghāzī, in *AO* 21 (1953), 288-300; G. Schoeler, *Charakter und Authentie der muslimischen Überlieferung über das Leben Mohammeds,* Berlin 1996; id., Mūsā b. ʿUqbas Maghāzī, in H. Motzki (ed.), *The biography of Muḥammad. The issue of the sources,* Leiden 2000, 67-97 [in Ger.]; id., ʿUrwa b. al-Zubayr, in *EI²*, x, 910-13; M. Schöller, *Exegetisches Denken und Prophetenbiographie. Eine quellenkritische Analyse der Sīra-Überlieferung zu Muḥammads Konflikt mit den Juden,* Wiesbaden 1998; M. Sells, Ascension, in *EQ,* i, 176-81; Sezgin, *GAS;* D. Spellberg, ʿĀ'isha bint Abī Bakr, in *EQ,* i, 55-60; J. Sperber, Die Schreiben Muhammads an die Stämme Arabiens, in *MSOS* 19 (1916), 1-93; J. von Stülpnagel, *ʿUrwa Ibn az-Zubair. Sein Leben und seine Bedeutung als Quelle frühislamischer Überlieferung,* PhD diss., Tübingen 1956; G. Vajda, Isrā'īliyyāt, in *EI²*, iv, 211-12; Wansbrough, *QS;* id., *The sectarian milieu. Content and composition of Islamic salvation history,* Oxford 1978; W.M. Watt, ʿAbbās b. ʿAbd al-Muṭṭalib, in *EI²*, i, 8-9; id., Ibn Hishām, in *EI²*, iii, 800-1; id., *Muhammad at Mecca,* Oxford 1953; id., *Muhammad at Medina,* Oxford 1956; id., The reliability of Ibn Isḥāq's sources, in T. Fahd (ed.), *La vie du prophète Mahomet. Colloque de Strasbourg (octobre 1980),* Paris 1983, 31-43; Wensinck, *Concordance;* Wild, *Text;* M. Zwettler, The poet and the prophet. Towards understanding the evolution of a narrative, in *JSAI* 5 (1984), 313-87.

Sirius

The brightest star in the night sky. Sirius *(al-shiʿrā)* is the only star mentioned by its proper name in the Qur'ān — Q 53, *al-Najm,* "the star," verse 49 says: "and he who is the lord of *al-shiʿrā.*" There are, in fact, two *al-shiʿrā*s, Sirius and Procyon, which are, in Arabic star-lore, both sisters of Suhayl (Canopus), and resided in the northern sky. After a failed courtship attempt, Suhayl had to flee to the southern sky (i.e. with respect to the Milky Way) and only one sister — the brighter Sirius — could follow. The other (Procyon) remained and cried until she became almost blind (*ghumayṣā* — hence her relative dimness). So we have one *shiʿrā* in the south *(al-yamāniyya)* and one in the north *(al-shāmiyya).* But there is consensus in qur'ānic exegesis that Q 53:49 refers to Sirius, *al-shiʿrā al-yamāniyya,* and when the name *al-shiʿrā* is used alone it refers to Sirius.

While the origins of the star's name are uncertain, it is the only star known with certainty in the Egyptian records — its hieroglyph (a dog, i.e. the companion of the hunter-hero Orion, an ancient association dating back to Mesopotamian times) is found on monuments throughout the valley of the Nile. The worship of Sirius — in conjunction with its helical rising at the summer solstice — is thought to have begun around 3000 B.C.E.; Ovid and Vergil referred to Sirius as Latrator Anubis: Egyptian Cahen Sihor. In Arabic, as in English, Sirius is also termed "the dog" (*al-kalb;* cf. the prophetic dicta relating to this name found in Ṭabarī, *Tafsīr,* ad Q 53:1). It is possible that the formal name of the star, "Sirius" (the root *sh-ʿ-r* means "to kindle fire" or "to shine"), and similar names in other languages (the Celts called the star Syr; the Greeks, Seirios aster, "the scorching star"; while in Sanskrit, it is termed Surya; cf. Heb. Sihor/Shihhor) derive from the Egyptian Sothis, the brightest star in the sky and the one directly linked with the Nile in Egyptian mythology. Among the other Arabic names for Sirius are *al-ʿabūr* (the crosser of the galaxy) and *barāqish* (the one of many colors).

As to why Sirius — albeit the brightest fixed star in the sky — was singled out from the hundreds of stars and the planets (see PLANETS AND STARS), a review of qurʾānic exegesis has revealed one line of reasoning common to all exegetes. This is that Sirius had been worshiped by some tribes of Arabia (as, incidentally, it was in its association with Isis by the ancient Egyptians, with the goddess Ishtar by the Sumerians), and God wanted to show them that he is the lord of their purported god (see PRE-ISLAMIC ARABIA AND THE QURʾĀN; IDOLS AND IMAGES; POLYTHEISM AND ATHEISM; SOUTH ARABIA, RELIGION IN PRE-ISLAMIC). One can, however, easily suppose that other stars, even more venerable than Sirius, were worshiped (see SUN; MOON).

A contemporary form of qurʾānic exegesis known as "scientific interpretation" *(tafsīr ʿilmī)* would stipulate that the significance of the mention of Sirius in the Qurʾān can only be understood when examined in the light of modern astronomical discoveries (see also SCIENCE AND THE QURʾĀN; EXEGESIS OF THE QURʾĀN: EARLY MODERN AND CONTEMPORARY). While appearing to be a single star, Sirius has a stellar companion as massive as the sun, which was only discovered in the mid-nineteenth century (1862). The two components of Sirius were found to revolve around their center of gravity every fifty years. The companion of Sirius is a collapsed star so dense that its size is equal to that of the earth. Studying the verse of Sirius and other related verses, the proponents of *tafsīr ʿilmī* perceive compatibility with modern scientific facts. By including the *basmala* (q.v.) as the first verse of sūra 53, the number of the Sirius verse (Q 53:49) becomes 50 — the same as the period of revolution of Sirius' two stars (which have an orbital period of 49.94 years). The first verse of the sūra ("By the star when it plunges," Q 53:1), is then deduced to refer to a collapsed star, and the Sirius verse to imply the existence of an extinct habitable planet (an earth). Other related verses, such as Q 43:37-9 and Q 55:17 confirm, for this form of interpretation, the existence of planets in binary stars, a recent astronomical discovery. Finally, the verse of Sirius together with the next verses (Q 53:49-50), relating the destruction of ʿĀd (q.v.; see also PUNISHMENT STORIES), is seen by such exegesis to hold a clue to what has been known as the "red Sirius mystery," namely that Sirius was described as a red star in ancient times while in modern times it is a white star.

Bassel A. Reyahi

Bibliography
R. Allen, *Star names. Their lore and meaning,* repr. New York 1963; K. Brecher and M. Feritag (eds.), *Astronomy of the ancients,* Cambridge, MA 1981; R. Burnham, *Burnham's celestial handbook,* New York 1978; J. Henninger, Über Sternkunde und Sternkult in Nord- und Zentralarabien, in

Zeitschrift für Ethnologie 79 (1954), 82-117; repr. J. Henninger, *Arabica sacra,* Freiburg 1981, 48-117, esp. 58 n. 17 (repr.), 66-9 (bibliography); B. Reyahi, *Najm al-shiʿrā fī l-Qurʾān al-karīm,* Amman 1998; id., *Sirius. A scientific and qurʾānic perspective,* Amman 1998; ʿA. al-R. al-Ṣūfī, *Kitāb Suwar al-kawākib,* Hyderabad-Deccan, 1373/1954.

Sister

A female who shares a mother and/or a father with a sibling. The term sister *(ukht)* appears in the Qurʾān in several ways, most frequently in this biological sense. It is also socially constructed in the case of a female who is suckled by a woman and thus becomes a "milk sister" (or foster sister) of the woman's biological children (q.v.; see also MILK; FOSTERAGE; WET-NURSING; KINSHIP; LACTATION). "Sister" is sometimes subsumed or included in the term for brothers *(ikhwa)* as evident from the context (see GENDER; BROTHER AND BROTHERHOOD). The term sister is also used metaphorically (see METAPHOR).

Qurʾānic verses relating to sister carry legal implications (see LAW AND THE QURʾĀN). Concerning marriage these apply equally to a biological sister and a "milk sister" (see MARRIAGE AND DIVORCE; PROHIBITED DEGREES). In Q 4:23 the man is told he may not marry his sisters (biological or foster), his father's sisters and mother's sisters, and his sister's (and brother's) daughters, nor may he take two sisters as wives (see WOMEN AND THE QURʾĀN; BLOOD AND BLOOD CLOT). From this it is clear those whom sisters must avoid as marriage partners. Legal implications concerning sisters and inheritance (q.v.) are restricted to biological sisters who alone are eligible as heirs. Sister is mentioned explicitly in Q 4:12 concerning her entitlements as an heir of a woman or man (along with any brother) leaving neither ascendants nor descendants. In Q 4:11, regarding entitlements in the case when the deceased leaves only parents (q.v.) and siblings, sisters are included in the term *ikhwa.*

Injunctions of modesty relating to sisters, both biological and milk-sisters, follow the pattern concerning marriage; they must not display their beauty to males who are not prohibited in marriage and must avert their gaze from them (and likewise such men must not gaze upon these women) as in Q 24:30-1. The exception in the prescription of modesty concerns sisters' sons as stated in Q 24:31 and Q 33:55. Sisters are explicitly included in the practice of family familiarity and conviviality as seen in Q 24:61, which enunciates a positive stance toward the sharing of meals in houses of kin (this constitutes a rejection of pre-qurʾānic notions and practices shunning such sociability).

The word sister appears once in relation to a named brother, as in Q 28:11, which mentions the "sister" of Moses (q.v.). This verse relates how the mother of Moses, after casting her son into the river, who is then taken in by the wife of Pharaoh (q.v.), despaired and sent his sister to look for him. When his sister (in the guise of a stranger) found her infant brother in the care of Pharaoh's wife and learned that he refused to suckle, she pointed the way to "a house that will nourish and bring him up for you." Thus did the sister of Moses restore her brother to his mother. The sister plays a pivotal role in this narrative of recovery and restoration and may be seen, by extension, as a defender of family and people. This story of the sister of Moses affirms the notion in Q 9:71 that women and men are supporters *(awliyāʾ)* of one another, in contradistinction to the idea that later became prevalent in juristic circles that men are the protectors of women (see CLIENTS AND CLIENTAGE; MAINTENANCE AND UPKEEP; PROTECTION; PATRIARCHY).

The term sister appears metaphorically

in Q 19:28 when Mary (q.v.) is called "the sister of Aaron" to establish her respectability by associating her with the lineage or tribe (people) of Aaron (q.v.). That she is referred to as "the sister of Aaron" and not the daughter of Aaron suggests the amplitude of meaning inhering in the idea of sister as conjuring family not only expressed in a directly descending biological line. Sister is also used abstractly to indicate closeness in Q 7:38, which refers to a "sister nation" or community *(ummatun la'anat ukhtahā)*, and to signal similarity or a like phenomenon in Q 43:48, "We showed them sign after sign (see SIGNS) each greater than its sister."

The qur'ānic *ikhwa*, as observed above, may include both female and male biological siblings and can also be understood in a wider metaphoric sense or as a social construct that includes women and men as brethren in religion (q.v.; see also FAITH; BELIEF AND UNBELIEF). Several verses attest to the notion of the brotherhood of believers such as Q 3:103, which relates that after the acceptance of the faith, "[God] joined your hearts (see HEART) together so that by his grace (q.v.), you became brethren." Clearly brethren in religion are not restricted to males. The deployment of the term "brethren" creates a sense of religious family (q.v.), bringing into the *umma* (religious community bound by faith) the sense of intimacy, loyalty (q.v.), and bonds implicit in family. If the mother is located, literally and figuratively, in the vertical line, the sister is positioned in a lateral line. In the Qur'ān, the sister is explicitly part of the adhesive of the religious collective.

The deployment of sister in the Qur'ān as both a biological category and as a social construction in the variant contexts of family, society, religious community, and people (see COMMUNITY AND SOCIETY IN THE QUR'ĀN), and the interchange between the explicit and the implicit, reveals the subtle and sophisticated interplay of terminology between text and context in signaling meaning and guidance. The term sister moves between "siblinghood" and a "wider fellowship."

Margot Badran

Bibliography
A. Yusuf 'Ali, *The meaning of the holy Qur'ān*, Johannesburg 2002 (new ed.) (for the commentary the work contains); A. Barlas, *'Believing women' in Islam. Unreading patriarchal interpretations of the Qur'an*, Austin, TX 2002; J. Esposito, *Women in Muslim family law*, Syracuse 2002; A. Wadud, *Qur'ān and woman*, New York 1999.

Skepticism see UNCERTAINTY; POLYTHEISM AND ATHEISM; BELIEF AND UNBELIEF

Skin see HELL AND HELLFIRE

Sky see HEAVEN AND SKY; NATURE AS SIGNS

Slander see LIE; GOSSIP

Slaughter

The act of slaying animals according to Muslim requirements, making them permissible as food. The act of slaughter (in Arabic, *dhakā, tadhkiya*) does not formally differ from the ritual of slaughtering the victims destined for immolation (*dhabīḥa;* see SACRIFICE; CONSECRATION OF ANIMALS).

The root *dh-k-w* occurs once in Q 5:3 regarding the prohibition of animals that have been strangled, killed by a blow or a fall, or by the horn of another beast, meaning that their flesh cannot be eaten (see FOOD AND DRINK; FORBIDDEN), unless they are slaughtered just before the last spark of life has disappeared (*illā mā dhakkaytum,* "except that you slaughtered"; see Ṭabarī, *Tafsīr* and Qurṭubī, *Jāmi'*, ad Q 5:3). According to al-Ṭabarī (d. 310/923), the act of *dhakā* purifies *(ṭahhara)* the flesh of the dying animals so that it becomes lawful (see LAWFUL AND UNLAWFUL).

Further qur'ānic interdictions concern blood (see BLOOD AND BLOOD CLOT), pork, what is dead *(mayta)* and what is sacrificed to idols (see CARRION; IDOLS AND IMAGES; IDOLATRY AND IDOLATERS), except in the case of extreme necessity *(ḍarūra):* "But if anyone in his hunger is forced *(fa-mani 'ḍṭurra)* [to eat of them] without wishing to commit sins (see SIN, MAJOR AND MINOR), God is merciful and indulgent" (Q 5:3; see also Q 2:173; 6:146; 16:115; see MERCY; GOD AND HIS ATTRIBUTES). The qur'ānic rules were further developed in *fiqh* literature (see LAW AND THE QUR'ĀN); according to these, there are a number of recognized means of *tadhkiya. Dhabḥ,* which applies particularly to smaller animals, like sheep and goats, consists of slitting the throat by cutting the windpipe, the gullet and the two jugular veins. If it becomes impossible to slaughter the animal in the specified manner, it is sufficient to cut the throat or to wound the animal at any place in order to cause its death by bleeding. The method called *naḥr* applies to camels, horses and cows and consists of slitting the throat, without it being necessary to cut it in the manner prescribed for the *dhabḥ.* At the moment of slaughtering by the method called *dhabḥ* the victim should be laid upon its left side facing the direction of the *qibla* (q.v.); if applying *naḥr* the animal remains upright facing the *qibla.*

According to all rites of Islamic law, the animal should be slaughtered by a sharp instrument, even with a stone or a piece of wood, without lifting it until the act is completed, in order to take the animal's life in the quickest and least painful way. It is forbidden to rend the throat by using unsuitable objects, like teeth or nails, since this will cause further pain to the animal (see ANIMAL LIFE; CREATION; CALIPH). The *tasmiya* (repeating the name of God) must accompany the act of slaughtering (*fa-kulū mimmā dhukira ism Allāh 'alayhi,* Q 6:118; cf. 6:119, 121), but there are differences of opinion among scholars about whether this is an essential condition in order to make the meat permissible to eat (see Ṭabarī, *Tafsīr* and *Jalālayn,* ad Q 6:118; see also BASMALA). According to al-Qurṭubī (d. 671/1272; *Jāmi'*, ad Q 6:118) who quotes a tradition related on the authority of 'Aṭā' b. Abī Rabāḥ (d. ca. 114/732), these words imply not only the duty of mentioning the name of God at the time of slaughter but also before drinking or eating food of any kind (see FOOD AND DRINK; SUSTENANCE). Moreover, a famous tradition narrated by 'Ā'isha (see ḤADĪTH AND THE QUR'ĀN; 'Ā'ISHA BINT ABĪ BAKR) suggests that God can also be invoked at the time of eating, if there is any doubt as to whether his name had been mentioned over the animal at the moment of slaughter.

The *'aqr,* the act of wounding prey in hunting (see HUNTING AND FISHING), also constitutes a legal method of *tadhkiya.* It must occur by shooting arrows or other sharp objects or by letting the dogs on the victims, and must be accompanied by the mention of the name of God (Q 5:4).

Some animals, like locusts and fish, do not require any special manner of slaughtering because they have no blood. Even the dead fish floating upon the surface of the water can be eaten, as it is said that, in this case, "the sea has performed the ritual slaughter." According to Mālikīs and Shāfi'īs the unborn animal can be eaten as well without any ritual slaughtering because "the slaughter of the mother is also the slaughter of the embryo."

Animals slaughtered by the ahl al-kitāb

Food prepared by the People of the Book (q.v.) is permitted for Muslims (Q 5:5), including what they slaughtered to eat, unless it is forbidden in itself, like blood or pork. According to the opinion of some jurists, however, the flesh of animals slaughtered for Christian festivals and churches is considered *ḥarām,* because it falls under the heading of what has been dedicated to other than God (see CHRISTIANS AND CHRISTIANITY; CHURCH).

There are some divergent views among scholars concerning animals slaughtered by Zoroastrians or Parsees (*majūs;* see MAGIANS). Some commentators forbid the eating of them because the words *wa-ṭaʿām alladhīn ūtū l-kitāb* refers only to the food of Jews (see JEWS AND JUDAISM) and Christians who were given the holy scripture (see, for example, Ṭabarī, *Tafsīr* and *Jalālayn,* ad Q 5:5; see BOOK). But a number of jurists do not consider the Zoroastrians polytheists (see POLYTHEISM AND ATHEISM), basing themselves on a tradition from the Prophet where he claims that they must be treated like the People of the Book. These jurists therefore allow Muslims to eat the flesh of an animal slaughtered by Zoroastrians.

The majority of jurists suggest that animals slaughtered by Christians are lawful for Muslims only if they have been slain according to Islamic procedures (cf. Ṭabarī, *Tahdhīb al-āthār. Musnad ʿAlī,* 230, on the basis of the Christian tribe of Taghlib; cf. Gilliot, Réalité et fiction, 192). On the other hand, a number of jurists admit that what the Christians consider religiously lawful to eat is allowed for Muslims, regardless of the manner in which the animal's life was taken. A step forward in this direction was made by a famous *fatwā* delivered by Muḥammad ʿAbduh, who was Egypt's Grand Muftī from 1899 until his death in 1905. From that pulpit he authorized the Muslims of the Transvaal to eat animals slaughtered by Christians, even though their way of killing animals might differ from the Muslims'. The chief point to be considered is that what is slaughtered by Christians should be regarded as food for the whole body of them (cf. Adams, Muḥammad ʿAbduh and the Transvaal *fatwā*). In the light of this ruling, meat originating from the People of the Book is lawful for Muslims, even though the animals may have been killed by means of electric shock or similar methods.

Ersilia Francesca

Bibliography
Primary: Qurṭubī, *Jāmiʿ;* Ṭabarī, *Tafsīr;* id., *Tahdhīb al-āthār. Musnad ʿAlī,* Cairo 1982, 223-32 (on the Taghlibī Christian tribes).
Secondary: A. ʿAbbādī, *al-Dhabāʾiḥ fī l-sharīʿa al-islāmiyya,* Ṣaydā (Lebanon) 1978; C.C. Adams, Muḥammad ʿAbduh and the Transvaal *fatwā,* in *The Macdonald presentation volume,* Princeton 1933, 13-29; B. Andelshauser, *Schlachten im Einklang mit der Scharia,* Freiburg 1996; E. Francesca, *Introduzione alle regole alimentari islamiche,* Rome 1995; Cl. Gilliot, Réalité et fiction dans l'utilisation des "documents" ou Tabari et les chrétiens taġlibites, in R.G. Khoury (ed.), *Urkunden und Urkundenformulare im klassischen Altertum und in den orientalischen Kulturen (Symposion über Urkunden. . ., Universität Heidelberg, 3.-5. November 1994),* Heidelberg 1999, 187-202; E. Gräf, *Jagdbeute und Schlachttier im islamischen Recht,* Bonn 1959; A.M. Karodia, The Muslim methods of animal slaughter and its scientific relevance, in *Journal of the Institute of Muslim Minority Affairs* 9 (1988), 173-85; Y. al-Qaraḍāwī, *The lawful and the prohibited in Islam,* Cairo 1997 (Eng. trans. of *al-Ḥalāl wa-l-ḥarām fī l-Islām*).

Slaves and Slavery

Persons incorporated into a family in a subordinate position who are subservient to a master who owns them and may sell them, and the institution of acquiring, keeping, selling, and freeing slaves. Slaves are mentioned in at least twenty-nine verses of the Qurʾān, most of these are Medinan and refer to the legal status of slaves. Seven separate terms refer to slaves, the most common of which is the phrase "that which your/their right hands own" *(mā malakat aymānukum/aymānuhum/aymānuhunna/yamīnuka)*, found in fifteen places. This phrase often refers to female concubines (q.v.), though it also serves as a general term for slaves. *ʿAbd*, the common word for slave in classical Arabic, is found in four places, and *ama*, a female slave, is mentioned twice. In several places, the Qurʾān refers to slaves in ambiguous terms: *fatayāt*, literally "female youths" (Q 4:25; 24:33); *rajul*, "a man" (cf. Q 16:76; 39:29); and *adʿiyā*, "adopted sons" (Q 33:4-5, 37). Finally, the Qurʾān uses *raqaba*, "the nape of the neck," several times as a synecdoche to mean slave, though captive may be a better interpretation for the plural form (*al-riqāb*, as in Q 2:177; 9:60). Slavery, *ʿubūdiyya* or *riqq*, is nowhere mentioned, though the Qurʾān recommends freeing of slaves and is obviously interested in regulating the institution.

The Qurʾān accepts the distinction between slave and free as part of the natural order and uses this distinction as an example of God's grace (q.v.) in Q 16:71: "God has preferred some of you over others in provision; but those that were preferred shall not give their provision to their slaves *(mā malakat aymānuhum)*, in order to make them equal therein. What, do they deny God's blessing (q.v.)?" The Qurʾān, however, does not consider slaves to be mere chattel; their humanity is directly addressed in references to their beliefs (Q 2:221; 4:25, 92), their desire for manumission and their feelings about being forced into prostitution (Q 24:33). In one case, the Qurʾān refers to master and slave with the same word, *rajul* (Q 39:29). Later interpreters presume slaves to be spiritual equals of free Muslims. For example, Q 4:25 urges believers to marry "believing maids that your right hands own" and then states: "The one of you is as the other" *(baʿḍukum min baʿḍin)*, which the Jalālayn interpret as "You and they are equal in faith (q.v.), so do not refrain from marrying them" (see MARRIAGE AND DIVORCE). The human aspect of slaves is further reinforced by reference to them as members of the private household, sometimes along with wives or children (q.v.; Q 23:6; 24:58; 33:50; 70:30) and once in a long list of such members (Q 24:31). This incorporation into the intimate family is consistent with the view of slaves in the ancient near east and quite in contrast to Western plantation slavery as it developed in the early modern period.

The legal material on slavery in the Qurʾān is largely restricted to manumission and sexual relations (see SEX AND SEXUALITY). Masters are encouraged to be kind to slaves (Q 4:36), manumit them and even marry them off but slaves have no corresponding right to demand such treatment (al-Ghazālī's [d. 505/1111] list of "slaves' rights" is based entirely on tradition; see Bousquet, Droits de l'esclave, 420-7). For example, Q 90:12-18, perhaps the earliest qurʾānic statement on slaves, addresses the master and emphasizes a religious motivation for manumission: "What will make you understand the steep path? Releasing a slave *(fakku raqabatin)* or giving food on a day of hunger to an orphan relative or a miserable poor person (see POVERTY AND THE POOR). [...] These are the companions of the right hand!" (see LEFT HAND AND RIGHT HAND; ORPHANS). Here, manumission is one way in which wealthy members of society can care for the less fortunate, but elsewhere, manumission is used to expiate sins such as oath-breaking (Q 5:89; 58:3; see SIN, MAJOR AND MINOR; BREAKING TRUSTS AND CONTRACTS). Q 24:33 is universally regarded by the interpreters as the origin of the *kitāba*, a "manumission contract," in which slaves buy their freedom from their masters in installments, though it is unlikely that such a contract was known in the qurʾānic period (Brockopp, *Early Mālikī law*, 166-8; Crone, Two legal problems, 3-21). Two exhortations to help *al-riqāb* (Q 2:177; 9:60) have been interpreted as urging believers to support slaves trying to pay off such contracts (e.g. *Jalālayn*), although these verses may also refer to ransoming of Muslims captured in battle (as implied in Qurṭubī, *Jāmiʿ*, ad loc.).

The second major category for qurʾānic rules on slavery is sexual relations. The Qurʾān condones the use of female slaves as concubines (Q 23:5-6; 70:29-30) and also marriage to believing slaves (Q 2:221; 24:32), although abstinence (q.v.) is touted as a better choice (Q 4:25; 24:30; see also CHASTITY). Within the rules on marriage to slaves, the punishment of married slave women is to be half that of married freewomen (Q 4:25), a rule that was later extended to all crimes committed by slaves. The Qurʾān also explicitly prohibits slave prostitution (Q 24:33; see ADULTERY AND FORNICATION).

There is strong evidence to suggest that the Qurʾān regards slaves and slavery differently from both classical and modern Islamic texts. First, the vocabulary is distinct. Several words for slave in classical Arabic (such as *mukātab*, *raqīq*, *qinn*, *khādim*, *qayna*, *umm walad*, and *mudabbar*) are not found in the Qurʾān, while others (*jāriya*, *ghulām*, *fatā*) occur but do not refer to slaves. Likewise, *ʿabd* (along with its plurals *ʿibād* and *ʿabīd*) is used over 100 times to mean "servant" (q.v.) or "worshipper" in the Qurʾān (see SERVANT; WORSHIP); in each occasion when it is used to refer to male slaves, a linguistic marker is appended, contrasting *ʿabd* to a free person (*al-ḥurr* in Q 2:178) or a female slave (*ama*, pl. *imāʾ* in Q 24:32) or qualifying it with the term "possessed" (*ʿabd mamlūk* in Q 16:75). Further, when the Qurʾān speaks of manumission, it does not use the classical *ʿitq*; nor does *walāʾ*, the state of clientage after manumission, appear (see CLIENTS AND CLIENTAGE).

Second, the institution of slavery changed dramatically in the seventh and eighth centuries C.E.: tens of thousands of captured slaves poured into Damascus and other urban centers, and Mecca (q.v.) and Medina (q.v.) became important centers of the luxury slave trade. The earliest legal texts have expansive chapters on slavery and manumission that depend very little on the Qurʾān. Pre-modern Islamic civilizations, with their eunuchs, slave armies and slave dynasties, were even further removed from qurʾānic concerns. Modern interpreters have used this disconnect to argue that the Qurʾān would not have condoned the slaving practices common in Islamic history, with some claiming that medieval interpreters subverted the Qurʾān's demand for manumission contracts (Rahman, *Major themes*, 48), while others argue that the Qurʾān's original intent, properly understood, was to eliminate slavery altogether (ʿArafat, Attitude; but compare Mawdudi, *Purdah*, 20).

It is possible, however, to delimit these interpretive constructs by analyzing early biographical dictionaries and historical accounts. While the biographies of certain famous individual slaves, such as Bilāl b. Rabāḥ (d. 20/642?) and Salmān al-Fārisī (d. 35/656?), were clearly enhanced or fabricated by later authors, the historical record is trustworthy regarding the general features of slavery in the qurʾānic period. According to these accounts, slavery was widely known but slaves were held in small numbers, with exceptionally rich persons owning no more than several dozen. Also, slaves appear to have been brought to Mecca and Medina through the caravan trade from Egyptian, Syrian, Persian and Ethiopian sources. In addition to importation, children of slaves were also considered slaves.

Among the earliest believers, slaves of non-Muslim masters reportedly suffered brutal punishments (see CHASTISEMENT AND PUNISHMENT). Sumayya bt. Kubbāṭ (d. before the *hijra;* see EMIGRATION) is famous as the first martyr of Islam, having been killed with a spear by Abū Jahl when she refused to give up her faith. Likewise, Bilāl was freed by Abū Bakr when his master, Umayya b. Khalaf, placed a heavy rock on his chest to force his conversion. In contrast, Muḥammad was kind to his slaves. Zayd b. Ḥāritha (d. 8/630), bought by Khadīja (q.v.) for the Prophet and one of the first to profess Islam, was adopted by Muḥammad as his son, though the adoption was later annulled (Q 33:5). Muḥammad was also very fond of Māriya (d. 16/638), a Coptic slave who bore him a son.

There is good evidence that slaves were freed for pious reasons; manumission is also mentioned as a reward for certain deeds. Many manumitted slaves remained dependent upon their masters (see Crone, *Roman law*) but some freed slaves attained positions of importance. Zayd b. Ḥāritha, general and confidant of Muḥammad, is perhaps the most famous example, although ʿAmmār b. Yāsir was governor of Kūfa, and Ṣuhayb b. Sinān served as interim caliph (q.v.) after ʿUmar's (q.v.) death (Dhahabī, *Taʾrīkh,* yrs. 11-40, p. 600). Other famous slaves include Sālim b. Maʿqil (d. 12/634), who is counted among the Emigrants (*muhājirūn;* see EMIGRANTS AND HELPERS) and was an important Qurʾān reciter (see RECITERS OF THE QURʾĀN) and Waḥshī b. Ḥarb (d. 41-50/662-70), a slave of Meccan owners who killed both the Prophet's uncle Ḥamza and, after his conversion, the pseudo-prophet Musaylima (q.v.).

These historical records agree with the Qurʾān on the following substantial points. Slaves were considered a part of the family, though of a status lower than that of free family members (see FAMILY; KINSHIP; TRIBES AND CLANS). Manumission of slaves was an act of piety (q.v.), though freed slaves remained dependent on their former masters. Female slaves were taken as concubines and marriage between free and slave was condoned. Neither the Qurʾān nor the historical record mentions any way of acquiring slaves other than through capture in war (q.v.; see also CAPTIVES; BOOTY), purchase or being born into slavery; this is significant given the persistence of debt slavery (see Schneider, *Kinderverkauf und Schuldknechtschaft*). Finally, the important role played by slaves as members of this community may help explain the Qurʾān's emphasis on manumission and kind treatment. Nonetheless, by the time of Muḥammad's death, slaves did not make up a large proportion of the believers.

While the institution of slavery in the Qurʾān shares many features with neighboring cultures, the use of alms for the manumission of slaves (see ALMSGIVING) appears to be unique to the Qurʾān (assuming the traditional interpretation of Q 2:177 and Q 9:60), as does the practice of freeing slaves in expiation for certain crimes (Pedersen, *Eid,* 196-8; but compare *Exod* 21:26-7). Other cultures limit a master's right to harm a slave but few exhort masters to treat their slaves kindly, and the placement of slaves in the same category as other weak members of society who deserve protection is unknown outside the Qurʾān (see OPPRESSION; OPPRESSED ON EARTH, THE). The unique contribution of the Qurʾān, then, is to be found in its emphasis on the place of slaves in society and society's responsibility toward the slave, perhaps the most progressive legislation on slavery in its time (see LAW AND THE QUR᾿ĀN).

Slavery continued as an important aspect of medieval Islamic culture but by the nineteenth century it was on the wane. The slave dynasties of Egypt and the Deccan had been dismantled and the famous Janissary corps of the Ottoman empire was no longer dependant on a slave levy *(devşirme)*. Pressure from European powers to end the slave trade was resisted in some areas but also found ready assent among Muslim jurists. In the Ottoman empire, east Africa and elsewhere, the manumission contract (*kitāba*, based on Q 24:33) was used by the state as a device to end slavery by giving slaves the means to buy their freedom from their masters. Some authorities made blanket pronouncements against slavery, arguing that it violated the qur᾿ānic ideals of equality and freedom (Shafiq, *L'esclavage;* see FREEDOM AND PREDESTINATION). The great slave markets of Cairo were closed down at the end of the nineteenth century and even conservative Qur᾿ān interpreters continue to regard slavery as opposed to Islamic principles of justice and equality (see JUSTICE AND INJUSTICE; EXEGESIS OF THE QUR᾿ĀN: EARLY MODERN AND CONTEMPORARY). This dramatic shift in Islamic attitudes toward slavery is a prime example of flexibility in interpreting qur᾿ānic norms (see also ETHICS AND THE QUR᾿ĀN).

Jonathan E. Brockopp

Bibliography

Primary: Dhahabī, *Ta᾿rīkh;* Ibn al-Athīr, ʿIzz al-Dīn Abū l-Ḥasan ʿAlī, *Usd al-ghāba fī maʿrifat al-ṣaḥāba*, Cairo 1970; Ibn Isḥāq, *Sīra;* Ibn Saʿd, *Ṭabaqāt; Jalālayn;* Qurṭubī, *Jāmiʿ*.

Secondary: W. ʿArafat, The attitude of Islam to slavery, in *IQ* 10 (1966), 12-8; D. Ayalon, Mamlūk, in *EI²*, vi, 314-21; G. Baer, Slavery and its abolition, in id. (ed.), *Studies in the social history of modern Egypt*, Chicago 1969, 161-89; C. Bosworth, Barda, in Ehsan Yarshater (ed.), *Encyclopaedia Iranica*, London 1982-, iii, 766; G.H. Bousquet, Des droits de l'esclave. Fragment extrait de l'*Iḥyā᾿* de Ghazālī, in *Annales de l'Institut d'Études Orientales* 10 (1952), 420-27; J. Brockopp, Competing theories of authority in early Maliki texts, in B. Weiss (ed.), *Islamic legal theory*, Leiden 2001, 3-22; id., *Early Mālikī law. Ibn ʿAbd al-Ḥakam and his major compendium of jurisprudence*, Leiden 2000; id., Slavery in Islamic law. An examination of early Mālikī jurisprudence, PhD diss., Yale University 1995; R. Brunschvig, ʿAbd, in *EI²*, i, 24-40; F. Cooper, *Plantation slavery on the east coast of Africa*, New Haven 1977; P. Crone, *Roman, provincial and Islamic law*, Cambridge 1987; id., Two legal problems bearing on the early history of the Qur᾿ān, in *JSAI* 18 (1984), 1-37; S. Marmon, *Eunuchs and sacred boundaries in Islamic society*, New York 1995; I. Mattson, *A believing slave is better than an unbeliever*, PhD diss, U. Chicago 1999; A. Mawdudi [Maududi], *Purdah and the status of woman in Islam*, Lahore 1992; J. Miller, Muslim slavery and slaving. A bibliography, in E. Savage (ed.), *The human commodity*, London 1992, 249-71; H. Müller, Sklaven, in *HO* [div. 1, vol. 6, sect. 6, pt. 1] (1977), 53-83; J. Pedersen, *Der Eid bei den Semiten*, Strassburg 1914; F. Rahman, *Major themes of the Qur᾿ān*, Minneapolis 1989; I. Schneider, *Kinderverkauf und Schuldknechtschaft. Untersuchungen zur frühen Phase des islamischen Rechts*, Stuttgart 1999; A. Shafiq, *L'esclavage au point de vue musulman*, Cairo 1891; trans. A. Zakī, *al-Riqq fī l-Islām*, Cairo 1892; E. Toledano, *The Ottoman slave trade and its suppression 1840-1890*, Princeton 1982; id., *Slavery and abolition in the Ottoman Middle East*, Seattle 1999.

Sleep

Natural and temporary periodic reduction of sensation and consciousness. Sleep *(nawm)* is mentioned a number of times in the Qur᾿ān. According to Q 25:47, "It is he [God] who appointed the night for you to be a garment and sleep for a rest, and day he appointed for a rising" (see DAY AND NIGHT). Sleep in the night is deemed to rest the body after a day's work and thus it is a gift from God almighty (see GRACE; GIFT AND GIFT-GIVING). The concept had found expression already in Q 78:9-11, "and we appointed your sleep for a rest and we appointed night for a garment and we appointed day for a livelihood" (see WORK).

That sleep is a gift from God is also alluded to in Q 30:23, which states that "of his signs (q.v.) is your sleep by night and day, and your seeking after his bounty." According to the exegetes (see EXEGESIS OF THE QUR'ĀN: CLASSICAL AND MEDIEVAL) this is a reference to God's omnipotent control (see POWER AND IMPOTENCE) over the passing of time (q.v.), in particular the alternation of day and night (Ṭabarī, *Tafsīr,* xxi, 32; see PAIRS AND PAIRING); since if there were no sleep, people would have no time to rest from the fatigues of the day (Muqātil, *Tafsīr,* iv, 558). The exegetes usually add that sleep is similar to death, since, like the dead, sleepers are neither conscious nor capable of thought (see DEATH AND THE DEAD; INTELLECT). This is alluded to in Q 39:42, according to which "God takes the souls at the time of their death (see SOUL), and that which has not died, in its sleep."

A different perspective is offered in another passage, where it is stated that "slumber seizes him [i.e. God] not, neither sleep" (Q 2:255; see SABBATH). This qualification underscores the same verse's earlier definition of God as the living and the eternal (see ETERNITY; GOD AND HIS ATTRIBUTES). The exegetes point out that sleep is a negative attitude *(āfa)* and cannot be attributed to God: as he is the conqueror (see VICTORY), he cannot, therefore, be conquered by sleep; just as he is the living, he cannot be overcome by rest and sleep, which are similar to death (Thaʿlabī, *Kashf,* ii, 231). Another qur'ānic passage alludes to sleep, in relation to the rather obscure "people of the cities" of Q 7:96-7. There it is asked: "Do the people of the cities feel secure [in the conviction] that our might shall not come upon them at night while they are sleeping?" (see CITY; PUNISHMENT STORIES; GENERATIONS; GEOGRAPHY). The occurrence of *manām* in Q 37:102, in the episode of Abraham's (q.v.) being commanded to sacrifice (q.v.) his son (see ISAAC; ISHMAEL), is connected to a vision during sleep, that is, a dream (see also Q 8:43; see VISION; DREAMS AND SLEEP).

Other episodes that Muslim tradition connects with sleep do not employ the common qur'ānic terminology for "sleep" *(nawm):* sleep *(nawm)* and vision in dream *(manām)* are not mentioned in the story of Joseph (q.v.) in Q 12, nor in the story of the Men of the Cave (q.v.) in Q 18 (see NARRATIVES; MYTHS AND LEGENDS IN THE QUR'ĀN). In the latter, although derivatives of *n-w-m* are not used, it is stated that God "smote their ears" (q.v.; Q 18:11; see also HEARING AND DEAFNESS) and then "raised them again" (Q 18:12; see RESURRECTION) and that they were lying asleep *(ruqūd,* Q 18:18) before God raised them (Q 18:19). The extent of this prodigious sleep, lasting more than three hundred years, is fully described in later reports.

In their exegesis of the verses just cited, qur'ānic commentaries seldom add any traditions regarding sleep. Muḥammad was asked if people in paradise (q.v.) sleep and he answered no, since sleep is the brother of death (Thaʿlabī, *Kashf,* ii, 231). According to another widespread report in the exegetical literature, Moses (q.v.) asked if God sleeps. In other versions Moses was prompted by the Israelites to ask this, or Moses asked the angels (see ANGEL; CHILDREN OF ISRAEL). God ordered him to take two glasses and when the end of the night came (or, according to some versions, after God ordered the angels to keep Moses awake for three days) he fell asleep and the glasses fell down and broke. The moral is that God never sleeps because otherwise the skies and earth (q.v.) and all creation (q.v.) would break apart (see HEAVEN AND SKY; COSMOLOGY). The explicit affirmation that God does not sleep and has no need for sleep is also mentioned in the major ḥadīth collections (see ḤADĪTH AND THE QURʾĀN), although in ḥadīth literature sleep is usually mentioned in connection with ritual laws relating to prayer (q.v.; see also VIGIL; RITUAL AND THE QURʾĀN). The question at hand in these cases generally centers on the requirement of ablution after sleep (see CLEANLINESS AND ABLUTION).

Roberto Tottoli

Bibliography
Primary: ʿAbd al-Razzāq, *Tafsīr,* i, 102; Abū l-Layth al-Samarqandī, *Tafsīr,* i, 233; ii, 462; iii, 439; Ibn Abī Ḥātim, *Tafsīr al-Qurʾān al-ʿaẓīm,* ed. A.M. al-Ṭayyib, 14 vols., Mecca 1997, repr. Beirut 1999², ii, 487 (ad Q 2:255); Ibn al-Jawzī, *Zād,* annot. A. Shams al-Dīn, i, 520-1 (ad Q 2:255); v, 86 (ad Q 18:18); vi, 19 (ad Q 25:47); Muqātil b. Sulaymān, *Tafsīr,* iii, 236; Ṭabarī, *Tafsīr,* ed. ʿAlī, iii, 7-8 (ad Q 2:255); xix, 20-1 (ad Q 25:47); xxx, 3 (ad Q 78:9); Thaʿlabī, *al-Kashf wa-l-bayān ʿan Tafsīr al-Qurʾān,* ed. Abū Muḥammad b. ʿĀshūr, 10 vols., Beirut 2002, ii, 231 (ad Q 2:255); vii, 140 (ad Q 25:47); x, 114 (ad Q 78:9).
Secondary: J.I. Smith, Concourse between the living and the dead in Islamic eschatological literature, in *History of religions* 19 (1980), 224-36 (on the interpretation of Q 39:42); Wensinck, *Concordance,* vii, 45-54.

Smell

Olfactory sense; pleasing or unpleasing odor. The verb "to smell" does not occur in the Qurʾān; the word for nose *(anf)* only occurs once, in the context of the *lex talionis* (see RETALIATION; LAW AND THE QURʾĀN; TEETH); the term *rīḥ,* usually "wind" (see AIR AND WIND), occurs at least once with the meaning "smell, odor, scent" (Q 12:94). Smell plays a significant role in qurʾānic images of paradise (q.v.) and in a scene in the Joseph (q.v.) story (see NARRATIVES). While the visual predominates, qurʾānic imagery also draws on smell, sound, taste and touch (see SEEING AND HEARING; VISION AND BLINDNESS; HEARING AND DEAFNESS; EARS; EYES; HANDS). The two main types of imagery which evoke the olfactory sense have to do with gardens (see GARDEN), particularly the garden of Eden or paradise, and drink (see FOOD AND DRINK). The sense of smell serves to heighten the effect of these depictions of delight (*naʿīm;* see JOY AND MISERY; GRACE; BLESSING). Garden imagery in the Qurʾān regularly depicts lush green foliage (see AGRICULTURE AND VEGETATION) and fruit-bearing trees (q.v.), including pomegranates and date-palms (see DATE PALM). Smell is evoked explicitly in references to the presence there of *rayḥān,* perhaps best rendered "scented, or sweet-smelling herbs": *wa-l-ḥabbu dhū l-ʿaṣfi wa-l-rayḥānu,* "grain with [full, plentiful?] leaves/ears [?] and scented herbs" (Q 55:12; see GRASSES). The same term occurs in Q 56:89: *fa-rawḥun wa-rayḥānun wa-jannatu naʿīmin,* "Then ease [or a light breeze], scented herbs, and a garden of delight." In keeping with the theme of sensory delight is the close association of smell with heavenly drink, the descriptions of which refer to perfumes. The drink of the inhabitants of heaven is described as pure wine *(raḥīq)* mixed with water of the heavenly spring of Tasnīm and "sealed" with musk (*misk,* Q 83:25-8; see SPRINGS AND FOUNTAINS; WATER; WINE; INTOXICANTS). In another passage, the righteous shall be rewarded in heaven (see REWARD AND PUNISHMENT) with wine mixed with *kāfūr,* "camphor" (q.v.), and water from another heavenly spring (Q 76:5-6). Dressed in silk (q.v.) and reclining on cool couches under shady trees with clusters of fruit hanging down above them, they will drink from shiny goblets of silver (see METALS AND MINERALS; CUPS AND VESSELS) wine mixed with ginger *(zanjabīl)* and water from the heavenly spring Salsabīl (Q 76:12-18). Missing are passages reminiscent of biblical references to the pleasant odor of burnt offerings, presumably because it would not be in keeping with the qurʾānic portrayal of God to suggest that he was delighted by sacrifices and felt hunger or need for them (see SACRIFICE; ANTHROPOMORPHISM). Missing also are references to women and their perfume which occur frequently in pre-Islamic poetry but which would not go along with the moral tenor of the qurʾānic text (see ETHICS AND THE QURʾĀN; WOMEN AND THE QURʾĀN; PRE-ISLAMIC ARABIA AND THE QURʾĀN; POETRY AND POETS).

Smell plays an important role in the scene in the Joseph story depicting the restoration of sight to the elderly Jacob (q.v.; Q 12:93-6), who had become blind out of grief at the loss of Joseph (Q 12:84). After revealing his identity to his brothers (see BROTHER AND BROTHERHOOD), Joseph orders them to return to Canaan and bring all their folk to Egypt (q.v.). He also instructs them to take his shirt with them and throw it over Jacob's face; this will enable him to see again. When they set out from Egypt, Jacob senses their approach. He claims to detect the "smell" *(rīḥ)* of Joseph (Q 12:94). Commentators, citing traditions from Ibn ʿAbbās (d. 68/686-8), say that he did so when the caravan (q.v.) was eight nights away, a distance comparable to that between Kūfa and Baṣra. Those present with Jacob think he is deluded (Q 12:95). When the brothers arrive, "the bearer of glad tidings" (*al-bashīr;* see GOOD NEWS), identified by commentators (see EXEGESIS OF THE QURʾĀN: CLASSICAL AND MEDIEVAL) as Jacob's son Judah (Yahūdhā), throws the shirt over Jacob's face and his sight is restored (Q 12:96). The suggestion is that smelling Joseph's odor proves to him that Joseph is indeed alive and restores his hope in being reunited with him. A pun here (see HUMOR; LITERARY STRUCTURES OF THE QURʾĀN) connects the "smell" *(rīḥ)* of Joseph with "the spirit/breath of God" *(rawḥ Allāh)* in Jacob's statement "Go, O my sons, and ascertain concerning Joseph and his brother, and despair not of the spirit of God. None despairs of the spirit of God save disbelieving folk" (Q 12:87; cf. alternate translation of "comfort or mercy of God"; see BELIEF AND UNBELIEF; SPIRIT; HOLY SPIRIT). Smell, like the dreams in the Joseph story (see DREAMS AND SLEEP), is one of God's methods for delivering messages. These messages are not apparent to everyone but only inspired or favored individuals notice them or understand their intent (see REVELATION AND INSPIRATION; MESSENGER; PROPHETS AND PROPHETHOOD).

According to exegetical traditions attributed to Anas b. Mālik (d. 91-3/710-12), Ibn ʿAbbās, Mujāhid (d. ca. 100/718) and others, Joseph's shirt originated in heaven. Gabriel (q.v.) had brought down this same shirt, or cloak, to Abraham (q.v.), whom it saved from burning at the hands of Nimrod (q.v.), and it had been passed down through the descendants of Abraham to Joseph. Joseph reportedly wore the shirt in a silver rod around his neck, as a type of amulet, and had it with him when he was thrown into the pit. The smell of heaven *(rīḥ al-janna)* which lingered in the shirt was what gave it the power to cure the ill and afflicted (Ṭabarī, *Tafsīr,* xvi, 249-52, ad Q 12:94; Zamakhsharī, *Kashshāf,* ii, 342-3, ad Q 12:93; Ṭabarsī, *Majmaʿ,* xiii, 115-16, ad Q 12:93; Ṭarafī, *Storie,* 226-8; Thaʿlabī, *Lives,* 228-9).

Devin J. Stewart

Bibliography

Ṭabarī, *Tafsīr,* ed. Shākir; Ṭabarsī, *Majmaʿ,* xiii, 115-16, ad Q 12:93; al-Ṭarafī, Abū ʿAbdallāh Muḥammad b. Aḥmad b. Muṭarrif al-Kinānī, *Storie dei profeti,* ed. and trans. R. Tottoli, Genova 1997; Thaʿlabī, *Qiṣaṣ,* trans. W. Brinner, *ʿArāʾis al-majālis fī Qiṣaṣ al-anbiyāʾ or "Lives of the prophets" as recounted by Abū Isḥāq Aḥmad Ibn Muḥammad ibn*

Ibrāhīm al-Thaʿlabī, Leiden 2002; Zamakhsharī, *Kashshāf,* 4 vols., Beirut 1979.

Smile see HUMOR; LAUGHTER

Smoke

Gaseous by-product of fire. Two words which occur in the Qurʾān — *dukhān* and *yaḥmūm* — are usually translated as "smoke" but their exact meaning in the text is uncertain: *dukhān,* though the contemporary Arabic word for "smoke," never occurs in the Qurʾān in connection with fire (q.v.), be it hellfire (see HELL AND HELLFIRE) or earthly fire. Actually, it can only be found twice, in Q 41:11, and in Q 44:10, to which latter sūra it lends its title (Sūrat al-Dukhān); both verses were revealed in Mecca (q.v.).

In the first of these verses, *dukhān* is mentioned in the context of the creation (q.v.) of heaven (see HEAVEN AND SKY) which was *dukhān* before God fashioned the seven heavens, assigned to each of them its proper order, and adorned the lower one with "lights" (*maṣābīḥ,* Q 41:12; see LAMP). According to a tradition which goes back to Ibn Masʿūd (d. 32/652-3), in the very beginning God's throne (see THRONE OF GOD) was set on the water (q.v.; *māʾ*). When he decided to create the universe, he first produced a *dukhān* from the water which rose; then he lifted it and called it "heaven" *(samāʾ).* It is likely that this *dukhān* resembles "mist," "fume," or "vapor," rather than "smoke." This interpretation is confirmed by al-Ṭabarī (d. 310/923), who comments on this *dukhān* in his remarks on Q 2:29 (Ṭabarī, *Tafsīr,* i, 425-6, no. 591), and also in his *Taʾrīkh* (i, 49-50; *History,* i, 219-20; cf. also the tradition of Ibn Isḥāq recorded in Ṭabarī, *Tafsīr,* i, 433, no. 590). In the same context, he quotes a tradition going back to Ibn ʿAbbās (d. 68/686-8) which explains that God "raised the water's vapor/ mist/ fume" *(rafaʿa bukhār al-māʾ)* and made the heaven(s) out of it (*Taʾrīkh,* i, 48; *History,* i, 218; see also Ṭabarī, *Tafsīr,* xxix, 14, ad Q 68:1; cf. Gilliot, Mythe, 165-6). In another version (Ṭabarī, *Taʾrīkh,* i, 52-3; *History,* i, 222) going back to Ibn Masʿūd, the same *dukhān* is said to have been the material out of which God created the earth *(arḍ)* as well as the heaven(s). According to the same tradition, the *dukhān* in question resulted from the breathing of the water (*min tanaffus al-māʾ ḥīna tanaffasa;* Ṭabarī, *Taʾrīkh,* i, 54-5; cf. Ṭabarī, *Tafsīr,* xxiv, 99, ad Q 41:12 for this same expression in a tradition of al-Suddī).

A similar problem concerning the meaning of *dukhān* arises in Q 44. Here, the Prophet is invited to watch for the day when heaven will bring forth a *dukhān* (Q 44:10) that will cover *(yaghshā)* the people, thus inflicting on them a painful torment (Q 44:11; see APOCALYPSE; CHASTISEMENT AND PUNISHMENT). The people then implore God to remove this torment, promising in exchange to become believers (Q 44:12; see BELIEF AND UNBELIEF; REWARD AND PUNISHMENT). But when God answers their prayer, they break their promise (see COVENANT; BREAKING TRUSTS AND CONTRACTS) and as a result God announces that he will have his revenge (see VENGEANCE) on the day of the "supreme disaster" (*al-baṭsha al-kubrā,* Q 44:16). A tradition going back to Ibn Masʿūd and accepted by most commentators (see EXEGESIS OF THE QURʾĀN: CLASSICAL AND MEDIEVAL), considers this passage to refer to a famine (q.v.). This famine is said to have affected the Quraysh (q.v.) and to have driven them to eat bones and carrion (q.v.), after the Prophet, exasperated by their insolence (see INSOLENCE AND OBSTINACY), had asked God to punish them with the "days of Joseph (q.v.)," i.e. to inflict on them seven years of famine. As for the "supreme disaster," it is believed to announce the future battle of Badr (q.v.) in which the Quraysh were defeated. In this context, *dukhān* is supposed to denote a sort of "haze" which dimmed the people's eyes as a consequence of their hunger. Contrary to this interpretation, some other traditions see in the *dukhān* mentioned in Q 44 one of the signs of doomsday. In these versions, *dukhān* actually seems to mean "smoke." This smoke is either supposed to enter the unbelievers' ears, so that their heads are like roasted meat (*ka-l-ra'ʾs al-ḥanīdh;* cf. Ṭabarī, *Tafsīr,* xxv, 113, ad Q 44:10, according to Ibn ʿUmar) or to dry up their heads and come out of their ears and nostrils. At the same time, the believers will only be affected by the smoke in the form of what resembles a head cold (*ka-hayʾat al-zakma/al-zukām; ka-l-zukām, ka-zakma;* Ṭabarī, *Tafsīr,* xxv, 111-13, ad Q 44:10). Of course, the commentators who adopt this interpretation consider the "supreme disaster" in Q 44:16 to refer to doomsday (see LAST JUDGMENT).

As for *yaḥmūm,* it only occurs once, namely in Q 56:43, in a Meccan sūra describing the environment of the damned (Q 56:41-4), where *yaḥmūm* qualifies the infernal shadow (*ẓill min yaḥmūm;* see DARKNESS; cf. also Ṭabarī, *Tafsīr,* xxvii, 189-93). Here again the exact significance of *yaḥmūm* is not absolutely sure. The word derives from a Semitic root meaning "intense heat." The corresponding Arabic root covers quite a large semantic field — it either means "to turn into coal," "to be very black," "to be very hot," or it qualifies boiling water *(ḥamīm)*. Yet, most commentators and lexicographers define *yaḥmūm* as a "very black smoke" *(dukhān aswad shadīd al-sawād)* or an "intense smoke" *(dukhān shadīd)* or a "hot smoke" *(dukhān ḥamīm)*. Whatever the exact meaning of *yaḥmūm* may be, in Q 56:43 it is obviously linked to hellfire and to the effect it produces on the whole infernal environment (see also ESCHATOLOGY).

Heidi Toelle

Bibliography

Primary: Ṭabarī, *Tafsīr,* ed. Shākir (to Q 14:27); ed. ʿAlī; id., *Taʾrīkh,* ed. de Goeje (ed. M.A. Ibrāhīm, i, 149-53); Eng. trans. F. Rosenthal, *The history of al-Ṭabarī.* i. *General introduction and From the creation to the flood,* Albany 1989.
Secondary: J. Berque, *Le Coran. Essai de traduction de l'arabe annoté et suivi d'une étude exégétique,* Paris 1990; Blachère; Cl. Gilliot, Mythe et théologie. Calame et intellect, predestination et libre arbiter, in *Arabica* 45 (1998), 151-92; Nöldeke, *GQ;* H. Toelle, *Le Coran revisité. Le feu, l'eau, l'air et la terre,* Damascus 1999.

Snake see ANIMAL LIFE

Snow see WEATHER

Social Interactions see ETHICS AND THE QURʾĀN

Social Relations see FAMILY; COMMUNITY AND SOCIETY IN THE QURʾĀN

Social Sciences and the Qurʾān

The rise and growth of the social sciences as we know them today coincided with the commercial and industrial revolutions that began in the eighteenth century. Formal economics, political science, and sociology emerged only with a differentiation between state and society and the ability to think abstractly about texts, social contexts, and institutional structures. For the Qurʾān or any other sacred text to be understood from a sociological perspective, language had to be developed to think abstractly about religion and text (see CONTEMPORARY CRITICAL PRACTICES AND THE QURʾĀN).

The social sciences began to take formal, disciplinary shape in the nineteenth century but they have always had two conflicting currents. One tendency has been to analyze and understand social forces and the relation of ideas and beliefs to society. The other tendency has been to hold the "modern" belief that societies, like physical structures, can be "managed" to engineer desired social outcomes. This idea of the social sciences often rests uneasily with the more analytical and philosophical goal of "understanding."

The tension between these two visions of social science was most evident in the colonial social sciences and in depicting the non-elite strata of society, such as the poor of Victorian London or Manchester, England, described in detail by Karl Marx and Fredrich Engels.

Text and society: pre-twentieth century approaches

Ideas of "good" social science have changed significantly since the nineteenth century, and these changes can be seen in the dynamic relation between understanding the Qurʾān and the social sciences. By the seventeenth century the plural "religions" became common English usage, and by the nineteenth century the idea of religion as an abstract category became connected with the rapid growth in knowledge about the historical development of rituals, beliefs, and practice of different religions over long periods of time (see RELIGION; RITUAL AND THE QURʾĀN; FAITH). Scholars and travelers began to seek out and organize information about religions. Such collected knowledge, when joined with reflection about religion as an abstract category, paved the way for what eventually came to be known as the history of religions. As a field of study, the history of religions used terms such as Islam, Christianity, Judaism, and Buddhism to connote organized systems of belief (see BELIEF AND UNBELIEF) that were differentiated from one another (Smith, *Meaning and end*).

The polymath biblical scholar W. Robertson Smith (1846-1894) may not have been the first scholar to see a close relationship between the stage of development of a social group and the nature of its intellectual, religious, and moral life, but by the late nineteenth century his *Religion of the Semites* became a foundational text for comparative religion. Smith's focus was on the relation of text to society in the study of the Hebrew Bible, but his travels to the Ḥijāz in 1880 and his monograph entitled *Kinship and marriage in early Arabia* allowed him to invoke qurʾānic texts alongside other religious texts as a means of advancing his principal argument on the structure of ancient Semitic society and the changing role of prophecy in it (see PROPHETS AND PROPHETHOOD; PRE-ISLAMIC ARABIA AND THE QURʾĀN). He saw a close relationship between what he viewed as the "stages" of development of a social group and the nature of its intellectual, religious, and moral life. Consequently, each prophet could speak only for his or her time and thus had to convey prophecy in terms that could be understood by members of that society.

In common with many other nineteenth century scholars, Smith judged some societies to be essentially holdovers from earlier historical areas. Hence when he traveled to western Arabia and neighboring Arab countries, his perception of Bedouin (q.v.) society was that it was relatively unchanged from the time of the Hebrew Bible and the time of the prophet Muḥammad (see also ARABS).

Such an ahistorical assumption was criticized even in Smith's time, but his efforts to relate the structure of social groups systematically to their representation in texts and to the structure of the texts themselves find strong parallels in the work of Smith's contemporaries, such as Ignaz Goldziher (1850-1921), whose primary interests were in early Islamic texts.

Context of qur'ānic revelation: twentieth century approaches

Although it is possible to find approaches in philological and historical writings that facilitate what later would be called a social scientific understanding of the Qur'ān in its initial setting, most such approaches focused not on the qur'ānic text itself but on the context of its revelation (see OCCASIONS OF REVELATION). This is the approach followed also by earlier sociologists. Joseph Chelhod's *Introduction à la sociologie de l'Islam* (1958) uses the Qur'ān, early Islamic sources (see TRADITIONAL DISCIPLINES OF QUR'ĀNIC STUDY), and sources in comparative religions to establish understandings of the sacred (see SACRED AND PROFANE), authority (q.v.), governance and ideas of the person. He also explored how conceptions of the Qur'ān as a text changed over subsequent centuries (see TEXTUAL HISTORY OF THE QUR'ĀN; COLLECTION OF THE QUR'ĀN; INIMITABILITY). His argument about Islam as a "national religion" for the Arabs is strained, but Chelhod's narrative has the advantage of juxtaposing qur'ānic passages in a way that facilitates placing them in a sociological context. In contrast, Rodinson's *Mohammed* is a more focused sociological biography that takes advantage of the earlier work on the sources for Muḥammad's life, using qur'ānic text to document the Prophet's life and the progression of the early Islamic movement from sect to nascent state, differentiating itself from the earlier religious ideas and organization prevalent in the Arabian peninsula (see ISLAM; POLITICS AND THE QUR'ĀN).

One issue that Rodinson and other sociologists addressed is the language and structure of the Qur'ān, less for an understanding of the text in itself but more to use it to determine the sociological context of seventh century Arabia (see LANGUAGE AND STYLE OF THE QUR'ĀN; FORM AND STRUCTURE OF THE QUR'ĀN). One issue with which they were concerned, for example, was how prophetic inspiration (see REVELATION AND INSPIRATION) was recognized and legitimized in seventh century Arabia. One indication was the use of *saj'* verse, short sentences in rhythmic prose (see RHYMED PROSE). A rival to Muḥammad who used such verse was Maslama, known in early Islamic sources as Musaylima (q.v.), the "little Muslim." He identified the source of his inspiration as "the Merciful One" (*al-raḥmān;* see GOD AND HIS ATTRIBUTES). There are some indications that Maslama's following was primarily related to his tribal origins, so that opposition to Muḥammad's claim to prophecy and the early Islamic movement would have been based on the understanding among the Banū Ḥanīfa, Maslama's tribal group, that prophecy was tribe-specific and did not transcend existing bonds of community (see TRIBES AND CLANS; KINSHIP).

Framing the question: Qur'ān and society

The sociological contribution to the understanding of the origins of Islam has been strongest in framing explicitly comparative questions. Writing in the 1960s, sociologist Robert Bellah *(Beyond belief)* argued that Islam in its seventh-century origins was, for its time and place, "remarkably modern... in the high degree of commitment, involvement, and participation expected from the rank-and-file members of the community." Its leadership positions were open, and divine revelation emphasized equality among believers. Bellah argues that the restraints that kept the early Muslim community from "wholly exemplifying" these modern principles underscore the modernity of the basic message of the Qurʾān, which exhorted its initial audience in seventh-century Arabia to break through the "stagnant localisms" of tribe and kinship. In making such statements, Bellah suggests that the early Islamic community placed a particular value on individual, as opposed to collective or group, responsibility (q.v.), so that efforts by contemporary Muslims to depict the early Islamic community as an egalitarian and participant one are not unwarranted.

Of course, these "stagnant localisms" offered powerful resistance to the qurʾānic vision of community in the seventh century (see COMMUNITY AND SOCIETY IN THE QURʾĀN). An often-cited qurʾānic verse emphasizes that there is "no compulsion in religion. Whoever... believes in God has grasped a firm handhold of the truth *(bi-l-ʿurwati l-wuthqā)* that will never break" (Q 2:256; see TOLERANCE AND COMPULSION). Other verses nonetheless appear to justify coercion and severe punishment (see CHASTISEMENT AND PUNISHMENT) for apostates (see APOSTASY), renegades (see HYPOCRITES AND HYPOCRISY), and unbelievers who break their agreement with the prophet Muḥammad (for example, Q 4:89, 9:1-16; see also CONTRACTS AND ALLIANCES; BREAKING TRUSTS AND CONTRACTS).

Some commentators (see EXEGESIS OF THE QURʾĀN: CLASSICAL AND MEDIEVAL) conclude that such coercion is specific to the context of the early Islamic community and grounded in "emergency conditions." In this view, coercion was needed to emphasize such "basic moral requirements" as keeping promises and treaties, and protecting a community's "basic welfare and security against aggression" (see ETHICS AND THE QURʾĀN). The overall emphasis is on voluntary consent to the will of God "which is prompted by the universal guidance that is engraved upon the human heart (q.v.)." The Qurʾān advises even the prophet Muḥammad to show tolerance toward his opponents (see OPPOSITION TO MUḤAMMAD): "If it had been your lord's (q.v.) will, they would all have believed, all who are on earth. Would you [O Muḥammad] then compel humankind [against their will] to believe?" (Q 10:99).

Of course, historians of religion use the same style of argument to interpret the qurʾānic text. Fazlur Rahman *(Major themes)* supports his view that Muḥammad "recognized without a moment of hesitation that Abraham (q.v.), Moses (q.v.), Jesus (q.v.), and other Old and New Testament religious personalities had been genuine prophets like himself" (see SCRIPTURE AND THE QURʾĀN; TORAH; GOSPEL) by invoking the Qurʾān: "I believe in whatever book (q.v.) God may have revealed" (Q 42:15). The idea of "book" *(kitāb),* as Rahman points out, is a generic term in the Qurʾān, denoting the totality of divine revelations.

In such interpretations, the Qurʾān is both a historical text and "good to think with." In 1999, the *Atlantic monthly* published an article, "What is the Koran?," that brought to the foreground issues regarding the interpretation of the Qurʾān. It made public a scholarly controversy surrounding the discovery of eighth-century manuscripts (see MANUSCRIPTS OF THE QURʾĀN) suggesting minor variant readings of the Qurʾān (q.v.) and the possibility of a stage at which the meaning and pronunciation of the Qurʾān was done "with no reference to a living oral tradition" (Rippin, *The Qurʾān,* xi; see ORALITY; RECITATION OF THE QURʾĀN). One of the developments emphasized in this article are those studies that treat the Qurʾān as a sacred text that can be analyzed through scholarly techniques that have been common since the nineteenth century (see POST-ENLIGHTEN-

MENT ACADEMIC STUDY OF THE QUR'ĀN). At one end of the spectrum of such studies are works in the classic philological tradition, such as the pseudonymous C. Luxenberg (2002), who argues that many otherwise inexplicable elements of qur'ānic orthography (q.v.), lexicon, and syntax can better be explained when understood in a Syriac (Christian Aramaic) linguistic context. In Luxenberg's hypossthesis, the Syriac palimpsest for many qur'ānic words and phrases helps to solve the problems of adding diacritical points to early Arabic orthography. Such arguments necessarily impute a particular social context in which the text was developed even when they do not develop this imputation. But studies that elaborate a sustained *sociological* idea of language use in the qur'ānic text are minimal.

The Qur'ān and sociolinguistics

At the other end of the interpretive spectrum is the use of a sociologically-informed linguistic analysis of the Qur'ān, such as the approach that Izutsu used in *God and man in the Koran* (1964). Izutsu's methodology assumes that the qur'ānic vision of the universe may be drawn from an analysis of how the basic concepts of the Qur'ān, such as *Allāh, islām, nabī* (prophet), *umma* (community), and *īmān* (belief) are interrelated, and how the text of the Qur'ān itself suggests the way in which qur'ānic usage of these terms differed from prior usage. The relationship between humankind and God, the idea of worship (q.v.) and community, and the implications of the "acceptance" and "rejection" of Islam are all embedded in a complex system of belief and practice. Izutsu's assumption is that Muslims may believe that divine revelation has nothing in common with ordinary human speech (q.v.), but understanding it requires that it possesses "all the essential attributes of human speech."

A similar approach underlies Naṣr Ḥāmid Abū Zayd's approach to an understanding of the qur'ānic text. Abū Zayd was significantly influenced by anthropology and sociology in his doctoral studies at the University of Pennsylvania, including the structural approach to the study of Islam developed by A. El-Zein (1977) at nearby Temple University. Abū Zayd's treatment of qur'ānic texts, like that of Muḥammad Shaḥrūr and Abdul Hamid El-Zein, also exemplifies the erosion of boundaries between "Muslim" and "non-Muslim" approaches to the social understanding of sacred texts. In El-Zein's structural approach, ideas of purity and impurity (see CLEANLINESS AND ABLUTION; RITUAL PURITY), sacralization and defilement (see CONTAMINATION) are embedded in relational constructs that people articulate with history and society in a variety of complex ways and possess "a logic which is beyond their conscious control" (El-Zein, Beyond ideology). Abū Zayd's hermeneutic methods for the study of the qur'ānic text follow a similar path, particularly in his seminal *Mafhūm al-naṣṣ* (1990), in which his textual concern is to trace how *waḥy* (inspiration) became the Qur'ān, the unlimited word of God (q.v.), expressed in human language and expressed as a text that can be understood like any other, as existing in particular social and historical contexts. Seen in this way, no text is a pure interpretation, but depends on webs of significance that are discussed, re-interpreted, and argued in a variety of contexts and for a variety of purposes.

The linguistic approach advocated by Muḥammad Shaḥrūr in his 1990 publication, *al-Kitāb wa-l-Qur'ān. Qirā'a mu'āṣira* ("The book and the Qur'ān: A contemporary reading"), like Abū Zayd's approach to the interpretation of qur'ānic text, stimulated considerable controversy when it first appeared because of what he said and how he said it. Although a civil engineer by training, the analytical method that he invokes is principally that of structural linguistics, thus contrasting significantly with conventional qurʾānic scholarship. Shaḥrūr refers to classic linguists such as Ferdinand de Saussure and Edward Sapir, but not to Toshihiko Izutsu's linguistic analysis of the Qurʾān.

Writing like an engineer, each chapter of his *al-Kitāb* begins with an outline, a procedure also followed in his subsequent books. Shaḥrūr argues that the chapters and verses of the Qurʾān do not change, but understanding of them in any given time and place is relative and part of the human heritage *(turāth)*. As Shaḥrūr writes, "What happened in the seventh century in the Arabian peninsula was the interaction of people in that time and place with the book. That interaction was the first fruit of Islam, not unique and not the last." Some elements were meant for all time, but others — "clothing (q.v.), drink (see FOOD AND DRINK), style of governance, and life style" — are the result of interaction with the "objective conditions" of specific times and places (*Kitāb*, 36).

Echoing Q 3:7 Shaḥrūr distinguishes between qurʾānic verses which are complete in themselves, representing the message of the Prophet and setting outer limits *(al-āyāt al-muḥkamāt)* and those verses *(al-āyāt al-mutashābihāt)* which become clear only when interpreted contextually and relative to time and place, such as dress codes (see MODESTY). All the verses are God's word, but their understanding requires the continuous exercise of human reason (see INTELLECT). Nor is there a contradiction between the Qurʾān and philosophy (see PHILOSOPHY AND THE QURʾĀN). Muslims have a responsibility to interpret the Qurʾān in light of modern linguistics and new scientific discoveries (see SCIENCE AND THE QURʾĀN; EXEGESIS OF THE QURʾĀN: EARLY MODERN AND CONTEMPORARY). "If Islam is sound *(ṣāliḥ)* for all times and places," then we must not neglect historical developments and the interaction of different generations. We must act as if "the Prophet just died and informed us of this book" and interpret his message anew (*Kitāb*, 44).

Consider how knowledge is passed between father and son, Shaḥrūr writes. Fathers pass knowledge little by little to their children, adapting content and style according to their age and experience. Likewise, in each historical era, the Qurʾān must be interpreted so that people can understand it. He writes that this purpose is defeated by the jurists, who have monopolized interpretation and imply that their heritage of interpretations are almost as sacred as the Qurʾān itself (see LAW AND THE QURʾĀN).

Shaḥrūr adapts the linguistic distinction between *langue* and *parole* to understanding the Qurʾān. Human thought requires language (q.v.). The qurʾānic text may be fixed, but its expressive and communicative side *(al-dhikr)* must be interpreted for each age and evolves like our understanding of the universe. The worst mistake of Muslims has been to rely heavily on inherited interpretations. Even relying on prophetic example can harm Muslims: if the Prophet's example was right for his own age, following it literally today would cause stagnation in knowledge (see KNOWLEDGE AND LEARNING) and science.

One of Shaḥrūr's primary examples is the treatment of women in Islam (*Kitāb*, 592-630; see WOMEN AND THE QURʾĀN; GENDER; FEMINISM AND THE QURʾĀN). Their status can be resolved only by distinguishing between qurʾānic understanding and later interpretations. In earlier historical eras, Muslims did not distinguish between qurʾānic verses intended to set outer limits *(ḥudūd)* and those limited to specific historical contexts *(taʿlīmāt)*. Nor should we blame our predecessors for failing to distinguish between the two, he argues. Just as the study of mathematical principles accelerated only with Isaac Newton's ideas, so too we have had to wait until now to understand the theory of outer limits *(ḥudūd)* and its compatibility with what we know of human nature today (see BOUNDARIES AND PRECEPTS). We should not assume that the liberation of women began with the Prophet's message and ended at his death. "If a woman wasn't a judge during the Prophet's lifetime or didn't attain a political position, this doesn't mean that she was forbidden from doing so for all time." As with slavery (see SLAVES AND SLAVERY), not all changes can occur at once. Islam drew the basic lines for freedom and liberation without ruining the existing means of production. If Syria, for example, tried to convert its economy to computer labor overnight, Syrian economic production would be destroyed. Women were full participants in the first acts of allegiance to the Islamic community and fought for Islam (see FIGHTING; PATH OR WAY); no one told them to stay at home and take care of the children (q.v.). Nonetheless, women's share in inheritance (q.v.) was initially less than that of men because of their relation to the means of production in the seventh century (see WORK; MAINTENANCE AND UPKEEP).

In Shaḥrūr's view, the qurʾānic verses related to women have been misunderstood. The inherited Islamic jurisprudence considers the [literal] interpretation of some qurʾānic verses, such as "Your women are a tillage for you" (Q 2:223) in isolation from other verses which suggest that women and men are equal in Islam, even if, in the time of the Prophet, men had a functional superiority over women. Thus in matters of clothing and modesty (q.v.), the qurʾānic injunctions apply equally to both genders (for example, Q 24:30-3).

Shaḥrūr argues that he is following a "scientific" method of qurʾānic analysis based on linguistic analysis, but his interpretive method is only loosely adapted to his approach to solving contemporary issues. Hence except for the unacceptable trades of "striptease" *(stribtīz)* and prostitution, which are sinfully immodest (see ADULTERY AND FORNICATION), he argues that women can practice any available occupation suitable to their social context and historical conditions, work alongside men, and participate in Friday prayers with men veiled or unveiled (*Kitāb,* 623; see VEIL; FRIDAY PRAYER). Some tasks may be more difficult for women to perform, but women, not traditional scholars *(ʿulamāʾ)*, should decide which tasks these are.

Shaḥrūr offers a similar argument, replete with qurʾānic citations and arguments against misinterpreted sayings of the Prophet (see ḤADĪTH AND THE QURʾĀN) for women to participate as full equals in politics, including parliament: "Muslim women should know that they have the right to elect and to be elected and to practice the highest responsibilities in the Islamic state, including its leadership, to participate in Friday prayers with men, and participate in all legislative and judicial activities" (*Kitāb,* 625-6).

Contemporary case studies

Two subjects under discussion in contemporary sociological and anthropological studies of the Qurʾān will suffice as a conclusion to this survey of social sciences and the Qurʾān.

Qurʾānic schooling: past and present

Among the topics that has attracted the attention of anthropologists who study Muslim societies is that of education. In its most traditional forms, Muslim education centers on the Qurʾān. The Qurʾān is omnipresent in daily life throughout the Muslim world (see EVERYDAY LIFE, THE QUR'ĀN IN), and the public recitation of the text reaffirms the idea of both divine and human ordering (see TEACHING AND PREACHING THE QUR'ĀN). Understood theologically, its recitation reaffirms the divine template for society as reiterated through a fixed and memorizable text. Even if most listeners cannot understand the Arabic words and phrases, accurate memorization and recitation take priority over understanding and interpretation and reaffirm the divine order and human community.

The paradigm of all knowledge is the Qur'ān (see TEACHING). Its accurate memorization in one or more of the seven conventional recitational forms is the first step in mastering the religious sciences through mnemonic possession. A distinctive feature of rural and urban community life is the presence of scholars versed in the Qur'ān who are present for all major life-cycle events and for major community occasions (see FESTIVALS AND COMMEMORATIVE DAYS; BURIAL; PRAYER FORMULAS). In Morocco, for example, every urban quarter and rural community maintains a mosque school in which a teacher *(fqīh)* conveys the basics of qur'ānic recitation and participates in recitations for both public ceremonies and private ones, such as birth (q.v.), circumcision (q.v.), marriage (see MARRIAGE AND DIVORCE), celebrations of school diplomas, and death (see DEATH AND THE DEAD).

Throughout the Muslim majority world, most males and a fair number of females, at least in towns, attend qur'ānic schools long enough to commit a few passages to memory, although these schools have long been characterized by a high rate of attrition. Most students leave before they acquire literacy and few remain the six to eight years generally required (at least in Morocco) to memorize the entire Qur'ān. In Morocco in the 1970s, according to one study, the average number of years spent in qur'ānic school ranged from almost two years in Marrakesh to only four months in small Middle Atlas mountain villages (Eickelman, *Knowledge and power*, 61).

The cognitive style associated with Qur'ān memorization is tied closely to popular understandings of Islam (see POPULAR AND TALISMANIC USES OF THE QUR'ĀN) and has important analogies in non-religious spheres of knowledge. *Ma'rifa* is the ordinary term for knowledge in contemporary Arabic: it can convey the technical religious connotation of esoteric spiritual insight but it also connotes knowledge related to commerce and crafts, including music and oral poetry. These arts share significant formal parallels with the religious sciences and are also presumed to be contained in fixed, memorized truths. Effective public speech involves the skillful invocation both of qur'ānic phrases and of the mundane but memorizable elements of knowledge drawn from poetry and proverbs (see POETRY AND POETS). A further parallel lies in the model for the transmission of knowledge. The religious sciences throughout the Islamic world are transmitted traditionally through a quasi-genealogical chain of authority that descends from master or teacher *(shaykh)* to student *(ṭālib)* to insure that the knowledge of earlier generations is passed on intact. Knowledge of crafts is passed from master to apprentice in an analogous fashion, with any knowledge or skill acquired independent of such a tradition regarded as suspect.

The formal features of qur'ānic schools have been frequently described, although the consequences of this form of pedagogy on how people think are not as well understood. The traditional emphasis on qur'ānic memorization, for example, is not unique to the Muslim world. Elaborate mnemonic systems existed in classical Greece and Rome to facilitate memorization through the association of material with "memory posts," "visual images like the columns of a building or places at a banquet table" (Yates, *Art of memory*, 2-7). Accompanying such techniques was the notion that mnemonic knowledge was more pure than that communicated through writing (see ORALITY AND WRITING IN ARABIA; MEMORY; REMEMBRANCE).

What is remarkable about memory in the context of Islamic education in Morocco is not the performance of prodigious mnemonic feats in qur'ānic memorization — such feats were fully paralleled in Europe. It is the insistence of former students that they employed no devices to facilitate memorization. Nonetheless, these same students recall visualizing the shape of the letters on their slates and the circumstances associated with the memorization of particular verses and texts. One study (Wagner, Memories, 14) suggests that patterns of intonation and rhythm systematically serve as mnemonic markers.

Even after the advent of print technology (see PRINTING OF THE QUR'ĀN), printed books were long neglected in *madrasa* education through the 1970s in many regions. This was partly because of the lack of printed or manuscript books, but also because of the cultural concept of learning implicit in Islamic education. A typical qur'ānic teacher (*fqīh* in Morocco) had between fifteen and twenty students, ranging in age from four to sixteen. Each morning the *fqīh* wrote the verses to be memorized on each student's wooden slate *(lūḥ)* and the student then spent the day memorizing the verses by reciting them out loud and also reciting the verses learned the previous day. Memorization was incremental, with the recitation of new material added to that already learned (for example, a, then a,b, then a,b,c). Students were not grouped into "classes" based on age or progress in memorization.

Qur'ānic studies have been culturally associated with rigorous discipline and the lack of clear explanation of memorized passages. Both these features are congruent with a concept of religious knowledge as essentially fixed and, in the Moroccan and other contexts, an associated concept of "reason" *(ʿaql)*, which is conceived as a human's ability to discipline his or her nature in accord with the arbitrary code of conduct laid down by God and epitomized by acts of communal obedience (q.v.), such as the fast of Ramaḍān (q.v.; Eickelman, *Moroccan Islam*, 130-8; see also FASTING). Firm discipline in the course of learning the Qur'ān is thus regarded as an integral part of socialization.

When a father handed his son over to a *fqīh*, he did so with the formulaic phrase that the child could be beaten. Such punishment was considered necessary for accurate qur'ānic recitation. Former students explained that the teacher (or the student's father, when he supervised the process of memorization) was regarded as the impersonal agency of punishment, which, like the unchanging word of God itself, was merely transmitted by him. Students were also told that the parts of their bodies struck in the process of qur'ānic memorization would not burn in hell (see REWARD AND PUNISHMENT; HELL AND HELLFIRE). The same notion applied to the beatings apprentices received from craftsmen and musicians. In practice, students were slapped or whipped only when their attention flagged or when they repeated errors, although the children of high-status fathers were struck much less frequently than other children.

Former students emphasize that they asked no questions concerning the meaning of qur'ānic verses, even among themselves, and it did not occur to them to do so. Their sole activity was properly recited memorization. Because the grammar and vocabulary of the Qur'ān are not immediately accessible to speakers of colloquial Arabic, and even less so to students from regions where Arabic is not the first language, former students readily admitted that they did not comprehend what they were memorizing until fairly late in their studies. "Understanding" *(fahm)* was not measured by the ability to explain particular verses, since explanation was considered a science to be acquired through years of study of the exegetical literature *(tafsīr)*. Any informal attempt to explain meaning was considered blasphemy (q.v.) and did not occur. Instead, the measure of understanding consisted of the ability to use qur'ānic verses in appropriate contexts.

In the first few years of Qur'ān school, students had little control over what they recited. They could not, for instance, recite specific chapters of the Qur'ān, but had to begin with one of the sixty principal recitational sections. Firmer control was achieved as students accompanied their father, other relatives, or occasionally the teacher to social gatherings, where they heard adults incorporate qur'ānic verses into particular contexts and gradually acquired the ability to do so themselves, as well as to recite specific sections of the Qur'ān without regard to the order in which they had been memorized. Thus the measure of understanding was the ability to make practical reference to the memorized text, just as originality was shown in working qur'ānic references into conversation, sermons, and formal occasions. Knowledge and manipulation of secular oral poetry and proverbs in a parallel fashion is still a sign of good rhetorical style; the skill is not confined to religious learning (see RHETORIC AND THE QUR'ĀN).

The high rate of attrition from qur'ānic schools supports the notion that mnemonic "possession" can be considered a form of cultural capital. Education was free aside from small gifts to the teacher, yet most students were compelled to drop out after a short period to contribute to the support of their families or because they did not receive familial support for the arduous and imperfectly understood process of learning. In practice, memorization of the Qur'ān was accomplished primarily by children from relatively prosperous households or by those whose fathers or guardians were already literate (see LITERACY). Nonetheless, education was a means to social mobility, especially for poor students who managed to progress through higher, post-qur'ānic education.

The notion of cultural capital implies more than possession of the material resources to allow a child to spend six to eight years in the memorization of the Qur'ān; it also implies a sustained adult discipline over the child. Students' fathers, elder brothers, other close relatives — including women in some cases — and peers, especially at later stages of learning, were integrally involved in the learning process. All provided contexts for learning to continue, since formal education did not involve being systematically taught to read and write outside the context of the Qur'ān, even for urban students from wealthy families. Students acquired such skills, if at all, apart from their studies in qur'ānic schools (Berque, *Maghreb*, 167-8), just as they acquired an understanding of the Qur'ān through social situations.

A student became a "memorizer" *(ḥāfiẓ)* once he knew the entire Qur'ān; this set him apart from ordinary society even without additional studies. In the pre-colonial era in Morocco, qur'ānic students often were the only strangers who could travel in safety through tribal regions without making prior arrangements for protection. The mnemonic "possession" of the Qur'ān set people apart from other elements of society.

The Qur'ān in daily life

Yet another aspect of qur'ānic studies that has generated interest among both anthropologists and sociologists is the integration of the Qur'ān within the social fabric of Muslim life. It may be correct to say that the Qur'ān continuously plays a central role in society, but *how* this is accomplished contextually points to significant differences that often are the product of incremental changes that frequently go unnoticed. One significant change is in the memorization of the Qur'ān. For an earlier generation of religious learning, it could be taken for granted that its recitation was known by heart. In courtrooms and in gatherings of the pious, those not engaged in conversation would continue its recitation *sotto voce,* using a rosary *(tasbīḥ)* to keep track of the parts recited. Among the most able and educated, apposite qur'ānic verses were dropped into conversation or sermons. With the spread of literacy and mass higher education, memorization of the entire Qur'ān has become less common. On occasions such as the commemoration of a deceased forty days after his or her death (the *arbaʿīn*), the reciters and guests who accompany the imām (q.v.) in most parts of the Muslim world are likely to recite from printed copies of the Qur'ān. This opens the art of recitation to more people, although the imām or other expert recitational leaders exercise the same care for the production of an *exact* recitation according to one of the established forms of recitation. In practice, the most skilled can exercise control over those at the core of such a gathering, occasionally correcting one another as a sign of authority but offering only example, not authoritative control, over the larger group. Governments offer qur'ānic recitation contests and commissions to ensure its proper style and encouraging it as an art (Nelson, *Art of reciting*). It remains popular, but other forms of public religious performance increasingly displace it.

Changes in media have tacitly displaced the predominance of the Qur'ān in daily life (see MEDIA AND THE QUR'ĀN). Several countries, including Saudi Arabia, Morocco, and Egypt, offer non-stop qur'ānic recitations on the radio and nearly all Muslim majority countries offer qur'ānic recitation for at least part of the day on radio and television. In an earlier era, such media recitations were central. The advent of the new media, including audio- and videocassettes and the Internet, offer many popular alternatives. The taxi driver in Cairo, Amman, or Fez who once would have listened to qur'ānic recitation on his radio is now more likely to listen to a popular religious preacher speaking in a direct, comprehensible, and forceful way in his own dialect. Ideally, listening to qur'ānic recitation is a complex activity, requiring a combination of intent, training, and discipline. The same is the case when listening to a cassette sermon, except that the speaker can build into his sermon calls for audience participation, such as asking the audience to recite "in the name of God" (*bi-smi-llāh;* see BASMALA) each time a qur'ānic verse is invoked, or to repeat certain key phrases from the sermon (Hirschkind, Ethics of listening, 637). Such interactivity is implicit, not explicit, in Qur'ān recitation. Qur'ānic recitation focuses attention on the beauty of recitation. Its meaning — as the word of God — is known in general, but except for a stock of commonly invoked passages for life-crises occasions, the meaning of specific phrases is the domain of scholars. Sermons are much more accessible to a wider public and one that increasingly anticipates the ability to participate in religious discussion and debate (Eickelman and Anderson, Redefining Muslim publics, 9-11).

The place of the Qurʾān in daily life can be highly variable. In places as varied as Bulgaria and North America, its presence in a room can be venerated and iconic if its recitation is limited to a handful of persons present. In other cases, its study, as in women's discussion groups in Iran (Torab, Piety as gendered agency, 296), can offer women a means of participation in the religious life of the wider community. In the contemporary world, the role played by the Qurʾān as a text, as the idea of a text, and as a physical object in printed or manuscript form continues to shift. Its character may be eternal, but its place in society contextually shifts. See also COMMUNITY AND SOCIETY IN THE QURʾĀN; EVERYDAY LIFE, THE QURʾĀN IN.

Dale F. Eickelman

Bibliography

N. Abū Zayd, *Mafhūm al-naṣṣ. Dirāsa fī ʿulūm al-Qurʾān*, Beirut 1990; id., *Voice of an exile. Reflections on Islam*, London 2004; R. Bellah, *Beyond belief. Essays on religion in a post-traditional world*, New York 1970; J. Berque, *Maghreb. Histoire et sociétés*, Gembloux 1974; J. Chelhod, *Introduction à la sociologie de l'Islam. De l'animisme á l'universalisme*, Paris 1958; D. Eickelman, *Knowledge and power in Morocco. The education of a twentieth-century notable*, Princeton 1985; id., *Moroccan Islam. Tradition and society in a pilgrimage center*, Austin, TX 1976; id. and J. Anderson, Redefining Muslim publics, in ids. (eds.), *New media in the Muslim world*, Bloomington, IN 2003², 1-18; A. El-Zein, Beyond ideology and theology. The search for the anthropology of Islam, in *Annual review of anthropology* 6 (1977), 227-54; C. Hirschkind, The ethics of listening. Cassette-sermon audition in contemporary Egypt, in *American ethnologist* 28 (2001), 623-49; J. Jomier, *L'islam vécu en Égypte*, Paris 1994; T. Lester, What is the Koran? in *Atlantic monthly* 283/1 (January 1999), 43-56; C. Luxenberg, *Die Syro-Aramäische Lesart des Koran. Ein Beitrag zur Entschlüsselung der Koransprache*, Berlin 2000; K. Nelson, *The art of reciting the Qurʾān*, Austin, TX 1985; F. Rahman, *Major themes of the Qurʾān*, Minneapolis, MN 1980; A. Rippin (ed.), *The Qurʾān and its interpretative tradition*, Aldershot 2001; M. Rodinson, *Muhammad*, trans. A. Carter, New York 1971 (Eng. trans. of *Mahomet*); M. Shaḥrūr, *al-Kitāb wa-l-Qurʾān. Qirāʾa muʿāṣira*, Damascus 1990; id., *Proposal for an Islamic covenant*, trans. D. Eickelman and I. Abu Shehadeh, Damascus 2000; W.C. Smith, *The meaning and end of religion. A new approach to the religious traditions of mankind*, New York 1963; W.R. Smith, *Kinship and marriage in early Arabia*, London 1903; id., *Lectures on the religion of the Semites*, Edinburgh 1889; S. Taji-Farouki, *Modern Muslim intellectuals and the Qurʾān*, Oxford 2004; A. Torab, Piety as gendered agency. A study of *Jalaseh* ritual discourse in an urban neighbourhood in Iran, in *Journal of the Royal Anthropological Institute* [N.S.] 2 (1996), 235-52; D. Wagner, Memories of Morocco, in *Cognitive psychology* 10 (1978), 1-28; F. Yates, *The art of memory*, London 1966.

Sociology see SOCIAL SCIENCES AND THE QURʾĀN

Solomon

The son of the biblical king David (q.v.) and heir to his throne. Solomon (Ar. Sulaymān) is presented in the Qurʾān as playing three important roles, although they are often interwoven in its narrative (see NARRATIVES). He was a ruler who inherited his father's knowledge as well as his kingdom (see KINGS AND RULERS; KNOWLEDGE AND LEARNING; POWER AND IMPOTENCE); a prophet (see PROPHETS AND PROPHETHOOD) who, despite occasional lapses in devotional practice (see PIETY; WORSHIP; RITUAL AND THE QURʾĀN), enjoyed divine protection (q.v.) and was assured an honored place in paradise (q.v.); and a person who possessed wide-ranging magical and esoteric powers which he used with divine sanction (see MAGIC). Solomon's life and accomplishments are described in Q 21:78-82, 27:15-44, 34:10-14 and 38:30-40 but many of these passages are written in a laconic and allusive style that stimulated the composition of glosses, commentaries and stories (see MYTHS AND LEGENDS IN THE QURʾĀN; EXEGESIS OF THE QURʾĀN: CLASSICAL AND MEDIEVAL). These sources often supply colorful details about him and his associates not mentioned in the Qurʾān. Solomon's unusual mixture of skills and characteristics also encouraged symbolic interpretations of his life and accomplishments (see SYMBOLIC IMAGERY).

Solomon in the Qurʾān

As a ruler Solomon was noted for his possession of knowledge *(ʿilm)* and wisdom (q.v.; *ḥikma*), characteristics that he inherited from his father, David, but in which he was believed to have surpassed him (Q 21:78-9; Ṭabarī, *Tafsīr*, xvii, 50-4; id., *Taʾrīkh*, i, 573; Thaʿlabī, *Qiṣaṣ*, 257-9). Another area in which the son was more accomplished than the father was as a builder. The Qurʾān alludes to the various objects and structures which were made for him, including mihrabs *(maḥārīb)*, images or sculptures *(tamāthīl)* and watering troughs (*jifān*, Q 34:12-13; Ṭabarī, *Tafsīr*, xxiii, 70-1; see ART AND ARCHITECTURE AND THE QURʾĀN; MOSQUE; IDOLS AND IMAGES). Another passage mentions the palace with a glass floor where he received the Queen of Sheba (q.v.; Q 27:44; Ṭabarī, *Tafsīr*, xix, 168-70; id., *Taʾrīkh*, i, 583; Thaʿlabī, *Qiṣaṣ*, 271, 275-6; see BILQĪS).

Descriptions of the structures and objects made for Solomon present them primarily as a demonstration of his power to force men, birds (see ANIMAL LIFE), jinn (q.v.) and *shayṭāns* to do his bidding (Q 21:82; 38:37-8; Ṭabarī, *Tafsīr*, xvii, 55-6; xxiii, 160; id., *Taʾrīkh*, i, 575-7; Thaʿlabī, *Qiṣaṣ*, 269-70; see DEVIL). Both Solomon and David are said to have had the ability to communicate with birds and animals (see LANGUAGE, CONCEPT OF). David charmed them with his mellifluous voice whereas Solomon was able to affect their behavior through his understanding of their speech (q.v.). His power to communicate with both ants and birds is specifically mentioned by the Qurʾān (Q 27:16-18; Ṭabarī, *Tafsīr*, xix, 141-2).

Solomon's ability to command the wind (see AIR AND WIND) and to make it transport him wherever he pleased is another manifestation of his special powers. This ability is referred to in three different qurʾānic passages affirming its importance as an aspect of Solomon's status (Q 21:81; 34:12; 38:36; Ṭabarī, *Tafsir*, xvii, 55-6; xxiii, 68-9, 160-1; id., *Taʾrīkh*, i, 573-5; Thaʿlabī, *Qiṣaṣ*, 260-1). A similar ability to travel miraculously is attributed to the jinn under his command because they are able to seize a throne belonging to the Queen of Sheba and bring it to Solomon in an instant (Q 27:23, 38-42; Ṭabarī, *Tafsir*, xix, 148, 159-68; id., *Taʾrīkh*, i, 580-1; Thaʿlabī, *Qiṣaṣ*, 279, 283-4; see TRIPS AND VOYAGES; JOURNEY).

Solomon in qurʾānic exegesis and the stories of the prophets

Muslim commentators provide anecdotes which demonstrate Solomon's wisdom and piety but they also delight in his regal pomp and magical powers. Stories about his magical levitating throne, his retinue of birds, animals, demons and men and his connection with the Queen of Sheba, identified as Bilqīs in Muslim sources, captured popular imagination. Solomon's temporal, religious and esoteric powers made him a model for both religious and secular personages (Melikian-Chirvani, Royaume). His mobility led Muslim commentators to link him with far-flung places; rulers distant from Jerusalem (q.v.) invoked his memory in the construction and decoration of their residences (Soucek, Throne; Koch, Jahangir). On a more popular level, his attributes and accomplishments are described in stories and depicted in paintings (Bagci, Divan; Milstein, Ruhrdanz and Schmitz, *Stories of the prophets*).

Priscilla Soucek

Bibliography
Primary: Kisāʾī, *Qiṣaṣ*, trans. W.M. Thackston, *Tales of the prophets of al-Kisāʾī*, Boston 1978, 288-96, 300-8, 313-21; Ṭabarī, *Tafsīr*, Cairo 1954; id., *Taʾrīkh*, ed. de Goeje, i, 571-97; trans. W.R. Brinner, *The history of al-Ṭabarī*. iii. *The Children of Israel*, Albany 1991, 150-74; Thaʿlabī, *Qiṣaṣ*, Beirut 1970, 257-393; trans. W.M. Brinner, *ʿArāʾis al-majālis fī Qiṣaṣ al-anbiyāʾ or "Lives of the prophets" as recounted by Abū Isḥāq Aḥmad Ibn Muḥammad Ibn Ibrāhīm al-Thaʿlabī*, Leiden 2002, 485-548; B. Wheeler (trans.), *Prophets in the Qurʾān. An introduction to the Qurʾān and Muslim exegesis*, London 2002, 266-79.
Secondary: S. Bagci, A new theme of the Shirazi miniatures. The divan of Solomon, in *Muqarnas* 12 (1995), 101-11; V. Gonzalez, The aesthetics of the Solomonic parable in the Qurʾān, in id., *Beauty and Islam. Aesthetics in Islamic art and architecture*, London 2001, 26-41; id., *Le piège de Salomon. La pensée de l'art dans le Coran*, Paris 2002; E. Koch, Jahangir and the angels. Recently discovered wall paintings under European influence in the Fort of Lahore, in id., *Mughal art and imperial ideology. Collected essays*, Oxford 2001, 27-37; J. Lassner, *Demonizing the Queen of Sheba. Boundaries of gender and culture in post-biblical Judaism and medieval Islam*, Chicago 1993; A.S. Melikian-Chirvani, Le royaume de Salomon, in *Le monde Iranien et l'Islam* 1 (1971), 1-41; R. Milstein, K. Ruhrdanz and B. Schmitz, *Stories of the prophets. Illustrated manuscripts of* Qiṣaṣ al-anbiyāʾ, Costa Mesa, CA 1999, 144-8; P. Soucek, Solomon's throne/Solomon's bath. Model or metaphor, in *Ars orientalis* 23 (1993), 109-36; id., The temple of Solomon in Islamic legend and art, in J. Gutmann (ed.), *The temple of Solomon. Archaeological fact and medieval tradition in Christian, Islamic and Jewish art*, Missoula, MT 1976, 73-111.

Soothsayer

One who foretells or interprets events. The Arabic term *kāhin*, related to Hebrew *kohen* ("priest"), designates a soothsayer, seer or diviner. It appears twice in the Qurʾān, reflecting one of several accusations directed at the prophet Muḥammad: that he was a madman (see INSANITY), poet (see POETRY AND POETS) or soothsayer or that he was instructed by someone else (*muʿallam;* see INFORMANTS). The text emphatically rejects such slurs:

> Therefore warn (humankind), for, by the grace of God, you are neither a soothsayer nor a madman" (Q 52:29; see WARNER). But nay! I swear by all that you see and all that you do not see that this is indeed the speech *(qawl)* of a noble messenger (q.v.). It is not the speech of a poet — how little you believe (see BELIEF AND UNBELIEF)! Nor is it the speech of a soothsayer — how little do you take heed! (Q 69:38-42).

The soothsayer was an important religious specialist in pre-Islamic Arabia who served several functions, showing some affinity with soothsayers in ancient Semitic traditions (see PRE-ISLAMIC ARABIA AND THE QURʾĀN; SOUTH ARABIA, RELIGION IN PRE-ISLAMIC; MAGIC). He was often the custodian *(sādin, ḥājib)* of a temple or shrine *(bayt, kaʿba)* within a sacred precinct (*ḥaram;* see SACRED PRECINCTS), in which capacity he maintained the shrine itself, supervised sacrifices (see SACRIFICE) and other rites and oversaw donations. As seer, he was called on to predict events (see FORETELLING; DIVINATION), interpret dreams (see DREAMS AND SLEEP) or provide advice regarding difficult decisions such as undertaking a journey (q.v.), going to war (q.v.), or sealing an alliance (see CONTRACTS AND ALLIANCES). He usually performed divination by casting lots consisting of marked rods or arrow shafts *(azlām, aqdāḥ)*. In an altered state, often enshrouded in a cloak, he also received oracular statements through inspiration from a familiar spirit *(tābiʿ)*. Purporting to be in the voice of the spirit, these statements addressed the soothsayer himself as "you" and were couched in rhymed and rhythmic cadences (*saj*ʿ; see RHYMED PROSE), drawing on obscure and ambiguous vocabulary and often prefaced by oaths (q.v.) sworn upon natural phenomena. They included omens, charms, prayers, blessings and curses (see CURSE; BLESSING; PORTENTS). The soothsayer received remuneration for his services in the form of an "honorarium" (*ḥulwān*).

In addition, the label soothsayer was applied to the "false prophets" active during the "wars of apostasy (q.v.)" both before and following the death of the prophet Muḥammad: al-Aswad al-ʿAnsī (d. 10/632) in Yemen, Ṭulayḥa b. Khuwaylid (d. 21/642) among the Banū Asad, Musaylima b. Ḥabīb in Yamāma and the prophetess Sajāḥ among the Banū Tamīm (see TRIBES AND CLANS). Musaylima (q.v.), known as "the liar" in Muslim sources, was the most important of these prophets historically; his religious movement showed many similarities to that of the prophet Muḥammad and may have been nascent Islam's most formidable rival. After crushing two Muslim armies, his forces were defeated by the Muslims under the general Khālid b. al-Walīd, and he himself was killed at the battle of ʿAqrabāʾ in 12/634.

As part of the pagan religion, soothsaying was rejected under Islam and survived only in marginal contexts. The soothsayers' claims of access to hidden knowledge (*ghayb*) went against the Islamic attribution of this power exclusively to God (see KNOWLEDGE AND LEARNING; HIDDEN AND THE HIDDEN); in the words of al-Bāqillānī (d. 403/1013), "soothsaying contradicts the prophecies" (*Iʿjāz*, 87). It is reported that the Prophet outlawed three fees: the price for a dog (q.v.), the payment (*mahr*) of a prostitute (see ADULTERY AND FORNICATION; TEMPORARY MARRIAGE) and the honorarium of a soothsayer (Bukhārī, *Ṣaḥīḥ*, *bāb thaman al-kalb*). A report known as "the ḥadīth of the fetus" is also cited to show that the Prophet rejected the use of rhymed prose because of its association with soothsaying. Transmitted in various versions, the ḥadīth relates a case concerning two co-wives (see MARRIAGE AND DIVORCE; WOMEN AND THE QURʾĀN; ḤADĪTH AND THE QURʾĀN), one from the tribe of Hudhayl and the other from the tribe of ʿĀmir. The Hudhaliyya struck the ʿĀmiriyya with a pole, killing her and also causing a miscarriage. When the Prophet ruled that the guilty woman's relatives had to pay blood money (q.v.) both for the ʿĀmiriyya and for the fetus, her guardian remonstrated, "O, messenger of God, have you ruled (that blood money be paid) for one who has neither eaten nor drunk, nor let out his first cry, when such as this should be left uncompensated?" (*qaḍayta fī man lā akala wa-lā shariba wa-lā ʿstahal[la] fa-mithlu dhālika yuṭal[l]*). The Prophet remarked, in disapproval, "*Saj*ʿ like the *saj*ʿ of the soothsayers?" (Jāḥiẓ, *Bayān*, i, 287-91; Abū Dāwūd, *Sunan*, iv, 190-3; ʿAskarī, *Ṣināʿatayn*, 261; Abū Nuʿaym al-Iṣbahānī, *Dhikr akhbār Iṣbahān*, ii, 97, 112). Some authorities argue, however, that the Prophet did not mean to condemn rhymed prose altogether but only its use as a rhetorical flourish designed to make an illegitimate point (Ibn al-Athīr, *al-Mathal al-sāʾir*, i, 274). Recommendations to avoid rhymed prose in prayers (Bukhārī, *Ṣaḥīḥ*, ii, 43 [34. *Buyu*ʿ, 113 (*bāb thaman al-kalb*)]; Fr. trans., ii, 5) also represent an attempt to distinguish Islamic prayers from those of the soothsayers (see PRAYER; RITUAL AND THE QURʾĀN; PRAYER FORMULAS).

Nevertheless, just as the pagan ritual of the pre-Islamic pilgrimage (q.v.) was accepted in Islam by being reinterpreted within a biblical framework, so, too, were elements of soothsaying adopted in the Qurʾān and Islamic tradition with similar modifications. It is curious that Ibn

Hishām's (d. 761/1360) *Sīra* uses a soothsaying tradition to legitimate the rise of Islam. It begins with two renowned south Arabian soothsayers, Shiqq and Saṭīḥ, predicting the Ethiopian invasion of Yemen and the rise of a great prophet who would reverse the invasion. In addition, many passages of the Qurʾān exhibit features related to the style of soothsayers' pronouncements. The Prophet receives revelation when enshrouded (Q 73:1; 74:1). He is also visited by a spirit (q.v.), though the familiar spirit of the soothsaying tradition is reinterpreted as the angel Gabriel (q.v.; cf. Q 53:1-18). The Prophet is regularly addressed as "you" (sing.). Rhymed prose is prevalent, particularly in the early Meccan sūras (see RHETORIC AND THE QURʾĀN; LANGUAGE AND STYLE OF THE QURʾĀN). In addition, many specific forms associated with soothsaying appear: oaths by celestial bodies (see PLANETS AND STARS) and natural phenomena (Q 37:1-3; 51:1-4; 52:1-6; 53:1; 74:32-34; 77:1-6; 79:1-5; 81:15-18; 84:16-18; 85:1-3; 86:1; 89:1-4; 90:1-3; 91:1-7; 92:1-3; 93:1-2; 95:1-3; 100:1-5; 103:1; see NATURE AS SIGNS), omens and predictions, often in the form "when" *(idhā)*... "then, on that day" (*yawmaʾidhin;* cf. Q 77:8-19; 81:1-14; 82:1-5; 84:1-15; 99), the *mā adrāka* construction (Q 69:1-3; 74:26-7; 77:3-4; 82:14-18; 83:7-8; 83:18-19; 86:1-2; 90:11-12; 97:1-2; 101:1-3; 104:4-5; see FORM AND STRUCTURE OF THE QURʾĀN), charms (Q 113; 114; see POPULAR AND TALISMANIC USES OF THE QURʾĀN), and curses (Q 104; 111). The content, though, has presumably shifted. For example, all omens or predictions in the Qurʾān, with the exception of Q 30:1-2 which are understood to predict a victory by the Byzantines (q.v.) over the Persians, have to do with the apocalypse (q.v.) and judgment day (see ESCHATOLOGY; LAST JUDGMENT).

Devin J. Stewart

Bibliography
Primary: Abū Dāwūd; Abū Nuʿaym al-Iṣbahānī, Aḥmad b. ʿAbdallāh, *Dhikr akhbār Iṣbahān,* ed. S. Dedering, 2 vols., Leiden 1931-4; al-ʿAskarī, Abū Hilāl al-Ḥasan b. ʿAbdallāh, *Kitāb al-Ṣināʿatayn. al-Kitāba wa-l-shiʿr,* Cairo 1952; Bāqillānī, *Iʿjāz;* Bukhārī, *Ṣaḥīḥ,* ed. Krehl; Fr. trans. O. Houdas and W. Marçais, *Les traditions islamiques,* 4 vols., Paris 1903-14 (repr. 1977); Ibn al-Athīr, Ḍiyāʾ al-Dīn Abū l-Fatḥ Naṣr Allāh, *al-Mathal al-sāʾir,* Cairo 1959-62; Ibn Qayyim al-Jawziyya, *Tibyān;* Jāḥiẓ, *Bayān;* Masʿūdī, *Murūj;* Ṭabarī, *Tārīkh.*
Secondary: R. Blachère, *Histoire de la littérature arabe des origines à la fin du XV siècle de J.-C.,* Paris 1964; id., *Introduction;* D. Eickelmann, Musaylima. An approach to the social anthropology of seventh century Arabia, in *JESHO* 10 (1967), 17-52; T. Fahd, *La divination arabe. Études religieuses, sociologiques, et folkloriques sur le lieu natif de l'Islam,* Leiden 1966; id., Sadjʿ. 1. As magical utterances in pre-Islamic Arabian usage, in *EI²,* viii, 732-4; L. Kandil, Die Schwüre in den mekkanischen Suren, in Wild, *Text,* 41-57; F.R. Müller, *Untersuchungen zur Reimprosa im Koran,* Bonn 1969; Nöldeke, *GQ;* D.J. Stewart, *Sajʿ* in the Qurʾān. Prosody and structure, in *JAL* 21 (1990), 101-39; J. Wellhausen, *Reste arabischen Heidentums,* Berlin 1927.

Sorcery see MAGIC

Sorrow see WEEPING; JOY AND MISERY

Soul

That which makes a creature animate, and to which individuality is attributed. From the second/eighth century until today, the vast majority of Muslims have believed that each human being has a soul. Opinion has varied regarding the soul's nature and its relationship to the body, though most Muslim scholars have envisioned the soul as a subtle form or substance infused within or inhabiting a physical body. Generally, Muslims have believed that souls are created by God, joined to a body at birth, taken from the body at death and reunited with the body on the resurrection day (see CREATION; BIRTH; BIOLOGY AS

THE CREATION AND STAGES OF LIFE; DEATH AND THE DEAD; RESURRECTION). Muslim theologians, philosophers and mystics have cited various verses from the Qurʾān in support of the soul's existence (see THEOLOGY AND THE QURʾĀN; PHILOSOPHY AND THE QURʾĀN; ṢŪFISM AND THE QURʾĀN). Yet, such readings appear indebted more to Aristotle, neo-Platonism and Christianity (see CHRISTIANS AND CHRISTIANITY) than to the Qurʾān, with its holistic view of the human being.

In Arabic, two words are used interchangeably for soul: *rūḥ*, "breath, spirit (q.v.; see also AIR AND WIND)," and *nafs*, "self." *Rūḥ* appears twenty-one times in the Qurʾān, always as a singular substantive, masculine noun. There, *rūḥ* often refers to the spirit of revelation (see REVELATION AND INSPIRATION) sent by God to his prophets (see PROPHETS AND PROPHETHOOD): "High of rank, possessor of the throne (see THRONE OF GOD), he casts the spirit of his command upon whomever he wills of his servants (q.v.), that they might warn of the day of meeting" (Q 40:15; see WARNER). The spirit (of God's command) may be accompanied by angels (see ANGEL) when bringing revelation, ascending to their lord (q.v.), and on judgment day (Q 16:2; 70:4; 78:38; 97:4; see LAST JUDGMENT). Using similar language, the Qurʾān speaks of *rūḥ al-qudus*, or "the holy spirit," sent by God to assist Jesus (q.v.; Q 2:87, 253; 5:110; see also HOLY SPIRIT) and to bring Muḥammad the qurʾānic revelation: "Say [Muḥammad]: Truly the holy spirit brought down [revelation] from your lord to strengthen those who believe (see BELIEF AND UNBELIEF), as guidance (see ERROR; ASTRAY) and glad tidings (see GOOD NEWS) for those who submit!" (Q 16:102; cf. 26:193; 42:52). The Qurʾān clearly identifies this spirit of revelation as Gabriel (q.v.; Q 2:97).

God's spirit also came, in the form of a man, to Mary (q.v.), to assist in her conception with Jesus (Q 19:17), about which the Qurʾān says: "And Mary daughter of Imrān (q.v.), who guarded her chastity (q.v.), we breathed into her from our spirit..." (Q 66:12; cf. 4:171; 21:91). Comparable to the prophets, who bring revelations from God, Mary conceived and gave birth to the prophet Jesus. Mary's story also parallels that of Adam's creation (see ADAM AND EVE): "Then [God] proportioned him and breathed into him of his spirit, and he assigned you hearing and sight and hearts, but little thanks you give!" (Q 32:9; cf. 15:29; 38:72; see SEEING AND HEARING; HEART; GRATITUDE AND INGRATITUDE). Yet, in the last two examples, the term *rūḥ* probably does not designate the spirit of revelation but, rather, the "breath of life" given by God (cf. Hebrew *ruaḥ; Gen* 2:7; *Ezek* 34:1-14). A related use of *rūḥ* is found in the verse of the pre-Islamic poet ʿAbīd b. al-Abraṣ (sixth century C.E.): "What are we but bodies that pass under the earth and breaths to the winds?" Nevertheless, many Muslims have taken the story of Adam's creation as proof of the existence of a soul within each human being. Some Muslim scholars have suggested that human beings may thus have a portion of divinity itself or, at the very least, a very special relationship with God. Clearly, the meaning of *rūḥ* in the Qurʾān has been a topic of discussion since Muḥammad's time, as the Qurʾān notes: "They ask you about the spirit. Say: 'The spirit is from the command of my lord, and you have been given little knowledge!'" (Q 17:85; see KNOWLEDGE AND LEARNING).

The second word found in the Qurʾān which has been read as soul is *nafs*. Like *rūḥ*, *nafs* is derived from a root involving air, breath and life; the verb *nafasa* means "to breathe," with *nafas* meaning "breath," though neither word appears in the Qurʾān. *Nafs* is a cognate of the Hebrew *nefesh* which, in the Bible, generally refers to the life force coursing through the blood of humans and animals (e.g. *Lev* 17:11; see BLOOD AND BLOODCLOT); by extension, *nefesh* may designate the appetites, a person or a slave (see SLAVES AND SLAVERY). Among the pre-Islamic Nabataeans, *napshā* referred to a tomb, the last resting-place of a human being, while in pre-Islamic Arabic poetry (see POETRY AND POETS; PRE-ISLAMIC ARABIA AND THE QURʾĀN), the feminine noun *nafs* and its plurals *anfus* and *nufūs* refer to living beings, in general, and to one's self or tribe (see TRIBES AND CLANS), in particular. This use of *nafs* as a reflexive particle is very common in the Qurʾān, where *nafs, anfus* and *nufūs* appear over 250 times:

As to those who argue with you about [the revelation] after what knowledge has come to you, say [to them]: "Come, let us call together our children (q.v.) and your children, our women and your women (see WOMEN AND THE QURʾĀN), ourselves *(anfusanā)* and yourselves *(anfusakum)*. Then we will humbly pray and call down God's curse (q.v.) upon the liars!" (Q 3:61; see also LIE).

Nafs may refer to humans, the jinn (q.v.), Satan (see DEVIL) and God: "God has prescribed mercy (q.v.) for himself" (*ʿalā nafsihi,* Q 6:12; cf. 6:130; 18:51; 21:43). As in this last example, *nafs* may imply an essential quality, a disposition or intentions: "Your lord knows what is within yourselves" (*fī nufūsikum,* Q 17:25; see HIDDEN AND THE HIDDEN). This calls attention to an important ethical aspect often found in the reflexive *nafs* (see ETHICS AND THE QURʾĀN) as the Qurʾān challenges its audience to choose between God's commands and their own desires (see WISH AND DESIRE): "Say: 'O people, the truth (q.v.) has come to you from your lord. Whoever is guided [by it], is guided for himself *(li-nafsihi),* while he who goes astray, strays against himself' " (*ʿalayhā,* Q 10:108). Use of the reflexive pronouns in such verses, then, underscores human responsibility for one's belief and actions: "What they spend on this worldly life is like a cold blast that strikes and destroys the fields of a people who oppress themselves (see PARABLE; SIMILES; LITERARY STRUCTURES OF THE QURʾĀN). God did not oppress them, but they oppress themselves!" (Q 3:117; see OPPRESSION; OPPRESSED ON EARTH, THE; FREEDOM AND PREDESTINATION; REWARD AND PUNISHMENT).

Here, *nafs* reflects a negative human trait, namely selfishness, against which the Qurʾān warns: "So be mindful of God as much as you can, listen and obey (see OBEDIENCE), and spend on charity to help yourselves. For those who are saved from their selfish greed *(shuḥḥ nafsihi),* they are the successful ones!" (Q 64:16; cf. 53:23; 59:9; see TRADE AND COMMERCE). This *nafs* corresponds to the appetites or the appetitive faculties discussed in ancient and Hellenistic philosophies. As such, the Qurʾān links *nafs* with greed (see AVARICE), envy (q.v.), and lust. Like Satan, selfishness whispers its desires to the individual and incites evil acts (Q 12:18; 20:96, 120; 47:25; 50:16; see EVIL DEEDS; WHISPER). As Joseph (q.v.) declares when faced with Potipher's wife and her scheme to seduce him: "I do not absolve myself, for, indeed, selfishness instigates evil *(al-nafsa la-ammāratun bi-l-sūʾi),* save where my lord has mercy. Indeed, my lord is forgiving and merciful!" (Q 12:53; cf. 4:128; 5:30; see FORGIVENESS). Thus, the Qurʾān declares that concupiscence must be fought and controlled if one is to obey God: "As for him who fears standing before his lord (see FEAR), and who restrains the self *(al-nafs)* from desire (see ABSTINENCE), indeed the garden (q.v.) will be the place of refuge!"

(Q 79:40-1). The believer resists his selfish impulses by heeding *al-nafs al-lawwāma,* his "blaming self" or conscience (Q 75:2), so that on the judgment day he may appear before God with a clear conscience and inner tranquility (*al-nafs al-muṭma'inna,* Q 89:27).

In these and similar instances, *nafs* and its plurals do not appear to designate a spiritual substance or soul but rather aspects of human character, including selfishness, concupiscence, personal responsibility and individual conscience. In other verses, however, *nafs* has a more general meaning as a living person or human life. When God called Moses (q.v.) to go to Egypt (q.v.), Moses replied: "Lord, I have killed a person *(nafs)* among them, and I fear they will kill me!" (Q 28:33; see MURDER; BLOODSHED; RETALIATION). Similarly, the Qur'ān declares: "And do not kill a person *(al-nafs),* which God has forbidden, save for a just cause" (Q 17:33; cf. 18:74; 25:68) and most explicitly: "And we decreed for them in [the Torah (q.v.)] a life *(al-nafs)* for a life (q.v.), an eye for an eye (see EYES), a nose for a nose…" (Q 5:45). Likewise, the Qur'ān calls Muslims to defend their faith (q.v.) with their property (q.v.) and lives: "Believe in God and his messenger *(rasūlahu)* and strive in the way of God with your property and lives *(anfus)*!" (Q 61:11; cf. 9:20, 41, 44, 81, 88; see PATH OR WAY). Such loss and death are an inevitable part of life's trials: "We will test you with something of fear and hunger, and loss of property, lives *(al-anfus),* and the fruits [of your labors]. Yet give good news to the patient ones" (Q 2:155).

The Qur'ān states emphatically that every human being will die: "Every person *(nafs)* will taste death, and your wages will be paid in full on the day of resurrection!" (Q 3:185; cf. 3:145; 21:35; 29:57). In several passages, angels seize the living at the time of death. Speaking of unbelievers, the Qur'ān says: "If you could only see when the oppressors are in the throes of death, as the angels stretch out their hands, pulling out their lives!" (*anfus,* Q 6:93; cf. 4:97). Some commentators have read this passage as referring to souls, though in a larger qur'ānic context, *anfus* might better be read as "lives." A related verse, however, is more ambiguous: "God gathers up persons *(al-anfus)* at their death and, for those who do not die, in their sleep (q.v.). He keeps those upon whom he has decreed death, and sends the others back until an appointed time…" (Q 39:42; cf. 6:60). The Qur'ān likens sleep to death for, as the commentator al-Zamakhsharī (d. 538/1144) points out, sleep suspends exterior movement and consciousness *(nafs al-tamyīz),* while, in death, consciousness, movement and life itself *(nafs al-ḥayā)* are ended. Al-Zamakhsharī makes a distinction here between reason and discrimination (*nafs al-ʿaql wa-l-tamyīz;* see INTELLECT) and the life force *(rūḥ)* that is characterized by breath and movement. Other commentators, however, including al-Ṭabarī (d. 310/923), al-Qushayrī (d. 465/1072) and al-Rāzī (d. 606/1210) go further, stating that in both sleep and death, God takes away a person's movement and consciousness, along with their soul *(rūḥ; jawhar mushriq rūḥānī).*

Commentators have also found reference to the soul in Q 81:7, which says that on judgment day, "the *nufūs* will be paired." They note that one possible meaning is that souls *(al-arwāḥ)* will be joined with their bodies. Yet some of these commentators, especially al-Ṭabarī, point out that the probable meaning is that each person *(al-insān)* will be gathered with people of a similar sort, as good persons enter paradise (q.v.), evil people, hell (cf. Q 56:7; 37:22; see GOOD AND EVIL; HELL AND HELLFIRE). This reading is consistent with the Qur'ān's many other references to the *nafs* on judgment day when individuals are called to account:

Every person *(nafs)* is held accountable for what she earned (Q 74:38).
We do not burden a person *(nafs)* beyond her capacity. We have a book (q.v.) that speaks the truth, and they will not be wronged! (Q 23:62; see also HEAVENLY BOOK).
[On a day] when a person *(nafs)* will know what she sent forward and what she left behind (Q 82:5).

Nafs in such passages probably means the person held responsible for his or her beliefs and actions and not the soul. This is suggested by nearly identical passages in which the feminine *nafs* is replaced, not by *rūḥ* or some other synonym for soul, but by the masculine noun *insān,* meaning human being. "On that day, the human being *(al-insān)* will be informed of what he sent forward and what he left behind" (Q 75:13; cf. 82:5; 91:7). Similarly, regarding the creation of the human race, the Qurʾān says: "He it is who created you from a single person *(nafs)* and made from her, her mate, that *he* might find rest in her" (Q 7:189; see PAIRS AND PAIRING). Though the feminine *nafs* is used here, this person clearly refers to Adam as reflected in the shift in gender within the verse (cf. Q 4:1; 38:71-2; 39:6).

Clearly, then, in accounts of creation and resurrection, the Qurʾān never states that the *nafs* is a soul that joins or enters a body. Rather, in the Qurʾān, it is the entire person in all of his or her physical, emotional and spiritual capacities that is created, dies and will be recreated on judgment day: "Your creation and resurrection are but like that of a single person *(nafs)*. Indeed, God hears and sees all!" (Q 31:28; see GOD AND HIS ATTRIBUTES).

Th. Emil Homerin

Bibliography
Primary: ʿAbīd b. al-Abraṣ, *Dīwān,* Beirut 1384/1964, 51; Bayḍāwī, *Anwār,* Beirut 1992 (reprint of the 1329/1911 Egyptian ed.), 184, 548, 612, 786; Qushayrī, *Laṭāʾif,* Cairo 1968-71, iii, 263, 283-4, 693; Rāzī, *Tafsīr,* Cairo 1352/1933, xiii, 85-6; xxvi, 283-4; xxxi, 69; Ṭabarī, *Tafsīr,* Cairo 1373-77/1954-7, vii, 182-3; xxi, 61; xxiv, 7; xxx, 44-5; Zamakhsharī, *Kashshāf,* Beirut 1366/1947, ii, 228; iii, 219-20, 349; iv, 188.
Secondary: ʿAbd al-Bāqī; J. Bemporad, Soul. Jewish concept, in *ER,* xiii, 450-5; R. Blachère, Note sur le substantif *nafs* "souffle vital", "âme" dans le Coran, in *Semetica* 1 (1948), 69-77; E.E. Calverley/I.R. Netton, Nafs, in *EI²,* vii, 880-4; S. Fraenkel, Miscellen zum Koran, in *ZDMG* 56 (1902), 71-3 (esp. 71-2, on Q 6:60, the soul during sleep); J.F. Healey, *The religion of the Nabataeans,* Leiden 2001, 169-71; T.E. Homerin, Echoes of a thirsty owl. Death and the afterlife in pre-Islamic Arabic poetry, in *JNES* 44 (1985), 165-84; Izutsu, *God,* 121-32; D.B. Macdonald, The development of the idea of spirit in Islam, in *MW* 32 (1932), 25-42, 153-68; A. Murtonen, The living soul. A study of the meaning of the word *naefaesh* in the Old Testament Hebrew language, in *Studia orientalia* 23/1 (1958), 3-105; T. O'Shaughnessy, *The development of the meaning of spirit in the Koran,* Rome 1953; F. Rahman, *Major themes of the Qurʾān,* Chicago 1980, 17-18, 95-7, 112; J.I. Smith and Y.Y. Haddad, *The Islamic understanding of death and resurrection,* Albany 1981.

South Arabia, Religions in Pre-Islamic

The religious history of south Arabia is divided into two periods of unequal length: polytheistic from its beginnings (eighth century B.C.E.) until around 380 C.E. (see POLYTHEISM AND ATHEISM), then monotheistic thereafter. Only the first is dealt with here; for the second, see YEMEN; JEWS AND JUDAISM; CHRISTIANS AND CHRISTIANITY. (For other aspects of pre-Islamic religious traditions of which the Qurʾān evinces knowledge, see e.g. ABYSSINIA; MAGIANS; MECCA; MEDINA; NAJRĀN; SABIANS; SHEBA; SOOTHSAYER; SYRIA.)

The main source for understanding the religions of pre-Islamic south Arabia consists of inscriptions, which are engraved on durable materials and are numbered in the thousands (see also EPIGRAPHY AND THE QURʾĀN). Archaeological investigation of ancient cult places complements the information taken from the texts (see also ARCHAEOLOGY AND THE QURʾĀN). By comparison, external sources, whether ancient works in classical or oriental languages or the rare pieces of information passed on by the Arab traditions of the Islamic era, provide us with very little (see ORALITY AND WRITING IN ARABIA; PRE-ISLAMIC ARABIA AND THE QURʾĀN). Such sources, which could clarify the religious conceptions of ancient south Arabians for us and give us an organized presentation of the divine cosmos (see COSMOLOGY), have not been preserved as literary texts (myths, epics, poems or rituals; see MYTHS AND LEGENDS IN THE QURʾĀN; POETRY AND POETS; RITUAL AND THE QURʾĀN). Most of the time, such sources simply mention the divinities, sanctuaries (see SACRED PRECINCTS; SACRED AND PROFANE; HOUSE, DOMESTIC AND DIVINE) or rituals.

The inscriptions deal only with a restricted range of subjects. The vast majority of them commemorate specific actions, setting out the rights of men or gods: building or construction operations which establish property (q.v.) rights; offerings to a divinity in order to obtain favor; rites carried out at important moments in the life of the community. These texts almost always provide important information for understanding religion (q.v.). The particular titles of their authors may make mention of a priestly office. The dedications quote the name of the intended divinity, particular titles (epithet, temple name) and, after the start of the Christian era, the reasons why the believer was making his offering. The dedications and texts which commemorate building or construction works normally end with "invocations," that is, a detailed list of the earthly and supernatural powers from whom the authors had obtained support or approval (see PRAYER FORMULAS). Prescriptive texts, which are few in number, are equally interesting. Some control access to the sanctuary, while others call upon divinities to grant greater weight to their prescriptions.

Gods and goddesses

The inscriptions name a whole host of divinities. Several, slightly dated works (Höfner, Die Stammesgruppen; id., Vorislamischen Religionen; Ryckmans, Religions arabes; id., *Religions arabes*) provide a list of these. Clearly this collection of divinities does not constitute a south Arabian pantheon as such. The first rule of classification is to identify those sites where a divinity is venerated or invoked: it is immediately clear that the majority of divinities have a special link with a particular family (q.v.), a named tribe (see TRIBES AND CLANS; KINSHIP), a tribal federation or a kingdom (see KINGS AND RULERS). These divinities may be termed "institutional" since they intervene in the life of the community at a certain level. It is these divinities that are invoked at the end of inscriptions.

Institutional divinities

Each kingdom had an official pantheon, made up of a small number of divinities, around five in total. This list of divinities is easy to determine for the kingdom of Sabaʾ (ʿAthtar, Hawbas, Almaqah, dhāt-Ḥimyam and dhāt-Baʿdān^{um}, *ʿṯtr, Hwbsʹ, ʾlmqh, ḏt-Ḥmym, ḏt-Bʿdn*^{m}; see SHEBA) and Qatabān (ʿAthtar, ʿAmm, Anbī, dhāt-Ṣanat^{um} and dhāt-Ẓahrān, *ʿṯtr, ʿm, ʾnby, ḏt-Ṣnt*^{m}, *ḏt-Ẓhr*^{n}) because the most solemn inscriptions always call upon them in that order (for the precise location of ethnic groups and place names, see Robin and

Brunner, *Map of ancient Yemen*). Elsewhere the list is much more a matter of conjecture. In the small kingdoms of al-Jawf, it is reconstructed from the rite celebrated by those in authority. Finally, for the Ḥaḍramawt there is almost no information at all.

Before the Christian era, the political cohesion of states was based upon the cult of divinities in the official pantheon; each divinity was the object of particular rites, which suggests a specific role, complementing the role of associated divinities. Changes in political organization, following conquests, annexations, secessions, alliances, etc., logically translated into change in the religious sphere also. For example, Sabaean domination of the city kingdom of Nashshān (in al-Jawf) led to the construction of a temple to the Sabaean god Almaqah in the town center; and when Saba' (Sheba) annexed the tribal federation of Samʿī, the great Samiʿyan god (Ta'lab) decreed that the federation should henceforth take part in the official Sabaean pilgrimage to Almaqah at Marib (today, Ma'rib; see AL-ʿARIM), in the month of dhū-Abhī (*ḏ-'bhy*, roughly July; see MONTHS; CALENDAR). The introduction to the Sabaean pantheon of a new god, Hawbas, around the sixth century B.C.E., may perhaps be explained by new alliances. This parallel political and religious organization broke up from the beginning of the Christian era, when the redrawing of the political map ceased to have a corresponding religious effect. Henceforth, whoever held power (whether sovereign or tribal leader) replaced the divinity as the basis of political entities and more and more often kingdoms and principalities were collections of tribes with different cults.

A large number of divinities were only worshipped by a single kingdom, such as Almaqah (Saba'), ʿAmm (Qatabān) or Sayīn (Ḥaḍramawt), others, such as Wadd^{um} *(Wd^{m})* or dhāt-Ḥimyam *(ḏt-Ḥmym)*, in many. Only one, ʿAthtar *(ʿṯtr)*, is common to the entire population of south Arabia. A single divinity common to several groups is often individualized by a qualifying name or title. ʿAthtar, for example, is always qualified by dhū-Qabḍ^{um} *(ḏ-Qbḍ^{m})* when describing the principal god of the kingdom of Maʿīn. The title often denotes the name or location of a sanctuary, and sometimes both, as with "Ta'lab Riyām^{um} lord (of the temple) of Qadmān (of the city) of Damhān" *(T'lb Rym^{m} bʿl Qdm^{n} ḏ-Dmh^{n})*.

For some uncommon divinities, the texts make explicit mention of their tribe of origin, such as dhū-(l)-Samāwī, "the heavenly one" *(ḏ- S^{1}mwy)*, who is often called "god (of the tribe) of Amīr^{um}," an Arab tribe (see ARABS) based between al-Jawf and Najrān (q.v.). His principal temple (called *ḏ-yġrw*) was located at the heart of Amir^{um} territory, in wādī l-Shuḍayf, (some sixty km north of al-Jawf), but some sanctuaries were also dedicated to him by other tribes elsewhere: at Haram (in al-Jawf), at Marib (capital of Saba'), at Tamnaʿ (capital of Qatabān) and at Sawā^{m} (22 km south of Taʿizz).

Some divinities are not exclusively Yemeni. There is evidence for the god Wadd^{um} in the Persian Gulf, and according to tradition, he was also worshipped by the Kalb at Dūmat al-Jandal. The gods Sayīn and Anbī had corresponding gods in Mesopotamia (Sīn and Nabū), the gods Saḥar and Rammān, just like the goddess Athirat, in the near east (Shaḥar and Athirat in Ugarit, Ashera in the Bible, Rammān as an epithet of the Aramaic god Hadad; Bron, Notes sur le culte; id., Divinités communes). The most widespread divinity was ʿAthtar, with a dual male and female aspect, as can be seen at Ugarit and Ḥaḍramawt, even if one of the two is very often dominant (the male aspect in south Arabia, except at Ḥaḍramawt, the female aspect in Mesopotamia).

A large number of divinities do not have a proper name as such, but are indicated by a quality (Wadd^um^, "Love"), a family relationship (ʿAmm, "Uncle on the father's side"), a locale (and perhaps sometimes by a quality or a function) introduced by the pronouns "He who ..., she who ..." (dhū-[l-]Samāwī, dhū-Qabḍ^um^, dhāt-Ḥimyam, dhāt Badān^um^, etc.). Most likely the real names of these divinities were taboo. The same phenomenon can be seen in the Arabian desert with al-Lāh ("the god"), al-Lāt ("the goddess"), al-ʿUzzā ("the most powerful"; cf. Q 53:19-20) and all the names with dhū- or dhāt- (dhāt Anwāṭ, dhū l-Kaʿbāt, dhū l-Khalaṣa, dhū l-Kaf-fayn or dhū l-Labaʾ).

The development of formal pantheons is most obvious at the level of kingdoms, which could be extremely varied in size, ranging from the simple city-tribe (like Kaminahū or Haram in al-Jawf) to the assembly of enormous collections of tribes (like Sabaʾ). But tribes, towns, clans, lineages and families had their own cults, too, and these were added to the collective rites of the kingdom. It follows from this that the structure of the divine world faithfully reflected the organization of society. The same phenomenon can be seen elsewhere in Arabia, for example in the Yathrib oasis when Muḥammad arrived there (Lecker, Idol worship; see MEDINA).

Some minor divinities, divided into four classes entitled *bʿl byt-*, *mnḏḥ*, *s²ms¹* and *rbʿ*, are entrusted with the protection of palaces, temples, family groups or individuals. The terms which denote these classes may be translated as "master of the palace of...," "household divinity," "genium (lit. sun)" and "protector."

Some divinities have a double name, like those of mere mortals, in which we can see a divine name, such as ʿIzazallāt ("Power of al-Lāt"), Hawfīʾīl ("Īl has saved"), Laḥayʿathat ("ʿAthtar shines"), Sumūyadaʿ ("His name knew") or Yadaʿismuhū ("He knew his name"). These are probably deified individuals, ancestors or heroes. Normally living human beings, including the sovereign, are not described thus. There is, however, one somewhat puzzling exception, a king of Awsān from the Hellenistic era, who is called "son of (god) Wadd^um^" and receives offerings, as if he were himself a god.

Non-institutional divinities

A relatively large number of divinities have no clear link with any political or tribal entity. These apparently include the "Daughters of Īl," mostly worshipped by women. Their name suggests that they were a class of supernatural entities acting as intermediaries between human beings and the assembly of gods. Other unnamed divinities can also be added, who may be identified by a parental relationship with a divinity: "Son of Hawbas," "Mother of ʿAthtar," or "Mother of goddesses." Instances of divinities particular to a place or sanctuary are more doubtful: e.g. "He who is at Raydān," the "Lord of Awran," the "Lord of Baḥr^um^," the "Lord of Yafʿān," the "Lord of Ḥadas^um^," the "Mistress of Ḥadath, she who is from Ẓarb^um^," the "god in the chapel (of worshippers) Kharīf at Mayfaʿ," etc. It is possible that these divinities, or some of them at least, provided individuals or non-tribal groups (women, those of the same age group, or in the same trade) the chance to meet with each other and express their solidarity.

Divinities borrowed from the Arabs

Several divinities of Arab origin were known and worshipped in south Arabia.

They were introduced after Arab tribes settled in the lowlands of Yemen from the second century B.C.E. Dhū-(l-)Samāwī, the Amīr^{um} god, has already been mentioned. Another god of the same sort is Kāhilān (who may perhaps be identified with the god Khl^{m} of Qaryat al-Fāw), known from the kingdom of Maʿīn (Bron, *Maʿīn*, 30). Above all, however, there are the three goddesses al-Lāt, Manāt and al-ʿUzzā, mentioned in Q 53:19-20 (cf. Robin, Filles de Dieu, 139 f.; see SATANIC VERSES).

Al-ʿUzzā, Sabaean ʿUzzayān *(ʿzy^{n})*, is the only Arab divinity, along with dhū-(l-) Samāwī, whose cult was widespread in south Arabia. There is evidence for her in twelve texts (two of which are fragmentary): five commemorate offerings in one of her temples; two, on amulets (q.v.), call upon her as a protectress; and three call upon her as the guardian divinity of the final royal palace of Qatabān. The name ʿUzzayān is also found in several theophoric anthroponyms, almost all relating to the same inscription. An onomastic, ʿUzzayān first appeared in south Arabia in the third century B.C.E. This was not far from Najrān, a region inhabited by north Arabian tribes. The first sign of a cult (a dedication in a sanctuary consecrated to the goddess) comes from Qatabān dating from the second century B.C.E.

Al-Lāt, Sabaean Lātān and Lāt (*Lt^{n}* and *lt*), who was popular in northwestern Arabia and among the Arabs of the near east, does not seem to have been the object of an organized cult in south Arabia. The only indications of veneration are two amulets. The name of the goddess is written once with the article *-n*, and once without. The goddess, however, seems to have been extremely popular among the Arab tribes on the northern borders of Yemen, then among the south Arabians themselves, judging by theophores with *-lt*, of which there are dozens. The appearance of these theophores in al-Jawf may be dated to the second century B.C.E.

Manāt, south Arabian Manawt *(Mnwt)*, whose cult is well documented among the Palmyrenians and in northwestern Arabia (notably at Taymāʾ and al-Ḥijr), makes almost no appearance in the epigraphic records of south Arabia. At present there is only a single reference in a text from Maʿīn dating from the fifth century B.C.E. (Bron, *Maʿīn*, 30). This occurrence, seemingly older than everything found elsewhere, suggests that Manawt was a divinity of Ragmat (the ancient name of Najrān). Similarly, the name Manawt appears in several anthroponyms from the Najrān region in its broadest sense.

These three goddesses, introduced by the Arabs, should be distinguished from the "Daughters of Īl," who are local divinities (Robin, Filles de Dieu). All these, however, are minor divinities, a fact which prefigures the compromise proposed by Muḥammad in the "satanic verses," namely the recognition of divinities which served Meccan interests, provided that they were reduced to the status of "Daughters of Allāh" (the local version of the south Arabian "Daughters of Īl"), that is, divine messengers (see MESSENGER).

Strangely enough, all the known south Arabian divinities had a positive or protective role. Evil powers are alluded to in invocations but are never personified. Magical thinking is afraid to name evil, lest it contribute to making it real (see MAGIC; GOOD AND EVIL).

Cult organization

Places of cult worship, whether of human design ("temples") or otherwise ("sanctuaries"), were quite varied in size. The plans, the quality of the building and the organization were incredibly diverse, even in the same tribe. This is equally true

[I] South Arabian inscription of Yūsuf Asʾar Yathʾar (*Yws*^{1}*f ʾs*^{1}*ʾr Yṯʾr*), a Jewish king of Ḥimyar to whom Christian sources attribute the early sixth-century C.E. persecution of the Christians of Najrān. The name of the king appears on the third line of the inscription. Photograph courtesy of Christian Robin.

[II] The walls of the southern Arabian ancient city of Najrān (today called al-Ukhdūd). Photograph courtesy of Christian Robin.

[III] The dam of the southern Arabian city of Ma'rib (Marib): northern sluice and canal. Photograph courtesy of Christian Robin.

[IV] The dam of the southern Arabian city of Ma'rib (Marib): view from the southern sluice. Photograph courtesy of Christian Robin.

[v] A south Arabian inscription of the Ḥimyarite king Abīkarib (Ar. Abū Karib); in about 380 C.E. he rejected polytheism and accorded Judaism a privileged position. Photograph courtesy of Christian Robin.

[VI] Part of the main monumental south Arabian rock inscription of al-Miʿsāl, from the third century C.E. Photograph courtesy of Christian Robin.

[VII] A votive south Arabian inscription on a bronze tablet (ca. first century B.C.E.). Photograph courtesy of Christian Robin.

for the locations, at the center of town, outside the walls, in the countryside or the steppe, at the top of a mountain or in the midst of the rocks (Jung, Religious monuments). The temple seems to have played an important economic role (see ECONOMICS; TRADE AND COMMERCE). It owned property (q.v.; *mbʿl*). Furthermore, at Sabaʾ and Ḥaḍramawt, the currency was placed under the control of the chief god (see MONEY). Certain temples and sanctuaries display features which can be found in the Meccan *ḥaram*. The temple of Ṣirwāḥ (90 km east of Ṣanʿāʾ), with a half-oval precinct, recalls the form of *ḥijr* and is bounded by a semi-circular cloister. The low walls which enclose the sanctuary of Jabal al-Lawdh (135 km north-east of Ṣanʿāʾ) seem comparable to the *ʿarīsh* (the building with no roof and with walls so low that cattle can step over them) which stood there, prior to the Kaʿba. The sacred perimeter of the sanctuary of Darb al-Ṣabī, near Barāqish (95 km northeast of Ṣanʿāʾ, ancient Yathill) is marked by boundary stones (nine are preserved, with the inscription "boundary of the sanctuary"), just like the Meccan *ḥaram*.

To the best of our knowledge, places of worship were not under the authority of an actual clergy, mediating between humans and the gods. Nonetheless, certain individuals were engaged in the service of the temples. They held titles such as *rs²w* ("priest"), *qyn* ("administrator"), *mrṯd* ("consecrated to a particular divinity") or *ʾfkl* (pl. *ʾfklt*, "priests," an Akkadian loan word, which is only found at a very early period).

Rituals

The most frequent ritual was apparently the presentation of offerings, commemorated by an inscription, which commends in a lasting manner the generosity of the person making the offering. In ancient times, these offerings consisted either of people (who seem to have entered into the service of the divinity) or of produce or various other objects. From the start of the Christian era, or a short time earlier, offerings of people were replaced by the dedication of small statuettes; such representations were called *ṣlm* (in Arabic *ṣanam*) when a man was represented and *ṣlmt* when a woman was concerned. By means of these statuettes, those individuals consecrated to the divinity were symbolically present in the temple, without actually performing any service as such.

The divinity was regularly honored by great pilgrimages (usually called *ḥḏr* and *mwfrt*, and less commonly *ḥg*; see PILGRIMAGE). For Sabaʾ, the most important was definitely the pilgrimage of Almaqah at Marib, in dhū-Abhī (roughly in July, the main period of rains). Another, the pilgrimage of Almaqah dhū-Hirrān at ʿAmrān (45 km northwest of Ṣanʿāʾ), is known because of two references. The principal god Samʿī, Taʾlab Riyām^{um}, was visited at Mount Turʿat (modern-day Jabal Riyām, 50 km north of Ṣanʿāʾ) and the Ẓabyān temple at Ḥadaqān (30 km north of Ṣanʿāʾ). Finally, a pilgrimage in honor of dhū(l-)Samāwī took place at Yathill. Apart from Sabaʾ, the only known pilgrimage is of Sayīn, at Shabwat.

The divinity provided oracles and issued commands — in an unknown manner (see DIVINATION; FORETELLING), and reveals itself via visions in the temple (see VISION; DREAMS AND SLEEP). He or she was asked to provide rain (a ceremony called *istisqāʾ* in Arabic) during particular ceremonies (see WATER; PRAYER FORMULAS). Several texts mention the practice of divination, although this is difficult to identify precisely. South Arabians definitely offered blood sacrifices, but there are few allusions to this, apart from some Minaean inscriptions (see BLOODSHED; BLOOD AND BLOOD CLOT). Ritual banquets accompanied certain celebrations. Fumigation with aromatic substances such as incense was common practice, to judge from the number of perfume burners found so far (see SMELL). Similarly, there would have been libations (consisting of what?) which were carried out on tables or altars (see TABLE; FOOD AND DRINK). Finally, several rites took place outside of the temple, such as ritual hunting (see HUNTING AND FISHING) or erecting memorials. (Regarding the cults of south Arabia, see Ryckmans, Rites du paganisme; Robin, Sheba. II, 1156-83.)

Representation of divinities

In south Arabia, human or animal representation was not taboo (see ICONOCLASM). Statues and historical tableaux adorned temples and palaces; images of the dead were placed in tombs (see BURIAL). It is worth noting, however, that in this large number of images, very few are definitely those of divinities. The most significative have been discovered very recently (Arbach, Audouin, Robin, La découverte). It is not certain whether the tentative identification of the young female figures on the temples of al-Jawf as the "Daughters of Īl" is indeed correct. The bust of a woman holding ears of corn in one hand and giving a blessing with the other, identified by Jacqueline Pirenne as the goddess Dhāt-Ḥimyam, or the young man whom she regards as Almaqah, represent believers, not divinities.

Representation of divinities in animal form is somewhat better documented. Large size coins from Ḥaḍramawt depict Sayīn, the kingdom's principal god, in the shape of an eagle attacking a serpent and there is an inscription which explicitly likens him to this powerful bird. Some coins of smaller size also depict Sayīn in the shape of a bull. Other divinities must also have appeared in the shape of a bull, such as Thawr-Baʿal^{um} ("Bull-Lord"), associated with and then identified as Almaqah or Samʿī, when he is called "Bull of Abḍuʿ^{um}."

Comparisons with the ritual practices of pre-Islamic Ḥijāz

The prohibitions entailed by the demand for ritual purity (q.v.; see also CONTAMINATION; CLEANLINESS AND ABLUTION) at Mecca and in south Arabia are often comparable. In the *ḥaram,* the area where the "idols" of Isāf and Nāʾila (see IDOLS AND IMAGES) stood was out of bounds for menstruating women (see MENSTRUATION), and this rule applied to all the "idols," if we are to believe Ibn al-Kalbī (d. ca. 205/820; *Kitāb al-Aṣnām,* 26). A south Arabian inscription from al-Jawf (Haram 34 = *CIH* 533) echoes an identical prohibition. Ibn al-Kalbī (*Kitāb al-Aṣnām,* 6) narrates that Isāf (son of Yaʿlā) and Nāʾila (the daughter of Zayd of Jurhum) were two young lovers who made love in the Kaʿba and had been turned to stone and joined in the Kaʿba (q.v.); this etiological story recalls the prohibition on sexual intercourse in the temple, set out in two other south Arabian inscriptions. According to some traditions, pilgrims coming to Mecca were given milk (q.v.) and honey (q.v.). In other temples, Ibn al-Kalbī (*Kitāb al-Aṣnām,* 40, 46) notes that flour and milk were used for the ritual. These are listed in the inscription Haram 13 = *CIH* 548/12-13: for some offence, the precise nature of which is unclear, the believer must hand over a bull to the temple of Arathat "and throughout the temple, flour, the cost of curds, honey, heart of palm and full expenses (imposed) on everyone." The practice of circumcision (q.v.) in the Arabian desert is mentioned by two external sources, Sozomen and the Talmud, and by Arab tradition. As regards Yemen, the information is contradictory. We have two representations of an uncircumcised male. First there is the bronze statue of a Ḥimyarī sovereign, depicted in Roman style, completely naked, and there is also a male member in relief on a small glass disc (Ghul, New Qatabāni inscriptions); these two artifacts are not decisive, however, since the first imitates a foreign model and the second may have been imported. Nonetheless, one external source remarks that the Ḥimyarīs practiced circumcision, at least in the middle of the fourth century C.E. (Philostorgius, *Kirchengeschichte,* iii, 4). The practice of covering the Kaʿba with hangings *(kiswa)* is not without parallel in Yemen. Three inscriptions from Qatabān commemorate the offering of *ks³wt* to lesser divinities. It is not known, however, whether these *ks³wt* were intended to cover the god or his dwelling place.

Development towards a supreme god?

In the third century C.E., the Sabaeans began to give the principal god, Almaqah, the title of "lord" (q.v.; *mrʾ*); in the same period, in the inscriptions dedicated to him in the temple of Awwām, they ceased to invoke the other divinities of the pantheon. This has been seen as the evolution towards henotheism, as it is surmised from this that a supreme divinity was beginning to emerge and take on the main functions of a chief god. In fact, the arguments put forward are not decisive. The Sabaeans gave the same title "lord" to other divinities. As for the fact that only Almaqah is mentioned by the invocations in the temple of Awwām, there are other possible explanations for this, such as clerical rivalry.

It nevertheless remains true that the greater divinities of every pantheon tended to assume the majority of functions from the start of the Christian era. An analysis of dedicatory inscriptions is illuminating. Their authors thank the divinity for the following reasons: political, military, diplomatic or hunting success (see VICTORY); help given in peril (sickness, misfortune or battle; see FIGHTING; WAR); protection (q.v.) bestowed upon their people and their goods; their well-being; their cure in case of illness; the birth of children, preferably male (see INFANTICIDE; PATRIARCHY); the abundance of agricultural produce and livestock (see AGRICULTURE AND VEGETATION; HIDES AND FLEECE); rainfall; the granting of visions or favorable oracles (see PORTENTS), etc. Petitions for the future are principally: humiliation of the enemy (see ENEMIES); good health, success and well-being; protection from various dangers, particularly sickness; good harvests; children, preferably male (see GRACE; BLESSING); the favor of the sovereign (see SOVEREIGNTY; KINGS AND RULERS), etc.

It does not, however, seem that any polytheistic divinity of south Arabia attained the status of supreme god. Until the rejection of polytheism, in the formulas which symbolize each kingdom, we note that two divinities are mentioned: Sayīn and Ḥawl for the Ḥaḍramawt; ʿAmm and Anbī for Qatabān; ʿAthtar and Almaqah for Sabaʾ; Wagl and Sumūyadaʿ for Ḥimyar, without exception. We may also add Balaw and Wadd^{um} for Awsān, even if the two gods are not mentioned in the same formula. It seems that one of the two divinities was the guardian of the throne (thus guaranteeing order and justice) and the other protected the tribe (watching over its growth and wealth). Anbī, ʿAthtar and Wadd^{um} are undoubtedly in the first category, ʿAmm, Almaqah and Balaw in the second.

South Arabian polytheism according to Islamic tradition

Islamic authors know little of the paganism of south Arabia. The most knowledgeable are Hishām b. al-Kalbī (ca. 120-204/737-819), who produced a work — *Kitāb al-Aṣnām* — entirely devoted to pre-Islamic paganism, and al-Ḥasan b. Aḥmad al-Hamdānī (d. 360/971), a Yemeni who spent his entire life on the Arabian peninsula. Al-Hamdānī's *Kitāb al-Iklīl* reflects his interest in the history and remains of pre-Islamic Yemen. Some information on south Arabia is also given by Ibn al-Kalbī in *Kitāb al-Aṣnām;* he mentions five Yemeni "idols": Yaghūth (venerated, according to him, by the Madhḥij tribe and the people of Jurash, that is by the peoples who were living at Najrān and in ʿAsīr in Ibn al-Kalbī's era), Yaʿūq (worshipped by Hamdān and their Yemeni allies at Khaywān, a small village 100 km north of Ṣanʿāʾ), Nasr (the eagle god, worshipped by the Ḥimyarites at Balkhaʿ, a location which has not been identified), Riʾām (in fact a temple, *bayt,* in the province of Ṣanʿāʾ) and Ammīʾanas, worshipped by the tribe of Khawlān-Ṣaʿda.

Yaghūth, Yaʿūq and Nasr are three of the five "idols" mentioned by Noah (q.v.) in Q 71:23 (see also IDOLATRY AND IDOLATERS). There is no mention of Yaghūth in the inscriptions of south Arabia; his name occurs only in the Safaitic inscriptions (of Syria and Jordan), where it is an anthroponym; elsewhere, we find *ʾmrʾyʿwt* as a man's name in three Nabataean inscriptions, consisting of *ʾmrʾ* (in Arabic *imruʾ*) and *yʿwt* (the Aramaic way of writing *yaghūth*). Finally, in pre-Islamic Arabic onomastica, such as that which Ibn al-Kalbī sets out in his *Jamharat al-nasab* (Caskel, *Ǧamharat*), the name ʿAbd Yaghūth reoccurs forty-two times (eighteen of these in the Madhḥij genealogies). It is possible that a god Yaghūth, apparently an individual who had been made a hero, existed and was commonly known among the Nabataeans and Madhḥij. The name Yaʿūq does not occur in Arabian epigraphy, except as the name of a synagogue *(mkrb)* built in January 465 C.E. (*ḏ-dʾw*^{n} 574 of the Ḥimyarite era), at Ḍulaʿ (twelve kilometers north-west of Ṣanʿāʾ). Nasr was indeed a divinity worshipped by the southern Arabs, especially in Ḥaḍramawt and at Sabaʾ (Müller, Adler und Geier), but the link with the mysterious Balkhaʿ made by Ibn al-Kalbī seems without foundation. Regarding Riʾām, Ibn al-Kalbī is a little better informed. He is aware that it is a temple in the province of Ṣanʿāʾ but he does not know the name of the god to whom this building is dedicated. The ancient temple was in fact called Turʿat and the god worshipped there was Taʾlab Riyām^{um}; his epithet eventually came to indicate both the building and the mountain upon which it was located (modern day Jabal Riyām, 50 km north of Ṣanʿāʾ).

Finally, there is no epigraphic evidence of ʿAmmīʾanas, but the existence of such a divinity cannot be ruled out because we know of a Khawlānite leader of this name in the third century C.E. ʿAmmīʾanas could have been an ancestor or a deified hero. Ibn al-Kalbī (or his source) thus provides more or less accurate information regarding four out of five divinities. That being said, two caveats should be borne in mind. First, Ibn al-Kalbī ignores all the major divinities of the ancient kingdoms, notably Almaqah (Sabaʾ), ʿAmm (Qatabān), Sayīn (Ḥaḍramawt), ʿAthtar dhū-Qabḍ^{um} (Maʿīn) and Balaw (Awsān); his knowledge is thus extremely incomplete. Secondly, he is more concerned with providing details of the idols mentioned in the Qurʾān or tradition (see ḤADĪTH AND THE QURʾĀN) rather than with researching first-hand information.

The second original author on south Arabian paganism was the Yemeni al-Ḥasan al-Hamdānī. In addition to a fairly accurate description of the temple of Riyām, he mentions the names of three south Arabian divinities, reinterpreted as anthroponyms: Sinān dhū-Ilīm, a king of Ḥaḍramawt in ancient times (Sayīn dhū-Ilīm in the Ḥaḍramawt inscriptions); Taʾlab Riyām b. Shahrān, who is supposed to have married Turʿa (a misunderstanding of the divine title "Taʾlab Riyām^{um} lord of Turʿat," in which the word *baʿal,* "lord," has been taken to mean "spouse"); Almaqah (the Sabaean god Almaqah) identified with Bilqīs (q.v.; the traditional name of the Queen of Sheba). Finally, in a short passage of *Kitāb al-Jawharatayn,* he observes: "The sun (q.v.), the moon (q.v.) and the stars (see PLANETS AND STARS) were depicted on the silver and gold coinage of the Ḥimyarites, because they worship them. They call them ʿAthtar, Hubas (the moon) and Alāmiqa (the stars), in the singular Almaq or Yalmaq. This is why Bilqīs is called 'Yalmaqa' and one speaks of Zuhra [i.e. Venus]." Al-Hamdānī not only knew that Almaqah was a divinity (and not a queen), he also knew the gods ʿAthtar and Hubas (Sabaean Hawbas), whose name appears in no other Islamic source (Robin, Sheba. II, 1184-9). Yemeni authors are thus a little better informed concerning the paganism of south Arabia than is the rest of Islamic tradition. They know the names of several important divinities, such as the principal gods of Sabaʾ, Ḥaḍramawt and Samʿī, whereas Ibn al-Kalbī only refers to minor divinities. Their knowledge is nonetheless limited to a few divine names and some uncertain identifications. Rather than vague recollections from memory, we are talking of names they have deciphered from inscriptions and interpreted more or less correctly. They were indeed able to read the south Arabian script, although they often confused letters of a similar shape and interpreted the text very freely. The feeble nature of such knowledge in traditional sources is undoubtedly explained by the fact that polytheism had been rejected by Ḥimyar almost 250 years before the appearance of Islam and that it survived only underground, except perhaps in certain outlying tribes.

Christian Julien Robin

Bibliography and abbreviations

Primary: al-Hamdānī, Abū Muḥammad al-Ḥasan b. Aḥmad, *Kitāb al-Jawharatayn al-ʿatīqatayn al-māʾiʿatayn aṣ-ṣafrāʾ wa-l-bayḍāʾ, Die beiden Edelmetalle Gold und Silber,* ed. and Ger. trans. Ch. Toll, Uppsala 1968; Ibn al-Kalbī, Abū l-Mundhir Hishām b. Muḥammad al-Kalbī, *Kitāb al-Aṣnām, Les idoles de Hicham ibn al-Kalbi,* ed. and Fr. trans. W. Atallah, Paris 1969; Philostorgius, *Kirchengeschichte,* ed. J. Bidez, rvw. of 2nd ed. by F. Winkelmann, coll. *Die Griechischen Christlichen Schriftsteller der ersten drei Jahrhunderte,* Berlin 1972.

Secondary: M. Arbach, R. Audouin, Ch.J. Robin, La découverte du temple d'Aranyadaʿ à Nashshān et la chronologie des Labuʾides, in *Arabia* 2 (2004), 23-41 (pl. 20-41 and 70: 205-16 and 234); J. Briend, Sheba. I. Dans la Bible, in *Supplément au Dictionnaire de la Bible, Fascicule* 70, *Sexualité — Sichem,* Paris 1996, col. 1043-6; F. Bron, Divinités communes à la Syrie-Palestine et à l'Arabie du Sud préislamique, in *Aula orientalis* 17-18 (1999-2000), 437-40; id., *Maʿīn,* Paris and Rome 1998; id., Notes sur le culte d'Athirat en Arabie du Sud préislamique, in Ch.-B. Amphoux, A. Frey and U. Schattner-Rieser (eds.), *...Études sémitiques et samaritaines offertes à Jean Margain,* Lausanne 1998, 75-9; W. Caskel, *Ǧamharat an-nasab. Das genealogische Werk des Hishām Muḥammad al-Kalbī,* 2 vols., Leiden 1966; M.A. Ghul, New Qatabāni inscriptions, in *BSOAS* 22 (1959), 1-22, 419-38; M. Höfner, Die Stammesgruppen Nord- und Zentralarabiens im vorislamischer Zeit, in H.W. Haussig (ed.), *Götter und Mythen im Vorderen Orient,* Stuttgart 1965, 407-81; id., Die vorislamischen Religionen Arabiens, in H. Gese, M. Höfner and K. Rudolph, *Die Religionen Altsyriens, Altarabiens und der Mandäer,* Stuttgart 1970, 233-402; M. Jung, The religious monuments of ancient southern Arabia. A preliminary typological classification, in *Annali dell'Istituto Orientale di Napoli* 48 (1988), 177-218 and pl. I-XII; M. Lecker, Idol worship in pre-Islamic Medina (Yathrib), in *Muséon* 106 (1993), 331-46; repr. in id., *Jews and Arabs in pre- and early Islamic Arabia,* Aldershot 1998, I, and in F.E. Peters (ed.), *The Arabs and Arabia on the eve of Islam,* Aldershot 1999, 129-44; W.W. Müller, Adler und Geier als altarabische Gottheiten, in I. Kottsieper et al. (eds.), *"Wer ist wie du, Herr, unter den Göttern?". Studien zur Theologie und Religionsgeschichte Israels für Otto Kaiser zum 70.*

Geburtstag, Göttingen 1994, 91-107; Ch.J. Robin, Les "Filles de Dieu" de Saba᾿ à la Mecque. Réflexions sur l'agencement des panthéons dans l'Arabie ancienne, in *Semitica* 50 (2001), 113-92; id., Sheba. II. Dans les inscriptions d'Arabie du Sud, in *Supplément au Dictionnaire de la Bible, Fascicule* 70, *Sexualité — Sichem,* Paris 1996, col. 1047-1254; id. and U. Brunner, *Map of ancient Yemen — Carte du Yémen antique, 1:1 000 000,* München 1997 (archaeological map, 70 x 100 cm, in three colors, with index); G. Ryckmans, Les religions arabes préislamiques, in M. Gorce and R. Mortier (eds.), *Histoire générale des religions,* iv, Paris 1947, 307-32, 526-34; id., *Les religions arabes préislamiques,* Louvain 1951²; J. Ryckmans, Rites du paganisme de l'Arabie méridionale avant l'islam, in *Bulletin de la Classe des Lettres et des Sciences Morales et Politiques (6e série)* 4/1-6 (1993), 125-42.
Sigla: *CIH: Corpus inscriptionum semiticarum.* Pars quarta. *Inscriptiones ḥimyariticas et sabaeas continens,* Paris 1889-; Haram 13 (= CIH 548) and 34 (= CIH 533): see *Inventaire des inscriptions sud arabiques,* 1, Paris and Rome 1992.

South Asian Literatures and the Qur᾿ān

With a Muslim population of over 300 million, south Asia (India, Pakistan, Bangladesh) is home to the largest concentration of Muslims in the world. Muslims in the region have employed a wide variety of languages to compose their literatures. Among these languages, Arabic and Persian have historically played a cosmopolitan role, for they have enabled south Asian elites to participate and share in literary cultures that extend well beyond the subcontinent to central Asia and the Middle East. In addition to these transnational languages, Muslims have employed a host of other languages that are indigenous to south Asia. Ranging from Baluchi and Bengali to Tamil and Urdu, these vernaculars, in contrast to Arabic and Persian, have been local, or regional, in their geographic significance. They encompass a broad spectrum of literary traditions that include folk songs sung by village women as well as sophisticated poems composed by erudite scholars. This article focuses on the interaction of the Qur᾿ān with literary cultures in the vernacular traditions. The corpus of these literatures is so vast and diverse that in this brief article we can only touch upon a few key ideas, citing examples from a limited range of linguistic traditions (see also LITERATURE AND THE QUR᾿ĀN).

It is hardly surprising that the Qur᾿ān, the sacred scripture of Islam, should have influenced Muslim poets and writers in south Asia. The nature of the Qur᾿ān's impact on the vernacular traditions varies, however. At its most obvious, it consists of the insertion of qur᾿ānic quotations into literary works, particularly poetry. Called *iqtibās,* this popular literary device assumes that every reasonably educated Muslim would know the Arabic Qur᾿ān well enough to understand a scriptural allusion, no matter how obscure it may be (see TEACHING AND PREACHING THE QUR᾿ĀN; RECITATION OF THE QUR᾿ĀN). The incorporation of a qur᾿ānic verse into a vernacular text served several purposes. First, it sanctified the text for both the author and the audience, thus making it more sublime. Second, the skill with which the Arabic sacred text (see BOOK; ARABIC LANGUAGE) was woven into the fabric of the vernacular demonstrated the author's literary prowess. Third, the verse could also serve as a proof text validating the author's religious beliefs and convictions. For instance, Q 7:172, *a-lastu bi-rabbikum? qālū balā shahidnā,* " 'Am I not your lord (q.v.)?' They said 'Yes we witness it'" (see WITNESSING AND TESTIFYING), is a particularly popular quote among mystically inclined Muslims, for it supports a concept that is pivotal to Ṣūfism: the existence of a primordial covenant (q.v.) of love (q.v.) between God and creation (q.v.; Schimmel, *Two colored brocade,* 57-8; see also ṢŪFISM

AND THE QUR'ĀN). To illustrate the insertion of this qur'ānic verse into a vernacular text, we may cite a verse in Sindhi by the poet Shāh ʿAbdu l-Laṭīf (d. 1752 C.E.) in which Maruī, a Sindhi folk heroine whom the poet uses to represent the human soul (q.v.), proclaims:

When I heard "Am I not your lord?"
Right there and then I said "Yes" with all my heart
At that time I made a promise [of loyalty] to my love
(Shāh ʿAbdu l-Laṭīf, *Risālo,* Sur Maruī, i, 1, 255).

Shīʿī writers, on the other hand, are more likely to quote those qur'ānic verses that best champion a Shīʿī perspective (see SHĪʿISM AND THE QUR'ĀN). Such is the case, for example, with Mīr Anīs (d. 1874 C.E.), a prominent Shīʿī poet, who embedded within his Urdu elegies those qur'ānic verses that could be interpreted as supporting the Shīʿī notion of the imāmate (for instance, Q 36:12 and its reference to the *imām mubīn,* "manifest imām"; Haider, *Rumūz,* 80-2; see IMĀM). In this manner, many a qur'ānic verse has been incorporated into south Asian vernacular literature, the choice of verse being determined by the author's religious worldview.

Frequently, a quotation from the Qur'ān may consist of only one or two words (see SLOGANS FROM THE QUR'ĀN); yet allusions to these isolated words, no matter how obscure they may seem, are sufficient to trigger a range of associations in the minds of those familiar with the scripture. Hence, in many vernacular poems in praise of the Prophet of Islam, Muḥammad may be referred to not by his name (see NAMES OF THE PROPHET) but by names or epithets that some Muslims claim to have discovered in the Qur'ān: *ṭā' hā* and *yā' sīn,* the unconnected letters that appear at the beginning of sūras 20 and 36 or *muzzammil* and *muddaththir,* divine addresses to the Prophet found in the introduction to Q 73: *yā ayyuhā l-muzzammil,* "O you enwrapped one," and Q 74: *yā ayyuhā l-muddaththir,* "O you covered one" (see REVELATION AND INSPIRATION; SOOTHSAYER).

Even more frequent than allusions to verses and words are references to figures mentioned in the Qur'ān, particularly prophets (see PROPHETS AND PROPHETHOOD), and events associated with them (see NARRATIVES). Abraham (q.v.), the ideal monotheist (see ḤANĪF) who destroyed the idols (see IDOLS AND IMAGES) made by his father Āzar (q.v.; cf. Q 6:74); Moses (q.v.) and the burning bush (Q 20:10f.); Jesus (q.v.) who could heal the sick and revive the dead, and give life to inanimate objects with his breath (Q 5:110; see DEATH AND THE DEAD; ILLNESS AND HEALTH; MIRACLES; MARVELS) are but a few examples from the rich prophetic lore of the Qur'ān to which many south Asian poets may refer (Schimmel, *Two colored brocade,* 62-79). In many instances, however, these figures are assigned interpretations and meanings that are not obvious in the original qur'ānic text. For instance, Q 21:69 mentions that when the tyrant Nimrod (q.v.) threw Abraham into a fire (q.v.), God saved him by commanding the fire to be cool and peaceful (see HOT AND COLD; PAIRS AND PAIRING). In the hands of many poets, Abraham becomes the symbol of a daring love that has the strength to accomplish the most miraculous feats. Hence, the seventh/thirteenth century poet Lāl Shāhbāz Qalandar alludes to this qur'ānic verse when he joyously sings: "[Because of] my friend's love, I dance every moment in the midst of fire!" (as quoted in Schimmel, *Two colored brocade,* 63).

Similarly, God's response to Moses "you shall not see me" (Q 7:143; see SEEING AND HEARING) becomes in vernacular poems the standard answer that a veiled or otherwise inaccessible beloved gives to a lover who yearns to see his/her face. The most dramatic reinterpretation of a qurʾānic figure, however, occurs in the case of ʿAzāzīl/Iblīs (Satan; see DEVIL), the angel who refused to bow to Adam (see ADAM AND EVE; BOWING AND PROSTRATION) and hence was cursed by God for disobedience (q.v.; Q 7:11 f.; see also INSOLENCE AND OBSTINACY; ARROGANCE). While it is true that in some south Asian literatures Iblīs is traditionally perceived as a character associated with rebellion (q.v.) and evil (see GOOD AND EVIL), he is viewed, in at least one powerful current of Muslim mystical poetry in the vernacular, as a positive figure — the paradigmatic lover who suffers for his unswerving loyalty to the one beloved (Schimmel, *Two colored brocade*, 60-1). Shāh ʿAbdu l-Laṭīf's memorable line in Sindhi bears eloquent testimony to this tendency:

ʿAzāzīl is the lover, all others are frauds
The cursed one was honored by way of love (Shāh ʿAbdu l-Laṭīf, *Risalo*, Sur Yaman Kalyān, v, 18, 32).

Although all major prophets named in the Qurʾān appear in south Asian literatures, perhaps the true favorite is Joseph (q.v.; Yūsuf), whose story is told in the twelfth sūra of the Qurʾān. The Joseph story, which the Qurʾān calls "the most beautiful of stories," has inspired epic narratives in several south Asian languages such as Bengali, Urdu, Panjabi and Sindhi. In some instances, the epic has even been illustrated with miniature paintings. Typically, these epics interpret the romance between Joseph and Potiphar's wife within a Ṣūfī framework. Potiphar's wife, identified in popular tradition as Zulaykha, represents the woman-soul at the lowest level of spiritual development — the *nafs ammara*, or "the soul inciting to evil" (*al-nafsa la-ammāratun bi-l-sūʾa*, Q 12:53), who must first be transformed into the *nafs lawwāma*, or "the blaming soul" (Q 75:2) and finally into "the soul at peace" (*al-nafs al-muṭmaʾinna*, Q 89:27) before she can be accepted by the divine beloved.

It is, perhaps, inevitable that the "most beautiful story" of the Qurʾān, when recast in the vernacular tradition, would be acculturated to the local environment, that is, the composers of the vernacular epic would set it within the geographical, social and cultural milieu of their region. A typical example would be the Bengali poet, Shāh Muḥammad Saghir (late thirteenth/early fourteenth century C.E.), who composed a version of the Yūsuf-Zulaykha epic set entirely in Bengal. In his version, he recreates the landscape of Egypt with the fauna and flora typical of Bengal, introduces the river Nile as the Ganges, gives the merchant who bought Joseph a typical Bengali name, and has Zulaykha send her female companions to Vrindavan, famed for being the location of the dalliance between Krishna and the *gopis*, "cow maids" (Roy, *The Islamic tradition*, 104-8).

The indigenization of the qurʾānic story of Joseph in the Bengali epic should also be seen within the larger context of Muslim Bengali literary culture and the development of a distinctive Bengali Muslim identity in medieval India that is reflected in the genre of the *puthi* literature. In this literature, the qurʾānic concept of *nabī/rasūl*, or "prophet/messenger (q.v.)," is identified with the local Hindu concept of *avatāra*, "divine descent or incarnation." This identification allowed authors to incorporate various Indian deities, particularly Krishna, into a long line of qurʾānic prophets that ends with Muḥammad (Roy, *The Islamic tradition*, 95-7). Just as Islam in the Middle Eastern context was seen as a culmination of Judeo-Christian monotheism (see JEWS AND JUDAISM; CHRISTIANS AND CHRISTIANITY), in medieval Bengal and several other Indian regions, the religion came to be seen as the continuation and culmination of the local Hindu tradition. Seen within this framework, the Qurʾān became the *Veda* (scripture) of the *Kali Yug,* the last chronological age of Hindu mythology.

Although such localized or acculturated understandings of the prophetology of the Qurʾān and the Qurʾān itself have frequently been characterized as syncretistic, mixed or heterodox, they are, perhaps, better understood as attempts to "translate" universal Islamic teachings within "local" contexts. The validity in approaching vernacular Muslim poetry through the lens of "translation theory," as proposed by Tony Stewart (In search of equivalence), is confirmed by the fact that communities who recite and sing vernacular religious poems frequently regard them as texts which encapsulate the teachings of the Arabic Qurʾān. Sindhi-speaking Muslims in southern Pakistan revere Shāh ʿAbdu l-Laṭīf's poetic masterpiece in the Sindhi language, the *Risālo,* as a book that contains within it the essence of the spiritual teachings of the Qurʾān. Through his exegetical remarks on dramatic moments and events in popular Sindhi folk romances, Shāh ʿAbdu l-Laṭīf is perceived to be conveying qurʾānic ideas on the spiritual significance of the human situation. In the Punjab, poems attributed to Punjabi Ṣūfī poets, such as Sulṭān Bahū (d. 1691 C.E.), Bullhe Shāh (d. 1754 C.E.) and Vāris Shāh (d. 1766 C.E.), are also commonly regarded as spiritual commentaries on qurʾānic verses. Similarly, the *ginān*s of the Khoja Ismāʿīlī communities of western India and Pakistan, composed in various vernacular languages such as Gujarati, Hindi, Punjabi and Sindhi and embodying the teaching of Ismāʿīlī preacher-saints (see SAINT), have also been regarded as texts embodying the inner signification of the Qurʾān (Asani, *Ecstasy and enlightenment,* 29-31).

The conception of some genres of vernacular poetry (such as the Sindhi *Risālo,* Punjabi Ṣūfī poems or the Ismāʿīlī *ginān*s) as secondary texts that provide non-Arabic speaking Muslims access to the inner *(bāṭin)* meaning of the Qurʾān (see POLYSEMY) is not without parallels. In Persian-speaking parts of the Muslim world, Mawlānā Jalāl al-Dīn Rūmī's *Masnawī,* popularly called the "Qurʾān in Persian," is regarded as a vast esoteric commentary on the Qurʾān, many of its verses being interpreted as translations of qurʾānic verses into Persian poetry (see PERSIAN LITERATURE AND THE QURʾĀN). Significantly, the mediating role that these vernacular texts play between the faithful and the Qurʾān provides evidence of a process that Paul Nwyia has so aptly called the "Qurʾānization of memory" (*Ibn ʿAṭāʾ Allāh,* 46). Referring specifically to early Ṣūfīs, he argues that, because they were constantly preoccupied with the Qurʾān as the word of God (q.v.), their memories were eventually "qurʾānized." Consequently, they saw everything in the light of the Qurʾān, interpreting their own experiences and contexts within the larger framework of the revelation (see REVELATION AND INSPIRATION). We may extend Nwyia's perceptive comments to include Muslim poets writing in the south Asian vernaculars, many of whom were influenced, directly or indirectly, by Ṣūfī ideas. Their worldviews were so thoroughly colored by qurʾānic ideas that even though they did not always cite specific qurʾānic verses in their compositions, many of their lines seem either to echo a qurʾānic concept or to be a literal translation of the qurʾānic text into the vernacular (see LANGUAGE AND STYLE OF THE QURʾĀN). This is why the student of south

Asian Muslim literatures, whether reading the highly philosophical Urdu poetry of Sir Muḥammad Iqbāl (d. 1938 C.E.) or listening to Punjabi songs attributed to the folk poet Bullhe Shāh, is often surprised to discover that a seemingly simple line in the vernacular is in fact inspired by a qurʾānic verse.

Ali S. Asani

Bibliography
Primary: Shāh ʿAbdu l-Laṭīf, *Shāh jo risālo,* ed. K. Advani, Bombay 1966.
Secondary: A.S. Asani, *Ecstasy and enlightenment. The Ismaili devotional literatures of south Asia,* London 2002; S.R. Haider, *Rumūz-i kalām-i anīs,* Allahabad 1997; P. Nwyia, *Ibn ʿAṭāʾ Allāh et la naissance de la confrèrie šādilite,* Beirut 1970; A. Roy, *The Islamic syncretistic tradition in Bengal,* Princeton 1983; A. Schimmel, *A two colored brocade. The imagery of Persian poetry,* London 1992; id., *As through a veil. Mystical poetry in Islam,* New York 1982; T. Stewart, In search of equivalence. Conceiving the Muslim-Hindu encounter through translation theory, in *History of religions* 40/3 (2001), 260-87.

Southeast Asian Qurʾānic Literature

This entry is meant to provide an overview of literature of the Qurʾān in southeast Asia, including both texts produced locally and those imported from elsewhere in the Muslim world that have been important to the region's religious and intellectual history.

Commentary in Arabic

As in many parts of the Muslim world, the most popular Arabic work of commentary *(tafsīr)* in southeast Asia from the seventeenth through the nineteenth centuries was the *Tafsīr al-Jalālayn*. In addition to being read and studied in its original Arabic, this text formed the primary basis of the most popular early modern work in Malay, the *Tarjumān al-mustafīd* of ʿAbd al-Raʾūf Singkeli. For three centuries, this work remained the standard work of *tafsīr* in the Malay-language curricula of the region's *pesantren* Islamic educational milieu. Other early Malay works of *tafsīr* drew on a range of Arabic texts, including those of al-Bayḍāwī (d. prob. 716/1316-17). Despite their openness to works of *tafsīr* from elsewhere in the Muslim world, however, southeast Asian scholars were not mere passive recipients of the Arabic tradition of *tafsīr.* For some attained the erudition and proficiency to produce Arabic works of their own. The most notable of this type is Muhammad al-Nawawī Jāwī (Banten's; 1813-97) *Marāh Labīd* (which draws in large measure on Fakhr al-Dīn al-Rāzī's [d. 606/1210] *Tafsīr al-Kabīr*; cf. Johns, Qurʾānic exegesis), which has been printed and distributed in the Middle East as well as in southeast Asia.

Translations into southeast Asian languages

The earliest textual evidence we have of qurʾānic exegetical activity in Muslim southeast Asia comes to us in a manuscript containing the Arabic text of Q 18, Sūrat al-Kahf ("The Cave"), written in red ink along with a Malay translation and running commentary, primarily following al-Baghawī (d. ca. 516/1122) and al-Khāzin (d. 740/1340), in black (Riddell, *Islam and the Malay-Indonesian world,* 139-67). The translation of such earlier commentaries appears to have been largely eclipsed by ʿAbd al-Raʾūf's *Tarjumān al-mustafīd* in the seventeenth century. While this work dominated the field of qurʾānic exegesis in southeast Asia for generations, in the early twentieth century an increasing amount of attention was given to other, more recent works of *tafsīr* in Arabic as well. This expansion of the curriculum of qurʾānic studies in the region was an important aspect of broader developments of Islamic reformism in modern southeast Asia. Among the works translated in these contexts were those of modern Muslim exegetes of various orientations, both from the Middle East and south Asia.

Indonesian translations of selections from the *Tafsīr al-Manār* (a work initiated by the Egyptian reformer Muḥammad ʿAbduh and continued after his death in 1905 by Rashīd Riḍā) by various translators appeared, starting in 1923. The Indonesian translation of Maulana Muḥammad ʿAlī's *The holy Qurʾān* and accompanying commentary by Tjokroaminoto began to appear in 1928 but the Muhammadiyyah and other Indonesian Muslim groups protested the project for its Aḥmadiyya (q.v.) orientation (see also TRANSLATIONS OF THE QURʾĀN). The pace of such translation activity increased dramatically as the century progressed, with economic development under the New Order supporting a vibrant publishing industry producing Indonesian translations of Arabic-language works of *tafsīr* by Maḥmūd Shaltūt, Muṣṭafā al-Marāghī and Sayyid Quṭb as well as thousands of other Muslim religious texts.

Commentaries in southeast Asian languages

Manuscript collections and library holdings in Indonesia and Europe contain a remarkable range of works on the Qurʾān written in a number of different southeast Asian languages. One striking example may be found in an early nineteenth-century Makassarese text that offers a paraphrase of the Qurʾān in that language. Another method of qurʾānic "translation" and interpretation can be found in Javanese literature, where a tradition developed of inserting an interlinear Javanese translation (written in *pegon,* or modified Arabic script) into the text of the Qurʾān itself. This tradition of *pegon*-script qurʾānic literature in Javanese continued into the twentieth century with works like the *Tafsīr al-Ibrīz* of Bisri Mustofa. An analogous work in the Arabic script, or *jawi,* an adaptation of the Arabic script used for writing Malay, can be found in Syekh Haji Abdul Karim Amrullah's *al-Burhān,* a commentary on the last thirtieth part of the Qurʾān *(juzʾ ʿam).*

Such works in *jawi* and *pegon* script were accessible only to *pesantren* students, and as the twentieth century progressed they were thus largely overlooked by the burgeoning ranks of new readers literate in the Roman, rather than Arabic script. Publishers catering to these growing markets produced an explosion of works in various fields of the Islamic religious sciences composed in modern Bahasa Indonesia. One of the first major original works of *tafsīr* to appear in this format was A. Hassan's *Tafsir al-Furqān,* which first appeared serially starting in 1928. This work by one of the leading figures of the radical reformist organization PERSIS is actually more of a "translation" than a *tafsīr* proper, as what little non-literal interpretation there is comes only in the form of short footnotes. Nonetheless, it also contains a fairly lengthy preface in which the author outlines his method of interpretation, laying out a set of radical and narrowly scriptural exegetical principles differing significantly from most works produced in southeast Asia before that time. When Hassan's work appeared, a parallel project was already in preparation by another Indonesian reformist, Mahmoed Joenoes. This work, begun in 1922, finally appeared in its first complete published edition in 1938 and contained a thirty-page indexed outline of "the summarized essence of the Qurʾān" for modern readers, in addition to an Indonesian translation of the text and explanatory footnotes.

From the 1950s on, one finds a steady increase in the number of new *tafsīr* works written in the modern Indonesian language with the Latin script. Among these the *Tafsir al-Azhar* of Hamka (Haji Abdul Malik Karim Amrullah) is one of the most enterprising endeavors of modern qurʾānic exegesis, not just in southeast Asia, but in the Muslim world as a whole. Although often described as a "Modernist," Hamka's thinking reflects a mixture of ideas and orientations to the tradition ranging from Ṣūfism to Salafism. Hamka's work of *tafsīr* runs to ten volumes totaling over 8,000 pages in its hardcover edition. The work began as a series of early morning lectures at the al-Azhar mosque in Kebayoran, Jakarta. The commentary expounded in these oral settings was first published serially in the magazine *Gema Islam*. Shortly after beginning the project, however, Hamka was imprisoned by the increasingly left-leaning government of Soekarno and the work was thus completed during his two years of incarceration. Hamka's copious commentary draws on a number of authorities with a heavy emphasis on modern Egyptian exegetes. The commentary is not, however, simply a rehashing of Egyptian modernism under the rubric of qur'ānic exegesis but rather incorporates select elements of Egyptian modernism and other aspects of Muslim tradition with considerable original material, including even a number of rather revealing personal anecdotes. This work continues to enjoy popularity not only in Indonesia but in other parts of southeast Asia as well, including Malaysia and Singapore, where the "deluxe edition" was published by Pustaka Nasional from 1982 to 1993.

With the establishment of Soeharto's New Order regime in 1965, the Indonesian government itself began to sponsor ambitious projects in the area of *tafsīr*. In 1967, the Ministry of Religious Affairs initiated a special foundation that was given the assignment of producing works of Qur'ān translation and commentary. This resulted in the publication of two major works: *Al Quraan dan terjemahannya*, "The Qur'ān and its translation," and *Al Quraan dan tafsirnya*, "The Qur'ān and its commentary." Both works may be seen as officially-sponsored attempts to provide Indonesian Muslims with "standard" works of reference and thus ensure a greater uniformity in national discourses on the sacred text. Nevertheless, over the course of the twentieth century the number of privately conceived and published works of translation and exegesis has continued to proliferate, thus offering a considerable range of interpretations of the text and its exegetical traditions. These range from the multi-volume works covering the entire qur'ānic text like that of Ash Shiddieqy's *Tafsir al-Quränul madjied "an-nur"* to a host of shorter works that deal only with certain sūras (especially Q 1, Sūrat al-Fātiḥa, "The Opening"; see FĀTIḤA) or selections from qur'ānic narrative (see NARRATIVES). Popular works of both of these latter genres are those by Bey Arifin: *Samudera al-Fatihah* and *Rangkaian tjerita dalam al-Quran*, respectively. Later editions of the latter relate embellished tales of Islamic prophets and the early Muslim community complete with illustrations (see PROPHETS AND PROPHETHOOD). There are likewise a number of handbooks on *tajwīd*, qur'ānic recitation, an art form in which Indonesian and Malay reciters have received international acclaim.

Just a few years after the completion of these works another Indonesian translation of the Qur'ān was published by the well-known literary critic H.B. Jassin. It was entitled *Bacaan mulia*, "the glorious reading," an Indonesian rendering of *al-Qur'ān al-karīm*, and met with strong criticism from conservative *'ulamā'* who objected to the fact that it claimed to be a "poetic" translation (see POETRY AND POETS; LANGUAGE AND STYLE OF THE QUR'ĀN). Critical responses appeared in a number of Indonesian magazines and newspapers and some even found their way into a number of polemic monographs. Jassin, however, seemed undeterred by all of this; some fifteen years later he published another edition of the Qur'ān, this one in Arabic rather than in Indonesian translation. This work, entitled *al-Qurʾān berwajah puisi,* did not alter the contents of the Qurʾān in any substantive way but rather experimented with new typographical arrangements of the Arabic text that highlighted its rhythmic and assonant qualities — giving it, in a sense, a "poetic" face (see FORM AND STRUCTURE OF THE QURʾĀN). Following the publication of this text, many of Jassin's earlier critics resurfaced to protest what they saw as his "deviation" from the established practice of printing the qurʾānic text (see PRINTING OF THE QURʾĀN), resulting in a new wave of public polemics and hampering the distribution of Jassin's text.

At about the same time that these developments were taking place in Indonesia, we see an unprecedented upsurge in the production of works of Qurʾān "translation" and exegesis in a wide range of southeast Asian languages beyond Malay/Indonesian. Prominent among them were a number of commentaries in Sundanese, including those of Qamaruddin Shaleh and Muhammad Ramli. Yet such activity was not even restricted to southeast Asian languages with predominantly Muslim speakers. For, at this time we find the first full Thai translation of the Qurʾān, completed by Direk Kulsiriswasd, a.k.a. Ibrahim Qureyshi. The translation of the Qurʾān into Vietnamese is an even more recent phenomenon, the first example of which the present writer is aware having been published not in southeast Asia but in southern California in 1997. Two of the first significant works on the Qurʾān in Tagalog date back to the early 1980s. The first, *Ang banal na Kuran,* is a fairly straightforward translation following the order of the standard arrangement of the text in Arabic. The second is a topically arranged treatment of legal categories and related concepts as illustrated by qurʾānic verses. In each section the verse is given first in English (text from Yūsuf ʿAlī's translation) and then followed by a Tagalog translation without further commentary.

This approach to topical *(mawḍūʿī) tafsīr* was also gaining popularity in Indonesia during the 1980s. Works of this kind appealed more to a modern lay Muslim readership than did works following the more traditional, verse-by-verse *(tartīb al-āyāt)* arrangement. One of the most ambitious works of this type is Dawam Rahardjo's 700-plus page *Ensiklopedi al-Qurʾān,* which is comprised of chapters dealing with topics like "justice," "mercy," "religion," "knowledge," etc. In addition to this, the work also contains important chapters on his interpretive methodology and his understanding of the "social vision" of the Qurʾān (see ETHICS AND THE QURʾĀN; SOCIAL SCIENCES AND THE QURʾĀN; COMMUNITY AND SOCIETY IN THE QURʾĀN). Other significant Indonesian works of this type include the work of Jalaluddin Rakhmat, a popular preacher from Bandung with a degree in communications from the University of Iowa.

With such work we enter a new period in the history of interpretive literature on the Qurʾān in Indonesia, one in which traditional methodologies have largely given way to works addressing the needs of a wider readership whose education has not been in the traditional Islamic sciences (see TOOLS FOR THE STUDY OF THE QURʾĀN; TRADITIONAL DISCIPLINES OF QURʾĀNIC STUDY). Over the past decade, these developments have been paralleled by a marked increase in Indonesian translations of works of modern qurʾānic scholarship that have been produced not in Arabic but in Western languages by Muslim scholars working in European and North American university contexts. Some of the most popular works of this type have been translations of Fazlur Rahman's *Major themes of the Qurʾān* and Muhammad Arkoun's *Lectures du Coran* (see CONTEMPORARY CRITICAL PRACTICES AND THE QUR'ĀN).

R. Michael Feener

Bibliography
ʿAbd al-Rāʾūf Singkeli, *al-Qurʾān al-karīm wa-bi-hāmīshih. Tarjumān al-mustafīd,* 2 vols., Cairo 1951 (in Jawi); *Al Quraan dan tafsirnya,* 11 vols., Jakarta 1975 (in Bahasa Indonesia); *Al Quraan dan terjemahannya,* Jakarta 1967 (in Bahasa Indonesia); M.M. Ali, *Qoer'an soetji, disertai salinan dan keterangan dalam bahasa melajoe,* Weltevreden 1928 (in Bahasa Indonesia); H.A.K. Amrullah, *Al-Burhān,* Sungai Batang/Manindjau 1935 (in Jawi); B. Arifin, *Rangkaian tjerita dalam al-Qurʾān,* Bandung 1963 (in Bahasa Indonesia); id., *Samudera al-Fatihah,* Bandung 1968 (in Bahasa Indonesia); A.R.H. Bruce, *Ang banal na Kuran,* Manila 1982 (in Tagalog); R. M. Feener, Notes toward a history of qurʾānic exegesis in southeast Asia, in *Studia Islamika* 3 (1998), 47-76; Hamka, *Tafsir al-Azhari,* Jakarta 1967-73 (in Bahasa Indonesia); A. Hassan, *Tafsir al-Furqän,* Bangil 1986 (in Bahasa Indonesia); H.B. Jassin, *Al-Quranu ʾl-karim. Bacaan mulia,* Jakarta 1977 (in Bahasa Indonesia); id., *Kontroversi al-Qurʾān berwajah puisi,* Jakarta 1995 (in Bahasa Indonesia); M. Joenoes, *Tafsīr Qurän Karim,* Jakarta 1954 (in Bahasa Indonesia); A.H. Johns, Qurʾānic exegesis in the Malay-Indonesian world. An introductory survey, in A. Saeed (ed.), *Approaches to the Qurʾān in contemporary Indonesia,* London (Oxford University Press) 2005 (forthcoming); id., Qurʾānic exegesis in the Malay world. In search of a profile, in Rippin, *Approaches,* 257-87; id., Qurʾānic exegetes and exegesis. A case study in the transmission of Islamic learning, in P. Riddell and T. Street (eds.), *Islam. Essays on scripture, thought and society,* Leiden 1997, 4-49; H.A. Karim, *Kinh Qurʾān,* Santa Ana, CA 1997 (in Vietnamese); S. Keijzer, De twee eerste Soera's van den Javaanschen Koran, in *Bijdragen tot de Taal-, Land- en Volkenkunde* 10 (1863), 314-66; I.M. al-L. de Leon, *The meaning of the holy Qurʾān in Tagalog on Islamic legislation,* Manila 1982; H.C. Millies, Inleiding. Proeven eener Makassarsche vertaling des Korans door B.F. Matthes, in *Bijdragen tot de Taal-, Land- en Volkenkunde* 3 (1856), 89-106; K.B. Mustofa, *al-Ibrīz li-maʿrifat tafsīr al-Qurʾān al-ʿazīz,* Kudus 1960 (in Javanese); Nawawī al-Jāwī, *Marāh Labīd li-kashf maʿnā Qurʾān majīd,* 2 vols., Beirut 1997; M.D. Rahardjo, *Ensiklopedi al-Qurʾān. Tafsir sosial berdasarkan konsep-konsep kunci,* Jakarta 1996 (in Bahasa Indonesia); J. Rakhmat, *Tafsir bil maʾtsur. Pesan moral Alquran,* Bandung 1994 (in Bahasa Indonesia); K.H.M. Ramli, *Al kitabul mubin. Tafsir al-Qurʾān basa sundai,* 2 vols., Bandung 1981 (in Sundanese); P. Riddell, *Islam and the Malay-Indonesian world. Transmissions and responses,* Honolulu 2001; H.Q. Shaleh, *Tardjaman Djuz Amma,* Bandung 1965 (in Sundanese); M.H. Shiddiqy, *Tafsir al-Qurānul madjied "an-nur",* Jakarta 1965 (in Bahasa Indonesia).

Sovereignty

(Sole) authority and power, rulership. In exploring the notion of sovereignty much care should be given to terminology. Sovereignty generally means authority (q.v.) and power (see POWER AND IMPOTENCE) but it lacks precise definition and has many divergent interpretations in English usage as do its cognates in other Western languages. The word *ḥākimiyya,* a derivative of the verb *ḥakama,* has been commonly used in modern Islamic thought to denote sovereignty. The form *ḥākimiyya* itself does not occur in the Qurʾān but *ḥakama* and other derivatives of *ḥ-k-m* are used in more than a hundred places. The verb *ḥakama* primarily means "to restrain from doing that which is desired." In Arabic dictionaries it signifies "to judge, decide order, exercise authority, rule and govern." An examination of the occurrences of the word and its derivatives in the Qurʾān reveals that they have been associated with both God and human beings but at varying levels and for varying types of authority (see also JUDGMENT; WISDOM).

The doctrine of God occupies a central position in the qurʾānic discourse, where God is portrayed with absolute authority over the world. Among the terms used to signify his divine authority is *ḥakama* and its derivatives. For instance, *ḥakam, ḥākim* and *ḥakīm* are all attributes of God that include his qualities as lord (q.v.) and ruler of the universe (see GOD AND HIS ATTRIBUTES; CREATION). The Qurʾān has also emphasized repeatedly that *ḥukm,* "command, judgment and decision," belongs ultimately to God (e.g. Q 95:8; 11:45; 12:40;

13:41; 18:26). The usage of the term in the Qurʾān has been understood to comprise several significant concepts. Theologically, it is understood to signify that God determines and causes all that happens in the universe (Q 4:78; 7:54; see FREEDOM AND PREDESTINATION) and that he is the sole adjudicator among humans on the day of the judgment (Q 22:55-7; see LAST JUDGMENT). On the other hand, God is also viewed as a lawgiver in the sense that he prescribes the rules that govern human affairs (see LAW AND THE QURʾĀN; BOUNDARIES AND PRECEPTS). On the basis of these understandings, it has been argued that sovereignty belongs to God, not only in the theological sense but also in the political and legal sense (Quṭb, *Ẓilāl*, 1191-9, 1213-34; see THEOLOGY AND THE QURʾĀN; POLITICS AND THE QURʾĀN).

But the Qurʾān does not confine *ḥukm* to God alone. It is assigned also to various humans: to the rabbis and scholars (q.v.) who judge, *yaḥkum*, applying the Torah (q.v.) code (Q 5:44; see JEWS AND JUDAISM); to David (q.v.) who was commanded to judge between people justly (Q 38:26; see JUSTICE AND INJUSTICE); to Muḥammad who must judge in accordance with the Qurʾān (cf. Q 4:65, 105). And, there are two further incidents where the authority of *ḥukm* is conferred: on the arbitrators who settle a marriage dispute (Q 4:35; see MARRIAGE AND DIVORCE) or estimate the compensation to be paid by a pilgrim as atonement (q.v.) for the sin (see SIN, MAJOR AND MINOR) of killing game during the pilgrimage (q.v.; Q 5:95; see also HUNTING AND FISHING).

Closely related to the term *ḥākimiyya* are two other terms relevant to the concept of sovereignty in the Qurʾān: *ulūhiyya* (divinity) and *mulk* (kingship). *Ulūhiyya* denotes, among other things, the absolute right of command over the creation (e.g. Q 7:54) and the authority to legislate for humankind (e.g. Q 42:21), both of which belong exclusively to God. Therefore, it appears that the term *ulūhiyya* comprises the meanings that those who assigned sovereignty to God wanted to attribute to him. On the other hand, human governance has been mostly denoted by derivatives of *m-l-k*, such as *mulk* (e.g. Q 2:102, 251, 258; 12:43, 50, 54, 72, 76, 101) though it has sometimes been used to refer to God's sovereignty (Q 3:26; 23:116; see KINGS AND RULERS). Ibn Khaldūn (d. 808/1406), the famous Muslim historian and sociologist, defines the nature of *mulk* in a way that is very similar to the Western concepts of political, legal and coercive sovereignty (see also TOLERANCE AND COMPULSION; OPPRESSION; OPPRESSED ON EARTH, THE). He says:

> *Mulk*, in reality, belongs only to one who dominates the subjects, subjugates the people, collects revenues (see TAXATION; POLL TAX), sends out military expeditions, and protects the frontiers; and there is no other human power over him. This is generally accepted as the real meaning of the true character of *mulk* (Ibn Khaldūn, *Muqaddima*, ii, 574).

Historically, the slogan of the Khārijīs (q.v.) that *ḥukm* belongs to God alone seems to be the earliest use of the term in politics. Modern Muslim reformers have attempted to find an Islamic equivalent to the Western concepts of political and legal sovereignty (see EXEGESIS OF THE QURʾĀN: EARLY MODERN AND CONTEMPORARY). A number of them, including Nāmiq Kemāl (d. 1888), Rashīd Riḍā (d. 1935) and Ḥasan al-Bannā (d. 1949), advocated the view that Islam approves of popular sovereignty. Others, among them Abū Aʿlā l-Mawdūdī (d. 1979) and Sayyid Quṭb (d. 1966), denied that sovereignty can be attributed to a human being and argued that it belongs exclusively to God. In spite of those differences about the type and location of sovereignty, it appears that many accept the principle of the supremacy of God's laws, the *sharīʿa,* the rights of the ruler and the role of the people in the collective decision-making process in Muslim politics.

Bustami Khir

Bibliography
Primary: Ibn Khaldūn, Abū Bakr ʿAbd al-Raḥmān b. Muḥammad, *al-Muqaddima,* trans. F. Rosenthal, 3 vols., London 1985; Quṭb, *Ẓilāl.*
Secondary: I. Ahmed, *Sovereignty, Islamic and modern. Conception of sovereignty in Islam,* Karachi 1965; D. Gimaret, *Les noms divins en Islam,* Paris 1988, 271-2, 347-9; B. Khir, *The concept of sovereignty in modern Islamic political thought,* Leeds 1996.

Sowing see AGRICULTURE AND VEGETATION

Spatial Relations

Relative physical and geographic placement (above, below, close, etc.). In Islamic tradition, the qurʾānic corpus is understood as consisting of two kinds of text units, Meccan sūras and Medinan sūras (see MECCA; MEDINA; SŪRA). While this division serves the juridical purpose of distinguishing earlier texts from later texts (see ABROGATION), by such geographic identification sūras are explicitly related to places (see GEOGRAPHY AND THE QURʾĀN) rather than time periods (see CHRONOLOGY AND THE QURʾĀN). This is in accord with a general qurʾānic trend to focus on space rather than time (q.v.). The Qurʾān furthermore displays a strong tendency to arrange essential phenomena of creation in pairs, sometimes antithetical, sometimes complementary (see PAIRS AND PAIRING; RHETORIC AND THE QURʾĀN). Although there occasionally occurs a similar kind of structuring speech in the Bible — see the passages about God's promise to Noah (*Gen* 8:22) or the sequence of antithetical mental dispositions (in *Koh* 3:1-8) — this tendency is much further developed in the Qurʾān (see Neuwirth, Qurʾānic literary structure revisited; see LITERARY STRUCTURES OF THE QURʾĀN; FORM AND STRUCTURE OF THE QURʾĀN). Among the many phenomena presented as coupled in the Qurʾān, spatial notions figure prominently. They are presented in some cases as related closely enough to constitute together one complete whole — linguistically reflected in the rhetorical figure of a *merismos* (see Lausberg, *Handbuch*). Although each part of the pair does exist by itself, it is always perceived as related to the other. Among these pairs, we find in the early sūras the figure of "present life/hereafter" (*al-ḥayāt al-dunyā/al-ākhira;* see ESCHATOLOGY; EARTH; TRANSITORINESS; ETERNITY), as well as that of paradise (q.v.) and hell (*al-janna* and *jahannam;* see HELL AND HELLFIRE; GARDEN). A less tightly connected pair in the early sūras is Mecca and the holy land (see SACRED AND PROFANE; SACRED PRECINCTS). It is exactly this pair, however, that will gain importance in the later sūras, where it appears emblematically coded as *al-masjid al-ḥarām/al-masjid al-aqṣā,* the first being a coded designation of Mecca, the second of Jerusalem (q.v.). In the later Meccan sūras, the biblical pair heaven and earth (q.v.; *al-samāʾ wa-l-arḍ/al-samāwāt wa-l-arḍ*) are frequently invoked (see HEAVENS AND SKY; SCRIPTURE AND THE QURʾĀN). A more marginal relation is that between Egypt (q.v.) and the holy land as portrayed in Q 12 (Sūrat Yūsuf, "Joseph") and in the story of the Children of Israel (q.v.; Banū Isrāʾīl), as narrated repeatedly throughout the developing revelation of the Qurʾān. Mecca and Medina are never juxtaposed explicitly in the Qurʾān, nor is the migration of the Prophet and his adherents portrayed in the Qurʾān (see EMIGRATION; EMIGRANTS AND HELPERS). Another relation between cities (see CITY) appears more significant: Mecca and, later, Medina are virtually related to a third, symbolic center — Jerusalem — a relation that develops into Mecca's absorption of Jerusalem's prerogatives (see Neuwirth, Spiritual meanings). Whereas a real journey is made from Mecca to Medina, a virtual and symbolic trajectory leads from Medina back to Mecca. In the following the three most prominent complementary (or antithetical) figures of spatial relations will be discussed, as well as some less explicit ones.

Earthly life and the hereafter, al-ḥayāt al-dunyā/al-ākhira

Since the early sūras are dominated by the imagination of eschatology, it is the antagonism of the present life and the hereafter (*al-ḥayāt al-dunyā* vs. *al-ḥayāt al-ākhira*) that appears first in the Qurʾān. Whereas the English translation of the pair might suggest a temporal rather than a spatial relation, the Qurʾān obviously views the two worlds as spatial units. This is all the more surprising since the likely rabbinical model for the idea of the two worlds (see JEWS AND JUDAISM; FOREIGN VOCABULARY), the Hebrew notion of *ha-ʿōlām ha-zeh* vs. *ha-ʿōlām ha-bā,* this world vs. the coming world, does presuppose a temporal sequence, *ʿōlām* being a temporal term in both Hebrew and Aramaic *(ʿalmā).* It is noteworthy, however, that with respect to terminology, the Hebrew discourse of the two temporally juxtaposed worlds did leave a trace in the Qurʾān, which from the middle Meccan sūras onward (the two first instances being still early Meccan, Q 81:29 and Q 83:6) employs the formula *rabb al-ʿālamīn* to express a crucial divine predicate, one that becomes a standard formula through the Fātiḥa (q.v.; see Neuwirth, Fātiḥa). Although *rabb al-ʿālamīn* reflects Hebrew *ribbōn ʿōlām* (in the sense of "lord [q.v.] of eternity [q.v.]"), the Arabic cognate of *ʿōlām,* i.e. *ʿālam,* which appears in the Qurʾān exclusively as *ʿālamīn* (see translation of 1 John 4:19), is not always used in a temporal sense but in some instances seems rather to denote the inhabited earthly world, represented by humans. *ʿĀlamīn* in this sense (which is reflected in various translations of the Qurʾān into western languages) could be explained as a contracted plural of an adjectival form *(nisba), ʿālamī.*

It appears, however, as if *ʿālamīn* was at first used in another sense: to denote something like "eternity," such as in the formula *rabb al-ʿālamīn* (early sūras, Q 56:80; 69:43; 81:29; 83:6) which is a loan from the Hebrew but is well isolated from the word *rabb* in *dhikrun lil-ʿālamīn* (Q 68:52; 81:27), perhaps in the sense of "a remembrance (q.v.) forever." Only later, from middle Meccan sūras onward, do contexts like *wa-faḍḍalnāhum ʿalā l-ʿālamīn* (Q 45:16; see GRACE; BLESSING) or *nisāʾ al-ʿālamīn* (Q 3:42; see WOMEN AND THE QURʾĀN), suggesting the meaning of "humans," occur. It is worth noting that the word *ʿālam* in Christian Arabic expresses a spatial notion (see 1 John 4:19), obviously reproducing the signification of the Greek *kosmos,* which is a spatial rather than temporal notion.

The qurʾānic structuring of the universe into two worlds is certainly inspired by the imagination of the Aristotelian-Ptolemaic edifice of the universe as made up of spheres viewed as encompassing each other (see COSMOLOGY). The lowest or closest of these is encompassed by the "nearest heaven," *al-samāʾ al-dunyā* (Q 67:5), which is the world, and by the last *(al-ākhira),* i.e. the most remote, which is the transcendent world, hosting the heavenly court. Since paradise is imagined in the Qurʾān to be situated in a higher place than the earth, *al-ākhira,* the "last," may well be alluding to the highest, the "last sphere."

Whereas in early and middle Meccan

texts *al-dunyā* is always positioned as an attribute to *al-ḥayāt,* and *al-ākhira* — though not directly connected to *al-dunyā* — refers back to *al-ḥayāt* as well, in late Meccan and Medinan sūras, *al-dunyā* becomes an independent designation of the earthly world, as does *al-ākhira* (which also appears as *dār al-ākhira,* Q 28:77) for the hereafter. In these texts the direct juxtaposition *al-dunyā wa-l-ākhira* (Q 12:101) marking a *merismos* — the earthly world and the hereafter equals reality in toto — becomes familiar.

Paradise versus hell, al-janna *vs.* jahannam (*or* al-nār, al-saʿīr, al-jaḥīm, al-ḥuṭama)

This pair, another major element of eschatology, does not appear in direct juxtaposition, though the two abodes are described almost always in close context with each other. *Jahannam* is the second most common (seventy-seven occurrences) designation of hell in the Qurʾān after *al-nār*. *Jahannam* originally denotes a site in Jerusalem, *Gē Hinnōm,* the valley of Bne Hinnom, the biblical locus of the immolation of human offspring to Moloch (*Jer* 7:31f.). The eschatological landscape of Jerusalem, which locates the diverse stages of the resurrection in single parts of the city (see Neuwirth, The spiritual meaning), is otherwise not reflected in the Qurʾān; it will come to the fore in early Umayyad times. The name is obviously already established as a geographically neutral term in Christian tradition and has possibly entered Arabic through Ethiopian (Jeffery, *For. vocab.*, 105-6; see CHRISTIANS AND CHRISTIANITY).

[Al-] janna is the counterpart of the biblical *gan* or *gan ʿeden*. As a designation for paradise, the primordial human abode, its biblical use does not denote the hereafter, eschatological thinking having emerged only after the completion of most biblical books. *[Al-] janna* is from middle Meccan times onward connected with the determination Eden (*ʿadn*) which, however, has no topographical reference in qurʾānic creation (q.v.) stories. In early sūras paradise and hell are often depicted with cognate literary devices, their respective attributes often matching each other, the one being extremely delightful, the other extremely abhorrent. Their depiction tends to be structured as constituting equal numbers of verses (e.g. Q 51:10-14, 15-19; five verses each) or as two verse groups displaying a proportional relation to each other (e.g. Q 69:19-24 as against 69:25-37, six and thirteen verses, respectively; see FORM AND STRUCTURE OF THE QURʾĀN). As such, they remind one of the closely juxtaposed pictorial representations of both forms of the hereafter that are familiar from Christian ecclesiastical iconography, thus suggesting the designation of "diptycha" (see Neuwirth, *Studien*). Both *janna* and *jahannam* share the presence of trees and abundant water, *janna,* however, being shady, *jahannam* being burning hot. Both are eternal abodes for their inhabitants. The most impressive depiction of paradise is presented in Q 55 (Sūrat al-Raḥmān, "The Merciful"; see GOD AND HIS ATTRIBUTES), one of the few cases where the negative counterpart *jahannam* is marginalized (see Neuwirth, Qurʾānic literary structure). The biblical characterization of paradise as a landscape where four mythic rivers are flowing is reflected in the Qurʾān in a more general way, the phrase "rivers flowing beneath it" (*tajrī min taḥtihā l-anhāru;* cf. Q 18:31) being often added to the mention of *janna* (see SPRINGS AND FOUNTAINS). A characteristic of the qurʾānic paradise that has no counterpart in the Bible is the existence of virtuous virgins destined to become the wives of the resurrected males (Q 44:54; 55:56-8; see HOURIS; MYTHS AND LEGENDS IN THE QURʾĀN). The banquets in which they participate have been interpreted by J. Horovitz (*Das koranische Paradies*) as magnifications of festal banquets familiar in

the circles of tribal elites and thus well-known to the Qurʾān's listeners from ancient Arabic poetry (see POETRY AND POETS; PRE-ISLAMIC ARABIA AND THE QURʾĀN). The hypothesis that the presence of virgins in the Qurʾān is due to a misreading of the text (see Luxenberg, *Die syro-aramäische Lesart*) is unfounded (see Wild, Lost in translation). These depictions are exclusively early and middle Meccan; later, once a community had been established where women played vital roles, the issue of transcendent happiness had to be rethought. In the course of that development, family members took the place of the houris as companions to the males in paradise. In the early sūras, paradise and hell appear to be juxtaposed; the antagonism between earth and paradise, resulting from the first couple's expulsion from *al-janna* (see FALL OF MAN), is introduced only in later texts, where, however, it does not play as momentous a role as in Christianity.

Mecca and the holy land

In their introductory sections, a few sūras focus on a place or a set of places held sacred in monotheistic tradition, to which Mecca has been added: Q 52:1-6 (Mount Sinai and Mecca), Q 95:1-3 (Mount Sinai, and, perhaps symbolically coded, Palestine — *wa-l-tīn wa-l-zaytūn,* "the fig and the olive," and Mecca — *hādhā l-balad al-amīn,* "this safe city"), whereas in Q 90:1-2 Mecca (*hādhā l-balad,* "this city") is mentioned alone. The places are obviously regarded as being related, Mecca thus being put in a position that allows it to share the blessing inherent in the other place(s). The relation between Mecca and the holy land is thus established from the beginning of the Qurʾān's development. In middle and late Meccan sūras the holy land, *al-arḍ al-muqaddasa* (Q 5:21), *al-arḍ allatī bāraknā ḥawlahā/fīhā,* literally, "the land that we have blessed" (Q 21:71; cf. 7:137; 17:1; 34:18), is evoked on different occasions. At this stage, the earlier reminiscences of Arabian salvation (q.v.) history, the sites of ʿĀd (q.v.), Thamūd (q.v.) and other ancient peoples are replaced by recollections of biblical history featuring the Children of Israel (see Speyer, *Erzählungen*). Local *lieux de mémoire* are substituted by geographically remote ones and a new *topographia sacra* emerges, adopted from the "others," not the genealogical, but the spiritual forebears. The community that was in late Meccan time urged to go into an inner exile yearned for a substitute for the emotionally alienated and politically hostile landscape of their origin. Through the adoption of the orientation in prayer, the *qibla* (q.v.), towards Jerusalem dating to the last years of Muḥammad's Meccan activities, a trajectory has been constructed. Q 17:1, the sole verse that connects the holy land directly with the biography of the Prophet (see Neuwirth, Sacred mosque; see SĪRA AND THE QURʾĀN; ASCENSION), is also a testimony of the establishment of the first *qibla* (see also GEOGRAPHY). This orientation taken by a community in spiritual exile towards the spiritual home is understood as an emulation of the practice of Moses (q.v.) who in Egypt, equally in a situation of external pressure, ordered the Children of Israel to adopt a *qibla* (Q 10:87) for their prayer (q.v.).

Only a few years later, in Medina, as a result of complex developments, the trajectory from the familiar but now banned and forbidden hometown Mecca to the "remote," imaginary sanctuary of Jerusalem is called into question. When, after the battle of Badr (q.v.), hostility between the community and the Medinan Jews broke out, the incompatibility of the rivaling *lieux de mémoire,* the two *topographiae sacrae,* Jerusalem with the holy land on the one hand and Mecca with the Ḥijāzī landscape on the other, became evident. The spiritual return of the worshippers to the

Kaʿba (q.v.) at Mecca is heralded in the verses that prescribe the realignment of the orientation in prayer, now directed towards Mecca (Q 2:142-4). In the prayer of Abraham (q.v.; Q 2:126f.), finally, the Kaʿba appears as the monument of a new divine foundation. According to Abraham's inaugural prayer, verbal worship (q.v.) and the reading of scripture shall take place in this sanctuary in addition to the constitutive rites of the ancient cult (see also RITUAL AND THE QURʾĀN) that reflects Solomon's prayer at the inauguration of his Temple (1 Kings 33-4). The prayer related in the Qurʾān reaches its fulfillment with the appearance of the prophet Muḥammad and the emergence of a scripture for the worshippers of the ancient cult (see BOOK; ḤANĪF). What had been a prerogative of Jerusalem to be the site of divine communication (*Isa* 2:3) is finally conferred on Mecca (see REVELATION AND INSPIRATION). Finally, both Mecca and the peninsula acquire biblical associations and become the site of monotheistic salvation history.

Various further spatial relations have been discussed in the context of other articles or in monographs: for heaven and earth *(al-samāwāt wa-l-arḍ),* see COSMOLOGY; for the hidden and the revealed (*al-ghayb* and *al-shahāda*), see HIDDEN AND THE HIDDEN and Izutsu, *God;* for earth and the two oceans, see BARRIER; BARZAKH; for world vs. underworld (the story of Moses in Q 18:60-82), see Francke, *Begegnung mit Khidr* (see also KHAḌIR/KHIḌR). See also LEFT HAND AND RIGHT HAND; SYMBOLIC IMAGERY.

Angelika Neuwirth

Bibliography
P. Francke, *Begegnung mit Khidr. Quellenstudien zum Imaginaeren im traditionellen Islam,* Beirut/Stuttgart 2000; J. Horovitz, *Das koranische Paradies. Scripta universitatis atque bibliothecae hierosolymitarum. Orientalia et Judaica volumen I,* Jerusalem 1923; Izutsu, *God;* H. Lausberg, *Handbuch der literarischen Rhetorik. Eine Grundlegung der Literaturwissenschaft,* Munich 1960; Ch. Luxenberg, *Die syro-aramäische Lesart des Koran. Ein Beitrag zur Entschlüsselung der Koransprache,* Berlin 2000; A. Neuwirth, From the sacred mosque to the remote temple. Sūrat al-Isrāʾ between text and commentary, in J.D. McAuliffe, B. Walfish and J. Goering (eds.), *With reverence for the word,* Oxford 2003, 376-407; id., Qurʾānic literary structure revisited. Sūrat al-Raḥmān between mythic account and decodation of myth, in S. Leder, *Story-telling in the framework of non-fictional Arabic literature,* Wiesbaden 1998, 388-420; id., The spiritual meaning of Jerusalem in Islam, in N. Rosovsky (ed.), *City of the great king. Jerusalem from David to the present,* Cambridge, MA 1996, 93-116, 483-95; id, *Studien;* id. and K. Neuwirth, *Sūrat al-Fātiḥa.* Eroeffnung des Text-Corpus Koran oder Introi tus der Gebetsliturgie?, in W. Gross, H. Irsigler and T. Seidl (eds.), *Text, Methode und Grammatik. Wolfgang Richter zum 65. Geburtstag,* St. Ottilien 1991, 331-58; Speyer, *Erzählungen;* S. Wild, Lost in translation. The virgins of paradise in the Qurʾān, in M. Marx, A. Neuwirth, N. Sinai (eds.), *The Qurʾān in context. Historical and literary investigations into the cultural milieu of the Qurʾān,* Leiden (forthcoming).

Speech

The act of speaking and the expression or communication of thoughts and feelings by spoken words. The Arabic word for "speech" is *kalām.* It is derived from the root *k-l-m,* just like the Arabic verbs "to speak," *kallama* and *takallama.* Several other qurʾānic verbs refer to the act of speaking, such as the verbs *qāla,* "to say," *naṭaqa,* "to articulate," and *nādā,* "to call or shout." Some verbs indicate the speaker's intention, such as *saʾala,* "to ask," *ajāba,* "to answer," *nabbaʾa,* "to inform" (see NEWS), *waʿada,* "to promise" (see REWARD AND PUNISHMENT), *nahā,* "to forbid" (see FORBIDDEN; VIRTUES AND VICES, COMMANDING AND FORBIDDING), and *amara,* "to command."

The most important speaking person in the Qurʾān is God. He brings things into existence by speaking to them and ordering them to exist. He says to a thing "Be!" *(kun),* whereupon the thing in question exists (Q 2:117; 3:47; 6:73; 16:40; 36:82; 40:68; see COSMOLOGY). After God had created Adam from dust (see ADAM AND EVE; CREATION; CLAY), he said to him "Be," whereupon Adam existed (Q 3:59). God may also speak to something and order it to change its quality. When Abraham's (q.v.) people intended to burn him, God said to the fire (q.v.) "Be cool!" (Q 21:69; see HOT AND COLD). Another example of a divine command that affects a change is God's ability to end people's lives, by ordering them: "Die!" (Q 2:243; see DEATH AND THE DEAD).

God speaks to the creatures he has created. There are some qurʾānic reports of conversations between God and the angels (see ANGEL). Before God created Adam, he informed the angels of that (Q 15:28; 38:71) and they commented on it (Q 2:30). After the creation of Adam, God ordered the angels to prostrate themselves to Adam (Q 2:34; 7:11; 15:29; 17:61; 18:50; 38:72; see BOWING AND PROSTRATION). Thereupon a discussion took place between God and Iblīs (see DEVIL) who refused to do so (Q 7:12-18; 15:32-42; 17:61-5; 38:75-85; see INSOLENCE AND OBSTINACY; ARROGANCE; PRIDE). Adam was the first human being to whom God spoke: "He taught Adam all the names" (Q 2:31; see TEACHING; KNOWLEDGE AND LEARNING). The exegetes disagree about whether God taught Adam the name of everything there is or simply the names of angels or humans (Ṭabarī, *Tafsīr,* ad Q 2:31; see EXEGESIS OF THE QURʾĀN: CLASSICAL AND MEDIEVAL). Some Arab grammarians (see GRAMMAR AND THE QURʾĀN; ARABIC LANGUAGE) referred to this verse to support their opinion that human speech finds its origin in revelation (see REVELATION AND INSPIRATION). They rejected the idea that language is the result of agreement between humans (Versteegh, *Arabic linguistic tradition,* 101-2). God also spoke to Adam and his wife when he told them to live in paradise (q.v.) but not to approach the tree [of immortality] (Q 2:35; see TREES; ETERNITY). After their disobedience (q.v.), God spoke to them again, when he told them to leave paradise (Q 2:38; 20:123).

These conversations took place in paradise (q.v.) but God also spoke to prophets (see PROPHETS AND PROPHETHOOD) who lived as human beings in this world. God spoke to Noah (q.v.; e.g. Q 11:46), Abraham (e.g. Q 2:124), Moses (q.v.; e.g. Q 7:143-4), Jesus (q.v.; e.g. Q 3:55) and Muḥammad (q.v.). In most accounts of these communications, the verb "to say" *(qāla)* is used, for instance, "God said" *(qāla llāhu),* "his lord (q.v.) said" *(qāla rabbuhu),* "he [God] said" *(qāla),* and "we [God] said" *(qulnā).* (For the use of personal pronouns with respect to God, see Robinson, *Discovering,* 224-55.) The whole Qurʾān is considered to be what God said to Muḥammad through the intermediation of Gabriel (q.v.), but when the Qurʾān refers to God's giving information to Muḥammad, the verb *qaṣṣa,* "to narrate," is repeatedly used (e.g. Q 40:78; 11:120; 12:3; see NARRATIVES; HEAVENLY BOOK; INIMITABILITY; CREATEDNESS OF THE QURʾĀN; COLLECTION OF THE QURʾĀN).

These reports about the prophets raise the question of whether they heard God's voice when he spoke to them (see SEEING AND HEARING). The answer is given in the Qurʾān itself. It is said that God speaks to humans only "by revelation, or from behind a veil (q.v.), or he sends a messenger (q.v.) who, with his permission, reveals what he wills" (Q 42:51). According to al-Zamakhsharī (d. 538/1144; *Kashshāf,* iv, 226-7), the first way means that God gives someone inspiration *(ilhām)* and "throws" something in his heart (q.v.) or in a dream (see DREAMS AND SLEEP). It is also possible that God creates a voice in some object *(baʿḍ al-ajrām)* without the listener seeing who speaks to him. The second way in which God speaks, i.e. from behind a veil, means that those who are addressed can hear his voice but cannot see him. According to al-Zamakhsharī, God spoke to Moses in this way. It is also the way in which God speaks to the angels. The other prophets did not hear God's voice. God spoke to them through an angel who acted as intermediary, bringing God's words to the prophet in question. This is the way in which God spoke to Muḥammad. The third way, according to al-Zamakhsharī's explanation, is that God speaks through the intermediation of a prophet. In this way, God speaks to the common people. They hear God's word from prophets who speak in their own languages (see LANGUAGE, CONCEPT OF).

"God really spoke to Moses" (*kallama llāhu Mūsā taklīman,* Q 4:164). Muslim scholars agree that Moses is the only prophet to whom God spoke directly. This does not become clear from Q 2:253, where it is said that God spoke to one (or some, *minhum man kallama llāhu*) of the messengers. According to al-Zamakhsharī (*Kashshāf,* i, 293), Moses is meant here. God said to Moses that he had chosen him above other people by means of his messages and his speech (*kalām,* Q 7:144; see ELECTION). A comparison of the verses about God's speaking to Moses indicates that not only the verb *kallama* but also other verbs are used to render God's speaking to Moses, such as *nādā,* "to call," as in "When his lord called him in the holy valley of Ṭuwā" (q.v.; Q 79:16, cf. 19:52; 26:10; 28:46). This verb is also used in the passive sense, although from the context it is evident that God is speaking. "When he [Moses] came to it [the fire], he was called *(nūdiya)* from the right side of the valley, in the blessed spot (see SACRED AND PROFANE), from the tree: 'Moses, I am God, the lord of the worlds' " (Q 28:30; cf. 20:11; 27:8).

In the Qurʾān it is reported that God spoke to humans who were not prophets, such as the apostles of Jesus (Q 5:115; see APOSTLE) and the Israelites (e.g. Q 5:12; 2:58; 17:104; see CHILDREN OF ISRAEL). As we have seen before, the explanation must be that he spoke to them through the intermediation of a prophet. It is not clear in which way God will speak to those who are brought back to life on the day of judgment (see RESURRECTION; LAST JUDGMENT). It is said that he will speak to them, including to the unbelievers (see BELIEF AND UNBELIEF). "Then I will inform you *(unabbiʾukum)* of what you did" (Q 31:15). God will not, however, speak *(yukallimu)* to people who have sold their covenant (q.v.) with him (Q 3:77; see TRADE AND COMMERCE) or the book (q.v.) he has sent down to them (Q 2:174). Only those will speak who have received permission (Q 11:105) and those who speak rightly (Q 78:38). Those who have declared the prophets to be liars will not be allowed to speak (e.g. Q 77:34-6; see LIE; GRATITUDE AND INGRATITUDE). Unbelievers will not be able to speak because God will seal up their mouths. Instead, their hands (q.v.) will speak *(tukallimu)* to God and their feet (Q 36:65), tongues (Q 24:24), ears (q.v.), eyes (q.v.) and skins (Q 41:20-3) will bear witness against them as to what they have done (see WITNESSING AND TESTIFYING). Probably, this is meant literally, as it is said that God can give each thing the power of speech (Q 41:21; see LITERARY STRUCTURES OF THE QURʾĀN).

In the Qurʾān some inanimate things are mentioned as speaking to God, such as the sky and the earth (q.v.; Q 41:11; see also HEAVEN AND SKY) and hell (Q 50:30; see HELL AND HELLFIRE). There are also written documents that can speak. "We have a book that speaks the truth" (*yanṭiqu bi-l-*

ḥaqq, Q 23:62; cf. 45:29). In this case, speaking may be understood metaphorically (see METAPHOR), just as in "This Qurʾān tells *(yaquṣṣu)* to the Israelites..." (Q 27:76) and "Did we [God] send them an authorization that speaks *(yatakallamu)?*..." (Q 30:35).

God's speech (kalām Allāh) *as a theological question*

The word *kalām* "speech" occurs four times in the Qurʾān. In all these cases it concerns God's speech. In Q 7:144 God says that he chose Moses above other people by means of the speech and messages that God revealed to him. In this case *kalām* may be understood as *taklīm,* "addressing someone," as al-Zamakhsharī says (*Kashshāf,* ii, 151), but it may also refer to the Torah (q.v.), which Moses received from God. In the other three cases, *kalām* cannot have the meaning of "addressing someone." It must mean God's message or the Qurʾān, as it is said that idolaters hear it (Q 9:6; see IDOLATRY AND IDOLATERS; POLYTHEISM AND ATHEISM) and people wish to change it (Q 48:15) or changed it after they had understood it (Q 2:75; see REVISION AND ALTERATION; FORGERY; CORRUPTION). Because of this, all Muslims agree that the Qurʾān is God's speech. Disagreement arose, however, about the nature of God's speech (see THEOLOGY AND THE QURʾĀN).

There is a close relationship between the discussions about the nature of God's speech and the discussions about the createdness of the Qurʾān (q.v.). Jahm b. Ṣafwān (d. 128/745-6) and his adherents asserted that God's speech is created but they denied that God speaks in the same way as humans do. They took into consideration the fact that human speech needs a special organ and movements of tongue and mouth. Because of their rejection of anthropomorphism (q.v.), they were convinced that God does not produce speech in this way. According to them, God does not really speak but when he wishes to "speak" to a creature, he creates the sound of speech, which is heard by this creature and is called "speech" (Madelung, *Origins,* 506-8).

The Muʿtazilīs (q.v.), too, were convinced that God's speech is created. The majority of the Muʿtazilīs defined speech as separately articulated sounds *(aṣwāt muqaṭṭaʿa).* For this reason they rejected the idea that speech is something that exists in the soul (q.v.; *nafs*). They acknowledged that God has the attribute of "speaking" and pointed out that someone is described as "speaking" *(mutakallim)* because he produces speech in accordance with his intentions. Depending on these intentions, speech occurs as information, command or prohibition. These Muʿtazilīs denied that speech can inhere in God but they deemed it possible that God creates speech directly in some substrate, in a tree, for instance, which explains how God spoke to Moses (see THEOPHANY). Another question is whether the Qurʾān in its recited, written and remembered form is identical to God's speech (see TEACHING AND PREACHING THE QURʾĀN; RECITATION OF THE QURʾĀN; MEMORY). According to the Muʿtazilī ʿAbd al-Jabbār (d. 415/1025), the Qurʾān is God's speech as he really produced it. When we hear a recitation *(qirāʾa)* of the Qurʾān, we hear a reproduction *(ḥikāya)* of God's speech as it was sent down to Muḥammad through his intermediary, the angel Gabriel.

Theologians who adhered to the opinion that God's speech is uncreated, such as the Ḥanbalīs, the Kullābīs and the Ashʿarīs, took into consideration that "speaking" is a divine attribute which can be equated with other essential attributes of God, such as his being knowing (see GOD AND HIS ATTRIBUTES). In their opinion, this implies that God is eternally "speaking" *(mutakallim).* Their opinion about speech differed from the Muʿtazilī definition of speech. Ibn Kullāb (d. ca. 240/854) declared that "God's speech *(kalām)* does not consist of letters and is not a sound. It is indivisible, impartible, indissectible and unalterable. It is one thing *(maʿnā)* in God" (Ashʿarī, *Maqālāt,* 584). This was the basis for the principle of "inner speech" *(kalām nafsī).* Probably, al-Ashʿarī (d. 324/935-6) himself did not speak about it but his adherents, al-Bāqillānī (d. 403/1013) and al-Juwaynī (d. 478/1085), used this term in reference to God's eternal uncreated speech. Inner speech is speech that is not yet expressed in words. In their opinion, the Qurʾān is an expression *(ʿibāra)* of God's inner speech but, as distinct from inner speech, it consists of sounds and letters. The expression may be Arabic or Hebrew. They declared that in the recitation *(qirāʾa)* of the Qurʾān, the pronunciation *(lafẓ)* is a human act but what we understand from the words is God's eternal speech.

The Ḥanbalīs declared that the Qurʾān, in whatever form, be it written, memorized, or recited, is God's uncreated speech. In their opinion, God's speech consists of sounds and letters and is identical to the letters of the Qurʾān (see PRESERVED TABLET; ARABIC SCRIPT; CALLIGRAPHY). The Ḥanbalīs rejected the idea that the Qurʾān is an expression or a reproduction of God's speech. They admitted that when the Qurʾān is recited, the pronunciation is a human act but they declared that what we hear and read is God's uncreated speech. H.A. Wolfson (*Philosophy,* 252-4) described this as the "inlibration" of God's uncreated speech (see also ORALITY; ORALITY AND WRITING IN ARABIA).

Margaretha T. Heemskerk

Bibliography

Primary: ʿAbd al-Jabbār [Ibn Mattawayh], *Kitāb al-Majmūʿ fī l-muḥīṭ bi-l-taklīf,* vol. i, ed. J.J. Houben, Beirut 1965, 316-46; id., *al-Mughnī fī abwāb al-tawḥīd wa-l-ʿadl.* vii. *Khalq al-Qurʾān,* ed. I. al-Abyārī, Cairo 1961; id., *Sharḥ al-uṣūl al-khamsa,* ed. A. ʿUthmān, Cairo 1965, 527-63; al-Ashʿarī, Abū l-Ḥasan ʿAlī b. Ismāʿīl, *al-Ibāna ʿan uṣūl al-diyāna,* ed. F.Ḥ. Maḥmūd, Cairo 1986 (1987²), 65-104; id., *Kitāb Maqālāt al-islāmiyyīn,* ed. H. Ritter, Wiesbaden 1929-30 (1980³), 191-4, 425-7, 516-17, 581-607; Bāqillānī, *Kitāb Tamhīd al-awāʾil wa-talkhīṣ al-dalāʾil,* ed. I.A. Ḥaydar, Beirut 1987, 268-84; al-Dārimī, ʿAbdallāh b. ʿAbd al-Raḥmān, *Kitāb al-Radd ʿalā l-jahmiyya,* ed. G. Vitestam, Lund 1960, 71-89; Ibn Abī Yaʿlā, *Ṭabaqāt al-Ḥanābila,* ed. M.Ḥ. al-Fiqī, 2 vols. in 1, Cairo 1952, ii, 295-6; al-Juwaynī, Abū l-Maʿālī ʿAbd al-Malik, *A guide to conclusive proofs for the principles of belief (K. al-Irshād ilā qawāṭiʿ al-adilla fī uṣūl al-itiqād),* trans. P.E. Walker, Reading 2000, 56-75.

Secondary: van Ess, *TG,* iv, 179-227, 604-30; id., Verbal inspiration? Language and revelation in classical Islamic theology, in Wild, *Text,* 177-94; L. Gardet, Kalām, in *EI²,* iv, 468-71; Izutsu, *God,* 151-97; W. Madelung, The origins of the controversy concerning the creation of the Koran, in id., *Religious schools and sects in medieval Islam,* London 1985, 504-25; J.R.T.M. Peters, *God's created speech. A study in the speculative theology of the Muʿtazilī Qāḍī l-Quḍāt Abū l-Ḥasan ʿAbd al-Jabbār bn Aḥmad al-Hamaḏānī,* Leiden 1976, 293-402; N. Robinson, *Discovering the Qurʾān. A contemporary approach to a veiled text,* London 1996, 224-55; A.S. Tritton, The speech of God, in *SI* 36 (1972), 5-22; K. Versteegh, *The Arabic linguistic tradition,* London 1977, 101-14; W.M. Watt, Early discussions about the Qurʾān, in *MW* 40 (1950), 27-40, 96-105; H.A. Wolfson, *The philosophy of the kalam,* Cambridge, MA 1976, 235-303.

Spell (to cast a)

see MAGIC

Sperm

see BIOLOGY AS THE CREATION AND STAGES OF LIFE

Spider

Creature whose body contains two main divisions: one with four pairs of walking legs, the other with two or more pairs of spinnerets for spinning the silk that is used in making the cocoons for its young, nests for itself or webs to entangle its prey. The word spider *(ʿankabūt),* which provides the name for Q 29, Sūrat al-ʿAnkabūt, occurs twice in the Qurʾān in one and the same verse, Q 29:41. In this verse, the spider exemplifies an agent for warning and threatening the infidels for their ungrateful conduct (see ANIMAL LIFE; BELIEF AND UNBELIEF; GRATITUDE AND INGRATITUDE). Those who choose for themselves benefactors other than God (see POLYTHEISM AND ATHEISM) are likened to the spider because this animal opts for the frailest of houses to live in. This qurʾānic passage alludes to the spider's web and its fragility and is one of the very few passages in the Qurʾān that refers to animal behavior. In reality, the spider's thread is strong enough for the spider itself and for its catch; so only from a human viewpoint can the web be considered weak.

In Arabic zoological literature, the spider's web plays an important role in describing the spider. (For other topics in connection with the descriptions of the spider in Arabic literature, e.g. its copulation, see Ruska, ʿAnkabūt; Eisenstein, *Einführung*, index.) It remains unclear for Arab authors whether it is the male or the female who fabricates the web in which the spider and its spittle wait for a catch. Although the spider's web is always described as weak it is also the reason for its reputation as a wonderful creature. For, according to the Arabic authors, the spider is able to spin its marvelous net immediately after its birth. Therefore, the spider is seen as one of the animals with inborn proficiencies, which do not have to be taught by parents. The spider only assumes its full shape, according to the Arabic sources, three days after birth. Among animals, the spider is considered impure and disgusting, and may therefore not be eaten. The prophet Muḥammad himself is said to have called the spider a *shayṭān* (devil) transformed by God and ordered it to be killed; this ḥadīth is, it should be noted, considered weak (al-Damīrī, *Ḥayāt*, ii, 223; see ḤADĪTH AND THE QURʾĀN).

In other words, contradiction and discrepancy determine the spider's image in Arabic literature. To make things more complicated, the spider and its web once saved the Prophet himself. According to tradition, the prophet Muḥammad and his Companion Abū Bakr had, on their way to Medina (q.v.) during the *hijra* (see EMIGRATION), taken refuge for three days in a cave (q.v.) located in the Thawr mountain. While they were in the cave, a spider built its web over the entrance of the cave protecting them from discovery by the Quraysh (q.v.) who were intent on harming them. A comprehensive account of this event may be found in Ibn Kathīr's (d. 774/1373) biography of the Prophet (Le Gassick, *Imām Abū l-Fidāʾ*, ii, 158f.; see SĪRA AND THE QURʾĀN), whereas in Ibn Hishām's account, the spider is not explicitly mentioned in this connection. (As an aside, other accounts have it that the Prophet was saved during the *hijra* not by a spider but by two doves.) At any rate, this event led to the conclusion that a spider could build its web very quickly. Moreover, the prophet Muḥammad was not the only one to be protected from danger by a quickly-built spider's web. Among the prophets, David (q.v.; Dāwūd) had the same experience. An account of this episode and a listing of other people saved by a spider are found in al-Damīrī's (d. 808/1405) book on animals.

Herbert Eisenstein

Bibliography

Primary: Damīrī, *Ḥayāt*, ii, 222-5; T. Le Gassick, *Imām Abū l-Fidāʾ Ismāʿīl ibn Kathīr, The life of the prophet Muḥammad. A translation of* al-Sīra al-nabawiyya, 2 vols, Reading 1998; al-Jāḥiẓ, ʿAmr b. Baḥr, *Kitāb al-Ḥayawān*, ed. ʿA.S.M. Hārūn, Cairo 1938-45 (rev. 1969²), vii, index.

Secondary: A.A. Ambros, Gestaltung und Funktion der Biosphäre im Koran, in *ZDMG* 140 (1990), 290-325; H. Eisenstein, *Einführung in die arabische Zoographie*, Berlin 1991; J. Ruska, ʿAnkabūt, in *EI²*, i, 509.

Spirit

Life force or supernatural being. In pre-Islamic poetry the Arabic word *rūḥ* refers to a blowing or breathing (see AIR AND WIND; POETRY AND POETS; PRE-ISLAMIC ARABIA AND THE QURʾĀN). In the Qurʾān, the word appears twenty-one times but in the sense of spirit rather than of blowing, in a manner analogous to its Hebrew cognate, *ruach*, in the Bible (see SCRIPTURE AND THE QURʾĀN). The qurʾānic *rūḥ* evokes spirit in passages related to the three boundary moments in the Qurʾān: creation (q.v.), the sending down of prophetic revelation (see REVELATION AND INSPIRATION; PROPHETS AND PROPHETHOOD), and the eschatology (q.v.) of the day of reckoning (*yawm al-dīn;* see LAST JUDGMENT). At divine behest or command *(amr),* spirit mediates the eternal and the temporal, coming down or rising up from one realm to another (see ETERNITY; TIME; WORLD). It comes down as the breath of life into Adam (see ADAM AND EVE; COSMOLOGY), as the conception of Jesus (q.v.) for Mary (q.v.), and with (or as) revelation to the prophets. It rises with the angels (q.v.) into the divine realm, bringing the temporal world to its conclusion and humans to their second creation (see RESURRECTION).

The qurʾānic concept of spirit is complicated by allusion, referential multivalence and theological allusion well beyond the issue of a possible equivalence of the spirit with Gabriel (q.v.; see also HOLY SPIRIT). These more subtle features are expressed through parallelism — in phrasing (see FORM AND STRUCTURE OF THE QURʾĀN), rhythm (see RHYMED PROSE), grammatical (see GRAMMAR AND THE QURʾĀN) and personal gender (q.v.) and key themes — which ties together passages across different sūras (q.v.) and allows disparate passages to reverberate semantically and sonically from one to the other (see LANGUAGE AND STYLE OF THE QURʾĀN; RHETORIC AND THE QURʾĀN). The result is that each boundary moment (creation, prophecy, reckoning) can be heard echoed within the others.

Spirit and creation

In the passages depicting the creation of Adam, the primordial human being (*insān* or *bashar*) is first shaped out of mud or clay (q.v.) and then brought to life as the creator breathes spirit into the shaped form (see BIOLOGY AS THE CREATION AND STAGES OF LIFE). God as creator speaks in the first person singular (Q 15:29; 38:72): "When I formed him and breathed into him some of my spirit" *(idhā sawwaytuhu wa-nafakhtu fīhi min rūḥī).* Other passages on the creation of Adam employ the exact same formula but in the third person (Q 32:9): "He formed him and breathed into him some of his spirit" *(sawwāhu wa-nafakha fīhi min rūḥihi).* The inbreathing actualizes and brings to life the material form of the creature after the shaping *(taswiya).* Before breathing into Adam, the creator shapes, kneads, molds, forms *(sawwā)* the substance of the creature into a form receptive of the spirit.

The formula used to depict spirit within creation found in the passages on Adam recurs in the passages depicting the conception of Jesus. Speaking about Mary, in one passage, God relates: "We breathed into her some of our spirit" (*nafakhnā fīhā min rūḥinā,* Q 21:91). Another passage is identical, except that the "into her" has been changed to "into it" *(fīhi):* "We breathed into it some of our spirit" (Q 66:12). The same verse had begun by referring to Mary as one who "guarded her private parts" *(farjahā)*. Thus some commentators interpret the "into it" as a reference to the breathing of the spirit directly into her vagina (see SEX AND SEXUALITY; MODESTY; CHASTITY). The most extended narrative concerning Jesus and Mary is found in Q 19:16-33. In Q 19:17 the divine voice relates that "We sent down to her our spirit which took on the likeness of a human being well formed *(basharan sawiyyan)*." Mary expresses shock and fear at the sight of the figure (interpreted in commentaries as Gabriel) and her reaction shows clearly that the figure is male in appearance. The figure (spirit in the likeness of a human form) replies that it is the messenger of her lord (q.v.; *rasūlu rabbiki*) sent to bestow on her a pious male child (for the efforts of commentators to distinguish the "our spirit" that God breathed into Mary from the "our spirit" that God sent down to Mary in the shape of a human, see MARY; and for a more philosophical discussion of the complex relationship of Mary to spirit, see Ibn al-ʿArabī, *Fuṣūṣ*, 138-67).

Spirit and revelation

With Jesus, the spirit is associated not only with creativity in his conception but with his prophetic mission as well. In three passages, Jesus, son of Mary, is depicted as being given the holy spirit *(rūḥ al-qudus)* as a support (Q 2:87, 253; 5:110). In the first two of those passages, the holy spirit's support is linked to Jesus' bringing of clear proofs (*bayyināt;* see PROOF). In the third passage, God speaks directly to Jesus, explaining how the holy spirit was sent as a support to him at the time he was prophesying while yet an infant. The passage goes on to remind Jesus how, with the permission of God, Jesus was able to shape birds from clay, breathe into them and bring them to life; this is a sequence that is precisely parallel to God's activity in bringing Adam to life. In yet another discussion of Jesus, he is identified with the spirit (Q 4:171). The different relations of Jesus to spirit can be summed up in the following way: Jesus was conceived through the spirit; prophesies with the support of the spirit; shapes creatures and brings them to life with divine permission by breathing into them in exactly the fashion through which God brought Adam to life; and is the spirit (see POWER AND IMPOTENCE; MIRACLES; MARVELS).

Spirit plays the central role in all prophecy which occurs through the spirit by the command *(amr)* of God (Q 16:2; 17:85; 40:15) and as a support for believers (Q 58:22). Other passages relate the spirit to the specific movement of the bringing down *(tanzīl)* and the coming down *(tanazzul)* of prophetic revelation. In a reference to the role of prophets as those who warn that there is no god but God (see WARNER; POLYTHEISM AND ATHEISM), the Qurʾān states (Q 16:2): "He sends down the angels with the spirit by his command to whichever of his servants (see SERVANT; WORSHIP) he wills." The spirit is sent down according to, through, or at the behest of the divine command. In a reference to the spirit sent to Muḥammad that empowers him to be a prophetic warner it is called the trustworthy *(amīn)* spirit.

In Q 16:102 it is the holy spirit that actively sends down *(nazzala)* the verses or signs *(āyāt)* of revelation. Most classical commentaries identify the holy spirit with Gabriel. Nowhere in the Qurʾān is such an identification made explicit and the name Gabriel appears in only two verses in the Qurʾān. The strongest evidence for assuming an identification between the spirit and Gabriel is found in Q 97:4, where the angels and the spirit descend *(tanazzalu)* by permission of their lord, a terminology and phrasing that relate to Q 16:102 on the role of the holy spirit. The Qurʾān refers neither to the spirit nor to Gabriel as an angel. The spirit does act in close proximity with the angels, leading to the common assumption that Gabriel and/or the spirit were the highest form of angel (see ANGEL; for further discussion and the alternative views of Ibn Zayd who interpreted the holy spirit as a reference to the Qurʾān and/or the Gospel, see Ayoub, *Qurʾān*, 124-5). In Q 81:19, the revelation to Muḥammad is referred to as the speech (q.v.) of a noble messenger (q.v.; *rasūl karīm*), which would fit the role of the spirit or that of Gabriel.

The spirit passages concerning Mary and Jesus tie creative activity to prophecy and revelation. Parallel constructions and vocabulary link those passages of the bringing to life of Adam to the act of prophetic inspiration (in the strong sense of inspiration). Q 97 recounts the sending down of revelation to Muḥammad. It begins with the divine voice announcing that "We sent him/it down *(anzalnāhu)* on the night of destiny (see NIGHT OF POWER)." If the pronoun *hu* is taken as indicative of a person, it is interpreted as Gabriel. When taken as indicative of a non-animate object, it is interpreted as the Qurʾān or associated with the revelatory vision(s) of Muḥammad depicted most famously in Q 53:1-18 and Q 81:19-24. Q 97:4 contains a complex formulation: The angels came down — the spirit — by the permission of their lord through/from every order. The central phrase, *wa-l-rūḥu fīhā*, is multivalent. The angels came down with the spirit among them; the angels came down with the spirit during it (the night of destiny or power, *qadr*); the angels came down upon the night (personified as female) of destiny. The grammatical and referential indetermination of the key phrase, its place at the rhythmic and semantic nexus of the verse and the dramatic placement of the verse in the larger sūra, heighten the sense of mystery and wonder surrounding the operation of the spirit (Sells, Sound).

Spirit and reckoning

The third boundary moment is the day of reckoning, a day when the angels will appear with the spirit in array (*ṣaffan;* see RANKS AND ORDERS). The spirit passages relating spirit to creation and prophecy parallel strongly the portrayal of the role of spirit in eschatology. In one case, the exact same wording is used stretched across disparate sūras concerning prophecy and reckoning. But the movement is reversed from downwards to upwards. In Q 97:4, "The angels come down with the spirit upon her/among them *(al-rūḥu fīhā)*." In Q 70:4, the angels rise with the spirit to him *(wa-l-rūḥu ilayhi)*. The link between these two passages and the events they depict is heightened by the stretching out of temporal limits in both prophecy and reckoning and by the inversion of night and day (see DAY AND NIGHT). Thus the night on which the spirit descends is "better than a thousand months" (q.v.; Q 97:3) while the day of reckoning is "a span of fifty-thousand years (see YEAR)." In addition, the grammatically feminine indirect object *(hā)* is balanced by the masculine indirect object *(hi)*. The intertwining of the two passages — one on the night of destiny, the other on the day of reckoning — intimate something undefined and perhaps indefinable hidden within the intensely lyrical imagery of daybreak (see DAWN; DAY, TIMES OF). The ambiguity in both passages concerning the role of the spirit in the rise and descent of the angels creates an openness of meaning that keeps the spirit from being limited to a particular finite being or form. The word "to breathe" or "to blow" *(nafakha)* intensifies the association of spirit with the day of reckoning. In the Qurʾān *nafakha* is used in only four contexts: the bringing to life of Adam; the conception of

Jesus; Jesus' bringing the material forms of birds to life; and (in twelve different places) the day on which the trumpet will be blown, that is, the day of reckoning and resurrection (see also APOCALYPSE).

Spirit and gender

Rūḥ is one of only a handful of nouns in Arabic that can be either masculine or feminine according to the grammatical gender (see ARABIC LANGUAGE). The way in which the differing spirit passages intersect and interweave with one another, particularly in the passages on the conception of Jesus and the descent of the spirit on or upon the night of destiny, suggest that spirit serves to mediate not only the temporal and eternal but also the male and female. The night of destiny is partially personified as female in a manner similar to the personification of the earth (q.v.) as giving birth to "her secret" in Q 99 (see SECRETS; HIDDEN AND THE HIDDEN). The implication of a personified animate being for the night would be especially pronounced in readings of verse one of Q 97 (Sūrat al-Qadr, "Destiny"), "we sent it/him down," as a reference to Gabriel, animate and conventionally male (at least in his appearance on earth). In its final verse, the sūra of Destiny closes with the emphatic "peace (q.v.) it is" or "peace she is" *(salāmun hiya)* "until the rise of dawn." The descent of the spirit upon or into Mary at the conception of Jesus strongly parallels the descent of the spirit on or into the night of destiny (Sells, *Approaching,* 183-207).

Michael Sells

Bibliography

Primary: Ibn al-ʿArabī, *Fuṣūṣ al-ḥikam,* ed. A.A. ʿAfīfī, Cairo 1946; Qurṭubī, *Tafsīr;* Rāzī, *Tafsīr;* Ṭabarī, *Tafsīr,* ed. Shākir (up to Q 14:27); ed. ʿAlī et al.

Secondary: M. Ayoub, *The Qurʾān and its interpreters,* vol. 1, Albany 1984; ʿAbd al-Bāqī; E.E. Calverley, Doctrines of the soul *(nafs* and *rūḥ)* in Islam, in *MW* 33 (1943), 254-64; Izutsu, *Concepts;* D.B. MacDonald, The development of the idea of spirit in Islam, in *AO* 9 (1931), 307-51; Th. O'Shaughnessy, *The development of the meaning of spirit in the Koran,* Rome 1953; M. Sells, *Approaching the Qurʾān,* Ashland 1999; id., A literary approach to the hymnic sūras of the Qurʾān. Spirit, gender, and aural intertextuality, in I. Boullata (ed.), *Literary structures of religious meaning in the Qurʾān,* London 2002, 3-25; id., Sound, spirit, and gender in *sūrat al-qadr,* in *JAOS* 111/2 (1991), 239-59.

Spiritual Beings

Supernatural creatures, either benevolent or malevolent. Within the Islamic world the expression "spiritual beings" carries different significations, depending on whether reference is made to the theological sphere (Qurʾān and ḥadīth; see ḤADĪTH AND THE QURʾĀN), or to the knowledge of the scholars or to local traditions. This wide world of chthonic spirits, that at first seems confused and undefined, consists of elements and cultural representations developed through the encounter with various ethnic groups and stratified throughout the course of history.

The belief in spiritual beings is already attested in the pre-Islamic period. The supernatural beings who survived the demise of Arab paganism, however, do not coincide with their status and significance in the animistic world of the Jāhiliyya (see AGE OF IGNORANCE; IDOLATRY AND IDOLATERS; POLYTHEISM AND ATHEISM). At first, they were utilized by some in the early Muslim community as more approachable entities who could intercede with God. The charges of *shafāʿa,* "intercession" (q.v.), in various sūras of the Meccan period are an indication of this utilization (Q 6:94; 10:18; 30:13; see MECCA). Subsequently, they were firmly rejected as impotent, or even changed into *shayāṭīn,* evil beings (see DEVIL; POWER AND IMPOTENCE).

As these preliminary remarks indicate, from its beginning, Islam has accepted the existence of subtle, non-human beings as part of God's creation (q.v.). In various passages the Qurʾān makes matter a metaphor (q.v.) of the spirit (q.v.; Q 42:49-53), whether this matter is fire (q.v.), air or light (q.v.; see also JINN; AIR AND WIND). Belonging to the world of the invisible (*ʿālam al-ghayb;* see HIDDEN AND THE HIDDEN), these spirits are characterized by their transient, volatile forms. They permeate the cosmos in order to direct the multifaceted variety of creation to the indivisible oneness of God (see GOD AND HIS ATTRIBUTES). But they are not thought to participate in God's transcendence; rather, the Qurʾān underscores their impotence and affords them a status not higher than humans (see ANGEL).

Qurʾānic and later references tend to distinguish malignant from benevolent spirits and to create a hierarchy within these categories. Whereas angels are considered to be benevolent, the scriptural conception of the jinn is somewhat more ambivalent. Angels *(malāʾika),* devils *(shayāṭīn)* and jinn, the largest gatherings of spiritual beings that appear in the Qurʾān, do not belong to the same cosmic sphere. All they share in common is being invisible; otherwise they are differentiated in terms of essence and nature, function, and place in the cosmos (see COSMOLOGY). The merciful angels are made of *nūr,* which can be translated as "cold light," while the angels of punishment are made of *nār,* "fire," indicating distinctions of both density and weight (cf. Q 66:6; Huart, *Livre de la création,* i, 169).

Whether they are "supervisors" *(al-mudabbirāt),* as in Q 79:5 or, expressed differently, "agents of beings" *(mawkūlāt bi-l-kāʾināt),* as al-Qazwīnī (d. 682/1283) says, or, again, spiritual entities *(rūḥāniyyūn),* as mentioned by the Ikhwān al-Ṣafāʾ, they govern the three realms of nature, "managing the mysterious development of life through their clever delicate hands" (Qazwīnī, *ʿAjāʾib,* 62). Among these innumerable creatures, some have proper names: *rūḥ al-qudus* (Q 16:102; see HOLY SPIRIT), Gabriel (q.v.; Jibrīl), Michael (q.v.; Mikāʾīl), Hārūt and Mārūt (q.v.; Q 2:102), Iblīs (see DEVIL). Others are identified only by their functions. There are the *ḥafaẓa,* honorable scribes, who attend human beings and record impartially their good or evil actions (see GOOD DEEDS; EVIL DEEDS; HEAVENLY BOOK; WRITING AND WRITING MATERIALS). There are the *kirām kātibīn,* as they are identified in Q 82:11 (cf. Q 43:80), who sit on a human's shoulders to note down his or her thoughts, and are termed *al-ḥafaẓa* in Q 6:61 or *ḥāfiẓ* in Q 86:4 (cf. Q 82:10). Their role is revealed by the epithets "observer" (*raqīb,* Q 50:18), "guide" *(sāʾiq)* and "witness" (*shāhid,* Q 50:21; see WITNESSING AND TESTIFYING).

The *muʿaqqibāt* (Q 13:11), "those who follow one upon the other," establish a continuous relationship between humankind and heaven (see HEAVEN AND SKY), coming down with divine grace and re-ascending *(ʿurūj)* with human actions (cf. Q 32:5; 34:2). This term has generated diverse interpretations and some commentators understood it to be a dual of the second verbal form *ʿaqqaba,* that here replaces the third form *ʿāqaba* (Ṭabarī, *Tafsīr,* xiii, 68). In function, however, these beings watch lovingly over every person: "Alike (to him) of you is he who conceals (his) words and he who speaks them openly, and he who hides himself by night and (who) goes forth by day (see DAY AND NIGHT). For his sake there are those who follow one another [*muʿaqqibāt,* angels, according to Ibn ʿAbbās], before him and behind him, who guard him by God's commandment" (Q 13:10-11).

The concept of "guardian angels" had already been developed throughout the

Semitic world. We find angels in charge of human souls and recording human actions in Enoch's *Book of secrets,* as well as in *Jubilees* (4:6 and 17:5), and in *Sabbat, Taʿanit, Hagigah* and *Berakot,* where two angels standing near every human being are mentioned. These figures may have been inspired by Thot, the scribal god in the Egyptian pantheon, who appears in funeral processions as the one who notes down the past actions, both good and bad (cf. Dubler, L'ancient orient, 71, who considers Q 101:5-8 to show a close resemblance to the Egyptian tradition concerning the last judgment). In reference to the judgment, Q 50:17 hints at two entities, *al-mutalaqqiyān,* "receivers," who are named *munkar* and *nakīr* in ḥadīth and the commentaries (see EXEGESIS OF THE QURʾĀN: CLASSICAL AND MEDIEVAL). "The two delegated to receive" carry out the torment of the grave *(ʿadhāb al-qabr),* repeatedly mentioned in the Qurʾān; it takes place after burial (q.v.). This idea recurs in rabbinic literature and its remote origins could be traced back to Iranian Mazdaism.

In the Qurʾān, as in other early sources, the angels are compared to the lightness of the wind. This is the element that best evokes the incorporeity of God but since it is still a substance it becomes identified with angels and spirits. Q 77:1, like Q 51:1, cites an oath by "those who have been sent one by one, and are blowing furiously," which affirms the similitude between winds and heavenly messengers (cf. Q 25:48; 27:63; 30:46). The connection of messenger and wind recurs in two lines of verse attributed to Umayya b. Abī l-Ṣalt, a contemporary of the Prophet and the linkage was maintained by the Islamic tradition, as the words of al-Maqdisī (d. 340/934) testify: "And we said that the wind is an angel as well as *al-rūḥ*" (cf. Huart, *Livre de la création,* i, 176). Such angels are also equated with the nineteen *al-zabāniya* (Q 96:18; cf. 74:30), under the leadership of one *mālik* (Q 43:77, possibly to be interpreted as the "owner of the doors of hell"; see HELL AND HELLFIRE), but there are other spiritual beings whose provenance is unspecified. The root of the word *qarīn* connotes the idea of a "double" — it is an adjectival form that indicates being one of a pair. This human "double," the companion or twin spirit, takes life upon the birth of a human being. Q 41:25 and its mention of *quranāʾ* can be understood to contain reference to the tempting spirit or *shayṭān* — synonymous with *muṣāḥib* (cf. *Lisān al-ʿArab,* s.v.) or *khidhn* (cf. Bayḍāwī, *Anwār,* ad Q 41:25) — to which Q 4:38 may allude. Commenting on Q 50:23, al-Suyūṭī (d. 911/1505) wonders whether the word *qarīn* denotes a *shayṭān* or an angel; but the author is sure that elsewhere in the same sūra (Q 50:27) it denotes a *shayṭān* (Suyūṭī, *Durr,* iv, 124). Al-Ṭabarī (d. 310/923), in his *Tafsīr* at Q 43:36, reports the tradition according to which every human has a *qarīn* or *shayṭān* and an angel, inciting evil and good respectively. These two beings are not to be confused with the two recording angels.

While a benevolent spirit in the pre-Islamic period, in which period the word indicated the spirit which follows a poet and inspires his verse (see POETRY AND POETS; RHYMED PROSE), this entity changes within the monotheistic orientation of Islam to a sort of keeper-demon who leads humans into temptation. The Islamic statements about *qarīn* recall the ancient Egyptian beliefs about *"ka,"* the abstract individuality of every human being, which in turn goes back to the Babylonian idea of an undefined personal god "walking beside man" (see Blackmann, *Karīn* and *karīneh;* Hornblower, Traces of a ka-belief).

In the Qurʾān, those who believe in *ṭāghūt,* along with *jibt* (q.v.), are said to be those who have received only a part of the scriptures (Q 4:51; see BOOK; PEOPLE OF THE BOOK; IDOLS AND IMAGES) and it contrasts belief in God with belief in the *ṭāghūt,* equating the latter with the leaders of the unfaithful (Q 2:257; see BELIEF AND UNBELIEF). The qurʾānic denunciation of those who "desire to go to judgment before the *ṭāghūt,* although they have been commanded not to believe in him; and Satan desired to seduce them into a wide error" (q.v.; Q 4:60; see also ASTRAY) indicates that *ṭāghūt* may refer to a spiritual entity or an idol (see also Atallah, Ǧibt and Ṭāghūt, for an interesting theory that relates these two words with magical practices in ancient Egypt). It is thus connected to the religious and political spheres of pre-Islamic society (see PRE-ISLAMIC ARABIA AND THE QURʾĀN). The meaning of the term *ṭāghūt,* however, remains a matter of speculation (for an Aramaic derivation — cf. Syr. *ṭāʿyē,* "planet/planet god" — see Köbert, Das koranische "ṭāġūt"; cf. Bukhārī, *Ṣaḥīḥ,* bk. 10, *K. Adhān,* 129 *[faḍl al-sujūd],* ed. Krehl, i, 207; trans. Houdas, i, 268: "Et il en est qui suivront le soleil, d'autres la lune, d'autres enfin les idoles"). Lexicographers and commentators have interpreted *al-jibt* and *al-ṭāghūt* as "everything that is adored instead of God," without identifying the origins of these words (see Fahd, *Le panthéon,* 240). According to both Qurʾān and ḥadīth, the Prophet recognized the existence of the heathen gods, but classed them among the demons.

In the Qurʾān, the word *jinn* acquires a connotation that is definitely pejorative, particularly in Medinan passages (see MEDINA). The original meaning of this term is probably "covert" (from the Semitic root *j-n-n*); another word for it is *jann* (to which the Ethiopic *ganen,* "demon," corresponds); it is sometimes used as a name of Iblīs (*al-jānn,* Q 15:27), or with the meaning of serpent (Q 27:10; 28:31), or as a synonym to jinn (Q 55:39; see also INSANITY).

An examination of the qurʾānic data reveals identification between *shayāṭīn* and jinn, as is the case in the Solomon (q.v.) legend (Q 2:102; 21:82; 38:37) or the abduction of human beings through the agency of spirits (Q 6:71). There are also several passages in which *shayāṭīn* means "pagan idols" (Q 2:14; 4:76; 5:90; 19:44) and a similar meaning is assigned to the word *jinn* in Q 6:100 and 34:41. This interpretation of their identity is a consequence of superimposing two different demonologies, one the outcome of monotheism, the other, previously known in the Arab world, arising from polytheism (see SOUTH ARABIA, RELIGIONS IN PRE-ISLAMIC). Nevertheless, in the qurʾānic purview, they are God's creatures and never appear as God's enemies (q.v.) or as an anti-divine power. The Qurʾān refers to the army of Iblīs (Q 26:95) and to Satan's party (Q 58:19), but these expressions have no dualistic flavor (see TROOPS; PARTIES AND FACTIONS; RANKS AND ORDERS). M. Iqbāl *(Reconstruction)* even considers Iblīs and the devils to be a necessary force in life because only by fighting them can one grow into a perfect human being. Though the jinn and *shayāṭīn* have no individuality, they fall into various classes, and some of them are mentioned as particularly harmful.

The most dangerous kind of harmful being is the *ghūl* (a feminine noun). This word, which comes from a root signifying "to destroy," does not appear in the Qurʾān except in the derivative form *ghawl* (Q 37:47), which refers to the dangerous effects of wine (q.v.). The *ghūl* is supposed to lie in wait at places where men are destined to perish; she entices them there, especially by night. Poets sometimes depict the *ghūl* as the daughter of the jinn (Qazwīnī, *ʿAjāʾib,* 370). Some words which are often understood as referring to demons actually have a different sense. *ʿIfrīt* (q.v.) in Q 27:39 is an epithet of somewhat doubtful meaning (it seems to have the general value of "skillful" with a shade of "rebel"; see REBELLION), which is applied to a jinn, but it is not the name of a particular class of demons.

As with other aspects of belief, the qurʾānic account of spiritual beings has generated a wide range of variations at the local level. For a large group of believers these spiritual beings are, at best, of philosophical importance only and of little practical concern as a sensible representation of the spiritual world. Others consider the veracity of their possible interference only in rare circumstances. But recent ethnographic research has shown that belief in spiritual beings persists as a regular ingredient of everyday life in various parts of the Muslim world.

Stefania Cunial

Bibliography

Primary: Bukhārī, *Ṣaḥīḥ;* trans. O. Houdas and W. Marçais, *Les traditions islamiques,* 4 vols., Paris 1977; Ibn al-ʿArabī, Muḥyi l-Dīn Abū ʿAbdallāh Muḥammad b. ʿAlī, *al-Futūḥāt al-makkiyya,* 4 vols., Cairo 1911; al-Ikhwān al-Ṣafāʾ, *Rasāʾil Ikhwān al-Ṣafāʾ,* Beirut 1957; al-Qazwīnī, Abū Zakariyāʾ, *ʿAjāʾib al-makhlūqāt wa-gharāʾib al-mawjūdāt,* Cairo 1956; Ṣuyūṭī, *Durr;* id., *al-Ḥabāʾik fī akhbār al-malāʾik,* Cairo 1990; id., *Laqṭ al-marjān fī aḥkām al-jānn,* Cairo 1908; Ṭabarī, *Tafsīr,* ed. Shākir.

Secondary: W. Atallah, Ǧibt and Ṭāghūt dans le Coran, in *Arabica* 17 (1970), 69-82; L. Berger, Esprits et microbes. L'interpretation des ğinn-s dans quelques commentaries coraniques du XX siècle, in *Arabica* 47 (2000), 554-62; W.S. Blackman, The *karīn* and *karīneh,* in *Journal of the Royal Anthropological Institute* 56 (1926), 163-9; C.E. Dubler, L'ancient orient dans l'Islam, in *SI* 7 (1957), 47-75; T. Fahd, Angeli, demoni e ginn in Islam, in D. Meeks et al., *Geni, angeli e demoni,* Roma 1994, 129-80; id., *Le panthéon de l'Arabie centrale à la veille de l'Hégire,* Paris 1968; G. Fartacek, Begegnungen mit Jinn, in *Anthropos* 97 (2002), 469-86; A. Gingrich, Spirits of the border, in *QSA* 13 (1995), 199-212; J. Henninger, Geisterglaude bei den vorislamischen Arabern, in *Festschrift Paul Schebesta zum* 75. *Geburtstag,* Vienna 1963, 279-316; repr. J. Henninger, *Arabica sacra,* Freiburg 1981, 118-69; G.D. Hornblower, Traces of a ka-belief in modern Egypt and old Arabia, in *IC* 1 (1927), 426-30; Cl. Huart, *Le livre de la création et de l'histoire,* 2 vols., Paris 1901; M. Iqbāl, *The reconstruction of religious thought in Islam,* ed. and annot. M.S. Sheikh, Lahore 1986; A. Khadir, *Mal, maladies, croyances et therapeutiques au Maroc,* PhD diss, Université de Bordeaux 1998; R. Köbert, Das koranische "ṭāġūt", in *Orientalia* n.s. 30 (1961), 415-16; repr. Paret (ed.), *Koran,* 281-2; G.J. Obermeyer, *Ṭāghūt, manʿ,* and *sharīʿa.* The realms of law in tribal Arabia, in W. al-Qāḍī (ed.), *Studia Arabica et Islamica. Festschrift for Iḥsān ʿAbbas on his sixtieth birthday,* Beirut 1981, 365-71; S.M. Zwemer, Animism in Islam (Hair, finger-nails and the hand), in *MW* 7 (1917), 245-55.

Spring see SEASONS

Springs and Fountains

Natural or artificial sources of water that issue from the earth and — in contrast to wells — provide running water (q.v.). There are several Arabic words for a natural spring. The most common designation is *ʿayn,* which occurs twenty-one times in the Qurʾān (with the respective dual and plural forms *ʿaynān* and *ʿuyūn;* e.g. Q 2:60; 15:45; 34:12; 55:50). The word *maʿīn* — probably of Syriac or Hebrew origin (see FOREIGN VOCABULARY) — is used four times (Q 23:50; 37:45; 56:18; 67:30); *yanbūʿ* (Q 17:90) and its plural *yanābīʿ* (Q 39:21) each appear only once. Although the Arabic term for hot springs, *ḥamma* (pl. *ḥammāt*), does not appear in the Qurʾān, *ḥamīm* is used fourteen times for the boiling water of hell (e.g. Q 6:70; 10:4; 22:19; see HELL AND HELLFIRE; REWARD AND PUNISHMENT). There is no special qurʾānic expression for artificial fountains, such as *fawwāra* (pl. *fawwārāt*) or *nāfūra* (pl. *nawāfīr*).

General characteristics

As objects of religious interest, springs are characterized above all by two aspects: on the one hand, with their life-giving water, they stand for vitality and purity; on the other hand, when considered as openings into the interior of the earth, they appear to be mysterious and strange. Especially when they are located in the immediate vicinity of other remarkable natural features, such as mountains, grottoes or trees (q.v.) — and even more so if they are hot or periodic — springs have attracted religious veneration and could persist as sacred locations even when the people living there changed (see NATURE AS SIGNS; AGRICULTURE AND VEGETATION).

The chthonic aspect often ascribed to springs appears in the widespread belief, held since time immemorial, that they are inhabited by spirits — a belief largely adopted in Islam as well (see SPIRITUAL BEINGS; JINN; DEMONS). Particularly when springs are situated in lonely, gloomy places, the inhabiting spirits are described as evil demons *(jinn; ghīlān)* who appear in the shape of animals or of seductive women. Yet other springs are associated in one way or another with saints (q.v.) and holy men, whether Christian or Muslim; in this case, the spirits *(arwāḥ)* who dwell there may be benevolent. In Greek antiquity, springs often stood under the patronage of particular gods, such as Apollo and Artemis. From Hellenistic times onward, however, hot springs were increasingly ascribed to the healing god Asclepius. According to Ibn al-Kalbī's (d. ca. 205/820) *Kitāb al-Aṣnām* (Book of Idols), it was after the legendary ʿAmr b. Luḥayy of pre-Islamic times had visited the spas of the Balqāʾ, which were associated with a cult of healing gods, that he introduced their idols in Mecca (q.v.; see also IDOLS AND IMAGES). And though Ibn al-Kalbī remains silent on this subject, it has been suggested that the female Arabic goddesses al-Lāt, Manāt and al-ʿUzzā — "the exalted cranes" *(al-gharānīq al-ʿulā)* according to the well-known story about a later abrogated Satanic inspiration (cf. commentaries on Q 53:19-20; see SATANIC VERSES; POLYTHEISM AND ATHEISM) — were originally venerated as water nymphs of some kind. Also, Ibn Isḥāq's (d. ca. 150/767) report of how ʿAbd al-Muṭṭalib, the Prophet's grandfather, found golden figurines, swords and coats of mail while excavating the shaft of the Zamzam spring can be seen as hinting at ritual offerings made at springs.

The idea of pure and vital spring water has its most influential expression in the mythical notion of the fountain of life, which provides those who drink from it with everlasting health and youth. The search for the fountain of life is the subject of countless tales and legends, including the late-antique legend of Alexander (q.v.). There is an allusion to this story in Q 18:60-4 (with Mūsā, Moses [q.v.], instead of Alexander) and it is retold at great length in several subsequent forms of Islamic literature, for example by the Persian poet Niẓāmī (fl. sixth/twelfth cent.) in his *Iskandarnāme*. The fountain of life is a familiar theme in the biblical tradition as well (see SCRIPTURE AND THE QURʾĀN; MYTHS AND LEGENDS IN THE QURʾĀN). The Psalms (e.g. *Ps* 36:9; 42:2-3) state that the fountain of life is with God; and the visions of Ezekiel 47, Zechariah 14 and John 22 describe the living water that issues from the temple in Jerusalem at the end of time. The early Christians frequently interpreted the baptismal font, the *piscina*, as *fons vitae* (cf. John 4:11 f.). The redemption obtained through baptism, on the other hand, is closely linked with the blood of Christ and, therefore, with the wine of the Eucharist. As a result, the predominant early-Byzantine symbol for the fountain of life is a goblet — itself an age-old symbol for the water-spring — with vine tendrils growing out of it, sometimes flanked by peacocks, which signify immortality. This imagery found its way into early Islam. In the mosaics in the Umayyad Dome of the Rock, goblets and tendrils adorned with pearls are one of the dominant motifs and can be read as metaphors for paradise (q.v.; for the symbolism of pearls, see Flood, *Great mosque*, 15f.). Finally, it should be remarked that these pictorial elements, viz. goblets (see CUPS AND VESSELS), pearls (see METALS AND MINERALS), vine tendrils and birds, are also features of the qur'ānic descriptions of paradise, although they appear there in a recontextualized manner — goblets *(akwāb)*: e.g. Q 43:71; 76:15; pearls *(lu'lu')*: e.g. Q 22:23; 56:23; clusters *(quṭūf)*: Q 69:23; 76:14; birds *(ṭayr)*: Q 56:21; cf. 52:22.

Springs and fountains in the qur'ānic paradise

In the Qur'ān, springs never appear as neutral natural phenomena. They are always connected with the idea of God's omnipotence (see POWER AND IMPOTENCE) and are predominantly symbols for his mercy (q.v.). This is especially clear in the qur'ānic descriptions of the landscape of paradise where springs appear as its most characteristic element. Several times, the Qur'ān promises that in the hereafter "those who show piety (q.v.) are among gardens (see GARDEN) and springs" (*inna l-muttaqīna fī jannātin wa-'uyūnin*, Q 15:45; 51:15; cf. 44:51-2; 55:50, 66; 77:41; 88:12; see ESCHATOLOGY). Still more often, paradise is referred to as "gardens underneath which rivers flow" *(jannātun tajrī min taḥtihā l-anhār)*. This usage appears some forty times (e.g. Q 2:25; 3:15; 4:13; 5:12) and implies the idea of springs as well.

The Qur'ān, however, does not give a clear picture of the design of this garden landscape, with its springs and rivers. Some passages suggest that there is only one — or at least only one distinctive — spring in paradise (Q 76:6, 18; 83:28; 88:12). For example, Q 83:25-8, in speaking about the beverage of the pious *(al-abrār)*, mentions one spring only: "They are given to drink of a wine (q.v.) sealed whose seal is musk so after that let the strivers strive and whose mixture is *tasnīm* *(wa-mizājuhu min tasnīm)*, a fountain *('ayn)* at which do drink those brought nigh *(al-muqarrabūn)*." While most commentators understand *tasnīm* as the fountain's proper name, al-Ṭabarī (d. 310/923) reports that Mujāhid (d. 104/722) and al-Kalbī (d. 146/763) explained the expression *min tasnīm* as meaning "from above." This explanation suggests a vertical concept of paradise, similar to the idea of the paradisiacal mountain, with the pious *(abrār)* dwelling below, above them "those brought nigh" *(al-muqarrabūn)*, and at the top the divine presence (see FACE OF GOD; SHEKHINAH).

This passage can be compared to Q 76:5-19. In the latter, verses 5 and 17 promise that the pious *(abrār)* will drink from a cup "whose mixture is camphor (q.v.)" and "ginger," respectively; whereas verse 6 seems to indicate that the "servants of God" *('ibād Allāh)* drink directly from that spring; and in verse 18, the spring is given the enigmatic name *salsabīl*. Although these verses contain no indication of a vertical structure of paradise, here, too, an implicit differentiation is made between the pious who drink mixed and strongly flavored beverages and another, privileged class of inhabitants of paradise, viz. the "servants of God," who have direct access to the pure divine spring (cf. Q 55:46, 62; 56:10, 27). In this context, it should be noted that only in Q 88 is the paradisiacal spring contrasted with a spring in hell: "Faces on that day humbled,... watered at a boiling fountain *('ayn āniya)*,... Faces on that day jocund,... in a sublime garden,... therein a running fountain (*'ayn jāriya*, Q 88:2-12)." Here, the dark side of springs appears as a symbol for evil and punishment (see GOOD AND EVIL; REWARD AND PUNISHMENT; CHASTISEMENT AND PUNISHMENT). This is remarkable because the polarity of paradise and hell, which is usually expressed in the Qurʾān through the polarity of water and fire (q.v.), appears here as the contrast between (cool) running and boiling (stagnant) water (see also PAIRS AND PAIRING).

Inspired by qurʾānic passages such as those mentioned above, Islamic culture commonly designates single fountains as symbols for paradise as a whole. This holds true, for example, for the basins or fountains that provide drinking water in the courtyards of mosques (see MOSQUE). (There are several designations for these basins, such as *ḥawḍ, birka* or *fisqiyya*, derived from the Latin *piscina*, the [baptismal] font, in contradistinction to the facilities for ablution, which are called *maṭāhir* or *mayāḍiʾ*; see CLEANLINESS AND ABLUTION.) It holds as well for the *asbila* (sing. *sabīl*), the public drinking fountains that were built and established as religious foundations from the sixth/twelfth century onward in some of the major cities of the Islamic world.

Q 55:46f. expresses the idea of a bipartite paradise and presents the vision of a double set of twin gardens. In describing the first pair of gardens it says: "therein two fountains of running water" (*fīhimā ʿaynāni tajriyāni*, Q 55:50). Referring to the second pair, which is situated *min dūnihim* (Q 55:62) — an expression that can either mean "below" or "besides these" two — it says: "therein two fountains of gushing water" (*fīhimā ʿaynāni naḍḍākhatāni*, Q 55:66). Although the qurʾānic text says nothing about it, the exegetical tradition (see EXEGESIS OF THE QURʾĀN: CLASSICAL AND MEDIEVAL) is nearly unanimous in declaring that a difference exists in rank between the two pairs of gardens and that the first pair is reserved for the *muqarrabūn*. According to al-Zamakhsharī (d. 538/1144), al-Ḥasan al-Baṣrī even identified the two springs therein as *salsabīl* and *tasnīm*. While it is possible that the continuous use of the dual in Q 55 is merely a stylistic means to intensify the meaning, the idea of four gardens indicated there exerted a very great influence upon later Islamic representations of paradise. This is especially true in painting and horticulture, where the *chahār bāgh* — the four-partite garden of the Achaemenid tradition, with its central basin and its four dividing canals — became the paradigm of paradise (see ART AND ARCHITECTURE AND THE QURʾĀN).

Q 47:15 contains a third important concept concerning the celestial springs and rivers: "This is the similitude of paradise (*mathalu l-jannati;* see PARABLE) which the godfearing have been promised: therein are rivers of water untainted, rivers of milk (q.v.) unchanging in flavor, and rivers of wine — a delight to the drinkers — rivers, too, of honey (q.v.) purified." The idea of four cosmic rivers that structure the world was already known to the Sumerians in the third millennium B.C.E. Genesis 2:10 adopts this notion and states that "a river went out of Eden to water the garden; and from thence it was parted, and became four heads." In the Genesis report, it is not clear whether the river's source is situated within the garden or whether the river divides into four inside of the garden or at its exit. The belief in the existence of four rivers inside paradise emerged, however, when, from exilic times onwards, the desired eschatological fate was described as a recovery of the garden of Eden. Later this became associated with the *pairidaeza* — the royal garden of the Achaemenids. In Hellenistic times, this conception was embellished by the idea that the four rivers were flavored with the tastes of milk, honey, wine and oil — sacred liquids in the ancient near east and symbols for the promised land (cf. *Lev* 2; *Num* 13:23f.). But while St. Ephraem the Syrian (fl. fourth century C.E.) mentions four kinds of paradisiacal springs, Q 47:15 speaks only of four kinds of rivers and leaves the question of their origin unanswered. Among the flavors of these rivers the "water untainted" now replaces the oil — certainly not because Muḥammad considered water necessary to dilute wine, as J. Horovitz suggested (*Das koranische Paradies*, 9), but rather because of the symbolic value inherent in living water. At any rate, the Qurʾān unmistakably characterizes this description of the rivers of paradise as a "similitude" *(mathal)* and emphasizes thereby its metaphorical dimensions (cf. Q 13:35; 24:35; see METAPHOR).

In this context, mention must be made of Q 108:1: "Surely we have given you *al-kawthar*." Many commentators understood the word *al-kawthar* to mean "the abundance" and interpreted this as "the plentitude of grace" *(al-khayr al-kathīr)* that God granted to his Prophet. According to a popular explanation (especially in connection with the story of the *miʿrāj*, Muḥammad's ascent to heaven; see ASCENSION), however, *al-kawthar* is said to be the proper name of a river in paradise or of the pool *(ḥawḍ)* into which this river flows. Of particular interest here is the way the river *al-kawthar* is usually described in exegesis: its water — more delicious than honey — is of a brighter whiteness than milk or snow, and runs over precious stones and pearls, with banks of gold (q.v.) and silver (cf. e.g. Ṭabarī, *Tafsīr;* Zamakhsharī, *Kashshāf;* Bayḍāwī, *Anwār,* ad Q 108:1). Q 37:45-6, too, clearly states that the non-intoxicating, pure paradisiacal beverage (Q 37:46-7; 56:19; 76:21) — which is wine, according to al-Ṭabarī and al-Rāzī (d. 606/1210) — has a white color *(bayḍāʾ)*.

It should be pointed out here that pearly whiteness is also the characteristic feature of the *qāṣirāt al-ṭarf ʿīn* and the *ḥūr ʿīn,* which have been traditionally understood as metaphors for the maidens awaiting the believers in paradise — "those of modest gaze, with lovely eyes" and as "fair ones with wide, lovely eyes," respectively (for an opposing interpretation, see Luxenberg, *Syro-aramäische Lesart,* 221f.; see HOURIS). The *qāṣirāt al-ṭarf ʿīn* are likened to hidden white objects (*bayḍ maknūn,* Q 37:49), pearls or eggs, and the *ḥūr ʿīn* are described "as the likeness of hidden pearls" *(al-luʾluʾ al-maknūn,* Q 56:23). In addition, the Arabic root *ḥ-w-r* that underlies the word *ḥūr* carries the meaning "whiteness," and *ʿīn* (derived from *ʿayn,* denoting either "spring" or "eye") implies the idea of shimmering and brightness as well. In ḥadīth and later Islamic literature (see ḤADĪTH AND THE QURʾĀN), this paradisiacal feature of pearly white shininess was enriched with the biblical vision of paradise as a garden of precious stones and metals (*Jes* 54:11-12; *Ez* 28:13-14; cf. *Rev* 21:10f.) — a vision that not only underscores the beauty of paradise but emphasizes its everlastingness as well (see ETERNITY). (In passing, reference can be made here to the use of rock-crystal in Islamic art: as a working material, it simultaneously stands for water and light and was therefore considered apt to symbolize God as the fountain of life and as the "light upon light" of Q 24:35; see LIFE; LIGHT.)

Given the varying glimpses of the paradisiacal landscape in the Qurʾān, it is not surprising that Islamic theology elaborated at least three different conceptions of it (see THEOLOGY AND THE QURʾĀN): paradise as one extensive park, paradise as four neighboring gardens, or paradise consisting of seven concentric and ascending circles. In each conception of paradise particular importance is imputed to its springs, which, by virtue of their hidden origin, point to another, transcendent dimension. One group of traditions locates the sources of the four rivers of paradise at the foot of the *sidrat al-muntahā,* the "lote-tree of the boundary," in the seventh heaven below God's throne (see al-Ṭabarī, *Tafsīr,* ad Q 53:14; see THRONE OF GOD). The idea of the divine origin of the paradisiacal springs also finds its appropriate expression in a later tradition that relates how, during the *miʿrāj,* the prophet Muḥammad is shown a huge cupola made from a white pearl *(min durra bayḍāʾ),* from whose four corners the four rivers of paradise flow. Entering the cupola, the Prophet sees that over its corners the *basmala* (q.v.) is written in such a way that the river of water springs from the letter *mīm* of the *bi-ism,* the river of milk from the *hāʾ* of *Allāh,* the river of wine from the *mīm* of *al-raḥmān* and the river of honey from the *mīm* of *al-raḥīm* (see Qāḍī, *Daqāʾiq,* 107f.; see GOD AND HIS ATTRIBUTES).

Qurʾānic cosmology and springs

Paradise is connected with earth (q.v.), and cosmology (q.v.) explains how. Following the ancient near east tradition all the way back to *Enuma elish,* the Babylonian myth of creation (q.v.; cf. also *Gen* 1:6-7), the Qurʾān assumes the existence of two oceans that surround the cosmos, one of sweet *(ʿadhb furāt),* the other of salt *(milḥ ujāj)* water (Q 25:53; 35:12; cf. 27:61). The clearest qurʾānic traces of the idea that the cosmos was created by dividing these primeval waters can be found in references to the deluge. There, it is stated that the destruction of the cosmos took place in reverse order of its creation, namely by the reuniting of the upper and lower ocean: "Then we opened the gates of heaven to water torrential, and made the earth gush with fountains *(wa-fajjarnā l-arḍa ʿuyūnan),* and the waters met for a matter decreed" (Q 54:11-12; cf. 11:44; 21:30 and *Gen* 7:11). According to two other verses (Q 11:40; 23:27) the flood began when "the oven boiled *(fāra l-tannūr).*" Most Muslim commentators explained this expression by saying that the water flowing out of his oven was the sign for Noah (q.v.) to embark; yet at its root lies the rabbinic conviction that the waters of the flood were boiling hot, like hell (cf. above at Q 88:5).

In the Ugaritic Baal mythology, the salty ocean represents the chaotic monster "Yamm," who threatens the gods (cf. *Ps* 93). Also, although the Qurʾān stresses that God exerts his control over both oceans by setting "between them a barrier (q.v.), and a ban forbidden" (Q 25:53), it may be considered a reminiscence of Ugarit, that the word *yamm* in the Qurʾān always denotes the sea in its negative aspects (e.g. Q 7:136; 20:39, 78, 97). Since, according to the qurʾānic cosmology, the salt-water ocean consists of the terrestrial sea, the sweet-water ocean must be located above the firmament where paradise is also situated, as H. Toelle (*Le Coran revisité,* 124-6) has pointed out. Even though the Qurʾān remains silent about the precise spatial relationship of paradise on the one hand and of the sweet water ocean on the other, paradise is characterized by the element of sweet water, and the celestial ocean in turn bears paradisiacal traits. From above, God sends down water which is blessed (Q 50:9; cf. 7:96), pure (Q 25:48) and purifying (Q 8:11) and which makes gardens flourish, whose description is reminiscent of the gardens of paradise (Q 23:19; 50:9-11). This is in contrast to Genesis 2:10-14, where the four rivers of paradise, especially the Tigris and the Euphrates, actually translate paradise to earth. Here, according to the Qurʾān, it is the rain that safeguards this connection. And since rain is the reason for springs to gush forth and for valleys to flow (Q 13:17; 23:18-20; 39:21), both springs and rivers are, although indirectly, of paradisiacal origin, too.

In the Islamic tradition, another concept for the connection of paradise and earth is that of the navel. This theory centers on the idea that one place on earth is distinguished as the point of contact to the upper world. In early Islam, this navel was identified as the rock in Jerusalem (q.v.); later on it was transferred to the Kaʿba (q.v.) in Mecca. Thus, according to Kaʿb al-Aḥbār (d. ca. 32/652-3), each source of sweet water on earth originates below the rock in Jerusalem. A similar idea evolved concerning Zamzam in the Kaʿba district. Yāqūt (d. 626/1229) relates that when Zamzam first gushed out to save Ishmael (q.v.; Ismāʿīl) and Hagar (Hājar), it was a spring, and had Hagar not built an enclosure around it, its waters would have flooded the whole earth. Ibn Jubayr (d. 614/1217; *Travels*, 139, ll. 12f.), in turn, reports that upon his visit to Mecca in 579/1183, pilgrims believed that on *laylat al-barāʾa*, the "night of repentance" following the 14th of Shaʿbān, when God descends to the lowest heaven to forgive the repentant sinners (see FORGIVENESS; REPENTANCE AND PENANCE), the water level of Zamzam will rise. Finally, Zamzam is thought to have a subterranean connection with other springs. Yāqūt reports the popular belief that each year on the day of ʿArafāt (q.v.), the 9th of Dhū l-Ḥijja, the spring in Sulwān, a spot in the environs of Jerusalem, is "visited" by the water of Zamzam. Likewise, at the beginning of the last century, it was still a widespread belief that on the 10th of Muḥarram, the day of ʿĀshūrāʾ (see FASTING; RAMAḌĀN), Zamzam water combines with the springs of Ḥammām al-Shifā in Palestine.

As symbols for paradise on earth, springs are considered signs of God's blessings for humankind (see BLESSING). Time and again, the Qurʾān admonishes people to be thankful for this (Q 2:74; 26:134, 147; 36:33-5; 39:21). If, however, man proves to be ungrateful (see GRATITUDE AND INGRATITUDE; BELIEF AND UNBELIEF), God may expel him from the springs or cause the springs to dry up (cf. Q 2:266; 18:32-46; 23:18-20; 26:57; 44:25; 67:30). In addition, springs appear as marks of distinction for persons important in salvation (q.v.) history (see HISTORY AND THE QURʾĀN): at God's command Moses (q.v.) strikes the rock with his staff (see ROD) and twelve springs gush out (*ʿayn*, Q 2:60; 7:160). God makes the "fount of molten brass" flow for Solomon (q.v.; *ʿayna l-qiṭr*, Q 34:12; cf. 1 *Kings* 7:23f.). When Mary (q.v.) — leaning against the trunk of a palm (see DATE PALM) and surprised by birth pangs — cries in despair (q.v.), [a voice] "below her" calls to her, "No, do not sorrow; [see] your lord (q.v.) has set below you a rivulet" (*sariyyan*, Q 19:24). Both Mary and Jesus (q.v.) are given refuge upon "a height with a secure abode and a spring" (*maʿīn*, Q 23:50). Finally, the unbelievers' demand that the Prophet legitimate his mission by making a spring gush (*yanbūʿ*, Q 17:90-1) can be seen in this context as well (see MIRACLES; MARVELS; OPPOSITION TO MUḤAMMAD; PROVOCATION).

Matthias Radscheit

Bibliography
Primary: Bayḍāwī, *Anwār;* J.Chr. Bürgel (trans.), *Nizami, Das Alexanderbuch. Iskandarname,* Zürich 1991, 369-87; Ibn Isḥāq, *Sīra,* ed. M.M. ʿAbd al-Ḥamīd, 4 vols., Cairo n.d., i, 154-8; Ibn Jubayr, *The travels of Ibn Jubayr. Edited from a manuscript in the University Library of Leyden,* ed. W. Wright, 2nd rvs. ed. M.J. deGoeje, Leiden 1907; Ibn al-Kalbī, Abū l-Mundhir Hishām b. Muḥammad, *Kitāb al-Aṣnām,* ed. A. Zakī, Cairo 1384/1965; al-Qāḍī, ʿAbd al-Raḥīm b. Aḥmad, *Daqāʾiq al-akhbār fī dhikr al-janna wa-l-nār,* ed. and German trans. M. Wolf, *Muhammedanische Eschatologie,* Leipzig 1872; Rāzī, *Tafsīr;* Ṭabarī, *Tafsīr;* Yāqūt, *Buldān,* ed. Wüstenfeld; Zamakhsharī, *Kashshāf.*
Secondary: M.A.S. Abdel Haleem, Water in the Qurʾān, in H. Abdel Haleem (ed.), *Islam and the environment,* London 1998, 103-17; A. Ambros,

Gestaltung und Funktion der Biosphäre im Koran, in ZDMG 140 (1990), 290-325; N. Ardalan, The paradise garden paradigm, in S.J. Ishtiyān et al. (eds.), *Consciousness and reality. Studies in memory of Toshihiko Izutsu*, Leiden 2000, 97-127; H.J.D. Astley, A sacred spring and tree at Hammam R'Irha, Algeria, in *Man* 10 (1910), 122-3; J. Brookes, *Gardens of paradise*, London 1987; T. Canaan, Haunted springs and water demons in Palestine, in *Journal of the Palestine Oriental Society* 1 (1920-1), 153-70; E. Clark, *Underneath which rivers flow. The symbolism of the Islamic garden*, London 1996; Clermont-Ganneau, La lampe et l'olivier dans le Coran, in *Revue de l'histoire des religions* 81 (1920), 213-59; J.H. Croon, Hot springs and healing gods, in *Mnemosyne* 4/20 (1967), 225-46; M. Eliade, *Die Religionen und das Heilige*, Frankfurt 1998, 219-48; G. Fartacek, *Pilgerstätten in der syrischen Peripherie*, Vienna 2003, 152f.; F.B. Flood, *The great mosque of Damascus. Studies on the making of an Umayyad visual culture*, Leiden 2001; P. Franke, *Begegnung mit Khidr. Quellenstudien zum Imaginären im traditionellen Islam*, Beirut 2000, 45-52; O. Grabar, The Dome of the Rock in Jerusalem, in S. Nuseibeh, *The Dome of the Rock*, New York 1996, 12-70; H. Halbfas, Der Paradiesgarten, in U. Heindrichs and H.-A. Heindrichs (eds.), *Zauber Märchen. Forschungsberichte aus der Welt der Märchen*, München 1998, 45-52; J. Horovitz, *Das koranische Paradies*, Jerusalem 1923; Jeffery, *For. vocab.*; I. Lichtenstaedter, A note on the "gharānīq" and related qurʾānic problems, in IOS 5 (1976), 54-61; Ch. Luxenberg, *Die syro-aramäische Lesart des Koran. Ein Beitrag zur Entschlüsselung der Koransprache*, Berlin 2000, 221-69; J.D. McAuliffe, The wines of earth and paradise. Qurʾānic proscriptions and promises, in R.M. Savory and D.A. Agius (eds.), *Logos Islamikos. Studia Islamica in honorem Georgii Michaelis Wickens*, Toronto 1984, 159-74; S.L. Mostafa, The Cairene *sabīl*. Form and meaning, in *Muqarnas* 6 (1989), 33-42; E.B. Moynihan, *Paradise as garden in Persia and Mughal India*, New York 1979; W. Müller, *Die heilige Stadt. Roma quadrata, himmlisches Jerusalem und die Mythe vom Weltnabel*, Stuttgart 1961; A. Neuwirth, Symmetrie und Paarbildung in der koranischen Eschatologie. Philologisch-stilistisches zu *Sūrat ar-Raḥmān*, in MFOB 50 (1984), 445-80; A. Petruccioli (ed.), *Der islamische Garten*, Stuttgart 1995; M. Radscheit, The iconography of the Qurʾān, in Chr. Szyska and Fr. Pannewick (eds.), *Crossings and passages in genre and culture*, Wiesbaden 2003, 167-83; A. Roman, *Une vision humaine des fins dernières. Le* Kitāb al-Tawahhum *d'al Muḥāsibī*, Paris 1978; M. Rosen-Ayalon, On Suleiman's *sabīls* in Jerusalem, in C.E. Bosworth et al. (eds.), *The Islamic world*, Princeton 1989, 589-607; B. Schrieke, Die Himmelsreise Muhammeds, in *Der Islam* 6 (1916), 1-30; N. Sed, Les hymnes sur le paradis de Saint Ephrem et les traditions juives, in *Muséon* 81 (1968), 455-501; A. Shalem, Fountains of light. The meaning of medieval Islamic rock crystal lamps, in *Muqarnas* 11 (1994), 1-11; Speyer, *Erzählungen*; H. Toelle, *Le Coran revisité. Le feu, l'eau, l'air et la terre*, Damascus 1999; P. Underwood, The fountain of life in manuscripts of the Gospels, in *Dumbarton Oaks papers* 5 (1950), 41-138; A.J. Wensinck, *The ideas of the western Semites concerning the navel of the earth*, Amsterdam 1916.

Staff see ROD

Stages of Life see BIOLOGY AS THE CREATION AND STAGES OF LIFE

Stars see PLANETS AND STARS; PARADISE

Station of Abraham see PLACE OF ABRAHAM

Statue see IDOLS AND IMAGES

Steadfast see TRUST AND PATIENCE

Steal see THEFT

Stone

Concreted earthy or mineral matter. Stone, *ḥajar* (pl. *ḥijāra*), attested in eleven verses of the Qurʾān, is never mentioned as part of the landscape or as a natural object; it is used as a symbol or a metaphor (q.v.) whose meaning is patterned by the intertextual relations between the stone motifs in the Qurʾān and the Bible (see SCRIPTURE AND THE QURʾĀN; SYMBOLIC IMAGERY). The image of the stone appears in the Qurʾān at the same time that biblical images, narratives (q.v.) and persons, which are virtually absent from the early sūras, flood the text (see CHRONOLOGY AND THE

QUR'ĀN). Most of the mentions are found in the late Meccan sūras and the Medinan sūras (see MECCA; MEDINA).

The *ḥajar*-contexts can be divided into two groups: 1) those related to the idea of stoning (q.v.; five occurrences); 2) those with a different symbolic weight (six occurrences). The first group is very homogeneous in meaning. All the contexts (Q 8:32; 11:82; 15:74; 51:33; 105:4) convey one and the same idea, that of God's direct punishment of sinners (see SIN, MAJOR AND MINOR) and infidels (see BELIEF AND UNBELIEF) by throwing stones from the sky. This has a clear biblical prototype (*Josh* 19:8-10; see CHASTISEMENT AND PUNISHMENT; PUNISHMENT STORIES). The main difference between the Bible and the Qur'ān with respect to this motif is that the qur'ānic stones for punishment are made of clay (q.v.). This would be impossible for the Hebrew Bible, where clay and stone constitute the opposition between a natural substance and a material symbolically intertwined with the idea of the chosen people (see ELECTION). The qur'ānic image of clay stones marked with inscriptions (*ḥijāratan min musawwamatan*, Q 51:33-4; *ḥijāra min sijjīl*, Q 11:82; 15:74; 105:4) recalls clay tablets with cuneiform inscriptions from Mesopotamia and hints at its Mesopotamian, not biblical, background. The second group of mentions is centered on the opposition between life (q.v.) and death (see DEATH AND THE DEAD; PAIRS AND PAIRING) — where stone is a metaphor for the dead matter — and the possibility of overcoming this opposition by God's omnipotence (see POWER AND IMPOTENCE). Two instances (Q 2:60; 7:160) are reminiscences of the biblical story of Moses (q.v.), who struck water (q.v.) from the stone with his rod (q.v.; *Exod* 17:5-6) and thus produced life (water) from dead matter with the lord's (q.v.) help. Conversely, Q 2:74, also placed within the framework of the story of Moses, asserts that live matter (e.g. the hearts of unbelievers; see HEART; BELIEF AND UNBELIEF) can turn into dead matter (stones) if they do not have faith (q.v.) and, on the contrary, stones can become alive and produce water if they fear (q.v.) God (cf. the motif of "hearts of stone" in the Bible: 1 *Sam* 20:37; *Job* 41:16; *Ezek* 11:19; 36:26; *Zech* 7:12; cf. also Q 2:264 for a very close motif in the Qur'ān but without stone). Along the same lines, Q 17:50 expressly asserts God's ability to resurrect people (see RESURRECTION) even if they became stones and has a direct parallel in the New Testament (*Matt* 3:9). The remaining instances (Q 2:24; 66:6) speak about people and stones as fuel for the fire of hell (see HELL AND HELLFIRE), and thus once more show that God's might is able to transcend such opposites (cf. a parallel to this motif in the Bible: 1 Kings 18:31-8).

Dmitry V. Frolov

Bibliography
Primary: Ibn Kathīr, *Tafsīr; Jalālayn; Lisān al-ʿArab* (for further details on the usage and meaning of the term); Suyūṭī, *Durr;* Ṭabarī, *Tafsīr;* Zamakhsharī, *Kashshāf.*
Secondary: J. Chabbi, *Le seigneur des tribus. L'Islam de Mahomet,* Paris 1997, 625-6; H. Toelle, *Le Coran revisité. Le feu, l'eau, l'air et la terre,* Damascus 1999, 111-12.

Stoning

A capital punishment for grave sins attested in the ancient Near East from time immemorial, representing part of the biblical legacy in the Qur'ān (see SCRIPTURE AND THE QUR'ĀN). The motif of stoning is expressed in two ways in the Qur'ān. It is either the verb *rajama*, "to stone" (equivalent to the biblical *ragam*), and its derivatives (thirteen occurrences); or verbs that convey the idea of "throwing, showering, sending down" *(ramā, amṭara, arsala),* with *ḥajar,* "stone" (q.v.), as an instrumental complement (five occurrences).

The punishment of stoning occurs in four different situations in the Qurʾān and the origin of most of them can be traced back to the Bible. The first is the punishment inflicted from the sky by the lord (q.v.) on his enemies (q.v.) expressed exclusively by a verbal phrase with *ḥajar* as a complement (see CHASTISEMENT AND PUNISHMENT; PUNISHMENT STORIES). It has evident biblical connotations as three of the five contexts which depict this are part of the story of Abraham (q.v.; Ibrāhīm) and Lot (q.v.; Lūṭ; Q 11:82-3; 15:74; 51:33) as well as a direct prototype in the Bible (*Josh* 19:8-10). The two remaining contexts are related to the biography and mission of Muḥammad (see Q 8:32; 105:4; see SĪRA AND THE QURʾĀN), including the episode of a miraculous punishment from the sky visited upon the "companions of the elephant," or the invaders from south Arabia who intended to conquer Mecca (q.v.; see also ABRAHA; PEOPLE OF THE ELEPHANT). In a second, variant occurrence God inflicts punishment by stoning not only people but also the devil (q.v.; *shayṭān*) and his army. This act of the lord, which has no parallels in the Bible, emerges as part of the story of the creation (q.v.) of humankind (Q 15:16-17; 67:5) and connotes the eternal condemnation of Satan. This narrative in turn gives birth to a well-known epithet of the devil, namely *rajīm* (stoned; Q 3:36; 16:98; 81:25) and to a ritual of stoning during the pilgrimage (q.v.) to Mecca. Its relation to the first situation is shown by the contexts where devils are stoned from the sky with projectiles in the form of the fallen stars (Q 15:17; 67:5). The third incident is opposed to the first two. The stoning or the threat of stoning of the prophets and the believers by the infidels is attested both in the Bible (*Exod* 8:25-6) and the Qurʾān, where this occurs not only in the story of Moses (q.v.; Mūsā; Q 44:20) but also in the story of Noah (q.v.; Nūḥ; Q 26:116), Abraham (Q 19:46) and Shuʿayb (q.v.; Q 11:91; see also Q 18:20; 36:18; see also BELIEF AND UNBELIEF; PROPHETS AND PROPHETHOOD). The most paradoxical situation has to do with the fourth situation which, according to Muslim tradition, is present in the qurʾānic text "virtually," not actually. Stoning as the capital punishment prescribed by the law for certain major crimes (see SIN, MAJOR AND MINOR), which is very frequent in the Bible, is absent from the *textus receptus* of the qurʾānic vulgate (see CODICES OF THE QURʾĀN; COLLECTION OF THE QURʾĀN). Muslim scholars nevertheless postulate the existence of a qurʾānic verse which has been "abrogated" *(mansūkh;* see ABROGATION) textually but still remains one of the foundations of Muslim law (see LAW AND THE QURʾĀN): "If a man or a woman commits adultery, stone them…" (on this "stoning verse," see Suyūṭī, *Itqān* [chap. 47], iii, 82; Nöldeke, *GQ*, i, 248-52; Burton, *Collection,* 70-80, 89-96 and passim; see also ADULTERY AND FORNICATION).

Dmitry V. Frolov

Bibliography
Primary: Ibn Kathīr, *Tafsīr; Jalālayn; Lisān al-ʿArab* (for further details on the usage and meaning of the term); Suyūṭī, *Durr;* id., *Itqān;* Ṭabarī, *Tafsīr;* id., *Tahdhīb al-āthār. Musnad ʿUmar b. al-Khaṭṭāb,* ed. M. Shākir, 3 vols., Cairo 1983, ii, 870-80 (for many traditions on the "stoning verse," *āyat al-rajm*); Zamakhsharī, *Kashshāf.*
Secondary: Burton, *Collection;* id., *The sources of Islamic law. Islamic theories of abrogation,* Edinburgh 1990; Nöldeke, *GQ.*

Storm
see WEATHER

Story
see NARRATIVES; JOSEPH

Straight Path

see PATH OR WAY; ASTRAY; ERROR; COMMUNITY AND SOCIETY IN THE QUR'ĀN

Strangers and Foreigners

Those who are away from their usual place of residence and find themselves among people who view them as outsiders. In this sense, stranger and foreigner are social categories whose referent cannot be fixed but will vary according to time, place and culture. In medieval Arabic, Persian and Turkish, both categories were best expressed by the term *gharīb*, which, however, does not occur in the Qur'ān. *Ajnabī*, a term that has come to mean "foreigner" in all three languages especially in the era of modern nation-states, is also absent from the Qur'ān but it is represented in the forms *al-jār al-junubi* and *al-ṣāḥib bi-l-janbi* in Q 4:36 mentioned among categories of people that are to be shown kindness (see LOVE; MERCY). Most commentators are agreed that the former phrase should be understood as the opposite of the phrase *al-jār dhī l-qurbā*, "near or related neighbor," that precedes it in the verse (see KINSHIP). Al-Ṭabarī (d. 310/923; *Tafsīr*, iv, 82-3) reports "unrelated neighbor" and "neighbor who is a *mushrik* (see POLYTHEISM AND ATHEISM)" as the two alternative readings for *al-jār al-junubi*, and he himself opts for "unrelated stranger" as the best reading (translation of key passage in Rosenthal, Stranger, 39-40). Al-Bayḍāwī (d. prob. 716/1316-17; *Anwār*, i, 214) and, following him, the modern Turkish exegete Elmalılı (*Kur'ān Dili*, ii, 1354-5) simply read the two phrases *al-jār dhī l-qurbā* and *al-jār al-junubi* to mean "near [i.e. related and/or close] neighbor" and "far [i.e. unrelated and/or far] neighbor" respectively, and linked them to the following ḥadīth (which does not appear in the six canonical collections [see ḤADĪTH AND THE QUR'ĀN], but is attributed to a Companion of the Prophet in a number of other works; see COMPANIONS OF THE PROPHET; cf. Zabīdī, *Itḥāf*, vii, 268; Daylamī, *Firdaws*, ii, 120, no. 2628; see also Ghazālī, *Iḥyā'*, ii, 231):

> There are three [kinds of] neighbors. The first [i.e. the Muslim who is both a neighbor and a relative] has three rights: the right of proximity, the right of relatedness, the rights accorded him on account of being a Muslim. The second [i.e. the non-related Muslim who is a neighbor] has two rights: the right of proximity and the right of being a Muslim. And the third [i.e. the neighbor who is neither Muslim nor a relative] has one right: the right of proximity, and these are *mushriks* [and *ahl al-kitāb*].

As for the qur'ānic phrase *al-ṣāḥib bi-l-janbi*, it is not clear whether it should be read in conjunction with what precedes it (which is the phrase *al-jār al-junubi*) or in isolation from what surrounds it. The first alternative would seem to be ruled out by the conjoined reading of the two preceding phrases as "near and far neighbors," while the second alternative is picked up by al-Ṭabarī (*Tafsīr*, iv, 83-4), who lists the meanings "travel companion (see TRIPS AND VOYAGES; JOURNEY)," "a man's female companion," and "friend, comrade," and endorses all of them. Whatever their exact meanings may be, however, it is clear that of the two phrases *al-jār al-junubi* and *al-ṣāḥib bi-l-janbi*, only the former may perhaps be slightly relevant to a discussion of strangers in the Qur'ān and neither expression really refers to those away from their usual place of residence.

Another qur'ānic locus for the concept of

foreignness might be the term *aʿjamī*, meaning "non-Arab" and "non-Arabic" (see ARABS). The term is used in Q 16:103, 41:44 and 26:198 but in all three instances the element of linguistic differentiation seems to be foregrounded and it is difficult to see anything other than an attempt to emphasize the inimitability (q.v.) of the Qurʾān. A better candidate for a qurʾānic approximation to the concept "stranger," however, is the phrase *ibn al-sabīl*, meaning "traveler," "wayfarer," or, though only secondarily, "guest," which is mentioned eight times in the Qurʾān (Q 2:177, 215; 4:36 [where it follows the phrase *al-ṣāḥib bi-l-janbi* discussed above]; 8:41; 9:60; 17:26; 30:38; 59:7) always as one of the many different social categories listed as recipients of charity. Arguably, the traveler is the stranger *par excellence;* the Qurʾān can be said to endorse travel (Q 20:53: "He spread out the earth for you and lined it up with roads," and Q 67:15: "It is he who has made the earth manageable for you, so travel its regions") and designates the traveler as deserving of charity and kind treatment. Thus it is possible to see here a genuine concern for the welfare of strangers, which would be in keeping with the qurʾānic insistence on social justice (see JUSTICE AND INJUSTICE; OPPRESSED ON EARTH, THE; OPPRESSION).

Finally, while not necessarily falling into the category of "strangers" as "outsiders," "guests" — and their proper treatment — also appear in the qurʾānic discourse (see VISITING; HOSPITALITY AND COURTESY). The "honored guests of Abraham" (*ḍayf ibrāhīm al-mukramīna,* Q 51:24; cf. 15:51) figure in four qurʾānic narratives (q.v.; Q 11:69f.; 15:51f.; 29:31f.; 51:24f.), in which Abraham (q.v.) is portrayed as the host *par excellence,* much as in the biblical account (see SCRIPTURE AND THE QURʾĀN). In these narratives, both Abraham and Lot (q.v.) fear lest their guests be dishonored and mistreated (cf. esp. Q 11:78; 15:68; 54:37), echoing the qurʾānic exhortation to proper treatment of visitors (and, by extension, foreigners).

Ahmet T. Karamustafa

Bibliography
Primary: Bayḍāwī, *Anwār;* Daylamī, Shīrawayh b. Shahradār, *al-Firdaws al-akhbār bi-maʾthūr al-khiṭāb,* ed. S. Zaghlūl, 5 vols., Beirut 1986; Elmalılı Muhammed Hamdi Yazır, *Hak Dīni Kurʾān Dili,* 9 vols., Istanbul 1935-9; al-Ghazālī, Abū Ḥāmid Muḥammad, *Iḥyāʾ ʿulūm al-dīn,* 5 vols., Beirut 1996; Ṭabarī, *Tafsīr,* 12 vols., Beirut 1992; Murtaḍā al-Zabīdī, Muḥammad b. Muḥammad, *Kitāb Itḥāf al-sāda al-muttaqīn bi-Sharḥ Iḥyāʾ ʿulūm al-dīn,* 14 vols., Beirut 1989; Zamakhsharī, *Kashshāf,* 4 vols., Beirut 1995.
Secondary: F. Rosenthal, The stranger in medieval Islam, in *Arabica* 44 (1997), 35-75.

Straw see GRASSES

Style (of the Qurʾān) see LANGUAGE AND STYLE OF THE QURʾĀN; RHETORIC AND THE QURʾĀN

Submission see FAITH; ISLAM

Suckling see CHILDREN; LACTATION; WET-NURSING

Suffering

Pain, distress or injury, and the endurance of pain, distress or injury. The noun "pain" (*alam* or *wajaʿ*) does not occur in the Qurʾān. The verb "to feel pain" *(alima)* is used only three times, all in the same verse (Q 4:104), in which it refers to suffering in warfare. The adjective "painful" *(alīm),* a derivation of the same root *(ʾ-l-m),* is more commonly used. It occurs seventy-two times, mostly in combination with the word "punishment" *(ʿadhāb).*

With the exception of Q 36:18, the

expression "painful punishment" (*ʿadhāb alīm*) relates to punishment from God (see CHASTISEMENT AND PUNISHMENT; REWARD AND PUNISHMENT). "My punishment is the painful punishment" (Q 15:50). Sometimes, the content of this punishment is mentioned. It is a wind that destroys everything (Q 46:24; see AIR AND WIND), smoke (q.v.) that covers the people (Q 44:10-11) or punishment in hell (Q 5:36; see HELL AND HELLFIRE). That the punishments in hell will be very painful can be concluded from their descriptions in the Qurʾān (e.g. Q 4:56; 9:35; 18:29; 22:19-21; 56:42-4). People in hell will undergo intense pain and suffering. They will sigh and groan (Q 11:106), distort their burnt faces (Q 23:104) and be distressed and despairing (Q 22:22; 43:75).

Part of God's punishment may be given in advance in this world (Q 24:19; 9:74). According to the qurʾānic punishment narratives (q.v.; see also PUNISHMENT STORIES), God has already punished unbelieving peoples by sending a flood (*ṭūfān*, Q 29:14), an earthquake (*rajfa*, Q 29:37), a violent storm (*ḥāṣib*, Q 29:40) or a roaring wind (*rīḥ ṣarṣar*, Q 69:6; see WEATHER). These calamities annihilated the unbelievers because of their persistence in unbelief after a prophet had warned them (see BELIEF AND UNBELIEF; PROPHETS AND PROPHETHOOD; WARNING). God's sending of a prophet may be accompanied by calamities that support the prophet's warning, so that the unbelievers will abandon their sins (Q 6:42; 7:94; 32:21-2; see SIN, MAJOR AND MINOR). This happened to the people of Egypt (q.v.). God sent them calamities as a warning, but when they did not heed these warnings and persevered in their sins, God drowned them in the sea (Q 7:133-6; see DROWNING).

Other afflictions and calamities are not meant to be punishments but trials (see TRIAL). God tests (*yablū*) the people's belief by giving them either welfare or adversity (Q 5:48; 6:165; 21:35; see GRACE; BLESSING; TRUST AND PATIENCE) because he wants to know how they behave in prosperity and in adversity (Q 47:31; 67:2). For this purpose, he has created earth (q.v.), life (q.v.), death (see DEATH AND THE DEAD), and people themselves (Q 11:7; 18:7; 67:2; 76:2; see CREATION). God tries them by restricting their sustenance (q.v.; Q 89:16). He imposes hunger (see FAMINE), poverty (see POVERTY AND THE POOR), and the loss of property (q.v.), lives and crops upon them to test them (Q 2:155). Being tried by these afflictions, people should show their belief in God by patient endurance (Q 2:156, 177; 22:35; 31:17).

Forms of suffering connected to human existence are the undergoing of illness, pain and infirmities (see ILLNESS AND HEALTH). In the Qurʾān some illnesses and infirmities are mentioned without being indicated as trials or punishments from God. Abraham (q.v.) referred to illness when he said that God gave him health when he was ill (Q 26:80). Leprosy and blindness are mentioned in Q 3:49 and Q 5:110, where it is said that Jesus (q.v.) healed the leper and those born blind (see SEEING AND HEARING; VISION AND BLINDNESS; MIRACLES; MARVELS). Q 22:5 refers to the infirmities of old age, stating that humans lose their knowledge (see KNOWLEDGE AND LEARNING) when they grow old (see YOUTH AND OLD AGE). The pains of childbirth are mentioned in Q 19:23, where it says Mary (q.v.) underwent them (see BIOLOGY AS THE CREATION AND STAGES OF LIFE). Blindness and other infirmities are mentioned when it is said that the blind, the cripple and the sick are excused for not being able to fulfill all their duties (e.g. Q 24:61; 48:17). There is no indication that these illnesses and infirmities are a punishment from God. An exception may be the blindness of Lot's (q.v.) people, whose eyes (q.v.) God effaced. This was a punishment and a warning (Q 54:37). The terms illness, blindness and deafness (see HEARING AND DEAFNESS) are, however, often used metaphorically in the sense of wavering in belief or failing to heed a prophet's message (see METAPHOR).

An example of suffering which is a trial imposed by God is that endured by prophets, a group who cannot have deserved punishment. We have already seen that Abraham suffered illness. An often-cited example of patient suffering is Job (q.v.), whose suffering was not from God but Satan (Q 21:83; 38:41; see DEVIL). According to the exegetes, however, this was done with God's permission. When Job endured affliction without losing his belief in God, God rewarded him by taking away the affliction, returning his family and doubling their number (Q 21:84; 38:42-3). Another prophet who suffered was Jacob (q.v.), who was told that his son Joseph (q.v.) had been killed by a wolf (Q 12:16-18). He patiently endured the loss of his son, although he became blind because of his distress (Q 12:84). Later he found out that Joseph had not died and he regained his sight (Q 12:96).

Job and Jacob suffered both mentally and physically but the suffering of other prophets was largely mental. They suffered distress, being called liars (see LIE) and being rejected by the unbelievers (Q 6:34; 14:12). This also happened to Muḥammad (see OPPOSITION TO MUḤAMMAD). He was distressed and depressed because of what the unbelievers said to him (Q 6:33; 15:97) and their unbelief caused him great sorrow. "Perhaps you [Muḥammad] will kill yourself with grief *(asaf)*, because they do not believe in this message" (Q 18:6; cf. 26:3; see JOY AND MISERY). God told him not to grieve (Q 5:41; 10:65; 27:70; 31:23; 36:76) but to endure patiently (Q 16:127; 20:130; 73:10). Just like Muḥammad, the believers should patiently endure distress and affliction (e.g. Q 3:200). If they hold out and keep to their belief in God in difficult situations, God will reward them (Q 23:111; 25:75; 33:35; 76:12). He will even double their reward (Q 28:54) and remit the bad actions of those who suffered because of their religion (Q 3:195).

More details about suffering can be found in the ḥadīth (see ḤADĪTH AND THE QUR'ĀN). It is reported that Muḥammad said that for each harm that a Muslim meets in the form of illness, tiredness, sorrow, distress and pain, "even if it were the prick of a thorn," God will grant remission of some of his or her sins (Bukhārī, *Ṣaḥīḥ,* bk. 75, *K. Marḍā,* 1/1, iv, 40; Fr. trans. iv, 50; and 2/2, iv, 41; trans. iv, 51). As God does not punish twice and some sins are already paid for by suffering imposed by him, they will not be counted on the last day (see LAST JUDGMENT). Suffering is also seen as a trial from God. Those who patiently endure it will be generously rewarded. A ḥadīth *qudsī* (prophetic dictum attributed to God that is not in the Qur'ān) says that when God tests a Muslim by depriving him of his eyes, and he patiently undergoes it, he will enter paradise (q.v.) as compensation (Bukhārī, *Ṣaḥīḥ,* bk. 75, 7, iv, 42; Fr. trans. iv, 52-3). God's imposition of illness and pain can be seen as a sign of his special attention or as a favor. Only those who suffer get the opportunity to practice patient endurance. Abū Hurayra (d. ca. 58/678) reported that Muḥammad said: "If God wants to do good to somebody, he afflicts him with trials" (Bukhārī, *Ṣaḥīḥ,* bk. 75, 1/5, iv, 41; Fr. trans. iv, 51, which contains an alternative reading of the final phrase: "Celui à qui Dieu veut du bien réussit toujours à l'obtenir"; cf. Ibn Ḥajar, *Fatḥ,* x, 108 for both readings). A closely related view is that those who are most loved by God suffer most. This finds its expression in the saying that the people who are most visited with afflictions are the prophets, then the most pious people (see PIETY), and so on. According to ʿĀʾisha (see ʿĀʾISHA BINT ABĪ BAKR), nobody suffers as much pain as Muḥammad did (Bukhārī, *Ṣaḥīḥ*, bk. 75, 2/1, iv, 41; Fr. trans. iv, 51).

Suffering is an important element in Islamic mysticism (see ṢŪFISM AND THE QURʾĀN). Patient endurance *(ṣabr)* of affliction *(balāʾ)* is one of the stations *(maqāmāt)* of the mystical path. It is closely related to *tawakkul*, "complete trust in God," and *riḍā*, "contentment about all that comes from God." According to the descriptions of the mystical path, the mystic's attitude to suffering changes in accordance with his mystical progress. First, he patiently endures affliction as a trial from God. Next, he willingly accepts it in the belief that affliction is a grace from God. At a still higher mystical level, he receives affliction with contentment and joy because God, the object of his love, sent it to him. Those who love God are happy to receive afflictions because they consider these as signs of divine love. The afflictions teach them that they are friends of God (see FRIENDS AND FRIENDSHIP), and that they are tested by him because he wishes to know the sincerity of their love.

The Imāmī Shīʿī (see SHĪʿISM AND THE QURʾĀN) doctrine of suffering focuses on the sufferings of Muḥammad and his descendants, the Imāms (see IMĀM), and in particular on the sufferings of Muḥammad's son-in-law ʿAlī b. Abī Ṭālib (q.v.; d. 40/661) and his grandson, al-Ḥusayn (d. 61/680). On the day of judgment, the Prophet, his daughter Fāṭima (q.v.), and the Imāms will be allowed to intercede for the faithful, as a reward for their sufferings (see INTERCESSION).

Suffering as a theological question

The view that suffering imposed by God is either a punishment or a trial raises the question of why innocent children (q.v.) and animals suffer. Adults of sound mind (see MATURITY) are considered to be *mukallaf*, which means that they are subject to God's imposition of obligations *(taklīf)*. They will be rewarded for fulfilling these obligations and will be punished for failing to do so. Children, the insane (see INSANITY), and animals (see ANIMAL LIFE) are not *mukallaf*, which means that their suffering cannot be a punishment, and cannot be a trial, either, because they are not eligible for a reward for patient endurance. Some theologians believed that children suffer as an advance punishment for sins they will commit as adults. This does not answer the question of the suffering of children who die before reaching adulthood, and the suffering of animals.

The Muʿtazilīs (q.v.) were convinced that the suffering of children, the insane, and animals cannot be intended to punish them because this would be in conflict with God's justice (see JUSTICE AND INJUSTICE). According to the Muʿtazilī scholar ʿAbd al-Jabbār (d. 415/1025), God imposes suffering upon children and animals because he wants to warn the adults near them. The children and animals will be compensated for this in the hereafter (see ESCHATOLOGY). For that reason, they will be revived on the last day (see RESURRECTION), together with those who were *mukallaf*. According to ʿAbd al-Jabbār, all those who are brought back to life will receive compensation for undeserved suffering, but they will have to give up some of this compensation in order to compensate for pain they themselves inflicted on other living beings without God's permission. The people of paradise will receive their compensation in addition to their reward, whereas the people of hell will receive it in the form of a temporal reduction of their punishment. Some adherents to parts of the Muʿtazilī doctrine, such as the Imāmī Shīʿīs al-Shaykh al-Mufīd (d. 413/1022) and al-Sharīf al-Murtaḍā (d. 436/1044) and the Karaite Yūsuf al-Baṣīr (fl. first half fifth/eleventh century) held largely similar opinions about suffering and its compensation.

The Ashʿarīs rejected the Muʿtazilī rationalizations about God's actions (see THEOLOGY AND THE QUR'ĀN). What counted for them was that everything in this world, good or bad, happens in accordance with God's will. God imposes suffering on his creatures but humans cannot know why he does so (see KNOWLEDGE AND LEARNING; FREEDOM AND PREDESTINATION; INTELLECT). The incomprehensibility of God's actions may be illustrated by the qur'ānic story of Moses' (q.v.) friend, whose name, according to the majority of the exegetes, was al-Khiḍr (or al-Khaḍir; see KHAḌIR/KHIḌR). He told Moses not to ask him about his actions, which included the killing of a boy (see MURDER; BLOODSHED). Nevertheless, Moses could not stop himself asking why he did such things. In the end, his friend explained his motives to him. Then it became clear to Moses that in reality his friend's actions were deeds of mercy (q.v.). The friend, however, left him because of his questioning (Q 18:66-82). This may explain why the Ashʿarīs and mainstream Sunnī Islam did not develop a theory about suffering in this world. Al-Bāqillānī (d. 403/1013) and al-Juwaynī (d. 478/1085) discussed suffering mainly in order to refute their opponents. Al-Juwaynī explained that there is no need to value pains imposed by God because we know that they are good, as they come from God (see GOOD AND EVIL). Al-Ghazālī (d. 505/1111) pointed out that humans do not have the right to ask God for an explanation of his actions (Q 21:23). As God is the master of all (see LORD; KINGS AND RULERS; SOVEREIGNTY), he is entitled to impose pain without it being deserved or compensated for (*Iḥyā'*, i, 99 [*kitāb* 2, *faṣl* 3, *rukn* 3: *al-ʿilm bi-afʿāl Allāh, al* 6]). He declared that although we cannot know the reasons for God's actions, believers should be convinced that all afflictions from God in this world may contain secret blessings (Ormsby, *Theodicy*, 256).

Margaretha T. Heemskerk

Bibliography
Primary: ʿAbd al-Jabbār b. Aḥmad Abū l-Ḥasan, *al-Mughnī fī abwāb al-tawḥīd wa-l-ʿadl*, various eds., 16 vols., Cairo 1960-9, xiii [*al-Luṭf* (ed. A. ʿAfīfī, 1962)], 229-568; Abū l-ʿArab b. Tamīm al-Tamīmī, *Kitāb al-Miḥan*, Beirut 1983; Bāqillānī, *Kitāb Tamhīd al-awā'il wa-talkhīṣ al-dalā'il*, ed. ʿI.A. Ḥaydar, Beirut 1987, 382-6; Y. al-Baṣīr, *al-Kitāb al-muḥtawī*, trans. and comm. G.Vajda, Leiden 1985, 335-86; Bukhārī, *Ṣaḥīḥ*, ed. Krehl; Fr. trans. O. Houdas and W. Marçais, *Les traditions islamiques*, 4 vols., Paris 1903-14, repr. 1977; al-Ghazālī, Abū Ḥāmid Muḥammad b. Muḥammad, *Iḥyā' ʿulūm al-dīn*, 4 vols., Cairo 1933 (repr. of Būlāq 1872 ed.); Ibn Mattawayh, Abū Muḥammad al-Ḥasan b. Aḥmad, *Kitāb al-Majmūʿ fī l-muḥīṭ bi-l-taklīf*, ed. J.J. Houben et al., 3 vols., Beirut 1962-99, iii [ed. J. Peters, 1999], 11-129 (the first volume has been wrongly attributed to ʿAbd al-Jabbār b. Aḥmad Abū l-Ḥasan); al-Juwaynī, Abū l-Maʿālī ʿAbd al-Malik, *A guide to conclusive proofs for the principles of belief (Kitāb al-Irshād ilā qawāṭiʿ al-adilla fī uṣūl al-iʿtiqād)*, trans. P.E. Walker, Reading 2000, 149-56.
Secondary: M. Ayoub, *Redemptive suffering in Islām. A study of the devotional aspects of ʿĀshūrā' in Twelver Shīʿism*, The Hague 1978; J. Bowker, *Problems of suffering in religions of the world*, Cambridge 1970, 99-122; M.T. Heemskerk, *Suffering in the Muʿtazilite theology. ʿAbd al-Jabbār's teaching on pain and divine justice*, Leiden 2000; M.J. McDermott, *The theology of al-Shaikh al-Mufīd (d. 413/1022)*, Beirut 1978, 181-7, 382-4; E.L. Ormsby, *Theodicy in Islamic thought. The dispute over al-Ghazālī's "Best of all possible worlds,"* Princeton, NJ 1984; B. Reinert, *Die Lehre vom tawakkul in der klassischen Sufik*, Berlin 1968, 90-140; H. Ritter, *Das Meer der Seele. Mensch, Welt und Gott in den Geschichten des Farīduddīn ʿAṭṭār*, Leiden 1978, 54-62, 228-52, 527-31; A. Schimmel, *Mystical dimensions of Islam*, Chapel Hill 1975; W.M. Watt, Suffering in Sunnite Islam, in *SI* 50 (1979), 5-19; H. Zirker, "Er wird nicht be- fragt..." (Sure 21,23). Theodizee und Theodizeeabwehr in Koran und Umgebung, in U. Tworuschka (ed.), *Gottes ist der Orient, Gottes is der Okzident. Festschrift für Abdoldjavad Falaturi zum 65. Geburtstag*, Köln 1991, 409-24.

Ṣūfism and the Qurʾān

Taṣawwuf, Islamic mysticism, is an ascetic-mystical trend in Islam characterized by a distinct life-style, values, ritual practices, doctrines and institutions. Ṣūfism emerged as a distinct ascetic and mystical trend in Islamic piety under the early ʿAbbāsids at about the same time as similar movements in Syria, Iran and central Asia which, though designated by different names, shared the same world-renouncing, inward-looking and esoteric attitude. By the fourth/tenth century, the Iraq-based trend in Islamic ascetic (see ASCETICISM) and mystical piety (q.v.) known as "Ṣūfism" *(taṣawwuf)* gradually prevailed over and integrated the beliefs and practices of its sister movements in the other regions of the caliphate (see CALIPH). By the end of the fourth/tenth century, leading representatives of this syncretic ascetic and mystical trend in Islam had generated a substantial body of teachings, practices and normative oral and literary lore that became the source of inspiration, life-orientation, ethos and identity for its subsequent followers, whose number continued to grow with every century. With the emergence first of Ṣūfī lodges, and, somewhat later, Ṣūfī "brotherhoods" (the fifth-seventh/eleventh-thirteenth centuries) or "orders" (*ṭuruq*, sing. *ṭarīqa*), Ṣūfism became part and parcel of the spiritual, social and political life of pre-modern Islamdom. With the advent of modernity in the thirteenth/nineteenth century Ṣūfism was subjected to strident criticism by Muslim modernists and reformers, and in the course of the fourteenth/twentieth century lost ground to competing ideologies, both religious and secular (see POLITICS AND THE QURʾĀN). Nevertheless, it has managed to survive both criticisms and overt persecutions and even won converts among some Western intellectuals.

Early Ṣūfī attitudes to the Qurʾān

From the outset, the Qurʾān was the principal source of contemplation and inspiration for every serious Muslim ascetic and mystic, whether formally Ṣūfī or not. In fact, many Ṣūfī concepts and terms have their origin in encounters with the qurʾānic text, endowing Ṣūfism with much-needed legitimacy in the eyes of both Ṣūfīs and Muslims not directly affiliated with it. Yet, from the very beginning Ṣūfī interpretations of the scripture (as well as Ṣūfī practices, values and beliefs) were challenged by influential representatives of the Sunnī and Shīʿī religious establishments (see TRADITIONAL DISCIPLINES OF QURʾĀNIC STUDY), occasionally resulting in persecution of individual mystics. Ṣūfīs were accused of overplaying the allegorical aspects of the Qurʾān, claiming privileged, esoteric understanding of its contents and distorting its literal meaning (see POLYSEMY; LITERARY STRUCTURES AND THE QURʾĀN). To demonstrate their faithfulness to the spirit and letter of the revelation (see REVELATION AND INSPIRATION) advocates of Ṣūfism drew heavily on the qurʾānic verses (q.v.) which, in their view, legitimized their brand of Islamic piety. Such verses usually emphasize the proximity and intimacy between God and his human servants (e.g. Q 2:115, 186; 20:7-8; 58:7; see SERVANT; WORSHIP; GOD AND HIS ATTRIBUTES). God's immediate and immanent presence among the faithful is forcefully brought home in Q 50:16, in which he declares himself to be nearer to man than "his jugular vein" (see ARTERY AND VEIN). The relationship of closeness and intimacy is occasionally presented in the Qurʾān in terms of mutual love (q.v.) between the maker and his creatures (see CREATION; COSMOLOGY), as, for instance, in Q 5:54 (cf. Q 3:31, 76, 134, 146, 148, 159; 5:93, which also describe different categories of believers deserving of divine affection). Deeming themselves paragons of piety and devotion to God and true "heirs" of his Prophet (see PROPHETS AND PROPHETHOOD; MUḤAMMAD), representatives of the early [proto-]Ṣūfī movements viewed such verses as referring primarily, if not exclusively, to them. With the emergence of mystical cosmology and metaphysics, which provided justification for the mystical experiences of the Ṣūfīs, they put the Qurʾān to new, creative uses. Thus, in the famous "Light Verse" (Q 24:35) God's persona is cast in the imagery of a sublime, majestic and unfathomable light, which renders it eminently conducive to gnostic elaborations on the theme of light (q.v.) and darkness (q.v.) and the eternal struggle between spirit (q.v.) and matter. According to early Ṣūfī exegetes, God guides whomsoever he wishes with his light (see ERROR; ASTRAY; FREEDOM AND PREDESTINATION) but has predilection for a special category of pious, god-fearing individuals (see FEAR) who devote themselves completely to worshipping him. In return, God assures them of salvation (q.v.) in the hereafter (Q 2:38, 262, 264; 3:170; etc.; see ESCHATOLOGY). As to those "who prefer the present life over the world (q.v.) to come," "a terrible chastisement" awaits them (Q 14:3; cf. 2:86; see REWARD AND PUNISHMENT). From the beginning, Muslim ascetics and mystics identified themselves with God's "protégés" *(awliyāʾ)* mentioned in Q 10:62 (cf. Q 8:34; 45:19; see CLIENTS AND CLIENTAGE; FRIENDS AND FRIENDSHIP). With time Ṣūfī exegetes came to portray them as God's elect "friends" and confidants who are able to intercede on behalf of the ordinary believers and guide them aright (see INTERCESSION; SAINTS). In Ṣūfī lore such "friends of God" were identified with authoritative Ṣūfī masters, both living and deceased. In Q 7:172, which figures prominently in early Ṣūfī discourses, the relations between God and his creatures are placed in a cosmic framework, as a primordial covenant (q.v.; *mīthāq*) between them. During this crucial event the human race presented itself before God in the form of disembodied souls (q.v.) to bear witness to the absolute sovereignty (q.v.) of their lord (q.v.) at his request (see WITNESSING AND TESTIFYING). Once in possession of sinful and restive bodies (see SIN, MAJOR AND MINOR), however, most humans have forgotten their promise of faithfulness and devotion to God and therefore have to be constantly reminded of it by divine messengers (see MESSENGER) and prophets. The goal of the true Ṣūfī is to return to the state of pristine devotion and faithfulness of the day of the covenant by minimizing the corruptive drives of his body and his lower soul — one that "commands evil" *(ammāra bi-l-sūʾ,* Q 12:53; see GOOD AND EVIL). If successful, the mystic can transform his lower, restive self into a soul "at peace" *(al-nafs al-muṭmaʾinna,* Q 89:27) that is incapable of disobeying its lord (see DISOBEDIENCE). This can only be achieved through the self-imposed strictures of ascetic life, pious meditation and the remembrance (q.v.) of God *(dhikr)* as explicitly enjoined in Q 8:45, 18:24 and 33:41 (see also REFLECTION AND DELIBERATION). Finally, on the level of personal experience, verses describing the visionary experiences of the prophet Muḥammad (namely, Q 17:1 and Q 53:1-18; see VISIONS) provided a fruitful ground for mystical elaborations and attempts by mystically minded Muslims to, as it were, "recapture the rapture" of the founder of Islam, all the more so because the Qurʾān and the sunna (q.v.) repeatedly enjoin the believers to imitate him meticulously. While all of these verses resonated well with the aspirations of early Muslim ascetics and mystics, there were also those that did not, in that they prescribed moderation in worship, enjoyment of family (q.v.) life and fulfillment of social responsibilities, while at the same time discouraging the "excesses" of Christian-style monasticism (Q 4:3-4, 25-8, 127; 9:31; 57:27; see CHRISTIANS AND CHRISTIANITY; MONASTICISM AND MONKS; ABSTINENCE). Yet, these passages, as well as numerous injunctions against the renunciation of this world found in the Prophet's sunna, could be either ignored or allegorized away, especially since some of them were inconclusive or self-contradictory (e.g. Q 5:82, which may be interpreted as praising the Christian monks for their exemplary righteousness). Eventually, however, the weight of scriptural evidence and social pressures forced most adherents of Ṣūfism to steer a middle course, which allowed them to participate in social life and raise families while not compromising their ascetic-mystical vocations. As the body of Ṣūfī lore grew with the passage of time and Ṣūfism became a distinct life-style and a system of rituals (see RITUAL AND THE QURʾĀN), practices and beliefs, there emerged a specific Ṣūfī exegesis aimed at justifying them (see also EXEGESIS OF THE QURʾĀN: CLASSICAL AND MEDIEVAL).

The rise and early development of Ṣūfī exegesis

The earliest samples of the Ṣūfī exegetical lore were collected by an eminent Ṣūfī master of Nīshāpūr, Abū ʿAbd al-Raḥmān al-Sulamī (d. 412/1021) in his *Ḥaqāʾiq al-tafsīr*. This work, which still awaits a critical edition (but cf. Böwering's ed. of Sulamī's *Ziyādāt*, an appendix to the *Ḥaqāʾiq*), is practically our only source for the initial stages of mystical exegesis in Islam. Its major representatives, al-Ḥasan al-Baṣrī (d. 110/728), Jaʿfar al-Ṣādiq (d. 148/765), Sufyān al-Thawrī (d. 161/778) and ʿAbdallāh b. al-Mubārak (d. 181/797) were not Ṣūfīs *stricto sensu*, since the Baghdād school of Ṣūfism was yet to emerge. Rather, these pious individuals were appropriated by Ṣūfism's later advocates, who presented them as paragons of Ṣūfī piety *avant-la-lettre*. While their preoccupation with the spiritual and allegorical aspects of the scripture is impossible to deny, the authenticity of their exegetical logia, which were collected and transmitted by al-Sulamī and some of his immediate predecessors more than a century after their death, is far from certain. The problem is particularly severe (and intriguing) in the case of the sixth Shīʿī *imām* (q.v.), Jaʿfar al-Ṣādiq (see also SHĪʿISM AND THE QURʾĀN). His role as a doyen of primeval mystical exegesis is difficult to prove, especially since his exegetical logia transmitted by al-Sulamī are devoid of any of the expected Shīʿī themes. Unless his other *tafsīr* transmitted in Shīʿī circles proves similar or identical to the one assembled by al-Sulamī, the matter will remain uncertain (for details see Nwyia, *Exégèse*, and Böwering, *Mystical vision*). One should not rule out the possibility of Shīʿī elements having been expunged from Jaʿfar's exegetical logia by Sunnī Ṣūfīs who transmitted them through separate channels (see THEOLOGY AND THE QURʾĀN). Alternatively, one may suggest that Ṣūfī and Shīʿī esotericism originated in the same pious circles (Jaʿfar al-Ṣādiq is frequently quoted in the standard Ṣūfī manual of Abū l-Qāsim al-Qushayrī; d. 465/1072), whereupon it took on different forms in the Sunnī and Shīʿī intellectual environments. The problem of authorship is less severe in the case of such ascetically minded individuals as al-Ḥasan al-Baṣrī, al-Thawrī, and Ibn al-Mubārak who were major exponents of Sunnī Islam in their age, although their role as the *bona fide* progenitors of the Ṣūfī tradition is problematic. If authentic, Jaʿfar's logia are probably the earliest extant expression of the methodological principles of mystical *tafsīr*, which were adopted and elaborated by subsequent generations of Ṣūfī commentators.

According to Jaʿfar's statement cited by al-Sulamī at the beginning of his *Ḥaqāʾiq al-tafsīr,* the Qurʾān has four aspects: *ʿibāra* (a literal or obvious articulation of the meaning of a verse); *ishāra* (its allegorical allusion); *laṭāʾif* (its subtle and symbolic aspects; see SYMBOLIC IMAGERY) and *ḥaqāʾiq* (its spiritual realities; cf. Böwering, Scriptural "senses"). Each of these levels of meanings has its own addressees, respectively: the ordinary believers *(al-ʿawāmm),* the spiritual elite *(al-khawāṣṣ),* God's intimate friends *(al-awliyāʾ)* and the prophets *(al-anbiyāʾ).* On the practical level, Jaʿfar and his Ṣūfī counterparts usually dealt with just two levels of meaning: the outward/exoteric *(ẓāhir)* and the hidden/esoteric *(bāṭin),* thereby subsuming the moral/ethical/legal meanings of a given verse (see ETHICS AND THE QURʾĀN; LAW AND THE QURʾĀN) under "literal" and its allegorical/mystical/anagogical subtext under "hidden." As demonstrated by P. Nwyia, Jaʿfar's exegetical interests were worlds apart from those of his contemporary Muqātil b. Sulaymān (d. 150/767) who pursued a more conventional (albeit imaginative) historical and philological *tafsīr* (see GRAMMAR AND THE QURʾĀN). For instance, unlike Muqātil, Jaʿfar shows no interest in the historical circumstances surrounding the battle of Badr (q.v.), as presented in the Qurʾān (see also OCCASIONS OF REVELATION). When the Qurʾān says that "God supported him [Muḥammad] with the legions you [his followers] did not see" (Q 9:40), Jaʿfar interprets the "legions" not as "angels" (as argued by Muqātil and other exoterically minded exegetes; see ANGEL; RANKS AND ORDERS; TROOPS) but as spiritual virtues that the mystic acquires in the course of his progress along the path to God *(ṭarīq),* namely, "certitude" *(yaqīn),* "trust in God" *(thiqa)* and a total "reliance" on him in everything one undertakes (*tawakkul;* see TRUST AND PATIENCE; VIRTUE). Likewise, the qurʾānic injunction to "purify my [God's] house (namely, the Kaʿba [q.v.]; see also HOUSE, DOMESTIC AND DIVINE) for those who shall circumambulate it" (Q 22:26) is interpreted by Jaʿfar as a call upon the individual believer to "purify [his] soul from any association with the disobedient ones and anything other than God" (see POLYTHEISM AND ATHEISM), while the phrase "those who stay in front of it [the Kaʿba]" is glossed as an injunction for the ordinary believers to seek the company of "the [divine] gnostics *(ʿārifūn),* who stand on the carpet of intimacy [with God] and service of him." The notion of the divinely bestowed "gnosis," or mystical knowledge *(maʿrifa),* which characterizes these elect servants of God figures prominently in Jaʿfar's logia (see e.g. his commentary on Q 7:143, 160; 8:24; 27:34). This was to become a central concept in later Ṣūfī epistemology, where it is usually juxtaposed with both received (traditional) wisdom *(naql)* and knowledge acquired through rational contemplation (*ʿaql;* see KNOWLEDGE AND LEARNING; INTELLECT). The Qurʾān was, for Jaʿfar and Ṣūfī commentators, a source of and a means towards the true realization *(taḥqīq)* of God (see TRUTH).

The next stage of the development of Ṣūfī exegesis, or, as Nwyia aptly calls it, *une lecture introspective du Coran,* is associated with a fairly large cohort of individuals who lived in the third/ninth-early fourth/tenth centuries. Their Ṣūfī credentials, a few exceptions apart (e.g. al-Ḥakīm al-Tirmidhī, fl. third/ninth cent.), do not raise any serious doubts. At least one of them, Aḥmad b. ʿAṭāʾ (d. 309/922), and possibly also Dhū l-Nūn al-Miṣrī (d. 246/861) were involved in the transmission of Jaʿfar's exegetical logia, which they amplified with their own elaborations. The others — namely Sahl al-Tustarī (d. 283/896), Abū Saʿīd al-Kharrāz (d. 286/899), Abū l-Ḥusayn al-

Nūrī (d. 295/907), Abū l-Qāsim al-Junayd (d. 298/910), Abū Bakr al-Wāsiṭī (d. 320/932) and Abū Bakr al-Shiblī (d. 334/946) — were frequently cited in Ṣūfī literature as authoritative sources of exegetical logia and, in the case of al-Tustarī, Ibn ʿAṭāʾ and al-Wāsiṭī, also as authors of full-fledged qurʾānic commentaries (Böwering, Ṣūfī hermeneutics; id., *Mystical vision*).

The centrality of the Qurʾān to Ṣūfī piety

The methods of Qurʾān interpretation characteristic of early Ṣūfī masters were examined by Nwyia (Jaʿfar al-Ṣādiq, Shaqīq al-Balkhī, Ibn ʿAṭāʾ, and al-Nūrī) and Böwering (al-Tustarī, al-Sulamī, and al-Daylamī). They should be viewed against the background of the practices, life-style, values and beliefs current among the members of the early Ṣūfī movement. On the practical level, the recitation of the Qurʾān (q.v.) was an indispensable part of quotidian Ṣūfī life. Thus, Ibn ʿAṭāʾ is said to have recited the entire text of the Qurʾān on a daily basis and thrice a day during the month of Ramaḍān (q.v.), which along with other rituals and supererogatory prayers (see PRAYER) left him only two hours of sleep; Sahl al-Tustarī (d. 283/896) learned the entire Qurʾān by heart when he was six or seven years old and kept reciting it throughout the rest of his life; Mālik b. Dīnār (d. 131/748) "was 'chewing' it for [the first] twenty years [of his life] only to take pleasure in its recitation *(tilāwa)* for the next twenty years" (Sarrāj, *Kitāb al-Lumaʿ*, 43); Ibn Khafīf (d. 371/981) recited Q 112:1 ten thousand times during just one prayer and occasionally recited the entire text of the Qurʾān in the course of one prayer, which took him an entire day and a good part of the night, etc.

In most cases, esoteric interpretations of the Qurʾān by the above-mentioned Ṣūfīs were the fruits of many years of incessant recitation in an attempt to grasp and "extract" its hidden meaning *(istinbāṭ)*. This term, which is derived from Q 4:83, became the hallmark of Ṣūfī methods of Qurʾān interpretation. Alerted to the presence of a hidden meaning in a given verse by its subtle "allusion" *(ishāra)*, the Ṣūfī felt obligated to "extract" it by means of *istinbāṭ*. This process is limited to those individuals who have fully engrossed themselves in the "sea" of the divine revelation after having purified their souls of any worldly attachments. Commenting on Q 4:83, al-Ḥallāj (d. 309/922) stated that a Ṣūfī's ability to exercise *istinbāṭ* corresponds to "the measure of his piety, inwardly and outwardly, and the perfection of his gnosis *(maʿrifa)*, which is the most glorious station of faith" (q.v.; *ajall maqāmāt al-īmān;* Sulamī, *Ḥaqāʾiq*, i, 157). The close link between one's ability to practice *istinbāṭ* and one's strict compliance with the precepts of the divine law is brought forth by Abū Naṣr al-Sarrāj (d. 378/988), a renowned collector and disseminator of early Ṣūfī lore. In his words, "extractions" *(mustanbaṭāt)* are available only to those who "act in accord with the book (q.v.) of God, outwardly and inwardly, and follow the messenger of God, outwardly and inwardly." In return, God makes them "heirs to the knowledge of subtle allusion *(ʿilm al-ishāra)*" and "unveils to the hearts of his elect [servants] carefully guarded meanings *(maʿānī madhkhūra)*, spiritual subtleties *(laṭāʾif)* and well-kept secrets" (*asrār makhzūna;* Sarrāj, *Kitāb al-Lumaʿ*, 105).

In the case of the early Ṣūfī exegete Sahl al-Tustarī, we find a deeply personal and experiential relationship of the Ṣūfī to the Qurʾān, which evolves within the framework of an oral recitation and reception of the divine word (see ORALITY; WORD OF GOD). On hearing or reciting a verse that resonates with the mystic's spiritual state he may occasionally find himself gripped by an intense ecstasy and even lose consciousness. According to Böwering (*Mystical,* 136), al-Tustarī's commentary can be seen as a product of such experiential encounters "between the qurʾānic keynotes and the mystical matrix of [the mystic's] world of ideas." Inspired by a certain verse, al-Tustarī spontaneously endeavored to communicate to his disciples his deeply personal and experiential understanding of it, which often had very little to do with its literal meaning. To sum up,

> The Ṣūfīs... read the Qurʾān as the word of God, and what they seek there is not the word as such (which may even become a veil between them and God), but a God who makes himself accessible [to his worshippers] by means of this word (Nwyia, *Trois oeuvres,* 29).

The themes of the first Ṣūfī commentaries on the Qurʾān are diverse and rather difficult to summarize. They usually deal with mystical cosmology, eschatology and the challenges faced by the human soul on its way to God (see TRIAL). After professing their allegiance to their divine sovereign on the day of the primordial covenant (Q 7:172) human beings have found themselves plunged into a world of false values, temptations and illusions designed to test the integrity of their pact with God. God created good and evil and arbitrarily imposed his command *(amr)* on his human servants in order to distinguish the blessed from the evildoers (see ELECT; EVIL DEEDS; BLESSING; GRACE). Within the former category he designated a special class of believers whom he endowed with an intuitive, revelatory knowledge of himself and his creatures *(maʿrifa),* leaving the rest of humankind to be content with the "externals" of religious faith and practice. These elect "friends of God" *(awliyāʾ Allāh)* carry divine light in their hearts (see HEART) and thus can be seen as embodiments of his immanent and guiding presence amidst humankind. By imitating the friends of God (who, in turn, imitate the godly ways of his Prophet) ordinary believers can hope to escape the allure and temptations of mundane existence and to achieve salvation in the hereafter. Attaining the status of God's friend and gnostic is not automatic, however, and requires painstaking efforts on the part of the aspirant *(murīd)* as well as God's continual assistance. The seeker's greatest challenge is the corruptive influences of his vile body and the base soul *(nafs),* which acts as a constant temptress and an ally of Iblīs (see DEVIL). Its machinations can only be overcome by constant remembrance of God *(dhikr),* including the recitation of God's word and remembrance of his "most beautiful names." This goal can only be achieved by the elect few who traverse the entire length of the path to God in order to enter into his presence (see PATH OR WAY; FACE OF GOD). In this state they become completely oblivious of the corrupt world around them, taking God as their sole focus and *raison d'être.* By any standard, since its inception Ṣūfī exegesis was thoroughly elitist and esoteric. Its practitioners implicitly and, on occasion, explicitly dismissed the concerns of mainstream Qurʾān interpreters (legal, historical, philological and theological) as inadequate and even misguided inasmuch as they focused on the Qurʾān's "husks," while ignoring its all-important spiritual "kernel." The Ṣūfīs regarded themselves as the sole custodians of that kernel and sought to protect it from outsiders by using subtle allusions and recondite terminology.

Some Muslim scholars were enraged by the Ṣūfī claim to a privileged knowledge of the scripture and denounced Ṣūfī exegesis as fanciful, arbitrary and not supported by the authority of the Prophet and his Companions (see COMPANIONS OF THE

PROPHET; ḤADĪTH AND THE QURʾĀN). Thus, a renowned Qurʾān commentator, ʿAlī b. Muḥammad al-Wāḥidī (d. 468/1076), not only refused to accord al-Sulamī's exegetical summa the status of *tafsīr* but even proclaimed it an expression of outright "unbelief" (see BELIEF AND UNBELIEF). Similar negative opinions of that work were voiced by Ibn al-Jawzī (d. 597/1201), Ibn Taymiyya (d. 728/1328) and al-Dhahabī (d. 748/1348), who declared it to be a collection of "distortion and heresy" (q.v.; *taḥrīf wa-qarmaṭa;* see also CORRUPTION; FORGERY) reminiscent of Ismāʿīlī exegesis *(taʾwīlāt al-bāṭiniyya)*. Yet, despite such criticism al-Sulamī's voluminous work, which contains more than twelve thousand glosses on some three thousand qurʾānic passages, gained wide popularity among Ṣūfīs of various stripes. As was the case with Jaʿfar, Ibn ʿAṭāʾ and al-Tustarī, al-Sulamī did not include in his compendium any conventional exegetical material, be it legal, philological or historical (Böwering, Ṣūfī hermeneutics). His position is clearly stated in the introduction to his magnum opus:

Upon discovering that — among the practitioners of exoteric sciences *(ʿulūm ẓawāhir)* [who] have compiled [numerous] works pertaining to [beneficial] virtues *(fawāʾid)* of the Qurʾān, such as methods of its recitation (*qirāʾāt;* see READINGS OF THE QURʾĀN), its [historical] commentaries *(tafsīr)*, its difficulties (*mushkilāt;* see DIFFICULT PASSAGES), its legal rulings *(aḥkām)*, its vocalization *(iʿrāb)*, its lexicological aspects *(lugha)*, its summation and detailed explanation *(mujmal wa-mufaṣṣal)*, its abrogating and abrogated verses (*nāsikh wa-mansūkh*; see ABROGATION), and so on — no one has cared to collect the understanding of its discourse *(khiṭāb)* in accordance with the language of the people of the true reality *(ahl al-ḥaqīqa)*... I have asked God's blessing to bring together some of it.

All told, al-Sulamī's exegetical methods and goals are similar to those of about a hundred of his authorities, who lived in the third/ninth and fourth/tenth centuries and whose foremost representatives have already been discussed. To quote the major Western expert on this work,

The *Ḥaqāʾiq al-tafsīr* is the crowning event of a long creative period of Ṣūfī terminology and ideology, developing in close relationship with its Koranic foundation and yet breaking through to a continuous process of inspired revelation by the methodological means of allusion (Böwering, Ṣūfī hermeneutics, 265).

The growth and maturity of Ṣūfī exegetical tradition (from the fifth/eleventh to the seventh/thirteenth centuries)

Al-Sulamī's monumental work, which played the same role in Ṣūfī *tafsīr* as al-Ṭabarī's (d. 310/923) *Jāmiʿ al-bayān* in traditional exegesis, laid the foundations for the subsequent evolution of this genre of Ṣūfī literature. With time there emerged several distinct trends within the body of Ṣūfī exegetical literature, which reflected the growing internal complexity of the Ṣūfī movement in the period leading up to the fall of the Baghdād caliphate in 656/1258. One such trend can be described as "moderate" or "*sharīʿa*-oriented." It is represented by such Ṣūfī luminaries as al-Qushayrī (d. 465/1074), Abū Ḥāmid al-Ghazālī (d. 505/1111) and Abū Ḥafṣ ʿUmar al-Suhrawardī (d. 632/1234).

Abū l-Qāsim al-Qushayrī of Nīshāpūr is famous first and foremost as the author of the popular tract *al-Risāla [al-Qushayriyya] fī ʿilm al-taṣawwuf* which combines elements of Ṣūfī biography with those of a Ṣūfī manual. Like the *Risāla*, al-Qushayrī's qurʾānic commentary *Laṭāʾif al-ishārāt* pursues a clear apologetic agenda: the defense of the teachings, values and practices of "moderate," Junayd-style Ṣūfism and the demonstration of its full compliance with the major precepts of Ashʿarī theology. Written in 410/1019, this exegetical work consistently draws a parallel between the gradual progress from the literal to the subtlest meanings *(laṭāʾif)* of the qurʾānic text and the stages of the Ṣūfī's spiritual and experiential journey to God. The success of this exegetical progress, as well as of the Ṣūfī journey, depends on the wayfarer's ability to combine the performance of pious works and feats of spirit with sound doctrinal premises. Giving preference to one over the other will result in failure. Even when this delicate balance is successfully struck, one still needs divine assistance in unraveling the subtleties of the divine revelation, which is equally true of the Ṣūfī seeker's striving toward God. Hence the notion of a privileged, esoteric knowledge of both God and this word that God grants only to his most intimate, elect "friends," the *awliyāʾ*. This idea is stated clearly in the introduction to *Laṭāʾif al-ishārāt:*

[God] has honored the elect *(aṣfiyāʾ)* among his servants by [granting them] the understanding of his subtle secrets (q.v.; *laṭāʾif asrārihi*) and his lights so that they can see the elusive allusions and hidden signs (q.v.) contained therein [in the Qurʾān]. He has shown their innermost souls hidden things so that by the emanations of the unseen (see HIDDEN AND THE HIDDEN) which he has imparted solely to them they can become aware of that which has been concealed from all others. Then they have started to speak according to their degrees [of attainment] and capabilities, and God — praise be to him — inspired in them things by which he has honored them. So, they now speak on behalf of him, inform about the subtle truths that he has imparted to them, and point to him... (*Laṭāʾif*, i, 53).

The exegete's progress toward the innermost meaning of the scripture is described by al-Qushayrī as a movement from the intellect (q.v.) to the heart, then to the spirit *(al-rūḥ),* then to the innermost secret *(al-sirr)* and, finally, to the secret of secrets *(sirr al-sirr)* of the Qurʾān. Al-Qushayrī's approach to the Qurʾān is marked by his meticulous attention to every detail of the qurʾānic word, from an entire verse to a single letter found in it (see ARABIC SCRIPT). Typical in this regard is his interpretation of the *basmala* (q.v.), in which each letter of this phrase is endowed with a symbolic meaning: the *bāʾ* stands for God's gentleness *(birr)* toward his friends *(awliyāʾ);* the *sīn* for the secret he shares with his elect *(aṣfiyāʾ);* and the *mīm* for his bestowal of grace *(minna)* upon those who have attained intimacy with him *(ahl wilāyatihi)*. In an attempt to achieve comprehensiveness al-Qushayrī marshals several alternative interpretations of the *basmala,* e.g. one in which the *bāʾ* alludes to God's freedom *(barāʾa)* from any fault; the *sīn* to the absence of any defect in him *(salāmatuhu min ʿayb);* and the *mīm* to the majesty of his attributes (*Laṭāʾif*, i, 56).

While such speculations are not unique to al-Qushayrī and can be found in exegetical works contemporary to his, both Ṣūfī and non-Ṣūfī alike, there is one feature that sets *Laṭāʾif al-ishārāt* apart from them. For al-Qushayrī, the *basmala* is not a simple repetition of the same set of meanings, for the divine word allows no repetition. Rather, the meaning of the *basmala* may change depending on the major themes contained in the sūras (q.v.) that it precedes. Thus, in discussing the symbolism of the letters of the *basmala* preceding Q 7, al-Qushayrī implicitly links them to the themes of submission *(islām),* humility and reverence requisite of the true believer as opposed to the rebellious behavior (see REBELLION) of Iblīs and his host (e.g. Q 7:11-15, 31-3, 35-6, 39-40, etc.) by arguing that the letter *bāʾ*

is of a small stature in writing and the dot [underneath it], which distinguishes it from other [letters] is single and, to boot, small to the extreme. Moreover, it [the dot] is positioned underneath the letter, [all of which] alludes to modesty and humility in all respects (*Laṭāʾif,* i, 211-12).

Likewise, the presence of the *sukūn* (absence of a vowel) over the letter *sīn* following the "humble" and "submissive" *bāʾ* alludes to its silent acceptance of the divine decree and complete contentment with it. Finally, the letter *mīm* points to "his [God's] bestowal of grace [upon you] *(minnatuhu),* if he so pleases, then to your agreement *(muwāfaqatuka)* with his decree and your satisfaction with it, even though he may not bestow anything [upon you] (ibid.).

Al-Qushayrī's interpretation of the *basmala* of Q 15 (Sūrat al-Ḥijr) is quite different. The omission of the *alif* in the *basmala* of that sūra without any rationally justifiable reason, either grammatically or morphologically, according to al-Qushayrī, symbolizes God's arbitrary "raising" of Adam (despite his "base" nature; see ADAM AND EVE) and his subsequent "humiliation" of the angels (despite their elevated status), as described in the main body of the sūra. In a similar vein, the omission of the *basmala* in Q 9 is interpreted by al-Qushayrī in the following manner:

God — praise be to him — has stripped *(jarrada)* this sūra of the *basmala,* so that it be known that he can endow *(yakhuṣṣ)* whomever and whatever he wants with whatever he wants. [In the same way,] he can single out whomever he wants with whatever he wants. His creation has no cause, his actions have neither a purpose nor a goal (*Laṭāʾif,* iii, 5; see FREEDOM AND PREDESTINATION).

This, of course, is an Ashʿarī stance formulated in implicit opposition to that of the Muʿtazilīs (see MUʿTAZILA) who advocated the underlying rationality and purposefulness of divine actions. Thus, as mentioned, in al-Qushayrī's commentary, Ṣūfī symbolism and the Ashʿarī dogma go hand in hand and are deployed to support each other.

Al-Qushayrī's interest in the symbolism of letters comes to the fore in his discussions of the "mysterious letters" (q.v.) that appear at the beginning of some qurʾānic chapters. Typical in this respect is his exegesis of the combination *alif lām mīm* that precedes Q 2. Upon stating that the *alif* stands for *Allāh,* the *lām* for *laṭāʾif* (the subtle realities; also one of the epithets of God, *laṭīf*) and the *mīm* for *majīd* (the glorious) and *malik* (the king; see KINGS AND RULERS), he proceeds to argue that

The *alif* is singled out from among the other letters by the fact that it is not connected to any letter in writing, while all but a few letters are connected to it. May the servant of God upon considering this feature become aware of the need of all creatures for him [God], with him being self-sufficient and independent of anything (*Laṭāʾif,* i, 41).

Furthermore, the *alif*'s singularity is evident from the fact that all other letters have a concrete site of articulation in the human speech (q.v.) apparatus, while it has none. In the same way, God cannot be associated with *(yuḍāf ilā)* any particular location or site. Finally, "The faithful servant of God is like the *alif* in its not being connected to any letter, in its constant uprightness and its standing posture before him" (ibid.).

As one may expect of a Ṣūfī master, al-Qushayrī showed little interest in the historical and legal aspects of the qurʾānic text. For him, they serve as windows onto the spiritual and mystical ideas and values characteristic of Ṣūfī piety. Thus, in discussing the spoils of war *(ghanīma)* mentioned in Q 8:41 (see BOOTY) al-Qushayrī argues:

Jihād (q.v.) can be of two types: the external one [waged] against the infidels and the internal one [waged] against [one's] soul and Satan. In the same way as the lesser jihād involves [the seizure of] spoils of war after victory, the greater jihād too has the spoils of war of its own, which involves taking possession of his soul by the servant of God after it has been held by his two enemies — [his] passions and Satan (*Laṭāʾif*, ii, 321).

A similar parallel is drawn between ordinary fasting (q.v.) which involves abstention from food, drink (see FOOD AND DRINK) and sex (see SEX AND SEXUALITY) and the spiritual abstention of the Ṣūfī from the allure of this world and from seeking the approval of its inhabitants. In a similar vein, al-Qushayrī likens the juridical notion of abrogation *(naskh)* to the initial strict observance of the divine law by the Ṣūfī novice, which is supplanted, or "abrogated," when he reaches the stage at which God himself becomes the guardian of his heart. In al-Qushayrī's commentary all ritual duties sanctioned by the Qurʾān are endowed with a deeper spiritual significance: the standing of pilgrims on the plain of ʿArafāt (q.v.) is compared to the "standing" of human hearts in the presence of the divine names and attributes (see PILGRIMAGE). Despite its overall "moderate" nature, the *Laṭāʾif al-ishārāt* is not devoid of the monistic and visionary elements that characterize what is usually described as the more "bold" and "esoteric" trend in Ṣūfī qurʾānic commentary. This aspect of al-Qushayrī's exegesis comes to the fore in his interpretation of Q 7:143, in which Moses (q.v.) comes to God at an appointed time *(li-mīqātinā)* and requests that God appear to him, only to be humbled by the sight of a mountain crumbling to dust, when God shows himself to it (see THEOPHANY). According to al-Qushayrī,

Moses came to God as [only] those passionately longing and madly in love could. Moses came without Moses. Moses came, yet nothing of Moses was left to Moses. Thousands of men have traversed great distances, yet no one remembers them, while that Moses made [only] a few steps and [school] children will be reciting until the day of judgment (see LAST JUDGMENT): "When Moses came…" (*Laṭāʾif*, ii, 259).

Despite such "ecstatic" passages, al-Qushayrī's book can still be considered a typical sample of "moderate" Ṣūfī exegesis because of its author's overriding desire to achieve a delicate balance between the mystical imagination and the respect for the letter of the revelation or, in Ṣūfī parlance, between the *sharīʿa* and the *ḥaqīqa*. One should point out that al-Qushayrī is also the author of a conventional historical-philological and legal *tafsīr* entitled *al-Taysīr fī l-tafsīr*, which is said to have been written before 410/1019. This is an eloquent testimony to his dual credentials as both a Ṣūfī and a conventional scholar *(ʿālim)*.

Another example of "moderate" Ṣūfī *tafsīr* is *al-Kashf wa-l-bayān ʿan tafsīr al-Qurʾān* by Abū Isḥāq Aḥmad b. Muḥammad al-

Thaʿlabī (d. 427/1035). Drawing heavily on *Ḥaqāʾiq al-tafsīr,* al-Thaʿlabī augmented the Ṣūfī exegetical logia assembled by al-Sulamī with conventional exegetical materials derived from ḥadīth as well as detailed discussions of the philological aspects and legal implications of the qurʾānic text (Saleh, *Formation*). Al-Thaʿlabī's work formed the foundation of the famous commentary *Maʿālim al-tanzīl fī tafsīr al-Qurʾān* by Abū Muḥammad al-Ḥusayn al-Baghawī (hence its better known title — *Tafsīr al-Baghawī*). He was born in 438/1046 in the village of Bagh or Baghshūr located between Herat and Marw al-Rūdh and distinguished himself primarily as a Shāfiʿī jurist and *muḥaddith,* whose thematically arranged collection of prophetic reports titled *Maṣābīḥ al-sunna* became a standard work of its genre. Although al-Baghawī was not considered a full-fledged Ṣūfī, he led an ascetic and pious way of life and avoided any contact with ruling authorities. His *tafsīr* is marked by his meticulous concern for the exegetical materials going back to the Prophet and his Companions *(al-tafsīr bi-l-maʾthūr)* and his desire to elucidate all possible aspects of the qurʾānic text. In seeking to achieve comprehensiveness he availed himself of diverse sources: from the leading Arab grammarians to the Shīʿī imāms and legal scholars. His Ṣūfī authorities include Ibrāhīm b. Adham (d. 160/777), Fuḍayl b. ʿIyāḍ (d. 188/803), al-Tustarī and al-Junayd (d. 298/910), whose ideas had probably reached him via al-Sulamī's *Ḥaqāʾiq al-tafsīr* and al-Thaʿlabī's *al-Kashf wa-l-bayān.* Al-Baghawī's use of this material was probably dictated by his drive to highlight all possible interpretations of the sacred text without privileging any one of them. Since by his age Ṣūfism had established itself as a legitimate and praiseworthy strain of Islamic piety he felt obligated to mention Ṣūfī views of the revelation, avoiding, however, their more controversial aspects. Thus, his inclusion of Ṣūfī exegesis did not necessarily reflect his own spiritual and intellectual priorities — a trend that we observe in many later exegetical works.

A typical representative of this trend in the later period is Abū l-Ḥasan ʿAlī b. Muḥammad al-Shīḥī al-Baghdādī, better known as "al-Khāzin" (d. 741/1341), whose *Lubāb al-taʾwīl fī maʿānī al-tanzīl* is an abridged rendition of al-Baghawī's *Maʿālim al-tanzīl.* As with al-Baghawī, Ṣūfī exegesis is just one of the aspects of the qurʾānic text that preoccupy al-Khāzin who explicitly states this in the introduction to his commentary. His other concerns include the rules of recitation, material transmitted by the Prophet and his Companions *(tafsīr bi-l-maʾthūr),* legal implications *(al-aḥkām al-fiqhiyya),* the "occasions of revelation," curious and unusual stories of past prophets and generations (q.v.; *al-qiṣaṣ al-gharība wa-akhbār al-māḍīn al-ʿajība*). Therefore, the reason why this *tafsīr* is sometimes classified as Ṣūfī (e.g. Ayāzī, *Mufassirūn,* 598-602; al-Baghawī's *tafsīr,* on the other hand, is not identified as such, ibid., 644-9) remains unclear. In any event, it is certainly indicative of the trend toward comprehensiveness that gradually led to the blurring of the borderline between "Ṣūfī" and "non-Ṣūfī" exegesis and the inclusion of Ṣūfī exegesis in conventional commentaries, both Sunnī and Shīʿī.

On the other hand, we observe the opposite tendency in approaching the Qurʾān, when renowned Ṣūfī masters produce quite conventional exegetical works that are practically devoid of any Ṣūfī elements. *Nughbat al-bayān fī tafsīr al-Qurʾān* by the influential Ṣūfī scholar and statesman under the caliph al-Qādir, Abū Ḥafṣ ʿUmar al-Suhrawardī (d. 632/1234), which is occasionally classified under the rubric of "moderate" Ṣūfī exegesis (e.g Böwering, Ṣūfī hermeneutics, 257), is a case in point.

This work, which remains in manuscript (see Düzenli, Şihabuddin), is characterized by a Western scholar as "a very standard, non-mystical commentary" that is "firmly situated in the type of philological and situational exegesis represented in the standard Sunni commentaries and exegetical tradition upon which al-Suhrawardī was drawing" (Ohlander, Abū Ḥafṣ). Indeed, even a cursory glance at the first dozen pages of its manuscript demonstrates an almost complete lack of any recognizable Ṣūfī motifs and methods. Moreover, the author explicitly states in the introduction that he has chosen to "stick to the basics" of the *tafsīr* genre and to abstain from composing a sophisticated and recondite esoteric commentary *(an ubriza min sawāniḥ al-ghuyūb mā yarwī ʿaṭash al-qulūb)* because of lack of time (fol. 2).

Our survey of "moderate" Ṣūfī exegesis would be incomplete without mentioning Persian *tafsīr*s by Abū l-Faḍl Rashīd al-Dīn Aḥmad al-Maybudī (d. 530/1135) and Abū Naṣr Aḥmad al-Darwājikī (d. 549/1154). The former is based on the exegetical work of the renowned Ḥanbalī mystic ʿAbdallāh al-Anṣārī l-Harawī (d. 481/1089), as the author explicitly states in the introduction. It is no wonder that it is sometimes referred to as *Tafsīr khawāja ʿAbdallāh al-Anṣārī*, but the title given to it by the author is *Kashf al-asrār wa-ʿuddat al-abrār*. Born of a family renowned for its learning and piety in a town of Maybud (the province of Yazd in Iran), al-Maybudī combined the traditional education of a Shāfiʿī jurist and *muḥaddith* with a propensity to mysticism and an ascetic life-style. Like the other "moderate" Ṣūfī commentaries discussed above, al-Maybudī's *Kashf al-asrār* combines conventional historical, philological and legal exegesis with Ṣūfī *ishārāt* and *laṭāʾif*. The former is usually expressed in Arabic and the latter in Persian, thereby setting a precedent to be followed by many Persophone Ṣūfī authors in Iran and India. The commentator describes his method as consisting of three "stages" *(nawba)*. The first involves a translation of selected verses from Arabic into Persian (see PERSIAN LITERATURE AND THE QURʾĀN; LITERATURE AND THE QURʾĀN); the second provides a conventional historical, philological and legal commentary; while the third deals with the mystical aspects of the revelation. The latter relies heavily on al-Anṣārī's mystical commentary, which in turn is based on al-Sulamī's *Ḥaqāʾiq al-tafsīr* and its Ṣūfī authorities such as Abū Yazīd al-Bisṭāmī (d. 234/848 or 261/875), al-Junayd, al-Tustarī, and al-Shiblī (d. 334/946), etc. As befits a "moderate" commentator, al-Maybudī avoids Ṣūfī interpretations that conflict with the literal meaning of the qurʾānic text. His treatment of the controversial issues of anthropomorphic features of God, the provenance of good and evil, and divine predetermination of all events is that of an Ashʿarī theologian (see FREEDOM AND PREDESTINATION).

Little is known about the other Persian *tafsīr* of that age by al-Darwājikī, nicknamed the "ascetic" *(zāhid)*, beyond a cursory mention of his work, which remains unpublished. Even the exact title of his *tafsīr* remains debated, although it is often referred to as *Tafsīr al-zāhid*. The author's sobriquet indicates his propensity for an ascetic life-style; however, in the absence of an available text of this work its exact character is impossible to determine.

A totally different vision of the qurʾānic revelation was presented by the celebrated Sunnī theologian and jurist Abū Ḥāmid al-Ghazālī, whose famous tract *Jawāhir al-Qurʾān* can hardly be defined as exegetical in the conventional sense of the word.

Nevertheless, its emphasis on the numerous layers of meaning embedded in qurʾānic chapters and verses and the idea that the most elusive and subtle of them constitute the exclusive domain of Ṣūfī gnostics gives it a distinctive Ṣūfī flavor. In this work al-Ghazālī undertakes a classification of several types of qurʾānic verses according to their contents. In so doing he establishes a hierarchy of verses by likening them to various types of precious stones, pearls and rare substances. Thus, the knowledge *(maʿrifa)* of God is symbolized by red sulfur (the precious substance which according to medieval alchemy could transform base metals into gold), while the knowledge of God's essence, attributes and works is likened to three types of corundum. Below this sublime knowledge lies what al-Ghazālī describes as "the definition of the path advancing to God," namely the verses of the Qurʾān that elucidate the major stages of the believer's progress to God. This progress is couched by al-Ghazālī in a typical Ṣūfī imagery of "polishing" the mirror of the heart and soul and actualizing the divine nature *(lāhūt)* inherent in every human being. Al-Ghazālī likens this category of qurʾānic verses to "shining pearls." The third category contains verses dealing with man's condition at the time of his final encounter with God, namely, resurrection (q.v.), reckoning, the reward and the punishment, the beatific vision of God in the afterlife, etc. According to al-Ghazālī, this category, which he dubs "green emerald," comprises "a third part of the verses and sūras of the Qurʾān." The fourth group includes numerous verses describing "the conditions of those who have traversed [the path to God] and those who have denied him and deviated from his path," namely, various prophetic and angelic figures and other mythological individuals mentioned in the Qurʾān (see LIE; GRATITUDE AND INGRATITUDE; MYTHS AND LEGENDS IN THE QURʾĀN). In al-Ghazālī's view, their goal is to arouse fear and give warning to the believers (see WARNER) and to make them consider carefully their own condition vis-à-vis God. He compares these verses to grey ambergris and fresh and blooming aloe-wood. The fifth group of verses deals with "the arguments of the infidels against the truth and clear explanation of their humiliation by obvious proofs." According to al-Ghazālī these verses contain the greatest antidote *(al-tiryāq al-akbar)*. The sixth category of verses deals with the stages of man's journey to God and the management of its "vehicle," the human body, by supplying it with lawful means of sustenance (q.v.) and procreation (see LAWFUL AND UNLAWFUL). All this presupposes the wayfarer's interaction with other human beings and their institutions, the rules of which, according to al-Ghazālī, are stipulated in the verses belonging to the sixth category. Al-Ghazālī likens it to the "strongest musk."

Upon establishing this hierarchy of qurʾānic verses, al-Ghazālī proceeds to classify the "outward" and "inward" sciences associated with the Qurʾān. To the former belong (a) the science of its recitation which is represented by Qurʾān readers and reciters (see RECITERS OF THE QURʾĀN); (b) the knowledge of its language and grammar which is handled by philologists and grammarians (see LANGUAGE AND STYLE OF THE QURʾĀN); and (c) the science of "outward exegesis" *(al-tafsīr al-ẓāhir)* which its practitioners, those scholars whose focus rests on the Qurʾān's "external shell" *(al-ṣadaf)*, mistakenly consider the consummate knowledge available to human beings. While al-Ghazālī recognizes the necessity of these "outward" sciences and their practitioners, he dismisses their claims to represent the ultimate knowledge about the Qurʾān. He attributes this honor to the "sciences of the kernels of the Qurʾān" *(ʿulūm al-lubāb),* which are subdivided into two levels: the lower and the higher. The former, in turn, is subdivided into three groups: (a) the knowledge of the stories of the qurʾānic prophets, which is preserved and transmitted by story-tellers, preachers and ḥadīth-transmitters (see TEACHING AND PREACHING THE QURʾĀN); (b) the knowledge of God's arguments against his deniers, which gave rise to theology *(al-kalām)* and its practitioners (the *mutakallimūn*); and (c) the knowledge of the legal injunctions of the Qurʾān, which is represented by the jurists *(fuqahāʾ).* The latter, according to al-Ghazālī, are more important than the other religious specialists because the need for them is "more universal." The upper level of the sciences that branched off of the Qurʾān includes the knowledge of God and of the world to come, followed by the knowledge of the "straight path and of the manner of traversing it."

Having established the hierarchy of sciences that have grown out of the Qurʾān, al-Ghazālī lays out his exegetical method, which hinges on the notion of the allegorical and symbolic nature of the revelation:

Know that everything which you are likely to understand is presented to you in such a way that, if in sleep you were studying the Protected Tablet (*al-lawḥ al-maḥfūẓ;* see PRESERVED TABLET) with your soul, it would be related to you through a suitable symbol which needs interpretation (Eng. trans. in Ghazālī, *Jewels,* 52).

Hence, "The interpretation of the Qurʾān *(taʾwīl),*" according to al-Ghazālī, "occupies the place of the interpretation of dreams" (*taʿbīr;* ibid.) and the exegete's task is to "comprehend the hidden connection between the visible world and the invisible" (Ghazālī, *Jewels,* 53) or unseen in the same way as the interpreter of dreams strives to make sense out of somebody's dream or vision (see DREAMS AND SLEEP). This idea is brought home in the following programmatic statement:

Understand that so long as you are in this-worldly life you are asleep, and your waking-up will occur only after death (see DEATH AND THE DEAD; SLEEP), at which time you become fit to see the clear truth face to face. Before that time it is impossible for you to know the realities except when they are molded in the form of imaginative symbols (Ghazālī, *Jewels,* 54).

The only way to gain the knowledge of the true reality of God and his creation is, according to al-Ghazālī, through the renunciation of this world and righteousness. Those who seek "the vanities of this world, eating what is unlawful and following [their] carnal desires" are barred from the understanding of the qurʾānic message. Their corrupt and sinful nature makes them see nothing in the Qurʾān but contradiction and incongruence. Hence, the perception of the qurʾānic allegories and symbols by different people correspond to their level of spiritual purity and intellectual attainment. In commenting on the special virtue of Q 1 (Sūrat al-Fātiḥa, "The Opening"; see FĀTIḤA), which many exegetes consider to be the key to paradise (q.v.), al-Ghazālī argues that a worldly individual imagines the qurʾānic paradise to be a place where he will satisfy his desire for food, drink and sex, while the perfected Ṣūfī gnostic sees it as a site of refined spiritual pleasures and "pays no heed to the paradise of the fools."

Apart from the Fātiḥa, al-Ghazālī singles out the following verses for a special discussion: Q 2:255, "The Throne Verse" (see

THRONE OF GOD), Q 112 (Sūrat al-Ikhlāṣ, "Purity of Faith"), Q 36 (Sūrat Yā Sīn), whereupon he declares the Fātiḥa to be "the best of all sūras" and the "Throne Verse" to be "the chief of all verses." In the subsequent narrative he enumerates 763 "jewel verses" and 741 "pearl verses." Al-Ghazālī never directly addresses the issue of how and why some divine statements can be better than others, although he profusely quotes prophetic reports that assert the special virtues of certain verses and sūras.

Like al-Qushayrī and earlier exegetes, al-Ghazālī is convinced that the depth of one's understanding of the Qurʾān is directly linked to one's level of spiritual purity, righteousness and intellectual progress. It is no wonder that in his ranking of exegetes the highest rank is unequivocally accorded to the accomplished Ṣūfī gnostic *(ʿārif)*. To him and only to him is disclosed the greatest secret of being. This is stated clearly in al-Ghazālī's *Mishkāt al-anwār* — an esoteric reflection on the epistemic and ontological implications of the "Light Verse" (Q 24:35):

The gnostics ascend from the foothill of metaphor (q.v.; *al-majāz*) to the way-station of the true reality *(al-ḥaqīqa)*. When they complete their ascension, they see directly that there is nothing in existence except God most high (Ghazālī, *Mishkat,* 58).

Therefore, for the gnostics, the qurʾānic phrase "Everything perishes save his face" (Q 28:88) is an expression of the existential truth, according to which "everything except God, if considered from the viewpoint of its essence, is but a pure nonexistence *(ʿadam maḥḍ)*," God being the only reality of the entire universe (*Mishkāt,* 58). This bold idea prefigures the monistic speculations of Ibn al-ʿArabī and his followers, who also were to make extensive use of esoteric exegesis in order to showcase their monistic vision of the world.

The blossoming of ecstatic/esoteric exegesis

The works of Persian Ṣūfīs Abū Thābit Muḥammad al-Daylamī (d. 593/1197) and Rūzbihān Baqlī (d. 606/1209) constitute a distinct trend in Ṣūfī exegetical literature that is characterized by "intense visions and powerful ecstasies interpreted in terms of a qurʾānically based metaphysics" (Ernst, *Rūzbihān,* ix). The prevalence of such elements in the exegetical works of these two writers prompted Böwering (Ṣūfī hermeneutics, 257) to describe them as being more "esoteric" than their "moderate" counterparts discussed above. Al-Daylamī, a little known, if original and prolific author, wrote a mystical commentary entitled *Taṣdīq al-maʿārif* (it is also occasionally referred to as *Futūḥ al-raḥmān fī ishārāt al-Qurʾān*). It creatively combines early Ṣūfī exegetical dicta borrowed from al-Sulamī's *Ḥaqāʾiq al-tafsīr* — they constitute about half of al-Daylamī's work — with the author's own elaborations. Surprisingly, al-Daylamī never mentions al-Qushayrī's *Laṭāʾif al-ishārāt,* which was composed some one hundred years before his own. As already mentioned, al-Daylamī's own texts reflect his overwhelming preoccupation with "the visionary world of the mystic," which "is seen as totally real and fully identical with the spiritual world of the invisible realm" (ibid., 270). In the absence of an edited and published text of this commentary — which seems to exist in a unique manuscript — one cannot provide a detailed analysis of its content. According to Böwering who discovered the manuscript in a Turkish archive, it is "a continuous yet eclectic commentary on selected koranic verses from all suras presented in sequence" which "consists of two parallel levels of interpretative glosses on koranic phrases, specimens of Ṣūfī sayings, and items of the author's own explanation." His work foreshadowed "ideas that emerged in the Kobrawi school" [of Ṣūfism] (Böwering, Deylamī), whose exegetical production will be discussed below.

Somewhat better known is the commentary of al-Daylamī's younger contemporary Rūzbihān [al-]Baqlī al-Shīrāzī (d. 606/1209) entitled *ʿArāʾis al-bayān fī ḥaqāʾiq al-Qurʾān*. This massive exegetical opus reflects Rūzbihān's overriding propensity for visions, dreams, powerful ecstasies and ecstatic utterances that "earned him the sobriquet 'Doctor Ecstaticus' *(shaykh-i shaṭṭāḥ)*" (Ernst, Rūzbihān). Like al-Daylamī's *Taṣdīq al-maʿārif*, *ʿArāʾis al-bayān* was written in Arabic and consists almost equally of earlier exegetical material — mostly borrowed from al-Sulamī — and of the author's own glosses. In contrast to al-Daylamī, Rūzbihān also availed himself of the materials borrowed from al-Qushayrī's *Laṭāʾif al-ishārāt*. Rūzbihān's uses of the Qurʾān in both his commentary and other works, however, are much bolder than those of the Ṣūfī exegetes already described. Not only does he constantly invoke the sacred text in describing his spiritual encounters with and visions of God, but he also claims to have symbolically eaten it (see POPULAR AND TALISMANIC USES OF THE QURʾĀN). Thus in his *Kashf al-asrār*, "Unveiling of secrets," he provides the following description of his visionary experiences:

When I passed through the atmosphere of eternity (q.v.), I stopped at the door of power (see POWER AND IMPOTENCE). I saw all the prophets present there; I saw Moses with the Torah (q.v.) in his hand, Jesus (q.v.) with the Gospel (q.v.) in his hand, David (q.v.) with the Psalms (q.v.), and Muḥammad with the Qurʾān in his hand. Moses gave me the Torah to eat, Jesus gave me the Gospel to eat, David gave me the Psalms to eat and Muḥammad gave me the Qurʾān to eat. Adam gave me the most beautiful names [of God] and the Greatest Name to drink. I learned what I learned of the elect divine sciences for which God singles out his prophets and saints (Ernst, *Rūzbihān,* 51).

One can hardly be any bolder than this. According to Ernst, this dream is deemed to symbolize Rūzbihān's "complete internalization" of the inspiration of these scriptures. The Qurʾān and its imagery figure prominently in the Ṣūfī's ecstatic visions. Thus he compares his condition in the presence of God with that of Zulaykha in the presence of Joseph (q.v.; Q 12:22-32), as described in the following passage:

He wined me with the wine (q.v.) of intimacy and nearness. Then he left and I saw him as the mirror of creation wherever I faced, and that was his saying, "Whereso-ever you turn, there is the face of God" (Q 2:109 [sic]). Then he spoke to me after increasing my longing for him... and [I] said to myself: "I want to see his beauty without interruption." He said: "Remember the condition of Zulaykha and Joseph..." (Ernst, *Rūzbihān,* 42).

Rūzbihān also draws a bold comparison between himself and Adam and has God say the following:

I have chosen my servant Rūzbihān for eternal happiness, sainthood *(wilāya)*, and bounty.... He is my vicegerent *(khalīfa)* in this world and all worlds; I love whosoever loves him and hate whosoever hates him..., for I am "one who acts when he wishes" (Q 107:11 [sic]; Ernst, *Rūzbihān,* 48).

This feeling of mutual love, intimacy and [com]passion between God and his

[I] Folio from an Ottoman manuscript (copied 1227/1812) of *Kashf al-sutūr fī tafāsīr āyat al-nūr* by Saʿd Allāh b. Ismāʿīl (Saʿīd Efendi, d. 1247/1831), that contains Ṣūfī interpretations extolling the "Light Verse" (Q 24:35). Reproduced with the kind permission of the manuscript collection at the University of Michigan, Ann Arbor (Mich.Isl.13, fol. 1a-b, Special Collections Library, University of Michigan).

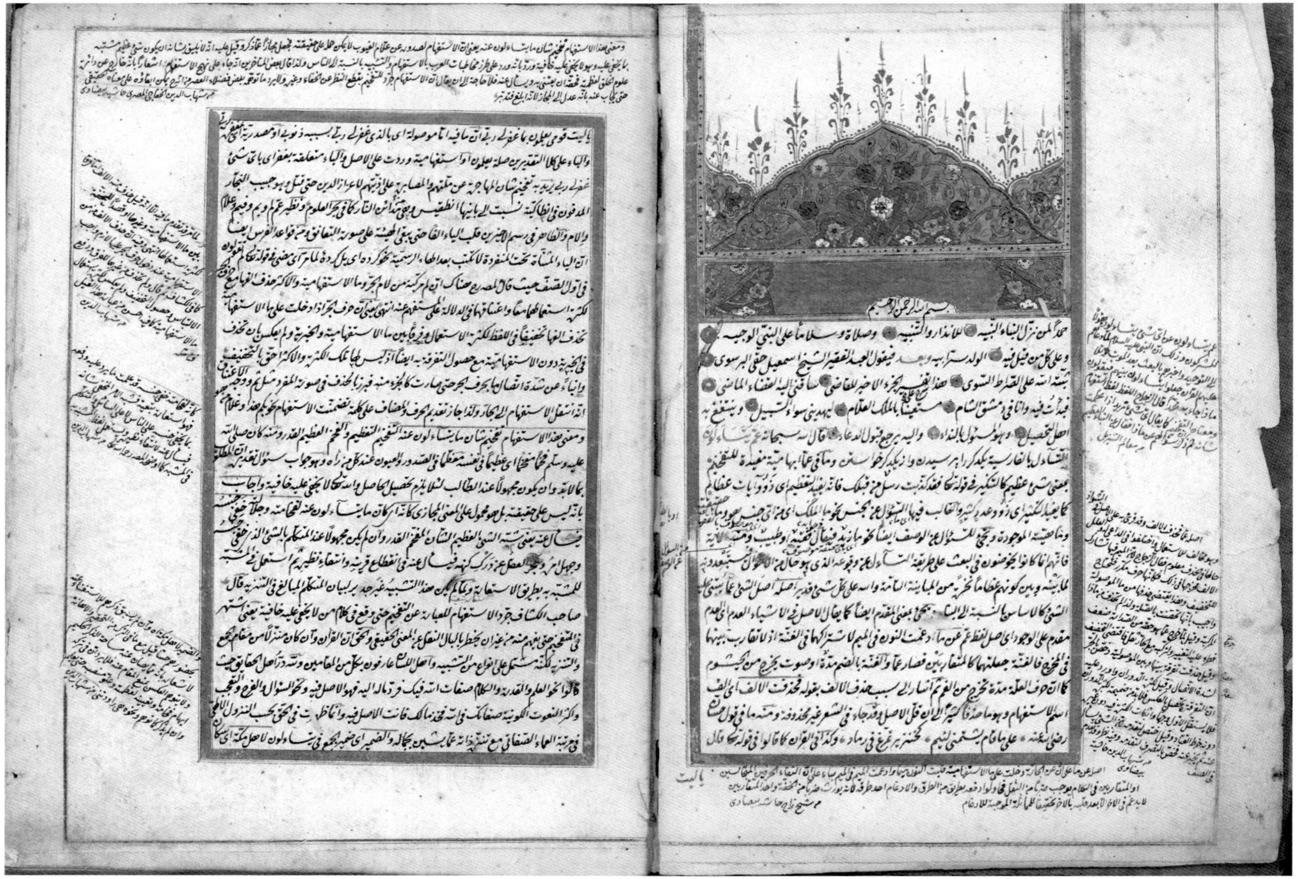

[II] Folio (ad Q 78:1) from a beautifully illuminated manuscript of *Rūḥ al-bayān*, a Qurʾān commentary by the Ottoman scholar and follower of Ibn al-ʿArabī (d. 638/1240), Ismāʿīl Ḥaqqī Brusāwī (d. 1137/1725). Reproduced with the kind permission of the manuscript collection at the University of Michigan, Ann Arbor (Mich.Isl.181, fol. 1a-b, Special Collections Library, University of Michigan).

mystical lover is the hallmark of Rūzbihān's entire mystical legacy. According to Ernst, the very title of Rūzbihān's commentary — *ʿArāʾis al-bayān,* "The brides of explanation" — "invokes the unveiling of the bride in a loving encounter as the model of initiation into the esoteric knowledge of God" (Ernst, *Rūzbihān,* 71). One can argue that Rūzbihān's visionary and ecstatic experiences are virtually permeated by qurʾānic language and imagery. As with early Ṣūfī masters, the Qurʾān serves Rūzbihān as a means of transforming himself and, eventually, achieving the ultimate intimacy with and knowledge of God.

Ibn al-ʿArabī and the Kubrawī tradition

According to Böwering's classification (Ṣūfī hermeneutics, 257), the subsequent stage in the development of Ṣūfī exegesis was dominated by its two major strains: Muḥyī l-Dīn Ibn al-ʿArabī (d. 638/1240) and his followers (mostly in the Muslim east) and Najm al-Dīn Kubrā (d. 618/1221) and the Kubrawī school of Ṣūfism.

One can say that Ibn al-ʿArabī's long-lasting influence on the subsequent Ṣūfī tradition springs from his role as an intellectual bridge between eastern and western strains of Ṣūfism. While Ṣūfī ideas initially spread westwards — from Sahl al-Tustarī and the Baghdādī school to Ibn Masarra al-Jabalī (d. 319/931) and his Andalusī and Maghribī successors — by the sixth/twelfth century western Ṣūfism acquired a distinctive character and was represented by such versatile and original thinkers as Ibn Barrajān (d. 536/1141), Ibn al-ʿArīf (d. 536/1141), Ibn Qasī (d. 546/1151), Abū Madyan (d. 594/1197) and Ibn al-ʿArabī, to name but a few (Gril, 'La lecture', 521-2). Of these Ibn Barrajān deserves special notice as the author of at least one, and possibly two, Ṣūfī commentaries that seem to have had a profound influence on Ibn al-ʿArabī and his numerous followers in the Muslim east.

As with earlier Ṣūfī exegetes, Ibn Barrajān envisioned the realization of the qurʾānic message by the mystic as his progressive immersion into its mysteries, which eventually results in what the Andalusī master called "the paramount reading" *(al-tilāwa l-ʿulyā)* of the Qurʾān. In the process, the very personality of the mystic is transformed by this encounter with the divine word as he passes from its literal message *(ʿibra; iʿtibār)* to its underlying, "crossed over to" truth *(al-maʿbūr ilayhi)* and from a physical perception *(baṣar)* of the sacred text to an interior, intuitive grasp of its inner reality (Gril, 'La lecture', 516). In other words, in the process of "remembering" *(dhikr)* and contemplating the Qurʾān the mystic develops a deep and genuine insight that allows him to realize its true meaning and implications. As a result, he is eventually transformed into the "universal servant" *(al-ʿabd al-kullī),* whose recitation of the sacred text is twice as effective as the recitation of the ordinary believer or the "partial servant" *(al-ʿabd al-juzʾī).*

Ibn Barrajān's exegesis displays the following characteristic features that set it apart from the mainstream interpretative tradition (whose elements are duly represented in his work): (1) the insistence that *dhikr* should serve as the means of achieving a total and undivided concentration on the sacred text; (2) the continual awareness of the subtle correspondences between the phenomena and entities of the universe and the "signs" embedded in the scripture; (3) the affirmation that the heart of the "universal servant" is capable of encompassing the totality of existence in the same way as it is contained in the Preserved Tablet; and (4) the notion that the divine word constitutes the supreme reality of human nature, which makes it possible to erase the boundary that separates the creature from its creator and thereby achieve a cognitive and experiential union between them (ibid., 520-1). Finally, Ibn Barrajān restricts this superior realization of the divine word to a small group of divinely elected individuals, whom he identifies as "the veracious ones" *(ṣiddīqūn)*. His bold ideas were elaborated upon and brought to fruition in the legacy of Ibn al-ʿArabī and his school.

Ibn al-ʿArabī's uses of the Qurʾān are rich and variegated. He claims to have composed a multi-volume commentary on the Qurʾān entitled *al-Jāmiʿ wa-l-tafṣīl fī asrār maʿānī l-tanzīl,* which seems to have been lost. On the other hand, his entire work, including his major masterpieces — *Fuṣūṣ al-ḥikam* and *al-Futūḥāt al-makkiyya* — may be seen as a giant running commentary on the foundational texts of Islam, the Qurʾān and the sunna of the Prophet. His overall approach to the Qurʾān must be considered in the general context of his thought which is characterized by the belief that the true realities of God and the universe are concealed from ordinary human beings behind a distorting veil of images and appearances. These true realities, however, can be rendered accessible to the elect few through a spiritual awakening and special intellectual insight or "unveiling" *(kashf)* bestowed upon them by God. Ibn al-ʿArabī calls the possessors of this insight "the people of the true reality" *(ahl al-ḥaqīqa),* or "divine gnostics" *(ʿārifūn)*. They and only they can decipher the true meaning of the symbols that constitute both the qurʾānic text and the entities and phenomena of the empirical universe, which are likened by Ibn al-ʿArabī to a giant book. For him, both the Qurʾān and the universe are but "books" of God — assemblages of symbols and images behind which lie the ultimate realities of existence that, in the final account, take their origin in and are somehow identical to the divine reality *(al-ḥaqq)*. The deciphering of these symbols and images becomes possible through God's revelatory manifestations *(tajallī)* to his elect "friends" and through their ability to perceive their hidden meaning by means of their imaginative faculties.

Since Ibn al-ʿArabī considered himself to be the greatest *ʿārif* of his age (and possibly of all times) and the spiritual "pole" *(al-quṭb)* of the universe, he saw no reason to legitimize his understanding of the meaning of the scripture or — as he put it, of its "spirit" *(rūḥ)* — by reference to any prior exegetical authority or tradition. In his opinion, he is absolved of such a justification because his "epistemic source" is nothing other than divine inspiration (Nettler, *Ṣūfī metaphysics,* 29). This attitude is evident from his poetic commentaries on selected qurʾānic sūras included in his poetic collection (*Dīwān,* 136-79). Here Ibn al-ʿArabī offers an exegesis aimed at bringing out the "spiritual quintessence" *(rūḥ)* of these sūras. In so doing, he deliberately relegates his role to that of a simple transmitter of the outpourings of divinely induced insights that are dictated to him in the "mystical moment" *(wārid al-waqt)* in which he happens to find himself. He is adamant that he has added nothing to what he has received from this divine source of inspiration (Bachmann, Un commentaire, 503). His use of poetry — an art associated with pre-Islamic paganism (see POETRY AND POETS; PRE-ISLAMIC ARABIA AND THE QURʾĀN) — and his occasional imitation of the meter and rhythm of qurʾānic chapters (see INIMITABILITY; PROVOCATION) no doubt raised many scholarly eyebrows, both during his lifetime and after his death. So did his radical departure from the conventions of traditional exegesis. Thus in elucidating the "spirit" of the Fātiḥa Ibn al-ʿArabī boldly and somewhat incongruously refers to God as "a light not like any other light" — a clear allusion to the Light Verse (*āyat al-nūr,* Q 24:35) — then proceeds to discuss its implications, which have little to do with the sūra that he is supposedly discussing (Bachmann, Un commentaire, 505).

His claim to be a simple mouthpiece of the divine inspirer absolves him, however, of the necessity to justify his exegetical method or to follow any conventional logic. This inspirational exegesis, according to Ibn al-ʿArabī, assures absolute certainty in interpretation of the divine word and overrules all alternative understandings of it. Ibn al-ʿArabī also revisits Q 24:35 in many passages of his magnum opus, *al-Futūḥāt al-makkiyya.* Here his interpretation of this verse reveals three distinct levels of understanding of its meaning: the metaphysical and cosmological, the analogical (built around the implicit correspondences between the universe and the human individual) and the existential-experiential based on the notion — so dear to Ibn al-ʿArabī — of the underlying unity (and union) of God, humankind and the universe (Gril, Le commentaire, 180). In *Fuṣūṣ al-ḥikam* — Ibn al-ʿArabī's controversial meditation on the phenomenon of prophethood and its major representatives — his uses of the qurʾānic text are particularly bold and challenging (the same is true of his uses of the sunna). The Qurʾān radically and dramatically reinterpreted by the Ṣūfī master serves as a showcase for his monistic metaphysics (see also PHILOSOPHY AND THE QURʾĀN). Moreover, for Ibn al-ʿArabī his monistic vision of God, humankind and the universe constitutes the very truth and ultimate meaning of the qurʾānic revelation (Nettler, *Ṣūfī metaphysics,* 13-14). In the *Fuṣūṣ,* the traditional exegetical lore associated with the prophets and other individuals mentioned in the qurʾānic text is inextricably intertwined with "an extremely abstruse 'Ṣūfī metaphysics,'" which for Ibn al-ʿArabī presumably reflected its inner, essential, truth (ibid., 14). This kind of exegesis is so distinctive and unique that it "may be considered an Islamic religious genre in its own right" that can be dubbed "Ṣūfī metaphysical story-telling" (ibid.).

As an example of Ibn al-ʿArabī's exegetical method, one can cite his audacious rendition of the story of Aaron (q.v.), Moses and the golden calf (Q 7:148-55 and Q 20:85-94; see CALF OF GOLD). Here — contrary to the literal meaning of the qurʾānic narrative — Aaron and the worshippers of the golden calf are portrayed as being wiser than Moses, who misguidedly scolds them for lapsing into idolatry (see IDOLATRY AND IDOLATERS). Unlike Moses, they realize that God can be worshipped in every object, for every object, including the golden calf, is but "a site of divine self-manifestation" (*baʿḍ al-majālī l-ilāhiyya; Fuṣūṣ,* 192; Nettler, *Ṣūfī metaphysics,* 53). In this interpretation, the original qurʾānic condemnation of idolatry is completely inverted: the idolaters become "gnostics," who

> *know the full truth* concerning idolatry, but are honor-bound not to disclose this truth, even to the prophets, the apostles and their heirs, for these all have their divinely-appointed roles in curbing idolatry and promoting the worship of God *in their time and their situation* (Nettler, *Ṣūfī metaphysics,* 67).

The ultimate truth, however, is that God is immanent to all things and can be worshipped everywhere. Here, and throughout the *Fuṣūṣ,* Ibn al-ʿArabī's unitive, monistic vision of God and the world is presented within the framework of qurʾānic narratives (q.v.) pertaining to the vicissitudes of the prophetic missions of the past (see PUNISHMENT STORIES). For him, however, this is not *his* personal vision but *the true and unadulterated* meaning of the divine word (ibid., 94).

The major themes of Ibn al-ʿArabī's legacy were explored and elucidated by his foremost disciple, Ṣadr al-Dīn al-Qūnawī (d. 673/1274), the author of numerous influential works on theoretical Ṣūfism. His major exegetical work, *Ijāz al-bayān fī ta'wīl al-Qur'ān,* is a lengthy disquisition on the metaphysical, epistemological and psychological implications of the first sūra of the Qur'ān based on the assumption that it constitutes the very gist of the revelation. The author's indebtedness to Ibn al-ʿArabī is obvious from the outset, when he states that

> God made the primeval macrocosm *(al-ʿālam al-kabīr)* — from the viewpoint of its [outward] form — a book carrying the images of the divine names... and he [God] made the perfect man — who is but a microcosm *(al-ʿālam al-ṣaghīr)* — an intermediate book from the viewpoint of [its] form, which combines in itself the presence of the names and the presence of the named [i.e. God]. He also revealed the great Qur'ān as a guidance to the human being — who is fashioned in his image — in order to explain the hidden aspect of his way, the secret of his sūra and of his rank (Qūnawī, *al-Tafsīr,* 98).

Al-Qūnawī identifies five levels and realms of existence and their correspondence to the five layers of meaning of the divine word. For the exegete, this task of identification is much more important than the minutia of conventional *tafsīr* with which he claims to have deliberately dispensed (ibid., 103). Al-Qūnawī's emphasis on the hierarchies of the divine names and their ontological counterparts (realms of existence) constitutes probably the most distinguishing feature of this highly technical and recondite mystical commentary, which came to characterize the intellectual legacy of Ibn al-ʿArabī's school of thought as a whole.

In ʿAbd al-Razzāq Kamāl al-Dīn al-Qāshānī (d. 730/1329), a native of the Iranian province of Jibāl, we find another scholar fully committed to Ibn al-ʿArabī's spiritual and intellectual legacy, while remaining an original mystical thinker in his own right. Not only did al-Qāshānī distinguish himself as an advocate of his great predecessor but also as an effective disseminator of the latter's mystical teaching which by that time had come to be known as "the doctrine of the unity/oneness of being/existence" *(waḥdat al-wujūd).* As a promoter of Ibn al-ʿArabī's ideas, his main achievement lies in his ability to strip them of their original ambiguity, and open-endedness and to present them in a lucid and accessible form to anyone who cared to learn them. Al-Qāshānī excelled in this task to such an extent that his popular mystical commentary, originally titled *Ta'wīl al-Qur'ān,* was for several centuries considered by many to be a work of Ibn al-ʿArabī himself. In fact, its latest edition, which appeared in Beirut in 1968, was entitled *Tafsīr al-Qur'ān al-karīm lil-shaykh al-akbar... Ibn ʿArabī.* A systematic and clear-headed thinker, al-Qāshānī provides a detailed self-reflective exposition of his exegetical method in the introduction to his commentary. Citing a famous prophetic ḥadīth according to which each qur'ānic verse has two aspects — the "outward" *(ẓahr)* and the "inward" *(baṭn)* — al-Qāshānī identifies the understanding of the former as *tafsīr* and of the latter as *ta'wīl* (Qāshānī, *Ta'wīl,* i, 4). His own interpretation is consistently identified as *ta'wīl* throughout the rest of his work. This indicates that by his time the rigid *tafsīr/ta'wīl* dichotomy, which does not seem to have existed in the earlier periods — both al-Ṭabarī and al-Bayḍāwī (d. prob. 716/1316) had no compunctions about applying the word *ta'wīl* to their conventional commentaries — had become widespread, at least in some Ṣūfī circles (cf. however, Shāh Walī Allāh, who defined *ta'wīl* as a regular historical and contextual commentary; Baljon, *Religion and thought,* 141). In a revealing passage from the introduction to his *Ta'wīl* al-Qāshānī describes his personal relationship with the qur'ānic revelation which, in a sense, epitomizes the Ṣūfī stance *vis-à-vis* the divine word:

For a long time I made the recitation *(tilāwa)* of the Qur'ān my habit and custom and meditated on its meaning with the [full] strength of my faith. Yet, despite my assiduousness at reciting passages from it *(al-awrād),* my chest was constrained, my soul troubled and my heart remained closed to it. However, my lord did not divert me from this recitation until I had grown accustomed and habituated to it and begun to taste the sweetness of its cup and its drink. It was then that I felt invigorated, my breast opened up, my conscience expanded, my heart was at ease, and my innermost self liberated... by these revelations. Then there appeared to me from behind the veil the meanings of every verse such that my tongue was incapable of describing, no capacity able to determine and count, and no power could resist unveiling and disclosure" (*Ta'wīl,* i, 4).

Unlike the authors of "moderate" Ṣūfī commentaries discussed above, al-Qāshānī consciously ignores those passages of the Qur'ān that, in his view, are not susceptible to esoteric interpretation *(kull mā lā yaqbalu al-ta'wīl 'indī aw lā yaḥtāju ilayhi).* With more than five centuries of Ṣūfī exegesis behind him, al-Qāshānī no longer feels obligated to pay tribute to the trivia of conventional *tafsīr* and focuses only on those aspects of the sacred text that resonate with his esoteric vision of the world. Even some favorite "Ṣūfī" verses such as Q 7:172 and Q 85:22 are passed over in silence, perhaps because al-Qāshānī feels that their interpretative potential has been exhausted by his predecessors (Lory, *Commentaires,* 31). Addressed to his fellow Ṣūfīs, "the people of [supersensory] unveiling" *(ahl al-kashf),* al-Qāshānī's exegesis brims with classical Ṣūfī terminology and themes borrowed from Ibn al-'Arabī's monistic ideas and imagery. In many cases, this terminology is not explained, presupposing its prior knowledge by the reader (ibid., 30). Al-Qāshānī is completely at home in dealing with all major levels of exegesis established by his predecessors: the monistic metaphysics with its tripartite division of being into the empirical realm *('ālam al-shahāda),* the intermediate realm of divine power *(al-jabarūt)* and the purely spiritual realm of divine sovereignty *(al-malakūt);* the parallelism and correspondence between the universe (the macrocosm) and its human counterpart (the microcosm); the major stages and spiritual states of the mystic's progress to God; the symbolism of the letters of the Arabic alphabet; numerology (q.v.); etc. As a typical example of his method one may his cite his glosses on Q 17:1:

"Glory be to him, who carried his servant," that is — [who] purified him from material attributes and deficiencies associated with [his] creation by means of the tongue of the spiritual state of disengagement [from the created world] *(al-tajarrud)* and perfection at the station of [absolute] servanthood... — "by night" — that is, in the darkness of bodily coverings and natural attachments, for the ascension and rise cannot occur except by means of a body — "from the holy mosque" — that is, from the station of the heart that is protected from the circumambulation of the polytheism of carnal drives… (*Taʾwīl,* i, 705).

In this passage and throughout, the correspondences between qurʾānic images and Ṣūfī psychology, epistemology and ontology are clearly and firmly established, leaving little room for the ambiguity of reference and referent and a general opacity of meaning that characterize the works of Ibn al-ʿArabī. One can thus conclude that in al-Qāshānī's commentary the esoteric exegesis of the previous centuries receives a succinct, systematic — perhaps overly-systematic — and lucid articulation. The exegetical method derived from Ibn al-ʿArabī and his predecessors has become stabilized. Its subsequent rearticulation by such later Ṣūfīs as Badr al-Dīn Simawī (d. 820/1420), Ismāʿīl Ḥaqqī (d. 1137/1725), Shāh Walī Allāh (d. 1176/1762), and Ibn ʿAjība (d. 1224/1809) — to name but a few — evinces a remarkable continuity that may be construed by some as a lack of originality. In the case of the last two authors, mystical exegesis is offered alongside other types of commentary, of which Ibn ʿAjība, for example, cites as many as eleven in his *al-Baḥr al-madīd* (i, 129-31). His *tafsīr* demonstrates his equal facility with both esoteric and exoteric commentary, without privileging either one of them (Michon, *Le soufi,* 88-9).

While the tradition of Qurʾān interpretation associated with the central Asian Ṣūfī master Najm al-Dīn Kubrā (d. 618/1221) and his followers Najm al-Dīn Dāya [al-]Rāzī (d. 654/1256) and ʿAlāʾ al-Dawla Simnānī (d. 736/1336) is often treated as a separate school of Ṣūfī exegesis (e.g. Böwering, Ṣūfī hermeneutics, 257), this perception has more to do with two different spiritual and intellectual lineages than with differences in their approaches to the Qurʾān. Unlike the Ṣūfī commentaries discussed above, we are dealing here with what amounts to a collective exegetical work that was started by Kubrā, continued by Dāya [al-]Rāzī and completed by Simnānī, although "it is possible that there are two different continuations to Kubrā's commentary, one by Simnānī and the other by Dāya" (Elias, *Throne carrier,* 205). "It is also conceivable that Dāya revised Kubrā's commentary" (ibid.). In any event, this commentary remains unpublished and our knowledge of its contents is derived from a recent Western study of Simnānī's oeuvre by Jamal Elias (ibid., 107-10).

As with earlier Ṣūfī exegetes, Simnānī spoke of "four levels of meaning [of the Qurʾān] corresponding to four levels of existence" (ibid., 108). Its exoteric dimension corresponds to the realm of "humanity" *(nāsūt);* its esoteric dimension to the realm of divine sovereignty *(malakūt);* its limit *(ḥadd)* relates to the realm of divine omnipotence *(jabarūt);* and its point of ascent, or *anagoge (maṭlaʿ/muṭṭalaʿ)* corresponds to the realm of divinity (*lāhūt,* ibid., 108). These realms, in turn, correspond to four levels of the human understanding of the Qurʾān — that of the ordinary believer *(muslim),* who relies upon his faculty of hearing (see SEEING AND HEARING; HEARING AND DEAFNESS); that of the faithful one *(muʾmin),* who relies on divine inspiration; that of the righteous one *(muḥsin),* who should not disclose what he understands except with divine permission *(idhn);* and, finally, the [direct] witness (*shāhid;* see WITNESS TO FAITH) whose understanding is so sublime that he should refrain from disclosing it to anyone for fear of confusion and sedition (ibid.). God's purpose in sending his revelation is to cleanse the hearts and souls of human beings from mundane distractions and thereby lead them to salvation. To this end, he has supplied them with special faculties or "subtle centers" *(laṭāʾif)* that orient them toward God and, eventually, lead the elect few of them to "a complete revelation of the true nature of reality" (ibid., 85).

Finally, mention should be made of the exegesis that combines esoteric exegesis and mystical metaphysics with Shīʿī theology. Here one thinks primarily of the exegetical works by Ḥaydar-i Āmulī (d. after 787/1385) — who consistently sought to integrate Ibn al-ʿArabī's ideas and exegetical methods into the Shīʿī intellectual universe — and Mullā Ṣadrā (d. 1050/1640) and his school, including what appears to be an extremely rare, if not unique, example of a mystical commentary written by a female scholar from Iran named Nuṣrat bt. Muḥammad Amīn, better known as Bānū-yi Iṣfahānī (d. 1403/1982; Ayāzī, *Mufassirūn,* 310-15, 629-33; Āmulī, *Jāmiʿ al-asrār;* Mullā Ṣadrā, *Asrār al-āyāt;* Amīn, *Tafsīr-i makhzan*).

This survey does not discuss the development of Ṣūfī exegesis in modern times, which in Western scholarship remains largely a terra incognita (see POST-ENLIGHTENMENT ACADEMIC STUDY OF THE QURʾĀN). For some representative works of this genre see Ayāzī, *Mufassirūn,* 833. See also WISDOM; SCIENCE AND THE QURʾĀN; TIME.

Alexander D. Knysh

Bibliography
Primary: N. Amīn (Bānū-yi Iṣfahānī), *Tafsīr-i makhzan al-ʿirfān,* 10 vols., Tehran 1982; H. Āmulī, *Jāmiʿ al-asrār,* ed. O. Yahya and H. Corbin, Tehran/Paris 1969; Baghawī, *Maʿālim;* al-Ghazālī, Abū Ḥāmid Muḥammad b. Muḥammad, *Jawāhir al-Qurʾān,* ed. M. al-Qabbānī, Beirut 1985, trans. M.A. Quasem, *The jewels of the Qurʾān,* London 1983; id., *Mishkāt al-anwār,* ed. S. Dughaym, Beirut 1994; Ibn ʿAjība, Abū l-ʿAbbās Aḥmad b. Muḥammad, *Tafsīr al-Fātiḥa al-kabīr al-musammā bi-l-Baḥr al-madīd,* ed. B.M. Bārūd, 2 vols., Abu Dhabi 1999; Ibn al-ʿArabī, Abū Bakr Muḥammad b. ʿAbdallāh, *Dīwān,* Beirut n.d.; id., *Fuṣūṣ al-ḥikam,* ed. A.ʿA. ʿAfīfī, Beirut 1980; id., *al-Futūḥāt al-makkiyya,* 4 vols., Beirut 1968; Khāzin, *Lubāb;* al-Maybudī, Abū l-Faḍl Rashīd al-Dīn Aḥmad, *Kashf al-asrār wa-ʿuddat al-abrār,* ed. ʿA.A. Ḥikmat, 10 vols., Tehran [1952-61]; Mullā Ṣadrā (Ṣadr al-Dīn Shīrāzī), *Asrār al-āyāt,* ed. M. Khvājavī, Beirut 1993; al-Qāshānī, *Taʾwīl;* al-Qūnawī, Ṣadr al-Dīn, *al-Tafsīr al-ṣūfī lil-Qurʾān. Ījāz al-bayān fī taʾwīl al-Qurʾān,* ed. A.Q.A. ʿAṭā, Cairo 1969; Qushayrī, *Laṭāʾif;* al-Sarrāj, Abū Naṣr ʿAbdallāh b. ʿAlī, *Kitāb al-Lumaʿ fī l-taṣawwuf,* ed. R.A. Nicholson, Leiden/London 1914; Sulamī, *Ḥaqāʾiq al-tafsīr,* ed. S. Imrān, 2 vols., Beirut 2001; id., *Ziyādāt.*
Secondary: S.M. Ayāzī, *al-Mufassirūn. Ḥayātuhum wa-manhajuhum,* Tehran 1414/1993; P. Bachmann, Un commentaire mystique du Coran, in *Arabica* 47 (2000), 503-9; J.M.S. Baljon, *Religion and thought of Shāh Walī Allāh Dihlawī, 1703-1762,* Leiden 1986; G. Böwering, Deylamī, Šams al-Dīn Abū Ṯābet Moḥammad b. ʿAbd al-Malek Ṭūsī, in *Encyclopedia Iranica,* vii, 341-2; id., *Mystical;* id. The scriptural "senses" in medieval Ṣūfī Qurʾān exegesis, in J.D. McAuliffe, B.D. Walfish and J.W. Goering (eds.), *With reverence for the word. Medieval scriptural exegesis in Judaism, Christianity, and Islam,* New York 2003, 346-65; id., Ṣūfī hermeneutics in medieval Islam, in *REI* 55-7 (1987-9), 255-70; Y. Düzenli, *Şihabuddin Sühreverdi ve Nuğbetü l-beyan,* PhD thesis, Marmara University, Istanbul 1994; J. Elias, *The throne carrier of God,* Albany, NY 1995; C. Ernst, Rūzbihān [al-Baḳlī], in *EI²,* viii, 651-2; id., *Rūzbihān Baqlī,* Richmond, Surrey 1996; D. Gril, 'La lecture supérieure' du Coran selon Ibn Barrajan, in *Arabica* 47 (2000), 510-22; id., Le commentaire du verset de la lumière d'après Ibn ʿArabī, in *Bulletin de l'Institut français d'archéologie orientale* 90 (1990), 179-87; A. Keeler, *Ṣūfī hermeneutics. Maybudī's Persian commentary on the Qurʾān, the Kashf al-asrār,* Oxford (forthcoming); J.-L. Michon, *Le soufi marocain Aḥmad Ibn ʿAjība (1746-1809),* Paris 1973; R. Nettler, *Ṣūfī metaphysics and qurʾānic prophets,* Cambridge 2003; Nwyia, *Exégèse;* id., *Trois oeuvres inédites de mystiques musulmans,* Beirut 1972; E. Ohlander, *Abū Ḥafṣ ʿUmar al-Suhrawardī and the institutionalization of Ṣūfism,* PhD diss., U. Michigan 2004; W. Saleh, *The formation of the classical* tafsīr *tradition,* Leiden 2004; K.Z. Sands, *Ṣūfī commentaries on the Qurʾān in classical Islam,* London 2005.

Suicide

The act of taking one's own life, killing oneself. Although several qurʾānic verses appear to be relevant to suicide, in particular Q 2:54, 4:66, 4:29 and 2:195, only the last two prove to be related to self-killing.

Moses (q.v.) said to his people, "My people, you have wronged yourselves by worshipping the calf (see CALF OF GOLD), so repent to your maker and kill yourselves; that is best for you in the eyes of your maker." Then he accepted your repentance: he is all-forgiving and most merciful (Q 2:54; see FORGIVENESS; MERCY; GOD AND HIS ATTRIBUTES).

The majority of the commentators (see EXEGESIS OF THE QUR'ĀN: CLASSICAL AND MEDIEVAL) are in agreement that the phrase "kill yourselves" *(fa-qtulū anfusakum)* means "those who have not worshipped the golden calf should kill those who worshipped it" (e.g. Ṭabarī, *Tafsīr,* i, 326-7). Some commentators, however, emphasize the metaphorical meaning (see METAPHOR; SYMBOLIC IMAGERY), that is, the Israelites are asked to repent through suppression of lustful desires *(bakh')* since such desire was the root cause of their sin (Bayḍāwī, *Anwār,* i, 62; Zamakhsharī, *Kashshāf,* i, 143; see CHILDREN OF ISRAEL; SIN, MAJOR AND MINOR). Another possible reading, collective suicide, is never mentioned by most commentators and is explicitly rejected by a few (e.g. Elmalılı, *Kur'ān Dili,* i, 355-6, who says that collective suicide is clearly not the intended meaning since that would have led to the extinction of the Jews; see JEWS AND JUDAISM; EXEGESIS OF THE QUR'ĀN: EARLY MODERN AND CONTEMPORARY).

The phrase "kill yourselves" also appears in Q 4:66, "If we had decreed to them [the hypocrites; see HYPOCRITES AND HYPOCRISY] 'kill yourselves' or 'leave your homes,' only a few would have done so" but, as in the case of Q 2:54, commentators normally see mutual killing in this verse and, even though collective suicide is mentioned by some as a possible reading (Elmalılı, *Kur'ān Dili,* ii, 1385-6), this is stated to be moot since the verse is not applicable to the Muslims who are commanded not to kill one another (see MURDER; BLOODSHED).

Q 4:29 is much more to the point: "You who believe (see BELIEF AND UNBELIEF), do not consume each other's property (q.v.) unjustly (see JUSTICE AND INJUSTICE), but trade through mutual goodwill is different (see TRADE AND COMMERCE; WEALTH), and do not kill yourselves, for God is the most merciful towards you." Al-Ṭabarī (d. 310/923; *Tafsīr,* iv, 38-9) reads the second part of this verse as a command against the believers' killing each other (see FIGHTING; WAR) and understands God's prohibition of unjust trade and believers' killing each other (except for a just reason) as a sign of his mercy. Al-Bayḍāwī (d. prob. 716/1316-17; *Anwār,* i, 211), however, sees here an injunction against self-killing through suppression of self *(bakh'),* placing oneself in danger, or through committing crimes that would incur death or abasement (presumably including usurious trade; see USURY; BOUNDARIES AND PRECEPTS; CHASTISEMENT AND PUNISHMENT), though he clearly does not view any of these as "intentional self-killing." In any case, the recommendation of the verse, he thinks, is for combined protection of self *(nafs)* and property *(māl),* which are joined as "halves." Al-Zamakhsharī (d. 538/1144; *Kashshāf,* i, 492) understands the verse as an injunction against the believers' killing each other and/or killing oneself (cf. Ibn al-Jawzī [d. 597/1200], *Zād,* ii, 61, ad Q 4:29, who maintains that the first meaning of *lā taqtulū anfusakum* is that God forbids his servant from killing himself). And, according to al-Qurṭubī (d. 671/1272; *Jāmi',* v, 156-7, ad Q 4:29), while the text itself *(lafẓ)* indicates that this phrase deals with (and urges against) killing oneself intentionally *(bi-qaṣdin minhu lil-qatl)* — by bringing him or herself to the folly that leads to destruction (as in the possible response to situations of boredom or anger: "do not kill yourselves") — the interpreters have agreed that this passage means that people should not kill one another. Elmalılı, a twentieth century Turkish interpreter (*Kurʾān Dili*, ii, 1343-4), rules out the apparent meaning (see POLYSEMY), which is suicide, and argues that the applicable meaning is "forbidding one to cause one's own destruction," which is possible in one of three ways (i) excessive asceticism (q.v.) — according to Elmalılı, this fits the context of the verse —; (ii) behavior that would lead to committing sins that call for killing, including illicit consumption of property of others; and (iii) placing oneself in harm's way, even if for a charitable purpose (see GOOD AND EVIL), where Elmalılı (like al-Ṭabarī) refers to the story of ʿAmr b. al-ʿĀṣ who refrained from taking major ablution with ice cold water on the basis of this verse (he resorted to *tayammum* instead) and the Prophet's acceptance of his practice (see CLEANLINESS AND ABLUTION; RITUAL PURITY).

The relevance of Q 2:195 to suicide is indirect but clear: "Spend in God's cause (see PATH OR WAY) and do not throw [yourselves] with your own hands to danger." Here, the question is about what the phrase "do not throw [yourselves] with your own hands to destruction/danger" means. In his extensive coverage of this question, al-Ṭabarī (*Tafsīr*, ii, 206-12) reports the following different readings: (i) spend in God's cause (no other meaning intended); (ii) spend in God's cause and do not jeopardize yourselves by fighting for God's cause unless there is (sufficient) provision and power; (iii) do not place yourself in harm's way, do not give yourself up to danger because you despair (q.v.) of God's forgiveness on account of your past sins (cf. Q 12:87: "Do not despair of God's mercy — only disbelievers despair of God's mercy," and Q 15:56: "Who except those who are astray despairs of his lord's mercy?"; see LORD); (iv) spend in God's cause and do not quit fighting; (v) a combination of the third and fourth: whoever does not give away in charity what he or she does not need places himself or herself in danger (see ALMSGIVING). Similarly, whoever is despondent because of past sins places herself or himself in danger because of the command in Q 12:87 and whoever quits fighting when fighting is clearly mandatory places herself or himself in danger of incurring God's punishment.

The reality of the temptation to end one's own life has not been denied by Islamic tradition. On the authority of Abū Hurayra (d. ca. 58/678), the Prophet himself is said to have said: "Whoever kills himself with an iron [instrument] *(bi-ḥadīdatin)*, his iron [instrument] would be in his hand, poking his belly with it in hellfire forever and ever (see HELL AND HELLFIRE; ETERNITY; REWARD AND PUNISHMENT). And whoever kills himself with poison, then his poison would be in his hand and he would sip from it in hellfire forever and ever. And whoever falls from a mountain killing himself, he would fall in hellfire forever and ever" (Ibn Ḥanbal, *Musnad*, xiii, 185; Muslim, *Ṣaḥīḥ*, i, 103-4, *bāb* 47, ḥadīth no. 175). And, although not qurʾānic, al-Ṭabarī (*Taʾrīkh*, i, 1150; Eng. trans. Watt and McDonald, *History*, vi, 71) preserves a tradition transmitted by Ibn Isḥāq (d. 150/767) that Muḥammad himself contemplated suicide when he first received the revelations (see REVELATION AND INSPIRATION): "I shall take myself to a mountain crag, hurl myself down from it, kill myself and find relief in that way."

In ethical discussions over both the qurʾānic positions on suicide and those developed in later Islamic thought, the motivations (e.g. despondency for one's own personal situation, vs. the decision to go into battle to defend one's community; see EXPEDITIONS AND BATTLES), as well as the results and means (killing oneself, killing others) of the action are considered. In both classical and contemporary discussions, no clear consensus has been reached and debated issues remain: does the benefit of a martyrdom outweigh the sin of killing oneself?; what, exactly, comprises an "unlawful" killing? Especially in the post-colonial period and with the use of suicide or martyr missions to secure political and social change have these questions become particularly pressing (cf. Malka, Must innocents die?; see also POLITICS AND THE QURʾĀN). While neither Q 4:29 nor Q 2:195 can be said to contain a clear injunction against suicide, it is safe to conclude that they may indeed be understood as ruling out killing oneself especially if they are considered in connection with one another. It is also possible to view suicide, at least from an ethical perspective (see ETHICS AND THE QURʾĀN), as a special case of murder, in which case all the qurʾānic verses that prohibit unlawful killing of a human being — in particular Q 6:151 and Q 17:33: "Do not take life that God has rendered sacred except for just cause," Q 5:32: "Whoever kills another, unless for murder or highway robbery (see THEFT; CORRUPTION), it is as though he has killed all humanity," and Q 4:93: "Whoever kills a believer intentionally, his punishment is to dwell in hell forever; God is angry with him (see ANGER), he curses (see CURSE) him and prepares a terrible punishment for him" — would also apply to suicide.

Ahmet T. Karamustafa

Bibliography
Primary: Bayḍāwī, *Anwār,* Beirut 1988; Elmalılı, Muhammed Hamdi Yazır, *Hak Dīni Kurʾān Dili,* 9 vols., Istanbul 1935-9; Ibn Ḥanbal, *Musnad,* ed. Shākir; Ibn al-Jawzī, *Zād,* 9 vols., Beirut n.d.; Muslim, *Ṣaḥīḥ;* Qurṭubī, *Jāmiʿ,* 20 vols., Beirut n.d.; Ṭabarī, *Tafsīr,* 12 vols., Beirut 1992; id., *Taʾrīkh,* ed. de Goeje et al., trans. W.M. Watt and M.V. McDonald, *The history of al-Ṭabarī.* vi. *Muḥammad at Mecca,* Albany 1988; Zamakhsharī, *Kashshāf,* Beirut 1995.
Secondary: H. Bleuchot, Le conflit des interprétations, le onze septembre et le droit musulman, in *Droit et cultures* 45 (2003), 241-76, 281; R. Denaro, Il suicidio nell'Islam medievale. Un'ipotesi di lettura della Sunna, in *Rivista degli studi orientali* 70 (1997), 23-34; H. Malka, Must innocents die? The Islamic debate over suicide attacks, in *Middle East quarterly* (Spring 2003), on http://www.brookings.edu/fp/saban/analysis/malka20030501.htm; F. Rosenthal, Intihār, in *EI²*, iii, 1246-8; id., On suicide in Islam, in *JAOS* 66 (1946), 239-59; repr. in id., *Muslim intellectual and social history,* Hampshire, UK 1990.

Summer see SEASONS

Sun

Star at the center of earth's solar system. The sun is the brightest and most powerful of all the celestial bodies orbiting — according to the geocentric cosmological view of the world current in antiquity and the Middle Ages (cf. Van Dalen, Shams) — the earth (q.v.; see also PLANETS AND STARS). Not inappropriately, it is mentioned thirty-three times in the Qurʾān. There are hints at its being worshipped in Babylonia (Q 6:74, 78) and in pre-Islamic Arabia (Q 41:37; see PRE-ISLAMIC ARABIA AND THE QURʾĀN; SOUTH ARABIA, RELIGIONS IN PRE-ISLAMIC), especially by the Sabaeans (Q 27:24; cf. Fahd, Shams; see SHEBA), and it is stressed that this was idolatry (see IDOLATRY AND IDOLATERS) and that, conforming to the order of God's creation, also the sun, like the other celestial bodies, is subject to God's supreme authority (q.v.; Q 22:18). A remnant of such earlier beliefs may be seen in the oath in Q 91:1, "By the sun and its light in the morning (q.v.)," after which the sūra (q.v.) was entitled *al-shams,* "The Sun" (see OATHS; FORM AND STRUCTURE OF THE QURʾĀN; LANGUAGE AND STYLE OF THE QURʾĀN; LITERARY STRUCTURES OF THE QURʾĀN).

The sun (like the moon [q.v.]) has been created to serve humankind (cf. Q 7:54; 13:2; 31:29; 35:13; 39:5; 14:33; 16:12; 29:61; see COSMOLOGY; CREATION). It is the great light (q.v.), *ḍiyāʾ* (Q 10:5) or *sirāj* (Q 25:61; 71:16; 78:13), by day (see LAMP). It was created *ḥusbānan* or *bi-ḥusbān* (cf. Q 6:96; 55:5), as a means for calculating time (q.v.) and organizing human life (see MEASUREMENT; WEIGHTS AND MEASURES). But its heat may become onerous (Q 18:90; 76:13; see HOT AND COLD). Elements of the physical behavior of the sun are well-known and mentioned on several occasions. Its course is firmly fixed (*li-ajalin/ilā ajalin musammā,* Q 13:2; 31:29; 35:13; 39:5); in its daily rotation, it reaches a resting place, *mustaqarr,* where it abides by night (Q 36:38; see NIGHT AND DAY). It moves in an orb, *falak,* like the moon (Q 21:33; 36:40), and these two can never touch *(tudrika)* each other (Q 36:40). It rises in the east and sets in the west (cf. Q 18:17, 86, 90). The sun has also been employed in the service of Islam as, notably, for the fixing of prayer (q.v.) times. Already in Muḥammad's lifetime, when the system of five daily ritual prayers *(ṣalāt)* had not yet been set up, prayers were prescribed at sunset, *dulūk,* and at dawn (q.v.), *fajr* (Q 17:78), as well as before the sun's rising, *ṭulūʿ,* and setting, *ghurūb* (Q 20:130; 50:39; see also DAY, TIMES OF; EVENING). Observation of the sun's shadow is also mentioned (Q 25:45), though not in connection with the fixing of prayer times. Later, Islamic legal scholars (see LAW AND THE QURʾĀN) developed several systems for fixing the times of prayer dependent on the sun's position and on shadow observation (cf. King, Mīḳāt). Still later, Muslim astronomers devised many more scientific methods for determining the times of prayer (cf. King, Mīḳāt; id., Mizwala; see SCIENCE AND THE QURʾĀN). Lastly, the Qurʾān mentions the sun in the eschatological (see ESCHATOLOGY) context of the day of resurrection (q.v.), when "the sun and the moon are joined [or fused]" (*wa-jumiʿa l-shamsu wa-l-qamaru,* Q 75:9 — perhaps in distinct contrast to Q 36:40, where it is said that these two can never touch each other) and when "the sun is wrapped up" (*idhā l-shamsu kuwwirat,* Q 81:1; on *kuwwirat,* cf. *WKAS,* i, 427b, 8-16).

In sum, it can be said that the Qurʾān covers the most important aspects of the sun's role in human life, in earlier history as well as for the Islamic community. Within the contemporaneous geocentric understanding of the world, the physical behavior of the sun is correctly described.

Paul Kunitzsch

Bibliography
B. van Dalen, Shams-2, in *EI²,* ix, 291-4; T. Fahd, *Le Panthéon de l'Arabie centrale à la veille de l'Hégire,* Paris 1968, 150-3; id., Shams-1, in *EI²,* ix, 291; D.A. King, Mīḳāt, in *EI²,* vii, 26-32; id., Mizwala, in *EI²,* vii, 210-11; H. Toelle, *Le Coran revisité. Le feu, l'eau, l'air et la terre,* Damascus 1999, esp. 97-100; A.J. Wensinck, *Tree and bird as cosmological symbols in western Asia* [in *Verhandelingen der Koninklijke Akademie van Wetenschappen te Amsterdam*], Amsterdam 1921 (on tree and sun, and bird and sun); *WKAS.*

Sunna

Arabic term for "way of acting." The ancient Arab concept *sunna* (pl. *sunan*) occurs eighteen times in the Qurʾān. Generally — that is to say outside the strict context of the Qurʾān — it is defined as a way of acting, whether approved or disapproved, and is normally associated with the people of earlier generations, whose example has to be followed or shunned by later generations. The concept occupies a crucial place in Islam. In the development of Islamic theology, it eventually came to be associated with orthodoxy, the bastion against heterodox innovation (*bidʿa;* see INNOVATION; THEOLOGY AND THE QURʾĀN; for a study of the first adherents of sunna, see Juynboll, Excursus on the *ahl as-sunna*).

As far as the qurʾānic context is concerned, the occurrences of the term can roughly be divided into two categories: "sunna" either denotes God's *way* of dealing with the as-yet unbelieving people of the world, or it is a word for the *behavior* of those rebellious unbelievers who refuse to comply with divine institutions by declining to submit to divine messengers (see INSOLENCE AND OBSTINACY; MESSENGER; BELIEF AND UNBELIEF; REBELLION). Examples of sunna within the first category comprise references to God's treatment of anonymous unbelievers in the Meccan verse Q 40:85 (see CHRONOLOGY AND THE QURʾĀN), or Qurashīs and/or the hypocrites (*munāfiqūn;* see QURAYSH; HYPOCRITES AND HYPOCRISY) in the Medinan verses Q 17:77, 33:38, 62 and 48:23. Examples of sunna within the second category refer in the Meccan sūras to anonymous peoples (cf. Q 15:13, 18:55, 35:43) and in a Medinan sūra to the prophet Muḥammad's Meccan adversaries among the Quraysh (cf. Q 8:38; see OPPOSITION TO MUḤAMMAD). Moreover, in the Medinan verse Q 3:137 the plural *sunan* is glossed by al-Ṭabarī (d. 310/923; *Tafsīr,* iv, 99) as *mathulāt,* i.e. the punitive measures meted out to pre-Islamic peoples like ʿĀd (q.v.) and Thamūd (q.v.), who refused to heed the preaching of prophets sent to them by God (see PROPHETS AND PROPHETHOOD), whereas in the other Medinan verse in which the plural occurs (Q 4:26) it stands for the pious "ways of life" of certain people and prophets of old (see GENERATIONS).

In addition to these uses of the term *sunna* in the Qurʾān, the concept of sunna can be traced along various lines, encompassing a number of different nuances. Some of these were later tentatively traced back to the Qurʾān, that is to say, to qurʾānic lexemes other than *sunna,* where it was thought that sunna was implied. Initially, *sunna* was a neutral term for good or bad precedents set by earlier generations, and it played a crucial role in the evolution of Islamic law, the *sharīʿa* (see LAW AND THE QURʾĀN). In the course of the second/eighth century, sunna came to be considered one of the roots *(uṣūl)* of Islamic law, indeed, after the Qurʾān, the second most important root. It was the legal theoretician al-Shāfiʿī (d. 204/820) who was especially instrumental in raising the concept of sunna to this unassailable level of legal authority. As a legislative source, the Qurʾān contains a fair number of injunctions that are pivotal in the formulation of laws dictating human behavior. But most of these injunctions are worded in terms that are either too broad, or ambiguous (q.v.) or downright opaque. Analyzing, and where possible elucidating, those terms became the task of early Islamic exegetes (see EXEGESIS OF THE QURʾĀN: CLASSICAL AND MEDIEVAL). These commentators acted in conformity with the gradually prevailing rule that, rather than an example set by any religious expert, a corroborative prophetic example had to be adduced. Thus these exegetes sought and disseminated reports *(aḥādīth)* which transmitted what the prophet

Muḥammad and the earliest learned authorities *(ʿulamāʾ)* had allegedly said concerning certain qurʾānic verses and, where relevant, their application in daily life (see SĪRA AND THE QURʾĀN; TRADITIONAL DISCIPLINES OF QURʾĀNIC STUDY). Among the earliest strata of authorities, the prophet Muḥammad was to play an increasingly important role. One indispensable need was clarification of obscure qurʾānic passages, and this need is reflected in a number of wide-ranging traditions, for which the introduction to the collection of al-Dārimī (d. 255/869) is especially famous. More than his fellow traditionists, it was al-Dārimī who brought together a number of ḥadīths that dealt with the issue of the inter-dependence of Qurʾān and sunna (see ḤADĪTH AND THE QURʾĀN). That most of these sayings are probably of his own making may be deduced from their absence from other early collections ascribed to his peers. Perhaps the most concise among the somewhat later sayings is the one that runs: "the Qurʾān needs [the elucidation contained in the] sunna more than the other way around" *(inna l-Qurʾān aḥwaju ilā l-sunna mina l-sunna ilā l-Qurʾān;* cf. the theologian al-Barbahārī [d. 329/941] in his *Kitāb al-Sunna,* which Ibn Abī Yaʿlā [d. 526/1131] extensively quotes in his *Ṭabaqāt al-Ḥanābila* [cf. ii, 25]).

The inter-relatedness of Qurʾān and sunna was transferred gradually to the delicate field of abrogation (q.v.; *naskh*). Initially it went without saying that a qurʾānic passage could abrogate a sunna; but eventually the question was raised whether a sunna laid down, for instance, in a prophetic ḥadīth, could perhaps abrogate a qurʾānic injunction. The statement "sunna may determine the Qurʾān but not vice versa" *(al-sunna qāḍiyatun ʿalā l-Qurʾān wa-laysa al-Qurʾān bi-qāḍin ʿalā l-sunna)* is ascribed to an early authority, Yaḥyā b. Abī Kathīr (d. 132/749) but is probably al-Dārimī's own handiwork (cf. his *Sunan,* i, 153, no. 587). This highly controversial issue kept theologians and jurisprudents occupied for a considerable period. In early *tafsīr* literature there are no discernible attempts to equate certain terms from scripture with sunna or, specifically prophetic sunna *(sunnat al-nabī)*. It was the aforementioned legal scholar al-Shāfiʿī who was the first to try to link an important qurʾānic term with sunna, in an attempt to provide scriptural evidence for his insistence that sunna should automatically be equated with *sunnat al-nabī*. The word chosen by him was *ḥikma,* "wisdom" (e.g. his *Risāla,* 32, 78, etc.); but even after his lifetime this identification does not seem to have caught on with other jurists. The only explanation early exegetes like al-Ḥasan al-Baṣrī (d. 110/728) and Qatāda b. Diʿāma (d. 117/735) are alleged to have offered for *al-ḥikma* was simply the gloss *al-sunna* without further specification (cf. *Tafsīr al-Ḥasan al-Baṣrī,* i, 115, Ṭabarī, *Tafsīr,* i, 557, ad Q 2:129). Then, at the hands of al-Shāfiʿī, that is extended to *sunnat rasūli llāh*. The verse that comes to mind most readily as providing a good opportunity for tracing the concept of sunna of the Prophet and/or that of his faithful followers in the Qurʾān, is Q 33:21: "You had (conceivably: have) in the messenger of God a perfect example…"; but al-Shāfiʿī did not even hint at this verse in his *Risāla*. It is the traditionist Aḥmad b. Ḥanbal (d. 241/855) who mentions the verse (cf. his *Musnad,* ii, 15 = ed. A.M. Shākir, no. 4641) in connection with sunna. The debate was couched in cautious terms, lest a sunna, which is after all a custom instituted by man, be too readily taken to be capable of abrogating or modifying the *prima facie* interpretation of scripture, which is, after all, of divine origin.

Another term bracketed with *al-sunna* next to the Qurʾān is the word *ḥabl,* "rope, cord," in Q 3:103 (cf. Ibn Ḥajar, *Fatḥ al-bārī,* xvii, 3, apud Bukhārī, *K. al-Iʿtiṣām,* 1). In exegetical literature, however, *ḥabl* is almost exclusively associated with the Qurʾān, or the religion, or the community *(jamāʿa)* of believers, but not with sunna.

The term *sunna* does not occur more often than in the verses dealt with above, whereas there are numerous qurʾānic passages in which *sunna* and/or its derivative *sunnat al-nabī* are quite clearly intended. The frequently repeated command that the believers must obey God and his messenger (cf. Kassis, *Concordance,* s.v. *aṭāʿa,* "to obey"; see OBEDIENCE) can virtually always be construed as pointing to submission to the exemplary behavior of the Prophet.

G.H.A. Juynboll

Bibliography
Primary: al-Dārimī, ʿAbdallāh b. ʿAbd al-Raḥmān, *Sunan,* ed. F.A. Zamarlī and Kh. al-Sabʿ al-ʿAlamī, 2 vols., Cairo 1987; al-Ḥasan al-Baṣrī, *Tafsīr,* ed. M. ʿAbd al-Raḥīm, Cairo [1992]; Ibn Abī Yaʿlā, *Ṭabaqāt al-Ḥanābila,* ed. Muḥammad Ḥāmid al-Fiqī, Cairo 1952; Ibn Ḥajar al-ʿAsqalānī, *Fatḥ al-bārī bi-sharḥ [Ṣaḥīḥ] al-Bukhārī,* Cairo 1959; al-Shāfiʿī, Muḥammad b. Idrīs, *Risāla,* ed. A.M. Shākir, Cairo 1940.
Secondary: G.H.A. Juynboll, An excursus on the *ahl as-sunna* in connection with van Ess, *Theologie und Gesellschaft,* vol. IV, in *Der Islam* 75 (1998), 318-30; id., Sunna, in *Dictionary of the Middle Ages,* ed. J.R. Strayer et al., 13 vols. to date, New York 1982-, xi, 510-13; id., Some new ideas on the development of *sunna* as a technical term in early Islam, in *JSAI* 10 (1987), 97-118; id., Sunna, in *EI²,* ix, 878-81; H.E. Kassis, *A concordance of the Qurʾan,* Berkeley 1983.

Sunrise see DAWN; DAY, TIMES OF

Sunset see EVENING; DAY, TIMES OF

Supererogation see ALMSGIVING

Supplication see PRAYER FORMULAS

Sūra(s)

A literary unit of undetermined length within the Qurʾān, often translated as "chapter." In the printed editions of the Qurʾān, but not in the earliest manuscripts (see MANUSCRIPTS OF THE QURʾĀN), it is marked as such by a title section that provides the name of the sūra, followed by a number that defines its place in the sequence of the 114 sūras of the entire corpus. Sūra names are not abbreviations of the content but "catchwords," taking up a particular lexeme from the text that is either a rare word in the Qurʾān (e.g. Q 80, Sūrat ʿAbasa, "He Frowned") and thus easy to remember, or a major issue discussed in the sūra (e.g. Q 4, Sūrat al-Nisāʾ, "The Women"), or, occasionally, the initial word of the sūra. There is no complete agreement about the names of the sūras, some sūras being known under more than one title. Whereas the naming and the ordering of the sūras are later textual adjustments (see MUṢḤAF; CODICES OF THE QURʾĀN), the arrangement of the text as a sequence of sūras goes back to the redaction of the Qurʾān itself, which tradition dates to the reign of the third caliph ʿUthmān b. ʿAffān (r. 23-35/644-56). Although that dating is not confirmed by external evidence, the redaction and official publication should have taken place some time before the Umayyad caliph (q.v.) ʿAbd al-Malik's reign (65-86/685-705), since it is attested among scholars of his time (see Hamdan, al-Ḥasan al-Baṣrī). Inasmuch as the somewhat mechanical arrangement of the sūras according to their length does not betray a particular historical or theological interest on the part of the redactors, but rather an awareness of the already achieved canonical status, the sūras as units should go back to a very early time (see FORM AND STRUCTURE OF

THE QURʾĀN). There is also no substantial contrary evidence to be gleaned from the findings of Qurʾān fragments at Ṣanʿāʾ, Yemen, whose analysis still awaits publication (Puin, Observations; but cf. ibid., 111 for the variations from the ʿUthmānic codex found in some of these fragments). Although there are no complete copies preserved, folios with overlapping sūra texts confirm the traditional sequence.

Etymologically, the term sūra is difficult to trace (see Jeffery, *For. vocab.*), but may have been derived from Hebrew *shūrah*, "line," as well as from Syriac *shūrayā*, "beginning," or short psalms that are sung before the reading of scripture. None of these etymologies, however, is totally convincing. In Arabic, the word makes its first appearance in the Qurʾān itself.

The word sūra is used ten times in the Qurʾān, all of which being rather late (see CHRONOLOGY AND THE QURʾĀN): The oldest evidence is Q 10:38, "Say, 'Bring a sūra like it and [for assistance] call upon whom you can besides God'" *(qul fa-ʾtū bi-sūratin mithlihi wa-dʿū mani staṭaʿtum min dūni llāhi)*, a verse belonging to the so-called *taḥaddī*-verses (see Radscheit, *Die taḥaddī-Verse*), i.e. the polemic discourse about the inimitability (q.v.) of qurʾānic speech (see also WORD OF GOD; PROVOCATION; CREATEDNESS OF THE QURʾĀN). The term "sūra" is part of that debate, and it reappears in Q 11:13 and Q 2:23. "Sūra" is employed in more general contexts to cover an unspecified text unit of the revelation (see REVELATION AND INSPIRATION), mostly in polemical contexts (like Q 9:64, 86, 124; see POLEMIC AND POLEMICAL LANGUAGE). It is only used once — in place of the more usual *kitāb* (see BOOK) — in a hymnal annunciation of a revealed text to be communicated (Q 24:1).

Thus, sūra certainly has to do with "text," but not necessarily with a written text (see ORALITY AND WRITING IN ARABIA). It seems to denote a recited text, more precisely, the quantity that is presented in public on a single occasion (see RECITATION OF THE QURʾĀN). It is, however, highly questionable if the term sūra was used during the Prophet's lifetime to denote the "chapters" of the Qurʾān in general which were only later designated as sūras.

It appears that the sūra in the qurʾānic context fulfills, to some degree, the function of textual subdivisions familiar from Judaism and Christianity (see below; see SCRIPTURE AND THE QURʾĀN; JEWS AND JUDAISM; CHRISTIANS AND CHRISTIANITY). But, whereas the canonical texts in those traditions have been subdivided for liturgical use only after the completion and canonization of the textual corpus, the arrangement of the qurʾānic text *grosso modo* seems to go back to the oral use of the text in the earliest community, a practice that preceded its codification as a whole (see ORALITY). A number of sūras display the character of intended literary units, composed as such for recitation; others seem to have been extended with repeated use; others again appear as collections of text units rather unrelated to each other that may not have had a *Sitz im Leben* in oral transmission. This complex problem still awaits evaluation. The sūra as an entity with a coherent unity has not yet been adequately studied (see LITERARY STRUCTURES OF THE QURʾĀN), although there have been, more recently, new approaches, often focusing on Q 12, Sūrat Yūsuf ("Joseph"; see Mir, Coherence; id., The sūra as a unity; id., The qurʾānic story of Joseph; Neuwirth, Zur Struktur; De Premare, Joseph et Muḥammad; Sells, *Approaching the Qurʾān;* id., Literary approach; Waldman, New approaches; see also JOSEPH; NARRATIVES).

In the following, an attempt will be made to trace the development of the sūra from early Meccan, to later Meccan and then to Medinan times (see MECCA; MEDINA; LANGUAGE AND STYLE OF THE QURʾĀN). Finally, a brief comparison to sections in other scriptures will be undertaken.

Early Meccan sūras

To embark on an analysis of the sūra as a literary form we must first define our stance vis-à-vis the Qurʾān as our textual basis. It is one task to discuss the sūra as a fixed textual unit within the transmitted text and an entirely different task to discuss it in its earlier function as an oral communication whose context was not the entire corpus of the Qurʾān but rather single, earlier qurʾānic communications (see OCCASIONS OF REVELATION) and — perhaps more importantly — individual religious debates (see DEBATE AND DISPUTATION) that must have taken place among the early followers of Muḥammad and their neighbors in their particular cultural milieu, Mecca and Medina. Revisionist scholarship has ruled out the possibility of exploring the situation of the first communications of qurʾānic texts, which are indeed impossible to re-construct in full (see POST-ENLIGHTENMENT ACADEMIC STUDY OF THE QURʾĀN). Still, to confine the analysis to the canonical shape of the Qurʾān, neglecting both its complex referentialities and its hints to the *Sitz im Leben* of particular text units, would render an insufficient reading. What qurʾānic scholarship still must do is consider systematically both intra-qurʾānic and extra-qurʾānic evidence on the religious situation at the time of the Prophet. Not least the largely blank map of the religious setting of central Arabia has made revisionist scholars look for a different milieu for the genesis of the Qurʾān, jumping over, however, the necessary step of a micro-structural reading of the Qurʾān itself. In what follows, a sketch of the pre-canonical development of the sūra as a literary genre will be attempted.

The earliest sūras must have been those that made use of the particular style related to the pre-Islamic *kāhin*, a soothsayer (q.v.) or seer, who claimed super-human origin for his enunciations. This literary form is known as *sajʿ*, and it consists of short syntactical units marked by an expressive rhyme, often ultima-stressed (see RHYMED PROSE). This pattern of phonetic correspondence between the verse endings *(fāṣila)* is not only more loose than the poetic rhyme *(qāfiya)*, but is also more flexible, thus allowing semantically related verses to be bracketed by a rhyme of their own and marked off by clearly distinct verse-groups (see VERSES). The highly sophisticated phonetic structures produced by this style have been evaluated by Michael Sells *(Approaching the Qurʾān)*. Among these earliest sūras should be counted the following, which are cited in an order that roughly follows the textual chronology: Q 111, 99-108, 77-97, 73-5, 68-70, 55-6, 51-3. As against those sūras that remain close to the *kāhin* speech model attesting the speaker's ecstatic disposition (e.g. Q 111, 101, 100, 99, 84, 82, 81, 79, 77, etc.), there are other early sūras that in their quiet and solemn mood (Q 95, 94, 93, 87, 74, 73, etc.) remind one of Christian hymns or adaptations of psalms (q.v.) rather than of a pagan ritual such as the performance of the *kāhin* (see also POLYTHEISM AND ATHEISM; IDOLATRY AND IDOLATERS). What they still have in common is the shortness of the verses, which do not exceed one syntactically complete sentence. In those sūras that remind one of the pagan model, the expression itself is often enigmatic, thus stressing the strangeness that adheres to a super-human communication. A striking characteristic of this style is the use of oaths (q.v.) and oath-clusters (see Neuwirth, Images, and also FORM AND STRUCTURE OF THE QUR᾽ĀN), conjuring heavenly bodies (see PLANETS AND STARS; SUN; MOON), thunderstorms (see WEATHER) and bands of inimical raiders, all of which are phenomena pertaining to the imagination of desert-dwellers rather than to the stock of images in the monotheistic tradition (see NOMADS; BEDOUIN; DESERT; CITY; NATURE AS SIGNS).

There are equally less menacing oaths that conjure sacred places — including monotheistic shrines — and sacred times, times of the day (see DAY, TIMES OF) that have been known as times of prayer (q.v.) in pre-Islamic times (see Neuwirth, Images and metaphors; see also TIME; SACRED PRECINCTS; SACRED AND PROFANE). These texts document a merger between a "pagan" form and a biblically inspired content. Sūras introduced by oath clusters, thus, are not necessarily imprinted by pagan thinking. On the contrary, the oath-cluster — a very dense and rhythmically dynamic section — is sometimes used to convey the urgency, the threatening closeness of the catastrophe that is the only thing that matters in the monotheistic context: the day of judgment (see LAST JUDGMENT; APOCALYPSE). The clusters here serve as a sign of alarm transposed into the language of the standard Arabian warners (see WARNER), the soothsayers. A comparable re-interpretation of pre-Islamic lore is observable with the other oath-clusters: "pagan" sacred times become ritually occupied by monotheistic cultic acts, a development that is mirrored in the text where praises and prayers continue the oath-cluster (see PRAISE; LAUDATION; PRE-ISLAMIC ARABIA AND THE QUR᾽ĀN). Moreover, many early sūras are replete with hymnal elements that are standard expressions in Christian and Jewish worship (q.v.; see Baumstark, Jüdischer Gebetstypus; Speyer, *Erzählungen*). The assumption of a strong Christian presence in Mecca and an equally strong Jewish one in its vicinity, at least since the emigration (q.v.; *hijra*), and the familiarity of the Prophet and his followers with Christian and Jewish pious texts of worship, are indispensable for the understanding of the early sūras. "Paganism" in the Qur᾽ān has to be understood not as a fixed system of beliefs but as the larger common denominator of a multiple and unstable set of elements, already strongly imbued with monotheist notions.

Qur᾽ānic texts and liturgy

Whereas the imperative to worship is always there (Q 96:1: "recite in the name of your lord who created" *[iqra᾽ bi-smi rabbika lladhī khalaq]*; Q 87:1: "glorify the name of your lord the most high" *[sabbiḥi sma rabbika l-aʿlā]*; Q 96:19: "and bow down and bring yourself closer" *[wa-sjud wa-qtarib]*; Q 73:2-4: "stand [for prayer] much of the night... and recite the Qur᾽ān" *[qumi l-layla illā qalīlan... wa-rattili l-qur᾽āna tartīlan]*) and God is always mentioned (in the wording "your lord [q.v.]," *rabbuka*), many texts do not seem to be, first and foremost, addressed to the Prophet, but could equally be addressed to the believer. This is a way of expression familiar from the Psalms where the first-person speaker is not necessarily the author of the psalm (see BELIEF AND UNBELIEF; FAITH). It is thus difficult to decide if a sūra like Q 93 is a reflex of the Prophet's biography or not (see SĪRA AND THE QUR᾽ĀN). There is an unambiguous paraphrase of a psalm (136) in Q 55, which, however, replaces the memory of salvation (q.v.) history with a focus on the eschatological future (Neuwirth, Qur᾽ānic literary structure; see ESCHATOLOGY). Still, the view, first presented by Lüling *(Urtext)*, later in a cruder form by Luxenberg *(Die syro-aramäische Lesart)* and taken into consideration again by Böwering (see CHRONOLOGY AND THE QUR'ĀN) that an existing Christian text may underlie some qur'ānic sections, appears to be merely a hypothesis. The familiar formulas do not make up entire sections or strophes — as Lüling would have it — but are embedded in exhortative (see EXHORTATIONS) or polemical contexts, that, in the early sūras, contrary to the later ones, frequently take the shape of projections of the scenario of the Qur'ān recitation itself, e.g. Q 53:59f.: "Do you wonder at this speech, will you laugh and not weep?... Bow down to God and adore [him]" *(a-fa-min hādha l-ḥadīthi ta'jabun wa-taḍḥakūna wa-lā tabkūn... fa-sjudū lillāhi wa-'budū)*. Particularly the cultic framework in which the Qur'ān was recited seems to have met opposition: Q 77:48-50: "and when it was said to them, 'Prostrate!', they did not do so... and what speech after that will they believe?" *(wa-idhā qīla lahumu rka'ū lā yarka'ūn... fa-bi-ayyi ḥadīthin ba'dahu yu'minūn)*; Q 107:4-5: "and woe to the worshipers who neglect their prayers" *(fa-waylun lil-muṣallīn alladhīna hum 'an ṣalātihim sāhūn)*; Q 96:9-10: "have you seen the one who prevents the servant from praying" (*a-ra'ayta lladhī yanhā 'abdan idhā ṣallā*; cf. Q 74:43; 75:31; see Neuwirth, Rezitationstext). The missing reference to the persona of the Prophet as the transmitter in early texts may be due to the still undeveloped consciousness of the speaker's own part in the communication.

There are at the same time unequivocal addresses to the Prophet, like Q 74:2 f.: "Arise and warn and magnify your lord" *(qum fa-andhir wa-rabbaka fa-kabbir)*, and his figure gradually becomes prominent in the sūras. Many early sūras end with an exhortation to the Prophet to worship God either in vigils (Q 52:48-9: "and glorify the praise of your lord as you stand and glorify him part of the night and at the setting of the stars" *[wa-sabbiḥ bi-ḥamdi rabbika ḥīna taqūm wa-mina l-layli fa-sabbiḥhu wa-idbāra l-nujūm]*; see VIGIL) or to praise him (Q 56:96: "and glorify in the name of your lord the mighty" *[fa-sabbiḥ bi-smi rabbika l-'aẓīm]*; Q 93:11: "and speak of the bounty of your lord" *[wa-ammā bi-ni'mati rabbika fa-ḥaddith]*; Q 108:2: "and pray to your lord and sacrifice" *[fa-ṣalli li-rabbika wa-nḥar]*). Sometimes he is admonished to worship at the very beginning of a sūra (Q 74:1 f.: "O enshrouded one, arise and warn and magnify your lord" *[yā ayyuhā l-muddaththir qum fa-andhir wa-rabbaka fa-kabbir]*). It appears that the early recitation took place in the framework of already existing rituals (see RITUAL AND THE QUR'ĀN), *ṣalāt*, made up of *rukū'* and *sajda* (see BOWING AND PROSTRATION), being evidently already a rite celebrated in Mecca before Muḥammad's mission (Q 53:62; 77:48). These may have taken place in privately held vigils as well as publicly performed rituals.

There is, then, an obvious convergence of the early qur'ānic text to liturgy. Some sūras sound like calls for repentance (see REPENTANCE AND PENANCE) in the face of the imminent coming of the day of judgment. This event is the topic of a number of sūras and is extensively elaborated: The catastrophic events that precede the judgment (q.v.) fill large sections of the early sūras, although the scene of judgment is less clearly described. The retribution — either in punishment by fire (q.v.) or in the admittance to lofty gardens (see GARDEN) — is of special interest (see REWARD AND PUNISHMENT). Indeed, the entire corpus of early texts pursue one task: to convince the listeners of the omnipresence of God (see GOD AND HIS ATTRIBUTES) and thus of the moral responsibility (q.v.) to which they will be held on the last day (see also FREEDOM AND PREDESTINATION). As with the Psalms, the theme of God's generosity and philanthropic concern enhances his claim to human gratitude (see GRATITUDE AND INGRATITUDE). Also as in the Psalms, events from salvation history are recalled: in Q 51 the story of Abraham (q.v.; Ibrāhīm) and Lot (q.v.; Lūṭ), and in Q 79 the story of Moses (q.v.; Mūsā) and Pharaoh (q.v.; Firʿawn). Both are presented as an exhortation (*ʿibra;* cf. Q 79:26) — and dramatize the divine punishment for transgressors (see SIN, MAJOR AND MINOR; BOUNDARIES AND PRECEPTS). Pharaoh's behavior clearly reflects that of the unbelievers, and his punishment is equally historical and eschatological (see CHASTISEMENT AND PUNISHMENT; HELL AND HELLFIRE).

The Qurʾān developed diverse motifs and structures not known from earlier Arabic literature (see FORM AND STRUCTURE OF THE QURʾĀN). Beside the eschatological prophecies (see PROPHETS AND PROPHETHOOD; FORETELLING) that abound in early Meccan sūras, the so-called *āyāt,* "signs" (q.v.; see also VERSES), are also prominent. Several descriptions of the "biosphere," of copious vegetation, fauna, an agreeable habitat for humans, the natural resources at their disposal, and the like, are incorporated into paraenetic appeals to recognize divine providence and accept divine omnipotence since all these benefits are signs *(āyāt)* bearing a coded message (see AGRICULTURE AND VEGETATION; GRACE; BLESSING). Properly decoded, they will evoke gratitude and submission to the divine will. The perception of nature, which in pre-Islamic poetry (see POETRY AND POETS) appears alien and threatening, provoking the poet's heroic defiance of its roughness, has crystallized in the Qurʾān into the image of a meaningfully organized habitat ensuring human welfare and arousing the awareness of belonging (see GEOGRAPHY).

"Signs" *(āyāt)* of divine omnipotence may also manifest themselves in history. Whereas extended narratives are prevalent in later Meccan texts, very short narratives — an invasion of Mecca (Q 105) repelled by divine intervention (see PEOPLE OF THE ELEPHANT), the Thamūd (q.v.) myth about a divine punishment of disbelievers (Q 91:11-15; see PUNISHMENT STORIES), the story of Pharaoh and Moses (Q 79:15-26) — or ensembles of narratives like that in Q 51 including Abraham and Lot, Moses and Pharaoh, the ʿĀd (q.v.), the Thamūd, and Noah (q.v.; Nūḥ) — or evocations of stories (Q 52, 53, 69), occur from the earliest sūras onward. The latter sometimes form lists (Q 89). Somewhat longer narratives are introduced by the formula known from *āyāt* on nature, "have you not seen" *(a-lam tara...),* later "and when..." *(wa-idh [faʿala]...),* i.e. they are assumed to be known to the listeners. It is noteworthy that the longer narratives from early Meccan texts onward are split into equal halves, thus producing proportionate structures (Q 51:24-37; 79:15-26; 68:17-34). Narratives then develop into retribution legends or punishment stories, serving to prove that divine justice (see JUSTICE AND INJUSTICE) is at work in history, the harassed just being rewarded with salvation, the transgressors and the unbelievers punished by annihilation. At the same time, legends that are located in the Arabian peninsula may be read as re-interpretations of ancient Arabian representations of deserted space. Sites no longer lie in ruins due to preordained natural processes, but because of an equilibrium, maintained by divine providence, that balances between human actions and human welfare. Deserted sites thus acquire a meaning; they carry a divine message (see GENERATIONS; GEOGRAPHY).

From the middle Meccan sūras onward, polemical and apologetic sections (see

APOLOGETICS) still do not refer to theoretical, let alone dogmatic, issues in the early sūras. In these middle Meccan texts, polemical utterances are more often than not directed against listeners who do not comply with the exigencies of the behavioral norms of the cult. These listeners are reprimanded by the speaker *in situ* (Q 53:59 f.). Sometimes curses are uttered against absent persons (Q 111:1 f.) or against humankind in general (Q 80:17; see CURSE). In other cases menaces are directed at the ungrateful or pretentious (Q 114:1; see ARROGANCE; INSOLENCE AND OBSTINACY), and these may merge into a catalogue of vices (Q 107:2-7; see VIRTUES AND VICES, COMMANDING AND FORBIDDING). Whereas in most of the early cases the adversaries are not granted an opportunity to reply, later sūras do present the voices of both sides.

Later Meccan surās

Sūras introduced by oath-clusters — the most graphic reference to the *kāhin* speech model — are no longer present once the sūra becomes complex and polythematic. A turn in paradigm occurs with Q 15, a text that triumphantly declares the achievement of another qurʾānic text: Sūrat al-Fātiḥa ("The Opening," Q 1; see Neuwirth, Referentiality; id., Sūrat al-Fātiḥa; see FĀTIḤA). Here, for the first time, an allusion is made to the existence of a particular form of service in which scripture functions as the cardinal section. In such sūras, the references to the Meccan sanctuary *(ḥaram)* as the central warrant for the social coherence of the community have been replaced by new symbols. Instead of introductory allusions to liturgical times and sacred space we encounter an evocation of the book, be it clad in an oath (Q 36:2; 37:3; 38:1; 43:2; 44:2; 50:1) or in a deictic affirmation of its presence (Q 2:2; 10:1; 12:1; 13:1, etc.).

Moreover, a new framework of the message in terms of space is recognizable. Later Meccan sūras broaden the scope of space for the listeners, who are transported from their local surroundings to a distant landscape, the holy land, familiar as the setting where the history of the community's spiritual forebears took place. The introduction of the direction of prayer towards Jerusalem (q.v.), the "first *qibla* (q.v.)," is an unequivocal testimony of this change in orientation (see Neuwirth, Spiritual meaning). The innovation is reflected in Q 17. In view of the increasing interest in the biblical heritage, it comes as no surprise that the bulk of the middle and late Meccan sūras seem to mirror a monotheistic worship service, starting with an initial dialogical section (apologetic, polemic, paraenetic) and closing with a related section, most frequently an affirmation of the revelation. These framing sections have been compared to the ecclesiastic *ecteniae*, i.e. initial and concluding *responsoria* recited by the priest or deacon and responded to by the community. The center of the monotheistic worship service and, similarly, of the fully developed sūra of the middle and late Meccan period is occupied by a biblical reminiscence — in the case of the service, a *lectio*, and in the case of the sūra, a narrative focusing on biblical protagonists. Ritual coherence has thus given way to scriptural coherence, with the more complex later sūras referring to scripture both by their transmission of scriptural texts and by their being themselves dependent on the mnemonic-technicalities of writing for their conservation. It is true, however, that already in later Meccan sūras the distinct tripartite composition often becomes blurred, with narratives gradually being replaced by discursive sections. Many compositions also display secondary expansions — a phenomenon that still requires further investigation. Yet, for the bulk of the middle and late Meccan sūras, the claim of a tripartite composition is sustainable (see Neuwirth, Vom Rezitationstext).

Salvation history

The Qurʾān is often criticized for lacking a chronological framework for the events of pre-qurʾānic history and for the repetitiveness of its narrative. While this accusation may hold true for the earliest qurʾānic discourse, that of eschatology, the situation changes substantially when a new paradigm is adopted. This new paradigm switches the focus from the deserted sites of the real homeland to the orbit of the messengers of the People of the Book (q.v.), whose discourse as intermediaries between God and man is much more sophisticated (see MESSENGER; HEAVENLY BOOK; PRESERVED TABLET).

Although initially embedded in catalogues of narratives of a partly extra-biblical tradition, stories about major biblical figures like Moses and a number of patriarchs known from the Book of Genesis gradually acquire a function of their own. They become the stock inventory of the central part of the longer Meccan sūras and only rarely do they appear in other positions. As mentioned earlier, sūras from the second Meccan period onward often form an ensemble that mirrors the enactment of a monotheistic service where the central position is occupied by the reading of scriptural texts. These sections are often explicitly related to a divine source labeled *kitāb*. In the qurʾānic context, they are embedded in a more extensive recital, whose initiatory and concluding sections may contain liturgical but also less universal elements such as debates about ephemeral community issues. The ceremonial function of the biblically inspired narrative as a festive presentation of the book is underlined by introductory formulas (Q 19:16: "and mention Mary in the book" *[wa-dhkur fī l-kitābi maryam]*). At a later stage, when the particular form of the revelation communicated to the Muslim community is regarded as a virtual scripture of its own, i.e. when community matters are acknowledged as part of salvation history, whole sūras figure as manifestations of *al-kitāb*.

The phenomenon of recurring narratives in the Qurʾān, retold in slightly diverging fashions, has often been interpreted as mere repetitions, i.e. as a deficiency of the Qurʾān. They deserve, however, to be studied as testimonies of the consecutive emergence of a community and thus reflective of the process of canonization. They point to a progressively changing narrative pact, to a continuing education of the listeners, and to the development of a moral consensus that is reflected in the texts. In later Meccan and Medinan sūras, when a large number of narratives are presupposed as being well known to the listeners, the position previously occupied by salvation history narratives is replaced by mere evocations of narratives and debates about them.

As was mentioned above, the early — and densely structured — parts of the Qurʾān reflect an ancient Arabic linguistic *ductus*, termed *sajʿ*, a prose style marked by very short and concise sentences with frequently changing patterns of particularly clear-cut, often phonetically expressive rhymes. Once this style has, in the later sūras, given way to a more loose flow of prose, with verses often exceeding one complete sentence, the rhyme end takes the form of a simple *-ūn* or *-īn* pattern, which in most cases is achieved through a morpheme denoting masculine plural. One wonders how this rather mechanically applied and inconspicuous ending should suffice to fulfill the listeners' anticipation of an end marker of the verse.

Upon closer examination, however, one discovers that the rhyme as such is no longer charged with this end-marker function, but there is instead another device to mark the end. The verse concludes with an entire syntactically stereotypical rhymed phrase, which one may term cadenza — in analogy to the final part of speech units in Gregorian chants which, through their particular sound pattern, arouse the expectation of an ending. In the Qurʾān what is repeated is not only the identical musical sound but a linguistic pattern as well: a widely stereotypical phrasing. The musical sound pattern comes to enhance the message encoded in the qurʾānic cadenza-phrase that in many instances introduces a meta-discourse. Many cadenza-phrases are semantically distinguished from their context and add a moral comment to it, such as "truly, you were one of the sinners" (*innaki kunti min al-khāṭiʾīn*, Q 12:29). They thus transcend the main narrative or argumentative flow of the sūra, introducing a spiritual dimension: divine approval or disapproval. They may also refer to one of God's attributes, like "God is powerful over everything" (*wa-kāna llāhu ʿalā kulli shayʾin qadīran*, Q 33:27; see POWER AND IMPOTENCE), which in the later stages of qurʾānic development become parameters of ideal human behavior. These meta-narrative insertions into the narrative or argumentative fabric which would, of course, in a written text, be meant for silent reading, appear rather disturbing, delaying the information process. They add, however, fundamentally to the impact of the oral recitation (see Neuwirth, Zur Struktur; see also VERSES; RECITERS OF THE QURʾĀN). The Qurʾān thus — as Nicolai Sinai has expressed it — consciously styles itself as a text evolving on different, yet closely intertwined, levels of discourse and mediality. Although it is true that not all multipartite verses bear such formulaic endings, cadenzas may be considered characteristic of the later Meccan and all the Medinan qurʾānic texts. The resounding cadenza, thus, replaces the earlier expressive rhyme pattern, marking a new and irreversible development in the emergence of the text and of the new faith. It immediately creates a new literary form within Arabic literature.

Types of Medinan sūras

In Medina, sūras not only give up their tripartite scheme, but they also display much less sophistication in the patterns of their composition. One type may be aptly termed the "rhetorical" sūra or sermon (Q 22, 24, 33, 47, 48, 49, 57-66; see RHETORIC AND THE QURʾĀN); they consist of an address to the community whose members are called upon directly by formulas such as *yā ayyuhā l-nās* (Q 22:1, "Oh people"). In these sūras, which in some cases (Q 59, 61, 62, 64) are stereotypically introduced by initial hymnal formulas strongly reminiscent of the biblical Psalms, the Prophet *(al-nabī)* no longer appears as a mere transmitter of the message but as one personally addressed by God (Q 33:28, "Oh Prophet" *[yā ayyuhā l-nabī]*) or as an agent acting synergistically with the divine persona (Q 33:22, "God and his Prophet" *[allāhu wa-rasūluhu]*). A particularly graphic testimony of the new self-positioning of the Prophet is Q 33, particularly Q 33:56.

As against these "monolithic" addresses, the bulk of the Medinan sūras are the most complex of the entire Qurʾān. Most of the so-called "long sūras" (*ṭiwāl al-suwar*, e.g. Q 2-10) cease to be neatly structured compositions, but appear to be the result of a process of collection that we can not yet reconstruct (see COLLECTION OF THE QURʾĀN). Initial attempts to claim an intended structure for some of these sūras have been made by Zahniser (Word of God); but a systematic study of all these sūras is still an urgent desideratum in the field.

Since we have to understand the Qurʾān's

development as one strain of a double process that will result in both a scripture and a cultus, the long sūras are most interesting as milestones of the development of the ritual backdrop of the qur'ānic communication process. Though their structure may be secondary, their message sheds important light on particular ritual changes whose symbolic value cannot be underestimated.

Although occasional regulations — mostly concerning cultic matters — do occur in Meccan sūras, more elaborate regulations about not only cultic but also communal affairs figure prominently in the Medinan context (see LAW AND THE QUR'ĀN). Their binding force is sometimes underlined by a reference to the transcendent source: "it is prescribed for you" (*kutiba ʿalaykum*, Q 2:183-7). Among the most important ritual rulings is the ruling concerning the new direction of prayer, the *qibla*, towards Mecca (Q 2:143f.). This ruling marks the separation of the community from the Jewish listeners who earlier had been among the receivers of the Qur'ān — a situation that had provoked a re-reading of earlier texts that had been done from the perspective of particular rabbinical discourses (Neuwirth, Oral scriptures). Other important rulings concern the three pillars of what was to become Islamic cultus and liturgy: the establishment of a weekly communal service, the *ṣalāt al-jumuʿa* (cf. Q 62:9; see FRIDAY PRAYER), the implementation of a fast (see RAMAḌĀN; FASTING), introduced with reference to the Jewish fast — both still preceding the exclusion of the Jews — and the introduction of the *ḥajj* ceremony into the festive canon (Q 2:196 f., 22:27 f.; see PILGRIMAGE). The Medinan regulations do not display any structured composition, nor do they form part of neatly composed units; they suggest, rather, later insertions into loosely connected contexts.

Time, thus, in the Medinan sūras becomes structured by an emerging Islamic cultus. Simultaneously, the historical flow of significant events starts to inform the consciousness of the community; indeed, they enter the Qur'ān as part of salvation history that is now perceived as encompassing the emerging Islamic community (see COMMUNITY AND SOCIETY IN THE QUR'ĀN). A new element appearing in Medinan sūras are accounts of contemporary events experienced or enacted by the community, such as the battle of Badr (q.v.; Q 3:123), Uḥud (Q 3:155-74), the expulsion of the Banū l-Naḍīr (Q 59:2-5; see NAḌĪR, BANŪ L-), the siege of Khaybar (Q 48:15), the expedition to Tabūk (Q 9:29-35; see EXPEDITIONS AND BATTLES) or the farewell sermon of the Prophet in Q 5:1-3 (see FAREWELL PILGRIMAGE). It is noteworthy that these reports do not display a special artistic literary shaping, nor do they betray any particular pathos. It comes as no surprise, then, that, unlike the situation in Judaism and Christianity, where biblical history has been fused to form a mythical drama of salvation, no such great narrative has arisen from the Qur'ān itself. A metahistorical blueprint of the genesis of Islam was constructed only later, through the *sīra*.

Sūra — *parashah* — *perikope*

The surely ancient division of the Qur'ān into sections, some of which may already have been called sūras during the Prophet's lifetime, has ruled out a later pericopization such as occurred in Judaism and Christianity (see Neuwirth, Three religious feasts). Both Judaic and Christian orthodoxy bind biblical texts to particular temporal frames. To quote Yerushalmi (*Jewish history*, 15 f.):

The Pentateuchal narratives, which brought the historical record up to the eve of the conquest of Canaan, together with the weekly lesson from the prophets, were read aloud in the synagogue from beginning to end. The public reading was completed triennially in Palestine, annually in Babylonia (as is the custom today), and immediately the reading would begin again.

In an analogous way, the Gospels (q.v.) in the Orthodox churches — having replaced in Christianity the Torah (q.v.) as the core of scriptures — are distributed over the course of the year, "cut" into pericopes (Greek *perikope*) and thus reflect the Jewish reading of weekly chapters of the Torah (Hebrew *parashah*). This cycle of readings from the core of the scripture is accompanied, as in Judaism, by a second sequence of texts taken from other parts of the scriptures. The Pauline letters (Greek *apostolos*) and additional readings from the historical or prophetic books of the Hebrew Bible (Greek *propheteia*) are meant to elucidate the pericopes from the core texts, the Gospels. This, of course, continues the tradition of the readings from the prophets in Judaism (Hebrew *haftarah*), a corpus undisputed in its rank as a vital complement and a necessary exegetical context for the Torah.

As against that, no annual cycle of scriptural reading exists in Islam; the qurʾānic text has never been divided into required weekly or daily portions to be read out in public services. That means that a continuous recollection of salvation history from creation (q.v.) to redemption, as in Christianity (see also FALL OF MAN), does not take place during the weekly ritual nor is the believers' predicants and salvation — their ever again being saved by divine intervention, as in Judaism —, made present through the weekly service. Sūras as such — even if arranged in an annual cycle of recitations — would not fulfill the task of the *parashah* or *perikope* to "represent" salvation history. Reflective as the sūras are of certain stages of the proto-Muslim communal development, they lack interest in an extended linear memorial representation of salvation history in its entirety. Yet the Qurʾān has been justly credited with having generated "a ceremonial of textual repetition with a pronouncedly obsessional character" (al-Azmeh, Muslim canon). This is, of course, due to its very structure, which predisposes it to be chanted. As the reciter with his chant re-enacts the practice of the Prophet's own recitation, he is — like the Prophet — free to select "whatever is easy for him to recite" (cf. Q 73:20, *mā tayassara mina l-qurʾāni*) be it an entire sūra or only a section of it.

Angelika Neuwirth

Bibliography
A. al-Azmeh, The Muslim canon from late antiquity to the era of modernism (unpublished paper presented at the Wissenschaftskolleg zu Berlin, 1997); A. Baumstark, Jüdischer und christlicher Gebetstypus im Koran, in *Der Islam* 16 (1927), 229-48; O. Hamdan, *Studien zur Kanonisierung des Koran. Al-Ḥasan al-Baṣrī und die Religionspolitik der Umayyaden,* Wiesbaden (Harrassowitz) 2005 (forthcoming); J. Horovitz, Jewish proper names and derivatives in the Koran, in *The Hebrew Union College annual* 2 (1925), 145-227; id., KU; Jeffery, *For. vocab.*; G. Lüling, *Über den Ur-Qurʾān. Ansätze zur Rekonstruktion vorislamishcer christlicher Strophenlieder im Qur'an,* Erlangen 1974; Eng. trans. *A challenge to Islam for reformation. The rediscovery and reliable reconstruction of a comprehensive pre-Islamic Christian hymnal hidden in the Koran under earliest Islamic reinterpretations,* Delhi 2003; reviewed by Ibn Rawandi, On pre-Islamic Christian strophic poetical texts in the Koran. A critical look at the work of Günter Lüling, in Ibn Warraq (ed.), *What the Koran really says,* Amherst 2002, 653-710; Ch. Luxenberg, *Die syro-aramäische Lesart des Koran. Ein Beitrag zur Entschlüsselung der Koransprache,* Berlin 2000; M. Mir, *Coherence in the Qurʾān. A study of Iṣlāḥī's concept of naẓm in Tadabbur-i Qurʾān,* Indianapolis 1986; id., The qurʾānic story of Joseph. Plot, themes and characters, in MW 76 (1986), 1-15; id., The sūra as a unity. A twentieth century development in Qurʾān exegesis, in Hawting and

Shareef, *Approaches*, 211-24; A. Neuwirth, Images and metaphors in the introductory sections of the Makkan suras, in Hawting and Shareef, *Approaches*, 3-36; id., Oral scriptures in contact. The biblical story of the Calf of Gold and its biblical subtext between narrative, cult, and communal debate, in S. Wild (ed.), *Self referentiality in the Qurʾān*, in preparation; id., Qurʾānic literary structure revisited. Surat al-Rahman between mythic account and decodation of myth, in S. Leder (ed.), *Story-telling in the framework of non-fictional Arabic literature*, Wiesbaden 1998, 388-421; id., Referentiality and textuality in *Sūrat al-ḥijr*. Some observations on the qurʾānic "canonical process" and the emergence of a community, in I. Boullata, *Literary structures of religious meaning in the Qurʾān*, Richmond 2000, 143-72; id., *Studien zur Komposition der mekkanischen Suren*, Berlin 1981; id., Three religious feasts between texts of violence and liturgies of reconciliation, in Th. Scheffler (ed.), *Religion between violence and reconciliation*, Beirut 2002, 49-82; id., Vom Rezitationstext über die Liturgie zum Kanon. Zur Entstehung und Wiederauflösung der Surenkomposition im Verlauf der Entwicklung eines islamischen Kultus, in Wild, *Text*, 69-105; id., Zur Struktur der Yusuf-Sure, in W. Diem and S. Wild (eds.), *Studien aus Arabistik und Semitistik. Anton Spitaler zum siebzigsten Geburtstag von seinen Schülern überreicht*, Wiesbaden 1980, 123-52; Nöldeke, *GQ*; A.-L. Premare, *Joseph et Muḥammad. Le chapitre 12 du Coran*, Aix-en-Provence 1998; G.R. Puin, Observations on early Qurʾān manuscripts in Ṣanʿāʾ, in Wild, *Text*, 107-11; M. Radscheit, *Die koranische Herausforderung. Die taḥaddī-Verse im Rahmen der Polemik-Passagen des Korans*, Berlin 1996; M. Sells, *Approaching the Qurʾān. The new revelations, selections, translations, and commentaries by Michael Sells*, London 1999; id., A literary approach to the hymnic suras in the Qurʾān. Spirit, gender and aural intertextuality, in I. Boullata (ed.), *Literary structures of religious meaning in the Qurʾān*, Richmond 2000, 3-25; id., Sound, spirit and gender in Sūrat al-Qadr, in *JAOS* 11 (1991), 239-59; N. Sinai, From qurʾān to kitāb, in M. Marx, A. Neuwirth and N. Sinai (eds.), *The Qurʾān in context. Historical and literary investigations into the cultural milieu of the Qurʾān*, Beirut (forthcoming); Speyer, *Erzählungen*; M.R. Waldman, New approaches to "biblical" materials in the Qurʾān, in W.M. Brinner and S.D. Ricks (eds.), *Papers presented at the Institute of Islamic-Judaic Studies. Center for Judaic Studies*, Atlanta 1986, 47-63; Wansbrough, *QS*; Y.H. Yerushalmi, *Zakhor. Jewish history and Jewish memory*, Seattle 1982; A.H.M. Zahniser, The word of God and the apostleship of ʿIsa. A narrative analysis of Al Imran (3:33-62), in *JSS* 37 (1991), 77-112.

Surrender

see WAR; FIGHTING

Suspicion

Feeling, thought or instance of tentative belief without ground or sufficient evidence; an inclination to accuse or doubt the innocence of someone or to question the genuineness or truth of something. The adjective "suspicious" denotes someone or something that arouses distrust, that appears to be neither sound nor trustworthy (see TRUST AND PATIENCE). The meaning of the English word suspicion and various other forms of the verb to suspect are conveyed by a number of Arabic words that can be derived from the roots *ẓ-n-n, r-y-b, sh-b-h, t-h-m, sh-k-k*. Some of these words, however, belong to the semantic field of suspicion only in a wider sense and when accompanied by particular other terms, since they originally denote acts of accusation, expressions of doubt and distrust or other kinds of thought (see UNCERTAINTY).

Suspicion — in the sense of entertaining thoughts without evidence or doubts about the existence of God and his power (see POLYTHEISM AND ATHEISM; GRATITUDE AND INGRATITUDE; POWER AND IMPOTENCE) or about the genuineness of his messengers (see MESSENGER; PROPHETS AND PROPHETHOOD; LIE) — is represented in various places in the Qurʾān as an attitude that displays or leads to unbelief (see BELIEF AND UNBELIEF). For example, in Q 41:22-3 the enemies (q.v.) of God are described as people who wrongly thought *(ẓanna)* that God would be unable to know what they were doing (see HIDDEN AND THE HIDDEN); such people will be punished on the day of final judgment for the wrongs they commited based on this suspicion (see LAST JUDGMENT; REWARD AND PUNISHMENT). Q 45:24 mentions the lack of knowledge (*ʿilm;* see KNOWLEDGE AND LEARNING;

IGNORANCE) that is compounded by suspicion and speculation *(yaẓunnūna)* as a trait of the atheists who believe that only time (q.v.) will determine their fate (q.v.). The followers of Muḥammad who failed to support him during his campaign against the enemies of God are described in Q 3:154 as temporarily entertaining suspicious thoughts about God *(yaẓunnūna bi-llāhi ghayra l-ḥaqqi)* that resemble those that are characteristic for the times of pre-Islamic paganism (see HYPOCRITES AND HYPOCRISY; AGE OF IGNORANCE; EXPEDITIONS AND BATTLES). In Q 6:116 the believer is enjoined not to adopt the opinion of the majority of those living on earth because they follow but their conjecture. Q 10:36 implies that the unbelievers replace firm reliance on the truth (q.v.; *ḥaqq*) as announced by God with pure conjecture *(ẓann)*. Also in other verses, words of the root *ẓ-n-n* are used to describe the suspicion of those who doubt the capacities of God or his messengers, as in Q 72:7, where Muḥammad, referring to a dream (see DREAMS AND SLEEP), puts those among the jinn (q.v.) who are of the opinion that God is not able to raise anyone on the day of final judgment in the context of unbelief (see RESURRECTION; DEATH AND THE DEAD; ESCHATOLOGY). In Q 12:110 even some messengers of God are described as losing faith (q.v.) and temporarily suspecting *(ẓannū)* that God has told them lies. There are other passages in the holy scripture where suspicion is mentioned without any reference to words that originate from the root *ẓ-n-n*. For example, this is the case in the episode of Q 24:11-20 in which the Prophet's wife, ʿĀʾisha (see WIVES OF THE PROPHET; ʿĀʾISHA BINT ABĪ BAKR), is suspected of an aberration without any justification and where the believers are enjoined not to speak of something of which they have no knowledge (see GOSSIP).

Firm and unquestioned belief in the power of God and in the truth of his messengers is an indispensible characteristic of the true believers, who distinguish themselves from the unbelievers in that they do not doubt *(lam yartābū)* the existence of God or his messengers (Q 49:15). Suspicion is identified also as ethically reprehensible in Q 49:12, where the believers are called upon to avoid undue suspicion *(ẓann)* as an act that in some cases is tantamount to a sin (*ithm;* see SIN, MAJOR AND MINOR; ETHICS AND THE QURʾĀN).

Lutz Wiederhold

Bibliography
Primary: ʿAbd-al-Bāqī; Arberry; Dāmaghānī, *Wujūh*, ed. al-Zafītī, ii, 61-2 *(ẓann, shakk, tuhma);* i, 371 *(rayb);* Lane; M. Sawār (ed.), *al-Qurʾān al-karīm bi-l-rasm al-ʿuthmānī wa-bi-hāmishihi Tafsīr al-Jalālayn*, Beirut n.d.
Secondary: T. Izutsu, *The structure of the ethical terms in the Koran*, Tokyo 1959, 128-9 (*ẓann* vs. *ʿilm*: Q 53:28-9; 10:37; 53:19-23; 10:67); 239-40 (on Q 48:12, *ẓanna l-sawʾi*).

Sustenance

Nutritional or financial support. In its various and numerous nominal-verbal forms, the root consonants *r-z-q* provide the key qurʾānic sense of "sustenance" understood more particularly as that which sustains life (q.v.) and health (see ILLNESS AND HEALTH) but in places suggests, too, that which provides a livelihood (see WEALTH). Another word signifying "sustenance" (*aqwāt*, sing. *qūt*) occurs once only (Q 41:10) in a description of God's creation (q.v.) of the world. The great provider or sustainer (Q 5:114; 22:58; 62:11) is, of course, God (see GOD AND HIS ATTRIBUTES), who orders people in Q 2:60 to "Eat and drink of God's sustenance" (and cf. Q 20:131 f.; see FOOD AND DRINK). In other places this sustenance *(rizq)* is described as "honorable" (*karīm,* Q 8:4; 22:50; 33:31) or "lawful" (*ṭayyibāt,* Q 7:32; see LAWFUL AND UNLAWFUL), or "goodly" (*ḥasan,* Q 16:67; see GOOD AND EVIL). It constitutes one of God's "signs" (q.v.; *āyāt,* Q 45:5; cf. 40:13); and it is even evidence of the genuineness of prophecy (Q 11:88; see PROPHETS AND PROPHETHOOD; REVELATION AND INSPIRATION). In one instance, a more strictly secular context is found in Q 18:19 where it means provisions purchased from a city (q.v.) market (see MARKETS).

The concept illustrates the central qur'ānic theme of the uniqueness of God over and against other mere pretensions to divinity (see POLYTHEISM AND ATHEISM) and the dependence of everything upon his power (see POWER AND IMPOTENCE), will (see FREEDOM AND PREDESTINATION) and mercy (q.v.). Having created the jinn (q.v.) and humankind to worship (q.v.) him, God has no need that they give him sustenance (Q 51:57). Indeed, Abraham (q.v.) warned his people (see WARNER) that the idols (see IDOLS AND IMAGES) they worshiped could not even provide their daily bread (q.v.), so they should seek instead the bounty of God (Q 2:22; 16:73; 29:17), whose sustenance was better and more abiding (Q 20:131). Compared to God, comments al-Ṭabarī (d. 310/923), idols could neither harm nor benefit, neither create nor provide for their followers. God's power, on the other hand, was such that he could increase or restrict the livelihood of whomsoever he wished (Q 13:26; 29:62; 30:37; 34:36). This applied equally to rewards in the afterlife as in this life (see REWARD AND PUNISHMENT; CHASTISEMENT AND PUNISHMENT; ESCHATOLOGY), as God possessed the keys to both (Q 42:12; also Q 65:1). Al-Ṭabarī observes that he who revelled in the life of this world was ignorant of the favor and felicity of the afterlife that God bestowed on those who believed (see BELIEF AND UNBELIEF) and obeyed (see OBEDIENCE). Yet, whosoever enjoyed God's bounty in greater abundance than others enjoy and was loath to share with those for whom he was responsible denied God's blessings (Q 4:8 f.; 16:71; also Q 22:28, on giving to the distressed and needy; see LIE; POVERTY AND THE POOR). The collections of al-Bukhārī (d. 256/870) and Muslim (d. 261/875) preserve the Prophet's saying that a dependent whom God has placed under one's authority (q.v.) must be fed and clothed in the same measure as one would treat himself (see MAINTENANCE AND UPKEEP; ORPHANS). If conditions of poverty caused fear that one's children (q.v.) could not be fed, clothed and sheltered, they must not be killed, for God would provide for all (Q 6:151; see INFANTICIDE).

The believer's proper response to God's munificence, as throughout the Qur'ān, is gratitude (Q 29:17; see GRATITUDE AND INGRATITUDE). In one passage (Q 36:47), however, the echo of debate with unbelievers (see DEBATE AND DISPUTATION; PROVOCATION) is found in their mocking rejoinder to being urged to spend on others from what God had provided them: "Shall we feed anyone whom, if (your) God had willed, he could have fed himself?"

Ibn Khaldūn (d. 784/1382), citing Q 29:17, "So, seek sustenance from God," distinguishes between God-given "sustenance" and "profit," the latter being that part of a person's livelihood obtained by one's own effort and strength (see WORK). He alludes to, but does not discuss, the Muʿtazilī argument of sustenance that they insist must be rightfully gained and possessed (see MUʿTAZILA; THEOLOGY AND THE QUR'ĀN).

David Waines

Bibliography

Primary: Bukhārī, *Ṣaḥīḥ;* Dāmaghānī, *Wujūh,* ed. al-Zafītī, i, 372-3 *(rizq);* Ibn Khaldun-Rosenthal, ii, 311-13; *Lisān al-ʿArab;* Muslim, *Ṣaḥīḥ;* Ṭabarī, *Tafsīr,* ed. Shākir (to Q 14:27); ed. ʿAlī et al.

Secondary: van Ess, *TG*, iv, 497-9 (on *rizq* in theology); A. Ghabin, Ṣināʿa, in *EI²*, ix, 625-9; D. Gimaret, *Les noms divins en Islam*, Paris 1988, 397-400 *(rāziq, razzāq)*; J.D. McAuliffe, Rizq (in the Ḳurʾān), in *EI²*, viii, 568.

Suwāʿ see IDOLS AND IMAGES

Swear see OATH; CURSE

Swine see LAWFUL AND UNLAWFUL; FOOD AND DRINK

Symbolic Imagery

The use of allusion and figurative language to produce vivid descriptions and complex levels of meaning. The symbolic imagery in the Qurʾān arises out of the symbolic imagery of previous revelations as well as out of the poetic conventions of pre-Islamic Arabia (see SCRIPTURE AND THE QURʾĀN; POETRY AND POETS; PRE-ISLAMIC ARABIA AND THE QURʾĀN). While a key verse in the Qurʾān (Q 3:7) has sometimes been read to suggest that Muslims should not attempt to interpret its more ambiguous (q.v.) or symbolic passages, most Muslim exegetes (see EXEGESIS OF THE QURʾĀN: CLASSICAL AND MEDIEVAL) have not shied away from examining the symbolic imagery that radiates from virtually every chapter of the sacred text. Since the Qurʾān is first and foremost an oral text (see ORALITY; ORALITY AND WRITING IN ARABIA; RECITATION OF THE QURʾĀN), studies of symbolic imagery should not be limited to its visual dimension but should also take into account its aural dimension. At this stage in qurʾānic studies, however, much more attention has been paid to the Qurʾān's visual symbolism and the discussion that follows will focus upon examples of this visual dimension of qurʾānic imagery with particular emphasis on its use of paired symbolic concepts (see PAIRS AND PAIRING).

Symbolic imagery of paradise and hellfire

Passages throughout the Qurʾān use rich figurative language, often employing symbols that refer to desert life (see BEDOUIN; ARABS) or to poetic conventions that would have been familiar to those who first heard the revelations in seventh century Arabia. For example, Angelika Neuwirth has shown how the Qurʾān combines oath statements (see OATHS) with symbolic allusions to tribal raids in order to construct meaning through what she calls a "matrix of images" or *Bildmatrix* (see Neuwirth, Images; see also RHETORIC AND THE QURʾĀN; FORM AND STRUCTURE OF THE QURʾĀN). The qurʾānic use of desert imagery takes place on a more mundane level as well, for instance in its juxtaposition of the heat of the open desert with the cool of the oasis (see HOT AND COLD), a contrast that would have been immediately comprehensible to anyone living in such an environment. Understanding this latter type of symbolic imagery helps one to understand the juxtaposition between the tortures of the fire (q.v.) of hell (see HELL AND HELLFIRE) and the pleasures of the garden (q.v.) of paradise (q.v.). In addition, the cool oasis evokes the trope of the fertile garden and the remembrance of the lost beloved that typically opens the early Arabian odes. The example of the garden thus illustrates how pre-existing associations serve as a vast repository of symbols that the Qurʾān draws upon in order to produce meaning in a new Islamic context.

The Qurʾān uses some of its most frequent symbolic imagery to refer to the two abodes of the next life, paradise and hellfire. Although different passages sometimes expand upon distinct aspects of paradise, this realm is almost invariably depicted as a garden of cool, luxurious abundance through which rivers flow (see WATER OF PARADISE; SPRINGS AND FOUNTAINS). Hellfire, on the other hand, becomes associated with a number of more complex depictions and allusions, evoked through Arabic terms such as *jahannam, jaḥīm, hāwiya, ḥuṭama,* and the most basic, *al-nār,* "the fire." Although these varied terms are connected to the idea of judgment (q.v.) and hellfire in some fashion, to collapse them into one collective term "hell" is to do violence to the subtleties of the qurʾānic symbolic discourse (Sells, *Approaching,* 24-6). The Qurʾān refers to fire in a personified form in a couple of cases (Q 21:40; 70:15-18) and in another as a metonym for idolatry (Q 40:41-2; see Sabbagh, *Métaphore,* 90; see IDOLATRY AND IDOLATERS). It is important to recognize, however, that the Qurʾān does not always use fire as synonymous with hellfire, idolatry or evil (see GOOD AND EVIL). For instance, a verse compares the light (q.v.) of a campfire a person builds to the light of guidance that God is able to take away (Q 2:17; cf. also the fire image in the famous "Light Verse" of Q 24:35).

Just as fire is a multivalent symbol in the Qurʾān, despite its frequent association with hellfire, so water (q.v.) expresses multiple values, despite its frequent association with paradise. As discussed above, references to the rivers of paradise are ubiquitous and the sending down of rain is often connected symbolically to God's sending down of revelations (Q 30:49; 31:34; 42:28; see Toelle, *Coran,* 115-20; cf. Lings, Qoranic symbolism; see REVELATION AND INSPIRATION) or blessings (see BLESSING; GRACE). Water also appears in the Qurʾān with reference to the flood, the treacherous seas and the destructive capacities of rain (see WEATHER; PUNISHMENT STORIES). The complex use of water symbolism also appears in pre-Islamic poetry and evokes the worldview of the desert environment in which the Qurʾān was first revealed.

Symbolic pairs that distinguish belief from unbelief

As with hellfire and paradise, the Qurʾān contains a number of other paired concepts whose symbolic meanings transcend their simple juxtaposition. One of the most important of these paired concepts is the distinction between belief and unbelief (q.v.). This binary relationship forms the basis for a whole series of symbolic binaries in the Qurʾān: from hearing and deafness (q.v.; see also ANATOMY and EARS) to sight and blindness (see VISION AND BLINDNESS; SEEING AND HEARING; EYES); from fertile and withered crops (see AGRICULTURE AND VEGETATION) to the split between humans and animals (see ANIMAL LIFE); from the distinction between the straight path and wandering lost (see ASTRAY; ERROR) to the ubiquitous imagery of light and darkness (q.v.). The juxtaposition between the believers and their adversaries (see ENEMIES) in the Qurʾān provides the basis for some of the most expressive of its similes (q.v.), metaphors (see METAPHOR), and parables (see PARABLE).

For instance, the aforementioned Light Verse (Q 24:35; see VERSES) offers an image of God as light and of God's light as of an oil lamp in a niche. These images form complex symbols that have generated multiple and diverse interpretations by Muslim exegetes. The images are followed by the idea of light as a symbol of God's guidance: "God guides to his light whom he wills, God strikes parables for people, and in all things God is most knowing" (see FREEDOM AND PREDESTINATION; KNOWLEDGE AND LEARNING). This equation between light and guidance is developed in a number of other passages (e.g. Q 2:257; 4:174; 14:5) and is sometimes explicitly associated with God's revelations of the scriptures (e.g. Q 5:15, 44, 46).

In addition to the "parables" *(amthāl)* mentioned in the Light Verse, the verses that immediately follow it contrast the believers who remember God with the disbelievers who presumably do not (see MEMORY; REMEMBRANCE; GRATITUDE AND INGRATITUDE), the latter of whom are described in a pair of expressive similes:

And [as for] those who disbelieve, their works are like a mirage in a level plain that the thirsty one considers water until he comes to it and finds nothing... Or like darkness in a fathomless sea, covered by wave upon wave, over which are dark clouds, some above others. When one puts out one's hand, one almost cannot see it. He for whom God does not make a light, he does not have a light (Q 24:39-40).

The first of these similes makes use once again of the imagery of the desert, where one who has gone astray and is dying of thirst believes his deeds are bringing him to water, while they are actually bringing him to nothing (cf. Q 13:14). In other passages, the Qur'ān employs different similes to suggest the futility of the deeds of those who deny the qur'ānic message, comparing their deeds to ashes (q.v.) blown about (Q 14:18; see GOOD DEEDS; EVIL DEEDS; AIR AND WIND) or to empty noises and gestures (Q 8:35). In the above passage, the water imagery derives from the idea of paradise as a garden in which rivers flow, a destination that this wayward traveler mistakenly believes is ahead of him. The second simile that follows the famous Light Verse is sometimes known as the Darkness Verse (Q 24:40) and it enriches the image of the light of God's guidance with a description of the darkness surrounding the unbeliever. Not only is such a person without a light but surging and billowing darkness encompasses him or her on all sides: the deep and dark waters below, the layers of wave upon wave all around, the layers of dark clouds above, resulting in darkness so complete that sight is practically impossible. The symbolism of this Darkness Verse not only refers back to the Light Verse that precedes it and the idea of guidance, but it also evokes the vision/blindness binary as a trope for the distinction between belief and unbelief, as mentioned previously.

While images of light and darkness are frequently associated with the idea of guidance or lack thereof, another qur'ānic symbol associated with this idea is that of the straight road or path *(al-ṣirāṭ al-mustaqīm;* see PATH OR WAY). This symbol implies that there are many ways to travel off the straight road, all of which will lead one to wander astray. The "opening" chapter of the Qur'ān, Sūrat al-Fātiḥa (see FĀTIḤA) mentions this trope in its verse, "Guide us on the straight road" (Q 1:6), and this same straight road appears in at least thirty other qur'ānic passages. In a few eschatological passages, this concept of a straight path takes concrete form in the image of the narrow bridge that spans the chasm between this world and the next (see ESCHATOLOGY).

In other passages, the symbol of the road or path appears in a related but somewhat broader symbolic context, for example when the Qur'ān describes righteous behavior as climbing the steep uphill pass *(al-ʿaqaba,* Q 90:11). The text explains the symbol in the following fashion:

What can tell you of the steep pass?
To free a slave (see SLAVES AND SLAVERY)
To feed the destitute on a day of hunger
(see FAMINE),
a kinsman orphan (q.v.),

or a poor man in need (see POVERTY AND THE POOR).
Be of those who keep the faith (q.v.), who counsel one another to patience (see TRUST AND PATIENCE), who counsel to compassion. They are of the right (see LEFT HAND AND RIGHT HAND). As for those who cast our signs (q.v.) away, they are of the left; over them a vault of fire (Q 90:12-20).

This passage begins with a mysterious symbolic reference, signaled by the use of the phrase "what can tell you of" *(mā adrāka mā)* which typically introduces terms that require further elaboration. The allusion to the "steep pass" *(ʿaqaba)* here is followed by an explanation of the term as a spiritual metaphor.

The description of the "steep pass" above illustrates another category of binary symbols found in the Qurʾān, the juxtaposition between left and right as morally-charged concepts. While this juxtaposition is obviously an ancient one, the qurʾānic discourse was revealed in the context of an Arabian culture in which the left hand was considered unclean and the right was used for swearing oaths (see CONTRACTS AND ALLIANCES). In addition, the Qurʾān refers to people "whom your right hand possesses" in reference to those people under one's control, such as war captives (q.v.) or slaves (e.g. Q 4:3, 24-5, 33-6; 24:33, 58; 30:28). The passage above, however, shows how other verses in the Qurʾān invest the categories of left and right with moral signification, associating the former with evil and the latter with good (see ETHICS AND THE QURʾĀN). The distinction between the "people of the right" *(aṣḥāb al-yamīn/al-maymana)* and the "people of the left" *(aṣḥāb al-mashʾama/al-shimāl)* in Q 90 above is elucidated at greater length in Q 56. Here the former are said to rest contentedly in a garden paradise, while the latter face punishment in a scorching hellfire (Q 56:8-9, 27-38, 41-56, 90-4; see REWARD AND PUNISHMENT). Yet other passages depict the blessed receiving their book of deeds in their right hands on the last day (see HEAVENLY BOOK; LAST JUDGMENT), as opposed to those unfortunate enough to be given their books in another fashion. Such examples illustrate the symbolic weight that the Qurʾān invests in the concepts of right and left, especially when it comes to eschatological judgment.

Imagery of the last day

Beyond the eschatological references discussed above, the Qurʾān presents graphic descriptions of what the world will be like on the last day (see APOCALYPSE). In these passages, those things thought to be stable are ripped apart, the graves are opened and the earth yields up its secrets as if a mother giving birth (e.g. Q 99). One particularly striking apocalyptic passage is found in Q 101, The Calamity (Sūrat al-Qāriʿa), in which the phrase "what can tell you" appears twice to introduce two presumably unfamiliar concepts:

The *qāriʿa*
What is the *qāriʿa*
What can tell you of the *qāriʿa*
A day humankind are like moths scattered *(ka-l-farāsh al-mabthūth)*
And mountains are like fluffs of wool *(ka-l-ʿihn al-manfūsh)*
Whoever's scales weigh heavy *(thaqulat mawāzīnuhu;* see WEIGHTS AND MEASURES)
His is a life that is pleasing *(rāḍiya)*
Whoever's scales weigh light *(khaffatun mawāzīnuhu)*
His mother is *hāwiya* (see PIT)
What can tell you what she is *(wa-mā adrāka mā hiya)*
Raging fire (*nārun ḥāmiyatun,* Q 101:1-11).

This sūra offers a pair of similes to help describe the "calamity" *(al-qāriʿa)* through symbolic images. The image of people becoming like "moths scattered" conjures up ideas of confused dispersion, rapid movement and mortal frailty. The image of mountains becoming like "fluffs of wool" illustrates how a thing that many humans see as a symbol of solidity and permanence transforms on the last day into something that will be cut from its roots and pliable. The concept of scales of judgment appears graphically in this sūra, offering a concrete visual image of deeds being literally weighed in the balance on the last day. Michael Sells has argued that the sound quality of the consonants that end the verses (see RHYMED PROSE) help to extend the similes "into more elaborate metaphors," and that the terms "are heavy" *(thaqulat)* and "are light" *(khaffat)* as used in the scale imagery "have onomatopoetic effects" (Sells, *Approaching*, 178). This insight reminds us that when examining the symbolic imagery of the Qurʾān, not only visual images but also aural images ("sound figures") help to generate layers of meaning that deserve scholarly attention.

Frederick S. Colby

Bibliography
Bint al-Shāṭiʾ (ʿĀʾisha ʿAbd al-Raḥmān), *al-Tafsīr al-bayānī lil-Qurʾān,* Cairo 1962; M. Lings, The qoranic symbolism of water, in *Studies in comparative religion* 2 (1968), 153-60; T. Lohman, *Die Gleichnisreden Muhammeds im Koran,* in *Mitteilungen des Instituts für Orientforschung* [Berlin] 12 (1966), 75-118; 416-69; A. Neuwirth, Images and metaphors in the introductory sections of the Makkan sūras, in Hawting and Shareef, *Approaches,* 3-36; T. J. O'Shaughnessey, God's throne and the biblical symbolism of the Qurʾan, in *Numen* 20 (1973), 202-21; R. Paret, *Symbolik des Islam,* Stuttgart 1958, completed by J. Chr. Bürgel and Fr. Allemann, *Symbolik des Islam,* Stuttgart 1975; T. Sabbagh, *La métaphore dans le Coran,* Paris 1943; W. Saleh, *Formation of the classical tafsīr tradition,* Leiden 2004, 119-24; M. Sells, *Approaching the Qurʾān. The early revelations,* Ashland, OR 1999; id., Sound and meaning in Sūrat al-Qāriʿa, in *Arabica* 40 (1993), 403-30; M. Siddiqi, *Who is who in the holy Qurʾān? Qurʾānic names and symbols,* Lahore 1994; M. Sister, Metaphern und Vergleiche im Koran, in *Mitteilungen des Seminars für Orientalische sprachen zu Berlin.* 2 Abt. *Westasiatische Studien* 34 (1931), 103-54; H. Toelle, *Le Coran revisité. Le feu, l'eau, l'air et la terre,* Damascus 1999; B. Wardī, *Ḥawla rumūz al-Qurʾān,* Casablanca 1983; Watt-Bell, *Introduction.*

Synagogue see JEWS AND JUDAISM; RELIGIOUS PLURALISM AND THE QURʾĀN

Synonyms see ARABIC LANGUAGE

Syria

In the larger sense, Syria (in Arabic *al-Shām*) extended from the Euphrates River/Amanus Mountains to the Gulf of Clysma/Suez. The region was known to the pre-Islamic Arabs (q.v.), especially the Meccans, whose caravans (see CARAVAN) traversed the spice-route, the two termini of which, Gaza and Buṣrā, were visited by them, as was the Sinai (q.v.) peninsula (see also PRE-ISLAMIC ARABIA AND THE QURʾĀN).

The term Syria or al-Shām does not appear in the Qurʾān but, as al-Shām included the holy land, references to it in the Qurʾān as the land of the biblical prophets and of the scenes of biblical history do occur, however allusively and anonymously (see SCRIPTURE AND THE QURʾĀN; HISTORY AND THE QURʾĀN; GEOGRAPHY). Such are *al-arḍ al-muqaddasa* (Q 5:21), Jerusalem (q.v.) by implication, where the *masjid* and the *miḥrāb* were located (Q 3:37, 39; 17:7; see MOSQUE; SACRED PRECINCTS); the Mount of Olives (Q 95:1); anonymously, the Jordan river (*nahr,* literally "river," Q 2:249; see WATER; SPRINGS AND FOUNTAINS); the villages of Lot (q.v.; *al-muʾtafika,* Q 53:53; cf. 69:9; see PUNISHMENT STORIES); Iram dhāt al-ʿImād, in present day Wādī Rumm in Trans-Jordan (Q 89:7; see IRAM); al-Raqīm (Q 18:9; see RAQĪM), possibly in al-Balqā᾽ in Trans-Jordan; and Sinai (Q 23:20). Although not mentioned by name, Jerusalem represented the strictly Islamic dimension of the holy land for two reasons: it was the destination of the *isrā᾽*, the nocturnal journey of the prophet Muḥammad (Q 17:1; see ASCENSION) and the gateway to his *miʿrāj*, ascent to the seventh heaven (see HEAVEN AND SKY); and it was the *qibla* (q.v.), the spot to which the Muslims turned in their prayers for twelve years before the direction of prayer was changed to Mecca (q.v.).

Al-Shām was known to the prophet Muḥammad before his call. According to tradition (see SĪRA AND THE QUR᾽ĀN), his great-grandfather, Hāshim, was buried in Gaza, and he accompanied his uncle, Abū Ṭālib, during the latter's journeys to al-Shām. Later he led the caravans of Khadīja (q.v.) after he married her — hence his references to places and areas in al-Shām during the twenty-two years of his prophethood: such, among others, were Ṣaffūriyya (Sepphoris) and Ḥabrūn (Hebron) in Palestine, Mu᾽ta and al-Balqā᾽ in Trans-Jordan and al-Dārūm in southern Palestine. After the campaign against Tabūk in 630 C.E. (see EXPEDITIONS AND BATTLES), the Prophet concluded treaties (see CONTRACTS AND ALLIANCES) with four of the towns of southern al-Shām, namely Ayla, Adhruḥ, Maqnā and Jarbā, places he had known before his prophetic call.

Al-Shām was the first target of the Muslim conquests. It was the region that Islam conquered immediately after the death of the Prophet. By 635 C.E., the holy land within al-Shām was already in Muslim hands after the two battles of Ajnādayn in Palestine and Fiḥl in Trans-Jordan. In 638 C.E. Jerusalem surrendered to none other than the caliph ʿUmar himself; its surrender clinched the possession of the holy land by Islam and opened the first chapter in the long struggle between Islam and Christianity (see CHRISTIANS AND CHRISTIANITY), which reached its climax in the crusades. The Muslim victory at Yarmūk in 636 C.E. decided the fate of the rest of al-Shām, the cities which surrendered one after the other being Damascus, Ḥims, Ḥamā and Antioch, among others.

The Muslim conquest of al-Shām and the holy land imparted a peculiarly new Islamic dimension to its holiness (cf. the several traditions on the "merits" of Syria/Damascus — and Jerusalem, for example "happy Syria... the angels of the merciful one spread their wings upon it," *ṭūbā li-Shām... inna malā᾽ikata l-raḥmān bāsiṭatun ajniḥatahum ʿalayhi*, in e.g. Ibn Ḥanbal, *Musnad*, xvi, 38, no. 21499; cf. Gilliot, Traditions, 18; Sivan, Beginning). Those who died in the battles were martyrs (q.v.) for the faith (q.v.) and many of them were *ṣaḥāba*, Companions of the Prophet (q.v.); such were the three commanders who died at Mu᾽ta and others who settled in the region. The conquest was initiated by the Prophet himself before he died, which imparted to it the religious tone of a holy war (q.v.; see also JIHĀD), especially as it was preceded and supported by letters which announced to their recipients the new Islamic kerygma.

It was, however, in the Umayyad period that al-Shām attained the acme of its importance as the metropolitan province of the first Arab dynasty of the Islamic empire. Furthermore, its character as a holy land was ratified by the first Umayyad caliph (q.v.), Muʿāwiya, who announced his caliphate and received allegiance in Jerusalem itself, as did Yazīd and ʿAbd al-Malik after him. But it was the Marwānid Umayyad branch that enhanced the Islamic component in the holy land, when

ʿAbd al-Malik built the Dome of the Rock and al-Walīd, his son, built the Aqṣā Mosque (q.v.), without which the Islamic presence in Jerusalem would have remained unclear, based on sūra 17 in the Qurʾān, entitled Sūrat al-Isrāʾ ("The Night Journey"). The two structures dwarfed architecturally all other structures in Jerusalem and reflected a powerful Islamic presence in the holy city. The future Umayyad caliph Sulaymān enhanced further the importance of the holy land when, during his governorship of Palestine, he built a new city, Ramla, and its White Mosque, and added to the Umayyad structures in Jerusalem. When he became caliph (r. 96-9/715-17), Palestine, the holy land, became the metropolitan province of the vast Muslim empire, which extended from India to Spain.

Islam raised to a higher level of importance not only Jerusalem but the sister city Hebron, where Abraham (q.v.) and his son Isaac (q.v.) and grandson Jacob (q.v.) were buried together with their wives. Hebron had been relatively obscure in the Byzantine period (see BYZANTINES) but Islam revived it, commensurately with the fundamental place of Abraham in the Qurʾān and in Islam.

It was also during the Umayyad period that the concept of the holy land experienced an extension of its boundaries from the old traditional ones to encompass practically the whole of al-Shām. The Umayyad Mosque of Damascus built by al-Walīd contributed to the veneration of the city as a Muslim center and Buṣrā was also venerated as the venue of Muḥammad's encounter with Baḥīrā (see MONASTICISM AND MONKS). The extension of the boundaries of the holy land had started in the Byzantine period, when other cities in the region acquired a certain holiness by association: such was Damascus with St. Paul, Emesa with the head of John the Baptist (q.v.), and Antioch as the place where the followers of Jesus (q.v.) of Nazareth were first called Christians. These *loca sancta* of Christianity were not difficult for the Umayyads to accept in view of the insistence of the Qurʾān on its close relation to Christianity (see POLEMIC AND POLEMICAL LANGUAGE; RELIGIOUS PLURALISM AND THE QURʾĀN; RELIGION), but still more in view of the strong Muslim-Christian symbiosis in al-Shām, accepted and promoted by the Umayyads after being initiated by Muʿāwiya, whose wife Maysūn was a Christian, the mother of his son and successor Yazīd I, who also married a Ghassānid Christian princess, Ramla. In a religious context this symbiosis is reflected in the fact that the mosque in Damascus has within its precinct the tomb of John the Baptist.

With the proliferation of *loca sancta* (see SACRED AND PROFANE), *mashāhīd* and *mazārāt*, in al-Shām, the whole region acquired a certain holiness — so much so that the medieval Muslim traveler, al-Harawī (d. 611/1215), devoted to al-Shām one third of his work on the *loca sancta* of the Islamic world.

Irfan Shahīd

Bibliography
Primary: al-Harawī, Taqī l-Dīn Abū l-Ḥasan ʿAlī b. Abī Bakr al-Mawṣilī, *Kitāb al-Ishārāt ilā maʿrifat al-ziyārāt*, ed. J. Sourdel-Thomine, Damascus 1953, 4-34; Ibn Ḥanbal, *Musnad*, ed. Shākir; Ibn Isḥāq-Guillaume, 532, 678; Ṭabarī, *Tārīkh*, ed. de Goeje, 2078-159.
Secondary: E.C. Bosworth, al-Shām, in *EI²*, ix, 261-75; Cl. Gilliot, Les traditions sur la composition ou coordination du Coran *(taʾlīf al-Qurʾān)*, in id. and T. Nagel (eds.), *Das Prophen ḥadīṯ. Dimensionen einer islamischen Literaturgattung* [Proceedings of the *Göttinger Kolloquium über das Ḥadīṯ*], Göttingen 2005, 14-39; Ph.K. Hitti, *History of the Arabs*, London 1981 (repr.), 147-54, 189-278; R. Lescot, Un sanctuaire des dormants en Jordanie, in *REI* 36 (1968), 3-9; M.M. Mandell, Syria, in A. Kazhdan (ed.), *Oxford*

dictionary of Byzantium, 3 vols., Oxford 1991, iii, 1997-2000; E. Sivan, The beginning of the *Faḍāʾil al-Quds* literature, in *IOS* 1 (1971), 263-71; S. Ward, Muḥammad said: You are only a Jew from the Jews of Sepphoris, in *JNES* 60 (2001), 31-42.

Syriac and the Qurʾān

see FOREIGN VOCABULARY; LANGUAGE AND STYLE OF THE QURʾĀN; CHRISTIANS AND CHRISTIANITY

T

Table

A supported horizontal surface that facilitates actions like working, writing or eating. There is no precise equivalent in classical Arabic for this English term. Words like *minḍada, sufra* and *simāṭ* only signify "table" by derivation; their basic meanings are respectively "a device where mats, carpets or cushions are piled up," "food provision for the traveler," and "a cloth or coat upon which the dishes are put." By contrast, several designations for "table" entered Arabic from neighboring, non-Semitic languages. These include *mēz* and *khiwān* from Persian, *ṭarabēza* from Greek, *ṭāwula* from Latin, and *māʾida* via Ethiopian, possibly originating from Latin as well (see FOREIGN VOCABULARY). Only this last term occurs in the Qurʾān, where it appears twice, namely in Q 5:112 and 114; it also gives the fifth sūra its title, *al-māʾida*, "The Table."

Strictly speaking, the table episode — a much debated issue in the Qurʾān — comprises verses Q 5:112 to 115 only. In order to understand the story properly, however, one must consider its broader context. The *leitmotif* of the whole passage is that God's messengers (see MESSENGER) have no knowledge of (see KNOWLEDGE AND LEARNING) — and therefore no responsibility (q.v.) for — the outcome of their missions (Q 5:109). This holds true for Jesus (q.v.) as well. God guided him throughout his lifetime, from when he spoke in the cradle supported by the spirit (q.v.) of holiness (see also HOLY SPIRIT), to his divine protection (q.v.) from the Israelites (Q 5:110; see CHILDREN OF ISRAEL). On God's prompting, the apostles (see APOSTLE) readily professed their belief in him and his messenger (Q 5:111). The passage then reads:

And when the apostles said, "O Jesus son of Mary (q.v.), is your lord able to send down on us a table *(māʾida)* out of heaven (see HEAVEN AND SKY)?" He said, "Fear you God, if you are believers" (Q 5:112; see BELIEF AND UNBELIEF; MIRACLES; MARVELS; FEAR).

They said, "We desire that we should eat of it and our hearts (see HEART) be at rest; and that we may know that you have spoken true to us, and that we may be among its witnesses" (Q 5:113; see TRUTH; WITNESSING AND TESTIFYING).

Said Jesus son of Mary, "O God, our lord, send down upon us a table out of heaven, that shall be for us a festival, the first and last of us, and a sign from you.

And provide for us; you are the best of providers" (Q 5:114; see SUSTENANCE). God said, "Verily I will indeed send it down to you; whosoever of you hereafter disbelieves, verily I shall chastise him with a chastisement such as I chastise no other being" (Q 5:115; see CHASTISEMENT AND PUNISHMENT).

It was not Jesus who deified himself and his mother Mary. During the time he lived among men, he exhorted them only to serve God alone, his lord and theirs (Q 5:116-17). It is God who punishes or forgives (Q 5:118; see REWARD AND PUNISHMENT; FORGIVENESS).

The broad scholarly consensus is that the qurʾānic table episode basically refers, in one way or another, to the Lord's Supper, although other biblical passages can be adduced as possible reference points as well, such as the feeding of the five thousand, Jesus' discourse on "the bread of life" (John 6: 22 f.), Peter's vision in Acts 10:10 f., or Psalms 78:19 and 23:5. But when it comes to understanding the meaning of the episode, opinions are divided. Are we dealing here with the demand for a miracle (Räisänen, *Jesusbild;* Gräf, Christlichen Einflüssen; Busse, *Theologischen Beziehungen;* and most of the Muslim commentators)? Is the table a sign of God's providence (Bowman, Debt of Islam; al-Nadjdjār, *Qiṣaṣ;* see SIGNS) or a simile (q.v.) for spiritual knowledge (the Ṣūfī interpretation according to al-Bayḍāwī)? Do the apostles want to celebrate a kind of thanksgiving (ʿAbd al-Tafāhum, Qurʾān and communion) or a commemorative meal (Beltz, *Mythen*)? Or is the whole episode finally nothing but confusion (Macdonald, ʿĪsā; Bell, *Origin of Islam;* cf. Comerro, Nouvelle alliance, 305f.; Radscheit, Iconography, 172f.)? The question of the meaning of the table motif in the Qurān has proved to be especially intractable.

Nevertheless, two explanations present themselves. On the one hand, as stated above, the word *māʾida* is borrowed from Ethiopian, where it signifies the lord's table (see CHRISTIANS AND CHRISTIANITY). This original usage probably had the double meaning of the altar of the Eucharist (which in early times was a simple table) and of the Eucharistic offering, viz. bread (q.v.) and wine (q.v.). If one assumes that this word still carried both meanings after its adoption in Arabic, it is possible that the apostles' request for *māʾida* sent down from heaven does not refer to "a table," but rather to "food" (see FOOD AND DRINK). In fact, the *Lisān al-ʿArab* even asserts that this is the basic meaning of *māʾida*. On the other hand, the table episode may be considered an instance of qurānic allusion to visual representations. In all the varying interpretations of the Lord's Supper in early Christian theology, the Eucharist is always regarded as closely related to Christ's being the son of God. Christian depictions of the Lord's Supper can therefore be considered to represent the core of Christian belief. The Qurʾān, however, categorically denies the divine nature of Jesus (see POLEMIC AND POLEMICAL LANGUAGE). Any qurʾānic reference to the Lord's Supper, then, can only occur in a polemic, i.e. a reinterpreting, form. Although the table motif is admittedly rather marginal in the Gospels' account of the Lord's Supper, the table is nevertheless one of the necessary elements in the Christian depictions of the event: it is the place where Jesus and the apostles reclined for the Passover meal. Yet in a Christian interpretation of such a picture, the table still has no function of its own; it merely serves to hold the food. Here one may argue that the Qurʾān, in a deliberate reinterpretation of the Lord's Supper, takes its visual elements — Jesus, the apostles and the table itself — at face value and re-contextualizes them in such a way that the element "table" receives a prominent place.

No matter whether the linguistic or the cross-media explanation for the presence of *mā'ida* is more likely, in order to understand the meaning of the table episode, it must be noted that the major theme in Q 5 is the notion of "covenant" (q.v.; cf. Comerro, Nouvelle alliance). Q 5:12 is a reminder of God's covenant with the Children of Israel (cf. Q 5:70); Q 5:14 mentions his covenant with "those who say 'We are Christians'" (cf. Q 5:111); and Q 5:7 recalls to mind the covenant God made with the actual community of believers (cf. Q 5:3, "Today I have perfected your religion [q.v.] for you, and I have completed my blessing [q.v.] upon you, and I have approved *al-islām* for your religion"; see ISLAM). But both the Israelites and the Christians broke their respective covenants, the first by disobeying God and his messengers (cf. Q 5:13, 20-6, 70; see DISOBEDIENCE), the latter by violating true monotheism (cf. Q 5:14, 17, 72-6; see POLYTHEISM AND ATHEISM; IDOLATRY AND IDOLATERS). Since the anti-Trinitarian argumentation in Q 5:116-17 (see TRINITY) stresses that the covenant with the Christians was broken only after God took Jesus to himself, it seems likely that the preceding verses also refer to this very covenant. Q 5:111, then, marks the moment the (twelve) apostles consent to this covenant (cf. the motif of the twelve chieftains of Israel in Q 5:12 and of the twelve men of the first ʿAqaba in the *Sīra* [see SĪRA AND THE QURʾĀN]; for references to the apostles' speech [q.v.] act, see Q 5:7 and, in a distorted form, Q 2:93). Seen in this light, Q 5:112-14 must be understood as a request to establish a commemoration feast *(ʿīd)* for this event. In the motif of the heaven-sent food one may detect the early Christian belief that the Holy Spirit comes down in the Eucharist. But what is more, the two ideas that food is a divine gift and that God sends down "tranquility into the hearts of the believers" are firmly rooted in the Qurʾān, too (cf. for the former Q 2:57; 50:9-11; 56:10-26, for the latter Q 48:4; see SHEKHINAH). Finally, since the early Church considered Judas to be the prototype of a traitor in the community, in the singular threat in Q 5:115 it is possible to see a transformation of Jesus' prophecy of woe for Judas (*Mt* 26:24; *Mk* 14:21) into a general verdict against all those who break the covenant (Q 5:13; cf. Gräf, Christlichen Einflüssen, who suggests a connection with 1 *Cor* 11:27-9).

To sum up, although the table episode carries strong biblical overtones (see SCRIPTURE AND THE QURʾĀN; NARRATIVES), it is basically a re-reading of the Lord's Supper. In this reinterpretation, the person of Jesus loses its paramount importance and his being the son of God is expressly denied. Instead, the Eucharist is interpreted as confirmation and remembrance of God's covenant with the apostles. With that, the Eucharist is added to the line of covenants God has made both with the Children of Israel previously and with the new community of believers afterwards.

Matthias Radscheit

Bibliography
Primary: Thaʿlabī, *Qiṣaṣ*, 397f.
Secondary: ʿAbd al-Tafāhum, The Qurʾān and the holy communion, in *MW* 49 (1959), 239-48; E. Beck, Die Eucharistie bei Ephraem, in *Oriens christianus* 38 (1954), 41-67; R. Bell, *The origin of Islam in its Christian environment,* London 1926[1], London 1968, 136; W. Beltz, *Die Mythen des Koran,* Düsseldorf 1980, 183; J. Bowman, The debt of Islam to monophysite Syrian Christianity, in *Nederlands Theologisch Tijdschrift* 19 (1964-5), 177-201; H. Busse, *Die theologischen Beziehungen des Islams zu Judentum und Christentum,* Darmstadt 1988, 130 f.; V. Comerro, La nouvelle alliance dans la sourate *al-māʾida,* in *Arabica* 48 (2001), 285-314;

L. Goppelt, Trapeza, in G. Friedrich (ed.), *Theologisches Wörterbuch zum Neuen Testament*, 10 vols., Stuttgart 1932-79, viii, 209-15; E. Gräf, Zu den christlichen Einflüssen im Koran, in *Al-Bahit. Festschrift Joseph Henninger*, St. Augustin 1976, 111-44; M. Kropp, Viele fremde Tische, und noch einer im Koran, in *Oriens christianus* 87 (2003), 141-4; K. Lüthi, Judas. i. Das Judasbild vom Neuen Testament bis zur Gegenwart, in *Theologische Realenzyklopaedie* 17 (1988), 296-304; D.B. Macdonald, ʿĪsā, in *EI*[1], ii, 562; ʿA. al-Nadjdjār, *Qiṣaṣ al-anbiyāʾ*, Cairo n.d.[5]; O. Pautz, *Muhammeds Lehre von der Offenbarung quellenmäßig untersucht*, Leipzig 1898; M. Radscheit, The iconography of the Qurʾān, in C. Szyska and F. Pannewick (eds.), *Crossings and passages in genre and culture*, Wiesbaden 2003, 167-83; H. Räissänen, *Das koranische Jesusbild*, Helsinki 1971, 43; A. Shalabī, *al-Masīḥiyya*, Cairo 1998[10], 50 f.

Tablet see BOOK; PRESERVED TABLET

Taboo see FORBIDDEN

Tābūt see ARK

Ṭāghūt see IDOLS AND IMAGES

Tale see NARRATIVES; JOSEPH

Talent

A gift, ability or propensity provided by God. There is no specific qurʾānic term for talent although meanings related to this concept may be associated with ideas such as degrees, ability, capacity and gifts (see GIFT AND GIFT-GIVING; GRACE; BLESSING). In modern Arabic, terms derived from the root *w-h-b*, "gifts," and *ʿ-d-d*, "preparation," refer to talent, but these roots and their derivations are not employed in this sense in the Qurʾān. In addition, *istiṭāʿa*, "ability, capacity," is an important theological concept in Islam (see THEOLOGY AND THE QURʾĀN), but it is usually discussed more in terms of the extent to which humans have the independent strength and ability to make choices and perform actions (cf. Gardet, Istiṭāʿa; see FREEDOM AND PREDESTINATION).

The concept of exceptional or distinctive abilities may be extrapolated from qurʾānic expressions regarding preferring *(faḍḍala)* or degrees and rankings *(darajāt)*. These terms usually convey the idea that certain people are raised by degrees both in this world and in the next life (see REWARD AND PUNISHMENT; ESCHATOLOGY), on the basis either of their effort (Q 4:95; see PATH OR WAY), belief (Q 58:11; see BELIEF AND UNBELIEF) or good deeds (q.v.; Q 46:19). Sometimes, however, this idea of degree seems to be innate, as in the passage asserting that males have been preferred above females (Q 4:34; see GENDER; WOMEN AND THE QURʾĀN; PATRIARCHY). This verse has attracted attention in the modern period on the part of modernists and Muslim feminists who interpret the words as indicating male responsibility (q.v.) derived on the basis of material resources (see WEALTH; PROPERTY; MAINTENANCE AND UPKEEP) rather than innate male superiority or talent (Wadud, *Qurʾān and woman*, 65-9; see FEMINISM AND THE QURʾĀN). Inasmuch as ultimately all guidance and provision (see SUSTENANCE; ERROR; ASTRAY) has a divine source according to the Islamic perspective, diversity in human talents, inclinations and abilities is understood as being part of God's plan. All of these degrees in livelihood arise from God's mercy (q.v.; *raḥma*) that is apportioned or measured (*q-s-m;* see WEIGHTS AND MEASURES; MEASUREMENT) by God alone (Q 43:32).

The idea of developing the inherent propensities or potentialities of each individual may be found in the thought of Ṣūfī mystics such as Ibn al-ʿArabī (d. 638/1240; see ṢŪFISM AND THE QURʾĀN). This is based on emanationist cosmology (q.v.), in which the pre-eternal creative act of God projects the divine names and attributes (see GOD AND HIS ATTRIBUTES) into creation (q.v.) and therefore into individuals as well. It is individual receptivity *(qabūl)* or preparedness *(istiʿdād)* that must be discerned and developed through appropriate contemplation and action (Chittick, *Ṣūfī path*, 91; see REMEMBRANCE).

Marcia Hermansen

Bibliography
W. Chittick, *The Ṣūfī path of knowledge*, Albany 1989; L. Gardet, Istiṭāʿa, in *EI²*, iv, 271-2; D. Gimaret, *Les noms divins en Islam*, Paris 1988, 389-91 *(dhū l-faḍl, mutafaḍḍil)*, 400-1 *(wahhāb)*; A. Wadud, *Qurʾān and woman*, New York 1999.

Talisman see AMULET; POPULAR AND TALISMANIC USES OF THE QURʾĀN

Talk see SPEECH; GOSSIP

Ṭālūt see SAUL

Tasnīm see SPRINGS AND FOUNTAINS

Tawrāt see TORAH

Taxation

Extraction of a part of communal wealth for its social redistribution and for its use in maintaining governing authority (q.v.), its various institutions, and public works. The Qurʾān offers no trace of the fiscal system first developed under ʿUmar b. al-Khaṭṭāb (r. 2-12/634-44), in substance a reformulation of Byzantine and Sasanian models (see Jeffery, *For. vocab.* and relevant *EI²* articles — e.g. Cahen, Djizya; Zysow, Zakāt; Cahen, Kharādj — for discussion of the foreign origins of taxation terminology in the Qurʾān; see also FOREIGN VOCABULARY). That fiscal system was a product of empire (see Dennett, *Conversion;* al-Dūrī, *Nuẓum;* Løkkegaard, *Islamic taxation*), itself the fruit of post-prophetic conquests (see CONQUEST), eventually being detailed by state servitors in administrative handbooks (e.g. Qudāma b. Jaʿfar's [d. 337/948] *Kitāb al-Kharāj wa-ṣināʿat al-kitāba*) or legal treatises (e.g. Abū Yūsuf's [d. 182/798] *Kitāb al-Kharāj*) and by religious scholars seeking to define imperial administration in Islamic terms (e.g. Abū ʿUbayd al-Qāsim b. Sallām's [d. 224/839] *Kitāb al-Amwāl*).

Taxation in the imperial context was oriented primarily towards the legal status of land (e.g. conquered, state, private); in contrast, the Qurʾān says nothing of a concept of land-based taxation, with only a single (and vague) reference at Q 23:72 to *kharāj* (the term later used to designate land tax) as the bounty of the lord (q.v.; cf. *Jalālayn*, ad loc., where it is referred to as *ajr*, "recompense"; see also BLESSING; GRACE). Nor is there any evidence in the ḥadīth that the Prophet instituted such a system of taxation. State control of communal wealth (q.v.) became a point of contention, Khārijīs (q.v.) seeing it as a threat to the sovereignty (q.v.) of God (Sayf b. ʿUmar, *Ridda*, i, 357) and Shīʿīs (see SHĪʿISM AND THE QURʾĀN) viewing it as a transgression of the authority of the Imāms (Madelung, Shīʿite; see IMĀM). Moreover, the Qurʾān's single reference to *jizya* at Q 9:29 suggests tribute and not poll tax (q.v.) in the sense of a tax per capita, as the term was to be defined in the imperial context (the Prophet may have instituted a poll tax of sorts, which was assessed according to the number of adults [*ḥālim*] but imposed on a subordinate group as a whole, e.g. Yaḥyā b. Ādam, *Kharāj*, 107f.). Finally, the Qurʾān makes no mention of the tithe *(ʿushr)* levied on Muslim-owned land (especially within the confines of the Arabian peninsula).

Rather, if taxation of any kind is to be read in the Qurʾān, it must be seen through two lenses: (1) a nascent Medinan polity attempting to extend its political authority and religious message over a largely tribally oriented society (see TRIBES AND CLANS; MEDINA) by managing the distribution of booty (q.v.); and (2) a charity-oriented economy of exchange, in which deserving groups (warriors, orphans [q.v.], the poor, etc.; see POVERTY AND THE POOR) were supported through almsgiving (q.v.) as a function of the qurʾānic call to renounce the luxuries of this world in favor of the one to come (cf. Rippin, Commerce; see also TRADE AND COMMERCE). Both lenses reflect a broader qurʾānic message, namely God's singular sovereignty and thus right to consume all material goods even if he permits their distribution to his "vassals," i.e. those faithful to his lordship — a message echoed in the Bible, which makes the similar claim that the spoils of war, even if designated for the communal good of the Israelites (see CHILDREN OF ISRAEL; ELECTION), belong ultimately to God in recognition of his exclusive sovereignty (e.g. *Josh* 6:17; see also *Josh* 7 which tells the tale of Achan and his kinsmen who, although Israelites, are wiped out for violating the holy ban instituted by God; cf. Q 9:79, which speaks of the punishment awaiting those who deride believers for their material and personal support of the cause of God; cf. also *Acts* 5:1-10; see also PATH OR WAY; CHASTISEMENT AND PUNISHMENT). If there is any connection between the "fiscal" message of the Qurʾān and the later imperial system of taxation, it may lie in this idea of religious sovereignty over (and potential consumption of) all material goods, represented in the Qurʾān by God and his messenger (q.v.) and later in the imperial context by the caliphal (or sultanic) ruler and his various military and administrative servitors.

The fiscal program of the Qurʾān was generally conceived in terms of material (and also personal) support *(nafaqa)* of the Islamic cause (i.e. as set by God and his messenger), to be given by Muslims (i.e. Companions of the Prophet [q.v.]) and their tribal allies (see Ṭabarī, *Tafsīr,* ad Q 9:103, who connects *nafaqa* [support of the Islamic cause], *jihād* [q.v.; struggle in the way of God] and *ṣadaqa* [charitable donation]). In support of this, later exegetes (see EXEGESIS OF THE QURʾĀN: CLASSICAL AND MEDIEVAL) note the strong rhetorical opposition in the Qurʾān between those who support *(munfiq)* the Islamic cause and those who support the enemy: al-Zamakhsharī (d. 539/1144, *Kashshāf,* ad Q 2:270) explains this as an option — given to the qurʾānic audience — of making expenditure in the path (or way) of God *(fī sabīl Allāh)* or in the path of Satan (*fī sabīl al-shayṭān;* see ENEMIES; PARTIES AND FACTIONS; DEVIL). The Constitution of Medina, an early attempt to define the nature of the first Muslim polity, also strongly exhorts its addressees to contribute *nafaqa* to the communal cause. This qurʾānic vision of communal wealth, reenacted in Medina, is detailed in later works on law and the prophetic tradition under three categories (see LAW AND THE QURʾĀN): division of booty, alms-giving and tribute. Discussion here will be limited to the first two categories (as these relate to the two fiscal lenses of the Qurʾān mentioned above). Tribute, later expanded into poll tax *(jizya)* and land tax *(kharāj),* is discussed elsewhere (see POLL TAX).

Division of booty

The legal *(fiqh)* and prophetic *(ḥadīth)* compendia treat division of booty as a distinct category, *qism al-fayʾ,* reflecting an attempt by piety-minded jurists and traditionists to keep intact the qurʾānic vision of communal wealth alongside state efforts to immobilize land under its own domain and extract taxes from those cultivating it. The fiscal message of the Qurʾān originated in the Prophet's practice of dividing the spoils of raids *(ghazawāt)* and expeditions (*maghāzī;* see EXPEDITIONS AND BATTLES), first as a means of livelihood and then as part of the struggle to preserve the Islamic cause (see, in general, the accounts of Ibn Isḥāq [d. 150/767] and al-Wāqidī [d. 207/822]), with a first share — later identified as the "choice" share *(al-ṣāfī)* — going to the Prophet as leader of the Muslim community and distributed to those whom the Qurʾān had defined as worthy recipients such as the Prophet's kin, orphans, the poor, wayfarers (cf. Q 59:7 and Q 8:41, although some scholars thought the latter verse abrogated the former).

The Qurʾān uses three terms for booty: *maghnam* (only in the plural, *maghānim,* Q 4:94; 48:15, 19, 20; and twice in verbal form, *ghanimtum,* Q 8:41, 69); *nafl* (also only in the plural, *anfāl,* Q 8:1, for which Q 8 — Sūrat al-Anfāl — is named); and *fayʾ* (only in verbal form, *afāʾa,* Q 33:50; 59:6, 7), which has the general sense of bounty bestowed by God upon those faithful to his cause (see BELIEF AND UNBELIEF; TRUST AND PATIENCE). Exegetes understood booty to function as an incentive (*taḥrīḍ;* see Ṭabarī, *Tafsīr,* ad Q 8:1) to work for the Islamic cause, as implied in the qurʾānic claim that Muslims can expect not merely earthly booty but heavenly-bestowed booty (Q 4:94, *fa-ʿinda llāhi maghānimu kathīra;* the three other instances of the term in reference to Ḥudaybiya [q.v.] also suggest an eschatological conception of booty, cf. Rippin, Commerce; see ESCHATOLOGY). In other words, the Qurʾān has reoriented a common tribal notion to the purposes of its prophetic message of God's final sovereignty in settling all accounts on judgment day (see LAST JUDGMENT).

The "tax" to be extracted from the division of booty and distributed by Medinan leadership is called the fifth *(khums),* as mentioned at Q 8:41:

> And know that whatever you take as booty *(ghanimtum),* a fifth [of it] is for God, the messenger, relations [of the messenger], orphans, the poor [or helpless] *(masākīn),* and the wayfarer *(ibn al-sabīl),* if you believe in God and that which we have revealed to our servant on the day of criterion (q.v.; *yawma l-furqān,* i.e. between right and wrong, but here in reference to the battle of Badr [q.v.]), when the two groups met [in battle]. God is master over all.

Income, then, is to play a significant role in the formation of the values of the Muslim community as a religio-political entity in which recognition of the sovereignty of God and the corresponding authority of his messenger is embodied in the redistribution of wealth to worthy recipients — those genealogically close to the Prophet and those in material need of some kind (see also PEOPLE OF THE HOUSE; OPPRESSED ON EARTH, THE). Emphasis on the redistribution of wealth is confirmed at Q 59:7. Since, however, this is not framed as "the fifth," Simonsen (*Studies,* 61-70) suggested that all booty — regardless of origin — was subject to division only in practice but fell entirely to the prophet Muḥammad in principle. He argued that the fifth is a post-prophetic innovation ascribed retroactively to prophetic decree in the battle of Badr to give Islamic legitimacy to the tribal practice of distributing the bulk of the booty, four-fifths in this case, to the warriors who captured it:

That which God has bestowed as booty upon his messenger from [the spoils of] the people of the villages [i.e. in the vicinity of Medina] is for God, the messenger, relations [of the messenger], orphans, the helpless, and the wayfarer, lest it circulate [only] among the wealthy among you. And take what the messenger gives you and refrain from what he forbids (see FORBIDDEN). Fear (q.v.) God, for God is severe in the infliction of punishment (see REWARD AND PUNISHMENT).

Finally, Q 8:1: "They ask you [Muḥammad] about the spoils *(anfāl)*. Say: The spoils belong to God and the messenger. So fear God, repair what is between you [i.e. communal disharmony] and obey God and his messenger (see OBEDIENCE), if you are believers." This is explained by al-Zamakhsharī (*Kashshāf,* ad Q 8:1) to mean that judgment (q.v.) in the division of the spoils is reserved for God and his messenger (in echo of the biblical vision; see SCRIPTURE AND THE QURʾĀN). Here, like Q 59:7, no mention is made of "the fifth"; this is explained by al-Zamakhsharī who defines *anfāl* as booty promised to a warrior beyond his normal share as an incitement to battle. So defined, such booty would not be subject to the fifth. If read on its own terms, however, this verse associates booty-division with communal harmony *(wa-aṣliḥū dhāta baynikum)*. Al-Ṭabarī (d. 310/923; *Tafsīr,* ad Q 8:1) cites a report that attributes the occasion for the revelation of this latter part of the verse (see VERSES; OCCASIONS OF REVELATION) to the complaint brought to the Prophet by the weaker members of the community *(ahl al-ḍaʿf)*, who protested that the strong had made off with the spoils *(dhahaba ahl al-quwwa bi-l-ghanāʾim)*, leaving the weaker members of the community with nothing (Zamakhsharī, *Kashshāf,* ad loc., echoes this by interpreting the verse as a call for a just/equitable distribution of communal wealth: *iqtasimū... bi-l-ʿadl*). The upshot of all this is the intimate link between claims of the Medinan leadership (i.e. the Prophet) to authority over the nascent community in general and its adjudication of the just distribution of communal wealth (see JUSTICE AND INJUSTICE) in a way that engendered communal solidarity between its various members, both rich and poor (cf. *Deut* 15:11 and *Rom* 15:25-9), strong (i.e. the fighting members of the community) and weak (i.e. the rest of the community; cf. *Num* 31:25-47).

It should be mentioned as an aside that the caliphal state (especially the ʿAbbāsid dynasty) and its scholarly servitors did turn to the Qurʾān to establish canonical justification for its fiscal system in general and the land tax specifically (see Heck, *Construction,* chap. 4; see CALIPH). The legal framework for the land tax drew a distinction between lands conquered by force *(ʿanwa)* and lands which submitted to the Muslim conquerors peacefully *(ṣulḥ),* a distinction of paramount importance for determining a region's tax terms and land ownership. Still, the Qurʾān and sunna (q.v.) had to be at least referenced to ensure Islamic legitimacy for this framework.

The belief that the Prophet had, in principle, divided the proceeds of conquest — both land and moveable property (q.v.), including captives (q.v.; see Q 8:67-71; cf. Paret, *Kommentar,* 192) — was met by the state position, based on Q 59:7-9, that the canon also made provision for Muslims yet to come, a recognition of the need to extend the idea of communal solidarity to future members. The community was ongoing (and no longer eschatological) and subsequent generations who would "emigrate" to Islam as had the first Emigrants *(al-muhājirūn)* were equally entitled to a share in the community's revenues (see EMIGRATION; EMIGRANTS AND HELPERS). This would be accomplished by immobilizing the land and levying a tax on those cultivating it, payable to the communal treasury *(bayt al-māl),* a practice initiated by the Companion (see COMPANIONS OF THE PROPHET) and second Rightly-Guided Caliph, ʿUmar b. al-Khaṭṭāb.

This qurʾānic justification of the land tax was eventually accepted by piety-minded circles (see PIETY), although when is not exactly clear. (Interestingly, Q 23:72, the sole qurʾānic attestation of *kharāj,* is not used as a rationale.) The distinction between poll tax and land tax is often attributed to the Umayyad caliph, ʿUmar b. ʿAbd al-ʿAzīz (r. 99-101/717-20; see Heck, *Construction,* 163-5), but Mālik b. Anas (d. 179/796) makes no mention of the land tax and understands taxation in Islam in strictly religious terms *(farīḍa).* For his part, al-Shāfiʿī (d. 204/820) is indecisive, first looking down upon the state's decision to immobilize the lands of conquest as extra-canonical but then deciding to leave the decision — to divide or immobilize — to the judgment of the leader (*Umm,* iv, 103, *bilād al-ʿanwa wa-bilād al-ṣulḥ*). ʿAbd al-Razzāq (d. 211/826) mentions the land tax in scattered places (e.g. *Muṣannaf,* entry 10,133) without treating it systematically. The canonical status of the land-tax, as mentioned above, never a dead issue, was at play especially in Sunnī-Shīʿī polemic (see Modarressi, *Kharāj*), partly as a function of competition over the share in communal wealth due to the successor of the Prophet (see Modarressi, *Crisis*).

Almsgiving

Almsgiving, the second important lens for qurʾānic notions of taxation, is charity extended mainly to those in need of some kind. It functions primarily in a ritual way, hence its inclusion as one of the five pillars of the religion, i.e. as a means by which the salvation (q.v.) of one's soul (q.v.) is sought. It is designated in the Qurʾān by two terms, *zakāt* and *ṣadaqa,* which are used interchangeably in the early period. The later distinction between them (although never decisively made; see Weir/Zysow, Ṣadaḳa) as obligatory and voluntary alms, respectively, is not specified in the Qurʾān. Yet they are never used in identical fashion or paired in a single verse. It is the exegetical tradition that for good reason (see below) defined *zakāt* as a religious duty (e.g. Ṭabarī, *Tafsīr,* ad Q 2:177, *al-zakāt al-mafrūḍa*), hence one of the five pillars of Islam (see RELIGION; RITUAL AND THE QURʾĀN).

In line with Q 59:7, which is concerned with the monopoly of wealth by the rich, almsgiving in the Qurʾān functions practically as a way to redistribute communal wealth, thus serving to define a charity-based economy with a particular interest in the poor, needy and dispossessed (see Bonner, Poverty; see ECONOMICS). It is not, however, simply a matter of charity but an eschatological-oriented charity for the sake of one's own salvation (or, in the case of its neglect, damnation; see Q 69:34; 89:17-20; 90:13-20; 107:3). *Zakāt,* mentioned thirty times, mainly in Medinan verses, is thus a way of purifying not merely one's wealth but one's soul, giving a ritual efficacy to its practice — charity in the function of gaining one's salvation. As Q 92:18 indicates, "Whoever gives from his wealth is made pure *(yatazakkā)*" — purification of one's soul (i.e. being made acceptable to God, *qurb*) through a religiously ordained exhortation to material giving (cf. Q 9:99). Those who give alms can expect a reward *(ajr)* from God (Q 2:277; 4:162; cf. 2:110) in the next life (Q 27:3; 31:4), effectively securing God's protection (q.v.; Q 22:78), which makes almsgiving an essential part of true religion, being included in the primordial covenant (q.v.; *mīthāq*) made between God and humankind (Q 2:83; 4:154; cf. 5:12 which speaks of it in terms of both reward and covenant). This is summed up in creed-like form at Q 2:177:

... the righteous are those who believe in God, judgment day, the angels (see ANGEL), scripture (*al-kitāb;* see BOOK), the prophets (see PROPHETS AND PROPHETHOOD), and give wealth *(māl)* out of love (q.v.) of him [or in spite of love for it, cf. Q 76:8 and Ṭabarī, *Tafsīr,* ad loc.], to relatives [presumably indigent ones; see FAMILY; KINSHIP], orphans, the helpless *(al-masākīn),* the wayfarer, beggars *(al-sāʾilīn),* and to ransom captives; and who undertake ritual prayer (q.v.) and give alms....

The religious quality of almsgiving here suggests association with the patriarchs of Israel (Q 21:73; see CHILDREN OF ISRAEL) and the life of Jesus (q.v.; Q 19:31). It enjoys sufficient religious status that its payment by a polytheist (*mushrik;* see POLYTHEISM AND ATHEISM) requires a Muslim to cease fighting (q.v.) him (Q 9:5; Ṭabarī, *Tafsīr,* ad loc., identifies it as repentance, *tawba,* on the part of the polytheist) and, instead, to consider him a brother in religion (Q 9:11; see BROTHER AND BROTHERHOOD). There is no clearer sign of the salvific (i.e. ritually efficacious) character of *zakāt* than its almost exclusive coupling (twenty-eight out of thirty occurrences) with ritual prayer, "undertaking prayer and giving alms" *(iqāmat al-ṣalāt wa-ītāʾ al-zakāt),* which constituted grounds for its later designation as a religious duty (*farīḍa;* see Ṭabarī, *Tafsīr,* ad Q 2:83, *mā kāna llāh faraḍa ʿalayhim fī amwālihim min al-zakāt;* cf. Siddiqui, Zakāt, who sees this coupling as epitomizing the religion itself, prayer representing the vertical relation of the love of God and alms the horizontal one of love of other). The connection was later to become the crux of the "wars of apostasy" (q.v.; see Shoufani, *Riddah*) conducted by the first caliph Abū Bakr (q.v.) against those tribes claiming that loyalty (q.v.) and tribute owed to Medina ceased upon the Prophet's death and that undertaking prayer was enough to make one a Muslim.

This raises many questions about the nature of almsgiving in early Islam: Was it conceived as tribal tribute in recognition of Medina as regional hegemon (for a more recent example of this, see Wilson, Hashemites, 216), making its payment a state concern (on the development of Islamic administrative institutions in general, see Sijpesteijn, *Shaping a Muslim state*)? Or was it a mark not of state authority over communal wealth but of communal/confessional solidarity? Q 58:13 mentions that tribal groups were expected to pay *zakāt* prior to an audience with the Prophet and, yet, as we have seen, *zakāt* in the Qurʾān is decidedly salvific. The two points of view, however, need not be viewed as mutually exclusive, especially when the Prophet, as messenger of God, is the foundational reference point in representing the pronouncements of God (see REVELATION AND INSPIRATION). So, if almsgiving is a means for seeking the face of God (q.v.; i.e. salvation, Q 30:39, in contrast to the practice of usury [q.v.] which yields no return from God), it is also a part of the process of binding men and women together in moral solidarity under the authority of God and his messenger (Q 9:71). It is partly for this reason that jurists later associated *zakāt* with the tithe *(ʿushr)* on agricultural produce, a "tax" only on Muslims, assessed at five or ten percent depending on irrigation method (natural or human). Q 6:141, known as "the verse of almsgiving" *(āyat al-zakāt),* was used to support this association: "And give [him] his due on the day of his harvest" (see Ibn Ādam, *Kharāj*, 146-51). The alms-tax, generally assessed at two and one-half percent of property, has a more complex formulation in the case of livestock and agricultural produce (see Aghnides, *Mohammedan theories*, 203-95).

Ṣadaqa (pl. *ṣadaqāt*, also occurring in verbal form, *taṣaddaqa*) shares the basic meaning of charity (e.g. Q 12:88, where Joseph's [q.v.] brothers ask him to be charitable to them in their need) and is used interchangeably with *zakāt* in exegetical and legal literature (e.g. equated with *zakāt* and treated as the tithe by Ibn Ādam, *Kharāj*, entry 356) and even with *nafaqa* (ibid., entry 428: *al-nafaqa fī l-Qurʾān hiya l-ṣadaqa*). Still, the term has its own semantic range in the Qurʾān. It is considered a voluntary offering (Q 9:79, the verse used by jurists to characterize it as voluntary in distinction from the obligatory *zakāt*), with the amount to be given left to the discretion of the benefactor. It also carries a religio-moral connotation, serving (1) to purify the benefactor (Q 9:103; Ṭabarī, *Tafsīr*, ad loc., says that it transforms belief from hypocrisy to sincerity, *wa-tarfaʿuhum fī khasīs manāzil ahl al-nifāq bihā ilā manāzil ahl al-ikhlāṣ;* see HYPOCRITES AND HYPOCRISY), (2) to test the right intent of those seeking the counsel *(najwā)* of the Prophet (Q 58:12) and (3) to expiate *(takfīr)* evil deeds (q.v.; *sayyiʾāt*, Q 2:271) or to compensate for the failure to perform — as a result of illness (see ILLNESS AND HEALTH) — the ritual obligation of not shaving while on pilgrimage (q.v.; Q 2:196). Debt (q.v.) forgiveness is also designated charity (Q 2:280; cf. 4:92 and 5:45 where remission of the blood-payment for murder [q.v.] is labeled charity; see BLOOD MONEY).

In other words, *ṣadaqa* signifies a proper response to God's abundant grace (*faḍl*, Q 9:75; cf. Bonner, Poverty), in the sense of gratitude (see GRATITUDE AND INGRATITUDE) for his sustenance (q.v.; *rizq*) embodied in care for others. Hence, *ṣadaqa* was never reduced to material gift (see GIFT AND GIFT-GIVING) but included recognition of a beggar with a smile when one had nothing to give, and also lawful sexual intercourse (*ṣadāq*, cognate with "righteous," *ṣiddīq;* see LAWFUL AND UNLAWFUL; SEX AND SEXUALITY). Its purposeful use for those in need implies distributive justice (Q 9:60; cf. 2:276 where it is contrasted to *ribā*, i.e. [self-] interest), but also — since its recipients at Q 9:60 include "those who work upon (for?) it" (understood as "collecting agents" but also likened, e.g. by Ibn Ādam, *Kharāj*, entry 354, to holy warrior *[mujāhid]*) and hearts to be reconciled (i.e. swayed to the prophetic cause, e.g. Meccan tribal leaders) — as a religious duty *(farīḍa)* set by God (cf. Q 2:273). Such charity, it is explained, should not be thought to relieve the benefactor of proper moral behavior (Q 2:263-4) and is better undertaken in secrecy (Q 2:272; 4:114; cf. *Prov* 21:14 and *Matt* 6:3-4; Zamakhsharī, *Kashshāf*, ad Q 2:271-2, says that *ṣadaqa* as a voluntary act is best done secretly whereas *zakāt* as an obligatory one should be done openly to avoid any accusation of failing to perform one's religious duty).

It should be noted that Simonsen (*Studies*, 32-5), largely on the basis of Q 58:12, strips *ṣadaqa* of any religious significance, viewing it as a payment required of Bedouin (q.v.; *aʿrāb*) for an audience with the Prophet. Once the social matrix shifts, he argues, from the tribally oriented caravan city of Medina (see CARAVAN; CITY) that was attempting to consolidate control of trade in the Arabian peninsula to a vast empire built upon the heritage of former empires, the logic of *ṣadaqa* as Bedouin tribute was tabled in view of richer sources of fiscal exploitation (lands of conquest), finally coming to be conflated with *zakāt* (cf. Sijpesteijn, *Shaping a Muslim state*). This hypothesis is borne out in certain passages in Ibn Saʿd's (d. 230/845) account of tribal delegations to the Prophet. He relates (*Ṭabaqāt,* e.g. i, 293) an incident where the Banū Tamīm renounce certain *ṣadaqa* conditions, forcing the collector to inform the Prophet, but not in others (ibid., i, 300, where a letter from the Prophet is read to the Banū Kilāb delegation, calling them, among other things, to respond to God and his messenger, who will take *ṣadaqa* from the rich and distribute it to the poor). In yet another passage (ibid., i, 307), the Prophet is depicted writing out *ṣadaqa* obligations (*farāʾiḍ al-ṣadaqa;* cf. Abū ʿUbayd, *Amwāl,* entry 1848, which shows al-Zuhrī [d. 124/742] recording the prophetic precedent *[sunna]* on *ṣadaqa* assessment for the Umayyad caliph ʿUmar b. ʿAbd al-Azīz).

The qurʾānic conceptualization of *ṣadaqa,* however, cannot be reduced to such a politico-economic view; its religious significance remained constant even if collection and distribution took on different forms in different times. As in the case of *zakāt* what stands out is its salvific role, not merely as charity but also as a sacrificial offering of sorts (see SACRIFICE) that indicates a penitent heart (q.v.). Q 9:104 states: "Do they not know that it is God who accepts repentance from his servants (see SERVANT) and takes alms *(ṣadaqāt)* and that it is God who grants repentance and mercy [q.v.; i.e. salvation]." Alms thus becomes an important soteriological stage in seeking the face of God (Q 2:271-3; cf. 30:39), making almsgiving a sub-category of gift-giving to God as ultimate recipient (the gift thus being irrevocable) and to his messenger as proxy in support *(nafaqa)* of God's cause. This is not to discount the tribal context but rather to note the close association of material sacrifice with a true desire to encounter the face of God as icon of salvation, for it is in sacrifice and self-denial that the will of the believer is humbled and God's glorified (e.g. Ṭabarī, *Tafsīr,* ad Q 2:271-3). To seek the face of God, one must prepare by purification — confirmed via alms payment — of one's sinfulness (Ṭabarī, *Tafsīr,* ad Q 9:103, where *ṣadaqa* removes the stain of sin; see SIN, MAJOR AND MINOR). Since, in the qurʾānic view, the rule of God and authority of the Prophet were so closely intertwined (see KINGS AND RULERS), sacrificial offering became part and parcel of building up the Medinan polity under the leadership of Muḥammad — sacrificial alms as a kind of "taxation" in support of God's cause.

Paul L. Heck

Bibliography

Primary: ʿAbd al-Razzāq, *Muṣannaf,* Beirut 1970; Abū ʿUbayd al-Qāsim b. Sallām, *Kitāb al-Amwāl,* ed. M.Ṣ. al-Fiqī, Cairo 1934; Ibn Saʿd, *Ṭabaqāt; Jalālayn;* Sayf b. ʿUmar, *Kitāb al-Ridda wa-l-futūḥ,* ed. Q. al-Sāmarrāʾī, 2 vols., Leiden 1995; al-Shāfiʿī, Muḥammad b. Idrīs, *Kitāb al-Umm,* ed. Būlāq, 7 vols., Cairo 1968; Yaḥyā b. Ādam, *Kitāb al-Kharāj,* ed. Ṣ Muʾnis, Cairo 1987.

Secondary: N.P. Aghnides, *Mohammedan theories of finance,* New York 1969 (reprint); S. Bashear, On the origins and development of the meaning of *zakāt* in early Islam, in *Arabica* 40 (1993), 84-113; M. Bonner, Poverty and economics in the Qurʾān, in *Journal of interdisciplinary history* 35 (2005), 391-406; Cl. Cahen, Djizya (i), in EI², ii, 559-62; id. et al., Kharādj, in EI², iv, 1030-56; D.C. Dennett, *Conversion and the poll tax in early Islam,* Cambridge, MA 1950; ʿA.ʿA. al-Dūrī, *al-Nuẓum al-islāmiyya,* Baghdad 1950; P.L. Heck, *The construction of knowledge in Islamic civilization,* Leiden 2002; F. Løkkegaard, *Islamic taxation in the classic period,* Copenhagen 1950; H. Modarressi, *Crisis and consolidation in the formative period of Shīʿite Islam,* Princeton 1993; id., *Kharāj in Islam,* London 1983; Paret, *Kommentar;* Y. al-Qaraḍāwī, *Fiqh al-zakāt,* 2 vols., Beirut 1969; A. Rippin, The commerce of eschatology, in Wild, *Text,* 125-35; J. Schacht, Zakāt, in EI¹, viii, 1202-5; E. Shoufani, *al-Riddah and the Muslim conquest of Arabia,* Toronto 1973; M.H. Siddiqui, Zakāt, in ER, xv, 550-1; P.M. Sijpesteijn, *Shaping a Muslim state. Papyri related to a mid-eighth-century Egyptian official,* PhD diss., Princeton 2004; J.B. Simonsen, *Studies in the genesis and early development of the caliphal taxation system,* Copenhagen 1988; T.H. Weir/

A. Zysow, Ṣadaḳa, in *EI²*, viii, 708-16; M.C. Wilson, The Hashemites, the Arab revolt, and Arab nationalism, in R. Khalidi et al. (eds.), *The origins of Arab nationalism*, New York 1991, 204-21; A. Zysow, Zakāt, in *EI²*, xi, 407-22.

Teaching

The act of instructing; imparting knowledge and information. Most of the numerous teaching-related passages in the Qurʾān are dedicated to the sound instruction of the believers in the faith (q.v.) and to their spiritual growth as individuals and members of the community (see BELIEF AND UNBELIEF; KNOWLEDGE AND LEARNING; IGNORANCE). These passages include instruction on the creed, worship and other aspects of religious life. Some passages in the Qurʾān, however, also provide detailed instruction on secular matters (human relations; political, social, and legal affairs, etc.; see ETHICS AND THE QURʾĀN; VIRTUES AND VICES, COMMANDING AND FORBIDDING; LAW AND THE QURʾĀN).

Matters related to teaching are dealt with in the Qurʾān in a wide variety of ways and are to be found in passages containing the following lexemes and concepts: 1) *ʿallama:* to teach, instruct, train; to make somebody know; 2) other terms implying the idea of teaching; 3) teaching principles; 4) certain approaches and techniques promoting the Qurʾān's teaching(s), such as: a) passages devoted to specific instructions; b) language signs and literary devices used as didactic tools (see PARABLE; SIMILES; METAPHOR; SYMBOLIC LANGUAGE; NATURE AS SIGNS; LITERARY STRUCTURES OF THE QURʾĀN); and 5) pedagogical and didactic elements significant for a more general context.

To teach, instruct, train

The verb *ʿallama* (with various subjects and objects) is found a total of forty-two times: as *ʿallama* (perfect active, twenty-two times), *yuʿallimu* (imperfect active, sixteen times), *ʿullima* (perfect passive, three times), and the passive participle *muʿallam* (once).

God teaches prophets

God "taught Adam the names of all [things]" (Q 2:31; see ADAM AND EVE; ANIMAL LIFE; CREATION; COSMOLOGY). After David (q.v.) slew Goliath (q.v.), David was given "the kingship, and the wisdom (q.v.), and he taught him such as he willed" (Q 2:251; see KINGS AND RULERS). David was also taught "the fashioning of [armor]..., to fortify [his people] against [the] violence [q.v.; they directed against each other]" (Q 21:80). David's heir, Solomon (q.v.), "said, 'People, we have been taught the speech of birds *(manṭiqa l-ṭayri)*'" (Q 27:16; for this topic and for relevant biblical passages, see Speyer, *Erzählungen*, 384-5). Jacob (q.v.), ancestor of all the Israelites, "was possessed of knowledge for that we had taught him" *(la-dhū ʿilmin li-mā ʿallamnāhu,* Q 12:68; see also ISRAEL). Joseph (q.v.), one of Jacob's sons, was taught the interpretation of tales and events (Q 12:6, 21, 101; see NEWS) and of dreams (Q 12:36-7; see DREAMS AND SLEEP). Moses' (q.v.) servant (*fatā,* associated by most commentators with al-Khiḍr; see KHAḌIR/KHIḌR) "had [been] given mercy (q.v.) from us, and... taught... knowledge proceeding from us" (Q 18:65); thus Moses asked his servant: "Shall I follow you so that you teach me of what you have been taught?" (Q 18:66; see also Wensinck, al-Khaḍir). Jesus (q.v.) had been taught "the book (q.v.) and the wisdom, the Torah (q.v.), and the Gospel" (q.v.; Q 5:110), in order to "be a messenger (q.v.) to the Children of Israel" (q.v.; Q 3:48-9). To Muḥammad, God revealed "the book and the wisdom, and taught [him] that which [he] knew not [before]" (Q 4:113; see UMMĪ; ILLITERACY; REVELATION AND INSPIRA-

TION). Muḥammad was "taught by one mighty in power" (Q 53:5), the archangel Gabriel (q.v.), "who brought [the Qurʾān] down upon [his] heart (q.v.) by the leave of God, confirming what was before it, and for a guidance and good tidings of the believers" (Q 2:97; see GOOD NEWS; ASTRAY). Muḥammad, however, had not been "taught poetry, [for] it [was] not seemly for him" (Q 36:69; see POETRY AND POETS).

God teaches humankind/common people

Q 96 (Sūrat al-ʿAlaq, "The Clot"), which the Islamic tradition usually considers to be the very first revelation to Muḥammad, gives priority to the fact that God "taught man that which he knew not" (Q 96:5) and that God did so "by [the use of] the pen" (Q 96:4), possibly indicating that God taught humankind "the holy scriptures" or "writing" (cf. also Q 2:282; see LITERACY; WRITING AND WRITING MATERIALS; ORALITY AND WRITING IN ARABIA; and Günther, Muḥammad, 4-5).

God taught humankind the Qurʾān (Q 55:2) and "the explanation" (*al-bayān*, Q 55:4; see also NAMES OF THE QURʾĀN), i.e. "articulated speech" (*nuṭq;* cf. *Jalālayn* and others on Q 55:4; see also Q 43:52, *wa-lā yakādu yubīnu*); or "the names of all things" *(asmāʾ kulli shayʾin)* or "all the languages" (*al-lughāt kullahā*; Qurṭubī, *Jāmiʿ*, xvii, 152-3; see LANGUAGE, CONCEPT OF; ARABIC LANGUAGE). It is said to "remember God, as he taught you the things that you knew not [before]" (Q 2:239; see REMEMBRANCE; MEMORY; REFLECTION AND DELIBERATION).

God orders Muḥammad to warn people about the previous generations (q.v.) who did not measure God "with his true measure" (see WARNER; PUNISHMENT STORIES; WEIGHTS AND MEASURES), denying that God had "sent the book… [to] Moses… as a light (q.v.) and a guidance to humankind *(bashar)*…" (see LIE). The unbelievers are addressed directly: "you were taught what you knew not, you and your fathers" (Q 6:91; see also Q 2:151, 239; 4:113; and Q 2:282; 96:4). That God taught humans how to train ("teach") animals is stated in Q 5:4.

God teaches the angels

God taught the angels (see ANGEL) so they said "We know not save what you have taught us" (Q 2:32). Nonetheless, the angels did not have Adam's knowledge, for God had taught him the names of all things — which resulted in God's setting Adam and humankind on the earth as his viceroy instead of the angels (see CALIPH).

Prophets teach

God's messengers (see PROPHETS AND PROPHETHOOD) were sent to the people to "teach them the book and the wisdom, and to purify them" (Q 2:129; cf. 2:151). Muḥammad was instructed "to recite his signs (q.v.) to them, and to purify them, and to teach them the book and the wisdom, though before that they were in manifest error" (q.v.; Q 62:2).

Pharaoh's (q.v.) accusation that Moses taught sorcery is implied in Pharaoh's threat to his sorcerers: "Have you believed him (Moses) before I gave you leave? Why, he is the chief of you, the same who taught you sorcery" (Q 20:71; cf. 26:49; see MAGIC; MIRACLES; MARVELS).

Humans teach

Certain humans (Muslims) are warned against wanting to "teach" God; this is evident in God's command to Muḥammad: "Say: 'What! Would you (people) teach God what your religion (q.v.) is…?'" (Q 49:16).

The *rabbāniyyūn*, "masters (in the scripture), people of the lord (q.v.)," are reminded of their twofold obligation: to teach and to continue studying. It is stated:

"Be you masters in that you teach the book [to your brethren in faith], and in that you [yourselves] study [it]" (*kūnū rabbāniyyīna bi-mā kuntum tuʿallimūna l-kitāba wa-bi-mā kuntum tadrusūna,* Q 3:79). According to Ibn ʿAbbās (d. 68/687-8), "the father of qurʾānic exegesis" (Veccia Vaglieri, ʿAbd Allāh b. al-ʿAbbās; see EXEGESIS OF THE QURʾĀN: CLASSICAL AND MEDIEVAL), the *rabbāniyyūn* are "scholars" and "teachers," for he remarks: "Be *rabbāniyyūn,* wise, erudite and learned men; and it is said that a [good] *rabbānī* is someone who [starts] instructing people in simple [things], before [dealing with] complex ones" (*kūnū rabbāniyyīna ḥukamāʾ, fuqahāʾ, ʿulamāʾ; wa-yuqālu: al-rabbānī lladhī yurabbī l-nāsa bi-ṣighāri l-ʿilmi qabla kibārihi;* cf. Bukhārī, *Ṣaḥīḥ, K. al-ʿIlm, bāb* 10; Khan, *Translation,* i, 59-60). *Rabbāniyyūn* is also a synonym for "erudite men" (*ḥukamāʾ;* see Dārimī, *Sunan,* n. 329). A different nuance in meaning is stressed by al-Rāzī (d. 606/1210) quoting Sībawayhi (d. ca. 180/796): "A *rabbānī* is [somebody] belonging to the lord, in the sense of his being knowledgeable of him and being persistent in obeying him" (*al-rabbānī l-mansūb ilā l-rabb, bi-maʿnā kawnihi ʿāliman bihi wa-muwāẓiban ʿalā ṭāʿatihi;* Rāzī, *Tafsīr,* xviii, 119; and the etymology offered in Horovitz, *Proper names,* 57; ed. Ohio, 201). In Q 5:44, 63, *rabbāniyyūn* is used in conjunction with the *aḥbār* (Jewish/non-Muslim doctors, teachers; see also Horovitz, *KU,* 63-4; *Proper names,* 53-4, 56-7; ed. Ohio, 197-8, 200-1; Paret, *Kommentar* 39, 122; for the Aramaic word *rabb, rabbī,* and the derived form *rabbūnī,* meaning "[my] master/teacher," also a title of a Palestinian scholar, see Sokoloff, *Aramaic,* 511, 513, 514; Buttrick, *Interpreter's dictionary,* iv, 522-4). In this context, it is worth noting that *al-rabb* in the Qurʾān — when referring to God, mostly translated as "the lord" — implies the meaning of the "supreme master, divine teacher," to whom humans feel close despite his omnipotence (see CLIENTS AND CLIENTAGE; POWER AND IMPOTENCE).

Humans shall "train, teach" animals as God has taught them before, as it is mentioned in the context of slaughtering animals and dietary rules (see SLAUGHTER; FOOD AND DRINK; LAWFUL AND UNLAWFUL): "The good things are permitted to you, and such hunting creatures you teach, training them as hounds, and teaching them as God has taught you (see HUNTING AND FISHING) — eat what they seize for you, and mention God's name over it!" (Q 5:4; see BASMALA).

Furthermore, mention is made of Muḥammad's opponents (see OPPOSITION TO MUḤAMMAD) and of their attempts to discredit him and his message by claiming that he had not been receiving revelations but was being "taught" instead by a human teacher: "And we know very well that they say, 'Only a human *(bashar)* is teaching him'" (Q 16:103) — perhaps an allusion to a monk known as Sergius (Sargis Baḥīrā; cf. Günther, Muḥammad, 25-6, n. 124; see CHRISTIANS AND CHRISTIANITY; MONASTICISM AND MONKS; INFORMANTS). Along these lines, Muḥammad was accused of being a man "tutored *(muʿallam)*, possessed" (Q 44:14; see INSANITY).

Angels/devils teach

The Qurʾān refutes the idea that Solomon knew and taught sorcery: "Solomon disbelieved not, but the satans *(al-shayāṭīn)* disbelieved, teaching the people sorcery, and that which was sent down [from heaven] upon the two angels in Babylon, Hārūt and Mārūt (q.v.); they [the two angels] taught not anyone [sorcery] without saying, 'We are but a temptation; do not disbelieve'" (Q 2:102), for Solomon was considered to be the originator of sorcery, an idea apparently prevalent among the Jews in Medina (q.v.; see Ṭabarī, *Tafsīr,* ii, 408; Fück, Das Problem, 5-6; Asad, *The message,* 21 n. 82; for *shayṭān* meaning satan, cf. Ṭabarī, *Tafsīr,* ii, 405, and passim; abr. Eng. trans. Cooper, *The commentary,* 475-91; see DEVIL; JEWS AND JUDAISM).

Other terms

This account of Solomon includes the only two qurʾānic references to *taʿallum,* "learning," the linguistic counterpart of *taʿlīm,* "teaching." It is said that the people in Babylon "learned [from the two fallen angels Hārūt and Mārūt] how they might separate a man from his wife…; and they learned what hurt them, and did not profit them…" (Q 2:102; see also Fahd, Siḥr).

Also relevant here is the concept of *dirāsa,* "to investigate, search [the scriptures]" (see Q 3:79; 6:105, 156; 7:169; 34:44; 68:37; also Horovitz, Proper names, 199, and the references given there; see also TRADITIONAL DISCIPLINES OF QURʾĀNIC STUDY; TEACHING AND PREACHING THE QURʾĀN).

Most of the numerous other expressions, implying more or less directly the idea of "teaching," relate to the notion of "God teaching the prophet(s)" and "the prophet Muḥammad instructing the people"; examples are *amara,* "to order" (cf. Q 3:80), *dhakara,* "to mention" (e.g. Q 7:2), *dhakkara,* "to remind" (cf. Q 14:5; 51:55), *qaraʾa* and *talā,* "to read aloud, recite" (e.g. Q 11:17; 18:27; see RECITATION OF THE QURʾĀN). *Adrā,* "to cause to know, to teach" (occurring seventeen times) is used in God's orders to Muḥammad and the Muslims to reply to those who doubt the message of the Qurʾān (see UNCERTAINTY): "Say, 'Had God willed, I would not have recited it to you, neither would he have taught you it'" (Q 10:16; see also the rhetorical questions introduced by *mā adrāka,* "What will teach you? What makes you conceive?" in Q 69:3; 74:27; 77:14; 82:17, 18; 83:8, 19; 86:2; 90:12; 97:2; 101:3, 10; 104:5; and *mā yudrīka,* Q 33:63; 42:17; 80:3; see EXHORTATIONS).

Further relevant terminology includes *tadabbara,* "to ponder, contemplate, seek to understand" (e.g. Q 4:82; 47:24), *istaftā,* "to ask for a legal opinion" (cf. Q 4:127), the indicative designation "those who were given knowledge" from God (*ūtū l-ʿilma,* Q 16:27; 17:107; 22:54; 28:80; 29:42; 30:56; 34:6; 47:16; 58:11), and terms for "explanation," such as *bayān, tabyīn, tafṣīl, tafsīr* and the like.

In addition, the Qurʾān often employs *ʿalima,* "to know," to mean "to gain knowledge of something, to receive knowledge of something." Its qurʾānic counterpart, *jahila,* connotes "to be ignorant, not to know" (see AGE OF IGNORANCE). *Darā* is often used figuratively in the Qurʾān to mean "to learn of something, to know," while *shaʿara* connotes "to know, to realize," and its counterpart *ghafala,* "not to know, to be unmindful" (for these latter terms, see Fück, Das Problem, 12-19). *Tadrīs,* "teaching," and *taʾdīb,* "educating," do not occur in the Qurʾān. While *sharḥ* can imply "explanation, explaining," in the Qurʾān, derivatives of *sh-r-ḥ* connote "acceptance, opening, expanding," so they are not included in this overview.

Teaching principles

The Qurʾān seems to suggest a number of teaching principles, such as to be patient (Q 17:11; 18:60-82; 75:16; see TRUST AND PATIENCE), and to be attentive (Q 7:204; 50:37) while receiving instruction; to train the mind and improve the memory by reading aloud, repeating and pondering (Q 4:82; 38:29; 47:24; 87:6); to instruct people in their native language (Q 12:2; 14:4); to dispute only in matters of which one is knowledgeable (Q 3:66; see DEBATE AND DISPUTATION); to argue in a courteous manner (Q 16:125; 29:46); and to instruct by use of examples and evidence, as the many biblical narratives (q.v.) in the Qurʾān illustrate (for instance, by suggesting that lessons be drawn from the past and the experiences of others; e.g. Q 5:32; 11:89); similarly for the passages teaching humans confidence (Q 11:38, 120; see also Speyer, *Erzählungen,* 87, 462-92; al-Gisr, Islamic education, 18-21; Jamālī, *Falsafa,* 13; Siddiqi, *Qurʾānic concept,* 1-10).

Methods and techniques

As for the question of what methods and techniques the qurʾānic text utilizes to promote its teaching(s), two points must be made. First, there are passages expressly dedicated to teaching; Q 2:282-3, for example, provides detailed instruction on how to handle legal matters:

O believers, when you contract a debt (q.v.) one upon another for a stated term, then write it down! And let a writer *(kātib)* write it down between you justly. And let not any writer refuse to write it down, as God has taught him (i.e. the art of writing). So let him write it down. And let the debtor dictate!... And if the debtor be a fool, or weak, or unable to dictate himself, then let his guardian dictate justly... (see MATURITY; GUARDIANSHIP). And be not loath to write it down, whether it (i.e. the amount) be small or great...! That is more equitable in God's sight... And take witnesses whenever you are trafficking one with another (see WITNESSING AND TESTIFYING)! And let neither a scribe nor a witness suffer harm.... And if you are upon a journey (q.v.), and you do not find a writer, then a pledge *(rihān)* in hand [should be required].

Second, there are textual characteristics and literary devices that emerge as sophisticated pedagogical and didactic tools. Examples are rhetorical questions, such as "Have you not seen...?" "Do you not know...?" (see RHETORIC AND THE QURʾĀN); textual elements that add force to already powerful passages (cf. Welch, Formulaic features, 77; see FORM AND STRUCTURE OF THE QURʾĀN); notions of forensic activity, such as proving (see PROOF), explaining, making manifest, and debating (cf. McAuliffe, Debate, 164); and literary signs, such as parallelism, repetition, metaphor, parable, simile (see also PAIRS AND PAIRING). The question as to how and to what extent the Qurʾān actualizes itself — as an aesthetic object — in the consciousness of its recipients seems to gain in significance in the context of "teaching and the Qurʾān" (see also Kermani, *Gott ist schön,* chap. 2; see LANGUAGE AND STYLE OF THE QURʾĀN; TEACHING AND PREACHING THE QURʾĀN).

Pedagogical and didactic elements

If "teaching (and learning)" were to be understood in a wider sense, the pedagogical and didactic elements in the Qurʾān extend to issues such as the developmental stages, habits and socialization of the human being (for the child, see Q 2:233; 40:67; 46:15; 65:6; see CHILDREN; PARENTS); ethical norms and values related to education (for orphans [q.v.], see Q 2:215; 76:8; 90:15-16; 89:17; for piety [q.v.] towards parents, see Q 2:83; 4:36; 6:151; 17:23-4; 18:80; 19:14; 29:8; 31:14-15; 46:15; see also Izutsu, *Concepts,* 207-10); human psychology (Q 3:135; 11:9-10; 12:53; 17:11; 21:37; 41:49; 96:6-7); and the appeal to the mind, reason and understanding (also in matters of faith) evident, for example, in the frequent phrase *a-fa-lā taʿqilūna,* "do you not understand?" (Q 2:44; see INTELLECT), and in the epitome of qurʾānic praise for the learned: "[Only] the erudite among his servants [truly] fear God" (Q 35:28).

Sebastian Günther

Bibliography
Primary: ʿAbd al-Bāqī; Bukhārī, *Ṣaḥīḥ*, ed. in Ibn Ḥajar al-ʿAsqalānī, *Fatḥ al-bārī bi-sharḥ Ṣaḥīḥ al-Bukhārī*, 13 vols., Beirut 1992; Dārimī, *Sunan*; *Jalālayn*; Qurṭubī, *Jāmiʿ*, Cairo 1952-67; Rāzī, *Tafsīr*, ed. ʿA. Muḥammad, 32 vols., Cairo 1357/1938; Ṭabarī, *Tafsīr*, 12 vols., Beirut 1412/1992; abr. Eng. trans. J. Cooper, *The commentary of the Qurʾān by Abū Jaʿfar Muḥammad b. Jarīr al-Ṭabarī. Being an abridged translation of* Jāmiʿ al-bayān fī taʾwīl al-Qurʾān, i, Oxford 1987.
Secondary: S. N. Al-Gisr, The Qurʾān on Islamic education, in IC 42 (1968), 1-24; M. Asad, *The message of the Qurʾān translated and explained*, Trowbridge 1997; I. J. Boullata (ed.), *Literary structures of religious meaning in the Qurʾān*, Richmond 2000; G. A. Buttrick (ed.) *The interpreter's dictionary of the Bible*, 5 vols., Nashville 1962; T. Fahd, Siḥr, in EI², ix, 567-71; J. Fück, Das Problem des Wissens im Qurʾān, in S. Günther (ed.), *Johann Fück. Vorträge über den Islam*, Halle (Saale) 1999, 1-26; S. Günther, Muḥammad, the illiterate prophet. An Islamic creed in the Qurʾān and qurʾānic exegesis, in *Journal of qurʾanic studies* 4/1 (2002), 1-26; ʿA.Y. Ḥamza, *Maʿālim al-tarbiyya fī l-Qurʾān wa-l-sunna*, Doha 1409/1989; L. Hicks, Teaching of Jesus, in G.A. Buttrick, *The interpreter's dictionary of the Bible*, 4 vols. plus Index, Nashville 1962, iv, 523-7; J. Horovitz, Jewish proper names and derivatives in the Koran, in *Hebrew Union College annual* 2 (1925), 145-227 [repr. Hildesheim 1964]; id., KU; Izutsu, *Concepts*; M. F. Jamālī, *al-Falsafa al-tarbawiyya fī l-Qurʾān*, n.p. 1966; H. E. Kassis, *A concordance of the Qurʾan*, Berkley 1983; N. Kermani, *Gott ist schön. Das ästhetische Erleben des Koran*, München 2000 (see also S. Günther's review in *Journal of Arabic and Middle Eastern literatures* 6/1 [2003], 113-17); M. M. Khan, *The translation of the meaning of Sahih al-Bukhari. Arabic-English*, [Beirut 1979 ?]; J. D. McAuliffe, 'Debate with them in a better way.' The construction of a qurʾānic commonplace, in A. Neuwirth et al. (eds.), *Myths, historical archetypes and symbolic figures in Arabic literature. Towards a new hermeneutic approach*, Beirut/Stuttgart 1999, 163-88; Paret, *Kommentar*; P. Parker, Teacher, in G. A. Buttrick, *The interpreter's dictionary of the Bible*, 4 vols. plus Index, Nashville 1962, iv, 522-3; M. Siddiqi, *The qurʾānic concept of history*, Karachi 1965; M. Sokoloff, *A dictionary of Jewish Palestinian Aramaic*, Ramat-Gan 1990; Speyer, *Erzählungen*; L. Veccia Vaglieri, ʿAbd Allāh b. al-ʿAbbās, in EI², i, 40-1; A. Welch, Formulaic features of the punishment stories, in I. Boullata, *Literary structures of religious meaning in the Qurʾān*, Richmond 2000, 77-116; A. J. Wensinck, al-Khaḍir, in EI², iv, 902-5.

Teaching and Preaching the Qurʾān

Since the earliest days of Islam, the Qurʾān has been considered the foundation of all knowledge and moral behavior. Originally, its study and transmission took place via lessons and sermons in the mosque from which the informal educational model of *madrasa* schools developed, as well as the master-student model, where students sought out teachers for their particular knowledge and studied with them for varying lengths of time. These two models formed a more or less uniform system that lasted for over a thousand years and actually still exists in modernized forms in various countries. There were no exams, no tables or chairs, and no distinction between religious and secular subjects. In some countries venerable mosque-universities developed, such as al-Azhar [University] in Cairo.

Students moved in and out of these educational structures and, depending on the years and intensity of their study, took up positions in the hierarchy of scholars (see KNOWLEDGE AND LEARNING; SCHOLAR). Some, wearing the mantle of their teacher's scholarship, became *ʿulamāʾ*: scholars of Islam who were qualified to participate in the science of interpreting the Qurʾān (*tafsīr*; see EXEGESIS OF THE QURʾĀN: CLASSICAL AND MEDIEVAL) and developing jurisprudence (*fiqh*; see LAW AND THE QURʾĀN). They were expected to have a deeper knowledge of the Qurʾān and its sciences than imāms (see IMĀM), leaders in the mosque who on Friday delivered the ritual sermon *(khuṭba)*, or held a variety of religious positions outside the mosque. The prophet Muḥammad was the first preacher, addressing his followers in his house-mosque in Medina (q.v.; beginning in 622 C.E.), and those preaching the Friday sermon *(khaṭīb)* still stand in the tradition of his religious authority (see also FRIDAY PRAYER).

By the nineteenth century, this traditional system of transmitting the Qurʾān and its sciences (see TRADITIONAL DISCIPLINES OF QURʾĀNIC STUDY) was more or less destroyed when, under colonial influences, Middle Eastern countries started to replace the *madrasas* with secular institutions that could produce teachers, medical doctors and engineers. This led not only to a crisis in the traditional educational system, forcing the classical institutions to re-invent themselves; it also involved a breakdown in the traditional authority of those considered the custodians of the Qurʾān.

Over time, those carrying the message of Islam graduated from secular institutions as well. This was, among others, facilitated by the reformist movement initiated by Muḥammad ʿAbduh (1849-1905) that allowed direct study of the Qurʾān and ḥadīth (see ḤADĪTH AND THE QURʾĀN) while bypassing the sources of jurisprudence *(fiqh)*. Several influential teachers and preachers of Islam, such as the philosopher of the Muslim Brotherhood Sayyid Quṭb (d. 1966), did not receive their training in the traditional schools that teach the classical qurʾānic sciences. Some of the most famous contemporary orators, such as the Egyptian Canadian Jamal Badawi and the Indonesian Abdullah Gymnastiar, hold graduate degrees in business, which they studied in addition to the Qurʾān.

Concomitant with changes in education, new media such as radio, TV, cassettes and the Internet developed, all contributing to what Patrick Gaffney has called a "fragmentation of Islamic religious authority" (*Prophet's pulpit,* 35).

As the media became a platform for non-ritual preaching and the educational level of Muslims in general rose, those delivering the message were no longer men only but also included women who had become more learned in religious topics (see WOMEN AND THE QURʾĀN). With Muslims emigrating to the West, converts to Islam such as the African American Siraj Wahaj and US-born Hamzah Yusuf gained prominence as charismatic preachers, especially among the second and third generation Muslims who were born in the West.

Through the activities of reformist Islamic movements, the act of preaching changed as well (see POLITICS AND THE QURʾĀN). Non-ritual preaching that is not constrained by the strict parameters of the mosque sermon *(khuṭba)* came to serve as a tool of mission or propagation (*daʿwa;* see INVITATION). In order to make the message more attractive, new methodologies and modes of delivering it developed. Some preachers chant or sing during their sermon, others allow room for remarks from the audience.

From the beginning of Islam, Friday worship has had more than just religious significance. Muslim believers also gathered in the mosque (q.v.) to intensify a sense of solidarity among the members of the community and to discuss public issues. The message of inspired preachers, inside and outside the mosque, can have profound spiritual, social and political ramifications. It can instill a strong sense of religious purpose in those within their audience, or bring them to the point of revolting against a regime or other power. In July 2004, the Yemeni firebrand preacher Ḥusayn Badr al-Dīn al-Hūthī caused an uprising that left 300 people dead. At the other end of the spectrum, the messages preached by Farid Esack and ʿAbdur Rashid Omar in South Africa promoted what they called "progressive Islam" among the black Muslim population which helped bring about the demise of the Apartheid regime. It also promoted gender equality (see GENDER; FEMINISM AND THE QUR'ĀN) and the development of an Islamic liberation theology.

Despite the fact that sermons, especially the Friday *khuṭba,* can be a barometer of social and political trends in Muslim societies, before the terrorist attacks in the United States on September 11, 2001, preaching had been largely ignored as a serious topic for study.

Terminology

The English term "preaching" has a variety of meanings in Arabic. The foremost act of preaching is the sermon, the *khuṭba,* that is delivered during the ritual of the Friday service, the two major feasts (see FESTIVALS AND COMMEMORATIVE DAYS) or during specific gatherings such as prayers for rain (see PRAYER FORMULAS). Preaching other than in the ritual Friday setting is called a *waʿẓ,* or *waʿẓa,* "sermon, lesson, moral warning," or *dars,* "lesson," in Arabic, but, depending on the local language, has many other translations. In Indonesia, for example, it is called *pengajian,* "the act of reciting the Qurʾān" (see also RECITATION OF THE QUR'ĀN), or *majelis ta'lim,* "educational meeting."

The art of preaching the Qurʾān took and takes place on several levels. By the fourteenth century, depending on the audience's literacy, there were different specialists delivering the qurʾānic messages for a variety of listeners. Apart from the ritual aspects (see RITUAL AND THE QUR'ĀN), there was and is little to distinguish the various types of preachers and their sermons and speeches from each other. The *khaṭīb,* delivering the *khuṭba* or *khuṭbat al-jumaʿ,* carried some of the authority of the Prophet. The *wāʿiẓ* told stories of the early heroes of Islam, while the *qāṣṣ* recited passages he had memorized from the Qurʾān and ḥadīth and encouraged his audience to fulfill their religious duties. Storytelling and preaching were mixed, and so were the roles of their performers; some were highly educated jurists, others based their knowledge on a few years of education in a *madrasa,* or had memorized the lessons of a *shaykh.*

Those preaching the Friday sermon continue to be called *khaṭīb* (preacher), while nowadays the words *imām* (leader of the ritual prayer, who also is the preacher) or (in the Middle East) *shaykh* are used as well. Influenced by trends of Islamic resurgence, *dāʿī* (one who performs *daʿwa,* a call or summons that invites or proselytizes) has become another term for those preaching non-ritual sermons. In the wake of the reformist movement the term *muballigh,* from *tablīgh* (to communicate, fulfill or implement a mission), which developed in response to colonialism and Christian missionary activities, has gained prominence as well.

Since the beginning of the twentieth century, preaching in general became identified as *daʿwa,* a qurʾānic term whose meaning has evolved over time and differs according to its context. "Preaching is *daʿwa,*" according to an Islamic scholar working at the Islam-online website. The basis for the call to exhort believers with the message of Islam is in the Qurʾān; a frequently-cited reference is Q 3:104, which refers to "A band of people *(ummatun)* inviting to all that is good, enjoining what is right and forbidding what is wrong" (see GOOD AND EVIL; VIRTUES AND VICES, COMMANDING AND FORBIDDING). Another is Q 16:125: "Invite (all) to the way of your lord (q.v.) with wisdom (q.v.) and beautiful preaching...."

The proliferation of *daʿwa* was further enhanced by the advent of the reformist movement that contributed to the democratization of knowledge by stressing the importance of education so that the text of the Qur'ān could become accessible to a general audience. Complex traditions of interpretation were bypassed and reading the original text was stressed. In countries where Arabic was not the local language (see ARABIC LANGUAGE), the reformists translated the text of the Qur'ān (see TRANSLATIONS OF THE QUR'ĀN) and stopped giving sermons in Arabic, as this language was understood by few.

Tablīgh

In the wake of the reformist movement, the term *tablīgh* (from *b-l-gh*, form II, "to inform, communicate a message"), became interchangeable with *da'wa*, including the phrase *tablīgh al-da'wa*. According to reformist interpretation, for example, as espoused by Muḥammad Rashīd Riḍā (1865-1935), *tablīgh* became the duty of every Muslim who had knowledge of the language and of Islamic laws. In non-ritual preaching it is the preacher's duty to communicate and warn others to follow the truth (q.v.) and thus its goal has ranged from strengthening Muslim believers to inviting non-Muslims to accept Islam (see BELIEF AND UNBELIEF).

Khuṭba and *khaṭīb*

Neither the term *khuṭba* nor *khaṭīb* is mentioned in the Qur'ān. The *khuṭba* is part of the ritual Friday service, during which it is delivered from a *minbar* (pulpit), precedes the *ṣalāt* (see PRAYER), and consists of two parts. Since it replaces two of the four customary *rak'āt* (see BOWING AND PROSTRATION) of the noon (q.v.) prayer, listening to it is considered an act of *'ibāda*, worship (q.v.), and hence should be observed with appropriate reverence.

In principle, the authority to deliver the *khuṭba* belongs to the successor of the Prophet and in the early years of Islamic history it was held by the caliph (q.v.) himself or his governor. As the Islamic domain expanded, the ruler appointed a scholar learned in religious matters to represent him as the official *khaṭīb*. *Khuṭba*s were of political importance and customarily mentioned the name of the ruler as a recognition of his legitimacy (see KINGS AND RULERS; AUTHORITY). As time went by, their function expanded to providing religious instruction and moral guidance. Depending on the political conditions, the *khuṭba* remained a political tool, and was, for example, used as a form of protest against colonialism in modern times.

The *khaṭīb* often serves as the imām of the mosque and leads the daily prayers; many of them used to be trained in a *madrasa*. Nowadays they are trained in one of the schools for traditional Islamic higher education such as al-Azhar in Egypt or IAIN (Institut Agama Islam Negeri, State Institute for Higher Islamic Studies) in Indonesia. Those working in state-owned mosques are part of the state bureaucracy. The state not only provides their salaries but also exercises a certain amount of control over the topics and contents of their sermons, and, via its publications, guides the *khaṭīb* in the preparation of his material. Especially because of the potentially important political ramifications of a sermon, local governments regularly interfere in its text, sometimes prescribing standard pre-screened sermons for state-owned mosques.

The preacher's authority is based on various definitions of knowledge (*'ilm*). In principle the *khaṭīb* is a scholar, gifted in oratory skills and drawn from among the religiously-trained scholars (*'ulamā'*). Since these have been the custodians of the Islamic tradition for more than a millennium, it is crucial that their authority be based on solid knowledge of the Qur'ān, Islamic doctrine, and traditional learning.

Teaching

In the pre-colonial era Islamic education took place mostly in *madrasa*s that ranged from the elementary to the university level, or via the master-student model. During the twentieth century, these traditional structures were replaced by modern institutions. As Muslims emigrated to non-Muslim countries, the complexity of teaching and preaching the Qurʾān increased. As many Muslims achieved higher levels of education, teaching went beyond the schooling of children and future religious leaders and expanded to include activities on the pre-school level, after-school mosque instruction and forms of continuing adult education. The Qurʾān (q 3:110) refers to the importance of teaching (q.v.) its injunctions, since they shape the character of a good and devout Muslim and since the Qurʾān is the foundation of all knowledge, its memorization becomes the cornerstone of Islamic learning.

After the traditional forms of education broke down, its institutions lost ground and became incorporated into the modernized national school systems. In many countries this not only interrupted the traditional teaching models of qurʾānic learning, but in places such as Morocco, led for a period of time to outright neglect of religious education. Other countries, such as Nigeria and Tanzania, were hardly affected by these trends and students continued to follow the model of seeking knowledge from a master or *shaykh*.

In the struggle to replace the classical models of Islamic education, some countries were more successful than others in creating contemporary alternatives. Nowadays, in many countries, kindergartens and private institutions continue to teach children the fundamentals of Islam. In countries such as Pakistan, Indonesia, Nigeria and Tanzania, *madrasa*s still exist and have incorporated the curriculum of elementary school subjects. Furthermore, in those countries, some *madrasa*s offer secondary and higher levels of education. Apart from these formal institutions of learning, informal programs in schools and mosques, Islamic organizations, and educational media such as websites play important roles in the formation and education of Muslims and of those who go on to become specialists in the Qurʾān.

While in earlier times education often ended at the *madrasa,* nowadays, depending on the accreditation of the *madrasa,* upon graduation students can continue their education in secular universities or in an Islamic institution for higher learning such as al-Azhar University in Cairo, the International Islamic Universities in Islamabad, Pakistan and Kuala Lumpur, Malaysia, and the IAIN and the Islamic State University networks in Indonesia.

Elementary education

Until the nineteenth century, the first level of traditional Islamic education in the Middle East took place in the *kuttāb, maktab* (Iran), or *mektep* (Turkey) where for a period of two to five years boys learned verses (q.v.) from the Qurʾān, a limited number of ḥadīths and some basic principles of Islamic law *(fiqh)*. Contemporary Islamic education on the elementary level takes different forms but Muslims agree that inculcation of Islamic values and knowledge should start as early in life as possible, especially nowadays when television and other media compete with religion in the formation of children. In many instances, teaching the children also provides an opportunity to include mothers in the educational process.

In her book about teaching qurʾānic recitation *(Perfection makes practice. Learning, emotion, and the recited Qurʾān in Indonesia),* Anna Gade provides several examples from

Indonesia, showing how a close connection is formed between preaching and Qurʾān recitation in order to create a new cadre of religious leaders. During the 1970s, when the reformists realized the lack of recitation skills among their preachers, they started a movement (AMM, Angkatan Muda Masjid dan Musholla, Youth groups for mosque and prayer house) that tried to counter the influence of television by teaching children Qurʾān recitation. This resulted in an extra-curricular schooling system for children under five (TKA, Taman Kanak-kanak Al-Quran), for elementary-school age children (TPA, Taman Pendidikan Anak-anak), and for youth. In order to instill enthusiasm for the Qurʾān in children, these educational institutions organized events such as mass recitations by children and a large pilgrimage (q.v.; *ḥajj*) simulation. The curriculum for these courses includes memorization of the ritual prayers, short sūras (q.v.), and daily non-ritual prayers; studying ḥadīth and the rules of Qurʾān recitation *(tajwīd);* writing Arabic and practicing rituals such as the ablution before prayer (*wuḍūʾ;* see CLEANLINESS AND ABLUTION; RITUAL PURITY). Mothers whose children participate in these courses often form their own groups to learn to read the Qurʾān.

*Madrasa*s

A *madrasa* is an endowed, private educational institution that originated in the Middle East around the eleventh century. Originally, it was an instructional center connected with a mosque, or a mosque complex where students could stay overnight. It evolved into an institution that until the nineteenth century came to preserve Islamic learning and orthodoxy. *Madrasa*s produced *ʿulamāʾ*, the cadre of religious scholars, judges and teachers, although, at their more elementary levels, an important aim was to inculcate the practices, knowledge and principles that shape the ethical and moral principles of a good Muslim (see ETHICS AND THE QURʾĀN). All students learned the reading and recitation of the Qurʾān in an accurate way (see READINGS OF THE QURʾĀN), since this is foundational to the transmission of the faith (q.v.).

In 459/1067 the first formally institutionalized *madrasa,* the Niẓāmiyya *madrasa,* opened in Baghdād. Its founder, Niẓām al-Mulk (d. 485/1092), vizier to the Saljūq sultans, envisioned a school that would teach orthodox Sunnī Islam in order to counter the prevailing heterodoxies, both theological and philosophical (see THEOLOGY AND THE QURʾĀN). The Niẓāmiyya *madrasa* served as the nucleus for the development of scores of *madrasa*s that provided education in Islamic sciences. In addition to study and memorization of the Qurʾān, the curriculum included traditionally transmitted sciences such as *tafsīr* (exegesis), ḥadīth, *uṣūl al-fiqh* (principles of jurisprudence); the ancillary Arabic-language sciences of grammar (see GRAMMAR AND THE QURʾĀN), rhetoric (see RHETORIC AND THE QURʾĀN) and literature (see LITERATURE AND THE QURʾĀN); theology; and the classical or "rational" sciences such as logic, philosophy (see PHILOSOPHY AND THE QURʾĀN), astronomy, and arithmetic (see SCIENCE AND THE QURʾĀN). Learning took place with the students sitting on the floor around a teacher while memorizing and repeating certain texts. Arabic was the primary medium of instruction, and students memorized the Qurʾān and ḥadīth and, lacking books, took notes while committing to memory the words of the teacher. There were no exams, but students were certified in particular texts when they reached a certain level of mastery of them. Other famous *madrasas* were al-Zaytūna in Tunis, al-Qarawiyyīn in Fez and al-Sulaymāniyya in Istanbul.

For the most part, *madrasa* education was traditionally for men only and guaranteed careers as religious leaders, as, for example, imāms in local mosques. Where they still exist *madrasas* continue to attract students from the poorer and middle classes because of their lower tuition fees. In Pakistan, for example, they offer a second chance and possible upward mobility to dropouts from state schools. Those who can afford it prefer to send their children, especially male children, to secular schools since its diplomas open to students a broader range of graduate programs or of job opportunities. For this reason, in certain *madrasas*, for example those in Indonesia, the number of female students has been gradually surpassing that of male students.

With the demise of the traditional institutions for Islamic education, private or state-owned mosques and institutes started to offer alternative religious curricula. Here children receive basic education in the Qurʾān. Some institutes such as al-Azhar University in Cairo continue to offer the elementary, middle and higher level courses that were the curriculum of the *madrasas*. In Morocco, the state has established religious institutes at the secondary and post-secondary level. Several renowned institutes of classical learning, such as the Yūsufiyya mosque-university, became integrated with the Qarawiyyīn University. In 1924, Turkey abolished its *medreses*, replacing them with a secular school system, and opening special secondary schools to train imāms and *khaṭībs*. This system proved unsatisfactory, and by the 1950s the *imam-hatip okullari* were established in order to provide comprehensive religious education while the Faculty of Theology at Ankara University became the most important institute for Islamic higher education.

Generally speaking, the *madrasa* system that offers a comprehensive Islamic education is still most vibrant in countries where Arabic is not the national language, such as in some sub-Saharan African countries, India, Pakistan, Malaysia, and Indonesia. In these places, children have to master Arabic as a second language before they can continue to study the Qurʾān-related sciences. In several African countries (e.g. Nigeria), new Islamic schools have proliferated; these combine traditional and modern features in their curriculum. Through teacher training colleges for male students they offer the traditional *madrasa* curriculum where students concentrate on Arabic and Islamic studies intensively for four years. In Kano, northern Nigeria, such a school exists exclusively for women.

Since the 1960s, the Indian and Pakistani governments have attempted to reform the religious curricula of the *madrasas* so that their students can meet the standards accepted by state schools and can enter the mainstream education. These efforts have been met with severe criticism from the established *ʿulamāʾ* who considered the introduction of secular subjects a threat to their religious authority and an attempt to weaken Islam. After it became known that leaders of the radical Taliban movement that ruled Afghanistan were trained in certain Deobandi *madrasas* (especially the Darul Uloom Haqqania; see DEOBANDIS), the Pakistani government tried to press more forcefully for the modernization of such institutions.

As secular models of education grew in prominence, an unresolved tension arose concerning the status of those graduating from *madrasas*. While these graduates possessed the traditional knowledge of Islam required for sustaining Islamic scholarship, they secured little respect in a society that had come to prefer professions, such as engineering or medicine, for which one had to have studied at secular schools. At the same time, *madrasa* graduates were no longer the sole custodians of Islamic knowledge, since "new" religious intellectuals emerged who had obtained their religious education elsewhere. Responding to this challenge that redefined the place of religion and religious authority in society, *madrasa*s and other institutions of Islamic learning all over the Muslim world started to introduce secular subjects into their curricula.

India and Pakistan

While there is evidence that *madrasa*s existed in north India since the twelfth century, the most vigorous *madrasa*s of the subcontinent grew out of reformist movements whose *daʿwa* activities needed trained workers. In 1867, this led to the establishment of the Dār al-ʿUlūm Deobandi *madrasa*s where those qualified to work in *tablīgh* were educated. This model became rapidly replicated in other parts of the country. One of the most prominent changes in reformist Deobandi *madrasa*s was increased attention to the study of ḥadīth in order to combat local, non-orthodox beliefs and rituals (see POPULAR AND TALISMANIC USES OF THE QURʾĀN; HERESY). The curriculum followed in most *madrasa*s in India and Pakistan derives from a corpus of texts referred to as *Dars-i Nizami* that was introduced by Mulla Nizam al-Din Muḥammad (d.1748). In most cases these texts were composed between the ninth and the eighteenth centuries by Iranian, central Asian and Indian scholars.

The Deobandi schools emulated the British educational system in introducing a set curriculum, a separation of academic levels, and examinations (Metcalf, *Islamic revival*, 87-137). Concurrent with the Deobandi movement, the organization of Nadwat al-ʿUlamaʾ set up the Dar al-ʿUlum *madrasa*s that aimed at producing scholars of Islam who could guide the believers in both religious and non-religious matters. Currently it is estimated that there are 30,000 *madrasa*s in India.

The strong Indian *madrasa*s did not expand to Pakistan with its establishment in 1947. There, religious leaders had to build a new system. Pakistan tried to reconfirm its commitment to Islam through opening and reforming the *madrasa*s. In Punjab alone, for example, the number of *madrasa*s (called *dini madaris*) grew from 137 in 1947, to 2,500 in 1994. State initiatives of 1962, 1979 and 2001 gradually introduced secular modern subjects while also reforming the religious subjects. President Muhammad Zia ul-Haq (1977-1988), in particular, tried to bring the *dini madaris* under government supervision and into the mainstream educational system while preserving their character as the custodians of Islamic learning. In 2001 the Pakistani state issued regulations that aimed at unifying the curriculum of the *dini madaris* in order to provide a comprehensive Islamic as well as a general education and so that the degrees these *madrasa*s granted could be recognized in the national system. As part of this effort, the new curriculum comprised subjects such as English, mathematics, computer science (see also COMPUTERS AND THE QURʾĀN), economics (q.v.), and political science (see also SOCIAL SCIENCES AND THE QURʾĀN).

Southeast Asia

Institutions of Islamic education in Singapore, Indonesia, Malaysia and Thailand not only serve to educate the Muslim populations but also provide a link to the Middle East where students often go to complete their religious education. This exchange guarantees a regular flow of Islamic thought between the Middle East and the Far East. Indonesia, the largest Muslim country with over 210 million Muslims, has a large and very efficient system of Islamic education that supplies preachers and teachers of the Qurʾān. Currently, many *madrasa*s offer levels of kindergarten *(Raudlatul Athfal)*, elementary *(Ibtidaʾiya)*, middle *(Tsanawiya)*, and high school *(Aliya)*. The current curriculum is divided into 70% general education and 30% religious education, although some *madrasa*s continue to offer religious education only. There are 37,362 *madrasa*s (85 percent of which are private) with nearly six million students. Almost fifty percent of the students are women, while more women than men study at the *Aliya* level (Jabali and Jamhari, *IAIN*, 130).

In southeast Asia an indigenous system of schools to teach Islamic sciences, called *pesantren*, developed and spread from Indonesia to the regions of Kedah and Kelantan in Malaysia and to southern Thailand. The *pesantren*, also called *pondok pesantren* (allegedly from *funduq*, hostel), is an Islamic boarding school where students (called *santri*) share cramped quarters in dormitories where they cook or buy their own food, wash their own clothes and spend the entire day following a discipline of studying or doing study-related activities. The majority of the *pesantren* are situated in the countryside. They are always independent and often set up by a charismatic teacher *(kiai)* who attracts students that can number into the thousands. Since the 1950s several *pesantren* have allowed female students who live in segregated dorms and have their own classes, often with female teachers. There are *pesantren* all over Indonesia; on the island of Java alone their number is nearly 10,000. Originally the *pesantren* curriculum was entirely religious. This changed in the 1980s, as a result of which 30 percent of the *pesantren* now offer three to four levels of mixed general and religious education. In many *pesantren* students attend state schools while studying the Qurʾān and related sciences for four to six hours a day before and after school. There are two types of *pesantren:* those belonging to the networks of the traditionalist Nahdlatul Ulama (NU) organization and the modernist ones. The Gontor *pesantren* on Java is a modernist *pesantren*, famous for an innovative curriculum that students can follow in English or Arabic. Around one quarter of the students of both types of *pesantren* continue their studies in the Middle East, mostly in Mecca, Medina and Cairo.

In the traditionalist *pesantren*, the daily schedule is organized around the cycle of ritual prayers. Apart from learning the Qurʾān by heart, there is emphasis on the study of the *fiqh* and on the practice of spiritual disciplines similar to those of *taṣawwuf* (see ṢŪFISM AND THE QURʾĀN). The topics studied can be classified into several groups: *qirāʾa* or *tilāwa*, the recitation of the Qurʾān with its subdivisions of syntax and morphology; jurisprudence *(fiqh);* the sources of jurisprudence; tradition (ḥadīth); Qurʾān interpretation *(tafsīr);* the unity of God (*tawḥīd;* see GOD AND HIS ATTRIBUTES); mysticism *(taṣawwuf)*, ethics, history of Islam and rhetoric. The texts in Arabic are called *Kitab Kuning*, "yellow books," and are made up of loose leaflets that can be taken out for study. *Pesantren* students are expected to become religious leaders who can deliver engaging sermons. In their "free time" students learn to give speeches *(pidato)* and practice the art of debating *(diskusi)*. The system is based on rote learning which leaves little room for creative thinking or questioning the *kiai*'s teachings. There are no final exams: when a *santri* masters a certain text she proceeds to the next, more complicated one. A major milestone is to become a *ḥāfiẓ* or *ḥāfiẓa*, i.e. someone who has memorized the Qurʾān (see MEMORY; RECITERS OF THE QURʾĀN). This is celebrated with much pomp in a "graduation" ceremony during which the public calls out random verses to be recited and assures itself that those graduating know the Qurʾān by heart.

Martial arts and other types of sports are especially popular among male *santri*. Apart from the academic curriculum, many *pesantren* organize vocational training courses and income-generating activities such as agricultural projects and business cooperations. To the surrounding communities, *pesantren* serve as centers for intensified expressions of religion. For example, during Ramaḍān (q.v.) the *santri* recite the entire Qurʾān daily following *tarwiya* prayers.

In Indonesia, the focus on memorizing the Qurʾān and becoming a *ḥāfiẓ* has produced unexpected results for women. As women learned the Qurʾān by heart, they asked that the Nahdlatul Ulama produce a *fatwā* allowing them to recite in public. As a result, the Nahdlatul Ulama decided in the 1970s that women had the same obligation to spread the faith of Islam as men, and they were allowed to recite the Qurʾān in public. Consequently, women started to compete in national Qurʾān recitation contests, and Maria Ulfa became the first woman to win the international Qurʾān recation contest in Malaysia in 1980. The following year she opened her own institute for Qurʾān studies for women (IIQ, Institut Ilmu Al-Qurʾān), which is modeled on al-Azhar University, with a subsequent division for men. Graduates from this institute perform regularly on television and radio (see MEDIA AND THE QURʾĀN) and among them there were two women who in 2000, and based on their religious scholarship, gained access to the official bodies of male religious authority. They were appointed members of the national councils of the Nahdlatul Ulama and Majelis Ulama Indonesia (MUI), both of which issue *fatwā*s. Although most *pesantren* are run by men, some women run their own. Tutty Alawiya is among the most famous preachers who heads her own *pesantren* in Jakarta.

Since the religious orientation of a *pesantren* depends on the views of its *kiai*, some have received ample press coverage because their *kiai*s' radical interpretations of Islam inspired students to join extremist groups such as those who were responsible for the Bali bombings in 2002. This event did not, however, precipitate a radical reformation of the *pesantren* system because such a transformation had already been going on since the 1970s. Especially *pesantren* within the Nahdlatul Ulama network had designed several projects in order to strengthen the Islamic learning of their graduates so that they could be custodians of the orthodox truth, while at the same time filling relevant positions in society. This reformation aimed at producing a counter discourse that could address urgent issues concerning human, women's and democratic rights. This movement was based on the re-interpretation of *fiqh* texts so that these could become a hermeneutical tool to negotiate social pluralism. A leader in this process is Abdurrahman Wahid, the long-time national chair of the Nahdlatul Ulama and former president of Indonesia. His innovative approach to the interpretation and teaching of the Qurʾān is based on his education as a classical scholar of Islam — he studied in Iraq and Egypt — combined with a rigorous training in Western philosophy and political science (see CONTEMPORARY CRITICAL PRACTICES AND THE QURʾĀN).

Through some of these projects, many

women studying and teaching in the *pesantren* began re-interpreting the *fiqh* texts concerning women. Among other consequences, this resulted in a unique effort to address women's reproductive rights as understood in Islam, including taboo topics such as marital rape, a phenomenon which Islamic scholars do not technically admit as a legal category (see MARRIAGE AND DIVORCE; SEX AND SEXUALITY).

The condition of the *pesantren* in Thailand illustrates the importance of the indigenous institutes of Islamic education. Since the early 1960s these schools have come under the control of the Thai state. As a result, future specialists in Islam receive their education mainly in Libya and Saudi Arabia. Upon their return these students propagate the ultra-conservative interpretations of Islam that are practiced in those countries.

Iran and Iraq

The town of Qom in Iran has long been among the leading centers for Shīʿī Islamic learning, with a *madrasa* tradition that provides the graduate levels of teaching necessary for a student to become a *mujtahid,* an authoritative doctor of the law. In the so-called *ḥawza ʿilmiyya* (center of religious learning), the most famous *madrasa*s are centered around ayatollahs or *marājiʿ taqlīd* who are the most authoritative religious authorities in the *ḥawza*. Their advice and learning spreads beyond Qom, and Shīʿites all over the world follow their opinions. These authorities give specialized lectures at advanced levels. Most *madrasa*s offer the traditional curriculum with courses in doctrine and jurisprudence. During the 1970s new *madrasa*s were added that introduced modern teaching methods and subjects such as English. Although by the nineteenth century Qom's educational system had lost its vigor, the Ayatollahs rehabilitated it and during the 1940s it had become a center of resistance to the Pahlavi monarchy. In the 1960s, reformist ayatollahs tried to modernize the traditional *madrasa*s by setting up institutes with alternative curricula. After the 1979 revolution of Ayatollah Ruhollah Khomeini, Qom served as the center of educational and political organizations of Shīʿī clergy.

In Iraq, the shrine cities of Najaf and Karbala became strongholds of Shīʿite Islam after the center of Shīʿite religious learning shifted from Iran to Iraq in the mid-eighteenth century. Until the 1920s, especially Najaf exercised both political and religious influence far beyond its borders. Its *madrasa*s produced experts in religious law and Iraqi literary figures of renown. By the 1920s these cities lost their prominence when Iranian scholars returned home and the number of pilgrims and amount of charitable income from Iran diminished. Nowadays the cities remain centers of religious study and leadership for Iraqi Shīʿite Muslims.

Western countries

Since the 1960s increasing numbers of Muslims have moved to the West in search of work, freedom of expression, and upward mobility. This has led to a proliferation of institutes, organizations and schools that teach children Islamic learning and values. Many offer religious classes during the weekend, in schools that are often called *madrasa,* where children learn the basics of the Qurʾān, Arabic and Muslim ethics. In several European countries, supported by state money, Muslims opened their own schools with mixed curricula of religious and non-religious subjects. In the United States and Canada four Muslim school organizations have established over one hundred private schools that provide education based on the Qurʾān and Islamic principles.

Beyond the middle school level, however,

there are limited options for further religious education. Few schools continue to the high school level, and there is little interest among students and their parents for more advanced study towards a career in religious education. In most countries the position of imām is not officially recognized, and that means that individual mosques take it upon themselves to hire their imāms. Hence the salaries of imāms and other religious specialists are very low. Following a new trend, the few who do graduate with advanced degrees in Islamic studies move into specialized professions and serve as imāms in prisons, hospitals or the army, while others become teachers and social workers. A lack of home-grown leadership, especially imāms, is the single most important concern facing Muslims in the West today.

The great shortage of western-born imāms in Europe and North America has prompted communities to invite imāms from various Muslim countries. Unfortunately, these leaders often lack knowledge of the local culture and language and are not familiar with problems and ethical issues that members of their community face in their new country. One of the main imāms in Copenhagen continues to preach in English and Arabic — after nearly two decades in Denmark — and that forces half of his audience to wear headphones for simultaneous translation. After the events of 11 September 2001 this problem has become more evident as governments have found that some clerics use their *khuṭba*s and Qurʾān lessons to incite violence (q.v.), while others espouse views that violate basic human rights, such as those concerning wife beating (see INSOLENCE AND OBSTINACY). In some cases this led to mandatory "integration" courses about the values of the host country. In December 2004, the French government decided that it would only accredit imāms trained in a French university.

Other governments are trying to create "Europeanized" imāms by encouraging local Islamic institutions of higher learning. For example, in the Netherlands the Turkish community opened the Islamic University of Rotterdam (IUR, 1997) that since 2001 has been dominated by the Nurculuk, a modern Turkish religious movement founded by Said Nursi (d. 1960). A break-off group from IUR started the Islamic University of Europe (IUE) in Schiedam and seeks neutrality and cooperation with all Muslim groups present in the Netherlands. The Dutch government has tried to provide for the needs of Muslim communities by launching the Godsdienst Islam, De Educatieve Faculteit Amsterdam (EFA), a community college where Muslim students are taught the basics of the Islamic sciences. Only a few who graduate from this school, however, become imāms; rather, the graduates seek teaching jobs or consider their education as an opportunity to enhance their personal Islamic knowledge. In 2005 the Dutch Ministry of Education decided officially to establish a program that provides BA and MA degrees in a combination of Islamic and Christian theology at the Free University of Amsterdam.

As a result of the diversity of Muslim populations in various western European countries, few Muslim communities in these countries have managed to find satisfactory solutions for the need to train local imāms. In several instances institutions such as the Muslim College in London have been funded and influenced by Libya, Algeria or Saudi Arabia.

In the United States, imāms who work with government and health care institutions are required to complete a master's degree. So far there are few schools where they can prepare for this type of chaplaincy. The School of Islamic and Social Sciences in Virginia offers a fledgling program for the training of imāms, while in a few cases Muslim programs cooperate with Christian schools to pool resources. Hartford Seminary in Connecticut has a program for Islamic chaplaincy in hospitals, the military and prisons, while some students of the American Islamic College in Chicago attend classes at the Lutheran School of Theology. (Few students were willing to commit to this College full-time and the College failed to obtain accreditation.) In an attempt to fill the gap of Islamic education, organizations such as the Islamic Society of North America (ISNA) organize part-time imām-training workshops. ISNA recently established a center to set standards for the education of imāms and chaplains. The struggle to create appropriate venues to educate Muslim teachers and preachers means that also in Western countries all roads lead to the Middle East where many Muslims return for graduate education at Islamic institutes for higher learning.

The institutes of higher learning

In most countries with significant Muslim populations students can pursue advanced degrees in Islamic studies at the undergraduate and graduate levels in state or private universities. The most illustrious of these graduate institutions is al-Azhar University in Cairo, set up in 361/972, initially to spread Fāṭimid Shīʿī doctrines. After Ṣalāḥ al-Dīn (d. 589/1193; Eng. "Saladin") and his Ayyūbid dynasty restored Sunnī Islam in Egypt, al-Azhar became one of the most important Islamic universities, educating students from all over the Muslim world. It developed satellite branches throughout Egypt and in several countries, such as Syria and Indonesia. Concurrent with the changes in the traditional educational systems, starting in 1872 it has undergone several reforms in efforts to streamline and modernize its curriculum. Since then, it has changed from an institution where students gathered at the feet of their professor as he lectured from a designated pillar in the mosque, to a modern school with classrooms, desks, grade-levels, exams and academic departments and administrators. After education in Egypt was gradually transferred to secular state schools, al-Azhar continued to offer religious curricula from the elementary to high school level, an undergraduate-level university degree, and specialized courses of study in Islamic law, theology, pedagogy and preaching and guidance.

Although pushed by reformers such as Muḥammad ʿAbduh (d. 1905) and Muṣṭafā al-Marāghī (d. 1945), reform did not come easily to al-Azhar because it had positioned itself as the conservative custodian of traditional knowledge and the methods of transmitting it. Reality overtook it several times when Egyptian authorities opened alternative schools that could train professionals more effectively. At the beginning of the twentieth century, the Egyptian government opened the Dār al-ʿUlūm teacher training college and the school for judges (*qāḍīs*), both of which offered severe competition to al-Azhar. This trend forced al-Azhar to become a university, and in 1961 the state passed a law that mandated the addition of secular subjects to its curriculum. Especially Maḥmūd Shaltūt (1893-1963), at that time al-Azhar's president, or Shaykh al-Azhar (1958-1963), envisioned an institute that would educate well-prepared scholars who could fight religious fanaticism and unite the global Islamic community. Under his auspices, al-Azhar opened non-religious colleges for engineering, medicine, commerce, science, agriculture, and education. Students at these colleges were obliged to take a preparatory year of religious studies. He tried to raise al-Azhar's international profile by instituting a Department of Culture and Islamic Missions *(Idārat al-Thaqāfa wa-l-Bu'ūth al-Islāmiyya)* which sent al-Azhar graduates to teach and preach in other countries. Primary and secondary Islamic institutions *(ma'āhid azhariyya)* graduated both men and women missionary preachers (*dā'īs*) to work inside and outside of Egypt. Finally, a Girl's College *(Kulliyyat al-Banāt)* was added; it offers degrees in Islamic, Arabic and social studies, as well as technical subjects and European languages.

Although nowadays many professors at al-Azhar send their own children to secular universities, al-Azhar continues to maintain its old aura of authority throughout the Muslim world. From the *pesantren* in Indonesia to the *madrasa*s in Tanzania or the USA, for many future *'ulamā'* the road to learning eventually leads to Cairo. The *Kulliyyat al-Da'wa* (Faculty for Islamic Mission) provides full-time programs and short courses in *da'wa* and trains many future teachers and preachers whose religious authority is socially and culturally reinforced for the Muslim audiences. Al-Azhar graduates can deliver their sermons in classical Arabic and a mediocre preacher from outside the Arabic-speaking countries, even after a cursory stay in the Middle East, can claim an exorbitant amount of religious authority upon return to the homeland. Al-Azhar ordinarily produces graduates who are conservative and moderate in their interpretation of Islam. Through its censorship activities, al-Azhar guards Islamic standards by banning books of those considered "heretics." In its ongoing efforts to keep pace with the times, in 2004 it chose Muḥammad Ṭanṭāwī as the Shaykh al-Azhar.

Some other institutes outside the Middle East that have become prominent institutes for Islamic learning are the International Islamic University at Kuala Lumpur, Malaysia, the International Islamic University of Islamabad, Pakistan, and the network of IAIN schools in Indonesia. They are not as international as al-Azhar University but do serve local and regional needs. The International Islamic University was set up by the Malaysian government in 1983 and is co-sponsored by seven other Muslim countries. Inspired by the recommendations of the first World Conference on Muslim Education (Mecca, 1977), it aims at the integration of Islamic knowledge and secular sciences. It offers a large number of non-religious disciplines, all infused with Islamic values and knowledge. In 1985, the International Islamic University of Islamabad established the Da'wa Academy, which publishes material on *da'wa* and organizes leadership programs, as well as courses and workshops to train *imām*s, community leaders, and professionals in Islamic knowledge.

The network of IAIN schools (Institut Agama Islam Negeri, State Institute for Higher Islamic Studies) in Indonesia was established in the 1950s to create a balance between traditional Islamic knowledge and indigenous modes of learning. Initially working with professors visiting from al-Azhar, these schools now have their own professors who have obtained Ph.D.'s from universities both in the West and in the Middle East. The curriculum is predominantly religious and provides a channel for advanced education and upward mobility for students from schools that do not offer the secular curriculum. Some of Indonesia's most prominent public scholars, such as Bahtiar Effendy and Komaruddin Hidayat, graduated from the IAIN network.

IAIN schools cooperate closely with

McGill University in Canada, Leiden University in the Netherlands and al-Azhar University. Unique to the IAIN are some undergraduate and graduate programs in comparative religions. Their founders stressed the application of Islam in society, and envisioned a well-rounded education in moderate Islam based on rationalism (see INTELLECT), modernity and tolerance of other religions (see TOLERANCE AND COMPULSION; RELIGIOUS PLURALISM AND THE QUR'ĀN). While it offers traditional subjects, its staff has ventured into new directions, which has led to innovative projects of learning and research. For example, IAIN Jakarta (the largest IAIN, which became a university in 2001) has an institute for research on Islam and society (PPIM) that is active in developing an Islamic discourse on civil society and democracy. IAIN Yogyakarta operates a Women's Study Center (PSW) which has prepared material that helps faculties of all IAIN's to re-evaluate their educational material from a gender-sensitive point of view. Several alumni and professors of IAIN have become well-known advocates for human rights and social justice based on Islam (see JUSTICE AND INJUSTICE).

Preaching

Ritual preaching: The khuṭba

While there are no rules for non-ritual preaching, there are several for the *khuṭba* and the one who offers it, the *khaṭīb*. Preferably, the *khaṭīb* or preacher stands on the *minbar* or, if this is not available, on any elevated place. Facing the people, he pronounces at the outset the greeting *al-salāmu ʿalaykum wa-raḥmatu llāh wa-barakātuhu*. After the response of the audience, he sits down to hear the call to prayer *(adhān)* before the *khuṭba*.

The *khuṭba* is encased in a formal ritual framework consisting of two parts. The first part, *al-khuṭba al-waʿẓiyya*, sermon of admonishing or warning, is longer than the second part. It begins with two repetitions of "Praise (q.v.) be to God" (the *ḥamdala;* see LAUDATION; GLORIFICATION OF GOD), the declaration of faith (*shahāda;* see WITNESS TO FAITH), the *ṣalāt* on the Prophet ("May God bless him and greet him with peace"); and must contain at least one verse from the Qurʾān. The second part, *al-khuṭba al-naʿtiyya*, the descriptive or qualifying sermon, should end with peace and blessings on the Prophet and his Companions (see COMPANIONS OF THE PROPHET) and prayer or supplication *(duʿāʾ)* on behalf of all the Muslims (see INTERCESSION). Prayer manuals teach that the sermon should be short in accord with the Prophet's saying: "Make your *ṣalāt* long and your *khuṭba* short." Traditionally, in the manner of the Prophet, the *khaṭīb* delivered the sermon standing while holding a staff in his hand, a pre-Islamic symbol of ceremony and authority (see ROD). In the Arabic-speaking countries the *khaṭīb* says "now then" *(ammā baʿd)* to indicate the beginning of his sermon.

The *khuṭba* admonishes and calls the believers to action. Although the contents of the sermons vary, there are certain recurring themes taken from the Qurʾān, tradition, Islamic history, the political situation and current events. To prepare the *khuṭba* preachers rely as sources, on the Qurʾān, ḥadīth, qurʾānic commentaries (for example, the *Tafsīr al-Jalālayn* written by Jalāl al-Dīn al-Maḥallī, d. 864/1459, and his student Jalāl al-Dīn al-Suyūṭī, d. 911/1505, is a popular source, and so is the *tafsīr* of al-Ṭabarī, d. 310/923), and writings by scholars such as al-Ghazālī (d. 505/1111) and Ibn Taymiyya (d. 728/1328). In his book describing the work of a rural preacher, Richard Antoun provides lists of titles from the preacher's library (*Muslim preacher*, 96-100) and remarks that the preacher does not use his many books on Islamic jurisprudence *(fiqh)* to prepare the *khuṭba* but reserves those books for other lessons on the Qurʾān.

Originally, Arabic was the language used for preaching *khuṭba*s all over the Muslim world. Since most people in many countries did not know Arabic they were unable to comprehend what they were hearing. During the medieval period, *khuṭba*s and other sermons or moral lessons formed a seamless part of Middle Eastern and other societies in which knowledge was transmitted orally (see ORALITY). By the nineteenth century, however, even in Arabic-speaking countries the *khuṭba* had become fossilized into forms of standardized discourse. The classical Arabic text for a sermon was often taken from a medieval source and repeated with minimal chance for comprehension by the mostly illiterate audience (see LITERACY; ILLITERACY). Influenced by the reformist movements this changed, although the sermons of medieval preachers such as Ibn al-Jawzī (d. 597/1200) are still readily available in the bookstalls around al-Azhar university.

There has been some debate about whether or not the *khuṭba* should be in Arabic. Some scholars consider it part of the ritual prayer *(ṣalāt)* and argue that it should. In 1975, hundreds of imāms and *ʿulamāʾ* at the World Conference of Mosques in Mecca agreed that it could be delivered in local languages. But the discussion continued and as late as 2001, the Mufti of Egypt (Shaykh Dr. Naṣr Farīd Wāṣil) ruled that it was admissible to deliver the Friday sermon in a language other than Arabic provided that qurʾānic verses were recited in Arabic, followed by translation. Even when the *khuṭba* is delivered in a language other than Arabic, it is still commonly laden with many Arabic quotes and expressions.

Medieval preaching

Collections of sermons of famous Muslim preachers from the medieval period inspired those coming after them and testify to the importance of preaching in the transmission of the Qurʾān during that time frame. The sermons of famous preachers such as Ibn Nubāta al-Fāriqī (d. 374/984-5) and ʿAbd al-Raḥmān b. ʿAlī b. al-Jawzī (d. 597/1200) were delivered by many minor preachers after them. Preaching often overlapped with what was taught in the *madrasa*s. Some preachers are reported to have attracted audiences of over thirty thousand while others so inspired listeners that they fought to touch the preacher after he had descended from the *minbar.*

Depending on the context and the time, sermons could be politically charged. Ibn Nubāta called for *jihād* (q.v.) when preaching in a court on the Byzantine frontier while ʿIzz al-Dīn b. ʿAbd al-Salām al-Sulamī (d. 660/1262) reprimanded the Ayyūbid sultan of Damascus for handing over property to the Crusaders. Preaching had potentially great impact. In the early centuries, while the legal schools were taking shape and theological battles raged, preachers contributed to the legitimization of Ashʿarite theology over and against Muʿtazilī teachings (see MUʿTAZILA). Sermons were a battleground about which interpretations of the Qurʾān should be considered the most authoritative. As the rapprochement between Ṣūfism and more formal Islam took shape, Ṣūfī preachers became among the most popular. At times this created tensions: for example, the sermons of famous Ṣūfī preachers such as Shaykh Shuʿayb al-Ḥurayfīsh (d. 801/1398-9) vexed the legalistic mind of many a jurist.

The Ḥanbalī jurist and theologian Ibn al-Jawzī not only drew crowds of thousands with his moving sermons, but was also moved to admonish the popular preachers (the *quṣṣāṣ;* sing. *qāṣṣ*) who in his view broke the conventional boundaries of religious authority. In his famous work *Kitāb al-Quṣṣāṣ wa-l-mudhakkirīn,* "The Book of Storytellers and Remonstrators," he reminds them of their potential power in transmitting and explaining religious knowledge, since their words reach all levels of society while the teachings of jurists are known only in limited circles. Preachers could jeopardize the Islamic heritage of knowledge by spreading false stories and unsound traditions, and by the ninth/fifteenth century famous scholars such as Jalāl al-Dīn al-Suyūṭī continued to write treatises against the "lies" spread by the *qāṣṣ*. Others were vexed by the salaries some preachers commanded. The themes of sermons were matters close to peoples' hearts: poverty (see POVERTY AND THE POOR), suffering (q.v.), death (see DEATH AND THE DEAD) and redemption (see SALVATION; FALL OF MAN). Also popular were the *qiṣaṣ al-anbiyā',* the stories about the pre-Islamic prophets (derived sometimes from *Isrā'īliyyāt;* see JEWS AND JUDAISM; SCRIPTURE AND THE QUR'ĀN; CHRISTIANS AND CHRISTIANITY), especially those about Moses (q.v.) and Joseph (q.v.). Preachers challenged the boundaries of religious authority and sometimes those of gender, especially when women flocked to the mosques to hear them as well. They could elicit raw emotions from their critics because, unless they uttered blasphemies (see BLASPHEMY), given the absence of a formal ecclesiastical structure in Islam, and short of direct interference by the sultan or state, their words were hard to control. In the end, the issue at stake was about legitimate religious knowledge and its corollary, religious authority.

Contemporary preaching

Debates about who holds the authority to interpret and preach Islam have never completely disappeared and have recently acquired the public's attention as governments in Muslim and non-Muslim countries have begun to realize the impact of sermons, formal or informal. Both in the West and in countries with a Muslim majority, or a substantial Muslim minority, there is an increasing tendency to control the mosques and the message.

Those bringing the message of the Qur'ān, be it in the *khuṭba* or other non-ritual forums, are expected to demonstrate high moral standards. Considered to be *du'āt* (sing. *dā'in*), propagandists or callers to Islam, Q 41:33 refers to them in its saying "Who is better in speech (q.v.) than one who calls [people] to God." The Prophet is reported to have said in a ḥadīth that "The best among you are those who study and teach the Qur'ān."

Based on their high calling, those preaching and teaching the Qur'ān are expected to practice the virtue of *ikhlāṣ,* sincerity and purity of intentions and actions. Secondly, having thorough knowledge of the topic discussed is an essential obligation for a preacher (cf. Q 12:108). Thirdly, they should imitate the Prophet's behavior and translate excellence of character into patience (see TRUST AND PATIENCE), tolerance and forbearance (Q 3:159; 16:125; 20:44). Preachers cannot be effective unless they possess excellent moral character and conduct: they should exemplify what they preach since the Qur'ān states (Q 61:2-3): "why do you say that which you do not do? Grievously odious is it in the sight of God that you say that which you do not do."

Standards of morality and learning are important because not all preachers are scholars of Islam. In principle, preachers or imāms can be of any background and many of them also have professional careers as engineers, economists or business men. Whatever their background, they practice *daʿwa,* calling others to Islam, and emphasize correct behavior and attitude. Scholars of Islam, the *ʿulamāʾ,* are expected to have a more advanced religious education. They are expected to have studied the Arabic language intensively and to use their deep knowledge of the Qurʾān, *fiqh* and *sharīʿa* to offer interpretation *(tafsīr)* and guide the believers, particularly through the *fatwā*s they issue. With their writings, scholars guide preachers who are not trained as *ʿulamāʾ* in the preparation of their messages. In the hierarchy of learning, *ʿulamāʾ* need deeper training in religion than *khaṭīb*s, and the demands of learning for those delivering non-ritual messages are less than those of the *khaṭīb*s. Perhaps this is the reason that in the 1990s the participation of women in non-ritual preaching began to grow rapidly in some Muslim countries.

Demanding strict moral and educational guidelines for preachers is also crucial, since in most countries they are woefully underpaid. This reality has forced preachers nowadays and in the past to find other means of income, for example, as merchants or schoolteachers. In Indonesia, it has long been held that the *kiai* in the *pesantren* should not benefit in material ways from preaching and teaching the Qurʾān. Hence many still offer their service for free, earning money by running a business, writing, and speaking engagements.

Frequent topics

Friday sermons often consist of a mix of Islamic teachings, exhortations and references to local and international events. The themes depend on the place and time a sermon is given. The Jordanian village-*shaykh* described by Antoun (*Muslim preacher,* 137) addressed mainly matters of belief, ethics, family (q.v.), society and the specific religious occasion, while his colleagues in Amman and Jerusalem referred regularly to colonialism, Jews and Zionism. Often the first part of the sermon contains the religio-spiritual message while the second part refers to political or other current issues, especially those concerning Palestine, Iraq and places where Muslims suffer oppression (q.v.; see also OPPRESSED ON EARTH, THE). In Indonesia and Malaysia, where non-Muslim minorities and pre-Islamic ideas still pervade society, preachers stress the centrality of the Qurʾān as a guide and tend to refer repeatedly to the need to behave correctly, to perform the ritual duties, and to the parents' (q.v.) role in raising children (q.v.). Occasionally they also discuss doctrinal points such as predestination (see FREEDOM AND PREDESTINATION) and the right to practice *ijtihād,* individual interpretation of the Qurʾān (inspired by the ongoing debate between modernists and traditionalists; see EXEGESIS OF THE QURʾĀN: EARLY MODERN AND CONTEMPORARY). Of course, other subjects such as Islam in the modern world, daily concerns and political themes are prevalent as well. Imāms preaching the *khuṭba* in Western countries face a complicated social environment that poses questions about moral and ethical issues such as dating, homosexuality (q.v.), and the relationship between Muslims and non-Muslims. Most of these topics are of little relevance in Muslim-majority countries.

During Shīʿī ritual preaching, the names of the Imāms have to be mentioned and *qunūt* prayers are pronounced on behalf of them. A Shīʿī preacher needs to communicate in a precise, attractive way in order to gain followers. Their sermons stress signs and symbols peculiar to Shīʿism. They refer to ʿAlī (his wisdom, ingenuity, and fairness in contrast to the behavior of the other three caliphs; see ʿALĪ B. ABĪ ṬĀLIB), the Prophet's daughter Fāṭima (q.v.), his granddaughter Zaynab and, of course, to the martyrdom of Ḥusayn b. ʿAlī (see SHĪʿA; FAMILY OF THE PROPHET; PEOPLE OF THE HOUSE). This last theme is especially popular during the month of Muḥarram when preachers also recount the sufferings of the Imāms, sometimes engaging in anti-Sunnī polemics.

For several decades, governments of Muslim countries have tried to influence the tone of sermons by sending around suggestions to preachers or, at times, complete texts. Not only do those suggestions aim to curb religious extremism, they are also a tool to familiarize the believers with government policies such as those on birth control (q.v.). Some groups of Muslim activists have started to emulate this governmental pattern. In an attempt to combat the increasingly aggressive attempts by Muslim conservatives to promote polygyny, an Indonesian women's group called YKF mined the Qurʾān, ḥadīth and *fiqh* sources for a counter discourse and sent texts for Friday sermons based on this research to every mosque in Java (see PATRIARCHY).

Star preachers

The influence of preachers who have risen to stardom is enormous. Sermons by Ibn al-Jawzī from the sixth/twelfth century were repeated for centuries. Nowadays, popular preachers (who preach ritual and non-ritual sermons) expand their audience through the media of newspaper columns, cassettes, CD's, DVD's, television and the Internet. Most of these preachers stand out because of the clarity and simplicity of their speech that directly connects with the audience, addressing issues of daily life (see EVERYDAY LIFE, THE QURʾĀN IN). During the 1990s several came on the scene who were especially popular with youth and women. Their messages are open to modern life and stress the individual responsibility to purify one's heart. The platforms of such preachers are no longer limited to mosques, and governments find it hard to control their activities.

It is impossible to mention all the star preachers operating in the Muslim world. Some, however, are noteworthy because they have strongly influenced other preachers and also public opinion. Others stand out for combining preaching with social action. The examples of three popular preachers from Egypt illustrate how the use of media and new types of education are influencing contemporary models of preaching and causing the centers of traditional religious authority to shift from the traditional, conservative al-Azhar graduates to a new type of lay preacher who does not follow classical paths of training. An important factor in the audio and visual media is that they convey the colloquial language and emotions of the preachers that cannot be transmitted via the written, edited sermons in which the colloquial is often replaced by classical Arabic.

The al-Azhar-trained blind shaykh, ʿAbd al-Ḥamīd Kishk (b. 1933), once called "the star of Islamic preaching," was immensely popular during the 1970s and 1980s. Early in his career he was barred from preaching in official state mosques in Egypt because he used his sermons to promote the ideology of the Muslim Brotherhood. Although boycotted by the Egyptian mass media during the Sadat era, his sermons were widely distributed via cassettes and pamphlets that served as what Gilles Kepel *(Prophet and pharaoh)* has called "antidotes to official discourse." Chanting his sermons, he stressed personal and private piety — a message attractive to Ṣūfīs as well. But his preaching also had strong political implications, for example when he attacked Jews and Christians (see CHRISTIANS AND

CHRISTIANITY; POLEMIC AND POLEMICAL LANGUAGE; APOLOGETICS).

Chronologically, Shaykh Muḥammad Mutawallī l-Shaʿrāwī's (1911-98) star rose as that of Shaykh Kishk waned. His sermons were televised on the Friday prime-time slot, immediately following the Friday prayers. Egyptians could see him in a mosque, surrounded by a male-only audience. Delivering a *khuṭba* or *dars,* he was cloaked in the mantle and ambiance of a traditional al-Azhar scholar. In his presentations he could switch from classical Arabic to pedestrian colloquial, explaining complex Islamic principles with simple language and examples drawn from everyday life. His speech and traditional views, interspersed with jokes, were especially attractive to the lower and middle classes. He attacked non-Muslims, exhorted actresses to halt their sinful work and, with one sermon in which he condoned the practice of female genital mutilation, he virtually destroyed years of activist work against it. After his death, his sermons and religious sessions were — and are still — televised, and can be found in the form of booklets and pamphlets on the streets of Cairo.

The star of the 1990s, ʿAmr Khālid is a lay preacher. Not trained at al-Azhar, the former accountant refrains from practicing *tafsīr* or issuing *fatwā*s. His informal preaching takes place on a talk show on television (*Kalām min al-qalb,* "Words from the heart"), and in mass gatherings that are not gender segregated. His speeches are available via MP3 recordings, DVD's, CD's, cassettes and booklets. He is a master of new media technologies and techniques, such as holding on-line dialogues with his audience. He is popular with youth and women from the elite classes, reminding them of the futility of life and the possibility of sudden death. Unlike Kishk and Shaʿrāwī he is not addressed as *shaykh* or *ustādh* ("university teacher") but is called a *dāʿiya*. Comparable to a born-again evangelical television preacher, he brings a moderate message that allows youth to moderate the injunctions of Islam with the demands of modern life. ʿAmr Khālid's influence is enormous and he has used his fame to launch a drive against smoking, for example. He embodies a new search and desire among young people to be good Muslims while remaining trendy. For challenging traditional notions of religious authority, the Egyptian government more or less exiled him in 2002.

These Egyptian preachers have counterparts all over the Muslim world. Before becoming a politician, the Indonesian H. Zainuddin M.Z. (b. 1951), nicknamed "*Daʿi* of Thousands" *(Daʿi Berjuta Umat)* rose to prominence during the 1980s. A graduate of IAIN and the Malaysian Universitas Kebangsaan, he delivered conservative, clear and straightforward messages laced with humor that at times were intolerant of religious pluralism. By the end of the 1990s, K.H. Abdullah Gymnastiar (b. 1962) came on the scene. Mixing his lessons with songs, this owner of fifteen media ventures preaches about "managing the heart." Using the style of evangelistic theatrics, he urges the faithful to improve themselves instead of blaming others. He brings crowds of both Muslims and Christians to tears and is one of the few Muslims ever to have preached in a church (in Palu, Sulawesi). It is said that he derived his knowledge from a three-day "direct inspiration" experience with a guru rather than through cumbersome years of learning.

A Canadian professor of economics, Jamal Badawi, was the *dāʿī* of the 1980s. His enormous conservative output, often about Muslim-Christian dialogue, consists of a 352-segment television series on Islam, and cassettes and lessons that are readily available on the Internet. His counterpart in Europe is Tariq Ramadan, the Swiss-educated grandson of Ḥasan al-Bannā, the founder of the Muslim Brotherhood. Nowadays, the US convert to Islam, Shaykh Hamza Yusuf (b. 1959), is influencing Muslim youth in the West with Ṣūfī-inspired talk about "purification of the heart" and how to live as a Muslim in the United States. He lived many years in the Middle East where he studied at universities and with individual *shaykh*s. Young Muslim adults born in the US consider him an antidote to conservative clerics from the Middle East whose message about the West they perceive to be too harsh. In the United States there are several charismatic African American preachers who arouse audiences to clapping and shouting responses. The charismatic Imam Siraj Wahhaj is an African-American convert to Islam who studied in Mecca. He currently leads a mosque in New York City where he has gained fame with his anti-drugs program.

In Shīʿī circles, various *marājiʿ* living in Qom, Najaf, or Kerbala, guide the believers from their respective countries of residence. They are considered the highest juridical authorities who can interpret the Islamic message to meet the challenges of modernity. Through their religious deputies, *marājiʿ* such as the Iraqi ayatollah, ʿAlī Ḥusaynī l-Sistānī, try to formulate answers for questions and needs of Shīʿīs living in the West. In 1999, al-Sistānī published a *Code of practice* for Muslims in the West.

The Lebanese *marjaʿ* ayatollah, Muḥammad Ḥusayn Faḍl Allāh, runs a website in Arabic and English where believers can read his Friday sermons. He holds conference calls by phone with believers in the West and his accessibility, pragmatism and leniency have made him popular with Shīʿī youth. His teachings about gender equality have also gained him an audience among women. Finally, the messages of a convert to Shīʿism from Sunnite Islam, Tunisian-born Muḥammad al-Tijānī al-Samāwī, have attracted many in prison to Shīʿite Islam.

Women teachers and preachers

In early and medieval Islamic works there are references to women who became specialists in ḥadīth and the names of women figure in some chains of transmission. Yet during most of Islamic history women's role in the transmission of the Qurʾān and its sciences was peripheral at best. Women were not allowed access to *madrasa*s, and this led to the demise of female activity in the transmission of ḥadīth and other forms of Islamic learning. Later, and in isolated cases they attended the *kuttāb* but were denied access to the institutes of higher Islamic learning. This began to change in the 1970s as the general level of education for women has risen as a result of mandatory public education for boys and girls in many countries. Limited numbers of women (less than five percent) were allowed to attend, for example, the Umm al-Qurā institute in Mecca. In Indonesia they obtained degrees in *pesantren* and the IAIN and Islamic State Universities. In Iran, the seminaries in Qom were opened for women between the ages of sixteen to twenty. Nigerian schools with a *madrasa* curriculum started to admit women during the 1980s-1990s. This is slowly producing women *ʿulamāʾ*.

In Western countries, Islamic education has become popular among women who want a career as teachers in Muslim elementary schools. Although some south Asian Deobandi and Tablighi-oriented mosques are still closed to women, in Europe mosques organize Qurʾān courses for women and girls, and some associations allow women to become imāms for other women. The Turkish Ṣūfī-oriented Süleymanlis, for example, encourage women to complete advanced religious studies in Turkey in order to serve as "madam imām" *(hoca hanım)*. During Ramaḍān, some of these women preachers conduct preaching tours in Western countries. In the past, many scholars allowed women to lead other women in the ritual prayers. Thus women are actually re-capturing their former leadership positions in worship.

Women's preaching and teaching activities take place outside the men's mosques, in prayer houses, homes, community centers or schools. For example, in central Asian countries (such as Kazakhstan, Uzbekistan and Tajikistan) the wives of imāms, called *Biblikhalifa*s, or *Bibiotun*s, organize religious educational circles for teenage girls. Several countries, such as China, Iran and Indonesia, have a history of women preachers who have had some basic knowledge of the Qurʾān, *tafsīr* and ḥadīth, and in some cases they have acquired the same level of knowledge as the male *ʿulamāʾ*.

Shīʿī women in Iran have long held religious meetings exclusively for women (forbidden to men). Since the Islamic revolution of 1979, the number of women with religious educations who could lead these meetings increased considerably. The meetings take place at home and are led by women preachers whose Islamic knowledge is gender specific. Apart from reciting the Qurʾān, the material discussed can be religious rituals, Islamic teachings, holy Shīʿī texts, *tafsīr*, special prayers, and readings on the occasion of Ramaḍān or feasts. Female preachers often have studied the Qurʾān with their fathers or other scholars. Nowadays they can study at religious schools or colleges. They need to have knowledge of Arabic, philosophy, logic, *fiqh*, and *tafsīr*, and to have studied for at least four years. The women preachers gain high social status among their followers because of their piety and dedication to religion. At times, some female *khaṭībāt* are invited to the United States to preach to women's groups, like during the major feasts.

In north, northwest and northeast China special mosques for women (*quinzhen nusi* or *nusi*) appeared as early as the nineteenth century. Adjacent to men's mosques, they are presided over by a female religious leader called *nu ahong* whose duties encompass teaching, ritual and worship guidance, sermons and counseling. The position of the *nu ahong* is controlled by the male leadership of the main mosque and is carefully mapped out within a system of strict gender segregation.

Women's agency is based on Chinese paradigms that were developed between the sixteenth and eighteenth centuries to promote women's virtuous and religious development. When adopted by Chinese Muslims, these values were translated into the call for Islamic education for women in order to construct an ideal of Muslim womanhood. Consecutive revival movements of Islamic reformism in the late nineteenth century and the 1980s stressed women's participation in religion. The level of training that female *ahong*s can obtain in the religious schools for women *(nuxue)*, however, is far inferior to that of the male leaders. Chinese Islamic colleges do not admit women, and this has perpetuated the limited education of women leaders.

Indonesian women connected to the reformist Muhammadiyya organization started preaching activities as early as 1917. During the 1920s they built their own prayer houses supervised and funded by women. Since women have started to graduate from *pesantren*, IAIN and other Islamic universities, there are women preachers and teachers who have reached the same level of knowledge as male scholars of Islam. Women preach not only in segregated gatherings, but also deliver sermons in mixed, non-ritual meetings. The cassettes of some women star preachers such as Tutty Alawiyah are sold widely. Female preachers appear on television regularly and many participate in talk shows and call-in shows.

All over the world, new classes of educated Muslim women have started to demand better religious education and more religious rights. This has resulted in a variety of initiatives, either mounted by women or orchestrated by the state. For example, the Turkish Diyanet, the government body that oversees the country's mosques, has appointed women preachers and women who act as deputies to muftis. The task of these deputies is to supervise the work done in mosques as that relates to women. Women in India recently announced that they want a mosque of their own, while women from the Progressive Muslims Union in the United States stated that the time has come for appointing women imāms. In 1994, the African American scholar of Islam, Amina Wadud-Muhsin, preached a Friday sermon at the South African Claremont Main Road Mosque. She delivered the text standing on the rostrum in front of the *minbar*, while afterwards the imām climbed the *minbar* and performed the required rituals for the liturgical sermon. The same pattern is now followed regularly in a mosque in Johannesburg. In March 2005, Wadud-Muhsin created a world-wide avalanche of comments and protests when in New York she led a group of women and men in Friday prayers. This immediately led to a *fatwā* by Yūsuf al-Qarḍāwī insisting that leadership in prayer is reserved to Muslim men only.

Women have more religious room to move in countries far from the Middle Eastern heartland of Sunnī Islam. Occasionally, we do hear of women, even in Saudi Arabia, holding Qurʾān circles in their houses but, on the whole, their preaching and teaching activities remain hidden from the public eye. Influenced by the Islamist trends within contemporary Egyptian society, women preachers there urge women to become more observant Muslims and to strengthen themselves in piety, patience and perseverance. These preachers obtain their religious knowledge from private institutes and Islamic voluntary associations that offer religious classes for women or from the al-Azhar College for Girls. They meet with women in buildings adjacent to mosques and at times earn bitter public criticism from those who find them inept and their sermons "futile."

Women preachers often address topics specific to women. Universal are basic teachings from the Qurʾān and guidance during the feasts and Ramaḍān. Furthermore, the correct execution of rituals connected to womanhood and children (see MENSTRUATION; BIRTH) as well as forms of ablutions, and issues of morality are important topics (see MODESTY). Depending on the local culture, sexual ethics and health care connected with the Islamic concepts of cleanliness and purity can be important as well.

Islamic organizations

During the twentieth century several organizations — mostly reformist — emerged that aimed at reviving and strengthening Islam via *daʿwa* and its manifold related activities. Through their courses, instructions, and handbooks, these organizations became influential gateways in recruiting and training missionary preachers. Nowadays their use of multimedia facilitates the dissemination of their material. Most organizations have their own web pages that provide support for preachers as well as model sermons, and on-line courses. Several organizations have set up their own schooling system from elementary to university level, thus providing informal and formal Islamic education. Some of these organizations have remained local while others have transformed themselves into global networks.

In 1912, inspired by the reformist teachings of Muḥammad ʿAbduh and Rashīd Riḍā, the Indonesian *kiai* Ahmad Dahlan (1868-1923) initiated the Muhammadiyya movement that currently counts around twenty million followers. Through its Department for Tabligh it trains thousands of male and female missionary preachers who are active all over the Archipelago. In 1927, Mawlānā Muḥammad Ilyās (1885-1944) started a movement that grew into the Tablīghī Jamāʿat that now counts several millions of followers. Reacting to increasingly aggressive Hindu efforts to convert Muslims, it aimed at reinvigorating Islamic beliefs and practices among the Muslims of the Indo-Pakistani subcontinent. Abū l-Aʿlā Mawdūdī (d. 1979), the founder of Jamāʿat-i Islāmī, elaborated on the method of *tablīgh,* stressing that it did not require coercion. By the 1960s, deliberate attempts were made to create comprehensive international networks such as the Higher Council of Islamic Affairs *(al-Majlis al-Aʿlā lil-Shuʾūn al-Islāmiyya)* that was founded in Cairo, in 1960. In 1961, an Islamic university opened in Medina to train missionaries who could work in minority communities, and in 1962, the transnational Muslim World League *(Rābiṭat al-ʿĀlam al-Islāmī)* was founded in Mecca. Its constitution states the wish to "spread the Muslims' word," and its training center produces *daʿwa* workers who operate all over the world.

The Muslim Brotherhood *(Jamʿiyyat al-Ikhwān al-Muslimīn)* set up in 1928 by the Egyptian Ḥasan al-Bannā (1906-49), together with the Jamāʿat-i Islāmī, became among the most influential forces guiding Muslims in Western countries. Both entered North America through the Muslim Student Association (MSA), which was founded in 1963. Naturally their ideas about *daʿwa* were heavily influenced by the philosophies of Ḥasan al-Bannā and Abū l-Aʿlā Mawdūdī. In 1981, the MSA merged into the large umbrella organization of ISNA (the Islamic Society of North America). Through national and regional conferences, publications and a website, ISNA has become instrumental in guiding Muslims in North America. Websites also serve as important transnational tools of guidance and education. The Islam-Online site, for example, has special sections in English and Arabic to serve preachers.

Nelly van Doorn-Harder

Selected bibliography

Primary: Abū ʿUbayd al-Qāsim b. Sallām, *al-Khuṭab wa-l-mawāʿiẓ,* Cairo 1986; [Ayatollah] Muḥammad Ḥusayn Faḍl Allāh, *World of our youth,* Montreal 1998; al-Ghazālī, Abū Ḥāmid Muḥammad b. Muḥammad, *Iḥyāʾ ʿulūm al-dīn,* book 9, *Kitāb al-adhkār wa-l-daʿawāt,* trans. K. Nakamura, *Invocations and supplications,* Cambridge 1973; Abdullah Gymnastiar, *Refleksi manajemen qolbu,* Bandung 2003; Ibn al-Jawzī, Abū l-Faraj ʿAbd al-Raḥmān b. ʿAlī, *Kitāb al-Quṣṣāṣ wa-l-mudhakkirīn,* ed. and trans. M.L. Schwartz, Beirut 1971; ʿAmr Khālid, *ʿIbādāt al-muʾmin,* Cairo 2003; [Shaykh] Mutawallī l-Shaʿrāwī, *Good and evil,* London 1995; [Ayatollah] al-Sayyid ʿAlī l-Ḥusaynī al-Sistānī, *A code of practice,* London 1999; H. Yusuf, *Purification of the heart. Signs, symptoms and cures of the spiritual diseases of the heart,* Chicago 2004.

Secondary: *Teaching:* H.N. Boyle, *Quranic schools. Agents of preservation and change,* London 2004; B. Dodge, *Al-Azhar. A millenium of Muslim learning,* Washington, DC 1974 (popularly written history that ends at the 1961 reform); Ch.A. Eccel, *Egypt, Islam, and social change. Al-Azhar in conflict and accommodation,* Berlin 1984 (a detailed, at times somewhat convoluted study on internal changes within al-Azhar and its role in Egyptian society); D.F. Eickelman, *Knowledge and power in Morocco. The education of a twentieth-century notable,* Princeton 1985 (description of a traditionally educated Moroccan scholar of Islam); A. Fathi, Preachers as substitutes for mass media.

The case of Iran, 1905-1909, in E. Kedourie and S.G. Haim (eds.), *Towards a modern Iran*, London 1980, 169-84 (provides examples of the role of preachers in agitating the people during the Constitutional Movement [1905-9] in Iran); M. Fischer, *Iran. From religious dispute to revolution*, Cambridge, MA 1980 (detailed descriptions of Shīʿī *madrasa* education and religious leadership in Qom); id. and M. Abedi, *Debating Muslims*, Madison 1990; N. Grandin and M. Gaborieau, *Madrasa. La transmission du savoir dans le monde musulman*, Paris 1997; K.M. Hassan, International Islamic University at Kuala Lumpur, in J.L. Esposito (ed.), *The Oxford encyclopedia of the modern Islamic world*, 4 vols., New York 1995, ii, 211-12; F. Jabali and Jamhari, *IAIN dan modernisasi Islam di Indonesia*, Jakarta 2002 (an analysis of the effects of IAIN education); J. Jomier, al-Azhar, in *EI²*, i, 813-21; J. Landau, Kuttāb, in *EI²*, v, 567-70; G. Makdisi, *The rise of colleges. Institutions of learning in Islam and the West*, Edinburgh 1981 (provides detailed descriptions of schools, how they were financed, what type of knowledge was transmitted, and the various categories of religious professions pursued by those "graduating" from these institutions); Y. Nakash, *The Shiʿis of Iraq*, Princeton 2003 (1994) (provides details on the influence and developments of the shrine cities of Karbala and Najaf and on the differences between Iraqi and Iranian Shīʿism); J. Pedersen et al., Madrasa, in *EI²*, v, 1123-54; D.M. Reid, al-Azhar, in J.L. Esposito (ed.), *The Oxford encyclopedia of the modern Islamic world*, 4 vols., New York 1995, i, 168-71; A.E. Sonbol, Shaltūt, Maḥmūd, in J.L. Esposito (ed.), *The Oxford encyclopedia of the modern Islamic world*, 4 vols., New York 1995, iv, 42-3; G. Starrett, *Putting Islam to work. Education, politics and religious transformation in Egypt*, Berkeley 1998; A. Talas, *La Madrasa Nizamiyya et son histoire*, Paris 1939 (study about the first official *madrasa*); A.L. Tibawi, Origin and character of *al-Madrasah*, in *BSOAS* 25/2 (1962), 225-38; M.Q. Zaman, Religious education and the rhetoric of reform. The madrasa in British India and Pakistan, in *Comparative studies in society and history* 41/2 (1999), 294-323; id., *The Ulama in contemporary Islam. Custodians of change*, Princeton 2002; M. Zeghal, *Gardiens de l'Islam. Les ulama d'al-Azhar dans l'Egypte contemporaine*, Paris 1995. *Preaching and preachers:* R. Antoun, *Muslim preacher in the modern world. A Jordanian case study in comparative perspective*, Princeton 1989; W. Armbrust, *Mass culture and modernism in Egypt*, Cambridge 1996; id., *Mass mediations. New approaches to popular culture in the Middle East and beyond*, Berkeley 2000; Th.W. Arnold, *The preaching of Islam. A history of the propagation of the Muslim faith*, London 1913² (analyzes the spread of Islam and the issues concerning *tablīgh*); J.P. Berkey, *Popular preaching and religious authority in the medieval Islamic Near East*, Seattle 2001 (a comprehensive analysis of medieval preachers, their message, the influence they wielded on the audiences and rulers of their time, and the issues concerning religious authority that surrounded their performance); id., *The transmission of knowledge in medieval Cairo*, Princeton, NJ 1992; B.M. Borthwick, The Islamic sermon as a channel of political communication, in *Middle East journal* 21/3 (1967), 299-313; P.D. Gaffney, The changing voices of Islam. The emergence of professional preachers in contemporary Egypt, in *MW* 81 (1991), 27-47; id., *The Prophet's pulpit. Islamic preaching in contemporary Egypt*, Berkeley 1994 (an important study that analyzes the discourses of several preachers in Upper Egypt); A.A. Ghalwash, *al-Daʿwa al-islāmiyya. Uṣūluhā wa-wasāʾiluhā* ("The principles and problems of Islamic mission"), Cairo 1978; T. Howarth, *The Twelver Shīʿa as a Muslim minority in India. Pulpit of tears*, London 2005; L.G. Jones, *The boundaries of sin and communal identity. Muslim and Christian preaching and the transmission of cultural identity in medieval Iberia and Maghreb (12th to 15th centuries)*, PhD diss., U. Santa Barbara, CA 2004; F.I. Khuri, The ulama. A comparative study of Sunni and Shiʿa religious officials, in *Middle Eastern studies* 23 (1987), 291-312; J. Pedersen, The criticism of the Islamic preacher, in *WI* 2 (1953), 215-31; id., Khaṭīb, in *EI²*, iv, 1109-12; B. Radtke and J.J.G. Jansen, Wāʿiẓ [1 and 2], in *EI²*, xi, 56-7; O. Roy, *Globalized Islam. The search for a new ummah*, New York 2004; M. ʿIzz al-Dīn Tawfīq, *Khuṭbat al-jumuʿa wa-dawruhā fī l-tawjīh al-tarbawī*, Casablanca 1994; L. Wise, *"Words from the heart". New forms of Islamic preaching in Egypt*, Oxford 2003 (engaging M.Phil. thesis about the phenomenon of the popular preaching of ʿAmr Khālid; available on line). *Africa:* A.M. Abdurrahman and P. Canham, *The ink of the scholar. The Islamic tradition of education in Nigeria*, Lagos 1978; R. Otayek (ed.), *Le radicalisme islamique au sud du Sahara. Daʿwa, arabisation et critique de l'Occident*, Paris 1993; S. Reese (ed.), *The transmission of learning in Islamic Africa*, Leiden 2004 (useful study that presents various articles about teaching the Qurʾān in sub-Saharan Africa); M.S. Umar, Mass Islamic education and emergence of female ʿulamāʾ in northern Nigeria. Background, trends, and consequences, in S. Reese (ed.), *The transmission of learning in Islamic Africa*, Leiden 2004, 99-120 (describes the process of granting women access to religious education in northern Nigeria and how this led to the emergence of women *ʿulamāʾ*); id., Profiles of new Islamic schools in northern Nigeria, in *The Maghreb review* 28 (Summer/Fall 2003), 146-69. *Indonesia and Malaysia:* M. van Bruinessen, Kitab Kuning. Books in Arabic script used in the pesantren milieu, in *Bijdragen Koninklijk Instituut voor de Tropen* 146 (1990), 226-69 (provides a detailed description of books used in Indonesian pesantren); Dh. Z. Dhofier, *The pesantren tradition. The role of the Kiai in the maintenance of traditional Islam in Java,* Tempe, AZ 1999 (provides detailed information and descriptions about the Tebuiring *pesantren* in Jombang, Java); A.M. Gade, *Perfection makes practice. Learning, emotion, and the recited Qurʾān in Indonesia,* Honolulu 2004; J. Nagata, *The reflowering of Malaysian Islam,* Vancouver, BC 1984; P. Riddell, *Islam and the Malay-Indonesian world. Transmission and responses,* Honolulu 2001 (chapter 13 is on preaching in Malaysia and Indonesia); K.H. Abdurrahman Wahid, Principles of pesantren education, in M. Oepen and W. Karcher (eds.), *The impact of pesantren in education and community development in Indonesia,* Jakarta 1988; G. Weix, Islamic prayer groups in Indonesia. Local forums and gendered responses, in *Critique of anthropology* 18/4 (1998), 405-20. *Europe and North America:* O. Cherribi, *Imams d'Amsterdam: À travers l'exemple des imams de la diaspora marocaine,* PhD diss., Amsterdam 2000; F. Fregosi (ed.), *La formation des cadres religieux musulmans en France. Approches socio-jurisdique,* Paris 1998; A. Ljamai, *Imams in tekst en context,* Zoetermeer 2004 (details and analyzes the sermons of three imāms working in the Netherlands); B. Metcalf (ed.), *Making Muslim space in North America and Europe,* Berkeley 1996; L. Poston, *Islamic daʿwah in the West. Muslim missionary activity and the dynamics of conversion to Islam,* New York 1992; M. Reeber, Islamic preaching in France. Admonitory address or political platform? in *Islam and Muslim-Christian relations* 4/3 (1993), 211-22; id., Les khutbas de la diaspora. Enquête sur les tendances de la predication islamique dans les mosques en France et dans plusieurs pays d'Europe occidentale, in F. Dassetto (ed.), *Paroles d'islam: Individus, sociétés et discours dans l'islam européen contemporain,* Paris 2000, 185-203; id., Les minbars de la diaspora. À propos de la prédication, in *Projet: Revue trimestrielle* 231 [special issue: Musulmans en terre d'Europe] (1992), 55-9; id., A study of Islamic preaching in France, in *Islam and Muslim-Christian relations* 2/2 (1991), 275-94; J.I. Smith, *Islam in America,* New York 1999; L. Walbridge, *Without forgetting the imam. Lebanese Shiʿism in an American community,* Detroit 1997; K. Vogt, Religious associations: Western Europe, in S. Joseph (ed.), *Encyclopaedia of women and Islamic cultures,* Leiden 2003-, ii, 451-4. *Women preaching:* N. van Doorn-Harder, *Women shaping Islam. Indonesian Muslim women reading the Qurʾān,* Urbana, IL 2006 (analyzes preaching and teaching activities by women belonging to the organizations of Nahdlatul Ulama and Muhammadiyya); Sh. Hafez, *The terms of empowerment. Islamic women activists in Egypt,* Cairo 2003; M. Jaschok and Sh. Jingjun, *The history of women's mosques in Chinese Islam. A mosque of their own,* Richmond, Surrey 2000; Z. Kamalkhani, *Women's Islam. Religious practice among women in today's Iran,* London 1998; S. Mahmood, *Politics of piety. The Islamic revival and the feminist subject,* Princeton 2004; L. Marcoes-Natsir, The female preacher as mediator in religion. A case study in Jakarta and West Java, in S. van Bemmelen et al. (eds.), *Women and mediation in Indonesia,* Leiden 1992, 203-28; id. Muslim female preacher and feminist movement, in A. Samiuddin and R. Khanam (eds.), *Muslim feminism and feminist movement. South-east Asia,* Delhi 2002, 253-89 (two detailed articles on the topics and sermons of several women preachers on Java). *Miscellaneous:* Shaykh ʿAbd al-ʿAzīz b. ʿAbdallāh b. Baz, Inviting towards Allāh and the qualities of the callers, on http://www. salafipublications.com/sps/sp.cfm?subsecID=DAW01&articleID=DAW010002&articlePages=1 (written by the former Grand Mufti of Saudi Arabia [d. 1999], this is one of many such treatises available via the Internet about the requirements for those preaching and teaching the Qurʾān); D.F. Eickelman and J.W. Anderson (eds.), *New media in the Muslim world. The emerging public sphere,* Bloomington, IN 1999 (discusses how the emergence of new media such as the Internet has contributed to the re-shaping of religious authority in the Muslim world); F. Esack, *Qurʾān, liberation and pluralism. An Islamic perspective of interreligious solidarity against oppression,* Oxford 2002[4] (describes Amina Wadud-Muhsin's Friday sermon and the preaching activities of the imāms leading progressive Muslims in South Africa); J.J.G. Jansen, *The neglected duty. The creed of Sadat's assassins and Islamic resurgence in the Middle East,* New York 1986 (provides detailed descriptions of the sermons of Shaykhs Kishk and Shaʿrāwī); G. Kepel, *The Prophet and the pharaoh,* London 1985 (provides the transcript of a sermon by Shaykh Kishk with an insightful analysis); id. and Y. Richard, *Intellectuals et militants de l'Islam contemporain,* Paris 1990 (essays about the tensions between traditionally Islamic and Western-trained intellectuals in contemporary Muslim society); B.D. Metcalf, *Islamic revival in British India. Deoband 1860-1900,* Princeton 1982 (a comprehensive study of the Deoband movement and the role of Muslim religious leaders in Indian politics); R. Schulze, *Islamischer Internationalismus im 20. Jahrhundert: Untersuchungen zur Geschichte der Islamischen Weltliga,* Leiden 1990; M. Sharon, *Black banners from the east,* Jerusalem 1983 (analyzes the evolving interpretations of the principle of *daʿwa,* first introduced by the ʿAbbāsids as a politico-religious principle used to bring them to power by re-creating the divine order). *Selected websites:* http://www.bayynat.org/(official website of Ayatollah Faḍl Allāh); http://www.isna.net/lilbrary/khutbahs/FridayKhutbahs.asp; http://www.IslamOnline.net.

Tears see WEEPING

Technology see MEDIA AND THE QURʾĀN; COMPUTERS AND THE QURʾĀN

Teeth

Hard bony appendages found in the mouths of vertebrates that assist in the chewing of food, as well as in defense and the capturing of prey. The word for tooth *(sinn)* occurs once in the Qurʾān, in a verse that refers to the biblical *lex talionis* (law of retaliation [q.v.]): "We prescribed for them [the Jews; see JEWS AND JUDAISM] therein [in the Torah (q.v.)]: life (q.v.) for life, eye for eye (see EYES), nose for nose, ear for ear (q.v.), tooth for tooth, and for injuries like retaliation. If someone forgoes (retaliation) out of charity, it shall be an expiation for him. Whoever judges not by that which God has revealed: such are wrong-doers" (Q 5:45; see JUDGMENT; REVELATION AND INSPIRATION; EVIL DEEDS; VIRTUES AND VICES, COMMANDING AND FORBIDDING). This statement occurs in the course of a passage discussing Jews and Christians (see CHRISTIANS AND CHRISTIANITY) who resort to the prophet Muḥammad for the adjudication of legal disputes (Q 5:42-50).

The basic principle established in the Qurʾān is that legal disputes within each religious community should be settled by reference to that community's sacred text. Disputes among Jews should be settled by reference to the Torah, disputes among Christians should be settled by reference to the Gospel (q.v.) and disputes among Muslims should be settled by reference to the Qurʾān, no matter who is acting as judge. This passage makes it clear that each community *(umma)* has its own law (Q 5:48) and that this law is contained in the scripture (see LAW AND THE QURʾĀN). The important role played by the sacred text in judgment is recognized in several ways. The Prophet or others are said to judge between disputants by that which God has revealed (Q 5:44, 45, 47). In other passages, the sacred text is personified and itself gives a verdict or judges between disputants: "Have you not seen how those who have been given a portion of the scripture invoke the scripture of God (in their disputes) that it may judge between them, then a faction of them turns away, opposed (to it)?" (Q 3:23; see PARTIES AND FACTIONS).

In addition, mention of the *lex talionis* shows an awareness in the Qurʾān of specific biblical legal rulings (see SCRIPTURE AND THE QURʾĀN): "Anyone who maims another shall suffer the same injury in return: fracture for fracture, eye for eye, tooth for tooth; the injury inflicted is the injury to be suffered" (*Lev* 24:20; see also *Exod* 21:24; *Deut* 19:21). The principle of like retaliation *(qiṣāṣ)* was adopted in Islamic law as well, but was supplemented by an alternative regime of monetary compensation. For the life of a free, adult male (see MURDER; BLOODSHED), compensation was set at one hundred camels and for the loss of limbs and other injuries, as well as for the death or injury of women (see WOMEN AND THE QURʾĀN), children (q.v.), and slaves (see SLAVES AND SLAVERY), various fractions of that amount were awarded (see VENGEANCE; REVENGE; BLOOD MONEY).

Devin J. Stewart

Bibliography
C. Carmichael, Biblical laws of talion, in *Hebrew annual review* 9 (1985), 107-26; J. Chelhod, *Les structures du sacré chez les Arabes,* Paris 1986, 155, 176; W.B. Hallaq, *A history of Islamic legal theories,* Cambridge 1997; B. Jackson, The problem of Exod. XXI 22-25 (Ius talionis), in *Vetus testamentum* 23 (1973), 273-304; S. Loewenstamm, Exodus XXI 22-25, in *Vetus testamentum* 27 (1977), 352-60; F. Rahman, Some key ethical concepts of the Qurʾān, in *Journal of religious ethics* 11 (1983), 170-85; R. Roberts, *The social laws of the Qorân,* London 1925, repr. London 1990 (Eng. trans. of *Familienrecht im Qorân*); R. Westbrook, Lex talionis and Exodus 21,22-25, in *Revue biblique* 93 (1986), 52-69.

Temperature see HOT AND COLD

Temple see SACRED PRECINCTS; HOUSE, DOMESTIC AND DIVINE

Temporary Marriage

Financial contract between a man and an unmarried woman permitting sexual relations for a fixed amount of time upon compensation of the woman. Although the Arabic term for this concept *(mutʿa)* does not occur in the Qurʾān, the tenth verbal form of the root *m-t-ʿ* is employed at Q 4:24, likely with reference to this practice as a pre-Islamic Arabian tradition (despite the explanations of many exegetes; cf. e.g. the traditions preserved in Ṭabarī, *Tafsīr,* ad loc., which identify *al-istimtāʿ* with *"nikāḥ"* or *"tazwīj";* cf. also Heffening, Mutʿa). This practice developed into a complex Shīʿī religious institution about which there has been much cultural and moral ambivalence, yet in Iran, since the revolution of 1979, it has become more commonplace (Haeri, *Law of desire*).

Literally "marriage of pleasure," *mutʿa* is a form of a pre-Islamic tradition in Arabia (Robertson-Smith, *Kinship and marriage;* see PRE-ISLAMIC ARABIA AND THE QURʾĀN) that still retains legitimacy among the Twelver Shīʿīs who live predominantly, though not exclusively, in Iran (see SHĪʿISM AND THE QURʾĀN). Legally, *mutʿa*-marriage is a contract *(ʿaqd)* in which a man and an unmarried woman decide how long they want to be married to each other and how much money, or bride-price, is to be given to the temporary wife (see CONTRACTS AND ALLIANCES; MARRIAGE AND DIVORCE; BRIDEWEALTH). Unlike in the case of permanent marriage *(nikāḥ)* a temporary wife is not legally entitled to financial support *(nafaqa)* above and beyond the bride-price, even in the event of pregnancy, unless it is agreed upon beforehand (see MAINTENANCE AND UPKEEP). Doctrinally, the Shīʿī jurists distinguish temporary marriage from permanent marriage by stating that the objective of *mutʿa* is sexual enjoyment, while that of *nikāḥ* is procreation (Ṭūsī, *Nihāya,* 497-502; Ḥillī, *Sharāʾiʿ,* 524; Kāshif al-Ghiṭāʾ, *Āyīn-i ma;* Ṭabāṭabāʾī, *Shiʿite Islam;* Muṭahharī, *Niẓām-i ḥuqūq-i zan,* 38; Khomeini, *Tawḍīḥ al-masāʾil;* id., Mutʿa; Levy, *Introduction;* Murata, *Temporary marriage;* Haeri, *Law of desire*).

According to Shīʿī literature, the second caliph ʿUmar (r. 13-23/634-44; see CALIPH) outlawed the custom of *mutʿa* marriage in the first/seventh century and threatened its practitioners with stoning (q.v.). The Shīʿīs have systematically contested the caliph's decision. They argue, on the basis of the qurʾānic reference to *mutʿa* (*mā stamtaʿtum bihi minhunna,* Q 4:24) and the lack of any unambiguous prophetic ḥadīth banning its practice (see ḤADĪTH AND THE QURʾĀN), that ʿUmar's *fatwā* lacks legitimacy (al-Amīnī, *al-Ghadīr;* Ṭabāṭabāʾī, *Shiʿite Islam;* Shafāʾī, *Mutʿa;* ʿĀmilī, *Mutʿa;* Haeri, *Law of desire,* 61-4; see LAW AND THE QURʾĀN).

Indeed the Shīʿīs point to the fact that temporary marriage was common at the time of the prophet Muḥammad and that many of the early converts were children of *mutʿa* marriages: ʿAdī, son of Ḥātim and Māwiyya, is an example (al-Amīnī, *al-Ghadīr,* vi, 129, 198-240; Robertson-Smith, *Kinship and marriage,* 81; cf. Ṭabāṭabāʾī, *Shiʿite Islam,* 227).

The Sunnīs and Shīʿīs have not ceased to dispute the religious legitimacy and moral propriety of temporary marriage. Although strongly opposed by the Sunnī *ʿulamāʾ* (see SCHOLAR), the custom of temporary marriage has apparently continued among some Sunnīs into modern times (Snouck Hurgronje, *Mekka,* 12-13).

Rules and procedures regarding *mutʿa* developed piecemeal and by analogical reasoning. Its present form is the result of dialogues and debates among Shīʿī scholars, the most prominent of whom was the sixth imām (q.v.), Jaʿfar al-Ṣādiq (d. 148/765; Ṭūṣī, *Nihāya,* 497-502; Ḥillī, *Sharāʾiʿ,* 515-28; Ghazanfarī, *Khudāmūz-i lumʿa,* ii, 126-34; Kāshif al-Ghiṭāʾ, *Āyīn-i ma,* 372-92; Khomeini, *Tawḍīḥ al-masāʾil;* Muṭahharī, *Niẓām-i ḥuqūq-i zan,* 21-54; Imāmī, *Ḥuqūq-i madanī;* Levy, *Introduction,* i, 131-90; Fayzee, *Outlines,* 117-21; Murata, *Temporary marriage;* Haeri, *Law of desire*).

Arabic in origin, the term *mutʿa* has multiple meanings: "that which gives benefits, for a short while," "enjoyment, pleasure" (i.e. to saturate), "to have the usufruct of something" (Dihkhudā, Ṣīgha, 318). Although the specified purpose of temporary marriage is sexual pleasure (specifically male pleasure), the religious language that describes it places — or misplaces — the emphasis on its marital aspect, thereby creating the impression that *mutʿa* is simply a form of marriage but with a built-in time limit. Outside of religious circles, everyday language in Iran has remained more faithful to the literal meaning of *mutʿa,* which has colloquially been substituted with the vernacular Persian term *ṣīgha.* Used in both nominal and verbal forms, properly speaking *ṣīgha* means "form" or "type" of a contract. It is a pejorative term that has been applied to a woman who is temporarily married but not to the man who engaged her services.

Primarily an urban phenomenon, temporary marriage is culturally stigmatized and is popularly perceived to be similar to "legalized prostitution." Ironically, it is also believed to be more prevalent around the pilgrimage centers in Iran than elsewhere in the country (cf. e.g. Haeri, *Law of desire,* 9-10). Temporary marriage is a form of contract that may be performed privately and in any language as long as the partners agree on the exact period the marriage shall last and the amount of bride-price to be given to the temporary wife *(ṣīgha).* A temporary marriage need not be witnessed or registered (Ṭūsī, *Nihāya,* 498). Presently, however, the Islamic state in Iran requires its registration, ostensibly to ascertain the legality of a woman's claim in case she may become pregnant.

At the end of the specified period, the temporary marriage automatically comes to an end without any divorce ceremony. Regardless of its length, women must keep a period of sexual abstinence, *ʿidda,* after it ends (see WAITING PERIOD). Also a feature of permanent marriage and divorce, the *ʿidda* of temporary marriage is shorter by one month. It is two menstrual cycles for women who menstruate regularly, and forty-five days for women who are at an age where they normally ought to menstruate but for some reason they do not. *ʿIdda* is not required of menopausal women. Temporary spouses do not legally inherit from each other, though theoretically they may negotiate such a condition in their contract. In addition to the four wives religiously allowed all Muslim men, a Shīʿī man may simultaneously contract as many temporary marriages as he wishes and renew any of them for as many times as the partners desire it, provided that certain conditions are met. A Shīʿī woman is permitted only one marriage at a time, be it temporary or permanent.

Temporary marriage is an institution in which the relationship between the sexes (see SEX AND SEXUALITY), marriage, sexuality, morality, religious rules, secular laws and cultural practices converge. At the same time it is a kind of custom that puts religion and popular culture at odds. Despite its legality and religious sanctity, temporary marriage has never enjoyed widespread support culturally, particularly among the more "secular" middle and upper middle classes in Iran, Iraq and Lebanon, where a substantial number of Shīʿīs live.

Shahla Haeri

Bibliography
ʿĀmilī, Sayyid Ḥusayn Yūsuf Makkī, *Mutʿa dar Islām* (Mutʿa in Islam), Damascus 1342/1963 [Pers. trans. of *al-Mutʿa fī l-Islām*]; A.A. al-Amīnī, *Tarjuma-i al-Ghadīr*, vols. 5-6, Tehran 1372/1952²; ʿA.A. Dihkhudā, Ṣīgha, in *Lughatnāma* (Dihkhudā dictionary), ed. M. Muʿīn, serial no. 204, Tehran 1338/1959, 315; A.A.A. Fayzee, *Outlines of Muhammadan law*, New Delhi 1974⁴; M. Ghazanfarī, *Khudāmūz lumʿa*, Tehran 1336/1957; A. Gribetz, *Strange bedfellows.* Mutʿat al-nisāʾ and mutʿat al-ḥajj. *A study based on Sunnī and Shīʿī sources of tafsīr, ḥadīth and fiqh*, Berlin 1994; Sh. Haeri, *Law of desire. Temporary marriage in Shiʿi Iran*, Syracuse 1989, 1993; W. Heffening, Mutʿa, in *EI²*, vii, 757-9; al-Ḥillī, Najm al-Dīn Abū l-Qāsim Jaʿfar, *Sharāʾiʿ al-Islām* (Islamic law), Pers. trans. A. Aḥmad Yazdī and M.T. Dānishpazhūh, vol. 2., Tehran 1347/1968; Sayyid Ḥ. Imāmī, *Ḥuqq-i madanī* (Civil law), 5 vols., Tehran 1350-3/1971-4; Kāshif al-Ghiṭāʾ, Muḥammad Ḥusayn, *Āyīn-i mā* (Our custom), trans. N.M. Shirāzī, Qom 1347/1968; Ruhollah Khomeini, Mutʿa, in *Mahjūba* 2/5 (1982), 38-40; id., *Tawḍīḥ al-masāʾil*, Mashhad 1977 [in Pers.]; R. Levy, *Introduction to the sociology of Islam*, 2 vols., London 1931-3; S. Murata, *Temporary marriage (*mutʿa*) in Islamic law*, London 1987; M. Muṭahharī, *Niẓām-i ḥuqūq-i zan dār Islām* (Legal rights of women in Islam), Qom 1353/1974⁸; id., The rights of women in Islam. Fixed-term marriage, part 3, in *Mahjūba* (Oct/Nov 1981), 52-6; W. Robertson-Smith, *Kinship and marriage in early Arabia*, Boston 1903; M. Shafāʾī, *Mutʿa wa-āthār-i ḥuqūq wa-ijtimāʿ-yiān* (Mutʿa and its legal and social effects), Tehran 1352/1973⁶ [in Pers.]; C. Snouck Hurgronje, *Mekka in the latter part of the 19th century*, trans. J.H. Monahan, London 1931; Ṭabāṭabāʾī, Muḥammad Ḥusayn, Mutʿa ya izdiwāj-i muwaqqat (Mutʿa or temporary marriage), in *Maktab-i Tashayyuʿ* 6 (1343/1964), 10-20; id., *Shiʿite Islam*, trans. (from Pers.) and ed. S.H. Nasr, Albany 1975; id., Zan dar Islām (Women in Islam), in *Maktab-i Tashayyuʿ* 1 (1338/1959), 7-30; id. et al., *Izdiwāj-i muwaqqat dār Islām* (Temporary marriage in Islam), Qom 1985; Ṭūsī, Abū Jaʿfar Muḥammad, *al-Nihāya fī mujarrad al-fiqh wa-l-fatāwā*, Pers. trans. M.T. Dānishpazhūh, Tehran 1343/1964.

Temptation see WHISPER; DEVIL

Ten Commandments see COMMANDMENT

Tents and Tent Pegs

Portable shelters for nomadic peoples and the means to affix them in the ground. Arabic lexicographical works and dictionaries provide us with a considerable variety of terms designating a tent (see TOOLS FOR THE STUDY OF THE QURʾĀN). Most of this vocabulary goes back to Arab philologists of the eighth/ninth centuries C.E. like al-Aṣmaʿī (d. 213/828), Abū ʿUbayda (d. 209/824-5) and Abū Zayd al-Anṣārī (d. 215/830) to whom later lexicographers owe most of their knowledge about pre-Islamic Arabs, their culture and language (see ARABS; PRE-ISLAMIC ARABIA AND THE QURʾĀN; ARABIC LANGUAGE; ARABIC SCRIPT). Only four of the terms designating a tent occur in the Qurʾān: *bayt, khayma, ẓulla,* and *surādiq*.

The Bedouin (q.v.) calls his tent a *bayt*. That is the common Semitic root for "dwelling," regardless if what is meant is the tent of the Bedouins or a house built of brick or stone for sedentary people (see NOMADS; CITY). The more precise term for a tent is *bayt shaʿr,* "hair tent," which indicates the material used for making it (see HIDES AND FLEECE). The preferred fiber for the Bedouin tent is goat hair the color of which gives the tent its characteristic "blackness," even though "black tents" are often not black at all but are dyed in other colors (Iṣfahānī, *Aghānī,* viii, 65 mentions red tents: *ahlu l-qibābi l-ḥumr*). Many tents are made of pure goat hair because it is stronger and warmer in winter than other sorts of wool. Furthermore, rain water slides off the surface of goats' hair so that the tent inside remains dry. Often sheep or camel wool or a plant fiber are added; a certain percentage of goat hair, however, is always needed because sheep wool stretches too much and camel wool is too short and weak (see CAMELS; ANIMAL LIFE).

The origin of the black tent is connected with the domestication of goats and sheep, the animals which provided the material for the tent cloth. The earliest mention of goat hair as tent material can be found in the Bible (*Exod* 26:7): "You shall also make the curtains of goats' hair for a tent over the tabernacle...." There are two basic types of black tent — the eastern or Persian type and the western or Arab type (according to Feilberg, *La tente noire*). The Persian black tent seems to be closer to the black tents of biblical times which are of the simple construction described in Exodus. The Arab black tent is used by the Bedouin tribes of Arabia, Iraq (q.v.) and Syria (q.v.) and the tribes to the west of them (Rackow, Beduinenzelt; see TRIBES AND CLANS). The shape of the Arab tent is an extended cube. The length of a tent can vary from 4-5 meters to about 40 or 50 meters. The more rooms the tent has, the more wooden center poles are erected. Secondary poles are used for supporting the side and the open front of the tent. The most important component of a tent is the cloth panels: For a two-room tent about eight panels are needed, each ten or twelve meters long and 60 or 70 centimeters wide, which are stitched together. In addition to the tent cloth of the Persian type, the Arab type has tension bands sewn across the cloth breadths. These tension bands serve as reinforcement of the tent cloth.

Pre-Islamic Arabic poetry gives only scanty information on the construction of tents and materials used for them (see the examples in Jacob, *Leben,* 41-3; see POETRY AND POETS). The Qurʾān itself does not describe the characteristics of the tent any further. The term *bayt* occurs only once in the sense of "tent," in Q 16:80, whereas in all other cases *bayt* denotes a holy place or "God's house" (see HOUSE, DOMESTIC AND DIVINE). The same verse mentions leather (skins) as the material used for making the tent: "God has appointed for you from your tents *(buyūt)* a rest, and from the skins of the cattle *(julūd al-anʿām)* he has appointed for you houses *(buyūt)* which were light for you on the day you strike them and the day you set them up...." The term *khayma,* interpreted by early Arabic lexicographers as some sort of tent-like shelter, occurs in Q 55:72 in the plural *(al-khiyām)* as tent for the houris (q.v.): "cloistered in (cool) pavilions." This term is found again in the same meaning in classical poetry (see also *Lisān al-ʿArab,* xii, 193; about a possible origin of the word from Ge'ez see Leslau, *Dictionary,* 269; see FOREIGN VOCABULARY). Al-Aṣmaʿī holds that a *khayma* is built only of branches of trees, and that otherwise it is called *bayt* (similarly in Muṭarrizī, *Mughrib,* 94); other lexicographers hold that it is made with pieces of cloth and tent ropes. The term *ẓulla* occurs in Q 7:171 and could denote some sort of unstable shelter:

"And when we shook the mountain above them as if it were a *ẓulla*" (cf. other translations of the term as "covering" or "shadow"). The commentators (e.g. Bayḍāwī, *Anwār,* ad loc.) conceive this passage to mean that God lifted the mountain like a roof. Arabic lexicographers interpret the term as a "thing that covers, or protects one, overhead" (Lane, 1916). According to A.S. Yahuda (Contribution, 285), the Jews in Arabia used *ẓulal* (pl. of *ẓulla*) for the "booths" (Heb. *sikkot*) that they erected for the Feast of Tabernacles (see JEWS AND JUDAISM). The *Lisān al-ʿArab* (xi, 416-17) says that *ẓulla* is of Aramaic ("Nabatean") origin. Yahuda therefore proposes as translation "booths of foliage made for shelter." In European translations of the Qurʾān the word is similarly translated as "canopy" (Arberry; Bell, *Qurʾān*) or "Hütte" (Paret, *Koran*), whereas Blachère has "dais." According to Arabic dictionaries, *surādiq* denotes a pavilion or a cloth tent of quite large dimensions. *Surādiq* is a Persian loanword *(sarāparda)* signifying a curtain, especially at the door of a pavilion (Jeffery, *For. vocab.,* 167; Asbaghi, *Persische Lehnwörter,* 157; see also Jawālīqī, *Muʿarrab,* 90). Arabic lexicographers interpret this word, besides the above-mentioned meaning, as an awning extended over the interior court of a house or as a tent-enclosure without a roof (e.g. Muṭarrizī, *Mughrib,* 130). The wording in Q 18:29, "We have prepared for the evildoers a fire (q.v.), whose *surādiq* encompasses them" (Arberry: "pavilion"; Bell, *Qurʾān:* "awnings"; Blachère: "flammes"; Paret, *Koran:* "Zeltdecke"), evokes the image of a wall of flames surrounding the sinners, indicating that the term should be understood rather in the sense of an enclosure or a surround (see also *Lisān al-ʿArab,* x, 157-8; see HELL AND HELLFIRE; REWARD AND PUNISHMENT; SIN, MAJOR AND MINOR; GOOD AND EVIL).

Of the components of a tent only tent-pegs (*awtād,* pl. of *watad*) are mentioned in the Qurʾān. The term occurs twice, in Q 38:12 and Q 89:10, in connection with Pharaoh (q.v.) where he is described as *dhū l-awtād,* "possessor of the pegs" (Bell, *Qurʾān:* "possessor of the stakes"; Blachère: "Maître des Épieux"; Paret, *Koran:* "der mit den Pfählen"). No satisfactory explanation of this epithet has been found; most of the commentators interpret the passage as a metaphor (q.v.) for power or grandeur (see POWER AND IMPOTENCE; SYMBOLIC IMAGERY). J. Horovitz (*KU,* 130) suggests that it refers to his buildings, and H. Speyer (*Erzählungen,* 238) sees in it an allusion to the tower of Babel. It is often supposed to refer to some form of torture (impale) practiced by Pharaoh, which seems to be the most acceptable explanation (see Bell, *Qurʾān,* ii, 451; also Kratchkovsky, *Koran,* 632). A third passage, Q 78:6, "Have we not made... the mountains as pegs?," reminds one of the biblical idea of the sky as tent (*Ps* 104:2; *Is* 40:12) stretched out (*Is* 40:22) and fitted out with pillars (2 *Sam* 22:8; see HEAVEN AND SKY). The concept of a pavilion as an image of the sky is widespread in Christian literature (see for Syriac and Coptic examples Lumpe and Bietenhard, Himmel, 207; see CHRISTIANS AND CHRISTIANITY) and plays also a role in the Persian symbolism of power. Plutarch (*Vit. Alex.,* 37:3) describes the golden pavilion of Alexander the Great (see DHŪ L-QARNAYN) representing the sky (other examples in L'Orange, *Studies,* 74f.). The Qurʾān seems to refer here obviously to common cosmological conceptions in the Near East (see COSMOLOGY).

Ute Pietruschka

Bibliography
Primary: Bayḍāwī, *Anwār;* Ibn Kathīr, *Tafsīr,* 4 vols., repr. Beirut 1980; Iṣfahānī, *Aghānī,* Cairo 1323/1905; Jawālīqī, *Muʿarrab,* ed. E. Sachau,

Leipzig 1867; *Lisān al-ʿArab;* al-Muṭarrizī, Burhān al-Dīn Abū l-Fatḥ Nāṣir b. Abī Makārim, *al-Mughrib fī tartīb al-muʿrib,* ed. M. Fākhūrī and ʿA. Mukhtār, Aleppo 1982, repr. Beirut 1999. Secondary: A. Asbaghi, *Persische Lehnwörter im Arabischen,* Wiesbaden 1988; T. Faegre, *Tents. Architecture of the nomads,* London 1979; C.G. Feilberg, *La tente noire. Contribution ethnographique à l'histoire culturelle des nomades,* Copenhagen 1944; Horovitz, KU; J.S. Jabbur, *The Bedouins and the desert. Aspects of nomadic life in the Arab east,* trans. L.I. Conrad, New York 1995, esp. 241-56; G. Jacob, *Das Leben der vorislâmischen Beduinen nach den Quellen geschildert,* Berlin 1895; A. Jaussen, *Coutumes des Arabes au pays de Moab,* Paris 1948, 74-7; Jeffery, *For. vocab.;* I.Y. Kratchkovsky, *Koran,* Moscow 1963; W. Leslau, *Comparative dictionary of Geʿez (classical Ethiopic),* Wiesbaden 1991; H. List, Notizen zu den Bezeichnungen von Zelt, Kleidung und Kochgeschirr bei nahöstlichen Beduinen, in ZAL 17 (1987), 69-90; H.P. L'Orange, *Studies in the iconography of cosmic kingship in the ancient world,* Oslo 1953; A. Lumpe and H. Bietenhard, Himmel, in *Reallexikon für Antike und Christentum* 15 (1991), 190-211; Plutarch, *Plutarch's Lives,* Eng. trans. B. Perrin, 11 vols., London 1919, repr. 1994 (tome vii); E. Rackow, Das Beduinenzelt. Nordafrikanische und arabische Zelttypen mit besonderer Berücksichtigung des zentralalgerischen Zeltes, in *Baessler-Archiv* 21 (1938), 151-69, 170-84; Speyer, *Erzählungen;* A.S. Yahuda, A contribution to Qurʾān and ḥadīth interpretation, in D.S. Löwinger and J. Somogyi (eds.), *Ignace Goldziher memorial volume,* 2 vols., Budapest 1948-58, i, 280-308.

Terror
see FEAR

Test
see TRIAL

Testifying
see WITNESSING AND TESTIFYING

Textile
see MATERIAL CULTURE AND THE QURʾĀN

Textual Criticism of the Qurʾān

Introduction

Anyone who writes on textual criticism should begin with definitions. So let it be said from the outset that textual criticism has nothing to do with the criticism of music, art or literature. In simplest terms, textual criticism is the correction of errors in texts. Classical scholars are, however, a bit more sophisticated. A. E. Housman (Application, 67) defines textual criticism as the "science of discovering error in texts and the art of removing it." But he goes on to say that it is not an exact science, so perhaps we might be justified in calling textual criticism "the art of discovering error in texts and the art of removing it." Regardless of how we define it, it is unfortunately true that qurʾānic studies have not profited much from it. Most Muslim scholars have been unwilling to "discover and remove error" in the qurʾānic text, and most non-Muslim scholars have followed suit, preferring to devote themselves to aspects of qurʾānic studies that do not impinge directly on the text. There have been, however, a few exceptions to this rule, some of which we shall mention later on. Classicists divide the process of textual criticism into three phases: recension, examination and emendation. Recension is the establishment of a preliminary text; one examines it to determine whether it is the best possible text and, where it is not, one tries to emend. If the work is well done, the result should be a revised version that is closer to the author's original. Since the standard Egyptian edition of the Qurʾān is quite good, there is no need to produce a recension of the qurʾānic text, which would be impossible in any case, since there is not sufficient manuscript material to prepare a fully documented recension (see MANUSCRIPTS OF THE QURʾĀN). It is, however, important to get an idea of just what this extant recension consists of, since it differs considerably from what we would expect in an ordinary literary text.

The Qurʾān began as a work of oral composition which took twenty-odd years to complete (see ORALITY; ORALITY AND WRITING IN ARABIA; RECITATION OF THE QUR'ĀN). Parts, if not all, of it were copied at the Prophet's dictation, but because the Arabic alphabet has no vowels, only the consonantal outline *(rasm)* of the words could be written (see ARABIC SCRIPT). Moreover, the diacritics that distinguish some consonants from others, though they existed at the time, were not used, probably because the copyists had to write quickly to keep up with the dictation. These features of the orthography (q.v.) can make the reading of individual words uncertain — although this difficulty is often exaggerated. The great majority of words in the Qur'ān can be read in only one way, determined by sense and syntax (see GRAMMAR AND THE QUR'ĀN). Oral transmission was the norm, however, and there is no evidence that anyone in the early years ever read the Qur'ān from a written text in public (see RECITERS OF THE QUR'ĀN). The oral tradition dominated until an official written version, known as the 'Uthmānic recension, was produced (see CODICES OF THE QUR'ĀN; COLLECTION OF THE QUR'ĀN). But even thereafter, the oral tradition remained of primary importance. Readers reciting in public, whether they were dependent on the 'Uthmānic recension or not, could not simply omit ambivalent words (see AMBIGUOUS), nor could they recite one or two variants of a single *rasm*. They had to make choices.

Qur'ānic recitation soon became professionalized and many reciters made collections of variants for their own use. The results were rather chaotic but gradually some order was introduced as the 'Uthmānic recension was accepted by more and more readers. Ultimately compatibility with the 'Uthmānic recension became a *sine-qua-non* for any acceptable reading (see MUṢḤAF; 'UTHMĀN; POLITICS AND THE QUR'ĀN). The sacrality of the 'Uthmānic recension for Muslims is demonstrated by the fact that it has been faithfully transmitted, including its errors, for over 1300 years (see EVERYDAY LIFE, THE QUR'ĀN IN; TEACHING AND PREACHING THE QUR'ĀN). One cannot really doubt that it was the 'Uthmānic recension that preserved the Qur'ān from complete disintegration. Competing recensions, ascribed to Ibn Mas'ūd (d. 32/652-3), Ubayy b. Ka'b (d. bet. 19/640 and 35/656), 'Alī (d. 40/660; see 'ALĪ B. ABĪ ṬĀLIB) and others, were eclipsed by the 'Uthmānic recension and were ultimately declared non-canonical. Likewise the variant readings that could be applied to the 'Uthmānic recension were much reduced, and in the early fourth/tenth century, a scholar named Ibn Mujāhid declared that only seven systems of readings were canonical; the others were *shādhdh*, "deviant," and could not be used for ritual recitations (see READINGS OF THE QUR'ĀN). Not everyone agreed with his decision but in the course of time even more of them fell out of use, so that today only two are in common use. Another progressive feature was the development of vowel signs and the regular use of diacritics (see ORNAMENTATION AND ILLUMINATION). These have been incorporated into the bare text so that a copy of the Qur'ān purchased today combines the 'Uthmānic recension with one particular reading. To be precise, the recension used today is the 'Uthmānic recension, to which has been affixed the reading of 'Āṣim b. Abī l-Najūd, a Kūfan scholar (d. 127 or 128/744-6), as transmitted by his student Ḥafṣ b. Sulaymān (d. ca. 190/805-6). The printed edition most frequently used, referred to as the Egyptian Qur'ān, or the Royal Egyptian Qur'ān, since it was produced under the sponsorship of

King Fuʾād of Egypt in 1342/1923-4, is much superior to all previous editions (see PRINTINGS OF THE QURʾĀN).

The next step is to examine the text with the purpose of isolating possible errors. The most important clue that an error may have occurred is the lack of good sense in the word or passage and the resulting variety of opinion among scholars as to what it means (see TRADITIONAL DISCIPLINES OF QURʾĀNIC STUDY; EXEGESIS OF THE QURʾĀN: CLASSICAL AND MEDIEVAL). Another clue is when the word is transmitted in more than one form. Different views about the meaning and/or form of a particular word make it likely that the word is wrong. Still another clue is when the word in question is said by the commentators to be dialectal or foreign (see DIALECTS; FOREIGN VOCABULARY). Such claims may indicate that the word was unfamiliar to the scribes and reciters and so probably could be a mistake. In proposing emendations of my own, and in judging the emendations of others, I have followed rules laid down by the classicists. In order to be acceptable, an emendation must make better sense than the received text; it must be in harmony with the style of the Qurʾān (see LANGUAGE AND STYLE OF THE QURʾĀN; FORM AND STRUCTURE OF THE QURʾĀN; RHETORIC AND THE QURʾĀN); it should be paleographically justifiable; and, finally, it should show how the corruption occurred in the first place. The most important of these is the semantic criterion.

The earliest generation of reciters and transmitters of the ʿUthmānic recension soon realized that it contained mistakes, some of which they claimed were copyists' errors. The problems of recitation presented by these mistakes were solved in three ways: Some simply corrected the text (i.e. emended it), others retained the text as it was and corrected only their recitation; still others — and this was the most common solution — recited the text as it was written. G. Bergsträsser (in Nöldeke, *GQ*, iii, 2f.) notes several of these early-identified mistakes. For example, in Q 20:63 we find the consonantal structure *(rasm) ʾn hdhn lsḥrn* read by Ḥafṣ as *in hādhāni la-sāḥirāni*. This is wrong since *in* in the construction *in... la-...* introduces verbs only, most of which begin with *kāf*, especially *kāna* and *kāda* (see Rabin, *Ancient West-Arabian*, 169f.). I prefer to read *inna hādhayni la-sāḥirāni*, accepting the emendation of Abū ʿAmr b. al-ʿAlāʾ (d. 154/771), a Baṣran scholar, and one of those approved by Ibn Mujāhid (Dānī, *Taysīr*, 151). The *yāʾ* was lost not because the scribe was ignorant of grammar but because of bad handwriting. *Yāʾ* before a final *nūn* and after a space is often minuscule and can easily be missed. More important, however, the same story — Moses (q.v.) before Pharaoh (q.v.) — is told twice again in the Qurʾān with the same construction but in the singular: *inna hādhā la-sāḥirun ʿalīmun* (Q 7:109; 26:34) and once more with reference to Muḥammad: *inna hādhā la-sāḥirun mubīnun* (Q 10:2; see NARRATIVES). Although *hādhā* does not change for the accusative, *inna* indicates that an accusative was understood, so there is no good reason to read Q 20:63 differently (see also Gilliot, *Elt*, 196-7 on Q 20:63). In the second chapter of his study (Zur Sprache des Korans), Th. Nöldeke deals with stylistic and syntactic peculiarities in the text. He points out a number of peculiarities in qurʾānic style but does not go so far as to note errors or propose emendations. A possible exception (p. 27) is the passage in Q 12:17 where Joseph's (q.v.) brothers (see BROTHER AND BROTHERHOOD) tell their father that he has been eaten by a wolf and then add: *wa-mā anta bi-muʾminin lanā wa-law kunnā ṣādiqīn*, "but you would not believe us even if we were telling the truth." Nöldeke calls this "zu ungeschickt," since they are in effect admitting that they are lying. What they really mean is "You do not believe us even though we are telling the truth." Despite this, Nöldeke tries to save the text by suggesting that Muḥammad might be putting his own condemnation of the speakers in their own mouths. One should note, however, that Reckendorf (*Arabische Syntax*, 494) gives several examples of *law* where, he says, it is not used to convey what is counter factual but only more strongly than *in*, gives "the mere mental object" (die blosse Gedachtheit) of the case, or sometimes, of the point in time, and so is related in sense and use to *idhā*. The statement by Nöldeke just quoted reveals very clearly the attitude of nineteenth-century scholars towards the qurʾānic text. If Muḥammad's audience was unaware of the flaws of expression, then he, too, must have been unaware of them. Consequently, no one admitted that they existed until they were discovered by later scholars and were rescued from this strange limbo of unawareness. Nöldeke was wise not to emend them, and one important lesson we can draw from his study is never to assume that flaws of expression are always errors.

Another method of emendation is employed by J. Barth (Studien zur Kritik und Exegese des Qorans), who tries to test the inner connections ("Zusammenhänge") of the sūras (q.v.) and their possible disjunctions, and to point out insertions in the original contexts as well as to make other critical and text-critical contributions. Most of Barth's proposals are based on the assumption that the text has been disarranged and that many verses, phrases and words are out of place and should be returned to their original locations. He thus inaugurates the method that was applied on a larger scale by R. Blachère, and was carried to an extreme by R. Bell (see POST-ENLIGHTENMENT ACADEMIC STUDY OF THE QURʾĀN). Few later scholars refer to Barth though Blachère cites him occasionally in the notes to his translation (see TRANSLATIONS OF THE QURʾĀN). An example of Barth's method can be seen in his treatment of Q 97:4-5: *tanazzala l-malāʾikatu wa-l-rūḥu fīhā* (i.e. *fī laylati l-qadri*) *bi-idhni rabbihim min kulli amrin; salāmun hiya ḥattā maṭlaʿi l-fajri*. He claims that *min kulli amr* cannot be construed since it cannot mean *bi-kulli amr*, nor "wegen jeder Sache," since this would be indicated by *min*. He proposes to read the last portion: *bi-idhni rabbihim ḥattā maṭlaʿi l-fajr; salāmun hiya min kulli amr*, "Sie ist ungefochten von jeder (bösen) Sache" (Barth, Studien, 19). In my view, if emendation is necessary, which is doubtful, it would be much simpler to emend *min* to *fī*, thus correcting a mistake that is frequently found in later manuscripts. Barth can, however, be given credit for one emendation which is undoubtedly correct. In Q 37:78, 108, 119, and 129 he reads, instead of *taraknā ʿalayhi fī l-ākhirīna*, which makes no sense, *bāraknā ʿalayhi fī l-ākhirīn*, "we blessed him among later generations." (Note that Q 37:113 correctly reads *bāraknā*.) Luxenberg (*Syro-Aramäische Lesart*, 138) also prefers *bāraknā* but does not note that Barth was the first to make this emendation.

Scholars, like Barth and Blachère, who try to restore the original by moving bits and pieces of text from one place to another have great difficulty in fulfilling the fourth requirement for an acceptable emendation, namely showing how the corruption came about. If they claim that these textual rearrangements are the Prophet's revisions and alterations (see REVISION AND ALTERATION; CORRUPTION; FORGERY), they must admit that in the end he did not really care whether the text made sense or not. If they ascribe them to the mistake of reciters, copyists, or editors, they argue for a level of corruption that cannot be admitted since the assumed dislocations run into the hundreds. Such a high level of corruption could have occurred with a written text only if someone had taken the original, i.e. correct, text and worked through it systematically, shifting passages to wrong locations, thus leaving it for later scholars to put right, something that no one would suggest. The simultaneous presence of oral and written transmissions of the qur'ānic text complicates this further and the most elaborate effort to explain textual misplacement — that of Richard Bell — remains unconvincing to me.

Almost from the beginning of Islamic studies in Europe, controversy arose between two groups of scholars, one of which believes that Judaism, the other that eastern (Syrian) Christianity, exercised the greater influence on Muḥammad, the Qur'ān and the subsequent development of Islam (see JEWS AND JUDAISM; CHRISTIANS AND CHRISTIANITY; RELIGIOUS PLURALISM AND THE QUR'ĀN). The supporters of Christianity have until now made little use of textual criticism in their arguments, although it has always been admitted that the Arabic of the Qur'ān contains a large number of borrowings from Syriac. Recently, however, a book has appeared under the name of Christoph Luxenberg, in which the author, who prefers to write under a pseudonym, deals critically with what he deems to be traces of Syriac in the qur'ānic text, which include single words, phrases and syntactic constructions. This work should be carefully reviewed by someone familiar with the methods of textual criticism and equally at home in both Arabic and Syriac. Here, in some of the examples that follow, I shall have to limit myself to citing a few instances of Luxenberg's emendations in order to contrast them with my own, so that the reader can get some idea of the type of textual criticism he is practicing.

Selected emendations

In the proposed emendations that follow, because of limitations of space, I have omitted most of the discussions that accompanied the original publications, which consisted by and large of proposals by Western scholars and the comments of Muslim commentators (see TOOLS FOR THE STUDY OF THE QUR'ĀN; CONTEMPORARY CRITICAL PRACTICES AND THE QUR'ĀN). This material is instructive for the history of *tafsīr* and displays the difficulties that scholars have had in coming to grips with the text, but in my judgment it is misguided and does not contribute much to the correction of the text. I shall, however, mention those comments of the commentators which are helpful in emending the text. For many, Arabic was their native language, so they could sometimes sense the correct meaning of a difficult passage (see DIFFICULT PASSAGES) and "redefine" the crucial word accordingly, even when this was lexically impossible. The modern textual critic has only to emend following their lead. There are several examples of this redefinition in the following emendations.

Ḥaṣab: fuel. Read *ḥaṭab,* with Ubayy b. Ka'b, in Q 21:98. *Ḥaṣab* cannot mean "fuel"; *ḥaṭab* occurs with this meaning in Q 111:4 and Q 72:15. The mistake was caused by a copyist omitting the vertical stroke of the *ṭā',* turning it into a *ṣād* (Bellamy, Some proposed emendations, 564).

Ummah: time, while, Q 11:8 and Q 12:45. Read *amad,* which has this meaning four times, in Q 3:30; 18:12; 57:16; 72:25. Final *dāl* was turned into *hā',* either because the copyist's pen fed too much ink or his hand was unsteady and twitched upward and to the right after the *dāl* was complete

(Bellamy, Some proposed emendations, 564).

Abban: fodder, pasturage, Q 80:31. Read *lubban,* "nuts." *Abb* has no acceptable meaning here but *lubb* fits in well with the other blessings that God has bestowed on humankind (Q 80:27-31; see GRACE; BLESSING). The copyist's pen as it turned to the left after the *lām* briefly ceased to flow, breaking the connection with the following *bāʾ* and converting the *lām* into *alif* (Bellamy, Some proposed emendations, 564).

Sijill: writer of a document, Q 21:104. Read *musjil* or *musajjil. Sijill* means only "document." In older hands, *mīm* after the definite article does not turn back under the *alif* as in later hands but is no more than a thickening of the line between the *lām* and the following letter. A leaky pen may have run the *mīm* into the first tooth of the *sīn,* causing the *mīm* to lose its identity; possibly one of the teeth of the *sīn* was indistinct, thus facilitating the misreading (Bellamy, Some proposed emendations, 566).

Ḥiṭṭah: forgiveness, Q 2:58; 7:161; read *khiṭatan.* This word has nothing to do with *ḥaṭṭa,* which means "put down," but comes from the verb *khaṭiʾa,* which in the Ḥijāzī dialect would become *khaṭiya* "commit a sin," with *maṣdar khiṭah,* omitting the *hamza.* The spelling is like that of *shṭh* = *shaṭʾahu* "its sprout" in Q 48:29. The people are appealing for forgiveness (q.v.), but they first must confess their sins (see SIN, MAJOR AND MINOR; REPENTANCE AND PENANCE). *Khiṭatan,* with the implied omission of the verb *khaṭīnā* < *khaṭiʾnā,* is the equivalent of "we have sinned" (Bellamy, Some proposed emendations, 566).

Ṣurhunna ilayka: incline them (the birds) toward you, Q 2:260. Read *jazzihinna (wa-) lbuk,* or *wa-labbik.* Abraham (q.v.; Ibrāhīm) is instructed by God, "Take four birds and incline them towards yourself *(fa-ṣurhunna ilayka)* then put a part of them on each mountain, then call them, and they will come to you flying." Al-Ṭabarī (d. 310/923; *Tafsīr,* iii, 35f.; cf. Gilliot, *Elt,* 107) cites the two major views on the meaning of *ṣur,* "incline" and "cut up," and chooses the latter because the majority of the exegetes accept it; he takes issue with a few Kūfan lexicographers who maintain that *ṣur* never means "cut up." Each group, however, is right in its own way. *Ṣur* never means "cut up" but the meaning must be "cut to pieces and mix them up." With the emendation suggested above the meaning would be, "make them into pieces and mix them up." Emending *ṣād* to *jīm* is simple; *jazzi* is the classical *jazziʾ,* since in the Ḥijāzī dialect, all the *hamza*s had been lost. The meaningless *ilayka* is removed by reading *ulbuk* with no change in the *rasm;* the *wāw* was dropped when the word was misread as *ilayka.* Another possibility is that the phrase originally read *wa-labbik,* which has the same meaning, on the assumption that the *wāw* was mistaken for an *alif* (Bellamy, Some proposed emendations, 567).

Sabʿan mina l-mathānī: seven *mathānī* (?). This and the following two emendations are of special interest since they depend on assuming the same mistake. One can argue that they were copied by the same scribe with a certain peculiarity in his handwriting. *Mathānī* occurs in Q 15:87: "We have given you seven *mathānī* and the mighty Qurʾān," and again in Q 39:23: "God has sent down the best account, a book (q.v.) alike (in its parts), *mathānī,* at which the skins of those who fear (q.v.) their lord (q.v.) creep...." Read: *matālīyi* and *matālīya,* the broken plural of *matlūw,* meaning "recitations," literally "something that has been or is to be recited." The copyist mistook the *lām* for a *nūn* because it was too short. We also emend *sabʿan* to *shayʾan.* The scribe wrote a small loop instead of the minim of the *yāʾ.* The next scribe, seeing what he took to be a *sīn* and an *ʿayn,* could hardly do anything but add the *bāʾ*. So Q 15:87 should read *wa-la-qad ātaynāka shayʾan mina l-matālīyi wa-l-qurʾāna l-ʿaẓīm,* "We have given you some recitations and the mighty Qurʾān" (Bellamy, Some proposed emendations, 567).

Tamannā; fī umniyatihi: to desire, in his desire. In Q 22:52 we read: "We have not sent down before you any messenger or prophet but that when he desired *(idhā tamannā)* Satan injected (something) into his desire *(fī umniyatihi)* but God cancels what Satan injects, then God makes his signs (q.v.) strong" (see ABROGATION; DEVIL; SATANIC VERSES). The word "desire" (verb and noun) makes little sense here; the sense required is recite, recitation, which was recognized by some commentators, who redefine *tamannā* to mean *qaraʾa,* even inventing *shawāhid* in support of this redefinition (Ibn Isḥāq, *Sīra,* 370 f.). The redefinition is correct. We emend *tamannā* to *yumlī* and *umniyatihi* to *imlāʾihi,* "dictates" and "in his dictation." The latter word was originally written *ʾmlyh,* with no *alif* for the long *ā*. The *nūn* was written for *lām* because it was too short as in *mathānī,* and one of the minims was lost. After *yumlī* was corrupted to *tamannā, umniyatihi* was inevitable (Bellamy, Some proposed emendations, 568).

Illā amāniyya: except desires. Read *amāliyya,* "dictations." Q 2:78 *wa-minhum ummiyyūna* (i.e. ignorant people who do not know the scriptures; see IGNORANCE; UMMĪ; SCRIPTURE AND THE QURʾĀN) *lā yaʿlamūna l-kitāba illā amāniyya wa-in hum illā yaẓunnūna,* "And among them are *ummiyyūna* who do not know the book except desires and they can only guess." The exegetes were not satisfied with *amāniyya,* and try to redefine it. Al-Ṭabarī (*Tafsīr,* i, 297f.) prefers the meaning "lies, falsehoods," but the best suggestion comes from al-Zajjājī (d. 311/923), who says plainly "They do not know the book except by recitation" (*illā tilāwatan, Lisān al-ʿArab,* xv, 294; Bellamy, Some proposed emendations, 569).

Ṣibghat Allāh: God's religion, Q 2:138. Read *ṣanīʿa* or *kifāya*. "But if they turn away, they are in schism, but God will take care of them for you [Muḥammad; *fa-sa-yakfīkahumu llāhu*] for he hears and knows (see SEEING AND HEARING; KNOWLEDGE AND LEARNING); the *ṣibgha* of God and who is better at *ṣibgha* than God" (Q 2:137-8). The word *ṣibgha* refers to the Christian baptism (q.v.), so the exegetes were obliged to redefine it. They take it to mean *dīn* or *īmān,* or they equate it with the *millat Ibrāhīm,* in Q 2:135, which they take to mean Islam (see RELIGION; FAITH). It seems inconceivable that one should find in the Qurʾān the name of a Christian sacrament used — even metaphorically — for Islam or *īmān*. The whole idea runs counter to the general attitude toward Christianity and Judaism in the Qurʾān (see POLEMIC AND POLEMICAL LANGUAGE; APOLOGETICS), and is so disturbing that the word practically announces itself as a mistake. In my view, *ṣibghat Allāh* refers to the words immediately preceding, *fa-sa-yakfīkuhum Allāh*. Taken thus, *ṣibgha* is an exclamatory accusative, used in praise of God's action in sparing the Prophet the trouble of dealing with his own enemies (q.v.; see also OPPOSITION TO MUḤAMMAD). There are two emendations that would give this sense. The first is to read *ṣanīʿa,* "favor." This emendation can be effected without altering the *rasm* if we assume that the original *ṣād* did not have the little nub on the left — this is often omitted in manuscripts — but that the next copyist took the *nūn* to be the nub. Otherwise it is possible to add a minim to the *rasm,* a minor change. The second possibility is to read *kifāya,* the *maṣdar* of *kafā,* which would have been spelled *kfyh,* the long *ā* without *alif.* In older manuscripts, *kāf* is often written without the diagonal stroke that we add separately, but is written first and then turns left and under to complete the letter. The copyist misread *kāf* as *ṣād,* and then took the loop of the *fāʾ* for a minim. Initially, it was my assessment that *ṣanīʿa* was preferable, since fewer changes were necessary to bring it into line (Bellamy, Some proposed emendations, 570), but *kifāya* is what should be expected, given *sayakfīkuhum* and good sense should take precedence over paleography.

Aṣḥāb al-aʿrāf: the People of the Heights (q.v.), Q 7:48 (cf. Q 7:46). The verses refer to a group of men who are situated in some vantage point from which they can observe both the blessed in heaven and the damned in hell (see REWARD AND PUNISHMENT; PARADISE; HELL AND HELLFIRE). "Between them is a curtain *(ḥijāb)*, and on the *aʿrāf* (*ʿalā l-aʿrāf*) are men who know each by their mark, and they call to the people of heaven… and the people of the *aʿrāf* call to men whom they know by their mark; they say 'Your collecting [of money] has not helped you nor has your arrogance (q.v.).'" The word *aʿrāf* is the plural of *ʿurf,* which means "mane" or "comb" of a cock, and it may not be incorrect. It could be used metaphorically of some high place on which these observers are located. What makes it a bit suspicious is that the metaphor (q.v.) does not appear to have been used either before or after the revelation of this passage. Furthermore, if the word refers to the top of the *ḥijāb* (see VEIL), as some think, one should expect *ʿalā aʿrāfihi.* Two emendations can be proposed here, neither of which has to be metaphorical, though the second may be. The first is *ajrāf,* pl. of *jurf* or *juruf,* which means "bank," specifically of a *wādi* that has been undercut by the current, or, simply, "a bank that rises abruptly from a torrent or stream" (Lane, 411). Paleographically there is no difficulty. Sometimes in early manuscripts and papyri initial *ḥāʾ* begins with a lead-in line like a small arc with the concavity facing right, which then continues toward the right completing the main body of the letter. If this arc is exaggerated the whole letter can be mistaken for an *ʿayn*. The other suggestion is *aḥruf,* pl. of *ḥarf,* which means, among other things, "point, ridge, brow, ledge, of a mountain" (Lane, 550). The same emendation, *ʿayn* to *ḥāʾ* is needed here as in *ajrāf,* and the *alif* presents no problem. It might have been introduced at the time of the ʿUthmānic recension, or it could have been added by ʿUbaydallāh b. Ziyād, who during his governorship of Kūfa (53-9/673-9) instituted a reform in qurʾānic spelling, which consisted of the introduction of about 2,000 *alif*s into the text (Nöldeke, *GQ*, iii, 255f.). Taken this way, *aḥruf* is not metaphorical but we find the singular *ḥarf* used metaphorically in Q 22:11: "And among the people there are those who serve God on a *ḥarf* and if good comes to them they are at ease with it but if trouble comes to them, they turn back to their (old) ways" (see GOOD AND EVIL; TRUST AND PATIENCE). These people who serve God on a ridge *(ḥarf)* are fence-sitters who are not sure which way they will jump since circumstances can vary. The same is true of the *aṣḥāb al-aʿrāf,* who are not sure whether they will end in heaven or hell, since it depends on God's will, which they do not yet know (see FREEDOM AND PREDESTINATION). The two usages are not exactly parallel, since *aʿrāf* is plural and definite and *ḥarf* is singular and indefinite; nevertheless the similarity is striking. In general, I prefer the reading *aḥruf* but would suspend judgment on whether it should be taken metaphorically or not (Bellamy, Some proposed emendations, 571).

Wa-inna kullan lammā la-yuwaffiyannahum rabbuka aʿmālahum, Q 11:111. The crux is the word *lammā,* for which we find the variants *la-mā, lamman* (acc.), which is said to mean "all" (*jamīʿan*); or, *inna* is changed into negative *in*, and *lammā* given the sense of *illā* "except." Barth (Studien, 136) must be correct in saying that *lammā* cannot be construed and ought to be deleted. Once this is done the sentence is good grammatical Arabic and fits perfectly in the context: "Surely to all, your lord will give full requital for their deeds" (see GOOD DEEDS; EVIL DEEDS; HEAVENLY BOOK). Barth does not explain, however, how *lammā* got into the text; that is, he ignores the fourth requirement for an acceptable emendation. The copyist's eye, after he had written *kullan*, strayed back to verse 108, where we find *wa-innā la-muwaffūhum naṣībahum*, "Indeed we shall give them their full portion." He proceeded to write *la-muwaffūhum* but caught his mistake after writing only *lām* and *mīm*, which he cancelled with a vertical stroke. This stroke was read by a later copyist as *alif* after the *mīm*, thus producing the meaningless *lammā* (Bellamy, More proposed emendations, 196).

The earliest version of the story of the prophet Shuʿayb (q.v.) is found in Q 26:177-89, in which it is told how he was sent to the People of the Thicket (q.v.; *aṣḥāb al-ayka*, cf. Q 26:176), whom he urged to obey God and the prophet. He was rejected by his people and they were punished by a day of shadow. There are two problems in the story: the form of the prophet's name, and the identity of the *aṣḥāb al-ayka*. The name Shuʿayb does not appear in pre-Islamic sources or in proto-Arabic inscriptions and it does not have a good Arabic etymology. It does, however, contain an *ʿayn*, which argues for a Semitic origin, so the natural place to look for the original is the Hebrew Bible. I believe that Shuʿayb is a mistake for Shaʿyā (spelled with final *alif*), the Arabic form of Isaiah. The difference between Shaʿyā and Shuʿayban (in the accusative) is only a single minim, so the name in the original (Arabic) source was probably in the accusative. The next step is to turn to the book of Isaiah to see if we can find any features common to the text of Isaiah and that of the Qurʾān that will corroborate our claim that the two are the same. In Isaiah 21:13-17 we find:

the oracle concerning Arabia. In the thickets of Arabia you will lodge, O caravans of Dedanites. To the thirsty bring water, meet fugitives with bread, O inhabitants of the land of Tema, for they have fled from the swords, from the drawn sword, from the bent bow, and from the press of battle. For the Lord said to me, "Within a year, according to the years of a hireling, all the glory of Kedar will come to an end; and the remainder of the archers of the mighty men of the sons of Kedar will be few, for the Lord, the God of Israel has spoken" (Oxford translation).

I believe that the *aṣḥāb al-ayka* are the Dedanite merchants who were driven into the thickets of Arabia by an incursion of the sons of Kedar, who are to be punished for their sins. That there is some confusion between the two versions over who the real sinners were is not serious enough to invalidate this piece of evidence, which, taken together with the emendation, is sufficient not only to identify the *aṣḥāb al-ayka*, but also to confirm that Shuʿayb and Isaiah are the same (Bellamy, More proposed emendations, 197).

Q 74:49-51 describes the rejection by the Meccans of Muḥammad's message: "Why do they turn away from the reminder (q.v.) as if they were frightened asses fleeing from a *qaswara?*" There is much uncertainty among the exegetes and lexicographers about this word, which is usually translated as "lion." I believe that it derives from the Syriac *pantōrā* "panther," which goes back ultimately to the Greek *panther*.

The Greek was transcribed into Syriac with the ambivalent letter *p/f*; this in turn was transliterated into Arabic with the ambivalent letter *f/q*, which closely resembles Syriac *p*, and which of course was left without dots. The only real mistake in the qurʾānic *rasm* is a minim error which occurred when a copyist wrote a *sīn* instead of *n-t*. Panther is a better comparison in this passage than lion, since it is unlikely that Arabs ever had the opportunity to see a lion chasing an onager. The cheetah, however, under the name *fahd*, which also means "leopard" and "panther," was well known to the Arabs as a hunting animal. *Fantūrah* does not present a perfect rhyme, probably because it derives from a written source that was neither pointed nor vocalized, so the reader who first attempted to pronounce the unfamiliar word changed the vowel *ū* to the consonant *w*, just as he read q for f. If *pantūrah* had been borrowed orally it would probably have been pronounced *bamtūrah*, since *p* in foreign words borrowed into Arabic becomes *b* (Bellamy, More proposed emendations, 198).

An alternative emendation is given by Luxenberg (*Syro-Aramäische Lesart*, 45f.) who derives *qaswarah* from the Syriac root *q-ṣ-r* (Arabic *qaṣura*, "be incapable"), from which a dialect word *qusrā*, also *quṣrā*, is found, which means "decrepit old ass unable to carry a load." The spectacle of asses fleeing from a tired decrepit ass is explained as a foolish action, unjustified because there is no real threat. Likewise there is no good reason for men to flee from the reminder. The Arabic has preserved the classical Syriac pattern *qasōrā*.

The name of the prophet or holy man Dhū l-Kifl (q.v.) appears twice in the Qurʾān: "And Ishmael (q.v.; Ismāʿīl) and Idrīs (q.v.) and Dhū l-Kifl were of those who were patient and we caused them to enter into our mercy" (Q 21:85-6); and "and remember Ishmael, Elisha (q.v.; al-Yasaʿ), and Dhū l-Kifl, they were all of the best" (Q 38:48). *Kifl* can mean "pledge, guarantee" and "double," but no satisfactory interpretation of the name has been offered. I think that Dhū l-Kifl is a copyist's error for Dhū l-Ṭifl, "he of the child," and that it, like the story of Shuʿayb and the *aṣḥāb al-ayka*, goes back ultimately to the book of Isaiah. In Isaiah 9:6 we read: "for to us a child is born, to us a son is given, and the government shall be upon his shoulder, and his name will be called 'wonderful counselor, mighty God, everlasting father, prince of peace'" and in Isaiah 11:6, "the wolf will dwell with the lamb, and the leopard shall lie down with the kid and the lion and the fatling together, and a little child shall lead them." These verses were regarded by Christians as foretelling the coming of Christ, so they would be the parts of Isaiah most likely to be widely circulated among Christians, and so most likely to be picked up by Muḥammad or his source. The use of the particle *dhū* is a bit puzzling, but since the child is mentioned in the book of Isaiah, the phrase Dhū l-Ṭifl probably refers to Isaiah himself. He was of course a prophet and so deserves to be mentioned along with Ishmael, Idrīs, and Elisha. Confusion of *ṭ* and *k* is a common mistake in Arabic manuscripts (Bellamy, More proposed emendations, 199).

In Q 44:23 God orders Moses to lead the Children of Israel (q.v.) through the Red Sea: "Make my servants travel by night *(fa-asri bi-ʿibādī laylan);* indeed you will be pursued; and leave the sea gaping wide *(wa-truki l-baḥra rahwan);* indeed they are an army that will be drowned" (Q 44:23-4; see DROWNING). The crux lies in the words of command which the exegetes assume God addressed to Moses after the Israelites had crossed over, although the first clause could only have been spoken before they started out. The word *rahwan* is taken by most exegetes to mean "gaping wide," and most translators accept this, though Blachère (170) notes that the phrase makes no sense to the commentators and that *rahwan* means only "marcher doucement." The necessary emendation is obvious. One should read *wa-nzili l-baḥra rahwan,* "and descend into the sea at an easy pace." There is no longer any need to shift the scene from before to after the crossing, and *rahwan* now has its most common meaning. Confusion of isolated *lām* and *kāf* is common in Arabic manuscripts (Bellamy, More proposed emendations, 198).

In Q 70:10-14 the Qurʾān describes the desperate situation of those sinners who are about to be punished on judgment day (see LAST JUDGMENT): "And friends will not ask friends *(wa-lā yasʾalu ḥamīmun ḥamīman);* they will be made to see them *(yubaṣṣarūnahum);* the sinner would like to rescue himself from the punishment of that day by his children (q.v.), his wife, and his brother, and his kinfolks (see KINSHIP) who give him refuge and everyone on earth, then (he thinks) this would save him." *Yubaṣṣarūnahum* makes little sense in the context. Blachère (94) and Paret (*Koran,* 482) note that the meaning is uncertain. Since *lā yasʾalu* requires a second object, the best emendation here is to read *yanṣurūnahum* without altering the *rasm,* and translating, "Friends will not ask friend to help them." Since they are willing to ransom themselves with the whole world, they would not consider asking mere friends for help (see FRIENDS AND FRIENDSHIP; INTERCESSION). The word *ḥamīm* may be used as a plural justifying the plural verb (Lane, 637). When *an* is omitted, the following verb is in the indicative. Another qurʾānic example is found in Q 39:64; *a-fa-ghayra llāhi taʾmurūnnī aʿbudu,* "Do you command me to worship (q.v.) other than God?" This construction is found after verbs of command, including *qāla,* refusing, forbidding, knowing, and in oaths and asseverations (Reckendorf, *Arabische Syntax,* 384). Since asking is a mild form of command, it is reasonable to admit the construction here, although I have not found another example with *saʾala* (Bellamy, More proposed emendations, 200).

The word *sūra* occurs nine times in the Qurʾān in the singular and once in the plural *suwar.* The word always refers to a portion of the divine revelation but not as yet a specific portion. The problem with *sūra* is not its meaning but its derivation, and on this point there is much variation among the Muslim exegetes and the non-Muslims scholars alike. For an extensive survey of the proposals by the latter, see Jeffery (*For. vocab.*, 180-2); none of them is convincing. The lexicographers are equally at a loss. They etymologize the word, trying to derive it from *s-w-r* or *s-ʾ-r.* The word *sūra* may mean "eminence of nobility, exalted state, rank," as well as "row of bricks or stones in a wall" (Lane, 1465). *Suʾra* means "a remnant of food or drink left in a vessel" or "remnant of youthful vigor." But one cannot really believe that Muḥammad would employ a word meaning "dregs" and "orts" or "row of bricks" as a metaphor for a divine revelation. In emending the text, the main consideration is to find a word that is fitting and appropriate for a revelation sent down by God from on high (see REVELATION AND INSPIRATION). I believe we can find it in the Heb. *beʿsôrāh,* which means "tidings, good tidings, news (q.v.; see also GOOD NEWS)." The mistake is another instance of a minim error in which the copyist wrote three minims instead of four. As in the case of Shuʿayb and *qaswara,* the error did not originate in the qurʾānic tradition, but was already present in the source from which *sūra* was taken. The borrowing must have been fairly old, since the word had already acquired a broken plural (Bellamy, More proposed emendations, 201).

In Exodus 3:1-5, the lord speaks to Moses from the burning bush: "Do not come near; put off your shoes from your feet (q.v.), for the place on which you are standing is sacred ground" (see SACRED AND PROFANE). In the story as retold in the Qur'ān (Q 20:12), the lord says: "I am your lord, so take off your sandals; verily you are in the sacred valley, Ṭuwā" (q.v.; *bi-l-wādi l-muqaddasi ṭuwan*). The best that the exegetes could offer is that *ṭuwan* is the name of the valley, but they do not know what it means. There is an episode in the Bible, however, that will give us a clue as to the meaning of *ṭuwan*. In Joshua 5:15 the commander of the lord's army comes to Joshua and says, "Put off your shoes from your feet, for the place where you stand is holy, and Joshua did so." The event occurred in a place near Jericho called Gilgāl, where the Israelites were encamped. The Bible, with a play on words, associates Gilgāl with the *g-l-l*, which in the *qal*-form means "to roll." By changing the vowel *ḍamma* in *ṭuwā* to *fatḥa* we get a verb *ṭawā*, which means among other things "to roll" (transitive), literally "he rolled." It is reasonable to assume that *ṭawā* is a translation of the exegetical definition of Gilgāl. The discrepancy between Mount Horeb and Gilgāl and between Moses and Joshua should not give us pause, since the Qur'ān in telling biblical stories often modifies them. No emendation of the *rasm* is necessary; however, the *ḍamma* in Ṭuwā may have been influenced by the fact that there is a locality near Mecca (q.v.) called Dhū Ṭuwā, where the pilgrims rest up before coming into the city (Bellamy, Textual criticism, 2; see PILGRIMAGE).

Q 4:51 states that those who have been given (only) a portion of the book believe in the *jibt* (q.v.) and the *ṭāghūt* (see IDOLS AND IMAGES). No one really knows who or what the *jibt* is or are. The Muslim commentators equate it with the *ṭāghūt*, that is "idol, priest, sorcerer" (see MAGIC; POLYTHEISM AND ATHEISM; PRE-ISLAMIC ARABIA AND THE QUR'ĀN). For the views of non-Muslim scholars, see Jeffery (*For. vocab.*, 99). If, however, we emend *jibt* very slightly, by moving the dot from beneath the *bā'* to above the letter, we get *al-jinnat*, which means the jinn (q.v.), a word that also occurs frequently in the Qur'ān. The only unusual thing about it is the use of the long *tā'*, instead of *tā' marbūṭa*, for the feminine singular ending. *Jinnah*, which also means "madness" (see INSANITY), occurs ten times in the Qur'ān, always spelled with *tā' marbūṭa*. G. Bergsträsser (in Nöldeke, *GQ*, iii, 27), however, lists thirty-six instances in the Qur'ān where feminine singular ending is long *tā'*, and a number of cases where it may be either singular or plural. The fact that all the other occurrences of the word have *tā' marbūṭa* may have been responsible for the readers' not recognizing the word here. In the time of Muḥammad the jinn or jinna were impersonal gods: "The Arabs of Mecca asserted the existence of a kinship *(nasab)* between them and Allāh (Ḳur'ān XXXVII, 158), made them companions of Allāh (VI, 100), offered sacrifices to them (VI, 128), and sought aid of them (LXXII, 6)" (Macdonald/Massé, Djinn, 547; see SACRIFICE; IDOLATRY AND IDOLATERS). Particularly close to the phrase "they believe in the *jibt* = *jinnat*" *(yu'minūna bi-l-jibt)* is Q 72:6, "there are people of mankind who seek refuge with the people of the jinn" *(ya'ūdhūna bi-rijālin mina l-jinni)*. Here again we do not need to emend the *rasm* (Bellamy, Textual criticism, 3).

In Q 6:74 Abraham asks his father Āzar (q.v.), "Do you take *(a-tattakhidhu)* idols as gods?" The problem is that in the Bible Abraham's father is not Āzar but Teraḥ. (See Jeffery, *For. vocab.*, 54f. for the opinions of Western scholars on this name.) More useful is the view of some Muslim exegetes who believe that Āzar is an expression of blame; it is like *yā aʿraj,* "O limper," as if he were saying to his sinful father, "O sinner, O dotard, O old man," or that it is a word of rebuke or forbidding wrong-doing (*Tāj al-ʿarūs,* x, 46f.). Although the canonical reading *(ʾ-r-r)* does not vary, there is an unusual *shādhdh* reading, ascribed to Ibn ʿAbbās, which takes the *alif* of the following word as the last letter of the previous word. Jeffery thinks the reading was originally *ʾa-ʾizran,* with the first *alif* representing two *hamza*s and the last the *tanwīn* of the accusative. This, he says, was the reading of Ismāʿīl al-Shāmī (Jeffery, Marginalia, 137). *Izr* is a variant of *wizr,* "burden," but it can hardly be correct; it does not occur in the Qurʾān, whereas *wizr* and its plural *awzār* occur twelve times, so it is clearly the form preferred by Muḥammad. Combining the insight of the Muslim exegetes noted above (that the word is some kind of reproach) with the deviant reading just mentioned, the result is the reading *ʾ-r-r-ʾ*, which can be vocalized *ʾizrāʾan,* and translated "contemptuously": that is, "when Abraham said to his father contemptuously 'You take idols as gods.'" The only objection that one might make is that *azrā* takes the prepositions *bi-* or *ʿalā* before the object; but one can argue here that the *maṣdar* is used absolutely, so it is not necessary to mention the object, which is clear from the context. No real change in the *rasm* is necessary (Bellamy, Textual criticism, 3).

Three names which have created difficulties for the Muslim exegetes and Western scholars alike are Idrīs, ʿUzayr (see EZRA), and al-Rass (q.v.). I believe that all three refer to the same person, Esdras or Ezra, the presumed author and protagonist of the Jewish apocalyptic book 2 Esdras (4 Esdras in the Catholic Bible). Idrīs is mentioned twice in the Qurʾān: "And mention in the book Idrīs; verily he was truthful and a prophet, and we raised him to an exalted place" (Q 19:56-7; see PROPHETS AND PROPHETHOOD), and again in Q 21:85-6, where he is mentioned along with Ishmael and Dhū l-Kifl. The Muslim commentators identify him with the biblical Enoch because "Enoch walked with God, and he was not, for God took him" (*Gen* 5:24), which seems to refer to his "exalted place" in Q 19:57. Among non-Muslim scholars, P. Casanova correctly suggested that the reference was to Esdras, and Bell in his translation of the Qurʾān (p. 288) agrees with Casanova that Idrīs is probably Esdras. The connection between Esdras and Idrīs is obvious. Arabic does not admit consonantal clusters, so when a foreign word is borrowed that has one, either an epenthetic vowel is inserted or one of the consonants is dropped, which reduces the cluster to two; in this case the *sigma* has been dropped. The following consonant *yāʾ* was pronounced *ōē* or *ē* as a result of the *imāla* of the *alif.* There is moreover in 2 Esdras 14:9 a clear statement that Esdras will be raised up. God says to him: "You shall be taken up from among men and henceforth you shall live with my son and with those who are like you until the times are ended." This is clearer than the statement in Genesis about Enoch. No emendation of the *rasm* is necessary.

In Q 9:30 we read: "The Jews say: 'Uzayr is the son of God,' and the Christians say, 'The Messiah is the son of God.'" Even more curious than the form of the name is the statement that ʿUzayr was believed by the Jews to be the son of God (see PEOPLE OF THE BOOK). I believe that we can solve both problems. Jeffery says that the form of the name is difficult but that it must come from the biblical ʿEzrā. "The form may be due to Muḥammad himself not properly grasping the name, or possibly giving it the contemptuous diminutive form" (Jeffery, *For. vocab.*, 214f.). The last statement is most unlikely since the Qurʾān does not elsewhere treat biblical figures with contempt. The first step in solving the textual problem is to take the *alif* from the beginning of *ibn* and attach it to ʿUzayr, as we did in the case of Āzar. This gives us ʿUzayrā, which could be the diminutive of ʿEzrā. It is, however, a feminine form (Howell, *Grammar*, i/3, 1232f.), and probably would not have been used of a prophet who was a man. Moreover, the Arabic diminutive form *fuʿayl* is used only when it is formed from a noun with three consonants and no long vowel, e.g. *faʿl*, *fuʿl*, etc. (see ARABIC LANGUAGE). So ʿUzayr could not be a diminutive of ʿEzrā. I do not believe, however, that a diminutive was intended, but that the *yāʾ* is intrusive, caused by a rough spot in the papyrus or vellum, or by an overflowing pen. Once this is eliminated, two possibilities present themselves. First we have *ʿ-z-r-ʾ*, an exact transliteration of the biblical ʿEzrā. We note, however, that the word *ibn* in the Qurʾān is always written with the *alif*, but in later texts the *alif* is often omitted contrary to the rules, and the orthography may have been standardized sometime after the original recording. A second, even more likely, possibility is that the long *ā* was shortened in recitation because of the cluster *bn* which follows. The scribe may simply have reproduced what he heard the Prophet say, which was *ʿazrabnu*, retaining, however, the conventional *alif* in *ibn*. The question why the Jews are said to believe that ʿUzayr is the son of God can be answered by again referring to 2 Esdras 14:9. There is, however, an even more pertinent reference in 2 Esdras 2:42-8. Esdras on Mount Zion sees a vision of a young man who is placing crowns on the heads of a multitude of people. He asks an angel who the young man is, and is told: "He is the son of God, whom they confessed in the world." It is clear that Muḥammad or his informant confused the name of the prophet Esdras, which is also the name of the book, with the son of God seen by Esdras in his vision.

The phrase *aṣḥāb al-rass* occurs in two lists of people who disbelieved in the prophets sent to them and so perished (Q 25:37-8; 50:12-14; see PUNISHMENT STORIES). The word *rass* has several meanings but the one adopted by most commentators, and consequently by some translators, is "well," so the *aṣḥāb al-rass* become the People of the Well. The commentators, however, do not agree on who they were, where the well was located, or precisely what the name of their prophet was. This is not surprising, since *al-rass* is nothing more than Idrīs misspelled. The *rāʾ* was written too close to the *dāl*, which was then read as a *lām*. The *yāʾ*, which has only one minim, was probably lost through a flattening-out of the minims. It may never have been there, however, since the following vowel could have been read as long *ā*, but pronounced without *imāla* and so not reproduced in the writing. The only other letter that could have been read instead of *dāl/dhāl* is *kāf*, but the roots *k-r-s* and *k-r-sh* gave no satisfactory meaning. So in sum, Idrīs and al-Rass go back to Esdras and ʿUzayr goes back to ʿEzrā, and in the apocryphal tradition Esdras and ʿEzrā are the same (Bellamy, Textual criticism, 4).

Perhaps the most mysterious textual problem in the Qurʾān is the name ʿĪsā, which is the name given to Jesus (q.v.). No one has yet satisfactorily explained why the Qurʾān should call Jesus ʿĪsā, since he is referred to by eastern Christians as Yasūʿ or Īsōʿ. ʿĪsā does not occur before the Qurʾān but Yasūʿ is used in personal names at an early period. The fact that ʿĪsā has no satisfactory derivation and no pre-qurʾānic history should have suggested to scholars that the word might be a mistake. I had originally emended the text to *m-s-y-y,* to be read Massīya, which I thought derived ultimately from the Greek *messias* without the nominative singular ending. I now prefer to derive it from the Arabic al-Masīḥ, from which the definite article has been dropped. This involves emending the *ʿayn* to *mīm,* and dividing the four minims into *sīn* and *yāʾ,* then emending the final *yāʾ* to final *ḥāʾ.* It is much more likely that the Prophet would have known the Arabic term than the Greek, so we do not have to assume that he vacillated between Greek and Arabic. The real problem is why Muḥammad would have rejected Yasūʿ for any alternative. I believe that his choice was dictated by the fact that Yasūʿ could have been turned into an obscene insult by his enemies. The verb *aswaʿa* and also apparently *sāʿa, yasūʿu* refer to the action of the two Cowper glands, which secrete a fluid when sexually stimulated (*Tāj al-ʿarūs,* xxi, 243). The *rasm*s of the two verbs are the same, *y-s-w-ʿ.* The phrases "Yasūʿ Yasūʿ" or "Yuswiʿ Yasūʿ" could have been used to ridicule Muḥammad's claim that Jesus was a prophet (Bellamy, Textual criticism, 6; id., Further note, 587-8). Luxenberg (*Syro-Aramäische Lesart,* 26f.), on the other hand, derives ʿĪsā from the biblical Īšay, (Jesse, in the English Bible) the father of David (q.v.). The eastern Syrians weaken initial *ʿayn* so that it is realized by *hamza,* and the final *ʿayn* vanishes completely. This agrees with Mandaean spelling in which *ʿayn* is used for *hamza,* and final *ʿayn* is dropped. The diphthong – *ay* – was eventually monophthongized to *ā,* a common feature in eastern Syriac.

The tale of the Seven Sleepers of Ephesus is told in Q 18 (see MEN OF THE CAVE). In Q 18:9 God speaks to the Prophet: "Or did you think that the companions of the cave and (of) al-Raqīm (q.v.; *anna aṣḥāba l-kahfi wa-l-raqīmi*) were one of our marvelous signs?" The word *al-raqīm* has not been satisfactorily explained, which makes it likely that the word is wrong. I suggest that it is a mistake for *al-ruqūd,* pl. of *rāqid,* "sleeping, sleeper," so the phrase should read *aṣḥāba l-kahfi l-ruqūdi,* "the sleeping companions of the cave." The corruption began with the loss of the final *dāl;* detached letters when final are sometimes omitted through carelessness. The other mistakes occurred because of the effort of a copyist to correct the text. The remaining letters *rqw* make no sense, so he mistook *w* for *m,* and added *y* to give the word a common nominal pattern, but since the new word does not fit with what precedes, he added the conjunction to make it a separate phrase. We note further that *ruqūd* is also found in Q 18:18, *wa-taḥsibuhum ayqāẓan wa-hum ruqūdun,* "you would think them awake but they are sleeping" (Bellamy, Al-raqīm, 115). Similarly, Luxenberg (*Syro-Aramäische Lesart,* 65f.) emends *al-raqīm* to *al-ruqād,* "sleep," taking the *yāʾ* as representing long *ā,* reading "the people of the cave and of the sleep." This goes against the orthography of the Qurʾān, in which *ā* after *qāf,* which occurs hundreds of times, is either omitted or is represented by *alif.* Exceptions occur when *alif* is *alif maqṣūrā,* as in *ʾ-sh-q-y* = *ashqā* (Q 87:11), and is retained when a suffix follows, e.g. *ʾ-sh-q-h-ʾ* = *ashqāha* (Q 91:12); this represents the pronunciation – *ay* (see Rabin, *Ancient West-Arabian,* 115f. and 160, who treats the matter in detail). In Q 3:28, however, we do find *t-q-y-h* = *tuqāt,* but in Q 3:102, with attached pronoun, *t-q-ʾ-t-h* or *t-q-t-h* = *tuqātihi* (Nöldeke, GQ, iii, 40). This word made difficulties for some readers: Yaʿqūb al-Ḥaḍramī and Ḥasan al-Baṣrā (d. 110/728) read *taqīyatan* (ibid., n. 4). This one exception, which is probably a mistake itself, is not sufficient to justify the reading *al-ruqād.*

In Q 101:6-11 we read "As for him whose scales are heavy (see WEIGHTS AND

MEASURES), he shall be in a pleasing way of life, as for him whose scales are light *fa-ummuhu hāwiyah*, but how should you know what that is? A hot fire." Even though the phrase in Q 101:9 is defined in verse 11, no one has been able to explain how the phrase can mean what it surely must mean (see PIT). The literal meaning is "his mother shall perish" or "his mother shall be bereft," but "hot fire" cannot explain it. Of the several Western scholars who have commented on this passage, Blachère (p. 26) comes close to solving the problem. He admits that the phrase does not make good sense; he translates it, "s'acheminera vers un abîme," but he thinks it would be simpler to take *umm* (perhaps to be read *amm*) as a verbal noun of *amma*, "se diriger vers, aller vers un but." I, however, believe that what is required is an ordinary feminine noun, which was supplied by *ummuhu*, but which is inappropriate here. Read instead, without changing the *rasm*, *ummatun* "path, way, course," and translate "then a steep course downward shall be his." *Ummatun hāwiyatun* is an incomplete nominal sentence, which can easily be completed by reference to the context. Such sentences are common in the Qurʾān; they occur most often in the apodoses of conditional sentences, as in this passage (see Q 2:265; 4:92; 56:88-94, for other examples; also Bellamy, Fa-ummuhu hāwiyah, 485).

James A. Bellamy

Bibliography
Primary: Abū ʿUbayd al-Qāsim b. Sallām, *Faḍāʾil al-Qurʾān wa-maʿālimuhu wa-ādābuhu*, ed. A. b. ʿA.al-W. al-Khayyāṭī, 2 vols., Rabat 1995, ii, 91-104 (traditions on mistakes in the codices); Dānī, *Taysīr;* Ibn Isḥāq, *Sīra; Lisān al-ʿArab;* Ṭabarī, *Tafsīr; Tāj al-ʿarūs*.
Secondary: J. Barth, Studien zur Kritik und Exegese des Qorans, in *Der Islam* 6 (1916), 113-48; Bell, *Qurʾān;* J.A. Bellamy, A further note of ʿĪsā, in *JAOS* 122 (2002), 587-8; id., Al-raqīm or al-ruqūd. A note on sūrah 18:19, in *JAOS* 111 (1991), 115-17; id., Fa-ummuhu hāwiyah. A note on sūrah 101:9, in *JAOS* 112 (1992), 485-7; id., More proposed emendations to the text of the Koran, in *JAOS* 116 (1996), 196-204; id., Some proposed emendations to the text of the Koran, in *JAOS* 113 (1993), 562-73; id., Textual criticism of the Koran, in *JAOS* 121 (2001), 1-6; Blachère; J. Burton, Linguistic errors in the Qurʾān, in *JSS* 33 (1988), 181-96; Gilliot, *Elt;* A.E. Housman, The application of thought to textual criticism, in *Proceedings of the Classical Association* 18 (1921), 67-84; M.S. Howell, *Grammar of the classical Arabic language*, repr. Delhi 1986; Jeffery, *For. vocab.*; id., Marginalia to Bergsträsser's edition of Ibn Khalawih, in *Islamica* 7 (1935-6), 130-55; Lane; Ch. Luxenberg (pseudonym), *Die Syro-Aramäische Lesart des Koran. Ein Beitrag zur Entschlüsselung der Koransprache*, Berlin 2000; D.B. Macdonald/ H. Massé, Djinn, in *EI²*, ii, 546-9; Nöldeke, *GQ;* id., Zur Sprache des Korāns, in id., *Neue Beiträge zur semitischen Sprachwissenschaft*, Strassburg 1904-10; repr. Amsterdam 1982, 1-30 (Fr. trans. G.-H. Bousquet, *Remarques critiques sur le style et la syntaxe du Coran*, Paris 1953); Paret, *Koran;* C. Rabin, *Ancient West-Arabian*, London 1951; H. Reckendorf, *Arabische Syntax*, Heidelberg 1921.

Textual History of the Qurʾān

see UNITY OF THE TEXT OF THE QURʾĀN; MUṢḤAF; TEXTUAL CRITICISM OF THE QURʾĀN; COLLECTION OF THE QURʾĀN; CODICES OF THE QURʾĀN

Thamūd

An ancient tribe, mentioned twenty-six times in the Qurʾān, counted among many peoples who rebelled against God and his messengers (see MESSENGER; PROPHETS AND PROPHETHOOD). The story of Thamūd forms part of a repeated trope of human rebellion (q.v.) and subsequent destruction (see PUNISHMENT STORIES; GENERATIONS) appearing in reference to other lost peoples such as the ʿĀd (q.v.) and the people of Lot (q.v.), Noah (q.v.), Midian (q.v.), Pharaoh (q.v.), Tubbaʿ (q.v.), Iram (q.v.) and the *aṣḥāb al-rass* (see PEOPLE OF THE THICKET; see also GEOGRAPHY).

Most often the Thamūd are mentioned along with the ʿĀd and represent lost pre-Islamic Arabian tribes (see TRIBES AND CLANS; PRE-ISLAMIC ARABIA AND THE QURʾĀN) that fit the pattern of rebellion and destruction. The Thamūd succeed the ʿĀd and live in homes hewn out of the earth (Q 7:74; 26:149). Ṣāliḥ (q.v.) is God's Thamūdic prophet (Q 7:73; 11:61; 26:141-2; 27:45) and the Qurʾān retains the oral memory (see ORALITY AND WRITING IN ARABIA): "And to Thamūd their brother Ṣāliḥ. He said: 'O my people! Serve God. You have no other god save him'" (Q 11:61; see WORSHIP; POLYTHEISM AND ATHEISM). Ṣāliḥ's people acknowledge his qualities (Q 11:62) but refuse to abandon the ancestral, polytheistic, tradition. They repudiate him because he is only mortal (Q 26:154; 54:24) and demand a sign (see SIGNS). He provides a she-camel, a camel (q.v.) of God (Q 7:73), and requires that she not be harmed or that both she and the people drink their well water on equal terms (Q 11:64; 26:155-6; 54:27-8). They respond by wounding or hamstringing her (Q 7:77; 11:65; 26:157; 54:29; 91:14); the term for this, *ʿ-q-r*, is far less common than *j-r-ḥ* and, in some of its forms (e.g. *ʿāqir*, a barren [woman]), connotes infertility. As a result the Thamūd are destroyed except for their messenger Ṣāliḥ, or Ṣāliḥ and a few righteous survivors (Q 11:66; 27:53; 41:18). The Thamūd are destroyed by an earthquake (*rajfa*, Q 7:78, associated with the last day in Q 79:6; see LAST JUDGMENT; APOCALYPSE), a thunderbolt (*ṣāʿiqa*, Q 41:13, 17; 51:44), a shout (*ṣayḥa*, Q 54:31), a terrible storm (*ṭāghiya*, associated linguistically with a common term for transgression, *t-gh-y*, Q 69:5) or by burying (*damdama ʿalayhim*, Q 91:14). It is interesting to note that these forms of destruction correlate with the *sajʿ* rhyme of the different passages in which the story is placed (see RHYMED PROSE; FORM AND STRUCTURE OF THE QURʾĀN; LANGUAGE AND STYLE OF THE QURʾĀN). In Q 27, the story blends into a narrative reminiscent of biblical and midrashic sources treating the destruction of Sodom, with nine evil, violent, plotting people who caused the destruction (Q 27:48-51), followed by direct reference to Lot (Q 27:54; see NARRATIVES; SCRIPTURE AND THE QURʾĀN).

The story is expanded in the exegetical traditions (see EXEGESIS OF THE QURʾĀN: CLASSICAL AND MEDIEVAL) in ways that provide meaning to obscure scriptural verses, but with some renderings (i.e. Kisāʾī, *Qiṣaṣ*, 117-28) utterly fantastic. The Thamūd was a mighty people living in al-Ḥijr (see ḤIJR) who served idols (see IDOLS AND IMAGES), were corrupt, and failed to heed the warnings of their prophet, Ṣāliḥ, unless he would show them a miracle (see WARNER; MIRACLES). He asked them to tell him what he should show them, so they called on him to bring forth a specific kind of pregnant camel from solid rock. When he did so, some immediately agreed to follow the prophet and encouraged others to join them but were forbidden by powerful tribesmen. The camel gave birth to a foal and would drink all the water in a certain well every other day, after which she would give huge amounts of milk to the people. On the other days, the Thamūd would drink abundantly and store enough until it was again their turn. The camel's behavior harmed some of the people's other flocks and Ṣāliḥ made enemies inadvertently in other ways as well. Certain women are included among the ringleaders in the plot to hamstring the camel, and nine people lead in the process that would result in the wounding and eventual destruction of the camel. When the prophet warns them of their impending doom, they try but fail to kill him. He warns them that their punishment would come in three days and that each morning they would awake to find the color of their skin changing to yellow, red and, on the final day, black. This terrified the Thamūd as they observed the changing color of their skin, but by that time it was too late, with horrific destruction as a result.

A people called Thamūd are mentioned in non-Arabian sources such as Ptolemy *(Geography)* and Pliny *(Natural history)*. The earliest mention is in a list of tribes defeated by the Assyrian Sargon II (721-705 B.C.E.). The name and other features of the qurʾānic story may be found in poetry attributed to Umayya b. Abī l-Ṣalt, a contemporary of Muḥammad.

According to Ibn Saʿd (d. 230/845; *Ṭabaqāt,* i, 37), the Thamūd were the Nabateans. Al-Bukhārī (d. 256/870; *Ṣaḥīḥ,* iv, 358-60) relates a tradition in which, when traveling northward through "the land of Thamūd, al-Ḥijr," Muḥammad forbade his troops from drinking the water from its wells or using it in food production. He further forbade them to enter the ruined dwellings "unless weeping, lest occur to you what happened to them." Some traditions find the Thaqīf tribe of Ṭāʾif to have derived from a Thamūdic survivor or slave of Ṣāliḥ. Popular legend associates the cliff dwellings, inscriptions and sculptures in or near the northern Ḥijāzī town of Madāʾin Ṣāliḥ ("The towns of Ṣāliḥ") with the Thamūd (see YEMEN; SOUTH ARABIA, RELIGIONS IN PRE-ISLAMIC). These "Thamudic inscriptions" reference a real community that is no longer extant.

Reuven Firestone

Bibliography
Primary: Bukhārī, *Ṣaḥīḥ,* trans. M. Khan, Lahore 1983, iv, 358-60; Ibn Kathīr, *Tafsīr,* Beirut 1985; Ibn Saʿd, *Ṭabaqāt,* 9 vols., Beirut 1997, i, 37; trans. S.M. Haq, *Ibn Saʿd's Kitāb al-Ṭabaqāt al-kabīr,* 2 vols., New Delhi n.d., i, 33-4; Kisāʾī, *Qiṣaṣ,* trans. W.M. Thackston, Jr., *Tales of the prophets of al-Kisaʾi,* Boston 1978, 117-28; Masʿūdī, *Murūj,* 7 vols., Beirut 1966-79, ii, 156-9 (sect. 929-35); ed. and trans. Ch. Pellat, *Les Prairies d'or,* 5 vols., Paris 1962-97, ii, 350-3; Ṭabarī, *Tafsīr,* Beirut 1984; id., *Taʾrīkh,* ed. de Goeje; Thaʿlabī, *Qiṣaṣ,* 57-63, trans. W.M. Brinner, *ʿArāʾis al-majālis fī qiṣaṣ al-anbiyāʾ, or Lives of the prophets,* Leiden 2002, 114-23; Umayya b. Abī al-Ṣalt, in F. Delitzsch, *Umajja ibn Abi ṣ-Ṣalt,* Leipzig 1911, xxxiii, 23-8 (101); Yāqūt, *Buldān,* Beirut 1990. Secondary: Horovitz, *KU,* 94 *(Aṣḥāb al-Ḥiğr),* 123 *(Ṣāliḥ);* R. Hoyland, *Arabia and the Arabs. From the Bronze Age to the coming of Islam,* London 2001; M.J. Kister and M. Plessner, Notes on Caskel's Ğamharat an-nasab, in *Oriens* 25-6 (1976), 48-68.

Thanksgiving see GRATITUDE AND INGRATITUDE

Theft

The unlawful taking of another's property (q.v.) entailing, in some cases, a punishment stipulated by the Qurʾān (see also CHASTISEMENT AND PUNISHMENT; LAW AND THE QURʾĀN; LAWFUL AND UNLAWFUL; SIN, MAJOR AND MINOR).

One of the better-known legislative passages in the Qurʾān provides: "As for the thief, whether male or female, for each, cut off the hands in punishment for what they did, as an exemplary punishment *(nakālan)* from God" (Q 5:38). The Arabic *wa-l-sāriq wa-l-sāriqa fa-qṭaʿū aydiyahumā* closely parallels the syntax of another qurʾānic legislative pronouncement concerning adultery: As for "the adulteress and the adulterer, whip each one of them..." (Q 24:2, *al-zāniya wa-l-zānī fa-jlidū kulla wāḥidin minhumā;* see ADULTERY AND FORNICATION). Muslim jurists came to include the crime of theft among the so-called *ḥudūd* (sing. *ḥadd,* "limit"), the small group of transgressions defined by the Qurʾān that constitute Islamic penal law (see Schacht, *Introduction,* 175-8; see also BOUNDARIES AND PRECEPTS). Although the Companion

ʿAbdallāh b. ʿAbbās (d. 68/687; see COMPANIONS OF THE PROPHET) is said to have declared the theft verse "unrestricted" in its application (*al-āya ʿalā l-ʿumūm*, Ṭabarī, *Tafsīr*, x, 296), the jurists rapidly undertook to ameliorate its harsh penalty by developing numerous exceptions that led to a narrow and highly technical definition of theft (*sariqa*). Discussions of specific exceptions are reported among early Meccan jurists such as ʿAṭāʾ b. Abī Rabāḥ (d. 115/733) and his student Ibn Jurayj (d. 150/767; see ʿAbd al-Razzāq, *Muṣannaf*, x, e.g. 195, 207, 232) and are also preserved in early compilations of Iraqi jurisprudence such as that attributed to Zayd b. ʿAlī (d. 122/740; *Corpus juris*, 817-20, probably before 184/800). Most jurists came to consider that the scope of the verse had been considerably narrowed by various prophetic ḥadīths (see ḤADĪTH AND THE QURʾĀN), making the verse itself "restricted" in its application (*khāṣṣ*, e.g. Ṭabarī, *Tafsīr*, x, 296, who objects to the characterization of Ibn ʿAbbās; for a summary of the jurisprudence, see Schacht, *Introduction*, 179-80, and for later legal-hermeneutical approaches, see Weiss, *Spirit*, 101-8). Legal reform and changing sensibilities led to a further decline in application of the *ḥudūd* punishments in later centuries (see e.g. Peters, Islamic and secular law).

With regards to forceful theft (robbery), Islamic jurisprudence has looked to another qurʾānic passage (Q 5:33) for penal guidelines. This passage decrees execution, crucifixion (q.v.), the amputation of the opposing hand and foot or exile for those who war against God and his messenger and strive to sow "corruption" (q.v.; *fasād*) throughout the land. This has been variously interpreted in the penalties for robbery found in Islamic law: for robbery that involved murder, execution or crucifixion; for simple robbery (i.e. in which no death is involved), amputation of the opposing hand and foot (cf. Heffening, Sariḳa; Carra de Vaux/Schacht, Ḥadd).

In addition to the aforementioned prohibition found in Q 5:38, the Qurʾān also contains a second though more oblique injunction against theft. After the treaty of Ḥudaybiya (6/628; see ḤUDAYBIYA), certain Meccan women are said to have come to Muḥammad to offer him allegiance (see WOMEN AND THE QURʾĀN; CONTRACTS AND ALLIANCES), and Q 60:12 stipulated that the Prophet should accept their pledge and also prescribed its form, which included an undertaking not to commit theft: "O Prophet, if believing women come to you to pay you homage, pledging not to associate anything with God (see POLYTHEISM AND ATHEISM), steal, commit adultery, kill their children (q.v.; see also INFANTICIDE), come up with a lie (q.v.) they invent between their hands and feet or disobey you in any honorable matter (see DISOBEDIENCE; OBEDIENCE), then accept their homage and ask God's forgiveness (q.v.) for them" (see Nöldeke, *GQ*, i, 219). Known as the "pledge of women" (*bayʿat al-nisāʾ*), this text is considered to be substantially identical to the first pledge of ʿAqaba, made to Muḥammad in 621 by a group of Medinans (Ibn Isḥāq, *Sīra*, i, 433; Ibn Isḥāq-Guillaume, 198-9; Watt, *Muhammad at Mecca*, 146; for affinities with the Decalogue, see Weiss, Law and covenant, 53-4).

Finally, a false accusation of theft plays a role in the qurʾānic (as in the biblical) story of Joseph (q.v.). When Joseph's brothers return to Egypt (q.v.) with Benjamin (q.v.), Joseph causes a goblet to be put in Benjamin's bag in order to create a pretense for detaining the brothers (episode beginning at Q 12:70; compare *Gen* 44). Joseph's subordinate accuses the brothers of being thieves (Q 12:70; *Gen* 44:4, not in the Hebrew) and they deny that they have stolen (Q 12:73; *Gen* 44:8). The subsequent qur'ānic elaboration of the narrative contains several intricacies not found in the biblical version (see SCRIPTURE AND THE QUR'ĀN; NARRATIVES).

Joseph E. Lowry

Bibliography
Primary: ʿAbd al-Razzāq, *Muṣannaf;* Ibn Isḥāq, *Sīra,* ed. al-Saqqā et al.; Ibn Isḥāq-Guillaume; Ṭabarī, *Tafsīr,* ed. Shākir; Zayd b. ʿAlī (attrib.), *Corpus juris,* ed. E. Griffini, Milan 1919.
Secondary: B. Carra de Vaux/J. Schacht, Ḥadd (a.), in *EI²*, iii, 20-1; M. Fakhry (trans.), *An interpretation of the Qur'ān,* New York 2004; W. Heffening, Sariḳa, in *EI²*, ix, 62-3; R. Peters, Islamic and secular law in 19th-century Egypt. The role and function of the qadi, in *Islamic law and society* 4 (1997), 70-90; J. Schacht, *An introduction to Islamic law,* Oxford 1965; S.S. Souryal and D.W. Potts, The penalty of hand amputation for theft in Islamic justice, in *Journal of criminal justice* 22/3 (1994), 249-65; W.M. Watt, *Muhammad at Mecca,* Oxford 1953; B. Weiss, Law and covenant in Islam, in E. Firmage et al. (eds.), *Religion and law,* Winona Lake 1990; id., *The spirit of Islamic law,* Athens 1998.

Theology and the Qur'ān

The Qur'ān displays a wide range of theological topics related to the religious thought of late antiquity and through its prophet Muḥammad presents a coherent vision of the creator, the cosmos and man. The main issues of Muslim theological dispute prove to be hidden under the wording of the qur'ānic message, which is closely tied to Muḥammad's biography (see SĪRA AND THE QUR'ĀN).

Preliminary remarks

Dealing with theology and the Qur'ān means looking in two different directions at the same time. On the one hand, the qur'ānic message plays an important role in the religious history of late antiquity, representing a specific step within the development of monotheism as derived from the Torah (q.v.) and its Hellenistic exegesis (see POLYTHEISM AND ATHEISM; IDOLATRY AND IDOLATERS; SCRIPTURE AND THE QUR'ĀN). On the other hand, one has to study the view of the creator and the universe (see CREATION; GOD AND HIS ATTRIBUTES) as expounded in a corpus of heterogeneous texts (see FORM AND STRUCTURE OF THE QUR'ĀN), which share the characterization of having been revealed to the prophet Muḥammad (see REVELATION AND INSPIRATION). Neither of these two aspects must be neglected, although it would be disadvantageous to combine them in this essay. Therefore, in the interest of a better understanding of the different issues, two separate lines of inquiry will be followed here. The first treats the place of qur'ānic monotheism in the religious history of the Middle East. This problem will be tackled by scrutinizing the qur'ānic narrative (see NARRATIVES) about Abraham (q.v.), one that indicates the far-reaching changes that the concept of the one god underwent after the age of the Torah. There is no need to discuss the parallels between the qur'ānic story and its presumed sources, since this kind of research has been done frequently and it is unlikely that substantially new results can be obtained. But beyond the field of literary history (see also LITERARY STRUCTURES OF THE QUR'ĀN; RHETORIC AND THE QUR'ĀN; MYTHS AND LEGENDS IN THE QUR'ĀN), the qur'ānic narratives offer valuable clues, which have rarely been used to deepen our understanding of how Muḥammad conceived the divine and of how his conceptions were related to those current in the Middle East of his time.

The answer to these questions will lead to the second major line of investigation, which will focus on the qur'ānic text itself (see COLLECTION OF THE QUR'ĀN; CODICES OF THE QUR'ĀN; MUṢḤAF; LANGUAGE AND

STYLE OF THE QUR'ĀN). This investigation will include a detailed review of the main theological topics of the Qur'ān, following an order determined by the emergence of particular concerns faced by the new community during the vicissitudes of the Prophet's career. In other words, this analysis of the theological contents of the Qur'ān will be conducted in close relationship to the material of the *sīra*. That religious arguments cannot be understood if divorced from their historical contexts is accepted as an indispensable hermeneutic principle in both Muslim and non-Muslim scholarship (see MUḤAMMAD; OCCASIONS OF REVELATION). In the sūras (q.v.) there is no theological concept that remains untouched by the circumstances under which it was pronounced by the Prophet (see SPEECH; RECITATION OF THE QUR'ĀN). The bulk of what the Qur'ān says about the creator and the role he assigned to humans as his viceregents in the world (Q 2:30; see CALIPH; ADAM AND EVE; CORRUPTION) seems to have been important at least to some of Muḥammad's contemporaries who were concerned with the divine and its meaning in human life. Research on the intellectual environment in which the Qur'ān was revealed has been overshadowed by the Muslim view that there was an abrupt change from the error (q.v.) of *jāhiliyya* (see AGE OF IGNORANCE) to the truth (q.v.) of Islam (q.v.). But if one takes the ample material on the pre-Islamic civilization of the Arabs (q.v.; see also BEDOUIN; NOMADS; PRE-ISLAMIC ARABIA AND THE QUR'ĀN) seriously — and there is no convincing reason to discard it in advance — one gets a distinct impression of a society in unrest, looking for some new and trustworthy guidance, and of a Prophet sensitive to that unrest who considers himself and his received revelations to be the remedy for what was felt to be going wrong. His personality and his strength of mind were the decisive additions that forged the Qur'ān out of a wealth of sundry ideas current in the Arabian peninsula of those days (see ORALITY AND WRITING IN ARABIA; ETHICS AND THE QUR'ĀN).

The Qur'ān within the theological thought of late antiquity

Although a great deal of research has been done on the question of whether the Qur'ān was influenced by Jewish or Christian theological conceptions (see CHRISTIANS AND CHRISTIANITY; JEWS AND JUDAISM), no certainty has been reached on this point. The issue requires a fresh approach, but is beyond the scope of this article. Even focusing the argument on matters of theology alone would not do justice to even the most important aspects of the problem. Nevertheless, a few tentative steps are necessary in order to gain some insight into the contributions of the Qur'ān to the religious history of the Middle East. As indicated above, the qur'ānic figure of Abraham will serve as a guide.

The Abraham portrayed in the Qur'ān is a Meccan citizen (see MECCA). Already in the earliest passages where he is mentioned the reader notices very close connections between Muḥammad's own reasoning and his idea of Abraham, whom he considers his most important predecessor. In Q 51:25-34, for example, Abraham welcomes three guests unknown to him; before leaving him they convey a warning to him or, rather, to his people (see WARNER): "We have been sent to a people who are sinners (see SIN, MAJOR AND MINOR) that we may let loose upon them stones of clay (q.v.; see also STONE), marked by your lord (q.v.) for the extravagant *(al-musrifīn)*." The Meccans would have recognized that the reproach of extravagance was directed against them, too, or even them primarily; extravagance, as Muḥammad understood it, was tantamount to a fatal lack of compliance with divine guidance (see ARROGANCE; INSOLENCE AND OBSTINACY; DISOBEDIENCE; OBEDIENCE), and God would punish the frivolous in the same way that he had annihilated those who a few decades ago had dared to wage war (q.v.) against Mecca (cf. Q 10:87; 21:9; 40:28, 34; 105:4; see also ABYSSINIA). There is much evidence showing how the Qurʾān's concept of the Meccan Abraham and the person of Muḥammad the Prophet were overlaid. It is sufficient to quote Q 14:35-8, where Abraham implores the lord to make Mecca a place of security and to prevent his children from worshipping idols (see IDOLS AND IMAGES): "O lord, I have caused some of my offspring to settle in an unfruitful valley, near your holy house... Grant therefore that the hearts of some men may be affected with kindness toward them; and bestow on them all sorts of fruits that they may give thanks (see GRATITUDE AND INGRATITUDE)...."

Most frequently, however, the Meccan revelations (see CHRONOLOGY AND THE QURʾĀN) deal with Abraham's struggle to convince his people to put an end to idolatry (Q 19:41; 21:51; 26:69; 29:16; 37:83; 43:26). These passages can be read to reflect Muḥammad's difficult experiences with his unbelieving countrymen (see BELIEF AND UNBELIEF), but they also reveal much about the theology behind the qurʾānic text, which sometimes seems strikingly simple to the modern non-Muslim reader. The most complete rendering of the story is to be found in Q 6:74-83 and dates back to the time shortly before the emigration (q.v.; *hijra*) to Medina (q.v.). It reads: "(Recall) when Abraham said to his father Āzar (q.v.): 'Do you take idols as gods? Verily, I think that you and your people are in manifest error.' Thus do we show Abraham [our] power *(malakūt)* over the heavens and the earth (q.v.; see also HEAVEN AND SKY; SOVEREIGNTY; POWER AND IMPOTENCE), and [it is] in order that he may be one of the convinced. When the night came down upon him (see DAY AND NIGHT), he saw a star (see PLANETS AND STARS); said he: 'This is my lord,' but when it vanished, he said: 'I love not the things which vanish.' Then when he saw the moon (q.v.) shining forth, he said: 'This is my lord,' but when it vanished, he said: 'Truly, if my lord guides me not, I shall be of the people who go astray (q.v.).' Then when he saw the sun (q.v.) shining forth, he said: 'This is my lord, this is greater,' but when it vanished, he said: 'O my people, I am quit of what you associate (with God). Towards him who opened up *(faṭara)* the heavens and the earth, I have set my face as a *ḥanīf* (q.v.), and I am not one of the polytheists.' But his people disputed with him; he said: 'Do you dispute with me in regard to God, though he has guided me; I fear not what you associate with him except [it be] that my lord will something [against me]; my lord's knowledge (see KNOWLEDGE AND LEARNING) is wide enough for everything; will you not then be reminded (see REMEMBRANCE; MEMORY)? How should I fear what you have associated (with him), when you are not afraid to associate with God what he has not sent you down any authority (q.v.) for? Which of the two parties is the better entitled to feel secure, if you have any knowledge?' Those who have believed and have not confused their belief with wrong-doing — theirs is the security, and they are the guided. That argument of ours we gave to Abraham against his people; we raise in rank whomsoever we will; verily, your lord is wise, knowing."

During the fifth century, Sozomenos [Sozomen], born at Bethelea near Gaza, wrote an ecclesiastical history covering the period from 324 to 422 C.E. In this work there is to be found the oldest evidence of some sort of popular veneration of Abraham: At the ancient holy place of Mamre near Hebron, Jews, Christians and pagan Arabs were accustomed to gather once a year. The pagans would commemorate the apparition of the angels (q.v.) to Abraham and they would sacrifice (q.v.) some animals like an ox or a cock. Furthermore, they would abstain from sexual intercourse (see SEX AND SEXUALITY; CHASTITY; ABSTINENCE) in order to avoid the wrath of the lord, whom they thought to be present at that holy place (Sozomène, *Histoire ecclésiastique,* 244-9). The scene of the angels announcing divine guidance to Abraham goes back to Genesis 18:1-16. The Bible tells us that Mamre was the place where Abraham was dwelling when a stranger with two companions visited him; they predicted that Sarah would give birth to a son, a prophecy that made Sarah laugh because she knew that she was barren (see ISAAC). In Q 51:24-34 the visitors add the words quoted above, which point to Mecca's recent past and to the moral deficiencies of its citizens. One might assume that those sentences are only a digression, but there is much more behind them. In a treatise entitled *De Deo,* Philo of Alexandria comments on Genesis 18:2. The passage can be summarized as follows: When (Abraham) raised his eyes, he saw a stranger with two companions: Those who study the holy scripture are given the capacity to perceive the hidden qualities of creation (see HIDDEN AND THE HIDDEN; SECRET); they gain insight into nature and its divine foundations and in this way they understand the true meaning of being God's creature. The creator, manifest in and through nature, bears witness to himself by the process of constantly creating. Calling Abraham's attention to this truth is the main reason for the visit those men pay him. They open his eyes and he can see how the creator "makes the earth and the water (q.v.), the air (see AIR AND WIND) and the heaven so that (these phenomena) would be suspended from himself... raising the world as if protecting it through guardians..." (Siegert, Abrahams Gottesvision, 82).

Thus Abraham is portrayed as a visionary whose experience testifies to God as the indefatigable creator; everything that exists in this world is dependent on his continuous activity. Philo's commentary points to a wide range of religious concepts which were alien to the original text of Genesis 18. Before going into more detail about Philo's understanding of this passage, it is worthwhile taking a look at the Book of Jubilees, which was composed a few decades before Philo's treatise. The author of this work, a revision of Genesis and Exodus, is convinced that he has reproduced the original text of the scriptures which Moses wrote down on Mount Sinai (q.v.), taking dictation from an angel or from God himself (see ORALITY). Nevertheless, the unknown author of the Book of Jubilees does not aim at replacing the Torah; he only wants to corroborate its text. In Exodus 19-24, Moses receives the Ten Commandments (see COMMANDMENT); in the Book of Jubilees God orders an angel to dictate, in addition, a complete record of the events from the beginning of creation until the erection of the sanctuary, which is to last for ever. Comparing these two accounts, the figure of Abraham undergoes some remarkable changes, too. In Genesis he is tempted by God who tells him to sacrifice Isaac. In the Book of Jubilees one reads about further temptations: When he is fourteen years old, Abraham recognizes the futility of idolatry; he forsakes his father and begins to venerate the one creator of the world and prays to him that he may save him from error. Without hesitating, he complies with God's order and leaves his country. While roaming through the holy land (see SYRIA; JERUSALEM), Abraham worships the creator in the way the Jews will do after Moses has delivered the tablets to them; he is a Mosaic Jew *avant la lettre* (Kratz, Wie Abraham Hebräisch lernte). Reflecting on what is expressed in the Book of Jubilees and what has been quoted above in a greatly abridged form, it is not surprising to note that Judaism does not accommodate itself to the Hellenistic Weltanschauung by referring to the figure of Moses; the divine law revealed to him on Mount Sinai obviously segregates Judaism from any other community and plays against the cosmopolitan ethos of Hellenism.

It is Abraham, therefore, father of a powerful people and the man chosen by God to bear witness to his will to bless humankind as a whole (see GRACE; BLESSING; ELECTION), who proves most attractive as a symbol of religious universalism compatible with the cosmopolitanism then penetrating Judaism. Whoever will be well-meaning towards Abraham and his offspring will pass his life in happiness (*Gen* 12:3). It is this interpretation of the figure of Abraham that Philo has in mind when writing his treatise *De Deo,* where he unfolds his ideas about the creator and his relationship to the universe. The God of the Pentateuch creates the world; he expels Adam and Eve (q.v.) from paradise (q.v.); later he annihilates the sinful, saving only Noah (q.v.) and his family to make a new start for human history, a history which culminates in Moses' encounter with him on Mount Sinai (see THEOPHANY). This is the internal logic of the events as narrated in Genesis and Exodus; taking possession of the holy land (see SACRED PRECINCTS) means the fulfillment of divinely-guided history and the god who has caused those events to happen is the god of Israel (see CHILDREN OF ISRAEL). But now, centuries after the composition of the Pentateuch, the perception of the world has changed and the image of the creator has changed, too.

The Septuagint refers to God as *kyrios* and as *theos*. Do these two names point to different beings? Philo asks himself in *De specialibus legibus*. He answers in the negative. It is due to God's remoteness from the world that people discern the different ways in which God's overwhelming creative power takes effect within the universe (see NATURE AS SIGNS). Therefore humans give him names with reference to the different ways of his acting, names that no longer point to Israel, his people, but to the cosmos as a whole, as Philo expounded in *De Deo*. The God of the Pentateuch has become a universal deity; he might still maintain a special relationship with Israel, but his never-ceasing creative actions pertain to the universe and to humanity as a whole, regardless of nationality or place of dwelling (see STRANGERS AND FOREIGNERS). When God reveals himself to Moses in the burning bush, the prophet asks him in whose name he is to accompany the Israelites out of Egypt and God answers: "I am,"or "I shall be," "who I shall be." In the Septuagint this sentence is rendered as *Ego eimi ho ōn,* "I am the existing one." This translation of the somewhat enigmatic Hebrew phrase of Exodus 3:14 is indicative of the changed conception of the creator that we have just outlined, and it is in this way that Philo interprets it in *De specialibus legibus*. God discloses his identity by stressing the personal character of himself — *ho ōn,* not *to on* — but at the same time he remains the hidden one, who himself cannot be perceived by man in this world (see FACE OF GOD; ANTHROPOMORPHISM). The fact that God is the existing one can only be known indirectly, by regarding the effects of his uninterrupted creative actions which constitute the cosmos, as Philo tells us in his treatise *De Deo* (Siegert, Abrahams

Gottesvision, 79). As the builder and indefatigable ruler of the cosmos the "existing one" is as near to the Israelites as to any other people regardless of their paganism, the history of Israel being just one sign among innumerable others of his being at work (see SIGNS; SHEKHINAH).

Attention can now be turned back to the Qur᾿ān. In the famous sūra "The Star" (Sūrat al-Najm, Q 53), Muḥammad relates the two visions (q.v.) he has had and connects them to his understanding of the divine. This sūra proved problematic for later Muslim commentators who grappled with the question of God's invisibility in this world and, as a rule, declared that it was the angel Gabriel (q.v.) who had appeared to Muḥammad — an interpretation that retrojects conceptions developed by the Prophet at a later date to an earlier time. In Q 53, the Qur᾿ān speaks frankly about Muḥammad's encounter with the one God, repudiating the reproaches of Muḥammad's fellow Meccan citizens who consider him a fool for what he relates (see OPPOSITION TO MUḤAMMAD). But what he relates is nothing but "an inspiration he is inspired with, taught by one, strong in power, forceful. He stood straight, upon the high horizon, then he drew near and let himself down, until he was two bow-lengths off or nearer and inspired to his servant what he inspired. The heart (q.v.) did not falsify what it saw. Do you debate with him as to what he sees? He saw him, too, at a second descent, by the lote tree at the nearest boundary, near which is the garden of the abode (see GARDENS; TREES; AGRICULTURE AND VEGETATION), when the lote tree was strangely enveloped. The eye turned not aside nor passed its limits. Verily, he saw one of the greatest signs (q.v.) of his lord" (q.v.; Q 53:4-18).

The following verses (q.v.) in the same sūra (Q 53:19-30), denouncing al-Lāt, al-ʿUzzā, and Manāt, three of the goddesses worshipped in pagan Mecca (see SOUTH ARABIA, RELIGIONS IN PRE-ISLAMIC), as powerless names, might be a later insertion, as Bell suggests. The argument made against their divine character is in keeping with the pagan milieu in which daughters were not much appreciated (see CHILDREN; INFANTICIDE; GENDER; WOMEN AND THE QUR᾿ĀN; PATRIARCHY). Thus ascribing daughters to God, the mighty one, is tantamount to giving offence to him. After this subject has been discussed at length, touching upon the male gender of the angels and emphasizing the incomparable power of the lord (see POWER AND IMPOTENCE), Muḥammad embarks on a description of the extent to which God governs the cosmos (Q 53:33-48): "Have you considered him who turns his back, gives little and is niggardly? Is knowledge of the unseen with him so that he sees? Or has he been told of what is in the pages of Moses, and Abraham who fully performed (his task; see BOOK; HEAVENLY BOOK)? That no burden-bearer bears the burden of another one; that man gets exactly (the result of) his striving; and that (the result of) his striving will in the end be seen; then he will be recompensed with the fullest recompense (see REWARD AND PUNISHMENT); that to your lord one comes at last; that it is he who causes laughter (q.v.) and weeping (q.v.); that it is he who causes to die and causes to live (see DEATH AND THE DEAD; LIFE; PAIRS AND PAIRING); that he created the pairs, male and female, from a drop emitted in desire; that upon him it rests to produce a second time (see RESURRECTION); that it is he who makes rich and gives possession (see WEALTH; PROPERTY)."

In the same manner the lord directs history (see HISTORY AND THE QUR᾿ĀN; GENERATIONS). It is he who destroyed the peoples of ʿĀd (q.v.) and Thamūd (q.v.) and who drowned the people of Noah (see DROWNING) after he had ordered him to warn them against their frivolous way of life (see PUNISHMENT STORIES; CHASTISEMENT AND PUNISHMENT). One cannot cast doubt on the overwhelming power of the lord, who now has summoned Muḥammad to warn his countrymen, for the day of judgment has drawn near (cf. Q 53:50-8; see LAST JUDGMENT; APOCALYPSE).

This is the content of Q 53, to the exclusion of the passages identified as late insertions by R. Bell. The text brings to the fore the main theological subjects of the Hellenistic interpretation of Abraham's religious experiences pointed out above: The lord reveals himself to Muḥammad as the mighty one, who not only determines every being's fate (q.v.; see also DESTINY) but also the history of humankind as a whole; his power cannot be resisted, therefore it is wise to comply with his ordinances. What is added to this conception of the divine is Muḥammad's prophetic self-confidence: he alludes to Noah as his predecessor, a topic which is displayed at some length in Q 71 (Sūrat Nūḥ, "Noah") with clear reference to his failure with the Meccans. Furthermore, it should be remembered that both Moses and Abraham are said to have received "pages." When one reflects on the following verses, one must conclude that those "pages" did not contain the divine law (see LAW AND THE QUR'ĀN), but were registers of events to come and, perhaps, of God's judgment (q.v.) on those who had lived sinful lives (see VIRTUES AND VICES, COMMANDING AND FORBIDDING; EVIL DEEDS). The seeds of the theological question about the extent of a human's capacity to determine his or her own actions (see FREEDOM AND PREDESTINATION) can be discerned in this qur'ānic passage; later on they will germinate in Medina, as shall be seen. Suffice it here to remark that Q 53:38-9 ("That no burden-bearer...") will later, in Khārijī polemics, be interpreted as evidence of human responsibility for actions — which, in Khārijī thought (see KHĀRIJĪS), originates in the human capacity to do so. This is a striking example of distorting the original meaning of a qur'ānic passage to accord with political circumstances (see POLITICS AND THE QUR'ĀN).

In comparison with Q 53 the verses of Q 6 quoted above do not, at first sight, prove to be indicative of the Qur'ān's identification of Muḥammad with Abraham. The story is told of how Abraham came to know the identity of the one creator, and there are themes in this passage that can be traced back to what is told in the Book of Jubilees: Abraham denounces idolatry, thereby kindling the wrath of his people. But there is another remarkable detail in this passage. Q 6:75 seems to be an enigmatic insertion interrupting the flow of the narrative: "Thus do we show Abraham (our) holding sway over the heavens and the earth, and (it is) in order that he may be one of the convinced." Such a guiding vision of God is the necessary condition for knowing him (see INTELLECT). This knowledge cannot be deduced from nature or from the course of history through human reflection (see REFLECTION AND DELIBERATION). On the contrary, humans must be guided by the creator to be open to deliberation of the kind expounded in the following verses. The cosmos as a whole is a sign of God's unceasing creative power, but humans are not able to decipher this sign without his assistance. That means that the creator is not an anonymous force asserting itself in this world in which humans must find access to some understanding of its nature; if the human mind were restricted to its own very deficient capacities, it would fail. The creator, as conceived of by Philo and as he reveals himself to Abraham in Q 6, is the existing one — *ho ōn* — i.e. he has an individuality, a personal character. Certainly his individuality is unfathomable, but because of this personal character God is characterized by volition, too. It was his intention to show Abraham his all-effecting being, as it is now his intention to reveal himself to Muḥammad. Were it not for God's intention, Abraham would not have been one of the guided ones; he would have gone astray like his countrymen. One must also admit that the creator's volition may be to the detriment of humanity; this possibly grievous consequence of the Abrahamic conception of God is hinted at in Q 6:81: idolatry is not forbidden because it proves futile; it must be dismissed from one's mind because God has not sent down any authority for it. Indirectly, the question of independent human reasoning is raised here and this shall be touched upon.

The last subject to mention when treating the position of Islam within the religious history of late antiquity is the cult of Abraham. As Sozomenos told us, there was a sort of pagan pilgrimage to the grove of Mamre. One might suppose that the cult of Mamre was emulated at Mecca; the sources on the — legendary — history of Mecca and the Quraysh (q.v.) abound in references to the influence of Palestine and Syria on the Ḥijāz, and tell us a lot about the Quraysh interest in the area on the northwestern fringe of the peninsula. Once more, it is necessary to look at Q 6: At that crucial moment when Abraham becomes aware of the futility of idolatry he sets "(his) face towards him who opened up *(faṭara)* the heavens and the earth, as a *ḥanīf*" (Q 6:79) and he dissociates himself from polytheism. Turning one's face towards the lord is the spontaneous corollary of knowing the creator. As a rule, this gesture is expressed in the Qurʾān by the verb *aslama,* and the person who has gained such knowledge is referred to as *ḥanīf:* "Who is better with regard to his religious practice *(dīn)* than he who surrenders *(aslama)* his face to God, doing good meanwhile (see GOOD DEEDS), and follows the creed *(milla)* of Abraham as a *ḥanīf*?" (Q 4:125; see also RELIGION). The *ḥanīf*s are men who transform into a ritual the singular gesture indicating their attainment of true knowledge (see RITUAL AND THE QURʾĀN); they reiterate that gesture several times a day, thus confirming that overwhelming truth and giving it a stability which is required in order to conduct their lives in keeping with it. The ritual prayer (q.v.), the center of Muslim religiosity, has its roots immediately in the history of Abraham, as it evolved in late antiquity. Except for the meager information in Sozomenos there seems to be no further evidence about the rites of the pagan cult of Abraham. But it is known for certain that the *ṣalāt* was not initiated by Muḥammad. It was the *ḥanīf* Zayd b. ʿAmr who used to practice it at Mecca. In al-Shām he had become acquainted with the Abrahamic veneration of the one God; back in Mecca, he preached against idolatry and performed a *ṣalāt* every evening (Nagel, Abraham in Mecca, 143).

Abraham is the key figure who leads us to a better understanding of the place of Islam in religious history. Using this key figure, fundamental theological conceptions of the Qurʾān can be related to an amalgam of ideas of Jewish and Hellenistic origin: God is the one creator and untiring governor of the cosmos; he determines everything; humanity is guided to know him according to his volition and after that people interpret everything in the universe with respect to this knowledge; the ritual of prayer is symbolic of the act of attaining that ultimate knowledge and testifies to an individual's willingness to live his life before the face of the One.

The main theological themes of the Qurʾān: God and creation

A very short summary of the qurʾānic idea of the divine is found in Q 112:1-3: "Say: 'He is God, one, God, the uniform one *(al-ṣamad)*; he brought not forth, nor has he been brought forth; co-equal with him there has never been any one.'" God is the one and uniform god; that means there is nothing with him or in him which is not of the divine, transcendent nature of his essence and for that reason he cannot be equal to any created being. The anti-Christian polemical tone of these verses is evident (see POLEMIC AND POLEMICAL LANGUAGE).

The almost dogmatic statement in Q 112 does not, however, mark the starting-point of qurʾānic theological reflection. In the earliest revelations pure monotheism is not called for. Those who listen to Muḥammad's preaching — one should avoid speaking of "the Meccans" at that stage of his career — are urged to pay veneration to the "lord, the most high." A human must purify himself (see CLEANLINESS AND ABLUTION), a very prominent demand, especially in the early sūras, because he is thought to have earned his wealth in an unlawful manner (see LAWFUL AND UNLAWFUL). Though one may do more than just one's duty with respect to this demand, one must not ask God for any compensation. One is to do good to the poor (see POVERTY AND THE POOR) simply "out of desire for the countenance of one's lord, the most high" (Q 92:20). The "countenance," literally the face of God, in this early revelation and also in later qurʾānic speech (e.g. Q 13:22) is the *pars-pro-toto* expression by which God's transcendent being is rendered conceivable in human thought. When the process of recognizing the oneness of the creator attains its aim, as has been demonstrated by Abraham, one turns one's face to God, thus establishing a face-to-face relationship with him, and this relationship is renewed every time one devotes oneself to one's ritual duties. "The lord, the most high," of course, still is not the One whom Q 112 preaches in uncompromising words. "The most high lord" implies there are "less high" divine beings. Muḥammad had to make his way to absolute clarity in this matter through painful struggles, which are echoed in Q 53 and in the famous story about the so-called Satanic verses (q.v.). Though Q 112 is an unmistakable plea for radical monotheism and untainted transcendence and therefore sheds at least some light on Q 92:20 — to which Q 87:1 should be added —, the face-to-face concept of that early revelation has been preserved and proves fundamental in the various kinds of Muslim ritual. There is thus a characteristic tension between a fully elaborated intellectual monotheism, on the one hand, and an eager search for some kind of immanence that is tolerable within the framework of sound theological reasoning and indispensable for an emotional experience of the ritual, on the other. This tension may be deduced from Muḥammad's career because he grew up in a polytheistic milieu; but it may also be due to the conception of the continuously acting creator that had evolved in late antiquity, as has been shown above. At any rate, this tension, present in the qurʾānic interpretation of deity, will encroach on Muslim theological speculation and will cause a rupture between pure metaphysics and the study of the *sharīʿa*, i.e. "applied theology."

"Glorify (see GLORY; GLORIFICATION OF GOD) the name of your lord (see BASMALA) the most high, who created and formed, who assigned power and guided, who brought forth the pasture, then made it blackened drift" (Q 87:1-4). Already the "lord, most high" is the one power that determines everything in this world, the good and the bad things. His image is that of a sovereign governor who rules without paying attention to the benefit of his subjects; or at least they are not in a position to discern the motives behind his decree. According to his volition, which is inaccessible to human reason, he created the world out of nothing, and since that time he has been caring for it, even looking after the tiniest details. The Qurʾān frequently stresses this idea, making use of the impressive picture of a ruler sitting on his throne (see THRONE OF GOD; KINGS AND RULERS): this is the posture befitting an omnipotent creator. By comparison with this idea, the reminiscence of creation in biblical history is rather shadowy: "We have created the heavens and the earth and what is between them in six days (see DAY; DAYS OF GOD), without being affected by fatigue (see SLEEP; SABBATH)." Thus reads Q 50:38. Here God's indefatigability is pointed out in order to encourage Muḥammad to perform the prayers assiduously. In other passages concerned with creation, God is referred to as "your lord" (Q 7:54; 10:3), "God" (Q 32:4), or "he" (cf. Q 11:7; 25:59; 57:4). In each of these six references we are told nothing more than that God created the world (q.v.) in six days; what God did on each of these days is passed over in silence. But in each case God's throne is mentioned, e.g. Q 7:54: "Verily your lord is God, who created the heavens and the earth in six days, then seated himself on the throne causing the night to cover the day, following it quickly, and the sun and the moon and the stars, subjected to service by his command; is it not his to create and to command? Blessed be God, lord of the worlds." Only in Q 11:7 is there a faint reminder of what the Bible says about creation: "He it is who created the heavens and the earth in six days, and his throne was upon the water...." But again it is the throne, symbol of God's unquestionable sovereignty, that Muḥammad bears in mind and the Qurʾān employs — not the biblical "spirit" (q.v.) of God, which seems less instrumental in portraying the creator as the ruler of an empire.

In the qurʾānic text the idea of continuous creation is closely connected with two further theological themes: the first is that God's incessant creative action is indicative of his all-embracing care for his world, and the second that human beings should consider this care as an irrefutable proof of the truth of resurrection and final judgment. To begin with the first theme, the Qurʾān says that God's creative action is tantamount to his unlimited mercy (q.v.); both are almost synonymous in the qurʾānic conception of the creator. The famous Q 55 (Sūrat al-Raḥmān, "The Merciful") bears witness to this most vividly: The merciful lord created this wonderful world to the benefit of humankind; neither they nor the jinn (q.v.) can deny this; everyone in this world will pass away, except "the face of your lord full of glory" (*dhū l-jalāli wa-l-ikrāmi,* Q 55:27); "Those in the heavens and the earth make request of him, each day he [is engaged] in something.... O company of jinn and men *(al-ins),* if you are capable of passing through any of the regions of the heavens and the earth, pass through; you will not pass through without authorization... There will be sent upon you a flame of fire and smoke, and you two will not find help... Then when the heaven is rent and becomes rosy like [burning] oil, which then of the benefits of your lord will you two count false?" (Q 55:29-38).

No creature can act without God's permission, and when he decides to destroy this world, thereby doing the utmost harm to humankind, even this will be to humanity's benefit; it will be part of God's mercy. In addition to that, God's capacity for incessant creative action is the Prophet's best argument to warn his unbelieving countrymen about resurrection and judgment; to quote Q 11:7 again, this time passing to its concluding phrases: "... and his throne was upon the water; that he might try you as to which of you is best in deed (see TRIAL; TRUST AND PATIENCE). If you say: 'Verily you will be raised up after death!' those who have disbelieved will say: 'This is only magic (q.v.) manifest....'"

We have already pointed to the contradiction which arises from the assumption that the totally transcendent creator to whom nothing is equal (Q 42:11) is simultaneously experienced as the omniscient and wise one who takes care of human welfare and is therefore "nearer to him [each person] than [his] jugular vein" (Q 50:16; see ARTERY AND VEIN). Is there anything bridging the gap between transcendence and immanence, which is felt already in Philo's idea of *ho ōn?*

"God it is who created the heavens and the earth and what is between them in six days, and then sat firm upon the throne — apart from him you have neither patron nor intercessor (see CLIENTS AND CLIENTAGE; FRIENDS AND FRIENDSHIP; INTERCESSION); will you not then be reminded? He manages the affair from the heaven to the earth, then it mounts up to him in a day, the length of which is a thousand years as you reckon" (Q 32:4-5). God knows everything, whether concealed or open; his creation testifies to his unsurpassable skill. These verses use the Arabic word *amr* that refers to an essence which is capable of linking God's creative power to the results of its activity, thus making his continuous determining of this world conceivable to humanity. Bell translates *amr* with "affair" (cf. Q 10:3; 16:1; 17:85; 97:4) or "command" (Q 7:54), a rendering which, in the opinion of the present writer, does not suit the qur᾿ānic meaning of the word. To grasp the idea expressed by the term let us look at the following two qur᾿ānic passages: "The *amr* of God has come, seek not to hasten it; glory be to him and exalted be he above all that they associate [with him]!" (Q 16:1). The *amr* of God has come; it is now present in his work and it is just for this *amr* that God is the exalted One. *Amr* is something like his decree, an uninterrupted influx of his volition into this world. There is no clear statement as to the ontology of *amr*. But as soon as the Prophet's understanding of the revelation becomes connected with the idea of transmitting a heavenly book, the term is interpreted as denoting God's all-embracing, incessant determination of things in this world. Part of this *amr* is the "spirit" manifest in the words of the qur᾿ānic revelation: "They ask you about the spirit; say: 'The spirit belongs to my lord's *amr*, but you have no knowledge bestowed upon you except a little'" (Q 17:85; see also HOLY SPIRIT). When dealing with prophecy below, this question will be revisited.

Humankind

The contradiction within Muḥammad's conception of the divine — the transcendent, inaccessible lord, essentially different from his creation versus the omnipresent and omniscient care-taker — reasserts itself within the qur᾿ānic understanding of humankind, and the twofold roots of qur᾿ānic theology become more palpable in this context. Q 32:5-9 can serve as a starting-point of analysis: "He manages the *amr* from the heaven to the earth... That is the knower of the hidden and the revealed, the sublime *(al-ʿazīz),* the compassionate, who has made well everything that he has created. He created man at the first from clay; then appointed his progeny to be from an extract of a base fluid. Then he formed him and breathed into him of his spirit, and gave you hearing and sight (see HEARING AND DEAFNESS; VISION AND BLINDNESS; SEEING AND HEARING; EYES; EARS) and hearts — little gratitude (see GRATITUDE AND INGRATITUDE) do you show." The shaping of humans means the natural process of procreation, as can be inferred from many other passages of the Qurʾān (see BIOLOGY AS THE CREATION AND STAGES OF LIFE; SEX AND SEXUALITY). Yet there seems to have been a remarkable development of this conception in the Qurʾān. In the very early sūras only natural procreation is mentioned (Q 53:45f.; 75:37-9; 77:20-3; 86:5-7); the growth of the embryo in the womb (q.v.) is the clearest evidence of God's creative power (Q 96:2). Then the Genesis account of the history of the creation of man finds its way into Muḥammad's revelations (see UMMĪ).

In addition to Q 32:5-9 quoted above, Q 18:37, 22:5, 23:12, and 40:67 must be considered; in each case God creates man from clay and immediately after that makes his "progeny from an extract of a base fluid *(nuṭfa)*." At the outset of Muḥammad's prophetic career, the natural world and course of nature are the best evidence of the creator's activity; there seems in the qurʾānic revelations to be no place for human singularity, which would separate humans to some extent from the rest of created beings. Then this idea is introduced into the qurʾānic reasoning by way of the biblical traditions that go back to Genesis: "At first" man is formed out of clay. God breathes the spirit into him, thus endowing him with "hearing and sight and a heart," i.e. with reason. It is this act of being created from clay which establishes humankind's special relationship with God, as expressed several times in the Qurʾān: By shaping the human being from clay before the beginning of mundane history God has honored him by giving him his special attention; no other beings were considered worthy of a primordial shaping before being initiated into the continuous process of creation. It is for this reason that God orders the angels to prostrate themselves before Adam (see BOWING AND PROSTRATION). All except Iblīs (see DEVIL), who deems himself nobler than Adam, obey; therefore God expels Iblīs from paradise (q.v.): "'Verily you are stoned *(rajīm;* see STONING) and upon you is the curse (q.v.) until the day of judgment.' (Iblīs) said: 'O my lord, grant me respite then till the day of their being raised up.' (God) said: 'You are one of the respited *(munẓarīn)* till the day of the time appointed.' (Iblīs) said: 'O my lord, as you have perverted me, I will make things appear beautiful to them in the earth, and I will pervert *(aghwā)* them all together, except those of them who are your single-hearted *(al-mukhlaṣīn)* servants" (Q 15:34-40; see SERVANT; FALL OF MAN). This is granted to Iblīs by God but his faithful servants will not be seduced; they will enjoy paradise in the hereafter, whereas the perverted will suffer eternal pain (see SUFFERING) in hell (*jahannam,* Q 15:28-40; cf. 38:71-85; see HELL AND HELLFIRE).

To what extent is the human being burdened with individual responsibility (q.v.)? This question arises when one reads the story in which humans are declared subject to a bet made by their creator and Satan. Those who are God's servants will resist the seducer's suggestions, the others will not — the individual's fate after the day of judgment seems to be predetermined. Here one should recall that for a human to know the one creator is due to God's volition, too. Thus humans are not just part of nature, whose growing and passing away is the manifestation of God's decree in this world; humans must do something about good and evil (q.v.), otherwise there would be no reason for judgment (q.v.), for eternal reward or punishment. A creator who withdraws from his work at least temporarily, thus asserting his transcendence, would be appreciated as a neutral judge of humans; but what about the "creator of everything" — the sinful acts of his creature included — a creator nearer to each human than his jugular vein? In fact, qur'ānic theology has no systematic conception of the human being as a responsible actor. One may suppose that this deficiency is due to the qur'ānic understanding of the divine as analyzed above. God's *amr,* permeating everything extant in the cosmos, reminds one of something like pagan animism or fatalism, as interpreted in the light of the belief in the one creator and further overshadowed by reminiscences of the biblical tradition, which tends to give prominence to individual responsibility.

In the *sīra,* the Prophet's Meccan enemies sometimes call him a Sabian (q.v.; see e.g. Balādhurī, *Ansāb,* v, 14; see also RELIGIOUS PLURALISM AND THE QUR'ĀN). Although this may be for polemical reasons, there is an interesting remark in al-Shahrastānī (fl. sixth/twelfth cent.) that comments on the religion of the ancient Sabians which, as must be inferred from the context, was well-known in Arabia in Muḥammad's time. The Sabians, al-Shahrastānī tells us, believe in the acquisition *(kasb)* of actions whereas the *ḥanīf*s "maintained the innate disposition of man" *(fiṭra).* Turning to the Qur'ān we find evidence of both ideas. The term *kasb* occurs very often, e.g.: "But how (will it be) when we gather them to a day of which there is no doubt, and each one will be paid in full what he has acquired *(kasabat),* without being wronged?"(Q 3:25; cf. 2:281 and many other references). Acquisition is not to be understood as the actions of human beings directed by their own will and performed according to their own deliberations. This absence of self-determination must be inferred from God's comprehensive care for his creation and creatures; it is also clearly pronounced in the Qur'ān itself: "They have no power over anything that they may have acquired, and God does not guide the people of the unbelievers" (Q 2:264). It is God who allots the means of subsistence *(rizq):* "My lord makes generous provision for whom he wills, or stints, but most of the people have no knowledge" (Q 34:36; numerous other references). Following the theological discussion that was to evolve in the first centuries after the Prophet's death, the "acquisition of actions" has to be interpreted as the manifestation of God's decree *(amr)* to be discerned when one observes a certain individual; in fact, the individual is nothing but the substance needed for making God's incessant acts of governing perceptible in this world and to its inhabitants. Insofar as it is the individual who makes perceptible a certain act wrought by God, this individual acquires the respective act. One might argue that in the Qur'ān the impersonal power of fate has assumed the character of a series of the personalized orders of the creator, tailored for the individual on his or her way through this life.

The second idea mentioned by al-Sharastānī claims a certain disposition which is innate and unchangeable in human beings; this *fiṭra,* says he, is part of the belief of the *ḥanīf*s, who, as can be concluded from the Qur'ān (cf. Q 16:120), are the followers of Abraham's ritual. *Fiṭra* only occurs once, in Q 30:30, and dates back to the middle or even late Meccan period of Muḥammad's career: "Set your face towards religious practice as a *ḥanīf* — the innate disposition laid down by God upon which he has created people *(nās)*; there is no alteration of the creation of God. This is the eternal religious practice, but most of the people do not know." Looking back at the story of how Abraham came to know the one creator (Q 6:74-83) and how he responded to the vision granted to him, we are now in a position to fathom its meaning: Of course, everything one does is wrought by God; this is borne out by the idea of acquisition; but the frightening consequences of this conception are warded off by the establishment of Islam, the face-to-face relationship between humans and their creator. This relationship, stabilized by ritual — "Set your face towards religious practice," has to occupy the center of human life; one has to be aware of God's untiring activity, has to suppress every impulse of self-conceit including the misperception that one's actions are one's own. Bearing this in mind, acquisition of good or evil will no longer be a cause of concern: Professing and living Islam is tantamount to preserving the innate disposition un-spoilt; Islam eclipses the perpetual challenge of right or wrong. The function of ritual in Muslim life and its preeminence over dogmatic ethics become apparent. What counts most is a human's trustful devotion to his creator, a behavior which almost automatically will save him from doing evil: "Recite what has been suggested to you of the book (q.v.), and observe the prayer, for the prayer restrains from indecency (*al-faḥshāʾ*; see ADULTERY AND FORNICATION) and what is disreputable (*al-munkar*), and surely the remembrance (*dhikr*) of God is greater..." (Q 29:45).

Muslim edifying literature dwells at length upon the importance of unlimited devotion to God's actions, on the necessity of strict observance of the ritual and on remembering the creator, which is developed into a refined skill of continuous spiritual presence before him. This leads us back to reason and its role in human life. In accordance with the concepts of *kasb* and *fiṭra*, reason could not serve as a tool to find one's way through the activities and dangers of this world. As must be inferred from the precedent of Satan's condemnation, the function of reason is only to justify and effect total obedience to God's orders: Satan refused to prostrate himself before Adam, who had been made of clay, explaining his refusal by pointing out that his own nature, made of fire, was nobler than Adam's (Q 38:76). Reasoning, in this case within the framework of analogy (see LITERARY STRUCTURES AND THE QURʾĀN), is subordinate to God's will, as has already been elucidated in the story of Abraham's way to the knowledge of the one creator. It is not because of Abraham's reasoning that idolatry is futile, but because God does not authorize human beings to practice idolatry. Keeping to the gist of this argument, humans could discern that their reasoning, if not immediately guided by God, may be successful as measured by the yardstick of mundane affairs, but its success according to the measure of the creator remains inherently doubtful. Success in mundane affairs may be tantamount to sin; for instance, a cunning businessman might multiply his profit by giving interest-bearing loans, thus trying to acquire more than the livelihood (*rizq*, e.g. Q 16:71) God had allotted to him (see USURY; TRADE AND COMMERCE). Such reasoning means to turn one's face away from God and to become entangled in passions for created things. It is from this point of view that usury (*ribā*) is prohibited. There is only one exception to this rule: fighting (q.v.) for the victory (q.v.) of God's Prophet and his community means lending to God a good loan (see DEBT), which he will double (Q 57:10-11; see also EXPEDITIONS AND BATTLES; JIHĀD). To encourage the believers to do so, Q 9:111 was revealed: "God has bought from the believers their persons and their goods at the price of the garden (q.v.; in store) for them, fighting in the way of God and killing and being killed (see BLOODSHED) — a promise (see also OATHS; CONTRACTS AND ALLIANCES; BREAKING TRUSTS AND CONTRACTS) binding upon him in the Torah (q.v.), the Gospel (q.v.), and the Qurʾān; and who fulfils his covenant (q.v.) better than God? So rejoice in the bargain you have made with him…."

Faith (q.v.; *īmān*) is proved by ruthless fighting against the non-Muslim enemies (q.v.). Those of the Prophet's adherents who do not protect their own lives will be superior to their fellows (e.g. Q 4:96) in the hereafter (see MARTYRS); they are sure to be rewarded with paradise, whereas normally God grants high ranks in the world to come according to his own impenetrable discretion (e.g. Q 12:76). In any case, during the decisive years of struggle the Qurʾān came to allude to the crucial theological subject of a person's justification by way of individual merit, an idea that proves substantially alien to the fundamental conception of the divine underlying Islam.

Prophecy

This is an illuminating example of the wide range within which the qurʾānic theological conceptions would oscillate according to the circumstances (see PROPHETS AND PROPHETHOOD). The same is true of the understanding of prophecy, which undergoes far-reaching changes over the life of the Prophet and the qurʾānic revelations. Here these changes will only be discussed as far as theology is concerned. A first step will embark on a short inquiry into the scope of knowledge transmitted to humankind through revelation; a second will attempt to explain the qurʾānic concepts of the relationship between transcendence and immanence in the context of the various stages of Muḥammad's prophetic career.

God creates Adam to be his vicegerent in this world. To fulfill this duty, Adam is dependent on a sufficient amount of skill, which, as has been shown, he cannot acquire on his own; he needs divine guidance. Accordingly, the creator does not withhold knowledge from him: "[God] taught Adam all the names. Then he mustered [all things created] before the angels and said: 'Tell me the names of these, if you speak the truth!' They said: 'Glory be to you! We have no knowledge but what you have taught us (see TEACHING; IGNORANCE). You are the knowing, the wise (see WISDOM).' He said: 'O Adam, tell them the names [of the things created]!' Then when Adam told them the names, God said: 'Did I not say to you that I know the secret [things] of the heavens and the earth?'…" (Q 2:31-3).

Adam, considered as the first prophet, received complete knowledge of everything in this world. Therefore he is capable of being the creator's vicegerent; he is to act within God's cosmos in accordance with the divine decree, continuously remaining face to face with God. As a prophet, Adam is granted the knowledge of which humanity is destined to make use. Revelation means the act of granting that knowledge, which is not specified as divine or theological but pertains to all mundane affairs as well as to ritual and eschatology (q.v.) and to those attributes of God that human beings are allowed to understand.

Knowledge transmitted by revelation is as all-embracing as God's decree and its effects are manifest everywhere in the cosmos (see COSMOLOGY AND THE QURʾĀN). We have already stated that in the qurʾānic view revelation is closely related to the concept of *amr.* This relationship becomes even more apparent if we analyze the meaning of the Arabic root *w-ḥ-y,* which is used throughout the Qurʾān, even at an early stage, to describe the event of revelation: Abraham was a *ḥanīf:* "We bestowed upon him in this world a goodly (portion), and verily, in the hereafter he is among the upright. Then we suggested *(awḥaynā)* to you: 'Follow the creed of Abraham, as a *ḥanīf,* and he was not of the polytheists!'" (Q 16:122-3; cf. 16:120). It should be noted that in this and related contexts (e.g. Q 12:15), translating *w-ḥ-y* as "suggestion," as Bell does, does not imply a specific fixed wording, suitable for a heavenly book (q.v.). In other cases (e.g. Q 7:117 and 160) the expression is followed by God's order reflecting an actual situation: "We suggested to [Noah]: Make the ship under our eye and according to our suggestion..." (Q 23:27; see ARK). Yet it is not only the prophets who receive divine suggestions: "(God) finished them (as) seven heavens and inspired *(awḥā)* each heaven [with] its command" (*amr,* Q 41:12).

From perhaps the beginning of the second half of the Meccan revelations, there is a remarkable change in the conception of prophecy, though the older concept is never completely abandoned: "Thus we have suggested to you a spirit *(rūḥ)* belonging to our affair *(amr).* You did not [formerly] know what the book and the faith were. But we have made it a light (q.v.) by which we guide whomsoever we please of our servants, and verily you will guide to a straight path, the path of God..." (Q 42:52-3; see PATH OR WAY). Here "suggestion" is more than a single command and more than God's decree; it has become the text of a law teaching humans to behave according to the creator's prescriptions, a text suitable to be written down in a book (see LITERACY; ILLITERACY). Still, "suggestions" have their origin in the realm of *amr* which is hidden from human senses (cf. Q 3:44; 11:49; 12:102), but part of this *amr* makes itself manifest as a holy message valid beyond time (q.v.). The creator, at work without interruption, becomes more and more personalized as the revelations progress; the human beings are gradually deprived of their shelter in the midst of nature, though they still remain completely dependent on God's determination; the feeling of existential insecurity arising from this loss of sheltering is compensated for by turning to God *(islām)* and this compensation may be enhanced by delivering oneself to fighting for the sake of God (Q 9:111) or to incessant remembrance of him (Q 29:45). At this critical stage of the evolution of qur'ānic theological conceptions, the Prophet is seen to become more than a warner — namely the transmitter of divine law, summoned by the creator to pronounce his legislation, his guidance of the obedient and his punishment of the disobedient. This legislation, together with the record of divine guidance and punishment, are to be recited as a heavenly book (see PRESERVED TABLET).

In the Qur'ān there are traces of a discussion between Muḥammad and the Meccans about such a heavenly book. The Prophet's enemies evidently argued that he should ascend to heaven in order to procure a divine message for them or for himself. In fact, al-Wāqidī (d. 207/822) relates that Muḥammad found himself raised into heaven (see ASCENSION) on the seventeenth of Ramaḍān (q.v.), some eighteen months before the *hijra,* which is dated to Ṣafar of the first year of the Muslim calendar (Ibn Saʿd, *Ṭabaqāt,* i/i, 143). "They say: 'We shall not give you credence till you cause a spring to bubble up for us from the earth (see SPRINGS AND FOUNTAINS; MIRACLES; MARVELS)... or you ascend into heaven; nor shall we give credence to your ascent until you bring down to us a writing *(kitāb)* which we may read'" (Q 17:90-3). It should be noted that now, near the end of Muḥammad's Meccan years, revelation tends to be conceived of as a sending down *(tanzīl)* of the divine message. The personalized God establishes personal relations with his messenger (q.v.); this is a very important innovation in the Prophet's view of himself and his mission. In Medina, where he is free of the sharp criticism of the Meccans, the far-reaching consequences of this innovation will be realized. The majority of the Meccans, it is true, were not much impressed by his claim to have received a divine book: "If we were to send down a book (written) upon parchment and they were to touch it with their hands, those who have disbelieved would say: This is nothing but magic manifest" (Q 6:7; see SCROLLS; SHEETS; WRITING AND WRITING MATERIALS). Even if God had made his messenger an angel, that angel must have assumed the shape of a human being in order to transmit the message, and therefore the Meccans would have rejected him as well. "Messengers have been mocked before you..." (Q 6:10; see MOCKERY).

Q 97 (Sūrat al-Qadr, "Night of Destiny/ Power"), celebrating the "Night of Power" (q.v.), seems to legitimate the new mode of revelation; in that night "the angels and the spirit (cf. Q 17:85) let themselves down, by the permission of their lord, [bringing] all kinds of divine decree" (*amr*, Q 97:4). In Medina, the month of Ramaḍān is chosen for commemorating the Prophet's vision which he had been granted eighteen months before leaving Mecca. As Q 2 (Sūrat al-Baqara, "The Cow") is said to have been revealed about eighteen months after his arrival in Medina, the famous verse of Q 2:185 may highlight the third anniversary of the event, now considered decisive for the Prophet's career. As an aside, the problem of the change in the understanding of revelation is closely related to the question of writing down the revealed texts, i.e. making a palpable book of "parchment" (see MUṢḤAF; MANUSCRIPTS OF THE QURʾĀN; EPIGRAPHY AND THE QURʾĀN). But since the focus here is the theological implications, it is only possible to discuss the last stage of Muḥammad's image of himself as a prophet.

It is evident that most of the qurʾānic texts dealing with divine legislation and with divine comments on actual situations the Prophet and his community endured are of Medinan origin. When reading these parts of the Qurʾān one gets the impression that the creator has become an alter ego of his Prophet. The formula "God and his messenger" is now smoothly incorporated in his speech. For instance, the Qurʾān enjoins his followers to pay unquestioned obedience to Muḥammad and to those he appoints to some duty or other: "O you who have believed, obey God and obey the messenger and those of you who have the command, and if you quarrel about anything, refer it to God and the messenger..." (Q 4:59; cf. 3:32, 132; 4:80; 8:24, 27). It is not surprising that this kind of revelation for a particular occasion (cf. Q 58:1; 59:2; 33:37-40) would be met with sharp criticism from the Medinan Jews (see NAḌĪR; QAYNUQĀʿ; QURAYẒA) — and on the part of some among the Aws and Khazraj (see TRIBES AND CLANS). It takes a considerable amount of credulity to believe in the divine origin of verses like those. But the Qurʾān stresses the certainty that Muḥammad is the messenger of the one personalized creator, whose *amr* has not ceased to be at work since time began and that part of this *amr* manifest in every affair has been transmitted to him through the spirit and thereby converted into human speech. The Qurʾān maintains this view against the Jews, who would have considered revelation an event which occurred in distant history, and against the skeptic pagans, by its praise for the one God of creation: "To God belongs what is in the heavens and the earth; verily God is the rich (*al-ghaniyy*), praiseworthy (see

PRAISE; LAUDATION). If all the trees in the earth were pens, and the sea with seven seas after it to swell it, the words of God (see WORD OF GOD) would not give out; verily God is sublime, wise" (Q 31:26-7; cf. 18:109).

Final remarks

Freeing oneself from the *petitio principii* that all Arabic literary tradition showing "qur'ānic" ideas and ascribed to authors prior or contemporary to Muḥammad must be a forgery (q.v.; see also CORRUPTION; MUSAYLIMA; PROVOCATION), one succeeds in setting into vivid relief the historical background of the intellectual world of early Islam as depicted in the Qur'ān. As expressed in the Qur'ān, Muḥammad's vision of God and the universe governed by him does not imply a history of salvation (q.v.). Therefore theology first of all is concerned with the cosmos and the creator manifesting himself in it and through it. His incessant creative activity may have been plausible even to the pagans; he revealed himself to Abraham, announcing the birth of a son to him, and it is for this impressive example of his all-embracing power, and perhaps for others similar to it, that humans should venerate him. Muḥammad felt that the Meccans fell short of this duty for several reasons, and when he was sure that he was summoned by the "lord, most high" to warn his countrymen against frivolous negligence towards the one power to which they owed their existence, he answered this call.

It is a reasonable assumption that in this situation Muḥammad would have looked for some elaborate theological tradition that could furnish him with a system of notions suitable to express his ideas. Eventually the belief of the *ḥanīf*s and their interpretation of Abraham's path to the knowledge of the one creator seemed to fit with his experiences. These tended to crystallize in the image of a highly personalized God who was on intimate terms with his Prophet, although he was to remain the transcendent omnipotent one. As for theology, this led to the contradictions outlined above, which lie at the base of later Muslim theological discussions. To attain to a more elaborate analysis of later discussions than has yet been achieved, a great deal of further research on the theological meaning of Muḥammad's message and its contemporary intellectual and spiritual background is necessary.

The following few lines may give an instructive, albeit superficial impression of what this means. Human beings cannot account for their actions because it is the one creator who makes them apparent in this world, and even if one were to endeavor to avoid a certain action, one could not escape God's decree. The *amr,* emanating from him into the cosmos, causes a human being to acquire *(kasaba)* that action. Later, Sunnī theology will discuss the problem of whether the capability of acquiring a certain action has been deposited in the individual human before that action comes about or whether it is granted to the individual by God simultaneously with the coming about of that action. The second view came to be preferred in Ash'arism, which is said to have carried predestination to its extreme. This, of course, is the opinion of the Westerner who has the problem of freedom of will in his mind; for him this is the idea which sets the standard for the evaluation of conceptions of humankind's position in this world. This is not the background of the Muslim view of the question. Their theological reasoning is based on the qur'ānic picture of the relationship between the creator and man. Nevertheless there are verses which seem to suggest one's responsibility for one's actions; therefore the freedom of will should be granted. "That day [the earth] will tell its news (q.v.), as your lord has prompted *(awḥā)* it; that day the people will come forward separately that they may be shown their works. Whoever has done a particle's weight of good, shall see it..." (Q 99:4-7; see WEIGHTS AND MEASURES; MEASUREMENT). This revelation dating from the early Meccan period can be considered valid evidence of each person's obligation to act according to his or her own decisions. Yet this line of argumentation is completely mistaken. The early Meccan passages of the Qurʾān do not plead at all for freedom of will. On the contrary, they advocate the all-embracing power of the creator's decree, and in Q 99 the believers are reminded of God's knowledge, which is all-embracing, too: On the day of judgment not a single action that has been "acquired" by a human being will be forgotten. "... No burden-bearer bears the burden of another;... man gets exactly [the result of] his striving" (Q 53:38f.). The one God "who causes to die, and causes to live... who makes rich and gives possession" (Q 53:44, 48) will look strictly into everybody's record of actions. It is only in Medina that the believers become responsible for a certain type of action, i.e. those greatly needed heroic deeds that would save Islam from annihilation. The believers now are summoned to sell their lives to God who will make them enter paradise as a recompense for fighting the enemies of Islam. It is remarkable that some Muslim scholars hold that Q 99 belongs to this Medinan period of Muḥammad's life. They seem to be conscious of the possibility of interpreting Q 99 as an allusion to one's responsibility for one's actions and one's fate in the hereafter. Nevertheless, the Westerner must be aware of the fact that verses like Q 99 or Q 53:38 do not aim at liberating the human being from divine decree; they only point to a rather limited range of actions left to human choice because God "has sent down authority" (cf. Q 6:81) for the individual to do them.

Therefore the question of human freedom of will in Muslim theology is neither concerned with some capacity of reason and power independent of God nor with ethics. It refers to the limits of "authority" granted to one by one's creator. This is even true of Muʿtazilī thought (see MUʿTAZILĪS) which does not confront the individual with the cosmos allowing each to find his or her own way, but rather obliges the creator to aim at the best *(aṣlaḥ)* for his creatures. Of course, under such conditions it is more plausible that God will do justice to the individual on the last day (see JUSTICE AND INJUSTICE); but, strictly speaking, God's authority still far surpasses human responsibility. This requires finally an examination of the human position in this world as intended by the personalized creator, who "each day [is engaged] in something" (Q 55:29). The Qurʾān confines itself to calling Adam God's vicegerent (*khalīfa*, e.g. Q 2:30). In the main, Islamic theological reasoning has conceived two different answers, both of them rooted in the qurʾānic message of the one God. The first answer is the elaborated system of *sharīʿa* law; if one keeps to all of its regulations scrupulously, seeing to the best for oneself and for the community of the believers, one will attain the rank of God's vicegerent on earth because God's volition and human action will be in perfect harmony (Shāṭibī, *Muwāfaqāt*, i, 251f.; see BOUNDARIES AND PRECEPTS). The second answer takes Q 51:56 into consideration: "I have not created jinn and men but that they may serve me (see WORSHIP)." The human being is God's servant, a fact that is reflected in the dependence of human reason on the creator's authority. A human being cannot act on his own but has to acquire every action, right or wrong, wrought by God. And it is this unquestioned compliance with God's decree *(amr)* that is looked upon as the quintessence of one's service to one's creator: By his incessant creative actions he realizes himself as the omnipotent one, and through the sinful (and righteous) actions he causes humans to acquire, he assures himself and humankind of his being the one legislator. Rendering this inestimable service to him, humans prove to be his indispensable vicegerents. This idea, elaborated in detail by Ibn al-ʿArabī (d. 638/1240) and his Sunnī interpreters, is the deepest understanding of qurʾānic theology ever arrived at. Both answers do not pertain to the Western concept of humankind hinted at above. The careful analysis of the qurʾānic message and its historical background will guide one, as has been demonstrated by this example, to a more appropriate understanding of Islam and Islamic theology and may be instrumental in establishing a reliable method of scientific hermeneutics.

T. Nagel

Bibliography
Primary: al-Balādhurī, Aḥmad b. Yaḥyā, *Jumal min Kitāb Ansāb al-ashrāf*, ed. S. Zakkār, 13 vols., Beirut 1996; Shahrastānī, *Milal*, ed. Cureton; al-Shāṭibī, Abū Isḥāq Ibrāhīm b. Mūsā, *al-Muwāfaqāt*, 4 vols., Beirut 1991.
Secondary: Bell, *Qurʾān;* I. Goldziher, *Introduction to Islamic theology and law*, trans. A. and R. Hamori, Princeton 1981 [Ger. orig. *Vorlesungen über den Islam*, Heidelberg 1910]; G. Kratz, Wie Abraham Hebräisch lernte, in id. and T. Nagel (eds.), *Abraham unser Vater*, Göttingen 2002, 53-65; id. and T. Nagel (eds.), *Abraham unser Vater*, Göttingen 2002; T. Nagel, Abraham in Mecca, in G. Kratz and T. Nagel (eds.), *Abraham, unser Vater*, Göttingen 2002, 143; id., *Geschichte der islamischen Theologie*, München 1994; id., *Islam. Die Heilsbotschaft des Korans und ihre Konsequenzen*, Westhofen 2001; id., *Medinensische Einschübe in mekkanischen Suren*, Göttingen 1995; A. Rippin, 'Desiring the face of God'. The qur'anic symbolism of personal responsibility, in I. Boullata, *Literary structures of religious meaning in the Qurʾān*, Richmond, Surrey 2000, 117-24 (for an alternative understanding of an element of qurʾānic theology); F. Siegert, Abrahams Gottesvision im hellenistischen Judentum, in G. Kratz and T. Nagel (eds.), *Abraham unser Vater*, Göttingen 2002, 142; Sozomène, *Histoire ecclésiastique*, ed. B. Grillet and G. Sabbah, Paris 1983.

Theophany

Visible appearance of God. In the Qurʾān, the closest one comes to a visible appearance of God is in Q 7:143. Moses (q.v.) expresses his wish to see God, who replies: "You shall not see me. Look at the mountain, though; if it stays in its place, then will you see me." The verse continues: "So, when his lord (q.v.) manifested himself *(tajallā)* to the mountain, he flattened it, and Moses, thunderstruck, collapsed. When he came to, he said, 'Glory to you! I turn toward you in repentance, and I am the first of the believers'" (see REPENTANCE AND PENANCE; GLORIFICATION OF GOD). The hairsplitting discussions (in the qurʾānic commentary of al-Rāzī, for example; see EXEGESIS OF THE QURʾĀN: CLASSICAL AND MEDIEVAL) over the possibility of humans seeing God represent attempts to vindicate theological positions staked out long after the revelation of the Qurʾān (see REVELATION AND INSPIRATION; THEOLOGY AND THE QURʾĀN; ANTHROPOMORPHISM; GOD AND HIS ATTRIBUTES). Both the letter and the spirit of Q 7:143 indicate that, according to the Qurʾān, in this world at least, human eyes (q.v.) cannot see God. Q 6:103, "Eyes cannot perceive him," makes the same point. The Qurʾān does say that God "actually spoke to Moses" but this does not mean that, in that conversation, Moses, in some sense, saw God (cf. *Exod* 33:11, which, using figurative language, says that God spoke to Moses "face to face"; see SPEECH; WORD OF GOD). Q 42:51 says that God speaks to human beings in one of three ways — in revelation, from behind a veil (q.v.) or through a messenger (q.v.; see also PROPHETS AND PROPHETHOOD). Thus, in reference to Q 7:143, the most one can say is that God did manifest himself on the mountain but that Moses was unable to see him; Moses' contrite "I turn toward you in repentance" upon regaining consciousness is proof of Moses' realization that he was a little too bold in making the request to see God.

Not only is there no mention in the Qurʾān of the several types of theophany found in the Bible, theophany probably would not have belonged in the theoretical framework of the Qurʾān (as we know, there is no history, in Islam, of any epiphany festival; see FESTIVALS AND COMMEMORATIVE DAYS; SCRIPTURE AND THE QURʾĀN). Q 4:153 cites disapprovingly the Israelites' demand to see God with their eyes (see CHILDREN OF ISRAEL). Also, theophany would be classed as a miracle and the Qurʾān is, in principle, averse to the idea of showing palpable miracles to establish the Qurʾān's veracity or Muḥammad's prophethood (see MIRACLES; MARVELS). According to the standard Muslim theological position, the Qurʾān is the miracle of Islam (see INIMITABILITY; CREATEDNESS OF THE QURʾĀN). In a sense, the Qurʾān — which is the speech of God and, as such, a manifestation of one of God's attributes — may be called the theophany of Islam but this would be a figurative use of that word, as Muslim theologians do make a distinction between God's being and his attributes, just as they distinguish between God and his signs (q.v.), the Qurʾān being one of those signs. In the same vein, the term "inlibration," which is sometimes used to distinguish the Qurʾān-event in Islam from the Christian doctrine of incarnation, has no more than a rhetorical value of highlighting a contrast between the two religions. For additional qurʾānic allusions to divine self-manifestation (albeit not a "visible appearance"), see SHEKHINAH; FACE OF GOD.

Mustansir Mir

Bibliography

Primary: Rāzī, *Tafsīr*.

Secondary: I. Abu Bakar, The Qurʾān and the beatific vision in Muslim rationalist and traditional theologies, in *Hamdard Islamicus* 27/1 (2004), 55-61; ʿA. Ahdal, *ʿIẓam al-minna fī ruʾyat al-muʾminīn rabbahum fī l-janna*, Mecca 1989; J. van Ess, Le *miʿrāǧ* et la vision de Dieu dans les premières spéculations théologiques en islam, in M. Amir-Moezzi (ed.), *Le voyage initiatique en terre d'islam*, Louvain 1996, 27-56; L. Goodman (ed.), *Maimonides and the philosophers of Islam. The problem of theophany*, Leiden 2000; ʿA. Salāma, *al-Samʿ wa-l-baṣar fī l-Qurʾān al-karīm*, Ṭarābulus 1986; A. Tuft, *The origins and development of the controversy over ruʾya in medieval Islam and its relation to contemporary visual theory*, PhD diss., UCLA 1979; id., The *ruʾyā* controversy and the interpretation of Qurʾān verse VII *(al-Aʿrāf)*: 143, in *Hamdard Islamicus* 6/3 (1983), 3-41; H. Wolfson, *The philosophy of the Kalam*, Cambridge 1976, chaps. 2 and 3.

Thicket see PEOPLE OF THE THICKET

Thief see THEFT

Thirst see FOOD AND DRINK

Thread, White and Black see RAMAḌĀN

Throne of God

Qurʾānic (and biblical) image related to God's sovereignty. The two terms used most commonly in the Qurʾān and exegetical literature for the throne of God are *ʿarsh* and *kursī*, although the latter has often been understood not as a seat but as a footstool or other accessory to the throne itself. The word *ʿarsh* appears twenty-five times in the Qurʾān with reference to God's throne, as well as the thrones of others: the seat on which Joseph (q.v.; Yūsuf) placed his parents (q.v.) is referred to as an *ʿarsh* (Q 12:100), as is the throne of Bilqīs (q.v.), the Queen of Sheba (q.v.; Q 27:23, 38, 41, 42). When referring to the throne of God, verses speak either of the throne itself or use it in a relational epithet to emphasize aspects of God's majesty. The latter category is the more common and God is referred to as the "lord (q.v.) of the throne" (*rabb al-ʿarsh,* Q 43:82) or "lord of the noble throne" (*rabb al-ʿarsh al-ʿaẓīm,* Q 9:129; cf. *rabb al-ʿarsh al-karīm,* Q 23:116). Elsewhere, God is referred to as "the one with the throne" (*dhū l-ʿarsh,* Q 40:15; cf. 17:42). A literal reading of the Qurʾān gives a clear sense of the throne of God as a concrete object (see LITERARY STRUCTURES AND THE QURʾĀN; METAPHOR; SIMILE; LANGUAGE AND STYLE OF THE QURʾĀN). Thus the angels (q.v.) are mentioned as circling God's throne (Q 39:75); elsewhere the Qurʾān describes the throne as being carried while it is being circled (Q 40:7). The image of the throne being borne by the angels appears explicitly in descriptions of eschatological events (see ESCHATOLOGY): "And the angels shall be ranged around (the heavens') borders (see HEAVEN AND SKY), eight of whom will be carrying above them, on that day, the throne of your lord" (Q 69:17). The term *kursī* is used for "throne" on two occasions. One of these refers to the throne of Solomon (q.v.; Sulaymān, Q 38:34). The other instance (Q 2:255) is the most famous reference to the throne of God in the Qurʾān, and may very well be the most popular verse in the Qurʾān (see VERSES), having come to be known as the "Throne Verse" (*āyat al-kursī*). Eight sentences long, the verse only refers to God's throne once: "His throne encompasses the heavens and the earth (q.v.), and their preservation does not burden him."

The throne of God, both as *ʿarsh* and *kursī,* has figured prominently in theological and mystical debates over God's transcendence and the status of anthropomorphic references in the Qurʾān (see THEOLOGY AND THE QURʾĀN; ṢŪFISM AND THE QURʾĀN; ANTHROPOMORPHISM). Ḥasan al-Baṣrī (d. 110/728) is said to have regarded the two terms as synonyms, as have some later scholars. A wide variety of writers have interpreted the throne of God metaphorically, beginning with both al-Ṭabarī (d. 310/923) and Ibn al-Jawzī (d. 597/1200) who credit Ibn ʿAbbās (d. ca. 68/686) with stating that *kursī* refers to divine knowledge (*ʿilm;* see KNOWLEDGE AND LEARNING). Al-Suyūṭī (d. 911/1505) takes a different approach and interprets the roof of heaven (*al-saqf al-marfūʿ,* literally "the upraised roof," Q 52:5) as a reference to God's throne.

In Ṣūfī literature the notion of God's throne has been a source of much speculation and interpretation, as has the Throne Verse mentioned above. In some schools of mystical philosophy, the throne of God (*ʿarsh*) is the lowest or seventh heaven. This is sometimes seen to coincide with the locus of divine self-manifestation (*tajallī*). Ibn al-ʿArabī (d. 638/1240) referred to the throne of God on many occasions in his writings and viewed the mystical heart (q.v.; *qalb*) as a microcosm of God's throne, in that it is capable of encompassing all things. This concept is perpetuated in Ṣūfī thought derived from Ibn al-ʿArabī, primarily through the influence of al-Jīlī's (d. 561/1166) understanding of the "perfect man" (*al-insān al-kāmil*).

The notion of a divine or supernatural throne is developed further in ḥadīth and *tafsīr* literature (see ḤADĪTH AND THE QURʾĀN; EXEGESIS OF THE QURʾĀN: CLASSICAL AND MEDIEVAL) where God's throne is described as possessing different designs and colors as well as being decorated with precious stones. The collections of al-Bukhārī (d. 256/870) and Muslim (d. ca. 261/875) refer to three celestial thrones, including those of Satan (see DEVIL) and Gabriel (q.v.; Jibrīl) along with that of God. Muslim and al-Tirmidhī (d. ca. 270/883) speak of Satan's throne floating on water and being surrounded by snakes, an image with important resonances in the study of comparative religion. See also SOVEREIGNTY; KINGS AND RULERS; POWER AND IMPOTENCE.

Jamal J. Elias

Bibliography
Primary: Bukhārī, *Ṣaḥīḥ,* 9 vols., Beirut 1980; al-Burūsawī, Abū l-Fidā' Ismāʿīl Ḥaqqī *Tafsīr rūḥ al-bayān,* 10 vols., Cairo n.d.; Ibn al-ʿArabī, Muḥammad b. ʿAbdallāh Abū Bakr, *al-Futūḥāt al-makkiyya,* 4 vols., Cairo n.d.; Ibn al-Jawzī, *Zād,* 9 vols., Beirut 1984; al-Kulaynī, Abū Jaʿfar Muḥammad b. Yaʿqūb, *al-Uṣūl min al-kāfī,* ed. ʿA.A. Ghifārī, 2 vols., Tehran 1968; Muslim, *Ṣaḥīḥ,* Cairo 1987; Suyūṭī, *Durr,* 6 vols., Tehran 1998; Ṭabarī, *Tafsīr,* 13 vols., Beirut 1999; Tirmidhī, *Sunan al-Tirmidhī,* 5 vols., Medina 1965; Zamakhsharī, *Kashshāf,* 4 vols., Beirut 1995.
Secondary: W.C. Chittick, *The self-disclosure of God,* Albany 1998; id., *The Sufi path of knowledge,* Albany 1989; J.J. Elias, *The throne carrier of God,* Albany 1995; Gilliot, *Elt,* 249-54 (on Muḥammad's sitting on the Throne, ad Q 17:79); D. Gimaret, *Dieu à l'image de l'homme. Les anthropomorphismes de la* sunna *et leur interprétation par les théologiens,* Paris 1997, 76-89 ("Sur Son Trône, ou Son Tabouret"); Cl. Huart and J. Sadan, Kursī, in *EI²,* v, 509; S. Uludağ, Arş, in *İslam Ansiklopedisi,* 27 vols. to date, Istanbul 1988-, iii, 410; Y. Şerki Yavuz, Arş, in *İslam Ansiklopedisi,* 27 vols. to date, Istanbul 1988-, iii, 406-9; id., Kursi, in *İslam Ansiklopedisi,* 27 vols. to date, Istanbul 1988-, xxvi, 572-3.

Throne Verse see VERSES; THRONE OF GOD

Thunder see WEATHER

Tidings see NEWS; GOOD NEWS

Time

The successive continuum of events and its measurement. The Qurʾān employs a rich terminology for aspects of time but uses these terms *ad hoc* and at random, in concrete and practical ways, rather than systematically and methodically addressing abstract and theoretical notions of time. This qurʾānic vocabulary does not include the principal technical terms for time, *zamān,* and eternity (q.v.), *qidam,* which are widely used in Islamic philosophy (see PHILOSOPHY AND THE QURʾĀN), nor does the Qurʾān contain typical philosophical terms such as *mudda* for extent of time and *dawām* for duration or *azal* and *abad* for eternity *a parte ante* and *a parte post* (though it uses the adverb *abadan,* "forever and ever," twenty-eight times). Three questions involving "time" and the Qurʾān will be excluded from this article because they are treated elsewhere: (1) the scholarly analysis of the text of the Qurʾān with regard to the sequence of the various stages of its composition and fixation as a normative text (see CHRONOLOGY AND THE QURʾĀN; CODICES OF THE QURʾĀN; COLLECTION OF THE QURʾĀN), (2) the vision of history embodied in the Qurʾān as well as the use of the Qurʾān as a historiographical source (see HISTORY AND THE QURʾĀN) and (3) the fixed times of ritual prayer cited in the Qurʾān (see PRAYER; cf. e.g. al-Ṭabarī's [d. 310/923] commentary on "the middle prayer," *al-ṣalāt al-wusṭā,* of Q 2:238, in his *Tafsīr,* ad loc.; cf. Gilliot, *Elt,* 149-50).

The qurʾānic day

Numerous references in the Qurʾān refer to the full twenty-four-hour cycle of the day by the term of *yawm* (see DAY, TIMES OF). The term is used 374 times as a singular noun *(yawm)* or a temporal adverb *(yawma),* three times in the dual *(yawmayn)* and twenty-seven times in the plural *(ayyām)* as well as seventy times in the form of the temporal adverb *yawma ʾidhin,* "on that day" (see FORM AND STRUCTURE OF THE QURʾĀN; RHETORIC AND THE QURʾĀN). The entire day, *yawm,* is understood in Semitic fashion as reckoned from sunset to sunset (see SUN; EVENING), beginning with the darkness of night followed by the brightness of daytime, namely "night" (collectively, *layl,* eighty-one times, singular, *layla,* eight times, plural, *layālin,* four times and never in the dual) and "day" (*nahār,* fifty-eight times, always in the singular; see DAY AND NIGHT). Likewise, the use of the term *sarmad* to signify the "continuous time" of night or day, which appears twice in Q 28:71-2, follows this precedence of night before day.

The word *yawm* may also refer to a historical event, such as "the day of deliverance" (*yawm al-furqān,* Q 8:41; see CRITERION; VICTORY) with reference to the battle of Badr (q.v.) in 2/624 or "the day of Ḥunayn" (Q 9:25) with reference to the battle of Ḥunayn (q.v.) in 8/630. Most frequently, however, it signals an eschatological event (see ESCHATOLOGY), such as "the day of resurrection (q.v.)" (*yawm al-qiyāma,* seventy times) or "the last day" (*al-yawm al-ākhir,* thirty-eight times), "the day of judgment" (*yawm al-dīn,* thirteen times; see LAST JUDGMENT), "the day of decision" (*yawm al-faṣl,* six times) and "the day of reckoning" (*yawm al-ḥisāb,* three times). This threatening and disastrous day of doom is further depicted by an abundance of apocalyptic and awe-inspiring attributes in the Qurʾān (see APOCALYPSE; FEAR; PIETY). Finally, *yawm* can signify a ritual event, such as "the day of assembly" (*yawm al-jumuʿa,* Q 62:9, referring to the congregational prayer on Friday; see FRIDAY PRAYER), "the day of the greater pilgrimage (q.v.)" (*yawm al-ḥajj al-akbar,* Q 9:3) or "the day of their Sabbath" (Q 7:163) with reference to the Jewish Sabbath (q.v.; see also JEWS AND JUDAISM).

Ayyām, the plural of *yawm,* is used in the Qurʾān in a sense congruent with the pre-Islamic combats of tribal prowess and battles of vengeance (q.v.), known collectively as "the days of the Arabs" (*ayyām al-ʿarab;* see TRIBES AND CLANS; PRE-ISLAMIC ARABIA AND THE QURʾĀN; ARABS). For example, *yawm buʿāth* names the battle between the Medinan tribes of Aws and Khazraj in 617 C.E. (see MEDINA). In the Qurʾān, however, the term is attributed to "the days of God" *(ayyām Allāh),* the *magnalia Dei,* manifested by God's intervention in human history through his acts of creation (q.v.), revelation (see REVELATION AND INSPIRATION) and retribution (see DAYS OF GOD). In this sense, the *ayyām Allāh* are explicitly compared to God's "signs" (q.v.; *āyāt*), revealed through Moses (q.v.), leading his people from darkness (q.v.) to light (q.v.; Q 14:5) and to God's final victories with their retribution of eternal gain or loss for what people's deeds have earned (Q 45:14; see GOOD DEEDS; EVIL DEEDS; REWARD AND PUNISHMENT). Similar to the biblical six day-work of creation, the Qurʾān (Q 7:54; 10:3; 11:7; 25:59; 32:4; 50:38; 57:4) understands God to have accomplished the creation of the heavens and the earth "in six days" *(fī sittati ayyām).* Further, God is seen to create the universe for a purpose, rather than for idle sport (Q 21:16-17; cf. 38:27; 44:38), in order to provide for the needs and wants of humans (Q 2:22 and passim) and to put their conduct to the test (Q 11:7; see TRIAL). In a peculiar passage (Q 41:9-12), the account of creation assigns two days to the creation of the earth (q.v.), then four days to setting it in order and, finally, two more days to the creation of the seven heavens (see HEAVEN AND SKY), while Q 71:14 asserts that God "created you in stages" (literally "times," *aṭwāran,* with reference to the stages of the embryo's growth; see BIOLOGY AS THE CREATION AND STAGES OF LIFE).

Other uses of the term *ayyām* include the incident when Zechariah (q.v.; Zakariyyāʾ) is struck dumb for "three days" (Q 3:41) or "those days" *(tilka l-ayyām)* when defeat is anticipated in Muḥammad's address before the battle of Uḥud in 3/625 (Q 3:140; see EXPEDITIONS AND BATTLES). The Thamūd (q.v.) were given the sign of a she-camel on an "appointed day" (*yawm maʿlūm,* Q 26:155) and hid "three days" in their dwellings before calamity overtook them (Q 11:65; see CAMEL; PUNISHMENT STORIES). The ʿĀd (q.v.) "were destroyed by a violent, roaring wind which [God] impelled against them seven nights and eight days, uninterruptedly" (Q 69:6-7; see AIR AND WIND), "in days calamitous" (*fī ayyāmin naḥisāt,* Q 41:16) or on "a day of constant calamity" (*fī yawmi naḥsin mustamirrin,* Q 54:19). Divine warnings are given to unbelieving people about "the like of the days of those who passed away before them" (*mithla ayyāmi lladhīna khalaw min qablihim,* Q 10:102; see WARNING; GENERATIONS; GEOGRAPHY) and the blessed of paradise (q.v.) are made the promise of "eating and drinking with relish for what you paid in advance in the days gone-by" (*fī l-ayyāmi l-khāliya,* Q 69:24; see FOOD AND DRINK).

Ritual observances apply on "a certain number of days" (*fī ayyāmin maʿdūdātin,* Q 2:203) or "days well-known" (*fī ayyāmin maʿlūmātin,* Q 22:28) of the pilgrimage (see RITUAL AND THE QURʾĀN). An exception is made for its performance in "two days" when one is in haste (Q 2:203) and, under certain circumstances, its ritual offering may be substituted by "a fast of three days in the pilgrimage, and of seven when you return, that is ten completely" (Q 2:196; see FASTING). Other ritual excuses with regard to the month of fasting (see MONTHS; RAMAḌĀN) are made through "a certain number of days" *(ayyāman maʿdūdātin)* for people who are sick or on a journey (q.v.; Q 2:184-5; see also ILLNESS AND HEALTH). In expiation for a wrong oath (Q 5:89; see OATHS) "three days" of fasting are required. The Jews claim that hellfire (see HELL AND HELLFIRE) shall not touch them except "for a certain number of days" (*ayyāman maʿdūdātin,* Q 3:24; see also POLEMIC AND POLEMICAL LANGUAGE).

The qurʾānic vocabulary of the times of day

Night and day are used antithetically in the Qurʾān (twenty-four times), e.g. "by night and day" (*laylan wa-nahāran,* Q 71:5; see PAIRS AND PAIRING). Night and day, created by God, are among the signs *(āyāt)* of divine power (Q 17:12; 41:37; see POWER AND IMPOTENCE) and put at the service of humankind (Q 14:33). God brings forth the day from the night (Q 35:13), "covering the day with the night it pursues urgently" (Q 7:54). Night and day are complementary (Q 6:60; 25:47; 27:86; 30:23; 34:33; 36:40; 40:61), mutually concurrent (Q 31:29; 39:5; 57:6) and succeed one another with regularity (Q 2:164; 3:190; 10:6; 23:80; 45:5). While *nahār* follows upon *layl* consistently in the Qurʾān, the order reverses as the sun, the asterism of the daytime, precedes the moon (q.v.), the asterism of the night when both are cited together (except in Q 71:16). This sequence of sun and moon is paralleled by *yawm* preceding *layla* in extra-qurʾānic literature, indicating that both lunar and solar reckonings of time were known to the Arabs (cf. Fischer, Tag und Nacht, 745–9; see CALENDAR). Notice, however, the switch of gender (q.v.), the sun being feminine and the moon masculine, while it is the opposite for *yawm* and *layla,* whereas *layl* and *nahār* are both masculine (see GRAMMAR AND THE QURʾĀN).

Specific terms in the Qurʾān identify a

number of regular time intervals and particular times of day and night. "Daybreak" *(al-falaq)* appears when God, "the lord of the daybreak" (Q 113:1), "splits the sky into dawn" (q.v.; *fāliq al-iṣbāḥ,* Q 6:96). The Qurʾān swears by the time of "dawn" (*fajr,* Q 89:1) when "the white thread becomes distinct to you from the black" (Q 2:187), a phenomenon defining the time of the "morning prayer" (*qurʾān al-fajr,* Q 17:78; *ṣalāt al-fajr,* Q 24:58) when god-fearing people ask forgiveness at "the times of dawn" (*bi-l-asḥār,* Q 3:17; 51:18; see MORNING). Lot's (q.v.) family was delivered "at dawn" (*bi-saḥar,* Q 54:34), their appointed time "in the morning" (*ṣubḥ,* Q 11:81), while his disloyal people were punished "in the early morning" (*bukratan,* Q 54:38). Muḥammad and Zechariah are bidden to give glory (q.v.) to God "in the evening and early morning" (*bi-l-ʿashī wa-l-ibkār,* Q 3:41; 40:55) and the latter signals his people to give glory "in early morning and evening" (*bukratan wa-ʿashīyan,* Q 19:11, cf. 19:62; see GLORIFICATION OF GOD). Muḥammad, exhorted to remember the name of his lord (q.v.) "in the early morning and evening" (*bukratan wa-aṣīlan,* Q 76:25; cf. 33:42; 48:9; see REMEMBRANCE; BASMALA), is accused of having ancient tales recited to him at those times (Q 25:5; see MYTHS AND LEGENDS IN THE QURʾĀN). The Qurʾān swears by the "morning" (*al-ṣubḥ,* Q 74:34; 81:18; cf. 100:3) and exclaims, "so glory be to God in your evening hour and in your morning hour" (*ḥīna tumsūna wa-ḥīna tuṣbiḥūn,* Q 30:17). But when punishment descends, "evil will be the morning *(ṣabāḥ)* of those who have been warned" (Q 37:177; see CHASTISEMENT AND PUNISHMENT; GOOD AND EVIL).

Generally, *ghadan* refers to "tomorrow" (Q 12:12; 18:23; 31:34; 54:26), yet every soul (q.v.) should consider "what it has forwarded for the morrow" (*ghad,* Q 59:18, possibly with reference to the last day). Muḥammad is bidden to remember his lord, without raising his voice, "at morn and eventide" (*bi-l-ghuduwwi wa-l-aṣāl,* Q 7:205), the times when the shadows bow to God (Q 13:15; see BOWING AND PROSTRATION) and God's name is glorified by people of prayer (Q 24:36), "calling upon their lord at morning and evening" (*bi-l-ghadāti wa-l-ʿashiyyi,* Q 6:52; 18:28). The folk of Pharaoh (q.v.) will be exposed to the fire (of hell) "morning and evening" (*ghuduwwan wa-ʿashiyyan,* Q 40:46) and the wind, subjected to Solomon (q.v.), blew in the morning and in the evening (Q 34:12). The Qurʾān swears "by the forenoon" (*ḍuḥā,* Q 93:1) and "by the sun and its morning brightness" (*ḍuḥāhā,* Q 91:1) and God brings out the "morning brightness" (*ḍuḥāhā,* Q 79:29; cf. 79:46). Adam (see ADAM AND EVE) does not have to "suffer the sun" *(wa-lā taḍḥā)* in the garden (q.v.) of paradise (Q 20:119) and Moses has the people mustered on the feast day *(yawm al-zīna)* at "the high noon" (*ḍuḥan,* Q 20:59). "The people of the cities" (*ahl al-qurā,* possibly Jewish villages around Medina; cf. Bell, *Commentary,* i, 243) are warned lest they are overcome by divine might at night and in "daylight" (*ḍuḥā,* Q 7:97-8). The "afternoon" (q.v.; *ʿaṣr,* Q 103:1), used in a qurʾānic oath, may actually be another term for time as destiny (q.v.; cf. Paret, *Kommentar,* 521; Brunschvig, Le culte et le temps, 168; see also FATE). "The twilight" (*shafaq,* Q 84:16) also appears once in the form of an oath in the Qurʾān while "the evening (q.v.) prayer" *(ṣalāt al-ʿishāʾ)* is cited in Q 24:58. Joseph's (q.v.) brothers (see BROTHER AND BROTHERHOOD) return to their father in the "evening" (*ʿishāʾ,* Q 12:16) and standing steeds are presented to Solomon in the evening (*bi-l-ʿashiyy,* Q 38:31), while the mountains join with David (q.v.) giving glory to God at evening and sunrise (*bi-l-ʿashiyyi wa-l-ishrāq,* Q 38:18).

Typical features of the qurʾānic language of time
The qurʾānic language of time commonly invokes particular times of day by random and mysterious oaths.

By the dawn *(fajr)* and ten nights *(layālin)*, by the even and the odd (see NUMERATION), by the night *(layl)* when it journeys on! (Q 89:1-4).
By the night *(layl)* enshrouding, by the day *(nahār)* in splendor! (Q 92:1-2).
By the bright forenoon *(ḍuḥā)*, by the brooding night *(layl)*! (Q 93:1-2).
By the sun and her morning brightness *(ḍuḥāhā)*, by the moon when it follows her, by the day *(nahār)* when it displays her, by the night *(layl)* when it enshrouds her! (Q 91:1-4).
By the heaven of the constellations, by the promised day *(al-yawm al-mawʿūd)*! (Q 85:1-2).
By heaven and the shooting star *(al-ṭāriq)*! (Q 86:1; see PLANETS AND STARS).
By the afternoon *(ʿaṣr)*! (Q 103:1) — an oath possibly invoking "time" in a more general sense (cf. Paret, *Kommentar*, 521).
By the snorting chargers, striking fire in sparks, storming forward in the morning *(ṣubḥan)*! (Q 100:1-4).
Nay! By the moon, by the night *(layl)* when it retreats and by the dawn *(ṣubḥ)* when it is white! (Q 74:32-4).
No! I swear by the day of resurrection *(yawm al-qiyāma)*! (Q 75:1).
On the day *(yawm)* when the first blast shivers and the second blast follows it! (Q 79:6-7).
By the night *(layl)* swarming, by the dawn *(ṣubḥ)* sighing! (Q 81:17-18).
No! I swear by the twilight *(shafaq)* and the night *(layl)* and what it envelops! (Q 84:16-17).

In one instance the seeking refuge from evil is related to an interval of time, i.e. a particular time of day, "I take refuge with the lord of the daybreak" *(rabb al-falaq*, Q 113:1).

References to intervals of day and night, expressed in succinct metaphorical phrases, are another typical feature. Examples include: "the ends of the day" *(aṭrāf al-nahār*, Q 20:130), referring to sunrise *(al-mashriq)* and sunset *(al-maghrib)*, frequently cited in tandem (whether in the singular Q 2:115, 142, 177, 258; 26:28; 73:9, in the plural, *mashāriq, maghārib*, Q 7:137; 70:40; cf. 37:5, or in the dual, as "the two easts," *al-mashriqayn*, Q 43:38; 55:17; and the "two wests," *al-maghribayn*, Q 55:17). Intervals of the night, "when it runs its course" *(idhā yasrī*, Q 89:4), are termed "the watches of the night" *(ānāʾ al-layl*, Q 3:113; 20:130; 39:9), while dusk is depicted as "the darkening of the night" *(ghasaq al-layl*, Q 17:78) and "the night of the night" *(zulafan min al-layl*, Q 11:114). *Zulafan*, which is plural, may refer not only to dusk but also to dawn, which another qurʾānic image calls "the withdrawal of the stars" *(idbār al-nujūm*, Q 52:49). The beginning of the day is likened to "the face of the day" *(wajh al-nahār*, Q 3:72) and "the rising of dawn" *(maṭlaʿ al-fajr*, Q 97:5). The sunrise is described by the images of "the sun shining forth" *(al-shams bāzighatan*, Q 6:78), the actual "rising" of the sun *(al-ishrāq*, Q 38:18), "the sun when it rises" *(al-shams idhā ṭalaʿat*, Q 18:17) and "experiencing the sunrise" *(mushriqīn*, Q 15:73; 26:60), while the early morning is the time when God "has stretched out the shadow" *(madda l-ẓilla*, Q 25:45). Noontime is marked by the "heat of noon" *(al-ẓahīra*, Q 24:58), "when you enter noontide" *(ḥīna tuẓhirūn*, Q 30:18), just as "you enter the evening and the morning" (Q 30:17). "The sinking of the sun" *(dulūk al-shams*, Q 17:78) follows the time "before the setting [of the sun]" *(qabla l-ghurūb*, Q 50:39) and the night covers like a "garment" *(libās*, Q 78:10; see CLOTHING) offering rest for sleep (q.v.).

The Qurʾān frequently uses temporal clauses, introduced by "when" *(idhā)* or "upon the day, when" *(yawma)*, especially in conjuring up the awe-inspiring phenomena of the last day and impressing these upon the listeners. Some examples for *idhā:*

When the sun shall be darkened, when the stars shall be thrown down, when the mountains shall be set moving, when the pregnant camels shall be neglected, when the savage beasts shall be mustered, when the seas shall be set boiling, when the souls shall be coupled, when the buried infant shall be asked for what sin she was slain (see INFANTICIDE), when the scrolls (q.v.) shall be unrolled, when heaven shall be stripped off, when hell shall be set blazing, when paradise shall be brought near, then shall a soul know what it has produced (Q 81:1–14).
When heaven is split open, when the stars are scattered, when the seas swarm over, when the tombs are overthrown, then a soul shall know its works, the former and the latter (Q 82:1-5).
When heaven is rent asunder and gives ear to its lord, and is fitly disposed, when earth is stretched out and casts forth what is in it, and voids itself (Q 84:1-4).
When the terror descends (Q 56:1).
When the earth shall be rocked (Q 56:4).
When the trumpet is blown with a single blast (Q 69:13).
When the trump is sounded, that day will be a harsh day (*yawm*, Q 74:8-9).
When the sight is dazed and the moon is eclipsed (Q 75:7-8).
When the stars shall be extinguished, when heaven shall be split, when the mountains shall be scattered and when the messengers' time is set *(uqqitat)*, to what day shall they be delayed? To the day of decision (*yawm al-faṣl*, Q 77:8-13).
When the great catastrophe comes upon the day *(yawm)* when man shall remember for what he has striven (Q 79:34-5).
When earth is shaken with a mighty shaking and earth brings forth her burdens (Q 99:1-2).
When comes the help of God and victory (Q 110:1).

A qurʾānic passage using *idhā,* "when it reaches the clavicles" (Q 75:26), introduces the moment of death, the soul departing from the body (see DEATH AND THE DEAD).

Some examples for *yawma:*

On the day when heaven shall be as molten copper (Q 70:8).
On the day when the trumpet is blown (Q 78:18).
On the day when a man shall flee from his brother (Q 80:34).
On the day when men shall be like scattered moths (Q 101:4).

The fixing of time in the Qurʾān

Fixing the divisions of time for the purpose of communal life is a qurʾānic preoccupation, which combines the pre-Islamic custom of reckoning time on the basis of the rising and setting of stars, called *anwāʾ* (a term absent from the Qurʾān, though appearing once in the verbal singular, *la-tanūʾu,* Q 28:76), with the observation of the lunar phases, called *manāzil,* "stations" (Q 10:5; 36:39), and the "mansions" *(burūj)* of the signs of the zodiac (Q 15:16; 25:61; 85:1). By and large, the pre-Islamic Arab year was lunisolar, with the year beginning in autumn and an intercalary month added in leap years (see SEASONS). The Qurʾān, however, opted for the lunar year (of 354 days) as established by God's creation. God created the sun and the moon as a pair for "reckoning" *(ḥusbān)* time (Q 6:96; 55:5), "stretching out the shadow" and appointing "the sun to be its guide" (Q 25:45). By divine ordainment, he has the sun return to its "fixed resting place" *(mustaqarr)* and has the moon marked by "its stations till it returns like an aged palm-bough" (Q 36:38-9; see DATE PALM; SYMBOLIC IMAGERY). The computation of years and months is rooted in the will of the creator, "who made the sun a radiance and the moon a light, and determined it by stations that you might know the number of the years *(ʿadada l-sinīn)* and the reckoning [of time]" (*ḥisāb*, Q 10:5; cf. 71:16). It is the creator who "determines the night and the day" (*yuqaddiru l-layla wa-l-nahār*, Q 73:20) and establishes their order: "We have appointed the night and the day as two signs; then we have blotted out the sign of the night and made the sign of the day to see, and that you may seek bounty from your lord, and that you may know the number of the years and the reckoning" (Q 17:12). Sun and moon have each their orbit, and night and day have each their measure, both assigned by God with neither intruding on the domain of the other: "It behooves not the sun to overtake the moon, neither does the night outstrip the day" (Q 36:40). Time moves in a regular mode, in the measurable rhythm of sun and moon, with the moon and its phases fixing the calculation of the months and years.

In the Qurʾān, the moon is the actual measurer of time, and the beginning of the month and the year is established by the observation of the new moon (*hilāl*, mentioned once in the Qurʾān in the plural, *ahilla*). Each lunar month begins with the sighting of the crescent in the clear sky: "They will question you concerning the new moons *(al-ahilla)*. Say, they are appointed times *(mawāqīt)* for the people, and the pilgrimage" (Q 2:189). The month, called *shahr* (twelve times in the singular, twice in the dual, and six times in the plural *ashhur*, and once in the plural *shuhūr*), is established by God who divided the year into twelve lunar months by divine decree: "The number of months *(shuhūr)*, with God, is twelve in the book of God, the day he created the heavens and the earth; four of them are sacred" (Q 9:36). The names of the pre-Islamic sacred months, Dhū l-Qaʿda, Dhū l-Ḥijja, al-Muḥarram and Rajab, are absent from the Qurʾān, but there are allusions to them in the qurʾānic phrases, "Journey freely in the land for four months" (Q 9:2) and "When the sacred months *(al-ashhur al-ḥurum)* have slipped away, slay the idolaters" (Q 9:5; see VERSES; IDOLATRY AND IDOLATERS; FIGHTING).

Of the twelve lunar months only the month of fasting is mentioned by name in the Qurʾān, "the month of Ramaḍān wherein the Qurʾān was sent down" (Q 2:185). This statement is frequently linked with the verse, "We [God] sent it down in the night of destiny" (*laylat al-qadr*, Q 97:1; see NIGHT OF POWER), with "it" explained as referring to the Qurʾān on the basis of the parallel passage, "By the clear book *(al-kitāb al-mubīn)*, we have sent it down in a blessed night" (Q 44:2-3). It is reasonably certain that Muḥammad first adopted the Jewish custom of the ʿĀshūrāʾ fast observed on the Day of Atonement and replaced it in 2/623-4 by the institution of the fast of Ramaḍān (Q 2:183-5) after the battle of Badr (cf. Q 3:123). This battle is usually understood to be the referent of Q 8:41, "What we sent down on our servant (q.v.; *ʿabdinā*) on the day of deliverance *(yawm al-furqān)*." It is probable that "a certain number of days" or "counted days" (*ayyāman maʿdūdātin*, Q 2:184) represents a ten-day fast as a stage of transition before the Qurʾān established the month-long fast of Ramaḍān (Goitein, Zur Entstehung, 101-9). It is disputed, however, whether the "night of destiny" refers to a night in the month of Ramaḍān when Muḥammad received his first revelation while practicing religious devotion (*taḥannuth;* see VIGILS) on mount Ḥirāʾ outside Mecca (cf. Ibn Isḥāq, *Sīra,* 151-2; Ibn Isḥāq-Guillaume, 105-6) or whether it signifies the sending down of the entire Qurʾān (a notion which is in conflict with verses stating that the Qurʾān was revealed gradually, cf. Wagtendonk, *Fasting in the Koran,* 87; see OCCASIONS OF REVELATION). Scholars also differ over whether the "night of destiny" was chosen against the background of the ancient Arabian new year, celebrated around the summer solstice and frequently identified with the 27th of Ramaḍān (cf. Wensinck, Arabic new year, 5-8) or whether the night of the 27th of Rajab should be determined as the night of Muḥammad's first revelation (Wagtendonk, *Fasting in the Koran,* 113; see YEAR).

The month of the pilgrimage is clearly called "the holy month" *(al-shahr al-ḥarām,* Q 2:194, 217; 5:2, 97) although, somewhat enigmatically, the pilgrimage *(al-ḥajj)* is said to fall in "months well-known" (*ashhur maʿlūmāt,* Q 2:197). The practice of adding an intercalary month *(nasīʾ)* to bring the lunar year in step with the seasons was expressly prohibited in the Qurʾān as "an increase of unbelief" (Q 9:37; cf. Moberg, *an-Nasīʾ*). The Qurān's fixing the number of months as twelve and its prohibition of intercalation prepared the way for Islam to adopt the lunar calendar, beginning with the 1st of Muḥarram of the year of the *hijra* (not the *hijra* itself; see EMIGRATION), in the caliphate of ʿUmar (r. 13-23/634-44; see CALIPH). A random reference to *shahr* in the Qurʾān refers to the wind that was subjected to Solomon and "blew a month's (journey) in the morning *(ghuduwwuhū shahrun)* and a month's (journey) in the evening" (*rawāḥuhā shahrun,* Q 34:12). Ritually, a fast of "two successive months" (Q 4:92; 58:4) can be substituted if one does not find the means to pay the bloodwit (see BLOOD MONEY). "A wait of four months" is recommended for those who forswear their women (Q 2:226; see ABSTINENCE; MARRIAGE AND DIVORCE; SEX AND SEXUALITY). Widows (see WIDOW) are to wait "four months and ten days" (Q 2:234) before they can remarry after the husbands' death, while the waiting period is reduced to "three months" (Q 65:4) for those whose menstrual periods have ceased (see MENSTRUATION). According to the Qurʾān, the bearing and weaning of a child lasts "thirty months" (Q 46:15; see MAINTENANCE AND UPKEEP; CHILDREN; WET-NURSING) and mothers are required to suckle their children "two years completely" (*ḥawlayn kāmilayn,* Q 2:233), a duration in step with Luqmān's (q.v.) instruction to his son that weaning a child lasts "two years" (*ʿāmayn,* Q 31:14). The week *(usbūʿ)* is not cited in the Qurʾān; Friday (*yawm al-jumuʿa,* Q 62:9) appears only once, and the Jewish Sabbath five times (Q 2:65; 4:47, 154; 7:163; 16:124).

For the year, the Qurʾān uses the terms *sana* (seven times in the singular, and twelve times in the plural *sinīn*) and *ʿām* (eight times in the singular and once in the dual) interchangeably. Noah (q.v.) remained among his people "a thousand years, all but fifty" (Q 29:14) and Pharaoh's people were struck with years of famine (q.v.; Q 7:130). Joseph explains the king's dream vision of seven fat and seven lean cows as meaning seven fertile and seven hard years (Q 12:47-9) and, forgetting a fellow-prisoner's wish, Joseph causes him to languish in prison for "some years" (Q 12:42). Moses also remained among the people of Midian (q.v.) for "some years" (Q 20:40) and, when sent to Pharaoh, is asked, "did you not tarry among us years of your life?" (Q 26:18). The people of Israel (q.v.; see also CHILDREN OF ISRAEL) wandered about the earth "for forty years" (Q 5:26). God sealed the ears of the seven sleepers for years (Q 18:11; see MEN OF THE CAVE) and "they remained in their cave (q.v.) three hundred years and nine more" (Q 18:25). The Meccans are told that a day *(yawm)* with God is "as a thousand years" (Q 22:47) and the unbelievers wish to live a thousand years (Q 2:96; see BELIEF AND UNBELIEF; OPPOSITION TO MUḤAMMAD). The last day is compared to a millennium, it is "one day *(yawm)* whose measure is a thousand years of your counting" (*miqdāruhu alfa sanatin mimmā taʿuddūn,* Q 32:5), while the angels (q.v.) and the spirit (q.v.) mount up to God in a day *(yawm),* "whereof the measure is fifty thousand years" (Q 70:4). Perhaps with reference to Ezekiel 27, the simile of a man who was dead for a hundred years and then finds himself raised up believing himself dead for only a day or part thereof is given in Q 2:259 (see SIMILES). A similar time argument against the resurrection is rejected by the rhetorical question of Q 23:112, "How long have you tarried in the earth, by a number of years?" According to the Qurʾān, a man reaches maturity (q.v.) at "forty years" (Q 46:15) and the believers are exhorted to go to war (q.v.) once or twice a year (Q 9:126) while the idolaters are debarred from the sacred mosque of the Kaʿba (q.v.) "after this present year" (Q 9:28). Although it is difficult to fix the particular event, Q 30:4 refers to the defeat of the Byzantine forces *(al-Rūm)* on the northern borders of Arabia in about 614 C.E. and promises them victory against the Persians in "a few years" (*fī biḍʿi sinīn;* see BYZANTINES).

Just as the Qurʾān pays no attention to fixing particular historical events in time, so it hardly betrays any awareness of historical epochs preceding its own advent, except perhaps with regard to the term *al-jāhiliyya,* which is generally taken as denoting the age of Arab pagan ignorance (q.v.) preceding the appearance of Islam (see AGE OF IGNORANCE). Rather than to a historical epoch of pre-Islamic lack of knowledge (see KNOWLEDGE AND LEARNING), this term primarily refers in the Qurʾān to an age of uncouth behavior as opposed to moderate conduct (*ḥilm,* cf. Goldziher, *MS,* 201-8; see MODERATION). This may be the primary meaning in Q 33:33, where Muḥammad's wives (see WIVES OF THE PROPHET) are admonished not to act in the immodest ways (see MODESTY) of "the former age of ignorance" *(al-jāhiliyya l-ūlā)*; in Q 5:50, where "the (mode of) judgment (q.v.) of the age of ignorance" *(ḥukm al-jāhiliyya)* is contrasted with God's judgment; in Q 48:26, where "the fierceness of the age of ignorance" *(ḥamiyyat al-jāhiliyya)* is overcome by the divine assurance of self-restraint; and in Q 3:154, where untrue "assumptions of the age of ignorance" *(ẓann al-jāhiliyya)* about God are defeated by those peacefully trusting in God (see TRUST AND PATIENCE).

The vision of time in the Qurʾān

Arabic, a Semitic language and the language of the Qurʾān, distinguishes two aspects of time, complete *(māḍī)* and incomplete *(muḍāriʿ),* lacking the morphological distinction into three tenses common to the Indo-European languages and operating without proper verbs for "to be" and "to become" (see ARABIC LANGUAGE; LANGUAGE AND STYLE OF THE QURʾĀN). Similarly, the Arabic Qurʾān does not exhibit a notion of time divided into past, present and future, but envisages time either as phases of time in the past or moments of time understood as instants whether present or future. Furthermore, the vision of time in the Qurʾān is firmly rooted in an Arabic vocabulary that betrays virtually no influence of foreign loanwords, unlike some of the ritual and religious terminology in the Qurʾān (see FOREIGN VOCABULARY; COSMOLOGY; SCRIPTURE AND THE QURʾĀN). Rather, the Qurʾān seems to intertwine a great variety of genuinely Arabic terms of time, combining them with a vision of God as the lord over time in the beginning and at the end of creation as well as during all of humanity's instants of time.

The Qurʾān rejects the pre-Islamic fatalism of impersonal time and destiny (*dahr,* Q 45:24; 76:1), also termed "fate's uncertainty" (*rayb al-manūn,* Q 52:30), which holds sway over everything and erases human works without hope for life beyond death (cf. Ringgren, *Studies,* 117-18; id., Islamic fatalism, 57-9). Rather than being forsaken to impersonal destiny, the Qurʾān emphasizes that "all things come home" *(taṣīru l-umūr)* unto God (Q 42:53) and "unto God is the homecoming" (*al-maṣīr,* Q 3:28; 24:42; 35:18; cf. 2:285; 5:18; 22:48; 31:14; 40:3; 42:15; 50:43; 60:4; 64:3), which for the wicked is an "evil homecoming" (*biʾsa l-maṣīr,* Q 2:126 and passim; *sāʾat maṣīran,* Q 4:97, 115; 48:6; cf. 25:15) to hellfire (Q 14:30; cf. Berque, l'Idée de temps, 1158). Proclaiming the creation of the universe by God and affirming the resurrection of the body in the world to come, the Qurʾān explains time from the perspective of a transcendent and omnipotent God, who obliterates the spell of fate and subdues the all-pervading power of time.

God begins the creation of the world and humanity with his creative command, *kun,* "Be!": "When he decrees a thing, he says to it, 'Be,' and it is" (Q 2:117; 3:47; 19:35; 40:68; cf. 3:59; 6:73; 16:40). God gave this command of creation when he formed the first human being (Q 3:59) and made the heavens and the earth (Q 6:73), fashioning them in six days (Q 7:54; 10:3; 11:7; 25:59; 32:4; 50:38; 57:4). "His are the creation *(khalq)* and the command" (*amr,* Q 7:54). God is not only creator at the beginning of creation and at the origin of a person's life, he also is judge at the end of the world and at the individual's death when humankind will hear "the cry in truth" (Q 50:42). In the final "hour" *(sāʿa),* the only perfect moment that there is, the divine command is revealed in "the twinkling of an eye" (*lamḥ bi-l-baṣar,* Q 54:50; cf. 16:77). In the Qurʾān, the divine creative command constitutes the beginning of time brought about by God who is beyond time. God brings it abruptly to its end in an apocalyptic termination when "the whole earth shall be his handful on the day of resurrection and the heavens will be rolled up in his right hand" (Q 39:67).

In the Qurʾān, the word *sāʿa,* "hour," generally denotes a brief lapse of time rather than the precise measure of one of the twenty-four hours of the day. The term appears forty-eight times, always in the singular, and predominantly designates the last hour. While the vivid imagery of apocalyptic signs, reversing the natural order and producing cataclysmic events (many of them quoted in the "when" passages, cited above), is depicted in reference to the *day* of doom, these terrifying happenings are rarely associated explicitly with the last *hour.* The hour is "coming" (*ātiya,* Q 15:85; 20:15; 22:7; 40:59) and comes with God's chastisement (Q 6:40; 19:75; 40:46). It "comes" (*taqūmu,* Q 30:12, 14, 55; 45:27), "there is no doubt of it" (Q 18:21; 45:32), and comes "suddenly" (Q 6:31; 12:107; 22:55; 43:66; 47:18) with its signs and "tokens" (*ashrāṭ,* Q 47:18). Only a few tokens of the last hour are cited in the Qurʾān, such as "the earthquake of the hour is a mighty thing" (Q 22:1), "the hour is their tryst, and the hour is very calamitous and bitter" (Q 54:46), and god-fearing people "tremble because of the hour" (Q 21:49). The unbelievers are in doubt of the hour (e.g. Q 42:18), are heedless of its coming (Q 18:36; 41:50) and do not seek to know the hour (Q 45:32), believing that it will never come to them (Q 34:3) and crying lies to the hour (Q 25:11; see LIE). On the last day humanity will be mustered as if they had not tarried in their graves "but an hour of the day" (*sāʿatan mina l-nahār,* Q 10:45; cf. 46:35), and the sinners will swear that they have not remained in their graves more than an hour (Q 30:55; see SIN, MAJOR AND MINOR). The term *(ajal)* of a nation can neither be put back "by a single hour" nor put forward (Q 7:34; 10:49; 16:61; 34:30), and the Meccan emigrants and Medinan helpers followed the Prophet "in the hour of difficulty" (*fī sāʿati l-ʿusra,* Q 9:117; see EMIGRANTS AND HELPERS).

The Qurʾān insists that only God knows the "hour" (Q 7:187; 33:63; cf. 31:34; 41:47; 43:61, 85) which is near (Q 33:63; 42:17; 54:1), as if in "a twinkling of the eye" (*ka-lamḥi l-baṣar,* Q 16:77; cf. 54:50). In the context of God's knowledge of the hour, the Qurʾān uses the term *waqt,* "moment, instant," which influenced the notion of an atomism of time in Ṣūfism (cf. Bowering, *Ideas,* 217–32; see ṢŪFISM AND THE QURʾĀN): "They will question you concerning the hour, when it shall berth. Say, the knowledge of it is only with my lord; none shall reveal it at its proper time *(waqt),* but he" (Q 7:187). Furthermore, the term appears twice as a description of the day of doom as "a day of a known time" (*al-waqt al-maʿlūm,* Q 15:38; 38:81), "when the messengers' time is set" *(uqqitat,* Q 77:11; see MESSENGER) and "when the former and later generations will be gathered to the appointed time of a known day" (*ilā mīqāti yawmin maʿlūm,* Q 56:50). "Surely, the day of decision is their appointed time *(mīqātu-hum),* all together" (Q 44:40). Another use of the term *mīqāt* refers to Moses' encounter with God, when he came "to our (God's) appointed time" (*li-mīqātinā,* Q 7:143; see THEOPHANY). In fact, "We (God) appointed with Moses thirty nights and we completed them with ten more, so the appointed time of his lord *(mīqāt rab-bihi)* was forty nights" (Q 7:142). "Moses chose of his people seventy men for our appointed time" (*li-mīqātinā,* Q 7:155), while Pharaoh's sorcerers were assembled for "the appointed time of a fixed day" (*li-mīqāti yawmin maʿlūm,* Q 26:38; see MAGIC). Both *waqt* and *mīqāt* denote a momentous instant whether it is the eschatological instant of the last hour or the moment of Moses' encounter with God.

Four times the Qurʾān uses the term *amad* for "space of time," considered with regard to its end. The believers are admonished to be unlike those to whom revelation had come before "and for whom the space of time was long" (*fa-ṭāla ʿalayhimu l-amad,* Q 57:16). Each individual wishes to have a "wide space of time" until the reckoning of a person's actions on judgment day (Q 3:30). The seven sleepers calculated the "space of time" they had tarried in the cave (Q 18:12) and Muḥammad professes not to know whether God has set a long "space of time" for the arrival of the last day (Q 72:25). The Qurʾān also employs the temporal clauses, *al-ams,* "yesterday, the day before" (Q 10:24; 28:18-19, 82) and, more prominently, *ḥīna,* "when" (once in the form *ḥīnaʾidhin*), *al-āna,* "now, at the present time" (Q 2:71, 187; 4:18; 8:66; 10:51, 91; 12:51; 72:9) and *ayyāna,* "when," with regard to the instant of the last hour and the day of resurrection (Q 7:187; 16:21; 27:65; 51:12; 75:6; 79:42). The indefinite noun denoting "an instant" *(ḥīn)* is used to manifest God's causality in its actual "efficacy" (e.g. Q 21:111; 26:218; 37:174; cf. Massignon, Time, 108). The Qurʾān's linguistic stress on the moment exerted an influence on the concept of temporal atomism that emerged in the theological occasionalism of Islam which, however, relied heavily on extra-qurʾānic nomenclature for its terminology (cf. Macdonald, Continuous re-creation, 328-37; van Ess, *TG,* iv, 474; see THEOLOGY AND THE QURʾĀN). Thinking atomistically, Muslim theologians envision time as a "galaxy" or constellation of instants rather than a continuous duration (cf. Massignon, Time, 108).

God ends the cosmos by setting a term *(ajal)* to his maintenance of the universe and human life. The Qurʾān differentiates between an irrevocable period of time assigned by God for each human being in this world *(dunyā)* and an endless period of time *(khulūd)* for his/her life in the world to come *(ākhira)*, whether in paradise or in hellfire. The term *ajal*, as designating "appointed time" of a person's life, carries the notion that the date of death is fixed for humans, who each have their "stated term" of death (*ajal musammā*, Q 11:3; 39:42). The Qurʾān uses the phrase *ajal musammā*, probably derived from the legal vocabulary of Muḥammad's time, to refer to the date when a debt (q.v.) is due (Q 2:282; cf. 2:231-5; 65:2, 4; see also TRADE AND COMMERCE; ECONOMICS; MONEY) or to Moses fulfilling the "term" of serving a period of years *(ḥijaj)* in order to obtain his wife (Q 28:27-9; see WOMEN AND THE QURʾĀN). The Qurʾān, however, ordinarily uses the word for God's setting a term to his own action. God creates humans from dust and appoints for each of them a stated term of death (Q 6:2). He determines the moment when each embryo leaves the womb (q.v.; Q 22:5) and, every day anew, wakes up each soul to life until humans reach their "appointed time" of death (Q 6:60; 39:42). All humanity will return to God when the stated term is completed on the last day (Q 6:60) and all those looking to encounter God will experience God's term *(ajal Allāh)* surely coming (Q 29:5). The *ajal* is "fixed" (*li-kulli ajalin kitāb*, Q 13:38; cf. 8:68) for both individuals (Q 6:2; 11:3; 63:11) and communities (Q 7:34; 15:5; 23:43). It can neither be anticipated nor deferred (Q 7:34; 10:49; 16:61; 35:11; 63:10-11), although God grants the repentant sinner a respite until a "stated term" (Q 14:10; 16:61; 35:45; 71:4; see REPENTANCE AND PENANCE). This is why the wicked are not punished at once and they do not find that sinning shortens their existence (Q 35:45; 63:10-11). Challenged to hasten the final punishment, Muḥammad declares himself unable to do so because it will come suddenly at its "appointed time" (Q 29:53; see PROVOCATION). Not only humans have their appointed time of existence, the whole universe was created by God with finality built into it. God created the heavens and the earth as well as all natural phenomena "between them," decreeing their duration until "a stated term" (Q 30:8; 46:3) and established the unchangeable course of the sun and the moon, "running to a stated term" (Q 13:2; 31:29; 35:13; 39:5; see NATURE AS SIGNS). God unambiguously enunciated the stated term through "a word" *(kalima)* that proceeded from him (Q 42:14; cf. 10:19; 11:110; 20:129; 37:171; 41:45; 42:21; see SPEECH; WORD OF GOD).

There is no place in the Qurʾān for impersonal time. God, rather than an impersonal agent, rules the universe. The destiny of human beings is in the hands of God who creates male and female, grants wealth (q.v.) and works destruction, and gives life (q.v.) and brings death (Q 53:44-54). God is active even in a person's sleep, for "God takes the souls unto himself *(yatawaffā l-anfus)* at the time of their death, and that which has not died, in its sleep. He keeps those on whom he has decreed death, but releases the others till a stated term" (*ajal musamman*, Q 39:42). Unless God has decreed a person's death, he sends back the soul and the human person wakes up. The divine command *(amr)* rules all of human life and resembles a judicial decision, proclaiming God's decree with authority and stating the instant that releases the acts which humans perform. Both human life and human action begin with the announcement of the divine *kun* ('Be!') and come to an end at the stated term (*ajal,* Q 40:67) as the irrevocable period of life assigned by God comes to an end at the moment of divine sanction. This appointed term of human life is fixed, it can neither be anticipated nor deferred. "No one has his life prolonged and no one has his life cut short except as [it is written] in a book [of God's decrees]" (Q 35:11; see HEAVENLY BOOK). The image-rich promise of the new human creation beyond time in paradise heightened the awareness that nothing escapes the grasp of God's perpetual presence. From the *kun* of his creation to the *ajal* of his death, individual human existence falls under the incessant decrees of God, which occur instantaneously. God is the lord of the instant. What God has determined happens.

G. Böwering

Bibliography
Primary: Ibn Isḥāq, *Sīra;* Ibn Isḥāq-Guillaume; Ṭabarī, *Tafsīr.*
Secondary: M. b. Mūsā Bābāʿammī, *Mafhūm al-zaman fī l-Qurʾān al-karīm,* Beirut 2000; J. Baljon, The 'amr of God' in the Koran, in *AO* 23 (1958), 7-18; Bell, *Commentary;* J. Berque, L'idée de temps dans le Coran, in *Homenaje al Profesor Jacinto Bosch Vilà,* 2 vols., Granada 1991, ii, 1155-64; G. Böwering, Ideas of time in Persian mysticism, in *Iran* 30 (1992), 77-89; R. Brunschvig, Le culte et le temps dans l'Islam classique, in id., *Études d'islamologie,* 2 vols., Paris 1976, i, 167-77; W. Caskel, Aijam al-ʿArab. Studien zur altarabischen Epik, in *Islamica* 4 (1931), 1-99; A. Falaturi, Experience of time and history in Islam, in A. Schimmel and A. Falaturi (eds.), *We believe in one God. The experience of God in Christianity and Islam,* New York 1979, 63-76; A. Fischer, "Tag und Nacht" im Arabischen und die semitische Tagesberechnung, in *Abhandlungen der Philologisch-historischen Klasse der königlichen Sächsischen Gesellschft der Wissenschaften, Leipzig* 27 (1909), 739-58; Gilliot, *Elt;* F. (S.D.) Goitein, Zur Entstehung des Ramaḍāns, in *Der Islam* 18 (1929), 189-96; id., The Muslim month of fasting, in S.D. Goitein, *Studies in Islamic history and institutions,* Leiden 1966, 90-110; I. Goldziher, Die Bedeutung der Nachmittagszeit in Islam, in *ARW* 9 (1906), 294-302; repr. in id., *GS,* v, 23-31; J. Horovitz, Bemerkungen zur Geschichte und Terminologie des islamischen Kultus, in *Der Islam* 16 (1927), 249-63; S. Kadi, *Ḥattā idhā in the Qurʾān. A linguistic study,* Beirut 1996; M. Ishaq Khan, Reflections on time and history vis-a-vis the Qurʾān, in *Hamdard Islamicus* 21 (1998), 7-14; D.B. Macdonald, Continuous re-creation and atomic time in Muslim scholastic theology, in *Isis* 9 (1927), 326-44; L. Massignon, Time in Islamic thought, in J. Campbell, *Man and time. Papers from the Eranos yearbooks,* Princeton 1957, 108-14; A. Moberg, *an-Nasīʾ in der islamischen Tradition,* Lund 1931; Paret, *Kommentar;* S. Pines, *Beiträge zur islamischen Atomenlehre,* Berlin 1936; H. Ringgren, Islamic fatalism, in id. (ed.), *Fatalistic beliefs,* Stockholm 1967, 52-62; id., *Studies in Arabian fatalism,* Uppsala 1955; F. Rosenthal, *Sweeter than hope,* Leiden 1983; K. Wagtendonk, *Fasting in the Koran,* Leiden 1968; Watt-Bell; A.J. Wensinck, Arabic new year and the feast of tabernacles, in *Verhandelingen der Koninklijke Akademie van Wetenschappen te Amsterdam, Afdeling Letterkunde, Nieuwe Reeks* 25/2 (1925), 1-41.

Tiring see SLEEP; SABBATH

Tithe see ALMSGIVING

Today see TIME

Tolerance and Coercion

Accepting attitude towards a plurality of viewpoints and the use of force to influence behavior or beliefs. Qurʾānic vocabulary lacks a specific term to express the idea of tolerance but several verses explicitly state that religious coercion *(ikrāh)* is either unfeasible or forbidden; other verses may be interpreted as expressing the same notion. Pertinent qurʾānic attitudes underwent substantial development during Muḥammad's prophetic career. The earliest reference to religious tolerance seems to be included in Q 109, a sūra that recognizes the unbridgeable gap between Islam (q.v.) and the religion of the Meccans (see POLYTHEISM AND ATHEISM; SOUTH ARABIA, RELIGION IN PRE-ISLAMIC) and concludes by saying: "To you your religion, and to me mine" (Q 109:6). This is best interpreted as a plea to the Meccans to refrain from practicing religious coercion against the Muslims of Mecca (q.v.) before the *hijra* (Zamakhsharī, *Kashshāf,* iv, 293; cf. Q 2:139; see EMIGRATION), but since it does not demand any action to suppress Meccan polytheism, it has sometimes been understood as reflecting an attitude of religious tolerance on the part of the Muslims (cf. Q 2:139; 28:55; see also RELIGIOUS PLURALISM AND THE QURʾĀN).

Q 15:85 and Q 43:89, dated by Nöldeke (*GQ*, i, 129, 131-2) to the second Meccan period (see CHRONOLOGY AND THE QURʾĀN), are also relevant. In contradistinction to Q 109:6, these verses clearly address the Prophet and enjoin him to turn away from those who do not believe (see BELIEF AND UNBELIEF). Q 15:85 reads: "Surely the hour is coming; so pardon, with a gracious pardoning" *(fa-ṣfaḥi l-ṣafḥa l-jamīl);* this injunction is related to the imminent approach of the last day (see LAST JUDGMENT). The verse seems to mean that the Prophet may leave the unbelievers alone because God will soon sit in judgment (q.v.) and inflict on them the just punishment (see REWARD AND PUNISHMENT). Then there is Q 10:99-100:

> And if your lord had willed, whoever is in the earth would have believed, all of them, all together. Would you then constrain the people, until they are believers? It is not for any soul (q.v.) to believe save by the leave of God; and he lays abomination upon those who have no understanding.

The verse seeks to convince the Prophet that matters of religious belief are in the hands of God and that any attempt to spread his faith by coercion would be an exercise in futility. It also sounds as though it were an attempt to allay the Prophet's distress at his initial failure to attract most Meccans to Islam: people believe only as a result of divine permission and the Prophet should not blame himself for their rejection of the true faith. Despite prophetic efforts to the contrary, most people opt for unbelief (Q 12:103; 16:37). The Qurʾān declares in numerous passages that prophets can only deliver the divine message (see PROPHETS AND PROPHETHOOD); it is not within their power to assure its acceptance or implementation (Q 16:35, 82; 28:56; 29:18 and elsewhere; cf. also Paret, Toleranz). This argument may be seen as compatible with the idea of predestination.

Moving to the period immediately following the *hijra,* we should consider the famous document known as the Constitution of Medina *(ʿahd al-umma)* which included a clause recognizing the fact that the Jews have a distinct — and legitimate — religion of their own (see JEWS AND JUDAISM): "The Jews have their religion and the believers have theirs" *(lil-yahūd dīnuhum wa-lil-muʾminīna dīnuhum;* Abū ʿUbayd, *Amwāl,* 204). Rubin (The constitution, 16 and n. 45) has already referred to the affinity between this passage and Q 109:6. Both accept the existence of religions other than Islam in the Arabian peninsula. It stands to reason that both passages reflect very early attitudes of nascent Islam, which had been willing, at that time, to tolerate the existence of other religions in the peninsula. This seems to have been the understanding of Abū ʿUbayd (d. 224/838-9) who thought that the *ʿahd al-umma* clause originated at a time when "Islam was not yet dominant and strong, before the Prophet was commanded to take *jizya* (see POLL TAX) from the People of the Book" (q.v.; *qabla an yaẓhara al-islām wa-yaqwā wa-qabla an yuʾmara bi-akhdh al-jizya min ahl al-kitāb,* Abū ʿUbayd, *Amwāl,* 207).

Q 2:256, "There is no compulsion in religion..." *(lā ikrāha fī l-dīni)* has become the *locus classicus* for discussions of religious tolerance in Islam. Surprisingly enough, according to the "circumstances of revelation" *(asbāb al-nuzūl)* literature (see OCCASIONS OF REVELATION), it was revealed in connection with the expulsion of the Jewish tribe of Banū l-Naḍīr (q.v.) from Medina (q.v.) in 4/625 (cf. Friedmann, *Tolerance*, 100-1). In the earliest works of exegesis (see EXEGESIS OF THE QURʾĀN: CLASSICAL AND MEDIEVAL), the verse is understood as an injunction *(amr)* to refrain from the forcible imposition of Islam, though there is no unanimity of opinion regarding the precise group of infidels to which the injunction had initially applied. Commentators who maintain that the verse was originally meant as applicable to all people consider it as abrogated *(mansūkh)* by Q 9:5, Q 9:29, or Q 9:73 (see ABROGATION). Viewing it in this way is necessary in order to avoid the glaring contradiction between the idea of tolerance and the policies of early Islam which did not allow the existence of polytheism — or any other religion — in a major part of the Arabian peninsula. Those who think that the verse was intended, from the very beginning, only for the People of the Book, need not consider it as abrogated: though Islam did not allow the existence of any religion other than Islam in most of the peninsula, the purpose of the jihād (q.v.) against the People of the Book, according to Q 9:29, is their submission and humiliation rather than their forcible conversion to Islam. As is well known, Islam normally did not practice religious coercion against Jews and Christians (see CHRISTIANS AND CHRISTIANITY) outside the Arabian peninsula, though substantial limitations were placed in various periods on the public aspects of their worship.

Later commentators, some of whom are characterized by a pronounced theological bent of thought, treat the verse in a totally different manner. According to them, Q 2:256 is not a command at all. Rather it ought to be understood as a piece of information *(khabar)*, or, to put it differently, a description of the human condition: it conveys the idea that embracing a religious faith (q.v.) can only be the result of empowerment and free choice *(tamkīn, ikhtiyār)*. It cannot be the outcome of constraint and coercion *(qasr, ijbār)*. Phrased differently, belief is "an action of the heart (q.v.)" in which no compulsion is likely to yield sound results *(li-anna l-ikrāh ʿalā l-īmān lā yaṣiḥḥu li-annahu ʿamal al-qalb)*. Religious coercion would also create a theologically unacceptable situation: if people were coerced into true belief, their positive response to prophetic teaching would become devoid of value, the world would cease to be "an abode of trial" (*dār al-ibtilāʾ*; Rāzī, *Tafsīr*, vii, 13; Ibn al-Jawzī, *Zād*, iv, 67; see TRUST AND PATIENCE; TRIAL) and, consequently, the moral basis for the idea of reward and punishment would be destroyed. This argumentation uses the verse in support of the idea of free will (see FREEDOM AND PREDESTINATION).

These tolerant attitudes toward the non-Muslims of Arabia were not destined to last. After the Muslim victory in the battle of Badr (q.v.; 2/624), the Qurʾān started to promote the idea of religious uniformity in the Arabian peninsula. Q 8:39 enjoins the Muslims "to fight... till there is no temptation [to abandon Islam; *fitna*] and the religion is God's entirely" (cf. Q 2:193). Once this development took place, the clauses in the *ʿahd al-umma* bestowing legitimacy on the existence of the Jewish religion in Medina had to undergo substantial reinterpretation. The clause stipulating that "the Jews have their religion and the believers have theirs" was now taken to mean that the Jewish religion is worthless (*ammā l-dīn fa-laysū minhu fī shayʾ*; Rubin, The constitution, 19-20, quoting Abū

ʿUbayd, *Amwāl,* 207). Similar was the fate of Q 109:6, which was declared abrogated by Q 9:5 *(āyat al-sayf)* or interpreted as a threat against the polytheists. This new attitude was also expressed in the prophetic tradition according to which "no two religions will coexist in the Arabian peninsula" (*lā yajtamiʿu dīnāni fī jazīrat al-ʿarab;* Friedmann, *Tolerance,* 91-3).

Despite the apparent meaning of Q 2:256, Islamic law allowed coercion of certain groups into Islam. Numerous traditionists and jurisprudents *(fuqahāʾ)* allow coercing female polytheists and Zoroastrians (see MAGIANS) who fall into captivity to become Muslims — otherwise sexual relations with them would not be permissible (cf. Q 2:221; see SEX AND SEXUALITY; MARRIAGE AND DIVORCE). Similarly, forcible conversion of non-Muslim children was also allowed by numerous jurists in certain circumstances, especially if the children were taken captive (see CAPTIVES) or found without their parents or if one of their parents embraced Islam (Friedmann, *Tolerance,* 106-15). It was also the common practice to insist on the conversion of the Manichaeans, who were never awarded the status of *ahl al-dhimma.*

Another group against whom religious coercion may be practiced are apostates from Islam (see APOSTASY). As a rule, classical Muslim law demands that apostates be asked to repent and be put to death if they refuse (see REPENTANCE AND PENANCE; BOUNDARIES AND PRECEPTS; CHASTISEMENT AND PUNISHMENT). It has to be pointed out, however, that the Qurʾān does not include any reference to capital punishment for apostasy. The Qurʾān mentions people who abandoned Islam and reverted to their former faith; those of them who did this willingly are condemned in a harsh and vindictive tone. There is a sense of resentment at the idea that someone who had perceived the truth of Islam and joined it only a short time ago could be swayed into reverting to idolatry or another false religion (see IDOLATRY AND IDOLATERS). The Qurʾān therefore asserts that the endeavors of the unrepentant apostates will fail, God will visit them with his wrath and will send valiant warriors against them; however, the main punishment of those who abandoned Islam will be inflicted upon them, according to the Qurʾān, in the hereafter (cf. Q 2:217; 3:86, 90; 4:137; 5:54; 9:74; 47:25). But in the ḥadīth and *fiqh* literature, the attitude toward the apostate became much harsher. It stands to reason that the Bedouin (q.v.) insurrection against the nascent Muslim state after the Prophet's death was the background for this development. The new attitude, which effectively transfers the punishment for apostasy from the hereafter (see ESCHATOLOGY) to this world, is reflected in utterances repeatedly attributed to the Prophet in the earliest collections of tradition. The most frequently quoted of these reads: "Whoever changes his religion, kill him" (*man baddala* or *man ghayyara dīnahu fa-qtulūhu* or *fa-ḍribū ʿunuqahu;* Mālik, *Muwaṭṭaʾ,* ii, 736). In another formulation, taking into account the idea that a person forced to abandon Islam is not considered an apostate, the Prophet is reported to have said: "Whoever willingly disbelieves in God after he has believed, kill him" *(man kafara bi-llāhi baʿda īmānihi ṭāʾiʿan fa-qtulūhu).* Most jurists maintain that the apostate should be given the opportunity to repent; there is a great variety of views concerning the time allowed for this purpose (Friedmann, *Tolerance,* 121-59; see REPENTANCE AND PENANCE).

Hence, the ideas of tolerance and coercion have undergone substantial development in the Qurʾān and are characterized by a great deal of variety in the literature of tradition and jurisprudence. Yet whatever the original meaning of Q 2:256 may have been, it is more compatible with the idea of religious tolerance than with any other approach. Any Muslim who wanted to practice religious toleration throughout the centuries of Islamic history could use Q 2:256, Q 10:99 and Q 109:6 as a divine sanction in support of his stance. On the other hand, Q 9:5, Q 9:29 or Q 9:73 may be interpreted as going a long way in the opposite direction.

Yohanan Friedmann

Bibliography
Primary (extensive primary documentation of all issues mentioned in this article is available in Friedmann, *Tolerance*): Abū ʿUbayd, al-Qāsim b. Sallām, *Kitāb al-Amwāl,* ed. M. Ḥāmid al-Fiqqī, Cairo 1353/1934; Ibn al-Jawzī, *Zād,* Damascus; Mālik, *Muwaṭṭaʾ,* Cairo 1951; Rāzī, *Tafsīr,* Beirut 1990; al-Sarakhsī, Abū Bakr Muḥammad b. Aḥmad, *Kitāb al-Mabsūṭ fī l-furūʿ,* 30 vols. (+ index, Beirut 1980), Beirut 1986, x, 98-124 (on the *murtadd*); Ṭabarī, *Tafsīr* (ad Q 2:256); Zamakhsharī, *Kashshāf.*
Secondary: M. Chokr, *Zandaqa et zindīqs en Islam au second siècle de l'hégire,* Damascus 1993; Y. Friedmann, *Tolerance and coercion in Islam. Interfaith relations in the Muslim tradition,* Cambridge 2003; F. Griffel, *Apostasie und Toleranz im Islam. Die Entwicklung zu al-Ġazālīs Urteil gegen die Philosophie und die Reaktionen der Philosophen,* Leiden 2000; id., Toleration and exclusion. Al-Shāfiʿī and al-Ghazālī on the treatment of apostates, in *BSOAS* 64 (2001), 339-54; W.B. Hallaq, Apostasy, in *EQ,* i, 119-22; A.M. Ḥūfī, *Samāḥat al-islām,* Cairo 1979; W. Kerber (ed.), *Wie tolerant ist der Islam?* Munich 1991; D. Little, J. Kelsay and A.A. Sachedina, *Human rights and the conflict of cultures. Western and Islamic perspectives on religious liberty,* Columbia, SC 1988; R. Mottahedeh, Toward an Islamic theology of toleration, in T. Lindhome and K. Vogt (eds.), *Islamic law reform and human rights. Challenges and rejoinders,* Copenhagen 1993, 25-36; Nöldeke, *GQ;* R. Paret, Innerislamischer Pluralismus, in P. Bachmann and U. Haarmann (eds.), *Die Islamische Welt zwischen Mittelalter und Neuzeit,* Beirut 1979, 523-9; id., Sure 2,256: Lā ikrāha fī d-dīni. Toleranz oder Resignation? in *Der Islam* 45 (1969), 299-300; id., Toleranz und Intoleranz im Islam, in *Saeculum* 21 (1970), 344-65; R. Peters and G.J.J. de Vries, Apostasy in Islam, in *WI* 17 (1976-77), 1-25; U. Rubin, The "Constitution of Medina." Some notes, in *SI* 62 (1985), 16 and note 45; A. Ṣaʿīdī, *al-Ḥurriyya al-dīniyya fī l-islām,* Cairo n.d.; A.A. Sachedina, *The Islamic roots of democratic pluralism,* New York 2001; S. Ward, A fragment from an unknown work by al-Ṭabarī on the tradition "Expel the Jews and Christians from the Arabian peninsula (and the lands of Islam)," in *BSOAS* 53 (1990), 407-20; A.L. Wismar, *A study in tolerance as practiced by Muḥammad and his immediate successors,* New York 1927.

Tolerance and Compulsion see TOLERANCE AND COERCION

Tomb see BURIAL; DEATH AND THE DEAD

Tomorrow see TIME

Tongue see ARABIC LANGUAGE; SPEECH

Tools for the Scholarly Study of the Qurʾān

The entire body of scholarship, both Muslim and non-Muslim, must be the foundation of any responsible scholarly study of the Qurʾān. Certain tools, however, form key elements of any scholarly library.

The text of the Qurʾān

The basic tool for the study of the Qurʾān is, of course, the text itself. Unlike the situation in scholarly study of some other scriptures, decisions regarding the base text to be used for analysis do not face scholars from the outset. We have a text of the Qurʾān before us, accepted by every Muslim. It is the text which is the well-known, well-established book, found between two covers in virtually every Muslim home, known for convenience as the ʿUthmānic text (see CODICES OF THE QURʾĀN; COLLECTION OF THE QURʾĀN; ʿUTHMĀN). That said, it must be admitted that this is a somewhat simplistic way of presenting the matter (see CONTEMPORARY CRITICAL PRACTICES AND THE QURʾĀN).

It is common to speak of the Royal

Egyptian edition of the Qurʾān published under the patronage of King Fuʾād I in 1342/1923 as being the modern standard text of the scripture (see PRINTING OF THE QURʾĀN). This edition has been criticized as not conveying the best rendition of the Ḥafṣ *ʿan* ʿĀṣim transmission which it purports to represent because it is based upon late Muslim sources for the details of the reading (see Bergsträsser, Koranlesung; see READINGS OF THE QURʾĀN). Some other copies of the Ḥafṣ *ʿan* ʿĀṣim tradition printed in the Muslim world — including a second edition of the Cairo text which appeared in 1952 — contain an additional (but small) number of minor variations especially in orthography (q.v.) and verse numbering (see VERSES). Printed copies of other established transmissions (e.g. that of Warsh) are available but their distribution is not widespread.

Still useful is the European edition of the Qurʾān produced by Gustav Flügel, which was published in 1834 and revised in 1841 and again in 1858. This edition maintains its value — it is typeset in a pleasant font, for example — but its verse numbering scheme, being at variance with any accepted Muslim tradition, has created an unfortunate complexity in scholarly referencing. To complicate matters further, Flügel constructed an eclectic edition of the text using undefined editorial principles. His edition has been subject to criticism on many grounds (see e.g. Ambros, Divergenzen; Spitaler, *Verszählung*).

Neither the Royal Egyptian text nor the Flügel edition may be considered a critically edited text in the sense that is understood in contemporary scholarly practice. Of course, such a concept may be thought redundant in the case of the Qurʾān, given the Muslim view of the authenticity of the written qurʾānic text and reliability of its transmission (see RECITERS OF THE QURʾĀN; TEXTUAL CRITICISM OF THE QURʾĀN; UNITY OF THE TEXT OF THE QURʾĀN). Even so, a substantial scholarly resource exists related to the establishment of such a critical text. Much of the material is the result of a project initiated in the 1930s which never achieved completion (see Nöldeke, GQ, iii *[Die Geschichte des Korantexts]*; Bergsträsser, *Plan;* Pretzl, *Fortführung;* Jeffery, Progress). In recent years a new effort has begun, one based on the critical analysis of texts written in the Ḥijāzī script, believed to be the oldest record of the text which we have available (see Noja, Note; see ARABIC SCRIPT; MANUSCRIPTS OF THE QURʾĀN; CALLIGRAPHY). Other manuscripts, epigraphy (see EPIGRAPHY AND THE QURʾĀN), scholarly emendations and related sources will also prove to be important elements in creating such a critical text, but attempts to gather these into a scholarly tool have yet to be made.

As a part of the effort to establish the critical text, attention has been paid to the variant readings and traditional codices of the Qurʾān. Jeffery's *Materials* was conceived as a major step along the way to the critical text edition, bringing together much of the data on variant readings *(qirāʾāt)* of the text. Such work needs considerable updating today in light of more extensive collections of variant readings that are becoming available (see ʿUmar and Mukram, *Muʿjam;* see also al-Khaṭīb, *Muʿjam;* the Qurʾān manuscripts discovered in 1973 in the Great Mosque of Ṣanʿāʾ present yet another potential source of information on the early history of the qurʾānic text; cf. Puin, Observations, 110-11).

The text of the Qurʾān is readily available in electronic form, following, for the most part, the tradition of the printed Egyptian edition (see COMPUTERS AND THE QURʾĀN). The text is available for downloading in fully voweled text format (for example, see www.al-kawthar.com/kotob/quran.zip [8 September 2005]); some unvoweled versions still linger at other sites, the result of limitations of early personal computer applications. The text is available for consultation on the Web in a variety of formats; the most useful ones are in text form rather than graphic images as the former facilitates the process of "cutting-and-pasting" into other applications.

Concordances

Even in this age of electronic texts, the study of the Qurʾān is substantially eased by the existence of printed concordances; the closest thing available (which displays great potential) is a project at the University of Haifa for creating a web-accessible tagged qurʾānic text (see http://www.cs.haifa.ac.il/~shuly/Arabic/; accessed 7 September 2005). Two works are especially worthy tools. ʿAbd al-Bāqī's *al-Muʿjam al-mufahras li-alfāẓ al-Qurʾān al-karīm* is a concordance of the Arabic text (in the Cairo edition) organized according to Arabic word roots. Hanna E. Kassis, *A concordance of the Qurʾān*, is a concordance based on the translation by Arberry but organized according to the Arabic word roots, indexed to their English meanings. Such concordances may not be perfect tools (as Ambros, Lexikostatistik, 11, has pointed out) in that the analysis of the root structure of some words (and other technical matters) is open to dispute and confusion. Until, however, a fully lemmatized and annotated computerized text is produced (which would have to allow the recognition of differences of opinion on grammatical issues), these works certainly have their place. The issues which Ambros raises illustrate the difficulty of the task. The concordance function of Paret, *Koran*, is not complete but its attention to thematic and phrase parallels makes it an essential and unique tool (cf. also the thematic concordance of Jules La Beaume, with a supplement by Edouard Montet). An additional merit of Paret's work is its inclusion of separate lists of sūra (q.v.) titles; those lists may be supplemented by Lamya Kandil, Surennamen. Since virtually every Arabic commentary on the Qurʾān uses the names of the sūras rather than their numbers to refer to chapters of the text, such listings can be essential in clarifying cross-references.

While the Arabic text of the Qurʾān is easily available electronically and is thus fully searchable, a morphologically tagged text of the Qurʾān does not currently appear to be available electronically for manipulation on one's computer. Neither does there appear to be an electronic version of a concordance such as that of ʿAbd al-Bāqī. The CD ROM *Jameʾ: Software of quranic tafsir*, produced by Nashr-e Hadith-e Ahl al-Bayt Institute in Iran, allows for text search of the Qurʾān by word roots as well as individual words (while also providing English and Persian translations of the text, Arabic recitation, and fifty-nine commentaries in Arabic or Persian; see RECITATION OF THE QURʾĀN; EXEGESIS OF THE QURʾĀN: CLASSICAL AND MEDIEVAL; EXEGESIS OF THE QURʾĀN: EARLY MODERN AND CONTEMPORARY). Only the results of such searches, however, may be printed; there is no facility for exporting the texts themselves. Another useful search facility is available online at altafsir.com [February 26, 2003] which allows searching by root; those results allow for successful "cut-and-paste" operations from one's web browser into other applications.

Dictionaries

Until recently there did not exist a complete dictionary of the Qurʾān in any European language that could be considered a true modern scholarly tool. Penrice, *Dictionary*, was first published in 1873 and was based almost completely upon al-Bayḍāwī's (d. prob. 716/1316-17) commentary. That work continues to be a convenient place to start lexical investigation, but it is very limited in scope. Other European languages have been no better served; works include F.H. Dieterici, *Handwörterbuch* (1881); S. Fraenkel, *Vocabulis* (1880); C.A. Nallino, *Chrestomathia* (1893). The recent publication of Arne Ambros and Stephan Procházka, *A concise dictionary of Koranic Arabic* (Wiesbaden 2004), improves the situation substantially; the work is compiled on the basis of an extensive analysis of the text of the Qurʾān and consideration of earlier scholarly etymological examinations; the lexical impact of variant readings is also documented.

Specialized works on aspects of qurʾānic vocabulary continue to provide some supplementary support for lexicographical purposes. While not a full dictionary, an extensive and useful work is Mir, *Verbal idioms*. For the most part, standard scholarly bilingual dictionaries, such as those of Lane and its ongoing completion by M. Ullmann, *Wörterbuch*, and the *Dictionnaire* of R. Blachère, are essential for determining the range of possible meaning of many qurʾānic words.

Foreign vocabulary (q.v.) and proper names have attracted a good deal of scholarly attention and there are a number of works that help in the etymological understanding of non-Arabic words: Jeffery, *Foreign vocabulary*, has an extensive bibliography of Qurʾān-related lexicographical studies and provides a summary of etymological data on many words. Such information is in need of substantial updating in light of modern philological principles and more recent research (see for example, Zammit, *Comparative*).

Additionally, there are a large number of scholarly articles that treat a more limited range of individual qurʾānic words, but the lack of an effective bibliographical tool in the field means that the material cannot always be utilized effectively. Paret's *Kommentar* provides one means of locating references in standard scholarly works to lexicographical studies but only those published before the last quarter of the twentieth century. Finally, there is no substitute for the critical use of the Muslim commentary *(tafsīr)* tradition and its subsidiary lexicographical works when it comes to determining the range of meanings that Muslims have ascribed to qurʾānic words. Some of the books that treat "difficult words" in the Qurʾān approach the dimensions of a full Arabic dictionary of the Qurʾān; the classic text by al-Rāghib al-Iṣfahānī (fl. early fifth/eleventh cent.), *Mufradāt*, is the best example (see DIFFICULT PASSAGES).

Grammars

The situation for studying the grammar of the Qurʾān is similar to that of vocabulary; the best sources for grammatical details remain standard grammars such as that of W. Wright, *Grammar*, T. Nöldeke's *Grammatik*, and R. Blachère and M. Gaudefroy-Demombynes, *Grammaire*. Once again, a large number of specialized studies must be consulted on individual issues of grammar, for example Bergsträsser, *Verneinungs- und Fragepartikeln;* M. Chouémi, *Le verbe;* F. Leemhuis, *D and H stems;* Reckendorf, *Arabische Syntax*. Analysis of qurʾānic grammar is, of course, a part of most *tafsīr* works but even in the tradition of Arabic grammarians, no extensive and synthetic grammar devoted to qurʾānic Arabic appears to exist (see also GRAMMAR AND THE QURʾĀN; DIALECTS).

Thematic indices

The bibliography of scholarly treatments of the contents of the Qurʾān is extensive. A few works attempt to provide synoptic overviews. Mir, *Dictionary*, is introductory but useful, as is F. Sherif, *Guide to the contents*. Older but still valuable is H.U. Weitbrecht Stanton, *Teaching of the Qurʾān*.

The punch card analysis, Allard, *Analyse*, is now primitive in its technology but its ability to provide access to what would now be termed "hyperlinks" between subjects within the Qurʾān has still not been replaced. One continuing value of the work resides in the analytic system that its author constructed; it is probably the most sophisticated and complete of any attempt to thematize the Qurʾān through its semantic worldview.

Commentaries

Translations of the Qurʾān (q.v.) may be considered valuable tools for research since such works provide access to interpretations of the meaning of the Qurʾān; it is important to remember, of course, that the nature of a translation is necessarily monovalent. Thus the more extensive commentaries that have been written to accompany various translations are more useful tools. Paret, *Kommentar,* is essential; certain elements of Bell, *Commentary,* are also helpful. A more recent project is A.T. Khoury, *Der Koran,* a twelve-volume commentary incorporating a translation. Such commentaries cannot match the wealth of information and analysis available in the Arabic (and Persian) *tafsīr* tradition, of course.

Approaches to the Qurʾān

A number of introductions to the study of the Qurʾān exist which can be used with great profit because they incorporate many of the basic resources needed to orient a scholarly reading. As well, in their presuppositions, they provide basic methodological orientations to the field. Nöldeke, *GQ;* Blachère, *Introduction;* Bell, *Introduction,* updated as Watt-Bell, *Introduction,* clearly stand out as "classics." Protracted and explicit discussions of the methods by which one approaches the Qurʾān in scholarly study have yet to appear; most such reflections have been limited to articles or introductions to books. The oeuvre of M. Arkoun is probably the most significant in trying to bring attention to the issue (for example, Arkoun, Bilan).

Four books can be singled out because of their impact on the field in setting models for how studies might proceed; they also speak about the general contents of the Qurʾān and thus provide significant overviews of major portions of the scripture. These works indicate the range of concerns of more contemporary scholars and each in its own way has had a significant impact on qurʾānic studies as a discipline. Few serious studies of the Qurʾān can proceed without some acquaintance with the following works: (1) Izutsu, *God,* and (2) Izutsu, *Concepts:* each of these works tries to define a semantic range of vocabulary central to religious discussion and to examine it in the context of Arabia (see SOUTH ARABIA, RELIGIONS IN PRE-ISLAMIC). Concepts in these books are defined broadly, and the two works in combination provide a significant view of the religious and cognitive structures of the Qurʾān. The attention to the workings of the semantic method that is contained in these books has had a lasting effect on the discipline. (3) F. Rahman, *Major themes,* approaches the scripture with a structure that reflects the central tenets of Muslim theology as conceived in the late twentieth century: God (see FAITH; GOD AND HIS ATTRIBUTES; BELIEF AND UNBELIEF), man as individual, man in society (see ETHICS AND THE QURʾĀN), nature (see NATURE AS SIGNS), prophethood and revelation (see PROPHETS AND PROPHETHOOD; REVELATION AND INSPIRATION), eschatology (q.v.), Satan and evil (see DEVIL; GOOD AND EVIL; FALL OF MAN; VIRTUES AND VICES, COMMANDING AND FORBIDDING), and the emergence of the Muslim community (see COMMUNITY AND SOCIETY IN THE QURʾĀN). Rahman's volume is thus able to provide a full overview of the Qurʾān while demonstrating a historical mode of analysis within the basic framework of Muslim assumptions. (4) Wansbrough, *QS*, deals with the content of the Qur'ān under the following rubrics: revelation and canon (the document, its composition), emblems of prophethood, and origins of classical Arabic (issues of language; see LANGUAGE AND STYLE OF THE QUR'ĀN). Attention in this book is primarily to the relationship between form and content (see FORM AND STRUCTURE OF THE QUR'ĀN). The work has been considered controversial in its treatment of the Qur'ān's contents because its use of a biblical-Jewish paradigm to contextualize the scripture is criticized as offering only a limited view of the contents of the text in all its dimensions. Methodologically his study draws attention to the need for contextualization of the Qur'ān as an essential part of the process of understanding it. His work demonstrates a reading of the text that could be constructed outside the framework traditionally established for it by Muslim historiography (see SĪRA AND THE QUR'ĀN; OCCASIONS OF REVELATION; HISTORY AND THE QUR'ĀN). Each of these four works, then, provides not only an overview of the contents of the Qur'ān but also a model by which the analysis of that content can proceed.

Bibliographical aids

The scholarly study of the Qur'ān has a long history, certainly not as long as the Bible, but significant nonetheless (see also PRE-1800 PREOCCUPATIONS OF QUR'ĀNIC STUDIES). The history of the study has not been written, although a number of bibliographically-oriented articles provide good introductions. Valuable contributions are W.A. Bijlefeld, Some recent contributions; A. Jeffery, Present status; A. Neuwirth, Koran. As mentioned previously, Paret, *Kommentar,* is the only comprehensive bibliographical tool available, although given its age its function is now limited to more "classic" works of scholarship. This *Encyclopaedia of the Qur'ān* will likely provide the best bibliographical tool for scholars for most purposes. See also POST-ENLIGHTENMENT ACADEMIC STUDY OF THE QUR'ĀN; TRADITIONAL DISCIPLINES OF QUR'ĀNIC STUDY.

Andrew Rippin

Bibliography

Primary: al-Rāghib al-Iṣfahānī, *Mufradāt.*

Secondary: ʿAbd al-Bāqī; M. Allard, *Analyse conceptuelle du Coran sur cartes perforées,* 2 vols., Paris 1963; A.A. Ambros, Die Divergenzen zwischen dem Flügel- und dem Azhar-Koran, in *WZKM* 78 (1988), 9-21; id., Eine Lexikostatistik des Verbs im Koran, in *WZKM* 77 (1987), 9-36; Arberry; M. Arkoun, Introduction. Bilan et perspectives des études Coraniques, in Arkoun, *Lectures,* v-xxxiii; translated as Introduction. An assessment of and perspectives on the study of the Qur'ān, in A. Rippin (ed.), *The Qur'ān. Style and contents,* Ashgate 2001, 297-332; Bell, *Commentary;* id., *Introduction to the Qur'ān,* Edinburgh 1953; G. Bergsträsser, Koranlesung in Kairo, in *Der Islam* 20 (1932), 1-13; id., *Plan eines Apparatus Criticus zum Koran,* München 1930, repr. in Paret (ed.), *Koran,* 389-97; id., *Verneinungs;* W.A. Bijlefeld, Some recent contributions to qur'ānic studies. Selected publications in English, French, and German, 1964-1973, Parts I-III, in *MW* 64 (1974), 79-102, 172-9, 259-74; Blachère, *Introduction;* id., M. Chouémi and C. Denizeau, *Dictionnaire arabe-français, français-arabe,* Paris 1967-; R. Blachère and M. Gaudefroy-Demombynes, *Grammaire de l'arabe classique,* Paris 1975[3]; M. Chouémi, *Le verbe dans le Coran,* Paris 1966; F.H. Dieterici, *Arabisch-deutsches Handwörterbuch zum Koran und Tier und Mensch vor dem König der Genien,* Leipzig 1881; G. Flügel, *Corani textus arabicus,* Leipzig 1834, 1858[3]; S. Fraenkel, *De vocabulis in antiquis arabum carminibus et in Corano peregrinis,* Leiden 1880; Izutsu, *Concepts;* id., *God;* Jeffery, *For. vocab.;* id., *Materials;* id., The present status of qur'ānic studies, in *Middle East Institute: Report on current research,* Spring 1957, 1-16; id., Progress in the study of the Qur'ān text, in *MW* 25 (1935), 4-16; repr. in Paret (ed.), *Koran,* 398-410; L. Kandil, Die Surennamen in der offiziellen Kairiner Koranausgabe und ihreVarianten, in *Der Islam* 69 (1992), 44-60; H.E. Kassis, *A concordance of the Qur'an,* Berkeley 1983; A.Th. Khoury, *Der Koran. Arabisch-Deutsch. Übersetzung und wissenschaftlicher Kommentar,* 12 vols., Gütersloh 1990-; J. La Beaume, *Le Koran analysé d'après la traduction de M. Kasimirski et les observations de plusieurs autres savants orientalistes,*

Paris 1878; Ar. trans. M.F. ʿAbd al-Bāqī, *Tafṣīl āyāt al-Qurʾān al-ḥakīm,* Beirut 1969; Lane; F. Leemhuis, *The D and H Stems in koranic Arabic. A comparative study of the function and meaning of the faʿʿala and ʾafʿala forms in koranic usage,* Leiden 1977; N. Kermani, *Gott ist schön. Das ästhetische Erleben des Koran,* Munich 1999; A. al-Khaṭīb, *Muʿjam al-qirāʾāt,* 11 vols., Damascus 2002; Mir, *Dictionary;* id., *Verbal;* C.A. Nallino, *Chrestomathia Qorani Arabica,* Leipzig 1893; K. Nelson, *The art of reciting the Qurʾān,* Austin 1985; A. Neuwirth, Koran, in *GAP,* ii, 96-135; S. Noja Noseda, Note esterne in margine al 1° volume dei "Materiale per un'edizione critica de corano," in *Istituto Lombardo: Rendiconti classe di lettere e scienze morali e storiche* 134 (2000), 3-38; Nöldeke, *GQ;* id., *Zur Grammatik des klassischen Arabischen,* Darmstadt 1963[2] (1897[1]); Paret, *Kommentar;* id. (ed.), *Koran;* Penrice, *Dictionary;* O. Pretzl, *Die Fortführung des Apparatus Criticus zum Koran,* München 1934; G.-R. Puin, Observations on early Qurʾān manuscripts in Ṣanʿāʾ, in S. Wild (ed.), *The Qurʾān as text,* Leiden 1996, 107-11; F. Rahman, *Major themes of the Qurʾān,* Minneapolis 1980; H. Reckendorf, *Arabische Syntax,* Heidelberg 1921; id., *Die syntaktischen Verhältnisse des Arabischen,* 2 vols., Leiden 1895; F. Sherif, *A guide to the contents of the Qurʾan,* London 1985; A. Spitaler, *Die Verszählung des Koran nach islamischer Überlieferung,* München 1935; H.U. Weitbrecht Stanton, *The teaching of the Qurʾān. With an account of its growth and a subject index,* London 1919; M. Ullmann, *Wörterbuch der klassischen arabischen Sprache,* Wiesbaden 1970-; A.M. ʿUmar and A. Mukram, *Muʿjam al-qirāʾāt al-qurʾāniyya,* 8 vols., Kuwait 1982-5, repr. Cairo 1997; Wansbrough, *QS;* W.M. Watt, *Companion to the Qurʾān,* London 1967; Watt-Bell, *Introduction;* W. Wright, *A grammar of the Arabic language,* 2 vols., Cambridge 1859-62; 1896-8[3]; M.R. Zammit, *A comparative lexical study of qurʾānic Arabic,* Leiden 2002.

Torah

The scripture revealed by God to Moses (q.v.) on Mount Sinai (q.v.). In the Qurʾān, it is mentioned by name (Ar. *Tawrāt*) eighteen times, but a number of other terms are used for the same revelation. The Arabic word *Tawrāt* clearly derives, if perhaps indirectly, from the Hebrew *Torah,* meaning law (see Jeffery, *For. vocab.,* 95-6; Lazarus-Yafeh, Tawrāt). In keeping, however, with the widespread belief that the Qurʾān does not contain words of foreign origin (see FOREIGN VOCABULARY), Muslim commentators traced it back to an Arabic root, viz. *w-r-y,* which means to strike fire (q.v.), a reference to the light (q.v.) said to be in the Torah (Q 5:44; 6:91; and cf. Q 3:184; 21:48; 35:25; see *Lisān al-ʿArab,* xv, 389). Some, like the exegetes al-Rāzī (d. 606/1210) and al-Zamakhsharī (d. 538/1144), rejected this etymology and admitted its non-Arabic origin. Although in the Qurʾān the name Torah is mostly used in its proper sense, i.e. the books of Moses or Pentateuch, it is often applied in post-qurʾānic Islamic literature to the entire Hebrew Bible, and even to Jewish extra-canonical literature. The rabbinical literature, too, is sometimes called Torah, which is not surprising considering the fact that Judaism considers these sources to be the "oral Torah."

References to the Torah in the Qurʾān

The word *Tawrāt* appears in the following verses: Q 3:3, 48, 50, 65, 93 (twice); 5:43, 44, 46 (twice), 66, 68, 110; 7:157; 9:111; 48:29; 61:6; and 62:5. In most of these cases it is mentioned in combination with the Gospel (q.v., Ar. *Injīl*), the sacred scripture of the Christians (see CHRISTIANS AND CHRISTIANITY). The Torah had earlier been confirmed by Jesus (q.v.; Q 3:50; 5:46; 61:6), and was now once again confirmed and clarified by the new revelation brought by Muḥammad (e.g. Q 3:3, and see also Q 2:89, 97, 101; 4:47; 5:15, 19, 48; 6:93; 46:12, 30; see REVELATION AND INSPIRATION; SCRIPTURE AND THE QURʾĀN). In addition to the instances of the word *Tawrāt,* the Qurʾān contains a much larger number of passages which clearly refer to this same scripture, describing it as the book brought by Moses, the book given to Moses, to Moses and Aaron (q.v.), or to the

Children of Israel (q.v.; Q 2:53, 87; 6:91, 154; 11:17, 110; 17:2; 23:49; 25:35; 28:43; 37:117; 40:53-4; 41:45; 45:16; 46:12). In numerous verses the Torah is subsumed under the collective rubric of the book (q.v.), possessed by the People of the Book (q.v.), which often indicates the Jews and the Christians together, but at times seems to refer to the Jews alone. Such verses are encountered in sūras (q.v.) from both the Meccan and the Medinan periods (e.g. Q 2:113, 121, 145, 146; 3:19, 23, 70, 71, 98, 110, 113, 199; 4:131; 5:59, 65; 6:20, 114; 13:36; 28:52; 29:46; see CHRONOLOGY AND THE QURʾĀN). All verses containing the word Torah seem to date from the period of the Prophet's preaching in Medina (q.v.), after he had come into close contact with Jews (see JEWS AND JUDAISM), although Q 7:157, which declares that Muḥammad can be found in the Torah and the Gospel, is assigned by many to the late Meccan period (see MECCA). Verses referring to the Torah as the Book of Moses, however, can be found in sūras from both periods of Muḥammad's preaching. Closely related to *Tawrāt* is another term: the *ṣuḥuf* or scrolls (q.v.; and see also SHEETS) of Moses, mentioned in combination with those of Abraham (q.v.; Q 53:36-7; 87:19), which form part of a set of ancient or previous scrolls (Q 20:133; 87:18). The question of whether these scrolls of Moses are identical with the Torah, or were revealed before it and constitute a separate set of revelations, is debated. Figures given for the total number of scrolls revealed by God vary between fifty and one hundred and sixty three; those given to Moses are said to number ten or fifty.

In a series of verses dealing with the revelation on the Mount, we also encounter the tablets (*alwāḥ;* see COMMANDMENTS) which God gave to Moses (Q 7:145, 150, 154), and which are believed to have contained the entire Torah. There is much speculation in post-qurʾānic literature about the kind of precious stone the tablets were made of, as well as about their color and their number: the familiar figure of two is given, as are three, seven, and ten. In two of the qurʾānic verses mentioning the term *furqān* (viz. Q 2:53; 21:48; see CRITERION) the revelation to Moses is intended. The term is ordinarily translated as criterion, and glossed as what distinguishes between true and false, right and wrong, allowed and prohibited. Two further terms that should be mentioned as belonging to the same semantic field are *dhikr* (remembrance [q.v.]) and *zabūr* (pl. *zubur,* revealed scriptures), which are occasionally interpreted as references to the Torah, although the *zabūr* is most often taken to mean the Psalms (q.v.; see Q 3:184; 16:43-4; 21:7; 26:196; 35:25). In what follows, a composite account will be given of the Qurʾān's treatment of the Torah, using the whole gamut of terms applied in the Qurʾān and its exegesis to the Mosaic law. A substantial portion of the verses relates to the period of Moses and the Children of Israel, while others refer to the Jewish contemporaries of Muḥammad. We shall not discuss textual parallels between the Qurʾān and the Torah (for these, see Speyer, *Erzählungen;* Thyen, *Bibel und Koran*), nor address the questions of Muḥammad's acquaintance with the Bible or the extent of Jewish or Christian influence on him, on which there is a host of scholarly and less scholarly literature. Suffice it to say that Muḥammad's opponents (see OPPOSITION TO MUḤAMMAD) accused him of listening to, or copying from, Jewish and Christian informants (q.v.), which is vigorously denied in the Qurʾān, namely in Q 16:103 and Q 29:48. Although the first verse seems to admit that Muḥammad did have interlocutors from among the People of the Book, their role is reversed in Muslim tradition to that of recipients of Muḥammad's teachings (see Gilliot, Les 'informateurs').

References to the book of Moses in the Qurʾān

God had given prophethood and scripture to the offspring of Abraham and Noah (q.v.; Q 4:54; 29:27; 57:26, and cf. 3:84; 6:83-90; see PROPHETS AND PROPHETHOOD). One of their descendants, Moses, was chosen to guide the Children of Israel (Q 2:53; 11:110; 17:2; 23:49; 32:23; 40:53-4). God summoned him to the Mount, where a conversation ensued (Q 7:142-3; see THEOPHANY). (This has given rise to the composition of a genre of texts called *Munājāt Mūsā,* the conversations of Moses with God; see Sadan, Some literary problems, 373-4, 395-6.) The meeting lasted forty nights, at the end of which God gave Moses the tablets, on which he had written admonitions and explained all things. This is taken as a reference to the Torah. (It is said that Moses could hear the squeaking of God's pen on the tablets; see *Lisān al-ʿArab,* ix, 192; x, 117.) In Moses' absence, the Children of Israel had made a calf which they worshiped (see CALF OF GOLD). Upon seeing this, he threw down the tablets, but once his anger abated, he took them up again. According to later sources, Moses had read in the tablets the description of an exemplary nation *(umma).* He asks God to make them his people, but is told that they are the people of Muḥammad. It is at this point that he shatters the tablets (see Rubin, *Between Bible and Qurʾān,* ch. 2). According to al-Suyūṭī (d. 911/1505; *Itqān,* i, 122f.), it is said that the tablets were originally seven in number, but that God kept six of them to himself, returning to Moses only one tablet. What is implied here is that God was saving the larger part of his heavenly book (q.v.) for a future occasion.

The verb used for God's revelation of the Torah is *anzala,* and that for the revelation of the Qurʾān *nazzala* (Q 3:3). The difference between these two forms of the same root, say the commentators, is that the Torah was revealed on a single occasion, whereas the Qurʾān was sent down piecemeal (see OCCASIONS OF REVELATION), and for a good reason: like the Israelites before them, the Muslims would have found it difficult to receive God's commandments all at once; it would be much easier to accept the new dispensation in small doses (Suyūṭī, *Itqān,* i, 121). Unlike the Qurʾān, the Torah was revealed directly by God (Q 4:164), without the mediation of an angel (q.v.). This, says al-Suyūṭī (*Itqān,* i, 122-3), is because the Torah was revealed to a prophet who could read and write (see LITERACY), whereas the Qurʾān was sent down in separate installments to an illiterate prophet (the most commonly accepted interpretation of the word *ummī* [q.v.] with which Muḥammad is described in Q 7:157; see also ILLITERACY). If Moses was grateful for this favor, the Children of Israel were not; they were reluctant to accept God's covenant (q.v.) contained in the Torah, and only accepted it after God held the Mount over their heads and threatened to send it crashing down on them (Q 2:63, 93; 4:154; 7:171; this motif is reminiscent of the Mishna: Sabbath, 80a, Avoda Zara, 2b). Soon, however, they broke their covenant (Q 2:64, 83, 93; 4:155; 5:13, 70), maligning and killing the prophets, uttering different words from the ones they were ordered to speak by God (Q 2:59; 7:162; see FORGERY; REVISION AND ALTERATION), and generally rejecting God's injunctions. The latter included both the duty to fight for God's cause (Q 9:111; see FIGHTING; PATH OR WAY) and the order to refrain from killing (Q 5:32; see MURDER; BLOODSHED). The commentators mention an additional violation of the covenant: the Israelites hid the description of Muḥammad *(naʿt Muḥammad),* which, according to Q 7:157, is found in their Torah and which they were under obligation to divulge (see also POLEMIC AND POLEMICAL LANGUAGE; INSOLENCE AND OBSTINACY).

The abrogation of the Mosaic law

The disobedience (q.v.) of the Israelites had grave consequences for themselves and their descendants, the Jews. Not only was their punishment in the afterlife assured, but in this life they were burdened with harsh laws (Q 4:160; see REWARD AND PUNISHMENT): much of what had earlier been allowed is now forbidden (q.v.) to them, especially in the realm of dietary law, where Israel (q.v.), i.e. Jacob (q.v.), had already imposed some restrictions on himself which did not originally form part of God's law (e.g. Q 3:93; 6:118-19, 146; see Wheeler, Israel and the Torah; see also LAWFUL AND UNLAWFUL). Jesus came to abrogate a number of these laws (Q 3:50), and further restrictions were later lifted by Muḥammad (Q 5:5; 7:157; see ABROGATION). There is obviously no contradiction between their confirming the earlier law and abrogating it. That the Torah was indeed abrogated and had lost its validity, inasmuch as it did not correspond with the teachings of Islam, was not doubted by any Muslim, although there apparently remained some who believed that certain Mosaic laws applied to them as well (see Adang, Ibn Ḥazm's critique; that God abrogated parts of his revelation or cast them into oblivion, only to replace them with something similar or better, is stated in Q 2:106, which is, however, mostly linked to the abrogation of one qurʾānic verse by another).

Rejection of the confirming scripture

In rejecting their covenant, the Israelites had behaved exactly like all the other nations to which God had sent messengers (see MESSENGER), and Muḥammad would encounter the same reaction during his mission (cf. Q 3:184; 35:25). When he began to preach his message, he was first opposed by the polytheists of Mecca (see POLYTHEISM AND ATHEISM), and later also by the People of the Book, especially the Jews among them. They denied that Muḥammad was receiving revelations (Q 6:92) and demanded that he bring a revelation like the one given to Moses, although they had not been impressed when Moses brought his book, wanting to see God instead (Q 4:153). Despite Muḥammad's overtures and attempts to point out the similarities between their religions (Q 29:46), and the fact that he believed in all the earlier prophets (Q 3:84), their reaction was negative, and there were only a few who believed (Q 3:110, 113; cf. 29:47, which is seen as a reference to the Jewish convert ʿAbdallāh b. Salām and the sympathetic king of Ethiopia; see ABYSSINIA). Yet they should have recognized this message (or perhaps the Prophet himself; see the commentaries to Q 2:144; 6:20) as they recognized their own sons. The People of the Book, more than anyone else, should embrace it. Instead, they fling the book behind their backs (Q 2:101; this is taken to mean either the Torah with its annunciations of Muḥammad, or God's revelations in general; see also Q 3:187 where it is the covenant that is discarded). Despite their overall hostility, Muḥammad is told to consult the People of the Book if he has any doubts about what God revealed to him (Q 10:94, and cf. Q 16:43-4; 21:7). Various commentators explain that it is only the believers among the People of the Book, like ʿAbdallāh b. Salām, who are intended here (see BELIEF AND UNBELIEF).

For all the skepticism with which they regarded Muḥammad, a group of Jews appealed to his judgment (q.v.; Q 5:42-3; cf. also Q 3:23). Post-qurʾānic sources are virtually unanimous about the circumstances which supposedly gave rise to the revelation of these verses: an adulterous Jewish couple was brought before Muḥammad, who was asked to pass judgment on them. This was a test to see whether he would apply the law of the Torah, which he claimed to confirm. Muḥammad asks the Jews what punishment is prescribed in the Torah (see CHASTISEMENT AND PUNISHMENT; BOUNDARIES AND PRECEPTS), so that he can apply it, following the example of the prophets, the rabbis and the scholars of the Jews (Q 5:44; see SCHOLAR). Taken aback, the Jews cover the passage which prescribes stoning (q.v.), and tell him that adulterers are to be flogged and their faces blackened — which is how they used to deal with the more prominent members of their community (see FLOGGING; ADULTERY AND FORNICATION). Muḥammad is unconvinced, and is proven correct when a convert to Islam points to the relevant passage in the Torah. The Prophet thereupon decides to have the couple stoned, much to the horror of the Jews. Q 5:43 expresses amazement at the fact that the Jews appeal to Muḥammad, when they possess the Torah in which God has given his ruling. And moreover, say the commentators, why should they turn to a prophet whose mission they utterly reject? Q 3:23, too, is cited as proof that the Jews were averse to the contents of the Torah. According to the exegetes, it was revealed after Muḥammad entered the *Bayt al-Midrās* and became embroiled in a discussion about Abraham. He told the Jews to bring the Torah to clinch the issue, but they refused. This story can in turn be connected with Q 3:65, in which the Jews and the Christians are criticized for claiming Abraham as one of their own although he predated the revelation of the Torah and of the Gospel and, therefore, the beginnings of their respective religions. (That the Jews and the Christians clashed with each other, despite the fact that they both read the scripture, is stated in Q 2:113.)

In two verses (Q 5:66, 68) the Jews are told that they will not be rightly guided unless they observe the Torah, and the same is true about the Christians and their scripture. The commentators tell us what they understood by "observing the Torah": accepting its teachings, such as the mission of Muḥammad, and its laws, which include a prohibition of taking interest (Q 4:161; see USURY). But the Jews deliberately ignore the revelation with which they have been entrusted, and do not apply the Torah. They have as much understanding as an ass carrying books (Q 62:5; see METAPHOR).

Tampering with the Torah

The Qurʾān more than once accuses the Israelites, the Jews, and the People of the Book in general, of having deliberately changed the word of God as revealed in the Torah and of passing off as God's revelation something they themselves wrote (Q 2:75-9; 4:46; 5:13). They are charged with confounding the truth (q.v.) with falsehood (Q 2:42; 3:71; see LIE), concealing the truth (e.g. Q 3:187), hiding part of the book (Q 6:91), or twisting their tongues when reciting the book (Q 3:78). In some verses we find a combination of allegations (e.g. Q 2:42; 3:71; 4:46). What may be at the root of these allegations is that the Jews denied that Muḥammad was mentioned in their scripture. Since the Qurʾān does not always explicitly state how, when, and by whom this misrepresentation (known as *taḥrīf*) was effected — some authors ascribe a major role to Ezra (q.v.) — different interpretations of the relevant verses soon arose. According to one, the Jews did not corrupt the text of their scripture, but merely misrepresented its contents. The other view, which developed somewhat later and seems to be held by the majority of Muslims, asserts that the Israelites and later the Jews changed the written text of the Torah, adding to and deleting from it as they pleased. Its most vocal and influential representative was Ibn Ḥazm of Cordoba (d. 456/1064), but several other polemicists took his cue, among them Jewish converts to Islam such as ʿAbd al-Ḥaqq al-Islāmī (wrote ca. 797/1395) and Samawʾal al-Maghribī (d. 570/1175), who sought to demonstrate the superiority of their adopted faith at the expense of Judaism. According to both interpretations of the tampering-verses, the Israelites and the Jews were motivated by a desire to delete or obscure the scriptural references to Muḥammad, as well as by their aversion to certain God-given commandments, such as stoning adulterers, as was seen. The allegation of textual corruption continues to be aired even in modern times. It has been used to delegitimize Jewish claims to Palestine, by stating that in the unadulterated Torah the land was promised not to the descendents of Isaac (q.v.), i.e. the Jews, but to those of Ishmael (q.v.), i.e. the Arabs (q.v.); the former just substituted the names (see Haddad, *Arab perspectives,* 89-122).

Ambivalent attitudes

Since the Qurʾān calls the Torah a divine scripture, Muslims must treat it with the respect due any one of God's books (Q 2:177, 285; 4:136) even if they have their doubts about the authenticity, and hence the sanctity, of the Torah which the Jews possess. The ambivalent attitude towards the Torah is well illustrated in a number of texts from the Muslim west. A *fatwā* from fourth/tenth century Qayrawān deals with the question of if and how to punish a Muslim slave who, in a fit of anger, reviled the Torah, if it can be proven that he only targeted the forged Jewish Torah and not the original divine scripture, in which case his offense did not constitute blasphemy (q.v.; al-Wansharīsī, *Miʿyār,* ii, 362-3, 525-6; see Adang, Tunisian mufti). In sixth/twelfth century Cordoba Ibn Rushd "the elder" (d. 520/1126) forbade Muslims to sell books supposedly containing the Torah or the Gospel, since there was no way to establish whether these were the true, uncorrupted scriptures, and it is unlawful to make a profit from such dubious transactions. But in any case, he adds, even the genuine scriptures have been abrogated, so that dealing in them is out of the question (Ibn Rushd al-Jadd, *al-Bayān,* xviii, 559-60). In Naṣrid Granada a *fatwā* was issued to the effect that despite doubts about the Torah's authenticity, Jewish litigants who appear before the Muslim *qāḍī* and are required to take an oath, should solemnly swear by their book, and preferably in the synagogue, for the fact that they hold the Torah to be true and sacred considerably reduces the risk of perjury (al-Wansharīsī, *Miʿyār,* x, 309 f.; Adang, Swearing).

Tracing Muḥammad in the Torah

Muslims who believed that the Jews possessed the original Torah, and merely interpreted it incorrectly assumed, naturally, that the references to Muḥammad of which Q 7:157 speaks could be found in the book (see Rubin, *Eye,* ch. 1, on early attempts to trace Muḥammad). Paradoxically, however, even commentators who regarded the Torah as a corrupted book that was not to be relied upon tapped it for references to Muḥammad, his nation and his religion (see McAuliffe, Qurʾānic context). That such references could still be found in an otherwise corrupted book was sometimes explained with the claim that God had preserved these specific passages from distortion. Muslim writers did not usually attempt to trace these passages in the Jewish scriptures themselves. First of all, they did not need to: lists of testimonies had been available at least since the late second/eighth century, when a number of them were included in an epistle sent on behalf of the caliph Hārūn al-Rashīd (r. 170-93/786-809) to the Byzantine emperor Constantine VI. They are clearly of Christian origin, being mostly Messianic passages made available to Muslim scholars by converts to Islam. Even Ibn Qutayba (d. 276/889), one of the few scholars to demonstrate some familiarity with the Torah, and especially the book of Genesis, apparently relied on a list of testimonies for his "Proofs of Prophethood" (*dalāʾil al-nubuwwa;* translated in Adang, *Muslim writers,* 267-77), which was used, among others, by Ibn Ḥazm and Ibn Qayyim al-Jawziyya (d. 751/1350). The testimonies cited most often by Muslim authors are Gen. 17:29; Deut. 18:18f.; Deut. 33:2f. and Isa. 21:6-10, the latter belonging to the Torah in its wider sense. These and other passages became a standard ingredient in tracts about the proofs of Muḥammad's prophethood (*dalāʾil* — or *aʿlām* — *al-nubuwwa;* see Stroumsa, The signs of prophecy). Secondly, apart from Jewish and Christian converts to Islam, few Muslims knew Hebrew, Syriac or Greek, and translations of the Torah and further parts of the Bible into Arabic were not readily available before the mid-ninth century: the claims of Aḥmad b. ʿAbdallāh b. Salām (active around the end of the second/eighth century) to have produced a full translation of the Torah, faithful to both the source and the target language is not altogether credible (Ibn al-Nadīm, *Fihrist,* 24; Adang, *Muslim writers,* 19-20), while the translations produced in the eighth and ninth centuries C.E. in some isolated monasteries in Palestine probably did not reach the Muslim public. The earliest Arabic translations accessible to Muslim readers seem to have been those by Ḥunayn b. Isḥāq (d. 260/873), which is referred to by al-Masʿūdī (d. 345/956; *Tanbīh,* 112-13) as the one considered most accurate, and al-Ḥārith b. Sinān, who seems to have been active in the latter part of the third/ninth and the first half of the fourth/tenth century. Both were translated not from the Hebrew, but from the Greek, first into Syriac and subsequently into Arabic. Further translations, based on the Hebrew, had been made by a number of Jewish scholars, Rabbanite and Karaite alike. The most influential one was that by Saʿadya Gaon (d. 942 C.E.). These translations, however, were clearly for internal consumption: since most Jewish scholars used the Hebrew script even for their Arabic writings, they would not have been easily accessible to the Muslims.

Pseudo-biblical quotations

Contrary to what might have been expected, the increased accessibility of the Torah did not lead to an increase in reliable quotations. In the case of the *kalām* theologians this is understandable: they preferred rational to scriptural arguments. But apart from some authors of works of an encyclopedic or comparative character, such as Ibn Qutayba, al-Masʿūdī (d. 345/956), al-Maqdisī (wrote ca. 355/966), and al-Bīrūnī (d. ca. 442/1050), and writers moved by polemical considerations, like Ibn Ḥazm, hardly anyone used the Torah (as distinguished from islamized versions of biblical accounts) as a source. This may be explained from the fact that many religious scholars were strongly opposed to consulting this book which was abrogated at best, and possibly corrupted as well. They were equally disapproving of seeking information from Jews about their beliefs, although the transmission of biblical narratives (q.v.) whose protagonists had become islamized, was permitted (see Vajda, Juifs et musulmans; Kister, Ḥaddithū). Spurious quotations from the Torah, intended to lend authority to certain views, proliferated, which shows that the theory of the scripture's corruption was not generally accepted. Because the Torah remained a closed book to most Muslims, it was possible to ascribe sayings to it whose connection with the actual scripture was tenuous at best. As is only to be expected, the popular genres of *Qiṣaṣ al-anbiyāʾ* and *Isrāʾīliyyāt,* which deal with the lives of the prophets and the Israelites, abound in pseudo- or semi-scriptural passages. They can be found, however, in smaller or larger quantities, in almost all genres of Muslim writing, ranging from ḥadīth (see ḤADĪTH AND THE QURʾĀN) and *tafsīr,* to historiography, geography, lexicography, and biography. A good example is *Ḥilyat al-awliyāʾ,* a biographical dictionary of pious and ascetic Muslims, which contains many statements ascribed to the elusive Kaʿb al-Aḥbār, Wahb b. Munabbih, Mālik b. Dinār and other putative specialists in the sacred books, on the pattern "it is written in the Torah" *(maktūb fī l-Tawrāt),* or "I have read in the Torah" *(qaraʾtu fī l-Tawrāt),* usually followed by some moral or ethical principle, or saying in praise of ascetical attitudes and practices (see ASCETICISM).

Apart from more or less universal ethical principles (see ETHICS AND THE QURʾĀN), which can be said to correspond at least to the spirit of the Jewish scriptures, less obvious things were traced to the Torah as well; the Greek theory of the four humors, for example, and the description of the second caliph, ʿUmar ("a horn of iron"; perhaps inspired by Dan. 7; see Abū Nuʿaym al-Iṣfahānī, *Ḥilyat al-awliyāʾ,* vi, 25), whose murder, too, was foretold in the Torah (al-Mālaqī, *Maqtal ʿUthmān,* i, 36). And Ḥaydara, one of the names of ʿAlī b. Abī Ṭālib (q.v.), could be encountered there (Khalīl b. Aḥmad, *Kitāb al-ʿAyn,* iii, 156). The Umayyad caliph ʿUmar b. ʿAbd al-ʿAzīz (r. 99-101/717-20) was allegedly described in the Torah as a righteous man, whose death was bewailed by the heavens for forty days (Abū Nuʿaym al-Iṣfahānī, *Ḥilyat al-awliyāʾ,* v, 339, 342); and not only Mecca, but also the city of Rayy is mentioned in the book of Moses in positive terms (Yāqūt, *Buldān,* iii, 118; iv, 225). At some point, however, someone must have decided that this was going too far: in an equally fictitious account, the (unnamed) Jewish exilarch told his Muslim interlocutors that what Kaʿb was telling them was a pack of lies, and that actually the Torah was very similar to their own scripture (Ibn Ḥajar, *Iṣāba,* v, 651).

Similar, yet different

The notion that there is a large degree of correspondence between the Qurʾān and the Torah is implicit in the qurʾānic statements that it confirms the earlier scriptures, that it constitutes a revelation like the Torah and the Gospel, and that it is contained in the earlier scriptures (Q 3:3; 26:196; 29:47). The exegetes state that certain passages from the Qurʾān correspond verbatim with the Torah. As proof they cite two passages which are assumed to occur also in the Torah, namely Q 5:45, which mentions the law of talion (see RETALIATION), and Q 48:29, which states that the believers are described in the Torah as having a mark on their foreheads as a result of their frequent prostration (see BOWING AND PROSTRATION).

ʿAbdallāh b. ʿAmr b. al-ʿĀṣ (whose father, incidentally, is said to have received permission from the Prophet, or from ʿUmar, to read the true Torah) said that Muḥammad is described in the Torah in the same way that he is described in the Qurʾān: as a witness (see WITNESSING AND TESTIFYING) and a bearer of good tidings (see GOOD NEWS) and a warner (q.v.; see Q 17:105; 25:56; 33:45; 48:8); he is not harsh nor rough nor does he cry in the streets. And Kaʿb al-Aḥbār attributed the following saying to the Torah: "Oh Muḥammad, I am revealing to you a new Torah, which will open blind eyes (q.v.), deaf ears (q.v.) and uncircumcised hearts" (Suyūṭī, *Itqān*, i, 115; see VISION AND BLINDNESS; HEARING AND DEAFNESS; HEART; CIRCUMCISION). These passages are reminiscent of Isaiah 42:2 and 35:5. The same man is credited with the information that the opening verse of the Torah corresponds with Q 6:1 ("Praise be to God, who has created the heavens and the earth, and has appointed darkness [q.v.] and light. Yet those who disbelieve ascribe rivals to their lord"), and that it ends with Q 17:111: "Praise be to God who has not taken a son [...] and magnify him with all magnificence." The saying that the final verse of the Torah is identical to the second half of the last verse of Q 11, Sūrat Hūd ("so worship him and put your trust in him. Your lord is not unaware of what you do," Q 11:123; see KNOWLEDGE AND LEARNING; HIDDEN AND THE HIDDEN), however, is also ascribed to Kaʿb, as is the statement that the first verses to be revealed in the Torah were ten verses from Q 6 (Sūrat al-Aʿnām, "Cattle"), starting with Q 6:151: "Say: Come, I will recite to you that which God has made a sacred duty for you" (*mā ḥarrama rabbukum ʿalaykum;* see SACRED AND PROFANE; LAW AND THE QURʾĀN). These verses bear a striking resemblance to the ten commandments (see Brinner, An Islamic Decalogue). Q 62:1 ("All that is in the heavens and all that is in the earth [q.v.] glorifies God, and he is the mighty, the wise"; see HEAVEN AND SKY; GLORIFICATION OF GOD) is said to appear 700 times in the Torah, and al-Raḥmān, the name by which God made himself known to Moses, is said to be found throughout the Torah (Suyūṭī, *Itqān*, i, 116), which contains an additional 999 names for God (Ibn Kathīr, *Tafsīr*, i, 20). It is said that while the contents of the two scriptures are essentially the same, their chapters bear different titles. Thus Q 50, Sūrat Qāf, is entitled in the Torah *al-Mubayyiḍa,* since it will whiten the face of he who believes in it on the day when faces will be blackened; Q 36, Sūrat Yā Sīn, appears in the Torah under the name *al-Muʿamma,* for it encompasses the good things of this life and of the afterlife. Many more examples of this kind could be cited. But not only isolated passages were attributed to the Torah: longer texts purporting to contain the true Torah were compiled, as were islamized Psalters. The texts in question appear to be ethical treatises which resemble the Qurʾān rather more than the Torah (see Sadan, Some literary problems; Jeffery, A Moslem Torah).

While the Torah, then, is believed to be very similar to the Qurʾān, the two scriptures are also said to differ on important points. Although it was important to emphasize that the Qurʾān stood at the end of a long line of venerated scriptures, which strengthened its authority, it was equally important to stress its unique nature and superiority (see Shnizer, *The Qurʾān*). It is said, for example, that Q 1, Sūrat al-Fātiḥa ("The Opening"; see FĀTIḤA), is unique to the Qurʾān, and unparalleled, and that neither in the Torah nor in the Gospel did God reveal anything like it. But the main difference was that unlike the Torah, the Qurʾān constituted an inimitable miracle and was matchless in style, composition and content (see INIMITABILITY; LANGUAGE AND STYLE OF THE QURʾĀN).

Translatable, therefore inferior

Many Muslim apologists and polemicists were aware that different versions of the Torah had existed even prior to its translation into Arabic, namely that of the Jews, the Samaritan Pentateuch and the Greek Septuagint. While some, like Ibn Ḥazm, pointed to the discrepancies between these versions as proof of the scripture's corrupted state, others, like Ibn Qutayba and al-Bāqillānī (d. 403/1013), argued — without playing the distortion card — that the existence of translations of the Torah was one of the clearest proofs of its inferiority to the Qur'ān which, because of its inimitable character, remained untranslated and untranslatable. For the Karaite al-Qirqisānī (fl. tenth cent. C.E.) the very fact that the Qur'ān only existed in one language weakened not the Jewish case, but the Muslim one, for, he said, only those fluent in Arabic could possibly appreciate the miraculous nature of the Qur'ān (Ben-Shammai, The attitude).

Further proof of the Qur'ān's superiority in the eyes of the Muslims is that it had been revealed in the presence of the entire nation, unlike the Torah, which had been given to Moses in the presence of a selected few only, and was not transmitted to the entire community, nor was it transmitted in uninterrupted succession from one generation to the other *(tawātur)*. Although hardliners like Ibn Ḥazm took the view that the Israelites and Jews had deliberately suspended the transmission of their (essentially unwanted) scripture, others, like the astronomer al-Bīrūnī, took a more charitable view: the Jews could not possibly have transmitted their Torah from generation to generation, because of the adversities they suffered, like expulsion and captivity.

Jewish reactions to attempts at discrediting the Torah

The Jews took up the defense of their scripture in polemical and apologetical tracts that were usually for internal consumption. In Iraq Saʿadya Gaon and his Karaite contemporary Yaʿqūb al-Qirqisānī, among others, tried to demonstrate, with rational and scriptural arguments, that the Torah had not been and would not be abrogated. They do not address the allegation of scriptural corruption, which was not usually raised by the Muslim *mutakallimūn* either; Muʿtazilī (see MUʿTAZILĪS) and Ashʿarī theologians attempted to refute the Jewish argument for the eternal validity of their scripture by rational means (see Sklare, Responses). Rabbanite and Karaite commentators did not deny that Islam was referred to in the Hebrew Bible: it was the last of the four kingdoms that subjugated Israel, according to the book of Daniel. Redemption will come when this kingdom ends. This should in no way, however, be taken as an endorsement of Muslim claims that Muḥammad is a true prophet. If anything, it was the falsity of his claims that could be demonstrated on the basis of the biblical text.

In later centuries it was formidable Jewish scholars like Jehudah ha-Levi (d. 1141 C.E.), Abraham b. Daud (d. 1181 C.E.), Moses Maimonides (d. 1204 C.E.), and Solomon Ibn Adret (d. 1310 C.E.), interestingly enough all Spaniards, who defended Judaism and its Torah against the attacks of the Muslim scholars. The influence of the arguments of their fellow-countryman, Ibn Ḥazm, can easily be discerned in their works.

Camilla P. Adang

Bibliography

Primary: ʿAbd al-Ḥaqq al-Islāmī, *al-Sayf al-mamdūd fī l-radd ʿalā aḥbār al-Yahūd*, ed. E. Alfonso, Madrid 1998; Abū Nuʿaym al-Iṣfahānī, *Ḥilyat al-awliyāʾ*, 10 vols., Beirut 1405/1984; Ibn Ḥajar, *al-Iṣāba fī tamyīz al-ṣaḥāba*, ed. A.M. al-Bajāwī, 8 vols., Beirut 1412/1992; Ibn Ḥazm, *Milal;* Ibn al-Jawzī, *al-Wafāʾ bi-aḥwāl al-Muṣṭafā*, ed. M. ʿAbd al-Wāḥid, Cairo 1386/1966; id., *Zād*; Ibn Kathīr, *Tafsīr;* Ibn al-Nadīm, *Fihrist*; Ibn Qayyim al-Jawziyya, *Kitāb Hidāyat al-ḥayārā min al-Yahūd wa-l-Naṣārā*, Cairo 1323/1905; Ibn Rushd (al-Jadd), *al-Bayān wa-l-taḥṣīl wa-l-sharḥ wa-l-tawjīh wa-l-taʿlīl*

fī l-masāʾil al-mustakhraja, ed. M. Ḥajjī et al., 20 vols., Beirut 1408/1988; *Jalālayn;* al-Khalīl b. Aḥmad, *Kitāb al-ʿAyn,* ed. M. al-Makhzūmī and I. al-Sāmarrāʾī, 5 vols., n.p. n.d.; Judah ha-Levi, *The Kuzari (Kitab al-Khazari). An argument for the faith of Israel,* trans. H. Hirschfeld, New York 1964; *Lisān al-ʿArab;* Moses Maimonides, *Epistle to Yemen,* in A.S. Halkin (trans.), *Crisis and leadership. Epistles of Maimonides,* Philadelphia 1985, 91-208; al-Mālaqī, Muḥammad b. Yaḥyā, *al-Tamhīd wa-l-bayān fī maqtal al-shahīd ʿUthmān,* ed. M.Y. Zayid, Doha 1405/2003; Masʿūdī, *Kitāb al-Tanbīh wa-l-ishrāf,* ed. M.J. de Goeje, Leiden 1894, 112; Muqātil, *Tafsīr;* al-Samawʾal al-Maghribī, *Ifḥām al-Yahūd. Silencing the Jews,* ed. and trans. M. Perlmann, in *Proceedings of the American Academy of Jewish Research* 32 (1964), 15-102; Suyūṭī, *Itqān;* Ṭabarī, *Tafsīr;* al-Wansharīsī, *al-Miʿyar al-muʿrib wa-l-jāmiʿ al-mughrib ʿan fatāwā ʿulamāʾ Ifrīqiyā wa-l-Andalus wa-l-Maghrib,* ed. M. Ḥajjī et al., 12 vols., Rabat/Beirut 1401-3/1981-3; Yāqūt, *Buldān.*
Secondary: M. Accad, Muḥammad's advent as the final criterion for the authenticity of the Judeo-Christian tradition. Ibn Qayyim al-Jawziyya's *Hidāyat al-ḥayārā fī ajwibat al-Yahūd wa-l-Naṣārā,* in B. Roggema et al. (eds.), *The three rings. Textual studies in the historical trialogue of Judaism, Christianity and Islam,* Leuven 2005, 217-35; C. Adang, A fourth/tenth century Tunisian *muftī* on the sanctity of the Torah of Moses, in N. Ilan et al. (eds.), *The intertwined worlds of Islam. Essays in memory of Hava Lazarus-Yafeh,* Jerusalem 2002, vii-xxxiv; id., Ibn Ḥazm's critique of some "Judaizing" tendencies among the Mālikites, in R.L. Nettler (ed.), *Medieval and modern perspectives on Muslim Jewish relations,* Oxford 1995, 1-15; id., *Muslim writers on Judaism and the Hebrew Bible. From Ibn Rabban to Ibn Hazm,* Leiden 1996; id., A reply to Ibn Ḥazm. Solomon b. Adret's Polemic against Islam, in M. Fierro (ed.), *Judíos y musulmanes en al-Andalus y el Magreb. Contactos intelectuales,* Madrid 2002, 179-209; id., Swearing by the *Mujaljala.* Jewish oaths in the Muslim west (forthcoming); H. Ben-Shammai, The attitude of some early Karaites towards Islam, in I. Twersky (ed.), *Studies in Medieval Jewish history and literature,* II, Cambridge, MA 1984, 3-40; W.M. Brinner, An Islamic Decalogue, in id. and S.D. Ricks (eds.), *Studies in Islamic and Judaic traditions,* Atlanta 1986, 67-84; R. Brunschvig, L'argumentation d'un théologien musulman du X siecle contre le judaïsme, in *Homenaje a Millás-Vallicrosa,* 2 vols., Barcelona 1954, i, 225-41; R. Caspar and J.M. Gaudeul, Textes de la tradition musulmane concernant le taḥrīf (falsification) des écritures, in *Islamochristiana* 6 (1980), 61-104; A.A. Dawud, *Muhammad in the Bible,* Kuala Lumpur 1969; T.A.M. Fontaine, *In defence of Judaism. Abraham ibn Daud. Sources and Structure of ha-Emunah ha-Ramah,* Assen 1990; Cl. Gilliot, Les 'informateurs' juifs et chrétiens de Muḥammad. Reprise d'un problème traité par Aloys Sprenger et Theodor Nöldeke, in *JSAI* 22 (1998), 84-126 (on the alleged source of any similarities between the Torah and the Qurʾān); I. Goldziher, Über muhammedanische Polemik gegen Ahl al-Kitâb, in *ZDMG* 32 (1878), 341-87, repr. in id., *GS,* ii, 1-47; M.Y.S. Haddad, *Arab perspectives of Judaism. A study of image formation in the writings of Muslim Arab authors, 1948-1978,* PhD diss., Rijksuniversiteit te Utrecht 1984; I. al-Ḥārdallū, *al-Tawrāt wa-l-Yahūd fī fikr Ibn Ḥazm,* Khartoum 1984; J. Horovitz, Tawrāt, in *EI[1]*, viii, 706-7; Jeffery, *For. vocab.;* id., A Moslem Torah from India, in *MW* 15 (1925), 232-9; id., *The Qurʾān as scripture,* New York 1952; S. Karoui, *Die Rezeption der Bibel in der frühislamischen Literature am Beispiel der Hauptwerke von Ibn Qutayba (gest. 276/889),* Heidelberg 1997; M.J. Kister, *Ḥaddithū ʿan banī isrāʾīla wa-lā ḥaraja.* A study of an early tradition, in *IOS* 2 (1972), 215-39 (on the ambivalent attitude toward material of Jewish origin); H. Lazarus-Yafeh, *Intertwined worlds. Medieval Islam and Bible criticism,* Princeton 1992; id., Taḥrīf, in *EI[2]*, x, 111-12; id., Tawrāt, in *EI[2]*, x, 393-5; J.D. McAuliffe, The prediction and prefiguration of Muḥammad, in J. C. Reeves (ed.), *Bible and Qurʾān. Essays in scriptural intertextuality,* Atlanta 2003, 107-31; id., The qurʾānic context of Muslim biblical scholarship, in *Islam and Christian-Muslim relations* 7 (1996), 141-58; G.D. Nickel, *The theme of "tampering with the earlier scriptures" in early commentaries on the Qurʾān,* PhD diss., Calgary 2004; M. Perlmann, The medieval polemics between Islam and Judaism, in S.D. Goitein (ed.), *Religion in a religious age,* Cambridge, MA 1974, 103-38; T. Pulcini, *Exegesis as polemical discourse. Ibn Ḥazm on Jewish and Christian scriptures,* Atlanta 1998; N. Roth, Forgery and abrogation of the Torah. A theme in Muslim and Christian polemic in Spain, in *Proceedings of the American Academy of Jewish Research* 54 (1987), 203-36; U. Rubin, *Between Bible and Qurʾān. The Children of Israel and the Islamic self-image,* Princeton 1999 (on the Torah in its wider sense as a source of vocabulary and themes found in ḥadīth literature); id., *The eye of the beholder. The life of Muḥammad as viewed by the early Muslims. A textual analysis,* Princeton 1995, ch. 1; J. Sadan, Some literary problems concerning Judaism and Jewry in mediaeval Arabic sources, in M. Sharon (ed.), *Studies in Islamic history and civilization in honour of Professor David Ayalon,* Jerusalem/Leiden 1986, 353-98; M. Schreiner, Zur Geschichte der Polemik zwischen Juden und Muhammedanern, in

ZDMG 42 (1888), 591-675, repr. in id., *Gesammelte Schriften. Islamische und jüdisch-islamische Studien*, ed. M. Perlmann, Hildesheim 1983, 75-159; A. Shnizer, *The Qurʾān. Aspects of its sacredness according to early Islamic tradition* (Hebrew), PhD thesis, Tel Aviv 2003; D. Sklare, Responses to Islamic polemics by Jewish *mutakallimūn* in the tenth century, in H. Lazarus-Yafeh et al. (eds.), *The Majlis. Religious encounters in medieval Islam*, Wiesbaden 1999, 137-61; Speyer, *Erzählungen;* S. Stroumsa, The signs of prophecy. The emergence and early development of a theme in Arabic theological literature, in *Harvard theological review* 78 (1985), 101-14; J.D. Thyen, *Bibel und Koran. Eine Synopse gemeinsamer Überlieferungen*, Cologne 1994; A.W. Ṭuwayla, *Tawrāt al-Yahūd wa-l-Imām Ibn Ḥazm*, Damascus 1425/2004; D. Urvoy, Ibn H̲aldun et la notion de l'altération des textes bibliques, in M. Fierro (ed.), *Judíos y musulmanes en al-Andalus y el Magreb. Contactos intelectuales*, Madrid 2002, 165-78; G. Vajda, Juifs et musulmans selon le ḥadīt, in JA (1937), 57-127 (on the ambivalent attitude toward material of Jewish origin); B.M. Wheeler, Israel and the Torah of Muḥammad, in J.C. Reeves (ed.), *Bible and Qurʾān. Essays in scriptural intertextuality*, Atlanta 2003, 61-85.

Torment

see SUFFERING; REWARD AND PUNISHMENT

Tornado

see WEATHER

Torture

see SUFFERING; REWARD AND PUNISHMENT

Touch

see HAND

Tower

see ART AND ARCHITECTURE AND THE QURʾĀN

Tower of Babel

see BABYLON

Towns

see GEOGRAPHY; CITY

Trace/Track

see AIR AND WIND; ASHES

Trade and Commerce

Economic activity focused on the exchange of goods among people. The language of the Qurʾān is imbued with the vocabulary of the marketplace both in practical, day-to-day references and in metaphorical applications (see METAPHOR; LITERARY STRUCTURES OF THE QURʾĀN). The way in which commercial activities are to be conducted among people is dealt with as a moral issue and a matter of social regulation (see ETHICS AND THE QURʾĀN). For example, rules governing contracts and trusts, and general economic principles find their place in the text and have been used within the *sharīʿa* to formulate the legal structures of society (see LAW AND THE QURʾĀN). Those aspects of this topic have been treated under many entries in this encyclopedia: see BREAKING TRUSTS AND CONTRACTS; CONTRACTS AND ALLIANCES; DEBT; ECONOMICS; MARKETS; MEASUREMENT; PROPERTY; SELLING AND BUYING; USURY; WEIGHTS AND MEASURES. Of particular interest in this entry are the terms which have sometimes been classified as constituting the commercial-theological terminology and which consist of a series of words linked to trade and commerce that are employed in order to provide a moral basis for the structures of society. Modern scholarship has understood this language as pivotal for reconstructing the nature of pre-Islamic society, the rise of Islam and Muḥammad's place in his community (see PRE-ISLAMIC ARABIA AND THE QURʾĀN; POST-ENLIGHTENMENT ACADEMIC STUDY OF THE QURʾĀN). The classic analysis by C.C. Torrey in his 1892 dissertation has set the basic dimensions of understanding the semantic field related to trade and commerce in the Qurʾān through an intuitive summary of relevant vocabulary; later works which provide a general treatment of metaphor have added some level of greater systematization to the definition (see Sabbagh, *Métaphore,* 212-16, and his classification of "Les termes se rapportant au commerce" under "Vie sédentaire," a sub-category of "La vie sociale"; and Sister, Metaphern, 141-2, "Das gesellschaftliche Leben" under "Der Mensch und sein Leben") but the basic scope of the concept has remained fairly stable.

Torrey spoke of the general "business atmosphere" of the Qurʾān and he saw the vocabulary which relates to this context falling into five main categories:

(1) Marketplace terminology: *ḥisāb,* "reckoning," used thirty-nine times plus many related verbal uses; *aḥṣā,* "to number or count," used ten times (see NUMBERS AND ENUMERATION); *wazana,* "to weigh," used seven times plus *mīzān,* "a balance," used sixteen times; *mithqāl,* "a weight," used eight times plus related verbal and adjectival instances.
(2) Employment terminology: *jazāʾ,* "recompense," used forty-two times plus many related verbal uses (see REWARD AND PUNISHMENT; CHASTISEMENT AND PUNISHMENT); *thawāb* and *mathūba,* "reward," used fifteen times plus related verbal usages; *ajr* (plural *ujūr*), "wage," used 107 times; *waffā,* "to pay what is due," used nineteen times usually with "wages"; *kasaba,* "to earn," used sixty-two times (see INTERCESSION).
(3) Negative trading terminology: *khasira,* "to lose," used sixty-five times in various verbal and nominal forms; *bakhasa,* "to defraud," used seven times in various forms; *ẓalama,* "to wrong," used frequently and has become, as *ẓālimūn,* a general ethical term for "wrongdoers"; *alata,* "to defraud, used once; *naqaṣa,* "to diminish," used ten times in various forms.
(4) Positive trading terminology: *sharā* and *ishtarā,* "to sell," used twenty-five times; *bāʿa,* "to sell, to bargain," used fifteen times in various forms; *tijāra,* "merchandise," used nine times; *thaman,* "price," used eleven times; *rabiḥa,* "to profit," used once.
(5) Finance: *qaraḍa,* "to provide a loan," used thirteen times in various forms; *aslafa,* "paid in advance," used twice; *rahīn* and *rihān,* "pledge," used three times.

The terminology is thus wide-ranging and the contexts in which it is employed are diverse, demonstrating the extent to which this range of language permeates the text. Three contexts may be isolated for the occurrence of the terms, in common with the overall themes of the Qurʾān but also illustrating the full range of the employment of the vocabulary: in recounting the stories of the prophets of the past (see NARRATIVES; GENERATIONS; PROPHETS AND PROPHETHOOD), in legislating the Muslim community and in describing the eschatological period (see ESCHATOLOGY). Many examples could be cited; the following is just a sampling.

Of the seven uses of "defraud," as derived from *bakhasa,* the first clearly deals with contemporary legal practice since the overall context relates to commercial transactions and the keeping of records. Q 2:282 contains the statement, "Let him fear (q.v.) God, his lord (q.v.), and not diminish [the debt] at all," when speaking of the scribe who will record the transaction (see WRITING AND WRITING MATERIALS; ORALITY AND WRITING IN ARABIA) where the verb *lā yabkhas* (translated here as "let him not diminish") takes on the sense of "he shall not defraud" (see CHEATING). In Q 7:85, the context is that of Midian (q.v.) and its prophet, Shuʿayb (q.v.), who is commanded to tell his people, "Do not undervalue (people's goods)," *lā tabkhas,* that is, "do not defraud them of its value." Q 11:85 puts the same phrase in Shuʿayb's mouth again as does Q 26:183 in which Shuʿayb addresses the "People of the Thicket" (q.v.). In Q 12:20, Joseph (q.v.) is sold by his brothers (see BROTHER AND BROTHERHOOD) for "a price which was fraudulent" *(bakhs)* because his brothers did not value him. In Q 11:15-16, the context is that of speaking of the reward and punishment in the voice of God: "If any [people] desire the life of this world with all its finery, we shall repay them in full in [this life] for their deeds — they will not be defrauded *(lā yubkhasūna)* — but such people will have nothing in the hereafter but the fire (q.v.)." Finally in Q 72:13, the jinn (q.v.) speak of the final reckoning being such that "whoever believes in his lord (see BELIEF AND UNBELIEF) need fear no fraud *(bakhs)* or injustice (see JUSTICE AND INJUSTICE)." The terminology thus spreads over the focal points of salvation (q.v.) history, past, present and future (see also HISTORY AND THE QURʾĀN).

The same observations can be made concerning the image of the "balance," *mīzān*. The statement in the Qurʾān, "Fill up the measure and the balance with justice," recurs as a regular motif with the end result that God is pictured as governing creation (q.v.) in the same way that humans should, if they are moral beings, run their own affairs: that is, with a full sense of justice. Q 11:84-5 has Shuʿayb preach, "O my people, serve God! You have no god other than him. Diminish not *(lā tanquṣū)* the measure *(al-mikyāl)* nor the balance *(al-mīzān)* [in weight]. I see you are prospering but I fear for you suffering on an encompassing day. O my people, fill up the weight *(al-mikyāl)* and the balance *(al-mīzān)* justly. Do not defraud the people of their things, and do not sow corruption (q.v.) in the land." The word *mīzān* also finds its place in passages of a legal nature addressed to the contemporary believing audience. In Q 6:152, Muḥammad is commanded to enunciate a rule for his followers using the same words as those used by Shuʿayb, "Fill up the measure and the balance with justice." Overall, however, the use of the word *mīzān* predominates as an image in eschatological passages which thereby invoke the references in the past (the time of the ancient prophets) and in the present (the present community of Muḥammad). Q 21:47 says, "We shall set up the scales *(al-mawāzīn)* of justice for the resurrection (q.v.) day, so that not one soul (q.v.) shall be wronged anything." Other passages which use the idea of a balance on the judgment day include Q 7:7-8, 23:102-3, 101:6-9, among others. It may also be noted that *wazana*, "to weigh," is used verbally in all three contexts as well.

The concept of *ajr* (plural *ujūr*), "wage(s)," is also widespread in the Qurʾān. In Q 11:51, Hūd (q.v.) says, "O my people, I do not ask of you a wage *(ajr)* for this; my wage *(ajr)* falls only upon him who originated me; will you not understand?" This is also found in the sequence of prophet stories in Q 26:105-91 where the same phrase occurs five times with Noah (q.v.), Hūd, Ṣāliḥ (q.v.), Lot (q.v.), and Shuʿayb in sequence. In terms of passages relating to regulations of the Muslim community, Q 4:24-5, 5:5, 33:50 and 60:10 all use "wages," *ujūr*, in reference to marriage in the sense of "dower," *mahr*, and also general subsistence (see MARRIAGE AND DIVORCE; BRIDEWEALTH; MAINTENANCE AND UPKEEP; SUSTENANCE). The eschatological uses of "wage" abound: "Their wage *(ajr)* awaits them with their lord" and variations on that phrase occur five times in sūra 2 alone (Q 2:62, 112, 262, 274, 277).

In the study of these words, many scholars have tended to emphasize, according to the principles of the historic-philological approach, how the language of the qurʾānic text must reflect the social situation at the time of Muḥammad (see LANGUAGE AND STYLE OF THE QURʾĀN;

FORM AND STRUCTURE OF THE QUR'ĀN; RHETORIC AND THE QUR'ĀN). Thus, the language is understood as being extended to the prophets of the past whose lives are retold in a manner which reflects the life circumstances of Muḥammad, even to the level of the vocabulary used to express common ideas and motifs (see ARABIC LANGUAGE; FOREIGN VOCABULARY). That understanding is also extended to eschatology, reasoning that language would have been used in a way in which the people in Muḥammad's time would best understand the concepts of the hereafter and judgment day (see LAST JUDGMENT). Torrey's work set the tone for much subsequent work when he declared, "Mohammed's idea of God, as shown us in the Koran, is in its main features a somewhat magnified picture of a Mekkan merchant. It could hardly have been otherwise" (*Commercial-theological*, 15). Torrey suggested that these words form a cluster of terms derived from actual commercial applications which have taken on theological overtones in the Qur'ān (see THEOLOGY AND THE QUR'ĀN). The full implications of the ideas underlying his work were developed later in works by H. Lammens, M. Rodinson and W.M. Watt, among many others, in their treatments of Muḥammad and the notion that economics and social revolutions are crucial to the rise of Islam. The evidence for those theories is, at least partially, to be found in the language of the Qur'ān and its commercial emphasis. For example, Watt's reading of the Qur'ān allows him to perceive a society in the throes of the impact of individualistic capitalism being challenged by a prophet of social justice. In Watt's seminal *Muhammad at Mecca* and *Muhammad at Medina* the theme is clear; Watt states, for example,

> The Qur'ān has ample evidence of the importance of voluntary "contributions" in the plans for the young community at Medina. Men are commanded to believe in God and his messenger and contribute of their wealth. Their contributions are a loan they lend to God; he knows more than they do; he will replay them the double and more (*Medina*, 252).

Watt clearly pictures the social environment and its regulations being reflected in the language which is used to talk about God, the essence of the notion of the "commercial-theological" terminology.

The critique of such a reading of the qur'ānic text has been raised primarily in the context of implications that underlie the debates about the pervasiveness and depth of commercial activity in pre-Islamic Arabia. P. Crone points out that there are only vague details for the model of a society in the throes of economic transformation within the Arab historical texts. Arguing that the view provided in the classical Greek texts of a flourishing trade throughout Arabia speaks of a situation some 600 years prior to the rise of Islam, Crone suggests that the later Muslim writers have been read rather imaginatively in light of the information provided about this earlier period. When the texts are read for what they say rather than for what is assumed, she says,

> such information as we have leaves no doubt that [the Meccans'] imports were the necessities and petty luxuries that the inhabitants of Arabia have always had to procure from the fringes of the Fertile Crescent and elsewhere, not the luxury goods with which Lammens would have them equip themselves abroad (*Meccan trade*, 150-1).

It is noteworthy that the body of early Arab poetry (see POETRY AND POETS), whether genuinely pre-Islamic or not, does not provide testimony to this commercial environment. As Peters comments (Quest, 292), the poetry "testifies to a quite different culture." The Meccans traded, certainly, but mainly within the confines of their own area and in response to their basic needs and not for "the commercial appetites of the surrounding empires" (Crone, *Meccan trade,* 151).

It is not clear, however, where such critiques leave our understanding of the qurʾānic vocabulary. The difficulties with the common interpretation have certainly been noted by writers such as K. Cragg, although the matter of how to resolve the issue has not been pursued. As Cragg notes,

> strangely, the word *tājir* (merchant) does not figure in the Qurʾān, and *tijāra* (merchandise) only on nine occasions, [yet] commerce is the central theme in the life it mirrors and in the vocabulary by which it speaks (*Event,* 98).

Further, the question must arise, when the issue is considered within the context of the entire debate concerning the nature of pre-Islamic trade, of whether we can read references to the goods of trade such as dates (see DATE PALM), gold (q.v.) and silver (see METALS AND MINERALS) which are mentioned in the Qurʾān as allowing us to infer historical evidence of the context of the time and place of Muḥammad (cf. Heck, Arabia without spices; see also MONEY; NUMISMATICS).

One answer might be found through a new investigation of the vocabulary in light of biblical and general near eastern religious metaphors (see RELIGIOUS PLURALISM AND THE QURʾĀN). One aspect of Torrey's argument regarding the reading of this vocabulary that justified his tying of these particular terms to the historical environment of Muḥammad is his assertion that "the mathematical accounting on the judgment day is alien to Judaism and Christianity" (*Commercial-theological,* 14; see JEWS AND JUDAISM; CHRISTIANS AND CHRISTIANITY). This statement may well have reflected the state of research at the turn of the twentieth century but such a position can no longer be maintained. Torrey himself notes (*Commercial-theological,* 17 n. 3) that he had been informed that the image of a balance being used at the final judgment was to be found in Egyptian religion. That, it is now well known, only scratches the surface of the extent to which it may be claimed that the Qurʾān shares in a near eastern mythic universe of judgment day symbolism (see SYMBOLIC IMAGERY). The eschatological vision is that of justice and the images used for that are ones which are common in near eastern religious language. God's justice on judgment day is the grounding image: all prophets, past and present, have urged that this must be reflected in human society (see also RELIGION; JUDGMENT). Ultimately, eschatological imagery may be seen to drive mundane symbolism and not vice-versa (Rippin, Commerce of eschatology). In that sense, the symbolism here is not necessarily a reflection of the state of affairs at the time of revelation (see REVELATION AND INSPIRATION). Rather, it expresses the aspirations of humans to achieve the moral standards of the eschaton, just as those standards are believed to have been enacted in the mythic past (as demonstrated by the earlier prophets; see MYTHS AND LEGENDS IN THE QURʾĀN) and just as implementation of those standards is urged in the present by the current prophet. The eschaton functions to assert the ultimate justice of the world while being the moral goal for human existence.

Andrew Rippin

Bibliography
K. Cragg, *The event of the Qurʾān. Islam in its scripture,* London 1971; P. Crone, *Meccan trade and the rise of Islam,* Princeton 1987; G.W. Heck, "Arabia without spices". An alternative hypothesis, in *JAOS* 123 (2003), 547-76; H. Lammens, *La Mecque à la veille de l'Hégire,* Beirut 1924; F.E. Peters, The commerce of Mecca before Islam, in F. Kazemi and R.D. McChesney (eds.), *A way prepared. Essays on Islamic culture in honor of Richard Bayly Winder,* New York 1988, 3-26; id., *Muhammad and the origins of Islam,* Albany 1994; id., The quest of the historical Muhammad, in *IJMES* 23 (1991), 291-315; A. Rippin, The commerce of eschatology, in Wild, *Text,* 125-35; T. Sabbagh, *La métaphore dans le Coran,* Paris 1943; M. Sister, Metaphern und Vergleiche im Koran, in *Mitteilungen des Seminars für Orientalische Sprachen* 34 (1931), 104-54; C.C. Torrey, *The commercial-theological terms in the Koran,* Leiden 1892; W.M. Watt, *Muhammad at Mecca,* Oxford 1953; id., *Muhammad at Medina,* Oxford 1956.

Tradition and Custom

The way things have been done, or are understood as having been done, in the past. In many societies the appeal to tradition and custom as the basis for current practice serves to legitimize the present. For a religion emerging in opposition to some of the beliefs and practices of its society, however, appeal to tradition or custom by its opponents is an obstacle to be overcome. At the same time, adherents of the new order may well attempt to justify it by reference to the past.

In Islam the positive value of tradition is most obviously manifest in the concept of *sunna* (q.v.), the accepted practice. The *sunna* of the Prophet is a model that all believers should strive to emulate and, according to the classical Sunnī theory of law, it is the most important source of the law alongside the Qurʾān (see LAW AND THE QURʾĀN). Innovations (*bidʿa, ḥawādith;* see INNOVATION) on the other hand, are commonly regarded as reprehensible. Naturally, the attitude towards custom and tradition may vary according to circumstances. A category of commendable innovation *(bidʿa ḥasana)* is recognized and what by many has been understood as the positive value of adherence to a tradition *(taqlīd)* may, in the hands of a religious reformer like Ibn Taymiyya (d. 728/1328), be reassessed as mere servile and blind imitation.

The Qurʾān reflects these tensions regarding tradition and custom. The prophet Muḥammad denies that he is anything new *(bidʿ)* among the messengers (Q 46:9; see MESSENGER) and references to preceding prophets (see PROPHETS AND PROPHETHOOD) and messengers emphasize their following in the footsteps *(āthār)* of their predecessors (e.g. Q 5:46; 57:27). One of the complaints made against the Christians, who are accorded some merits (see CHRISTIANS AND CHRISTIANITY), is that they had "invented" *(ibtadaʿū)* monasticism (Q 57:27; see MONASTICISM AND MONKS).

What is "known" or "recognized" *(maʿrūf)* is good or honorable in contrast to what is reprehensible (*munkar,* Q 3:104, etc.; see VIRTUES AND VICES, COMMANDING AND FORBIDDING; LAWFUL AND UNLAWFUL). Although some commentators gloss *maʿrūf* as "known or recognized by reason or revelation" (see INTELLECT; REVELATION AND INSPIRATION), the related word *ʿurf* in Q 7:199 (where it is contrasted with "ignorance" [q.v.; *jahl*] and understood to mean simply "goodness" or "kindness") is in Islamic law one of the most common words for traditional practice or custom, which has a limited role as a legal principle.

On the other hand, following the footsteps *(āthār)* of predecessors and ancestors is reprehensible if that means following the wrong path (see PATH OR WAY; ASTRAY; ERROR). In its arguments against those who refuse to accept its message, the Qurʾān frequently presents them as appealing to the tradition of their fathers in justification of their refusal to accept the truth (q.v.).

Those opponents (see OPPOSITION TO MUḤAMMAD), like the opponents of previous prophets, are portrayed as using the justification that their fathers' beliefs and practices were good enough for them and there is no reason why they should go against their customs. "We found our fathers attached to a religious community and we are guided by their footsteps *(wa-innā wajadnā abāʾanā ʿalā ummatin wa-innā ʿalā āthārihim muhtadūna/muqtadūna),*" as they are reported as saying in Q 43:22 and 23. This sentiment, repeated sometimes with relatively minor variations of wording and usually involving reference to the "fathers," recurs frequently throughout the Qurʾān, in the mouths of the opponents of its prophet and of earlier ones like Moses (q.v.; e.g. Q 2:170; 5:104; 6:148; 7:28; 10:78; 21:53; 26:74; 31:21). In a slightly different manner, reference is made to this assertion in the account of the primordial covenant (q.v.) that God made with humans prior to their earthly lives. Q 7:172-3 affirms that the conclusion of the covenant by all mankind should rid the nonbelievers from claiming on the day of judgment (see LAST JUDGMENT) that it was only their "fathers" who ascribed partners to God and that they were their "seed" after them (see PARENTS; POLYTHEISM AND ATHEISM): "So will you destroy us on account of that which the falsifiers did (see LIE)?"

The social setting is presumably one in which a high value is placed on loyalty (q.v.) to one's ancestors. Q 2:200 urges people to "remember God as you remember your fathers" (see REMEMBRANCE). In such a society loyalty to the family tradition would be a major hindrance to proselytism. Q 9:23 commands the believers not to take their fathers or brothers as friends *(awliyāʾ)* if they take pleasure in disbelief (see BELIEF AND UNBELIEF; FRIENDS AND FRIENDSHIP; CLIENTS AND CLIENTAGE), and the account of Abraham's (q.v.) break with his father and his father's religion would presumably be especially resonant (see IDOLATRY AND IDOLATERS).

In the Qurʾān, *sunna* never has the sense of the exemplary custom of the Prophet. When scholars sought a qurʾānic support for that notion they commonly found it in the phrase "the book (q.v.) and the wisdom" (q.v.; *al-kitāb wa-l-ḥikma;* e.g. Q 2:231; 4:113; cf. 33:34; see also SIGNS; VERSES), which they interpreted as indicating the Qurʾān and the sunna of the Prophet (see TRADITIONAL DISCIPLINES OF QURʾĀNIC STUDY). In the Qurʾān *sunna* nearly always refers to God's exemplary and customary punishment of earlier nations to whom he had sent his messengers only for them to be rejected (see PUNISHMENT STORIES). The believers are exhorted, when they travel in the land (see JOURNEY; GEOGRAPHY), to take note of the sunna of those earlier peoples *(sunnatu l-awwalīn, sunanu lladhīna min qablikum)* or of the sunna of God regarding them *(sunnatu llāhi fī lladhīna khalaw)*. God's sunna in this respect is not subject to change or variation *(tabdīl, taḥwīl;* Q 33:62; 35:43; 48:23). In such passages *sunna* usually appears in collocation with either God or the earlier generations (q.v.; *al-awwalīn* or *alladhīna min qablikum*).

Another word signifying "custom" or "habit" is *daʾb*. In the Qurʾān this occurs three times in the expression "as was the *daʾb* of the people of Pharaoh (q.v.) and those [who were] before them" *(ka-daʾbi āli firʿawna wa-lladhīna min qablihim,* Q 3:11; 8:52, 54) and once (Q 40:31) in a similar expression: "like the *daʾb* of the people of Noah (q.v.) and ʿĀd (q.v.) and Thamūd (q.v.) and those [who came] after them" *(mithla daʾbi qawmi nūḥin wa-ʿādin wa-thamūda wa-lladhīna min baʿdihim)*. In each case it is not easy to see what force *daʾb* adds to the preceding preposition "like" *(ka-, mithla)* but on each occasion the passage refers to the divine punishment (see CHASTISEMENT

AND PUNISHMENT) that befell the peoples mentioned (those of Pharaoh, Noah, ʿĀd, Thamūd and others) and it is likely that *daʾb* is the equivalent of *sunna* in the passages mentioned above. Commentators (see EXEGESIS OF THE QURʾĀN: CLASSICAL AND MEDIEVAL) sometimes gloss *daʾb* by the relatively neutral word "deeds" *(ṣanīʿ, fiʿl)* but one also finds it understood as equivalent to *sunna*. Its other occurrence (Q 12:47) is in the adverbial form *daʾban* and clearly means "as usual" or "as is customary."

Commentators frequently explain parts of the Qurʾān as referring to the traditions and customs of the pre-Islamic Arabs (q.v.; see also PRE-ISLAMIC ARABIA AND THE QURʾĀN). Sometimes, as with infanticide (q.v.; e.g. Q 6:137, 140, 151; 16:57-9; 81:8-9) or "entering houses from their backs" (Q 2:189; see HOUSE, DOMESTIC AND DIVINE), the alleged tradition of the *jāhilī* Arabs is rejected (see AGE OF IGNORANCE). Sometimes, as with the circumambulation of Ṣafā and Marwa (q.v.; Q 2:158) or engaging in commerce while making the pilgrimage (q.v.; *ḥajj*, Q 2:198), it is confirmed (see also TRADE AND COMMERCE; MONTHS; SACRED AND PROFANE). Cumulatively, such interpretations help to substantiate the image of a revelation addressed in the first instance to the society of the pre-Islamic period *(jāhiliyya)*.

On the whole, therefore, the Qurʾān does not have the strongly positive evaluation of tradition and custom that Islamic culture later displays. It portrays the past negatively as a series of episodes in which various communities have rejected God's message and messengers, and those whom it addresses have to break the pattern by dissociating themselves from the tradition of their fathers. Only God's tradition and custom — his sending of messengers and his destruction of those who do not heed them — is consistently good (see also GOOD AND EVIL; HISTORY AND THE QURʾĀN).

G.R. Hawting

Bibliography

Primary: al-Shāfiʿī, Muḥammad b. Idrīs, *Risāla fī uṣūl al-fiqh*, ed. M. Shākir, Cairo 1940; trans. M. Khadduri, *al-Shāfiʿī's* Risāla, Baltimore 1961; Shawkānī, *Tafsīr;* Ṭabarī, *Tafsīr*.

Secondary: M.M. Bravmann, *Sunnah* and related concepts, in id. (ed.), *The spiritual background of early Islam*, Leiden 1972, 123-98; M. Cook, *Commanding right and forbidding wrong in Islamic thought*, Cambridge 2000, 25-6; Goldziher, *MS*, i, 41f.; trans. i, 46f.; R. Gwynne, *Logic, rhetoric and legal reasoning in the Qurʾān. God's arguments*, London 2004, chap. 3 ("The *sunna* of God"); J. Schacht, *Introduction to Islamic law*, Oxford 1964, 62, 136 (on *ʿurf*); J. Wansbrough, *The sectarian milieu*, London 1978, 67.

Traditional Disciplines of Qurʾānic Studies

In Islamic theological representation the Qurʾān is considered *the* "knowledge/science" *(ʿilm)*, so it is not surprising that the understanding and exegesis *(tafsīr)* of this text were considered the most excellent kinds of knowledge (see KNOWLEDGE AND LEARNING). Thus in a tradition attributed to Muḥammad (see ḤADĪTH AND THE QURʾĀN), transmitted by the Companion Ibn Masʿūd (see COMPANIONS OF THE PROPHET), we read: "Whoever wants knowledge, has to scrutinize the Qurʾān, because it contains the knowledge of the first and last (generations)" (Ibn Abī Shayba, *Muṣannaf*, vi, 127, no. 30,009; Abū ʿUbayd, *Faḍāʾil*, 41-2, no. 79; Abū l-Layth al-Samarqandī, *Tafsīr*, i, 71; Bayhaqī, *Shuʿab*, ii, 332, no. 1960; Ghazālī, *Iḥyāʾ [8, Ādāb tilāwat al-Qurʾān]*, i, 254, l. 18; Zabīdī, *Itḥāf*, v, 94; Qurṭubī, *Tafsīr*, i, 446-53; Zarkashī, *Burhān*, i, 8). Or in another tradition attributed to Muḥammad: "The best of you is he who learns the Qurʾān and teaches it" (Bukhārī, *Ṣaḥīḥ*, iii, 402 [66, *Faḍāʾil al-Qurʾān*, 21]/trans. iii, 534; see TEACHING AND PREACHING THE QURʾĀN). The superiority of the Qurʾān's language vis-à-vis every other language is similar to the superiority of God vis-à-vis his creatures (in some versions: because it comes from him; Baghdādī, *Faṣl,* i, 234-6; Ibn Ḍurays, *Faḍāʾil,* 77-8, nos. 132-40; Ājurrī, *Akhlāq,* 61-8; Rāzī, *Faḍāʾil,* 70-1, nos. 26-7; Ibn Rajab, *Mawrid,* 75-6; Suyūṭī, *Itqān,* iv, 124; cf. Biqāʿī, *Maṣāʿid,* i, 378-9, then 298-301, and Fīrūzābādī, *Baṣāʾir,* i, 57-64, both with other traditions; *UQM,* i, 69-86). Or according to a tradition attributed to ʿAlī: "God has sent down in this Qurʾān 'the exposition of all things' (an echo of Q 16:89), but our knowledge is too limited for it" (Biqāʿī, *Maṣāʿid,* i, 379, from the commentary of ʿAbd b. Ḥamīd, d. 249/863; Sezgin, *GAS,* i, 113). For Muslim scholars: "The book of God and the traditions of his Prophet are the exposition of every knowledge" (*bayān li-kulli maʿlūm;* Ibn al-ʿArabī, *Qānūn,* 180). In time, the science derived from the Qurʾān or applied to it, was divided into many "sciences," "the sciences of the Qurʾān" (*ʿulūm al-Qurʾān),* called in the above title "traditional disciplines of qurʾānic studies."

The Qurʾān, the noblest of the sciences?

As noted above, according to Islamic representation, the Qurʾān contains all science and particularly all legal knowledge, *expressis verbis* or virtually (see LAW AND THE QURʾĀN; see also SCIENCE AND THE QURʾĀN; MEDICINE AND THE QURʾĀN). The locus classicus for this conviction is Q 16:89: "And we reveal the scripture unto you as an exposition of all things *(tibyānan li-kulli shayʾin)*" (see the interpretations below; see BOOK; TEACHING). Sometimes Q 6:38, "We have neglected nothing in the book," is also quoted in the same spirit (Suyūṭī, *Itqān,* iv, 28 [chap. 65]). The theme of the "seven aspects (*aḥruf,* sing. *ḥarf;* in a later context *ḥarf* sometimes corresponds to what French linguists call 'articulation')" in which the Qurʾān is supposed to have been delivered also played a major role in that theological representation, as can be seen in the use of this prophetic tradition by the Andalusian jurist Abū Bakr Ibn al-ʿArabī (d. 543/748; *Qānūn,* 70, 189-95; see OFT-REPEATED; POLYSEMY). For him, "The sciences of the ḥadīth are sixty, but the sciences of the Qurʾān are more" (op. cit., 193), and for him the sciences of the Qurʾān are 77,450, i.e. the number of the words he said it contained (op. cit., 226-7; Zarkashī, *Burhān,* i, 16-17; Suyūṭī, *Muʿtarak,* i, 23; id., *Itqān,* iv, 37 [chap. 65; cf. chap. 19, i, 242, for the number of words: 77,435, 77,437, or 77,200]; Rosenthal, *Knowledge,* 20: ca. 78,000). This last declaration seems to come from Ṣūfī scholars (see ṢŪFISM AND THE QURʾĀN); it was already in *The revival of the religious sciences* of al-Ghazālī (d. 505/1111; *Iḥyāʾ,* Cairo 1939, i, 290: 77,200 sciences).

In a later period, the Ḥanbalite traditionist Ibn Rajab (d. 795/1395) wrote a book, now lost, entitled *Bayān al-istighnāʾ bi-l-Qurʾān fī taḥṣīl al-ʿilm wa-l-īmān* ("The exposition showing that the Qurʾān is sufficient for acquiring science and faith"; Ḥājjī Khalīfa, *Kashf,* i, 273, no. 613); he mentioned it in his treatise against singing and his other treatise on submission to God during prayer (q.v.; *Nuzhat al-asmāʿ,* in Ibn Rajab, *Majmūʿ rasāʾil,* ii, 463: against singing the Qurʾān and singing in general; *al-Dhull wa-l-inkisār* or *al-Khushūʿ fī l-ṣalāt,* in *Majmūʿ rasāʾil,* i, 298: on people who died of pleasure on hearing the Qurʾān; see RECITATION OF THE QURʾĀN; WEEPING). This last work is usually mentioned with the title *al-Istighnāʾ bi-l-Qurʾān* ("That the Qurʾān is sufficient"; quoted by Biqāʿī, *Maṣāʿid,* i, 379). In the introduction to his *Nafaḥāt al-Raḥmān fī tafsīr al-Qurʾān wa-tabyīn al-furqān* ("Fragrances of the merciful and elucidation of the evidence"), the Shīʿī Muḥammad b. ʿAbd al-Raḥīm al-Nihāwandī (born 1289/1871; see SHĪʿISM AND THE QURʾĀN) provides an impressive list of all the knowledge supposed to be found in the Qurʾān, which "contains everything" (quoted in *UQM,* i, 179-81). ʿAlī is purported to have said, "The Qurʾān was sent down in four parts: a part concerning us (i.e. the people of the family of the Prophet), one part concerning our enemies, one part obligations and regulations *(farāʾiḍ wa-aḥkām),* and one part permitted and prohibited *(ḥalāl wa-ḥarām).* And the exalted *(karāʾim)* passages concern us" (Furāt al-Kūfī, d. ca. 310/922, *Tafsīr,* 45-6, no. 1, with other versions, 46-50; Bar-Asher, *Scripture,* 88-9).

Thus studying the Qurʾān is the most sublime duty. According to Ibn al-Jawzī (d. 597/1200): "The holy Qurʾān, being the noblest of the sciences, the insight into its meanings is the most complete of insights *(kāna l-fahmu li-maʿānīhi awfā l-fuhūm)* because the nobility of a science depends upon the nobility of the subject of this science" (*Zād,* i, 3; cf. Ibn Abī Shayba, *Muṣannaf,* vi, 125-6 [22, *Faḍāʾil al-Qurʾān,* 16]).

The origins and development of the sciences of the Qurʾān

To enforce recognition of the new religion, Muḥammad and/or Islam used a kind of competitive mimeticism (French *mimétisme concurrentiel,* an expression used by anthropologists) in viewing the Qurʾān *("al-kitāb")* as superior to the other sacred books. They based this claim on the well-known tradition attributed to Muḥammad: "The first scripture came down according to a single *ḥarf* [mode, face, edge, letter, passage, meaning or reading? in other versions *bāb,* i.e. gate], while the *Qurʾān* came down according to seven [other versions have four or five]" (Ṭabarī, *Tafsīr,* i, 21-71; Eng. trans. i, 16-30; Mahdawī, *Bayān,* 24-8; Gilliot, Lectures, i; id., *Elt,* 111-33). The alleged limitation of the prior scriptures and the polysemy of the word *ḥarf* opened the way to an interpretation such as the following:

By the first Book coming down from one gate he (Muḥammad) meant the Books of God which came down on his prophets to whom they were sent down, in which there were no divine ordinances and judgments, or pronouncements about what was lawful and what was unlawful, such as the Psalms of David, which are invocations and exhortations, and the Evangel of Jesus, which is glorification, praise and encouragement to pardon and be charitable, but no legal ordinances and judgments besides this, and scriptures like these which came down with one or seven meanings, all of which are contained in our Book which God conferred on our Prophet, Muḥammad and his community (Ṭabarī, *Tafsīr,* i, 71; Eng. trans. i, 30; Gilliot, Lectures, ii, 56).

The theme of "seven *ḥarf*s" (in the Sunnī tradition; cf. UQM, ii, 127-207) has probably been borrowed from Judaism or Christianity, and their notion of the quadruple sense/meaning of scripture (Heb.: *peshat, remez, derash, sod;* Lat: *sensus litteralis, sensus spiritualis,* divided into: *littera/historia, allegoria, tropologia/moralis, anagogia;* Wansbrough, QS, 243; Böwering, *Mystical,* 139-40; Gilliot, *Elt,* 120-1; see Gilliot/Larcher, Exegesis, 100b). The tradition on the seven (three, four or five; Biqāʿī, *Maṣāʿid,* i, 382-8) "meanings/faces" *(aḥruf)* of the Qurʾān was interpreted in different ways (16 or 35 interpretations in the Sunnī tradition, which we have reduced to seven kinds; Gilliot, Lectures, i, 18).

Imāmī Shīʿa (UQM, ii, 209-38), especially the "rationalists" *(uṣūliyya),* also discuss the Sunnī way of interpreting these traditions but early Shīʿism and the group of those who were called later "traditionists/traditionalists" (*akhbāriyya;* Amir-Moezzi and Jambet, *Qu'est-ce que le chiisme,* 221-3) reject the theme of the seven *aḥruf,* in accordance with their doctrine of the falsification of the Qurʾān by the Companions (see also SHĪʿA). They use as their authority a declaration attributed to Jaʿfar al-Ṣādiq (d. 148/765): "The Qurʾān was only sent down in one *ḥarf*, and the disagreement comes from the transmitters" (UQM, ii, 237-8). But the tradition was also explained as seven possibilities of interpretation, so according to Jaʿfar al-Ṣādiq: "The Qurʾān was sent down in seven *aḥruf*, and the most suitable for the imām *(adnā mā li)* is to deliver his opinions *(an yuftiya)* in seven ways *(wujūh)*. Then he said: 'This is our gift, so bestow, or withhold, without reckoning'" (Q 38:39; Ibn Bābawayh, d. 381/991, *Khiṣāl*, 358; UQM, ii, 212).

One of these interpretations is especially interesting for our subject. According to Ibn Masʿūd, Muḥammad should have said: "The first Book came down from one gate according to one *ḥarf*, but the Qurʾān came down from seven gates according to seven *ḥarf*s: prohibiting and commanding (see FORBIDDEN; VIRTUES AND VICES, COMMANDING AND FORBIDDING), lawful and unlawful (q.v.), clear and ambiguous (q.v.), and parables" (Ṭabarī, *Tafsīr*, i, 68, no. 67; Eng. trans. i, 29; Abū Shāma, *Murshid*, 107, 109, 271-4; Suyūṭī, *Itqān*, i, 170-1; Gilliot, Lectures, i, 20; cf. Abū ʿUbayd, *Faḍāʾil* [44], i, 278-9, no. 87: different, and from another Companion; see also PARABLE). Or in another version the seven are "command and reprimand (*zajr*; or prohibition, *nahy*), encouragement of good and discouragement of evil (*targhīb wa-tarhīb;* see GOOD AND EVIL), dialectic (*jadal;* see DEBATE AND DISPUTATION), narratives (q.v.; *qiṣaṣ*) and parable (*mathal;* Ṭabarī, *Tafsīr*, i, 69, no. 68; trans. i, 29, modified by us; Māwardī, *Nukat*, i, 29). We are not at all sure that Muḥammad ever uttered such a declaration, but what interests us here is that this tradition with the symbolic number seven (see NUMBERS AND ENUMERATION; NUMEROLOGY), which relates to perfection, was one way to express the conviction that the Qurʾān contains all knowledge. The word knowledge *(ʿilm)* does not appear in it nor does it use substantives, but only participles and adjectives; yet the way was opened to creating categories from these, i.e. different "genres" or "sciences." This is exemplified in a declaration attributed to the same Ibn Masʿūd: "God sent down the Qurʾān according to five *aḥruf:* lawful and unlawful, clear and ambiguous, and parables" (Ṭabarī, *Tafsīr*, 69, no. 70; trans. i, 29).

The early exegete Muqātil b. Sulaymān (d. 150/767; Gilliot, Muqātil) has summarized in two lists, a shorter and a longer, the various aspects or genres contained in the Qurʾān (see LITERARY STRUCTURES OF THE QURʾĀN). He does not refer to the prophetic traditions on the *aḥruf* of the Qurʾān but his lists clearly relate to that subject. They are also an attempt to establish some exegetical or hermeneutical principles (see EXEGESIS OF THE QURʾĀN: CLASSICAL AND MEDIEVAL). He does not speak of "science" *(ʿilm)*, but we can see in these lists an indication for what will become in the future the "sciences of the Qurʾān." In the first list, he says: "The Qurʾān was sent down according to five aspects/modes/genres (*awjuh*, pl. of *wajh;* Goldziher, *Richtungen*, 84-5): its command *(amruhu)*, prohibition, promise, threat *(waʿīd)*, and account of the ancients" (Muqātil, *Tafsīr*, i, 26; Nwyia, *Exégèse*, 67; Gilliot, *Elt*, 118). This declaration should be compared with that attributed to the Companion Ibn ʿAbbās (d. 69/688) and transmitted by al-Kalbī (d. 146/763), since both al-Kalbī and Muqātil have numerous exegetical interpretations in common and are considered the heirs of the exegesis of the Companion Ibn ʿAbbās:

The Qurʾān was [revealed] in four aspects *(wujūh): tafsīr* [the literal meaning?] which scholars know; Arabic with which the Arabs (q.v.) are acquainted (see ARABIC LANGUAGE); lawful and unlawful *(ḥalāl wa-ḥarām)* of which it is not permissible for people to be unaware; [and] *taʾwīl* [the deeper meaning?], that which only God knows.

Where a further explanation of *taʾwīl* is demanded, it is described as "what will be" (*mā huwa kāʾin;* Muqātil, *Tafsīr,* i, 27; see Gilliot/Larcher, Exegesis, 100b).

Muqātil's second list is a considerable expansion of his first one:
The Qurʾān contains references that are: (1) particular and (2) general; (3) particular to Muslims; (4) particular to certain idolaters, particular to one idolater (see IDOLATRY AND IDOLATERS); (5) general to all people; (6) ambiguous and (7) well-established (or clear, univocal); (8) explained (*mufassar*) and (9) obscure (or unexplained, *mubham*); (10) implicit (*iḍmār*) and (11) explicit (*tamām*); (12) connections (*ṣilāt*) in the discourse. It also contains (13) abrogating and (14) abrogated [verses (q.v.); see ABROGATION]; (15) anteposition (*taqdīm*) and (16) postposition (*taʾkhīr;* Gk. *hysteron* vs. *proteron*); (17) synonyms/analogues (*ashbāh*), with many (18) polysems/homonyms (*wujūh*), and with apodosis (*jawāb*) in another sūra (see SŪRAS). [It contains also] (19) parables (*amthāl*) by which God refers: to himself, (20) to unbelievers and idols (see IDOLS AND IMAGES), (21) to this world (q.v.), (22) to resurrection (q.v.), and to the world to come (see ESCHATOLOGY); (23) report (or history; *khabar*) about the ancients, (24) about paradise (q.v.) and hell (see HELL AND HELLFIRE); (25) particular to one idolater; (26) duties (*farāʾiḍ*, or perhaps here: inheritance? [q.v.]), (27) legal rules (*aḥkām*) and (28) punishments (*ḥudūd;* see BOUNDARIES AND PRECEPTS; CHASTISEMENT AND PUNISHMENT); (29) accounts of what is in the hearts of the believers, (30) or in the hearts of the unbelievers; (31) polemics (*khuṣūma*) against the Arab idolaters; then (32) interpretation (*tafsīr*), and (33) the interpretation which has an interpretation (Muqātil, *Tafsīr,* i, 27; Gilliot, *Elt,* 118-19; Versteegh, *Arabic grammar,* 104-5).

This list could be compared to the list of thirty aspects attributed to "ancient" scholars by al-Suyūṭī (*Itqān,* iii, 117-18 [chap. 51]).
As for Q 16:89, "And we reveal the scripture unto you as an exposition of all things" (see above), it played a role comparable to the traditions of the "seven *aḥruf*" in preparing the way for the establishment or creation of "qurʾānic sciences." Indeed, this verse was interpreted by an early exegete, Mujāhid (d. 104/722), as: "What is permitted and what is forbidden" (Ṭabarī, *Tafsīr,* xiv, 162). For one of the first theorists of the methodology of law, al-Shāfiʿī (d. 204/820):

God has revealed the scripture as an exposition of all things, and this clarification (*tabyīn*) has several forms: Either he has clearly stated duties (*mā bayyana farḍahu fīhi*), or he has given general revelations (*mā anzala jumlatan;* see REVELATION AND INSPIRATION), and in this case he has elucidated how it should be, through the tongue of his prophet, or he has given a ruling on duties in a general way (*jumlatan*) and ordered to investigate it, but giving indications (*ʿalāmāt*) which he has created... (Shāfiʿī, *K. Jimāʿ al-ʿilm,* in id., *al-Umm,* vii, 277; ix, 15; trans. according to this latter, better ed.; Suyūṭī, *Itqān,* i, 16; cf. ibid., iv, 29 [chap. 65]; Ibn ʿĀdil, *Lubāb,* xii, 140-1, commenting on Q 16:89, adds: consensus, analogy, information coming from a single traditionist, etc.).

For al-Shāfiʿī, "the Qurʾān virtually contains all the modes of the *bayān*" (Yahia, *Contribution,* 310). It should be noted that *bayān* cannot be translated as a single word because it is "the manifestation of the divine meanings, the intentions of the Creator who conveys them by the acts of his will, the *aḥkām*" (i.e. rules). "It is a theophany of the meaning" (Yahia, *Contribution,* 362).

But the same al-Shāfiʿī related the interpretation of Q 16:89 with the tradition on the "seven *aḥruf*" and its interpretations, opening the way to a representation of "the science (then sciences) of the Qurʾān," in ca. 189/805, when he appeared before the caliph Hārūn al-Rashīd, in the presence of the famous Ḥanafī jurist, Muḥammad b. al-Ḥasan al-Shaybānī, who defended him. The caliph asked al-Shāfiʿī about his "knowledge/science" of the "book of God" *(kayfa ʿilmuka bihi),* and al-Shāfiʿī answered:

About what science do you ask, Commander of the Faithful? Is it the science of its descent (revelation, *tanzīl*) or of its interpretation *(taʾwīl)*? The science of what is clear (*muḥkam,* or well established) or ambiguous (*mutashābih,* or similar) in it? What is abrogating *(nāsikh)* or abrogated *(mansūkh)* in it? Its narratives *(akhbār)* or rules *(aḥkām)*? Its Meccan or Medinan (sūras or verses; see MECCA; MEDINA; CHRONOLOGY AND THE QURʾĀN)? What was sent down in the night or during the day? During a journey (q.v.; *safar;* see also TRIPS AND VOYAGES) or at home *(ḥaḍarī)*? The elucidation of its description *(tabyīn waṣfihi)*? The arrangement of its forms (?) *(taswiyat ṣuwarihi)*? Its synonyms/analogues *(naẓāʾir)*? Its good pronunciation (or grammatical pronunciation/explanation; *iʿrāb;* see GRAMMAR AND THE QURʾĀN)? The modes of its reading (*wujūh qirāʾatihi;* see READINGS OF THE QURʾĀN)? Its words *(ḥurūfihi)*? The meanings of its manners of speaking *(maʿānī lughātihi)*? Its legal punishments *(ḥudūdih)*? The number of its verses?

Hārūn al-Rashīd said, "You claim that you have a great knowledge of the Qurʾān" (Bayhaqī, *Manāqib,* i, 136; Zurqānī, *Manāhil,* i, 26: an abridged report without references, of which the beginning does not seem authentic: "The sciences of the Qurʾān are numerous…").

This list of al-Shāfiʿī is not unconnected to that of Muqātil b. Sulaymān because he knew Muqātil's exegesis and held it in high esteem, and he reportedly declared that, "All people are dependent on *(ʿiyāl)* three men: on Muqātil b. Sulaymān for exegesis…" (Ibn Khallikān, *Wafayāt,* v, 255; Abbott, *Studies,* ii, 100).

Books on the topic or with the term "sciences of the Qurʾān" in their title

The emergence of the technical expression "sciences of the Qurʾān" has been credited to the sixth/twelfth or seventh/thirteenth century (*UQM,* i, 10), or seventh/thirteenth century (Zurqānī, *Manāhil,* i, 27), or even to the beginning of the fifth/eleventh century (ibid., i, 28). A precise determination, however, depends on the state of our knowledge, and to date no complete study in Arabic or any other language exists concerning this subject.

What can be said is that this technical term already occurs in the title of a book from the second half of the third/ninth or the beginning of the following century: Ibn al-Marzubān (Abū Bakr Muḥammad b. Khalaf al-Muḥawwalī al-Baghdādī al-Ājurrī, d. 309/921; Brockelmann, *GAL,* i, 125; S i, 189-90; Samʿānī, *Ansāb,* v, 221) wrote a large book in twenty-seven parts *(ajzāʾ)*, entitled *al-Ḥāwī fī ʿulūm al-Qurʾān* ("The compendium in the sciences of the Qurʾān"; Ibn al-Nadīm, *Fihrist,* 149; Ibn al-Nadīm-Dodge, 328; Yāqūt, *Irshād,* vi, 2645, no. 1115, has: Muḥammad b. al-Marzubān Abū l-ʿAbbās al-Dīmiratī, *leg.* al-Dīmīratī; Dhahabī, *Siyar,* xiv, 264; Dāwūdī, *Ṭabaqāt,* ii, 141, no. 486; Ṣāliḥ, *Mabāḥithi,* 122). We know nothing about the content of this book, which could be a Qurʾān commentary. The author was primarily a man of letters and he translated more than fifty books from Persian into

Arabic. One of his students, Ibn al-Anbārī (d. 328/940; Brockelmann, *GAL*, i, 119; S ii, 182; Sezgin, *GAS*, viii, 148, ix, 144-7) is said to have composed *ʿAjāʾib ʿulūm al-Qurʾān* ("The marvels of the sciences of the Qurʾān"; Sezgin, *GAS*, ix, 147 *op.* 4: ms. Alexandria), in which he dealt with the excellent qualities *(faḍāʾil)* of the Qurʾān, its descent in seven modes, the writing of its codices (see CODICES OF THE QURʾĀN), the number of its sūras, verses and words, etc. (Ṣāliḥ, *Mabāḥith*, 122). This title does not appear in the list of his works (Ibn al-Anbārī, *Ẓāhir*, i, 21-7), but since a presumed manuscript of it has been preserved, this manuscript should be examined thoroughly to establish authenticity. On the other hand, we are sure that he wrote *al-Mushkil fī maʿānī l-Qurʾān* ("The obscure in the meanings of the Qurʾān") which he dictated over the years but only completed up to Q 20 (Sūrat Ṭā Hā; Sezgin, *GAS*, viii, 153).

An author who was accused of extremist Shīʿī tendencies, al-Ruhnī (Muḥammad b. Baḥr, fl. early fourth/tenth century; Yāqūt, *Irshād*, vi, 2434-6, no. 1004; Kohlberg, *Medieval Muslim*, no. 441) wrote *Muqaddimat ʿilm al-Qurʾān* ("The introduction to the science of the Qurʾān," not extant) in which he emphasized that ʿAlī (see ʿALĪ B. ABĪ ṬĀLIB) and the People of the House (q.v.; i.e. the family of the Prophet; see FAMILY OF THE PROPHET) are the sole authority (q.v.) for the interpretation of the Qurʾān, stating also that the copies of the Qurʾān which ʿUthmān (q.v.) sent to the great cities of the empire differed from each other in their reading of certain passages, etc. (see also RECITERS OF THE QURʾĀN).

The Muʿtazilī philologist al-Rummānī al-Ikhshīdī (d. 384/994) wrote several books on various qurʾānic topics (see Qifṭī, *Inbāh*, 295), among them a huge qurʾānic commentary, of which parts 7, 10 and 12 are extant (part 12 in 150 folios, from Q 14:17 to Q 18:37!) — namely *al-Jāmiʿ fī ʿilm (ʿulūm) tafsīr al-Qurʾān* ("The comprehensive treatise on the science [or sciences] of the exegesis of the Qurʾān"; Sezgin, *GAS*, viii, 112-13, 270; for both, see Mubārak, *Rummānī*, 93-9). It seems to be identical with his *al-Tafsīr al-kabīr* ("Great commentary").

A confusion was made in some sources (Ibn al-ʿArabī, *Qānūn*, 119; id., *ʿAwāṣim*, 97-8) between two works of Abū l-Ḥasan al-Ashʿarī (d. 324/935), *al-Mukhtazan* ("The depository"), a book on dialectic theology, and *Tafsīr al-Qurʾān* ("Commentary of the Qurʾān," in 500 volumes!) in which he refuted his opponents and especially the Muʿtazilite Abū ʿAlī l-Jubbāʾī and al-Kaʿbī. Ibn al-ʿArabī claims that only one copy (!) of this work existed in the fourth/tenth century, for which al-Ṣāḥib Ibn ʿAbbād (d. 385/995) is reported to have paid 10,000 dinars to put it in the Dār al-Khilāfa, but the copy was destroyed in a fire (Gimaret, Bibliography d'Ashʿarī, 255-6, 260-2). Ibn Fūrak (d. 406/1015) tells us that there existed only rare copies of this commentary and that it was unknown by most of the Ashʿarites (Ibn Fūrak, *Mujarrad*, 165, 325).

In the second half of the fourth/tenth century or the beginning of the following, a great exegete of Khurāsān, the Karrāmite Ibn Ḥabīb al-Nīsābūrī (d. 406/1016; Gilliot, Exégèse, 139), who became a Shāfiʿī, wrote *al-Tanbīh ʿalā faḍl ʿulūm al-Qurʾān* ("The exhortation on the precedence of the sciences of the Qurʾān"; not in the list of his works, but quoted in Suyūṭī, *Itqān*, i, 36), and *Kitāb al-Tanzīl wa-tartībihi* ("The book of the descent and its arrangement"), which are extant (Saleh, *Formation*, 45-7, 88). His well-known student, the Nīsābūrian exegete Abū Isḥāq al-Thaʿlabī (d. 427/1035) composed *al-Kāmil fī ʿilm al-Qurʾān* ("The complete work in the qurʾānic science"); one of his most noted disciples Abū l-Ḥasan al-Wāḥidī (d. 468/1076) read it in his presence (Yāqūt, *Irshād,* iv, 1663; Gilliot, Exégèse, 140; Saleh, *Formation,* 51). These three books are not extant.

But the works of these Nīsābūrians were possibly preceded by those of the Karrāmites of Nīsābūr (Saleh, *Formation,* 87-8: on al-Thaʿlabī's fourteen hermeneutical aspects). Another testimony of their great activity in the qurʾānic disciplines is *The book of foundations* (*Mabānī,* in Jeffery, *Muqaddimas,* 5-250; Gilliot, Sciences coraniques) of Ibn Bisṭām (Abū Muḥammad Ḥāmid b. Aḥmad b. Jaʿfar b. Bisṭām al-Ṭuḥayrī, or al-Ṭakhīrī? Ṣarīfīnī, *Muntakhab,* 211, no. 638; Gilliot, Sciences coraniques, 19-20, 59). This book on qurʾānic sciences was completed in 425/1034, as an introduction to Ibn Bisṭām's qurʾānic commentary. We had previously attributed it erroneously to Abū Muḥammad Aḥmad b. Muḥammad b. ʿAlī l-ʿĀṣimī (Gilliot, Théologie musulmane, 183) but the right attribution has recently been definitively established (Anṣārī, Mulāḥaẓāt-i, 80). This Karrāmī tradition in qurʾānic sciences, however, is earlier and comes from the great Karrāmī master of Nīsābūr, al-Ḥakīm Ibn al-Hayṣam al-Nabī (d. 409/1019; van Ess, *Ungenützte Texte,* 60-74), who had a *Kitāb Iʿjāz al-Qurʾān* ("Book on the inimitability of the Qurʾān") and from important elements going back to Ibn Karrām (d. 255/869) himself, as seen in the *Kitāb al-Īḍāḥ* of another Karrāmī, Aḥmad b. Abī ʿUmar al-Zāhid al-Andarābī (d. 470/1077) who was a student of Ibn Bisṭām (Gilliot, Théologie musulmane, 18-19, 57-8). Al-Andarābī had also collected in a manuscript written by his own hand (extant in Mashhad, Maktaba Riḍawiyya, ms. 12405 with a *waqf* signed by al-Andarābī) five books or treatises on the qurʾānic sciences pertaining to the Karrāmī legacy, like *Qawāriʿ al-Qurʾān* ("The book on the verses containing maledictions against Satan," copied by al-Andarābī in 429/1038, with certificates of audition; edited in Iran but not on the basis of the manuscript of al-Andarābī; Anṣārī, Mulāḥaẓāt-i, 69-71). The leader of the Nīsābūrian Karrāmites at his time, Abū Bakr ʿAtīq b. Muḥammad al-Sūrābādī (d. 494/1101; van Ess, *Ungenützte Texte,* 73-4), composed a commentary on the Qurʾān which has been edited. Numerous manuscripts of the Karrāmite productivity in the field of qurʾānic sciences are extant, above all in Iranian libraries.

Al-Bāqillānī (d. 403/1013), the Mālikī and Ashʿarī scholar, who lived first in Baṣra and then Baghdād, was the author of *Iʿjāz al-Qurʾān* ("The inimitability of the Qurʾān"). He also wrote *[Nukat] al-Intiṣār li-naql al-Qurʾān* ("The victory for the transmission of the Qurʾān"), which contains much material on qurʾānic disciplines, such as: the names of the Qurʾān (q.v.), sūra, verse (see FORM AND STRUCTURE OF THE QURʾĀN); its transmission and arrangement (see MANUSCRIPTS OF THE QURʾĀN; MUṢḤAF); refutation of the Shīʿīs and others on it, the seven aspects *(al-aḥruf al-sabʿa);* its language and style (see LANGUAGE AND STYLE OF THE QURʾĀN); the satanic verses (q.v.); its collection (see COLLECTION OF THE QURʾĀN); the variants and the seven readers; etc.

The Egyptian grammarian and exegete al-Ḥawfī (Abū l-Ḥasan ʿAlī b. Ibrāhīm, d. 430/1039) wrote a qurʾānic commentary in thirty volumes, called *al-Burhān fī tafsīr al-Qurʾān* ("The proof concerning the exegesis of the Qurʾān"; Brockelmann, *GAL,* ii, 411; S i, 729; Ḥājjī Khalīfa, *Kashf,* ii, 46-7, no. 1794; i, 241; Yāqūt, *Irshād,* iv, 1343-4, no. 713; Zarkashī, *Burhān,* i, 301; iii, 222). It is extant in about fifteen volumes. It is a commentary that follows the order of the text but with subdivisions according to the "sciences of the Qurʾān": the syntax of the verse and its sense in the context (i.e. *al-naẓm,* "the arrangement"; cf. Biqāʾī, *Naẓm;* Suyūṭī, *Tanāsub:* on the relation between the sūras), then the grammatical and lexical points, or *"prononciation grammaticale"* (*iʿrāb;* Silvestre de Sacy, Muqniʿ, 307). Al-Zarkashī (d. 794/1392; *Burhān,* i, 301, puts this book in the list of the best books on that subject). This commentary treats the meaning and the exegesis *(maʿnā, tafsīr)* of the verse, then issues concerning the recitational pause or its impossibility *(al-waqf wa-l-itmām),* then the textual variants *(qirāʾāt),* then, if necessary, the legal rules *(aḥkām),* the occasions of revelation *(asbāb al-nuzūl),* the abrogation *(naskh),* etc. (Zurqānī, *Manāhil,* i, 27-8; according to al-Zurqānī, al-Ḥawfī had originally entitled his commentary *al-Burhān fī ʿulūm al-Qurʾān,* "The proof concerning the sciences of the Qurʾān").

In the fifth/eleventh century, the man of letters and poet Abū ʿĀmir al-Faḍl b. Ismāʿīl al-Tamīmī l-Jurjānī (d. after 458/1066) wrote *al-Bayān fī ʿilm/ʿulūm al-Qurʾān* ("The exposition on the science or sciences of the Qurʾān"; Yāqūt, *Irshād,* 2166, 2170; Ḥājjī Khalīfa, *Kashf,* ii, 82, no. 2012). It was probably a commentary with special emphasis on the philological and literary aspects of the Qurʾān, like *Durj al-durar* ("The drawer of pearls"; Brockelmann, GAL, S i, 504, *op.* viii) of his colleague, the philologist and rhetorician ʿAbd al-Qāhir al-Jurjānī (d. 471/1078; see RHETORIC AND THE QURʾĀN), if the attribution of this title to al-Jurjānī is true (Ḥājjī Khalīfa, *Kashf,* iii, 222, no. 5043, expresses a doubt).

The Shāfiʿī jurist, judge and Ashʿarī theologian of Baghdād (who was originally from Jīlān, which was noteworthy for an Ashʿarī), Shaydhala (Abū l-Maʿālī ʿAzīzī/ʿUzayzī b. ʿAbd al-Malik al-Jīlī: d. 494/1100; Brockelmann, GAL, i, 433; S i, 775; Ibn Khallikān, *Wafayāt,* iii, 259-60), wrote *al-Burhān fī mushkilāt al-Qurʾān* ("The proof about the difficult passages of the Qurʾān"). Al-Suyūṭī (*Itqān,* i, 31-2; 177-81) puts this book on the list of handbooks on the sciences of the Qurʾān that do not provide exhaustive coverage of the constitutent topics of this discipline. It is also quoted by al-Zarkashī, especially concerning the "inimitability" (q.v.) of the Qurʾān (*Burhān,* ii, 90; iii, 375).

In the sixth/twelfth century, the Khurāsānī Shāfiʿī of Marw al-Rūdh, al-Zāghūlī (Muḥammad b. al-Ḥusayn al-Aruzzī, d. 559/1164), is said to have written a work in 400 volumes, *Qayd al-awābid,* "The fettering of the fleeing (animals)"/ "The registration of the fleeting (ideas)," a kind of huge encyclopedia on the sciences of exegesis, tradition, law and language, which is not extant (Dhahabī, *Siyar,* xx, 492-3; Ahlwardt, *Verzeichnis,* i, no. 450/2; Ḥājjī Khalīfa, *Kashf,* iv, 590, no. 9688, has "four volumes"; ed. Yaltkaya, ii, 1367 has "400 volumes").

The Ḥanbalī polymath from Baghdād, Ibn al-Jawzī (d. 597/1201), wrote several books on the subject, e.g. *ʿAjāʾib ʿulūm al-Qurʾān* ("The wonders of the sciences of the Qurʾān"; Brockelmann, GAL, i, 504, *op.* 30; ʿAlwajī, *Muʾallafāt,* no. 324), which is edited (Gilliot, Textes arabes, in MIDEO 19, no. 29). The title mentioned by Brockelmann (GAL, *op.* 32), *al-Mujtabā fī ʿulūm al-Qurʾān* ("The selection on the sciences of the Qurʾān"), extant in one volume, deals not only with qurʾānic knowledge (like variants), but also with other matters, ḥadīth, etc. (ʿAlwajī, *Muʾallafāt,* no. 383). Ibn al-Jawzī also wrote an abridgment of it, *al-Mujtabā min al-mujtabā* ("The selection of the selection"; Brockelmann, GAL, S i, 918, *sub op.* 32; ʿAlwajī, *Muʾallafāt,* no. 384). A third work, *al-Mudhish* ("The marvellous"), also called *al-Mudhish wa-l-muḥāḍarāt* ("The marvellous and the lectures," or "The marvellous on exhortations and sermons," etc.), completed in 591/1194, treats some qur'ānic matters in the first chapter (2-22), then language, ḥadīth, historiography, and parenetics, such as legends of the prophets, etc., in the remaining four chapters (Brockelmann, *GAL*, i, 506, *op.* 81; S i, 920; Ḥājjī Khalīfa, *Kashf*, v, 477, no. 11704; ii, 1640; ʿAlwajī, *Muʾallafāt*, no. 329). But the book which is the closest to the genre of the later voluminous and exhaustive handbooks on the sciences of the Qurʾān, like those of al-Zarkashī and al-Suyūṭī, is Ibn al-Jawzī's *Funūn al-afnān fī ʿajāʾib ʿulūm al-Qurʾān* ("The disciplines of the branches in the wonders of the sciences of the Qurʾān"; Brockelmann, *GAL*, i, 504; S i, 918; ʿAlwajī, *Muʾallafāt*, no. 167). It is also extant with other titles like *Fann al-afnān fī ʿuyūn ʿulūm al-Qurʾān* ("The discipline of the branches in the sources of the sciences of the Qurʾān"). But the relation between the first and the last of these works should be checked, taking into account the content of the different manuscripts of both. Finally, it should be noted that Ibn al-Jawzī, like other scholars, also wrote separate books on various sciences of the Qurʾān (see below; cf. also Fanīsān, *Āthār al-ḥanābila*, 94-9).

In the seventh/thirteenth century at least two handbooks were composed on the sciences of the Qurʾān: *Jamāl al-qurrāʾ wa-kamāl al-iqrāʾ* ("The beauty of the Qurʾān reciters and the perfection of the recitation"; Gilliot, Textes arabes, in *MIDEO* 19, no. 24) by ʿAlam al-Dīn al-Sakhāwī (d. 643/1246). It is divided into ten books: the sūras and verses of the Qurʾān; its inimitability; its meritorious qualities; its divisions; the number of its verses; non-canonical variants; abrogation; readers and readings; recitation *(tajwīd);* pause and beginning *(al-waqf wa-l-ibtidāʾ)*. It is one of the sources of another handbook: *al-Murshid al-wajīz ilā ʿulūm tataʿallaq bi-l-kitāb al-ʿazīz* ("The brief guide to sciences connected with the august book"; Ḥājjī Khalīfa, *Kashf*, v, 494, no. 11,801) by the Damascene historian Abū Shāma al-Maqdisī (d. 665/1267); it falls in six chapters: revelation *(nuzūl)*, collection, seven modes *(aḥruf)*, recognized readings, irregular readings, and useful sciences of the Qurʾān.

The eighth/fourteenth century witnessed the most complete handbook on the subject yet produced: *al-Burhān fī ʿulūm al-Qurʾān* ("The proof concerning the sciences of the Qurʾān") of the Egyptian Badr al-Dīn al-Zarkashī (d. 794/1392). It was made up of forty-seven chapters (Brockelmann, *GAL*, ii, 91-2; S ii, 108, *op.* 20; Anawati, Textes arabes, in *MIDEO* 4, no. 18; no. 15 in *MIDEO* 6).

The work of the Andalusian Ibn Juzayy al-Kalbī l-Gharnāṭī (d. 741/1340), entitled *al-Tashīl li-ʿulūm al-tanzīl* ("The facilitation in the sciences of revelation"), is a commentary, but with a long introduction on these sciences (op. cit., i, 4-29). Another book, *al-Durr al-maṣūn fī ʿulūm/ʿilm al-kitāb al-maknūn* ("The protected pearls on the sciences or science of the covered book") of al-Samīn (or Ibn al-Samīn) al-Ḥalabī (d. 756/1355), which has been edited in six volumes, is in fact a commentary limited to grammatical and lexical explanations supported by numerous poetical quotations (see POETRY AND POETS). For this reason it is also called *Iʿrāb al-Samīn* ("The grammatical commentary of al-Samīn"; Brockelmann, *GAL*, ii, 111; S ii, 137-8, *op.* 1; Ḥājjī Khalīfa, *Kashf*, iii, 190, no. 4870).

The genre thrived in the ninth/fifteenth century, a century that can be called the century of the great handbooks on the qurʾānic sciences. Thus we have the author of a well-known Arabic dictionary *(al-Qāmūs)*, al-Fīrūzābādī (d. 817/1415), writing his *Baṣāʾir dhawī l-tamyīz fī laṭāʾif al-kitāb al-ʿazīz* ("Insights of those having discernment in the subtleties of the holy book"). Then *Mawāqiʿ al-ʿulūm fī mawqiʿ al-nujūm*

("The positions of the sciences in relation to the places from which the stars set") is written by the Egyptian Jalāl al-Dīn ʿAbd al-Raḥmān al-Bulqīnī (d. 824/1421; Brockelmann, *GAL*, ii, 112; S ii, 139). This title is inspired by the concept of *nuzūl/tanzīl* (descent) which is one of the terms used for the Islamic concept of "revelation." The book of Bulqīnī, together with that of al-Zarkashī, is one of the numerous sources of the *Itqān* of al-Suyūṭī who was a student of the former's younger brother ʿAlam al-Dīn al-Bulqīnī (Ḥājjī Khalīfa, *Kashf*, vi, 233-4, no. 13,351; Suyūṭī, *Itqān*, i, 17-18, with the introduction of al-Bulqīnī; id., *Taḥbīr*, 27-8).

The Ḥanafī of Bergama who settled in Cairo, Muḥammad b. Sulaymān al-Kāfiyajī (d. 879/1474; Brockelmann, *GAL*, ii, 144-5, *op.* 1), one of al-Suyūṭī's teachers, wrote a small handbook entitled *al-Taysīr fī qawāʿid ʿilm al-tafsīr* ("The facilitation of the principles of the science of exegesis"), which was completed in 856/1452. It is said that the author "was very proud of his book, thinking that nobody had produced such a good one before him. But he had probably not seen *al-Burhān* ("The proof") of Zarkashī, otherwise he would have been ashamed" (Ḥājjī Khalīfa, *Kashf*, ii, 487, no. 3813). It is divided into two chapters: 1. The technical terms of the qurʾānic sciences necessary for exegesis. 2. The rules of exegesis and various related questions.

The Egyptian polymath Jalāl al-Dīn al-Suyūṭī (d. 911/1505) succeeded in writing the most complete handbook on the genre. When he read the book of his master al-Kāfiyajī on the sciences of the Qurʾān, he was disappointed. Then he read the *Mawāqiʿ* of Jalāl al-Dīn al-Bulqīnī, as per the advice of the brother of the author, his own master, ʿAlam al-Dīn al-Bulqīnī; he found it to be informative and well-organized, but thought it needed to be completed on a large number of important points and to be reorganized. He thus compiled *al-Taḥbīr fī ʿilm al-tafsīr* ("The refinement of the science of exegesis"; often called *al-Takhbīr*, "The index"; Ḥājjī Khalīfa, *Kashf*, ii, 248, no. 2729), which was written in 872/1467-8, in 102 chapters (Suyūṭī, *Itqān*, i, 16-23). Still unsatisfied, he wanted to do better and to write an exhaustive work. At this point, he discovered al-Zarkashī's *Burhān*, which pleased him greatly. He decided to reorganize it in a better way, and to add chapters and questions to it. This resulted in his writing *al-Itqān fī ʿulūm al-Qurʾān* ("The perfection of the sciences of the Qurʾān"; *Itqān*, i, 23-31), which was completed in 878/1474, in eighty chapters, as an introduction to his major qurʾānic commentary, *Majmaʿ al-baḥrayn wa-maṭlaʿ al-badrayn*, which he had already begun (Ahlwardt, *Verzeichnis*, i, no. 423, on the genesis of the *Itqān;* Brockelmann, *GAL*, ii, 144; S ii, 179, *op.* 1). In spite of the smaller volume of the *Burhān*, it contains things which are not in the *Itqān*. Before his *Itqān*, al-Suyūṭī had written *Muʿtarak al-aqrān fī iʿjāz al-Qurʾān* ("The gymnasium of the equal [plurivocal words] about the inimitability of the Qurʾān"; Ḥājjī Khalīfa, *Kashf*, v, 620, no. 12,346), on the rhetorical and stylistic aspects of the Qurʾān. Although it does not deal with all the sciences of the Qurʾān, this book has numerous chapters in common with the *Itqān* (e.g. *Itqān* chapters 22-7/*Muʿtarak* chapter 10; 37-8/13; 43/9; 44/11; 45/14; 47/8; 48/7; 55/12; 60/5; 62/4; 63/6; 65/1; 67/29; 68/30, etc.).

The Shāfiʿī Ṣūfī of Damascus, Ibn ʿArrāq (Muḥammad b. Aḥmad b. ʿAbd al-Raḥmān, d. 933/1526) wrote a kind of anthology in 138 folios entitled *Jawharat al-ghawwāṣ wa-tuḥfat ahl al-ikhtiṣāṣ* (Brockelmann, *GAL*, ii, 332, *op.* 1; Ahlwardt, *Verzeichnis*, i, no. 427), on the sciences of the Qurʾān, the Prophet, legends, the Companions, and mystical notions. In it he copied Ibn al-Jawzī's *Risāla fī ʿilm al-mawāʿiẓ* ("Treatise on the science of religious exhortations"; Brockelmann, GAL, S i, 919, *op.* 75a; ʿAlwajī, *Muʾallafāt,* no. 168, not extant apart from this ms.), in four chapters: sciences of the Qurʾān, Qurʾān and philology, the sciences of tradition, historiography. He also copied *Radd maʿānī al-āyāt al-mutashābihāt,* or *Radd al-mutashābih ilā l-muḥkam* ("The meanings of the ambiguous passages of the Qurʾān") by al-Labbān al-Miṣrī (d. 749/1349; Brockelmann, GAL, i, 111, *op.* 3; Ahlwardt, *Verzeichnis,* i, no. 716). Ibn ʿArrāq followed this with his own *Nawḥ al-qulūb* ("The intention of the heart") on the Prophet and Companions, etc., which has nothing to do with qurʾānic sciences, and then included a small treatise on special qurʾānic expressions coming from dialects (q.v.), according to the order of the sūras (ff. 14-30), transmitted by Abū Ṭāhir al-Silafī (d. 576/1180), in 572/1176, which is in reality *Kitāb Lughāt al-Qurʾān* ("The dialectal expressions in the Qurʾān"), attributed to Ibn ʿAbbās, transmitted to al-Silafī by al-Wazzān (Rippin, Ibn ʿAbbās, 19; Biqāʿī, *Kitāb Lughāt al-Qurʾān,* 137-8). Ibn ʿArrāq ends his collection with Ṣūfī explanations of a hundred qurʾānic expressions, drawn from the beginning of the qurʾānic commentary written by Abū l-ʿAbbās al-Būnī (d. 622/1225; Brockelmann, GAL, i, 497-8).

In his *Miftāḥ al-saʿāda wa-miṣbāḥ al-siyāda fī mawḍūʿāt al-ʿulūm* ("The key of happiness and the lamp of mastership on the subjects of the sciences"), an encyclopedic bio-bibliographical work on the classification of the sciences, Abū l-Khayr Ṭāshkubrīzādah (d. 968/1561) devotes the sixth chapter to the legal sciences (vol. ii), i.e. Qurʾān, ḥadīth and law *(fiqh),* in which the qurʾānic sciences receive considerable attention: exegesis of the Qurʾān, particularly the books written about this discipline (ii, 62-128); the branches of the [variant] readings (*furūʿ al-qirāʾāt;* 369-77); the branches of exegesis (*furūʿ al-tafsīr;* 380-595). That means that for him most of the qurʾānic sciences center on exegesis. Others consider them to be studies about the Qurʾān, except those devoted to "the meanings *(maʿānī)* and exegesis *(tafsīr)* of its verses" (UQM, i, 9).

The writing of handbooks on qurʾānic sciences continued in the following centuries, until the present day. We have thus *Maḥāsin al-taʾwīl* ("The beauties of exegesis") of Jamāl al-Dīn al-Qāsimī (d. 1914), which is a qurʾānic commentary containing much information on the sciences of the Qurʾān; *Tibyān al-furqān fī ʿulūm al-Qurʾān* ("The exposition of the discrimination of the sciences of the Qurʾān") of the Damascene Ṭāhir al-Jazāʾirī (d. 1920); *Manāhil al-ʿirfān fī ʿulūm al-Qurʾān* ("The springs of the knowledge of the sciences of the Qurʾān") of the Azharī scholar of the first half of the twentieth century, Muḥammad ʿAbd al-ʿAẓīm al-Zurqānī, published in 1943, and quoted by some scholars as a source, although it is devoid of references; *Manhaj al-furqān fī ʿulūm al-Qurʾān* ("The method of the discrimination of the sciences of the Qurʾān") of M.ʿA. Salāma; *Fī ʿulūm al-qirāʾāt* ("On the sciences of the qurʾānic readings") of S.R. al-Ṭawīl, etc. And recently an anonymous collection was published under the title *ʿUlūm al-Qurʾān ʿinda l-mufassirīn* ("The sciences of the Qurʾān according to the exegetes," which has been abbreviated to UQM in this article) in three volumes, and also *al-Tamhīd fī ʿulūm al-Qurʾān* ("The facilitation of the sciences of the Qurʾān") of Ayatollah Muḥammad Hādī Maʿrifa.

It should be also noted that several exegetes wrote introductions to their commentaries which include different aspects of the sciences of the Qurʾān (UQM, i, 12), e.g. al-Ṭabarī (d. 310/923; *Tafsīr,* i, 3-110; Eng. trans. i, 5-51); al-Thaʿlabī (d. 427/

1035; *Kashf,* i, 73-87); al-Ṭūsī (d. 460/1067; *Tibyān,* i, 1-21); Rāghib al-Iṣfahānī (d. prob. 502/1108; *Muqadimma* to his *Jāmiʿ al-tafāsīr,* 27-109); Ibn ʿAṭiyya al-Andalusī (d. 541/1147; *Muḥarrar,* i, 33-57; Jeffery, *Muqaddimas,* 251-94); al-Shahrastānī (d. 548/1153; *Mafātīḥ al-asrār,* i, f. 1ᵛ-27ʳ; Monnot, Introduction); al-Ṭabarsī (d. 548/1153; *Majmaʿ,* i, 17-34); al-Qurṭubī (d. 671/1273; *Jāmiʿ,* i, 1-107); Niẓām al-Dīn al-Ḥasan b. Muḥammad b. al-Ḥusayn al-Nīsābūrī l-Aʿraj (d. after 730/1329; *Tafsīr,* i, 1-48; Gilliot, Exégèse, 142-3, with reference to the studies of Monnot); Ibn Juzayy (d. 741/1340; *Tashīl,* i, 4-29); Abū Ḥayyān al-Gharnāṭī (d. 745/1344, *Baḥr,* i, 3-14: sources, masters and disciplines of exegesis); Ibn Kathīr (d. 774/1373; *Faḍāʾil,* as an independent book but also as a part of his commentary in some manuscripts (at the end; *Faḍāʾil,* 3-4; and perhaps in some editions); however, the introduction of the *Tafsīr* (i, 11-18) is different from that in his *Faḍāʾil;* al-Biqāʿī (d. 885/1480; *Maṣāʿid,* i, 97-478); Maḥmūd al-Ālūsī (d. 1854; *Rūḥ,* i, 22-85), etc. Some scholars, however, considered a general introduction, without detailed treatment of the qurʾānic sources, to be sufficient, while others would write a few pages on the necessity of exegesis, e.g. al-Māturīdī (d. 333/944, *Taʾwīlāt,* ed. Jubūri, 5-6; ed. Vanioğlu, i, 3-4: on *tafsīr* and *taʾwīl*), Abū l-Layth al-Samarqandī (d. 373/983; *Tafsīr,* i, 71-113), or al-Māwardī (d. 450/1058; *Nukat,* i, 23-43), on the names of the Qurʾān, the sūra, the seven aspects *(aḥruf),* "inimitability" and exegesis.

We should also mention the great books of traditions *(ḥadīth),* many of which have a "chapter on exegesis" *(Kitāb al-Tafsīr),* e.g. Saʿīd b. Manṣūr al-Khurāsānī (d. 227/842; in his *Sunan,* ii-iv, up to Q 5); al-Bukhārī (d. 256/870; in his *Ṣaḥīḥ,* iii, 193-390 [bk. 65]; Fr. trans. iii, 249-519); Ibn Ḥajar, in his *Fatḥ* (viii, 155-744); Muslim (d. 251/875; *Ṣaḥīḥ,* iv, 2312-23 [bk. 54]); al-Nasāʾī (d. 303/915; in his *Sunan,* vi, 282-526 [bk. 82]); Ḥākim al-Nīsābūrī (d. 405/1014; in his *Mustadrak,* ii, 220-541), etc. Many of them also have a *Faḍāʾil al-Qurʾān* ("Book on the meritorious qualities of the Qurʾān"), e.g. Saʿīd b. Manṣūr, in his *Sunan* (i, 7-232), one of the sources of al-Suyūṭī (*Itqān,* i, 48); Ibn Abī Shayba (d. 235/849, in his *Muṣannaf,* vi, 117-56 [bk. 22]); al-Bukhārī, in his *Ṣaḥīḥ* (iii, 391-410 [bk. 66]; Fr. trans. iii, 520-43); Ibn Ḥajar, in his *Fatḥ* (ix, 3-103); Muslim, in his *Ṣaḥīḥ* (iv, 543-66, within book 6, on the prayer of the travelers; see PRAYER FORMULAS); al-Nasāʾī, in his *Sunan* (v, 3-34 [bk. 75], or in an independent book such as Ḥākim al-Nīsābūrī, *Mustadrak,* ii, 220-57, i.e. at the beginning of *Kitāb al-Tafsīr*).

A survey of qurʾānic sciences based on the Itqān *of al-Suyūṭī*

Of course, before handbooks covering "all" qurʾānic disciplines were compiled and written, independent works on each of these qurʾānic disciplines were already in circulation. Yet we still have no exhaustive study, either in Arabic or in other languages, on the genesis and development of each of the so-called "qurʾānic sciences or disciplines." We shall thus attempt to provide here some ordering of this topic, based on the chapters of al-Suyūṭī's *Itqān,* and to give a brief chronological survey of books written on some of these disciplines (Nolin's *Itqān and its sources* is be used with caution because it contains many mistakes in proper names and titles as well as other errors). The eighty chapters of the *Itqān* can be divided into nine sections (Suyūṭī-Balhan, *Révélation,* 23-9; for all these disciplines, see also Ṭāshkubrīzādah, *Miftāḥ,* 380-595).

I. *Where and how the Qurʾān was sent down (inzāl, tanzīl, nuzūl;* Gilliot, Le Coran, fruit d'un travail collectif?): 1. What was sent down in Mecca (q.v.) or in Medina (q.v.; UQM, i, 303-20). ʿIzz al-Dīn al-Dīrīnī (d. 697/1297; Brockelmann, GAL, i, 451-2, *op.* 3; Ahlwardt, *Verzeichnis*, i, no. 466-7) wrote a poem of thirty-three verses, *Fī tartīb nuzūl al-Qurʾān al-ʿaẓīm*, on the arrangement of the sūras according to the place of their revelation. The question was also treated by the Mālikī Makkī b. Abī Ṭālib al-Qaysī l-Qayrawānī l-Andalusī (d. 437/1045), but al-Suyūṭī (*Itqān*, i, 36) does not include the title of his book. The interpolation of Medinan verses into Meccan sūras is treated in this discipline (Nagel, *Einschübe*, according to Ibn ʿAbd al-Kāfī's [d. after 400/1009] book without a title).

What was sent down: 2. At home or on a journey (or during a campaign; Ḥājjī Khalīfa, *Kashf*, i, 75 no. 4358; see EXPEDITIONS AND BATTLES). 3. During the day or at night. 4. In the summer or in the winter (see SEASONS). 5. In bed and while sleeping (see DREAMS AND SLEEP; VISION). 6. On the earth (q.v.) or in the sky. 7. First revealed, chronologically, either generally or on a particular subject (e.g. on wine [q.v.] or food; see FOOD AND DRINK; SUSTENANCE). 8. Last revealed.

9. The occasions of revelation. It is said that the earliest book on this subject was composed by ʿAlī b. al-Madīnī (d. 264/849; Sezgin, GAS, i, 108; Suyūṭī, *Itqān*, i, 177), but *al-Tafṣīl li-asbāb al-tanzīl*, attributed to Maymūn b. Mihrān (d. 117/735), although probably a later redaction with material coming from him, is extant in manuscript (introduction of the edition of Ibn Ḥajar, *ʿUjāb*, i, 80, with a list of twenty-two titles on this subject, 80-4).

10. Revelations (literally "descent") which coincided with the speech of one of the Companions. 11. Revelations which were repeated. 12. Revelations containing legal rules which were not applied immediately or revelations which were revealed after the application of a legal rule. 13. What was sent down in fragments or as a whole (*jumʿan*). 14. What was sent down accompanied (by angels; see ANGEL) or unaccompanied. 15. What had (already) been sent down to a prophet or was not sent down before the Prophet. 16. The modalities of the revelation (trans. Suyūṭī-Balhan, *Révélation*, 30-88).

II. *Its edition:* 17. The names of the Qurʾān (UQM, i, 21-52) and of the sūras (UQM, i, 321-34): In Shaydhala Abū l-Maʿālī ʿAzīzī's (d. 494/1100) *al-Burhān fī mushkilāt al-Qurʾān* ("The proof about the difficult passages of the Qurʾān"), it has fifty-five names (*Itqān*, i, 178-81). 18. Its collection (*jamʿ*; UQM, i, 335-412; Gilliot, Le Coran, fruit d'un travail collectif?, 195-9, on Zayd b. Thābit; on its collection and the problem of its falsification from a Shīʿī point of view, see Amīn, *Dāʾirat*, ix, 122-8) and arrangement (*tartīb*; Gilliot, Traditions). 19. The number of its sūras and verses (Pretzl, Koranlesung, 239-41, for both; Nöldeke, GQ, iii, 237-8: verses; Amīn, *Dāʾirat*, ix, 133a: 6236 verses), words and letters.

III. *Its transmission:* 20. Those who have memorized (Gilliot, Traditions) or transmitted it (see MEMORY). 21-27. The character of the various chains of authorities (*isnāds*) through which the different qurʾānic readings (variants) were transmitted (Nöldeke, GQ, iii, 116-231: readings, readers and books; Pretzl, Koranlesung, 17-47, 230-45; books: Ḥājjī Khalīfa, *Kashf*, iv, 506-8).

On readings and readers: Mahdawī (d. after 430/1039), *Bayān* (justification of the different readings); Andarābī (d. 470/1077), *Qirāʾāt*. On the seven canonical readings: Ibn Mujāhid (d. 324/936), *Sabʿa*; Ibn Khālawayh (d. 370/980), *Ḥujja*; Abū Manṣūr al-Azharī (d. 370/980), *Maʿānī l-qirāʾāt*; Abū ʿAlī l-Fārisī (d. 377/987),

Ḥujja; Abū l-Ṭayyib b. Ghalbūn (d. 389/999), *Istikmāl;* Ibn Shurayḥ al-Ruʿaynī l-Ishbīlī (d. 476/1083), *al-Kāfī;* Ibn Siwār al-Baghdādī (d. 496/1103), *Mustanīr;* Ibn al-Bādhish al-Gharnāṭī (d. 540/1145; Pretzl, Koranlesung, 28-9, no. 11: where *leg.* Bādhish, not Bādhash), *Iqnāʿ,* held in high esteem by Abū Ḥayyān al-Gharnāṭī (*Baḥr,* i, l. 11-12). On the eight (see their names and ways of transmission in Gilliot, Textes, in *MIDEO* 25-6, no. 78), i.e. the seven canonical readers and Yaʿqūb b. Isḥāq al-Ḥaḍramī (d. 205/821): Ibn Ghalbūn (Ṭāhir, d. 399/1009, the son of the previous Ibn Ghalbūn), *Tadhkira;* Ahwāzī (d. 446/1055), *Wajīz,* 63-76 (Kohlberg, *Medieval Muslim,* no. 643); Abū Maʿshar al-Ṭabarī (d. 478/1085), *Talkhīṣ.* On the ten readings: Abū Bakr b. Mihrān (d. 381/991), *Ghāya;* id., *Mabsūṭ,* which is a commentary on his larger work, *al-Shāmil fī l-qirāʾāt al-ʿashr* (not extant); Makkī b. Abī Ṭālib, *Tabṣira;* Abū l-ʿIzz al-Wāsiṭī l-Qalānisī (d. 521/1127; Pretzl, Koranlesung, 40, no. 28), *Irshād;* Ibn al-Jazarī (d. 833/1429), *Nashr,* i, 2-192, with a list of books on readings in general. On the fourteen readings and ways of transmission: Bannāʾ al-Dimyāṭī (d. 1117/1705), *Iḥtāf,* i, 75-9 (see Khaṭīb, *Muʿjam al-qirāʾāt;* Hamdan, *Koranlesung;* id., Nichtkanonische Lesarten; Muḥaysin, *Qirāʾāt,* on the influence of the readings on Arabic grammar and philology; Gilliot, *Elt,* 135-64). Of course, most qurʾānic commentaries quote a great number of variants, but this is done above all by the great Andalusian grammarian Abū Ḥayyān al-Gharnāṭī (d. 745/1344) in *al-Baḥr al-muḥīṭ* (see Khān, *Lahjāt,* a study on this commentary).

On the differences in the consonantal ductus between the so-called "codex of ʿUthmān" and other codices we have: Ibn Abū Dāwūd (d. 316/929), *Maṣāḥif;* Ibn al-Anbārī, *Marsūm al-khaṭṭ;* id., *al-Maṣāḥif* (Sezgin, *GAS,* ix, 147, *op.* 7, one of the sources for al-Suyūṭī, e.g. *Itqān,* ii, 320); id., *al-Radd ʿalā man khālafa muṣḥaf ʿUthmān* (Suyūṭī, *Itqān,* ii, 322; Sezgin, *GAS,* ix, 147, *op.* 6); Ibn Ashta (d. 360/971), *al-Maṣāḥif* (not extant; one of the sources of al-Suyūṭī, *Itqān,* chapter 18, i, 205; chapter 41, ii, 323-4, 327-9); Abū l-ʿAbbās al-Mahdawī, *Hijāʾ;* Ibn al-Bannāʾ al-ʿAdadī l-Marrākushī (d. 721/1321), *ʿUnwān;* Farmāwī, *Rasm al-muṣḥaf;* Qannawjī, *Abjad,* ii, 299; Ḥamad, *Rasm al-muṣḥaf.*

IV. *Its recitation:* for all forms of pronunciation (Silvestre de Sacy, Alcoran, 76-110; Ḥamad, *Dirāsāt ṣawṭiyya*) we have Dānī (d. 444/1053), *Taysīr* (summarized in Pretzl, Koranlesung, 291-331); Makkī b. Abī Ṭālib, *Riʿāya.* 28. The pause and the "beginning" (*al-waqf wa-l-ibtidāʾ/al-iʾtināf,* called also *al-Maqāṭiʿ wa-l-mabādiʾ,* the title of the book of Ibn Mihrān, which is not extant; Nöldeke, *GQ,* iii, 234-7; Pretzl, Koranlesung, 234-8; Silvestre de Sacy, Repos de voix; id., Pauses). 29. The exposition of what is connected *(mawṣūl)* according to the wording but separated *(mafṣūl)* in meaning. 30. Vocalic inflexion of *a* (*imāla;* Nöldeke, *GQ,* iii, 197, 37; Pretzl, Koranlesung, 318-26; Grünert, Imâla). 31-33. Other phenomena of pronunciation (Pretzl, Koranlesung, 293-318). 34-35. On memorization and the learning of reading *(tilāwa)* and recitation (*tajwīd;* Nöldeke, *GQ,* iii, 231-4; Pretzl, Koranlesung, 232-4, 290-1).

V. *Its linguistic aspects:* 36. Uncommon or rare words or words acquiring special meaning in particular contexts (all of this is called *gharīb;* Ḥājjī Khalīfa, *Kashf,* iv, 322-32: Science of the lexical rarities of Qurʾān and ḥadīth). Lists on that subject had been established very early or attributed to early scholars (Rippin, Ibn ʿAbbās's *Gharīb al-Qurʾān;* id., Ibn ʿAbbās's *al-Lughāt fī l-Qurʾān;* Neuwirth, Der Koran, 125-6). A list of eighty-five titles, including, however, also some *Maʿānī* ("meanings") *al-Qurʾān* titles, has been collected (Marʿashlī, introduction to Makkī b. Abī Ṭālib, *ʿUmda,* 19-37). Very early in Islam the vocabularly of ancient poetry was used to explain words of the Qurʾān, as evidenced by the *Responsa* to the Khārijī Nāfiʿ b. al-Azraq (see KHĀRIJĪS) attributed to Ibn ʿAbbās (d. 69/688), which were collected in various versions (Suyūṭī, *Itqān,* ii, 67-105; *Masāʾil Nāfiʿ b. al-Azraq;* Neuwirth, Die *Masāʾil;* Gilliot, Textes, in *MIDEO* 23 [1997], no. 44, with bibliography).

37. Words that are not in accordance with the manner of speaking *(lugha)* of the Ḥijāz. 38. Words that do not pertain to the Arabic language (see FOREIGN VOCABULARY). 39. Polysemy/homonymy and synonymy *(al-wujūh wa l-naẓāʾir).* Under *al-wujūh wa-l-naẓāʾir* should be listed kinds of concordances of the Qurʾān, such as: Muqātil, *Ashbāh;* Hārūn b. Mūsā (d. 170/786), *Wujūh;* Yaḥyā b. Sallām (d. 200/815), *Taṣārīf;* Dāmaghānī, *Wujūh;* Ibn al-Jawzī, *Nuzha;* Samīn, *ʿUmda,* one of the best in this genre.

40. Knowledge of the particles, letters and special words (*adawāt, ḥurūf,* etc.) which is necessary for the exegete (ʿUmayra and al-Sayyid, *Muʿjam al-adawāt wa l-ḍamāʾir fī l-Qurʾān;* Sharīf, *Muʿjam ḥurūf al-maʿānī fī l-Qurʾān*). 41. Case and mood (*iʿrāb;* Ḥājjī Khalīfa, *Kashf,* i, 352-7, no. 926; Qannawjī, *Abjad,* ii, 80-2; Shantarīnī, *Tanbīh al-albāb*). Among the books on this subject mentioned by al-Suyūṭī (*Itqān,* ii, 309, partly repeating, as usual, al-Zarkashī, *Burhān,* i, 301): Makkī (d. 437/1047), *Mushkil;* al-Ḥawfī (d. 430/1039) who had a book in ten volumes on this subject; Abū l-Baqāʾ al-ʿUkbarī (d. 616/1219), *Tibyān;* al-Samīn al-Ḥalabī (d. 756/1355), *Durr,* also called *Iʿrāb al-Samīn;* the commentary *(Baḥr)* of Abū Ḥayyān al-Gharnāṭī, which contains much on *iʿrāb.* 42. The morphological rules (Gilliot, *Elt,* 165-203), e.g. the pronouns, masculine and feminine, affirmation and negation, singular and plural, false synonymy, question and answer, etc.

VI. *Its normative (legal) aspect:* 43. Clear and ambiguous or similar verses (al-Kisāʾī, d. 189/805, *Mutashābih;* al-Khaṭīb al-Iskāfī, d. 421/1030, *Durrat al-tanzīl;* al-Kirmānī, d. ca. 500/1106, *Burhān,* which includes a list of books on the subject, 61-4; Ḥājjī Khalīfa, *Kashf,* v, 370, no. 11350-1; *UQM,* iii, 11-165). 44. Anteposition *(muqaddam)* and postposition *(muʾakhkhar).* 45. General and particular. 46. Synoptic or ambiguous *(mujmal)* and elucidated or clear *(mubayyan).* 47. Abrogating and abrogated. 48. What poses a problem (*mushkil;* Ḥājjī Khalīfa, *Kashf,* v, 559-60, no. 12,093-16) and suggests disagreement *(ikhtilāf)* or contradiction. The grammarian Quṭrub (d. 206/821) is said to have written a book on this subject; it is probably *Kitāb Quṭrub fī mā saʾala ʿanhu l-mulḥidūn min āy al-Qurʾān* (Sezgin, *GAS,* viii, 65); Ibn Qutayba (d. 276/889) composed *Taʾwīl mushkil al-Qurʾān* ("The interpretation of the difficult passages [q.v.] of the Qurʾān"). 49. Absolute and restricted statements *(muṭlaq, muqayyad).* 50. Expressed or understood statements *(manṭūq, mafhūm).*

Special books on the legal content or the exegesis of the legal verses of the Qurʾān have been composed, and are entitled *Aḥkām al-Qurʾān* ("The legal rules of the Qurʾān"; Ḥājjī Khalīfa, *Kashf,* i, 173-4, no. 156). The following book should be added to our list (see Gilliot, Exegesis, 113-14): Ibn Faras al-Gharnāṭī (d. 599/1202), *Aḥkām al-Qurʾān* (Brockelmann, *GAL,* S i, 734; Suyūṭī, *Itqān,* i, 49, 54, etc.).

VII. *Its rhetorical and stylistic aspects and its inimitability:* 51-64 (see also LITERATURE AND THE QURʾĀN).

VIII. *Various aspects:* stylistic again, the proper names in the Qurʾān, its meritorious qualities *(faḍāʾil),* the writing of the Qurʾān, etc. 65. Knowledge drawn from the Qurʾān. 66. The parables *(amthāl).*

Māwardī (d. 450/1058) has collected these parables in *al-Amthāl wa-l-ḥikam* (see also Ibn al-ʿArabī, *Qānūn,* 261-96). 67. The oaths (q.v.). 68. Dialectic, argumentation and polemics *(jadal):* according to al-Suyūṭī (*Itqān,* iv, 60), Sulaymān ʿAbd al-Qawī l-Ṭūfī (d. 716/1316) wrote a book on this topic. 69. The proper names.

70. The unidentified individuals (*al-mubham;* Ḥājjī Khalīfa, *Kashf,* v, 367, no. 11, 342-3): Suhaylī, d. 581/1185, *Taʿrīf;* Ibn ʿAskar of Malaga, d. 636/1239, *Takmīl* (correct Suyūṭī, *Itqān,* iv, 93, and Suyūṭī, *Mufhamāt,* 7, both of which have erroneously Ibn "Asākir"); Suyūṭī, *Mufhamāt.* In numerous cases this discipline is related to the occasions of revelations. 71. The names of those upon/about whom the Qurʾān was sent down (cf. chapters 70 and 9).

In the literature numerous books were written on this topic, in particular concerning ʿAlī, the subsequent imāms (see IMĀM), and the family of the Prophet (Kohlberg, *Medieval Muslim,* no. 83, 107-8, 149, 488, 623). But deciphering anonymous and obscure expressions to uncover them *(taʿyīn al-mubham, tasmiya)* was also a focus of interest during the earlier stage of Shīʿī exegesis on "positive" and "negative" verses, the former referring to members of the Prophet's family, the latter to enemies like Abū Bakr, ʿUmar, or ʿĀʾisha (see ʿĀʾISHA BINT ABĪ BAKR), e.g. on Q 15:44 (Bar-Asher, Scripture, 106-10; Amir-Moezzi, *Guide,* 217-20; Amir-Moezzi and Jambet, *Qu'est-ce que le chiisme,* 91-3); also with words and expressions which are not in the ʿUthmānic text, for both positive and negative verses: Q 2:225; 4:63, 65-6; 20:115; 33:71; 42:13 (Amir-Moezzi and Jambet, *Qu'est-ce que le chiisme,* 92-3).

72. The meritorious qualities of the Qurʾān (*Faḍāʾil al-Qurʾān,* see also above and below).

73. The best of the Qurʾān and what makes it so (*afḍal, fāḍil;* Ḥājjī Khalīfa, *Kashf,* i, 373, no. 1022). This issue is a matter of disagreement among scholars: al-Ashʿarī, Ibn Ḥibbān (d. 354/965), al-Bāqillānī, probably already Mālik b. Anas (d. 179/795), etc., did not find this topic acceptable. They argued that since the Qurʾān is the speech (q.v.) of God (see WORD OF GOD), everything in it is excellent. Yet, others did discuss this topic: Isḥāq b. Rāhawayh (d. 238/853), al-Ghazālī (*Jawāhir,* 37-8), Abū Bakr b. al-ʿArabī (*Qānūn,* 230-40, on Q 1 and 112, also referring to al-Ghazālī), etc.

74. Selected passages *(mufradāt)* of the Qurʾān. This chapter is connected with the previous one, but instead of saying "the best of...," it discusses expression(s) or verse(s) that are "the most sought" *(arjā),* for one reason or another. 75. Its prophylactic and propitiatory properties *(khawāṣṣ).* According to the *Itqān,* al-Tamīmī wrote *Khawāṣṣ al-Qurʾān.* He was a physician of Jerusalem called Abū ʿAbdallāh al-Tamīmī (d. last quarter of the fourth/tenth century; Ḥājjī Khalīfa, *Kashf,* iii, 180, no. 4814; Sezgin, *GAS,* iii, 318, *op.* 2: *Manāfiʿ khawāṣṣ al-Qurʾān*). Al-Ghazālī also wrote a book on the subject (*Kitāb al-Dhahab al-abraz [al-ibrīz] fī asrār khawāṣṣ kitāb Allāh al-ʿazīz;* cf. Bouyges, *Chronologie,* 127-8, no. 199).

76. The calligraphic form (*marsūm al-khaṭṭ;* see ORTHOGRAPHY OF THE QURʾĀN) and the discipline of writing the Qurʾān. Among those who wrote on this subject, al-Suyūṭī mentions the treatises of al-Dānī on orthography (*Muqniʿ;* Silvestre de Sacy, Muqniʿ) and "punctuation" (*Naqṭ;* Silvestre de Sacy, Mémoire, 320-49; id., Traité de ponctuation; id., De différents traités); Ibn Wathīq al-Ishbīlī (d. 654/1256), *Jāmiʿ;* Ibn al-Bannāʾ al-Marrākushī, *ʿUnwān* (see above, chapters 21-7).

IX. *Exegesis and exegetes* (chapters 77-80; see Gilliot, Exegesis; add: Amir-Moezzi and Jambet, *Qu'est-ce que le chiisme,* 139-74: on symbolic interpretation, *taʾwīl,* in Shīʿism; *UQM,* iii, 169-587; French translation of passages of several commentaries in

Borrmans, *Commentaire*): The early commentator Yaḥyā b. Sallām (d. 200/815) had listed twelve qualities *(khaṣla)* requisite for the exegete, namely the knowledge of what is Meccan and Medinan, the abrogating and the abrogated, the anteposition and the postposition, what is separated *(maqṭūʿ)* and what is connected (*mawṣūl;* cf. Suyūṭī, *Itqān,* chap. 29), the particular and the general, ellipsis *(iḍmār)* and the Arabic language (that is, the technical knowledge of this language; Ibn Abī Zamanīn, d. 399/1008, *Tafsīr,* i, 114).

It can be said that al-Zarkashī's *Burhān* and al-Suyūṭī's *Itqān* represent the result of centuries of Islamic studies on the Qurʾān. Up to the present day they remain the main sources, especially the *Itqān,* for those who write "new" handbooks in Arabic on the sciences of the Qurʾān, e.g. Qaṭṭān, *Mabāḥith,* a sort of abridgment of the *Itqān,* also to a certain extent Ṣāliḥ, *Mabāḥith.*

Final remarks

It should be emphasized that several authors have written much on various qurʾānic sciences, e.g. the reader and grammarian of Kūfa, al-Kisāʾī (d. 189/805), was the author of more than ten books on qurʾānic philology (Sezgin, *GAS,* ix, 130-1), and materials from his *Maʿānī l-Qurʾān* have been recently collected. One of his students, the grammarian and author of *Maʿānī l-Qurʾān,* al-Farrāʾ (d. 207/822), wrote several other books on qurʾānic philology (Sezgin, *GAS,* ix, 133). The grammarian Ibn Khālawayh (d. 370/980) wrote some fifty books, five of which were on qurʾānic disciplines (see the introduction of ʿUthaymīn to *Iʿrāb al-qirāʾāt,* i, 62-85). Makkī b. Abū Ṭālib (d. 437/1045) produced about 100 books, sixty-seven pertaining to qurʾānic sciences. These include twenty-five on the readings, a qurʾānic commentary in seventy *ajzāʾ (al-Hidāya fī bulūgh al-nihāya),* another in fifteen volumes (*mujallads*; *Mushkil al-maʿānī wa-l-tafsīr*), a book on recitation *(Riʿāya),* several on the pause, etc. (Marʿashlī, ed. of Makkī, *ʿUmda,* 50-4). Among the more than forty books that Abū ʿAmr al-Dānī (d. 444/1053) composed, twenty-nine were on qurʾānic sciences, of which fifteen were on readings or readers, others on qurʾānic philology, like *al-Idghām al-kabīr* ("The great book of assimilation in the Qurʾān"), *Taḥdīd* (on recitation; see the introduction of the edition of *Muktafā,* 35-42; introduction to *Naqṭ,* 15-19, listing only twenty-eight books). Ahwāzī (d. 446/1055) wrote some thirty books (introduction to *Wajīz,* 31-7), of which sixteen were on readings and readers. Ibn al-Jawzī (d. 597/1200) wrote more than 200 books (list of Ibn Rajab, ʿAlwajī, *Muʾallafāt,* 20-8, who lists in his book 574 titles, of which many are actually the same book but with variant titles), twenty-eight of which were on qurʾānic sciences: two on abrogation, one on occasions of revelation, one on the seven readings, one on interpretative constants (*al-Wujūh wa-l-naẓāʾir,* i.e. *Nuzha*), two on rare or strange words *(gharīb),* several on exegesis (*Zād, al-Mughnī, Taysīr al-bayān;* ʿAlwajī, *Muʾallafāt,* 269-70; Ibn al-Jawzī, *Funūn,* 9-11, introduction of the edition), etc.

Mention has been made several times in this article of the "genre" known as the "meritorious qualities of the Qurʾān" *(Faḍāʾil al-Qurʾān).* This title is often used for books or chapters of major ḥadīth collections containing traditions attributed to Muḥammad or the Companions, or coming from scholars of the first two centuries of Islam or later. Some of them are small handbooks of qurʾānic sciences in general with chapters on: (1) learning, teaching and recitation of the Qurʾān; (2) those who know and recite the Qurʾān and what is required of them; (3) the sūras and verses, and the merits attached to the recitation of the different sūras; (4) the collection of the Qurʾān, words contradicting the ductus of the so-called ʿUthmānic codex and the various codices; (5) linguistic problems (dialects, etc.); (6) Meccan and Medinan sūras; (7) the readers; (8) its exegesis; (9) the orthography of the Qurʾān, etc. (see Abū ʿUbayd's, Ibn Kathīr's, and also, but to a lesser degree, ʿAbd al-Raḥmān al-Rāzī's *Faḍāʾil,* and Ibn Rajab's *Mawrid*). Other books have little or nothing about the history of the text (see TEXTUAL HISTORY OF THE QURʾĀN), but more about the merits acquired through its recitation, audition and occupying oneself with it (*taʿāhud;* cf. Ibn Abī Shayba, *Muṣannaf* [bk. 22, *Faḍāʾil,* ch. 13], vi, 124: *Fī taʿāhud al-Qurʾān*), e.g. Firyābī's *Faḍāʾil.* In the arrangement of the collection of traditions of Ibn Ḥibbān (d. 354/965) by Ibn Balbān al-Fārisī (d. 729/1329), the equivalent of the *Faḍāʾil* is the chapter on the recitation of the Qurʾān, a part of the *Book of subtleties* (Ibn Ḥibbān, *Ṣaḥīḥ* [bk. 7, *Raqāʾiq,* ch. 7, *Qirāʾat al-Qurʾān*], iii, 5-83).

According to Franz Rosenthal, over time there was a tendency in Islam to give preference "to a disjunctive juxtaposition of individual data as against a continuous and integrated exposition" of science. He further explained, "It can also be assumed to have contributed to the growing tendency of constantly adding to the number of what was considered to constitute independent scientific disciplines" (*Knowledge,* 44) until they reached the number of 150, or even 316 (Ṭāshkubrīzādah, *Miftāḥ,* i, 74-5). This statement about sciences in general is even truer for the "sciences of the Qurʾān" whose specification and proliferation was a matter of ultimate importance because they are supposed to lead to salvation (q.v.) in the hereafter. According to a declaration attributed to Muḥammad: "The believer will never become surfeited with beneficial *(khayr)* [religious knowledge] until he reaches paradise" (Tirmidhī, *Ṣaḥīḥ* [42, *ʿIlm,* 19], v, 50-1, no. 2686; Rosenthal, *Knowledge,* 89). But some of these disciplines have also contributed to several "profane" fields of knowledge, like grammar, lexicography, stylistics, rhetoric, etc., which became, for many scholars, ancillary disciplines for the study of the Qurʾān.

Claude Gilliot

Bibliography

Primary: Abū Ḥayyān, *Baḥr,* Cairo 1328-9/1911; Abū l-Layth al-Samarqandī, *Tafsīr,* ed. Muʿawwaḍ; Abū Manṣūr al-Azharī, *Maʿānī l-qirāʾāt,* ed. ʿI.M. Darwīsh and ʿA. b. Ḥ. al-Qawzī, 3 vols., Cairo 1991-3; Abū Maʿshar al-Qaṭṭān al-Ṭabarī, *al-Talkhīṣ fī l-qirāʾāt al-thamān,* ed. M.Ḥ. ʿAqīl Mūsā, Cairo 2001; Abū Shāma, *Murshid,* ed. T. Altikulaç/W.M. al-Ṭabāṭabāʾī, Kuwait 1993[2]; Abū ʿUbayd, *Faḍāʾil al-Qurʾān,* ed. Khāwajī/A. b. ʿA. al-Khayyāṭī, 2 vols., Rabat 1415/1995; Ahwāzī, Abū ʿAlī al-Ḥasan b. ʿAlī al-Muqriʾ, *al-Wajīz fī sharḥ qirāʾāt al-qaraʾa l-thamāniya aʾimmat al-amṣār al-khamsa,* ed. D.Ḥ. Aḥmad, Beirut 2002; al-Ājurrī, Abū Bakr, *Akhlāq ahl al-Qurʾān,* ed. M.ʿA. ʿAbd al-Laṭīf, Beirut 1407/1987[2] (1986[1]); Ālūsī, *Rūḥ,* 17 vols., ed. Ṭ. ʿAbd al-Raʾūf Saʿd, Cairo 1418/1997; ʿAlwajī, ʿAbd al-Ḥamīd, *Muʾallifāt Ibn al-Jawzī,* Kuweit 1992; Andarābī, Aḥmad b. Abī ʿUmar, *Qirāʾāt al-qurrāʾ al-maʿrūfīn bi-riwāyāt al-ruwāt al-mashhūrīn,* ed. A.N. al-Janābī, Beirut 1407/1986[3]; Bannāʾ al-Dimyāṭī, *Itḥāf fuḍalāʾ al-bashar bi-l-qirāʾāt al-arbaʿat ʿashar,* ed. Sh. M. Ismāʿīl, 2 vols., Cairo 1407/1987; Bāqillānī, *Intiṣār;* al-Bayhaqī, Abū Bakr Aḥmad b. al-Ḥusayn, *Manāqib al-Shāfiʿī,* ed. S.A. Ṣaqr, 2 vols., Cairo 1391/1971; id., *Shuʿab al-mīn,* ed. H.M.S. al-Basyūnī Zaghlūl, 7 + 2 vols., Beirut 1410/1990; Biqāʿī, *Maṣāʿid al-naẓar lil-ishrāf ʿalā maqāṣid al-suwar,* ed. ʿAbd al-Samīʿ M.A. Ḥasanayn, 3 vols., Riyadh 1408/1987, i, 161-478 (some aspects of qurʾānic sciences); id., *Naẓm,* ed. ʿA. Ghālib al-Mahdī, 8 vols., Beirut 1415/1995; Bukhārī, *Ṣaḥīḥ,* ed. Krehl; trans. O. Houdas and W. Marçais, *El-Bokhāri. Les traditions islamiques,* 4 vols., Paris 1903-14; Dāmaghānī, *wujūh,* ed. Zafītī; Ḥ.Ṣ. Ḍāmin (ed.), *Arbaʿat kutub fī ʿulūm al-Qurʾān,* Beirut 1418/1998; Dānī, *al-Idghām al-kabīr fī l-Qurʾān,* ed. Z.Gh. Zāhid, Beirut 1993; id., *al-Muktafā fī l-waqf wa-l-ibtidāʾ,* ed. J.Z. Mukhlif, Baghdad 1403/1983; id., *Muqniʿ;* id., *Naqṭ;* id., *al-Taḥdīd fī l-itqān wa-l-tasdīd fī ṣanʿat al-tajwīd,* ed. A.ʿA. al-Fayyūmī, Cairo 1993; id., *al-Taʿrīf fī ikhtilāf al-ruwāt ʿan Nāfiʿ,* ed. T. al-Rājī al-Hāshimī, Muhammadiyya 1403/1982; id., *Taysīr;* Dāwūdī, *Ṭabaqāt,* ed. ʿUmar; Dhahabī, *Siyar;* Fārisī, *Ḥujja;* Fīrūzābādī, *Baṣāʾir;* Firyābī, Jaʿfar b. Muḥammad, *Faḍāʾil al-Qurʾān,* ed. I.ʿU.F. Jibrīl, Riyadh 1989; Furāt al-Kūfī, *Tafsīr,* ed. M. al-Kāẓim, Tehran 1410/1990; al-Ghazālī, Abū Ḥāmid Muḥammad b. Muḥammad, *Iḥyāʾ ʿulūm al-dīn,* 4 vols., Cairo

1289/1872, repr. Cairo 1933, i, 244-64[bk.8]/ Zabīdī, *Itḥāf al-sādat al-muttaqīn bi-sharḥ Iḥyā' 'ulūm al-dīn,* 15 vols., Beirut 1409/1989, v, 4-181; id., *Jawāhir al-Qur'ān,* Beirut 1974[4] (Cairo 1933[2]); id., *Kitāb al-Dhahab al-abraz (al-ibrīz) fī asrār khawāṣṣ kitāb Allāh al-'azīz,* ed. 'A.Ṣ. Ḥamdān, Cairo [2000]; Ḥājjī Khalīfa, *Kashf;* Ḥākim al-Nīsābūrī, Ibn Bayyi', *al-Mustadrak 'alā l-Ṣaḥīḥayn fī l-ḥadīth,* ed. M. 'Arab b. M. Ḥusayn et al., 4 vols., Hyderabad 1915-23, repr. Riyadh n.d.; Hārūn b. Mūsā, *al-Wujūh wa-l-naẓā'ir,* ed. Ḥ.Ṣ. al-Ḍāmin, Baghdad 1409/1988; Ibn 'Abbās (attrib.), *Masā'il Nāfi' b. al-Azraq 'an 'Abdallāh b. 'Abbās* (recension of al-Khuttalī, d. 365/975), ed. M.A. al-Dālī (ms. Damascus Ẓāhiriyya), Limassol 1412/1992; Ibn Abī Dāwūd al-Sijistānī, *Kitāb al-Maṣāḥif,* ed. in Jeffery, *Materials;* Ibn Abī Shayba, Abū Bakr, *al-Muṣannaf fī l-aḥādīth wa-l-āthār,* ed. M.'A. Shāhīn, 9 vols., Beirut 1416/1995; Ibn Abī l-Zamanīn, *Tafsīr,* ed. A.Ḥ. Ibn 'Ukāsha and M.M. al-Kanz, 5 vols., Cairo 1423/2002; Ibn 'Ādil, Sirāj al-Dīn 'Umar al-Dimashqī al-Ḥanbalī, *al-Lubāb fī 'ulūm al-Kitāb,* ed. 'A.A. 'Abd al-Mawjūd and 'A.M. Mu'awwaḍ, 20 vols., Beirut 1419/1998; Ibn al-Anbārī, *Kitāb Īḍāḥ al-waqf wa-l-ibtidā' fī Kitāb Allāh 'izz wa-jall,* ed. M. Ramaḍān, Damascus 1971; id., *Marsūm al-khaṭṭ,* ed. I.'A. 'Arshī, New Delhi 1977; id., *al-Ẓāhir fī ma'ānī kalimāt al-nās,* ed. Ḥ.Ṣ. al-Ḍāmin, i, Baghdad 1979; Ibn al-'Arabī, *Aḥkām;* id., *al-'Awāṣim min al-qawāṣim (fī taḥqīq mawqif al-ṣaḥāba),* ed. 'A. Ṭālibī, Algiers 1981 (1974[1]); id., *Qānūn al-ta'wīl fī 'ulūm al-tanzīl,* ed. M. al-Sulaymānī, Beirut 1990; Ibn 'Askar, *Takmīl;* Ibn Bābawayh al-Qummī, Abū Ja'far Muḥammad b. Abū l-Ḥasan, *al-Khiṣāl,* ed. 'A. Akbar al-Ghaffārī, Beirut 1410/1990; Ibn al-Bādhish, Abū Ja'far, *al-Iqnā' fī l-qirā'āt al-sab',* ed. 'A. Qaṭāmish, 2 vols., Mecca 1422/2001[2] (1403/1983); Ibn al-Bannā' al-'Adadī al-Marrākushī, *'Unwān al-dalīl min marsūm khaṭṭ al-tanzīl,* ed. H. Shalabī, Beirut 1990; Ibn Ḍurays, *Faḍā'il;* Ibn Fūrak, *Mujarrad maqālāt al-Shaykh Abī l-Ḥasan al-Ash'arī (min imlā' al-Shaykh al-Imām Abī Bakr Muḥammad b. al-Ḥasan b. Fūrak),* ed. D. Gimaret, Beirut 1987; Ibn Ghalbūn, Abū l-Ṭayyib 'Abd al-Mun'im, *al-Istikmāl li-bayān mā ya'tī fī Kitāb Allāh fī madhhab al-qurrā' al-sab'a,* ed. 'A. Buḥayrī Ibrāhīm, Cairo 1412/1991; Ibn Ghalbūn, Ṭāhir, *al-Tadhkira fī l-qirā'āt al-thamān,* ed. A.R. Suwayd, Jeddah 1991; Ibn Ḥajar al-'Asqalānī, *Fatḥ al-bārī bi-sharḥ Ṣaḥīḥ al-Bukhārī,* ed. 'A. b. 'A. Bāz, numbering of the traditions according to M.F. 'Abd al-Bāqī, under the direction of Muḥibb al-Dīn Khaṭīb, 13 vols. plus introduction, Cairo 1390/1970, repr. Beirut n.d.; id., *al-'Ujāb fī bayān al-asbāb,* ed. 'A.M. al-Anīs, 2 vols., Dammām 1418/1997, i, 6f.; Ibn Ḥibbān, Abū Bakr Muḥammad, *Ṣaḥīḥ, Tartīb* of 'Alā' al-Dīn Alī b. Balbān al-Fārisī, ed. Sh. al-Arna'ūṭ, 18 vols., Beirut 1984-91; Ibn al-Jawzī, *'Ajā'ib 'ulūm al-Qur'ān,* ed. 'A. 'Āshūr, Cairo 1986; id., *Funūn/Fann al-afnān fī 'uyūn 'ulūm al-Qur'ān,* ed. A. al-Sharqāwī and I. al-Marrākushī, Rabat 1970; id., *al-Mudhish,* ed. M.T. al-Samāwī, Baghdad 1348/1929, repr. Beirut, n.d.; ed. F.F. al-Jundī, Riyadh 2002; id., *Nuzha;* id., *Zād;* Ibn al-Jazarī, *Nashr;* Ibn Juzayy, al-Kalbī al-Gharnāṭī, *al-Tashīl li-'ulūm al-tanzīl,* ed. 'A. Yūnus and I.'A. 'Awaḍ, 4 vols. in 1, Cairo 1976, repr. Beirut 1973; Ibn Kathīr, *Faḍā'il,* Beirut 1979; ed. A. al-Ḥuwaynī al-Athīr, Cairo and Jedda 1416/1996; id., *Tafsīr;* Ibn Khālawayh, *Ḥujja;* id., *I'rāb al-qirā'āt;* Ibn Khallikān, *Wafayāt,* ed. I. 'Abbās; Ibn Mihrān, Abū Bakr, *al-Ghāya fī l-qirā'āt al-'ashr,* ed. M.Gh. al-Junbāz, Riyadh 1411/1990[2] (1985[1]); id., *al-Mabsūṭ fī l-qirā'āt al-'ashr,* ed. S.Ḥ. Ḥākimī, Damascus 1407/1986; Ibn Mujāhid, *Sab'a;* Ibn al-Nadīm, *Fihrist,* ed. Flügel; Ibn al-Nadīm-Dodge; Ibn al-Naqīb, *Muqaddima;* Ibn Qutayba, *Gharīb;* id., *Ta'wīl;* Ibn Rajab, Abū l-Faraj 'Abd al-Raḥmān b. Aḥmad, *Majmū' rasā'il al-Ḥāfiẓ Ibn Rajab al-Ḥanbalī,* ed. A. Ṭal'at b. Fu'ād al-Ḥulwānī, 2 vols., Cairo 1423/2002; id., *Mawrid al-ẓam'ān ilā ma'rifat faḍā'il al-Qur'ān,* ed. B.'A. al-Bushrā, Cairo 1990; Ibn Shurayḥ al-Ru'aynī al-Ishbīlī, *al-Kāfī fī l-qirā'āt al-sab',* ed. J.M. Sharaf, Tanta 2004; Ibn Siwār al-Baghdādī, *al-Mustanīr fī l-qirā'āt al-'ashr,* ed. J.M. Sharaf, Tanta 2002; Ibn Taymiyya, *Muqaddima,* ed. 'A. Zarzūr, Beirut 1979 (1971[1]); Ibn Wathīq al-Ishbīlī, *al-Jāmi' li-mā yuḥtāj ilayhi min rasm al-muṣḥaf,* ed. Gh. Qaddūrī Ḥamad, Baghdad 1988; Jaṣṣāṣ, *Aḥkām;* Kāfiyajī, Muḥammad b. Sulaymān, *al-Taysīr fī qawā'id 'ilm al-tafsīr,* ed. N. b. M. al-Maṭrūdī, Damascus 1410/1990; [al-Khaṭīb] al-Baghdādī, Abū Bakr Aḥmad b. 'Alī, *al-Faṣl lil-waṣl al-mudraj fī l-naql,* ed. M. Naṣṣār, 2 vols., Beirut 1424/2003; al-Khaṭīb al-Iskāfī, *Durrat al-tanzīl wa-ghurrat al-ta'wīl fī bayān al-āyāt al-mutashābihāt fī Kitāb Allāh al-'azīz,* Beirut 1977; Kirmānī, Maḥmūd b. Ḥamza, *al-Burhān fī tawjīh mutashābih al-Qur'ān,* ed. A.'I.'A. Khalaf Allāh, Beirut 1996[2] (1991[1]); Kisā'ī, *Ma'ānī l-Qur'ān,* collected by 'Īsā Shaḥāta 'Īsā, Cairo 1998; al-Mahdawī, Abū l-'Abbās, *Bayān al-sabab al-mūjib li-ikhtilāf al-qirā'āt wa-kathrat al-ṭuruq wa-l-riwāyāt,* in Ḥ.Ṣ. Ḍāmin (ed.), *Arba'at kutub fī 'ulūm al-Qur'ān,* Beirut 1418/1998, 9-42; id., *Hijā' maṣāḥif al-amṣār,* ed. M.M. Ramaḍān, in RIMA 19/1 (1973); also in M.S.Ḥ. Kamāl (coll.), *Majmū'at al-rasā'il al-kamāliyya. i. Fī l-maṣāḥif wa-l-Qur'ān wa-l-tafsīr (5 rasā'il),* Taif 1407/1986, 115-202 (this last edition is a bad one, the editor could not identify the author); Makkī, *Ibāna;* id., *Kashf;* id., *Mushkil,* ed. Ḥ.Ṣ. al-Ḍāmin, Beirut 1407/1987[3] (Baghdad 1973[1]); id., *al-Ri'āya li-tajwīd al-qirā'a wa-taḥqīq lafẓ al-tilāwa,* ed. A.Ḥ. Farḥāt, Damascus 1393/1973; id., *al-Tabṣira fī l-qirā'āt al-'ashr,* ed. M. Ghawth al-Nadwī,

Bombay 1402/1982; id., *al-ʿUmda fī gharīb al-Qurʾān,* ed. Y.ʿA. al-Marʿashlī, Beirut 1984 (1981¹); Māturīdī, *Taʾwīlāt,* ed. Jubūrī; ed. F.Y. Khaymī, 5 vols., Beirut 2004 (the complete text, but a somewhat uncritical ed.); *Taʾwīlāt al-Qurʾān,* ed. A. Vanlioğlu and B. Topaloğlu, 1 vol. to date (Q 1 and 2), Istanbul 2005- (a good, critical ed.); al-Māwardī, *al-Amthāl wa-l-ḥikam,* ed. F. ʿAbd al-Munʿim Aḥmad, Alexandria 1985; id., *Nukat;* Nasāʾī, *Faḍāʾil;* id., *Sunan (al-kubrā);* al-Nīsābūrī, Niẓām al-Dīn al-Ḥasan b. Muḥammad b. al-Ḥusayn al-Qummī al-Aʿraj, *Tafsīr,* on the margin of Ṭabarī, *Jāmiʿ al-Bayān;* al-Qannawǧi, Abū l-Ṭayyib M. Ṣiddīq Khān, *Abjad al-ʿulūm,* ed. ʿA. Zakkār, 3 vols., Damascus 1978; Qasṭallānī, *Laṭāʾif,* i, 5-86; Qurṭubī, *Jāmiʿ,* ed. al-Bardūnī; al-Rāghib al-Iṣfahānī, *Muqaddamat Jāmiʿ al-tafsīr,* Kuweit 1984; al-Rāzī, ʿAbd al-Raḥmān, *Faḍāʾil al-Qurʾān wa-tilāwatihi wa-khaṣāʾiṣ tulātihi wa-ḥamlatihi,* ed. ʿĀ.Ḥ. Ṣabrī, Beirut 1994; Saʿīd b. Manṣūr, *al-Sunan,* ed. S. b. ʿA. b. ʿA. Ḥumayyid, 5 vols., Riyadh 2000; Sakhāwī, *Jamāl;* Samīn al-Ḥalabī, Shihāb al-Dīn, *al-Durr al-maṣūn fī ʿulūm al-kitāb al-maknūn (Iʿrāb al-Samīn),* ed. M.ʿA. Muʿawwaḍ et al., 6 vols., Beirut 1414/1994; id., *ʿUmdat al-ḥuffāẓ fī tafsīr ashraf al-alfāẓ,* ed. ʿA.A.T. al-Ḥalabī, 4 vols., Tripoli, Libya 1995; Ṣarīfīnī, *al-Muntakhab min al-Siyāq li-taʾrīkh Nīsābūr,* ed. M.A. ʿAbd al-ʿAzīz, Beirut 1989; Shāfiʿī, *Aḥkām;* id., *K. al-Umm,* ed. M.Z. Najjār, 7 vols. in 4, Beirut n.d.; ed. R.F. ʿAbd al-Muṭṭalib, 11 vols., Mansourah 1422/2001; al-Shahrastānī, *Mafātīḥ al-asrār wa maṣābīḥ al-abrār,* facsimile ed. and introduction A. Ḥāʾirī, 2 vols., Tehran 1989; Shantarīnī, Ibn al-Sarrāj Abū Bakr Muḥammad b. ʿAbd al-Malik, *Tanbīh al-albāb ʿalā faḍāʾil al-iʿrāb,* ed. M. b. M. al-ʿAwfī, Cairo 1410/1989; Suhaylī, *Taʿrīf;* Sūrābādī, *Tafsīr-i Sūrābādī,* 5 vols., Tehran 1381 Sh./2002; Suyūṭī, *Itqān,* Cairo 1974; id. (attrib.), *Maqālīd al-ʿulūm fī l-ḥudūd wa-l-rusūm,* ed. M.I. ʿUbāda, Cairo 1424/2004; id., *Muʿtarak al-aqrān fī iʿjāz al-Qurʾān,* ed. ʿA.M. al-Bijāwī, 3 vols., Cairo, 1939-72; id., *Taḥbīr;* id., *Tanāsub;* Suyūṭī-Balhan = J.-M. Balhan, *La Révélation du Coran selon al-Suyūṭī, Traduction annotée du chapitre seizième de [...]* al-Itqān *[...],* in *Etudes arabes* 97 (2001); Ṭabarī, *Tafsīr;* trans. J. Cooper, *The commentary on the Qurʾān,* Oxford 1987; Ṭabarsī, *Majmaʿ;* Ṭāsh-kubrīzādah, Abū l-Khayr, *Miftāḥ al-saʿāda,* ed. K.K. al-Bakrī and ʿAbd al-Wahhāb Abū l-Nūr, 4 vols., Cairo 1969; Thaʿlabī, Abū Isḥāq Aḥmad b. Muḥammad, *al-Kashf wa-l-bayān ʿan tafsīr al-Qurʾān,* ed. A.M.ʿA. ʿĀshūr, 10 vols., Beirut 2002; Tirmidhī, *Ṣaḥīḥ;* Ṭūsī, *Tibyān;* ʿUkbarī, *Tibyān;* UQM = (anon.), *ʿUlūm al-Qurʾān ʿinda l-mufassirīn,* 3 vols., Tehran 1374 Sh./1995 (compiled from sources, both Shīʿī and Sunnī); Wāsiṭī, Abū l-ʿIzz al-Qalānisī, *Irshād al-mubtadī wa-tadhkirat al-muntahī fī l-qirāʾāt al-ʿashr,* ed. ʿU. Ḥamdān al-Kabīs, Mecca 1984; Yaḥyā b. Sallam, *Tafsīr* [Q 16-37], ed. H. Shalabī, 2 vols., Beirut 2004; id., *Taṣārīf;* Yāqūt, *Irshād,* ed. I. ʿAbbās.

Secondary: Abbott, *Studies II;* id., *Studies III: Studies in Arabic literary papyri, III, Language and literature,* Chicago 1972; W. Ahlwardt, *Verzeichnis der arabischen Handschriften der Königlichen Bibliothek zu Berlin,* 10 vols., Berlin 1887-99; Ḥ. Amīn, *Dāʾirat al-maʿārif al-islāmiyya al-shīʿiyya,* 11 vols., Beirut 1412-18/1992-8; M.A. Amir-Moezzi, *Le Guide divin dans le shīʿisme originel. Aux sources de l'ésotérisme en Islam,* Lagrasse 1992; id. and Ch. Jambet, *Qu'est-ce que le chiisme?,* Paris 2004; G. Anawati, Textes arabes anciens édités en Egypte au cours de l'année 1957, in *MIDEO* 4 (1957), 203-46 (esp. no. 18); id., Textes arabes anciens édités en Egypte au cours des années 1959 et 1960, in *MIDEO* 6 (1961), 227-80 (esp. no. 15); Ḥ. Anṣārī (Qummī), Mulāḥaẓāt-i chand darbārih mīrāth barge mandeh karramiyye (in Persian), in *Kitāb Mah Dīn* (Tehran) 56-7 (1380 Sh.), 69-80; M.M. Ayāzī, *al-Mufassirūn. Ḥayatuhum wa-manhajuhum,* Tehran 1414/1993-4; M.M. Bar-Asher, *Scripture and exegesis in early Imāmī Shiism,* Leiden 1999; M.K. al-Biqāʾī, Kitāb Lughāt al-Qurʾān, in *Journal of the Jordan Academy of Arabic* 18 (1994), 131-46; M. Borrmans et al., Le Commentaire coranique. Première partie: le tafsīr ancien, in *Etudes arabes,* 67-68 (1984-5); M. Bouyges, *Essai de chronologie des œuvres de al-Ghazali,* Beirut 1959; Brockelmann, *GAL;* van Ess, *TG;* id., *Ungenützte Texte zur Karrāmīya. Eine Materialsammlung,* Heidelberg 1980; S.A. al-Fanīsān, *Āthar al-ḥanabila fī ʿulūm al-Qurʾān. Al-maṭbūʿ, al-makhṭūṭ, al-mafqūd,* Cairo 1989; A. Fedeli, Early evidences of variant readings in qurʾānic manuscripts, in K.-H. Ohlig and G.-R. Puin, *Die Dunklen Anfänge. Neue Forschungen zur Entstehung und frühen Geschichte des Islam,* Berlin 2005, 295-316; Cl. Gilliot, Le Coran, fruit d'un travail collectif?, in D. de Smet et al. (eds.), *al-Kitāb. La sacralité du texte dans le monde de l'Islam, Actes du Symposium international tenu à Leuven et Louvain-la-Neuve du 29 mai au 1 juin 2002, Bruxelles, Louvain-la-Neuve,* Leuven 2004, 185-231; id., L'exégèse du Coran en Asie Centrale et au Khorasan, in *SI* 89 (1999), 129-64; id., *Elt;* id., Exegesis of the Qurʾān: Classical and medieval, in *EQ,* ii, 99-124; id., Muqātil, grand exégète, traditionniste et théologien maudit, in *JA* 279 (1991/1-2), 39-92; id., Les sciences coraniques chez les Karrāmites du Khorasan. Le livre des fondations, in *JA* 288 (2000), 15-81; id., Les sept "lectures" [i and ii]. Corps social et écriture révélée, [i], in *SI* 61 (1985), 5-25; [ii] 63 (1986), 49-62; id., Textes arabes anciens édités en Egypte, in *MIDEO* 19 (1989)-25-6 (2004); id., La théologie musulmane en Asie centrale et au Khorasan, in *Arabica* 49 (2002/2), 135-203; id., Les traditions sur la mémorisation et la composition/coordination du

Coran *(ğamʿ* et *taʾlīf)* et leur ambiguïté, in Cl. Gilliot and T. Nagel (eds.), *Das Propheten ḥadīṯ. Dimensionen einer islamischen Literaturgattung* [Proceedings of the *Göttinger Kolloquium über das ḥadīṯ*, Göttingen, Seminar für Arabistik, 3-4 November 2000], Göttingen 2005, 14-39; D. Gimaret, Bibliographie d'Ašʿarī. Un réexamen, in *JA* 273 (1985), 223-92; Goldziher, *Richtungen;* TH. Grünert, Die Imāla, der Umlaut im Arabischen, in *Sitzungsberichte der Akademie der Wissenschaften zu Wien, Phil.-hist. Classe* 81 (1876), 447-542; Gh. Qaddūrī al-Ḥamad, *al-Dirāsāt al-ṣawtiyya ʿinda ʿilm al-tajwīd,* Amman 2003; id., *Rasm al-muṣḥaf. Dirāsa lughawiyya tarkhiyya,* Baghdad 1982; O. Hamdan, Können die verschollenen Korantexte der Frühzeit durch nichtkanonische Lesarten rekonstruiert werden, in Wild, *Text,* 27-40; id., *Die Koranlesung des Ḥasan al-Baṣrī (110/728). Ein Beitrag zur Geschichte des Korantextes,* PhD diss., Tübingen 1995; ʿĀ. Ḥulw, *Muʿjam al-dirāsāt al-qurʾāniyya ʿinda l-shīʿa l-imāmiyya,* Beirut 1992; M. al-Fāḍil Ibn ʿĀshūr, al-Tafsīr wa-rijāluhu, in M.S.Ḥ. Kamāl (coll.), *Majmūʿat al-rasāʾil al-kamāliyya,* i, *Fī l-maṣāḥif wa-l-Qurʾān wa-l-tafsīr (5 rasāʾil),* Taif 1407/1986, 307-495; Ibyārī, *al-Mawsūʿa al-qurʾāniyya,* 6 vols., Cairo 1388/1969; M. Khān, *al-Lahjāt al-ʿarabiyya wa-l-qirāʾāt al-qurʾāniyya. Dirāsa fī l-Baḥr al-muḥīṭ,* Cairo 2002; ʿAbd al-Karīm al-Khaṭīb, *Min qaḍāyā l-Qurʾān. Naẓmuhu, jamʿuhu, tartībuhu,* Cairo 1393/1973; ʿAbd al-Laṭīf al-Khaṭīb, *Muʿjam al-qirāʾāt,* 11 vols., Damascus 1422/2002; E. Kohlberg, *A medieval Muslim at work. Ibn Ṭāwūs and his library,* Leiden 1992; M.Sh. Lāshīn, *al-Laʾālī l-ḥisan fī ʿulūm al-Qurʾān,* Cairo 1423/2002; M. Hādī Maʿrifa, *al-Tafsīr wa-l-mufassirūn,* 2 vols., Mashhad 1418/1997; id., *al-Tamhīd fī ʿulūm al-Qurʾān,* Qom 1378 Sh./1999; G. Monnot, Islam. Exégèse coranique. L'introduction de Shahrastānī à son commentaire coranique inédit, in *Annuaire. Résumé des conférences et travaux, EPHE, Ve Section Sciences religieuses* 93 (1984-5), 305-15; M. Mubārak, *al-Rummānī al-naḥwī fī ḍawʾ sharḥihi li-Kitāb Sībawayh,* Beirut 1974²; M.S. Muḥaysin, *al-Qirāʾāt wa-atharuhā fī l-ʿulūm al-ʿarabiyya,* Cairo 1984-6; K. Mūsā, *al-Tibyān fī ʿulūm al-Qurʾān,* Beirut 1412/1992; Nagel, *Einschübe;* A. Neuwirth, Der Koran, in *GAP,* ii, 96-135; id., Die *Masāʾil Nāfiʿ b. al-Azraq.* Éléments des "Portrait mythique d'Ibn ʿAbbās" oder ein Stück realer Literatur? Rückschlüsse aus einer bisher unbeachteten Handschrift, in *ZAL* 25 (1993), 233-50; Nöldeke, *GQ;* K.E. Nolin, *The Itqān and its sources. A study of al-Itqān fī ʿulūm al-Qurʾān by Jalāl al-Dīn al-Suyūṭī with special reference to al-Burhān fī ʿulūm al-Qurʾān by Badr al-Dīn al-Zarkashī,* PhD diss., Hartford Seminary Foundation 1968; O. Pretzl, Die Wissenschaft der Koranlesung, in *Islamica* 6 (1933-35), 1-47, 230-246, 290-331; Pickthall, *Koran;* A. Rippin, Ibn ʿAbbās's *Gharīb al-Qurʾān,* in *BSOAS* 46 (1983), 332-3; id., Ibn ʿAbbās's *al-Lughāt fī l-Qurʾān,* in *BSOAS* 44 (1981), 15-25; F. Rosenthal, *Knowledge triumphant. The concept of knowledge in medieval Islam,* Leiden 1970; I.M. al-Ṣaffār, *Muʿjam al-dirāsāt al-qurʾāniyya,* Mosul 1984; W. Saleh, *The formation of the classical* tafsīr *tradition. The Qurʾān commentary of al-Thaʿlabī (d. 427/1035),* Leiden 2004; Sezgin, *GAS;* A. Shaḥāta, *ʿUlūm al-tafsīr,* Cairo 1986; M.Ḥ. al-Sharīf, *Muʿjam ḥurūf al-maʿānī fī l-Qurʾān,* 3 vols., Beirut 1996; A.-I. Silvestre de Sacy, Mémoire sur l'origine et les anciens monuments de la littérature parmi les Arabes, in *Mémoires tirés des registres de l'Académie royale des inscriptions et belles lettres* 50 (1785), 247-441; id., in *Notices et Extraits des Manuscrits de la Bibliothèque Impériale* 8 (1810), 290-332 (Du manuscrit arabe n° 239 de la Bibliothèque Impériale, contenant un traité sur l'orthographe primitive de l'Alcoran, intitulé: *Kitāb al-Muqniʿ fī maʿrifat maṣāḥif al-amṣār...,* 290-306; Traité de ponctuation, 306-32); 333-54 (Commentaire sur le poème nommé Raïyya); 355-9 (De différents Traités relatifs à l'orthographe et à la lecture de l'Alcoran); 360-2 (Traité des repos de voix dans la lecture de l'Alcoran); id., in *Notices et Extraits...* 9 (1813), 1-116 (De la prononciation des lettres arabes, extrait du manuscrit arabe n° 260, 1-75; Alcoran = D'un manuscrit arabe de l'Alcoran, accompagné de notes critiques et de variantes [ms. 189], 76-110; Pauses = D'un Traité des pauses dans la lecture de l'Alcoran, 111-16); S.R. al-Ṭawīl, *Fī ʿulūm al-qirāʾāt,* Mecca 1405/1985; I.A. ʿUmayra and ʿA.M. al-Sayyid, *Muʿjam al-adawāt wa-l-ḍamāʾir fī l-Qurʾān,* Beirut 1986 (1988²); K. Versteegh, *Arabic grammar and qurʾānic exegesis in early Islam,* Leiden 1993; Wansbrough, *QS;* Wild, *Text;* M. Yahia, *La contribution de l'Imam aš-Šāfiʿī à la méthodologie juridique de l'islam sunnnite,* PhD diss., Paris 2003; M.ʿA. Zurqānī, *Manāhil al-ʿirfān fī ʿulūm al-Qurʾān,* 2 vols., Cairo 1943.

Transitoriness

Being subject to change, departure or destruction. The Qurʾān contrasts the transitoriness of this world (q.v.; see also GENERATIONS; HISTORY AND THE QURʾĀN; AIR AND WIND; ASHES) with the eternally enduring quality of the hereafter (see ESCHATOLOGY) and also with the eternity (q.v.) of God (see GOD AND HIS ATTRIBUTES). The Qurʾān often states that whereas this life *(al-ḥayāt al-dunyā)* will pass away (e.g. Q 10:24; 18:45) and both its pleasures (e.g. Q 57:20) and its trials (e.g. Q 7:94-5; see TRIAL; TRUST AND PATIENCE) are transitory, the realities to come in the hereafter *(al-ākhira)* will endure forever. More emphasis is laid on the latter point as the Qur'ān repeatedly emphasizes the everlasting destinies of believer and unbeliever in the garden (q.v.) and hellfire, respectively (see BELIEF AND UNBELIEF; REWARD AND PUNISHMENT; PARADISE; HELL AND HELLFIRE); "abiding in it forever" *(khālidīna fīhā)* is one of the most distinctive qur'ānic refrains (e.g. Q 2:81-2; 98:6, 8). Believers should therefore not be deceived, as unbelievers are, by the alluring quality of this world's attractions (Q 2:212, on which see Paret, *Kommentar*, for numerous other references) but rather are to be schooled in a perspective that sets greater store by that which is eternal than by that which is transitory. "You prefer this life *(al-ḥayāt al-dunyā)* but the hereafter *(al-ākhira)* is better and more enduring" (*abqā*, Q 87:16-17); "that which you have wastes away *(yanfadu)*; that which is with God endures" (*bāqin*, Q 16:96; cf. 28:60; 38:54; 42:36). The unbeliever, failing to grasp this truth, seeks to confer immortality upon himself in ways doomed to failure: Q 104:3 speaks of an unbeliever who believes that wealth (q.v.) will make him immortal; the construction of impressive defensive buildings *(maṣāni')* can also appear as a misguided human attempt to escape the transitoriness of this life (Q 26:129; see CITY; HOUSE, DOMESTIC AND DIVINE).

In terms of frequency of reference this is the main emphasis in the qur'ānic perspective on the transitory quality of this life: a contrast between this life and the life to come. The Qur'ān does, however, also contrast the transience of this world with God himself. "Everyone who is thereon [on the earth] will pass away *(fānin)*; there endures *(yabqā)* only the face of your lord (q.v.), possessor of might and glory" (q.v.; Q 55:26-7; see also FACE OF GOD; POWER AND IMPOTENCE). Although this passage is not obviously echoed elsewhere in the Qur'ān (Paret, *Kommentar*, indicates no parallels) it memorably encapsulates the qur'ānic insistence on the gulf between creator and creation (q.v.). Only God is inherently eternal; everything else is transitory. The wider qur'ānic context supplements this theological foundation (see THEOLOGY AND THE QUR'ĀN) with the message that in the hereafter God will bestow eternity on the destinies that human beings earn for themselves (see FATE; DESTINY).

David Marshall

Bibliography
Izutsu, *God*, 85-9, 123-32; Paret, *Kommentar*, 44-5 (ad Q 2:212).

Translations of the Qur'ān

Translations of the Qur'ān did not have the same significance during the early spread of Islam that, for example, translations of the Bible had during the spread of Christianity. This is connected to the role of Arabs (q.v.) as the original target audience and bearers of Islam, as well as to the increasing importance of the Arabic language in the newly conquered territories. An additional role was played by the conviction of the stylistic inimitability (q.v.) of the Qur'ān. In the Qur'ān itself, its Arabic nature is repeatedly emphasized (cf. Q 41:2-3; 12:2; 13:37; 20:113; 39:28; 41:2-3; 42:7; 43:3; see also ARABIC LANGUAGE). Herein lies the deeply rooted conviction among Muslims that a "valid" recitation of the Qur'ān (q.v.) is possible only in the Arabic language. Only the Ḥanafite law school (see LAW AND THE QUR'ĀN; THEOLOGY AND THE QUR'ĀN) allows for exceptions in this regard, as set forth in detail in 1932 by the Ḥanafī Azhar scholar al-Marāghī (d. 1945).

In the Islamic world up to the early twentieth century

The question of qurʾānic recitation should be kept separate from that of the conveyance of its contents, i.e. its "meaning" (Ar. *maʿānī*) in Islamic vernaculars. Commensurate with the paramount significance of the oral tradition of delivering the Qurʾān (see RECITERS OF THE QURʾĀN), sermons also played an important role (see TEACHING AND PREACHING THE QURʾĀN). The Qurʾān was always recited and then, afterwards, paraphrased (and hence, explained) from the Arabic text into the vernacular. From al-Zamakhsharī's (d. 538/1144) exegesis of Q 14:4, it becomes clear that he not only sanctioned the translation of the Qurʾān from the Arabic, but also that such translations actually existed. Even the annotation (Ar. *tafsīr*) of the Qurʾān's text (see EXEGESIS OF THE QURʾĀN: CLASSICAL AND MEDIEVAL) could only be meaningfully conveyed to non-scholarly non-Arabs in their respective mother tongues (see TRADITIONAL DISCIPLINES OF QURʾĀNIC STUDY). The oldest example for this is the translation of al-Ṭabarī's monumental commentary *Jāmiʿ al-bayān* into Persian (see PERSIAN LITERATURE AND THE QURʾĀN), which was prepared for the Sāmānid ruler Abū Ṣāliḥ Manṣūr b. Nūḥ (r. 349-63/961-74). An ancient Turkish version was produced, almost simultaneously, on the basis of the Persian version (see TURKISH LITERATURE AND THE QURʾĀN). Numerous Ottoman annotations exist for the most important commentaries, such as al-Bayḍāwī's (d. prob. 716/1316-17) *Anwār al-tanzīl;* however, thus far, the question of circulation of the most important commentaries in the vernacular remains largely unexamined. Evidence for the secondary significance of vernacular translations with respect to the Arabic original may be found in the form of the interlinear version, which is extant in numerous manuscripts. It frequently gives simply the isolated meaning of the individual words, and rarely indicates a coherent text. The latter becomes common only later, mainly after the widespread introduction of the printing press in the Islamic world in the nineteenth century (see PRINTING OF THE QURʾĀN).

Important impetuses for the translation of the Qurʾān arose through the confrontation between the Islamic and Christian worlds (see PRE-1800 PREOCCUPATIONS OF QURʾĀNIC STUDY). This happened initially in Spain, as a result of the Christian *reconquista,* and in India as a result of English colonization. In Spain, as of the fifteenth century, translations of the Qurʾān arose in Aljamiado (that is, in old Spanish dialects), which were written in Arabic script; however, a complete translation written in Latin script, dating from the year 1606, is also preserved (cf. Lopez-Morillas, *Six Morisco-versions,* 20). Although not probable, it cannot be ruled out that the majority of the remaining fragmentary Aljamiado texts of the Qurʾān were influenced by the old-Castilian translation prepared by the jurist Yça of Segovia (that is, ʿĪsā dhā Jābir, also known as Yçā Gidelli) between 1454 and 1456 in Aiton/Savoy at the request of Cardinal John of Segovia (see below, under *"Qurʾān translations outside the Islamic world until ca. 1700"*). Traces of an Aragonite translation of the Qurʾān can be found in the polemical work of the convert Juan Andres, *Confusion dela secta mahomatica* (Valencia 1515). In India, it was Shāh Walī Allāh Dihlawī (1114-76/1703-62) who, in conjunction with his pursuit of modernization, called for the translation of the Qurʾān and, with his Persian-language work, *Fatḥ al-Raḥmān bi-tarjamat al-Qurʾān* (1737), delivered a Persian translation of the Qurʾān that is still meaningful today (first printed in Delhi, in 1283/1866). His two sons, Shāh Rafīʿ al-Dīn (1749-1818) and Shāh ʿAbd al-Qādir (1753-1814), translated the Qurʾān into

Urdu (printed in Calcutta in 1840, Delhi 1829; see SOUTH ASIAN LITERATURE AND THE QUR'ĀN).

Actually, since the emergence of the printing press, numerous translations have appeared in India in various regional Indian languages such as Urdu (first in 1828, by ʿAbd al-Salām Badayūnī), Sindhi (1876), Punjabi (1870), Gujarati (1879), Tamil (1884), and Bengali (1886; incidentally, this translation was produced and repeatedly reprinted at the initiative of Girish Chandra Sen [1835-1910], a follower of the neo-Hindu reformer Keshab Chandra Sen [1838-84]; see also LITERATURE AND THE QUR'ĀN).

Even in the nineteenth century, the Qur'ān and qur'ānic translations were very influential throughout the Islamic world. The first printed Qur'ān in a Turkish translation appeared in Cairo in 1842, and a Turkish translation of the *Tafsīr al-Jalālayn* in 1877. In Istanbul, Turkish translations have only been printed since 1865. The first printed Persian translation appeared in Tehran in 1855 and the first Pashtu edition in Bahupal in 1861. The first Serbo-Croatian translation (based on a French translation) was published in Belgrade in 1895.

In the Islamic world during the twentieth century

In the first half of the twentieth century, printed translations of the Qur'ān were still being published for the most important languages used by Muslims. In Asia, this necessitated translations into Balochi (1911), Brahui (1916), Telugu (1938), Malayan (1923), Indonesian (1928), Chinese (1927) and Japanese (1920; see SOUTHEAST ASIAN QUR'ĀNIC LITERATURE). In Africa, a translation into Yoruba appeared in 1906. A translation into the Zanzibar dialect of Swahili (printed 1923), produced by Godfrey Dale and G.W. Broomfield, was deemed unacceptable for Muslims due to an added Christian apologetic text, despite the quality of its language (see AFRICAN LITERATURE). At this time, two other factors became very significant: the missionary activities of the Aḥmadiyya (q.v.) movement and the efforts of the government of Kemal Atatürk in Turkey to put the Qur'ān into Latin script, aiming to publish only the Latin transcription without further publication of the Arabic Qur'ān text (see ARABIC SCRIPT; CALLIGRAPHY).

Both existing branches of the Aḥmadiyya movement valued above all spreading the Qur'ān in European languages (such as English, Dutch, and German). There is therefore an unmistakably rationalistic tendency in the older Aḥmadiyya translations (Maulvi Muhammad ʿAli, 1917). Thus, for example, in the English version of 1920 (a text identical to the London first edition of 1917), the word *naml*, "ants," appears in Q 27 as the description of a clan and "by hudhud is not to be understood the *lapwing*, but a person of that name" (see ANIMAL LIFE; NATURE AS SIGNS). The explanatory statement that follows says: "The verses that follow show clearly that Solomon (q.v.) was speaking of one of his own officers: the infliction of severe punishment on a small bird by such a mighty monarch as Solomon, and the exposition of the great religious doctrine of Unity by the lapwing, are quite incomprehensible" (p. 747, n. 1849). A comprehensive study of the different Aḥmadiyya translations is lacking. The debate over the Qur'ān in the Turkish Republic led to important discussions in al-Azhar, and in its journal these debates coalesced into multiple, significant essays (cf. Paret/Pearson, Translations, 429f.). In an essay from the year 1936, the later Rector of al-Azhar, Maḥmūd Shaltūt (1893-1963), expressly embraced the use of translation for non-Arabs, arguing that even translations contain the meaning of

God's word (see SPEECH; WORD OF GOD).

In contrast, the British author and convert, Marmaduke Pickthall (1875-1936), took a considerably more conservative position. In 1930, he published a translation of the Qurʾān bearing the title *The meaning of the glorious Koran,* "the first English translation of the Koran by an Englishman who is a Muslim" (p. vii). In the foreword, he wrote: "The Koran cannot be translated. That is the belief of old-fashioned Sheykhs and the view of the present writer. The Book is here rendered almost literally and every effort has been made to choose befitting language. But the result is not the Glorious Koran, that inimitable symphony, the very sounds of which move men to tears and ecstasy. It is only an attempt to present the meaning of the Koran — and peradventure something of the charm — in English. It can never take the place of the Koran in Arabic, nor is it meant to do so" (ibid.). Pickthall's translation, which contains exceedingly few annotations, had enormous success among Muslims and continues to be reprinted today (for example, in Istanbul, 1996f.). Another prominent convert was the Austrian journalist and, later, acting diplomat for Pakistan, Leopold Weiss (1900-92), who took the name Muhammad Asad after his conversion in 1926. He published an English translation of the Qurʾān in Gibraltar in 1980.

Four years after Pickthall (1934), a further translation appeared, which is still common today. It stems from the Indian scholar ʿAbdallāh Yūsuf ʿAlī (1872-1951) and is explicitly a response to Pickthall's work. In its introduction, "Translations of the Qur-an," ʿAlī writes of Pickthall's translation, that it is " 'almost litteral': it can hardly be expected that it can give an adequate idea of a Book which (in his own words) can be described as 'that inimitable symphony, the very sounds of which move men to tears and ecstasy.' Perhaps the attempt to catch something of that symphony in another language is impossible. Greatly daring, I have made that attempt." In the numerous notes to his bilingual edition (the Arabic text in calligraphy by Pir ʿAbdul Ḥamīd), ʿAlī strives for a contemporary exegesis that seeks primarily to answer the question: "What guidance can we draw for ourselves from the message of God?"

After the Second World War, intensified efforts to make the Qurʾān accessible in as many languages as possible can be discerned — always with the theologically motivated condition that the main concern be with translating, i.e. explaining, the meaning of the Qurʾān. Henceforth, translations by Muslims outnumber those by non-Muslims. In the English language, numerous new translations were published; notable are the translations by Abdul Majid Daryabadi (Lahore 1957) and, that favored by the Aḥmadiyya movement, the translation of Muhammad Zafrullah Khan (first published in London, 1971), both of which contain detailed commentaries. The first American translation derives from T.B. Irving (Vermont 1985). In 1959, the scholar Muhammad Hamidullah (1908-2002), who came from Haydarabad in India, published an excellent French translation. This edition underwent more than twelve editions and was also translated into Turkish. Preceding the translation itself is an extremely valuable survey of earlier Qurʾān translations. In 1972, Sheikh Si Hamza Boubakeur published a French translation with detailed commentaries based on traditional sources; it is particularly popular among north African migrants. In Germany, several translations by Muslims first appeared in the 1990's, independently from one another.

The increasing number of Muslim immigrants from various Islamic countries has been of great importance in different European countries. Because of this phenomenon, the task of translating the Qurʾān into the languages of their new host countries was set before Muslims themselves. At the same time, intensified Islamic missionary efforts are discernible worldwide, particularly in African countries south of the Sahara. In this context, the "King Fahd Complex for the Printing of the Holy Qurʾān" (Ar. *Mujammaʿ al-Malik Fahd li-ṭibāʿat al-Qurʾān al-karīm;* founded 1982, opened 1984; www.qurancomplex.org) in Medina acquires a very specific importance. The ultimate goal of this institution is to make the Arabic text of the Qurʾān, together with "the translation of the meaning of the Qurʾān," freely accessible worldwide. Presently, translations in 44 different languages (23 Asian, 11 African, and 10 European) are available. All of these editions, produced with an excellent quality of typographic technique and binding, are bilingual, and some even have additional, relatively extensive commentaries. In the meantime, however, editions not containing the Arabic text have also appeared.

Qurʾān translations outside the Islamic world until circa 1700

In the Middle Ages and in pre-modern times, translations of the Qurʾān by non-Muslims initially originated from the polemical conflict with Islam (see POLEMIC AND POLEMICAL LANGUAGE; APOLOGY). A complete translation of the Qurʾān into Greek is not preserved. Remnants of this translation can, however, be found in polemical works by Byzantine theologians such as Niketas of Byzantium (third/ninth century; cf. Versteegh, *Greek translations*). References to a possible Syriac translation of the Qurʾān can be found in the west Syrian theologian Barṣalībī's (d. 565/1170; cf. Mingana, Ancient Syriac translation) polemical tract against Jews, Nestorians, and Muslims (see JEWS AND JUDAISM; CHRISTIANS AND CHRISTIANITY). The complete Qurʾān was repeatedly translated into Latin; however, only two of these translations were also printed, namely that by Robert of Ketton (1142/43, printed in Basel, 1534) and that by Ludovico Marracci (printed together with the Arabic text in Padua, 1698; the Latin text only in Leipzig, 1721, published by Christian Reineccius). The oldest complete Latin translation of the Qurʾān was produced in Spain in the years 1142/43, at the instigation of the Abbot of Cluny, Peter the Venerable (1092-1156). The translator was the English scholar Robert of Ketton (Robertus Ketenensis, or Robert of Chester, Robertus Cestrensis; exact lifespan unknown), who availed himself of the assistance of a native "Moorish" speaker named Muḥammad. This translation, together with several non-qurʾānic Islamic texts, found a remarkable circulation in Europe, possibly because of its association with Cluny. The quality of this translation, however, was sharply criticized as early as the fifteenth and sixteenth centuries, and by none other than Juan of Segovia in the Prologue to his own translation (see below), Martin Luther (1483-1564) in his German adaptation of Ricoldo's *Contra legem Sarracenorum* (1542), as well as, eventually, by Justus Joseph Scaliger (1540-1609; cf. Bobzin, Reformation, 38 n. 127). Above all, the typical qurʾānic first-person speech of God is completely obscured by merely referential paraphrase. Nevertheless, this translation had great influence well into the seventeenth century, because of its printing in 1543 as a reference work. Incidentally, the first completely preserved translation into the Italian vernacular was based upon this version (see below).

A second complete Latin translation belongs in the realm of the polemical conflict with the doctrine of the Almohads (al-Muwaḥḥidūn, r. in north Africa and Spain in the sixth-seventh/twelfth-thirteenth cents.). Supported by the Archbishop Don Rodrigo Jiménez de Rada (ca. 1170-1247), Mark of Toledo (Canon Marcus of Toledo, exact lifespan unknown) produced a new, fairly literal translation, apparently in total ignorance of the earlier work by Robert of Ketton. This translation, however, was not widespread outside of Spain (cf. d'Alverny and Vajda, *Marc de Tolède*).

A third Latin translation was produced by John of Segovia (Juan de Segovia; ca. 1398-1458); it was, however, basically just an accessory to an old-Castilian Qur᾿ān translation, which he composed between 1454 and 1456 in the Monastery of Aiton in Savoy, together with the Muslim scholar ʿĪsā dhā Jābir (alias Yçā Gidelli). Both translations have been lost, with the exception of the Latin prologue (cf. Gázquez, Prólogo). A fourth Latin translation was produced by Johannes Gabriel Terrolensis (exact lifespan unknown) for the Roman curial cardinal Aegidius of Viterbo (Egidio da Viterbo; 1470-1532). What is valuable about this work, available in two recensions, is a column of notes, based on the Muslim exegesis of the Qur᾿ān (cf. Burman, *Latin-Arabic Qur᾿ān edition*), next to the Latin transcription of the Arabic text. Another Latin translation, of which two manuscripts are known, is attributed to the Byzantine patriarch Kyrillos Lukaris (1572-1638). Two manuscript recensions also remain of the translation of the Franciscan, Dominicus Germanus de Silesia (1588-1670; cf. Devic, *Traduction inédite*).

The translation by the Italian Fr. Ludovico Marracci (1612-1700), which appeared in 1698, ushered in an entirely new era. For his translation, Marracci was able to rely on the collection of Arabic manuscripts belonging to the Bibliotheca Vaticana, which was rather substantial for the time (cf. Nallino, *Fonti arabe*). In it, he found the most important Islamic commentaries to the Qur᾿ān, which he used extensively for his translation and from which he had numerous excerpts printed in Arabic with a Latin translation. Because of its accuracy, Marracci's translation can be used profitably to this day. Of Marracci's Qur᾿ān edition, Edward Denison Ross quite rightly says: "It represents a most remarkable feat of scholarship, greatly in advance of most Orientalism of the period" (Ross, *Marracci*, 118).

Like the printed Latin precursor translation, Marracci's translation was also used as a template, that is, as a reference work, for further translations into the vernacular. The German translation by the Nuremberg pastor, David Nerreter (1649-1726), refers directly and explicitly to Marracci's text. Nerreter revised *Pansebeia* (1653), the work in comparative religion, by the Scottish author Alexander Ross (1590-1654), and contributed his own extensive volume about Islam, titled *Neu eröffnete Mahometanische Moschea* (Nuremberg, 1703). After a general description of Islam based on the sources known at the time, the German text of the Qur᾿ān followed in a second tract, translated according to Marracci's Latin version. Nerreter's work is still fully immersed in the tradition of anti-Islamic polemics of the previous century; he translates the Qur᾿ān in order that every individual can see for themselves the "corruptive teachings of Mohammad" (schädliche Lehre Mohammeds). Nerreter's work, chronologically the third German translation of the Qur᾿ān, had no noteworthy repercussions. The first Hungarian translation of the Qur᾿ān (1831), by Imre Buzitai Szedlmayer and György Gedeon (born 1831), is also based on Marracci's translation.

The oldest complete translation into a

European vernacular, namely the Italian, is in the Qurʾān edition issued by the Venetian publisher Andrea Arrivabene in 1547. Although the title asserts that the Qurʾān was "newly translated from the Arabic," the translation is actually based exclusively on the 1543 Latin Qurʾān by Theodor Bibliander, as noted by the two great Leiden philologists, Justus Joseph Scaliger and Thomas Erpenius (1584-1624). Arrivabene divides his Qurʾān edition into three books, with the text of the Qurʾān being contained only in the second and third books. The first book contains three treatises, *Chronica mendosa et ridiculosa Sarracenorum, De generatione Mahumet et nutritura eius,* as well as *Doctrina Machumeti,* which were published alongside a translation of the Qurʾān in the "Corpus Toletanum" (cf. Bobzin, Reformation, 264f.). The first German translation of the Qurʾān, by the then-pastor of Nuremberg, Salomon Schweigger (1551-1622), is based on Arrivabene's edition. In the foreword to the book, which first appeared in 1616, he wrote that he had come to know of Arrivabene's translation of the Qurʾān during his travels as a missionary preacher to Istanbul in Turkey (1578-81). Schweigger's edition is entirely dependent upon Arrivabene's in its composition and, astonishingly, lacks any acknowledgement of the Latin edition of the Qurʾān by Bibliander. In the year 1659, an edition of Schweigger's works, with a substantially expanded commentary section, appeared in Nuremberg in the prominent printing office of Endters', without, however, naming Schweigger as the translator (reprinted 1664). The first Dutch translation of the Qurʾān, printed in 1641, also goes back to Schweigger's text, whose name appears as "Swigger" on the title page; the name of the Dutch translator is unknown and the place of publication given there ("Hamburg") is false.

The oldest French translation (Paris 1647) comes from André du Ryer, "Sieur de la Garde Malezair" (d. 1672). Supported by the French diplomat, François Savary de Bréves (d. 1618), du Ryer studied Turkish, Arabic and possibly also Persian from 1616-21 in Egypt. His path as a diplomat led him first to an appointment as vice-consul to Alexandria and Cairo, and then, as interpreter and ambassador, to Istanbul. He published one of the first studies of Turkish grammar (1630; 1633) and translated one of the most famous works of Persian literature, the "Flower garden" *(Gulistān),* by Saʿdī, into French (1634). Du Ryer's translation of the Qurʾān is the oldest complete translation of the Qurʾān into a European vernacular and became an unparalled literary success, to which reprints in France and even more numerous reprints in the Netherlands during the seventeenth and eighteenth centuries testify. The easy availability of the Qurʾān accompanied a newfound interest in the Orient; additionally, du Ryer's translation lacked the polemical tone of previous editions, an orientation which arose mainly in ecclesiastical contexts. Du Ryer used Islamic commentaries such as al-Bayḍāwī's *Anwār al-tanzīl,* the *Tafsīr al-Jalālayn* by al-Maḥallī (d. 864/1459) and al-Suyūṭī (d. 911/1505), or an excerpt from al-Rāzī's (d. 606/1210) great commentary made by al-Rāghī l-Tūnisī (d. 715/1315) entitled *al-Tanwīr fī l-tafsīr,* quite casually in his translation, merely noting them in the margins. The deprecatory tone present in the introductory chapter, "Sommaire de la religion des Turcs," can be understood as an attempt at camouflage (cf. Hamilton and Richard, *André du Ryer,* 94f.). The success of du Ryer's translation, despite its philological shortcomings, which were already recognized by his contemporaries, rests on its use as a basis for the production of further translations.

Already two years after the first French edition, in 1649, the Scottish author Alexander Ross, previously mentioned in connection with Marracci and Nerreter, published an English translation, whose author is unknown. Ross prefaced his translation with a very traditional view of Muḥammad's life and an extensive presentation of Islam. That problems with censorship existed is evidenced by the subtitle: *With a Needful Caveat, or Admonition, for them who desire to know what use may be made of, or if there be danger in Reading the Alcoran*. The success of the book arose from the fact that it was reissued in the year of its initial publication, 1649, as well as in 1688. Eventually, the translation was incorporated as a fourth volume in *The Compleat History of the Turks from the Origin in the Year 755 to the Year 1718*, by David Jones (London 1718). It appears, without mention of Ross's name, after the biography of Muḥammad titled *The True Nature of Imposture fully Display'd in the Life of Mahomet*, by Humphrey Prideux (1648-1724). It is of particular interest to note that the first translation printed and published in America was that published by Ross (Springfield 1806), not the translation by Sale (see below), which, at the time, had already completely displaced Ross's work in Britain.

The second language into which du Ryer's Qur'ān was translated was Dutch. The Mennonite Jan Hendricksz. Glazemaker (d. 1682) worked as a professional translator of Latin, French, German, and Italian; the list of works he translated (among them, works by Descartes and Spinoza) is impressive. His Qur'ān translation is "an elegant piece of prose which was obviously intended for a public more interested in literature than in the theological study of Islam" (Hamilton and Richard, *André du Ryer*, 115). Glazemaker's Dutch translation appeared first in Amsterdam in 1658. The translation was printed together with a life of Muḥammad from Thomas Erpenius's Latin translation of the *Historia Saracenica* by the Coptic historian al-Makīn (Jirjis b. al-ʿAmīd, d. ca. 1273), as well as with excerpts from the works of various ecclesiastical authors who wrote about Muḥammad (cf. Hamilton and Richard, *André du Ryer*, 115f.). Furthermore, a text about Muḥammad's ascension (q.v.) to heaven, as well as a version of the so-called *Masāʾil ʿAbdallāh b. Salām* (cf. Bobzin, Reformation, p. 334, n. 310 and 312), which had already appeared in the earlier Toledo collection, was added. Glazemaker's translation of the Qur'ān was extraordinarily successful and a total of six reprints were issued up to 1734. Glazemaker based the second German translation of the Qur'ān upon the Dutch translation. It appeared, however, not as an independent work, but rather as part of the collected edition *Thesaurus Exoticorum* (Hamburg 1688), published by the late-baroque professional writer Eberhard Werner Happel (1647-90). In this version, the Qur'ān was embedded in the framework of an all-encompassing cosmographic presentation, in which the "Asiatic, African and American nations" were presented. In this extensive encyclopedic volume, the translation of the Qur'ān follows a detailed illustrated description of the Ottoman empire. Yet, the impact of du Ryer's translation does not end with the third German translation, but with two Russian translations of the French edition. The first appeared at the command of czar Peter the Great in 1716 in St. Petersburg; the translator was Petr Vasilyevic Pos(t)nikov. This translation contains numerous misinterpretations. The second translation, penned by the litterateur Mikhail Ivanovic Verevkin (1733-95), appeared in 1790, shortly after the first Arabic edition of the Qur'ān, which was printed in St. Petersburg in 1787 at the behest of the empress Catherine II (cf. Hamilton and Richard, *André du Ryer*, 117f.).

18th century translations outside the Islamic world

In contrast to all previously presented Christian translations, the history of the impact of the translation done by the English jurist and Orientalist George Sale (d. 1736) endures until today. According to J. Fück, "through a somewhat prosaic neatness, it illustrates that what matters is to reflect the contents of the work clearly and effectively" ("zeichnet sie sich durch eine etwas nüchterne Sauberkeit aus, welcher es nur darauf ankommt, den Inhalt des Werkes klar und deutlich wiederzugeben," Fück, *Studien*, 104). In his discussion of Marracci's translation, Sale writes, "This translation... is very exact; but adheres to the Arabic idiom too literally to be easily understood." Undoubtedly, Sale's own translation is based on the Arabic text, for the interpretation of which Sale regularly drew on the commentary by al-Bayḍāwī. But he continuously looked at Marracci's interpretation of the text and used Marracci's work copiously in his extensive notes: "So much had been achieved by Marracci that Sale's work might also have been performed with a knowledge of Latin alone, as far as regards the quotations from Arabic sources" (E.D. Ross in the foreword to his edition of Sale, ix). Of particular significance, however, is the detailed "Preliminary Discourse"; herein Sale gives a detailed description of the history and religion of the pre-Islamic Arabs, supporting himself above all with the *Specimen Historia Arabum*, by Edward Pococke (1604-91), which appeared in 1650. To this, he adds a general introduction to the Qur'ān, as well as an overview of the most important Islamic sects. Sale's translation had extraordinary success. In the eighteenth century itself four additional editions appeared, and in the nineteenth, well over 60. This translation is still on the market. Since 1825, editions preceded by a "sketch of the life of George Sale," penned by Richard Alfred Davenport (d. 1852) are available, with expanded notes based on translations such as the French translation by Savary (see below). In 1882-6, Elwood Morris Wherry (d. 1927) republished the work under the title *A comprehensive commentary on the Quran* without adding anything essentially new to the edition. Additionally worth noting is the edition of 1921, to which the British Orientalist Edward Denison Ross contributed an insightful introduction, pointing out the manner in which Sale was indebted to Marracci's work (see above).

The fourth German translation is based on Sale's translation. It was composed by Theodor Arnold (1683-1761), an English teacher who also composed a widely used study of English grammar (Leipzig 1736) and translated numerous English works into German, among them Ockley's *History of the Saracens*. Arnold's German translation appeared in Lemgo in 1764. Although not widely circulated, Goethe used it for his *West-östlichen Divan* and its accompanying *Noten und Abhandlungen*. Furthermore, the third Russian translation of the Qur'ān (St. Petersburg 1792) goes back to Sale's text by way of Alexej Vasiljevic Kolmakov, as does the first Hungarian (1854) translation, by way of Istvan Szokoly (1822-1904).

The first German translation produced directly from the Arabic was published in 1772 by the Frankfurt scholar David Friederich Megerlin (1699-1778). From the fact that an etching of "Mohammad, the false Prophet," faces the title page, one can infer that Megerlin remained entirely attached to the traditional Christian polemic against Islam. With respect to this translation, Goethe spoke of an "elende Produktion" (wretched production). Only one year later (1773), a further translation directly from the Arabic appeared. It was composed by the Quedlinburg clergyman Friedrich Eberhard Boysen (d. 1800). A contemporary reviewer criticized the translation for its tendency to paraphrase improperly. In 1775, a second print run was issued. In 1828, a revision that attempted to rebut the scathing critique by the most important German Arabic scholar of the time, Fleischer (1801-88), was issued by the Orientalist Samuel Friedrich Günther Wahl (1760-1834), who, at the time, was teaching in Halle/Saale.

Claude Etienne Savary (1750-88) produced a new French translation in 1783. It originated during an extended stay in Egypt (cf. *Lettres sur l'Egypte*), quasi "sous les yeux des Arabes," as Savary wrote in the foreword. Consequently, Savary can be viewed as the first translator of the Qur'ān who had a feel "for the perfection of the style and the grandeur of the imagery" (für die Perfektion des Stils und die Großartigkeit der Bilder) of the Qur'ān. For this reason, he can rightly characterize du Ryer's translation as a mere "rhapsodie plate et ennuyeuse;... en lisant sa traduction, on ne s'imagerinait jamais que le Koran est le chef-d'oeuvre de la langue arabe." Accordingly, in his translation, Savary tried to preserve precisely the linguistic character of the Qur'ān's style: "To the extent of my abilities, I have imitated the concision, energy and grandeur of its style" ("J'ai imité autant qu'il a dépendu de moi la concision, l'énergie, l'élévation de son style"). Above all, a certain stylistic obscurity should not be smoothed out in the translation. Savary preceded his translation with a "life of Muḥammad," compiled from different Arabic authors. The notes to the text are rather sparse, although nevertheless substantive; they were later incorporated into a part of Sale's editions. Savary's translation, of which there are a total of seventeen different editions, is still read to this day and is still on the market. Incidentally, Savary was the first to give up the until-then common European usage of "Alkoran" (Alcoranus) in favor of "Koran." The Spanish translations by Joaquin Garcia-Bravo (1907) and A. Hernandez Cata (1913), as well as an anonymous Italian translation (1882), draw on Savary's text.

19th century translations outside the Islamic world

A further translation of the Qur'ān, likewise still available today, was produced by Albin de Biberstein Kazimirski (d. 1887), a Polish immigrant to France. He was a student of Silvestre de Sacy (d. 1838) and worked as an interpreter of Arabic and Persian. Kazimirski's translation first appeared in 1840, as part of the three-volume collection entitled *Les livres sacrés de l'Orient*, published by the Sinologist Jean Pierre Guillaume Pauthier (d. 1873), which also contained translations of the *Shi King* and the laws of the *Manu*. This juxtaposition is significant in the history of ideas in that the Qur'ān was thereby placed on an entirely new plane of understanding, as the document of a world religion, that is, of an independent culture. In the same year (1840), a separate edition, which was frequently reprinted, appeared. The translation was certified as preserving "the poetic vapor of numerous passages of the Qur'ān" ("le soufflé poétique de nombreux passages du Coran," G.C. Anawati). Another testament to its quality is certainly the fact that scholars such as G.H. Bousquet (1959), Mohammed Arkoun (1970), and Maxime Rodison (1981) reissued the translation, adding a new introduction each time. The Spanish editions by Jose Garber de Robles (1844) and Vicente Ortiz de la Puebla (1872), as well as the Russian translation by K. Nikolajev (1864), are all based on Kazimirski's translation. In addition to further translations from other languages, Kazimirski's constitutes the basis for the two Dutch translations by L.J.A. Tollens (1859) and Salome Keijzer (1860).

A German translation was put out in 1840 as well, by the Rabbi Lion (Ludwig) Baruch Ullmann of Krefeld (d. 1843). Ullmann was inspired in his work by the dissertation of the important Jewish scholar Abraham Geiger (1810-74), *Was hat Mohammed aus dem Judenthume aufgenommen?* (Bonn 1833), and emphasized in the preface to his translation his conviction that "what this translation will have above and beyond all others is the exact observation and documentation of everything that Muḥammad borrowed from Judaism" ("Was diese Übersetzung vor anderen voraushaben wird, ist die genaue Beachtung und Nachweisung alles dessen, was Muhamed aus dem Judenthum entlehnt hat"). Although this translation was sharply criticized for its philological shortcomings by such important scholars of Arabic as H.L. Fleischer (1801-88) and Th. Nöldeke (1836-1930), a ninth edition was issued in 1897. A revision (1959) by Leo Winter did nothing to improve the quality of the translation; nevertheless, this edition, though linguistically deficient, remains widely popular in Germany to this day.

A few years before Ullmann, the German poet and Orientalist Friedrich Rückert (d. 1866), using the newly published Arabic edition of the Qurʾān by Gustav Flügel as his basis, attempted a poetic rendition of the Qurʾān that simultaneously observed the philological standards of the time, but not in the form of a complete translation. Rückert's work was first published after his death. Annemarie Schimmel wrote of the translation, "Rückert spürte mit dichterischem Instinkt die poetische Kraft und Schönheit weiter Parteien des Textes und suchte sie so wiederzugeben, daß der Originalcharakter- sei er stärker poetisch oder prosaisch- gewahrt blieb" (Rückert felt with a poet's instinct the poetic power and beauty of sections of the text and attempted to render them in such a manner that the original character- whether strongly poetic or prosaic- remained preserved).

The first Swedish translation of the Qurʾān stems from the linguist and diplomat J. Fredrik S. Crusenstolpe (1801-82) and appeared together with a historical introduction in 1843. It was followed in 1874 by the translation by Carl Johan Tornberg (1807-77), a student of de Sacy, who had been teaching Orientalism in Lund since 1847. Tornberg prefaced this with a Swedish translation of Nöldeke's *Das Leben Muhammeds* (Hannover 1863).

The first Italian translation of the Qurʾān directly from the Arabic is by Cavaliere Vincenzo Calza (1847). The first Polish edition of the Qurʾān was published by Jan Murza Tarak Buczacki, together with a *Life of Mahomet* (London 1849/50) by Washington Irving (d. 1859), information about various aspects of the relationship between Poland and the Turks and Tartars, and about the pre-Islamic Arabs and the Qurʾān (from Sale's "Preliminary Discourse"). Eventually, a few of the prayers, translated from the Arabic, were added. This edition was reprinted in 1985 and 1988.

The 1857 Hebrew translation by the Jewish scholar Hermann (i.e. Zvi Chajjim) Reckendorf (d. ca. 1875) is noteworthy; additionally, it even contains three essays about the pre-Islamic Arabs, the life of Muḥammed, as well as about the Qurʾān. Yosef Yoel Rivlin made another Hebrew translation (1937), which is still viewed as the most popular such translation; several editions have been published over the years. Aaron Ben Shemesh published a third Hebrew translation in 1971. To this list should be added the 2005 Hebrew translation by Uri Rubin.

In 1861, a new English translation of the Qur'ān by the clergyman John Meadows Rodwell (d. 1900), who was an old friend of Darwin's, appeared. It is unusual in that, for the first time in a translation of the Qur'ān, the sūras were arranged by taking into consideration their chronological order. Rodwell could resort to the prior works of Gustav Weil (*Mohammed der Prophet,* Stuttgart 1843), William Muir (*The life of Mahomet,* London 1858f.), and Theodore Nöldeke, *GQ* (first ed. 1860); he nevertheless followed his own ideas about arrangement, compiling the older sūras according to thematic considerations rather than historical allusion. Particularly noteworthy is Rodwell's perception of the significance of the originally oral character of the Qur'ān: "Of all the Suras it must be remarked that they were intended not for *readers* but for *hearers*- that they were all promulgated by public recital- and that much was left, as the imperfect sentences shew, to the manner and suggestive action of the reciter" (Preface). G. Margoliouth, who revised the translation for the "Everyman's Library" in 1909, characterized it in his introduction as "one of the best that have as yet been produced. It seems to a great extent to carry with it the atmosphere in which Muhammed lived, and its sentences are imbued with the flavour of the east." In 1875, the first Spanish translation from the Arabic prepared by a Christian, Benigno de Murguiondo y Ugartondo, appeared. Like the translation by Marracci, it included an extensive refutation on the basis of the doctrine of the Catholic church. This is amply expressed by the title. Three years later (1878), the first modern Greek translation, by Gerasimos I. Pentakes, appeared; by 1887, three further editions had been published.

The first Russian translation of the Qur'ān from the Arabic (first appearance 1877/9) was prepared by the Orientalist Gordij Semjonovic Sablukov (d. 1880) from Kazan on the basis of the so-called Petersburg Qur'ān (1787; see above; see also PRINTING OF THE QUR'ĀN). As of the third edition (1907), the Arabic text, set in the Kazan Arabic typeface, was printed on the opposing page. Reprints of this edition still appeared after the second World War, but without exact dates of publication.

To produce the Qur'ān translation for the well-known series, Sacred Books of the East, the publisher, F. Max Müller (d. 1900), engaged the services of the Cambridge Orientalist Edward Henry Palmer (d. 1882), who completed the task in a short period of time. The two sections appeared in 1880 as the sixth and ninth volumes in the series. Palmer added a historical introduction (pp. ix-lxxx), as well as an "Abstract of the contents of the Qur'an" (pp. lxxxi-cxviii), to the book. The short period of time allowed for completion of the translation led to what Stanley Lane-Poole (1854-1931) described as "the grave fault of immaturity." H.A.R. Gibb (1895-1971) judged the translation to be "rather literal and inadequate." Nevertheless, Palmer's translation was reissued numerous times and, as of 1928, was even incorporated into the renowned serial "World's Classics," with the addition of an "Introduction" by Reynold Alleyne Nicholson (1868-1945).

Two years later (1882), the first Portuguese translation appeared in Rio de Janeiro. A translator is not named.

20th century translations beyond the Islamic world

Progress in Arabic philology in the nineteenth century initially had hardly any effect on the translation of the Qur'ān. In the festschrift for Theodor Nöldeke

(Bezold, *Orientalische Studien*, i, 34 n. 1), the German Arabist August Fischer wrote, "daß unter allen vorhandenen, vollständigen wie partiellen, Qoran-Übertragungen keine einzige strengen philologischen Anforderungen genügt" (of all the Qurʾān translations available, whether complete or partial, not a single one satisfies the stringent standards of philology). This statement makes clear that philologically weak translations could still be exceedingly successful, even in the twentieth century. A good example of this is the German translation by Max Henning (d. 1927), who was certainly not an Arabist. This version first appeared in 1901 as a volume in the popular and highly circulated "Universal-Bibliothek," published by Ph. Reclam in Leipzig. In 1960, this edition was republished in the West German branch of Reclam in Stuttgart, slightly revised by Annemarie Schimmel (d. 2003). In 1968, another revision of this translation was published by the Leipzig historian of religion, Kurt Rudolf, in the East German branch of Reclam in Leipzig. This version distinguished itself through its particularly meticulous and comprehensive commentary. Henning's translation is easy to read but philologically unreliable; it is noteworthy that it was republished by Turkish authorities for migrants from Turkey. The translation experienced a last, considerably more incisive revision by the Muslim convert Murad Wilfried Hofmann (first published in Istanbul, 1998).

More decisive philological advances than those made by Henning's translation are present in three other translations, which are still reissued to this day, although with partially new introductions. These are the Swedish translation (1917; expanded reprint 1971 and more recently) by Karl Vilhelm Zetterstéen (1866-1953), the Italian translation (1929; numerous reprints) by Luigi Bonelli (1865-1947), and the French translation (1929; expanded reprint 1998) by Edouard Montet (1865-1934). Three other translations stand out because of enduring scholarly qualities: the English version by Richard Bell, the French version by Régis Blachère, and the German version by Rudi Paret.

Rodwell was the first translator of the Qurʾān to arrange the sūras (q.v.) according to chronological principles (see CHRONOLOGY AND THE QURʾĀN). The Scottish Arabist Richard Bell (1876-1952) went one step further down this path. Although he held to the traditional order of the sūras in his translation of the Qurʾān (1937-9), in the sūras themselves, he followed a "re-arrangement" according to the origin of the individual components of the sūras. Underlying this is a concept of "three main periods" of the composition of the Qurʾān (Bell, *Qurʾān*, i, vii), as explained in the preface: "(a) an early period from which only fragments survive consisting mainly of lists of 'signs' and exhortations to the worship of Allah; (b) the Qur'an period, covering the latter part of Muhammad's activity in Mecca (q.v.), and the first year or two of his residence in Medina (q.v.), during which he is producing a Qur'an giving in Arabic the gist of previous revelation; (c) the Book-period, beginning somewhere about the end of the year II, during which Muhammad is definitively producing a Book, i.e. an independent revelation." In his translation, these composition processes are also visualized within the individual sūras. Even if one cannot follow Bell's analysis in all its points, his very exacting translation is an asset to the historical understanding of the text of the Qurʾān. No other researcher of the Qurʾān put as much thought into the inner coherence of the sūras as did Bell (see FORM AND STRUCTURE OF THE QURʾĀN; UNITY OF THE TEXT OF THE QURʾĀN;

TEXTUAL CRITICISM AND THE QURʾĀN). The many notes and explanatory statements which Bell produced were mostly left out of the printed version. In 1991, two volumes of Bell's *Commentary on the Qurʾān* drawn from materials left in his estate (admittedly in unsatisfactory typographical form) were published by C.E. Bosworth and M.E.J. Richardson.

In 1947-9, the French Arabist Régis Blachère (1900-73) brought forth a three-volume introduction to the Qurʾān *(Introduction au Coran)*, as well as a new translation of the Qurʾān itself, in which the sūras (similarly to Rodwell's edition) were presented in the order Nöldeke had suggested, with only slightly modified chronological changes. Blachère's translation is, as far as I know, the first scholarly translation of the Qurʾān that uses the Cairene Qurʾān text of 1342/1923 as its foundation. Furthermore, Blachère's careful and exacting translation is notable for its continuous observance of important ways of reading the Qurʾān (see READINGS OF THE QURʾĀN), which every now and again lead to translations that depart from the traditional perception of the text. The two extensive commentaries by al-Ṭabarī (d. 310/923) and al-Rāzī are constantly taken into account, as well as those by al-Bayḍāwī and al-Nasafī (d. 710/1310; *Madārik al-tanzīl wa-ḥaqāʾiq al-taʾwīl*), although only for grammatical issues. In 1957, a revised edition of the translation appeared which, however, followed the traditional arrangement of the sūras.

Already in 1935, Rudi Paret (d. 1983) had published his "Plan einer neuen, leicht kommentierten wissenschaftlichen Koranübersetzung." In this article, Paret developed his concept of a historically grounded translation, the main purpose of which should be to "render the text in the same manner as contemporaries heard it from the Prophet's mouth" ("daß sieden Wortlaut so wiedergibt, wie ihn die Zeitgenossen aus dem Munde des Propheten gehört haben," Paret, *Übersetzung*, 1). Therefore, the Arabic commentaries, "which are full of later, ahistorical interpretations of the text" ("die voll sind von späteren, unhistorischen Auslegungen des Textes," Paret, Plan, 122), are to be used only with great reservation. Instead, one must "seek the key to understanding difficult sections in the Qurʾān itself" ("im Koran selber den Schlüssel zum Verständnis schwieriger Stellen zu suchen"; ibid). Above all, Paret's translation, which appeared in 1962 after much preparatory work, is marked by these two principles which he implemented rigorously throughout. Addenda necessary to understanding the text, which presents "an effectively condensed historical commentary" ("gewissermaßen einen kondensierten historischen Kommentar"; ibid.), are parenthetically inserted into the text. In the relatively sparse critical apparatus, the literal translation is often given; aside from that, alternative translations are provided. The complementary volume *Kommentar und Konkordanz*, published in 1971, painstakingly and exhaustively lists parallels within the Qurʾān and gives historical explanations for selected sections. With regard to the style of the translation, Paret emphasizes that it is not intended "für erbauliche Zwecke" (for edifying purposes), and that he therefore did not aim for a lofty style ("gehobene Ausdrucksweise"). In a second edition (1982), Paret carried out a series of alterations, and, above all, occasionally considering alternative readings (such as that by Ibn Masʿūd [d. 32/652-3]).

The German translation by Adel Theodor Khoury (1987) is entirely dependent on Paret's concept of the text, but with hardly any indication of alternative translation possibilities. Khoury published a twelve-volume commentary (1990-2001) on the basis of this translation which, unfortunately, does not present a real step forward in historical and literary scholarship on the Qurʾān because it only selectively engaged contemporary research literature. In 2004, the same translator published a brief one-volume commentary with text and translation.

Paret's translation, of which, incidentally, reprints published in Iran are available (for example Qom 1378/2000), had a wide-reaching effect on the German-speaking world. Many of the translations into various European languages that have appeared since Paret's are unthinkable without the philologically pioneering work of his translation.

Among the numerous English translations, that by the Cambridge Arabist Arthur John Arberry (1901-69) holds a special place. The very title, *The Koran interpreted,* hints that Arberry follows the concept, first emphasized in the English-speaking world by Pickthall, that the Qurʾān is actually untranslatable. In noticeable contrast to Bell, Arberry intends "to imitate, however imperfectly, those rhetorical and rhythmical patterns which are the glory and the sublimity of the Koran," and beyond that, "to show each Sura as an artistic whole, its often incongruent parts constituting a rich and admirable pattern" (p. 25). Particularly among Muslims, Arberry's translation is held in special esteem because of its linguistic form. Also widely popular is the translation by N.J. Dawood that first appeared as a Penguin paperback (1956). Among the French translations, that by Denise Masson (Paris 1967) stems from the ambit of Louis Massignon and is indebted to a dialogical attitude towards Islam. In 1990, two new translations appeared simultaneously. With his very biblical language, André Chouraqui, who also translated the Bible, tried to emphasize the continuity of the three monotheistic religions. Jacques Berque is primarily concerned with rendering the Arabic text in a stylistically fitting linguistic manner, while at the same time providing scholarly justification for the translation. The aforementioned Italian translation by Bonelli has, since 1955, been joined by a very academically valuable work by Alessandro Bausani. Among the Spanish translations, both that by Juan Vernet (1963) and that by Julio Cortes (1980) deserve special notice. Of the academically significant translations into Slavic languages, the following two are noteworthy: the Russian edition by Ignatij Julianovic Krackovskij (1963) and the Czech edition by Ivan Hrbek (1972).

Hartmut Bobzin

Bibliography

Bibliographies: I. Binark and H. Eren, *World bibliography of translations of the meanings of the holy Qur'an: Printed translations 1515-1980*, Istanbul 1986; V. Chauvin, *Bibliographie des ouvrages arabes ou relatifs aux Arabes publiés dans l'Europe Chrétienne de 1810 à 1885*. x. *Le Coran et la tradition*, Liège/Leipzig 1907; M. Cunbur, *Kur'an-ı Kerīm-in Türk dilinde basılmım tercüme ve tefsirleri*. Diyanet İşleri Başkanlığı Dergisi 1961/62, 123-41; id., Türkçe Kur'an tefsir ve çevirileri bibliyografyası, in *Yeni Yayınlar* 4 (1959), 111-24; M.-E. Enay, *Mohammed und der Heilige Koran*, Hamburg 1995; M. Hamidullah, Liste des traductions du Coran en langues européennes, in id., *Le saint Coran. Traduction intégrale et notes*, Paris 1986[12], lx-llii; E. İhsanoğlu and M.N. Seferciоğlu (eds.), *World bibliography of the translations of the holy Qurʾān in manuscript form*, Istanbul 2000; M.H. Khan, English translations of the holy Qurʾān. A bio-bibliographical study, in *IQ* 30 (1986), 82-108; J.D. Pearson, Bibliography of translations of the Qurʾān into European languages, in Beeston, *CHAL*, i, 502-20; H.M. Said, *Qur'an in Pakistan. A bibliographical survey*, New Delhi 1982; C.F. de Schnurrer, *Bibliotheca arabica*, Halae ad Salam 1811 (repr. Amsterdam 1968); C.A. Storey, *Persian literature. A bio-bibliographical survey*. i. *Qur'anic literature. History and biography* (pt. 1), London 1970; W.S. Woolworth, A bibliography of Koran texts and translations, in *MW* 17 (1927), 279-89; A. Yarmolinsky, *The Koran in Slavonic. A list of translations*, New York 1937; J.Th. Zenker, *Bibliotheca orientalis*, vols. 1-2, Leipzig 1846-61

(repr. Amsterdam 1966); S.M. Zwemer, Translations of the Koran, in *MW* 5 (1915) 244-49.
Primary: *Alcorán. Traducción castellana de un morisco anónimo del año 1606,* Barcelona 2001; A.Y. Ali, *The holy Qur'an. An interpretation in English, with the original Arabic text in parallel columns, a running rhythmic commentary in English, and full explanatory notes*, Lahore 1934; M.M. Ali, *The Holy Qur'ān containing the Arabic text with English translation and commentary*, Lahore 1920^{2}; *Al-Koranum Mahumedanum. Das ist / Der Türcken Religión/Gesetz und Gotteslästerliche Lehr...*, Nürnberg 1659 (1664^{2}); Arberry; Th. Arnold, *Der Koran, Oder insgemein so genannte Alcoran des Mohammeds, Unmittelbahr aus dem Arabischen Original in das Englische übersetzt, und mit beygefügten, aus den bewährtesten Commentatoribus genommenen Erklärungs-Noten, Wie auch einer Vorläuffigen Einleitung versehen von George Sale, Gent. Aufs treulichste wieder ins Teutsch verdollmetschet*, Lemgo 1746; A. Arrivabene (ed.), *L'Alcorano di Macometto, nel qual si contiene la doctrina, la vita, i costumi, e le leggi sue. Tradotto nuevamente dall'Arabo in lengua italiana*, [Venice] 1547; M. Asad, *The message of the Qur'an*, Gibraltar 1980; A. Bausani, *Il Corano. Introduzione, traduzione e commento*, Firenze 1955; R. Bell, *A commentary on the Qur'ān*, ed. C.E. Bosworth and M.E.J. Richardson, 2 vols., Manchester 1991; id., *The Qur'ān. Translated, with a critical re-arrangement of the Surahs*, 2 vols., Edinburgh 1937-9; J. Berque, *Le Coran. Essai de traduction de l'arabe annoté et suivi d'une étude exégétique*, Paris 1990; Th. Bibliander [Buchmann] (ed.), *Machumetis Sarracenorum principis, eiusque successorum vita, ac doctrina, ipseque Alcoran...*, 3 vols., Basel 1543, 1550^{2}; R. Blachère, *Le Coran. Introduction au Coran. Traduction nouvelle*, 3 vols., Paris 1947-50; id., *Le Coran (al-Qor'ân) traduit de l'arabe*, Paris 1957; L. Bonelli, *Il Corano. Nuova versione letterale italiana, con prefazione e note critico-illustrative*, Milan 1929; S.H. Boubakeur, *Le Coran. Traduction française et commentaire d'après la tradition, les différentes écoles de lecture, d'exégèse, de jurisprudence et de théologie, les interprétations mystiques, les tendances schismatiques et les doctrines hérétiques de l'Islam, et à la lumière des théories scientifiques, philosophiques et politiques modernes*, 2 vols., Paris 1972; new rev. ed., with foreword by his son, D. Boubakeur, Paris 1995; F.E. Boysen, *Der Koran, oder das Gesetz für die Muselmänner, durch Muhammed, den Sohn Abdall, nebst einigen feyerlichen koranischen Gebeten, unmittelbar aus dem Arabischen übersetzt*, Halle 1773; J.M.T. Buczacki, *Koran, z arab. Przeklad*, Warsaw 1858; V. Calza, *Il Corano. Versione italiana... con commenti, ed una noticia biografica di Maometto*, Bastia 1847; A. Chouraqui, *Le Coran-L'appell. Traduit et présenté*, Paris 1990; J. Cortes, *El Corán. Edición, traducción y notas*, Madrid 1979; J. Fredrik S. Crusenstolpe, *Koranen, öfversatt fran arabiska originalet jemte en historisk inledning*, Stockholm 1843; A.M. Daryabadi, *The holy Qur'an*, Karachi 1957; N.J. Dawood, *The Koran translated*, Harmondsworth 1956; A. Du Ryer, *L'Alcoran de Mahomet. Translaté d'arabe en François*, Paris 1647; J.H. Glazemaker, *Mahomets Alkoran, door de Heer Du Ryer uit d'Arabische in de Fransche taal gestelt; beneffens een tweevoudige beschryving van Mahomets leven; en een verhaal van des zelfs reis ten hemel, gelijk ook zijn samenspraak met de Jood Abdias*, Amsterdam 1658; M. Hamidullah, *Le Coran. Traduction intégrale et notes*, Paris 1959; M. Henning, *Der Koran. Aus dem Arabischen übertragen und mit einer Einleitung versehen*, Leipzig n. d. [1901]; I. Hrbek, *Korán*, Prague 1972; A. Kasimirski [Kazimirski], *Le Koran. Traduction nouvelle faite sur le texte arabe*, Paris 1840; Z. Khan, *The Qur'an.The eternal revelation vouchsafed to Muhammad, the seal of the prophets. Arabic text with a new translation*, London 1971; I.J. Kračkovskij, *Koran. Perevod i kommentarij*, Moscow 1963; J. Lange, *Vollständiges Türckisches Gesetz=Buch / Oder Des Ertz=Betriegers Mahomets Alkoran. Welcher vorhin nimmer vollkommen herauszgegeben / noch im Druck außgefertiget worden. Auß der Arabischen in die Frantzösische Sprach übergesetzet Duch Herrn du Ryer. Aufl dieser aber in die Niederländische Durch H.J. Blasemacker [sic]. Und jetzo Zum allerersten mahl in die Hochteutsche Sprache versetzet*, in E.W. Happel (ed.), *Thesaurus Exoticorum, Oder eine mit Außländischen Raritäten und Geschichten Wohlversehene Schatz=Kammer Fürstellend Die Asiatische / Africanische und Americanische Nationes...*, Hamburg 1688; L. Marracci (ed.), *Alcorani textus universus. Ex correctioribus Arabum exemplaribus summa fide, atque pulcherrimis characteribus descriptus, Eademque fide, ac pari diligentia ex Arabico idiomate in Latinum translatus, Appositis unicuique capiti notis, atque refutatione*, Padua 1698; D.F. Megerlin, *Die türkische Bibel, oder des Korans allererste teutsche Übersetzung aus der arabischen Urschrift selbst verfertiget*, Frankfurt-am-Main 1772; E. Montet, *Le Coran. Traduction nouvelle*, Paris 1929; B. de Murguionde y Ugartondo, *El Alcorán, traducido fielmente al español, anotado y refutado segun el dogma, la doctrina santa y la moral perfecta de la Santa Religion Católica, Apostolica, Romana, nica verdadera*, Madrid 1875; D. Nerreter, *Neu eröffnete Mahometanische Moschea/worinn nach Anleitung der VI. Abtheilung von unterschiedlichen Gottes-Diensten der Welt/Alexander Rossens/Erstlich Der Mahometanischen Religion Anfang/Ausbreitung/Secten/Regierungen/mancherley Gebräuche/und vermuthlicher Untergang/Fürs andre/Der völlige Alkoran/Nach der besten Edition Ludovici Marraccii, verteutscht/und*

kürzlich widerlegt wird, Nürnberg 1703; E.H. Palmer, *The Qur'ân translated*. Parts I-II, Oxford 1880 (= Sacred Books of the East, vols. vi and ix); R. Paret, *Der Koran. Kommentar und Konkordanz*, Stuttgart 1971; id., *Der Koran. Übersetzung*. Stuttgart 1962 (1982²); G.I. Pentakes, *Koranion, metafrasthen ek tou Arabikou keimenou*, Alexandria 1878; Pickthall, *Koran*; H. Reckendorf, *Al-Qurân ô ha-Miqrâ*, Leipzig 1857; Ch. Reineccius (ed.), *Mohammedis filii Abdallae pseudo-prophetae Fides islamitica, i. E. Al-Coranus ex idiomate Arabico, quo primum a Mohammede conscriptus est, Latine versus per Ludovicum Marraccium... et ex ejusdem animadversionibus aliorumque observationibus illustratus et expositus*, Lipsiae 1721; J.M. Rodwell, *The Koran, translated from the Arabic, the Surahs arranged in chronological orders, with notes and index*, London 1861; A. Ross (ed.), *The Alcoran of Mahomet, Translated out of Arabick into French. By the Sieur du Ryer... And Newly Englished, for the satisfaction of all that desire to look into the Turkish Vanities. To which is prefixed the Life of Mahomet, The Prophet of the Turks, and Author of the Alcoran. With a Needful Caveat, or Admonition, for them who desire to know what use may be made of, or if there be danger in Reading the Alcoran*, London 1649; id. (without mentioning his name), *The Life of Mahomet: Together with The Alcoran at large...*, London 1718; F. Rückert, *Der Koran in der Übersetzung von F.R.*, ed. H. Bobzin (with explanatory notes by W. Fischer), Würzburg 1995; G.S. Sablukov, *Koran. Perevod s arabskago jazyka*, Kazan 1877; G. Sale, *The Koran, Commonly called The Alcoran of Mohammed, Translated into English immediately from the Original Arabic; with Explanatory Notes, taken from the most approved Commentators. To which is prefixed A Preliminary Discourse*, London 1734; Cl.E. Savary, *Le Coran, traduit de l'arabe, accompagné de notes, et précédé d'un abrégé de la vie de Mahomet, Tirés des Ecrivains Orientaux les plus estimés*, tomes 1-2, Paris 1783; id., *Lettres sur l'Egypte*, 3 vols. in 2, Paris 1785-6; S. Schweigger, *Alcoranus Mahometicus, Das ist: Der Türcken Alcoran/Religion und Aberglauben*. Nürnberg 1616 (1623²); S. Swigger, *De Arabische Alkoran*, Hamburg 1641 [Dutch]; I.B. Szedlmayer and G. Gedeon, *Alkoran*, n.p. 1831; C.J. Tornberg, *Korânen, ifran Arabiskan öfversatt. Med en inledande biografi öfver Muhammed*, Lund 1874; L. Ullmann, *Der Koran. Aus dem Arabischen wortgetreu neu übersetzt und mit erläuternden Anmerkungen versehen*, Crefeld 1840; J. Vernet, *El Corán. Traducción y notas*, Barcelona 1963; S.F.G. Wahl, *Der Koran oder das Gesetz der Moslemen durch Muhammed den Sohn Abad'as. Auf den Grund der vormaligen Verdeutschung F.E. Boysen's von neuem aus dem Arabischen übersetzt*, Halle 1828; K.V. Zetterstéen, *Koranen, översatt från Arabiskan*, Stockholm 1917.

Secondary: N. Abbott, Arabic-Persian Koran of the late fifteenth or early sixteenth century, in *Ars Islamica* 6 (1939), 91-4; M.A.M. Abou Sheishaa, The translation of the Qur'ān. A selective bibliography (07/12/2003), on http://www.quran.org.uk/articles/ieb_quran_european_studies.htm; R.D. Abubakre, *Linguistic and non-linguistic aspects of Qur'ān translating to Yoruba*, Hildesheim 1986; M. Ali, Dottrine e attività dei Musulmani Ahmadiyya di Lahore, in *Oriente moderno* 6 (1926), 108-23; M.-Th. d'Alverny, Deux traductions latines du Coran au Moyen Age, in *Archives d'histoire doctrinale et littéraire du Moyen Age* 22/23 (1947/48), 69-131 (repr. in id., *La connaissance de l'Islam dans l'Occident médiéval*, Aldershot 1994, no. I); id., Quelques manuscrits de la "Collectio Toletana" in G. Constable (ed.), *Petrus Venerabilis 1156-1956*, Rome 1956, 202-18 (repr. in id., *La connaissance de l'Islam dans l'Occident médiéval*, Aldershot 1994, no. III); id. and G. Vajda, Marc de Tolède, traducteur d'Ibn Tûmart, in *al-Andalus* 16 (1951), 100-40, 259-307; 17 (1952), 1-56 (repr. in id., *La connaissance de l'Islam dans l'Occident médiéval*, Aldershot 1994, no. II); M. Asad, *Kann der Koran übersetzt werden?* Genf 1964; F. Aubin, Les traductions du Coran en Chinois, in *Etudes Orientales — Dirāsāt Sharqiyya* 13-14 (1994), 81-8; M. Ayoub, Translating the meanings of the Qur'an: Traditional opinions and modern debates, in *Inquiry* 3 (1986), 34-9; A. Bausani, On some recent translations of the Qur'ān, in *Numen* 4 (1957), 75-81; C. Bezold (ed.), *Orientalische Studien: Theodor Nöldeke zum siebzigten Geburtstag (2 März 1906) gewidmet von Freunden und Schülern und in ihrem Auftrag*, 2 vols. in 1, Gieszen 1906; J.K. Birge, Turkish translations of the Koran, in *MW* 28 (1938), 394-9; E. Birnbaum, On some Turkish interlinear translations of the Koran, in *Journal of Turkish studies* 14 (1990), 113-38; H. Bobzin, Latin Translations of the Koran. A short overview, in *Der Islam* 70 (1993), 193-206; id., *Reformation;* A. Bodrogligeti, The Persian translation of the Koran in Latin letters, in *AO-H* 13 (1961), 261-76; T.E. Burman, The Latin-Arabic Qur'ān edition of Egidio da Viterbo and the Latin Qur'āns of Robert of Ketton and Mark of Toledo, in M. Barceló and J. Martínez Gázquez (eds.), *Musulmanes y cristianos en Hispania durante las conquistas de los siglos XII y XIII*, Bellaterra 2005, 103-17; id., Tafsīr and translation. Traditional Arabic Qur'ān exegesis and the Latin Qur'āns of Robert of Ketton and Mark of Toledo, in *Speculum* 73 (1998), 703-32; D. Cabanelas Rodriguez, Juan de Segovia y el primer Alcorán Trilingüe, in *al-Andalus* 14 (1949), 149-73; id., *Juan de Segovia y el problema islámico*, Madrid 1952; T.I. Chinniah, The holy Qur'ān in Telugu, in *Islam in*

India 1 (1982), 143-54; G. Dale, A Swahili translation of the Koran, in *MW* 14 (1924), 5-9; E. Dammann, Die von der Ahmadiyyah herausgegebene Übersetzung des Korans in das Suaheli, in *ZDMG* 106 (1956), 135-44; R. Dankoff, Some notes on the Middle Turkic glosses, in *Journal of Turkish studies* 5 (1981), 41-4; P.P. Das, Zur ersten bengalischen Koranübersetzung, in *Der Islam* 59 (1982), 122-4; C. De Frede, *La prima traduzione italiana del Corano sullo sfondo dei rapporti tra Cristianità e Islam nel Cinquecento*, Naples 1967; J.B. Derost, Notice sur André du Ryer, in *Bulletin de la Société d'Etudes du Brionnais* (1935), 237-52; M. Devic, Une traduction inédite du Coran, in *JA* 8 (1883), 343-406; J. Eckmann, Eastern Turkish translations of the Koran, in L. Ligeti (ed.), *Studia turcica*, Budapest 1971, 149-59; id., *Middle Turkic glosses of the John Rylands interlinear Koran translation*, Budapest 1976; A. Fischer, *Der Wert der vorhandenen Koran-Übersetzungen und Sure III*, Leipzig 1977 (= Berichte über die Verhandlungen der Sächsischen Akademie der Wissenschaften, Phil.-hist. Klasse 89 [1937], 2); J. Fück, *Die arabischen Studien in Europa bis in den Anfang des 20. Jahrhunderts*, Leipzig 1955; id., Zur Frage der Koranübersetzung, in *OLZ* 47 (1944), 165-68 (repr. in id., *Arabische Kultur und Islam im Mittelalter*, Weimar 1981, 116-18); J.M. Gázquez, Finalidad de la primera traducción Latina del Corán, in M. Barceló and J. Martínez Gázquez (eds.), *Musulmanes y cristianos en Hispania durante las conquistas de los siglos XII y XIII*, Bellaterra 2005, 71-7; id., Observaciones a la traducción Latina del Corán (Qur'an) de Robert de Ketton, in J. Hamesse (ed.), *Les traducteurs au travail. Leurs manuscripts et leurs methods*, Turnhout 2001, 115-27; id., Los primeros nombres de Allāh en la traducción Latina del Alchoran de Robert de Ketton, in *Euphrosyne* NS 33 (2005), 303-13; id., El Prólogo de Juan de Segovia al Corán *(Qur'ān)* trilingüe (1456), in *Mittellateinisches Jahrbuch* 38 (2003), 389-410; id., Trois traductions medievales latines du Coran. Pierre le Venerable — Robert de Ketton, Marc de Tolède et Jean de Segovia, in *Revue des études latines* 80 (2003), 223-36; Cl. Gilliot, Le Coran. Trois traductions récentes, in *SI* 75 (1992), 159-77 (on the translations of J. Berque [Paris 1990], A. Chouraqui [Paris 1990] and R. Khawam [Paris 1990]); P.A. Gryaznevich, Koran v Rossi (Izuchenie, Perevody i Izdaniya), in id. and S.M. Prozorov (eds.), *Islam: Religiya. Obshchestvo, Gosudarstvo*, Moscow 1984, 76-82; A. Hamilton and F. Richard, *André du Ryer and Oriental studies in seventeenth-century France*, London 2004; J.D. Holway, The Qur'ān in Swahili. Three translations, in *MW* 61 (1971), 102-10; M.M. Husine, The rendering of the holy Quran into Kannada, in *Islam in India* 1 (1982), 155-60; E. İhsanoğlu, A study on the manuscript translations of the meanings of the holy Qur'ān, in J. Cooper (ed.), *The significance of Islamic manuscripts. Proceedings of the Inaugural Conference of al-Furqān Islamic Heritage Foundation*, London 1992, 79-105; M. Karimnia, Bibliography. European studies on translation of the holy Qur'ān, on http://www.quran.org.uk/articles/ieb_quran_european_studies.htm; M. Keyser (ed.), *Glazemaker 1682-1982. Catalogus bij een tentoonstelling over de vertaler Jan Hendriksz. Glazemaker*, Amsterdam 1982; M.H. Khan, A history of Bengali translations of the holy Qur'ān, in *MW* 72 (1982), 129-36; id., Translation of the holy Qur'ān in African languages, in *MW* 77 (1987), 250-8; M.Y. Kokan, The holy Quran in Tamil translation, in *Islam in India* 1 (1982), 135-42; M.M. Koyakutty, Malayalam renderings of the holy Qur'ān, in *Islam in India* 2 (1985), 229-36; G. Lazard, Lumières nouvelles sur la formation de la langue Persane. Une traduction du Coran en Persan dialectal et ses affinités avec le Judéo-Persan, in S. Shaked and A. Netzer (eds.), *Irano-Judaica II. Studies relating to Jewish contacts with Persian culture throughout the ages*, Jerusalem 1990, 184-98; C. López-Morillas, Lost and found? Yça of Segovia and the Qur'an among the Mudejars and Moriscos, in *JIS* 10 (1999), 277-92; id., The *Qur'an in sixteenth century Spain. Six Morisco versions of Sura 79*, London 1982; H. Ma'ayergi, History of translations of the meanings of the holy Qur'an into the Polish language, in *Journal of the Institute of Muslim Minority Affairs* 7 (1986), 538-46; id., History of the works of qur'anic interpretation (tafsir) in the Kurdish language, in *Journal of the Institute of Muslim Minority Affairs* 7 (1986), 268-74; id., Translations of the meanings of the holy Qur'an into minority languages. The case of Africa, in *Journal of the Institute of Muslim Minority Affairs* 14 (1994), 156-80; S.P. Manzoor, The Swedish translations of the holy Qur'ān, in *Proceedings of the Symposium on Translations of the Meanings of the Holy Qur'ān*, Istanbul 1986; N. Matar, *Alexander Ross and the first English translation of the Qur'ān*, in *MW* 88 (1998), 81-92; G.M. Meredith-Owens, Notes on an old Ottoman translation of the Kur'an, in *Oriens* 10 (1957), 258-76; J.E. Merrill, *Dr. Bell's critical anlysis of the Qur'an*, in *MW* 37 (1947), 134-48 (repr. in Paret [ed.], *Koran*, 11-24); A. Mingana, An ancient Syriac translation of the Ḳur'ān exhibiting new verses and variations, in *Bulletin of the John Rylands Library* 9 (1925), 188-235; id., An important old Turki manuscript in the John Rylands Library, in *Bulletin of the John Rylands University Library* 2 (1915), 129-38; V. Monteil, Un Coran Ahmadi en Swahili, in *Bulletin de l'Institut Fundamental d'Afrique Noir* 29

(1967), 479-95; A. Morimoto, A brief history of the holy Qur'an translation into Japanese, in *Islamic cultural forum* 9-10 (1978), 22-6; 18-23; K. Nait-Zerrad, Un essai de traduction du Coran en Berbère, in *Etudes et documents berbères* 10 (1993/4), 241-6; C.A. Nallino, Le fonti arabe manoscritte dell'opera di Ludovico Marracci sul Corano, in M. Nallino (ed.), *Raccolta di scritti editi e inediti*, 6 vols., Roma 1940, ii, 90-134; N. Nazifoff, The Bulgarian Koran, in *MW* 23 (1933), 187-90; R. Paret, *Grenzen der Koranforschung*, Stuttgart 1950; id., Der Plan einer neuen, leicht kommentierten wissenschaftlichen Koranübersetzung, in id. (ed.), *Orientalistische Studien E. Littmann zu seinem 60. Geburtstag überreicht*, Leiden 1935, 121-30; id. and J.D. Pearson, al-Kurʾān. 9. Translations of the Ḳurʾān, in *EI²*, v, 429-32; N. Petrus I. Pons, Marcos de Toledo y la segunda traducción Latina del Corán, in M. Barceló and J. Martínez Gázquez (eds.), *Musulmanes y cristianos en Hispania durante las conquistas de los siglos XII y XIII*, Bellaterra 2005, 87-94; A. Popovic, Sur une "nouvelle" traduction du Coran en Serbo-Croate, in *Arabica* 20 (1973), 82-4; M.G. Qureshi, The Gujarati editions of the Qur'ān, in *Islam in India* 1 (1982), 161-7; D. Rahbar, Aspects of the Qur'an translation, in *Babel* 9 (1963), 60-8; N. Robinson, Sectarian and ideological bias in Muslim translations of the Qur'an, in *Islam and Christian-Muslim relations* 8 (1997), 261-78; E.D. Ross, Ludovico Marracci, in *BSOAS* 2 (1921/3), 117-23; V. Salierno, Le edizioni Italiane del "Corano," in *L'Esopo* 13 (1982), 6, 7, 29-38; S.A. Sanabas, Translations of Qurʾān in Malayalam, in *Islam and the modern age* 24 (1993), 271-9; A. Schimmel, Die neue tschechische Koranübersetzung, in *WO* 7 (1973/4), 154-62; id., A new Czech translation of the Qur'an, in *Studies in Islam* 15 (1978), 171-6; id., Translations and commentaries of the Qur'an in Sindhi languages, in *Oriens* 16 (1963), 224-43; M. Seth, A manuscript Koran in classical Armenian, in *Journal and proceedings of the Asiatic Society of Bengal* NS 19 (1923), 291-4; M. Shākir, *al-Qawl al-faṣl fī tarjamat al-Qurʾān al-karīm ilā l-lughāt al-aʿjamiyya*, Cairo 1925; S.A. Sharafuddīn, *A brief survey of Urdu translations of the Qurʾān*, Bombay 1984; E. Teza, Di un compendio del Corano in espagnolo con lettere arabiche (manoscritto fiorentino), in *Rendiconti della Reale Accademia dei Lincei. Cl. di scienze morale, storiche e filologiche*, Ser. 4, no. 7 (1891), 81-8; Z.V. Togan, The earliest translation of the Qurʾān into Turkish, in *İslâm Tetkikleri Enstitüsü Dergisi* 4 (1964), 1-19; J. Tolan, Las traducciones y la ideología de reconquista: Marcos de Toledo, in M. Barceló and J. Martínez Gázquez (eds.), *Musulmanes y cristianos en Hispania durante las conquistas de los siglos XII y XIII*, Bellaterra 2005, 79-85; J. Vernet, Traducciones moriscos de El Corán, in W. Hoenerbach (ed.), *Der Orient in der Forschung, Festschrift für Otto Spies*, Wiesbaden 1967, 686-705; id. and L. Moraleda, Un Alcorán fragmentario en aljamiado, in *Boletín de la Real Academia de Buenas Letras de Barcelona* 33 (1969-70), 43-75; K. Versteegh, Greek translations of the Qurʾān in Christian polemics (9th century A.D.), in *ZDMG* 141 (1991), 52-68; P. Wexler, Christian, Jewish and Muslim translations of the Bible and Koran in Byelorussia: 16th-19th centuries, in *Journal of Byelorussian studies* 6 (1989), 12-19; J. Yijiu, The Qur'an in China, in *Asian studies* 17 (1982), 95-101; K.V. Zetterstéen, Some chapters of the Koran in Spanish transliteration, in *MO* 5 (1911), 39-41.

Transportation see SHIPS; VEHICLES AND TRANSPORTATION; CARAVAN

Travel see JOURNEY; TRIPS AND VOYAGES

Treasure see WEALTH; BOOTY

Tree(s)

A perennial woody plant with a main trunk. The *Lisān al-ʿArab* defines the term *shajar* as the "kind of plant that has a trunk or stem." In the Qurʾān, the denominative *shajara (nomen unitatis)* is the form used most frequently (nineteen times) to designate this concept. The nominal *shajar* is found generally in a collective sense of trees, bushes or plants; in two instances (Q 56:52; 36:80), however, it refers to specific trees, of which more below. For mention of other trees (date palm [q.v.], olive, etc.) see AGRICULTURE AND VEGETATION.

The contexts in which the collective sense of *shajar* appears depict the creative, supreme power of the one, unique deity (see CREATION; POWER AND IMPOTENCE). For example, "It is he who sends down water (q.v.) from the skies for you (see HEAVEN AND SKY; GRACE; BLESSING); from it is drink and from it is foliage *(shajar)* upon which you pasture [your beasts]" (Q 16:10; see SUSTENANCE; ANIMAL LIFE). The following verse mentions specific plants such as the olive tree, date palm, grape vine and many (unnamed) fruits, as portents for those who reflect upon God's creation. In two similar passages (Q 22:18; 55:6), all things in heaven and on earth prostrate before God (see BOWING AND PROSTRATION), including the sun (q.v.), moon (q.v.), stars (see PLANETS AND STARS), mountains, trees and beasts (see ANIMAL LIFE). Whereas God alone causes splendid orchards or gardens (see GARDEN) to spring forth, humans cannot produce (the seeds of) the trees (Q 27:60; see also Q 56:72). The ḥadīth collector Muslim (d. ca. 261/875) records a tradition in which God is said to have created trees on the third day, Monday, after the earth (q.v.) and the mountains (cf. Tibrīzī, *Mishcàt,* ii, 691-5 [chap. 7]).

One of the two instances of the nominal form referring to a particular tree is the "green tree" (*al-shajar al-akhḍar,* Q 36:80). Al-Zamakhsharī (d. 538/1144) explains this as one of the marvels of God's creation, the wood of such a tree containing the opposite qualities of fire (q.v.) and water. A proverb claims that "In every tree there is fire *(nār),* the best species being the *markh* and the *ʿafār*" (cf. Zamakhsharī, *Kashshāf,* ad Q 36:80). A green twig the size of a tooth stick *(siwāk)* cut from both trees, each of which secretes drops of water, would be rubbed together. Underlying the proverb is the notion of fertility since the male twig *(markh)* rubbed against the female twig *(ʿafār)* ignites fire with God's permission.

The second instance refers to *shajar min zaqqūm* (Q 56:52), a term that appears in two other verses as *shajarat al-zaqqūm* (Q 37:62; 44:43). Ibn Manẓūr (d. 711/1311-12) in the *Lisān* offers the explanation that, when Q 44:43-4, "Verily the tree of Zaqqūm is the food of sinners" (see SIN, MAJOR AND MINOR; FOOD AND DRINK; HELL AND HELLFIRE; REWARD AND PUNISHMENT), was revealed, the Quraysh (q.v.) did not understand what tree it referred to as it did not grow in the region. Abū Jahl enquired if anyone could identify it. A north African replied that in the dialect of Ifrīqiya it meant a dish of dates and fresh butter (*al-zubd bi-tamr;* the qurʾānic commentator al-Zamakhsharī attributes the food to the Yemenis). Abū Jahl ordered a plate of it for his companions and, having sampled it, they mockingly exclaimed, "Is this what Muḥammad has tried to scare us with in the hereafter?" God then revealed Q 37:62-5 in which the Zaqqūm is described as a tree that grows in the depths of hell, the fruits thereof being like the heads of devils or, according to al-Bayḍāwī (d. prob. 716/1316-17), like terrible serpents foul in aspect, having manes. In Q 56:52 the tree feeds the "companions of the left hand" (see LEFT HAND AND RIGHT HAND), unbelievers tormented in the afterlife who drink boiling water to quench their thirst (see HOT AND COLD). Hence, from being the food of the people of the fire, the word was extended to apply to any deadly food. Combining other lexicographical explanations, the tree might have been an import to the Middle East (possibly from India) known for its pungent odor or astringent and bitter qualities. The tree is alluded to in Q 17:60 as the "cursed tree in the Qurʾān." In this context al-Zamakhsharī presents a rejoinder to the unbelievers' scoffing scepticism that a tree that did not burn could possibly exist in hell. He cites the example of an animal's fur skin used by the Turks as a "table cloth." When it became dirty it was thrown onto the fire, the dirt vanished and the table cloth remained unaffected by the fire. The real purpose of the passage, he notes, is that God revealed it to frighten the Prophet's followers who feared the earthly punishment of death at the battle of Badr (q.v.). Among the multiple symbolic functions of trees in the world's religions, there is a notably infrequent occurrence of the tree as a direct source of danger, or as an instrument of punishment. The tree of Zaqqūm is one such symbol which, as an integral part of God's creation, reflects the divine control over both destinies in the afterlife, hell as well as heaven. In the post-biblical *Book of Zohar,* the fruit of the tree of knowledge is said to have brought death to the whole world.

With the story of the forbidden tree in paradise (q.v.), the qurʾānic narrative falls well within the earlier biblical tradition, although with certain significant differences. The first reference occurs in Q 2:35 where God permits Adam and his wife to dwell in the garden (see ADAM AND EVE), saying, "Eat freely of its plenty wherever you wish, but do not go near this tree, or you will be wrongdoers." The tree is unidentified in this passage and al-Ṭabarī's (d. 310/923) sources suggest it referred to wheat or the vine, among others. Al-Ṭabarī himself concludes that God had indicated to them by name which tree he meant. In the next passage (Q 7:19-22), the tree is again unidentified. Iblīs (Satan), whom God had already expelled from the garden for his refusal to bow to Adam (see BOWING AND PROSTRATION; INSOLENCE AND OBSTINACY; ARROGANCE), secretly re-enters it and deceitfully *(bi-ghurūrin)* advises the pair of God's intention behind his prohibition. This was to prevent their becoming angels (see ANGEL) or one of the immortals (see ETERNITY). In Q 20:120 the tree is explicitly named. Here Iblīs (Satan) whispers (see WHISPER) to Adam, "Shall I lead you to the tree of immortality *(shajarat al-khuld)* and a kingdom that does not decay?" Satan's real purpose was to expose the couple to their own nakedness (of which they had previously been unaware) and shame in their disobedience (q.v.) of God (see NUDITY; FALL OF MAN). In his *History,* al-Ṭabarī presents several overlapping accounts of these events. In one, originating with Wahb b. Munabbih (d. ca. 110/728), the tree is described as having intertwining branches which bore fruit of which the angels ate in order to live eternally. Then, addressing Adam after his sin of disobedience, God says, "Neither in paradise nor on earth was there a tree more excellent than the acacia *(ṭalḥ)* and the lote-tree *(sidr),*" a pointed allusion to these mentioned in Q 56:28-9.

Lane says the denominative form *(sidra)* denotes a species of lote-tree called by Linnaeus *rhamnus spina Christi* and by Forskal *rhamnus nabeca,* its fruit known as *nabiq.* The (thornless) lote and acacia in the collective sense appear in Q 56:28-9 in a description of the day of judgment (see LAT JUDGMENT), where the companions on the right hand (of God), the faithful, dwell among the shade of the trees, gushing water and abundant fruit. The lote-tree *(nomen unitatis sidra)* is also mentioned in Q 53:14, 16, but here it is a unique tree, the *sidrat al-muntahā,* the lote tree of the furthermost boundary near the garden of refuge *(jannat al-maʾwā).* Al-Zamakhsharī notes that here ends the knowledge of the angels and others and no one knows what lies beyond the tree, and that the spirits of the martyrs end here (see MARTYR). In the ḥadīth literature (see ḤADĪTH AND THE QURʾĀN), details from the two qurʾānic passages appear to be conflated. In one, the Prophet said, "In paradise there is a tree in whose shade a horseman would be able to ride for a hundred years." In another, also preserved in al-Tabrīzī's (fl. eighth/fourteenth cent.) *Mishkāt al-Maṣābīḥ* (Tibrīzī, *Mishcàt,* i, 24) as a citation from al-Bukhārī (d. 256/870) and Muslim (cf. Bukhārī, *Ṣaḥīḥ,* i, 306-7 [bk. 59, *K. Badʾ al-khalq,* 6]; Fr. trans. ii, 428-31; Muslim, *Ṣaḥīḥ,* i, 145-7, no. 259 [bk. 1, *K. al-Īmān,* 74]), the Prophet describes his night journey and ascension (q.v.) through the heavens where, in the seventh sphere (in another version, the sixth), he is taken to the *sidrat al-muntahā*. Its fruits were as large as earthenware pots and its leaves like elephants' ears. His companion, the angel Gabriel (q.v.), tells him of the four rivers he witnessed; the two concealed which were in paradise and the two manifest which were the Nile and the Euphrates. As the *sidrat al-muntahā* figured in the ascension stories, it proved an attractive symbol in the Ṣūfī tradition (see ṢŪFISM AND THE QUR'ĀN). For example, al-Tustarī (d. 283/896) links this qur'ānic passage about the celestial tree with the light of Muḥammad when it appeared before God a million years prior to creation. There was unveiled "the mystery by the Mystery Itself, at the Lote Tree of the Boundary, that is the tree at which the knowledge of everyone comes to an end" (Schimmel, *Muhammad*, 125; see INTELLECT; KNOWLEDGE AND LEARNING).

Historians of religion have seen in this account of the lote tree parallels with shamanic visions of the world-tree. N.R. Reat has argued that the most common name of the Islamic world-tree is taken from a ḥadīth in Ibn Ḥanbal's (d. 241/855) *Musnad*. To the question, "What is bliss *(ṭūbā)?*", the Prophet answered that it is a tree in paradise called *shajarat al-ṭūbā*, the like of which does not exist on earth. In the Shī'ī tradition (see SHĪ'ISM AND THE QUR'ĀN), Muḥammad Bāqir al-Majlisī's (d. 1110/1698) life of the Prophet contains several references to the same tree. Jesus (q.v.) inquired about it and was told by God that he had planted it himself; that its "trunk and branches are gold and its leaves beautiful garments. Its fruit resembles the breasts of virgins and is sweeter than honey and softer than butter and it is watered by the fountain of Tesneem" (Majlisī, *Life*, 92; see SPRINGS AND FOUNTAINS). Muḥammad, on his ascension journey, describes the tree as so immense that a bird could not fly around its trunk in seven hundred years; that its roots lay in 'Alī's celestial palace (see 'ALĪ B. ABĪ ṬĀLIB; SHĪ'A) and "there was not a residence in that blessed world to which a branch of that tree did not extend." In this account, Gabriel tells Muḥammad that God has referred to the tree in Q 13:29: "Those who believe and do what is right (shall enjoy) bliss *(ṭūbā)* and a happy resurrection (q.v.)." It is clear from Majlisī's account, however, that *ṭūbā* was a tree distinct from the *sidrat al-muntahā*, lying beyond the former and "every leaf of which shaded a great sect." Al-Ṭabarī's sources are more equivocal in his discussion of Q 13:29. Some exegetes argue for the abstract notion of "bliss" or "bounty," while others claim it is a garden in Ethiopia or India or a tree in paradise, for which last meaning he provides lengthy discussion.

Of the remaining references to trees in the Qur'ān, the most notable occurs in the famous "Light Verse" (Q 24:35): "A blessed olive tree, of neither east nor west, whose oil gives light (q.v.), though fire (q.v.) touches it not," forming part of a simile of God (see SIMILES) as "the light of the heavens and earth." Prayer rugs may be designed with a niche, a lamp and a stylised tree appearing to feed it with its oil. Al-Zamakhsharī explains that the best olive tree with the purest oil grows in Syria and that the rising and setting sun should fall upon it, hence it is both of the "east and west."

Finally, in Q 14:24, 26, there occurs the parable (q.v.) of the good word which is like a good tree *(shajara ṭayyiba)* with firm roots and high branches while an evil word is like an evil tree *(shajara khabītha)* uprooted and unstable (see SPEECH; GOOD AND EVIL). Q 37:147 refers to Jonah (q.v.) and how he was cast up from the sea upon the shore and a gourd vine *(shajara min yaqṭīn)* was caused to grow over him for protection. A historical allusion is found in Q 48:18, that "God was well pleased with the believers when they swore allegiance to you under the tree." This is a reference to the 1500 persons who declared themselves for the Prophet at Ḥudaybiya (q.v.; see also CONTRACTS AND ALLIANCES). Robertson Smith, citing Yāqūt (d. 626/1229), says this tree was visited by pilgrims seeking its blessing until the caliph (q.v.) ʿUmar cut it down to avoid its being worshipped like al-Lāt and al-ʿUzzā (see POLYTHEISM AND ATHEISM; SOUTH ARABIA, RELIGIONS IN PRE-ISLAMIC). Among the numerous references to God's causing vegetation to grow from the rain he sends down, there is the lone mention (Q 23:20) of "a tree that issues from Mount Sinai (q.v.) yielding oil *(duhn)* and seasoning *(ṣibgh)* for all to eat." At Q 28:30 God speaks to Moses (q.v.) from a bush *(al-shajara)* on blessed ground. In contrast to the examples discussed above (with the possible exception of the "green tree"), the trees mentioned in this last paragraph are all terrestrial rather than supernatural (see also ESCHATOLOGY).

David Waines

Bibliography
Primary: Bayḍāwī, *Anwār;* Bukhārī, ed. Krehl; Fr. trans. O. Houdas and W. Marçais, *Les traditions islamiques,* 4 vols., Paris 1903-14; Ibn Ḥanbal, *Musnad;* Lane; *Lisān al-ʿArab;* Majlisī, ʿAllāma Muḥammad Bāqir, *The life and religion of Muhammad (Ḥayat al-qulūb),* trans. J. Merrick, Boston [1850] 1982; Muslim, *Ṣaḥīḥ;* Ṭabarī, *Tafsīr;* id., *Taʾrīkh;* al-Tibrīzī, Muḥammad b. ʿAbdallāh, *Mishcàt-ul-maśábiḥ,* trans. Capt. A.N. Matthews, 2 vols., Calcutta 1809-10; Zamakhsharī, *Kashshāf.*
Secondary: Th. Barnes, Trees and plants, in *ERE,* xii, 448-57; M.I.H. Farooqi, *Plants of the Quran,* Lucknow 1989 (1992[2]); P.R. Frese and S.J.M. Gray, Trees, in *ER,* xv, 26-33; G. Lechler, The tree of life in Indo-European and Islamic cultures, in *Ars islamica* 4 (1937), 369-416; Nöldeke, *GQ,* i, 135 n. 5 (for further references); N.R. Reat, The tree symbol in Islam, in *Studies in comparative religion* 9 (1975), 164-82; W. Robertson Smith, *The religion of the Semites,* New York 1956; A. Schimmel, *And Muhammad is his messenger,* Chapel Hill 1985; A.J. Wensinck, *Tree and birds as cosmological symbols in western Asia,* Amsterdam 1921, esp. pp. 1-35.

Trench see PEOPLE OF THE DITCH; EXPEDITIONS AND BATTLES; MUḤAMMAD

Trial

Challenge to be endured. Some one hundred verses in the Qurʾān deal directly or indirectly with trial, in particular as a trial or test of true belief. Four verbs and/or their verbal nouns are especially used, of which the first two constitute the vast majority of these references: *balāʾ, ibtilāʾ* (e.g. Q 2:49; 3:186; 47:31; 89:16), *fatana, fitna* (e.g. Q 8:28; 64:15), *maḥḥaṣa* (only in Q 3:141 and 154) and *imtaḥana* (only in Q 49:3 and 60:10; Q 60 is additionally entitled *al-Mumtaḥana,* literally, "she who was tested," but its main concern is relations between believers and non-believers, which is tangential to this article; see BELIEF AND UNBELIEF). For trial in the sense of inquisition, see INQUISITION.

Yet the meaning of the Qurʾān in its entirety can be taken as a trial or test since it affords humankind the way to salvation (q.v.) if people choose to follow God's commands (see COMMANDMENT; OBEDIENCE) presented in it. Trials serve the purpose of distinguishing between those who do right and those who do not (Q 2:152-7; 47:31; 60:10; 67:2; see GOOD DEEDS; EVIL DEEDS; VIRTUES AND VICES, COMMANDING AND FORBIDDING) or between believers and unbelievers. In his exegesis of a qurʾānic verse dealing with the issue of coercion in religious matters (Q 2:256; see TOLERANCE AND COMPULSION), the exegete al-Rāzī (d. 606/1210; see EXEGESIS OF THE QURʾĀN: CLASSICAL AND MEDIEVAL) actually speaks of this world as a place of trial *(dār al-dunyā hiya dār al-ibtilāʾ)* with reference to the fact that people have a choice to believe or not (see FREEDOM AND PREDESTINATION; GRATITUDE AND INGRATITUDE). Carrying the argument further, he says that, had there been no choice and all were true believers, the world would be a perfect place and the notion of later punishment or reward would cease to have any meaning (see REWARD AND PUNISHMENT). Believers are subjected to trials in this world, both materially and spiritually (e.g. Q 2:155; 3:186; 5:48; 6:165; 21:35; 89:16). Hope (q.v.) and endurance (patience; see TRUST AND PATIENCE) help a believer during moments of trial (Q 4:104; 31:17). God gives signs (q.v.) as a test to people (Q 44:33) and God rewards those who stand in the face of adversity (Q 2:155-7). Even God's prophets (see PROPHETS AND PROPHETHOOD) are not exempt from these tests: "Thus we have appointed for every prophet an adversary (see ENEMIES; OPPOSITION TO MUḤAMMAD): the demons of humankind or of jinn (q.v.), who inspire to one another pleasing speech intended to lead astray (q.v.) through guile" (Q 6:112; cf. also Q 22:52; see DEVIL).

In light of the above, trials of past prophets and communities serve as examples for humankind. Abraham (q.v.), for instance, endured trials but in the end succeeded because he accepted God's commandments (Q 2:124; 37:104-7). The story of Joseph (q.v.) recounts his torment but final victory (Q 12) and that of his father Jacob (q.v.) who had lost his sight as a result of his distress over the loss of his son (Q 12:84), only to regain it later after learning that, true to his inner belief, his son was indeed not dead (Q 12:96). The Children of Israel (q.v.) suffered persecutions under the people of Pharaoh (q.v.; Q 2:49) but were delivered from this shame by the lord (q.v.; Q 44:30; see also DELIVERANCE). God grants mercy (q.v.) to those who are faithful in the face of numerous trials, illustrated, for example, by the initial childlessness of Zechariah (q.v.), and the allegations of Mary's (q.v.) immoral behavior — both of whom were ultimately rewarded and/or exonerated (Q 19:2-33; see CHASTITY; ADULTERY AND FORNICATION). Satan, too, may tempt and hence test people by raising doubt in sick hearts (Q 22:53; see HEART) and Satan brought agony to the prophet Job (q.v.) which was taken away after Job asked God for help (Q 38:41f.).

The qurʾānic emphasis on the trials of this world is reflected in the theological gloss given to the struggles of the Islamic community, particularly in its early years. This is especially evident in the portrayal of social and political upheavals of the first generations as rebellion (q.v.) against the divine law (see LAW AND THE QURʾĀN), leading to schism which could threaten the purity of the faith (q.v.) of the believers (cf. Gardet, Fitna). Disturbances such as that between ʿAlī and Muʿāwiya were often labeled as eras of *fitna*, or trial, for the believing community (see also POLITICS AND THE QURʾĀN).

John Nawas

Bibliography
Primary: al-Ghazālī, Aḥmad b. Muḥammad, *Iḥyāʾ ʿulūm al-dīn*, 4 vols., Cairo 1933 (repr. of Būlāq 1289/1872), iv, 53-123 (*K. al-Ṣabr wa-l-shukr*, esp. 110f., for discussion of *al-balāʾ* in the life of humans); Nuʿaym b. Ḥammād, *al-Fitan*, ed. M. b. M. al-Shūrī, Beirut 1997 (particularly for the trial of the afterlife, or *ʿadhāb al-qabr*); Rāzī, Tafsīr.
Secondary: J. Aguadé, *Messianismus zur Zeit der frühen. Das Kitāb al-Fitan des Nuʿaym Ibn Hammad*, diss. U. Tübingen 1979 (another work important for the trial of the afterlife); L. Gardet, Fitna, in EI², ii, 930-1.

Tribes and Clans

The social units that constituted Arabian society in pre-Islamic and early Islamic times (see PRE-ISLAMIC ARABIA AND THE QURʾĀN). As the Muslim polity developed, Muslim society became more complex and tribes ceased to be the sole constituent element. Nonetheless, Arab tribes did not disappear altogether (see ARABS; BEDOUIN). Modern historians of Islam understand the word "tribe" as a social unit larger than a "clan," but there is no consensus about the definition of either of these terms. Other words are occasionally used as synonyms of "clan," such as "sub-tribe," "branch," "faction," and "subdivision," but all of these lack a fixed meaning. Anthropologists, in contrast, use such terms in a much more technical and precise fashion. The Arabic designations of social units, such as *qabīla, ḥayy, ʿashīra, qawm, baṭn,* etc., also lack precision and the sources often use them interchangeably (see also KINSHIP). The common practice among modern Islamicists is to translate *qabīla* as "tribe."

Four terms in the Qurʾān express the notion of a social unit: *ʿashīra, asbāṭ, shuʿūb* and *qabāʾil.* The first of these, *ʿashīra,* occurs three times (Q 9:24; 26:214; 58:22) and seems to denote an extended family (q.v.) rather than a tribe. The second, *asbāṭ,* occurs five times, invariably referring to the tribes of the Children of Israel (q.v.; Q 2:136, 140; 3:84; 4:163; 7:160). Medieval Muslim exegetes (see EXEGESIS OF THE QURʾĀN: CLASSICAL AND MEDIEVAL) explain that the word *asbāṭ* is used to denote the tribes of the descendants of Isaac (q.v.; Isḥāq) in order to distinguish them from the descendants of Ishmael (q.v.; Ismāʿīl); the latter, the Arabian tribes, are referred to as *qabāʾil.* As for etymology, certain exegetes derive the term *asbāṭ* from *sibṭ* in the sense of "a grandchild," for the Children of Israel are like grandchildren to Jacob (q.v.; Yaʿqūb). Others assign to *sibṭ* the meaning of "succession," explaining that the generations (q.v.) of the Children of Israel succeeded one another and therefore they are *asbāṭ.* Yet another derivation of *asbāṭ* is from *sabaṭ,* a certain tree; the exegetes explain that the father is likened to a tree and the descendants to its branches (Ibn al-Hāʾim, *Tibyān,* i, 111; Qurṭubī, *Jāmiʿ,* ii, 141; vii, 303; Ibn Kathīr, *Tafsīr,* i, 188; Shawkānī, *Fatḥ,* i, 147). The word *asbāṭ,* however, seems to be a loan word from the Hebrew *shevaṭim* (sing. *shevet*), "tribes."

The third and the fourth terms, *shuʿūb* and *qabāʾil,* occur in the Qurʾān once, in the famous verse that served the Shuʿūbiyya movement (see below), "O people, we have created you male and female, and made you groups and tribes *(shuʿūban wa-qabāʾila)* so that you may know one another; the noblest among you in the sight of God is the most pious" (Q 49:13). *Shaʿb* (pl. *shuʿūb*) probably was the South Arabic term parallel to the Arabic *qabīla* (pl. *qabāʾil;* see Beeston, Some features; al-Sayyid, *al-Umma,* 29). There were, however, important differences. First, the Arabian social units called *qabāʾil* were based on common descent, whereas the south Arabian units called *shuʿūb* were not; secondly, the latter were sedentary, whereas the former included both nomads (q.v.) and settled people. Muslim exegetes, however, interpreted the qurʾānic *shuʿūb* and *qabāʾil* according to the needs of their own days. The various interpretations reflect the dispute about equality between Arab Muslims and other Muslims, the ideas of the Shuʿūbiyya movement and the response of their rivals (see POLITICS AND THE QURʾĀN). One line of interpretation conceives of the two words as applying to north and central Arabian social units of different size and different genealogical depth. According to this interpretation a *qabīla* is a tribe, such as the Quraysh (q.v.), whereas a *shaʿb* is a "super tribe," that is, the framework that includes several tribes, such as Muḍar. Another line of interpretation endows the two words with an ethnic coloring. According to this, *qabāʾil* refers to Arabs, whereas *shuʿūb* means non-Arabs or *mawālī* (clients; see CLIENTS AND CLIENTAGE) or social units based on territory rather than on genealogy (which again amounts to non-Arabs, see e.g. Ibn Kathīr, *Tafsīr,* iv, 218; for a detailed discussion and references, see Goldziher, *MS,* i, 137-98; Mottahedeh, Shuʿūbiyya; Marlow, *Hierarchy,* 2-3, 96-9, 106; al-Sayyid, *al-Umma,* 26-36).

The scarcity of resources in Arabia on the one hand and the tribal structure of the society on the other, led to incessant competitions and feuds between the Arabian social units. These facts of life were idealized and became the basis of the social values of the Arabs (Goldziher, *MS,* i, 18-27; Obermann, Early Islam; al-Sayyid, *al-Umma,* 19-25). Naturally, when the Prophet sought to establish a community of believers, he hoped to achieve unity among all Muslims (Goldziher, *MS,* i, 45-9). Many prophetic traditions (ḥadīths; see ḤADĪTH AND THE QURʾĀN) were circulated, denouncing tribal pride, tribal feuds and tribal solidarity that disrupted the overall unity of the Muslim community. The Qurʾān, however, advocates unity among Muslims (e.g. Q 3:103; 8:63; 49:10) without denouncing tribal values. Indeed, the Qurʾān does not even reflect the fact that pre-Islamic Arabian society was a tribal society. It is nevertheless important to understand the structure and the social concepts that constituted the setting prior to the advent of Islam.

Arabian society of pre-Islamic and early Islamic times may be schematically described as consisting of hierarchies of agnatic descent groups that came into being by a process of segmentation. As a rule, the major part of any given group considered itself the descendants in the male line of a single male ancestor, thus differentiating itself from other descent groups (see PATRIARCHY). At the same time, it considered itself part of ever larger descent groups because its members were also the offspring of ancestors further and further removed up the same male line. Any given descent group referred sometimes to a closer, at other times to a more distant ancestor, according to its interests. When referring to a distant ancestor, a descent group ignored the dividing lines between itself and those segments which, like itself, descended from the same distant ancestor. Thus, the more distant the ancestor, the larger the descent group and the greater the number of segments included in it. All Arabs considered themselves to be ultimately descended from two distant ancestors, in two different male lines, so that the genealogical scheme may be represented approximately as two pyramids. Descent groups are typically called "*Banū* so-and-so," i.e. "the descendants of so-and-so." It should, however, be noted that not every name mentioned in the genealogies stands for a founder of a descent group and that the recorded genealogies are not always genuine (some would even say are never genuine). Groups were sometimes formed by alliances, not by segmentation; but such groups, too, were eventually integrated into the genealogical scheme by fabricated genealogies and considered to be agnatic descent groups.

The sources preserved the names of many agnatic descent groups, which varied greatly in size and in their genealogical depth or level of segmentation. It is often clear that a given descent group was an entity of considerable genealogical depth that comprised a great number of independent segments. In the genealogies, the ancestor of such a comprehensive descent group would be far removed up the male line; the constituent segments of the group would be called after various descendants in the male line of that distant ancestor. Modern scholars of Arabia and Islam commonly refer to the comprehensive descent groups as "tribes" although, technically speaking, the term is perhaps not entirely appropriate. A descent group (comprehensive or not) consists of all descendants in the male line of a single male ancestor. A tribe, usually having a descent group at its core, includes others as well (clients, confederates; see BROTHER AND BROTHERHOOD). It is in fact difficult to determine whether the familiar names such as Quraysh, Tamīm, ʿĀmir, Ṭayyiʾ, Asad, etc., stand for tribes or for comprehensive descent groups. Obviously, the sources do not make this distinction (although they may include various specifications); neither do Islamicists who refer to these entities as tribes. As far as the medieval books of genealogy are concerned, these names stand for comprehensive descent groups. The records of Quraysh, Tamīm, etc., in these sources only include descendants in the male line of the respective distant ancestors. The genuineness of the genealogies is often disputed but no confederate or client is included as such in the record of any given group. On the other hand, it stands to reason that, in practice, a descent group and its confederates and clients counted as one entity, at least for certain purposes. Were it not so, there would have been no point to the existence of categories such as confederates and clients. This ambiguity is reflected in the way the historical sources record details of groups such as participants in a given battle (see EXPEDITIONS AND BATTLES). The names of the genuine members of each tribe are recorded first, followed by a separate list containing the names of the clients and the confederates. The same analysis applies to the segments that constituted the tribes. For the genealogical books they are descent groups but in practice they included outsiders as confederates and clients, so that they were not in fact descent groups; they may be referred to as "sections." The processes of segmentation and alliance effected constant changes in the composition of descent groups, tribes and sections. Because of this fact and the fluidity of the genealogical references, the distinction between tribes and sections is often blurred.

There is no dispute about the tribal nature of Arabian society before and after the advent of Islam; yet we do not know what the members of any given tribe had in common other than the name and perhaps some sense of solidarity (see an example of such solidarity in Ṭabarī, *Taʾrīkh,* vii, 175). Defining features such as those that exist for modern Bedouin tribes cannot be discerned for the period under discussion. A modern Bedouin tribe in the Negev and Sinai may be defined by a common name, common leadership, common territory, sometimes common customary law, and external recognition, both legal and political (see Marx, *Bedouin,* 61-3, 95, 123-4; id., Tribal pilgrimages, 109-16; Stewart, *Bedouin boundaries;* id., ʿUrf, 891). By contrast, the defining features of the tribes of old are far from clear. The members of a given tribe sometimes occupied adjacent territories but the legal significance of this fact, if any, is unknown (see al-Jāsir, Taḥdīd). As often as not, sections of one and the same tribe were scattered over large, non-adjacent areas. It is therefore not possible to define a tribe by its territory. Customary law seems to have constituted a factor uniting all Arabian tribes rather than a boundary differentiating between them. A pre-Islamic tribe certainly had no common leadership and its sections did not usually unite for common activities. Political division within one and the same tribe was the rule rather than the exception. When the sources seem to be reporting a joint activity of a tribe, it often turns out that the report is misleading. The confusion arises from the fluidity of the genealogical references. Apparently following the practice of the tribesmen themselves, the sources call sections interchangeably by the names of their closer and more distant ancestors. Obviously, a designation by a more distant ancestor applies to a more comprehensive segment. As a rule, a smaller section may be designated by the name of one of the larger ones to which it belongs but not vice versa (except when a specific name becomes generic, such as Qays, which came to designate all the so-called "northern tribes"). Thus when various versions of one and the same account refer to a given group by different names, the smallest framework mentioned is probably the one that was really involved in the events related in that account (Landau-Tasseron, Asad; id., Ṭayyiʾ). We are thus left with no real definition of an Arabian tribe in the period discussed here, except its name and a measure of solidarity. The concept of *ʿaṣabiyya,* commonly rendered as "tribal solidarity," was too vague and too fluid to bind all the men of any given tribe or section.

ʿAṣabiyya should not be confused with the concept of shared legal responsibility. The latter was a factor that drew precise boundaries between groups; the groups thus defined, however, were neither tribes nor sections because they consisted of adult males only. In pre-Islamic and early Islamic society the adult male members of certain agnatic descent groups shared legal responsibility. They were accountable for each other's offenses. At its most extreme manifestation, this rule meant that they jointly sought revenge or received blood money (q.v.; see also RETALIATION) when one of them was killed by an outsider (see MURDER; VIOLENCE); conversely, they were all exposed to vengeance (q.v.) or obliged to pay blood money when one of them killed an outsider. The obligation of mutual assistance applied not only in matters of blood revenge but also in less extreme situations. Such a group of men sharing legal responsibility may be called a co-liable group (see Marx, *Bedouin,* chaps. 7 and 8). The rules by which co-liable groups were formed in the past are unknown. The material at hand does not disclose whether they came into being on the basis of a certain genealogical depth, mutual consent of the members, a decision by the elders, external public opinion or any combination of these or other factors (cf. Stewart, *Texts,* i, 26-122; id., Thaʾr; id., Structure of Bedouin society; Marx, *Bedouin,* 63-78, 180-242).

Agnatic descent groups often accepted outsiders into their ranks. The male adults from among these outsiders shared liability with the male adults of the descent group that they had joined. It should be noted that, as a rule, a section bore the name of the descent group that formed its core; the co-liable group based on a given descent group, or on the section that crystallized around it (if any), bore the same name. Obviously, great confusion ensues when one and the same name designates three groups of different kinds (a descent group, the section that crystallized around it and the male adult members thereof, i.e. the co-liable group).

Co-liable groups were thus based either on descent groups or on sections, but not every descent group and every section constituted the framework of a single co-liable group. The actual boundaries of liability, that is, the lines dividing the various co-liable groups, are unknown. We may be certain that the men of a tribe never constituted a single co-liable group; we cannot tell, however, which sections within each tribe fulfilled this function at any given point in time.

In conclusion, we know thousands of names of tribes and sections but we cannot describe the defining features of a tribe or a section. We can define the phenomenon of the co-liable groups that were based on tribal sections but we cannot draw the lines dividing them.

Ella Landau-Tasseron

Bibliography
Primary: Ibn ʿAbd Rabbihi, Aḥmad b. Muḥammad, *al-ʿIqd al-farīd*, ed. A. Amīn, A. al-Zayn and I. al-Abyārī, 8 vols., Cairo 1942, iii, 312-417; Ibn al-Hāʾim, Aḥmad b. Muḥammad, *al-Tibyān fī tafsīr gharīb al-Qurʾān*, Cairo 1992; Ibn Ḥazm, ʿAlī b. Aḥmad, *Jamharat ansāb al-ʿarab*, ed. ʿA.M. Hārūn, Cairo 1962; Ibn Kathīr, *Tafsīr*, Cairo n.d.; al-Nuwayrī, Shihāb al-Dīn Aḥmad b. ʿAbd al-Wahhāb, *Nihāyat al-arab fī funūn al-adab*, 6 vols., Cairo 1924, ii, 291-375; al-Qalqashandī, Aḥmad b. ʿAlī, *Qalāʾid al-jumān fī l-taʿrīf bi-qabāʾil ʿarab al-zamān*, ed. I. al-Abyārī, Cairo 1383/1963; id., *Ṣubḥ al-aʿshā fī ṣināʿat al-inshā*, ed. M.Ḥ. Shams al-Dīn, 14 vols., Beirut 1407/1987, i, 359-420; Qurṭubī, *Jāmiʿ*, Cairo 1952-67; al-Shawkānī, Muḥammad b. ʿAlī, *Fatḥ al-qadīr*, 5 vols., Beirut n.d.; Ṭabarī, *Taʾrīkh*, Cairo 1960-9, vii.
Secondary: A.F.L. Beeston, Some features of social structure in Sabaʾ, in *Sources for the history of Arabia*, 2 vols., Riyadh 1979, i, 115-23; E. Braunlich, Beiträge zur Gesellschaftsordnung der Arabischen Bedouinenstämme, in *Islamica* 6 (1934), 68-111, 182-229; W. Caskel, The bedouinization of Arabia, in G.E. von Grunebaum (ed.), *Studies in Islamic cultural history* [*The American anthropologist* (n.s.) 56/2 pt. 2 (April 1954)], Menasha, WI 1954, 36-46; id., *Ǧamharat an-nasab. Das Genealogicsche Werk des Hišām b. Muḥammad al-Kalbī*, Leiden 1966; J. Chelhod, *Introduction à la sociologie de l'islam*, Paris 1958, chap. 2; id., Ḳabīla, in *EI²*, iv, 334-5; P. Crone, Tribes and states in the Middle East, in *JRAS* 3/3 (1993), 353-76; F. Gabrielli (ed.), *L'antica societa beduina*, Roma 1959; Goldziher, *MS*, trans.; Ḥ. al-Jāsir, Taḥdīd manāzil al-qabāʾil al-qadīma ʿalā ḍawʾ ashʿārihā, in *Majallat al-ʿArab* 7 (1972-3), 321-57, 421-8, 515-22, 597-602, 653-68, 759-70, 829-38, 898-922; 8 (1973-4), 29-34, 104-14; ʿU.R. Kaḥḥāla, *Muʿjam al-qabāʾil al-ʿarabiyya al-qadīma wa-l-ḥadītha*, Damascus 1949; Ph.S. Khoury and J. Kostiner (eds.), *Tribes and state formation in the Middle East*, Berkeley 1990, part 1; M.J. Kister and M. Plessner, Notes on Caskel's *Ǧamharat an-nasab*, in *Oriens* 25-6 (1976), 48-68; E. Landau-Tasseron, Alliances among the Arabs, in *al-Qanṭara* 26/1 (2005), 141-73; id., Asad from Jahiliyya to Islam, in *JSAI* 6 (1985), 1-28; id., The participation of Ṭayyiʾ in the *ridda*, in *JSAI* 5 (1984), 53-71; *Majallat al-ʿArab* 1 (1966-7), 111-120 (a survey of literature on genealogy, both ancient and modern); L. Marlow, *Hierarchy and egalitarianism in Islamic thought*, Cambridge 1997; E. Marx, *Bedouin of the Negev*, Manchester 1967; id., Tribal pilgrimages to saints' tombs in south Sinai, in E. Gellner (ed.), *Islamic dilemmas. Reformers, nationalists and industrialization*, Berlin/New York/Amsterdam 1985, 105-32; R. Mottahedeh, The Shuʿūbiyya and the social history of early Islamic Iran, in *IJMES* 7 (1976), 161-82; J. Obermann, Early Islam, in R.C. Dentan (ed.), *The idea of history in the ancient Near East*, New Haven 1955, 239-310; W. al-Qāḍī, The conceptual foundation of cultural diversity in pre-modern Islamic civilization, in A.A. Said and M. Sharify-Funk (eds.), *Cultural diversity and Islam*, New York 2003, 85-106; R. al-Sayyid, *Mafāhīm al-jamāʿāt fī l-Islām*, Beirut 1984; id., *al-Umma wa-l-jamāʿa wa-l-sulṭa*, Beirut 1984; F. Stewart, *Bedouin boundaries in central Sinai and the southern Negev*, Wiesbaden 1986; id., On the structure of Bedouin society in the Negev, in *Ha-mizraḥ He-ḥadash* 33 (1991), 132-44 (in Heb.); id., *Texts in Sinai Bedouin law*, 2 vols., Wiesbaden 1988-90; id., Thaʾr, in *EI²*, x, 442-3; id., ʿUrf, in *EI²*, x, 887-92.

Tribute

see TAXATION; POLL TAX; BOOTY; CAPTIVES; POLITICS AND THE QURʾĀN

Trick

see LAUGHTER; LIE; MOCKERY; MAGIC; HUMOR

Trinity

The distinctive Christian doctrine of one God in three persons, directly alluded to three times in the Qurʾān. The overwhelmingly powerful assertion in the Qurʾān that God is absolutely one rules out any notion that another being could share his sovereignty (q.v.) or nature (see GOD AND HIS ATTRIBUTES). The text abounds with denials that there could be two gods (Q 16:51) and that he could have partners (e.g. Q 6:163; 10:18, 28-9; 23:91; see POLYTHEISM AND ATHEISM) or relations (Q 6:100; 16:57; 17:111; 25:2; 112:3) and explicitly repudiates the idea that he took Jesus (q.v.) as his son (Q 4:171; 19:34-5). This is the context in which its rejection of belief in the Trinity is to be understood. Whether it does, in fact, reject the doctrine has been contested, though from a very early date there has been little doubt of this among Muslims.

The three direct references to triple deity occur in the two late sūras, Q 4 and 5, which number 100 and 114 respectively in the chronological order suggested by Nöldeke, *GQ*. What appears to be the most straightforward of the three is Q 5:73: "Certainly they disbelieve (see BELIEF AND UNBELIEF) who say: God is the third of three *(thālith thalātha)*, for there is no god except one God." It has been suggested that this verse criticizes a deviant form of Trinitarian belief which overstressed the distinctiveness of the three persons at the expense of their unity as substance (Masson, *Coran*, 93; Watt-Bell, *Introduction*, 158). It has also been noted that, in fact, this is not a reference to the Trinity but to Jesus, who in Syriac literature was often called "the third of three" (Griffith, Christians and Christianity, 312-13). By this reading Q 5:73 must be seen as constituting part of a sustained criticism of the belief in the divinity of Christ that occupies the whole of Q 5:72-5, i.e. an emphatic repetition of the criticism in verse 72 that God and Christ are identical (see CHRISTIANS AND CHRISTIANITY; POLEMIC AND POLEMICAL LANGUAGE). But it is equally plausible to read this and the preceding verse, which is evidently intended as a pair with this since it begins with the same formula *(laqad kafara lladhīna qālū inna...)*, as intentional simplifications of the two major Christian beliefs in the humanity and divinity of Christ and the Trinity, simplifications that expose the weaknesses they each contain when analyzed from the strictly monotheistic perspective of the Qurʾān. Thus, Q 5:72 attacks what it portrays as the eternal God (see ETERNITY) and the human born of Mary (q.v.) being identical, while Q 5:73 attacks the notion that God could have partners in his divinity. The teaching in this verse is certainly that Christians place other beings alongside the true God. If it is taken in its context, the implication can be drawn from Q 5:72 and 75 that one of these is Jesus, while from the firm emphasis on his and his mother's human needs in Q 5:75 ("Christ the son of Mary was no more than a messenger [q.v.]... and his mother was a woman of truth [q.v.]; they had both to eat food"; see FOOD AND DRINK; PROPHETS AND PROPHETHOOD), it is even possible to infer that the other was Mary (*Jalālayn*, ad loc.).

Whether or not this is the intention in Q 5:73, the second reference in the Qurʾān to three deities makes such an accusation explicit. This is in Q 5:116: "And behold! God will say: 'O Jesus, the son of Mary! Did you say to people *(al-nās)*, "Take me and my mother for two gods beside God?"' He will say, 'Glory to you (see GLORIFICATION OF GOD)! Never could I say what I had no right [to].'" In what is intended as an eschatological interrogation of Jesus (see Q 5:109; see ESCHATOLOGY), God brings up a claim evidently associated with him, that he encouraged people to regard himself and Mary as gods besides God *(min dūni llāh)*. The implication is that Christians made him the source of the wrong belief they hold. Strictly speaking, this verse need not be read as a reference to a version of the Trinity but rather as an example of *shirk*, claiming divinity for beings other than God (see IDOLATRY AND IDOLATERS). As such, it could be understood as a warning against excessive devotion to Jesus and extravagant veneration of Mary, a reminder linked to the central theme of the Qurʾān that there is only one God and he alone is to be worshipped (see WORSHIP). Nevertheless, this verse has been read in relation to the Trinity and linked with others such as Q 6:101, which denies that God has a consort and therefore a son, to assert that Christians believe in a godhead comprising God, Mary and Jesus.

It has been argued that this accusation, which is remote from orthodox Christianity, may be directed at a particular form of deviant belief, such as that associated with the Collyridians, a female sect who sacrificed cakes, *kollyrídes,* to Mary (Masson, *Coran,* 93; Parrinder, *Jesus,* 135). They are described by the fourth century heresiographer Epiphanius (d. 403 C.E.) as a sect that "came to Arabia from Thrace and northern Scythia" (*Panarion* LXXIX). This suggestion is helpful in linking the accusation with a historical referent but it raises the problem of why the Qurʾān should take this comparatively little-known belief as a representative formulation of the Trinity. To accept such a link may have some attraction on historical grounds (though firm proof is entirely lacking), but it entails acknowledging that the Qurʾān is not addressing mainstream Christian beliefs. If, on the other hand, there is no sectarian version of Christian doctrine being addressed in this verse, it need not be read as a rejection of a deviant doctrine of the Trinity but as a denial that Jesus and Mary are equal with God, and a warning (q.v.) against making excessive claims about them. Thus, it can be understood as an instance of the warning against the divinization of Jesus that is given elsewhere in the Qurʾān and a warning against the virtual divinization of Mary in the declarations of the fifth-century church councils that she is *theotókos,* "God-bearer." The vehement opposition of Nestorius (d. ca. 451) and his followers to this title as incompatible with the full humanity of Christ may be part of the historical context from which the polemics of this verse arise. It is not farfetched to think that ecclesiastical extravagances as related by groups of Christians to whom they were distasteful, combined with the constant emphasis in the Qurʾān on the uniqueness of God, produced this dramatically conceived denial that other beings could be divine besides him.

The third clear reference to triple deity occurs in Q 4:171:

> O People of the Book (q.v.)! Commit no excesses in your religion (q.v.), nor say of God anything but the truth. Christ Jesus the son of Mary was only God's messenger and his word (see WORD OF GOD) which he bestowed on Mary, and a spirit (q.v.) from him. So believe in God and his messengers and do not say "Three"; desist, it will be better for you. For God is one God, far removed is he in his glory from having a son.

When read as part of the whole verse, the reference here to "three" is most obviously connected with the rejection of the related claims that Jesus was more than a human messenger and that God had a son. So a straightforward interpretation would be that here as in Q 5:73 the Qurʾān warns against both divinization of Christ and Trinitarian exaggerations because no other beings should be placed beside God in divinity. (There is a curious reminiscence of the classical Christian doctrine in the immediately preceding mention of Jesus as word and spirit of God, though also a clear denial of it on the grounds that the titles hypostasised into persons of the godhead by Christians are no more than qualities to be ascribed to the human Jesus.) Like the other two, this third qur'ānic reference to tripleness in deity is, then, really directed against associating creatures with God, though it must be taken as intended to refute the central Christian doctrine of the Trinity, and, as such, as a radical deconstruction of that doctrine in its essential formulation of three discrete beings who share in divinity.

It appears that unless they are naïve misunderstandings of the doctrine, all of these three references to the Trinity are directed from the context of the uncompromising insistence in the Qur'ān upon the unity of God against claims that challenge this. (It is, however, worth recalling that in their discussions of these verses early commentators often noted that for Christians the "three" was an internal characteristic of the godhead in the form of the persons rather than a series of external beings placed together with God.) The lack of detail about what these claims actually consist of suggests that the Qur'ān has no concern to analyze and evaluate them but simply to deny them as distortions of its central teaching of divine unicity.

The undeviating denial in the Qur'ān of any god besides God has not prevented Christians over the centuries from detecting in it hints of the Trinity. As early as the mid-second/eighth century the anonymous treatise entitled *Fī tathlīth Allāh al-wāḥid* alludes to the plural forms of self-address in such verses as Q 90:4, 54:11 and 6:94 as indications of a triune godhead (Gibson, Triune nature, 77; trans., 5; for dating of this work see Samir, Arab apology, 61-4). A little later the Nestorian patriarch Timothy I in his dialogue with the caliph al-Mahdī, dated to 165/781, refers to such verses as Q 19:17 and Q 21:91 for the same purpose, as well as to the groups of three letters at the start of some sūras (Mingana, Apology, 201-4; see MYSTERIOUS LETTERS). And some years after him the Jacobite Ḥabīb b. Khidma Abū Rā'iṭa also refers to the evidence of the plural forms of address (Graf, *Schriften*, 20). This motif can be traced through the medieval period and is employed as late as 1461 C.E. by the German cardinal Nicholas of Cusa in his *Cribratio Alkorani*, where he also regards Q 42:52, 4:171; 26:192-5; and 16:102 as open references to the three persons of the godhead (Hopkins, *Nicholas of Cusa*, 119, 126-7; see PRE-1800 PREOCCUPATIONS OF QUR'ĀNIC STUDIES). Just as provocatively, the Melkite bishop Paul of Antioch (thought to have been active towards the end of the sixth/twelfth century), who knew the Qur'ān more thoroughly than most earlier Christians, sees a Trinitarian allusion in the Throne Verse (see VERSES; THRONE OF GOD), "God, there is no god but he, the living, the self-subsisting" (Q 2:255) and also marshals mentions of God's word and spirit in Q 5:110, 37:171, 40:68, and 66:12 into an argument that supposedly supports the doctrine from the Qur'ān itself (Khoury, *Paul d'Antioche*, 69-71; trans., 177-8).

Needless to say, Muslim polemicists unanimously rejected such attempts to base the doctrine on the Qur'ān and took what they read as the denial of the Trinity in their scripture as the basis of their own arguments against it. As early as the beginning of the third/ninth century the Zaydī Imām al-Qāsim b. Ibrāhīm (see IMĀM; SHĪ'ISM AND THE QUR'ĀN) describes the doctrine in tritheistic terms as "three separate individuals" *(thalāthat ashkhāṣ muftariqa)*, which are "one compacted nature" (*ṭabī'a wāḥida muttafiqa*, di Matteo, Confutazione, 314-15, trans., 345) and goes on to argue that the names "Father" and "Son" cannot refer to the eternal being of God since they derive from the temporal act of begetting (di Matteo, Confutazione, 318-9; trans., 349-50). A little later the philosopher Abū Yūsuf al-Kindī (see PHILOSOPHY AND THE QUR'ĀN) also describes the persons as *ashkhāṣ* who are each distinguished by particular properties and argues that they cannot be eternal since they are composite and, according to the Aristotelian system, must be categories of existents which may contain other categories of existents within them or themselves be members of categories (Périer, Traité). At about the same time the independent thinker Abū ʿĪsā al-Warrāq (fl. third/ninth cent.), in the most searching examination of the Trinity that survives from a Muslim author, painstakingly demonstrates that the Christian doctrine cannot be reconciled with monotheism as long as it also itemizes a number of constituents in the godhead (Thomas, *Polemic*).

Arguments such as these which exposed the tritheistic nature of the Trinity set the pattern for later Muslim approaches towards the doctrine. Despite their differences in detail, they all acknowledge the lead of the Qurʾān in focusing on the accusation that the doctrine imports plurality into the godhead.

David Thomas

Bibliography

Primary: M.D. Gibson (ed. and trans.), *Fī tathlīth Allāh al-wāḥid,* On the triune nature of God, in *Studia sinaitica* 7 (London 1899), 2-36, 74-107; G. Graf (ed. and trans.), *Die Schriften des Jacobiten Ḥabīb Ibn Khidma Abū Rāʾiṭa,* 2 vols., Louvain 1951; J. Hopkins, *Nicholas of Cusa's De Pace Fidei and Cribratio Alkorani. Translation and analysis,* Minneapolis 1994[2]; P. Khoury, *Paul d'Antioche, évêque melkite de Sidon (xii*[e] *s.),* Beirut 1964; I. di Matteo, Confutazione contro i Cristiani dello zaydita al-Qāsim b. Ibrāhīm, in *RSO* 9 (1921-2), 301-64; A. Mingana (ed. and trans.), The apology of Timothy the patriarch before the caliph Mahdi, in *Bulletin of the John Rylands Library* 12 (1928), 137-298; A. Périer, Un traité de Yaḥyā ben ʿAdī, in *ROC* 22 (1920-1), 3-21; S.Kh. Samir, The earliest Arab apology for Christianity, in id. and J.S. Nielsen (eds.), *Christian Arabic apologetics during the Abbasid era (750-1258),* Leiden 1994, 57-114; D. Thomas, *Anti-Christian polemic in early Islam. Abū ʿĪsā al-Warrāq's "Against the Trinity",* Cambridge 1992.

Secondary: S. Griffith, Christians and Christianity, in *EQ*, i, 307-16; R. Haddad, *La Trinité divine chez les théologiens arabes (750-1050),* Paris 1985; Y. Khūrī et al., *ʿĪsā wa-Maryam fī l-Qurʾān wa-l-tafāsīr,* Amman 1996; D. Masson, *Le Coran et la révélation judéo-chrétienne. Etudes comparées,* 2 vols., Paris 1958; G. Parrinder, *Jesus in the Qurʾān,* London 1965; D. Thomas, The doctrine of the Trinity in the early ʿAbbasid era, in L. Ridgeon, (ed.), *Islamic interpretations of Christianity,* Richmond, Surrey 2001, 78-98.

Trips and Voyages

Travel episodes of long or short duration. Instances and descriptions of travel may be real, e.g. trips undertaken by qurʾānic characters, or figurative, e.g. following the straight path (see PATH OR WAY) to earn God's pleasure. Both feature prominently in the Qurʾān. Common also are references to modes of and motives for travel and allusions to the journeys (see JOURNEY) undertaken by Muḥammad (e.g. the night journey; see ASCENSION) and by the early Muslim community (e.g. the *hijra* from Mecca [q.v.] to Medina [q.v.]; see EMIGRATION).

The Qurʾān acknowledges the fact that the course of human activity includes the undertaking of trips and voyages. Among God's gifts to humanity is the ability to travel upon the earth (q.v.): "And he has set upon the earth... rivers and roads *(anhāran wa-subulan)* that you may guide yourselves, and sign-posts too; and stars by which to be guided" (Q 16:15-16; see PLANETS AND STARS; GRACE; BLESSING; NATURE AS SIGNS). These trips may be commercial, military, diplomatic, religious or political (see EXPEDITIONS AND BATTLES; MARKETS; CARAVAN). Indeed, in the context of certain ritual practices (see RITUAL AND THE QURʾĀN), this translates into explicit provisions. Fasting (q.v.) in the month of Ramaḍān (q.v.), for instance, is enjoined on believers (see BELIEF AND UNBELIEF) but those on a trip (*ʿalā safarin,* also identified as wayfarers, *ʿābirī sabīl,* in Q 4:43) and the sick (see ILLNESS AND HEALTH) are exempt from this obligation (Q 2:184, 185; see also CLEANLINESS AND ABLUTION). Ritual prayers may also be curtailed by reason of travel (*wa-idhā ḍarabtum fī l-arḍ…,* Q 4:101; cf. 5:106; see PRAYER). The hazards of travel are the reason for such provisions and are frequently invoked by the Qurʾān. One danger facing travelers in the late antique world was ambush, either on the road or at sea. This helps explain the Qurʾān's harsh view of pirates and highway robbers (see THEFT), the threat of the latter being mentioned in one place together with sexual relations between men (see HOMOSEXUALITY; SEX AND SEXUALITY) and the giving of wicked counsel (Q 29:29; see also BOUNDARIES AND PRECEPTS).

The danger posed by weather (q.v.) conditions (sometimes evoked directly, as in Q 77:1-4) and the vagaries of nature are implicit in the Qurʾān's frequent reference to the fact that God's grace is what allows ships (q.v.; in twenty-three places) to travel without difficulty and for humanity's profit upon the seas (Q 17:66; cf. 2:164; 17:70). From God's bounty also come the means by which to navigate: "He is the one who placed the stars so you may be guided by them through the darkness (q.v.) of land and sea" (*wa-huwa l-ladhī jaʿala lakumu l-nujūma li-tahtadū bihā fī ẓulumāti l-barri wa-l-baḥri,* Q 6:97) — although it should be noted that in some Shīʿī commentary these stars are identified as the imāms (see Ṭabarsī, *Majmaʿ,* iv, 132; see SHĪʿISM AND THE QURʾĀN; IMĀM). The most famous ship mentioned in the Qurʾān is Noah's (q.v.) ark (q.v.), which God instructs him to build to save himself, his kin and the righteous from the flood he will send as punishment (Q 11:36-49; see CHASTISEMENT AND PUNISHMENT; PUNISHMENT STORIES). Noah's appeals to God to save his unbelieving son (Q 11:45-7) are rejected by God; Noah's wife, too, is not spared (Q 66:10) and so neither makes the momentous trip to safety and grace (see Zamakhsharī, *Kashshāf,* ii, 218-19; iv, 118). There is one instance of a journey in the belly of a fish: the prophet Jonah (q.v.; Yūnus, also called Dhū l-Nūn) is thrown overboard, swallowed by a fish and cast forth on a barren shore (Q 37:139-48).

Danger during trips also helps explain the Qurʾān's use of safe passage and of public safety as a metaphor (q.v.). At Q 14:35, Abraham (q.v.) prays for a secure land; at Q 95:3 God swears by a safe city (q.v.; *wa-hādha l-baladi l-amīn*); and at Q 34:18, God tells the people of Sheba (q.v.), "Travel *(sīrū)* between [the cities] in all security *(āminīn),* day or night." Sheba is the place to which Solomon's (q.v.) hoopoe travels and returns, bringing news of its people and queen (Q 27:22; see BILQĪS). Solomon then dispatches both a human and jinn (q.v.) embassy (Q 27:37-40) prompting the queen's visit (Q 27:42). Her people are the ones who had covetously asked God to place greater distances between their way stations (Q 34:19) because they wished to monopolize trade and benefit from the hardship to others (*Jalālayn,* 430; see TRADE AND COMMERCE). The latter is one of countless references to trade in the Qurʾān, a revelation vouchsafed, it should be remembered, to a merchant of the Quraysh (q.v.) tribe (see e.g. Q 35:29 for a metaphorical use of *tijāra,* commerce; see also TRIBES AND CLANS).

The Quraysh and their caravans are described in Q 106, a short early Meccan revelation (see REVELATION AND INSPIRATION; CHRONOLOGY AND THE QURʾĀN). Although this sūra (q.v.) does not explicitly mention the animals used in the caravans, they are enumerated elsewhere (see ANIMAL LIFE): Q 16:5-8, for example, mentions the creation of cattle *(anʿām)* which "carry your heavy loads (see LOAD OR BURDEN) to lands that you would not otherwise reach except with great distress." Animals are beneficial also because their skins can be used to make tents, in particular for use on trips (*yawma ẓaʿnikum wa-yawma iqāmatikum,* Q 16:80; see HIDES AND FLEECE). Horses, mules and donkeys (*wa-l-khayl wa-l-bighāl wa-l-ḥamīr,* Q 16:8) are also identified. Q 59:6 makes reference to the use of horses and camels in battle, and in Q 105, a short Meccan sūra which describes the unsuccessful attempt of the Abyssinian governor Abraha (q.v.) to besiege Mecca and take the Kaʿba (q.v.), war elephants are mentioned (see also CAMEL; PRE-ISLAMIC ARABIA AND THE QURʾĀN; ABYSSINIA; PEOPLE OF THE ELEPHANT).

That humankind may be involved in struggles, both unarmed and armed, is evoked in formulations such as "go forth lightly or heavily equipped and struggle with your wealth (q.v.) and your persons in the cause/way of God" (*infirū khifāfan wa-thiqālan wa-jāhidū bi-amwālikum wa-anfusikum fī sabīli llāhi,* Q 9:41; see EXPEDITIONS AND BATTLES; JIHĀD). Of special significance here is the use of the term *sabīl Allāh* — *sabīl* (way, cause), and its plural *subul,* occur in 176 places in the Qurʾān. At Q 4:94, the Qurʾān addresses those who do God's work *(fī sabīl Allāh),* such as those calling people to Islam (q.v.; see also INVITATION). These righteous and pious folk are occasionally specifically described, like *sāʾiḥāt* (Q 66:5), women who travel for faith (q.v.; cf. *al-sāʾiḥūn* at Q 9:112; see also PIETY; VISITING; FASTING).

Q 16:9 reads: "And unto God leads straight the way" *(wa-ʿalā llāhi qaṣdu l-sabīl),* highlighting the fact that one's very life is a journey (cf. Gimaret, *Jubbāʾī,* 543 for a reading of this as God's imparting of knowledge; see KNOWLEDGE AND LEARNING) and that life's destination is God: *innā lillāhi wa-innā ilayhi rājiʿūn* (Q 2:156). The path to [God] is called by the Qurʾān *al-ṣirāṭ al-mustaqīm.* Though typically described as straight, most famously at Q 1:6 (*ihdinā l-ṣirāṭa l-mustaqīm,* "guide us to the straight path"), it is also described as "the path of [God], the mighty, the praised" (*ṣirāṭ al-ʿazīz al-ḥamīd,* Q 14:1; see GOD AND HIS ATTRIBUTES; PRAISE; POWER AND IMPOTENCE), contra the path to hellfire (*ṣirāṭ al-jaḥīm,* Q 37:23; see HELL AND HELLFIRE; REWARD AND PUNISHMENT) and contra the path of those who have earned God's wrath (*al-maghḍūb ʿalayhim,* Q 1:7; see Āzād, *Tarjumān al-Qurʾān,* i; see ANGER). The possibility that one can be led astray (q.v.) is in one instance expressed by the righteous (see GOOD AND EVIL) who ask whether they should be "like the one whom the demons have made into a fool (see IGNORANCE), wandering bewildered through the earth" *(ka-lladhī istahwathu l-shayāṭīnu fī l-arḍi),* averring that God's guidance is the only guidance (*inna hudā llāhi huwa l-hudā,* Q 6:71; cf. 10:23). The human need for guidance on earth even extended to Muḥammad: God asks the despairing Prophet (see DESPAIR; HOPE) in Q 93:7, "did he not find you wandering and guide you" *(wa-wajadaka ḍāllan fa-hadā)* — though this is understood by some commentators to mean that Muḥammad was ignorant of God's law (see e.g. Zamakhsharī, *Kashshāf,* iv, 219; see LAW AND THE QURʾĀN).

In this worldly life, one desirable destination is God's house, i.e. the Kaʿba in Mecca (see HOUSE, DOMESTIC AND DIVINE). When the prophet Abraham leaves his home in Mesopotamia because of the idol worship there (see IDOLATRY AND IDOLATERS), he travels to Mecca where he rebuilds God' house, first erected by the prophet Adam (cf. Q 3:96; see ADAM AND EVE) and by the angels (see ANGEL) before him (*Jalālayn,* 62), where worship (q.v.) of the one true God then resumes (Q 2:125).

The pilgrimage (q.v.) to Mecca is enjoined on believers several times (e.g. Q 2:196). And blocking the path to God or that of the pilgrims to the holy precincts (see SACRED PRECINCTS; FIGHTING) is described as a grave offence (*wa-ṣaddun ʿan sabīli llāhi wa-kufrun bihi wa-l-masjid al-ḥarām*, Q 2:217). The peril associated with the trip to Mecca is suggested in the following appeal at Q 22:27: "And proclaim the pilgrimage among people: they will come to you on foot *(rijālan)* and on every kind of mount *(wa-ʿalā kulli ḍāmirin),* from distant mountain highways *(min kulli fajjin ʿamīq).*"

Many of the messengers and prophets in the Qurʾān travel about the earth on foot (see MESSENGER; PROPHETS AND PROPHETHOOD), calling people to belief or leading their people to safety, such as Moses (q.v.; see also MYTHS AND LEGENDS IN THE QURʾĀN). Moses' own life begins with a fateful trip when his mother places him in a basket upon the river to protect him from Pharaoh (q.v.; Q 20:39) who is killing newborn boys (Q 28:4); but Moses is saved when he is picked up and adopted by Pharaoh's wife (identified in commentary as Āsiya, Q 28:9). Moses will in adult life lead the Israelites (see CHILDREN OF ISRAEL) away from Egypt to the holy and promised land (Q 5:21; see also e.g. Q 28:29). That trip includes surviving another body of water (Q 7:138; 10:90), namely the Red Sea; traveling by night (Q 20:77; see DAY AND NIGHT); and wandering in the desert for forty years (Q 5:26; cf. 28:29). Joseph (q.v.; see Q 12) is also cast out (by his plotting brothers; see BROTHER AND BROTHERHOOD). He is picked up by a caravan and transported to Egypt (q.v.), where he eventually rises to a position of authority (q.v.). He is later reunited with his brothers and father who had traveled to Egypt to seek food and sustenance (q.v.) in times of difficulty (see Beeston, *Baiḍāwī's commentary*).

Though less momentous for the religious history of the Israelites, Moses takes another well-known trip in the Qurʾān when he sets out on a journey in search of one of God's elect (Q 18:60-82). He eventually finds this man — unnamed but identified as al-Khaḍir/Khiḍr (q.v.) by Muḥammad — at a confluence and implores him to let him accompany him (Q 18:66). The man reluctantly agrees and they journey along a river (see Q 18:71 for a boat and its passengers) and then on to an unnamed town. Their trip comes to an end when Khiḍr demonstrates to Moses that he (Moses) is unable to abide him and his actions. Earlier, the sūra recounts the story of the companions of the cave (*aṣḥāb al-kahf*, Q 18:9-26; see MEN OF THE CAVE), whose trip is the earliest example of "time travel" in Arabic literature (see TIME; SPATIAL RELATIONS). Later in the same sūra (Q 18:83-101) are described the travels of Dhū l-Qarnayn, many features of whose story resemble those of Alexander (q.v.). In the qurʾānic account, he journeys to the east to deal with Gog and Magog (q.v.), building an iron wall to contain them (Q 18:94). The terrestrial travels of Jesus (q.v.) are not described in the Qurʾān but the fact that he was not captured or crucified but rather raised alive to be with God is mentioned (Q 3:55; see CRUCIFIXION; POLEMIC AND POLEMICAL LANGUAGE; RESURRECTION).

A number of the trips taken by Muḥammad are mentioned in the Qurʾān (see SĪRA AND THE QURʾĀN). His *hijra* or emigration, together with the small Muslim community, north from Mecca to Yathrib/Medina is explicitly mentioned at Q 48:11 where those who opted out of the trip for selfish reasons *(al-mukhallafūna mina l-aʿrābi)* are criticized. At Q 59:8-9 and elsewhere those who did emigrate are praised, as are those who strive in the way of God (Q 2:218; see EMIGRANTS AND HELPERS; HYPOCRITES

AND HYPOCRISY). On his way to Yathrib/ Medina, Muḥammad is reported to have hidden in a cave (q.v.), together with Abū Bakr, to escape Meccan pursuers. This is alluded to at Q 9:40 and foreshadows the reference a few verses later to unbelievers and hypocrites desperately seeking caves in which to hide from God (Q 9:57; see Suyūṭī, *Durr,* iii, 436, 447). Of all Muḥammad's voyages, the most spectacular is the nocturnal one from Mecca to Jerusalem (q.v.), called the *isrāʾ* (and thence to heaven [see HEAVEN AND SKY], called the *miʿrāj*). The *isrāʾ*, or night journey, is the subject of a whole chapter (Q 17, Sūrat al-Isrāʾ), which opens "Glory to God who took his servant for a journey by night *(asrā bi-ʿabdihi laylan)* from the sacred mosque (Mecca) to the farthest mosque" (Jerusalem; Q 17:1; see GLORIFICATION OF GOD).

At Q 29:20, God asks believers to proclaim, "Travel through the earth and see how God originated creation" (q.v.; *qul sīrū fī l-arḍi fa-nẓurū kayfa badaʾa l-khalq;* see Ghazālī, *Jewels,* 126; and cf. e.g. Q 3:137 for travel that reveals the consequences of those who rejected God's messengers; see TRIAL). And at Q 55:33 God urges "O company of jinn and men, if you are able to break through the regions of the heavens and the earth (q.v.), then break through, but (know that) you will not do so without our sanction." This has been interpreted by certain modernists to be an invitation to space travel (see e.g. Haeri, *Keys,* iv, 73; see EXEGESIS OF THE QURʾĀN: EARLY MODERN AND CONTEMPORARY; SCIENCE AND THE QURʾĀN). Terrestrial or otherwise, the prophet Muḥammad recommended the following passage be recited when setting out on a journey: "Glory be to the one who has subjected these [modes of travel] to our use because we could not have accomplished this by ourselves" (*subḥāna lladhī sakhkhara lanā hādhā wa-mā kunnā lahu muqrinīn,* Q 43:13). The possibility that one may die (see DEATH AND THE DEAD) on a trip is adumbrated at Q 31:34: "and no soul (q.v.) knows in what land it will die" (*wa-mā tadrī nafsun bi-ayyi arḍin tamūt;* see also FAREWELL PILGRIMAGE; FESTIVALS AND COMMEMORATIVE DAYS; HOSPITALITY AND COURTESY).

Shawkat M. Toorawa

Bibliography
Primary: A. Azad, *The Tarjumān al-Qurʾān,* vol. 1, trans. S. Abdul Latif, Hyderabad 1978; A.F.L. Beeston, *Baiḍāwī's commentary on sūrah 12 of the Qurʾān,* Oxford 1963; al-Ghazālī, Abū Ḥāmid Muḥammad b. Muḥammad, *The jewels of the Qurʾān. Al-Ghazālī's theory,* trans. M. Abul Quasem, London 1983; Gimaret, *Jubbaʾī;* F. Haeri, *Keys to the Qurʾān,* 5 vols., Reading, UK 1993; *Jalālayn;* Suyūṭī, *Durr;* Ṭabarsī, *Majmaʿ;* Zamakhsharī, *Kashshāf.*
Secondary: C.E. Bosworth, Travel literature, in J. Meisami and P. Starkey (eds), *Encyclopedia of Arabic literature,* London 1998, 778-80; M. Cooperson, Remembering the future. Arabic time travel literature, in *Edebiyat* 8 (1998), 171-89; D. Eickelman and J. Piscatori, Introduction, in ids. (eds.), *Muslim travelers. Pilgrimage, migration and the religious imagination,* Berkeley 1990, 3-25; J.E. Montgomery, Salvation at sea? Seafaring in early Arabic poetry, in G. Borg and E. de Moor (eds.), *Representations of the divine in Arabic poetry,* Amsterdam 2001, 25-48; I.R. Netton, *Seek knowledge. Thought and travel in the house of Islam,* Richmond, Surrey 1996; S.M. Toorawa, Travel in the medieval Islamic world, in R. Allen (ed.), *Eastward bound. Travel and travellers 1050-1550,* Manchester 2004, 86-120; H. Touati, *Islam et voyage au Moyen Age. Histoire et anthropologie d'une pratique lettrée,* Paris 2000; B.M. Wheeler, *Prophets in the Qurʾān. An introduction to the Qurʾān and Muslim exegesis,* London 2002.

Triumph see VICTORY

Troops

Individuals massed together, often to form an army. Qurʾānic references to "troops" in the military sense fall second to those in which "forces" or "hosts" are meant in a more general sense. The military sense also is usually obscured by an emphasis on the

[1] A segment of a contemporary *ḥajj* mural containing qur'ānic verses (e.g. Q 113:1, "Say, 'I seek refuge in the lord of the dawn,'" *qul aʿūdhu bi-rabbi l-falaqi*), composed upon return from the pilgrimage to Mecca. This particular mural is found on the wall of an alabaster shop in Gurna, Egypt (near the Valley of the Kings). Photograph courtesy of Juan Campo.

eschatological thrust of a given reference (e.g. Q 10:90 on Pharaoh's "armies"; see ESCHATOLOGY; PHARAOH). In the second category, a distinction is to be made between temporal and other-worldly "forces" (see also RANKS AND ORDERS).

The relevant terms are principally the hapax legomenon *shirdhima,* and/or *zumar, fawj* and *jund.* The first term, usually translated as "band," occurs in Q 26:54, in Pharaoh's dismissive reference to the Children of Israel (q.v.; *shirdhimatun qalīlūna,* "a worthless little band"). Al-Ṭabarī (d. 310/923; *Tafsīr,* xix, 74) treats it as a small group or "the remnant" of a larger whole. *Zumar* (sing. *zumra*), the usual name of the thirty-ninth sūra (q.v.), occurs there twice as "groups" or "throngs," in the one case (Q 39:71) in reference to those destined for hell (see HELL AND HELLFIRE), and in the second case (Q 39:73) for paradise (q.v.; see also REWARD AND PUNISHMENT). *Fawj* (pl. *afwāj*) occurs synonymously; al-Ṭabarī defines it as "group" *(jamāʿa).* One occurrence (Q 27:83) speaks of the host (of evil-doers) drawn from each community and arranged in ranks. The relevant verbal phrase *yūzaʿūna,* "kept in ranks," has a distinct military ring (see, as Paret suggests, Q 27:17; 41:19).

Jund (pl. *junūd*), the most frequent of the terms, occurs in roughly three ways and, as a result, occasions some debate among early exegetes (see EXEGESIS OF THE QURʾĀN: CLASSICAL AND MEDIEVAL). References to military forces include those to Pharaoh's armies (Q 10:90; 20:78; 28:6, 8, 39-40; 44:24; 51:40; 85:17-18), and to those respectively of Saul (q.v.; Ṭālūt) and Goliath (q.v.; Jālūt; Q 2:249), and of Solomon (q.v.; Q 27:37). On the passage concerning Saul's troops at the river's edge, see M.M. Ayoub (*Qurʾān,* i, 241-3). Less specific occurrences are understood by the exegetes in reference to the Quraysh (q.v.) and others of the Prophet's opponents in battle (see OPPOSITION TO MUḤAMMAD; FIGHTING). Al-Ṭabarī (*Tafsīr,* xxiii, 126), commenting on Q 38:11, puts it in relation to the battle of Badr (q.v.), and Q 33:9 in relation to the Quraysh and their allied forces arrayed against Medina (q.v.) at the battle of the Trench (Ṭabarī, *Tafsīr,* xxi, 126-7; see EXPEDITIONS AND BATTLES). The reference to military forces *per se* is incidental: the forces of Pharaoh are mostly on display to demonstrate the certainty of destruction through divine retribution (e.g. by drowning [q.v.]; see also CHASTISEMENT AND PUNISHMENT; PUNISHMENT STORIES). In addition, these references to "armies" appear to be only loosely connected to the patterns and rules of warfare dealt with at some length elsewhere in the Qurʾān (see WAR). *Jund* also occurs in two references to earthly "forces." Q 37:173 speaks of those aligned with God as inevitably victorious (*ghālibūn;* see VICTORY; PARTIES AND FACTIONS). Q 36:75 seems to refer to the forces of those devoted to idols and false gods who are thus misled (see IDOLS AND IMAGES; ERROR; ASTRAY; POLYTHEISM AND ATHEISM; ENEMIES). Al-Ṭabarī notes a disagreement among his sources on the occasion of the idols' intervention on behalf of their followers (see INTERCESSION). He sides with those who see it as a reference to the forces aligned with the *mushrikūn* on earth and not, in the opposing view, at the day of judgment (see LAST JUDGMENT). A final set of references concerns other-worldly "forces." A sole reference (Q 26:95, using *jund*) refers to the "gathered hosts" of hell led by Iblīs (*junūdu iblīsa ajmaʿūna;* see DEVIL). The remaining examples treat the celestial "hosts" at God's disposal. Q 36:28, 48:4 and 48:7 speak in general of these hosts (respectively, *min jundin mina l-samāʾi, junūdu l-samāwāti wa-l-arḍi*). Q 9:26, 9:40 and 33:9 refer to "hosts that you perceive not" *(junūdan lam tarawhā)* sent down, as is consistently understood by the exegetes, as divine intervention on behalf of the prophet Muḥammad. Al-Ṭabarī (*Tafsīr,* xxiii, 1-2), referring to an early debate over Q 36:28, argues that *jund* is to be understood in terms of "forces" and not, as some suggested, as reference to a new scripture (*risāla;* see REVELATION AND INSPIRATION; SCRIPTURE AND THE QURʾĀN). As for the intervention of the celestial hosts, considerable discussion in the exegetical literature surrounds the angels of Q 3:124-5 (see Ayoub, *Qurʾān,* ii, 314-17; see ANGEL).

Matthew S. Gordon

Bibliography
Primary: Ṭabarī, *Tafsīr,* ed. Shākir (up to Q 14:27); ed. ʿAlī et al.
Secondary: M.M. Ayoub, *The Qurʾān and its interpreters,* 2 vols., Albany 1984, 1992; Paret, *Kommentar.*

Trumpet see ESCHATOLOGY; LAST JUDGMENT; APOCALYPSE

Trust and Patience

Belief in another's integrity, justice or reliability, and forbearance in the face of adversity. According to the Qurʾān, trust and patience are two distinguishing virtues (see VIRTUES AND VICES, COMMANDING AND FORBIDDING) of the "faithful" person (i.e. *muʾmin;* see BELIEF AND UNBELIEF). There are two qurʾānic concepts typically translated by the English word "trust." The first, *tawakkul (ʿalā),* is a *maṣdar* (abstract noun expressing action) derived from the fifth form of the Arabic root *w-k-l,* meaning "to give oneself over to" *(istaslama ilayhi),* "to rely/depend on" *(iʿtamada ʿalayhi),* or "have confidence in" *(wathiqa bihi)* another as *wakīl,* that is as one's "guardian" or "protector" (i.e. *ḥāfiẓ; Lisān al-ʿArab,* xv, 387; Bustānī, *Muḥīṭ,* 984; see CLIENTS AND CLIENTAGE). Evidence from classical Arab grammarians (see GRAMMAR AND THE QURʾĀN; ARABIC LANGUAGE) suggests that, in pre-Islamic usage, the word *wakīl* was nearly synonymous to the word *rabb* (a qurʾānic term applied to God and most commonly translated as "lord" [q.v.]) in the sense that both imply a position, not primarily of ownership, but of responsibility (q.v.) to nurture to its fullest potential the thing, animal, or person over which the *wakīl/rabb* has charge (*Lisān al-ʿArab,* ibid.; Bayḍāwī, *Anwār,* ad Q 1:2). Although the word *tawakkul* does not itself occur in the Qurʾān, the fifth-form verb meaning "to trust [in God]" (in various tenses and moods, i.e. *tawakkala, yatawakkalu, tawakkal*), and the fifth-form active participle from the root *w-k-l (mutawakkil)* meaning "entrusting oneself [to God]" are attested a total of forty-four times.

The second qurʾānic concept understood to mean "trust" is *amāna,* a *maṣdar* derived from the root *ʾ-m-n* and ordinarily used to refer to something given "in trust" *(wadīʿa)* with the expectation that it will be cared for diligently and faithfully by the trustee. (*Lisān al-ʿArab,* i, 223 and 224; Bustānī, *Muḥīṭ,* 17). This word *(amāna)* occurs in the Qurʾān a total of six times. In only one of these six occurrences (Q 33:72) does the word "trust" (i.e. *al-amāna*) have cosmic significance as the 'covenant (q.v.) of obedience' (q.v.; *ṭāʿa*) that is the foundation of the divine-human relationship (see Ṭabarī, *Tafsīr;* Bayḍāwī, *Anwār,* ad Q 33:72).

The qurʾānic concept typically translated by the English word "patience" is *ṣabr,* a *maṣdar* from the first form of the Arabic root *ṣ-b-r* originally having to do with binding or "restraining a living creature" *(ḥabs al-rūḥ)* for prolonged slaughter or execution (see also SACRIFICE; CONSECRATION OF ANIMALS), but also coming to mean — especially in a qurʾānic context — to exercise "self-restraint" *(ḥabs al-nafs),* "to be persistent," and/or "to endure great adversity" (*Lisān al-ʿArab,* vii, 275; Bustānī, *Muḥīṭ,* 496). *Ṣabr* — along with other derivatives of the same root, including: the first-form verb meaning "to have patience" (in various tenses and moods, i.e. *ṣabara, yaṣbiru, iṣbir*); the third-form verb *(ṣābara)* meaning "to excel in patience" or "compete with one another in forbearance"; the eighth-form verb *(iṣṭabara)* meaning "to be patient"; the first-form active participle *(ṣābir)* meaning "having patience"; and the first-form intensive noun *(ṣabbār)* meaning "of the utmost patience" — is attested in the Qurʾān a total of 103 times. It is important to note that, although in one hundred of these 103 attestations *ṣabr* and other derivatives from the same root carry the virtuous connotation of "patient endurance," in the remaining three cases *ṣabr* does connote the vice of "stubborn persistence" in the worship of ancestral deities (Q 25:42; 38:6; see POLYTHEISM AND ATHEISM) as well as in other errant behaviors (Q 41:24; see ERROR; ASTRAY).

Tawakkul

In the Qurʾān, God is the only proper object of *tawakkul.* Thus, in a qurʾānic context, *tawakkul* is best understood as a human being's "absolute trust in," or "unmitigated reliance upon," God *(tawakkul ʿalā llāh).* In this sense, *tawakkul* is, as Izutsu notes (*Concepts,* 62), a fundamental component of *īmān,* the qurʾānic term for "faith" (q.v.). This is particularly evident in those five verses which make it explicitly incumbent on the faithful to place their absolute trust in God: "And it is in God that the faithful must place their absolute trust" (*wa ʿalā llāhi fa-l-yatawakkali l-muʾminūn,* Q 3:122; 5:11; 14:11; 58:10; 64:13). Of these five verses, two (Q 5:11; 64:13) speak about *tawakkul* as a general moral and spiritual imperative, with each verse drawing an essential connection between *tawakkul* and a specific component of faith. In the case of Q 5:11 this component is *taqwā* or "God-consciousness" (Asad, *Message,* passim; see FEAR), and in the case of Q 64:13 this component is *ṭāʿa* or "obedience" to both God and God's messenger (q.v.; i.e. Muḥammad [q.v.]; cf. Q 64:12). The remaining three verses refer to specific instances of extreme duress in the context of which *tawakkul* becomes the key to survival for the person of faith. Each of these instances involves a confrontation with powerful enemies (q.v.) whose goal is the ultimate dissolution of their would-be victim's faith. In Q 3:122 there is the implication that it was the faithful's absolute trust in God that yielded the miraculous victory (q.v.) of the vastly outnumbered Muslim army at Badr (q.v.), and that it was Muḥammad's absolute trust in God that prevented the ultimate desertion of the Banū Salima and the Banū Ḥāritha clans at Uḥud, and thus forestalled the Meccans from completely decimating the Muslim forces that day (Ṭabarī, *Tafsīr;* Bayḍāwī, *Anwār,* ad Q 3:122; see EXPEDITIONS AND BATTLES; MECCA). In Q 14:11 we find the trope of the *tawakkul* of God's messengers as their only real source of resistance against those who deny the validity of their message (*innā kafarnā bi-mā ursiltum bihi,* Q 14:9) and who seek to do harm to God's messengers. And finally, in Q 58:10 *tawakkul* is presented as the best defense against the most powerful enemy of all — Satan (*al-shayṭān;* see DEVIL) — who insinuates himself into the "private" or "secret conversations" *(munājāt)* of human beings, threatening to destroy the faithful and their community, not from without, but from within.

The mainstream theological rationale for the centrality of *tawakkul* to the life of faith is rooted in the important qurʾānic teaching regarding the divine power of determination over everything *(qadar)* and the divine "decree" *(qaḍāʾ*; see FREEDOM AND PREDESTINATION). There are, for example, two verses (Q 33:3, 48) in which God warns Muḥammad never to yield to "those who deny God" *(al-kāfirīn;* see LIE; GRATITUDE AND INGRATITUDE) and to the "hypocrites" *(al-munāfiqīn;* see HYPOCRITES AND HYPOCRISY) — especially when, at one point, they seek reconciliation by pressuring him to compromise the integrity of the divine message and recognize the intercessory role of certain pagan deities before God (Bayḍāwī, *Anwār,* ad Q 33:1-2). Even when such a compromise appears to be the sine qua non of Muslim survival in an overwhelmingly pagan environment, Muḥammad is told that compromise is not an option. Instead, both verses (Q 33:3, 48) go on to enjoin the Prophet — and, by implication, all the faithful — to place absolute trust in God *(tawakkal ʿalā llāh)* precisely because "God is the guardian *(wakīl)* who never fails" *(wa-kafā bi-llāhi wakīlan).* For classical Sunnī exegetes (see EXEGESIS OF THE QURʾĀN: CLASSICAL AND MEDIEVAL) such as al-Bayḍāwī (d. prob. 716/1316-17), the statement, "God is the guardian who never fails" (Q 33:3, 48) is synonymous with the statement in Q 39:62, "God is the guardian of everything" *(wa-huwa ʿalā kulli shayʾin wakīlun);* each statement means that "all matters are in God's charge" *(mawkūlan ilayhi l-umūru kulluhā;* Bayḍāwī, *Anwār,* ad Q 33:3), or that God "has absolute power of disposal [over all things]" *(yatawallā l-taṣarruf;* Bayḍāwī, *Anwār,* ad Q 39:62).

Modern translators and exegetes (see EXEGESIS OF THE QURʾĀN: EARLY MODERN AND CONTEMPORARY) such as Muḥammad Asad (d. 1412/1992) agree and point out that the qurʾānic references to God as *wakīl* (i.e. the only proper object of *tawakkul*) allude "to God's exclusive power to *determine the fate* of any created being or thing" (Asad, *Message,* ad Q 17:2). In general, therefore, the qurʾānic imperative that the faithful place their absolute trust *(tawakkul)* in God, and the corollary imperative that they adopt no one other than God as the ultimate guardian of their affairs (e.g. Q 17:2) have a deep semantic and theological connection to the well known qurʾānic refrain, attested a total of thirty-five times: "God has the power of determination over everything" *(Allāh* [or simply *huwa*] *ʿalā kulli shayʾin qadīrun).* In other words, the only proper human response to the absolute and limitless nature of God's power of determination over all things *(qadar)* is an equally absolute and limitless trust in, and reliance upon, God. Anything less would necessarily imply the sin of *shirk* — ascribing a partner to the partner-less God — and would thus seriously compromise one's faith.

Ṣabr

Reference to Job (q.v.) as a paradigmatic embodiment of the virtue of patience is as deeply qurʾānic as it is biblical. Of the four appearances of the prophet Ayyūb (i.e. the biblical "Job") in the Qurʾān (Q 4:163; 6:84; 21:83-5; 38:41-4) two are substantive and make reference to Ayyūb's legendary afflictions (i.e. Q 21:83-5; 38:41-4). There is, however, at least one important difference between the biblical portrait of Job and the qurʾānic portrait of Ayyūb (see SCRIPTURE AND THE QURʾĀN; NARRATIVES; MYTHS AND LEGENDS IN THE QURʾĀN). Though both are portrayed as enduring great adversity, unlike Job, Ayyūb is not depicted as being plagued by the problem of theodicy. Not only does Ayyūb refrain from cursing the day he was born (cf. Job 3:1-12), but he not once — as does Job — attributes his travails to God (cf. Job 6:4; 8:17-18; 10:3, 8, 16; 13:24; 16:7, etc.); nor does he ask God for the reason he is suffering (q.v.; cf. Job 6:24; 10:2b); nor does he protest that "there is no justice" (cf. Job 19:7b; see JUSTICE AND INJUSTICE); nor does he witness to his own "righteousness" (cf. Job 29:14-20; 31:5-40). In keeping with the highly idealized qurʾānic presentation of the prophets (see PROPHETS AND PROPHETHOOD) and messengers of God as nearly perfect in their submission (i.e. *islām*) to God's will, Ayyūb merely mentions his tribulations (*annī massaniya l-ḍurru* and *annī massaniya l-shayṭānu bi-nuṣbin wa-ʿadhābin*, Q 21:83 and 38:41, respectively), and in the very same breath — without ever explicitly asking for deliverance — praises God as "the most merciful of the merciful ones" (*wa-anta arḥamu l-rāḥimīn*, Q 21:83; see MERCY; GOD AND HIS ATTRIBUTES). Thus, in both the Bible and the Qurʾān, neither Job nor Ayyūb ever curses God (see CURSE); in their respective literary traditions both are regarded as paragons of patience because of their ability to endure great adversity without cursing God. The one significant difference, however, is that the Qurʾān seems to set the threshold of "patience" a bit higher for Ayyūb than the Bible does for Job. Whereas Job's patience allows him to question God, including asking God why he should be patient (Job 6:11); and whereas Job is only silenced in humility when God speaks to him "out of the whirlwind" (Job 38), Ayyūb's patience has no questions for God — only praise and dutiful silence.

This difference is significant because it underscores the degree to which the qurʾānic proclamation of Ayyūb's *ṣabr* or paradigmatic "patience" (*[ayyūb] wa-ismāʿīl wa-idrīsa wa-dhā l-kifli kullun mina l-ṣābirīn*, Q 21:85 and *innā wajadnāhu ṣābiran*, Q 38:44) is predicated, not only on his endurance, but quite specifically on his *unquestioning* and presumably placid acceptance of suffering and adversity (see also ISHMAEL; IDRĪS; DHŪ L-KIFL). Nowhere is this link between *ṣabr* and a thoroughly unquestioning and tranquil disposition more apparent than in the story of the prophet Moses (q.v.; Mūsā) and the mysterious 'servant of God' (see SERVANTS) known to traditions of qurʾānic exegesis as "Khiḍr" (Q 18:65-82; see KHAḌIR/KHIḌR). Here, although the adversity is not his own (perhaps we are to presume that, as a prophet, Moses did indeed have the patience of Ayyūb when it came to his own personal suffering?), Moses cannot abide the seemingly antinomian acts (i.e. Q 18:71, 74, 77) of his newfound teacher without asking for a reason or justification. In so doing, however, Moses loses the privilege of discipleship which was originally established on the basis of the stipulation that the prophet would bear patiently (i.e. unquestioningly — *fa-lā tasʾalnī ʿan shayʾin ḥattā uḥditha laka minhu dhikran*, Q 18:70) with Khiḍr. The first two times Moses impatiently asks a question of Khiḍr, the latter chastises the former with the words, "Did I not say, 'You will not be able to bear with me patiently'?" (*a-lam aqul innaka lan tastaṭīʿa maʿiya ṣabran*, Q 18:72; cf. 18:75). The third time Moses breaks his vow of patience, Khiḍr finally declares "This is the parting of the ways between me and you" (*hādhā firāqu baynī wa-baynika*, Q 18:78). Although Khiḍr is willing to give Moses a third and final justification for the former's third antinomian act, he makes it clear to Moses that he has not yet cultivated the patience necessary to receive the special "knowledge learned through intimacy" with God (i.e. *ʿilm ladunnī* from *wa-ʿallamnāhu min ladunnā ʿilman*, Q 18:65; see Schimmel, *Dimensions*, 193), knowledge that he might otherwise have received from Khiḍr had he been able "to bear patiently what he did not comprehend" (*wa-kayfa taṣbiru ʿalā mā lam tuḥiṭ bihi khubran*, Q 18:68). This connection between unquestioning patience (*ṣabr*) and special knowledge (*ʿilm laddunī*) — a connection which is made quite explicit in the narrative of the encounter between Moses and Khiḍr — comes to play a central role in Ṣūfī (see ṢŪFISM AND THE QURʾĀN) understandings of "patience" (see below).

Tawwakul *and* ṣabr

In three instances (Q 14:12; 16:42; 29:59) the Qurʾān makes it clear that, on a foundational level, the concepts of *ṣabr* and *tawakkul* belong to what Izutsu refers to as a single "semantic category" (Izutsu, *Concepts*, 9). In all three of these instances, the qurʾānic concepts of trust *(tawakkul)* and patience *(ṣabr)* are understood as defining and informing each other. In Q 14:12, we find one of the many qurʾānic accounts of how all of God's messengers at one time or another faced great adversity, especially in the form of persecution at the hands of those who refused to accept their messages (see OPPOSITION TO MUḤAMMAD). Yet all of these messengers "patiently endured" whatever harm might come their way, "placing absolute trust in God." The messengers are quoted as having said to themselves and their persecutors, "Why should we not place absolute trust in God when he has guided us along our ways? We shall patiently endure whatever harm you might bring us! Let those who trust place absolute trust in God [and God alone]!" In Q 16:42, the original group of Meccan faithful who emigrated with Muḥammad to Medina (q.v.; i.e. the *muhājirūn*) in the year 1/622 are described as "those who have patiently endured and place absolute trust in their lord" *(alladhīna ṣabarū wa-ʿalā rabbihim yatawakkalūn;* see EMIGRATION). For al-Bayḍāwī, these émigrés endured "adversities such as the persecution of those who deny God and separation from their homeland" *(ṣabarū ʿalā l-shadāʾidi ka-adhā l-kuffār wa-mufāraqati l-waṭan)* precisely by "keeping their exclusive attention on God, realizing that every matter is in his charge" *(munqaṭiʿīn ilā llāh mufawwiḍīn ilayhi l-amra kullahu*; Bayḍāwī, *Anwār*, ad Q 16:42). In Q 29:59, "those who are faithful and do righteous deeds" *(alladhīna āmanū wa-ʿamilū l-ṣāliḥāt*, Q 29:58; see GOOD DEEDS; GOOD AND EVIL) are promised paradise (q.v.) and are declared to be "those who have patiently endured, and place absolute trust in their lord" (cf. Q 16:42).

In addition to pairing "patience" and "trust" into a single semantic category, the Qurʾān does the same with "patience" and "thankfulness" *(shukr)*. There are, in fact, four occurrences of an identical refrain in which an intensive noun-form *(ism al-mubālagha)* of both roots (i.e. *ṣabbār* and *shakūr*) are placed in apposition to each other (i.e. Q 14:5; 31:31; 34:19; 42:33). Each of these verses mentions an astonishing occurrence (e.g. the deliverance of the Hebrews from bondage and ships cruising on the seas; see CHILDREN OF ISRAEL; SHIPS), and in reference to the occurrence declares: "Surely in that there are signs (q.v.) for every truly patient and thankful person" *(inna fī dhālika la-āyātin li-kulli ṣabbārin shakūrin)*. This qurʾānic pairing of the concepts of the "patient" and the "thankful" person eventually becomes the basis for Ṣūfī teaching that while patience in adversity is undoubtedly a virtue, an even greater virtue lies in the capacity to go beyond patience and actually express genuine thankfulness to God for the purgative opportunities inherent in every trial (q.v.; see Schimmel, *Dimensions*, 124-5).

Ṣūfī interpretations of tawakkul *and* ṣabr

The *Tafsīr al-Qurʾān al-karīm* (published under the name of the great Ṣūfī master and mystical theologian Ibn al-ʿArabī [d. 638/1240], but actually the work of ʿAbd al-Razzāq al-Kāshānī [d. 730/1329]) draws a direct connection between "patience" *(ṣabr)* and "courage" (q.v.; *shajāʿa*), while at the same time rooting both of them in the deepest profession of the oneness of God *(tawḥīd Allāh)*. In his exegesis of Q 3:145-51, a set of verses discussing the "patience" of the many prophets who fought for the sake of God (see FIGHTING; PATH OR WAY; JIHĀD) without ever "flagging" or "growing weak" in either body or spirit *(mā wahanū... wa-mā ḍaʿufū)*, the author argues that the "terror" *(ruʿb)* that eventually erupts in the hearts of the enemies of God's prophets "is a result of their ascribing partners to God" *(musabbaban ʿan shirkihim)*. The exegete goes on to explain that "courage and the other virtues [such as absolute trust in God] emerge out of the proper balance of the faculties of the lower self when it exists beneath the [luminous] shadow of the divine oneness; that is, when it is illuminated by the light of the heart enlightened by the light of the divine oneness. [Courage], therefore, truly attains its fullness only when the one who professes the oneness of God [in thought, word, and deed] has attained certitude in his or her profession" (ibid.). In this passage, the author is attempting to convey the deeper meaning of a legend regarding the state of the great Ṣūfī Shaqīq al-Balkhī's heart. According to Shaqīq's longtime companion, Ḥātim b. al-Aṣamm, one day — in the midst of an intensifying battle — Shaqīq put down his weapon, put his head on his shield, and fell asleep on the battlefield to the point that Ḥātim could hear him snoring. "This," al-Kāshānī [pseudo. Ibn al-ʿArabī] writes, "is the ultimate state of reliance on God and confidence in him; it belongs to the faculty of absolute certitude" *(wa-hādhā ghāyatun fī sukūni l-qalbi ilā llāhi wa-wuthūqihi bihi li-quwwati l-yaqīn;* ibid.).

It is no coincidence that al-Kāshānī (pseudo. Ibn al-ʿArabī) reflects on the attainment of absolute certitude in professing God's oneness in his exegesis of a qurʾānic passage which, at one point, proclaims God's "love" (q.v.; *ḥubb* or *maḥabba*) for the "patient" *(wa-llāhu yuḥibbu l-ṣābirīn,* Q 3:146). Just thirteen verses later, in the very same chapter, the Qurʾān also proclaims God's love for those who have absolute trust in him *(inna llāha yuḥibbu l-mutawakkilīn,* Q 3:159). Since, for the Ṣūfīs, love is the medium par excellence for the purification of the soul (q.v.), any quality in the human being which occasions divine love must be a quality which is indispensable for the perfection of the human heart. Therefore, as a Ṣūfī, al-Kāshānī (pseudo. Ibn al-ʿArabī) understands patience and trust not only to be "distinguishing marks of the person of faith" (*ʿunwān al-muʾmin;* see Bayḍāwī, *Anwār,* ad Q 14:5), but as stations *(maqāmāt)* and states *(aḥwāl)* of the interior mystical journey to the goal of unqualified profession of divine oneness (i.e. *tawḥīd*). For this author, as for many Ṣūfīs before and after him, trust and patience become two of the key ingredients in the alchemy of spiritual purification and the achievement of human perfection.

In his magnum opus, *The Revivification of the religious sciences (Iḥyāʾ ʿulūm al-dīn),* the renowned medieval Sunnī jurist, theologian, and mystic, Abū Ḥāmid al-Ghazālī (d. 505/1111), devotes an entire book to the subject of the "profession of divine oneness and absolute trust in God" (bk. 35, *Kitāb al-Tawḥīd wa-l-tawakkul*) and another entire book to the subject of "patience and thankfulness" (bk. 32, *Kitāb al-Ṣabr wa-l-shukr*). In his treatment of *tawakkul,* al-Ghazālī articulates the thesis, later developed by (the real) Ibn al-ʿArabī and others, that absolute trust in God is "[not only] one of the stations of those who possess certitude, but it is also indicative of one of the highest ranks of those who are drawn near to God" *(wa-maqāmun min maqāmāti l-mūqinīn bal huwa min maʿālī darajāti l-muqarrabīn*; Ghazālī, *Iḥyāʾ,* xiii, 154/2490). Al-Ghazālī argues that because the profession of the divine oneness *(tawḥīd)* is the source or root *(aṣl)* of *tawakkul*, the perfection of both are coterminous. This is why al-Ghazālī correlates the attainment of absolute trust in God with what he refers to as the "fourth [and highest] degree" *(al-rutba l-rābiʿa)* of the profession of divine oneness. It is the state in which the one who has attained it "does not perceive anything in existence, but one being.... [This is the person] whom the Ṣūfīs designate as [having attained the state of] 'passing away in the divine oneness' from whence he or she perceives nothing but one being, and thus does not even perceive him or herself" (Ghazālī, *Iḥyāʾ*, xiii, 158/2494).

From al-Ghazālī's perspective, however, the problem with *tawakkul* is not the understanding that, as a spiritual state, it is coterminous with complete realization of the divine oneness. The problem, rather, is with erroneous understandings that the attainment of *tawakkul* is marked by a radical trust in God which eschews all purposive action on the part of the human person (Ghazālī, *Iḥyāʾ*, xiii, 154/2490). ʿAbd al-Qādir al-Jīlānī (d. 561/1166) deals with this very same issue in his "Satisfaction for those who seek the path of truth" *(Kitāb al-Ghunya li-ṭālibī ṭarīqi l-ḥaqq)* where he quotes a well-known ḥadīth (see ḤADĪTH AND THE QURʾĀN), reported on the authority of Anas b. Mālik (d. ca. 92/711), which appears to be a scriptural *locus classicus* for reflecting on the relationship between absolute trust in God and responsible purposive action on the part of the human being (see Ibn Abī l-Dunyā, *Tawakkul*, n. 11, 46). According to al-Jīlānī's version of this ḥadīth, a man arrives riding on a she-camel which belongs to him and says, "O messenger of God, shall I just leave her [i.e. unattended] and place my trust [in God]?" *(adiʿuhā wa-atawakkalu)*. To which Muḥammad replies, "Tie her up, and then

place your trust [in God]" *(iʿqilhā wa-tawakkal;* Jīlānī, *Ghunya*, 219). Both al-Ghazālī and al-Jīlānī represent mainstream Ṣūfī teaching that the attainment of *tawakkul* should have no effect on whether one responsibly fulfills one's duties to God and to others, but simply on how attached one is to outcomes.

As for *ṣabr*, al-Ghazālī quotes two ḥadīth that have been attributed to the Prophet. The first is a report with a weak chain of transmission and which states plainly, "Faith has two halves: patience and thankfulness" *(fa-inna l-īmāna niṣfāni niṣfu ṣabrin wa-niṣfu shukrin;* Ghazālī, *Iḥyāʾ*, xii, 32/2176), and in doing so echoes the original qurʾānic coupling of *ṣabr* with *shukr* (see above). The second has a much stronger chain than the first and simply reads, "Patience is half of faith" *(al-ṣabru niṣfu l-īmān;* Ghazālī, *Iḥyāʾ*, xii, 33/2177). As al-Ghazālī sees it, the other half of faith to be coupled with "patience" can be construed to be either "certitude" *(yaqīn)* or "thankfulness" *(shukr)*, depending on one's perspective on faith. If one thinks of faith primarily from the perspective of belief, then "'certitude' refers to those definitive types of knowledge (see KNOWLEDGE AND LEARNING) that come through God's guidance of his servant to the fundamental principles of religion (q.v.), and 'patience' refers to action on the basis of that certitude" (Ghazālī, *Iḥyāʾ*, xii, 42/2186). Thus certitude is the first half and patience the second half of faith. If, however, one thinks of faith primarily from the perspective of states of being that give rise to various types of practice — and one identifies one state as appropriate for that which benefits the servant in this life and the next, and another for that which harms the servant in this life and the next, then "'patience' is the state that correlates with what is harmful and 'thankfulness' the state which correlates with what is beneficial" (*wa lahu bi-l-iḍāfati ilā mā yaḍurruhu ḥālu l-ṣabri wa bi-l-iḍāfati ilā mā yanfaʿuhu ḥālu l-shukr;* Ghazālī, *Iḥyāʾ,* ibid.; see GOOD AND EVIL; REWARD AND PUNISHMENT). Whichever perspective one might prefer, patience remains one of the necessary and paramount virtues of the faithful person. As al-Ghazālī writes, "The majority of the virtues of faith enter through [the door of] patience" (*fa-aktharu akhlāqi l-īmāni dākhilun fī l-ṣabr;* Ghazālī, *Iḥyāʾ,* xii, 43/2187).

As for mainstream Ṣūfī teaching on the relationship between "trust" and "patience" — not so much as cardinal virtues of the faithful person, but as stations and states on the mystical path — the following anecdote communicates one of the dominant perspectives: "Abu ʿAlī al-Rūdhbārī... said, 'With respect to absolute trust in God *(tawakkul),* there are three levels. The first is [the servant of God's] thankfulness *(shukr)* when [something he or she wants] is bestowed upon him or her, and patience *(ṣabr)* when he or she is denied. The second is when it is one and the same whether the servant is denied [what he or she wants] or it is bestowed upon him or her. The third is when the servant meets denial with thankfulness — denial being more dear to him or her [than bestowal] because of his or her knowledge that this is God's choice for him or her'" (Jīlānī, *Ghunya,* 217).

Scott C. Alexander

Bibliography

Primary: ʿAbd al-Bāqī; M. Asad, *The message of the Qurʾān,* London 1980; Bayḍāwī, *Anwār,* 2 vols., Beirut 1420/1999; B. Bustānī, *Muḥīṭ al-muḥīṭ,* Beirut 1867, repr. 1998; *The Holy Bible (NRSV),* Catholic ed., Oxford 1999; al-Ghazālī, Abū Ḥāmid Muḥammad, *Iḥyāʾ ʿulūm al-dīn,* Cairo 1938 (vols. xii and xiii); Ibn Abī l-Dunyā, *Kitāb al-Tawakkul ʿalā llāh,* ed. J.F. al-Dawsarī, Beirut 1987; Ibn al-ʿArabī, *Tafsīr;* al-Jīlānī, ʿAbd al-Qādir, *Kitāb al-Ghunya li-ṭālibī ṭarīq al-ḥaqq,* Beirut 1996; *Lisān al-ʿArab,* Beirut 1977 (vols. i, vii, and xv); Ṭabarī, *Tafsīr,* ed. Shākir.

Secondary: D. Burrell (trans.), *Al-Ghazali. Faith in divine unity and trust in divine providence,* Louisville 2001; Izutsu, *Concepts;* H. E. Kassis, *A concordance of the Qurʾān,* Berkeley 1983; Lane; H.T. Littlejohn (trans.), *al-Ghazali on patience and thankfulness. Book XXXII of the Revival of the religious sciences (*Iḥyāʾ ʿulūm al-dīn*),* Cambridge 2005; B. Reinert, *Die Lehre vom tawakkul in der älteren Sufik,* Berlin 1968; A. Schimmel, *Mystical dimensions of Islam,* Chapel Hill, NC 1979; W. Wright, *A grammar of the Arabic language,* Cambridge 1859-1862, repr. 1981.

Truth

That which is established by evidential or experiential proof. A number of qurʾānic lexemes convey this significance *(ḥaqq, qayyim, ṣawāb, ṣadaqa/ṣidq), ḥaqq* being the most prevalent. Evidence abounds in the Muslim tradition to support a multivalent understanding of *ḥaqq* as alternatively "true" or "real," yet that is only the beginning of a story with a pre-history. "The original meaning of the Arabic root *ḥ-q-q* has been obscured but can be recovered by reference to the corresponding root in Hebrew with its meanings of (a) 'to cut in, engrave' in wood, stone or metal, (b) 'to inscribe, write, portray'" (Macdonald and Calverley, Ḥaqq). From this it can be inferred that "the primary meaning of *ḥaqq* in Arabic is 'established fact'..., and therefore 'truth' is secondary; its opposite is *bāṭil* [vain] (in both readings)" (ibid.). Yet as one of the ninety-nine canonical "names of God" (see GOD AND HIS ATTRIBUTES), *ḥaqq* will exploit both of these meanings as well as the original notions of forming or inscribing. Besides the five times the term is introduced formally as a divine name, it is found 247 times in the Qurʾān.

Beyond these philological considerations, we must attend to our understanding of "true," and even of "real," in order to grasp the import of this term in the Qurʾān and hence for Muslims. To appreciate the complexities involved, let us canvas the transformations needed in our prima facie grasp of these notions. At least since the development of Hellenic philosophy, reinforced by medieval scholars and in a peculiar way by modernity, "true" is properly applied to statements rather than to things, whereas "real" is paradigmatically said of things. The crucial difference presented by qurʾānic use centers on the creator, one of whose proper names — *al-ḥaqq* — should remind us that whatever be true or real about everything else, the created universe derives from this One who is paradigmatically true and real (see CREATION; COSMOLOGY). Since the concept of a free creator is shared by all Abrahamic faiths (see RELIGION; ABRAHAM), Western medieval scholars also underlined this difference, introducing a novel notion of the "truth of things," whereby things (as created) can be said to conform to the creator's intent, much as statements conforming to what is the case can be said to be true. So if God, the free creator, is paradigmatically true, then events or things will be true (or false) as they conform (or fail to conform) to the creator's intent. Yet that intent cannot be discerned from creatures themselves, whose derived status is hardly perspicuous, so humankind has been gifted with the Qurʾān (see REVELATION AND INSPIRATION). While the primacy of creation can hardly be gainsaid, without the guidance of the Qurʾān there can be no access to things-as-created, nor *a fortiori* to the creator. So while the creator's intent is what makes things be, and be what they are, it is the Qurʾān which makes that intent known, in the measure that it can be made manifest at all, giving to the notion of truth in the Qurʾān a radical coherence (with divine intent) as well as correspondence with what is.

Hence the very One "who sent down upon you the book with the truth" (Q 3:3), "verifies the truth by his words" (Q 8:7; 10:82). If the creating word makes things to be, "it is he who created the heavens and the earth (q.v.) in truth" (Q 6:73; see HEAVEN AND SKY), and that same word in the Qurʾān becomes the "call to the truth" (Q 13:14) and the ground by which a people "guide [others] in the truth" (Q 7:159, 181) and to the truth. Hence the centrality of promise "be patient; surely God's promise is true" (Q 30:60; cf. 31:33; see TRUST AND PATIENCE); indeed the Qurʾān is given "that they might know that God's promise is true" (Q 18:21), even though the truth asserted there remains to be fulfilled. For with promise comes faith (q.v.), "those who believe follow the truth from their lord" (q.v.; Q 47:3), which is the Qurʾān "guiding to the truth and to a straight path" (Q 46:30; see PATH OR WAY). Notice how "truth" can never be anyone's possession; it remains a lure yet with definite parameters for the search: the "straight path" (Q 1:6) of the Qurʾān together with the sunna (q.v.) or traditions of the Prophet (see ḤADĪTH AND THE QURʾĀN), enshrined in and interpreted by the community or *umma* (see COMMUNITY AND SOCIETY IN THE QURʾĀN). So the truth revealed in the Qurʾān becomes a path to discovering the "truth of things" as created, by which one can hope to find one's way to the creator. Only then, according to the Ṣūfīs (see ṢŪFISM AND THE QURʾĀN), will the promise, the hope and the faith, be transmuted in such a way that one could begin to say with al-Ḥallāj (exec. 309/922): *Anā l-ḥaqq,* "I am the truth" (Massignon, *Passion,* 216-18). Yet however coherently and properly it may be expressed, the very fact that *ḥaqq* is one of the names which God gives himself in the Qurʾān assures us that the path which is the Qurʾān and the sunna will lead us from the term to the divine name by a process designed to transform us. As emphasized in Ṣūfī thought, this is one more manifestation of the way in which the exoteric can meld into the esoteric in Islam (see POLYSEMY), as believers who walk the path come to realize its transforming power.

The Qurʾān consistently contrasts those who accept the truth in faith with those who reject it: "We brought you the truth but most of you were averse to the truth" (Q 43:78; see LIE; BELIEF AND UNBELIEF), where the reference is to Jesus' (q.v.) followers who placed him on a level with God (see CHRISTIANS AND CHRISTIANITY; POLYTHEISM AND ATHEISM; POLEMIC AND POLEMICAL LANGUAGE). Yet here, too, the truth will emerge when "they encounter their day promised them" (Q 43:83; see LAST JUDGMENT; ESCHATOLOGY). So any denial of the truth — especially the truth of creation — will be short-lived, for when "the promised truth draws near, then the unbelievers, their eyes wild with terror, will say: 'Woe betide us! We were heedless of this!'" (Q 21:97). Moreover, such a denouement is perfectly reasonable, for such is the nature of things: "to return to us is the destiny of each and all. Whoever has done good deeds (q.v.), being a believer, will not find his endeavors denied" (Q 21:93-4). So the truth which things owe to their being created freely by a wise God will be realized in those who believe the truth revealed to them, while the reverse side of the same truth will be realized for those who reject that revelation (see REWARD AND PUNISHMENT). Since there is no escaping this creating truth, it is best to follow the "straight path" to its benign realization. Yet if the revelation of the Qurʾān is the precondition for human beings to realize their true reality, the community engendered by that revealed truth will offer them the way to attain it. So "true" and "truth" in the Qurʾān have an inescapably "performative" dimension, on God's part as well as ours: "God meant to verify the truth of his words by the total rout of the truth-rejecters, demonstrating how true the truth is and how vain the falsehood" (Q 8:7-8). "This is truth, certain truth" (Q 56:95; 69:51), or alternatively, the "truth of certainty," *ḥaqq al-yaqīn*, where *yaqīn* carries more metaphysical than epistemological connotations: the truth which stands fast. The Qurʾān is less concerned with our hold on what is true than with truth's hold on us; and rightly so, since we cannot "hold onto" a truth meant to be realized in and through our "return" to it as our source. That is why the final consequence of that return is less individual reward than it is human access to the divine manifestation, even though justice (see JUSTICE AND INJUSTICE) demands that believers be recompensed, positively or negatively, for an act which is theirs. Accepting the offer would not be free were we not able to refuse it, so the truth the Qurʾān insists will be realized bears no hint of determinism (see FREEDOM AND PREDESTINATION). The human capacity to accept or reject is internally linked with the "graceful" offer which the Qurʾān extends (see GRACE; BLESSING).

Yet just as our access to the truth of creation is dependent upon our accepting the truth revealed in the book (q.v.), so our grasp of that revealed truth will be shaped by the community which embodies it. Because for Muslims, the Qurʾān is inextricably linked with the sunna, the meaning of "truth" in the Qurʾān will be unveiled in practices characteristic of that community. Greeting each other, Muslims will invariably end their exchange with *al-ḥamdu lillāh*, "God be praised" (see LAUDATION; GLORIFICATION OF GOD). Even when a cliché, it remains an illuminating one. As Eric Ormsby has noted, in explicating al-Ghazālī's (d. 505/1111) insistence that the world as it stands is "the best possible," there is nothing Panglossian here, primarily because al-Ghazālī is not claiming that we could know what the best would be, such that this world conforms to it. It rather states the conviction that we do not know what "best" would be like but that to those who believe, the world discloses unsuspected ways of realizing the divine wisdom (q.v.) that directs its unfolding. That is closer to the qur'ānic insistence that God's truth will be realized, even in the case of scoffers. The divinely ordained context of our lives — what William Chittick and Sachiko Murata *(Vision of Islam)* translate as "the measuring out" *(qudra)* — reflects the truth as the Qur'ān sees it: the outworking of what is divinely ordained. Such an operative notion of truth demands that we let go of any pretension to control what will happen, which in fact only makes good sense (see FATE; DESTINY).

At this point, we are bound to ask: what kind of truth can the Qur'ān be expounding? One that is certain, yet unveiled only as one's life unfolds; one more akin to coming to understand a wisdom initially hidden, than to knowing straightforwardly what is the case (see KNOWLEDGE AND LEARNING; IGNORANCE). So the truth of the Qur'ān is of a paradoxical sort: it turns on accepting as true what the Qur'ān reveals, and then on following the "straight path" it prescribes to allow that truth to be realized, and so confirm one's original acceptance. Recourse to metaphor (q.v.) signals our inability to say anything directly about this "truth," since it embodies the ineffable relation of creation to the creator:

> the thing which most deserves to be [called] true is the One whose existence is established by virtue of its own essence, forever and eternally; and its knowledge as well as the witness to it is true forever and eternally (al-Ghazālī, *Ninety-nine names,* 124, commenting on *al-ḥaqq* as a name of God).

But note how al-Ghazālī's exposition follows the performative ethos of the Qur'ān itself (see ETHICS AND THE QUR'ĀN), appending the following counsel:

> Man's share in this name lies in seeing himself as false, and not seeing anything other than God — great and glorious — as true. For if a man is true, he is not true in himself but true in God — great and glorious — for he exists by virtue of him and not in himself; indeed he would be nothing had the Truth not created him.

By tracing the abiding Ṣūfī sentiment of one's proper nothingness to the originating act of creating, al-Ghazālī seeks to align the conclusions of *kalām* with Ṣūfī convictions (Gimaret, *Les noms divins,* 142; see THEOLOGY AND THE QUR'ĀN; TRADITIONAL DISCIPLINES OF QUR'ĀNIC STUDY). While this reconciling move is characteristic of al-Ghazālī, it is illuminating as well, signaling that the relation of creatures to their creator, which allows us to speak of them as true, exceeds our capacity for articulation; and so opens the way for Ibn al-ʿArabī's (d. 638/1240) insistence that the creator/creature relation be utterly unlike any relation which obtains between creatures themselves (Chittick and Murata, *Vision,* 61). For creation is the founding or grounding relation, allowing things to be true in their dependent existence. And if this be recondite philosophy, it can be found implicit in the paradoxical uses of "true/real" in the Qur'ān itself.

David B. Burrell

Bibliography
Primary: Dāmaghānī, *Wujūh,* ed. al-Zafītī, 284-5 (for eleven meanings of *al-ḥaqq*); al-Ghazālī, Abū

Ḥāmid Muḥammad, *The ninety-nine beautiful names of God,* trans. D. Burrell, Cambridge 1995. Secondary: W. Chittick and S. Murata, *Vision of Islam,* Minneapolis 1994; D. Gimaret, *Les noms divins en Islam,* Paris 1988; D.B. Macdonald/E.E. Calverley, Ḥaqq, in *EI²*, iii, 82-3; L. Massignon, *Passion of al-Hallaj,* trans. H. Mason, Princeton 1982; E. Ormsby, Creation and time in Islamic thought with special reference to al-Ghazali, in D. Burrell and B. McGinn (eds.), *God and creation,* Notre Dame, IN 1990, 246-64; M. Rāwī, *Kalimat "al-ḥaqq" fī l-Qurʾān al-karīm. Mawriduhā wa-dalālatuhā,* Riyadh 1995.

Tubbaʿ

"The people of Tubbaʿ" *(qawm tubbaʿ),* an extinct community mentioned twice in the Qurʾān. Among other pre-Islamic groups, they were punished because they refused to believe God or obey God's prophets (see BELIEF AND UNBELIEF; OBEDIENCE; PROPHETS AND PROPHETHOOD). Q 44:37 compares Muḥammad's detractors (see PROVOCATION; OPPOSITION TO MUḤAMMAD), who challenged him to prove resurrection (q.v.) by himself reviving the dead (see DEATH AND THE DEAD), with the people of Tubbaʿ, who were destroyed for their sins (see SIN, MAJOR AND MINOR; PUNISHMENT STORIES): "Are they better, or the people of Tubbaʿ and those before them? We destroyed them, for they were sinners." In Q 50:14, the people of Tubbaʿ are listed along with other lost communities (see GEOGRAPHY): the people of Noah (q.v.), those of al-Rass (q.v.), and the Thamūd (q.v.), the ʿĀd (q.v.), Pharaoh (q.v.) and the brethren of Lot (q.v.): "And the dwellers in the wood (see PEOPLE OF THE THICKET), and the people of Tubbaʿ: all denied the messengers (see MESSENGER; LIE), so [my] threat took effect."

Arab lexicographers (see ARABIC LANGUAGE; GRAMMAR AND THE QURʾĀN) define the term *tubbaʿ* as a title of rulership among the kings (see KINGS AND RULERS) of Yemen (q.v.) and specifically among the Ḥimyar. The title is explained from the root meaning "to follow": every time one *tubbaʿ* died, he was followed immediately by one who took his place. Specifically, *tubbaʿ* was the royal title of the kings of the second Ḥimyarite kingdom (ca. 300-525 C.E.). According to Ibn Isḥāq (d. ca. 150/767), Ibn al-Kalbī (d. ca. 205/820), al-Yaʿqūbī (fl. third/ninth cent.), al-Ṭabarī (d. 310/923) and others (with differences in detail), the Tubbaʿ Asʿad Abū Karib returned from Iraq (q.v.; or Yathrib [see MEDINA]) with two rabbis (*ḥabrayn min aḥbār al-yahūd;* see JEWS AND JUDAISM), who convinced him to destroy the image of the idol (see IDOLS AND IMAGES) or place of sacrifice (q.v.) called Riʾām, located in Medina, Mecca (q.v.) or in Yemen (see also SOUTH ARABIA, RELIGIONS IN PRE-ISLAMIC). "Thereupon they demolished it, and the Tubbaʿ, together with the people of Yemen, embraced Judaism" (Faris' translation of Ibn al-Kalbī). Beeston questions whether the Ḥimyar actually became Jewish or practiced some heterodox indigenous pre-Islamic expression of monotheism. The Ḥimyar are known in legend to have remained Jewish for a century until the time of their last great king, Yūsuf, also known as Dhū Nuwās, who was killed according to legend after his massacre of the Christians of Najrān (q.v.) and the subsequent invasion of the Christian Abyssinians to destroy him (see ABYSSINIA; CHRISTIANS AND CHRISTIANITY).

According to most commentators, the Tubbaʿ referenced in the Qurʾān was good and a believer but his subjects were not. They (the qurʾānic "people of *tubbaʿ*") are destroyed while he is saved. The role of the two Jewish learned men includes (1) proving the future coming of Muḥammad through the esoteric knowledge of the Jews and thus convincing the Tubbaʿ not to destroy Yathrib, the future home of the Prophet, and (2) proving the original monotheistic purity of the Kaʿba (q.v.) even before Muḥammad. They affirm that "it is indeed the temple (see SACRED PRECINCTS) of our forefather Abraham (q.v.)... but the local people... set up idols around it." They instruct the Tubbaʿ how to perform the pilgrimage (q.v.) rituals at the Kaʿba and he subsequently learns in a dream (see DREAMS AND SLEEP) that he should make for it a beautiful *kiswa* or covering. In an oft-repeated legend, when the Tubbaʿ returns to Yemen with the two Jewish learned men, the people of Ḥimyar refuse him entry because he abandoned their ancestral religion. The Tubbaʿ calls them to his new religion and the Ḥimyarites propose that the conflict should be settled by their traditional ordeal of fire (q.v.), through which the guilty are consumed while the innocent remain unscathed. The idolaters (see IDOLATRY AND IDOLATERS) came with their idols and offerings (see CONSECRATION OF ANIMALS) while the (Jewish) learned men came with their texts *(maṣāḥif)* hanging from their necks (see SCROLLS; SHEETS). The idolaters are consumed along with their idols but the wise men are not. The Ḥimyarites are convinced and thus accept Judaism, the Tubbaʿ's religion. The Ḥimyarites were said to have claimed that there were seventy Tubbaʿ kings.

Tubbaʿ is a name as well as a title. Al-Thaʿlabī (d. 427/1035) cites Wahb b. Munabbih (d. ca. 114/732), who narrates how Solomon (q.v.) married Bilqīs (q.v.) to Tubbaʿ the great, king of Hamdān, and brought him back to Yemen, and conflates this with Dhū Tubbaʿ, who ruled over Yemen with the support of King Solomon and the help of the Yemeni jinn (q.v.). In al-Kisāʾī's *Qiṣaṣ*, Kaʿb al-Aḥbār (d. 32/652-3) is made to include a Tubbaʿ among the twelve male children of ʿĀd b. ʿŪṣ b. Aram b. Sām b. Nūḥ.

A pre-Islamic alabaster stele made by "Layaʿathat the Sabaean" (see SHEBA) on behalf of "Abibahath wife of Tubbaʿ son of Subh" for the goddess Shams depicts a male figure with bow, spear and dagger, presumably Tubbaʿ, making an offering with his wife to the goddess. See also PRE-ISLAMIC ARABIA AND THE QURʾĀN.

Reuven Firestone

Bibliography

Primary: Ibn Isḥāq, *Sīra*, 2 vols., Beirut n.d., i, 19-28; Ibn Isḥāq-Guillaume, 6-12; Ibn al-Kalbī, Hishām b. Muḥammad b. al-Sāʾib, *Kitāb al-Aṣnām*, trans. N.A. Faris, Princeton 1952; Ibn Kathīr, *Tafsīr*, Beirut 1985; Kisāʾī, *Qiṣaṣ;* trans. W.M. Thackston, Jr., *The tales of the prophets of al-Kisāʾī*, Boston 1978, 109; *Lisān al-ʿArab*, viii, 31; Ṭabarī, *Tafsīr*, Beirut 1984, xiii, 128-9, 154-5; id., *Taʾrīkh*, ed. de Goeje, 684, 901-10; trans. M. Perlmann, *The history of al-Ṭabarī. iv. The ancient kingdoms*, New York 1987, 79; C.E. Bosworth, *The history of al-Ṭabarī. v. The Sāsānids, the Byzantines, the Lakhmids, and Yemen*, New York 1999, 164-76; Thaʿlabī, *Qiṣaṣ*, 286; trans. W.M. Brinner, *ʿArāʾis al-majālis fī qiṣaṣ al-anbiyāʾ or "Lives of the prophets"*, Leiden 2002, 536; Wahb b. Munabbih, *Kitāb al-Tījān fī mulūk Ḥimyar*, Sanʿāʾ 1979; Yaʿqūbī, *Taʾrīkh*, 222-4.

Secondary: A.F.L. Beeston, Ḥimyarite monotheism, in *Studies in the history of Arabia. ii. Pre-Islamic Arabia*, Riyadh 1984, 149-54; Horovitz, *KU*, 102-3; R. Hoyland, *Arabia and the Arabs. From the Bronze Age to the coming of Islam*, London 2001; M. Lecker, The conversion of Ḥimyar to Judaism and the Banū Hadl of Medina, in *WO* 26 (1995), 129-36; id., Judaism among Kinda and the *ridda* of Kinda, in *JAOS* 115 (1995), 635-50; C.A. Nallino, *Raccolta di scritti editi e inediti*, 6 vols., Rome 1941, iii, 88-9.

Ṭūr see SINAI

Turkish Literature and the Qurʾān

The acceptance of Islam in Anatolia towards the end of the third/ninth century brought new beliefs and social norms, and began to create a new linguistic and literary climate which would dramatically reshape the Turkish language and its literary traditions. The literary language was eventually enriched with a large number of borrowings from Arabic, the sacred language of the Qurʾān (see ARABIC LANGUAGE), and from the court poetry of Persia. In their effort to be pious Muslims, the new converts adopted the script of the qurʾānic language as well (see ARABIC SCRIPT). Regardless of the degree to which Turkish-speaking peoples have, or have not, had access to the semantic content of the Qurʾān, its iconographic power has been extremely influential on their cultural outpourings (see MATERIAL CULTURE AND THE QURʾĀN). The Arabic script, in its association with the Qurʾān, conveys an aura of spirituality and provides a calligraphic and symbolic entry into the Islamic world (see REVELATION AND INSPIRATION; CALLIGRAPHY).

The pre-Islamic Turkic epics went through a striking transformation in Anatolia after the acceptance of Islam and its holy book. The birth of the romantic epic *(hikaye)* with new dimensions of love (q.v.) began to manifest Islamic references but at the same time kept the pre-Islamic (particularly Shamanistic) rituals and symbols. In these epics, one can observe a remarkable intertextuality of different and often contrasting religious practices and references. While a troubadour or bard played his *saz*, a stringed instrument, performing his epic to his audience, he would not hesitate to talk about wine (q.v.) or his character's sexual life (see SEX AND SEXUALITY), while at the same time citing a verse from the Qurʾān. In some cases, the epic-teller would address his audience through a digression, saying that he knows it is not right to cite from the Qurʾān while he is holding a musical instrument in his hands (see LAWFUL AND UNLAWFUL; RITUAL PURITY; RECITATION OF THE QURʾĀN). Linguistically speaking, these quotations from the Qurʾān are often highly corrupt and out of context. Since the audience would not know Arabic, immediately after the qurʾānic quote the epic-singer would offer his own Turkish translation and commentary.

Turkish hagiographic legends exhibit a similar use of the Qurʾān and ḥadīth (see ḤADĪTH AND THE QURʾĀN). Though no scholarly treatment of the qurʾānic verses in these compositions exists, in the great majority of the manuscripts, the composers do not cite the Arabic verses correctly, and their Turkish renderings are rather more like approximations than accurate translations. This is typical of folk literature, whether its transmission was written or oral. Just as the peoples of Anatolia created their own version of folk Islam, their folk literature created its own version of Islam, the Qurʾān, and Muḥammad.

The treatment of the Qurʾān finds a new level of sophistication in Turkish, or more properly Ottoman, court literature. It functioned as one of the major sources of this classical literary tradition (thirteenth-nineteenth centuries C.E.). Although the subjects and vocabulary of *taṣawwuf*, Islamic mysticism (see ṢŪFISM AND THE QURʾĀN), dominate those aspects of Turkish court literature that carry religious themes, the Qurʾān also has a very special place, both in terms of its vocabulary and direct quotations from it, as well as reworkings of some famous qurʾānic stories (see NARRATIVES; MYTHS AND LEGENDS IN THE QURʾĀN). One important reworking of such stories is Şeyyād Ḥamza's (fl. seventh/thirteenth century) retelling of the Joseph story. This narrative of Joseph (q.v.) was widely used in Ottoman literature. Also known as "the most beautiful of stories" (cf. Q 12:3), the tale has more or less the same plot in Turkish court poetry: Joseph (Ar. Yūsuf; T. Yusuf) was one of the twelve sons of the prophet Jacob (q.v.; Ar. Yaʿqūb; T. Yakub/Yakup). He was more loved by his father than his other siblings (see BENJAMIN; BROTHER AND BROTHERHOOD). One day he saw in a dream (see DREAMS AND SLEEP) that eleven stars (see PLANETS AND STARS) and the sun (q.v.) and the moon (q.v.) worshipped him. He recounted his dream to his father. Jacob interpreted these eleven stars as his brothers. He believed that what Joseph saw in his dream was a divine message from God to announce that Joseph had been chosen to be a prophet (see PROPHETS AND PROPHETHOOD). He told his son to be careful and not to tell his dream to his brothers. He was afraid that jealousy would invade the hearts of his eleven other sons and, indeed, his worries turned out to be true. Joseph's brothers plotted against him, threw him into a well, and told their father that a wolf had eaten him. When Jacob heard the devastating news, he cried, from that moment on, day and night; Jacob's dwelling came to be known as "the house of grief." In fact, his brothers had sold Joseph into slavery to a merchant for a couple of silver coins. The merchant took Joseph with him to Egypt (q.v.) where he was bought at the slave market by an Egyptian notable named ʿAzīz (T. Aziz; see KINGS AND RULERS). When his wife, Zulaykha (T. Züleyha; see WOMEN AND THE QURʾĀN), saw Joseph, she was drawn to him sexually as he had unrivaled physical charm. She did everything to attract his attention. One day, Zulaykha entered Joseph's room and tried to seduce him. While he was struggling to escape from her, Joseph's shirt was torn. When he went out, he found ʿAzīz in front of him. Zulaykha seized this opportunity to take revenge on Joseph for rejecting her. She told her husband that Joseph had attacked her. His resistance to her desires brought him disgrace and imprisonment. In prison, Joseph stayed with two other men. He interpreted their dreams correctly. One of his fellow prisoners was released and became the king's cup-bearer. Through this man, the king of Egypt found out the truth about the Joseph-Zulaykha relationship and released the innocent man. Joseph interpreted one of the king's dreams, too. He was later appointed a minister by the king. After a while, his brothers came to Egypt and were warmly welcomed by Joseph. They did not know that he was an important man. In the end, Joseph forgave all of his brothers (see FORGIVENESS) and also brought his father from Canaan to Egypt. Extra-qurʾānic details elaborate the narrative. For example, in the meantime, great misfortunes had befallen Zulaykha. Her husband had died, and she had become desperate. She had also lost her beauty (q.v.). When Joseph found this out, he felt sorry for her, and decided to marry her. Having done so, God bestowed her former beauty upon her and happiness was restored to the family.

The practice of citing from the Qurʾān and ḥadīth was usually called *iktibas* (Ar. *iqtibās*), and is similar to another common figure of speech known as *irsal-i mesel,* "providing a proverb and its application in a single distich." The main purpose of these quotes was to reinforce the poet's discourse on a subject, on the assumption that no one would challenge the word of God (q.v.) or that of the Prophet, thus giving more credibility to the poet's own statements. Often times, the poets use a figure of speech called *telmih* (Ar. *talmīḥ*), "allusion," to a particular verse of the Qurʾān or a ḥadīth (see also LITERATURE AND THE QURʾĀN). A scholarly examination of these quotes and allusions in Turkish literary texts and their contextualization (and in many cases decontextualization) has not been undertaken.

While the authors of folk narratives would often provide their audience with a Turkish translation or approximation of the qurʾānic passages they were citing (see TRANSLATIONS OF THE QURʾĀN), Ottoman court poets did not engage in such practice. Indeed, there was no practical reason for it. Generally speaking, court poetry assumed an educated audience, an audience usually literate in Turkish, Persian and Arabic, and with an adequate education in the Islamic sciences (see TRADITIONAL DISCIPLINES OF QURʾĀNIC STUDY). Not translating such quotes, and not providing any explicit source for the quotes, also challenged the capacities of the audience and added to the overall liveliness of this tradition.

Despite the tremendous efforts of modern Turkish philologists since the founding of the Turkish republic to decipher and publish the major Ottoman literary sources, unfortunately a great majority of the existing sources remain in manuscript form, and have not been studied. Thus, any attempt to write an overview of the Qurʾān and Turkish literature is necessarily incomplete. Based on some of the most significant studies on Ottoman literature, the following list of the most frequently cited verses of the Qurʾān in Turkish court poetry can be composed (cf. Levend, *Divan;* Onay, *Eski Türk;* Pala, *Ansiklopedik dīvān;* Tarlan, *Fuzūlī divani*): Q 21:22; 95:4; 14:34; 36:69; 2:47; 89:27-8; 61:13; 2:82; 13:23; 16:31; 20:76; 39:73; 111:4; 6:2; 17:1; 2:224; 12:87; 11:70; 20:21-68; 27:10; 28:25-31; 29:33; 7:172; 43:32; 2:1; 29:1; 30:1; 31:1; 32:1; 2:225; 7:206; 13:15; 16:49; 17:107; 19:58; 22:18; 25:60; 27:25; 32:15; 38:24; 78:40; 24:36; 8:17; 3:14; 35:33; 39:73; 24:35; 2:2; 81:1; 95:4; 2:256; 5:45; 9:25; 93:1; 68:1; 56:30; 28:88; 56:29; 33:4; 20:6; 92:1; 93:2; 21:107; 30:50; 55:1; 24:35; 93:2; 17:1; 31:77; 39:73; 2:115; 53:9; 17:37; 31:18; 71:5; 35:1; 37:35; 47:119; 13:30; 39:6; 59:22; 27:30; 26:224; 36:69; 2:115; 78:40; 65:7; 84:5-6; 48:1; 39:22; 20:12; 2:285; 4:46; 5:7; 24:51; 96:19; 21:30; 61:13; 50:20; 87:1; 27:7; 28:29; 24:36; 8:17; 3:14; 9:72; 13:23; 16:31; 18:31; 19:61; 20:76; 38:50; 61:12; 39:73; 24:35; 81:1; 95:4; 2:256; 5:45; 9:25; 56:30; 28:88; 33:4; 20:4; 53:9; 15:72; 26:88; 25:53; 83:26; 21:23; 7:179; 25:44; 75:40; 14:7; 65:10; 5:100; 3:13; 59:12; 43:32; 55:26; 33:41; 39:53; 3:103-12; 20:66; 26:44; 21:107; 93:2. Many of these verses were commonplace in the collections of Turkish poetry and for centuries poets have alluded to them repeatedly. Ottoman Turkish court poetry was highly technical, linguistically cumbersome, and rhetorically charged, but at the same time it had a limited lexicon. Thus it is not surprising to see the repetition of these verses in collections (*divans*) written centuries apart. The established literary tradition dictated the vocabulary of the medieval poet, as did the limited number of canonical books, the Qurʾān being the most significant of all. Generally it was viewed by the Ottoman poet as the supreme example of "poetic perfection" (see INIMITABILITY).

In Turkish court poetry, the Qurʾān is equated with the beauty of the beloved: his or her beautiful face, tall stature, long and dark hair, eyes, eyebrows, cheek fuzz, and mole. Sometimes it is designated as the *kitap*, "book" (q.v.), *mushaf* (see MUṢḤAF), "book, volume," *ayet* (pl. *ayat*), "verses" (q.v.; see also SIGNS; MIRACLES; MARVELS), *fürkan*, "that which distinguishes truth (q.v.) from error (q.v.)" (see also CRITERION), and *nur*, "light" (q.v.). In the majority of the *divans*, it is the absolute truth with utter perfection, and thus it is referred to with utmost respect (see also NAMES OF THE QURʾĀN).

In the eighteenth century, Ottoman court poetry (together with other arts of the empire, such as miniature painting) went through a dramatic change in its language, themes, representation of the real world, manifestation of human sexuality, and depiction of the place of religious discourse in poetry. Indeed, the whole society began to display signs of a Turkish "renaissance," one that emphasized a more secular state of mind. The clash between the *rind,* "the epicurean poet," and *zahid,* "zealot," had long dominated the pages of Turkish *divans*, but in eighteenth century poetry, serious challenges to religion and religious authorities were evident, but without the previous centuries' reliance upon mysticism to mediate this clash. The poet Nedim (1681-1730) was one of those Ottoman authors who openly confronted some of the strongest proscriptions of Islam, such as drinking alcohol and consuming opium (see INTOXICANTS; FORBIDDEN) during the holy month of Ramaḍān (q.v.), refusing to write a single *tevhid,* "composition praising the unity of God" (see GOD AND HIS ATTRIBUTES), *münacat,* "poem which calls upon God for help, communicates with God," or *naʿt,* "poem in honor or praise of Muḥammad" (see PRAYER FORMULAS; NAMES OF THE PROPHET), and provocatively disparaging the Qurʾān itself:

Oh zealot, excuse me but your face seems rather homely (literally "there is some heaviness on your skin")
your ugliness can be perceived even by the thickness of your book!

This secular or anti-religious posture in literature became much stronger in the nineteenth and twentieth centuries with the advance of modernist movements in Turkey (see CONTEMPORARY CRITICAL PRACTICES AND THE QURʾĀN). The positivist mentality of modern Ottoman and Turkish literature emphasized critical thinking, belief in positive sciences (see SCIENCE AND THE QURʾĀN), and a desire to free the human mind from the dogmas of Islam and its holy book. Among the foremost figures of this literature of the Turkish enlightenment were Tevfik Fikret (1867-1915), Reşat Nuri Güntekin (1889-1956), Nāzım Hikmet (1902-1963), and Aziz Nesin (1915-1995).

The philosophy exemplified in Fikret's poem entitled "Halūk's credo" (written for his son Halūk, and translated by Walter G. Andrews; Silay, *Anthology,* 259-60) occupied the pages of Turkish literature until the 1980s. A few lines can convey some sense of this philosophy:

There is a universal power, supreme and limitless
Holy and sublime, with all my heart, so
do I believe
The earth is my homeland, my nation all humankind;
A person becomes human only by knowing this, so
do I believe
We are Satan, and jinn (q.v.), there's no devil (q.v.), no angels (q.v.)
Human beings will turn this world into paradise (q.v.), so
do I believe
The perfect is immanent in creation (q.v.); in that perfection
By way of the Torah (q.v.), of the Gospels (q.v.), of the Koran
do I believe

The military coup in Turkey on September 12, 1980 not only reshaped the whole political, cultural and economic nature of the country but its literature as well. Whether Marxist-Leninist or Kemalist, the positivist character of Turkish literature began to go through a remarkable "postmodern" transformation and thus reflected a much more positive image of the so-called "Ottoman times" in general and Islam and its icons in particular (see also POLITICS AND THE QURʾĀN).

Kemal Silay

Bibliography

Ahmet Refik, *Lāle devri,* Istanbul 1331/1912; K. Akyüz, La littérature moderne de Turquie, in J. Deny et al. (eds.), *Philologiae turcicae fundamenta,* 3 vols., Wiesbaden 1959-2000, ii, 465-634; W.G. Andrews, *The age of beloveds. Love and the beloved in early-modern Ottoman and European culture and society,* Durham, NC 2005; id., *An introduction to Ottoman poetry,* Minneapolis 1976; id., *Poetry's voice, society's song. Ottoman lyric poetry,* Seattle 1985; O. Aslanapa, Türk minyatür sanatının gelişmesi, in *Erdem. Atatürk Kültür Merkezi Dergisi* 2/6 (1987), 851-66; N. Berkes, *The development of secularism in Turkey,* Montreal 1964; A. Bombaci, *Histoire de la littérature turque,* trans. I. Melikoff, Paris 1968; P.N. Boratav, *Türk halk edebiyatı,* Istanbul 1969; M. Çavuşoğlu, *Necāti Bey dīvānı'nın tahlili,* Istanbul 1971; C. Dilçin, Divan şiirinde gazel, in *Türk Dili* 415-17 (1986), 78-247; id., *Örneklerle Türk şiir bilgisi,* Ankara 1983; R. Ettinghausen, *Turkish miniatures from the thirteenth to the eighteenth century,* New York 1965; A.Ö. Evin, The tulip age and definitions of "westernization," in O. Okyar and H. İnalcık (eds.), *Social and economic history of Turkey (1071-1920),* Ankara 1980, 131-45; F. İz (ed.), *Eski Türk edebiyatnda nazīm. XIII. Yüzyīldan XIX. Yüzyīl ortasna kadar yazmalardan seçilmi metinler* [vol. i], Istanbul 1966; L. Karahan, *Erzurumlu darir, kıssa-i Yūsuf (Yūsuf u Züleyhā). İnceleme, metin, dizin,* Ankara 1994; C. Kurnaz, *Hayālī Bey dīvānī (tahlili),* Ankara 1987; A.S. Levend, *Divan edebiyatī. Kelimeler ve remizler, mazmunlar ve mefhumlar,* Istanbul 1943; id., *Türk dilinde gelişme ve sadeleşme evreleri,* Ankara 1972; G.M. Meredith-Owens, *Turkish miniatures,* London 1963; A. Nedīm, *Nedīm dīvānī,* ed. H. Nihad, Istanbul 1338-40 [1919-21]; A.T. Onay, *Eski Türk edebiyatında mazmunlar,* ed. C. Kurnaz, Ankara 1993; İ. Pala, *Ansiklopedik dīvān siiri sözlüğü,* Ankara 1992; Sir J.W. Redhouse, *New Redhouse Turkish-English dictionary,* Istanbul 1968; id., *A Turkish and English lexicon,* Beirut 1974; Ş. Sāmī, *Ḳāmūs-ı Türkī,* 2 vols., Istanbul 1317-18/1899-1900; K. Silay (ed.), *An anthology of Turkish literature,* Bloomington, IN 1996; id., *Nedim and the poetics of the Ottoman court. Medieval inheritance and the need for change,* Bloomington, IN 1994; id. (ed.), *Turkish folklore and oral literature. Selected essays of İlhan Başgöz,* Bloomington, IN 1998 (for a sampling of works by one of the most noted contemporary names in Turkish folklore); F. Steingass, *A comprehensive Persian-English dictionary,* London 1988[8]; A.N. Tarlan (ed.), *Ahmed Paşa divanı,* Istanbul 1966; id. *Fuzūlī divanı şerhi,* 3 vols., Ankara 1985; id., *Hayālī Bey Dīvānı,* Istanbul 1945; id., Kadı Burhaneddin'de tasavvuf, in *Türk Dili ve Edebiyatı Dergisi* 8 (1958), 8-15; id., Kadı Burhaneddin'de tasavvuf. İkinci gazelin şerhi, in *Türk Dili ve Edebiyatı Dergisi* 9 (1959), 27-32; id., Kadı Burhaneddin'de tasavvuf III. Bir gazelinin şerhi, in *Türk Dili ve Edebiyatı Dergisi* 10 (1960), 1-4; id., *Necati Bey divanı,* Istanbul 1963; id., *Şeyhī divanı'nı tetkik,* Istanbul 1964; H. Tolasa, *Ahmet Paşa'nın şiir dünyası,* Ankara 1973; S.L. West, The *Qiṣṣa-i Yūsuf* of ʿAlī. The first story of Joseph in Turkic Islamic literature, in *AO* 37 (1983), 69-84.

Ṭuwā

An enigmatic term mentioned in the Qurʾān, denoting a place or a concept of holiness. The term's semantic origins are obscure — a place name, a term meaning "twice done," even a misreading of the Syriac *ṭūr/ṭūrā* ["mountain"] have been suggested (cf. Bell, *Commentary,* i, 523 [ad Q 20:12]; cf. also Horovitz, *KU,* 125). The sacred place called *ṭuwā* is found in two sūras (Q 20 and 79), both of which speak of a holy valley and mention Moses (q.v.), but which are quite different otherwise. While Q 20 consists of 135 verses and Q 79 of only forty-six verses, they include only slight similarity (see SŪRAS).

Q 20, entitled Ṭāhā (see MYSTERIOUS LETTERS), begins with "We did not reveal to you [Muḥammad] the Qurʾān that you should be distressed, but to admonish the God-fearing" (Q 20:2-3; see PIETY; FEAR; WARNER). Verses 9-12 tell what Moses did, after which God spoke to him and mentioned *ṭuwā:* "Have you heard the story of Moses? When he saw a fire (q.v.) he said to his people: 'Stay here, for I can see a fire. Perchance I can bring you a lighted torch, or find guidance at the fire.' When he came near, a voice called out to him: 'Moses! I am your lord. Take off your sandals, for you are in the sacred valley of *ṭuwā.*'" In verse Q 20:15 God speaks strongly, that "the hour is surely coming (see TIME; LAST JUDGMENT; ESCHATOLOGY). But I will keep it hidden so that every soul may be rewarded for its striving (see REWARD AND PUNISHMENT; PATH OR WAY)." Then God frightens Moses by telling him to throw down his staff (see ROD) which becomes a serpent. He then tells him to take it with no fear, for it will return to its former state, and promises that he will show him most wondrous signs (q.v.). God tells Moses that he has chosen him to serve him (see WORSHIP; SERVANT), to recite his prayers (see PRAYER; RITUAL AND THE QURʾĀN) in remembrance of him and warns that the hour (of doom) has come. God continues (Q 20:16), "Let those who disbelieve in the hour (see BELIEF AND UNBELIEF) and yield to their desires not turn your thoughts from it, lest you perish (see DEATH AND THE DEAD)." Moses asks God to put courage (q.v.) into his heart (q.v.), free his tongue from impediment, and to appoint his brother Aaron (q.v.) to strengthen him and share his task. God agrees and tells the story of the birth and early years of Moses, then goes on with the story of Pharaoh (q.v.).

Q 79 is called al-Nāziʿāt, a title that is little understood, and translated by various English names such as "The Soul-Snatchers," "Those Who Pull and Withdraw," "Those Who Drag Forth," and "The Pluckers" (see, for instance, the translations of A. Ali, A.J. Arberry, N.J. Dawood, M. Pickthall, J.M. Rodwell and M.H. Shakir). Q 79 briefly notes the story of Pharaoh, with a mention of the fire and the hour (of doom) as in Q 20, and includes a few final words of future events that threaten humanity (see APOCALYPSE). The two first words of this sūra *(nāziʿāt/sābiḥāt)* are difficult to understand and have been the subject of considerable exegetical discussion. Q 79 contains the brief verses 15 and 16: "Have you heard the story of Moses? His lord (q.v.) called out to him in the sacred valley of *ṭuwā*."

Although exegetes differ as to the meaning of the term *ṭuwā*, the most plausible tradition is that which maintains that *ṭuwā* is the name of a sacred place, the one that was entered by Moses (but cf. SACRED PRECINCTS). *Ṭuwā(n)* has also been defined as something "twice done," as though folded, and medieval writers (see EXEGESIS OF THE QURʾĀN: CLASSICAL AND MEDIEVAL) have said that *ṭuwā* is "twice sanctified, twice blessed and twice called," as God calls Moses.

William M. Brinner

Bibliography
Primary: Yāqūt, *Buldān*, ed. Wüstenfeld, iii, 553.
Secondary: Bell, *Commentary;* Horovitz, *KU*.

Twelvers
see SHĪʿISM AND THE QURʾĀN

Twilight
see EVENING

Tyrant
see OPPRESSION; KINGS AND RULERS

U

Uḥud see EXPEDITIONS AND BATTLES

[Al-]Ukhdūd

Substantive (or proper name) found in the qurʾānic expression *aṣḥāb al-ukhdūd* (Q 85:4):

> [They] were destroyed, the men of the furnace *(aṣḥāb al-ukhdūd)*, a fire (q.v.) abundantly fed, while they were sitting by it, and they were witnesses of what they did to believers (see BELIEF AND UNBELIEF), and they ill-treated them for no other reason than that they believed in God (Q 85:4-9).

Islamic tradition is almost unanimous in identifying these *aṣḥāb al-ukhdūd* with those involved in the persecution at Najrān (q.v.; a large oasis in southern Saudi Arabia, on the border with Yemen [q.v.]), in November 523 C.E. (regarding this event and the sources dealing with it, see Beaucamp et al., La persécution), but quite often without specifying whether they mean the Jewish persecutors (directed by the king Zurʿa dhū-Nuwās Yūsuf, the Yūsuf Asʾar Yathʾar of Ḥimyarite inscriptions; see JEWS AND JUDAISM) or their Christian victims (see CHRISTIANS AND CHRISTIANITY). For Wahb b. Munabbih (d. ca. 114/732; *Tījān*), Ibn Ḥabīb (d. 245/860; *Muḥabbar*) or Nashwān al-Ḥimyarī (d. 573/1178; *Mulūk Ḥimyar*), they are the persecutors, since these authors call the king Yūsuf *ṣāḥib al-ukhdūd,* but others remain rather vague (Ibn Isḥāq, *Sīra,* followed by Ṭabarī, *Taʾrīkh;* Nashwān al-Ḥimyarī, *Shams al-ʿulūm,* ad *ḫ-d-d,* etc.)

As a consequence of this identification, tradition interprets al-Ukhdūd as a place name of the Najrān oasis (Bakrī, *Muʿjam mā staʿjama,* i, 121, ad "al-Ukhdūd"; al-Ḥasan al-Hamdānī, *Ṣifat jazīrat al-ʿArab,* specifies that "the ancient city is the site of 'al-Ukhdūd'"). In pre-Islamic sources (principally the inscriptions of south Arabia, but also external sources such as Christian hagiographies relating to the persecution, written in Greek and Syriac), however, no evidence is available for such a place name; in inscriptions, the oasis and main city are first of all called *Rgmt*^{m} (RES 3943/3; Maʿīn 9/5; M 247/2; in Hebrew *Raʿmā,* in Greek *Ragma,* in *Gen* 10:7 = *I Chron* 1:9, and *Ezek* 27:22), then, after the start of the Christian era, *Ngr*^{n} (in Arabic Najrān; see ARABIC SCRIPT). There is good reason to believe that the name "al-Ukhdūd" bestowed upon the ruins of Najrān (already indicated in the tenth century C.E. by al-Hamdānī and still used nowadays, see Philby, *Arabian highlands*) postdates Islam and is derived from an interpretation of Q 85.

Other observations have led the majority of contemporary scholars to doubt the identification of the *aṣḥāb al-ukhdūd* with those responsible for, or the victims of, the Najrān persecution. While the Qurʾān speaks of a ditch filled with fire (for R. Blachère, a furnace), since the meanings given to the Arabic *ukhdūd* (pl. *akhādīd*) are "ditch, cavity, pit" (for references in Yemeni dialects, see Serjeant, Ukhdūd), scholars note that, according to Christian hagiographies, those executed were not thrown into a furnace but put to the sword. Besides, the text of the Qurʾān, which gives no indication of location or time, at no point suggests that the "believers" were Christians (see PEOPLE OF THE DITCH).

For al-Ṭabarī (d. 310/923), followed by some Islamicists, most recently Régis Blachère, the Qurʾān is alluding to the "fiery furnace" (Daniel 3:6, 11, 15, 17, 20, 21, 23 and 26) into which the three young men are thrown. Other scholars, such as Rudi Paret, following Hubert Grimme and Joseph Horovitz, prefer an eschatological interpretation (see ESCHATOLOGY): the *aṣḥāb al-ukhdūd* will be the wicked cast into hell (see HELL AND HELLFIRE) at the time of the last judgment (q.v.) because of their crimes against believers, even if it is very unusual to use the term "ditch" to describe hell (see REWARD AND PUNISHMENT).

This last objection has disappeared following the publication of texts from Qumrān, in which Sheol is constantly referred to by the Hebrew *šaḥat*, "ditch." Marc Philonenko, who stresses this point, equally notes the expressions *bny h-šḥt*, "sons of the ditch," and *ʾnšy h-šḥt*, "men of the ditch," to denote the wicked, the damned or rather those who suffer punishment (see CHASTISEMENT AND PUNISHMENT; GOOD AND EVIL) on judgment day. The qurʾānic expression *aṣḥāb al-ukhdūd* could be an exact equivalent of the expressions from Qumrān.

Christian Julien Robin

Bibliography and abbreviations
Primary: al-Bakrī, al-Wazīr Abū ʿUbayd ʿAbdallāh b. ʿAbd al-ʿAzīz al-Andalusī, *Muʿjam mā staʿjama*, ed. M. al-Saqqā, 4 vols. in 2, Cairo 1945, repr. Beirut 1983[3]; R. Blachère, *Le Coran. Traduction selon un essai de reclassement des sourates*, 3 vols., Paris 1947-51, ii, 119-20, no. 43; al-Hamdānī, Abū Muḥammad al-Ḥasan b. Aḥmad b. Yaʿqūb, *Ṣifat jazīrat al-ʿArab*, 2 vols., ed. D.H. Müller, *al-Hamdānī's Geographie der arabischen Halbinsel*, Leiden 1884-91, repr. Leiden 1968, 169f.; Ibn Ḥabīb, Abū Jaʿfar Muḥammad, *Muḥabbar*, ed. I. Lichtenstädter, Hyderabad 1942, repr. Beirut n.d., 367-8; Ibn Isḥāq, *Sīra*, 24-5; Ibn Isḥāq-Guillaume, 15-16; Nashwān b. Saʿīd al-Ḥimyarī, *Mulūk Ḥimyar wa-aqyāl al-Yaman*, ed. ʿA. al-Jarāfī, Cairo 1378/1958-9, 148 (poem with commentary); id., *Shams al-ʿulūm. Die auf Südarabien bezüglichen Angaben Našwān's im Šams al-ʿulūm*, Leiden/London 1916, 31-2; Ṭabarī, *Taʾrīkh*, ed. de Goeje et al., i, 919/922-5; trans. C.E. Bosworth, *The history of al-Ṭabarī. v. The Sāsānids, the Byzantines, the Lakhmids, and Yemen*, Albany 1999, 191, 198-202; Thaʿlabī, *Qiṣaṣ*; trans. W.M. Brinner, *ʿArāʾis al-majālis fī qiṣaṣ al-anbiyāʾ or "Lives of the prophets"*, Leiden 2002, 728-32; Wahb b. Munabbih, *Kitāb al-Tījān fī mulūk Ḥimyar*, Ṣanʿāʾ 1347/1928-9, 323-501.
Secondary: J. Beaucamp, F. Briquel-Chatonnet and Ch. Robin, La persécution des chrétiens de Nagrān et la chronologie ḥimyarite, in *Aram* 11/12 (1999-2000), 15-83; H. Grimme, *Mohammed*, 2 vols., Münster 1892-5, ii, 77 n. 4; Horovitz, *KU*, 12; R. Paret, Aṣḥāb al-Ukhdūd, in *EI*[2], i, 692 (complete bibliography); H. Philby, *Arabian highlands*, New York 1976[2], esp. chap. 14, Ukhdud, 254-5 (map of the Najrān wādī and al-Ukhdūd area); 266-7 (sketch of the site between); M. Philonenko, Une expression qoumrânienne dans le Coran, in *Atti del Terzo Congresso di Studi Arabi e Islamici (Ravello, 1-6 September 1966)*, Napoli 1967, 553-6 (complete bibliography); R. Serjeant, Ukhdūd, in *BSOAS* 22 (1959), 572-3. Sigla: M: *Iscrizioni sudarabiche*. i. *Iscrizioni minee*, Naples 1974; Maʿīn 9: Ch. Robin and G. Gnoli, *Inventaire des Inscriptions sud arabiques*, iii, Paris/ Rome 1998; *RES*: *Répertoire d'épigraphie sémitique*.

Ulema see SCHOLARS

ʿUmar see CALIPH; COMPANIONS OF THE PROPHET

Umm Ḥabība see WIVES OF THE PROPHET

Umm Salama see WIVES OF THE PROPHET

Umma see COMMUNITY AND SOCIETY IN THE QURʾĀN; RELIGION

Ummī

A qurʾānic epithet for the prophet Muḥammad that acquired significantly different interpretations in the course of Islamic history. Traditionally, Muslims understand *ummī* as "illiterate" and as unequivocally identifying Muḥammad as "the illiterate Prophet" *(al-nabī l-ummī)* — a view that has come to constitute an article of orthodox faith and spirituality in Islam (see ILLITERACY). Recent research, however, recovering some of the earliest exegetical glossing, has suggested that *ummī* in the Qurʾān signifies the ethnic origin (being an Arab, Arabian) and the originality of the Prophet of Islam (coming from among a people, the Arabs [q.v.], who had not yet received a revelation; see REVELATION AND INSPIRATION).

Terms in the Qurʾān and their interpretations

The term *ummī* occurs only in Q 7:157 and 158; its plural, *ummiyyūn*, is found in Q 2:78; 3:20, 75 and 62:2. In Q 7:157 and 158, God proclaims:

My mercy (q.v.),... I shall ordain it for those who are God-fearing,... those who believe in our signs (q.v.; Q 7:156), [those] who follow the messenger (q.v.), the *ummī* Prophet, whom they find mentioned in their [own scriptures, the] Torah (q.v.) and the Gospel (q.v.; see also SCRIPTURE AND THE QURʾĀN), who bids them to what is just (see JUSTICE AND INJUSTICE) and forbids them what is reprehensible (see VIRTUES AND VICES, COMMANDING AND FORBIDDING; FORBIDDEN), and who makes lawful for them the good things and unlawful for them the corrupt things... (Q 7:157; see LAWFUL AND UNLAWFUL; GOOD AND EVIL). Say: "O humankind, I am the messenger of God to you all...." Therefore, believe in God and in his messenger, the *ummī* Prophet who believes in God and his words. Follow him! Perhaps, you will [then] be guided (Q 7:158; see ERROR; ASTRAY).

In commenting on these verses, the classical Muslim exegetes (see EXEGESIS OF THE QURʾĀN: CLASSICAL AND MEDIEVAL) offer several interpretations for *ummī*, including "unable to read (and write; see LITERACY; ORALITY AND WRITING IN ARABIA)," Arab/Arabian (derived from *umma*, "nation, the people of the Arabs"), Meccan (from *umm al-qurā*, "Mother of all Cities," an epithet for Mecca [q.v.]), and, "pure, natural," like a newborn from its "mother" *(umm)*, thus incorporating the notions of being "unlettered," "untaught," "intellectually untouched" (see KNOWLEDGE AND LEARNING), and "spiritually virgin," by virtue of which Muḥammad became the receptacle for the divine revelation. (For references and discussion of these and the following derivations, see Günther, Illiteracy, esp. 493-9; and id., Literacy, esp. 188.) Despite these various possible meanings, the classical commentaries stress that *ummī* in the two verses characterizing the prophet Muḥammad means "unable to read (and write)." Presenting a threefold argument, they suggest (1) that *ummī* most likely relates to *umma*, "the people of the Arabs" who, (2) at the time of Muḥammad, were mostly an "illiterate nation" *(umma ummiyya),* "neither reading nor writing," and, (3) since Muḥammad belonged to this nation, he neither read nor wrote, or was unable to do so.

Western scholars have contested, in particular, the idea that *ummī* means "illiterate." While some scholars suggest the meaning of "ethnically Arab/Arabian," others argue in favor of "untaught" or "ignorant" (of the scriptures, as opposed to being "learned," "knowledgeable" about them) or "not having received a revelation" and, strictly speaking, "pagan" and "heathen," or "gentile" (see Günther, Illiteracy, 496; see POLYTHEISM AND ATHEISM; SOUTH ARABIA, RELIGIONS IN PRE-ISLAMIC).

Analysis of the qurʾānic expressions *ummiyyūn* and *umma* (the latter being the noun from which *ummī* is most likely derived, as both classical exegetes and contemporary scholars agree) highlights above all two things. First, *umma* in the Qurʾān means "a people" or, more specifically, "the nation [of the Arabs]" (notwithstanding its other meanings, which are not relevant here; see Günther, Illiteracy, 496-8). Second, the term *ummiyyūn* in the Qurʾān identifies "Arabs who have not [yet] been given a divinely inspired scripture" (cf. Q 3:20, 75; 62:2). On one occasion, however, a certain group among the Jews (see JEWS AND JUDAISM) is called *ummiyyūn,* "not knowing the scripture," or "not being well-versed in the book [q.v.; because they are not reading in it]" (Q 2:78). When the terms *ummī* and pl. *ummiyyūn* are examined in conjunction with the previous two remarks, it becomes clear that in the Qurʾān they do not represent a single meaning. Rather, they suggest a spectrum of ideas, which includes (a) someone belonging to a people *(umma)* — the Arabs — who were a nation without a scripture as yet; (b) someone without a scripture and thus not reading it; and (c) someone not reading a scripture and, therefore, not being taught or educated [by something or somebody] (cf. Günther, Muḥammad, 15-16). Although this spectrum of ideas does not include the meaning of "illiterate" as such, it apparently formed the basis upon which the idea of *ummī* meaning "illiterate" was developed.

The dogma of the Prophet being ummī, *"illiterate"*

The fact that questions surrounding the possibility of Muḥammad's literacy were already an issue of considerable significance at the time of the revelation seems to be evident, for example, in Q 25:5. This passage echoes attempts made by "unbelievers" (polytheists in Mecca) to discredit Muḥammad by claiming that he was not communicating divine revelations, but "stories taken from writings of the ancients (*asāṭīr al-awwalīn;* see GENERATIONS), which he has written down (see WRITING AND WRITING MATERIALS; OPPOSITION TO MUḤAMMAD) and which were dictated to him *(tumlā ʿalayhi)* at dawn (q.v.) and in the early evening" (q.v.; see also Günther, Illiteracy, 492-3). In contrast, Q 29:47-8 states: "We have sent down to you [Muḥammad] the book *(al-kitāb)*.... Not before this did you read *(tatlū)* any book, or inscribe it with your right hand..." (for *talā* referring to "reading [the holy scriptures]," see Günther, Literacy, 190).

The concept of the Prophet's illiteracy, however, "seems to have evolved in some circles of Muslim learning not before the first half of the second century of the *hijra* (see EMIGRATION; CALENDAR)," i.e. the first half of the eight century C.E. (Goldfeld, Illiterate prophet, 58). Furthermore, it seems that Muḥammad's illiteracy had already become dogma by the end of the third/ninth century when al-Ṭabarī (d. 310/923) summed up much of the learning of previous generations of Muslims (see Goldfeld's research into certain exegetical works, which al-Ṭabarī used as sources and quoted in his comments on *ummī* and *ummiyyūn;* see THEOLOGY AND THE QURʾĀN). The famous theologian al-Ghazālī (d. 505/1111), for example, advocates this creed on numerous occasions in his *The revival of the religious sciences (Iḥyāʾ ʿulūm al-dīn),* his greatest and most authoritative work. Here he states that: "He (the Prophet) was *ummī;* he did not read or write.... God [himself] taught him all the virtues of character, the praiseworthy ways of behaving and the information about the ancients and the following generations" (*Iḥyāʾ,* ii, 364 [ch. 11]).

In the course of time, the notion of the illiterate Prophet of Islam came to be a central argument in defending Islam against opponents who attempted to discredit the prophet Muḥammad and his message. Moreover, for the exegete al-Rāzī (d. 606/1210), and other orthodox Muslim scholars in medieval and modern times, this concept also underscores the inimitability and uniqueness of the Qurʾān in terms of content, form and style (*iʿjāz;* see INIMITABILITY), its miraculous nature (*muʿjiza;* see MIRACLES) and the outstanding place Islam and its Prophet deserve within the canon of the monotheistic religions (see LANGUAGE AND STYLE OF THE QURʾĀN; FORM AND STRUCTURE OF THE QURʾĀN). In other words, Muḥammad's illiteracy came to be seen as a particularly excellent sign and proof of the genuineness and nobility of his prophethood (see al-Rāzī's lengthy statement in Günther, Illiteracy, 495-6). The Ṣūfī (see ṢŪFISM AND THE QURʾĀN) ʿAlī b. Muḥammad al-Baghdādī, known as al-Khāzin (d. 741/1340), for example, says:

> The Prophet was *ummī;* he did not read, write, or count.... His being *ummī* is one of the greatest and most magnificent miracles. Had he mastered writing and then come forward with this magnificent Qurʾān, he could have been accused of having written and transmitted it from others (*Lubāb,* ii, 147).

To expand on this tenet could result in trouble, as seen in the example of Abū l-Walīd al-Bājī al-Mālikī (d. 474/1081), a distinguished theologian and man of letters in eleventh-century Spain. The controversy began in the city of Denia, during a teaching session on al-Bukhārī's (d. 256/870) famous collection of "Sound prophetic traditions," which includes an account of the events in 6/628 at al-Ḥudaybiya, when a peace treaty was agreed on between Muḥammad and the Meccan tribe of Quraysh (q.v.). As al-Bukhārī has it: "the messenger of God took the document and wrote this (his name)," *fa-akhadha rasūl Allāh... al-kitāba fa-kataba hādha* (no. 2700), although "he did not write well...," *wa-laysa yuḥsinu yaktubu* [sic] *fa-kataba hādha* (no. 4251; Dārimī, *Sunan,* no. 2507; *wa-laysa yuḥsinu an yaktuba fa-kataba...,* Ibn Ḥanbal, *Musnad,* no. 18,161). Al-Bājī explained the significance of the event and stated furthermore that this tradition was authentic and a proof that the Prophet wrote on that day. Because of his explanation, al-Bājī was accused of heresy and atheism. At a specifically organized public disputation, however, he convinced the learned audience that his opinion did not contradict the Qurʾān — and its notion of the *ummī*/illiterate Prophet — because Q 29:47-8, as al-Bājī argued, indicates (only) that Muḥammad did not write any scripture before he received the revelation *(al-kitāb)* and became a prophet. Al-Bājī later wrote an epistle on this subject to justify his doctrinal position (edited in Bājī, *Taḥqīq,* 170-240), which in turn gave rise to treatises, for and against his position, written by Muslim scholars in Spain, north Africa and Sicily (cf. Bājī, *Taḥqīq,* 115-16, 119; Abū Ḥayyān, *Baḥr,* vii, 155; Sprenger, *Mohammad,* ii, 398; and esp. Fierro, Polémicas, 425). A similar argument is made by the influential Twelver-Shīʿī scholar (see SHĪʿISM AND THE QURʾĀN) and legal authority (see LAW AND THE QURʾĀN), ʿAllāma Majlisī (d. 1110/1698), after he surveyed for his Persian readership the various interpretations of *ummī* common among Muslim scholars. Basing himself also on Q 29:47-8, he supports the idea that Muḥammad was "never taught to read and write" before he became a prophet. He says, however:

whether [or not] he [actually] read and wrote after he became prophet,... there can be no doubt of his ability to do so, inasmuch as he knew all things by divine inspiration, and so by the power of God was able to perform things impossible for all others to do.... How could the Prophet be ignorant [of reading and writing] when he was sent [by God] to instruct others (cf. Majlisī, *Ḥayāt,* ii, 155).

It appears that Q 29:47-8 was instrumental in harmonizing the doctrinal concept of Muḥammad's "illiteracy" with the data given, for example, in historical and biographical sources (see SĪRA AND THE QURʾĀN), according to which Muḥammad seems to have had (some) knowledge of reading and writing at a later stage of his life. Nonetheless, the well-attested incident that reportedly took place on Thursday, June 4, 632 C.E. — i.e. four days before Muḥammad's death — also provides no conclusive answer to the question as to whether or not the prophet Muḥammad was able to read and write at the end of his life. The accounts given by Ibn Saʿd (d. 230/845) relate that the prophet Muḥammad was lying on his sick-bed when he said: *"iʾtūnī* [sic] *bi-dawāt wa-ṣaḥīfa aktubu lakum kitāban lā taḍillū baʿdahu,"* which seems to mean, "Bring me writing instruments and a piece of parchment (or papyrus). I will write (i.e. dictate?) a will for you, after which you will not go astray," rather than, simply, "... I will draft for you a writing...." (cf. Ibn Saʿd, *Ṭabaqāt,* ii, 244-5; for the entire passage, see pp. 242-55, the chapter entitled *al-Kitāb alladhī arāda rasūl Allāh an yaktubahu li-ummatihi;* see furthermore Ghédira, Ṣaḥīfa; Sprenger, *Mohammad,* ii, 400-1; for *kataba [li]* meaning in the Qurʾān also "to decree, to ordain [a will, or law]," see Günther, Literacy, 190-1; similarly, Lane, vii, 2590; on the verbal use of the root *k-t-b* in the Qurʾān in general, see Madigan, *Qurʾān's self-image,* 107-24; on the importance that writing and political documents generally had for Muḥammad in Medina [q.v.] after he had become a statesman, see Hamidullah, *Six originaux,* 23-38, 48-51; Margoliouth, *Mohammed,* 5; see POLITICS AND THE QURʾĀN; for the frequent occurrence of the expressions *al-nabī l-ʿarabī,* "the Arab/Arabian Prophet," in biographical and historical Muslim sources, see for example Wāqidī, *Futūḥ,* ii, 42, 54, 164; Ibn Saʿd, *Ṭabaqāt,* i, 19, 259; Dhahabī, *Siyar,* i, 375; Ibn Khaldūn, *Muqaddima,* 3; Ibn Kathīr, *Bidāya,* ii, 16, 85; Maqqarī, *Nafḥ,* vii, 340, 427; Kātib Chelebi, *Kashf al-ẓunūn,* ii, 1523 and 1718). In conclusion, one notes two things: While the meaning of the terms *ummī* and *ummiyyūn* in the Qurʾān can be determined as indicated above, the question as to whether or not the prophet Muḥammad knew how to read and write (at the end of his life) is another matter that cannot be decided conclusively on the basis of the textual evidence available today.

Sebastian Günther

Bibliography
Primary: Abū Ḥayyān, *Baḥr,* Riyadh 1968; al-Bājī al-Mālikī, Abū l-Walīd Sulaymān b. Khalaf, *Taḥqīq al-madhhab. Yatlūhā ajwibat al-ʿulamāʾ bayna muʾayyid wa-muʿāriḍ ḥawla daʿwā kitābat al-rusūl li-ismihi yawm Ṣulḥ al-Ḥudaybiya,* ed. A.A. al-Ẓāhirī, Riyadh 1403/1983; Bukhārī, *Ṣaḥīḥ,* ed. in *Fatḥ al-bārī bi-sharḥ Ṣaḥīḥ al-Bukhārī... li-Ibn Ḥajar al-ʿAsqalānī,* 13 vols., Beirut 1992; Dhahabī, *Siyar,* i, 375; al-Ghazālī, Abū Ḥāmid Muḥammad, *Iḥyāʾ ʿulūm al-dīn,* 4 vols., Beirut n.d.; Ibn Kathīr, *Bidāya,* ii, 16, 85; Ibn Khaldūn, *Muqaddima,* Beirut 1984; Ibn Saʿd, *Ṭabaqāt;* Kātib Chelebi, *Kashf al-ẓunūn,* 2 vols., Beirut 1413/1992, ii, 1523, 1718; al-Khāzin, ʿAlāʾ al-Dīn ʿAlī b. Muḥammad al-Baghdādī, *Tafsīr al-Qurʾān al-jalīl al-musammā Lubāb al-taʾwīl fī maʿānī al-tanzīl,* Cairo [1910]; Majlisī, Muḥammad Bāqir b. Muḥammad Taqī, *Ḥayāt al-qulūb,* 2 vols., Qom [1952-54]; trans. J.L. Merrick, *The life and religion of Mohammed, As contained in the Sheeāh traditions of the Hyât-ul-Kuloob,* Boston 1850 (chapter "Mohammed's names, possessions, person and character," 85-107); al-Maqqarī, Aḥmad b. Muḥammad, *Nafḥ al-ṭīb,* ed. I. ʿAbbās, 8 vols. (+ 1 vol. Index), Beirut 1968, vii, 340, 427; al-Wāqidī, Abū ʿAbdallāh b. ʿUmar, *Futūḥ al-Shām,* 2 vols., Beirut n.d., ii, 42, 54, 164.
Secondary: Arberry; A. al-Baghdadi, Muhammad, The ummi prophet, in *Arab review* 1/4 (1993), 38-40, esp. 40; N. Calder, The *ummī* in early Islamic juristic literature, in *Der Islam* 67 (1990), 111-23; M. Fierro, Polémicas, in R.M. Pidal (ed.), *Historia de España* [viii, 1], Madrid 1994, 413-54; D.V. Frolov, The spread of literacy in Mecca and Medina at the time of Muḥammad, in *The Humanities in Russia: Soros Laureates. The 1994 all-Russia competition of research projects in humanities,* Moscow 1997, 133-7; A. Ghédira, Ṣāḥīfa, in *EI*[2], viii, 834-5; I. Goldfeld, The illiterate prophet *(nabī ummī).* An inquiry into the development of a dogma in Islamic tradition, in *Der Islam* 57 (1980), 58-67; S. Günther, Illiteracy, in *EQ,* ii, 492-500; id., Literacy, in *EQ,* iii, 188-92; id., Muḥammad, the illiterate prophet. An Islamic creed in the Qurʾān and qurʾānic exegesis, in *Journal of qurʾanic studies* 4/1 (2002), 1-26; M. Hamidullah, *Six originaux des lettres du prophète de l'Islam. Étude paléographique et historique des lettres du prophète,* Paris 1986; Lane; D.A. Madigan, *The Qurʾān's self-image. Writing and authority in Islam's scripture,* Princeton and Oxford 2001; D.S. Margoliouth, *Mohammed,* London [1939], esp. 2-5; O. Pautz, *Muhammeds Lehre von der Offenbarung, quellenmäßig untersucht,* Leipzig 1898 (includes a survey of nineteenth century scholarship on *ummī,* esp. 257-64); H.G. Reissner, The ummī prophet and the Banu Israil of the Qurʾān, in *MW* 39 (1949), 276-81; G. Schoeler, *Charakter und Authentie der muslimischen Überlieferung über das Leben Mohammed,* Berlin and New York 1996, 59-117 (with a comprehensive study of the various reports regarding the first revelation to the prophet Muḥammad, the *iqraʾ*-account); L. Shāyib, *Hal Kāna Muḥammad Umiyyan? Al-ḥaqīqa al-dāʾiʿa bayna aghlāṭ al-muslimīn wa-Mughālaṭāt al-Mustashriqīn,* Beirut 1423/2003; A. Sprenger, *The life of Mohammad from original sources,* Allahabad 1851 (esp. 101-2); id., *Mohammad,* ii, 398-402; S.M. Zwemer, The "illiterate" prophet. Could Mohammed read and write, in *MW* 11 (1921), 344-63.

ʿUmra see PILGRIMAGE

Unbelief/Unbelievers see BELIEF AND UNBELIEF; POLYTHEISM AND ATHEISM; FAITH

Uncertainty

Questioning the truth or existence of something. In the Qurʾān, this is a quality often attributed to those peoples, past and present, who do not believe or trust the messengers (see MESSENGER) or signs (q.v.) of God (see LIE; BELIEF AND UNBELIEF; OPPOSITION TO MUḤAMMAD; TRUST AND PATIENCE). And, like its first auditors, Islamic tradition (and certainly non-Muslims) has grappled with how to understand — and interpret — the word of God (q.v.).

According to the tradition, Islam began with Muḥammad's uncertainty and panic (*fa-akhadhatnī rajfa; al-nashiʾ ʿan al-ruʿb;* Suyūṭī, *Itqān,* i, 93; see FEAR) after a very early revelation (most authorities claim that Q 96:1-5 was the first revelation; see Zarkashī, *Burhān* [*Nawʿ* 10], i, 264; followed by Suyūṭī, *Itqān,* i, 93; see REVELATION AND INSPIRATION) in, or shortly after leaving, the cave (q.v.) of al-Ḥirāʾ (see SĪRA AND THE QURʾĀN; CHRONOLOGY AND THE QURʾĀN; OCCASIONS OF REVELATION; for the archetypical theme of the mythic hero and the cave, see Jung, *Memories,* 160-1; Dreifuss and Riemer, *Abraham,* 6; see also Schub, *"Hakim al-balad..."*). He rushed home to his wife Khadīja (q.v.) in such an agitated state that she threw cold water on him (see e.g. Zarkashī, *Burhān,* i, 264); he then told her to wrap him in a mantle to soothe him (Khadīja was the first *umm al-mu'minīn,* "mother of the faithful"; for a discussion of Muḥammad's revelation in the context of their relationship, cf. Dreyfuss and Riemer, *Abraham,* 89; see WIVES OF THE PROPHET; WOMEN AND THE QUR'ĀN; BELIEF AND UNBELIEF). She reassured him that he was indeed worthy, being an exemplary upright individual (*tu'addī al-amāna...*, literally "you [always] return the surety to its rightful owner..."; on *amana,* cf. Dreyfus and Riemer, *Abraham,* 30); this is the *sabab al-nuzūl,* the occasion for the revelation, of Q 73, Sūrat al-Muzzammil, "The Enshrouded One," and Q 74, Sūrat al-Muddaththir, "The Cloaked One."

The Qur'ān describes itself as a "book in which there is no doubt *(rayb)* [whatsoever]" (Q 2:2; the word *rayb* is glossed by al-Qurṭubī [d. 671/1272; *Jāmi',* i, 119] in his commentary as: (1) equivalent to *shakk,* "doubt"; (2) *tuhma,* "suspicion" [q.v.]; or (3) *ḥāja,* "want"); as *al-yaqīn,* "certainty" (Q 15:99; 74:47); *ḥaqq al-yaqīn,* "certain truth" (q.v.; Q 69:51); *'ilm al-yaqīn,* "certain knowledge" (Q 102:5; see KNOWLEDGE AND LEARNING); *'ayn al-yaqīn,* "certainty itself" (Q 102:7), etc. (for discussion of biblical struggles over questions of faith [q.v.], see Gries, Heresy, 341). Its truth (q.v.) is sempiternal; it is inscribed on the heavenly "preserved tablet" (q.v.; *al-lawḥ al-maḥfūẓ*). The Sunnīs believe that it is uncreated *(ghayr makhlūq)* and coterminous with God (see CREATEDNESS OF THE QUR'ĀN); the medieval Mu'tazilīs (q.v.) demurred, pointing to a resulting diminution of God's unicity (see GOD AND HIS ATTRIBUTES; THEOLOGY AND THE QUR'ĀN).

Despite the qur'ānic assertions of its indubitable nature, the received text of the Qur'ān was subject to scrutiny (see TEXTUAL HISTORY OF THE QUR'ĀN; MUṢḤAF; UNITY OF THE TEXT OF THE QUR'ĀN; COLLECTION OF THE QUR'ĀN; CODICES OF THE QUR'ĀN) by the early Muslim community, and elements such as the foreign vocabulary (q.v.) of the Arabic Qur'ān had to be explained (see ARABIC LANGUAGE; LANGUAGE AND STYLE OF THE QUR'ĀN; GRAMMAR AND THE QUR'ĀN):

From Abū Bakr, the eminently veracious *(al-siddīq),* [is related] that when asked about the meaning of *abb* [Q 80:31, a word, probably from Syriac, that is usually translated as "herbage"], he said: "Which heaven would cover me and which earth would support me if I were to say that there is something in the Book of God that I know not?" [A correct translation: "If I were to say about the book of God what I know not."]

From 'Umar [is related] that when asked about the meaning of *abb,* he said that he once recited this verse and said: "We all know that. But what is *abb?*" Then he threw away a stick which he had in his hand, and said: "By the eternal God! That is artificiality. What does it amount to for you, son of the mother of 'Umar, if you do not know what *abb* is?" And then he added: "Obey what is clear to you in this Book and leave aside what is not clear!" (Gätje, *Qur'ān,* 64, translating Zamakhsharī, *Kashshāf,* ad Q 80:31).

It should be noted, however, that neither Shī'īs nor Sunnīs doubt the authenticity and veracity of the received text of the Qur'ān although some Shī'ī scholars have questioned its integrity (see INIMITABILITY).

The therapeutic antidote to uncertainty/doubt and its resulting anxiety is to invoke the *sakīna* (e.g. Q 2:248; 9:40; 48:4, 18, 26; see SHEKHINAH) through "patience and prayer" (Q 2:45, 153; see TRUST AND PATIENCE; PRAYER) in order to be able to grasp *al-ʿurwa al-wuthqā* (Q 2:256; 31:22, lit. "the firm hand-hold on the camel-saddle"; see METAPHOR).

Michael B. Schub

Bibliography
Primary: Qurṭubī, *Jāmiʿ*, Beirut 2002; Suyūṭī, *Itqān;* Zarkashī, *Burhān*, Beirut 2001.
Secondary: A.Y. ʿAlī, *The meaning of the holy Qurʾān*, Beltsville, MD 1989; M. Cook, *Muhammad*, Oxford 1983; G. Dreifuss and J. Riemer, *Abraham. The man and the symbol*, Wilmette, IL 1995; H. Gätje, *The Qurʾān and its exegesis*, trans. A. Welch, Berkeley 1976; Z. Gries, Heresy, in A.A. Cohen and P. Mendes-Flohr (eds.), *Contemporary Jewish religious thought*, New York 1972, 339-52; C. Jung, *Memories, dreams, reflections*, Garden City, NY 1963; S. Murata and W. Chittick, *The vision of Islam*, New York 1994; Pickthall, *Koran;* D. Powers, The exegetical genre *nāsikh al-Qurʾān*, in Rippin, *Approaches*, 138; M. Schub, *"Hakim al-balad..."*, in *ZAL* 38 (2000), 88-90; id., Review of H. Berg, *The development of exegesis in early Islam. The authenticity of Muslim literature from the formative period*, Richmond, Surrey 2000, in *JAL* 33/3 (2002), 293-4; Watt-Bell, *Introduction*.

Uncle see FAMILY; KINSHIP

Unclean see CONTAMINATION

Unction see BAPTISM

Unity of God see GOD AND HIS ATTRIBUTES; WITNESS TO FAITH

Unity of the Text of the Qurʾān

As a subject of study, the unity of the qurʾānic text assumes special importance because the Qurʾān does not always seem to deal with its themes in what most readers would call a systematic manner (see FORM AND STRUCTURE OF THE QURʾĀN). Western scholars of Islam have often spoken of the "disconnectedness" of the Qurʾān (see PRE-1800 PREOCCUPATIONS OF QURʾĀNIC STUDIES; POST-ENLIGHTENMENT ACADEMIC STUDY OF THE QURʾĀN). Historically, most Muslim exegetes have not raised the issue at all (see EXEGESIS OF THE QURʾĀN: CLASSICAL AND MEDIEVAL). Of those who have, some have offered the apologetic explanation that a text revealed in portions (see REVELATION AND INSPIRATION) over more than two decades cannot have a high degree of unity (see CHRONOLOGY AND THE QURʾĀN; OCCASIONS OF REVELATION). But a few others, notably Fakhr al-Dīn al-Rāzī (d. 606/1210) and Ibrāhīm b. ʿUmar al-Biqāʿī (d. 885/1480), present the Qurʾān as a well-connected text (for further discussion of the concept of *tanāsub/munāsaba*, see TRADITIONAL DISCIPLINES OF QURʾĀNIC STUDY). A distinction must, however, be made between connection and unity: the former may be defined as any link — strong or weak, integral or tangential — that is seen to exist between the components of a text (see LITERARY STRUCTURES OF THE QURʾĀN; LANGUAGE AND STYLE OF THE QURʾĀN), whereas unity arises from a perception of a given text's coherence and integration and from its being subject to a centralizing perspective. In the second chapter of *al-Burhān fī ʿulūm al-Qurʾān*, al-Zarkashī (d. 794/1392) seems to make this distinction, but most of his illustrative examples bear upon the Qurʾān's connectedness rather than upon its unity. The attempts of al-Rāzī and others also do not go beyond demonstrating that the Qurʾān is, in the above-noted sense, a connected text. In modern times, however, a number of Muslim scholars from various parts of the Muslim world have, with varying degrees of cogency, argued that the Qurʾān possesses a high degree of thematic and structural unity, and this view seems to represent a modern consensus in the making (see CONTEMPORARY CRITICAL PRACTICES AND THE QURʾĀN; EXEGESIS OF THE QURʾĀN: EARLY MODERN AND CONTEMPORARY). In the introduction to his *Tafhīm al-Qurʾān*, Abū l-Aʿlā Mawdūdī (d. 1979) maintains that one can appreciate the unity of the qurʾānic text if one notes that nowhere does the Qurʾān depart from its subject (humankind's ultimate success and failure; see ESCHATOLOGY; REWARD AND PUNISHMENT), its central thesis (the need for humans to take the right attitude in life — that is, to accept God's sovereignty [q.v.] in all spheres of life and submit to him in practice; see VIRTUES AND VICES, COMMANDING AND FORBIDDING) and its goal (to invite man to adopt that right attitude). One of Sayyid Quṭb's (d. 1966) premises in *Fī ẓilāl al-Qurʾān* is that each sūra (q.v.) of the Qurʾān has a *miḥwar* (pivot, axis) that makes the sūra a unified whole. But perhaps the most sustained effort to bring out the unity of the qurʾānic text has been made by two exegetes of the Indian subcontinent, Ḥamīd al-Dīn al-Farāhī (d. 1930) and his student Amīn Aḥsan Iṣlāḥī (d. 1997). Developing his teacher's ideas, Iṣlāḥī in his *Tadabbur-i Qurʾān* shows that the Qurʾān possesses unity at several levels: the verse-sequence in each sūra deals with a well-defined theme in a methodical manner (see VERSES); the sūras, as a rule, exist as pairs, the two sūras of any pair being complementary to each other; and the sūras are divisible into seven groups, each dealing with a master theme that is developed systematically within the sūras of the group. The Farāhī-Iṣlāḥī thesis would seem to constitute a serious challenge to the theories that view the Qurʾān as a disconnected text.

Mustansir Mir

Bibliography
Primary: Amīn Aḥsan Iṣlāḥī, *Tadabbur-i Qurʾān,* 9 vols., Lahore 2000; Abū l-Aʿlā Mawdūdī, *Tafhīm al-Qurʾān,* 6 vols., Lahore 1949-72; Quṭb, *Ẓilāl;* Zarkashī, *Burhān.*
Secondary: M. Mir, *Coherence in the Qurān. A study of Iṣlāḥī's concept of* naẓm *in* Tadabbur-i Qurʾān, Indianapolis 1986; id., The sura as a unity. A twentieth-century development in qurʾānic exegesis, in Hawting and Shareef, *Approaches,* 211-24.

Universe

see COSMOLOGY; CREATION; NATURE AS SIGNS

Urination and Defecation

see CONTAMINATION

Usury

[Unlawful] profit gained as interest charged when loaning money. The Qurʾān refers to both interest and usury as *ribā* and renounces evil effects on the equal, just and productive distribution of resources. The denunciation of *ribā* applies to excesses in both financial contracts *(ribā l-faḍl)* and fungibles *(ribā l-nasīʾa)*. It also applies to all forms of interest — nominal, real, effective, simple and compound (see also ECONOMICS; MONEY; TRADE AND COMMERCE).

Q 30:39 provides the general definition of *ribā* relating to all forms and measures of gifts (see GIFT AND GIFT-GIVING) and exchanges:

And that which you give in compensation *(wa-mā ātaytum min riban)* in order that it may increase [i.e. your wealth (q.v.)] from other's property (q.v.), has no increase with God; but that which you give in charity seeking God's countenance (see FACE OF GOD), then those they shall have manifold increase (Q 30:39).

In marked contrast with the qurʾānic encouragement and praise of the charitable distribution of wealth, such as almsgiving (q.v.; cf. Schacht, Ribā), we can infer the unacceptability of all forms of interest from the following qur'ānic verse by using the idea of the term structure of interest rates. The Qur'ān says: "O you who believe! Devour not *ribā*, doubled and multiplied; but fear (q.v.) God, that you may prosper" (Q 3:130). Although a few Islamicists do not concede to a uniform implication of the qur'ānic *ribā*-law in all forms of interest (i.e. usury versus interest, compound versus simple interest), this differentiation is untenable. It is well-known from the theory of the term structure of interest rates that any simple (i.e. one period) interest rate can be expressed as the compound rates over many smaller time-periods within a given time horizon. Besides, because nominal rates are abolished in the *ribā* rule, real rates cannot exist. The real rate is the nominal rate net of the rate of change in price level (inflation rate). Nominal rate is abolished by the financial and real economic interrelationship, which also, by means of the direct productivity consequence of such an interrelationship, causes the rate of increase in money to equal the rate of increase in real economic returns. Consequently, inflationary conditions caused by a mismatch of the above-mentioned two rates cannot exist. The inappropriateness of the equation in terms of nominal, real and inflation rates is therefore non-existent in Islamic economic relations, and the reason behind this is both the complementary relationship between money and real economy and the institutional and policy action towards realizing such complementarities.

Regarding the qur'ānic principle of just measure (see WEIGHTS AND MEASURES; MEASUREMENT) in gifts and exchanges there is the following in Q 2:279:

> And if you do not do it [i.e. give up *ribā*], then receive a declaration of war (q.v.) from God and his messenger (q.v.), but if you repent (see REPENTANCE AND PENANCE), you will have your *capital sums (ru'ūs amwālikum)*. Deal not unjustly and you will not be dealt with unjustly (see JUSTICE AND INJUSTICE).

The Qur'ān strongly forbids *ribā* on the grounds that it fosters the unjust acquisition of wealth at the expense of social justice, the equitable distribution of wealth and the well-being of the community. According to the Qur'ān, these important values are achieved through solidarity, co-operation and active production of the good things of life (see GOOD AND EVIL; BLESSING; GRACE; ETHICS AND THE QUR'ĀN). The jurist al-Shāṭibī (d. 790/1388) explains the concept of the good things of life as a combination of necessities *(ḍarūriyyāt)*, comforts *(ḥājiyyāt)* and refinements *(taḥsīniyyāt)*, all of which belong to the hierarchy of positive, life-fulfilling goods.

Several verses testify to this interconnection between the abolition of *ribā* and the promotion of trade, charity and social well-being. On the causal linkage among charity, trade, prosperity and social well-being, the Qur'ān declares:

> Those who (in charity) spend of their goods by night and day (see DAY AND NIGHT), in secret and in public (see SECRETS; HIDDEN AND THE HIDDEN), have their reward with their lord (q.v.): On them shall be no fear, nor shall they grieve (see JOY AND MISERY). Those who devour *ribā* will not stand except as stands one whom the evil one by his touch has driven to madness (see INSANITY; DEVIL). That is because they say: "Trade is like *ribā*'. But God has permitted trade and forbidden *ribā*..." (Q 2:274-5).

Q 2:265 makes the connection between spending on the good things of life and social well-being:

And the likeness of those who spend their substance, seeking to please God and to strengthen their souls (q.v.), is as a garden (q.v.), high and fertile (*jannatin bi-rabwatin;* see also PARABLES): heavy rain (see WATER) falls on it and makes it yield a double increase of harvest, and if it receives not heavy rain, light moisture [suffices it]. God sees well whatever you do (Q 2:265; see SEEING AND HEARING).

This interrelationship between the abolition of *ribā* and the productivity and well-being attained through trade and charity is important to note. There are clear connections between the abolition of *ribā* and the implementation of co-operative and participatory financial instruments for resource mobilization, such as profit sharing, equity participation and trade. These generate and mobilize productive spending on the good things of life and allow economic participation for all ranks of society, thereby creating social and political empowerment (see KINGS AND RULERS; OPPRESSED ON EARTH, THE; OPPRESSION; POLITICS AND THE QURʾĀN). Q 2:267 speaks to these issues of production, consumption, exchange and distribution:

O you who believe (see BELIEF AND UNBELIEF)! Give of the good things which you have [honorably] earned, and of what we have produced for you from the ground (see AGRICULTURE AND VEGETATION), and do not aim at [getting anything which is] bad, in order that you may give away some of it, when you yourselves would not receive it except with closed eyes. And know that God is free of all wants *(ghaniyyun),* and worthy of all praise (q.v.; Q 2:267; see also GOD AND HIS ATTRIBUTES).

While the full implication of these interrelationships mentioned above are too detailed to be elaborated in this brief entry, the salient feature can be stated: the abolition of *ribā* can activate the mobilization of financial resources through its linkage with real resource development. This causes employment, profitability, equity and efficiency, entitlement, empowerment and social security to emerge as elements of the total social well-being (see WORK). These gains ratify, in turn, the judgment to abolish *ribā* and generate a continuing cycle of socially beneficial economic development.

Masudul Alam Choudhury

Bibliography

R.Ḥ. ʿAbd al-Raḥmān, *al-Ribā,* Cairo 1978; ʿA.J. Abū Zayd, *Fiqh al-ribā. Dirāsa muqārana shāmila lil-taṭbīqāt al-muʿāṣira,* Beirut 2004; M.S. al-Ashmāwī, *al-Ribā wa-l-fāʾida fī l-islām,* Cairo 1988; R. Brunschvig, Conceptions monétaires chez les jurists musulmans, in *Arabica* 14 (1967), 113-43; add. in *Arabica* 15 (1968), 316; repr. in id., *Etudes d'islamologie,* 2 vols., Paris 1976, ii, 271-301; M.A. Choudhury, *The Islamic world-system. Polity-market interaction,* London 2003; id., *Money in Islam,* London 1997; id. and U.A. Malik, *The foundations of Islamic political economy,* London 1992, chap. 4; Th.W. Juynboll, *Handbuch des islāmischen Gesetztes,* Leiden 1910, 270-6; R. Lohlker, *Schariʿa und Moderne. Diskussionen über Schwangerschaft, Versicherung und Zinsen,* Stuttgart 1996, 107-39; F. Rahman, Riba and interest, in *Islamic studies* 3 (1964), 1-43; E. Sachau, *Muhammedanisches Recht nach schafiitischer Lehre,* Stuttgart 1897, 279-81 (sects. 3-4); 284-7 (sects. 6-9); 298-9 (sect. 15); D. Santillana, *Istituzioni di diritto musulmano malichita,* 2 vols., Rome 1926-38, ii, 60-6; J. Schacht, Ribā, in *EI²*, viii, 491-3; A. Sen, *On ethics and economics,* Oxford 1987 (on the contemporary conception of social well-being); al-Shāṭibī, Abū Isḥāq Ibrāhīm b. Mūsā, *al-Muwāfaqāt fī uṣūl al-sharīʿa,* trans. A. Draz, Cairo n.d. (on the Islamic conception of social well-being, *al-maṣlaḥa*).

Uterus see WOMB

ʿUthmān

Abū ʿAbdallāh ʿUthmān b. ʿAffān, third caliph (q.v.; r. 23-35/644-55) and first "rightly guided" *(rāshid)* caliph from the Umayyad clan, an early convert to Islam and emigrant (*muhājir;* see EMIGRANTS AND HELPERS) to both Abyssinia (q.v.) and Medina (q.v.; see also EMIGRATION). These pious credentials (see PIETY) are tainted by his absence at the battle of Badr (q.v.), his flight at Uḥud (see EXPEDITIONS AND BATTLES), his absence at Ḥudaybiya (q.v.; see Bukhārī, *Ṣaḥīḥ,* 66, *Faḍāʾil al-Qurʾān,* 3; ed. Krehl, iii, 93; trans. Houdas, iii, 522-3) and his alleged impiety during the latter six years of his caliphal rule (Masʿūdī, *Murūj,* iii, 76). He was stabbed to death while reading from the Qurʾān (supposedly from the *muṣḥaf* [q.v.] now known as the Samarqand codex) by insurgents from Egypt. ʿUthmān is often credited with standardizing and codifying the present qurʾānic text, which is therefore called the ʿUthmānic codex (see also COLLECTION OF THE QURʾĀN; CODICES OF THE QURʾĀN).

The historicity of the ʿUthmānic codex narrative is, for the most part, accepted by scholars in preference to narratives attributing the collection to Abū Bakr or other early caliphs (Caetani, ʿUthmān; Nöldeke, *GQ,* ii, 11-27, 47-62; Jeffery, *Materials,* 4-9; pace Mingana, Transmission). This narrative relates that one of ʿUthmān's generals (Ḥudhayfa), alarmed at disputes between his Syrian and Iraqi soldiers over qurʾānic recitation (see RECITATION OF THE QURʾĀN; SYRIA; IRAQ) during the conquests (see CONQUEST), asked the caliph for guidance, imploring: "O Commander of the Faithful, inform this community what to do before we are divided in our reading (see PARTIES AND FACTIONS; READINGS OF THE QURʾĀN) like the Jews (see JEWS AND JUDAISM) and the Christians" (Bukhārī, *Ṣaḥīḥ,* 62, *Faḍāʾil aṣḥāb al-nabī,* 7; ed. Krehl, ii, 430-1; trans. Houdas, ii, 601-2; see also CHRISTIANS AND CHRISTIANITY). In response, ʿUthmān secured the Qurʾān materials already gathered by Abū Bakr from Ḥafṣa (q.v.; who had received them via Abū Bakr's successor, her father ʿUmar; see also WIVES OF THE PROPHET). With this as reference, and with a committee made up of the pro-Qurayshite Medinan Zayd b. Thābit (also protagonist of the Abū Bakr collection narrative) and three Qurayshites (see QURAYSH), ʿUthmān had a *muṣḥaf* written in the dialect of the Quraysh (see DIALECTS; ARABIC LANGUAGE). He sent copies of it to Baṣra, Kūfa, Damascus and Mecca (q.v.; Yaʿqūbī, *Taʾrīkh,* ii, 160, adds Egypt, Bahrain, Yemen and the Jazīra) and ordered that all variant versions be destroyed, an order that met with resistance from many (see RECITERS OF THE QURʾĀN; TEACHING AND PREACHING THE QURʾĀN) and outright refusal from the Companion Ibn Masʿūd in Kūfa (see COMPANIONS OF THE PROPHET). Al-Balādhurī (fl. third/ninth cent.; *Ansāb,* v, 36) has Ibn Masʿūd declare the caliph's blood licit in response, while al-Yaʿqūbī (d. early fourth/tenth cent.; *Taʾrīkh,* ii, 160) relates that the two came to blows in the mosque at Kūfa.

The historicity of this narrative, however, is not beyond dispute. A number of factors — conflicts between different versions, redundancies with the Abū Bakr collection narrative and the temporal distance of sources from events — suggest that it is more the product of speculation and apology than historical dictation (in fact, early Muslim scholars disputed how to reconcile the redundant and contradictory reports; Khaṭṭābī [d. 386/996] concludes that God inspired *[alhama]* all of the "rightly guided caliphs," *al-khulafāʾ al-rāshidūn;* see Suyūṭī, *Itqān,* 202 [beginning of chap. 18]).
J. Burton (*Collection,* 202-39) argues that the narrative is meant to conceal the fact that Muḥammad himself compiled the Qurʾān, thus justifying the absence from the *muṣḥaf* (that is, the Qurʾān in book form; see ORALITY AND WRITING IN ARABIA) of certain elements argued to be in the revealed

Qurʾān (e.g. the stoning [q.v.] verse, *āyat al-rajm*). Burton also points out that alternate codices continued to be used in legal disputes after they were supposedly destroyed by ʿUthmān's orders, suggesting that they were actually "posterior, not prior, to the ʿUthman text" (ibid., 228; see ABROGATION; LAW AND THE QURʾĀN). J. Wansbrough (*QS*, 45), meanwhile, noting the absence of extant variations to the ʿUthmānic codex and considering it unlikely that the caliph could have done such a complete job of destroying other versions, suggests that the story is meant to conceal the late origins of the Qurʾān. A recently edited work, however, further complicates this hypothesis (cf. Crone and Zimmermann, *Epistle*).

Thus scholarly opinion differs in its estimation of ʿUthmān: some see him as the one who established, with pious meticulousness, the *textus receptus ne varietur* of the Qurʾān; others regard him as a semi-legendary figure of Islamic salvation history. This much seems clear: many traditions surrounding ʿUthmān's codification of the Qurʾān come from a period when Islamic religious development was fueled by apologetical and polemical concerns (see APOLOGETICS; POLEMIC AND POLEMICAL LANGUAGE). In the third and fourth Islamic centuries texts on the proofs *(dalāʾil)* of Muḥammad's prophecy (see PROPHETS AND PROPHETHOOD; MIRACLES), the inimitability (q.v.; *iʿjāz*) of the Qurʾān and the refutation *(radd)* of other religions proliferated (see TOLERANCE AND COERCION; RELIGIOUS PLURALISM AND THE QURʾĀN). The ʿUthmānic codex narrative serves a clear purpose in this context: it confirms to Muslims that their *muṣḥaf* is indeed the Qurʾān sent down from heaven (see BOOK; HEAVENLY BOOK; THEOLOGY AND THE QURʾĀN; CREATEDNESS OF THE QURʾĀN). Further work on early Qurʾān manuscripts (such as the find in Ṣanʿāʾ; see MANUSCRIPTS OF THE QURʾĀN; TOOLS FOR THE STUDY OF THE QURʾĀN) — not excluding the study of the orality (q.v.) and variety of readings of the qurʾānic text (see POST-ENLIGHTENMENT ACADEMIC STUDY OF THE QURʾĀN) — remains a desideratum for a fuller understanding of the historicity of the narratives concerning the formation of the ʿUthmānic codex (see also TRADITIONAL DISCIPLINES OF QURʾĀNIC STUDY; VERSES; SŪRAS).

Gabriel Said Reynolds

Bibliography
Primary: Ibn ʿAsākir, *Taʾrīkh*, ed. ʿAmrawī; al-Balādhurī, Aḥmad b. Yaḥyā, *Ansāb al-ashrāf*, ed. S. Goitein, 5 vols., Jerusalem 1936; Bukhārī, *Ṣaḥīḥ*, ed. Krehl; trans. O. Houdas and W. Marçais, *Les traditions islamiques*, Paris 1908; P. Crone and F. Zimmermann (eds.), *The epistle of Sālim ibn Dhakwān*, Oxford 2001; Suyūṭī, *Itqān;* Yaʿqūbī, *Taʾrīkh*, ed. M. Ṣādiq, Najaf 1964.
Secondary: Burton, *Collection* (alternative visions of the development of the qurʾānic text); L. Caetani, ʿUthmān and the recension of the Koran, in *MW* 5 (1915), 380-90; M. Hinds, The murder of the caliph ʿUthmān, in *IJMES* 3 (1972), 450-69; Jeffery, *Materials;* Ch. Luxenberg, *Die Syro-Aramäische Lesart des Koran*, Berlin 2000 (alternative visions of the qurʾānic text); W. Madelung, *The succession to Muḥammad*, Cambridge 1998, chap. 3; A. Mingana, The transmission of the Koran, in *MW* 7 (1917), 223-32, 402-14; H. Motzki, The collection of the Qurʾān, in *Der Islam* 78 (2001), 1-35 (a defense of the historicity of the ʿUthmān narrative); Nöldeke, *GQ;* A.-L. de Prémare, *Les fondations de l'Islam*, Paris 2002, 278-316; Wansbrough, *QS* (alternative visions of the qurʾānic text).

ʿUzayr see EZRA

al-ʿUzzā see IDOLS AND IMAGES; SATANIC VERSES

V

Vainglory see PRIDE

Valley see GEOGRAPHY

Variant Readings see READINGS OF THE QURʾĀN

Vegetation see AGRICULTURE AND VEGETATION

Vehicles

Objects used to carry people or things from place to place, on land or sea or through the air. The Qurʾān mentions several kinds of vehicles while attributing their existence to God's bounty (see BLESSING; GRACE), as stated, for example, in Q 17:70: "And surely we have honored the children of Adam, and we carry them in the land and the sea (see EARTH; WATER), and we have given them of the good things (see SUSTENANCE)...." The same idea recurs in Q 10:22: "He it is who makes you travel by land and sea" (see also TRIPS AND VOYAGES; JOURNEY).

The vehicles operating on land are beasts of burden, and their kinds are enumerated in Q 16:8: "And (God made) horses and mules and asses that you might ride upon them...." The camel (q.v.; *baʿīr*) is mentioned separately as a vehicle carrying wheat (Q 12:65, 72; see AGRICULTURE AND VEGETATION). Q 59:6 implies that camels (called here *rikāb*), as well as horses, were used also in military campaigns (see EXPEDITIONS AND BATTLES; FIGHTING; WAR).

God's creation of beasts on which people can ride and of which they eat (see FOOD AND DRINK; HIDES AND FLEECE) is praised in Q 36:72 as a manifestation of the things that God has subdued to them for their own benefit (see also Q 40:79). Beasts of burden carry not only people but also cargo: They "carry your heavy loads to regions which you could not reach but with distress of the souls" (Q 16:7; see also Q 6:142; see SOUL; LOAD OR BURDEN). On the other hand, sacred kinds of such animals were considered by the idolaters forbidden (q.v.) for usage as vehicles (Q 6:138).

Ships (q.v.), too, signify God's benevolence toward humankind, and they are mentioned alongside of riding animals in Q 43:12-13: "He who created pairs of all things (see PAIRS AND PAIRING), and made for you ships and beasts of burden such as you ride, that you may firmly sit on their backs, then remember the favor of your lord when you are firmly seated thereon, and say: Glory be to him (see GLORIFICATION OF GOD) who made this subservient to us and we were not able to do it" (see also Q 2:164; 23:22; 40:80).

The imposing shape of sailing ships signifies God's creative powers, as stated in Q 42:32: "And among his signs (q.v.) are the ships that ride on the sea like landmarks" (see also Q 55:24). The glory (q.v.) of ships as representing divine blessing comes out most clearly in the fact that in Q 51:3 God swears by them, calling them "the smooth runners" (*fa-l-jāriyāti yusran;* see OATHS).

The idea that God is the one who has put ships under human command means that people should be thankful to him (Q 14:32; 16:14; 17:66; 22:65; 30:46; 31:31; 35:12; 45:12; see GRATITUDE AND INGRATITUDE). Noah's (q.v.) ark (q.v.) was the first manifestation of God's kindness in providing transport on sea and all ships have preserved the beneficence of this original model of divine salvation (q.v.). This parallelism comes out in Q 36:42 in which God alludes to the ark saying: "And we have created for them the like of it, whereon they ride." Most commentators hold that by "the like of it" ships are meant but some contend that the allusion is to camels (see SYMBOLIC IMAGERY).

Vehicles operating in the air (see AIR AND WIND) occur in the legendary sphere, in the commentaries on Q 21:81. This verse states that God has made the wind subservient to Solomon (q.v.) and it was "blowing violent and pursuing its course by his command to the land which we have blessed." Tradition has it that the wind would carry Solomon from place to place and then bring him back to his home in the holy land (see SACRED PRECINCTS; SACRED AND PROFANE). See also ANIMAL LIFE for further discussion, and bibliography.

Uri Rubin

Bibliography

Rāzī, *Tafsīr;* Ṭabarī, *Tafsīr;* Zamakhsharī, *Kashshāf.*

Veil

Device that creates separation or privacy. The concept of veiling associated with a woman covering her body (see NUDITY) appears in no definitive terms in the Qurʾān. Instead the Qurʾān contains various verses (q.v.) in which the word *ḥijāb,* literally a "screen, curtain," from the root *ḥ-j-b,* meaning to cover or screen, is used to refer to a sense of separation, protection and covering that has both concrete and metaphorical connotations (see METAPHOR). *Ḥijāb* has, however, evolved in meaning and is most commonly used to denote the idea of a Muslim woman's veil, either full or partial, and more generally to denote a level of segregation between the sexes (see GENDER; WOMEN AND THE QURʾĀN). The word appears seven times in the Qurʾān (according to the traditional chronological sequence of revelation, Q 19:17; 38:32; 17:45; 41:5; 42:51; 7:46; 33:53; see CHRONOLOGY AND THE QURʾĀN) and has a common semantic theme of separation (Stowasser, *Women,* 168), albeit not primarily between the sexes. In Q 19:17, Mary (q.v.) withdraws from her family and "places a screen *(ḥijāb)* [to screen herself] from them." In Q 17:45, when the believers (see BELIEF AND UNBELIEF) recite the Qurʾān (see RECITATION OF THE QURʾĀN), God "places a thick/invisible veil *(ḥijāban mastran)* between them and those who do not believe in the hereafter" (see ESCHATOLOGY). Similarly, in Q 41:5, those who do not wish to listen to or accept Muḥammad's message say that there is a distance, *ḥijāb*, between them and the Prophet (see OPPOSITION TO MUḤAMMAD). In Q 7:46, for those people who deliberately lead others

[1] Contemporary Pakistani truck, decorated with talismanic slogans, among which are Qur'ān passages. Photograph courtesy of Jamal J. Elias.

astray (q.v.) from God's path (see PATH OR WAY) or do not believe in the hereafter, "there will be a veil/screen *(ḥijāb)* between them and... those who know" (see KNOWLEDGE AND LEARNING). In Q 42:51, God claims that he sends revelation to humankind in one of three ways: inspiration (see REVELATION AND INSPIRATION), messengers (see MESSENGER; PROPHETS AND PROPHETHOOD) or from behind a veil/curtain *(min warāʾi ḥijāb)*. Commentators (see EXEGESIS OF THE QURʾĀN: CLASSICAL AND MEDIEVAL) have drawn on traditions from Muslim's (d. ca. 261/875) ḥadīth collection (see ḤADĪTH AND THE QURʾĀN) to the effect that this veil refers to a veil of light. In these verses, *ḥijāb* carries various metaphorical levels of meaning, specifically as something that separates truth (q.v.) from falsehood (see LIE) and light (q.v.) from dark (see DARKNESS). This idea has been elaborated significantly by the mystics (see ṢŪFISM AND THE QURʾĀN) who see *ḥijāb* as the curtain or barrier (q.v.) that lies between them and God, the object of their devotion.

The most common meaning of screen or veil as implied in *ḥijāb* has, however, become synonymous with the various forms of clothing (q.v.) that a Muslim woman wears to cover either her hair, her hair and face or her full body when in public or when in the company of those outside close kinship (q.v.) bonds (see also PROHIBITED DEGREES). Although the Qurʾān itself enjoins modest behavior for both men and women (see MODESTY; SEX AND SEXUALITY) and contains no precise prescriptions as to how a woman's body should be covered in public, arguments in favor of such modes of covering stem from a literal as well as historical interpretation of various verses (see FEMINISM AND THE QURʾĀN; PATRIARCHY). Some of the verses deal specifically with items of clothing, some refer more generally to behaving modestly. The verse most famously known as the *ḥijāb* verse itself refers more specifically to the observance of certain manners when in the company of the Prophet and/or his wives (see WIVES OF THE PROPHET). Q 33:53,

O believers, do not enter the Prophet's houses unless permission is given to you for a meal... and if you ask them [the Prophet's wives] for something you need, ask them from behind a *ḥijāb*, that is purer for your hearts and their hearts (see HEART).

There are variances in opinion as to the exact context in which this verse was revealed (see OCCASIONS OF REVELATION) but many of the *tafsīr* accounts identify the occasion as Zaynab bt. Jahsh's marriage to the Prophet. The guests invited to the wedding outstayed their welcome but they also failed to observe the proper etiquette when in proximity to the Prophet's wives. The concept of *ḥijāb* here is actually a literal curtain/screen which the Prophet let fall between his chambers and his companions so as to afford his wives privacy and protection. It also prescribes a level of seclusion for the Prophet's wives away from the public gaze by virtue of their special and specific status. In fact, the verses soon after in Q 33:55 give a list of individuals with whom it is permissible for the wives to associate face to face ("their fathers, their sons, their brothers, their brothers' sons, their sisters' sons, their women, the [slaves] whom their right hands possess"). The subsequent revelation in Q 33:59, known as the "mantle verse," addresses itself to the Prophet that he should "tell his wives and daughters and the women of the believers" that they should cover themselves in a mantle or a cloak *(jalābībihinna)* when outside. The verse explains that this is so that believing women are recognized in the streets by virtue of their outer covering and not molested in the streets of Medina (q.v.). The advice on preserving modesty is contained in Q 24:30 which tells the believing men to "lower their gaze and guard their private parts" *(yaghuḍḍū min abṣārihim wa-yaḥfaẓū furūjahum)*. Q 24:31 goes on to address Muslim women:

And tell the believing women to lower their gaze and guard their private parts, and to not display their adornments *(zīna)* except for what is apparent, and let them draw their coverings (*khumur*, sing. *khimār*) over their bosoms (*juyūb*, sing. *jayb*), and not display their adornments except to their husbands, their fathers (see FAMILY; MARRIAGE AND DIVORCE)....

Both these verses deal directly with the external appearance of all believing women, urging them to adopt a certain decorum in both their posture and clothing when outside the home. The verses are not concerned with restricting women's movement nor secluding women within the home. Q 33:33, however, which instructs the Prophet's wives to "stay in your houses" as befitting the wives of God's messenger, has also become part of the whole segregation/modesty debate. The internal domestic space for the wives of the Prophet becomes the ideal space for all righteous women.

The concept of veiling then develops between the two distinct but related concepts of clothing that hides and space that secludes. In both cases, the conceptual framework is one where gender boundaries are already assumed within the predominant cultural context and the issue at hand is that of determining the basis upon which these boundaries can be further established. The use of these three words, *ḥijāb, jilbāb* and *khimār* in the Qurʾān and the subsequent *tafsīr* and legal debate (see LAW AND THE QURʾĀN) have led to a diversity of opinion about the exact nature and context of female covering or veiling. To some extent the discussions have revolved around the distinction made between those verses that address the wives of the Prophet in particular, for whom both physical covering and physical seclusion with the advent of the *ḥijāb* verse reflects their special status, and those verses that advise all believing women to adopt some level of concealing dress. Scholars have argued on both sides; either that whatever has been prescribed for the Prophet's wives must naturally be applied to all believing women or from the opposite perspective that it was precisely because the Prophet's wives were seen as a privileged group of women that they were advised to assume a greater level of seclusion from public gaze for their own protection.

Classical commentaries go into very little discussion about the precise nature of female dress but do discuss specific issues such as what parts of her body a woman is permitted to show. In so doing, they debate the very nature of a woman's *ʿawra*, literally, genitalia or pudendum. For al-Ṭabarī (d. 310/923), as women pray (see PRAYER) and perform the pilgrimage (q.v.; *ḥajj*) with their face and hands exposed, it would be correct to argue that these parts of a woman's body are not *ʿawra* and therefore can and should be left exposed. He argues that it is therefore the hands and the face that are alluded to in Q 24:31, "except that which is apparent" (Ṭabarī, *Tafsīr*, v, 419). Al-Bayḍāwī (d. prob. 716/1316-17; *Anwār*, ii, 20), however, argued that a woman's whole body is *ʿawra* and must therefore be concealed from the eyes of men outside the permitted degrees of kinship. This discussion continued well into the legal tradition, but aside from a general consensus that women should be covered in public, no form of dress is prescribed. For the Shāfiʿīs and the Ḥanbalīs, the concept of *ʿawra* was applied to the entire female body, including the face, hands and below the ankles; the Mālikīs and the Ḥanafīs, however, excluded the face and the hands from *ʿawra* on the basis that the Prophet's own instructions to the "believing women" was to bare their face and hands.

The ḥadīth canons also vary on the issue of female veiling. Despite mention of technical terms such as *khimār* and *jilbāb* in al-Bukhārī (d. 256/870) and Abū Dāwūd (d. 275/889; cf. Wensinck, *Concordance*, s.vv.), the scant references to any specific type of veiling give the overall impression that adult females covered themselves to some extent in public and that this continued to be encouraged as a form of public modesty after the arrival of Islam; once again, however, no exact dress form is prescribed.

During the last two centuries, the issue of female veiling has become one of the most contentious religious and cultural debates in the Muslim world and also in Western societies where there are relatively large communities of Muslims (see EXEGESIS OF THE QURʾĀN: EARLY MODERN AND CONTEMPORARY; POLITICS AND THE QURʾĀN). Female veiling is very often used as the distinguishing factor between "traditional" and "modern" societies. The word *ḥijāb* has shifted in meaning from delineating physical boundaries between men and women to becoming very much a boundary reflected through various types of modest clothing, most specifically in the form of headscarves. But it symbolizes far more than a simple head-covering, chador (cloak mainly worn in Iran) or *niqāb*, face veil. Women who cover or veil in loose clothing much of their bodies when in public or in mixed company feel that this is the manner of dressing most in conformity with the spirit if not the literal prescription of the Qurʾān and the associated ḥadīth references. The fact that the Qurʾān does not specifically refer to veiling as understood and practiced in a variety of ways today is of little consequence, for the Qurʾān could take for granted the social practices of its time or modify them slightly (see PRE-ISLAMIC ARABIA AND THE QURʾĀN). Conservatism has generally tended to see this type of covering as synonymous with a woman's expected social and domestic role. Many women, however, in both Islamic societies and in non-Muslim countries have in recent years turned to wearing the headscarf as a sign of reaffirming their religious devotion. This has often been done in variance to the prevailing female dress in their particular cultures, and the veil represents at times a political as well as religious position. For many, veiling in its various forms offers a kind of liberation from the fashion expectations of modern life; it does not signify coercion or oppression within any patriarchal system. As more and more Muslim women take up public professions, or are schooled in mixed educational spaces, the issue of male/female segregation is perhaps not as significant as it once was in many societies. The idea, however, that modesty has to be preserved between the sexes is most apparent in the frequent preoccupation with female dress and more importantly, female covering. For Islamists in countries such as Saudi Arabia and Iran, the issue of female dress remains significant in terms of how a society perceives its own religious values. In many other parts of the Muslim world, female veiling may no longer be central to a country's Islamic identity, but it remains at the margins of what is still considered an ideal of an Islamic society.

Mona Siddiqui

Bibliography
Primary: Bayḍāwī, *Anwār;* Ṭabarī, *Tafsīr,* Beirut 1994.
Secondary: ʿA. Ibn Bāz, *Masāʾil al-ḥijāb wa-l-sufūr,* Beirut 1986; M. Fakhri, *Taḥrīr al-marʾa wa-l-sufūr,* Cairo 1920; T. Haddad, *Notre femme, la législation islamique et la société,* Tunis 1978, 207-17; F. Mernissi, *Beyond the veil. Male-female dynamics in a modern Muslim society,* Cambridge, MA 1975; B. Stowasser, *Women in the Qurʾān, traditions and interpretation,* Oxford 1994; Wensinck, *Concordance.*

Vein see ARTERY AND VEIN

Veneration see WORSHIP

Vengeance

Punishment inflicted in return for an injury or offense, closely related to the concept of retaliation (q.v.), i.e. "to return like for like." In some dozen qurʾānic passages the eighth verbal form of the Arabic root *n-q-m* is employed to describe God as "taking vengeance" upon sinners (i.e. Q 30:47; 32:22; see SIN, MAJOR AND MINOR), repeat-violators of the regulations relating to the pilgrimage (q.v.; i.e. Q 5:95) and people who reject his signs (q.v.; i.e. Pharaoh [q.v.] and his people, cf. Q 7:136; see also LIE; BELIEF AND UNBELIEF; GRATITUDE AND INGRATITUDE). In addition to being an attribute of God (cf. Q 3:4; 5:95; 14:47; 39:37; see GOD AND HIS ATTRIBUTES), vengeance is also the provenance of humans, although different lexemes are utilized (see REWARD AND PUNISHMENT and PUNISHMENT STORIES for further discussion of God's vengeance).

The first murder (q.v.) and the fear of revenge in human history occurred soon after the creation (q.v.) of humankind (see also BLOODSHED; BLOOD MONEY). According to the Hebrew Bible, after being punished for the murder of his brother Abel, Cain said, "My punishment is too great to bear... anyone who meets me may kill me" (*Gen* 4:13-14; see CAIN AND ABEL). The second commandment states, "You shall not murder" (*Exod* 20:13). There is also a sanction for murder, "He who fatally strikes a man shall be put to death" (*Exod* 21:12) and "... a life (q.v.) for a life" (ibid., 23; see also BOUNDARIES AND PRECEPTS; CHASTISEMENT AND PUNISHMENT). The continuation of that biblical verse specifies different types of murder, including "eye for an eye" and "tooth for a tooth," etc. (see TEETH; EYES). Also in the Hebrew Bible a distinction is made between murder or premeditated murder and killing, and there is mention of cities of refuge for murders committed unintentionally (*Num* 35:10-31). It is worth comparing those verses with Q 5:45 (Sūrat al-Māʾida, "The Table Spread"): "And in it [the Torah] we prescribed for them life for the life, the eye for the eyes, the nose for the nose and the ear for the ear...."

In the *jāhiliyya* period (see AGE OF IGNORANCE), Arabic poetry (see ARABS; POETRY AND POETS) is disdainful of mercy (q.v.), moderation (q.v.) and compromise. The early poetry glorifies force, even to the point of murder, and a desire for battle and revenge. The poet ʿAmr b. Kulthūm, from the tribe of Taghlib, is cited in the *Muʿallaqāt:* "Hatred as a result of hatred will overcome you" (verse 32); "Because our blood was spilled, their blood was made to flow" (verse 42); and "A person who will harm you will be injured twice as severely" (verse 51). Even after the advent of Islam, the poet al-Mutanabbī (d. 354/955) said, "You killed me, God will kill you. Attack the enemy and kill." He said, "God will kill you," but in fact the deed will be carried out by humans (Goren, *Ancient Arabic poetry,* 17; cf. 30-4; Pellat, al-Ḥakam b. ʿAbdal; see also Fākhūrī, *Taʾrīkh,* 602-50).

The Qurʾān, by contrast, refers to murder-killing eight times (Q 4:29, 92, 93; 5:32; 6:151; 17:33; 25:68; 50:74) and the general instruction is not to kill. Vengeance, *al-qiṣāṣ,* is mentioned four times (Q 2:178, 179, 194; 5:45). Commentary on these verses clarifies the concept of vengeance and the notion of using blood money instead of revenge as well as how the issue should be handled (see TRADITIONAL DISCIPLINES OF QURʾĀNIC STUDY; EXEGESIS OF THE QURʾĀN: CLASSICAL AND MEDIEVAL). An example of such legal explication would be Ibn Qayyim al-Jawziyya (d. 751/1350; *Iʿlām,* ii, 78-9) who claims that without a system of punishments it is impossible to have a properly-functioning society. According to him, such punishments have a deterrent effect.

The method of avenging the murder has also been discussed. Ibn al-Qayyim states that the murderer has to be killed by a sword, which supposedly causes him less suffering, while others insist that a murderer should be executed in the same way as he murdered his victim. Ibn al-Qāsim (d. 191/806), the Mālikī jurist, specifies the mode of retribution depending on whether the murderer used a stick, a stone, fire or drowned the victim. Ibn Qayyim al-Jawziyya (*Iʿlām,* ii, 195 and 196) cites authorities who refer to Q 2:194, "And one who attacks you, attack him in the manner as he attacks you" and Q 16:126, "If you punish [them] punish with the like of that wherewith you were afflicted"). Further, Q 2:178 states that vengeance for murder of a free man is the murder of a free man and likewise a slave for a slave and a woman for a woman (see SLAVES AND SLAVERY; WOMEN AND THE QURʾĀN).

There are, however, differences of opinion about how to punish a person who murdered a woman. Some say that he must be executed. Others say that he has to pay the *diya,* blood money, instead. Another approach emphasizes that, although murder deserves the punishment of death, the woman's family must pay the murderer's family the *diya* for the "difference" — the man being considered more "valuable" than the woman (Aḥmad b. Ḥanbal [d. 241/855] and the Baṣran jurist ʿUthmān b. Sulaymān al-Battī [d. 143/760; cf. van Ess, *TG,* ii, 156f.] as well as ʿAṭāʾ [d. ca. 114/732] in Shinqīṭī, *Aḍwāʾ,* 49). Yet another view insists that only the sultan or the imām (q.v.), who represent religious authority in Islam, can decide in an individual case whether the punishment is execution or payment of the *diya* (Sarakhsī, *Mabsūṭ,* v, 219; a similar approach can be found in Shinqīṭī, *Aḍwāʾ,* iii, 375). There is a common agreement among the scholars that when *diya* is paid instead of execution as revenge, a need to conduct a *ṣulḥ* is called for, a reconciliation ceremony (Shinqīṭī, *Aḍwāʾ,* iii, 3). The *ṣulḥ* ceremony is performed upon receiving the *diya,* which is based on Q 2:178 "and for him who is forgiven somewhat by his (injured) brother (see BROTHER AND BROTHERHOOD; FORGIVENESS), prosecution according to usage and payment unto him in kindness. This is an alleviation and a mercy from your lord."

A ban on punishing a sleeping man who killed someone exists, a ban which is also applicable for a minor or an insane person (see SLEEP; MATURITY; INSANITY). There is no capital punishment for a master who killed his slave or a father who murdered his son (Ibn Qudāma, *Mughnī,* ix, 349). The murder of one of the "People of the Book" (q.v.; *ahl al-kitāb*) i.e. a Jew or Christian (see JEWS AND JUDAISM; CHRISTIANS AND CHRISTIANITY), is, however, punishable by death (ibid.); the Prophet executed a Muslim who murdered a person from the

People of the Book, saying "I am the first one who has to fulfill my duties towards the People of the Book. If a Muslim or a person of the People of the Book murders a non-believer *(kāfir)* he will not be punished and will not have to pay *diya* either" (ibid., 341).

The modern jurist Shurayḥ al-Khuzāʿī al-Shinqīṭī (d. 1913) summarizes the classical jurisprudence on the response to murder by offering three options: to execute in revenge, to receive *diya,* and the third is to forgive without any payment (Ibn Qudāma, *Mughnī,* ix, 381).

Bedouin (q.v.) and semi-rural Arab societies have behavioral norms which do not always correspond with the instruction of the Qurʾān. Execution as revenge can be carried out by killing any individual adult in the *khams,* the collective responsibility unit of five generations (cf. Marx, *Bedouin,* who introduced the term "co-liable group" to define this collective responsibility unit of five generations). Collective responsibility means that each member of the co-liable group knows that if he murders someone or even if he kills someone unintentionally without any premeditation, he creates a conflict with the injured co-liable group that might lead to blood revenge, the exile of his co-liable group, or, at the very least, payment of *diya.* The blood dispute is not ended until there is a reconciliation ceremony or revenge is taken. It is not always the individual who caused the murder upon whom revenge is taken. It can be any member of the murderer's co-liable group — somebody who is completely innocent and not involved in the original argument may be murdered in revenge in the name of collective responsibility. Although any member of the group can be killed in revenge, members of the injured group will usually try to kill a close relative of the murderer (see Ginat, *Blood revenge,* 26-30; for *diya* see al-ʿĀrif, *Qaḍāʾ;* ʿAbbādī, *Min al-qiyam;* see also TRIBES AND CLANS; KINSHIP; EVERYDAY LIFE, THE QURʾĀN IN).

In contrast to the Qurʾān and the ḥadīth instructions, in contemporary Bedouin societies the murder of a woman is revenged by the murder of four men in the case where a man kills a woman. In most such cases there is an attempt to solve the conflict by payment of *diya* in an amount equal to the *diya* of four men.

A group whose economy is based on wage labor will be anxious to resolve a blood quarrel quickly as compared to tent dwellers whose economy is based on raising herds (see TENTS AND TENT PEGS). More and more Bedouin are now entering the wage labor market on a permanent basis (see WORK). In undertaking such work a Bedouin accepts a certain responsibility to attend work regularly. If, for reasons of a blood dispute, he decides one morning that it is unsafe for him to attend, it is highly likely that his job will not be waiting for him when he decides that it is safe to return. The wish to keep one's job and the benefits of a regular income are strong reasons to make sure that blood disputes are settled quickly. The major factor affecting revenge or settlement is the political "condition" of the avenging group. A leader anxious to promote cohesiveness within the group will encourage revenge. Mutual responsibility (q.v.) constitutes the ultimate obligation of members of a co-liable group. By deliberately increasing tension a leader can make his group aware of their collective responsibility, thus promoting group cohesiveness (cf. Marx, Organization). Even if the leader does not advocate revenge he can achieve cohesion by not permitting a cease-fire agreement. There are also political circumstances where it is in the interest of the injured group to agree to a settlement (see Ginat, *Blood revenge*, 25-6).

While the Qurʾān and the ḥadīth are the basic laws that govern the determination of punishment for murder, throughout the generations the values, the norms, the *ʿurf* (tradition) have widened the gap between the original rules and the existing reality.

Joseph Ginat

Bibliography
Primary: Ibn Qayyim al-Jawziyya, *Iʿlām al-muwaqqiʿīn ʿan rabb al-ʿālamīn*, 4 vols., Beirut 1993; Ibn Qudāma al-Maqdisī, Muwaffaq al-Dīn and Muḥammad b. Aḥmad Shams al-Dīn, *al-Mughnī wa-l-sharḥ al-kabīr*, 11 vols. (+ 2 vol. Index), Beirut 1983; al-Sarakhsī, Abū Bakr Muḥammad b. Aḥmad Shams al-Aʾimma, *Kitāb al-Mabsūṭ*, 30 vols. in 15, Beirut 1989; al-Shinqīṭī, al-Shaykh Muḥammad al-Amīn b. Muḥammad al-Mukhtār al-Jakanī, *Aḍwāʾ al-bayān fī īḍāḥ al-Qurʾān bi-l-Qurʾān*, Beirut 1966, 49.
Secondary: A.ʿU. al-ʿAbbādī, *Min al-qiyam wa-l-ādāb al-badawiyya*, Amman 1976; ʿĀ. al-ʿĀrif, *al-Qaḍāʾ bayna l-badw*, Jerusalem 1933; S. Bar-Zvi, *The tradition of justice among the Bedouin of the Negev*, Tel Aviv 1991 (in Hebrew); Y. Ben-David, *Jabaliyya. A Bedouin tribe in the shadow of the monastery*, Jerusalem 1981 (in Hebrew); van Ess, *TG*; Ḥ. al-Fākhūrī, *Taʾrīkh al-adab al-ʿarabī*, Harisa, Lebanon 1953, 1966²; J. Ginat, *Blood revenge. Family honor, mediation, and outcast*, Brighton 1997; A. Goren, *Ancient Arabic poetry*, Jerusalem 1970 (in Hebrew); ʿA. al-Ḥashshāsh, *Qaḍāʾ al-ʿurf wa-l-ʿāda*, Amman 1991; H. Lammens, *L'Arabie occidentale avant l'hégire*, Beirut 1928, 181-236; G. Lüling, Das Blutrecht (die Blutrache) der archaisch-mythischen Stammesgesellschaft. Zum schriftkulturellen Staatsrecht, in *Zeitensprünge* 11/2 (1999), 217-27; E. Marx, *Bedouin of the Negev*, Manchester 1967; id., The organization of nomadic groups in the Middle East, in M. Milson (ed.), *Society and political structure in the Arab world*, New York 1973, 305-35; Ch. Pellat, al-Ḥakam b. ʿAbdal b. Djabala al-Asadī, in *EI²*, iii, 72-3; E.L. Peters, Some structural aspects of the feud among the camel herding Bedouin of Cyrenaica, in *Africa* 37 (1967), 262-82; O.C. Procksch, *Über die Blutrache bei den vorislamischen Arabern und Mohammeds Stellung zu ihr* (Leipziger Studien aus dem Gebiet der Geschichte), Leipzig 1899.

Verdict

see JUDGMENT

Verse(s)

The smallest formally and semantically independent qurʾānic speech units, marked by a final rhyme. The qurʾānic word *āya* (pl. *āyāt*, probably from Syriac *āthā*, cf. Heb. *ōth;* see Jeffery, *For. vocab.*), "sign," has become the technical term used to denote a verse of the Qurʾān. Like the term *sūra* (q.v.), however, which also entered the Arabic language (q.v.) through the Qurʾān, in the qurʾānic corpus itself the word *āya* means a literary unit undefined in extent, perhaps at no stage identical with the qurʾānic verse (see LITERARY STRUCTURES AND THE QURʾĀN). During the process of the qurʾānic communication *āya* figures primarily as part of the discourse of scriptural authority that the Prophet and his listeners engaged in through the entire period of the emergence of the Qurʾān (see REVELATION AND INSPIRATION). This discourse involves the notions of *āya, sūra, qurʾān* and *kitāb* (see BOOK; NAMES OF THE QURʾĀN). It is only in the *muṣḥaf* (q.v.), the canonical codex of the Qurʾān codified after the death of the Prophet (see COLLECTION OF THE QURʾĀN; CODICES OF THE QURʾĀN), that the word *āya* comes unequivocally to denote a qurʾānic verse. In this entry, first the qurʾānic discourse that occurred in the course of Muḥammad's career will be sketched. In the second part, evocations and quotations of early verses in later qurʾānic texts will be discussed (see CHRONOLOGY AND THE QURʾĀN) and, finally, various manifestations of the literary unit "verse," *āya*, in the canonical text will be surveyed.

The qurʾānic imagination of āya

Āya in the Qurʾān is not a descriptive term but rather a functional designation that in the early sūras primarily denotes non-scriptural signs (q.v.) of divine omnipotence (see POWER AND IMPOTENCE), such as

those visible in nature (Q 76:6-16; 77:25-7; 79:27-32; etc.; see NATURE AS SIGNS) or remembered from history (Q 51:34-46; 79:15-26; etc.; see HISTORY AND THE QUR᾿ĀN; FORM AND STRUCTURE OF THE QUR᾿ĀN). In the vast majority of instances, the word *āya,* thus, is not connected to a text. In one rather early sūra, Q 83:13, however, it appears to cover an undefined textual unit: "when our signs are recited to him he says: mere legends of the ancients" (*idhā tutlā ʿalayhi āyātunā qāla asāṭīru l-awwalīn;* see GENERATIONS). In this sūra, one that already reflects the bifurcated categorization of the listeners into believers (*alladhīna āmanū*) and transgressors, unbelievers (*alladhīna ajramū,* Q 83:29; see BELIEF AND UNBELIEF), the "signs" are unambiguously presented as texts that are recited and that function as proofs of divine power. The context is polemical (see POLEMIC AND POLEMICAL LANGUAGE): the hermeneutic value of the recited texts (see RECITATION OF THE QUR᾿ĀN) is not recognized by a group of listeners who try to distance themselves from the message, claiming to know it from of old, and who do not acknowledge the function of the *āyāt* as signs of authority (q.v.). The qur᾿ānic speaker, however, through the use of the word *āyāt,* which recalls the much more frequently discussed visual and often miraculous signs of divine omnipotence observed in nature and history, claims a miraculous and immediately convincing character for the texts being recited (see MIRACLES; MARVELS; INIMITABILITY).
It is first and foremost their linguistic guise, their particularly poetic code (see RHETORIC AND THE QUR᾿ĀN; LANGUAGE AND STYLE OF THE QUR᾿ĀN), that substantiates the claim of the qur᾿ānic text sections to miraculous signs of divine power. The closeness of early qur᾿ānic texts to poetry (see POETRY AND POETS) or the equally artistic speech of the soothsayers (q.v.) is, more than once, indirectly acknowledged by the Prophet's adversaries (see OPPOSITION TO MUḤAMMAD). Indeed, the poeticity of the early qur᾿ānic texts seems to have triggered attempts at disqualifying him as a messenger (q.v.) by connecting him typologically to poets (Q 69:40-1: *innahu la-qawlu rasūlin karīmin wa-mā huwa bi-qawli shāʿirin... qalīlan mā tu᾿minūn,* "it is the speech [q.v.] of a noble messenger, and it is not the speech of a poet! How little do you believe!" cf. Q 52:29 f.; 68:2; 81:22, where *shāʿir,* "poet," is represented by *majnūn,* "possessed, mad"; see INSANITY; PROVOCATION; REFLECTION AND DELIBERATION) and soothsayers, the *kāhins* (Q 52:29: *fa-dhakkir fa-mā anta bi-niʿmati rabbika bi-kāhinin wa-lā majnūn,* "so remind them, for you are not, by the grace of your lord [q.v.], a soothsayer or a madman"; see Neuwirth, Der historische Muhammad). His speech — perhaps not least in view of the claim to a supernatural source occasionally raised for it — appeared closest to the enunciations of those speakers, familiar in ancient Arabia, who are themselves under the spell of a superhuman power (see PRE-ISLAMIC ARABIA AND THE QUR᾿ĀN; SOUTH ARABIA, RELIGIONS IN PRE-ISLAMIC). It has been justly underscored, however, that the qur᾿ānic claim to truth (q.v.) in the early texts relies less on extra-textual reference than on its very medium, the poetic character of its language.

The early sūras' claim to validity is not anchored in something beyond the text; rather, it is the truth of what is being said within the text, as made evident through a variety of poetic devices, that grounds its claim to validity: One might speak of a poetic, rather than a theological truth-claim (see THEOLOGY AND THE QUR᾿ĀN). Thus, in sūras such as Q 89, 91, 99 or 100 the question on whose authority the recitations can legitimately demand their listeners to mend their ways is nowhere posed. Their normative claim on the audience rests on the fact that artful rhetoric, such as the oath clusters (see OATHS), functions like an artfully ground lens which allows one to glimpse something distant, yet visibly real, namely, the imminent nature of divine judgment (see LAST JUDGMENT). Rhetoric, then, is conceived of not primarily as an instrument of deception, as modern prejudice would have it, but rather as an instrument of making manifest that which is, and can be seen to be, the case. Exploring the lens metaphor more might say that knowing who has produced the lens is of much less importance than simply looking through it. In a sense, then, it would be entirely amiss to pose the question on whose authority one ought to acknowledge what one sees (Sinai, From qurʾān to kitāb, forthcoming).

It is initially the linguistic code, then, that warrants the character of qurʾānic text units as signs of divine authority. The gradual self-theologization of qurʾānic discourse — to refer again to Sinai's survey — continues with the third-person authorizations of Muḥammad.

In response to scathing polemics and sarcastic objections, Muḥammad's recitations are forced to provide some account of whence and how they reach their audience. The Qurʾān is thus driven into a rudimentary form of prophetological reflection, as attested by 81:19-25: *innahu la-qawlu rasūlin karīm/dhī quwwatin ʿinda dhī l-ʿarshi makīn/ muṭāʿin thumma amīn/wa-mā ṣāḥibukum bi-majnūn/wa-laqad raʾāhu bi-l-ufuqi l-mubīn/ wa-mā huwa ʿalā l-ghaybi bi-ḍanīn/wa-mā huwa bi-qawli shayṭānin rajīm,* "it is the speech of a noble messenger, who has power with the lord of the throne and is highly placed, obeyed and trustworthy. Your companion is not mad. He saw him upon the luminous horizon; he is not regarding the unseen, niggardly. And it is not the speech of a devil, accursed." Cf. Q 53:2f. where Muḥammad's unspecific claim to divine inspiration is now with greater terminological precision qualified as "revelation," in *huwa illā waḥyun yūḥā/ ʿallamahu shadīdu l-quwā,* "it is only a revelation being revealed. The mighty one taught him" (Q 53:4-5; Sinai, From qurʾān to kitāb, forthcoming).

One might count the identification of Muḥammad's recitation with divine signs, *āyāt,* among these stratagems of indirect authorization (see Q 46:7; 34:43; 31:7; 2:252). The more or less systematic employment of the "prophetical you," datable to early Meccan times, may be regarded as a second step, reflecting development on the level of literary technique.

Nicolai Sinai identifies a third step along the same lines in those early Meccan passages, in which the qurʾānic discourse is traced back to a written heavenly archetype (see HEAVENLY BOOK). Most probably, this step, too, was triggered by polemics. As Q 74:52 implies, the orality (q.v.) of Muḥammad's recitations was seen as betraying their human origin: "rather each one of them wishes to be given scrolls (q.v.) unrolled" *(bal yurīdu kullu mriʾin minhum an yuʾtā ṣuḥufan munashshara).* Elsewhere, and probably by way of reaction to similar charges, such *ṣuḥuf,* "scrolls," are presented as indeed forming some kind of written draft of which Muḥammad's recitations are but the oral promulgation or reading (Q 80:10-16): "Yet, it is only a reminder, whoever wishes, will remember it, in scrolls highly honored, lifted up and purified, by the hands of scribes, honorable and pious" *(kallā innahā tadhkira fa-man shāʾa dhakarahu fī ṣuḥufin mukarramatin marfūʿatin muṭahharatin bi-aydī safaratin kirāmin barara,* Q 80:11-16;

see MEMORY; REMEMBRANCE; PIETY). Since the performative orality of Muḥammad's revelations, which appear to have been viewed as incompatible with their claim to divine authorship, could not very well be simply denied, it is at least counterbalanced.

Finally, in yet another passage, the term *kitāb* instead of *ṣuḥuf* or *lawḥ*, "tablet" (as in Q 85:22; see PRESERVED TABLET; WRITING AND WRITING MATERIALS), is used: "it is indeed a noble *qur'ān*, in a hidden book, that only the purified shall touch, a revelation from the lord of the worlds" (*innahu la-qur'ānun karīm fī kitābin maknūn lā yamassuhu illā l-muṭahharūn tanzīlun min rabbi l-ʿālamīn*, Q 56:77-80). Thus, first Muḥammad's revelations are qualified either from a functional viewpoint — they serve as *tadhkira*, i.e. admonition — or from a performative one — they are presented as *qur'ān*, recitation — then they are said to be "in" (*fī*), something else: *ṣuḥuf, lawḥ, kitāb*. This latter entity is most likely viewed as a kind of transcendent storage medium to which the basic message of Muḥammad's preaching is traceable. In Q 56:80, this bipartite self-predication is expanded upon by a third element, namely, reference to the process by which the heavenly writing is transformed into an earthy recitation, i.e. *tanzīl*, "revelation."

Where is the notion of āya *as verse to be located in this process?*

The word appears first, and only once, in a text from the end of early Meccan times, serving as an indirect authorization of the Prophet (Q 83:13). The accusation of not respecting the signs presented here becomes, in later Meccan and Medinan sūras, a stock argument (Q 31:7; 34:5, 38). This argument is further enhanced by the qualification of the signs as *bayyināt*, "made clear," by the divine sender himself ("we have made clear the signs for people who firmly believe," *qad bayyannā l-āyāti li-qawmin yūqinūn*, Q 2:118; "look, how we make clear the signs for them, then look how they are perverted," *unẓur kayfa nubayyinu lahumu l-āyāti thumma nẓur annā yu'fakūn*, Q 5:75; cf. 2:99; 5:89; 45:25, 46).

The idea that the recitation is particularly adapted to fit the listeners' capacities for understanding is further developed in texts that attest to additional acts of clarification, first through the structuring of the texts (*taḥkīm*), then through their expounding them (*tafṣīl*): the late Meccan sūra Q 11 (Sūrat Hūd) starts thus: "*Alif lām rā*. A book with sections which are elaborately formulated and clearly expounded from the wise, the all-aware" (*alif lām rā. kitābun uḥkimat āyātuhu thumma fuṣṣilat min ladun ḥakīmin khabīr*, Q 11:1; see GOD AND HIS ATTRIBUTES; WISDOM; KNOWLEDGE AND LEARNING; HIDDEN AND THE HIDDEN). Such clarification of the texts is even considered as the decisive factor for the constitution of an emerging Arabic scripture: "a book whose sections have been well expounded, an Arabic *qur'ān* addressed to a people who know" (*kitābun fuṣṣilat āyātuhu qur'ānan ʿarabiyyan li-qawmin yaʿlamūn*, Q 41:3; for the intra-qur'ānic and exegetical debates about the Arabic character of the text, see FOREIGN VOCABULARY). At a still later stage, *āyāt* made clear and unambiguous (see AMBIGUOUS) are explicitly contrasted to others that allow for more than one understanding — see the Medinan verse Q 3:7: "it is he who sent down to you the book, with sections that are precise in meaning, and which are the mother of the book, and others that are ambiguous" (*huwa lladhī anzala ʿalayka l-kitāba, minhu āyātun muḥkamātun hunna ummu l-kitābi wa-ukharu mutashābihātun*). Equally Medinan is the idea put forward in Q 2:106 that an *āya* may, during the communication process, occasionally become the object of modification or be forgotten and replaced:

"whatever verse we abrogate or cause to be forgotten, we will bring instead a better or similar one" (*mā nansakh min āyatin aw nunsihā naʾti bi-khayrin minhā aw mithlihā;* see ABROGATION). From late Meccan times onwards, the term *āya* loses its connotation of a sign that exerts a particular appeal and comes to mean simply "text unit, section."

In this late understanding, the term *āya* is employed in the context of an argument of central importance that had been aroused by the unique situation of the qurʾānic revelations. The unbelievers raised the provocative question of why Muḥammad's revelation had not come down in one piece but in small parts: "the unbelievers say, if only the Qurʾān had been sent down to him all at once?" (*wa-qāla lladhīna kafarū law lā nuzzila ʿalayhi l-qurʾānu jumlatan wāḥida,* Q 25:32), i.e. as a complete book, as in the case of Jews and Christians (see JEWS AND JUDAISM; CHRISTIANS AND CHRISTIANITY; SCRIPTURE AND THE QURʾĀN). The qurʾānic response to that challenge was: "that is how [it is revealed] because we wanted to strengthen your heart (q.v.) with it and we have recited it in a distinct way" (*ka-dhālika li-nuthabbita bihi fuʾādaka wa-rattalnāhu tartīlan,* Q 25:32). The fact that, because of the Qurʾān's situatedness, the scripture to be recited is not under the control of the transmitter, is presented as the result of divine wisdom. What had been viewed by adversaries as an embarrassing shortcoming was turned "into a precondition for God himself assuming the hitherto human activities of recitation *(qurʾān)* and exegesis *(bayān)*. Hence, Judaism and Christianity are trumped by an ingenious redescription of the Qurʾān's '*ad rem* mode of revelation'" (Madigan, *Qurʾān's self-image,* 68) transforming it from a liability into an asset. There is no better illustration of how the dynamics of inter-communal polemics can bring about a true revaluation of values: that which one party considers an appalling flaw is elevated by the other party, "through a blend of spite and theological cunning, to the rank of a veritable hallmark of its self-definition" (Sinai, From qurʾān to kitāb, forthcoming). This *tafṣīl al-āyāt,* the expounding of the qurʾānic text sections (Q 41:3), qualifies the revelation to pose as an Arabic text speaking to the hearts in an understandable way. At the end of this development, the *āya* is established as a term to designate relevant, though undetermined, units of the qurʾānic text. Thus the qurʾānic text that attests to both the emergence of a scripture and a community (Abraham [q.v.] and Ishmael's [q.v.] prayer [q.v.] of consecration of the Kaʿba [q.v.]) can refer to the *āyāt* shape of the revelations as an achievement that enables Mecca (q.v.), its place of origin, to rival Jerusalem (q.v.) in its most prominent prerogative: to be recognized as the birthplace of divine communications (*Isa* 2:3: The law will go out from Zion and the word of the lord from Jerusalem; see Neuwirth, Spiritual meaning). Q 2:128-9 says: "Our lord, cause us to submit to you, and make of our posterity a nation that submits to you. Show us our rites and pardon us (see RITUAL AND THE QURʾĀN; FORGIVENESS), you are indeed the pardoner, the merciful (see MERCY). Our lord, send them a messenger from among themselves who will recite to them your signs and teach them the book and the wisdom and purify them (see CLEANLINESS AND ABLUTION; RITUAL PURITY); you are the mighty, the wise" *(rabbanā wa-jʿalnā muslimīna laka wa-min dhurriyyatinā ummatan muslimatan laka wa-arinā manāsikanā wa-tub ʿalaynā innaka anta l-tawwābu l-raḥīmu. rabbanā wa-bʿath fīhim rasūlan minhum yatlū ʿalayhim āyātika wa-yuʿallimuhumu l-kitāba wa-l-ḥikmata wa-yuzakkīhim innaka anta l-ʿazīzu l-ḥākīm).*

Verses alluded to and verses quoted in the Qurʾān: basmala *and Fātiḥa*

Although during the communication process there appears to have been no term to designate "verse," from early on the notion of verse was strongly developed in the Qurʾān. Verses are neatly structured and unambiguously delimited often through phonetically expressive rhymes (see RHYMED PROSE). Though identical verses sometimes recur in the Qurʾān — such as the phrase *waylun yawmaʾidhin lil-mukadhdhibīn,* "woe on that day to those who denounce," that figures as a refrain in Q 77 (Sūrat al-Mursalāt; Q 77:15, 19, 24, etc.) and recurs in Q 83:10 — their repetition does not usually convey a sense of textual quotation, in view of the strongly oral character of the Qurʾān (see ORALITY AND WRITING IN ARABIA). Some verses from earlier texts, however, seem to be quoted or evoked in later qurʾānic contexts, thus shedding light on the self-referentiality of the Qurʾān. A case in point is the *basmala* (q.v.), the formula "in the name of God, the compassionate, the merciful." Thus, in Q 27:30 a letter dispatched by Solomon (q.v.) to the queen of Sheba (q.v.) is quoted: "it is from Solomon and it says: 'in the name of God the compassionate, the merciful' " (*innahu min sulaymāna wa-innahu bi-smi llāhi l-raḥmāni l-raḥīm;* see also BILQĪS). What is demonstrated here, according to the most plausible hypothesis, is that the custom of starting written documents with the *basmala* is a dignified ancient custom, applied already by an ancient prophet to his written message (see PROPHETS AND PROPHETHOOD). It is usually assumed that qurʾānic texts were successively put into writing in the middle and late Meccan periods, when verses became more complicated structurally and through that procedure were connected to the *basmala.* That formula, which displays the divine name *al-raḥmān* in a prominent position, most probably originated from the time when this divine name had replaced others. Since in Q 27:30 the divine name *al-raḥmān* figures only in the *basmala,* the formula should be considered a quotation in that text. But, of course, the *basmala* that was promulgated through the Fātiḥa (q.v.) is also a proper introduction to orally conveyed sacred speech. In the Qurʾān it precedes the texts of all sūras with the sole exception of Q 9. The *basmala* is counted as an ordinary verse in the first sūra (Sūrat al-Fātiḥa, "The Opening"), although when the text is recited in ritual prayer it is separated from the bulk of the text of the Fātiḥa through other formulas (see Neuwirth, Sūrat al-Fātiḥa; see also PRAYER FORMULAS). Its consideration as an ordinary verse is due, as will be shown, to the peculiar recognition that the Fātiḥa has found in the qurʾānic text itself (see EVERYDAY LIFE, THE QURʾĀN IN).

Q 15:87 triumphantly states that, besides his scriptural recitation, there are now at the disposal of the Prophet a particular group of verses fit to be repeated over and again — the "seven litany-verses": "verily we gave you seven litany-verses *(mathānī)* and the mighty recitation" (*wa-laqad ātaynāka sabʿan mina l-mathānī wa-l-qurʾāna l-ʿaẓīm;* see OFT-REPEATED). Although no particular term is mentioned, the units counted as *sabʿ* (seven) are certainly verses. The allusion is to the Fātiḥa — an interpretation already held by a major group of classical exegetes (see Neuwirth, Referentiality). The alternative interpretation advocated by some scholars like R. Paret (*Koran;* Rubin, Exegesis) and A. Welch (Ḳurʾān), that *mathānī* should point to the punishment legends (see Horovitz, *KU*) is untenable (see PUNISHMENT STORIES) since these stories were not yet composed at the time the Qurʾān is emerging. The word *mathānī,* a plural form of *mathnā* ("in double number," Q 4:3; 35:1; 34:46), occurs in

Q 39:23 where it is used to denote not an individual partial corpus apart from the Qurʾān, made up of seven units, but appears as a qualification of the *kitāb* in toto: "God has sent down the best discourse in a book with similar, repeated texts, from which the skins of those who fear their lord shiver; then their skins and hearts mellow at the mention of God" *(allāhu nazzala aḥsana l-ḥadīthi kitāban mutashābihan mathāniya, taqshaʿirru minhu julūdu lladhīna yakhshawna rabbahum thumma talīnu julūduhum wa-qulūbuhum ilā dhikri llāhi)*. "*Mathānī*" here refers to similarly repeated units of texts that appear to be larger than single verses, and, in view of the psychological effect ascribed to them, perhaps refer to punishment stories. This meaning is, however, deduced from the particular context of late Meccan polemic and is completely incompatible with the earlier situation of Q 15, when no plurality of punishment stories had yet existed, let alone seven such stories (see Neuwirth, Sūrat al-Fātiḥa). The Fātiḥa, in its canonical form, indeed consists of seven verses, a number achieved through the counting of the *basmala* that is usually not considered a verse but an introductory invocation. The fact, however, that the Fātiḥa "originally" did not consist of seven, but of six, verses does not contradict its identification with the seven *mathānī*, "seven" being often understood in the sense of a small, "round" number, not necessarily numerically seven (see NUMBERS AND ENUMERATION). A strong argument in favor of *sabʿ mina l-mathānī* meaning the Fātiḥa is the fact that the entire sūra (Q 15) is replete with short evocations of the text of the Fātiḥa, thus marking the emergence of this particular text as a significant development. The Fātiḥa indeed marks a turn of the liturgical practice of the community since its text was, originally, not considered to be part of the *qurʾān*, the recitation, but was rather used as a communal prayer, and as such was often repeated, thus deserving of the label of *sabʿ mina l-mathānī* (see Neuwirth, Referentiality). Eventually, the Fātiḥa came to complete the liturgical service which, until then, must have consisted in a *qurʾān* (see Q 15:87; *al-qurʾān al-ʿaẓīm*) and the inherited ritual gestures. At that point, the Fātiḥa was presumably known under one of its alternative designations, namely *al-ḥamd* (alluded to as such in Q 15:98; see PRAISE; LAUDATION).

Typology of the qurʾānic verses

The poetical structure of the Qurʾān is marked by the rhyme endings of the verses. A classification of the rhymes has been undertaken for the Meccan parts of the Qurʾān in Neuwirth, *Studien*. It was shown that semantically determined verse groups in early sūras are regularly bracketed by a joint rhyme pattern; thus eschatological introductions like Q 101:1-3 are distinguished from the ensuing prediction of the events on the last day (Q 101:4) and again from the description of the judgment (q.v.; Q 101:6-11) by individual rhyme patterns (see also ESCHATOLOGY; LAST JUDGMENT; APOCALYPSE). There is a significant difference between those sūras classified as early Meccan whose endings comprise no less than eighty types of rhyme, those classified as middle Meccan with seventeen types of rhyme endings, and those classified as late Meccan with only five types of rhyme endings. The scope of diversity among the rhymes is related to the general style of the Qurʾān. The sūras commonly considered the oldest, i.e. those that display *sajʿ* rhymed prose in the strict sense — short units rhyming in frequently changing sound patterns reiterating the last consonants and based on a common rhythm — are made up of monopartite verses containing one colon each. (For the colon, a text unit borrowed from classical rhetoric, see Norden, *Kunstprosa;* Neuwirth, *Studien;* loosely construed, a colon equals a single phrase. This, however, is not sustained indefinitely. As soon as the topics become less expressive, turning from immediate appeal to description or more sophisticated argument, verses tend to become longer and more complex.)

Monopartite verses

Principally, two types of monopartite verses can be distinguished, verses of the *sajʿ al-kāhin* type (oath clusters, *idhā*-phrase-clusters, etc.; see FORM AND STRUCTURE OF THE QURʾĀN) and others reminiscent of monotheistic hymns (*sabbiḥi sma rabbika l-aʿlā*, "praise the name of your lord, the exalted," Q 87:1). The earliest verses thus are not necessarily modeled after *kāhin* speech but often seem to echo monotheistic hymnal texts. One has also to keep in mind that *kāhin* style verses have changed their function: the enigmatic speech does not prepare the way for the disclosure of a truly unknown danger, as is often the case in *kāhin* predictions (see Neuwirth, Der historische Mohammad), but the solution of the enigma built up by the short verses of oath clusters (see Neuwirth, Images) and *idhā*-phrase clusters comes as no real surprise: it is the news of the imminent day of judgment. Still, from a rhetorical point of view, a tension is generated in these texts by means not found in the existing literary genres, thus extending the spectrum of literary forms substantially. The clusters of particular syntactic structures as presented in the short verses are remote from functional ordinary speech; nor are they familiar from poetry either. It is noteworthy that the qurʾānic *saj*ʿ sometimes inverts the ordinary sequence of syntagmata in order to facilitate the achievement of expressive rhymes; thus in the qurʾānic *idhā*-phrase clusters the verb stands in the final position, contrary to ordinary prose (for the aesthetic impact of the monopartite verses, see Sells, *Approaching*). On the other hand, short hymnal verses would have been familiar from the liturgical language in Christian use (see Baumstark, Jüdischer und christlicher Gebetstypus). Indeed the typological similarity of the qurʾānic hymnal sections to Christian hymns has inspired Günther Lüling's hypothesis of a Christian origin of the Qurʾān (*Über den Urkoran;* see POST-ENLIGHTENMENT ACADEMIC STUDY OF THE QURʾĀN). One has, however, to bear in mind that qurʾānic hymns are mostly functionally employed, serving as introductions to longer texts or as personal exhortations to the Prophet to perform liturgical tasks. These verse groups are not infrequently followed by a report concerning the acceptance of their recitation, thus bringing them into a scenario of debate (see Neuwirth, Vom Rezitationstext; see DEBATE AND DISPUTATION). Only in one case can a specific model for a hymnal text, Q 55 (Sūrat al-Raḥmān, "The Merciful"), be determined, namely Psalm 136 (see Neuwirth, Qurʾānic literary structure; see also PSALMS). Still, through its re-casting the psalm has been thoroughly islamized and indeed turned into a new text altogether. Similarly, the doxological introductory verses that become familiar with the mid-sized sūras in Medina (q.v.; Q 59, 61, 62, 64) are not to be read as drawing on a pre-existing "*Ur*-text" from another religious tradition but rather as rephrasings of formulas derived from psalms that were current in monotheistic liturgical use of the time.

Whereas early *kāhin*-style and hymnal verses are usually monopartite, more discursive sections, such as the description of paradise (q.v.) in Q 52:17-28 and the debate in Q 52:29-44, usually display bipartite or even pluripartite verse structures, i.e. verses made up of an entire sentence, mostly paratactically structured. The transition attested in early Meccan texts from *sajʿ* speech with monopartite verses to a more ordinary, though still poetically tinted, articulation attests to the transformation of an adherence to standard pre-Islamic tradition into a novel literary paradigm. This can be considered to be a genuine qurʾānic development marking a new stage in the history of the Arabic literary language (see LITERATURE AND THE QURʾĀN).

Pluripartite verses

Even the structure of pluripartite verses remains extremely conducive to recitation (see Nelson, *The art of reciting*). The colometric structure of qurʾānic style, comparable to that familiar from ancient rhetoric (see Norden, *Kunstprosa*), facilitates the oral performance of texts. A comparison between the shape of biblical narratives (q.v.) narrated in the Qurʾān and in poetry contemporary to the Qurʾān, e.g. that of Umayya b. Abī l-Ṣalt, supports this argument strongly (see also MYTHS AND LEGENDS IN THE QURʾĀN). A comparison between qurʾānic recitation and the — equally chanted — recitations of Hebrew Bible and New Testament texts confirms the unique predisposition of qurʾānic verses for recitation. In Jewish and Christian traditions, the scriptural texts, most of which were originally not composed to be recited, were, at a later stage, structured by musical notation to ensure the preservation of the meaning and to facilitate recitation (see Neuwirth, Three religious feasts). Though in later tradition the Qurʾān is also furnished with additional markers to prevent mistaken readings through problematic connecting or disconnecting of units of meaning (see READINGS OF THE QURʾĀN; ORNAMENTATION AND ILLUMINATION; MANUSCRIPTS OF THE QURʾĀN), it is not comparably dependent on additional regulations since the text is largely free of overlong phrases and complex hypotactic periods.

It is noteworthy that two multipartite verses have acquired particular popularity among Muslims, the Throne Verse (*āyat al-kursī*, Q 2:255; see THRONE OF GOD) and the Light Verse (*āyat al-nūr*, Q 24:35; see LIGHT), both outstanding examples of especially meditative qurʾānic texts. It is *āyat al-nūr* in particular ("God is the light of the heavens and the earth," *allāhu nūru l-samāwāti wa-l-arḍ;* see EARTH; HEAVEN AND SKY) that through its complex similes (q.v.) and metaphors ("his light is like a niche in which there is a lamp [q.v.], the lamp is in a glass, the glass is like a glittering star," *mathalu nūrihi ka-mishkātin fīhā miṣbāḥ/al-miṣbāḥu fī zujāja/al-zujājatu ka-annahā kawkabun durrī;* see also PLANETS AND STARS; SYMBOLIC IMAGERY) simultaneously discloses the paths leading to the knowledge of the divine and upholds their mystery. The description of the nature of the divine light contained in its mysterious receptacles (colons 2-8) is followed by a call for interpretation; colons 9-10 identify the image of the lamp as an example, a *mathal*, that demands from the reader the hermeneutic task of de-coding (see PARABLES). Finally, colon 11 comes to confirm God's wisdom in a hymnal clausula, a fit conclusion for a section about an epistemic issue. Multipartite verses like this — no longer spontaneous addresses to the immediate listeners only but composed to consider later readers as well — describe the full circle of communicating knowledge to the reader and challenging the reader's response.

Clausula verses

Any similarity to *sajʿ* is abandoned when verses exceed the bipartite structures. In these cases, the rhyming end of the verses follows the stereotypical *-ūn, -īn*-pattern that would hardly suffice to fulfill the listeners' anticipation of a resounding conclusion. A new mnemonic technical device that enters the picture is the rhymed phrase, a syntactically stereotyped colon that is distinguished from its context inasmuch as it does not participate in the main strain of the discourse but presents a kind of moral comment on it. One might term this concluding phrase a "cadenza" — in analogy to the final part of the speech units in Gregorian chant, which through their particular sound pattern arouse the expectation of an ending — or, more modestly, a "clausula." The musical sound pattern of the often stereotypically structured clausula phrase enhances the message encoded in it, which in many cases introduces a meta-discourse entailing a moral judgment on the behavior of the protagonists of a narrative, as in Q 12:29, "verily, you were one of the sinners" (*innaki kunti min al-khāṭiʾīn;* see SIN, MAJOR AND MINOR). They thus transcend the main — narrative or argumentative — flow of the sūra, introducing a spiritual dimension: divine approval or disapproval. Indeed, their most typical manifestation is the reference to one of God's attributes, as in Q 3:29, "verily God has power over everything" *(wa-llāhu ʿalā kulli shayʾin qadīr)*. These meta-narrative insertions into the narrative or argumentative fabric of the qurʾānic text would, of course, in a written text meant for silent reading, appear rather disruptive of the larger argument or narrative. They add, however, substantially to the impact of the oral recitation. The Qurʾān thus consciously styles itself as a text evolving on different, yet closely intertwined, levels of discourse. Although it is true that not all multipartite verses bear such formulaic endings, cadenzas may be considered characteristic for the later Meccan and all the Medinan qurʾānic texts. The resounding cadenza, thus, replaces the earlier expressive rhyme pattern, marking a new and irreversible development in the emergence of the text and of the new faith.

The cadenza is a characteristically qurʾānic device that connects story and commentary, making the divine sender of the message also its exegete. The story is told as a representation of human interaction, the cadenza functioning to relate that interaction to the divine authority in an interplay of horizontal and vertical vectors. The opening up of a communication between the divine speaker and his human audience, which is celebrated in the early sūras as a novel achievement, bestows on the here and now the vision of an attainable equilibrium between the opposites governing reality (see PAIRS AND PAIRING). Two textual stratagems contribute to this breakthrough in qurʾānic hermeneutics: (i) the self-referential technique of reflecting the narrated world through diverse layers of the textual structure, both the worldly and the transcendent, and (ii) the genre-transcending stratagem of introducing two strands of speech, one communicated through the main text, the other through the clausula. We are confronted here with a unique kind of intrinsic qurʾānic commentary, through both self-reference and exhortation, which invites the listener to explain, to practice *bayān,* and to make apparent the hidden dimension of meaning (see POLYSEMY; EXEGESIS OF THE QURʾĀN: CLASSICAL AND MEDIEVAL). The listener does so by interpreting the information conveyed in the narrative strand as tokens of divine faculties, divine promises, and divine demands — that is, social rulings (see LAW AND THE QURʾĀN; ETHICS AND THE QURʾĀN). The listener's exegetical semiotization of the words received is thus an indispensable part of the text itself, its intrinsic exegesis.

Angelika Neuwirth

Bibliography
A. Baumstark, Jüdischer und christlicher Gebetstypus im Koran, in *Der Islam* 16 (1927) 229-48; J. Horovitz, Jewish proper names and derivatives in the Koran, in *The Hebrew Union College annual* 2 (1925), 145-227; id., *KU*; Jeffery, *For. vocab.*; G. Lüling, *Über den Ur-Qurʾān*, Erlangen 1972; D. Madigan, *The Qurʾān's self-image. Book, writing and authority in Muslim scripture*, Princeton 2001; K. Nelson, *The art of reciting the Qurʾān*, Austin 1985; A. Neuwirth, Der historische Muḥammad im Spiegel des Koran — Prophetentypus zwischen Seher und Dichter?, in W. Zwickel (ed.), *Biblische Welten. Festschrift für Martin Metzger zu seinem 65. Geburtstag*. Freiburg/Goettingen 1992, 83-108; id., Images and metaphors in the introductory sections of the Makkan suras, in Hawting and Shareef, *Approaches*, 3-36; id., Qurʾānic literary structure revisited. Sūrat al-Raḥmān between mythic account and decodation of myth, in S. Leder (ed.), *Story-telling in the framework of non-fictional Arabic literature*, Wiesbaden 1998, 388-421; id., Referentiality and textuality in *Sūrat al-Ḥijr*. Some observations on the qurʾānic "canonical process" and the emergence of a community, in I. Boullata, *Literary structures of religious meaning in the Qurʾān*, Richmond 2000, 143-72; id., Vom Rezitationstext über die Liturgie zum Kanon. Zur Entstehung und Wiederauflösung der Surenkomposition im Verlauf der Entwicklung eines islamischen Kultus, in Wild, *Text*, 69-105; id., The Spiritual meaning of Jerusalem in Islam, in N. Rosovsky (ed.), *City of the great king. Jerusalem from David to the present*, Cambridge, MA 1996, 93-116, 483-95; id., *Studien*; id., Three religious feasts between texts of violence and liturgies of reconciliation, in Th. Scheffler (ed.), *Religion between violence and reconciliation*, Beirut 2002, 49-82; id. and K. Neuwirth, Sūrat al-Fātiḥa: "Eröffnung" des Text-Corpus Koran oder "Introitus" der Gebetsliturgie? in W. Gross, H. Irsigler und T. Seidl (eds.), *Text, Methode und Grammatik. Wolfgang Richter zum 65. Geburtstag*, St. Ottilien 1991, 331-58; Nöldeke, *GQ*; E. Norden, *Die antike Kunstprosa*, Leipzig 1898, Darmstadt 1958²; Paret, *Kommentar*; U. Rubin, Exegesis and ḥadīth. The case of the seven *mathānī*, in Hawting and Shareef, *Approaches*, 141-56; M. Sells, *Approaching the Qurʾān. The new revelations, selections, translations, and commentaries*, London 1999; id., A literary approach to the hymnic suras in the Qurʾān. Spirit, gender and aural intertextuality, in I.J. Boullata (ed.), *Literary structures of religious meaning in the Qurʾān*, Richmond 2000, 3-25; id., Sound, spirit and gender in Sūrat al-Qadr, in *JAOS* 11 (1991), 239-59; N. Sinai, From qurʾān to kitāb, in M. Marx, A. Neuwirth and N. Sinai (eds.), *The Qurʾān in context. Historical and literary investigations into the cultural milieu of the Qurʾān*, Leiden (forthcoming); Wansbrough, *QS*; A. Welch, Kurʾān, in *EI²*, v, 400-13.

Versions of the Qurʾān see TEXTUAL HISTORY OF THE QURʾĀN; READINGS OF THE QURʾĀN

Vessels see SHIPS; VEHICLES AND TRANSPORTATION; CUPS AND VESSELS

Vestment see CLOTHING

Vice see VIRTUES AND VICES, COMMANDING AND FORBIDDING

Vicegerent/Viceroy see CALIPH

Victory

Success, often in the face of military aggression. The principal meanings of "victory" in the Qurʾān are conveyed by derivatives of the verbal roots *f-t-ḥ*, *n-ṣ-r*, *f-w-z*, and *gh-l-b*. Particularly in the case of *fatḥ*, a specific military meaning can pertain to the defeat of one's foes in battle (see EXPEDITIONS AND BATTLES; FIGHTING; ENEMIES) and, by extension, conquest, as in the opening verses of Q 48, entitled "Victory" (Sūrat al-Fatḥ), and referring to the conquest of Mecca in 8/630 by the Prophet and the early Muslims. More often than not reference to aspects of an eschatological "triumph" is intended (see ESCHATOLOGY). On *f-t-ḥ*, see CONQUEST.

The many occurrences of *n-ṣ-r* nearly always refer to divine "support," the backing necessary to the success of God's cause and its partisans (see PATH OR WAY). Specific contexts in which *n-ṣ-r* occurs include references to Badr (q.v.; Q 3:123) and Ḥunayn (q.v.; Q 9:25), and the "help" provided by God to Noah (q.v.; e.g. Q 21:76-7), Jesus (q.v.; e.g. Q 3:52; see also APOSTLE) and the prophets as a group (e.g. Q 6:34; see PROPHETS AND PROPHETHOOD). A more general meaning is the "help" provided by those who remain true to God's cause. In this sense, God is the provider *(naṣīr),* a term frequently coupled with "protector" (*walī,* e.g. Q 9:74, 116; see FRIENDS AND FRIENDSHIP; CLIENTS AND CLIENTAGE). It follows that the unbelievers (see BELIEF AND UNBELIEF) are those who, seeking "help" from other sources, be they false gods or armed conflicts, will inevitably fail (e.g. Q 7:197; 21:43; see IDOLS AND IMAGES; POLYTHEISM AND ATHEISM). The term *anṣār,* "helpers," occurs both in reference to Muḥammad's Medinan supporters (e.g. Q 9:117; see MEDINA; EMIGRANTS AND HELPERS) and, more generally, to those who perpetuate God's way by siding with Jesus or other prophets (e.g. Q 61:14).

Most occurrences of *f-w-z* are in the nominal form *(fawz),* always joined by one of three modifiers: *mubīn,* "clear, obvious" (Q 6:16; 45:30); *kabīr,* "great, mighty" (Q 85:11) and, most often, *ʿaẓīm,* "supreme" (Q 9:72 and elsewhere). *Fawz* designates the final reward, the "victory" as it were, of God's activity on behalf of humankind (see REWARD AND PUNISHMENT). Thus, in Q 6:16, it is the avoidance of damnation (see HELL AND HELLFIRE), what Muḥammad Asad (*Message,* 173) calls "a manifest triumph." Similarly, in Q 9:72, alongside the "physical" pleasures of paradise (q.v.), God's satisfaction *(riḍwān)* occurs as "the supreme felicity" (Yūsuf ʿAlī, *Meaning,* 459). Four verses (Q 9:20; 23:111; 24:52; 59:20) speak of those sure to be victorious *(al-fāʾizūn).*

Gh-l-b and derivatives, as in the case of *f-t-ḥ,* carry both the general sense of "to overcome" and the more specific meaning of military victory (or defeat). An example in the first category is the evildoers of Q 23:106 (see EVIL DEEDS; VIRTUES AND VICES, COMMANDING AND FORBIDDING), who are described as "overwhelmed" by their own misfortune *(shiqwa),* or in Q 41:26, about those who seek by continuous chatter to drown out or overwhelm the sound of the Qurʾān so as to "gain the upper hand" (see RECITATION OF THE QURʾĀN; OPPOSITION TO MUḤAMMAD). In the second category, an example is Byzantium *(al-rūm)* in Q 30:2-5 which, as most exegetes understand it, nearly fell to the Sasānids only to rally as the prediction here would have it (see BYZANTINES). The "party of God" (*ḥizb Allāh,* Q 5:56; see PARTIES AND FACTIONS) are "the true victors" *(al-ghālibūn).* Some disagreement surrounds the pronominal suffix in *wa-llāhu ghālibun ʿalā amrihi* (Q 12:21), as noted by Paret (*Kommentar,* 249).

Matthew S. Gordon

Bibliography
Primary: Ṭabarī, *Tafsīr,* Beirut 1972.
Secondary: ʿA. Yūsuf ʿAlī, *The meaning of the holy Qurʾān,* Brentwood, MD 1989; M. Asad, *The message of the Qurʾān,* Gibraltar 1980; Paret, *Kommentar.*

Vigil

Wakefulness at night for religious observance. There are a number of places in the Qurʾān where night prayer (q.v.) is mentioned. The term which came to be used for it in Islam is *tahajjud,* the verbal noun *(maṣdar)* of *tahajjada.* In one place in the Qurʾān the imperative of this verb is used: "And in a part of the night, perform a vigil *(tahajjad)* with it (*bihi,* i.e. with the Qurʾān) voluntarily (*nāfilatan*, Q 17:79). In Q 3:113 we find a reference to the People of the Book (q.v.) who perform this rite: "They are not all alike; among the People of the Book is a steadfast community *(ummatun qāʾimatun)* that recites the signs (q.v.) of God during the night, prostrating themselves" (see BOWING AND PROSTRATION). Probably Christians are meant (see CHRISTIANS AND CHRISTIANITY) as influence from Byzantine orthodox Christianity, from monophysite Ethiopia (see ABYSSINIA) or from Nestorian Christians in al-Ḥīra appears to have been present in seventh-century Arabia. Priests and monks are positively mentioned in the Qurʾān (Q 5:82; but cf. 9:31, 34; see MONASTICISM AND MONKS), and were likely known to Muḥammad. From the beginning of his mission Muḥammad practiced nightly prayer (cf. Q 73:1-4, "O enfolded one, stand up [in prayer] during the night, except a small portion of it, the half or rather less, or rather more, and recite the Qurʾān with accuracy *[tartīlan]*"), although nightly vigil was never a prescribed rite for his followers (see RECITATION OF THE QURʾĀN; RITUAL AND THE QURʾĀN). Also in another early Meccan verse (see VERSES; MECCA; CHRONOLOGY AND THE QURʾĀN) it is Muḥammad himself who is addressed: "And mention the name of your lord (q.v.) in the morning (q.v.) and in the evening (q.v.) and in the night prostrate yourself before him and praise (q.v.) him the livelong night" (Q 76:25f.; see DAY, TIMES OF; DAY AND NIGHT; REMEMBRANCE; BASMALA); "And perform the *ṣalāt* at both ends of the day and in the stations *(zulafan)* of the night" (Q 11:114). Eventually, pious followers joined him (Q 73:20). The righteous sleep (q.v.) little and pray at night, says the Qurʾān (Q 51:15f.). In Medina (q.v.), when Muḥammad and those who followed him in night-vigils were not in a position to pray at night because circumstances had changed, he was granted dispensation from it: "Your lord knows that you stand (in prayer) nearly two-thirds of the night... and a party of those with you.... He knows that you will not count it precisely, so he has relented towards you. So recite of the Qurʾān what may be convenient; he knows that some of you will be sick and others are traversing the land seeking the bounty of God and others striving in the way of God (see PATH OR WAY; JIHĀD; FIGHTING; GRACE; BLESSING; JOURNEY; ILLNESS AND HEALTH). So recite of it what is convenient" (Q 73:20).

One night is especially mentioned in the Qurʾān, the Night of Power (or, better, "measuring-out"; *laylat al-qadr;* see Wagtendonk, *Fasting*, 83f.; Wensinck, *Arabic new year*, 1-13; see NIGHT OF POWER), an ancient Arabian new-year's night (Q 97:1-5). It is not known in which way this night was celebrated in Muḥammad's time but later generations held vigils in it as the night of the beginning of the revelation of the Qurʾān to the Prophet (see REVELATION AND INSPIRATION; PRE-ISLAMIC ARABIA AND THE QURʾĀN). Although vigils are not a communal obligation, and there is no set time for the pious practice of a protracted stay in a mosque (*iʿtikāf*, i.e. retreating to a mosque for a specified period of time, including nights, and not leaving except for the performance of natural functions and ablutions; cf. Bousquet, Iʿtikāf), such extended retreat vigils are particularly popular in the last ten days of Ramaḍān (q.v.).

K. Wagtendonk

Bibliography
Primary: Ibn Abī l-Dunyā, *al-Tahajjud wa-qiyām al-layl*, ed. M. ʿAbd al-Ḥamīd M. al-Saʿdānī, Cairo 1994.
Secondary: T. Andrae, *Der Ursprung des Islams und das Christentum*, Uppsala 1926; id., Zuhd und Moenchtum. Zur Frage von den Bezeihungen zwischen Christentum und Islam, in *Monde*

oriental 25 (1931), 296-327; S.A. Ashraf, The inner meaning of the Islamic rites. Prayer, pilgrimage, fasting, jihād, in S.Ḥ. Nasr (ed.), *Islamic spirituality. Foundations*, London 1987, 111-30; C. Bell, *Ritual theory, ritual practice*, Oxford 1992; G.H. Bousquet, Iʿtikāf, in *EI²*, iv, 280; I.K.A. Howard, Some aspects of the pagan Arab background to Islamic ritual, in *Bulletin of the British Association of Orientalists* 10 (1978), 41-8; *Muṣḥaf al-tahajjud*. An edition of the Qur'an for night prayers, in *Journal of qur'anic studies* 1 (1999), 158-61; Wagtendonk, *Fasting*; A.J. Wensinck, *Arabic new year and the feast of tabernacles* [in *Verhandelingen der Koninklijke Akademie van Wetenschappen te Amsterdam*], Amsterdam 1925.

Vines see AGRICULTURE AND VEGETATION

Violate see SACRED AND PROFANE

Violence

Aggression; use of physical coercion against others. How does the concept of violence emerge from the qurʾānic corpus? To answer this question simply identifying the qurʾānic vocabulary concerning violence is not enough. One needs to identify, if possible, the social, political and religious status of violence, without, of course, permitting oneself to make the usual extrapolations from synchronic analysis to diachronic extrapolation or, conversely, devising an Islamic doctrine of violence (see ETHICS AND THE QURʾĀN; POLITICS AND THE QURʾĀN; VIRTUES AND VICES, COMMANDING AND FORBIDDING).

Let us begin with some negative observations. The usual term employed in present-day Arabic for violence is *ʿunf*. It is not found in the Qurʾān. In the biblical corpus, violence is designated by the Hebrew word *hamas*, which, as an acronym, has strong political overtones in contemporary Arabic. *Ḥams* in early and present-day Arabic covers the semantic fields of force, constancy, bravery and courage (q.v.) in combat: anger (q.v.) and rage are also covered by the term. This implies momentary violence in interpersonal relations but, above all, war-like violence, which is always accorded added value by each group participating in the combat (see WAR; FIGHTING; EXPEDITIONS AND BATTLES). The root word is similarly absent from the qurʾānic corpus. To the extent that we can make use of a corpus of authentic texts, particularly poetic ones (see POETRY AND POETS), that are contemporary with the Qurʾān, it would be useful to ascertain the use made of the roots *ʿ-n-f* and *ḥ-m-s*. It would be seen, in fact, that the Qurʾān is never interested in violence in itself, whereas today, a focus on violence has become a major anthropological theme (see SOCIAL SCIENCES AND THE QURʾĀN; CONTEMPORARY CRITICAL PRACTICES AND THE QURʾĀN).

Among the qurʾānic roots from which are derived terms implying violence, one finds *j-h-d, q-t-l, ḥ-r-b, q-ṣ-ṣ, q-s-r, ʿ-d-w, f-s-d, ʿ-q-b, ḍ-r-b, b-gh-y, ẓ-l-m*. The two dominant notions are *ẓ-l-m*, oppression (q.v.), injustice (see also JUSTICE AND INJUSTICE; OPPRESSED ON EARTH, THE), and *q-t-l*, fighting the enemy, killing (see ENEMIES; MURDER; BLOODSHED). *Ẓ-l-m* and its derivatives are used 319 times (with ninety-one times for *ẓālimīn* and forty times for *ẓalamū*). *Q-t-l* is found 173 times; *ʿ-d-w*, to attack (without provocation), to transgress the limits (see BOUNDARIES AND PRECEPTS; MODERATION), is found 106 times, with fifty-six recordings for *ʿaduww*, enemy; *f-s-d*, meaning corruption (q.v.), disorder, is found fifty times; *ʿ-q-b*, to punish, chastise, twenty-seven times (see CHASTISEMENT AND PUNISHMENT; REWARD AND PUNISHMENT); *b-gh-y*, to cause wrong, to go against correct norms, thirty times. But *ḥ-r-b*, to wage war, is found only six times, *jihād* (q.v.) four times, *mujāhidūn* four times, *jāhada* twenty times, and *qiṣāṣ*, meaning retaliation (q.v.), six times.

The disproportion between the number of times *z-l-m* appears (319) and the number of times *ʿ-d-l* (only thirteen) is observed, throws light on the strategy of qurʾānic discourse (see LANGUAGE AND STYLE OF THE QURʾĀN); it is concerned with stigmatizing, rejecting and condemning unjust conduct, by referring to it insistently (see RHETORIC AND THE QURʾĀN). Likewise, the numerous appearances of *q-t-l* aim to fix strict conditions for recourse to deadly combat, to define the merits of those who struggle to protect the true faith (q.v.; *dīn al-ḥaqq;* see also RELIGION; TRUTH; RELIGIOUS PLURALISM AND THE QURʾĀN), and to disqualify the attitude of those who retreat or refuse to give their lives to protect truth, justice and the common welfare, such as they are redefined when confronting different agents who "cannot clearly distinguish" *(yaʿqilūn)* between just and unjust combat (see HYPOCRITES AND HYPOCRISY). The designations of the forms and shapes of "violence" are never named as such but always aiming at an attitude, or at intolerable conduct that rejects values, knowledge (see KNOWLEDGE AND LEARNING), and the "limits" *(ḥudūd)* fixed by God and his envoy (see MESSENGER; PROPHETS AND PROPHETHOOD; LAW AND THE QURʾĀN). The processes of composition and the arguments of qurʾānic discourse strive to instill the idea of a legitimate "violence," humanized in the sense of "making sacred the human individual" *(taḥrīm al-nafs),* and to protect him from arbitrary domination, or pointless killing in the pursuit of mere power (see POWER AND IMPOTENCE), booty (q.v.), and conquest of territory, etc. (see also KINGS AND RULERS; CONQUEST). On this essential point, the Qurʾān continues, in its own style and in a different context, the work of the Bible and the Gospels (q.v.; see also TORAH; SCRIPTURE AND THE QURʾĀN), which convert archaic usages of "violence" in tribal societies into a "violence" contained in a new symbolism (see TRIBES AND CLANS; ARABS; PRE-ISLAMIC ARABIA AND THE QURʾĀN). While this symbolism seeks to be spiritual, its inner dynamic is to consider sacred (see SACRED AND PROFANE), without realizing it, the rituals of violence it was in search of "transcending." For specific examples of qurʾānic allusions to violent acts, see — in addition to the articles cross-referenced above — MARTYRS; CONSECRATION OF ANIMALS; AGE OF IGNORANCE; ARBITRATION; BYZANTINES; CRUCIFIXION; DROWNING; FLOGGING; ḤUNAYN; INFANTICIDE; JEWS AND JUDAISM; NIMROD; OPPOSITION TO MUḤAMMAD; PHARAOH; POVERTY AND THE POOR; PRISONERS; PROVOCATION; PUNISHMENT STORIES; REBELLION; SACRIFICE; SIN, MAJOR AND MINOR; SLAUGHTER; SLAVES AND SLAVERY; STONING; SUFFERING; SUICIDE; TOLERANCE AND COMPULSION; VENGEANCE; WOMEN AND THE QURʾĀN.

M. Arkoun

Bibliography

M. Arkoun, *The unthought in contemporary Islamic thought,* London 2002; M. Dousse, *Dieu en guerre. La violence au coeur des trois monothéismes,* Paris 2002; J.Y. Lacoste, Violence, in *Dictionnaire de théologie catholique,* Paris 1998.

Virgins see HOURIS; CHASTITY

Virtue

Moral excellence. Qurʾānic terminology has no exact equivalent to "virtue" or to the Greek word *areté* but it deals with how moral excellence is taught, the noble ideals of the righteous person and the virtues of a God-fearing society (for virtue in the sense of sexual propriety, see MODESTY; CHASTITY). Ethical reflection as such, including the question of what constitutes a virtuous act, was taken up by Muslim thinkers over time in a variety of genres (see ETHICS AND THE QURʾĀN). Yet the Qurʾān's message is steeped in moral categories: "God poured out his favor on the believers by sending to them a messenger (q.v.) from their midst to recite to them his signs (q.v.), to purify them, and to teach them the book (q.v.) and wisdom (q.v.), though they had previously been in manifest error" (q.v.; Q 3:164). This message was proclaimed by Muḥammad in an Arabic dialect easily intelligible to his hearers (Q 26:195; see DIALECTS; LANGUAGE AND STYLE OF THE QURʾĀN). At the same time, it provoked hostility and opposition from the leaders of pagan Mecca (q.v.; see also OPPOSITION TO MUḤAMMAD). As contemporary theories of semantics and hermeneutics necessarily raise issues of sociology and anthropology (see CONTEMPORARY CRITICAL PRACTICES AND THE QURʾĀN), one would have to look at the social, cultural and political implications of this hostility to fully grasp the Qurʾān's ethical vision.

The Qurʾān exhorts its hearers to cultivate virtues that were also prized by Arab Bedouin (q.v.) culture — but always with a twist (Hourani, Ethical presuppositions, 24; Izutsu, *Concepts*, 74-104): generosity (see GIFT AND GIFT-GIVING) and charity (see ALMSGIVING), not for show but out of submission to God (Q 2:264) and without recklessness (Q 17:26, 27); courage (q.v.) in battle, not for personal or tribal glory, but for God (Q 9:5, 13, 44-5, etc.; see EXPEDITIONS AND BATTLES); loyalty (q.v.; *wafāʾ*, also as keeping covenant [q.v.], expressed in the Qurʾān through the verb *awfā*) directed to God and, beyond the tribe (see TRIBES AND CLANS), to one's fellow Muslims (Q 2:40; 48:10); truthfulness (these related words appear ninety-seven times: *ṣadaqa, ṣidq, ṣādiq, ṣiddīq*) as a virtue the believer acquires because God himself is truthful (e.g. Q 3:152; 9:119; 29:3; 33:24) and abhors lying (over 200 instances of the root *k-dh-b;* see LIE); patience (*ṣabr,* steadfastness and endurance) in battle (Q 2:249-50; 3:146) and in the face of opposition to God's cause (Q 2:153-6; 6:34; 7:128; 73:10; see TRUST AND PATIENCE; TRIAL; PATH OR WAY).

At the same time, the Qurʾān is no stranger to the Greek virtue of moderation (q.v.): "Those who, when they spend, are not extravagant and not niggardly, but hold a just [balance] between those [extremes]" (Q 25:67). Ibn Kathīr (d. 774/1373) explains, "they are not wasteful by spending over that which they need, and they are not stingy with regard to their family by withholding what is theirs by right and thus making them needy, but act justly and kindly, and the best of options is the middle ground" (*wa-khayru l-umūr awsaṭuhā;* Ibn Kathīr, *Tafsīr,* x, 322). The prophet Muḥammad and his Companions (see COMPANIONS OF THE PROPHET) displayed this virtue, affirms al-Suyūṭī (d. 911/1505), quoting from a ḥadīth: "Those are the Companions of God's apostle, who would not eat food out of a desire for pleasure from it, and would not wear clothes out of a desire for beauty from them, but they were of one heart" (Suyūṭī, *al-Durr,* vi, 77). Besides presenting us with a fuller version of the above ḥadīth (see ḤADĪTH AND THE QURʾĀN), al-Shawkānī (d. 1255/1839) quotes the third/ninth century Baṣran grammarian Abū ʿUbayda (see GRAMMAR AND THE QURʾĀN) who wrote that this median between excessive largesse and miserliness means to stay "within the bounds of what is right" *(al-maʿrūf),* and cites a parallel passage, Q 17:29 (*Tafsīr,* iv, 109). Fazlur Rahman (*Major themes,* 29) expresses a consensus among modern commentators when he avers that this virtue of the middle path is at the heart of the qurʾānic message and it is best portrayed in the qurʾānic term, *taqwā:* "to be squarely anchored within the moral tensions, the 'limits of God,' and not to 'transgress' or violate the balance of those tensions" (see PIETY; FEAR; BOUNDARIES AND PRECEPTS).

One might ask: what would this virtue of self-restraint in obedience (q.v.) to God have meant to Muḥammad's contemporaries? The chief characteristic of the *jāhilī* mindset (see AGE OF IGNORANCE) is described in the Qurʾān (Q 48:26) as *ḥamiyya,* "passion, violence (q.v.), arrogance (q.v.)." By contrast, "God brought down serenity (*sakīna;* see SHEKHINAH) upon his messenger and imposed on believers the word of self-restraint" (*kalimata l-taqwā,* Q 48:26). Commentators are unanimous about the circumstances under which this passage (indeed, the whole Q 48, Sūrat al-Fatḥ ["Victory"]) was revealed (see OCCASIONS OF REVELATION; REVELATION AND INSPIRATION): Muḥammad's Ḥudaybiya (q.v.) treaty of 628 C.E. (see CONTRACTS AND ALLIANCES). On the impulse of a dream (see DREAMS AND SLEEP), Muḥammad set off from Medina (q.v.) with a group of about 1,500 men to perform a pilgrimage (q.v.) to Mecca (*ʿumra).* At Ḥudaybiya, on the outskirts of Mecca, a Meccan armed delegation refused to let them pass. Negotiations began but seemed to falter. At this tense moment, the Qurʾān informs us that the Muslims made a pledge of loyalty to Muḥammad, "the pledge under the tree" (Q 48:18), which pleased God who sent down his peace or tranquility upon them (again, *sakīna,* the second of three instances in this sūra, the first is in verse 4). Finally, an agreement was reached, in which the Muslims would be obliged to sacrifice (q.v.) their animals, at Ḥudaybiya this time (see also CONSECRATION OF ANIMALS), but would be allowed to perform their pilgrimage to Mecca the following year. In the context of this passage, therefore, the tranquility God sent was in large measure an affirmation of Muḥammad's controversial decision and a calming of those among the Muslims who would rather have fought the Meccans then and there — after all, was not their behavior going against the accepted Arabian customs of the time?

What then is this *ḥamiyya* that took hold of the unbelievers' hearts (see HEART; BELIEF AND UNBELIEF) at this time? Al-Ṭabarī (d. 310/923) says, without specification, that it was what made them act in this way, and that "all of this sprung from the nature (or ethics, *akhlāq*) of the people of unbelief, and none of it was permitted for them — neither by God, nor by any of his messengers" (Ṭabarī, *Tafsīr,* xxvi, 104). Al-Zamakhsharī (d. 538/1144) defined *ḥamiyya* as *anafa,* "pride, or disdain," and *sakīna* as *waqār,* "sobriety, dignity, a composed demeanor." Following al-Ṭabarī, and in concert with most other commentators, he sees the Meccans' *ḥamiyya* as their refusal to allow Muslim wording in the compact (the *basmala* [q.v.] and the *shahāda* [see WITNESS TO FAITH]) and this, mainly because of the phrase *kalimat al-taqwā* which is invariably seen as the *shahāda* or, in some cases, Sūrat al-Ikhlāṣ ("Purity," Q 112; e.g. Ibn Kathīr, *Tafsīr,* xiii, 112-13; Qurṭubī, *Jāmiʿ,* xvi, 275-6). Even if we grant the historicity of the theological squabbles over the wording of the treaty (see THEOLOGY AND THE QURʾĀN), it is likely that later commentators tended to over-spiritualize the term *ḥamiyya.* More in line with al-Zamakhsharī, al-Shawkānī (*Tafsīr,* iv, 67) quotes the early commentator Muqātil b. Sulaymān (d. 150/767) in saying that the *ḥamiyya* of the Age of Ignorance *(jāhiliyya)* was in the Meccans' reasoning: "They have killed our sons and brothers and now they will attack us in our homes and the Arabs will say that they have entered [our city] to humiliate us." The main issue was whether Muḥammad would respond in kind and enter by force or whether he would express God's *sakīna* by offering the kind of peaceful terms that would allow a greater victory for Islam in the years to come (Quṭb, *Ẓilāl*, vi, 3325-9).

Ironically, the *jāhilī* Arabs (q.v.) themselves contrasted "unbridled passion for honor" *(jahl)* with forbearance, shrewdness, and self-control (*ḥilm;* Goldziher, *MS*, i, 201-8) but it was always the prerogative of the powerful (Izutsu, *God*, 203-15; see POWER AND IMPOTENCE; IGNORANCE). The Qurʾān espouses this same ideal but teaches that *ḥilm* can only blossom in a soul (q.v.) that gratefully receives God's bounty and mercy (q.v.; the root meaning of *kāfir* is "ungrateful"; see GRATITUDE AND INGRATITUDE; BELIEF AND UNBELIEF; BLESSING). Muḥammad cares for the orphan and the poor because he himself had been an orphan, wandering and poor (Q 93; see ORPHANS; POVERTY AND THE POOR). This ethic of showing mercy to the most vulnerable and needy is to be the hallmark of the emerging Muslim community (Q 28:77; 59:7; 80:1-10; 107; see OPPRESSED ON EARTH, THE).

The greatest break with *jāhilī* culture is seen in the Qurʾān's assertion that virtue is not determined by this-worldly considerations but rather in light of the awesome reality of divine judgment (q.v.) in the life to come (see LAST JUDGMENT). The primary meaning of the key qurʾānic term *taqwā* (especially in the early Meccan sūras) is "trembling in fear of God" or "trembling with piety before God" (e.g. Q 12:1). In contrast to the fierce arrogance of the *jāhilī* Arab, the Qurʾān calls for submission and surrender to God (*islām*, e.g. Q 3:19, 52, 64, 67). Thus only the pious *(taqī)* who has surrendered his will to God can be truly righteous (*ṣāliḥ* appears thirty-three times; *bārr*, a close synonym, nine times) and produce the good deeds (q.v.; *ṣaliḥāt*, ninety-eight times) that God will reward. The centrality of the root *taqwā/ittaqā* (almost 200 instances) and its connection to the qurʾānic ethical ideal is best illustrated by the verse "Surely the noblest among you in God's sight is the most pious of you" (*atqākum*, Q 49:13). See also VIRTUES AND VICES, COMMANDING AND FORBIDDING.

David Johnston

Bibliography

Primary: Ibn Kathīr, *Tafsīr*, ed. M.S. Muḥammad et al., 15 vols., Jiza, Egypt 2000; Qurṭubī, *Jāmiʿ*, ed. M.I. al-Hifnāwī, 22 vols., Cairo 1994; Quṭb, *Ẓilāl;* Shawkānī, *Tafsīr*, ed. H. al-Bukhārī and Kh. ʿUkkārī, 5 vols., Beirut 1997; Suyūṭī, *Durr;* Ṭabarī, *Tafsīr*, Cairo 1954-68; Zamakhsharī, *Kashshāf.*

Secondary: M. Fakhry, *Ethical theories in Islam*, Leiden 1991; Goldziher, *MS*, trans.; A. Hourani, Ethical presuppositions of the Qurʾān, in *MW* 70 (1980), 1-28; Izutsu, *Concepts;* id., *God;* F. Rahman, *Major themes in the Qurʾān*, Minneapolis 1994[2]; W.M. Watt, *Muhammad at Mecca*, Oxford 1960.

Virtues and Vices, Commanding and Forbidding

Forms of the phrase *al-amr bi-l-maʿrūf wa-l-nahy ʿani l-munkar*, literally "commanding right and forbidding wrong" (hereafter usually abbreviated as "forbidding wrong") appear eight times in the Qurʾān. Just what is intended in the relevant qurʾānic passages is somewhat unclear, and the exegetes interpret them in more than one way. By far the most widespread interpretation relates them to the duty of the individual Muslim to forbid wrong as developed in classical Islamic thought (see GOOD AND EVIL; SIN, MAJOR AND MINOR; BOUNDARIES AND PRECEPTS; ETHICS AND THE QURʾĀN).

The qurʾānic attestations

In the context of an appeal for the unity of the community of believers, Q 3:104 enjoins "Let there be one community *(umma)* of you, calling to good, and commanding right and forbidding wrong." This strongly suggests that forbidding wrong is a duty to be performed by the community as a whole; but we are not told to whom the commanding and forbidding are to be addressed and there is no further specification of the right and wrong to which they are to relate. The same is true of some further references to forbidding wrong. One that follows a few verses later in Q 3:110 speaks of forbidding wrong in similar terms (though with no explicit indication that it is a duty): "You are *(kuntum)* the best community *(khayra ummatin)* ever brought forth to people, commanding right and forbidding wrong." Q 9:71 states that "the believers, the men and the women (see BELIEF AND UNBELIEF), are friends one of the other; they command right, and forbid wrong." (This contrasts with Q 9:67, in which the terms are transposed: "The hypocrites [see HYPOCRITES AND HYPOCRISY], the men and the women, are as one another; they command wrong, and forbid right.") Q 22:41 refers to "those who, if we establish them in the land..., command right and forbid wrong." This latter verse may, however, relate to believers engaged in holy war (q.v.; see also FIGHTING; JIHĀD; EXPEDITIONS AND BATTLES; PATH OR WAY) rather than to the believers at large, if the reference is to "those who fight because they were wronged" in Q 22:39. The same may be true of Q 9:112, which speaks of "those who repent (see REPENTANCE AND PENANCE; FEAR; FORGIVENESS), those who serve (see WORSHIP), those who pray (*ḥāmidūn;* see PRAYER; LAUDATION),... those who command right and forbid wrong, those who keep God's bounds," if the people in question are in fact identical with those who wage holy war in the preceding verse; but the relationship between the two verses poses a serious syntactical problem in the standard text of the Qur'ān (see GRAMMAR AND THE QURʾĀN; TEXTUAL HISTORY OF THE QURʾĀN). Even if in Q 9:112 and Q 22:41 it is only a subset of the believers who forbid wrong, it is nevertheless the most significant part of the community. Q 3:114 belongs with the verses discussed so far inasmuch as it speaks of a community forbidding wrong; however, the "upstanding community" (*ummatun qāʾimatun,* Q 3:113) in question is part of the People of the Book (q.v.; *ahl al-kitāb*).

In contrast to these passages, two verses refer to forbidding wrong as something done by individuals. One is Q 7:157, which refers to "those who follow the gentile prophet (*al-rasūl al-nabī l-ummī;* see UMMĪ; ILLITERACY; PROPHETS AND PROPHETHOOD; MESSENGER) whom they find inscribed in their Torah (q.v.) and Gospel (q.v.; see also SCRIPTURE AND THE QURʾĀN)"; it is stated that, among other things, he "commands them right and forbids them wrong." This verse is also the only one in which it is specified to whom the commanding and forbidding are addressed, and the reference is clearly to Jewish or Christian followers of the gentile prophet (see JEWS AND JUDAISM; CHRISTIANS AND CHRISTIANITY). The other verse in which forbidding wrong appears as something done by an individual is Q 31:17, in which the pre-Islamic sage Luqmān (q.v.) tells his son to "perform the prayer, and command right and forbid wrong, and bear patiently whatever may befall you (see TRUST AND PATIENCE)."

To sum up the data presented so far, we can say the following: forbidding wrong is usually referred to as something done by the community as a whole or a significant part of it but occasionally as something done by individuals. Only one verse tells us to whom the commanding and forbidding is addressed, in that instance the Jewish or Christian followers of the gentile prophet. No verses give further indications regarding the content of the commanding and forbidding.

It may be noted that the two components of the phrase — "commanding right" and "forbidding wrong" — scarcely appear separately in the Qurʾān, although there are a couple of references to "forbidding indecency and wrong" (Q 16:90; 29:45, and cf. Q 24:21; the possible relevance of Q 5:79 will be discussed below). The term "right" (*maʿrūf,* literally "known," hence "recognized, approved of") appears frequently in the Qurʾān (Q 2:178, 180, 228, 229, etc.), normally as a substantive but occasionally as an adjective (for the latter, see for example Q 2:235; 24:53). It usually, though not always, appears in legal contexts but does not seem to be a technical term; it appears to refer rather to performing a legal or other action in a decent and honorable fashion, and a few verses suggest that it may be synonymous with "kindliness" (*iḥsān,* see Q 2:178, 229, and cf. Q 2:236; see GOOD DEEDS). The word "wrong" (*munkar,* literally "unknown," hence "not recognized, disapproved of") is much less common (Q 22:72; 29:29; 58:2), and its appearances do not help to limit the scope of the term. The words "command" (*amara)* and "forbid" *(nahā)* are, of course, of common occurrence in the Qurʾān (see FORBIDDEN).

As an indication of the scope of forbidding wrong, it is perhaps worth noting the kinds of themes that appear in conjunction with it in the relevant verses: performing prayer (Q 9:71, 112; 22:41; 31:17); paying alms (Q 9:71; 22:41; see ALMSGIVING); believing in God (Q 3:110, 114), obeying him and his Prophet (*rasūlahu,* Q 9:71; see OBEDIENCE), keeping his bounds (Q 9:112), reciting his signs (q.v.; *āyāt,* Q 3:113; see also VERSES); calling to good (Q 3:104), vying with each other in good works (Q 3:114), and enduring what befalls one (Q 31:17). There is nothing here to narrow the concept of the duty.

Two further passages require discussion, though it is not clear that either refers to forbidding wrong. One is Q 5:78-9. After stating that those of the Children of Israel (q.v.) who disbelieved were cursed by David (q.v.) and Jesus (q.v.) for their sins, the passage continues: *kānū lā yatanāhawna ʿan munkarin faʿalūhu*. This is the only qurʾānic occurrence of the verb *tanāhā*. Etymologically it would be possible to interpret this form in a reciprocal sense derived from *nahā,* "to forbid"; the meaning would then be that the Children of Israel "forbade not one another any wrong that they committed." This would suggest that forbidding wrong is something individual believers do to each other. Yet there seems to be no independent attestation of such a sense of the verb, and in normal Arabic usage *tanāhā* is a synonym of *intahā;* this verb, common in the Qurʾān and elsewhere, means "refrain" or "desist" (as in Q 2:275 and Q 8:38). Thus the sense would be that "they did not desist from any wrong that they committed," and the passage would then have no connection with forbidding wrong. There is in fact a variant reading (see READINGS OF THE QURʾĀN), with *yantahūna* in place of *yatanāhawna,* that would provide further support for this (in a text written with *scriptio defectiva,* the two forms would be distinguishable only by the pointing of the second and third consonants; see ORTHOGRAPHY; ARABIC SCRIPT).

The other passage is Q 7:163-6. These verses tell a story about God's punishment of the people of a town by the sea who fished on the Sabbath (q.v.; see also PUNISHMENT STORIES). The context implies that a part of this community had reproved the Sabbath-breakers; another part *(ummatun)* then asked the reprovers why they took the trouble to admonish people whom God would punish in any case (see REWARD AND PUNISHMENT; CHASTISEMENT AND PUNISHMENT). God then saved those who forbade evil (*alladhīna yanhawna ʿani l-sūʾi*, Q 7:165), and punished those who had acted wrongly. Here we have a clear conception of forbidding evil as something done by members of a community toward each other, and we learn in concrete terms what the evil in question was. The passage, however, speaks of forbidding "evil" *(sūʾ)*, not "wrong" *(munkar)*.

What is the origin of the qurʾānic phrase "commanding right and forbidding wrong"? To judge from *jāhilī* poetry (see AGE OF IGNORANCE; PRE-ISLAMIC ARABIA AND THE QURʾĀN; POETRY AND POETS), the terms here rendered "right" and "wrong" were well-known in pre-Islamic Arabic, and might be paired; but there is no worthwhile evidence that people spoke of "commanding" and "forbidding" them. The phrase finds a parallel in Hellenistic Greek, which might be its source; but the similarity could be accidental, inasmuch as a similar phrase can be found in classical Chinese (for the question of origins, see Cook, *Commanding right*, chap. 19).

The pre-modern exegetical tradition

It will be evident from the survey given above that the relevant qurʾānic passages left wide latitude to the exegetes (see EXEGESIS OF THE QURʾĀN: CLASSICAL AND MEDIEVAL). Often they take some verse, usually Q 3:104, as an occasion to set out a classical doctrine of forbidding wrong reflecting the traditions of their sect or school (see LAW AND THE QURʾĀN). Such discussions are likely to have much in common with accounts of the duty in other genres and to have little bearing on the exegetical problems raised by the verse in question. In this article we will be concerned only with the treatment by the exegetes of properly exegetical questions.

With regard to the question as to who is obligated by the duty, a major focus of exegetical attention is an ambiguity of Q 3:104 (see AMBIGUOUS). The verse states that there should be a "community of you *(minkum ummatun)*" forbidding wrong. The issue is the sense of "of" *(min)*. Does it mean "consisting of," or does it mean "from among"? In the technical language of the exegetes, the first would be an instance of "specification" *(tabyīn)* and would imply that all members of the community had the duty of forbidding wrong; the second would be an instance of "partition" *(tabʿīḍ)* and would imply that only some members were obligated (for this terminology, see, for example, Zamakhsharī, *Kashshāf*, ad loc.; Rāzī, *Tafsīr*, ad loc.). The prevalent view among the exegetes was the second (see, for example, Zamakhsharī, *Kashshāf*, ad loc.; Qurṭubī, *Jāmiʿ*, ad loc.; Abū Ḥayyān, *Baḥr*, ad loc.; Ibn Kathīr, *Tafsīr*, ad loc.). The minority view, however, was held by a scholar as distinguished as the philologist al-Zajjāj (d. 311/923) who held that "Let there be one community of you" meant "Let all of you be a community" (*Maʿānī*, ad loc.; see also Māturīdī, *Taʾwīlāt*, ad loc.). The position of al-Ṭabarī (d. 310/923) is unclear (*Tafsīr*, ad loc.) and Fakhr al-Dīn al-Rāzī (d. 606/1210) sits on the fence (*Tafsīr*, ad loc.). Exegetes often link the issue to the highly technical question whether forbidding wrong is a "collective duty" *(farḍ ʿalā l-kifāya)* or an "individual duty" (*farḍ ʿalā l-aʿyān;* see, for example, Zamakhsharī, *Kashshāf*, ad. loc; Rāzī, *Tafsīr*, ad loc.; Qurṭubī, *Jāmiʿ*, ad loc.; Bayḍāwī, *Anwār*, ad loc.). (To say that a duty is collective means that when one person undertakes it, others are thereby dispensed from it, whereas in the case of an individual duty there is no such dispensation.) The exegetes may also adduce as people unable to perform the duty women, invalids and the ignorant (see, for example, Abū l-Layth al-Samarqandī, *Tafsīr*, ad loc.; Zamakhsharī, *Kashshāf*, ad loc.; Rāzī, *Tafsīr*, ad loc.; Bayḍāwī, *Anwār*, ad loc.; Nīsābūrī, *Tafsīr*, ad loc.; Abū Ḥayyān, *Baḥr*, ad loc.;

see WOMEN AND THE QUR'ĀN; GENDER; ILLNESS AND HEALTH; IGNORANCE). Here the occasional exclusion of women seems odd in the light of the reference to "the believers, the men and the women" in Q 9:71.

The exegetes have little to say about the question to whom the commanding and forbidding is addressed. Occasionally they supply "people" *(al-nās)* as the object of the verb "command" in Q 3:104 (Ṭabarī, *Tafsīr,* ad loc.) or Q 3:110 (Muqātil, *Tafsīr,* ad loc., echoing the use of the word earlier in the verse).

The most interesting divergence concerns the scope of the duty. One line of interpretation limits the duty to enjoining belief in God and his Prophet. This early trend is particularly well established in the *wujūh* genre, that is to say in a tradition of works devoted to setting out the senses of qur'ānic terms that have more than one meaning (see POLYSEMY). According to the earliest of these works, that of Muqātil b. Sulaymān (d. 150/767-8), "commanding right" in Q 3:110, 9:112, and 31:17 means enjoining belief in the unity of God *(tawḥīd),* while "forbidding wrong" in these verses means forbidding polytheism (*shirk;* see POLYTHEISM AND ATHEISM); at the same time, in Q 3:114 and Q 9:71, "commanding right" refers to following *(ittibā')* and affirming belief *(taṣdīq)* in the Prophet, and "wrong" refers to denying *(takdhīb)* him (*Ashbāh,* 113-14 no. 13; for the most part these interpretations also appear in the commentary to the relevant verses in his *Tafsīr;* see LIE). This analysis recurs in later works of the same genre (Yaḥyā b. Sallām, *Taṣārīf,* 203 no. 42; Dāmaghānī, *Wujūh,* 113; Ibn al-Jawzī, *Nuzha,* 544 no. 270, 574 no. 286). Interpretations of this type are also ascribed to yet earlier authorities. Thus there is a view attributed to Abū l-'Āliya (d. 90/708-9) according to which, in all qur'ānic references to "commanding right" and "forbidding wrong," the former refers to calling people from polytheism to Islam, and the latter to forbidding the worship of idols and devils (Ṭabarī, *Tafsīr,* ad Q 9:71 and Q 9:112; and see Mujāhid, *Tafsīr,* ad Q 31:17; Abū Ḥayyān, *Baḥr,* ad Q 3:110 and Q 9:71; Suyūṭī, *Durr,* ad Q 3:104 and Q 9:67; see IDOLS AND IMAGES; IDOLATRY AND IDOLATERS; JINN; DEVIL). Similar views are ascribed to Sa'īd b. Jubayr (d. 95/714; Māwardī, *Nukat,* ad Q 9:112; Suyūṭī, *Durr,* ad Q 31:17) and Ḥasan al-Baṣrī (d. 110/728; Ṭabarī, *Tafsīr,* ad Q 9:112). Such interpretations are likewise an element in the mainstream exegetical tradition, but we do not find them adopted consistently there (see, for example, Zajjāj, *Ma'ānī,* ad Q 9:67, 112; Māturīdī, *Ta'wīlāt,* ad Q 3:114).

The more usual interpretation does not limit the scope of forbidding wrong in this way. Thus al-Ṭabarī in his commentary on Q 9:112 explicitly rejects such limitation, declaring that "commanding right" refers to all that God and his Prophet have commanded, and "forbidding wrong" to all that they have forbidden (*Tafsīr,* ad loc.). Likewise Fakhr al-Dīn al-Rāzī in commenting on Q 3:114 emphasizes that the terms "right" and "wrong" are to be understood without restriction — they refer to all "right" and all "wrong" (*Tafsīr,* ad loc.; see also Abū Ḥayyān, *Baḥr,* ad Q 3:104). This approach justifies the common understanding of the duty as extending to such everyday sins as drinking liquor (see WINE; INTOXICANTS) and making music.

There is a significant tendency among the exegetes to construe as references to forbidding wrong verses which make no explicit reference to it. A striking example of this is found in the commentary of al-Qurṭubī (d. 671/1273), who takes the reference to "those who command justice *(qist)*" in Q 3:21 as an invitation to embark on his major discussion of forbidding wrong (*Jāmi',* ad loc.); most commentators would have waited till Q 3:104. Another such case is Q 5:79, where the exegetes favor the interpretation of *yatanāhawna* as "forbid one another" rather than "desist." For example, Fakhr al-Dīn al-Rāzī notes both interpretations but describes the first as that of the mainstream (*Tafsīr,* ad loc.) and many exegetes simply omit to mention the second (see, for example, Wāḥidī, *Wasīṭ;* Baghawī, *Maʿālim;* Ibn al-Jawzī, *Zād;* Qurṭubī, *Jāmiʿ;* Ibn Kathīr, *Tafsīr; Jalālayn,* ad loc.). Likewise the exegetes regularly take the story of the Sabbath-breakers (Q 7:163-6) to be about forbidding wrong, despite the fact that the passage speaks rather of forbidding "evil" (*sūʾ;* see, for example, Zajjāj, *Maʿānī;* Ṭabarī, *Tafsīr;* Wāḥidī, *Wasīṭ;* Zamakhsharī, *Kashshāf;* Ibn Kathīr, *Tafsīr,* ad loc.). Their main concern in interpreting the passage is with the group who saw no point in admonishing people whom God would punish anyway: were they saved with those who spoke out, or damned with those who had violated the Sabbath? (see Zajjāj, *Maʿānī,* ad loc.). The Qurʾān provided no clear guidance on the question, inviting division among the exegetes. There are, for example, traditions ascribing three different views to ʿAbdallāh b. al-ʿAbbās (d. 68/687-8): that those who kept silent were saved, that they were damned and that he did not know (Ṭabarī, *Tafsīr,* ad loc.). This issue was related to a question regularly discussed in formal accounts of forbidding wrong: does the duty lapse where it is known that performing it would not achieve anything?

In commenting on Q 31:17, the exegetes often stress that one should be willing to endure the unpleasant consequences of forbidding wrong. This reflects the fact that, immediately after telling his son to command right and forbid wrong, Luqmān goes on to say that he should "bear patiently" whatever befalls him *(wa-ṣbir ʿalā mā aṣābaka).* This is related to another doctrinal issue: is one dispensed from performing the duty in cases where this would put one in harm's way? Most exegetes took the patience enjoined by Luqmān to refer to the consequences of forbidding wrong (see, for example, Muqātil, *Tafsīr;* Ṭabarī, *Tafsīr;* Abū l-Layth al-Samarqandī, *Tafsīr;* Wāḥidī, *Wasīṭ;* Rāzī, *Tafsīr;* Ibn Kathīr, *Tafsīr,* ad loc.). The alternative interpretation, that the verse refers to the trials and tribulations of life in general, is mentioned by some exegetes but does not find much favor with them (Māwardī, *Nukat;* Zamakhsharī, *Kashshāf;* Qurṭubī, *Jāmiʿ;* Bayḍāwī, *Anwār;* Abū Ḥayyān, *Baḥr,* ad loc.). In this context it is worth noting a variant reading for Q 3:104 which adds after "forbidding wrong" the words "and they seek God's help against whatever may befall them" (*wa-yastaʿīnūna llāha/bi-llāhi ʿalā mā aṣābahum;* Jeffery, *Materials,* 34); some exegetes draw the same moral from this textual variant, even while rejecting it (Ibn ʿAṭiyya, *Muḥarrar,* ad loc.; Abū Ḥayyān, *Baḥr,* ad loc.). Some verses, though making no mention of forbidding wrong, may be interpreted to refer to incurring death in the course of it. One example is Q 2:207, which falls in a passage contrasting sincere and insincere adherents of the Prophet; here the sincere follower is described as one "who sells himself desiring God's good pleasure." Among the traditions quoted regarding the circumstances in which this verse was revealed, there is one from ʿUmar b. al-Khaṭṭāb (d. 23/644) according to which it referred to a man who forbad wrong and was killed (Ṭabarī, *Tafsīr,* ad loc.; Wāḥidī, *Asbāb,* ad loc.; Ibn al-ʿArabī, *Aḥkām,* ad loc.; see MURDER; BLOODSHED). Al-Ṭabarī takes the wider view that the verse includes both forbidding wrong and holy war (Ṭabarī, *Tafsīr,* ad loc.).

A verse that posed a problem for the exegetes, though it made no mention of forbidding wrong, was Q 5:105: "O believers, look after your own souls (*ʿalaykum anfusakum*). He who is astray (q.v.) cannot hurt you, if you are rightly guided." The plain sense of this verse clearly undermines the idea that the believer has a duty to forbid wrong. The exegetes therefore sought to inactivate the verse, either by referring it to some future time when the duty of forbidding wrong would indeed lapse, or by insisting that those who fail to forbid wrong cannot be considered "rightly guided." In an extensive commentary on the verse, al-Ṭabarī adduces earlier authorities in support of both views, and states his preference for the second (*Tafsīr,* ad loc.). Some went so far as to entertain the idea of abrogation (q.v.) within the verse (see, for example, Abū ʿUbayd, *Nāsikh,* 98).

All that has been said so far about exegesis relates to the Sunnī tradition. The exegetical literature of the major sectarian traditions is for the most part similar in character: it draws on the same pool of material, and presents its results in the same kind of way. This is true of such Ibāḍī and Zaydī commentaries as are easily available and also of much Imāmī commentary. Thus the relevant discussion in the exegetical works of Abū Jaʿfar al-Ṭūsī (d. 460/1067) and al-Ṭabrisī (d. 548/1153) is more strongly colored by Muʿtazilī than by Shīʿī thought (see MUʿTAZILA; SHĪʿISM AND THE QURʾĀN). There is, however, a strongly Shīʿī tradition of exegesis that is particularly well-represented in Imāmī sources and construes certain verses on forbidding wrong as references to the (Shīʿī) imāms (see IMĀM). Thus the commentary attributed to ʿAlī b. Ibrāhīm al-Qummī (alive in 307/919) interprets Q 9:111-12 to refer to them — those who command right are those who know all that is right, as only the imāms do (*Tafsīr,* ad loc.; and see ʿAyyāshī, *Tafsīr,* ad loc.). In commentary to Q 3:110 this is linked to a variant reading transmitted by the Imāmīs, in which "the best community" (*khayra ummatin*) becomes "the best *imāms*" (*khayra aʾimmatin;* Qummī, *Tafsīr,* ad loc.; ʿAyyāshī, *Tafsīr,* ad loc.). These views appear in Imāmī commentaries down the centuries, though they are almost absent from that of al-Ṭūsī (see, for example, Abū l-Futūḥ Rāzī, *Rawḍ,* ad Q 3:110; Kāshānī, *Manhaj,* ad Q 3:110; Baḥrānī, *Burhān,* ad Q 3:104; and cf. Ṭūsī, *Tibyān,* ad Q 3:110).

Modern exegesis

The exegetes of the thirteenth/nineteenth century remained overwhelmingly traditional in their approach to the relevant verses (see EXEGESIS OF THE QURʾĀN: EARLY MODERN AND CONTEMPORARY). Thus there is nothing even incipiently modern about the treatment of Q 3:104 in the commentaries of the Yemeni Shawkānī (d. 1250/1834) or the Iraqi Maḥmūd al-Ālūsī (d. 1270/1854; Shawkānī, *Tafsīr;* Ālūsī, *Rūḥ,* ad loc.).

It is with the *Tafsīr al-manār* of Muḥammad ʿAbduh (d. 1323/1905) and Rashīd Riḍā (d. 1354/1935) that modernity floods in (see CONTEMPORARY CRITICAL PRACTICES AND THE QURʾĀN). Their commentary on Q 3:104 is a good example of this (Rashīd Riḍā, *Manār,* ad loc.). Thus it sets out an elaborate curriculum of study for Islamic missionaries, including political science (*ʿilm al-siyāsa),* by which is meant the study of contemporary states; this missionary enterprise requires organization, and should be in the hands of what these days is called an association *(jamʿiyya),* with a leadership *(riyāsa)* to direct it. In a similar vein, Riḍā was able to find in this verse a basis for government by a representative assembly such as is found in republics and limited monarchies.

Another area in which modern concerns are manifested in discussions of forbidding wrong is an increased interest in the role of women (see FEMINISM AND THE QURĀN). On the whole, however, this has little impact on Sunnī commentaries on Q 9:71. Nevertheless, the Palestinian Muḥammad ʿIzzat Darwaza (d. 1404/1984) understands the verse to establish the equality of the sexes, in particular with regard to forbidding wrong (*Tafsīr,* xii, 186).

Perhaps the most original approach to forbidding wrong in modern Sunnī exegesis is that of Sayyid Quṭb (d. 1386/1966) in his commentary on Q 5:79 (*Ẓilāl,* ad loc.). At first he seems to align himself with traditional views: he observes that the Muslim community is one in which no one who sees someone else acting wrongly can say "what's that to me?" and that a Muslim society is one in which a Muslim can devote himself to forbidding wrong, without his attempts being reduced to pointless gestures or made impossible altogether, as is regrettably the case in the *jāhilī* (i.e. neo-pagan) societies of our times. The real task is accordingly to establish the good society as such, and this task takes precedence over the righting of small-scale, personal and individual failings through forbidding wrong; such efforts can only be in vain as long as the whole society is corrupt. All the sacred texts bearing on forbidding wrong, he argues, are concerned with the duty of the Muslim in a Muslim society — that is to say, in a form of society that does not exist in our time.

Modern Imāmī discussions of forbidding wrong have tended to be more innovative than Sunnī ones. This contrast has little to do with qurʾānic exegesis but it finds echoes in Imāmī commentaries. Modern Imāmī exegetes are significantly more likely than their Sunnī counterparts to take Q 9:71 as an occasion to discuss the role of women in forbidding wrong (see, for example, Akbar Hāshimī Rafsanjānī, *Tafsīr,* ad loc.). While Sunnī exegetes rarely quote Imāmī commentaries, Imāmī exegetes have a liking for the discussion of Q 3:104 in the *Tafsīr al-manār* (see, for example, Muḥammad Riḍā Āshtiyānī and others, *Tafsīr,* ad loc.).

Modern exegetes, whether Sunnī or Shīʿī, have little that is new to say about the properly exegetical questions raised by the relevant verses.

Michael Cook

Bibliography

Primary (almost every commentary on the Qurʾān touches on the subject under the relevant verses, in particular Q 3:104): Abū l-Futūḥ Rāzī, *Rawḍ;* Abū Ḥayyān, *Baḥr;* Abū l-Layth al-Samarqandī, *Tafsīr;* Abū ʿUbayd, *Nāsikh;* Ālūsī, *Rūḥ;* Muḥammad Riḍā Āshtiyānī et al., *Tafsīr-i numūna,* Tehran 1353-8 Sh.; ʿAyyāshī, *Tafsīr;* Baghawī, *Maʿālim;* Baḥrānī, *Burhān;* Bayḍāwī, *Anwār;* Dāmaghānī, *Wujūh;* Darwaza, *Tafsīr;* Ibn al-ʿArabī, *Aḥkām;* Ibn ʿAṭiyya, *Muḥarrar;* Ibn al-Jawzī, *Nuzha;* id., *Zād;* Ibn Kathīr, *Tafsīr; Jalālayn;* Kāshānī, *Manhaj;* Māturīdī, *Taʾwīlāt;* Māwardī, *Nukat;* Mujāhid, *Tafsīr;* Muqātil, *Ashbāh;* id., *Tafsīr;* Nīsābūrī, *Tafsīr;* Qummī, *Tafsīr;* Qurṭubī, *Jāmiʿ;* Quṭb, *Ẓilāl;* Akbar Hāshimī Rafsanjānī, *Tafsīr-i rāhnumā,* Qummī 1371 Sh.; Rashīd Riḍā, *Manār;* Rāzī, *Tafsīr;* Shawkānī, *Tafsīr;* Suyūṭī, *Durr;* Ṭabarī, *Tafsīr;* Ṭūsī, *Tibyān;* Wāḥidī, *Asbāb;* id., *Wasīṭ;* Yaḥyā b. Sallām, *Taṣārīf;* Zajjāj, *Maʿānī;* Zamakhsharī, *Kashshāf.*

Secondary: M. Cook, *Commanding right and forbidding wrong in Islamic thought,* Cambridge 2000, especially chap. 2, with fuller references (for forbidding wrong in Qurʾān and exegesis; the data in the present article are mostly taken from this chapter); id., *Forbidding wrong in Islam. An introduction,* Cambridge 2003 (for a general account of forbidding wrong); Jeffery, *Materials;* W. Madelung, Amr be maʿrūf, in E. Yarshater (ed.), *Encyclopaedia Iranica,* 13 vols. to date, London 1982- (for general accounts of forbidding wrong), i [1985], 992-5.

Vision

The perception of reality through the eyes, or — for immaterial realities or future events — also the "mind's eye." Two main semantic fields converge in the notion of "visions": one is oneiric, referring to dreams (*ru'yā;* see DREAMS AND SLEEP) and the other is sensory, meaning the actual faculty of sight (*baṣar,* pl. *abṣār*). In both cases divine action plays a central role (see REVELATION AND INSPIRATION). When associated with dreams, visions appear as processes forced upon humans by divine stimulation. Most prominent of these are: the dream of Abraham (q.v.) that involves the sacrificing of his son (Q 37:102-5; see SACRIFICE); Joseph's (q.v.) dream that eleven stars (see PLANETS AND STARS), the sun (q.v.) and the moon (q.v.) bow before him (Q 12:4-6; see BOWING AND PROSTRATION); and Muḥammad's dream that precipitates his night journey (Q 17:60; see ASCENSION). In all these instances, the dreams are premonitions that intimate a divine plan rather than random somatic or mental activities (see FORETELLING; DIVINATION). In fact, Joseph's father tells his son that God will teach him the skill of dream interpretation (Q 12:6), recognizing at the outset the significance of such experiences within the revelatory order. Most exegetes (see EXEGESIS OF THE QUR'ĀN: CLASSICAL AND MEDIEVAL), however, focus on the possible names of the planets and stars and/or their meaning, thus engaging in the intricacies of dream interpretation and acknowledging that Joseph's father was fully aware of the significance of such divine interventions (Ṭabarī, *Tafsīr;* Kāshānī, *Ṣāfī;* Ibn Kathīr, *Tafsīr*). In certain instances, exegetes point out that *ru'ya* (the visual faculty) is not to be confused with *ru'yā* (dream), especially in the case of Joseph's experience (Kāshānī, *Ṣāfī;* Zamakhsharī, *Kashshāf*). Al-Ṭabarī (d. 310/923), however, does recognize the double entendre in Q 17:60 which evokes *r-'-y* as possibly dreaming and/or seeing (see SEEING AND HEARING; VISION AND BLINDNESS), and he reports divergent opinions on this matter. Here, God announces that he has induced a dream *(ja'alnā l-ru'yā)* so that he could show *(araynāka)* Muḥammad a test for the people (see TRIAL; TRUST AND PATIENCE). Similarly, in Q 48:27, in reference to the signing of the peace of Ḥudaybiya (q.v.) and taking control of Khaybar (see EXPEDITIONS AND BATTLES), God confirms the fulfillment of Muḥammad's dream about entering Mecca (q.v.) with his people (Kāshānī, *Ṣāfī;* Ibn Kathīr, *Tafsīr,* ad loc.). Dreams, then, belong to the category of God's signs (q.v.) through which he communicates with humankind, although it is not clear that all dreams are to be viewed as such.

In the semantic field of the root *b-ṣ-r,* God gives human beings the capacity to see (Q 76:2), which throughout the Qur'ān is directly linked to the cognitive and psychological potential of human beings to recognize and accept God (see BELIEF AND UNBELIEF; KNOWLEDGE AND LEARNING). In that way, the sensory and other human faculties interrelate as the criteria of faith (q.v.). God thus characterizes his prophets, specifically Abraham, Isaac (q.v.) and Jacob (q.v.), as possessing vision *(abṣār).* In Q 59:2, God addresses the believers as "people of vision!" *(yā ūlī l-abṣār),* that is, those, according to Ibn Kathīr (d. 774/1373; *Tafsīr,* ad loc.), on whom God has bestowed clarification for his actions. But just as God creates vision, he can disable or remove it (Q 6:46, 110), seal it (Q 2:7), seize it (Q 2:20-2), or restore it (Q 12:96; 50:22; see POWER AND IMPOTENCE; VEIL). In turn, those who refuse God are accused of turning away their vision (Q 24:37; see LIE; GRATITUDE AND INGRATITUDE). The true vision is one that, even if it does not perceive God, learns to perceive his signs and results in submission. After all, unlike the divine, human vision is limited, as per Q 6:103: "No vision can comprehend him; but he comprehends all visions" *(lā tudrikuhu l-abṣār wa-huwa yudriku l-abṣār).* Al-Suyūṭī (d. 911/1505; *Durr,* ad loc.) explains that, according to the tradition (see ḤADĪTH

AND THE QUR'ĀN; SUNNA), this means that, while in this world (q.v.) God can never be seen (see THEOPHANY; FACE OF GOD), in the afterlife one will be able to see him on the horizon the way one now sees the moon rise in the night sky (see ESCHATOLOGY). The ability to see is understood at once as a physical and ethical capacity (see ETHICS AND THE QUR'ĀN) whereby vision is opposed to blindness, figuratively as well as literally, as per Q 35:19-20: "The one who is blind is not the same as the one who can see *(al-baṣīr)*, just as the darkness (q.v.) and the light (q.v.) are not the same" (see also PAIRS AND PAIRING; SYMBOLIC IMAGERY; METAPHOR).

Amila Buturovic

Bibliography
Primary: Ibn Kathīr, *Tafsīr*, Beirut 1980; Jalālayn; Kāshānī, *Ṣāfī*; Suyūṭī, *Durr*; Ṭabarī, *Tafsīr*, Beirut 1984; Zamakhsharī, *Kashshāf*.
Secondary: L. Kinberg, Dreams as a means to evaluate ḥadīth, in *JSAI* 23 (1999), 63-80; id., Literal dreams and prophetic ḥadīth in classical Islam. A comparison of two ways of legitimation, in *Der Islam* 70/2 (1993), 279-300; M. Maroth, The science of dreams in Islamic culture, in *JSAI* 20 (1996), 229-36; M. Mir, The qur'ānic story of Joseph. Plots, themes, and characters, in *MW* 76 (1986), 1-15.

Vision and Blindness

Ability, or lack thereof, to perceive physical objects and, when used metaphorically, ideas and concepts.

Witnessing the unseen

The Qur'ān divides existence into this world (q.v.) and the next, followed by a second division into the seen *(shāhid)* and the unseen *(ghayb)*, as in Q 59:22, "He is God, besides whom there is no god, the one who knows the unseen and the seen" (see HIDDEN AND THE HIDDEN). The two dichotomies overlap in an important way. The next world is entirely unseen but this world consists of elements seen and elements unseen. God is not visible (see GOD AND HIS ATTRIBUTES), as in Q 7:143, "Moses (q.v.) said, 'My lord, show yourself to me and let me gaze upon you!' God said, 'You will never see me'" (see THEOPHANY). Elements of the unseen world are made visible, however, in miracles (q.v.) granted to prophets (see PROPHETS AND PROPHETHOOD) and saints (see SAINT), like Muḥammad's ascension (q.v.; *mi'rāj*). Q 53:1-18 asserts that "The heart [of Muḥammad] never denied what he saw" (*ra'ā*, Q 53:11) and "[his] vision *(al-baṣar)* never swerved nor did it transgress" (Q 53:17; see also ERROR; ASTRAY; SEEING AND HEARING). The term for Prophet, *nabī*, is derived from a verbal root meaning to be lofty and command a far-reaching overview *(n-b-y)*, connoting the ability to inform others of what is beyond the horizon of their sight. A ḥadīth report (see ḤADĪTH AND THE QUR'ĀN) clarifies that "Truthful vision *(al-ru'yā al-ṣāliḥ)* is one fortieth part of prophecy" (see also VISION; TRUTH).

Seeing is believing

God's signs in the world can be seen and can prompt people to have faith (q.v.) in what is beyond routine perception. Angels (see ANGEL) and jinn (q.v.) are normally unseen but can be manifest to human sight, forming two important conduits between the world of human habitation and the ambiguities beyond. For example, Mary (q.v.) sees an angel who announces the birth of Jesus (q.v.) in Q 19:17: "Then we sent our spirit (q.v.) to her, and it appeared to her [vision] *(tamaththala lahā)* exactly like a man." In this way, the Qur'ān gives profound depth to the truism that "seeing is believing." Physical vision is a powerful metaphor (q.v.) for faith *(īmān)*: faith is the vision of the heart (cf. e.g. Q 58:22) rather than the eyes (q.v.; cf. e.g. Q 6:103). Conversely, blindness is a metaphor for deliberate disbelief (see BELIEF AND UNBELIEF; LIE; GRATITUDE AND INGRATITUDE) when confronted with the truth or spiritual insensitivity, and is often linked to deafness (e.g. Q 7:179; 11:20; 47:23; see HEARING AND DEAFNESS).

The Qurʾān links true vision to perception of the prophets and acceptance of the covenant (q.v.; *mīthāq*) they offer. Q 5:78-9 says that whenever a prophet came to Israelite tribes (see CHILDREN OF ISRAEL) with a message that contradicted their desires (see MESSENGER), a part of them called the prophet's mission a lie and fought against the prophet: "They estimate that there will be no trial (q.v.)? Thus they go blind and deaf. Yet God turns to them accepting repentance (see REPENTANCE AND PENANCE), still many of them remain blind and deaf. But God is the one who sees *(baṣīr)* all they do."

The Qurʾān often informs the prophet Muḥammad of what he sees or will see in the future and clarifies the spiritual importance of what Muḥammad sees or provides prognostic visions (e.g. Q 17:60; 48:27; see FORETELLING; DIVINATION). The Meccan revelations often stress eschatological vision (e.g. Q 99 and 102; see ESCHATOLOGY; FORM AND STRUCTURE OF THE QURʾĀN), while the Medinan revelations frequently allude to what the community will see in the near earthly future (see CHRONOLOGY AND THE QURʾĀN; MECCA; MEDINA). The Qurʾān often equates Muḥammad's revelation with vision as well as audition, as in Q 4:105: "We have caused the message *(al-kitāb;* see BOOK) to descend upon you in truth (see REVELATION AND INSPIRATION), so that you judge between the people (see JUDGMENT) by means of what God has shown you *(arāka)*."

The Qurʾān expresses ambivalence toward routine vision. It challenges people to see the signs (q.v.) of God in nature, human history and individual experience (see also HISTORY AND THE QURʾĀN; GEOGRAPHY; GENERATIONS; NATURE AS SIGNS). Q 67:3-4 challenges, "Do you see *(tarā)* any imbalance in the creation (q.v.) of the compassionate one? So turn your vision to it again — do you see any flaw?" Q 24:41 asks, "Have you not seen *(a-lam tara)* that all beings in the heavens and the earth glorify God (see GLORY; GLORIFICATION OF GOD), even the birds in flight (see ANIMAL LIFE)?" In these examples, seeing is a test, not simple perception. It is witnessing the truth (*shahāda;* see WITNESS TO FAITH) if sight causes the heart to recognize God's presence but it is ignoring or covering the truth *(kufr)* if sight urges the heart toward denying God's presence or aggrandizing the ego. Q 96:6-8 pronounces, "No indeed, the human being transgresses the limits, and sees *(raʾāhu)* him/herself as independent (see ARROGANCE) — [but no indeed,] to your lord all things return." Ṣūfī commentaries (see ṢŪFISM AND THE QURʾĀN) understand "returning" as "remembering" the primordial moment of witnessing the truth (see REMEMBRANCE; WITNESSING AND TESTIFYING), when each human before creation witnessed *(sh-h-d)* God directly in seeing, hearing and being present, as in Q 7:172 (see COSMOLOGY).

Deceptive appearances

Vision can misconstrue the truth; seeing something from one's own perspective can mean holding an opinion that may be false. In this way, the Qurʾān often uses the verbal root "he saw" *(r-ʾ-y)* as synonymous with the verbal root "he imagined" *(z-ʿ-m)* or "he thought" (*n-ẓ-r;* see SUSPICION; KNOWLEDGE AND LEARNING; INTELLECT). Q 6:46 provides an example: "Say, 'Do you think *(a-raʾaytum)* that when God snatches away your hearing and your sight *(abṣārukum)* and seals up your hearts that there is any other god (see POLYTHEISM AND ATHEISM) that could return [them] to you?" Seeing could be disbelieving if the heart's spiritual vision is obscured by darkness (q.v.; cf. e.g. Q 6:25; 17:46; 22:46), impaired by disease (cf. e.g. Q 2:10; 5:52; 8:49; see ILLNESS AND HEALTH), or sealed up with rust (cf. e.g. Q 83:14; cf. 42:24; 47:24 see HEART).

From the contrary perspective, blind people can have intense spiritual insight. Q 80 describes an incident when Muḥammad turned away from a blind man who sought spiritual guidance. The blind man had interrupted the Prophet's meeting with a tribal leader who, if he converted to Islam, would bolster the early Muslim community. Q 80:1-6 states,

> He frowned and turned away, when the blind man *(al-aʿmā)* came to him. And what might let you know if he would increase in purity, or if he were bearing [God] in mind that he might benefit from the reminding? But as for him who considers himself independent, you turn to him to attend his needs!

This is the only qurʾānic passage to mention an actual blind person and in it, the Qurʾān chastises Muḥammad. According to Muslim tradition he remained ashamed of this incident throughout his life, to the point of wishing that if any phrases of the Qurʾān could be erased, these are the ones he would like to see eliminated. This is because the Qurʾān condemns hypocrites for their deceptive appearance (and judging people by how they appear; see HYPOCRITES AND HYPOCRISY): in Q 63:4, "When you see them *(raʾaytahum)*, their external appearance *(ajsāmuhum)* pleases you, but when they speak, you hear them speak it is as if they are hollow timber propped up."

Metaphorical blindness

Despite this example of an actual blind man, the Qurʾān mainly refers to the blind in a metaphorical sense (see SYMBOLIC IMAGERY). The blind are those whose hearts have no spiritual perception, and they are the subject of critique, ridicule and threat of punishment. Q 13:16 (cf. Q 6:50) rhetorically contrasts the blind to those with sight (see RHETORIC AND THE QURʾĀN): "Say, 'Is the blind person equal to one endowed with vision, and is the darkness equal to the light?'" Q 35:19 answers the question negatively (those with sight are better); and Q 40:58 offers a further comparison to clarify the ethical importance of the question (see ETHICS AND THE QURʾĀN): "Not equal are the blind and those who see *(al-aʿmā wa-l-baṣīr)*! Nor are those who believe, performing good works (see GOOD DEEDS), and those who perpetrate evil actions (see EVIL DEEDS; GOOD AND EVIL)!" Those who believe have true vision because their hearts perceive the spiritual reality of the unseen consequence of action. In contrast, those who do evil are truly blind: the arrogance and waywardness of their hearts blinds them, rather than the vision of their eyes. Q 22:46 clarifies that "It is not their eyes that are blind *(lā taʿmā l-abṣār)*, but rather the hearts in their breasts that are blind." Abū Ḥāmid al-Ghazālī (d. 505/1111) provided a profound commentary on physical vision and spiritual vision in his treatise *Mishkāt al-anwār*, "Niche for lights."

S. Kugle

Bibliography

F. Colby (trans.), *Subtleties of the ascension. Early mystical sayings on Muḥammad's heavenly journey as compiled by Abū ʿAbd al-Raḥmān Sulamī*, Louisville, KY: Fons Vitae 2006; F. Esack, *A short introduction to the Qurʾān*, Oxford 2002; J. van Ess, Vision and ascension. Sūrat al-Najm and its relationship with Muḥammad's *miʿrāj,* in *Journal of qurʾanic studies* 1 (1999), 47-62; W.H.T. Gairdner (trans.), *Al-Ghazzālī's Mishkāt al-anwār ("The niche for lights"),* London 1924; S. Kugle, Heaven's witness. The uses and abuses of Muḥammad Ghawth Gwaliori's ascension, in JIS 14 (2003), 1-36 (for discussion of the appropriation of the religious experience of a sixteenth century Indian Ṣūfī of the Shaṭṭāriyya *ṭarīqa*); S. Murata and W. Chittick, *The vision of Islam,* St. Paul 1994; M. Sells, *Early Islamic mysticism,* New York 1996.

Visiting

Traveling to another place and staying there for a period of time. The terms that usually come to mind when considering the concept of visiting are derived from the root *z-w-r.* These terms occur in ḥadīth literature (see ḤADĪTH AND THE QURʾĀN) in reference to visiting graves (see BURIAL), usually in order to pray for the deceased (see Wensinck, *Handbook,* 89-90; see DEATH AND THE DEAD; PRAYER FORMULAS). In popular parlance, *ziyāra* came to be identified with spiritual practices (see ṢŪFISM AND THE QURʾĀN) involving the visitation of saints' tombs (see SAINT) so that pilgrims could acquire blessings, request miracles (q.v.) and benefactions, or seek mediation for sins (see SIN, MAJOR AND MINOR; INTERCESSION). The term, in this sense, does not occur in the Qurʾān. Words stemming from the root *z-w-r,* which pertain to the concept of visiting, occur only once, in Q 102:2, "until you come *(zurtum)* to the graves." According to al-Ṭabarī (d. 310/923), the term *"zurtum"* is a metaphor (q.v.) for death that ends the struggle for material wealth (q.v.; *Tafsīr,* xii, 678-9). The more common term used in the Qurʾān for visiting or visitation is *ʿumra,* as in Q 2:196 that refers to the minor pilgrimage to the Kaʿba (q.v.). The verb *iʿtamara* also occurs in Q 2:158 which specifies what *ʿumra* entails and serves as the qurʾānic basis for legal rules outlining pilgrimage (q.v.; see Ṭabarī, *Tafsīr,* ii, 47-55, 212-19). An example of how far later legal discourse moved away from the Qurʾān as a basis of law (see LAW AND THE QURʾĀN) is the rather lengthy discussion of *ḥajj* and *ʿumra* in the *al-ʿAzīz sharḥ al-Wajīz* (iii, 456-523) by Abū l-Qāsim al-Rāfiʿī (d. 623/1226), the most important Shāfiʿī legal text of the late medieval period, which does not refer to the two qurʾānic passages but bases its entire discussion on ḥadīth.

Mathāba, as a place of visitation, is mentioned in Q 2:125 although there appears to have been a dispute as to the specific boundaries of the area around the Kaʿba to which it refers. Al-Ṭabarī said that it could refer to the whole of Mecca (q.v.), the *ḥaram,* or more specifically to the immediate area of the Kaʿba itself. Finally, the term *ṭāʾif,* or *ṭāfa,* came to be interpreted as a kind of visitation from a supernatural entity. In Q 7:201 Satan (Shayṭān; see DEVIL) visits humans, although the nature of the visitation was, according to al-Ṭabarī, a matter of some dispute. He argued that some theologians held that the visitation *(ṭāʾif)* came in the form of a whisper (q.v.) or a low voice that the individual heard and was thus prompted into action. Others held that Satan came over the person in the form of emotions such as anger (q.v.) or jealousy (see ENVY). In Q 68:19, a variation of this occurs, which states "So there came *(ṭāfa)* on it a visitation *(ṭāʾif)* from your lord (q.v.) [all around], while they slept" (see SLEEP). In this instance, al-Ṭabarī maintains that *ṭāʾif* refers to the command *(amr)* of God as embodied by Muḥammad. According to Ibn Kathīr (d. 774/1373; *Tafsīr,* viii, 214), however, the "it" refers to the Quraysh (q.v.) who rejected Muḥammad and *ṭāʾif* refers to their destruction. In other words, God visited [destruction on] the people of Quraysh who rejected Muḥammad as a prophet (see OPPOSITION TO MUḤAMMAD;

PROPHETS AND PROPHETHOOD). For visitors in the sense of "guests," see HOSPITALITY AND COURTESY; ABRAHAM.

R. Kevin Jaques

Bibliography
Primary: Ibn Kathīr, *Tafsīr*, ed. M.Ḥ. Shams al-Dīn, 8 vols., Beirut 1998; al-Rāfiʿī, Abū l-Qāsim ʿAbd al-Karīm b. Abī Saʿīd Muḥammad, *al-ʿAzīz sharḥ al-Wajīz*, ed. ʿA.M. Muʿawwaḍ and ʿĀ.A. ʿAbd al-Mawjūd, 13 vols., Beirut 1997; Ṭabarī, *Tafsīr*, 13 vols., Beirut 1999;
Secondary: Wensinck, *Handbook*.

Vocabulary

see LANGUAGE AND STYLE OF THE QURʾĀN; FOREIGN VOCABULARY

Vow

A promise made to God to undertake an act of piety (q.v.). It differs from an oath (q.v.) which is not a promise to do something but a solemn declaration of truth (hence, its essential role as a form of juridical evidence; see WITNESSING AND TESTIFYING) performed by an act of swearing (often but not necessarily by God; but for overlap in juristic discourse on oaths and vows, see Calder, Ḥinth, esp. 220-6). A vow, which in Islam can only be made to God (for vows in pre-Islamic Arabia and non-religious vows after Islam, see Pedersen, Nadhr; see PRE-ISLAMIC ARABIA AND THE QURʾĀN), may or may not include an act of swearing (*aqsama* and *ḥalafa* in Arabic), but does imply a pledge of oneself — one's honor and credibility — i.e. it places one in a state of self-dedication. Thus, failure to fulfill a vow in Islam carries the same requirement for the performance of "penance" (i.e. expiation, *kaffāra;* see REPENTANCE AND PENANCE) as does breaking an oath. This usually entails feeding or clothing ten poor (see POVERTY AND THE POOR; FOOD AND DRINK), releasing a slave (see SLAVES AND SLAVERY), or, in case of hardship, fasting (q.v.) for three days (on the basis of Q 5:89). There is also the possibility of releasing oneself from a vow that one could perform but no longer feels it good to do so, through the performance of expiation.

A vow (*nadhr*, pl. *nudhūr*), a self-imposed promise to carry out a religious act not required by the law *(ilzām al-nafs bi-qurba),* is understood as obligatory (in effect, the vow renders the supererogatory act of piety a required individual duty, *wājib ʿaynī*, to God). Those who do not fulfill their vowed religious pledges *(ʿahd)* are hypocrites (Q 9:75-8; cf. 48:10; and Bukhārī, *Ṣaḥīḥ*, no. 6695, where the Prophet declares that Muslims in the third generation after him will begin to break their vows; see HYPOCRITES AND HYPOCRISY; ḤADĪTH AND THE QURʾĀN), while righteous servants of God fulfill their vows (Q 76:5-7). The mother of Mary (q.v.), in an echo of 1 Samuel 11, vowed to God what was in her womb (q.v.; Q 3:35) and Mary herself, the Qurʾān reports, made a vow to fast and to speak to no human for a day (Q 19:26). Finally, vows are associated with involuntary alms (see ALMSGIVING) at Q 2:270, supporting evidence for defining vows as religious acts above and beyond what is prescribed by law.

That humans had made vows before the coming of Islam was recognized by the first Muslims (e.g. Bukhārī, *Ṣaḥīḥ*, no. 6697, where ʿUmar b. al-Khaṭṭāb asks the Prophet whether he should fulfill a vow he made before his conversion; Q 3:35 and Q 19:26 are also cited in this regard), as was the fact that they had made them for purposes of religion (q.v.), e.g. before idols (Q 6:136; 39:3; see IDOLS AND IMAGES). Given this recognition, it was important to establish an understanding of vow-making acceptable to Islam: the consensus eventually established this as a vow capable of being fulfilled and freely made as an act of obedience (q.v.) to God by a Muslim of legal majority (Abū Fāris, *Aymān,* 138-40; the Ḥanbalī school, however, recognized as valid the vow of non-Muslims; see LAW AND THE QURʾĀN; RELIGIOUS PLURALISM AND THE QURʾĀN). The vow must stipulate the act to be performed, i.e. a supererogatory act with its origin in the ritual duties of Islam *(furūḍ al-islām).* It is thus permitted to vow to give alms, spend the night in prayer (q.v.; see also VIGIL), fast, go on (additional) pilgrimage (q.v.; both *ʿumra* and *ḥajj*), sacrifice (q.v.) an animal (see also CONSECRATION OF ANIMALS), but not to do something forbidden (q.v.; e.g. consume pork or alcohol; see INTOXICANTS; WINE) or even something permitted (see LAWFUL AND UNLAWFUL) that is not ritual in nature (e.g. divorce one's wife, eat food, sleep [q.v.] at night; Abū Fāris, op. cit., 140-5; however, a condition commonly used in vow-making has been the promise to divorce one's wife, see Pedersen, Nadhr; see also MARRIAGE AND DIVORCE).

A vow, then, was equated with obedience *(ṭāʿa)* to God in the sense of ritual acts *(ʿibādāt),* by which one might draw close to God (see RITUAL AND THE QURʾĀN). Any other element in the formulation of a vow was incidental. For example, a vow to walk to Iraq or Morocco has no meaning; in contrast, a vow to walk to Mecca (q.v.), with the goal being the performance of pilgrimage, is acceptable. The vow to walk, however, is itself incidental, while the performance of pilgrimage, an act of piety, is the element of the vow that renders it meaningful (see Calder, Ḥinth, 226-32). There is no set formula for a vow, although it must be uttered aloud. It need not be accompanied by a condition (e.g. if X happens, I will do Y) but can be simply a formal statement of ritual intention (e.g. I will fast tomorrow), and it is invalidated if accompanied by the phrase "if God wills" (*in shāʾa llāh,* Abū Fāris, *Aymān,* 145-7). A vow is also invalidated if it involves pledging goods belonging to someone else (on the basis of a ḥadīth in which a woman of the Anṣār, held captive by enemy tribes, wrongfully vowed to sacrifice the Prophet's camel upon the back of which she made her escape; Muslim, *Ṣaḥīḥ,* no. 4245; see PROPERTY) but it is recommended that one fulfill a vow made by a deceased relative (Bukhārī, *Ṣaḥīḥ,* nos. 6698-9; see DEATH AND THE DEAD; KINSHIP).

The prophetic tradition is careful to downplay any magical dimension of vows (i.e. the idea that a vow might cause the deity to carry out the condition of the vow; see MAGIC; POPULAR AND TALISMANIC USES OF THE QURʾĀN), essentially declaring vows to be useless since they cannot influence God (see POWER AND IMPOTENCE). Thus, excessive piety of the kind that hopes to influence the divine will was discouraged. The Prophet ordered a man who had vowed to go on foot to the Kaʿba (q.v.) to mount his riding animal, since God "has no need of this [man's] chastisement of himself" (*ghanī ʿan taʿdhīb hadhā nafsahu,* Muslim, *Ṣaḥīḥ,* no. 4247) and "has no need of you or your vow" (*ghanī ʿanka wa-ʿan nadhrika,* Muslim, op. cit., no. 4248). A vow is therefore incidental to God's foreordained decree *(qadar),* acting only as a pious supplement to it on the part of the votary — a means not to hasten or delay divine decree but to extract some good from the miserly (Bukhārī, *Ṣaḥīḥ,* nos. 6692-4; see GOOD AND EVIL; FREEDOM AND PREDESTINATION). A vow, then, is a spur to piety, the condition of which, if it is accomplished, merely coincides with the foreordained decree of God (Muslim, *Ṣaḥīḥ,* no. 4025). It is in this sense that a vow generally was understood in Islam, as a mechanism to encourage believers (see BELIEF AND UNBELIEF) to strive towards a life of piety and to help them to persevere in it.

Paul L. Heck

Bibliography

Primary: Bukhārī, *Ṣaḥīḥ*, Riyadh 1999; ed. Krehl, iv, 257-81 (bk. 83, *K. al-Aymān wa-l-nudhūr*); Ibn Ḥazm, *al-Muḥallā*, ed. A.M. Shākir, 11 vols., Cairo 1928; repr. Beirut n.d., viii, 30-64 *(K. al-Aymān)*, 65-76 *(K. Kafārāt)*; Muslim, *Ṣaḥīḥ*, Riyadh 1998; ed. ʿAbd al-Bāqī, iii, 1260-5 (bk. 26, *K. al-Nudhūr*); iii, 1266-90 (bk. 27, *K. al-Aymān*).
Secondary: M.ʿA. Abū Fāris, *Kitāb al-Aymān wa-l-nudhūr*, Amman 1988[3]; N. Calder, Ḥinth, birr, tabarrur, taḥannuth. An inquiry into the Arabic vocabulary of vows, in *BSOAS* 51 (1988), 214-39; J. Pedersen, Nadhr, in *EI*[2], vi, 846-7; ʿA. al-Ṭaḥṭāwī, *Bidaʿ al-nudhūr wa-l-dhabāʾiḥ wa-l-tasawwul wa-l-duʿāʾ wa-l-ḥilf bi-ghayr Allāh taʿālā*, Beirut 2000; M.S. ʿUbaydāt, *Fiqh al-aymān wa-l-nudhūr wa-ḥukm al-islām fī l-dhabāʾiḥ*, Amman 1992.

Voyage

see TRIPS AND VOYAGES; JOURNEY

W

Wadd see IDOLS AND IMAGES

Wage see REWARD AND PUNISHMENT

Wahhabism and the Qurʾān

The eighteenth century revival and reform movement founded by the scholar and jurist Muḥammad b. ʿAbd al-Wahhāb (d. 1206/1792), in the Arabian peninsula. Based on the central qurʾānic concept of *tawḥīd* (absolute monotheism), Wahhabism called for a direct return to the Qurʾān and ḥadīth for study and interpretation (see SUNNA; ḤADĪTH AND THE QURʾĀN; TOOLS FOR THE STUDY OF THE QURʾĀN).

Ibn ʿAbd al-Wahhāb considered the Qurʾān and ḥadīth to be the only infallible (see IMPECCABILITY) and authoritative sources of scripture with the Qurʾān, as the revealed word of God (q.v.), holding absolute authority (q.v.) in cases of conflicting views (see ABROGATION; INIMITABILITY). Other source materials, including legal opinions (see LAW AND THE QURʾĀN) and qurʾānic commentary (*tafsīr;* see EXEGESIS OF THE QURʾĀN: CLASSICAL AND MEDIEVAL), could be consulted, but could not contradict the Qurʾān or ḥadīth. Ibn ʿAbd al-Wahhāb's Qurʾān interpretation was based on historical contextualization of the revelation and on consideration of the use of both terms and concepts within the broader context of the entire Qurʾān in order to know which prescriptions were universal as opposed to those that were limited to specific historical conditions (see OCCASIONS OF REVELATION). This methodology was then combined with legal concepts like *maṣlaḥa* (consideration of public welfare) to interpret Islamic law. For example, although the Qurʾān requires payment of *zakāt* (almsgiving [q.v.]), Ibn ʿAbd al-Wahhāb used *maṣlaḥa* to allow delay of payment during times of public hardship, such as the aftermath of a natural disaster.

Ibn ʿAbd al-Wahhāb also sought to determine broad qurʾānic values, such as the obligation to preserve human life (q.v.; see also MURDER; BLOODSHED) as a higher priority than obedience (q.v.) to Islamic law or ritual (see RITUAL AND THE QURʾĀN), for application in both private and public life. Examples of the application of this value include the limitation of violence (q.v.) and killing during jihād (q.v.; see also FIGHTING; PATH OR WAY; EXPEDITIONS AND BATTLES; WAR) and the command that women (see WOMEN AND THE QURʾĀN) should seek medical care when ill or injured, even when this means sacrificing modesty (q.v.).

Ibn ʿAbd al-Wahhāb believed that the Qurʾān assigned equal responsibilities to men and women with respect to God, accompanied by a balance of rights in their human relations. He held both genders responsible for carrying out the five pillars of Islam and for studying and interpreting the Qurʾān (see TRADITIONAL DISCIPLINES OF QURʾĀNIC STUDY; EXEGESIS OF THE QURʾĀN: EARLY MODERN AND CONTEMPORARY). He declared a balance of rights in matters of marriage and divorce (q.v.), guaranteeing the woman the right to divorce by *khulʿ* through repayment of the dower (*mahr;* see BRIDEWEALTH) to the husband upon her recognition that she could no longer fulfill the requirements of marriage. This interpretation assured the woman the practical right to assert *khulʿ* unfettered by the husband in the same way that the husband has the right to divorce by *ṭalāq* unfettered by the woman. He balanced the husband's rights in marriage by granting the woman the right to stipulate conditions favorable to her in the marriage contract relating both to the contracting and the continuation of the marriage (see CONTRACTS AND ALLIANCES; BREAKING TRUSTS AND CONTRACTS).

By the twentieth century, Wahhabism had become synonymous with literal interpretations of the Qurʾān and ḥadīth that did not appear to take context into consideration (see SĪRA AND THE QURʾĀN). The result was a more legalistic interpretation of Islam. At the turn of the twenty-first century, however, as interest in Ibn ʿAbd al-Wahhāb's methodology was renewed, Wahhābī legal scholars in Saudi Arabia re-initiated a more context-sensitive interpretation of the Qurʾān, combined with greater attention to legal tools like *maṣlaḥa* and recognition of the Qurʾān's gender balance of rights and responsibilities.

Natana J. DeLong-Bas

Bibliography
Primary: Muḥammad Ibn ʿAbd al-Wahhāb, *Muʾallafāt al-Shaykh al-Imām Muḥammad Ibn ʿAbd al-Wahhāb,* 5 vols., Riyadh 1983; id., *Muʿāmalāt al-Shaykh al-Imām Muḥammad Ibn ʿAbd al-Wahhāb. Mulḥaq al-muṣannafāt,* Riyadh 1983; id., *Muʿāmalāt al-Shaykh al-Imām Muḥammad Ibn ʿAbd al-Wahhāb. Qism al-ḥadīth,* 4 vols., Riyadh 1983.
Secondary: *Buḥūth Usbū al-Shaykh Muḥammad b. ʿAbd al-Wahhāb: Raḥimahu llāh,* 2 vols., Riyadh 1980; N.J. DeLong-Bas, *Wahhabi Islam. From revival and reform to global jihad,* New York 2004; R. Firestone, *Jihad. The origin of holy war in Islam,* New York 1999; H. Laoust, *Essai sur les doctrines socials et politiques de Taḳī-d-dīn Aḥmad b. Taimīya canoniste ḥanbalite,* Cairo 1939, 506-40; E. Peskes and W. Ende, Wahhābiyya, in *EI²,* xi, 39-47; ʿA.Ṣ al-ʿUthaymin, *al-Shaykh Muḥammad Ibn ʿAbd al-Wahhāb. Ḥayātuhu wa-fikruhu,* Riyadh 1992.

Waiting Period

The period that must be observed by a married couple after separation. Waiting periods are known in many cultures. Within the Qurʾān this concept is expressed by two Arabic words: *tarabbaṣa* or *tarabbuṣ,* literally "waiting," and by *ʿidda,* literally "number." The first word appears in Q 2:226, 228, 234 and seems to be the earlier expression because the verses in which the term *ʿidda* is used (Q 33:49; 65:1, 4) answer questions that must have been raised from rules stipulated in Q 2 (see LAW AND THE QURʾĀN). The clear relation between the two groups of verses shows that the word *ʿidda* in this context has to be interpreted as *ʿiddat al-tarabbuṣ,* i.e. "waiting period."

There are three different causes of separation that necessitate a waiting period: (i) death of the husband (Q 2:234), (ii) divorce (Q 2:228; 65:1) — except in the case in which the marriage has not been consummated (Q 33:49; see MARRIAGE AND DIVORCE) — and (iii) the oath of the husband to stop intercourse with his wife (Q 2:226; see OATHS; SEX AND SEXUALITY). The length of the waiting period differs accordingly. It is (i) four (lunar) months (q.v.) and ten days in the case of death of the husband (Q 2:234); (ii) three menstrual periods *(qurūʾ)* for menstruating women or three months for non-menstruating women after divorce has been pronounced provided that the marriage had been consummated (Q 2:228; 65:4; see MENSTRUATION), or until the birth of the child in the case of a divorced pregnant woman whose divorce has become definite (Q 65:4; see BIRTH); and (iii) four months after the oath of continence (Q 2:226; see ABSTINENCE).

The waiting period has different functions. First, in the case of a revocable divorce and that of an oath of continence, it gives time to the man to think over his decision that could have serious personal and financial consequences for himself, his wife and their children (q.v.; see also FAMILY; WOMEN AND THE QURʾĀN). He can return to his wife during the waiting period. Second, the waiting period after divorce has been pronounced and after the death of the husband serves as a means to establish whether the wife is pregnant. A prerequisite is, on the one hand, that no sexual intercourse with the husband (or anyone else) take place during the waiting period after the divorce has been pronounced — a condition implied but not expressly stipulated in the qurʾānic rules, and, on the other hand, that the wife does not conceal a pregnancy that becomes apparent during this period (Q 2:228). This is important for two reasons: pregnancy and thus the prospect of offspring may influence the husband's decision to separate from his wife; the ruling prevents the wife from remarrying and then giving birth to a child whose father's identity is doubtful (see PATRIARCHY; PARENTS). Consequently, there is no need for a waiting period in the case of divorce before consummation (Q 33:49). Third, the waiting period after the husband's death has, in addition, the function of a period of mourning that should be respected by men wishing to marry the widow (q.v.; see also DEATH AND THE DEAD; BURIAL). Hence, it is strictly forbidden to propose a marriage to a widow or to arrange for it during the waiting period (Q 2:235). The Qurʾān is silent on the question of whether a husband whose wife has died must observe a mourning period of similar length.

Several responsibilities are combined with the waiting period. First, the responsibility for its correct observance. The responsibility is given partly to the wife (Q 2:228, 231, 234), partly to the husband (Q 2:226; 33:49; 65:1, 4). In the case of divorce, the end *(ajal)* of the waiting period must be established in the presence of two witnesses (Q 65:2; see WITNESSING AND TESTIFYING). Second, the husband is obliged to provide maintenance *(matāʿ, nafaqa, rizq,* Q 2:241; 65:1, 6, 7) for his wife during the waiting period and to let her remain in her house (Q 65:1) without doing any harm to her (Q 65:6; see MAINTENANCE AND UPKEEP). The widow has the right to maintenance and housing at her former husband's expense even for a whole year (Q 2:240). The woman is obliged to live chastely (see CHASTITY) during the waiting period; otherwise she forfeits her rights (Q 65:1).

It seems that the qurʾānic rules concerning the waiting period changed the existing customs of pre-Islamic Mecca (q.v.) and Medina (q.v.). According to Muslim traditions the mourning period of a widow in pre-Islamic times was a year (Muslim, *Ṣaḥīḥ,* 18:146; Bukhārī, *Ṣaḥīḥ,* 68:46; see ḤADĪTH AND THE QURʾĀN; PRE-ISLAMIC ARABIA AND THE QURʾĀN). Whether there had been a custom of a waiting period for divorced women at all is doubtful. Yet the new rules of the Qurʾān provided only a basic framework and gave rise to many questions concerning details. The answers are found in ḥadīth compilations as well as in exegetical and legal literature (see EXEGESIS OF THE QURʾĀN: CLASSICAL AND MEDIEVAL).

Harald Motzki

Bibliography
Primary: ʿAbd al-Razzāq, *Muṣannaf,* vii; Bukhārī, *Ṣaḥīḥ; Jalālayn;* Mālik, *Muwaṭṭaʾ;* Muslim, *Ṣaḥīḥ;* Ṭabarī, *Tafsīr,* ed. Shākir.
Secondary: Y. Linant de Bellefonds, ʿIdda, in *EI*², iii, 1010-13; H. Motzki, *The origins of Islamic jurisprudence,* Leiden 2002 (index); J. Wellhausen, Die Ehe bei den Arabern, in *Nachrichten von der Königlichen Gesellschaft der Wissenschaften und der Georg-Augusts-Universität zu Göttingen* 11 (1893), 431-81, esp. 453-5.

Wall (between Heaven and Hell) see BARZAKH; PEOPLE OF THE HEIGHTS

Wander see JOURNEY; ASTRAY

War

A state of open, armed and often prolonged conflict between states, tribes or parties, frequently mentioned in the Qurʾān. It is usually referred to by derivatives of the third form of *q-t-l,* "fighting" (q.v.), sometimes with the qualification *fī sabīl Allāh,* "in the path of God" (see PATH OR WAY); but we also hear of *ḥarb,* "war," both against God and the messenger (q.v.; e.g. Q 5:33; 9:107; cf. 5:64) and by or for them (Q 2:279; 8:57; cf. 47:4). Derivatives of *j-h-d* are used for efforts which include fighting without being reducible to it (see JIHĀD).

Wars mentioned

Past wars are rarely mentioned (see HISTORY AND THE QURʾĀN). The vanished nations are destroyed by brimstone, fire and other natural disasters (see PUNISHMENT STORIES), not by conquest (q.v.), though the messenger expects to punish his own opponents by military means (Q 9:14, 52). Of the Israelite conquest of the holy land we are only told that when Moses (q.v.) ordered the Israelites (see CHILDREN OF ISRAEL) to enter this land, all except two refused on the grounds that it was inhabited by mighty men *(jabbārīn);* the Israelites thus had to wander in the desert for another forty years (Q 5:21-6; cf. *Num* 13:31-14:34). But elsewhere we learn that many prophets were accompanied in battle by large numbers, who never lost heart when they met disasters (Q 3:146). There is also an obscure reference to thousands who went out from their homes: God told them to die (so they did), whereupon he revived them. This is told in encouragement of fighting in God's path (Q 2:243f.), followed by an account of the Israelite demand for a king (Q 2:246-51; see KINGS AND RULERS): they wanted a king so that they could fight in the path of God (cf. *1 Sam* 8:5, 19; *Judg* 8:22), having been expelled from their homes and their families; but when fighting was prescribed for them, they turned back, except for a small band. Worse still, when their prophet announced that God had appointed Ṭālūt, i.e. Saul (q.v.), as their king, they disputed his authority (q.v.); and when Saul set out to fight Goliath (q.v.), most of them failed the test he set for them (cf. *Judg* 7:4-7; see TRIAL; TRUST AND PATIENCE); but the steadfast uttered the famous words, "How many a small band has vanquished a mighty army by leave of God," and David (q.v.) slew Goliath. No further Israelite wars are mentioned down to Nebuchadnezzar, whose destruction of Jerusalem (q.v.) is briefly alluded to, as is the Roman destruction of the Temple, in both cases without any names being named; the two disasters are presented as punishment for Israelite sins (see JEWS AND

JUDAISM), with a period of wealth and power in between and a possibility of better times ahead (Q 17:4-8). Another sūra (Q 30:2-4) notes that the Byzantines (q.v.) have been defeated, predicting that they will soon win (over the Persians) or, alternatively, that the Byzantines have been victorious, predicting that they will soon be defeated (by the believers).

Most warfare in the Qurʾān is conducted by the believers in the present. One verse regulates fighting among the believers themselves: one should make peace (q.v.) between the two parties or fight the wrongdoers (Q 49:9; see ARBITRATION). Another threatens war against the believers when they take usury (q.v.; Q 2:278f.). But most encourage the believers to fight others, variously identified as "those who fight you" (Q 2:190), unbelievers (e.g. Q 4:84; 9:123; 47:4), the polytheists altogether (Q 9:36), People of the Book (q.v.) who do not believe in God and the last day (Q 9:29; see LAST JUDGMENT), hypocrites (Q 9:73), friends of Satan (Q 4:76), and imāms of unbelief (Q 9:12), without it being clear how far these groups are identical or distinct. The hypocrites side with the believers when the latter win but not when they lose (Q 4:141) and once appear in alliance with unbelieving People of the Book (Q 59:11). All war is assumed to involve religious issues.

The moral status of war

Fighting is declared legitimate in self-defense, by way of preemption (Q 9:8; cf. 60:2), for the rescue of fellow believers (Q 4:75) and for the righting of wrongs, including the punishment of the wrongdoers (Q 9:13-14). The basic principle is that one should treat other communities as they treat one's own (see ETHICS AND THE QURʾĀN). "As for the person who defends himself after having been wronged, there is no way of blaming them" (Q 42:41); God would help those who had always met like with like, only to be wronged (Q 22:60), for a bad deed called for another like it (Q 42:39-42; see GOOD DEEDS; EVIL DEEDS). "Fight in the path of God those who fight against you, but do not transgress" (Q 2:190); "a sacred month for a sacred month… whoever aggresses against you, aggress against him in a like manner" (Q 2:194; see MONTHS); "fight the polytheists all together as they fight you altogether" (Q 9:36). Where the principle of like for like is abandoned (see RETALIATION), the claim is that bloodshed (q.v.) is the lesser evil ("kill them wherever you come upon them, expel them from where they expelled you, for *fitna* is worse than killing," Q 2:191; cf. 2:217; see GOOD AND EVIL). The famous "sword verse" ("kill the polytheists wherever you find them, take them, seize them, besiege them, and lie in wait for them," Q 9:5), seems to be based on the same rules, given that it is directed against a particular group accused of oath-breaking and aggression (Q 9:1-23; cf. 8:56-60; see BREAKING TRUSTS AND CONTRACTS; OATHS) and that polytheists who remain faithful to their treatises are explicitly excepted (Q 9:4). Here as elsewhere, it is stressed that one must stop when they do (Q 2:193; 4:90; 8:39f., 61; 9:3, 5, 11) and, though the language is often extremely militant, the principle of forgiveness (q.v.) is reiterated in between the assertions of the right to defend oneself (Q 42:37-43).

Justifying war appears to have been hard work. The exhortations (q.v.) are addressed to a people who were not warlike ("prescribed for you is fighting, though you dislike it," Q 2:216), who assumed warfare to be forbidden (q.v.; "permission has been granted to those who fight/are fought, because they have been wronged," Q 22:39), and who had to be persuaded that it could be morally right ("if God did not drive back some people by means of others, cloisters, churches/synagogues *[biyaʿ]*, oratories *[ṣalawāt]*, and mosques in which God's name is much mentioned would be destroyed," Q 22:40; "the earth would be ruined," Q 2:251). Only the *jizya* verse (Q 9:29; see POLL TAX) seems to endorse war of aggression. If read as a continuation of Q 9:1-23, however, it would be concerned with the same oath-breaking "polytheists" (cf. Q 9:30f.) as the sword verse.

Mobilization

Orders to fight came down in "sūras" (q.v.), apparently on an ad hoc basis (Q 9:86; 47:20) and always in what appears to be a mobilizing rather than a legislative vein (for Q 2:216, an apparent exception, compare Q 2:246; 4:77). Exhortations to fight abound (Q 2:244; 4:71, 84; 8:65; 9:36, 41, 123; 61:4, etc). Those who emigrate (see EMIGRATION; EMIGRANTS AND HELPERS) and strive for the cause with their wealth (q.v.) and their lives are promised rich rewards, not least when they fall in God's path (e.g. Q 2:154; 9:20; 22:58f., see MARTYRS; REWARD AND PUNISHMENT). They rank higher than those who sit at home (Q 4:95), just as those who joined the fighting before the victory rank higher than those who joined after it (Q 57:10; cf. 9:20; see RANKS AND ORDERS). Fighting and/or striving in God's path is described as selling the present life to God for the hereafter (Q 4:74; 9:111), a loan that will be repaid many times over (Q 2:245; 57:11; cf. 57:18; 73:20) and a commerce that will deliver from painful chastisement (Q 61:10f.; see TRADE AND COMMERCE; ESCHATOLOGY). Whatever one spends, God will repay in full (Q 8:60).

The response to these appeals is frequently deemed inadequate. "How is it with you that you do not fight in God's path?" (Q 4:75; cf. 4:72); "What is the matter with you, that when you are told to go forth in the path of God you sink heavily into the ground?" (Q 9:38). Some people are apparently happy to pray and pay alms but protest when fighting is prescribed for them, asking for postponement (Q 4:77). Some hope for a sūra but would look faint if one were to come down mentioning fighting (Q 47:20; cf. 9:86). Some plead ignorance of fighting or turn back, wishing that their brethren who have fallen in battle had done the same (Q 3:155f., 167f.). Others ask for permission to leave before a battle, pleading that their own homes are exposed (Q 33:13) or ask not to be put in temptation (by being asked to fight against kinsmen?; Q 9:49; cf. Q 60; see KINSHIP). Bedouin (q.v.) shirkers plead preoccupation with their flocks *(amwāl)* and families (Q 48:11; see FAMILY). Some turn their backs in actual battle (Q 3:155; 8:15f.; 33:15f.).

All lack of martial zeal is debited to base motives. The blind, sick, weak and destitute are of course exempted (Q 9:91; 48:17; see POVERTY AND THE POOR; ILLNESS AND HEALTH) but shirkers are sick of heart (q.v.; Q 47:20), unwilling to be inconvenienced by long journeys (Q 9:42) or heat (Q 9:81), keen to stay at home with their women (Q 9:87, 93), reluctant to contribute even though they are rich (Q 9:81, 86, 93), cowards who anticipate defeat (Q 48:12; see COURAGE; FEAR), who are scared of death (cf. Q 33:18f.; 47:20) and who would boast (q.v.) of their luck if the expedition were hit by disaster but wish that they had been present when things went well (Q 4:72f.); if they were Bedouin (q.v.), they are only interested in booty (q.v.; Q 48:15). Such people are liars (Q 9:42; cf. 48:11), hypocrites (Q 3:167), cursed by God for only obeying part of what he sent down (Q 47:26), closer to unbelief than to faith (Q 3:167), indeed outright unbelievers (Q 3:156; 33:19; cf. 9:44f.), who are really fighting for *ṭāghūt* (Q 4:76, cf. 4:72; see IDOLS AND IMAGES; JIBT); they will be cast into a blazing fire (q.v.; Q 48:13) and hell is to be their abode (Q 9:95; see HELL AND HELLFIRE). Some people who have been granted permission to stay behind, a decision now regretted, are singled out for particular attention in increasingly sharp terms (Q 9:43-88). But the Bedouin who stayed behind are promised a second chance: they will be called against a mighty people and rewarded if they obeyed (Q 48:16). The believers in general are told that if they would not go forth, God will punish them and choose another people (Q 9:39). If they think their fathers, sons, brothers, wives, kinsmen, trade and houses are more important than God, his messenger, and *jihād fī sabīl Allāh,* then they will eventually learn otherwise (Q 9:24). There is no need to be afraid. Death will come at its appointed time, wherever one may be (Q 4:78), and God might restrain the power of the unbelievers (Q 4:84); in any case, unbelievers, hypocrites and People of the Book are all cowards who will turn their backs (cf. Q 3:110f.; 48:22; 59:11f.).

Attempts are also made to shame the believers into fighting by construing war as a test: God could have avenged himself on his opponents but he wants the believers to do it so that he and they can see their true worth (Q 47:4, 31). Most people have failed the test, as they had done back in the time of Moses and Saul and David (q.v.; above), whose experiences clearly reflect the messenger's own (see NARRATIVES). Misfortunes in battles are likewise cast as tests (Q 3:166f.; 33:10f.). God alternates good and bad days to purify the believers and to destroy the unbelievers, i.e. to weed out those of little faith (Q 3:140f.). Here as so often, the unbelievers seem to be members of the party deemed lacking in commitment to the cause.

The objectives of war

Opponents have wronged the believers by breaking their oaths and plotting to expel or kill the messenger (Q 8:30; 9:13; 17:76) and by actually expelling both him (Q 60:1; 9:40) and the believers without right, just for saying "God is our lord" (q.v.; e.g. Q 22:40; cf. 60:1, 8f.); they have also blocked access to the sanctuary (Q 2:217; 48:25; see SACRED PRECINCTS). The objective of war is to avenge these wrongs, to help the weak men, women and children left behind (Q 4:75; see OPPRESSED ON EARTH, THE), to expel the people in control of the sanctuary as they expelled the believers (Q 2:191), to put an end to *fitna* (trial or test, traditionally understood as persecution, more probably communal division), to make the religion entirely God's (Q 2:193; 8:39), to make his religion prevail even if the polytheists dislike it (Q 9:33; 61:9; cf. 48:2) and to punish the opponents: one should fight them so that God might chastise them "at your hands" (Q 9:14); God will chastise them either on his own (*min ʿindihi,* presumably meaning by natural disasters; see WEATHER; COSMOLOGY) or "at our hands" (Q 9:52); he would have exacted retribution himself (see VENGEANCE) if he had not decided to do it through the believers to let them test one another (Q 47:4). The *jizya* verse stands out by enjoining fighting until unbelieving People of the Book are reduced to tributary status (Q 9:29). That the opponents will be destroyed is treated as certain: "How many a city (q.v.) stronger than the one that expelled you have we destroyed," God says (Q 47:13); "are your unbelievers better than they?" (Q 54:43). And the objectives are in fact achieved: God has expelled the unbelieving People of the Book from their homes and their fortresses, banishing them (Q 59:2f.); and he has fulfilled the vision he had granted the messenger by allowing the believers to enter the sanctuary (Q 48:27), though the presence of believing men and women there has caused him to withhold his punishment (Q 48:25).

Exegesis

The exegetes understood the qur'ānic verses on war as legislation regarding the Islamic duty of jihād and typically treated each verse as an independent unit for which the context was to be found in the tradition rather than the Qur'ān itself. For the result, see CONQUEST, JIHĀD, JEWS AND JUDAISM, and the further cross-references given there.

Patricia Crone

Bibliography
(in addition to the classical commentaries on the verses cited above): H. Busse, The Arab conquest in revelation and politics, in *IOS* 10 (1980), 14-20; R. Firestone, *Jihād. The origin of holy war in Islam,* New York 1999; M.K. Haykal, *al-Jihād wa-l-qitāl fī l-siyāsati l-sharʿiyya,* Beirut 1996; A.A. Jannatī, Defense and jihad in the Qur'an, in *al-Tawḥīd* 1 (1984), 39-54; M.J. Kister, *ʿAn yadin* (Qur'ān IX/29). An attempt at interpretation, in *Arabica* 11 (1964), 272-8; A. Morabia, *Le Ǧihād dans l'Islam médiéval. Le "combat sacré" des origines au XIIe siècle,* Paris 1986; M. Muṭahhari, Jihad in the Qur'ān, in M. Abedi and G. Legenhausen (eds.), *Jihād and shahādat. Struggle and martyrdom in Islam,* Houston 1986, 81-124; A. Noth, *Heiliger Krieg und heiliger Kampf in Islam und Christentum,* Bonn 1966; H.T. Obbink, *De heilige oorlog volgens den Koran,* Leiden 1901; ʿAbdallāh b. Aḥmad al-Qādirī, *al-Jihād fī sabīli llāh. Ḥaqīqatuhu wa-ghāyatuhu,* Jeddah 1992; U. Rubin, *Barā'a.* A study of some quranic passages, in *JSAI* 5 (1984), 13-32; A. Sachedina, The development of jihād in Islamic revelation and history, in J.T. Johnson and J. Kelsay (eds.), *Cross, crescent and sword,* New York 1990, 35-50; A. Schleifer, Jihād and traditional Islamic consciousness, in *IQ* 27 (1983), 173-203; F. Schwally, Der heilige Krieg des Islam in religionsgeschichtlicher und staatsrechtlicher Beleuchtung, in *Internationale Monatsschrift für Wissenschaft, Kunst und Technik* 6 (1916), 689-714; W.M. Watt, Islamic conceptions of the holy war, in T.P. Murphy (ed.), *The holy war,* Columbus, OH 1976, 141-56.

Warmth see HOT AND COLD

Warner

One who foretells the (negative) consequences of actions. The Arabic word *nadhīr* (pl. *nudhur*) appears no fewer than fifty-eight times in the Qur'ān, scarcely less frequently than the verb *andhara* (including nominal and adjectival forms, particularly *mundhir*) from which it derives, and nearly always in the sense of "warner" (cf. *Lisān al-ʿArab,* xiv, 100). As Watt puts it (*Muhammad at Mecca,* 71), the verb "describes the action of informing a person of something of a dangerous, harmful, or fearful nature, so as to put him on his guard against it or put him in fear (q.v.) of it" (see also CHASTISEMENT AND PUNISHMENT; REWARD AND PUNISHMENT). Particularly in the language of the *sīra* (see SĪRA AND THE QUR'ĀN), *andhara* is also used to describe the Prophet's foreknowledge — his "giving notice" — of future events (see FORETELLING; MIRACLES; MARVELS) and as such can be counted as one of the signs (q.v.; see also PROOF) of his prophethood (Ibn Isḥāq, *Sīra,* i, 134; Ibn Ḥazm, *Jawāmiʿ al-sīra,* 10f.; see PROPHETS AND PROPHETHOOD).

The primary sense of *nadhīr* in pre-qur'ānic Arabic seems to have been connected to warfare: the *nadhīr al-jaysh/al-qawm* is usually described as the scout who warned the main force of the enemy's presence (see WAR; ENEMIES), a usage that continues in the Islamic period (see Bevan, *Naḳā'iḍ,* 12, "one who gives the alarm," and 517, "a warner"; Ibn Qutayba, *ʿUyūn,* i, 109; Wensinck, *Concordance,* s.v. *andhara*). It is apparently this sense that lies behind the prophetic ḥadīth in which Muḥammad identifies himself as the "naked warner" (*al-nadhīr al-ʿuryān;* cf. Wensinck, *Concordance,* iv, 203), who waves his shed garments in order to raise the alarm (see ḤADĪTH AND THE QURʾĀN). Unlike *bashīr* (and its cognate, *mubashshir,* "the bearer of good news"; see NEWS; GOOD NEWS) or, for that matter, *nadhr* ("vow"), which have parallels in pre-Islamic Semitic languages (see Jeffery, *For. vocab.,* 79f. and 278; Widengren, *Muḥammad,* 13f.), usage of the term *nadhīr* apparently becomes monotheistic only in the Qurʾān itself (see FOREIGN VOCABULARY; GRAMMAR AND THE QURʾĀN). Although the jinn (q.v.) can occasionally warn people (see Q 46:29 and Ibn Isḥāq, *Sīra,* i, 130), here as elsewhere God, acting out of his mercy (q.v.), usually sends men. The *bashīr,* with which *nadhīr* is frequently paired (at least in part for reasons of rhyme; see RHYMED PROSE; PAIRS AND PAIRING; RHETORIC AND THE QURʾĀN), promises good news for those who believe (see BELIEF AND UNBELIEF), but God's warners invariably promise bad news for those who do not (see, for the two antonyms, al-Rāghib al-Iṣfahānī, *Mufradāt,* s.v. *n-dh-r;* and on Q 34:28, Muqātil b. Sulaymān, *Tafsīr,* iii, 533). In this respect, *andhara* and *nadhīr* lie close to the qurʾānic *dhakkara* "to remind, admonish" (on which see Bravmann, *Spiritual background,* 87 n. 1; see REMEMBRANCE; MEMORY; REFLECTION AND DELIBERATION). As the last of the prophets, Muḥammad seems to have been construed as the last of the *nadhīr*s, and exhorting the faithful to fear would later fall to preachers of varying status, some of whom took their name from the far less common qurʾānic term *mudhakkir* (for examples, see Ibn al-Jawzī, *Quṣṣāṣ,* 42f.; see TEACHING AND PREACHING THE QURʾĀN).

Attempts to assign fairly precise dating to the "warner" passages (thus Horovitz, *KU,* 47; Speyer, *Erzählungen,* 34f.; Andrae, *Mohammed,* 43f.; see CHRONOLOGY AND THE QURʾĀN) are only as persuasive as the schemes upon which they otherwise rely. But if one holds to the traditional and modern consensus that Q 74:2 ("Rise and warn!") is among the earliest lines — indeed, perhaps the earliest — revealed to Muḥammad, then his role as God's warner is at least as old as that (thus Ṭabarī, *Tafsīr,* xxix, 143f.; id., *Taʾrīkh,* i, 1153f.; Rubin, Shrouded messenger; see OCCASIONS OF REVELATION). Even if one does not, Muḥammad's role as warner is still attested in Q 26:214 ("And warn your nearest relatives..."; see KINSHIP), which is held to signal the beginning of his public preaching, an event conventionally dated three years after his first revelation (thus Ibn Isḥāq, *Sīra,* i, 166; Ṭabarī, *Taʾrīkh,* i, 1169; Nöldeke, *GQ,* i, 129). In the traditional literature, the imagery is one of the battlefield (see Rubin, *Eye,* 130f.), which may suggest a relatively early date (see EXPEDITIONS AND BATTLES). That this verse marks the concept's point of entry into the Qurʾān is also suggested by echoes of the parochialism (cf. also Q 42:7) that characterizes earlier warners, who had warned their communities of their own particular fates: the thunderbolt that fell upon ʿĀd (q.v.) and Thamūd (q.v.) in Q 41:13, the blow delivered to the people of Lot (q.v.) in Q 54:36 and the "painful chastisement" promised by Noah (q.v.; Q 71:1), which is glossed in tradition as the flood (thus Ṭabarī, *Tafsīr,* xxix, 91; see PUNISHMENT STORIES).

Muḥammad is certainly portrayed as one of a line of monotheistic warners (thus Q 28:46; 32:3), "there is not a community but that it has had a warner" (Q 35:24), and warning sometimes appears to have been intrinsic to prophecy itself (see especially Q 6:48 and Q 18:56: "We have not sent messengers save as bearers of good news and warners"; see MESSENGER). Unlike his predecessors, however, Muḥammad is frequently given to warn through a scripture that was revealed to him (e.g. Q 6:19; 7:2; 42:7; 46:12; see BOOK; REVELATION AND INSPIRATION); he is also given to warn "all humankind" (Q 34:28), and whereas Noah's "painful chastisement" (*ʿadhāb ʿalīm,* Q 71:1) was the flood, Muḥammad warns of nothing less than the eschaton itself: "the day of meeting" (Q 40:15; cf. 40:18; see ESCHATOLOGY) and "the flaming fire"(q.v.; Q 92:14; see also HELL AND HELLFIRE). At least once (Q 78:40), this day of chastisement is said to be near to hand, but the precise timing of the end probably held more interest for later Muslims than it did for Muḥammad himself (see Bashear, Muslim apocalypses; see APOCALYPSE). In sum, "this is a warner of the warners of old" (Q 53:56), but the Prophet brings together an altogether unprecedented combination of vision, scripture and political action (cf. Cook, *Muhammad,* 35f.; Cook and Crone, *Hagarism,* 16f.; see SCRIPTURE AND THE QURʾĀN; POLITICS AND THE QURʾĀN).

Chase F. Robinson

Bibliography
Primary: A. Bevan (ed.), *The Nakāʾid of Jarīr and al-Farazdak,* Leiden 1905; Ibn Ḥazm, ʿAlī b. Aḥmad b. Saʿīd, *Jawāmiʿ al-sīra,* Cairo 1956; Ibn Isḥāq, *Sīra,* ed. Wüstenfeld; Ibn al-Jawzī, Abū l-Faraj ʿAbd al-Raḥmān b. ʿAlī, *Kitāb al-Quṣṣāṣ wa-l-mudhakkirīn,* ed. M. Swartz, Beirut 1971; Ibn Qutayba, *ʿUyūn al-akhbār,* Cairo 1925; *Lisān al-ʿArab,* Beirut 1988; Muqātil, *Tafsīr;* al-Rāghib al-Iṣfahānī, *Mufradāt;* Ṭabarī, *Tafsīr,* Cairo 1954-7; id., *Taʾrīkh,* Leiden 1879-1901.
Secondary: T. Andrae, *Mohammed. Sein Leben und sein Glaube,* Göttingen 1932; S. Bashear, Muslim apocalypses and the hour. A case study in traditional interpretation, in *IOS* 13 (1993), 75-99; M.M. Bravmann, *The spiritual background of early Islam. Studies in ancient Arab concepts,* Leiden 1972; M. Cook, *Muhammad,* Oxford 1983; id. and P. Crone, *Hagarism. The making of the Islamic world,* Cambridge 1977; Horovitz, *KU;* Jeffery, *For. vocab.;* Nöldeke, *GQ;* U. Rubin, *The eye of the beholder. The life of Muḥammad as viewed by the early Muslims,* Princeton 1995; id., The shrouded messenger. On the interpretation of *al-muzzammil* and *al-muddaththir,* in *JSAI* 16 (1993), 96-107; Speyer, *Erzählungen;* W.M. Watt, *Muhammad at Mecca,* Oxford 1953; Wensinck, *Concordance;* G. Widengren, *Muḥammad, the apostle of God and his ascension,* Uppsala and Wiesbaden 1955.

Warning

see WARNER

Wars of Apostasy

see APOSTASY

Washing

see CLEANLINESS AND ABLUTION; RITUAL PURITY

Waṣīla

see CONSECRATION OF ANIMALS; CAMEL; IDOLS AND IMAGES

Waswās

see DEVIL

Watcher

see GOD AND HIS ATTRIBUTES; SEEING AND HEARING

Water

The compound of oxygen and hydrogen on which every form of life depends. Of the four Heraclean elements, water has the highest number of attestations in the Qurʾān and appears in the greatest variety of forms. In its general sense, it is designated by the Arabic word *māʾ*. It subsists in the sky as clouds *(saḥāb, muzn, muʿṣirāt, ghamāma, ʿarḍ),* falls to the earth as rain *(māʾ min al-samāʾ, wadq, maṭar),* or hail (*barad;* see WEATHER) or is condensed from the atmosphere as dew *(ṭall).* It rises from within the earth as springs *(ʿayn, yanbūʿ)* and is also accessible as wells (*biʾr, jubb;* see SPRINGS AND FOUNTAINS). It flows across the land as rivers (*nahr,* pl. *anhār*) and foaming torrents *(sayl)*. It comprises the great aqueous mass of the sea (*yam, baḥr,* pl. *biḥār*), and its surges are waves *(mawj)*. Often explicit mention of it is elided *(maḥdhūf)* and its presence indicated by context, through such verbs as *ghasila,* "to wash," or *saqā,* "give to drink" (see FOOD AND DRINK). There is the water of bodily fluids, such as semen (*nuṭfa, māʾ mahīn, māʾ dāfiq;* see BIOLOGY AS THE CREATION AND STAGES OF LIFE) and tears (*damʿ;* see WEEPING). Finally, there is in hell scalding water *(ḥamīm)* and putrid liquid *(ṣadīd)* among the torments of the damned (see REWARD AND PUNISHMENT; HELL AND HELLFIRE).

Water in all these forms has a part in the divine economy of creation (q.v.). The words that designate it interact with each others' meanings, creating what Frithjof Schuon calls a spiritual geometry that yields structures of religious meaning characteristic of qurʾānic rhetoric (see RHETORIC AND THE QURʾĀN). They occur individually but are also combined to form images of power and beauty (q.v.). Water is a sign of God's power (see NATURE AS SIGNS; POWER AND IMPOTENCE). It reveals aspects of the dependence of creation on him, his dealings with it, and its duty to serve him.

God created water before the heavens (see HEAVEN AND SKY) and the earth (q.v.) — this is how the commentators (al-Ṭabarī, al-Rāzī, al-Nasafī), understand the verse "[God] created the heavens and the earth in six days, when his throne was above the water *(māʾ)*" (Q 11:7), and "He raised up the dome [of the sky], then perfected it; he made dark its night and made bright its day (see DAY AND NIGHT), he laid out the earth, and drew forth from it its water *(māʾ)* and its pasturage" (Q 79:28-31; see AGRICULTURE AND VEGETATION). It is life-giving. Further God says, "We made every living thing of water *(māʾ)*" (Q 21:30; cf. 24:45) and, as seminal fluid, in phrases such as *māʾ mahīn* (Q 77:20), and *māʾ dāfiq* (Q 86:6), water passes on life (q.v.) from one generation to the next.

From above the earth

"Water from the sky" *(min al-samāʾ māʾ),* a regular periphrasis for rain, is among the gifts celebrated in hymnic pericopes (see LANGUAGE AND STYLE OF THE QURʾĀN; GIFT AND GIFT-GIVING) such as: "He has set the earth for you as a resting place, and placed across it paths for you, and sent down from the sky water by which we have brought forth in profusion greenery of various kinds" (Q 20:53). It is one reason for humankind to worship (q.v.) God (see also GRATITUDE AND INGRATITUDE). Water is a single entity, but it produces a variety of wonderful things. "In the earth are neighboring tracts of land and gardens, of grapes, land with sown crops, date palms in clusters (see DATE PALM), sprung from a single root, or standing singly, though irrigated by one water" (*māʾ,* Q 13:4; cf. 80:25). By it "he makes grow for you your crops, olives, dates, grapes and fruits of every kind" (Q 16:10-11; cf. 50:9-10). Humankind depends totally on God's bounty, "Have you reflected on the water *(māʾ)* you drink? Did you make it come from the cloud *(muzn)* or did we?" (Q 56:68-9; cf. 67:30; see REFLECTION AND DELIBERATION; GRACE; BLESSING).

Water may be taken away (Q 23:18), and without it, everything withers. "We send down [water] from the sky. The greenery of the earth blends with it, but then becomes dry grass that the wind scatters" (Q 18:45). Water is carried by the clouds *(saḥāb)*. The winds *(riyāḥ lawāqiḥ)* impregnate them (with water), and by them "We send water *(māʾ)* down from the sky, then give it to you as drink. It is not you who hold it in store" (Q 15:22). The winds drive the clouds to carry water wherever God wills.

Clouds may portend blessings. "We spread over you clouds *(ghamāma),* and sent upon you manna and quails" (Q 2:57). The winds carry them, "... you see rain *(wadq)* come from the midst of them," and "his servants (see SERVANT)... who receive it rejoice" (Q 30:48). They may, however, contain thunder and lightening, and send down hail *(barad),* and threaten punishment (Q 24:43; see CHASTISEMENT AND PUNISHMENT).

The wonderful effect water has on drought-stricken earth is proof of God's power to resurrect the dead. "Among his signs (q.v.) is [this]: That you look on the earth [and see it] barren, yet when we send down upon it water *(māʾ),* it is stirred and becomes fecund. Indeed, he who brings it back to life restores to life the dead" (Q 41:39; cf. 7:57; 16:65; see DEATH AND THE DEAD; RESURRECTION).

On earth

Water is given to humankind in wells, rivers and torrents *(sayl)* flowing through the valleys (Q 13:17) and springs. Wells are mentioned in Q 12:10, 15 as *jubb,* and as *biʾr* in Q 22:45. The miraculous appearance of the well of Zamzam near Mecca (q.v.), is implied in Q 2:158, that prescribes the *saʿy* between Ṣafā and Marwa (q.v.), and is the scriptural basis for the story of Ishmael (q.v.; Ismāʿīl) and Hagar (Hājar).

Rivers provide water for irrigation, are a means of travel and transport and are sources of food and ornaments. Like rain they are celebrated in hymnic pericopes of great beauty (cf. Q 13:3; 14:32; 16:15; 27:61). The unbelievers (see BELIEF AND UNBELIEF) say to Muḥammad that they will not believe unless "You provide for us a garden (q.v.) of date palms and grapes, and rivers *(anhār)* gush through it" (Q 17:91; see OPPOSITION TO MUḤAMMAD). On two occasions, *yamm* replaces *nahr* to identify the river Nile, when the infant Moses (q.v.) was left to float in a box to be carried by its waters to safety (Q 20:39; 28:7).

Springs have a place in the canon of divine blessings: "he has caused you to have abundance of cattle and sons, of gardens and springs" (Q 26:133-4). And "we set [upon the earth] gardens of date palms and grapes, and we make gush from it springs" (Q 36:34). Yet springs only gush from the earth because God so wills (Q 67:30). Like God's other gifts they may be taken back due to people's wickedness (see GOOD AND EVIL). Ṣāliḥ (q.v.) warned his people that, if they did not accept his message, the "gardens, springs, tilled fields, and date palms with heavy sheaths" (Q 26:147-8) they enjoyed would be taken away from them (see WARNER; PUNISHMENT STORIES).

So precious are they that the unbelievers said to Muḥammad, "We will not believe you until you make a spring *(yanbūʿan)* gush forth for us" (Q 17:90). Moses had performed such a miracle (q.v.). When he asked God for water in the desert, God replied, "'Strike the rock with your staff (see ROD),' and twelve springs gushed from it" (Q 2:60).

The sea

There are two words for sea: *baḥr* and *yamm,* the latter of which is attested only eight times in the Qurʾān. In four places, *yamm* refers to the sea in which Pharaoh (q.v.) drowned (Q 7:136; 20:78; 28:40; 51:40; see DROWNING), and once to the sea in which were thrown the ashes of al-Sāmirī's idol (Q 20:97; see SAMARITANS; CALF OF GOLD). The sea *(baḥr)* is mighty. God swears by Mount Sinai (q.v.), by the Torah (q.v.), by the heavenly Kaʿba (q.v.), by the vault of the sky, and by the ever brimful sea (Q 52:1-6) that the punishment he threatens will come about (Q 52:7; see OATHS). The water of the sea is salty. The Qurʾān contrasts it with the fresh water of springs and rivers, speaking of the two seas *(baḥrayn):* "It is he who has let flow the two seas, one sweet and one salty and set a barrier (q.v.) between them" (Q 25:53-4; cf. 55:19-20; see also BARZAKH). The point of meeting of the two seas is apotheosized in the Qurʾān as the place at which Moses meets the prophet al-Khiḍr (Q 18:60-5; see KHAḌIR/KHIḌR). Though different, both serve humankind: "From each you can eat fresh fish and find ornaments. You can watch the ships (q.v.) cleaving them with their prows as they seek his bounty" (cf. Q 14:32; 16:14; 17:66; 22:65; 31:31; 35:12; 45:12; see HUNTING AND FISHING). Especially vivid is "his are the ships on the sea with sails aloft like mountains" (Q 55:24).

The sea is also a place of terror and darkness (q.v.). God gives protection against these perils: "God has set the stars to guide you in the darknesses of land and sea" (Q 6:63, 97; 27:63; see PLANETS AND STARS). It is at its most terrifying when mariners are threatened by a tempest: "When waves are suspended over them like a canopy, they call on God, in total sincerity, but when he has brought them safely to land, their faith (q.v.) grows feeble" (Q 31:32; cf. 10:22; 17:67).

Water as punishment

Water may be an instrument of punishment. One occasion, in historical time, is referred to in Q 34:16: "Then they turned away from us, so we sent to overwhelm them the torrent *(sayl)* of the great dam (*al-ʿarim* [q.v.])," referring to the devastation of Sabaʾ (see SHEBA) after the collapse of a dam above the city. On a greater scale is the flood sent to punish the people of Noah (q.v.), wiping out all of humankind apart from Noah and his family. "So we opened the gates of the sky to let water *(māʾ)* pour forth, then we made springs *(ʿuyūn)* gush from the earth until the water *(māʾ)* [from above and below] met to accomplish what had been decreed" (Q 54:11-12; cf. 69:11). The waves *(mawj)* drowned Noah's son (Q 11:43), who put his trust in a mountain instead of God. The waters of the sea drowned Pharaoh and his armies (Q 10:90; 44:24). God has total power over the waters. He saved Noah, "By God's help, the ark (q.v.) sailed safely amid [waves] like mountains" (Q 11:42). God saved Moses from Pharaoh by dividing the sea (Q 2:50; 7:138; 20:77; 26:63).

In paradise

A surging up of the sea (Q 81:6; 82:3) is a sign of judgment day but it is no longer mentioned in the hereafter (see ESCHATOLOGY; LAST JUDGMENT). Water, however, still has a role. In the gardens of paradise (q.v.) are springs (Q 15:45; also Q 44:52; 55:50; 77:41-3) and from them the blessed are given drinks of wonderful taste (Q 37:45-7; 76:6), including *zanjabīl* from a spring called *salsabīl* (Q 76:17-18). Those brought close to the divine presence drink from water called *tasnīm* (Q 83:27-8; see FACE OF GOD). Through these gardens flow rivers (Q 64:9; 65:11; cf. 2:266; 98:8), the water of which will never run brackish (Q 47:15). For those enjoying them is assurance of forgiveness (q.v.), the ending of hostilities and peace (q.v.; Q 47:12; 48:17; see also ENMITY).

In hell

Water is also part of the torments of the damned. The most terrible form of it is *ḥamīm*. It is a scalding, seething fluid, with a terrible taste (Q 38:57; 44:46). There are other liquid torments. The damned who cry out calling for cooling water (Q 7:50) are given water like fused brass, like the dregs of oil (Q 18:29; see SMELL; HOT AND COLD). It is foul and purulent, and can scarcely pass their throats (Q 56:42). There are springs that add to their agony such as one that spouts scalding water (Q 88:5).

In God's design

Water plays a direct role in the dispositions of divine providence. One example is the vignette of Moses, after his flight from Egypt, helping the two daughters of Jethro water their flocks (cf. Q 28:23-4). This was a critical moment in his career, for it set the stage for his return to Egypt as a prophet (see PROPHETS AND PROPHETHOOD). Another is the pivotal role played by "water from the sky" the evening before the battle of Badr (q.v.), rain making the soft and shifting sand firm underfoot for the Muslims, and providing a stream to furnish drink and from which to take water for ritual ablutions (cf. Q 8:11; see CLEANLINESS AND ABLUTION; RITUAL PURITY).

In purification

Q 8:11 alludes to the nexus between water and the ritual purity necessary for the valid performance of the ritual prayer (q.v.), and by extension, progress in the spiritual life. Q 4:43 and Q 5:6 prescribe the ritual of *wuḍūʾ* and the circumstances that render it necessary. Q 38:42 shows water as an agent of healing, sanctifying and restoring. After Job (q.v.) has suffered for many years, God says to him, "Scuff [the earth] with your foot! This is [a spring]. A cool place to bathe, and [it is] drink" (Q 38:42), the words "water" and "spring" being understood. The water this miraculous spring provides quenches Job's thirst, cleanses him from disease, and is a sign that everything taken from him is to be restored. It is a cue to the spiritual dimensions of water in the Qurʾān, richly exploited in the Ṣūfī tradition (see ṢŪFISM AND THE QURʾĀN), notably in the thought of al-Ghazālī (d. 505/1111) and Ibn al-ʿArabī (d. 638/1240).

In rhetoric

Metaphors in which water plays a part highlight its connotations (see METAPHOR). Unbelieving hearts are harder than stone (for nothing good can come from them; see HEART), whereas from some stones rivers gush forth, others shatter, and water flows from them (Q 2:74). The unbeliever is totally ignorant and blind (see IGNORANCE; VISION AND BLINDNESS). He is "in the darkness of a vast sea; waves envelop him, above them further waves, above them clouds, [forming] layers of darkness, one upon the other" (Q 24:40). Finally, even the plenitude of the sea is little compared to the words of God, for if all the trees of the world were pens, and the seas seven times over were ink, they would not suffice to write them (Q 18:109; 31:27; see WRITING AND WRITING MATERIALS; WORD OF GOD).

Conclusion

Water, in its primal position in the order of creation, the variety of its forms and uses, its literal and symbolic significances (see SYMBOLIC IMAGERY), has a dominant position in the Qurʾān's presentation of natural phenomena. In it is an inherent dynamism that makes it unique. It is one, but fecundates life in diverse forms. The movement of the life-cycle from the germination of a seed depends on it. It brings the dead earth back to life and is thus an image of God's power to resurrect the dead. The frequent periphrasis "water from the sky" instead of rain *(wadq, maṭar)* highlights water as substance, untrammeled by any accident.

Every attestation elaborates the spiritual economy of the qurʾānic revelation (see REVELATION AND INSPIRATION). Like the Qurʾān *(tanzīl),* it is sent down *(nazala)* from the sky, as a mercy (q.v.) to humankind. It is essential to every form of life and a symbol and agent of spiritual purity. Mystics have found in it an infinity of aspects and significances.

Anthony H. Johns

Bibliography
Primary: Bayḍāwī, *Anwār;* Jalālayn; Nasafī, *Tafsīr;* Rāzī, *Tafsīr;* Ṭabarī, *Tafsīr.*
Secondary: T. Burckhardt, The symbolism of water, in W. Stoddart (ed. and trans.), *Mirror of the intellect. Essays on traditional science and sacred art,* Albany, NY 1987, 124-31; A.H. Johns, Narrative, intertext and allusion in the qurʾānic presentation of Job, in *Journal of qurʾanic studies* 1 (1999), 1-25; M. Lings, The qoranic symbolism of water, in *Studies in comparative religion* 2 (1968), 153-60; F. Schuon, *Understanding Islam,* London 1976; H. Toelle, *Le Coran revisité. Le feu, l'eau, l'air et la terre,* Damascus 1999.

Water of Paradise

Rivers and springs found in the paradisiacal garden, as described in the Qurʾān. The phrase "rivers of paradise," *anhār al-janna,* occurs forty-six times, while the terms *ʿayn,* spring, and its plural, *ʿuyūn,* occur nine times only (see also WATER; SPRINGS AND FOUNTAINS). There are four kinds of rivers in paradise (q.v.): Rivers of milk (q.v.) whose taste never alters, rivers of pure honey (q.v.), rivers of delightful wine (q.v.) which causes neither drunkenness nor heaviness (see INTOXICANTS) and, finally, rivers of water that are always gushing, as in Q 47:15.

Where are these rivers and springs located? Al-Qurṭubī (d. 671/1272) mentions that the qurʾānic expression "underneath them" means that rivers flow "under the dwellers of paradise's couches and under their chambers" (*Jāmiʿ,* viii, 312). A much earlier commentator, al-Ṭabarī (d. 310/923), had offered an expanded explanation: "God means the trees, fruits, and plants in the garden (q.v.; see also AGRICULTURE AND VEGETATION), not the ground. That is why he has said 'underneath which rivers flow,' because it is clear that he wanted to say that the water of the rivers therein flowed under the trees, plants, and fruits, not under the ground. For, when water flows under the ground, it is not the lot of someone above it to see it unless the cover between it and him is removed. According to the description of the rivers of the garden, they do not flow in underground channels" (*Tafsīr,* ad loc.). Al-Qurṭubī delves into the location of these rivers. He cites al-Bukhārī's (d. 256/870) *Ṣaḥīḥ:* "If you asked God, then ask him to dwell in *al-firdaws* which is in the middle of the garden. It is located in the highest place. On top of it is placed the Throne of God (q.v.), the merciful (see MERCY; GOD AND HIS ATTRIBUTES). It is from *al-firdaws* that the rivers of paradise flow" (*Jāmiʿ,* ix, 311).

Islamic tradition (see TRADITIONAL DISCIPLINES OF QURʾĀNIC STUDY) has ascribed various names of qurʾānic origin to these rivers (e.g. Kawthar, Kāfūr, Tasnīm, Salsabīl; cf. Smith and Haddad, *Islamic understanding,* 88, esp. n. 76). One of them, *al-kawthar,* occurs only once in the Qurʾān. Ibn Qayyim al Jawziyya (d. 751/1350) cites a ḥadīth of the Prophet (see ḤADĪTH AND THE QURʾĀN) from Muslim (d. ca. 261/875): "*al-kawthar* is a river in paradise that my God promised me" (*Ḥādī l-arwāḥ,* 314). Abū Nuʿaym al-Iṣfahānī (d. 430/1038) quotes the following ḥadīth: "Then *sidrat al-muntahā* (the lote-tree of the boundary; see TREES; ASCENSION) was uncovered for me, and I saw four rivers: two internal and two external; I said: 'What are these rivers, O Gabriel (q.v.)?' He said, 'The internal ones are in paradise and the external are the Nile and the Euphrates'" (*Ṣifat al-janna,* iii, 157-8; see GEOGRAPHY).

In Q 76:18, we read that the faithful will drink from a source called *salsabīl.* Its water is flavored with ginger (Q 76:17) and the calyx of sweet-smelling flowers (cf. Q 76:5; see CAMPHOR; SMELL; FOOD AND DRINK).

Water of paradise purifies literally and metaphorically (see METAPHOR; CLEANLINESS AND ABLUTION; RITUAL PURITY). Al-Qurṭubī (*Jāmi*ʿ, x, 33) interprets Q 15:45 as follows: "when the people of paradise enter paradise, two springs are offered to them. They drink from the first one, and God erases all hatred and desire for vengeance (q.v.) from their hearts (see HEART). Then, they enter into the second spring and wash themselves. Their faces (q.v.) become serene."

Inasmuch as the water of paradise purifies, it was connected to light (q.v.). Light, like water, renews and regenerates. Thus, al-Qurṭubī interprets the term *nahar* in Q 54:54 as light rather than river (*Jāmi*ʿ, xvii, 149). These two meanings of radiance and refinement can be understood in a highly esoteric way, as expressed in the commentary published under the name of the great Ṣūfī (see ṢŪFISM AND THE QURʾĀN) Ibn al-ʿArabī (d. 638/1240) as "the sources of the esoteric sciences and their branches" (*Tafsīr*, i, 234; see POLYSEMY).

Amira El-Zein

Bibliography
Primary: Abū Nuʿaym Aḥmad b. ʿAbdallāh al-Iṣfahānī, *Ṣifat al-janna*, 4 vols., Damascus 1987; Ibn al-ʿArabī, *Tafsīr;* Ibn Qayyim al-Jawziyya, *Ḥādi l-arwāḥ ilā bilād al-afrāḥ*, al-Dammām, Saudi Arabia 1997; Qurṭubī, *Jāmi*ʿ; Ṭabarī, *Tafsīr*.
Secondary: E. Clark, *Underneath which rivers flow. The symbolism of the Islamic garden*, London 1996 (2004); Ṣ. El-Ṣaleḥ, *La vie future selon le Coran*, Paris 1971; E.J. Jenkinson, The rivers of paradise, in *MW* 19 (1925), 151-5; M. Lings, *Symbol & archetype. A study in the meaning of existence*, Cambridge, UK 1991, 67-82 (ch. 7, The qurʾānic symbolism of water); J. Macdonald, Paradise, in *IS* 5 (1966), 331-83; J. Smith and Y. Haddad, *The Islamic understanding of death and resurrection*, Albany 1981.

Weakness

see OPPRESSED ON EARTH, THE

Wealth

Worldly possessions and property. In this sense, "wealth" occurs often in the Qūrʾan. The most common term for it, *māl* and its plural *amwāl*, prevails in the later (Medinan) sūras (q.v.; see also CHRONOLOGY AND THE QURʾĀN). Additional terms include *ghināʾ* and other words derived from its root, especially in the early (Meccan) sūras. Sometimes property (q.v.) seems taken for granted as a simple fact of life: God "has made it a support for you" (*allatī jaʿala llāhu lakum qiyāman*, Q 4:5); one reason for men's control over women is "the expenditure they make [for them] out of their property" (Q 4:34; see MAINTENANCE AND UPKEEP; WOMEN AND THE QURʾĀN; PATRIARCHY). For the most part, however, wealth is considered permissible and even desirable under certain conditions but a dangerous thing overall.

To begin with, God is *ghanī*, which means both "wealthy" and "able to dispense with" something or someone (see GOD AND HIS ATTRIBUTES). He has no need of creation (q.v.) and the world (q.v.; *ghaniyyun ʿani l-ʿālamīn*, Q 3:97; 29:6). Human beings, however, need at least a bare minimum of the goods of this world, which can only come from God. God combines his wealth with mercy (q.v.; Q 6:133), providing humans with property to satisfy their needs (Q 53:48, *aghnā wa-aqnā*). Accordingly, we have the famous passage Q 35:15, "Oh you people! You are the (poor) ones in need of God (*al-fuqarāʾu ilā llāhi;* see POVERTY AND THE POOR), while God is the wealthy and praiseworthy one (*al-ghaniyyu l-ḥamīd;* see PRAISE; LAUDATION; GLORIFICATION OF GOD)." God's gifts (see GIFT AND GIFT-GIVING) may be related to the sustenance (q.v.; *rizq*) which he provides, as for instance in the quickening rain (see WATER; BLESSING). More to the point here, however, is the fact that the divine beneficence is often called *faḍl,* which means "grace" (q.v.) but, also, in many cases, something more like "surplus" (see Bravmann, Surplus of poverty). "So if you fear (q.v.) poverty, God will make you wealthy out of his *faḍl"* (Q 9:28); those who lack the means for getting married should wait chastely for God's *faḍl* to arrive (Q 24:33; see MARRIAGE AND DIVORCE; CHASTITY).

God's generosity contrasts with the hoarding and greed of certain people (Q 10:58; see AVARICE). It is especially blameworthy to respond to God's *faḍl* with vengeful behavior (cf. Q 9:73-4; see VENGEANCE). Yet many people are misled by or through their material goods. In the days of old, the Children of Israel (q.v.; Bānū Isrāʾīl) rejected their prophet's designation of Saul (q.v.; Ṭālūt) as king over them, because they did not consider him rich enough (Q 2:247; see KINGS AND RULERS). The people of Midian (q.v.) asked Shuʿayb (q.v.) if his religion would require them "to cease doing whatever we like with our property" (Q 11:87). The dazzling splendor and wealth of the present life which God permitted to Pharaoh (q.v.) and his chiefs caused them to lead people astray (q.v.) from God's path (Q 10:88; see PATH OR WAY). In Muḥammad's own time, the unbelievers spent their wealth in precisely the same way (Q 8:36; see BELIEF AND UNBELIEF). Acquisition of wealth is repeatedly described as useless (e.g. Q 15:84; 69:28; 92:11; 111:1-2, etc.). In a great many verses, worldly wealth is paired with children (q.v.), together constituting a vain enticement or temptation away from God (Q 3:10, 116; 8:28; 9:55, 69, 85; 17:6, 64; 18:34, 39, 46; 19:77; 23:55-6; 26:88; 34:35, 37; 57:20; 58:17; 63:9; 64:15; 71:21; see TRIAL; TRUST AND PATIENCE).

Hoarding, avarice and arrogance (q.v.) all go together (see Q 57:23-4; 4:36-8, "God does not love the arrogant and vainglorious, nor those who are stingy and who hide the benefits that God has bestowed on them... nor those who spend of their substance so as to be conspicuous before others"). Every time a warner (q.v.) appears before a people, its well-off members *(mutrafūhā)* say, "We do not believe...; we have more in wealth and children, and we cannot be punished" (cf. Q 34:34-5). Of course they are proved wrong; and in the afterlife, the saved will call down to the damned (see REWARD AND PUNISHMENT): "Of what profit to you were your hoarding and arrogant ways?" (Q 7:48; cf. 14:21). The basic problem with avarice is its claim to self-sufficiency (Q 92:8, *man bakhila wastaghnā*). Avarice thus comes at the cost of one's own soul (q.v.; Q 47:38) and to be saved from the "covetousness of one's soul" is to achieve true "prosperity" (Q 64:16). Similarly, greed is a form of ingratitude: the creature whom God created and to whom he granted abundant goods and sons, and whose life he made comfortable, is now greedy for more (Q 74:11-15). Man, though created for toil and struggle (see WORK), still boasts, "I have squandered abundant wealth" (Q 90:4-6).

A great many passages in the Qurʾān speak of arrogance and the arrogant *(alladhīna stakbarū),* rather than of wealth and the wealthy. These two groups (the arrogant and the wealthy) are related, if not identical. Interestingly, the Qurʾān, like the New Testament (Mark 10:25; Matthew 19:24; Luke 18:25) talks of a camel (q.v.) going through the eye of a needle yet here the object of comparison is not the wealthy man seeking entrance to heaven (see PARADISE) but rather "those who reject our signs (q.v.) and consider them with arrogance" (Q 7:40; see LIE; GRATITUDE AND INGRATITUDE).

Despite its many dangers for us, we can purify our wealth by giving it away without any thought for favors in return (Q 92:18-19). We should not mar our acts of charity (see GOOD DEEDS; ALMSGIVING) with reminders of our generosity or with unkind remarks (Q 2:264). In this way, our wealth may come to resemble God's original gift to humankind (*rizq* or *faḍl*), which was likewise given without any expectation of its being restored to the original donor. This reciprocity between God and the donor becomes clear when we are called upon to help meritorious *mukātab* slaves (see SLAVES AND SLAVERY): "give them some of God's wealth *(min māli llāhi)* which he has given you" (Q 24:33). Many passages specify how to take alms from property and the right or claim *(ḥaqq)* for "the needy and the deprived" that inheres within the property itself (Q 51:19; 70:24-5; see OPPRESSION; OPPRESSED ON EARTH, THE).

Wealth becomes an aid to salvation (q.v.) when it has not only been "purified," but also spent "in the path of God" (Q 2:261-5). Repeatedly, the believers are enjoined to struggle with their possessions and their persons *(bi-amwālihim wa-anfusihim)*; often (as at Q 4:95; 8:72; 9:44, 81, 88) this refers specifically to fighting (q.v.) and warfare (see WAR), though in other cases perhaps not (see JIHĀD). God has purchased the possessions and persons of the believers in return for the garden (q.v.; Q 9:111). Here, through war and conquest (q.v.), material wealth becomes a positive value: "He made you heirs of the lands, houses and goods [of the People of the Book (q.v.)], and of a land which you did not frequent previously" (Q 33:27).

There are also many passages that deal with the management of property. Orphans' estates must be handled honestly (see ORPHAN; GUARDIANSHIP). Money is prescribed for dowries (Q 4:24; see BRIDEWEALTH) and should not be made over to the weak of understanding (Q 4:5; see MATURITY; INTELLECT). You should not devour your own substance and that of others by spending it on vanities or on bribes (?) for judges (e.g. Q 2:188; 4:29). The alternative to such spending on vanities is commerce based on mutual good-will (*tijāratan ʿan tarāḍin minkum,* Q 4:29). Similarly, *ribā* denotes a kind of bad transaction, contrasted with alms (Q 30:39), and permissible trade (Q 2:274; see USURY).

Regarding the historical context for references to wealth in the Qurʾān, in one place, Q 48:11, the term *amwāl* is used to refer to the herds of nomadic desert-dwellers (see NOMADS). Otherwise, we seem to be in a world consisting largely of town-dwellers, perhaps one in a process of intense social change, as Watt *(Muhammad at Mecca; Muhammad at Medina),* Ibrahim *(Merchant capital)* and Bamyeh *(Social origins)* have variously proposed (see CITY). It is not often clear, however, whether or to what extent the references to wealth in the Qurʾān have to do with moveable or immoveable property. Clear references to money (q.v.) are lacking altogether. Only rarely does the Qurʾān provide much context for these matters. One example may be Q 4:160-1, where the Jews (see JEWS AND JUDAISM) are mentioned together with *ribā* (usury?); however, this may fit within a well-established thematic of monotheist debate (see DEBATE AND DISPUTATION), as Rippin (Commerce) has suggested regarding the commercial vocabulary of the Qurʾān (see TRADE AND COMMERCE; POLEMIC AND POLEMICAL LANGUAGE).

Despite the variety among them, these qurʾānic themes relating to wealth and property together constitute a coherent view. A summary of this view, at Q 47:36-8, makes it clear that if people believe and do the right things (see VIRTUES AND VICES, COMMANDING AND FORBIDDING; ETHICS AND THE QURʾĀN), if they are generous and open-handed, and if they remember that this life is mere play and frivolity, then God will allow them to keep their worldly property after all. Among the classical exegetes (see EXEGESIS OF THE QURʾĀN: CLASSICAL AND MEDIEVAL), al-Ṭabarī (d. 310/923) had a particularly strong sense of the qurʾānic moral economy regarding property and wealth.

Michael Bonner

Bibliography
M. Bamyeh, *The social origins of Islam,* Minneapolis 1999; M. Bonner, The *Kitāb al-Kasb* attributed to al-Shaybānī. Poverty, surplus, and the circulation of wealth, in *JAOS* 121 (2001), 410-27; id., Poverty and economics in the Qurʾān, in *Journal of interdisciplinary history* 35/3 (2005), 391-406; M.M. Bravmann, The surplus of property. An early Arab social concept, in *Der Islam* 38 (1962), 28-50; repr. in id., *The spiritual background of early Islam,* Leiden 1972, 229-53; M. Ibrahim, *Merchant capital and Islam,* Austin, TX 1990; A. Rippin, The commerce of eschatology, in Wild, *Text,* 125-35; W.M. Watt, *Muhammad at Mecca,* Oxford 1953; id., *Muhammad at Medina,* Oxford 1956.

Wean see LACTATION

Weapons see INSTRUMENTS; FIGHTING; WAR; HUNTING AND FISHING

Weariness see SLEEP; SABBATH

Weather

In general terms, the state of the atmosphere at a given time and place, involving the variables of heat, cold, moisture, wind and pressure, and referring both to beneficial and destructive consequences. In the Qurʾān there are a number of words covering many of these aspects, some phenomena having more than one term. In the vast majority of contexts, the agency of God is explicit (e.g. Q 30:48).

Rain, for example, is expressed in several ways. The most frequent is the mention of God's "sending down water from the sky" thereby giving life (q.v.) to or restoring it on earth (q.v.; see also AGRICULTURE AND VEGETATION). The word *ghayth* is also employed in a bountiful sense in Q 42:28 and Q 57:20 (see GRACE; BLESSING). The two occurrences of *wadq* (Q 24:43; 30:48) mean a heavy rain falling from a cloud; *ṣayyib* (Q 2:19) is also rendered heavy rain or rainstorm. A neutral sense is conveyed in Q 4:102 where fighters are allowed to set aside their arms (see FIGHTING; EXPEDITIONS AND BATTLES; WEAPONS) if sick (see ILLNESS AND HEALTH) or discomfited by rain *(maṭar).* The causative verbal form IV of this root *(m-ṭ-r)* is used exclusively to express divine punishment, as in Q 25:40 where it "rained an evil rain" *(umṭirat maṭara l-sawʾi)* upon Sodom. The same occurred to the people of Lot (q.v.; Q 7:84; 26:173; 27:58), although in Q 11:82 and Q 15:74 (see also Q 8:32) "stones" *(ḥijār)* were rained down upon them, possibly a metaphor (q.v.) for a volcanic eruption (see STONE).

A series of related weather terms, wind (sing. and pl.; see AIR AND WIND), storm (*ʿāṣif,* Q 14:18), and cloud may be treated together. In Q 22:31, ascribing partners to God (see POLYTHEISM AND ATHEISM) is likened to a wind *(rīḥ)* that carries someone far away. Another simile (q.v.) compares those who devote themselves to the life of this world to a biting icy wind (*rīḥ fīhā ṣirr,* Q 3:117) that destroys the harvest. Solomon (q.v.) is granted a fair wind by God by which he could safely set sail at sea (Q 21:81; 38:36). On the other hand, the ungrateful (see GRATITUDE AND INGRATITUDE) may feel a sense of security but God could drown them in a mighty storm or hurricane (*qāṣifan mina l-rīḥi,* Q 17:69; see DROWNING). A fierce roaring wind (*rīḥ ṣarṣar ʿātiya,* Q 69:6; cf. also Q 41:16; 54:19;

al-rīḥ al-ʿaqīm, Q 51:41) destroyed the people of ʿĀd (q.v.) for their disobedience (q.v.). The faithful (see FAITH; BELIEF AND UNBELIEF) are reminded of God's favor that when they were besieged at Medina (q.v.) by the Quraysh (q.v.), he sent against them a strong wind *(rīḥan,* Q 33:9) and hosts they could not see (see RANKS AND ORDERS; ANGEL). God sends winds *(al-riyāḥ bushran,* Q 7:57; see also Q 25:48; 27:63; cf. 30:46) that herald his mercy (q.v.) by bringing clouds to water a scorched earth (see WATER).

Two words for cloud, *ʿāriḍ* and *saḥāb,* the latter used in a collective sense as well, naturally occur along with mention of wind(s) (Q 2:164; 46:24) and rain. One splendid passage (Q 24:43) contains numerous signs of God's lordship as creator and sustainer of the natural order in the clouds, rain, hail *(barad)* and lightning *(barq;* see CREATION; SUSTENANCE; LORD; NATURE AS SIGNS). Thunder *(raʿd)* and lightning appear naturally together in Q 2:19-20 along with thunderbolts *(ṣawāʿiq;* see also Q 13:12-13). The people of Thamūd (q.v.) were destroyed (Q 69:5) by a divine punishment which appeared to combine the qualities of thunder and lightning *(ṭāghiya),* a term occurring only in this context (see PUNISHMENT STORIES). Lane notes that it is synonymous with *ṣāʿiqa* (pl. *ṣawāʿiq*) meaning "thunderbolt" (Q 41:13), although translators render it as "lightning" as well. Thunder *(raʿd)* is also the title of the thirteenth chapter of the Qurʾān (see SŪRA).

David Waines

Bibliography
Lane; *Lisān al-ʿArab;* H. Toelle, *Le Coran revisité. Le feu, l'eau, l'air et la terre,* Damascus 1999.

Wedding see MARRIAGE AND DIVORCE

Weeping

Shedding of tears as a result of a heightened emotional state. Weeping out of piety (q.v.) or the fear (q.v.) of God is considered an expression of great devotion and several ḥadīths relate that this is what the Companions of the Prophet (q.v.) used to do when they heard sermons and preaching (see TEACHING AND PREACHING THE QURʾĀN). According to a ḥadīth reported by Abū Hurayra (d. ca. 58/678; see ḤADĪTH AND THE QURʾĀN), among "the seven people to whom God gives his shade on the day" of resurrection (q.v.), there is "a man who remembers God in solitude and his eyes become tearful" (Bukhārī, *Ṣaḥīḥ, K. Adhān* 14; Tirmidhī, *Ṣaḥīḥ, K. Zuhd,* 53; see REMEMBRANCE; VIGILS). Another ḥadīth, reported by ʿAbdallāh b. al-Shikhkhīr (fl. fourth/tenth cent.), says that the Prophet himself, "when he was performing prayers, would sob and his chest sound like a boiling kettle" (Abū Dawūd, *Sunan, K. Ṣalāt,* 22, 157; see PRAYER). In the Qurʾān, some verses say that the believers (see BELIEF AND UNBELIEF) are those who, listening to the holy book, "fall down on their faces in tears" (Q 17:109; see RECITATION OF THE QURʾĀN), and the same is said about the ancient prophets who "would fall down in prostrate adoration and in tears" (Q 19:58; see BOWING AND PROSTRATION). These verses are among the eleven, according to al-Qayrawānī (d. 385/996, *Risāla;* most traditional schools speak of fourteen or fifteen occasions) that, when recited, Muslims are commanded to perform *sujūd* (see RITUAL AND THE QURʾĀN). Al-Bukhārī (d. 256/870) and Muslim (d. ca. 261/875) report that Muḥammad ordered Abū Bakr (q.v.) to lead the prayer, but ʿĀʾisha (see ʿĀʾISHA BINT ABĪ BAKR) said that he could not because he "will not be able to recite the noble Qurʾān to the people on account of weeping" (Bukhārī,

Ṣaḥīḥ, K. Faḍāʾil al-ṣaḥāba, 3; Muslim, *Ṣaḥīḥ, K. Faḍāʾil al-ṣaḥāba,* 2). In spite of that, the Prophet re-affirmed his order. The question of whether it is permitted to weep for the dead is more complex (see DEATH AND THE DEAD; BURIAL). Muslim scholars agree that weeping for the dead is permissible, whereas lamenting and wailing are not (cf. Halevi, Wailing; Rippin, Sadjda). Many narrations report that in particular ʿUmar admonished those who wail for the dead, recalling that the Prophet had said: "A dead person is tormented by the wailing of the living people" (Bukhārī, *Ṣaḥīḥ, K. Janāʾiz,* 33; Muslim, *Ṣaḥīḥ, K. Janāʾiz,* passim). After the death of ʿUmar, ʿĀʾisha said, in reply to the son who had admonished those who were crying for his father, that, on the contrary, "The messenger of God did not say that a believer is punished by the weeping of his relatives. But he said that God increases the punishment of a non-believer because of the weeping of his relatives" (Bukhārī, *Ṣaḥīḥ, K. Janāʾiz,* 32; Muslim, *Ṣaḥīḥ, K. Janāʾiz,* passim). She further added, quoting the Qurʾān: "Nor can a bearer of burdens bear another's burdens" (Q 35:18). Ibn ʿAbbās (d. ca. 68/686-8) then recited: "It is he who grants laughter and tears" (Q 53:43). After that, Ibn ʿUmar did not say anything. On the other hand, it is related that the Prophet himself wept on the death of his son Ibrāhīm and said: "The eyes shed tears and the heart feels pain, but we utter only what pleases our lord. O Ibrāhīm! We are aggrieved at your demise" (Sayyid Sābiq, *Fiqh al-sunna,* iv, 21). The verb "to weep" recurs only rarely elsewhere in the Qurʾān. Regarding those who were congratulating themselves on having successfully avoided taking part in the expedition of Tabūk (see EXPEDITIONS AND BATTLES; HYPOCRITES AND HYPOCRISY), it is said: "Let them laugh a little: much will they weep" (Q 9:82; see LAUGHTER). Joseph's (q.v.) brothers also pretend to weep on their return to their father after having sold their sibling (Q 12:16; see BROTHER AND BROTHERHOOD; BENJAMIN). Those who make fun of the announcement of the end of the world (see ESCHATOLOGY) are rebuked for laughing instead of weeping (Q 53:60). Lastly, we are told that neither heaven nor earth shed tears for the people of Pharaoh (q.v.), after being punished by God for not having listened to Moses (q.v.; Q 44:29; see also CHASTISEMENT AND PUNISHMENT; REWARD AND PUNISHMENT; JOY AND MISERY).

Paolo Branca

Bibliography
Primary: Abū Dawūd; Abū ʿUbayd, *Faḍāʾil,* 63-6 (for early treatment of weeping in response to the Qurʾān); al-Ansārī, Abū ʿAbdallāh, *Sharḥ ḥudūd Ibn ʿArafa,* Morocco 1992; Bukhārī, *Ṣaḥīḥ,* ed. M.D. al-Baghā, 6 vols., Beirut 1987; Ibn Hibbān, *Ṣaḥīḥ,* ed. Sh. al-Arnaʾūt, 18 vols., Beirut 1993; Ibn Hishām, *al-Sīra al-nabawiyya,* ed. Ṭ. ʿAbd al-Raʾūf Saʿd, 6 vols., Beirut 1411/1990-1; Ibn Kathīr, *Tafsīr,* Beirut 1980; Mālik, *Muwaṭṭaʾ;* al-Maqdisī, Muḥammad b. ʿAbd al-Wāḥid, *al-Aḥādīth al-mukhtāra,* ed. ʿAbd al-Malik b. ʿAbdallāh b. Duhaysh, 10 vols., Mecca 1410/1989-90; Muslim, *Ṣaḥīḥ;* Qurṭubī, *Jāmiʿ;* Sayyid Sabiq, *Fiqh al-sunna,* Eng. trans. 4 vols., Indianapolis 1989 (orig. 5 vols., Cairo 1954-5); Ṭabarī, *Tafsīr,* Beirut 1984; Tirmidhī, *Ṣaḥīḥ,* 13 vols., Cairo 1931-4.
Secondary: L. Halevi, Wailing for the dead. The role of women in early Islamic funerals, in *Past and present* 183 (May 2004), 3-39; A. Rippin, Sadjda, in *EI²*, viii, 740.

Weights and Measures

Means for making quantitative evaluations. Information about weights and measures in the Qurʾān must be derived from symbolic discourse (see SYMBOLIC IMAGERY; SIMILES; METAPHOR). This is true even for very concrete weights and measures and is reflected in the exegetical literature (see EXEGESIS OF THE QURʾĀN: CLASSICAL AND

MEDIEVAL), which contains often divergent information and explanations about weights and measures in the Qurʾān. What follows is a closer examination of the qurʾānic (1) measures of length; (2) measures of weight; (3) mixed measures; and (4) measures of time. The Qurʾān makes no mention of explicit measures of area.

Measures of length

Dhirāʿ, "cubit," appears only in Q 69:32, in "a chain of seventy cubits reach." It is equivalent to "the part of the arm from the elbow to the tip of the middle finger" (see Hinz, Dhirāʿ, on its concrete early Islamic, not qurʾānic, dimension). Al-Ṭabarī (d. 310/923) simply says "God knows best the span of its length" (*Allāhu aʿlamu bi-qadri ṭūlihā; Tafsīr,* xii, 220). He also mentions the opinion that "one *dhirāʿ* corresponds to seventy *bāʿ*." The term *bāʿ* does not occur in the Qurʾān but in early Islamic times it corresponded to about two meters (see Hinz, *Islamische Masse,* 54). Following al-Ṭabarī, one *bāʿ* can also represent — symbolically, of course — a distance that is supposed to be longer than the distance between Kūfa and Mecca (q.v.).

Qāb denotes "a short span" and appears only in Q 53:9, in combination with *qaws,* "bow," or "cubit" (see Lane, vii, 2575) as *qāba qawsayn,* literally the "distance of two bow-lengths," meaning "very close." Al-Ṭabarī (*Tafsīr,* xi, 507-9) reports opinions on the length of *qāba qawsayn,* including, among others, "half the length of a finger" or "length of a finger." He also explains the phrase as referring to either the distance between the archangel Gabriel (q.v.) and God or between Muḥammad and God.

Measures of weight

Mithqāl, "(an undefined) weight," appears eight times, six occurrences of which (Q 4:40; 10:61; 34:3, 22; 99:7-8) are in a genitive construction with *dharra. Dharra* (e.g. "God does not do a grain's weight of wrong," Q 4:40) denotes something tiny, a speck (e.g. an ant — a hundred of them weigh one grain of barley; see Lane, iii, 957), or, in modern Arabic usage, an atom. Following al-Ṭabarī (*Tafsīr,* x, 574) with regard to Q 10:61, *mithqāl dharra* denotes the weight of one single, small speck. With regard to Q 34:3, al-Ṭabarī says: "God misses nothing in heaven (see HEAVEN AND SKY) and on earth (q.v.), even if it has only the weight of a *dharra* (*Tafsīr,* x, 346) and at Q 34:22 he comments: "There are no gods but God, so they do not even own something of the weight of a *dharra* in heaven and on earth" (ibid., x, 371; see POLYTHEISM AND ATHEISM; IDOLS AND IMAGES; POWER AND IMPOTENCE).

Kayl appears repeatedly for "measure" in general. In just one place the Qurʾān uses *kayl baʿīr,* "camel-load" (see CAMEL), as the definition of a weight which is, following the verse itself, "an easy measure": "We shall… get an extra measure of a camel(-load). That is an easily acquired measure" (*nazdādu kayla baʿīrin dhālika kaylun yasīrun,* Q 12:65). Apart from that, whenever *kayl* appears — ten places in all — it never refers to a defined weight (see MEASUREMENT).

Some other expressions belong to the sphere of measures of weight. Twice, *mithqāl* appears in connection with *ḥabba min khardal,* "grain of mustard" (Q 21:47; 31:16): "… if it be the weight of a grain of mustard, and it be in a rock,… God will produce it" (Q 31:16). In all other places where *ḥabba,* "grain," occurs alone, it is a mere metaphor (cf. the metaphorical "grain of a mustard seed" of the Bible, e.g. in Mark 4:31).

Ḥiml, "load," serves in three places as a periphrasis for a weight: as "camel-load" (*ḥiml baʿīr,* Q 12:72, synonymous to the above-mentioned *kayl baʿīr*); one burdened soul (q.v.) will not bear the burden of another (Q 35:18; see also INTERCESSION; REWARD AND PUNISHMENT); some will bear a burden on the resurrection (q.v.) day (Q 20:101; the same meaning is denoted by *wizr*, "load," in the preceding verse, Q 20:100).

Similarly metaphorical are *waqr*, "heaviness," which occurs four times (Q 6:25; 17:46; 18:57; 31:7), and *wiqr*, "burden," where once (Q 51:2) it denotes metaphorically the burden of water (q.v.) that clouds carry (see also AIR AND WIND; WEATHER).

Mixed measures

Some terms of measure in the Qurʾān signify simultaneously weight and value (see also TRADE AND COMMERCE; MARKETS; MONEY; NUMISMATICS).

Dirham denotes the early Arabic silver coin, and, at the same time, a weight as a coin was understood to be of a particular weight. It appears only once, in the plural *darāhim* (Q 12:20). From there, it simply follows that it is a measure for a small value: "They sold him [Joseph (q.v.)] for a low price, a certain number of *dirhams*, for they thought little of him." At the time of the prophet Muḥammad, one *dirham* was supposed to have the value of a tenth or a twelfth of a *dīnār* (Miles, Dirham).

Dīnār denotes the early Islamic gold coin and appears only once, too. It is of a lesser value than the *qinṭār* (Q 3:75). It is said that Christians and Jews who had borrowed *dīnār*s from Muslims would sometimes not give them back (Miles, Dīnār; see JEWS AND JUDAISM; CHRISTIANS AND CHRISTIANITY).

Qinṭār, mostly understood as "talent," appears three times (Q 3:75; 4:20; pl. *qanāṭīr*, Q 3:14). It is apparently derived from the Latin *centenarius* (Ashtor, Mawāzīn). In Q 3:14 "talents of gold (q.v.) and silver" are listed as earthly enticements, in addition to women (see WOMEN AND THE QURʾĀN), children (q.v.), excellent horses, cattle (see ANIMAL LIFE) and land (see also GRACE; BLESSING; PROPERTY; WEALTH). Commentaries on this verse list many different opinions on the meaning of *qinṭār*. Al-Ṭabarī (*Tafsīr*, iii, 199-202) says repeatedly that it means "a lot of property (*māl*) of gold and silver" and that it cannot be defined by weight. The other interpretations al-Ṭabarī lists range from 1200 *ūqiyya*, "ounce" (not in the Qurʾān; in early Islam it denoted a weight of 125 grams; see Hinz, *Islamische Masse*, 35) to over 1200 gold *dīnār*s; or 1200 *dīnār*s and 1200 *mithqāl* (see above) in silver; or 12,000 *dirham*, or 1000 *dīnār*; until the equally unclear "as much gold as a sack made of bull hide can contain" (*milʾu maski thawrin dhahaban*). Ibn Kathīr (d. 774/1373; *Tafsīr*, ii, 17-18, 57) concedes that the opinions of the interpreters differ. He understands *qinṭār* simply as "money" or "property" (*māl*), although he has heard opinions that it is worth 40,000, 60,000, and 80,000 *dīnār*s. He refers to the Prophet who is said to have assigned to a *qinṭār* the weight of 12,000 *ūqiyya* (see above): each single *ūqiyya* is supposed to be more valuable than everything between heaven and earth (*kullu ūqiyyatin khayrun mimmā bayna l-samāʾi wa-l-arḍ*).

Again for the sake of completeness, two metaphorical expressions for something of little value should be noted: *qiṭmīr*, "skin of a date-stone," which denotes symbolically very little value and appears only in Q 35:13: "Those whom you call upon, apart from him, have not power over the skin of a date-stone"; and *qabḍa*, "a handful," which occurs twice, as in Q 39:67: "The earth as a whole will be his handful on the day of resurrection" (also Q 20:96). Al-Ṭabarī (*Tafsīr*, viii, 451-2) says with regard to Q 20:96: "A handful (of dust) from the track, which the hoof of the horse of the archangel Gabriel (who came to reveal the Qur'ān to the prophet Muḥammad) had left."

Measures of time

A number of terms are used with the meaning "eternity, unlimited period of time" (for further discussion of measurements of time, see ETERNITY; TIME): *dahr* (twice, in Q 45:24; 76:1), also with the meaning of "fate" (q.v.; see Watt, Dahr); *sarmad* (twice, in Q 28:71-2), meaning "incessant continuance" (see Lane, iv, 1353); *abad,* always in the accusative case, *abadan* (twenty-eight times), fourteen of which are with the meaning of "forever," e.g. Q 64:9: *khālidīna fīhā abadan,* "to abide therein forever." In the remaining places, *abadan* is not a measure of time in the strict sense, because it appears as a negation meaning "never."

In contrast, *amad* denotes a clearly limited period of time (four times, in Q 3:30; 18:12; 57:16; 72:25): "Time, considered with regard to its end" (Lane, i, 95; Ṭabarī, *Tafsīr,* xii, 275, with regard to Q 72:25). Al-Ṭabarī (*Tafsīr,* iii, 231) gives the term a different gloss at each occurrence: he acknowledges with regard to Q 3:30 the interpretation "period of time" as well as "place" *(makān),* meaning an undefined measure of dimension or space. Then, he compares the *amad* of Q 18:12 (Ṭabarī, *Tafsīr,* viii, 187) with *ghāya,* "extreme limit," noting that it can denote both a temporal and a spatial dimension. He knows also the interpretation "number" *('adad)* for *amad.* Moreover, al-Ṭabarī (*Tafsīr,* xi, 682) narrates an opinion about Q 57:16 in which *amad* is synonymous to *dahr* (see above).

Not much more concrete are the synonymous terms *sana* and *'ām,* both meaning "year," because they are used either metaphorically or for the vague description of longer periods of time. *Sana* appears seven times in the singular and twelve in the plural *sinīna; 'ām* appears nine times (see YEAR). Q 2:189 and 10:5 indicate that time-fixing follows the new moon (q.v.). The calculation of the year according to the lunar calendar (in which one year is ca. 354 days) thus has a qur'ānic basis (see CALENDAR). The Qur'ān, however, knows a year longer than the lunar year because it mentions a leap month (Q 9:37, see below; see MONTHS).

This leads us to the next smallest unit of time, *shahr,* "month," of which twelve make one year (Q 9:36). *Shahr* appears twenty-one times, twelve of which are in the singular, twice in the dual, once in the plural *shuhūr,* six in the plural *ashhur.* One month is indicated by its name: Ramaḍān (q.v.; Q 2:185). Sacred months in general (see SACRED AND PROFANE) are mentioned eight times (in Q 2:194, 197, 217; 5:2, 97; 9:2 — here the four months during which one can travel safely in the country, because feuds are forbidden [q.v.]; see also FIGHTING; LAWFUL AND UNLAWFUL; JOURNEY). A travel distance of two months corresponds to the distance that the wind, which was made to serve Solomon (q.v.), covered in one day (Q 34:12; see below at *yawm*).

Shahr is also used metaphorically: "The Night of Power (q.v.) is better than a thousand months" (Q 97:3). When God created the heavens and the earth (see CREATION; COSMOLOGY), he simultaneously created twelve months, four of which are sacred (Q 9:36). Thirty months are the time for a woman to become pregnant and wean her child (Q 46:15; see BIOLOGY AS THE CREATION AND STAGES OF LIFE; WET-NURSING; FOSTERAGE; LACTATION; MILK). Other regulations in connection with the measure of months can be found in Q 4:92 (about fasting [q.v.] for the sake of repentance; see REPENTANCE AND PENANCE),

Q 58:4 (about remarriage; see MARRIAGE AND DIVORCE; LAW AND THE QUR'ĀN), Q 2:226 and 65:4 (about the woman's waiting period [q.v.] after divorce and before remarriage), Q 2:234 (about a widow's [q.v.] waiting period before she may be remarried after her husband's death). If we assume that the Arabs (q.v.) at the time of the revelation followed the lunar calendar (see PRE-ISLAMIC ARABIA AND THE QUR'ĀN), a qur'ānic month has an average duration of around 29.5 days (see De Blois, Ta'rīkh, 258). The length of the leap month, *al-nāsī'*, whose insertion is prohibited (Q 9:37; see CALENDAR; MONTHS; cf. De Blois, Ta'rīkh, 260), is unclear.

The next smallest unit of time is *yawm*, "(an entire) day (between sunset and sunset)." *Layl* and *layla*, "night" (pl. *layālin*), stands for the first half of the twenty-four hour day, *nahār*, "day," for its second half. The times of the day generally denote vaguely defined periods of time (for more details see DAY AND NIGHT; DAY, TIMES OF). For example, two terms describing times of the day signify a short period of time in relation to the (metaphorical) hour of the last judgment (q.v.): *'ashiyya* (late, dark evening) and *ḍuḥā* (forenoon): *ka-annahum yawma yarawnahā lam yalbathū illā 'ashiyyatan aw ḍuḥāhā*, "On the day when they see it, it will be as if they had not tarried more than an evening, or its morning" (only Q 79:46; see MORNING; EVENING).

Two other terms appear in connection with the time or the distance which the wind that was made to serve Solomon covered in one day: *ghuduww* (morning) and *rawāḥ* (evening, or "afternoon [q.v.], from the declining of the sun [q.v.] from the meridian until night"; see Lane, iii, 1182); both terms appear only in Q 34:12: "And to Solomon (we subjected) the wind which blew a month's (journey) in the morning, and a month's (journey) in the evening...." Al-Ṭabarī (*Tafsīr*, x, 353) repeats the opinion that the wind covers in one day the distance that one travels in two months (a distance equal to that between Kābul and an unidentified place).

The smallest unit of time in the Qur'ān is *sā'a*, commonly translated as "hour." *Sā'a* appears forty-eight times. It denotes a period of the day shorter than its second part, *al-nahār;* as in Q 10:45 (cf. Q 46:35): *lam yalbathū illā sā'atan min al-nahār*, "On the day when we round them up as if they had not remained (in the grave; see BURIAL; DEATH AND THE DEAD) an hour of the day." Therefore, it can also be understood as "a time, a (little) while, a space, a period, an indefinite short time" (Lane, iv, 1467).

Stephan Dähne

Bibliography
Primary: 'Abd al-Bāqī; Ibn Kathīr, *Tafsīr;* Ṭabarī, *Tafsīr*, 12 vols., Beirut 1420/1999.
Secondary: E. Ashtor, Mawāzīn, in *EI²*, vi, 118-21; F.C. de Blois, Ta'rīkh, in *EI²*, x, 257-64; W. Hinz, Dhirā', in *EI²*, ii, 231-2; id., *Islamische Masse und Gewichte*, Leiden 1970; Lane; G.C. Miles, Dīnār, in *EI²*, ii, 297-9; id., Dirham, in *EI²*, ii, 319-20; W.M. Watt, Dahr, in *EI²*, ii, 94-5.

Wells

see SPRINGS AND FOUNTAINS

Wet-Nursing

Breastfeeding — voluntary or for payment — of an infant by a woman other than its own mother, or by the latter, following divorce (see MARRIAGE AND DIVORCE). *Murḍi'a* (pl. *marāḍi'*) in the Qur'ān denotes in general "suckling female" (Q 22:2, Bell; "nursing mother," Pickthall) and, more specifically, a "foster-mother" (Q 28:12, Arberry) or a "wet-nurse." In Q 65:6 the root *r-ḍ-'* in the fourth form describes the act of wet-nursing, and in Q 2:233 the tenth form of this root denotes "seeking, or demanding, a wet-nurse" (see Lane, 1097). The term *ẓiʾr,* "one that inclines to, or affects, the young one of another, and suckles or fosters it" (Lane, 1907-8), which became very common in Islamic legal and medical writings from the classical through the medieval periods (Giladi, *Infants,* esp. 106-14), was in use already in early qurʾānic exegesis (Muqātil, *Tafsīr,* ad Q 2:233) but has no qurʾānic roots (see LAW AND THE QURʾĀN; MEDICINE AND THE QURʾĀN).

Inasmuch as it assumes a connection between a nurse's blood and her own milk, Q 4:23 makes ties created by suckling similar to ties of blood kinship (q.v.; see also BLOOD AND BLOOD CLOT) and therefore explicitly forbids sexual relations (see SEX AND SEXUALITY; PROHIBITED DEGREES) between men and their (non-biological) milk-mother(s) and milk-sister(s). In ḥadīth (see ḤADĪTH AND THE QURʾĀN) and *fiqh* writings these impediments were gradually widened to include the nurse's husband and his relatives — a development based on the idea that the nurse's milk is created by the man who made her pregnant (Benkheira, Donner le sein, 5-52).

Q 28:12 furthermore points out that infants sometimes reject the milk of women other than their own mothers (see LACTATION; FOSTERAGE). The Qurʾān, however, sanctions in principle (in the specific context of divorce) mercenary nursing of an infant either by its divorced mother or, if the divorced parents "find mutual difficulties" (Q 65:6), i.e. disagree on the fee, by "some other woman" (see also Q 2:233). Both verses (as well as Q 65:7) encourage men to be both fair and even generous towards women hired to nurse their own infants (and see e.g. Muqātil, *Tafsīr,* ad Q 65:6-7).

The Qurʾān itself gives almost no hint about actual wet-nursing practices in seventh century Arabia or neighboring areas — e.g. in which circumstances they were applied, how popular they were, how gender (q.v.) relations within the nursling's family and that of its wet-nurse both affected and were affected by these practices, what the common criteria were for selecting wet-nurses and the physical and moral demands with which these women had to comply, etc. (see PRE-ISLAMIC ARABIA AND THE QURʾĀN). Suggestions, e.g. that it was the accepted custom to send a child to foster-parents in Mecca (q.v.) but not in Medina (q.v.; Stern, *Marriage,* 96), are based on the interpretation of post-qurʾānic sources and are, in any case, debatable (see Benkheira, Le commerce, 3-6). From later exegetical and legal writings, however, one gleans that in the Islamic classical and medieval periods wet-nursing was practiced in vast areas of the Muslim world.

Muslim scholars who interpreted Q 2:233 as pertaining to parents (q.v.) in general (see e.g. Jaṣṣāṣ, *Aḥkām, bāb al-raḍāʿ;* Rāzī, *Tafsīr,* ad Q 2:233), distilled from this verse a great number of rules (see LACTATION; Giladi, *Infants,* 53-6, 106-14). As they clearly viewed breastfeeding as a maternal instinct and the preferable way of feeding infants (see LACTATION; MILK), Muslim scholars generally regarded it as a natural right of the mother (see e.g. Ṭabarī, *Tafsīr,* ad Q 2:233 and 65:6; Jaṣṣāṣ, *Aḥkām, bāb al-raḍāʿ*) but often insisted that no mother could be forced to suckle her baby unless the nursling's health would otherwise be endangered (see e.g. Ṭabarī, *Tafsīr;* Zamakhsharī, *Tafsīr;* Rāzī, *Tafsīr,* ad Q 2:233). Wet-nursing is a legitimate option when the mother is unable or refuses to breastfeed. In these and similar circumstances (specified e.g. in Ṭabarī, *Tafsīr* and Rāzī, *Tafsīr,* ad Q 2:233; see also Ibn al-ʿArabī, *Aḥkām,* ad Q 2:233), it is the father's duty to look for a wet-nurse and pay for her services (Muqātil, *Tafsīr,* ad Q 2:233; Jaṣṣāṣ, *Aḥkām, bāb al-raḍāʿ;* Rāzī, *Tafsīr,* ad

Q 2:233; see MAINTENANCE AND UPKEEP; CHILDREN). In the same context such other questions are discussed, as the father's duty versus his economic ability (see e.g. Ṭabarī, *Tafsīr,* ad Q 2:233), the hiring of a woman by her own husband to breast-feed their infant (see e.g. Zamakhsharī, *Tafsīr,* ad Q 65:6), the duties of the wet-nurse, both concerning her own way of life and health (see Benkheira, Le commerce; Giladi, *Infants,* 53-6, 106-14) as well as the proper treatment she should extend to the infant and other legal aspects of the hire agreement (see e.g. Ibn Qudāma, *al-Mughnī,* vi, 73-5; on the detailed chapter in al-Sarakhsī's *al-Mabsūṭ* in this regard, see Shatzmiller, *Women and wage,* 182-8; Giladi, *Infants,* 106-14). The core of the Islamic attitude towards wet-nursing is perhaps best characterized by the insistence of legal-moral authorities to try if at all possible not to separate nurslings from their mothers (see e.g. Jaṣṣāṣ, *Aḥkām, bāb al-raḍāʿ,* passim).

Avner Giladi

Bibliography
Primary: Ibn al-ʿArabī, *Aḥkām;* Ibn Qudāma, ʿAbdallāh b. Aḥmad b. Muḥammad, *al-Mughnī,* Beirut 1972; Jaṣṣāṣ, *Aḥkām;* Muqātil, *Tafsīr;* Rāzī, *Tafsīr;* Ṭabarī, *Tafsīr;* Zamakhsharī, *Tafsīr.*
Secondary: Arberry; Bell, *Qurʾān;* M.H. Benkheira, Le commerce conjugal gâte-t-il le lait maternel? Sexualité, médecine et droit dans le sunnisme ancien, in *Arabica* 50 (2003), 1-78; id., Donner le sein c'est comme donner le jour. La doctrine de l'allaitement dans le sunnisme médiéval, in *SI* 92 (2001), 5-52; A. Giladi, *Infants, parents and wet nurses. Medieval Islamic views on breastfeeding and their social implications,* Leiden 1999; Lane; M. Omidsalar and Th. Omidsalar, Dāya, in E. Yarshater (ed.), *Encyclopaedia Iranica,* London 1983-, vii, 164-6; Pickthall, *Koran;* M. Shatzmiller, Women and wage labour in the medieval Islamic west, in *JESHO* 40 (1997), 174-206; G. Stern, *Marriage in early Islam,* London 1939.

Wheat
see GRASSES; AGRICULTURE AND VEGETATION

Whip
see FLOGGING

Whisper

Barely audible speech or sound, often with sibilance. The Qurʾān is a text to be heard *(samʿ)* more than to be read and within the text there are many allusions to aurality and its different degrees (see BOOK; RECITATION OF THE QURʾĀN; ORALITY; ORALITY AND WRITING IN ARABIA). In the most common qurʾānic scenario one hears a noise without discerning its source. This is the meaning of *ḥasīs* in Q 21:102. Those who will escape the tortures of hell (*jahannam;* see HELL AND HELLFIRE; REWARD AND PUNISHMENT) on the day of promise *(waʿd)* will be saved by discerning (aurally) the presence of the brazier near them. They will thus escape the terror (initially not visible) which will grip the damned.

The auditory contents can be positive but also entirely negative. A positive inspiration *(waḥī),* perceived as a distant and persistent noise like a roll of thunder, is contrasted to a category of very different noises (see REVELATION AND INSPIRATION). These are unexpected, furtive, worrying sounds which take one's hearing unawares. Even before Islam, they were to be classed as negatively supernatural. These collective obsessions are linked to a parallel world, conceived as dangerous, of jinn (q.v.) and desert beings (Wellhausen, *Reste,* 148-59; Eichler, *Die Dschinn,* 8-39; Niekrens, *Die Engel,* 65-7; see SPIRITUAL BEINGS). In the Qurʾān the collective representations of the jinn conclude by coalescing into the extremely negative form of *shayṭān,* the devil (q.v.). As for people who give themselves over to secret intrigues and assemblies, they, too, will be seen as participating in a jinn-like and diabolical activity. The Qurʾān therefore uses a largely recycled terminology ("une terminologie largement de remploi") relating to earlier usages which seem to be hardly changed.

The following roots link directly with the jinn and the diabolical world: *w-s-w-s,* from the connotation of a light, intermittent wind sound (see AIR AND WIND), the concealed approach of hunters laying an ambush (see HUNTING AND FISHING), or the muted jingling of jewelry worn by a woman, shifts to the confused and pernicious murmurs of Q 114:4-5. With a form of conspiracy, a jinn-like murmurer, *waswās,* passes furtively *(khannās)* after implanting an evil proposition in the breasts (the center of understanding; see HEART; KNOWLEDGE AND LEARNING; INTELLECT) of people *(nās).* But God, whom nothing escapes, as the Qurʾān emphasizes constantly, is there to oppose this. In the later passages of Q 7:20 and 20:120, the association of *w-s-w-s* with the devil, *shayṭān,* becomes explicit (cf. Ṭabarī, *Tafsīr,* ed. Shākir, xii, 346-7, ad Q 7:20, *fa-waswasa lahumā*).

The concealed whisper is negative, as in Q 20:108 (*hams,* the murmur), with respect to the damned (in this context, Q 20:108 must be read in conjunction with the preceding verses, esp. Q 20:103; cf. Ṭabarī, *Tafsīr,* ed. ʿAlī, xvi, 214, ad Q 20:103, *yatakhāfatūna baynahum*). Connected to the sphere of the secret word (*sirr;* see SECRETS) it is opposed to *jahr,* the word spoken clearly to be heard by everyone. But God knows both (i.e. Q 67:13). The *rikz,* however, the voice heard from so far away as to be almost imperceptible, is linked in a more neutral way to the very rich terminology of hearing in the desert world. In this environment one must listen constantly and alertly to protect oneself from danger. Q 19:98 indicates that one does not hear the least murmur *(rikz)* of the people in the past whom God destroyed (cf. Ṭabarī, *Tafsīr,* ed. ʿAlī, xvi, 134; see PUNISHMENT STORIES; GENERATIONS; GEOGRAPHY). It is a way of saying that no survivor has remained of them.

The theme of a hostile secret assembly looms large in qurʾānic discourse. It concerns both people and the devil simultaneously. The *takhāfut bayna,* a precise expression that designates the transferring of secrets, and so of offering a word that divides rather than unifies, occurs only twice, both in entirely negative contexts: Q 20:103, the damned who whisper, thinking they are not heard by God, and think they can escape punishment, and Q 68:23, the futile secret assembly of two greedy men whose plans God frustrates.

The terminology that conveys notions of dissimulation (q.v.; *katama, asarra* versus *aʿlana, jahara*) occurs most frequently. A commonly found meaning is that of voluntarily suppressing the truth, *katm al-ḥaqq,* and is applied often to the adversaries of Muḥammad in Medina (q.v.; i.e. Q 2:159; 21:110). The secret word (v. *asarra,* n. *sirr*) among men, against God, or that which is concealed by the individual (a thought formed in secret) — is in the same category (see also HIDDEN AND THE HIDDEN). But *sirr* and its cognates also has a wider meaning, both in Meccan and Medinan sūras (q.v.; Q 2:77; 16:19, etc.; see also CHRONOLOGY AND THE QURʾĀN). These words or secret thoughts cannot escape God (Q 64:4). More rarely one meets *ajwā, tanājī, najwā* (to speak into someone's ear in order to weave a plot, often in association with *asarra, sirr,* cf. Q 17:47; 20:62; 21:3). As for the terms linked to ruse and the intent to deceive *(makr, kayd, khadʿ, ibrām),* they refer to the whole process of deceit (see MAGIC) and leading astray (*ḍalāl, taḍlīl;* see ERROR; ASTRAY). The devil, *shayṭān,* is associated with deceit but also with divinity; he has the same supreme power of deceiving any enemy, human or demon (Q 86:16; 13:42), and of foiling the most cunning plots hatched against him (e.g. Q 52:42; 4:76).

Jacqueline Chabbi

Bibliography
Primary: Ibn Abī l-Dunya, Abū Bakr ʿAbdallāh b. Muḥammad, *Kitāb al-Hawātif,* ed. M.S. Ibrāhīm, Cairo 1988 (61-71 on the exclamations or shouts and calls of the jinn); id., *Makāyid al-shayṭān,* ed. M.S. Ibrāhīm, Cairo 1991; Ṭabarī, *Tafsīr,* ed. Shākir; ed. ʿAlī.
Secondary: G. Calasso, Note su *waswasa,* 'sussurrare', nel Corano e nei *hadit,* in *Annali Istituto Orientale di Napoli* (n.s.) 23 (1973), 233-46; P.A. Eichler, *Die Dschinn, Teufel und Engel im Koran,* PhD diss., Leipzig 1928; W. Eickmann, *Die Angelologie und Dämonologie des Korans im Vergleich zu der Engel- und Geisterlehre der Heiligen Schrift,* New York/Leipzig 1908; W. Niekrens, *Die Engel- und Geistervorstellungen des Korans,* PhD diss., Rostock 1906; J. Wellhausen, *Reste arabischen Hiedentums,* Berlin 1887, 1897².

White see COLORS; WEEPING; EYES

Wicked see GOOD AND EVIL

Widow

A woman whose husband has died. The Qurʾān speaks of the widow by addressing the male believers in Q 2:234-5 (see BELIEF AND UNBELIEF), who die leaving behind wives *(yadharūna azwājan).* The term itself has no Arabic equivalent in the Qurʾān though it is implied in the status of the *thayyibāt* in Q 66:5, which refers to any woman who is not a virgin (see CHASTITY; ABSTINENCE), a woman who has had sexual intercourse (see SEX AND SEXUALITY) either as a previously married woman, a divorced woman (see MARRIAGE AND DIVORCE) or a widow. In this particular verse, the wives of the Prophet (q.v.) are admonished for their jealousies and told that they could be replaced by other women (see WOMEN AND THE QURʾĀN). There follows a long list of desirable virtues (see VIRTUE; VIRTUES AND VICES, COMMANDING AND FORBIDDING) with the words *thayyibātin* and *abkāran,* virgins, at the end of the verse. The juxtaposition of the two words signifies that these qualities could belong to both sorts of women, "the women who are deflowered and whose virginity has gone and the virgins" (Ṭabarī, *Tafsīr,* ad loc.).

The first reference to the specific status of the widow is made in the context of verses pertaining to marriage and divorce. Inasmuch as every dissolution of a marriage that has been consummated, or even where there has been a presumption of consummation, requires the wife to observe a waiting period *(ʿidda),* so it is for the widow. The Qurʾān states specifically four months and ten days as the widow's *ʿidda.* This is longer than the *ʿidda* for the divorced woman, which is three menstrual cycles (Q 2:228; see MENSTRUATION). The primary legal concern (see LAW AND THE QURʾĀN) in the case of both the widow and the divorced woman is to ascertain whether or not the woman is pregnant with her husband's child (see CHILDREN). In such cases, the widow should not remarry until she has given birth (q.v.) to the child. Once she has given birth, she is free to remarry and the full period of *ʿidda* need not be observed (see WAITING PERIOD).

In the case of the widow, the time of *ʿidda* is longer, as it is also a time of mourning for the deceased husband (see BURIAL; DEATH AND THE DEAD). There is, however, no indication in the Qurʾān that the woman's position as a widow should be seen as either a social stigma or a disadvantage to her. Widowhood is understood to be a temporary situation. Q 2:235 speaks immediately to those men who would wish to ask for the widow's hand in marriage. It is appropriate that they do so openly and not in secret once the woman has observed her period of *ʿidda.*

Q 2:240 explains what men should bequeath to their widows in terms of financial and residential support (see INHERITANCE; MAINTENANCE AND UPKEEP). A widow should be entitled to a year's maintenance and full residence in the husband's home. If, however, she herself chooses to leave the home, she is entitled to do so. Q 4:12 refers to inheritance rights in which the widow is entitled to a quarter of her husband's property (q.v.) if he leaves no children and an eighth if he leaves children.

In the legal discussions on *mahr* (dower paid to the wife on marriage; see BRIDEWEALTH), widowhood is one of the three situations, along with consummation and divorce, which confirms the payment of the full *mahr* to the wife. Even if the husband dies before the marriage has been consummated, the widow is entitled to the full *mahr* because "by the death of the husband, the marriage is rendered complete. For everything becomes established and confirmed by its completion, and becomes established with respect to all its effects" (Marghinānī, *Hidāya,* i, 204).

Mona Siddiqui

Bibliography
Primary: al-Marghinānī, Abū l-Ḥasan ʿAlī b. Abī Bakr, *al-Hidāya sharḥ bidāyat al-mubtadiʾ*, 4 vols., Cairo 1908-9, i, 204; Ṭabarī, *Tafsīr.*
Secondary: J.I. Smith and Y.Y. Haddad, Eve. Islamic image of woman, in *Women's Studies international forum* 5 (1982), 135-44; G. Stern, *Marriage in early Islam,* London 1939; B. Stowasser, *Women in the Quran, tradition and interpretation,* New York 1994; A. Wadud-Muhsin, *Qurʾān and woman,* Kuala Lumpur 1992.

Wife see MARRIAGE AND DIVORCE

Will see FREEDOM AND PREDESTINATION; INHERITANCE

Wind see AIR AND WIND

Wine

Intoxicating beverage made from fermented grapes or other substances. The most common word for wine in the Qurʾān is *khamr,* a term prevalent in early Arabic poetry, although the Arabs of the peninsula customarily drank *nabīdh,* a fermented beverage made, for example, from barley, honey, spelt or different kinds of palms. While the climate and geography of much of "Arabia" is not suitable for wine production, parts of the Yemen, as well as areas such as Medina and Ṭāʾif, would have had the necessary conditions for the cultivation of grapes. Wine was also imported from Syria and Iraq, particularly through the agency of the Jewish and Christian communities in the peninsula (the Arabic *khamr* may derive from the Syro-Aramaic *ḥamrā*).

The qurʾānic *khamr* marks both earthly and paradisiacal vintages (see FOOD AND DRINK; PARADISE). Unlike later Islamic exegetes (see EXEGESIS OF THE QURʾĀN: CLASSICAL AND MEDIEVAL), who privileged a limited set of wine references to support its strict prohibition, the Qurʾān expresses a highly nuanced and largely ambivalent attitude towards this beverage and its effects (see INTOXICANTS; LAW AND THE QURʾĀN). *Khamr* is linked with gambling (q.v.) and identified as a source of both sin and profit (Q 2:219; see SIN, MAJOR AND MINOR), with gambling, idol worship (see IDOLS AND IMAGES; POLYTHEISM AND ATHEISM) and divination (q.v.) arrows, and labeled an abomination (Q 5:90-1). Joseph's dreams (see DREAMS AND SLEEP) in prison feature *khamr* (Q 12:36, 41), and dwellers of paradise delight in rivers of wine (Q 47:15; see McAuliffe, Wines). In addition to *khamr, sakar* appears as an inimical earthly intoxicant (cf. Q 4:43) that undermines prayer (q.v.) but also serves as a divine gift (Q 16:66-9; see GIFT AND GIFT-GIVING), a sign (*āya;* see SIGNS) for those who understand (see INTELLECT; KNOWLEDGE AND LEARNING). Also mentioned is *raḥīq,* the purest, most excellent of heavenly wines (Q 83:25) and a celestial goblet (see CUPS AND VESSELS) with liquid from a pure spring *(maʿīn)* mirroring its earthly counterpart in every way but its ability to intoxicate (Q 37:45; 56:18-19). Throughout the shorter sūras (q.v.) of the Qurʾān, a chaotic, intoxicated madness that marks the day of judgment (see LAST JUDGMENT) contrasts sharply with the tranquil, perfected garden of repose (see GARDENS), where righteous ones imbibe as much wine as they please without the drunken effects. This tension between the real and the ideal may also account for the Qurʾān's sober portrayals of Noah (q.v.) and Lot (q.v.), men all too familiar with the pleasures of the vine in their Jewish and Christian contexts (see JEWS AND JUDAISM; CHRISTIANS AND CHRISTIANITY) but pillars of abstinence (q.v.) in the Islamic revelation (see REVELATION AND INSPIRATION; SCRIPTURE AND THE QURʾĀN), where their actions must match the integrity of the message they bear. Even servants of God (see SERVANT; WORSHIP) may fall prey to wine's earthly enticements. The Qurʾān's ambivalent treatment of wine was resolved by early exegetes, who determined the historical "occasion" upon which God revealed each wine passage (see OCCASIONS OF REVELATION). By examining such passages sequentially, qurʾānic commentators noted a gradual diminution in tolerance toward wine consumption (see ABROGATION; FORBIDDEN; LAWFUL AND UNLAWFUL). Al-Ṭabarī (d. 310/923; *Tafsīr,* v, 58) records how God allowed humans to enjoy his gift until they proved incapable of drinking responsibly. After a series of such atrocities, like the Prophet's uncle mutilating ʿAlī's camel in a fit of drunkenness, God finally prohibited wine. While both Sunnī and Shīʿī schools of law assert the prohibition of wine (a position that critiques the pre-Islamic, libertine position; see AGE OF IGNORANCE; PRE-ISLAMIC ARABIA AND THE QURʾĀN), dissensions over what constitutes "wine," or whether the substance itself or only its effects are prohibited, can be detected in legal discussions surrounding this beverage. The Ḥanafīs, for example, note that since the Qurʾān only condemns *khamr,* the prohibition of *khamr* should not extend to other alcoholic beverages. Contrary to this view, the majority opinion emphasizes a drink's potential to intoxicate over and above its composition and forbids intake of any amount of liquid if it causes (or may potentially cause) one to become drunk. The law extends well beyond mere consumption to include the production and sale of alcoholic beverages under penalty of punishment (see BOUNDARIES AND PRECEPTS; CHASTISEMENT AND PUNISHMENT). Despite its prohibition, wine becomes a favorite metaphor of mystics (see ṢŪFISM AND THE QURʾĀN), who exploit the Qurʾān's ambivalence towards this potent substance to confuse the boundaries that separate sobriety from intoxication, licit from illicit, human from divine and, ultimately, real from ideal.

Kathryn Kueny

Bibliography
Primary: Ibn Qutayba, Abū Muḥammad ʿAbdallāh b. Muslim al-Dīnawarī, *Ashriba,* ed. Y.M. al-Sawwās, Beirut 1998; Rāzī, *Tafsīr;* Ṭabarī, *Tafsīr,* ed. Shākir.
Secondary: A.J. Arberry, *The mystical poems of Ibn al-Fāriḍ,* Dublin 1956; Goldziher, *MS;* R.S.

Hattox, *Coffee and coffeehouses,* Seattle 1985; P. Heine, Nabīdh, in *EI²*, vii, 840; K.M. Kueny, *The rhetoric of sobriety. Wine in early Islam,* Albany 2001; J.D. McAuliffe, The wines of earth and paradise. Qurʾānic proscriptions and promises, in R.M. Savory and D.A. Agius (eds.), *Logos islamikos. Studia islamica in honorem Georgii Michaelis Wickens,* Toronto 1984, 159-74; F. Rosenthal, *Gambling in Islam,* Leiden 1975; A.J. Wensinck and J. Sadan, Khamr, in *EI²*, iv, 994-7.

Winter see SEASONS

Wisdom

Ability to understand deeply and judge soundly. God is wise *(ḥakīm).* He is, however, never described by this characteristic alone, but always in conjunction with another characteristic. *Ḥakīm* is most frequently connected with *ʿazīz,* "almighty" (forty-seven times; see POWER AND IMPOTENCE), and almost as frequently is God described as *ḥakīm* and *ʿalīm,* "omniscient" (thirty-six times; see KNOWLEDGE AND LEARNING; INTELLECT). *Ḥakīm* with *khabīr,* "knowing," is rare (three times) and even rarer are the occurrences of *ḥakīm* with "forgiving" *(tawwāb),* "all-embracing" *(wāsiʿ),* "praiseworthy" *(ḥamīd),* and "exalted" (*ʿalī;* see GOD AND HIS ATTRIBUTES).

God possesses wisdom *(ḥikma),* which he can give "to whom he wishes" (Q 2:269), mainly to the prophets (see PROPHETS AND PROPHETHOOD; MESSENGER): Abraham (q.v.) and his family (Q 4:54), David (q.v.; Q 2:251; 38:20), Jesus (q.v.; e.g. Q 5:110; 43:63) and Muḥammad (Q 4:113), but also to Luqmān (q.v.; Q 31:12). Wisdom is a revelation (e.g. *awḥā,* Q 17:39; see REVELATION AND INSPIRATION) and the Qurʾān is also "wise" (*al-Qurʾān al-ḥakīm,* Q 36:2; see NAMES OF THE QURʾĀN), for wisdom stands on an equal footing with scripture (*kitāb;* see BOOK; SCRIPTURE AND THE QURʾĀN), including the Torah (q.v.) and the Gospel (q.v.; Q 3:48; 5:110). God teaches scripture and wisdom (e.g. Q 3:48; see TEACHING): he sends down scripture and wisdom (Q 2:231). It remains unclear whether in such collocations "wisdom" means another holy scripture or is a summative reference to the contents of those holy books just mentioned. The task of the messenger or prophet is to deliver the scriptures together with wisdom to the people (cf. Q 2:151; 43:63), or to recite the scripture and wisdom to the people (cf. e.g. Q 33:34; 62:2; see RECITATION OF THE QURʾĀN; ORALITY AND WRITING IN ARABIA). Qurʾān commentators understand *ḥikma* as knowing and understanding the Qurʾān, or as understanding and reflecting on the religion, or even as fear (q.v.) of God (godliness, devoutness, piety [q.v.]; *khaysha, waraʿ,* Ṭabarī, *Tafsīr,* iii, 60f.; Qurṭubī, *Jāmiʿ,* iii, 330; Ibn Kathīr, *Tafsīr,* i, 571f.).

God is the omnipotent, omniscient creator of the world (q.v.; see also CREATION; COSMOLOGY), in which the wisdom of God reveals itself, the recognition of which is the task of the wise. *Ḥikma,* as human wisdom, is understood in two ways. First, Greek philosophy *(falsafa),* natural science and medicine in its Arabic-Islamic form are *ḥikma.* Thus the biographical lexicons for philosophers, natural scientists, physicians, etc. are called *taʾrīkh al-ḥukamāʾ* — for example, Ibn al-Qifṭī's (d. 646/1248) *Taʾrīkh al-ḥukamāʾ;* additionally, accounts and collected works are called *ṣiwān al-ḥikma* (e.g. al-Bayhaqī's *Tatimmat ṣiwān al-ḥikma;* see SCHOLARS; SCIENCE AND THE QURʾĀN; MEDICINE AND THE QURʾĀN; PHILOSOPHY AND THE QURʾĀN).

In devout-mystic circles, *ḥikma* is wisdom delivered through the pronouncements of wise men *(ḥukamāʾ)* mostly anonymously: edifying, devout and mystic aphorisms. In this context, in the third/ninth century, *ḥikma* becomes mystical wisdom and also theosophy (see ṢŪFISM AND THE QURʾĀN). Of this, the best example is the east Iranian mystic al-Ḥakīm al-Tirmidhī (who died between 318/936 and 320/938). For him, *ḥikma* is the mystic knowledge of the soul (q.v.) and the world. A further step was the syncretic mingling of the more mystical *ḥikma* — theosophy — with Greek philosophy and non-Islamic religious concepts. This occurred in the systems of Suhrawardī (d. 587/1191) and Ibn al-ʿArabī (d. 638/1240).

Lastly, for the gloss of *al-ḥikma* (in *al-kitāb wa-l-ḥikma* of e.g. Q 2:129) as *sunnat al-nabī,* see SUNNA.

Bernd Radtke

Bibliography
D. Gimaret, *Les noms divins en Islam,* Paris 1988, 99, 271-2; A.M. Goichon, Ḥikma, in *EI²*, iii, 377-8; B. Radtke, Theosophie (Ḥikma) und Philosophie (Falsafa). Ein Beitrag zur Frage der *ḥikmat al-mašriq/al-išrāq,* in *Asiatische Studien* 42 (1988), 156-74.

Wish and Desire

The act of hoping for or wanting something and the object of that act. There are three main agencies through which wish and desire are exercised in the Qurʾān: one is divine, another human, and the third satanic (see DEVIL). The manifestations and the interplay of the three create an ethical tension (see ETHICS AND THE QURʾĀN) that evokes questions of accountability, responsibility (q.v.) and justice (see JUSTICE AND INJUSTICE). In that sense, wish and desire become the principles whereby the subject and the object are placed into a value-laden relationship. Be it an act of God, Satan, or the human being, wish and desire are a function of the subject's awareness and expectations of the object. Among the three, God's wishes are mentioned most frequently. The phrase "God willing" *(in shāʾa llāh)* is both common and varied, indicating that God's wishes are exercised at both cosmic and everyday levels (see COSMOLOGY). Like many other passages, Q 5:17 affirms that it was through God's wish/will that the world came into being *(yakhluqu mā yashāʾu)* in such a way that associates his wishing with his infinite power (*wa-Allāh ʿalā kulli shayʾin qadīrun;* see POWER AND IMPOTENCE; FREEDOM AND PREDESTINATION). As divine wish is inextricably linked with divine omnipotence, it is continuously carried out within and beyond worldly limits (see WORLD). No wonder then that the verb *shāʾa* and its derivatives appear over 500 times in the Qurʾān, mainly in reference to God.

Although at first glance God's wishes appear volatile and unpredictable, the Qurʾān ascertains that their function and purpose can be appreciated only after the human mind accepts its own limitations (see INTELLECT; KNOWLEDGE AND LEARNING). In Q 18:23-4, the Qurʾān warns: "And do not say anything like 'I will surely do this tomorrow.' Unless God wishes, and remember your lord (q.v.) when you forget (see REMEMBRANCE; MEMORY) and say, 'Maybe my lord will guide me (see ASTRAY) to a nearer way to truth (q.v.) than this.'" Historically understood as a response to Muḥammad's negligence when he answered a Qurayshī inquirer (see QURAYSH) with inappropriate self-confidence — "Come tomorrow and I will surely give you an answer" but without adding the phrase *in shāʾa llāh* — this verse was ostensibly intended to highlight the unpredictability of divine volition even in the context of Muḥammad's own prophetic mission (see PROPHETS AND PROPHETHOOD). Reflecting upon this essential dependability on, yet inaccessibility to, divine wishes, classical Muslim exegetes (see EXEGESIS OF THE QURʾĀN: CLASSICAL AND MEDIEVAL) interpret the ubiquitous *in shāʾa llāh* phrase in relation to their theological positions on free will and predetermination. Al-Rāzī (d. 606/1210), for example, develops a lengthy argument by contrasting the Muʿtazilī (see MUʿTAZILA) and his own Ashʿarī positions and concludes that: one, we can never be sure that we will/can do anything until God gives us permission; and, two, we should never anticipate future events because, if they prove to be different, we will be deemed liars (see LIE; FORETELLING; THEOLOGY AND THE QURʾĀN). He charges the Muʿtazila with transferring the agency of wishes and desire to human beings rather than leaving it with its divine source. When God asks for belief (see BELIEF AND UNBELIEF) and obedience (q.v.) and his servants disobey (see DISOBEDIENCE), al-Rāzī continues, God's wishes are not fulfilled. In contrast, he holds that everything that God wills must happen: for example, if a man says, "Tomorrow I will return the debt I owe, if God wills," and if he fails to do it, he cannot be blamed because this was clearly God's wish and we can either understand it or not. He contrasts this interpretation with that of the Muʿtazila, according to which it is the man who is to blame if the debt is not returned because man's evil nature (see GOOD AND EVIL; FALL OF MAN) prevents him from doing what he has promised (Rāzī, *Tafsīr*). Al-Rāzī's interpretation poignantly relates to Q 81:27-9 which says, "This is surely a reminder to all human beings *(lil-ʿālamīna),* and those among them who wish to change their ways *(an yastaqīma);* you cannot wish but what God, the lord of all worlds, wishes" (the wording almost identical to Q 76:29-30).

In addition to *shāʾa,* God's wishes are also expressed through the verb *arāda.* Although often used synonymously with *shāʾa, arāda* evokes more strongly divine intentionality, as in Q 2:26: "What does God intend/mean *(mādhā arāda)* by this parable (q.v.)?" Reflecting thus with divine deliberation, *arāda* attempts to lay out the inner workings of the divine order in the implementation of God's desires, as per Q 16:40: "Truly, when we refer to a thing, if we want it to be *(idhā aradnāhu),* we just tell it 'Be!' and it is." God does not desire without a purpose but the speculations of what that purpose might be yields different theological possibilities.

While continuously attesting to the power of divine desire, both *shāʾa* and *arāda* place human beings in a direct and dynamic relationship with it. But the nature of that relationship is far from simple. In fact, its complexity has created a theological conundrum and the rise of several scholastic positions on the questions of free will and predestination. Can human beings act on their own wishes and desires? Do these desires predate them in accordance with the divine plan? Notwithstanding the theological and political implications of such questions in Islamic history, it is clear that the Qurʾān keeps the tension among different possibilities alive, placing divine and human wishes simultaneously in harmony and conflict, and perpetuating sharp ethical differentiations between the wishes and desires of believers and those of nonbelievers. There are no simple answers in the Qurʾān or in the later intellectual tradition, even though the message seems rather straightforward, as Q 6:125 states (similarly, in Q 5:41; 6:17, 125; 7:176; 10:107; etc.): "Whomever God wishes to guide, he opens his heart (q.v.) to Islam; whomever God wishes to lead astray, he restricts his heart, as if he is rising to heaven (see HEAVEN AND SKY). This is how God inflicts punishment (see CHASTISEMENT AND PUNISHMENT) on those who do not believe."

In this sense, because the relational function of divine desire necessitates reciprocity, many qurʾānic passages posit human beings not only as objects of God's wishes and intentions but as subjects/agents exercising their own desires. It is here that the Qurʾān draws a sharp distinction between believers and nonbelievers. Believers surrender to God's wishes and, in turn, become conscious of, and act on, their desires for divine grace (q.v.) and mercy (q.v.). Nonbelievers, on the other hand, reject God and direct their desires elsewhere, for which they become eternally condemned, as in Q 18:29, "Say, The truth comes from your lord; whoever so wishes, let them believe; whoever wishes, let them disbelieve," upon which the Qurʾān details the difference in the outcome of the two choices for the condition in the hereafter (Q 18:30-44; see ESCHATOLOGY; REWARD AND PUNISHMENT). Human desire directly reflects both one's knowledge of God and one's system of belief (see FAITH; RELIGION). Those who lived in the pre-Islamic Age of Ignorance (q.v.; *jāhiliyya*) are accused not only of their ignorance (q.v.) of the creator (see CREATION) but of the stubborn, blinding urge to fulfill their desire for material and visible goods (see WEALTH; INSOLENCE AND OBSTINACY): "There is only our life in the present world; we die (see DEATH AND THE DEAD), we live (see LIFE), and only fate (q.v.)/time (q.v.; *al-dahr*) destroys us" (Q 45:24). The pursuit of this-worldly desires is a pursuit for self-realization that reflects the pre-Islamic teaching that all sensations and experiences belong to the physical world only, in contrast to the qurʾānic cosmos in which the greatest self-fulfillment comes in the hereafter, as worded in Q 87:16-17: "No, you prefer the life of this world; whereas the hereafter is superior and lasting" (see TRANSIENCE; ETERNITY). Human desires are thus bifurcated into those that are low and worldly, characteristic of a conduct inspired by one's whims and fancies (*ahwāʾ* [sing. *hawā*], appearing numerous times, e.g. Q 3:14; 18:28; 20:16; 25:43; 28:50; 42:15; 45:18), and those that are ethically sound and inspire to behave and do one's duty as a servant (q.v.) of God. An example of this distinction is those incidents at the early stages of Muḥammad's career when pagan Arabs hurled accusations at him and the Qurʾān responded (Q 53:2-3): "No, your companion has not strayed away nor has he erred, and he does not speak on a whim (*mā yanṭiqu ʿani l-hawā;* see OPPOSITION TO MUḤAMMAD; PRE-ISLAMIC ARABIA AND THE QURʾĀN)."

In addition to the ethics of desire-driven behavior, the issue of human wishes and yearning acquires another interpretative trajectory, associated with the Ṣūfī worldview (see ṢŪFISM AND THE QURʾĀN). For the Ṣūfīs, a *ḥadīth qudsī* (see ḤADĪTH AND THE QURʾĀN) exemplifies the principle of the relationship between God and human beings: "I was a hidden treasure and I longed to be known, so I created the world." The desire for self-reflection is believed to inspire the very act of creation. Focusing on the language of love (q.v.) and yearning that permeates much of the Qurʾān (e.g. Q 2:165, 195; 49:9; 57:19, 23; 60:1, 8; etc.), the mystics define desire as a spiritual propeller that allows the wayfarer (see JOURNEY) to achieve closeness with God. The wayfarer is often referred to as the *murīd* — the active participle form of *arāda* — in accordance with the aforementioned double-entendre of *arāda,* to want and to intend. The desire for God is personalized as both affection and primordial yearning for beatific vision (see FACE OF GOD), in accordance with not only the *ḥadīth qudsī* mentioned above, but also with the qurʾānic phrase *ibtighāʾa wajhi llāh,* "out of yearning for God's face," that appears in Q 2:272, 6:52 and 92:20. After all, it is only God's face that lasts forever while everything else perishes (Q 28:88). Desiring it (both *arāda* and *ibtaghā* are used in the Qur'ān) is therefore the only ultimate kind of desire and yearning a believer can have in this self-reflective genesis of creation.

Finally, in the ethical triangle of wishing/desiring, Satan's role in splitting humankind into believers and nonbelievers is instrumental: *wa-yurīdu l-shayṭānu an yuḍillahum ḍalālan baʿīdan* (Q 4:60; see PARTIES AND FACTIONS; ENEMIES). The Qur'ān repeatedly mentions Satan's desire to confuse and lead humankind astray as a vindictive reaction against his expulsion from heaven. Satan's rebelliousness (see REBELLION; ARROGANCE) is thus expressed through his desires to intervene at the level of human action. Because metaphysically speaking Satan is neither superior nor equal to God, his desires do not pose a competition to God's nor do they overrun them. Rather, being more powerful than inferior human beings, Satan desires to confuse them about the nature of divine commands, leading them away from God's path (e.g. Q 4:48, 60; 22:52; see PATH OR WAY), making them forget God (Q 5:91), tempting them with various promises which he never fulfills (Q 4:120; 7:20; 8:48; 14:22, etc.) and ever deceiving them (Q 4:76; 24:21; 58:10; see JOY AND MISERY). Satan thus redirects human desire from God to himself, turning himself into the false object of desire: "God made a true promise to you (see COVENANT). I too made promises, but did not keep them. I had no authority over you, but when I called out to you, you answered. Do not blame me; blame yourselves." Those who, against God's warnings (e.g. Q 7:27, "Children of Adam, do not let Satan seduce you"; see ADAM AND EVE; OATHS; BREAKING TRUSTS AND CONTRACTS), respond to Satan, are doomed, as in Q 43:36: "And whoever turns away from remembrance of the compassionate (see GOD AND HIS ATTRIBUTES), we shall assign Satan to be his companion."

Divine wishes thus tower over both human and Satanic ones, keeping the two in a tension that creates a range of possibilities that people can choose once they are offered the knowledge of God's path. This interplay functionally separates the three agents only in the realm of individual action, laying out specific guidelines for practical judgments as well as inducing divergent theological debates on the issues of accountability, justice and responsibility. In the cosmic scheme of things, however, divine wishes prevail and reflect the integrity and omnipotence of God's plan to make all human beings aware of the ways to realize their ultimate desires. Regarding the theological matters of agency, Muslim orthodoxy eventually found a middle ground that, no matter what the subjective reasons for acting on one's desires through the principles of acquisition *(kasb)* may be, the epistemic frame of reference is unwavering, stable, and clear. The Ashʿarīs sum up this position in the following terms:

His will is one, everlasting, connected to all willing from his own actions, and the actions of his servants insofar as they are created for him, not insofar as they are acquired from them. From that, he said that he willed everything, good and bad, beneficial and harmful, just as he willed and knew it to be. He willed from his servants what he knew and what he commanded his pen (see WRITING AND WRITING MATERIALS) to write on the preserved tablet (q.v.). That is his decree, ruling, and predetermination which never changed and can never be replaced. It is impossible for anything to be against what is known and predetermined in form in this manner (from Shahrastānī, *Milal,* i, 66-9; trans. M. Sells, *Early Islamic mysticism,* 320).

Amila Buturovic

Bibliography
Primary: Rāzī, *Tafsīr,* Beirut 1981; Shahrastānī, *Milal.*
Secondary: M. Fakhry (trans.), *An interpretation of the Qurʾān,* New York 2004; F. Denny, The will in the Qurʾān, in *JNES* 40/3 (1981), 253-7; I. Goldziher, *Introduction to Islamic theology and law,* Princeton 1981; H. Kassis, *A concordance of the Qurʾān,* Berkeley 1983; M. Sells (trans. and ed.), *Early Islamic mysticism,* New York 1996; M. Watt, *Free will and predestination in early Islam,* London 1948; T.J. Winter, Desire and decency in the Islamic tradition, in *Islamica* (London pub.) 1/4 (1994), 9-12.

Wit

see HUMOR; INTELLECT

Witness to Faith

Arabic *shahāda,* i.e. the statement "I testify that there is no god but God and I testify that Muḥammad is the messenger of God," *ashhadu an lā ilāha illā llāh wa-ashhadu anna Muḥammadan rasūlu llāh.* The utterance of the statement in Arabic is required of all Muslims to signify acceptance of Islam and thus it must be said at least once, with full intention, in a lifetime. The *shahāda* also plays a central role in the structure of the daily prayer (q.v.; *ṣalāt*) as well as in other life-cycle occasions and thus is repeated frequently in a Muslim's life. In the Qurʾān the statement itself is not found as a formula nor is there indication of the ritual act which later Islam has made it (as one of the five pillars; see RITUAL AND THE QURʾĀN). The content of the statement, however, and the phraseology of the two elements (known as the *shahādatāni*) of the *shahāda* are in the Qurʾān, as is a very strong sense of the role of "witnessing" one's faith (q.v.; see also BELIEF AND UNBELIEF; WITNESSING AND TESTIFYING).

Proclaiming the unity of God

"There is no god but God" is found in the Qurʾān in the exact phrasing of the *shahāda* only in Q 37:35 and Q 47:19. The first of these passages is especially interesting given the development of the ritual *shahāda,* since it speaks of an oral profession of the statement in front of unbelievers (see ORALITY; GOD AND HIS ATTRIBUTES). Verses 34 through 36 of Q 37 state: "Even so it is with the sinners (see SIN, MAJOR AND MINOR). When it is said to them, 'There is no god but God,' they wax proud (see PRIDE; ARROGANCE) saying, 'What, shall we forsake our gods for a poet possessed (see POETRY AND POETS; INSANITY; JINN)?'" Q 47:19 is a command to believers but not one entailing ritual testimony: "Know therefore that there is no god but God and ask for forgiveness [q.v.; of your sin]." Given this, it would be accurate to suggest that the performative aspect of the statement of the oneness of God as it is expressed in the *shahāda* is clearly post-qurʾānic. That said, it is worth remembering that the statement, "There is no god but he," *lā ilāha illā huwa,* is a constant refrain in the Qurʾān, found over forty times with some variations, including "There is no god but I" and "There is no god but you" (e.g. Q 2:163; 16:2; 21:87). Sometimes (e.g. Q 2:255) this is prefaced by the word "God," *Allāh lā ilāha illā huwa,* "God, there is no god but he!" In Q 3:62 and Q 38:65 the phrasing of the negative in the statement "There is no god but God" is another variant of the ritual *shahāda,* using *wa-mā min ilāhin* rather than the particle of absolute negation, *lā* (see GRAMMAR AND THE QURʾĀN). The theological position of "There is no god but God" is a major theme of the Qurʾān, even if the precise way in which that is ritually expressed in Islam is, at best, latent in the text.

The non-qurʾānic status of the precise phrasing (as well as some variability in how the statement was to be expressed in the early centuries of Islam — on which see below) has led some to seek the background to the phrase outside the Islamic context. Attention has been drawn to the Samaritans (q.v.) as having a parallel formulation (Baumstark, Herkunft; Macuch, Vorgeschichte).

Proclaiming Muḥammad's status

The figure of the "messenger of God" is a constant presence in the Qurʾān with phrases such as "He is the messenger of God" in Q 49:3 and proclamations such as "I am the messenger of God" in Q 7:158 (see MESSENGER). References to "God and his messenger" with variants such as "me and my messenger" also abound (e.g. Q 4:13, 136; 5:111, with Jesus as the messenger; 9:62). The precise phraseology "Muḥammad is the messenger of God" is, however, included in scripture only once, in Q 48:29. The context there is a statement of fact and not of ritual enunciation: "Muḥammad is the messenger of God and those who are with him are hard against the unbelievers, merciful to one another (see MERCY)." The other three instances of the use of the proper name Muḥammad (q.v.; see also NAMES OF THE PROPHET) in the Qurʾān (Q 3:144; 33:40; 47:2) do not suggest any notion of a ritual formula.

The emergence of the formula of the shahāda

Within the early Islamic period the *shahāda* and variations on it emerged as identifiers of Islamic allegiance, being found on coins and in inscriptions dating from the first Muslim century (see EPIGRAPHY AND THE QURʾĀN; NUMISMATICS; MONEY). It is during this period that the *shahāda* clearly gained status and, eventually, a set formulation. The precise phrasing of the statements displays some variation over time. Commonly the word "alone" (*waḥda* or *wāḥid*), is added after *Allāh,* perhaps picking up on the phrasing of Q 6:19 (cf. Q 18:110, etc.), which states, *huwa ilāhun wāḥidun,* "He is one god." This phrase, as found in coins and inscriptions, is often followed by "He has no partner," *lā sharīka lahu* (as found in Q 6:163; see POLYTHEISM AND ATHEISM). A typical example of this formulation is found in the wall mosaic located in the ruins of some Umayyad shops in Baysān (today, Bet Shean, in Israel) dating from earlier than 131/749 (when the town was destroyed by an earthquake). This inscription reads, "In the name of God, the merciful, the compassionate. There is no god but God alone; he has no partner. Muḥammad is the messenger of God" (Khamis, Two wall mosaic inscriptions, 163). The examples of coins with the phrasing "There is no god but God alone" from the post-ʿAbd al-Malik monetary reform period are well known. Examples still exist from as early as the years 77/696 and 78/697. Those coins often add the phrase "Whom he sent with guidance (see ASTRAY) and the religion (q.v.) of truth (q.v.), that he might make it victorious (see VICTORY) over all religions" (cf. Q 9:33; 48:28; 61:9; for examples see Walker, *Catalogue*). The existence of these phrases on coins might suggest that, at this time, the ritual status and formulation of the *shahāda* had not yet been reached. The same observation may be made for the inscriptions in the Dome of the Rock in Jerusalem (q.v.) dating from the same period. Even in the ḥadīth literature of the third Muslim century/ninth century C.E. (see ḤADĪTH AND THE QURʾĀN), the place and the formulation of the *shahāda* as an independent ritual activity (outside of its incorporation into the prayer ritual) appears to be not yet completely fixed (see Rippin, *Muslims,* 98-100; Wensinck, *Muslim creed,* 27-35).

"Witnessing" as a qurʾānic theme

The Qurʾān uses the root *sh-h-d* some 200 times in a variety of senses, some of which may be connected with the sense of "giving witness to faith," thus providing impetus, it may be thought, to the development of the *shahāda* as a ritual activity.

There are two main senses of witnessing in the Qurʾān. One relates to matters of faith and the other, to various legal matters (see LAW AND THE QURʾĀN). While it may be argued that there is a relationship between those two, especially since God is described as *al-shahīd,* the witness over everything (e.g. Q 58:6; 85:9), the emphasis on a notion of testifying specifically to one's faith, a notion which is not present in the legal "witness" passages, suggests that at least a theoretical separation is possible.

On the legal side, the Qurʾān speaks of witnesses as needing to be involved in various commercial and personal transactions (see CONTRACTS AND ALLIANCES). Such witnessing is deemed evidence and the words *bayyina,* "evidence," and *shahāda,* "witnessing," are often used interchangeably. The Qurʾān (e.g. Q 2:282; 4:15; 24:4) requires such witness-evidence from people in a number of situations, including lawsuits, matters regarding the status of persons (marriage, divorce, manumission, bequest; see MARRIAGE AND DIVORCE; SLAVES AND SLAVERY; INHERITANCE), financial matters and *ḥadd* offences (i.e. those which involved prescribed penalties such as fornication, adultery, manslaughter and so on; see BOUNDARIES AND PRECEPTS; CHASTISEMENT AND PUNISHMENT; ADULTERY AND FORNICATION; MURDER; BLOODSHED).

Of its religious uses the first thing to note is that witnessing is not passive but active. It is a demand to "bear witness" or to "testify." Q 3:64 states, "If they [the People of the Book (q.v.)] turn back, say, 'Bear witness that we are Muslims.'" Q 2:143 has biblical resonances in stating, "Thus we have made you a middle nation that you might be witnesses to the people and the messenger a witness to you." It is relevant to the development of the *shahāda* as a spoken ritual activity that God bears witness to his oneness in Q 3:18, "God bears witness that there is no god but he," and believers bear witness to the truth of Muḥammad's message in Q 3:86, "How can God guide those who disbelieve after they have accepted faith and testified that the messenger was true and that the clear signs (q.v.; see also VERSES) had come to them?" Statements close to both elements of the *shahāda* are thus found in the Qurʾān in a context which suggests an active process of witnessing.

Martyrdom as witnessing faith

The semantic link between "witnessing faith" (being a *shāhid*) and being a "martyr" *(shahīd)* — two terms and usages clearly separated in later Islamic times — is not evident in the Qurʾān (see MARTYRS). Goldziher (*MS,* ii, 350-4) argued that the development from witness to martyr derived from Christian Syriac usage of the cognate *sāhdā* in translating the Greek *martus*. Those who are spoken of as "witnesses to faith" in the Qurʾān (either *shuhadāʾ,* the plural of *shahīd,* as in Q 3:140; 4:69; 39:69; 57:19, or *shāhidūn* in Q 3:53; 5:83, etc.) fit within the meaning sketched above of those who "testify" to their faith in God and Muḥammad (the plural uses of the word as "legal witnesses" are clearly separated). Many commentaries, however, interpret *shuhadāʾ,* especially in Q 3:140, in the sense of "martyr" by connecting it to the context of the battles of Badr (q.v.) and

Uḥud which occurred during the lifetime of the Prophet (see EXPEDITIONS AND BATTLES). The early authority Ibn Jurayj is reported by al-Ṭabarī (d. 310/923; *Tafsīr*, vii, 243, report no. 7915) to have said regarding "So that God may know those who believe and may take witnesses/martyrs from among you" (Q 3:140), that the Muslims used to petition their lord (q.v.) by saying, "Our lord, show us another day like the day of Badr in which we can fight the polytheists, strive well in your cause, and seek therein martyrdom." That prayer was said to have been answered at Uḥud because, on that day, the Muslims met the polytheists in battle and God chose martyrs from among them. Such readings of these verses are also found in very early exegetical works; the meaning of the *shuhadāʾ* as "those martyred in the path of God" is, for example, the fourth of six meanings given to the word by Muqātil b. Sulaymān (d. 150/767) in his *al-Ashbāh wa-l-naẓāʾir fī l-Qurʾān al-karīm* (148-9) connected to Q 4:69 and Q 57:19 (see PATH OR WAY). As Goldziher has pointed out, however, the more standard qurʾānic phrase for referring to the martyrs who die in battle is "those killed in the path of God" (e.g. Q 3:169, "Think not of those who are slain in the path of God as dead! They live, finding sustenance [q.v.] with their lord"; see DEATH AND THE DEAD; REWARD AND PUNISHMENT; PARADISE). Be that as it may, it is clear that by the time of the ḥadīth literature, *shahīd* as "martyr" is well established, with martyrdom understood in a very broad sense, not limited to those killed in battle, and often carrying an implicit criticism of those who seek death in order to gain the status of the martyr.

The shahāda *in theology*

The ritual repetition of the *shahāda* is often treated as the core or ground level of faith, *īmān*, as a whole. In many discussions, the profession of the *shahāda* is the one action required for someone to be considered a Muslim. Questions about the status of works beyond that required profession produced the debates about the role of works in the life of the believer in Islam (see GOOD DEEDS; THEOLOGY AND THE QURʾĀN). Most famously, this related to the discussion of the status of the "believing sinner" which, in the extreme case, applied to someone who only said the *shahāda* but whose actions were otherwise not in keeping with Islamic requirements. In later Muslim times, likely starting with al-Ghazālī (d. 505/1111), the *shahāda* was understood as the creedal statement of Islam, providing the basis for the discussion that characterized all theology as an explanation of the two sentences of the *shahāda* (Wensinck, *Muslim creed*, 270-6).

Andrew Rippin

Bibliography

Primary: Muqātil, *Ashbāh;* Ṭabarī, *Tafsīr*, ed. Shākir.

Secondary: A. Baumstark, Zur Herkunft der monotheistischen Bekenntnisformeln im Koran, in *OC* 37 (1953), 6-22; Goldziher, *MS*, trans; E. Khamis, Two wall mosaic inscriptions from the Umayyad market place in Bet Shean/Baysān, in *BSOAS* 64 (2001), 159-76; E. Kohlberg, Shahīd, in *EI²*, ix, 203-7; R. Macuch, Zur Vorgeschichte der Bekenntnisformel *lā ilāha illā llāhu*, in *ZDMG* 128 (1978), 20-38; C.E. Padwick, *Muslim devotions. A study of prayer-manuals in common use*, Oxford 1996 (original 1961), chaps. 10a and 10b; A. Rippin, *Muslims, their religious beliefs and practices*, London 2001²; J. Walker, *A catalogue of the Muhammadan coins in the British Museum. ii. Arab-Byzantine and post-reform Umaiyad coins*, London 1956; A.J. Wensinck, *The Muslim creed. Its genesis and historical development*, London 1932; id., The Oriental doctrine of the martyrs, in *Mededeelingen der Koninklijke Akademie van Wetenschappen, Afdeeling Letterkunde*, Deel 53, Serie A, No. 6, Amsterdam 1921.

Witnessing and Testifying

Perceiving something and giving evidence of it. These two notions are distinct from each other but interrelated, insofar as the one is the prerequisite of the other. Also, the act of perception results in knowledge that can later be passed on, and so may be considered to be oriented towards the future; bearing evidence, by contrast, refers to the past. Thus, witnessing and testifying establishes a chain of information, with the witness serving as a connecting link between a past event and a person inquiring about it. From an epistemological point of view, however, this chain consists of two different relationships. On the one hand, the witness' relationship to the event in question is normally characterized by trust in his own perception; the inquirer, on the other hand, must always decide whether the witness is credible and, therefore, whether the information he is obtaining is true. Since the practice of witnessing and testifying is one of the most important methods of arriving at a decision in the field of law, formulating criteria to ensure the credibility of the witness has always been of pivotal importance.

The Arabic counterpart to the English notion of "witnessing and testifying" is derived from the root *sh-h-d,* which occurs 160 times in the Qurʾān, mainly in the first verbal form. The verb *shahida* (44 times) covers a set of notions that includes: first, "to be present (at)" or "to be (eye)witness (of)" (with acc.: e.g. Q 2:185; 12:26; 27:49; 43:19); second, "to bear evidence of something" (*bi-,* seldom *ʿalā*), or "against someone or oneself" (*ʿalā;* e.g. Q 6:130; 12:81; 41:20; 46:10); and, third, "to declare" or "to profess" (with acc. or *anna,* "that"; e.g. Q 3:81; 7:172; 11:54; 25:72; with even God as its subject: Q 3:18). Likewise, the active participle *shāhid* (21 times, including its plural forms *shāhidūn, shuhūd* and *ashhād*) and the verbal adjective *shahīd* (56 times, including the dual *shahīdān* and the plural *shuhadāʾ*) mostly refer to the eyewitness of deeds and events (e.g. Q 4:72; 12:26; 28:44), to the witness who gives evidence in the court either in this world or in the hereafter (e.g. Q 4:166; 24:4; 40:51; see JUDGMENT; LAST JUDGMENT) and to the witness who attests to his faith (q.v.) or beliefs (e.g. Q 3:53; 6:150; 46:10; not *shahīd*).

Finally, the verbal noun *shahāda* (26 times) signifies the "manifest" in contrast to *al-ghayb,* "the hidden" (see HIDDEN AND THE HIDDEN), in the recurrent formula *ʿālim al-ghayb wa-l-shahāda* ("[God] knower of the unseen and the visible"; e.g. Q 6:73; 9:94; cf. 6:19). It also denotes witnessing the conclusion of an agreement (e.g. Q 2:282; 5:106; see CONTRACTS AND ALLIANCES) and testifying to one's knowledge (e.g. Q 2:140; 24:4; see KNOWLEDGE AND LEARNING), while in Q 24:6, 8 its meaning comes close to that of an oath (see OATHS). There are, however, several instances where it is not easy to determine in which sense words derived from the root *sh-h-d* should best be understood (e.g. Q 3:18, 99; 11:17; 46:10; 74:13; 83:21).

At any rate, due to its complex shades of meaning, the term *shahāda* with its derivations gained central importance in three different fields of Islamic culture. It refers, first, to witnessing in a judicial context, second, to the credo statement, "I confess *(ashhadu)* there is no god except God, Muḥammad is the messenger of God" (see WITNESS TO FAITH) and third, to martyrdom (see MARTYRS).

Two types of witnesses: attesting and testifying

In the Qurʾān, the notion of witnessing is a main issue in the description of events on judgment day, on the one hand, and in the prescriptions for procedural rules in penal and civil law cases in this life, on the other (see LAW AND THE QURʾĀN; CHASTISEMENT

AND PUNISHMENT). These two usages should be treated separately.

To give an idea of the impending divine judgment at the end of time, the Qurʾān — aside from referring to the metaphor (q.v.) of the mechanical and hence impartial scale (e.g. Q 7:8-9; 21:47; see WEIGHTS AND MEASURES) — evokes above all the imagery of a great trial. The Qurʾān, however, hardly talks about the course of events at this trial; rather, it focuses on the impact of two kinds of evidence that will be presented there: 1) written documents (see ORALITY AND WRITING IN ARABIA; WRITING AND WRITING MATERIALS), and 2) the testimony of witnesses. Both draw their authority from the close surveillance to which human beings are subject during their lifetime. Nothing that happens on earth escapes God (cf. Q 50:16; 58:7; see POWER AND IMPOTENCE). Therefore: "God is sufficient as witness" (*shahīd,* Q 4:79; cf. 3:98; 4:33; 6:19; 13:43; and sometimes God is called *raqīb,* "watcher," e.g. Q 5:117; 33:52; both designations belong to his "most beautiful names," *al-asmāʾ al-ḥusnā;* see GOD AND HIS ATTRIBUTES). Also he (Q 3:181; 19:79; 36:12), or rather some angelic beings who are mostly called "our messengers" (*rusulunā;* e.g. Q 10:21; 43:80; see ANGEL) or "guardians" (*ḥāfiẓīn,* Q 82:10; *ḥafaẓa,* Q 6:61; cf. 4:166; 13:11; 50:17-18), write down the deeds of every human being (see HEAVENLY BOOK).

According to some verses (q.v.), on judgment day there will be one comprehensive book (q.v.; *kitāb*) for all (Q 18:49; 39:69; cf. 36:12); according to others, there is one book for the sinners and one for the pious (Q 83:7, 18; see SIN, MAJOR AND MINOR), one for each community (*umma,* Q 45:28-9; see COMMUNITY AND SOCIETY IN THE QURʾĀN), or one record for each individual (Q 17:13-14, 71; 69:19, 25; 84:7, 10). Be that as it may, the notion of celestial registers of deeds belongs to the common religious heritage of the Near East (see SCRIPTURE AND THE QURʾĀN). In the Qurʾān, as well as in biblical texts (cf. Malachi 3:16-17; Daniel 7:10; Revelation 20:12), written documents, whether collective or individual, are the decisive evidence in the last judgment. In fact, due to their precision and comprehensiveness, these writings themselves dictate unmistakably the final fate of the souls (see SOUL; REWARD AND PUNISHMENT). The events on judgment day do not themselves serve to determine the verdict — since God is all-knowing, this is already clear — but rather to demonstrate that the divine verdict is just (see JUSTICE AND INJUSTICE). Therefore, on judgment day the records of deeds will be made public: they will be spread open before the souls (Q 17:13; 18:49; 39:69); they will be handed over to them (Q 17:71; 69:19, 25; 84:7, 10); everyone has to read his own register aloud (Q 17:14, 71; 69:19). Thus the pious as well as the sinners, after gaining insight to the records of their deeds, will acknowledge the supreme divine justice (Q 17:14; 18:49; 69:19f.).

The second piece of evidence that plays a major role on the day of judgment, the testimony of witnesses, is only ever mentioned in connection with evil-doers (Q 50:21 might appear to be an exception, but as the context shows, the sinner is the focus of attention here, too; see EVIL DEEDS). Those who are summoned to appear as witnesses before the tribunal include first of all the messengers of God, who are to testify against the peoples to whom they have been sent (e.g. Q 4:41, 159; 5:116-17; 16:84, 89; 28:75). Q 2:143 is relevant here, too. Concerning the Muslim community, it says: "… that you may be witnesses against humankind *(shuhadāʾa ʿalā l-nās),* and that the messenger may be a witness against you *(ʿalaykum shahīdan)…."* Here, as well as in Q 22:78 where nearly the same formula recurs, the context in which it appears has to do with Muslim ritual duties, especially prayer (q.v.; *ṣalāt;* see also RITUAL AND THE QURʾĀN). Thus, it could be argued that these verses imply that the believers, while performing their duties, are considered to act as witnesses for God in face of the unbelievers (see BELIEF AND UNBELIEF). The mainstream of Muslim exegesis, however (see EXEGESIS OF THE QURʾĀN: CLASSICAL AND MEDIEVAL), relates this expression to the role of Muḥammad's community on the day of judgment: Relying on what their Prophet taught them, the members of the community will testify that God's messengers indeed conveyed their message to the nations. And the nations in turn, impressed by the Muslims' privileged status, will exclaim: "This community, they all were nearly prophets!" (see Ṭabarī, *Tafsīr,* ad loc.)

Another important group who will be gathered to give evidence are the *shurakāʾ* — the associates (whom the unbelievers venerated beside God; see POLYTHEISM AND ATHEISM). When they are asked whether they led the unbelievers astray (q.v.), they will renounce them and give the unbelievers full responsibility (q.v.) for their conduct (Q 25:17-19; 28:62-6; cf. 11:18; 16:86; 37:22-32; 39:69; 40:51). The unbelievers will be called upon to produce witnesses for their own claims, but they will be unable to comply (Q 41:47; cf. 6:94; 10:28; 30:13; etc.) — a motif that also recurs in the polemical passages of the Qurʾān (e.g. Q 2:23; 11:13-14; 68:41; see POLEMIC AND POLEMICAL LANGUAGE) and that can be traced back to God's tribunal on the heathen nations in Isaiah 43:8 f. In this context, mention must also be made of Q 50:20-9. It says that on judgment day "every soul shall come, and with it a driver *(sāʾiq)* and a witness" (*shahīd,* Q 50:21): "... And his comrade *(qarīnuhu)* shall say, 'This is what I have, made ready'" (Q 50:23); and, "'Our lord (q.v.), I made him not insolent, but he was in far error'" (q.v.; Q 50:27; see also INSOLENCE AND OBSTINACY). The question of who the "driver," the "witness" and the "comrade" are, is not easy to answer. Aside from other, partly metaphorical interpretations, Islamic exegesis usually takes the "driver" to be a kind of heavenly court usher; while the "witness" is generally understood as the angels who record the human deeds. These angels, however, are nowhere else expressly called "witnesses" (see above). As for the soul's "comrade" who denounces him, al-Zamakhsharī (d. 538/1144; *Kashshāf,* ad loc.) explains that it is a satan (see DEVIL) who was sent to seduce him (cf. Q 4:38; 6:112; 25:31; 41:25; 43:36). This "comrade," then, is reminiscent of the Judaic conception of Satan as an angel of God whose office it is to tempt human beings on earth and to act as heavenly prosecutor against them before the last judgment (Zechariah 3:1; Job 1:6 f.; Ps. 109:6). Finally, God will also enable the limbs and sense organs of the unbelievers to testify to their actions (Q 41:20-2; 24:24; 36:65). Thus, left alone without any witness for the defense, the unbelievers — human beings and jinn (q.v.) — will give evidence against themselves and end up in hell (Q 6:130; 7:37; see HELL AND HELLFIRE).

Now, while the qurʾānic view anticipating the events of the last judgment is characterized by trust in the triumph of divine justice, the qurʾānic attitude towards legally relevant matters in worldly affairs takes a rather more realistic tone. This is demonstrated clearly in the prescriptions related to the attesting and testifying witnesses. (As to terminology, in the Qurʾān, both *shāhid* and *shahīd* signify both the attesting and the testifying witness [see above]. But since *shahīd* later acquired the meaning of "martyr," Islamic jurisprudence then began using the term *shāhid* exclusively for the witness in legal matters.) The Qurʾān expressly demands the presence of witnesses for five kinds of acts — four of them belonging to civil law, one to penal law. These include: the agreement on a financial obligation (Q 2:282; see DEBT), the delivery of property (q.v.) to orphans (q.v.) by their guardian (Q 4:6; see GUARDIANSHIP), the drafting of the last testament (Q 5:106-8; see INHERITANCE), the decision on the continuation or dissolution of a marriage after the prescribed waiting period (q.v.; Q 65:1-2; see also MARRIAGE AND DIVORCE), and the execution of the *ḥadd*-punishment for fornication (Q 24:2; see ADULTERY AND FORNICATION). (It could be argued that Q 2:185, *man shahida… al-shahr* implies that witnesses are required to attest to the new moon [q.v.], as well, but this is not at all clear. For the discussion concerning the *ruʾyat al-hilāl* — "attesting of the new moon" — see Lech, *Geschichte*, i, 73-105; see also MONTH; RAMAḌĀN). As for the last-named act, i.e. punishing a fornicator, the reason for the attendance of witnesses lies in the special character of the qurʾānic *ḥadd*-regulations. Because they are prescribed by God, they cannot be altered, and it is the duty of the community of believers to implement them duly if the accused is found guilty (see BOUNDARIES AND PRECEPTS). The execution of the punishment is therefore a public concern, and the witnesses represent the community. In this respect, Muslim commentators speak of *tashhīr* — public exposure. But since Q 24:2 simply says: "Let a party *(ṭāʾifa)* of the believers witness their punishment," the teachings from the scholars diverge as to the minimum number of witnesses required. According to al-Ṭabarī's (d. 310/923) commentary, Mujāhid (d. bet. 100/718 and 104/722) considered the presence of only one person to be sufficient; the majority, however, prefer at least three, but better four, witnesses, analogous with the prescriptions concerning fornication (see below).

In contrast, the other instances mentioned above (Q 2:282; 4:6; 5:106-8; 65:1-2) deal with private-law agreements. There, the number of the witnesses has to be (at least) two. Q 2:282, the extremely long *āyat al-dayn* — the verse of debt — deals with witnessing agreements concerning financial obligations. It lays down the following: first, that a scribe has to fix such agreements in writing; and, second, that two witnesses must be called in to attest to the drafting of the contract, in order to be able to give evidence of its proper course in case of future legal contest. Now, this prescription conforms generally with the corresponding regulations in Talmudic law. In the Talmud, however, women are excluded from acting as attesting and testifying witnesses (cf. Josephus, *Antiquities*, bk. 4, chap. 8, par. 15) except in the case of typically female matters. The Qurʾān, on the other hand, stipulates the rule: "If the two be not men, then one man and two women, such witnesses as you approve of *(mimman tarḍawna mina l-shuhadāʾ)*, that if one of the two women errs the other will remind her" (see WOMEN AND THE QURʾĀN; GENDER). According to the Ḥanafīs, this means that the testimony of two women and one man may be accepted for all cases, except for *ḥadd* and *qiṣāṣ* (retaliation [q.v.]). The other Islamic schools of law, however, restricted this possibility mainly to financial transactions and otherwise conceded women the right to testify in matters within their special realm of knowledge. In such matters, the judge could confine himself to the testimony of women only — although the required number of female witnesses in these cases differed from school to school.

Q 65:2 stipulates that after the *ʿidda* — the waiting time of three menstural periods *(qurūʾ*; cf. Q 2:228; see MENSTRUA-

TION) — the husband's decision whether to retain his wife or to part from her must be attested to by "two men of equity from among yourselves *(dhaway ʿadl minkum)*." It continues: "and perform the witnessing to God *(wa-aqīmū l-shahādata lillāh)*." Q 5:106 uses the same notion, i.e. "two men of equity" should be present when a testament is made. Both should come "from among yourselves *(minkum)*," but if the testator faces death away from home, two others *(ākharāni min ghayrikum)* will do as well. For the Shāfiʿī and Mālikī jurists (just as for the Ḥanafī exegete al-Zamakhsharī), this differentiation between "from yourselves" and "from others" refers to the relatives of the testator and to strangers. Scholars of the Ḥanafī tradition (and also the Shāfiʿī commentator al-Suyūṭī [d. 911/1505]), however, explain it as referring to Muslims on the one hand, and to non-Muslims on the other, allowing the "People of the Book" (q.v.) thereby to witness in this special case, when no Muslims can be found. (As a rule, the testimony of the "People of the Book" is admissible only when it concerns their own religious communities.) In the continuation of Q 5:106, the wording leaves space for interpretation, as well. It says the witnesses should be detained after prayer *(ṣalāt)* and, in case of doubt, made to swear by God *(fa-yuqsimāni bi-llāh)*: "We will not sell it for a price, even though it were a near kinsman (see KINSHIP), nor will we hide the testimony of God *(lā naktumu shahādata llāh)*, for then we would surely be among the sinful." Here, it is neither entirely clear whether the prescriptions mentioned refer to the first pair of witnesses, those "from among yourselves," or to the second pair, the "two others"; nor whether the moment of drafting the last testament or giving evidence of this act at a later time is intended.

As to the criteria of witness credibility, *ʿadl* — equity — is the only one expressly mentioned in the Qurʾān (Q 5:106; 65:2). There, this term sometimes implies a certain legal competence (cf. Q 5:95; 42:15); in later times, however, it was usually understood as referring generally to a good reputation. Al-Shāfiʿī (d. 204/820) defined it as "acting in obedience (q.v.) to God" and added that one's surface impression of a person suffices to attest to his *ʿadl*. In addition to *ʿadl*, later Islamic scholars also drew up lists of further criteria for both the attesting and the testifying witness. These criteria include the following: the witness should be a Muslim (thus, Jews and Christians are normally excluded from witnessing, see above; see JEWS AND JUDAISM; CHRISTIANS AND CHRISTIANITY), a free man (*ḥurr;* see SLAVES AND SLAVERY), in full possession of his mental faculties (*ʿāqil;* see INSANITY), have attained the age of majority (*bāligh;* see MATURITY), not be suspected of having personal interests in the case (*nafy al-tuhma;* the classical definition of the testimony is *ikhbār bi-ḥaqqin lil-ghayri ʿalā ākhar*), and not have been previously punished by *ḥadd* because of defamation (*ghayr maḥdūd fī l-qadhf;* cf. Q 24:4). The judge (*qāḍī*, pl. *quḍāt*) is responsible for examining whether the witnesses meet these conditions before the court. Now, while the external conditions can easily be checked, the verification of the *ʿadāla* is problematic. (Since *ʿadl* can also be used as an adjective, it is often replaced by "*ʿadāla*" as a noun.) According to the procedure of *taʿdīl* — declaring one's equity — it is incumbent upon the judge to make secret enquiries about a candidate's reputation and private life, and to question him in public, before accepting him as a witness.

ʿAdāla understood as good reputation is, however, an extremely flexible notion and can be interpreted arbitrarily. Therefore, one finds in the sources that not only the belief in the doctrine of free will (see

FREEDOM AND PREDESTINATION), but also eating in the streets or breeding pigeons and the like could disqualify someone from acting as a witness. Due to the subjective nature of interpreting this term, private-law agreements could easily be contested later on by denying the *ʿadāla* of the witnesses that attested to the act. To minimize this risk, already in the second/eighth century, judges started to confer a permanent status of *ʿadāla* to a limited group of persons, who were then regularly examined. The presence of these officially approved witnesses at the closing of contracts and passing of sentences secured the legality of these acts. In this way, a class of notarial witnesses, the *shuhūd ʿudūl* (sing. *shāhid ʿadl*), evolved. They belonged to the judge's entourage, but could also work independently as notaries, attesting and testifying legal acts, drawing up deeds and documents. The notary profession (which was called *ʿadāla,* as well) required specialist knowledge of law and legal jargon — the *ṣināʿat al-wirāqa,* arithmetic, calligraphy (q.v.) and so on, and was the subject of the treatises of *ʿilm al-shurūṭ* — the discipline pertaining to the conditions (of the notary profession). Conversely, the evidentiary weight conceded to written documents — although recommended in Q 2:282 (and decisive in the hereafter; see above; see ESCHATOLOGY) — was originally very limited, at least in theory: Those witnesses who attended the drafting of a document had to reappear before the court in order to testify to its validity. It was only for practical reasons that written documents eventually became fully admissible as evidence — chiefly by a revaluation of the witnesses' signatures on the document — except in cases of *ḥadd* and *qiṣāṣ*.

Concerning the role of witnesses testifying before a worldly court, the Qurʾān contains very little information (cf. Q 21:61, the trial against Abraham [q.v.; Ibrāhīm], and Q 12:26-8, the acquittal of Joseph [q.v.] through circumstantial evidence). Only in two passages are precise prescriptions given: Q 4:15 says: "Such of your women as commit indecency *(al-fāḥisha),* call four of you to witness against them *(fa-stashhidū ʿalayhinna arbaʿatan)*; and if they bear witness *(fa-in shahidū),* then detain [the women] in [their] houses until death takes them or God appoints for them a way." Q 24:4, too, demands the testimony of four witnesses: "And those who accuse honorable women but bring not four witnesses *(bi-arbaʿati shuhadāʾ),* scourge them with eighty lashes (see FLOGGING) and never afterward accept their testimony *(shahāda)*." While this verse deals with the accusation of fornication *(zinā),* the delict in Q 4:15 is interpreted either as lesbian sex (*siḥāq;* see HOMOSEXUALITY) or fornication, as well. In the latter case, the difference between the penalty in Q 4:15 (house arrest or a divine decision) and the one in Q 24:2, where a hundred lashes are prescribed for the fornicator, is clarified by taking recourse to the supposed order of revelation (see REVELATION AND INSPIRATION; CHRONOLOGY AND THE QURʾĀN; OCCASIONS OF REVELATION): first, Q 4:15 came down; it was then replaced by Q 24:2; this in turn was superseded by the notorious verse of stoning (q.v.), the *āyat al-rajm,* "whose recitation is abrogated but not its validity" (*mā nusikha tilāwatuhu dūna ḥukmihi;* Suyūṭī, *Itqān, nawʿ* 47; see ABROGATION).

Be that as it may, two items deserve mention here: First, Islamic jurisprudence has always restricted the necessity of the testimony of four (male) witnesses to *zinā* (and *siḥāq*) only. For all other cases, murder (q.v.) and manslaughter included (see BLOODSHED), two witnesses suffice — a rule which is in accordance with Mosaic law (cf. Deuteronomy 17:6; 19:15 f.). The witness' statement before the judge has to be introduced by the formula, "I testify by God" *(ashhadu bi-llāh),* or simply "I testify" and is considered an oath *(qasam)*. Second, he who cannot call four witnesses to support his charge is guilty of defamation *(qadhf)* and risks not only losing his right to give evidence, but also a corporal punishment, one which is only slightly milder than the punishment for the fornicator. (It is characteristic of the qur'ānic *ḥadd*-prescriptions that they are followed by restrictive clauses, which gave rise to discussions about their respective fields of application; besides Q 24:4-5, see Q 3:86-9; 5:33-4, 38-9.) Within the sphere of marriage, however, in Q 24:6-9 the Qur'ān allows the procedure of *li'ān,* which entitles the husband, instead of calling four witnesses, to swear four oaths that his accusation is true. And because the truth of these oaths normally cannot be verified, he then has to declare in a fifth oath that, in case of perjury, he should be subject to God's curse (q.v.). In order to evade punishment, the accused wife in turn must invalidate her husband's oaths, swearing four times that he is a liar and a fifth time that she, too, if lying, should incur the wrath of God (see ANGER). Insofar as in the *li'ān* each of them is invoking an ordeal, it can be compared with the *mubāhala,* the mutual curse in Q 3:61.

There are yet other instances in Islamic law where an oath may replace the testimony of a witness. Except for the Ḥanafīs, all other schools accept the oath *(yamīn)* of the plaintiff together with the testimony of another man as valid in financial matters. It is also valid the other way round: if the plaintiff's testimony is not based on sufficient evidence, the defendant can reject the accusation by means of an oath. Finally, in a situation where there is strong, but not sufficient, evidence against a person suspected of killing someone else, i.e. when there are neither two eye-witnesses nor the confession of the culprit, the practice of *qasāma* is allowed as supplementary evidence. This consists in the swearing of fifty oaths, either by fifty men or by fewer persons who then have to swear more than once in order to make up the required number. According to the Ḥanafīs, the *qasāma* on the part of the relatives of the suspect, swearing that they were neither involved in the crime nor do they know the culprit, prevents the mechanism of retaliation. For the Mālikīs, however, the *qasāma* is an instrument for the relatives of the victim. Their fifty-fold oath that the suspect is doubtless the offender increases the weight of the available, legally insufficient evidence to a sufficient degree.

As a rule, giving evidence is a duty for the Muslim community, but if someone can thereby be exonerated, the duty is individual (cf. Q 2:282). Nevertheless, in cases of *ḥadd*-delicts, it is laudable to keep one's knowledge to oneself in order to spare the suspect the corporal punishment.

The profession of faith

In its second meaning, the term *shahāda* refers to the credo statement of Islam. Although there exist some slight variations in wording (see Fischer, Gestalten; 'Alī, *ṣalāt,* 57 f., 136 f.), the *shahāda* essentially consists in the bipartite slogan "There is no god except God *(lā ilāha illā llāhu)*" and "Muḥammad is the messenger of God *(Muḥammadun rasūlu llāhi)*." It is therefore also called "the two words" — *al-kalimatān* — its first part being the *kalimat al-tawḥīd* — the word of God's oneness — (or, with respect to its sound, the *tahlīl*), its second part the *kalimat al-rasūl* — the word of the Prophet. For the Shī'a (q.v.) it is commendable, though not indispensible, to add a third phrase, namely: "'Alī is the friend of god" (*'Aliyyun waliyyu llāh;* as to the alleged 'Alawite *shahāda* see Guyard, Fetwa, 182; Firro, ʿAlawīs, 5f.; see also SHĪʿISM AND THE QURʾĀN; ʿALĪ B. ABĪ ṬĀLIB). In Islam, the *shahāda* is considered a performative utterance: Saying it intentionally in the presence of a Muslim audience means embracing Islam or emphasizing one's affiliation to it. By speaking the formula "I confess *(ashhadu)*" that precedes the whole declaration and that may be repeated before its second — and, as far as the Shīʿites are concerned, also its third — part, the performative nature of the *shahāda* is made explicit. In the philological tradition of Islam, this special character is mostly refered to as *inshāʾī*, what can be rendered approximately as "declarative," in contrast to pure statements, which are classified as *ikhbārī*, i.e. "informative" (see the discussion in Ālūsī, *Kanz*, 32f.).

As a performative, the *shahāda* requires publicity. This public nature of the *shahāda* shows above all in its prominence in the whole complex of the Islamic common prayer, the *ṣalāt:* First of all, it is part of the *adhān* — the call to prayer — which means that it can be heard loudly from above the minarets (see MOSQUE) five times a day in artistic rendering, sometimes even collectively performed (Damascus) or with instrumental accompaniment (Mashhad). It thereby became one of the most noticeable features of the Islamic world. It then figures in the *ijāba* — the individual Muslim's response to the *adhān* — and in the *iqāma* — the repetition of the *adhān* immediately before the prayer starts. In addition, at the end of every two *rakʿas* — series of ritual acts in the *ṣalāt* (see BOWING AND PROSTRATION) — and at the end of each *ṣalāt* itself, the believer utters the *tashahhud* — a set of phrases which includes the *shahāda*, too. (Because one has to raise the forefinger of the right hand while saying *lā ilāha illā llāhu* in the *tashahhud*, this finger is also called the *shāhid* — the confessor.) But beyond this importance in daily ritual, the *shahāda* accompanies the Muslim literally throughout his or her whole life: It is a custom to whisper it into the ear of the new-born child, a Muslim should die with it on his lips (see DEATH AND THE DEAD), and the deceased, before being buried (see BURIAL), is reminded of it so that he or she may know what to answer when asked in the grave by the two angels Munkar and Nakīr (q.v.).

These practices illustrate that the *shahāda* is considered the essential message of Islam. Accordingly, al-Ghazālī (d. 505/1111) used it as his starting point to unfold Islamic dogma *(ʿaqīda)* in his "Revival of the religious sciences" (*Iḥyāʾ ʿulūm al-dīn*, i, 160f.), and the 9th/15th century theologian al-Sanūsī concludes his creed (q.v.), saying: "The meanings of all these articles of belief are brought together in the words, 'There is no god exept God; Muḥammad is the messenger of God'" (see Watt, *Islamic creeds*, 94). Therefore, every Muslim is admonished to remember the two words constantly; according to the Shāfiʿite scholar al-Bayjūrī (d. 1276/1860), the Islamic teachers of law — the *fuqahāʾ* — recommended that one should repeat it at least three hundred times a day.

Generally, the first part of the *shahāda*, the *kalimat al-tawḥīd*, is considered to imply the second part, the *kalimat al-rasūl*, as well (see e.g. Shaʿrānī, *Fatḥ*, 24). But not only for this reason do the words *lā ilāha illā llāhu* hold a great fascination. Theology discusses the logical structure of its phrasing as an exception clause and the philosophical implications of this (cf. Bayjūrī, *Ḥāshiya*, 35f.; see THEOLOGY AND THE QURʾĀN; PHILOSOPHY AND THE QURʾĀN). With its distinctive rhythm and sound, it became a prefered formula for the *dhikr*-exercises of the mystics (see REMEMBRANCE; ṢŪFISM AND THE QURʾĀN) and for exorcisms (cf. Schimmel, Sufis). The graphical shape of its letters made it a favorite motif for calligraphic embellishments (see ARABIC SCRIPT). The number of these letters and the existing symmetries among them invite to further speculations about hidden harmonies (cf. Canteins, *Mirroir;* see also NUMEROLOGY). And popular imagination all along was able to decipher it in natural phenomena like flowers, trees or swarms of bees. Thus, the *shahāda* is one of the most important constituents of communal identity in Islam. This is clearly expressed in a prophetic saying that calls the believers the "people of *lā ilāha illā llāhu*" (cf. Ghazālī, *Iḥyāʾ,* i, 505). Despite this popularity, however, the origins of the *shahāda* remain rather obscure.

In order to express the core idea of monotheism, the Qurʾān uses various formulations, e.g. the statement of Q 42:11: *laysa ka-mithlihi shayʾun,* "Like him there is naught," the rhetorical question Q 35:3: *hal min khāliqin ghayru llāhi,* "Is there any creator apart from God?" (see CREATION; RHETORIC AND THE QURʾĀN), and the command in Q 112:1: *qul huwa llāhu aḥadun,* "Say: He is God, one." Two kinds of formulas, however, are especially prominent. There is, on the one hand, the positive statement *ilāhukum ilāhun wāḥidun,* "Your god is one god" (six times, e.g. Q 2:163; 18:110; 21:108; 41:6) with the variations "He *(huwa)* is one god" (three times: Q 6:19; 14:52; 16:51) and "God *(allāhu)* is one god" (once only: Q 4:171). As A. Baumstark pointed out (Zur Herkunft), this formula can be traced back indirectly — via a supposed Jewish-Arabic version of Aramaic translations (see FOREIGN VOCABULARY) — to Deuteronomy 6:4, the opening verse of the *shᵉmaʿ* — the Judaic creedal prayer: "Hear, O Israel: The lord *(yhwh)* our God, the lord *(yhwh)* is one." In its historical context, Deuteronomy 6:4 originally demanded Israel's exclusive cultic veneration of Yahweh alone, while implicitly conceding the existence of other gods for other nations. In exilic times, however, after Israel's turn to exclusive monotheism, i.e. to the negation of the existence of other gods, this verse could no longer be understood in its original sense, and the predicate "one" had to be interpreted in an absolute way (cf. Rechenmacher, *"Außer mir gibt es keinen Gott!,"* 195 f.). The same holds true, of course, of the qurʾānic formula as well, and, thus, the Muslim commentators explain the predicate *wāḥid* as meaning "one in essence" or "the unique one," etc. (cf. Ṭabarī, *Tafsīr*, ad Q 2:163 and compare the different translations of this formula).

On the other hand, there is the exception clause, "There is no god but he" *(lā ilāha illā huwa,* thirty times, e.g. Q 2:163, 255; 3:18; 9:31; 73:9) with the alternative endings "but I" *(illā anā,* three times: Q 16:2; 20:14; 21:25), "but God" *(illā llāhu,* twice: Q 37:35; 47:19) and "but you" *(illā anta,* only Q 21:87). According to Baumstark (Zur Herkunft), the wording *lā ilāha illā huwa* ultimately echoes Deuteronomy 4:35, 39 and must have been part of a pre-Islamic Jewish-Arabic cult prayer. In fact, many passages where this phrase figures exhibit a distinctive Jewish-Christian coloring, e.g. when combined with Hebrew or Aramaic borrowings like *al-qayyūm* — "the everlasting" (Q 2:255; 3:2) and *rabb al-ʿālamīn* — "the lord of all being" (Q 40:64-5), in connection with the biblical motif of the throne (Q 2:255; 9:129; 20:5-8; 27:26; see THRONE OF GOD) or in juxtaposition to *al-raḥmān* — "the all-merciful" — the name under which God was venerated in pre-Islamic times by the Jews of the Yemen (q.v.), e.g.: "Your god is one god; there is no god but he, the all-merciful, the all-compassionate" *(al-*

raḥmān al-raḥīm, Q 2:163; cf. 13:30; 59:22). Thus, it must be assumed that the phrase *lā ilāha illā huwa* was, at the time the Qurʾān originated, a popular slogan in Arabian Jewish or Christian circles. But then, the way the Arabic proper name "God," *Allāh,* becomes connected with this phrase in the Qurʾān, shows how the new religious movement first adopted and, later on, started to monopolize it. There are verses where the word *Allāh* simply precedes the *lā ilāha illā huwa* (e.g. Q 2:255; 3:2; 4:87; cf. 3:18), while in others, *Allāh* is almost defined by means of it (Q 20:98; cf. 6:102; 39:6; 40:62, 64-5). After a short hymn to *al-raḥmān* on the throne, Q 20:8, which runs "God *(Allāhu),* there is no god but he, his are the most beautiful names *(lahu l-asmāʾu l-ḥusnā),*" may be read as a justification for the use of the Arabic *Allāh* in connection with the exception clause (cf. Q 17:110). One may discern another attempt to justify this connection in Q 3:18, where the praxis of confessing *lā ilāha illā huwa* is somewhat illogically attributed to *Allāh* himself. Finally, in two verses the name *Allāh* enters the exception clause itself and constitutes the *kalimat al-tawḥīd.* And it is especially noticeable that in both instances the preceding verbs indicate that the resulting slogan *lā ilāha illā llāhu* was already in use for purposes of teaching and proselytizing (see TEACHING AND PREACHING THE QURʾĀN): "When it was said to them *(idhā qīla lahum):* There is no god but God *(Allāh),* they were scornful" (Q 37:35; cf. 47:19).

A central motif in the Qurʾān is the emphasis on the authority (q.v.) of the prophetic duty (see PROPHETS AND PROPHETHOOD). One of the means to effect this, is to equate the belief in and the obedience (q.v.) to God with the belief in and the obedience to the messenger (*rasūl;* the term "prophet," *nabī,* by contrast, is seldom used: Q 2:177; 5:81; 7:158). This principle is clearly stated in Q 4:80: "Whosoever obeys *(man yuṭiʿ)* the messenger *(al-rasūl),* thereby obeys God" (cf. Q 4:64). And thus, many qurʾānic orders and regulations are enforced with formulations like "Those only are believers, who believe in *(āmanū bi)* God and his messenger and who, when they are with him upon a common matter, go not away until they ask his leave" (Q 24:62; cf. 49:15; 61:11) or with the imperative "Obey God and obey the messenger!" (e.g. Q 4:59; 5:92; cf. 24:47). And although there are some short catechisms which add further elements, like the belief in angels and the scriptures of revelation or the performance of the prayer and the payment of the alms (*zakāt;* e.g. Q 2:285; 4:136; 9:71; see ALMSGIVING), verses like Q 48:17 suggest that obedience is in the end the decisive criterion for salvation (q.v.): "Whosoever obeys God and his messenger, he will admit him into gardens underneath which rivers flow" (cf. Q 33:71; see GARDEN). It is characteristic, however, not only of these passages, but of the Qurʾān as a whole, that this messenger remains without a name, except for four verses — Q 3:144; 33:40; 47:2 and 48:29 (see NAMES OF THE PROPHET) — which identify *Muḥammad* (q.v.) as the messenger of God and as a recipient of revelations. It has been suggested that these verses were later insertions into the Qurʾān; Islamic tradition, too, doubted the genuineness of at least Q 3:144 (see Suyūṭī, *Itqān, nawʿ* 10; Nöldeke, *GQ,* ii, 81f.; van Ess, *TG,* i, 3 n. 3). Anyway, at the end of Q 48 — after the divine promise to his messenger: "You (pl.) shall indeed enter the inviolable place of worship (*al-masjid al-ḥarām;* see SACRED PRECINCTS)" in verse 27 and after the assurance that God sent his messenger to make the "religion (q.v.) of truth" (q.v.; *dīn al-ḥaqq*) prevail over all religion in verse 28 — the final verse (Q 48:29) identifies this messenger and extols his supporters. This is the only qurʾānic instance of what later was to become the second part of the *shahāda:* "Muḥammad is the messenger of God."

In the Qurʾān can be found at least three ways to declare one's belief in and obedience to God and his prophet: first, the formula "We hear and we obey (*samiʿnā wa-aṭaʿnā;* see also SEEING AND HEARING)" with which the believers accepted the covenant (q.v.) with God (Q 5:7) and with which they submit to the decisions of the prophet (Q 24:51; this formula ultimately goes back to Deuteronomy 5:27, and therefore, the Qurʾān especially connects it with the Israelites, although in a deliberately distorted form; cf. Q 2:93; 4:46; see CHILDREN OF ISRAEL). Second, there is the confession of faith "We believe" (*āmannā,* Q 2:14, 76; 29:2; 49:14; sometimes with additions such as "in God and the last day" or "in God and the messenger, and we obey": Q 2:8; 24:47; cf. 40:84). That this is not merely an expression of an inner conviction, but should rather be understood as a performative utterance which confers upon its speaker a privileged status, is clear from verses like Q 40:84-5 and 49:14 (this latter verse plays exactly on the possible double use of *āmannā;* cf. Q 9:97). Finally, the verb *shahida* is used to signal the consent of the children of Adam (see ADAM AND EVE), of the prophets and of the Children of Israel in the covenant *(mīthāq)* with God (Q 2:84; 3:81; 7:172). But there are also instances where it obviously signifies a formal declaration of loyalty (q.v.) to the messenger of God, e.g.: "How shall God guide a people who have disbelieved after they believed, and bore witness *(shahidū)* that the messenger is true?" (*anna l-rasūla ḥaqqun,* Q 3:86; cf. 63:1; as for Q 3:86, see above).

Opinions differ considerably about when and how the *shahāda* as credo statement developed. According to K. Cragg (Shahādah), it was used in the Prophet's Medinan period (see MEDINA) as a formula for conversion, but its wording probably belonged to an even earlier time. M.J. Kister (Study) connects the origin of the twofold *shahāda* with the experiences of the wars of apostasy (q.v.; *ḥurūb al-ridda)* after the death of the Prophet. A.J. Wensinck (Tashahhud) argues that the *shahāda* must be comparatively early since it is part of the *ṣalāt*-rite and that it was customary to proclaim it at conversion to Islam in the second half of the first century A.H. — a view largely adopted by W.M. Watt *(Formative period),* too. By contrast, T. Nagel (Inschriften) thinks that from 72/691-2 onwards the Umayyad caliph (q.v.) ʿAbd al-Malik (r. 65-86/685-705) propagated especially the second part of the *shahāda* against the inner-Islamic opposition of the Zubayrids in order to legitimize the prophetic tradition, the ḥadīth (see ḤADĪTH AND THE QURʾĀN), as an authoritative source of its own. Finally, A. Rippin *(Muslims)* assumes that the *shahāda* "received its final shape fairly late" and that it gained acceptance as the first of the five pillars of Islam not before the third Islamic century.

Thus, the problem of the early history of the *shahāda* can be summarized in three questions: First, at what time were the two *kalima*s combined with each other? Second, what was the underlying intention thereby? And, third, when did the *shahāda* gain general acceptance as a set phrase to express Muslim identity? To start with, there is no evidence that the two parts of the *shahāda* were combined with each other before the second half of the first century A.H. Both formulas were originally independent from each other. When, for instance, the phrase "Muḥammad is the messenger of God" begins to appear on coins (see EPIGRAPHY AND THE QURĀN), from 66/685-6 onwards, it is introduced by the *basmala* (q.v.), but not accompanied by the *kalimat al-tawḥīd*. There exist several variations, especially to this latter phrase. For example, a south Jordanian graffiti (see also ARCHAEOLOGY AND THE QURʾĀN), probably from the first century A.H., runs: "O God, I do call you to witness that you are God. There is no god but you *(allāhumma innī ushhiduka annaka llāhu lā ilāha illā anta)*." The favorite wording, however, of the Umayyads — still preserved in the *tashahhud* — is: "There is no god except God alone, he has no associate *(waḥdahu lā sharīka lahu)*." From the seventies of the first Islamic century onwards, both words of the *shahāda* appear together. In 72/691-2, a drachma was issued in Sistan which on its reverse bears a Pahlavi text very close in meaning to the *shahāda* (see NUMISMATICS). And from 73/692 on, there are Arab-Sasanian and Arab-Byzantine coins with both the *basmala* and *shahāda* on the margin. These examples, however, are still tentative efforts to link the notion of the exclusiveness of God with the claim that Muḥammad is his messenger. Both words of the *shahāda* were freely combined with other religious phrases, too. There is, for example, the outer inscription of the ambulatory of the Dome of the Rock (see ART AND ARCHITECTURE AND THE QURʾĀN) from 72/691-2. In five sections, the text emphasizes the two basic ideas of the *shahāda*, and in each of these sections, both *kalimas* appear. They do not, however, make up a distinct unit, but are rather divided from each other by additional formulas. Likewise, in the standard legend on the Umayyad coins from ʿAbd al-Malik's reform (77/696-7 onwards), the two *kalimas* are separated from each other and are given different weight: The obverse has the Umayyad version of the first *kalima* as cited above, and the reverse gives the text of Q 112 (without the initial "Say: He"), while the legend on the margin runs: "Muḥammad is the messenger of God. He sent him with the guidance and the religion of truth, that he may uplift it above every religion, though the unbelievers be averse" (cf. Q 9:33; 61:9; also Q 48:28; see above). Only when the ʿAbbāsids came to power and struck new coins, did the *kalimat al-rasūl* take the place of Q 112 on the reverse and thereby became the true counterpart of the *kalimat al-tawḥīd* on the obverse (see also POLITICS AND THE QURʾĀN).

This epigraphic and numismatic material suggests that it was in the period from the reign of ʿAbd al-Malik (r. 65-86/685-705) until the ʿAbbāsid assumption of power in 132/750, that both words of the *shahāda* first became combined with each other and finally coalesced into a set phrase expressing Muslim identity. Therefore, it is not likely that the *shahāda* should have been used before ʿAbd al-Malik's reign as a slogan for conversion. By contrast, there is plenty of evidence that at least throughout the first/seventh century allegiance to Islam was expressed — besides many other formulations — by a declaration of the type: "I believe" (*āmantu;* see Ory, Aspects; Abbott, Ḳaṣr Kharāna). In addition, it seems that before the seventies of the first century A.H./ the end of the seventh century C.E., none of the rival factions in early Islam — Zubayrids, ʿAlids, Khārijīs (q.v.) and Umayyads — explicitly mentioned the Prophet in their creedal formulas (see below). But then, the decision of ʿAbd al-Malik to promote the *kalimat al-rasūl* hardly had an inner-Islamic background. Since the phrase "Muḥammad is the messenger of God" ascribes God-given authority to the Arab Muḥammad, it is more likely that it was originally directed towards the non-Arab, non-Muslim subjects in the new empire and emphasized the Umayyad dominance in the field of religion, too. This becomes especially evident in the inscriptions of the Dome of the Rock. In any case, ʿAbd al-Malik's propagation of the two words of the *shahāda* created for him serious diplomatic tensions with the Byzantines (q.v.; see Walker, *Catalogue of the Arab-Byzantine and post-reform Umaiyad coins,* liv).

The discussion of the term *islām,* as preserved in the medium of the ḥadīth — the prophetic tradition — shows how the *shahāda* started to play a role in theology. Given the fact that eventually *islām* was defined by five "pillars" (*arkān,* sing. *rukn*), A.J. Wensinck (*Creed,* 17f.) argued that definitions, which are less complex, can be considered preliminary stages belonging to an earlier date. Besides a tradition that defines *islām* solely by five daily prayers, obedience and the fast of Ramaḍān (e.g. Muslim, *Ṣaḥīḥ, K. Īmān,* 8), three principal groups of ḥadīths can be distinguished: first, traditions that emphasize the exclusive veneration of God and add three further, mostly ritual duties (e.g. Muslim, *Ṣaḥīḥ, K. Īmān,* 5, 7, 12, 14, 15); second, traditions where a catalogue of five pillars is established, which, however, do not include any declaration of loyalty towards the Prophet (e.g. Muslim, *Ṣaḥīḥ, K. Īmān,* 19, 20, 22); and, third, the kind of tradition where the bipartite *shahāda* figures as the first of the five pillars of *islām,* either in answer to Gabriel's (q.v.) examination of the Prophet or introduced by the formula, "Islam is built upon five" (e.g. Muslim, *Ṣaḥīḥ, K. Īmān,* 1, 21). Wensinck rightly called this type "a masterpiece of early Muslim theology." Its importance lies in the fact that it holds the middle position between the Murjiʾī thesis that the public confession of faith *(īmān)* alone establishes one's status as a believer, on the one hand, and the Khārijī rigorism with its emphasis on works, on the other (see GOOD DEEDS; EVIL DEEDS). All the traditions of this type go back to ʿAbdallāh b. ʿUmar (d. 73/693), a personality famous for his neutrality during the Umayyad civil wars and therefore a suitable candidate for the attribution of such a compromise solution. The names in the *isnād*s — the chains of transmitters — point, however, to the milieu of proto-Sunnī traditionalists of the second/eighth century who, equally opposed to Murjiʾīs, ʿAlids, Khārijīs and Qadarīs, formulated these traditions and put them in circulation.

Now, the instruction in these ḥadīths to testify to both *kalima*s ("Islam is the testimony *[shahāda]* that there is no god but God and that Muḥammad is the messenger of God…"), signals, first, that, at that time, they both belonged together and, second, that they were used as a performative utterance. This strongly suggests that the *shahāda* must already have been part of the *adhān* and the *tashahhud* in the *ṣalāt*-rite. It is of great interest to know when the *ṣalāt* got its final shape but this is still an open question. Wensinck's argument, that the *ṣalāt* must have been standardized shortly after the Prophet's death "since there are no traces of deviation from the common ritual of the *ṣalāt* among the sects" (*Creed,* 32), as plausible as it seems at first sight, is after all an argument *ex nihilo.* We do not even know at what time the five daily prayers were introduced (cf. Alverny, Prière; Rubin, Morning; Monnot, ṣalāt). What we do know is, on the one hand, that according to Muslim tradition the Prophet was taught the *adhān* either during his ascension (q.v.) to heaven or while sleeping in the lap of ʿAlī (cf. Ibn Bābawayh, *Man lā yaḥḍuruhu,* 280f.), and that he taught the *tashahhud* "the way he used to teach us a sūra (q.v.) of the Qurʾān" (Muslim, *Ṣaḥīḥ, K. Ṣalāt,* 60). On the other hand, there are indications that the Umayyads more than once enforced alterations in the rite of the *ṣalāt*. During the revolt of Ibn al-Ashʿath (80-3/699-702), for example, their opponents reproached them with the demise of the *ṣalāt*, and, at Dayr al-Jamājim, the battle cry of the *qurrāʾ* (see RECITERS OF THE QURʾĀN; READINGS OF THE QURʾĀN) runs: "Revenge for the *ṣalāt!*" What they meant by this, however, is not at all clear; further research is neccessary. For use of the term *shahāda* to mean "martyrdom," see MARTYRS.

Matthias Radscheit

Bibliography

Primary: Ālūsī, *Kanz al-saʿāda fī sharḥ al-shahāda*, Beirut 1411/1991; al-Bayjūrī (al-Bājūrī), Ibrāhīm b. Muḥammad, *Ḥāshiya ʿalā matn al-Sanūsiyya*, Cairo 1315/1897-8; al-Ghazālī, Abū Ḥāmid Muḥammad, *Iḥyāʾ ʿulūm al-dīn*, 4 vols., Aleppo 1419/1998, i, 160-7; Ibn Bābawayh al-Qummī, *Man lā yaḥḍuruhu l-faqīh*, 4 vols., Tehran 1392/1972-3, i, 281-300; Ibn Rushd, Muḥammad b. Muḥammad, *Bidāyat al-mujtahid*, 2 vols., Cairo 1969, ii, 499-513; Khalīl b. Isḥāq al-Jundī, *al-Mukhtaṣar*, Paris 1318/1900, 211-19; Jurjānī, *Kitāb al-Taʿrīfāt*, ed. G. Flügel, Leipzig 1845, Beirut 1985, 135; al-Kaffawī, Abū l-Baqāʾ Ayyūb b. Mūsā, *al-Kulliyyāt*, Beirut 1413/1993², 527f.; Muslim, *Ṣaḥīḥ;* Shāfiʿī, *al-Risāla*, ed. A.M. Shākir, Cairo 1940, 25, 493; al-Shaʿrānī, ʿAbd al-Wahhāb b. Aḥmad, *al-Fatḥ al-mubīn*, Beirut 1420/1999; Fīrūzābādī al-Shīrāzī, Abū Isḥāq Ibrāhīm b. ʿAlī b. Yūsuf, *al-Muhadhdhab fī fiqh al-imām al-Shāfiʿī*, 2 vols., Beirut 1410/1990, ii, 324-44; Suyūṭī, *Itqān;* Ṭabarī, *Tafsīr;* Tahānawī, Muḥammad Aʿlā b. ʿAlī, *al-Kashshāf fī ṣṭilāḥāt al-funūn*, Calcutta 1863, 737-41; Ṭūsī, *al-Istibṣār*, 4 vols., Tehran 1390/1970-1, i, 305-7, 340-1; Zamakhsharī, *Kashshāf;* Zayd b. ʿAlī, *Majmūʿ al-fiqh*, ed. E. Griffini, *Corpus iuris di Zaid ibn ʿAlī*, Milan 1919, 186-94.

Secondary: N. Abbott, The Ḳaṣr K͟harāna inscription of 92 H. (710 A.D.). A new reading, in *Ars islamica* 11-12 (1946), 190-5; Kh.S. ʿAlī, *al-Ṣalāt ʿalā l-madhāhib al-arbaʿa*, Damascus 1461/2000²; A. d'Alverny, La prière selon le Coran, in *Proche-Orient chrétien* 10 (1960), 212-26, 303-17; 11 (1961), 3-16; Ṭ. al-ʿAlwānī, The testimony of women in Islamic law, in *American journal of Islamic social sciences* 13/2 (1996), 173-96; H.F. Amedroz, The office of the kadi in the Ahkam Sultaniyya of Mawardi, in *JRAS* (1910), 761-96; J.L. Austin, *How to do things with words*, Oxford 1962 (for a philosophical analysis of the category "performative utterance"); A. Baumstark, Zur Herkunft der monotheistischen Bekenntnisformeln im Koran, in *OC* 37 (1953), 6-22; C.H. Becker, Zur Geschichte des islamischen Kultus, in *Der Islam* 3 (1912), 374-99; repr. in id., *Islamstudien. Vom Werden und Wesen der Islamischem Welt*, 2 vols., Hildesheim 1967, i, 472-500; G. Bergsträsser, Review of *The governors and judges of Egypt*, in *ZDMG* 68 (1914), 395-417; R. Brunschvig, Le système de la preuve en droit musulman, in id., *Etudes d'islamologie*, 2 vols., Paris 1976, ii, 201-18; J. Canteins, *Mirroir de la shahāda*, Paris 1990; Carra de Vaux, S͟hahāda, in *EI¹*, iv, 278; B. Cohen, Testimonial compulsion in Jewish, Roman and Moslem law, in S. Löwinger (ed.), *Ignace Goldziher memorial volume*, 2 vols., Jerusalem 1958, ii, 50-70; H.H. Cohn, Witness, in *Encyclopedia Judaica*, xvi, coll. 584-90; K. Cragg, Shahādah, in *ER*, xiii, 198-9; P. Crone and M. Hinds, *God's caliph*, Cambridge 1986, 24-6; van Ess, *TG;* K.M. Firro, The ʿAlawīs in modern Syria, in *Der Islam* 82 (2005), 1-31; A. Fischer, Gestalten, Gebrauch, Namen und Herkunft der muslimischen Bekenntnisformel, in *Islamica* 5 (1932), 97-110; id., The pronounciation of the formula of the Muhammadan declaration of faith, in *JRAS* (1931), 845-55; id., Zur Syntax der muslimischen Bekenntnisformel, in *Islamica* 4 (1931), 512-21; D. Gimaret, S͟hahāda, in *EI²*, ix, 201; S.D. Goitein, *Studies in Islamic history and institutions*, Leiden 1966, 73-89; St. Guyard, Le Fetwa d'Ibn Taimiyyah sur les Nosairies, in *JA* [6ᵉ sér.] 18 (1871), 158-98; F. Hoerburger, Gebetsruf und Qorʾān-Rezitation in Kathmandu (Nepal), in *Baessler-Archiv* 23 (1975), 121-37; id., *Volksmusik in Afghanistan nebst einem Exkurs über Qorʾān-Rezitation und Thora-Kantillation in Kabul*, Regensburg 1969, 95-100; J. Horovitz, Bemerkungen zur Geschichte und Terminologie des islamischen Kultus, in *Islam* 16 (1927), 248-63; A. Jeffery, The Qurʾān as scripture, in *MW* 40 (1950), 41-55, 106-33, 185-206, 257-75; J. Jomier, *Dieu et l'homme dans le Coran*, Paris 1996, 117-38; id., Le nom divin "al-Raḥmān" dans le Coran, in *Mélanges Louis Massignon*, 3 vols., Damascus 1956-, ii, 361-81; Fl. Josephus, *The antiquities of the Jews*, in. W. Whiston (trans.), *The complete works of Josephus*, Grand Rapids 1981; M. Kaser, Testimonium, in A.F. von Pauly, *Paulys Real-encyclopädie der classischen Altertumswissenschaft*, ed. G. Wissowa, Stuttgart 1893-19-, vol. vA, pt. 1, coll. 1021-61; Ch. Kessler, ʿAbd al-Malik's inscription in the Dome of the Rock. A reconsideration, in JRAS (1970), 2-14; M.J. Kister,... *Illā bi-ḥaqqihi*...: a study of an early *ḥadīth*, in JSAI 5 (1984), 33-52; R. Köbert, Die *shahādat az-zūr*, in *Der Islam* 34 (1959), 194-5; D. Künstlinger, *Shuhūd* in Sūra 74,13, in OLZ 40 (1937), col. 273-4; K. Lech, *Geschichte des islamischen Kultus*. i. *Das ramaḍān Fasten*, Wiesbaden 1979, 73-105; D.S. Margoliouth, Omar's instructions to the kadi, in JRAS (1910), 307-26; K. Massey and K. Massey-Gillespie, A dialogue of creeds, in *Islamochristiana* 19 (1993), 17-28; G.C. Miles, Miḥrāb and ʿanazah. A study in early Islamic iconography, in id. (ed.), *Archeologica orientalia in memoriam Ernst Herzfeld*, Locust Valley, NY 1952, 156-71; Mir, *Dictionary*, 155, 216f.; id., *Verbal*, 191-3; E. Mittwoch, *Zur Entstehungsgeschichte des islamischen Gebets und Kultus*, Berlin 1913; M.I. Mochiri, A Pahlavi forerunner of the Umayyad reformed coinage, in JRAS (1981), 168-72; M. Momen, *An introduction to Shi'i Islam*, New Haven 1985, 178-9; G. Monnot, Ṣalāt, in EI[2], viii, 925-34; S. Mowinckel, Die Vorstellungen des Spätjudentums vom heiligen Geist als Fürsprecher und der johanneische Paraklet, in *Zeitschrift für die neutestamentliche Wissenschaft* 32 (1933), 97-130; Z. al-Muḥaysin, Nuqūsh jadīda min janūb al-Urdunn, in *Anbāʾ maʿhad al-āthār wa-l-anthrūbūlūjiyā, Jāmiʿat al-Yarmūk* 1 (1988), 6-8; T. Nagel, Die Inschriften im Felsendom und das islamische Glaubensbekenntnis — der Koran und die Anfänge des Ḥadīth, in *Arabica* 47 (2000), 329-65; id., *Das islamische Recht. Eine Einführung*, München 2001, 112-21; E. Neubauer and V. Doubleday, Islamic religious music, in S. Sadie (ed.), *The New Grove dictionary of music and musicians*, 29 vols., London 2001[2], xii, 599-610; Nöldeke, GQ; S. Ory, Aspects religieux des textes épigraphiques du début de l'Islam, in REMMM 58 (1990), 30-9; Th. O'Shaughnessy, *Muhammad's thoughts on death*, Leiden 1969, 65f.; C.E. Padwick, *Muslim devotions. A study of prayer-manuals in common use*, London 1961, 126-51; J. Pedersen, *Der Eid bei den Semiten*, Strassburg 1914; id./[Y. Linant de Bellefonds], Ḳasam, in EI[2], iv, 687-90; R. Peters, Shāhid, in EI[2], ix, 207-8; M. Radscheit, *Die koranische Herausforderung*, Berlin 1996; H. Rechenmacher, *"Ausser mir gibt es keinen Gott!" Eine sprach- und literaturwissenschaftliche Studie zur Ausschliesslichkeitsformel*, St. Ottilien 1997; A. Rippin, The commerce of eschatology, in Wild, *Text*, 125-35; id., *Muslims. Their religious beliefs and practices*, London 2002[2], 98-100, 248-9; U. Rubin, Morning and evening prayers in early Islam, in JSAI 10 (1987), 40-64; R. Sayed, *Die Revolte des Ibn al-Ašʿaṯ und die Koranleser*, Freiburg 1977, 342-3; J. Schacht, Liʿān, in EI[2], v, 730-2; A. Schimmel, The Sufis and the *shahāda*, in R.G. Hovannisian and Sp. Vryonis, Jr. (eds.), *Islam's understanding of itself*, Malibu 1983, 103-25; W.C. Smith, *On understanding Islam*, The Hague 1981, 162-73; J.K. Sollfrank, *Spuren altarabischer Rechtsformen im Koran*, Freiburg 1963; G. Stemberger, *Midrasch. Vom Umgang der Rabbinen mit der Bibel*, München 1989, 75-81; A. Subhan, The significance of the shahāda recalled, in IC 22 (1948), 233-6; S. Supomo, From *śakti* to *shahāda*. The quest for new meanings in a changing world order, in P.G. Riddell and T. Street (eds.), *Islam. Essays on scripture, thought and society. Festschrift Anthony H. Jones*, Leiden 1997, 219-36; E. Tyan, ʿAdl, in EI[2], i, 209-10; id., Le notariat et le regime de la preuve par ecrit dans la pratique du droit musulman, in *Annales de la Faculté de Droit de Beyrouth* 2 (1945), 3-99; J. Walker, *A catalogue of the Arab-Byzantine and post-reform Umaiyad coins*, London 1956; id., *A catalogue of the Arab-Sassanian coins*, London 1941; id., Some early Arab and Byzantine-Sasanian coins from Susa, in G.C. Miles (ed.), *Archeologica orientalia in memoriam Ernst Herzfeld*, Locust Valley, NY 1952, 235-43; W.M. Watt, *The formative period of Islamic thought*, Edinburgh 1973, 126-9; id., *Islamic creeds. A selection*, Edinburgh 1994; A.J. Wensinck, *The Muslim creed*, London 1932, 1-35; id., Tashahhud, in EI[1], iv, 742; J. Wirsching, *Allah allein ist Gott*, Frankfurt 2002; W. al-Zuḥaylī, *al-Mawsūʿa l-qurʾāniyya l-muyassara*, Damascus 2002[2].

Wives of the Prophet

The Prophet is usually said to have had thirteen wives or concubines, of whom nine survived him. But there is some dispute as to the identity of the thirteen. Some modern Muslim biographers have linked the large size of the Prophet's harem to the fact that all of the Prophet's marriages had been concluded by the time that the early Medinan revelation of Q 4:3 limited the number of wives to four (Haykal, *Life of Muḥammad*, 293; see MARRIAGE AND DIVORCE). Conversely, an Orientalist historian of the qurʾānic text has suggested that the Prophet had only four wives at the time of the revelation of Q 4:3 (Stern, *Marriage*, 78-81; see POST-ENLIGHTENMENT ACADEMIC STUDY OF THE QURʾĀN).

In ḥadīth (see ḤADĪTH AND THE QURʾĀN) and classical qurʾānic exegesis (*tafsīr;* see EXEGESIS OF THE QURʾĀN), the Prophet's right to less restricted polygamy is presented as a prerogative that *sunnat Allāh,* God's "law" for the world (see SUNNA; LAW AND THE QURʾĀN), had always granted to God's prophets and apostles (see PROPHETS AND PROPHETHOOD; MESSENGER). Furthermore, the classical sources found the scriptural legitimization of the Prophet's larger household (see FAMILY OF THE PROPHET) in Q 33:50, a late Medinan revelation that enumerated the "categories of females" lawful to the Prophet for marriage as follows (see LAWFUL AND UNLAWFUL; PROHIBITED DEGREES; WOMEN AND THE QURʾĀN): wives with whom the Prophet contracted marriage involving payment of "hires" (dowers; see BRIDEWEALTH); female prisoners of war (slaves) who fell to him as part of his share of the spoils (see SLAVES AND SLAVERY; BOOTY; CAPTIVES); paternal and maternal cousins who had migrated to Medina (q.v.; see also EMIGRANTS AND HELPERS; KINSHIP; FAMILY); and

a believing woman (see BELIEF AND UNBELIEF), if she gives herself to the Prophet, if the Prophet should wish to marry her. Especially for you, exclusive of the believers. We know what we have imposed upon them concerning their wives and slaves. So that there be no restriction on you. And God is forgiving, compassionate (see FORGIVENESS; MERCY; GOD AND HIS ATTRIBUTES).

The interpretation of the verse has presented difficulties because it appears to relate to a social system that had ceased to exist within a century after the Prophet's death (Watt, *Muhammad at Medina,* 393). Especially problematic within the changing code of early Islamic marriage law was the institution of *hiba,* possibly a pre-Islamic form of marriage, by which a woman "offers herself" to a man without a guardian (*walī;* see GUARDIANSHIP) to negotiate the union and without expectation of a dower. Later Muslim interpreters were uncomfortable with the institution of *hiba* and some opined that it was not a lawful form of marriage for anyone with the sole exception of the Prophet himself. Consequently, they used Q 33:50 primarily as an aid to classify the Prophet's consorts; but it also provided them with scriptural proof that Muḥammad's marriages — even though more than four — were divinely sanctioned.

Ḥadīth reports agree overall that the Prophet was married to the following women:

1. Khadīja bt. Khuwaylid (Quraysh [q.v.] — Asad; see KHADĪJA). She was married to Abū Hāla Hind b. al-Nabbāsh of Tamīm with whom she had two sons, Hāla and Hind, and to ʿAtīq b. ʿĀbid of Makhzūm, with whom she had a daughter, Hind. Twice widowed (see WIDOW), Khadīja was a wealthy merchant woman who is said to have employed Muḥammad in a business enterprise in 595 C.E. and then proposed marriage to him (see MARKETS; CARAVAN). He was twenty-five years old at that time and she was forty. They had two or three sons, named Qāsim, ʿAbdallāh al-Ṭāhir al-Muṭahhar (and Ṭayyib?), and four daughters, Zaynab, Ruqayya, Umm Kulthūm, and Fāṭima (q.v.). All the male children died in infancy. When the revelations began (see REVELATION AND INSPIRATION), Khadīja was the first person or, some say, the first woman to accept Islam from the messenger of God. Khadīja died three years before the migration to Medina (see EMIGRATION) and was buried in Mecca (q.v.).
2. Sawda bt. Zamʿa (Quraysh — ʿĀmir).

She was married to Sakrān b. ʿAmr, an early Muslim, and made the *hijra* (emigration) to Abyssinia (q.v.) with him. He died after their return to Mecca and she married the Prophet around 620 C.E. when she was about thirty. She migrated with his household to Medina where she died in 54/673-4.

3. ʿĀʾisha bt. Abī Bakr (q.v.; Quraysh — Taym), married in 1/623 when she was nine. She was the only virgin Muḥammad married. She remained childless and died in Medina in 58/677-8.

4. Ḥafṣa bt. ʿUmar b. al-Khaṭṭāb (Quraysh — ʿAdī) was the widow of Khumays b. Ḥudhāfa, a Muslim killed at Badr (q.v.). She married the Prophet in 3/625 at age eighteen. She died in 45/665 (see ḤAFṢA).

5. Umm Salama (Hind) bt. al-Mughīra (Quraysh — Makhzūm) married the Prophet in 4/626 at age twenty-nine. Her husband Abū Salama had died of a wound received at Uḥud and had left her with several small children (see EXPEDITIONS AND BATTLES). She died in 59/678-9.

6. Zaynab bt. al-Khuzayma (ʿĀmir b. Ṣaʿṣaʿa — Hilāl) was first married to al-Ṭufayl b. al-Ḥārith (Quraysh — al-Muṭṭalib) who divorced her. Then she married his brother ʿUbayda who was killed at Badr. Her marriage to the Prophet took place in or around 4/625-6 when she was about thirty. She died just a few months later.

7. Juwayriyya (al-Musṭaliq — Khuzāʿa), daughter of the chief of the tribe, was captured in the attack on her tribe in 5/627, married by Muḥammad on her profession of Islam and set free. She was about twenty years old at the time. Some say that she was at first only a concubine (see CONCUBINES) but that she had become a full wife before the Prophet's death. Juwayriyya died in 50/670.

8. Zaynab bt. Jaḥsh (Asad b. Khuzayma) married Muḥammad in 5/626-7 at age thirty-eight after her divorce from Zayd b. Ḥāritha. She was a granddaughter of ʿAbd al-Muṭṭalib, and Muḥammad's first cousin on his mother's side. Her father was a client of the clan of ʿAbd Shams of the Quraysh tribe (see CLIENTS AND CLIENTAGE). Zaynab bt. Jaḥsh died in 20/640-1.

9. Māriya the Copt (see CHRISTIANS AND CHRISTIANITY) was a slave-concubine whom the ruler of Egypt (q.v.) sent to the Prophet as a gift in or around 6/627-8. She bore Muḥammad a son called Ibrāhīm who died when he was less than two years old. She remained a concubine. She died in 16/637.

10. Umm Ḥabība (Ramla) bt. Abī Sufyān (Quraysh — ʿAbd Shams) was about thirty-five when the Prophet married her on his return from Khaybar in 7/628. She was the widow of ʿUbaydallāh b. Jaḥsh with whom she had made the emigration to Abyssinia. She died in 46/666.

11. Ṣafiyya bt. Ḥuyayy (of the Jewish al-Naḍīr tribe; see JEWS AND JUDAISM; NAḌĪR, BANŪ L-) was captured at Khaybar in 7/628 and assigned to the Prophet. She was seventeen. Perhaps she was at first a concubine, but later accepted Islam, was set free, and became a wife. She died in 52/672.

12. Maymūna bt. al-Ḥārith (ʿĀmir b. Ṣaʿṣaʿa — Hilāl) became Muḥammad's wife at age twenty-seven in the year 7/629 during or right after the lesser pilgrimage (q.v.). She died in 61/680-1.

13. Rayḥāna bt. Zayd (of the Jewish al-Naḍīr tribe) was captured in 5/627 during the attack on the Banū Qurayẓa (q.v.) to whom her husband had belonged. With the Prophet, she had the status of concubine which she apparently retained until her death in 10/631-2.

In addition to these thirteen women generally acknowledged to have been either regular wives or concubines, there is some information on a number of others whose names are linked with the Prophet, but the accounts are truncated, often contradictory, and on the whole quite dubious. The Prophet is said to have married several women whom he divorced (or some of whom divorced him?) before the marriage was consummated; mentioned are Fāṭima bt. al-Ḍahhāk b. Sufyān of the Kilāb tribe and ʿAmra bt. Yazīd of the Kilāb tribe (often assumed to be one and the same person), Asmāʾ bt. al-Nuʿmān of the Kinda tribe, Qutayla bt. Qays of the Kinda tribe, and Mulayka bt. Kaʿb of the Banū Layth. To some additional women, marriage was proposed but the marriage contract was not concluded (see CONTRACTS AND ALLIANCES; BREAKING TRUSTS AND CONTRACTS). The identity of the women who "gave themselves to the Prophet" by way of *hiba* is likewise quite obscure, as the list contains some additional names but also the names of several of the established wives.

When the Prophet died in 11/632, three of his thirteen consorts — Khadīja bt. Khuwaylid, Zaynab bt. Khuzayma, and Rayḥāna bt. Zayd — were already dead. Māriya retained her rank of concubine. The other nine were recognized as rightful bearers of the honorific title "Mothers of the Believers" (cf. Q 33:6, a late Medinan revelation; see CHRONOLOGY AND THE QURʾĀN).

The Prophet's wives in the Qurʾān

The Qurʾān specifically addresses the Prophet's wives on numerous occasions; many other revelations are linked with members of their group in the ḥadīth literature. They are clearly the elite women of the community of the faithful whose proximity to the Prophet endows them with special dignity. But this rank is matched by more stringent obligations. While the Qurʾān (Q 33:32) says of the Prophet's wives that they "are not like any [other] women," their peerlessness also entails those sharper rebukes for human frailties and more stringent codes of private and public probity, with which the scripture singles out the Prophet's consorts (see VIRTUES AND VICES, COMMANDING AND FORBIDDING). By linking dignity with obligation and elite status with heightened moral responsibility (q.v.; see also ETHICS AND THE QURʾĀN), their example defines two aspects of *sunnat Allāh,* God's "law" for the world. On the one hand, the Prophet's wives emerge in the qurʾānic context as models of the principle of ethical individualism. On the other hand, the dynamic of the revelations when read in chronological order moves toward increasing emphasis on the perfection of the Prophet's household as a whole; it is this collective entity that the revelations ultimately mean to strengthen and elevate to model status, even if it be at the expense of individual ambitions and the idiosyncrasies of some of its members.

The Prophet's wives figure unequally in qurʾānic exegesis, which is to say that only a small number of their group are consistently presented as key figures in the ḥadīth accounts of contexts of specific revelations (*asbāb al-nuzūl,* "occasions of revelation"). The following presents the qurʾānic revelations commonly linked with one, or several, or all of the members of the Prophet's household in the traditional chronology of revelation.

1. Q 33:37-8, *Lawfulness of marriage with former wife of adopted son,* and Q 33:4, 40, *Adopted sons are not sons*

Muslim scholarship dates these revelations to the fifth year after the *hijra* and commonly links them with the figure of Zaynab bt. Jaḥsh. The Prophet had arranged her marriage with Zayd b. Ḥāritha, a former Arabian slave of Khadīja's whom the Prophet had freed and adopted as a son. The marriage was not harmonious and Zayd desired a divorce. The Prophet is then said to have begun to feel an attraction for Zaynab; he concealed it because at that time adopted sons were regarded as the full equals of legitimate natural sons, which rendered their wives unlawful for the adopting father. The revelations of Q 33:37-8 commanded the Prophet to marry Zaynab, and Q 33:4, 40 abolished the inherited notion of legal equality between real sons and adopted sons.

2. Q 33:53, *The* ḥijāb *verse,* and Q 33:55, *exemptions thereto*

Zaynab bt. Jaḥsh's marriage to the Prophet, likewise said to have occurred during the fifth year after the *hijra,* is identified in the majority of ḥadīth and *tafsīr* accounts as the occasion of God's legislation of the *ḥijāb,* "curtain, screen," imposed by God to shield the Prophet's women from the eyes of visitors to his dwellings (see VEIL; MODESTY). Many traditions maintain that this revelation was vouchsafed after some of the wedding guests had overstayed their welcome at the nuptial celebration in Zaynab's house. Another strand of traditions mentions ʿUmar b. al-Khaṭṭāb in the role of counselor who urged the Prophet to conceal and segregate his wives as a protective measure. For some of the later medieval exegetes, such as al-Bayḍāwī (d. prob. 716/1316-17) and Ibn Kathīr (d. 774/1373), ʿUmar's vigilance for the good of the Prophet's wives rates greater consideration as an occasion of revelation of Q 33:53 than do the accounts of the Prophet's annoyance at the guests who lingered in Zaynab's house on the wedding eve. The *ḥijāb* verse is followed by a revelation that establishes the classes of relatives and servants with whom the Prophet's wives were permitted to deal face-to-face rather than from behind a partition (Q 33:55). The qurʾānic directive to the Prophet's wives in Q 33:33 to stay in their houses and avoid strutting about is dated later than Q 33:53 (cf. below; see HOUSE, DOMESTIC AND DIVINE).

Self-protection of "the Prophet's wives, his daughters, and the women of the believers" was thereafter enjoined in Q 33:59-60 by way of God's demand that Muslim women cover themselves in their "mantles" *(jalābīb)* when abroad, so that they would be known (as free women) and not molested. Once again, classical exegesis has here identified ʿUmar b. al-Khaṭṭāb as the main spokesman in favor of a new clothing (q.v.) law. An additional legislative item on female modesty, directed at Muslim women in general, was revealed at a later date in Q 24:31 which prescribed use of their "kerchiefs" (*khumur,* sing. *khimār*) as a means to cover up "their bosoms" *(juyūb)* and their finery *(zīna)* except in the company of their husbands, other males to whom marriage is taboo and female friends and relatives, slaves, and the small children. It was on the basis of Q 33:53 (*ḥijāb,* "curtain" or "partition"), Q 33:59 (*jalābīb,* "mantles"), Q 24:31 (*khumur,* "kerchiefs") and Q 33:33 ("stay in your houses and avoid self-display") that classical law and theology (see THEOLOGY AND THE QURʾĀN) thereafter formulated the medieval Islamic ordinance for overall female veiling and segregation. Muḥammad's wives' domestic seclusion behind a partition *(ḥijāb)* merged with the clothing laws to such an extent that the very garments which Muslim women were commanded to wear in public came to be called *ḥijāb.*

3. Q 24:11-26, *The qurʾānic injunction against slander*

In chronological terms, the next block of qurʾānic legislation consistently linked in the ḥadīth with a member of the Prophet's household is Q 24:11-26, the injunction against slander (see GOSSIP). The verses are dated into the fifth or sixth year after the *hijra* and are said to have been occasioned by ʿĀʾisha bt. Abī Bakr's involvement in "the affair of the lie (q.v.)," *al-ifk*.

The medieval ḥadīth describes ʿĀʾisha as the Prophet's favorite wife. The only virgin among Muḥammad's brides, she was betrothed to the Prophet three years before the *hijra* when she was six or seven years old, and the marriage was concluded and consummated when she was nine. The "affair of the lie" thus occurred when she was eleven, twelve, or thirteen. Returning from a military expedition on which she had accompanied the Prophet, ʿĀʾisha was inadvertently left behind at the last camping ground when the army departed for Medina in the darkness of early morning. She was rescued and returned to Medina by a young Arab Bedouin (q.v.; see also ARABS; NOMADS). A scandal broke that was mainly instigated by the Prophet's enemies (q.v.) but also tore the Prophet's followers apart (see OPPOSITION TO MUḤAMMAD). A full month later, the revelation of Q 24:11-26 was vouchsafed which established ʿĀʾisha's innocence, severely reprimanded the believers for their unrighteous behavior, and announced grievous penalties for all who would perpetrate unfounded slander of chaste women (see BOUNDARIES AND PRECEPTS; CHASTITY). Additional legislation on slander is found in Q 24:4-5. The transgression was later classified in Islamic jurisprudence as one of the *ḥudūd* offenses ("canon law cases with unalterable punishments"; see CHASTISEMENT AND PUNISHMENT).

4. Q 33:28-9, *The verses of choice*

Ḥadīth accounts do not reflect a consensus on the incident or incidents that led to the Prophet's seclusion from all of his wives for a month until he received the revelation of Q 33:28-9 that instructed him to have his wives choose between "the life of this world and its glitter" and "God, his Prophet, and the abode in the hereafter." This revelation has been dated to the late fifth, seventh, or ninth year after the *hijra*. The ḥadīth sources mention several different episodes of household disagreement caused by the women's (or some of the women's) insubordination and backtalk (see INSOLENCE AND OBSTINACY; OBEDIENCE), material demands that the Prophet was unable to fulfill (see MAINTENANCE AND UPKEEP), and mutual jealousy (see ENVY), that may all have fed into one major crisis. By all accounts, the domestic turmoil was of significant proportions and when the Prophet secluded himself for a month, there was fear in the community that he would divorce his wives.

When the Prophet returned, he repeated the newly-revealed "verses of choice" to each of them. Thereupon each of the women, beginning with ʿĀʾisha, declared that she chose God and his Prophet and the abode in the hereafter over the world and its adornment. It is said that ʿĀʾisha reached her decision swiftly and without consulting her father (or parents), and that the Prophet was gladdened by her choice.

5. Q 33:30-1, *Double punishment and double reward for the Prophet's women,* Q 33:32, *Peerlessness of the Prophet's women and injunction against complaisant speech,* Q 33:33-4, *Command that they stay in their houses, avoid displaying their charms, and be pious, charitable, obedient, and mindful of God's verses and wisdom recited in their houses*

These verses are generally thought to have been revealed soon after the crisis that had led to the Prophet's seclusion from his wives. They acknowledge the peerlessness of the Prophet's consorts and also impose specific and far-reaching restrictions on the women's accessibility, visibility, and manner of comportment. Q 33:30-1 establish double punishment in the case of clear immoral behavior, and double reward for obedience to God and his apostle and godly acts (see GOOD DEEDS). In Q 33:32, the Prophet's women are then told that they are "not like any (other) women," and are enjoined to abstain from submissive speech that might be misunderstood. In the verses immediately following, Q 33:33-4, the expression "O women of the Prophet" does not appear, but both verses are syntactically tied to the four that precede them. Because of the context, qurʾānic exegesis has traditionally understood Q 33:33-4 as having been addressed to the wives of the Prophet. The question of context is here especially significant because the verses include important pieces of legislation. In Q 33:33, the Prophet's wives (or, a plurality of women?) are commanded to stay in their houses, avoid *tabarruj*, "strutting-about," in the manner of *al-jāhiliyya l-ūlā*, "the first age of unbelief" (see AGE OF IGNORANCE; IGNORANCE), perform the prayer (q.v.), give alms (see ALMSGIVING), and obey God and his Prophet. In Q 33:34, they are commanded to be mindful of God's signs (q.v.; or verses [q.v.]) and the wisdom (q.v.) that is recited in their houses (see RECITATION OF THE QURʾĀN).

In terms of Islamic legal-theological institution building, when Q 33:33 was later applied to Muslim women in general it enjoined them to stay at home and also be indistinguishable from all other females when abroad, as *tabarruj* came to mean a woman's display of her physical self in all manners of speaking that would include the wearing of revealing garments, the use of cosmetics, unrestricted gait and the like. While the exact definition of *tabarruj* has varied over the ages, its condemnation by the custodians of communal morality has always included the qurʾānic reference that it is un-Islamic, a matter of *jāhiliyya* and therefore a threat to Islamic society. *Tabarruj*, forbidden to the Prophet's wives in Q 33:33, eventually came to signify the very antithesis of the *ḥijāb* imposed on the Prophet's wives in Q 33:53, both in its qurʾānic sense of seclusion qua "partition" and also its extended meaning of a concealing garment worn outside the house. In their totality, the three qurʾānic commands to Muḥammad's wives of Q 33:53 and 33:33 thus became the scriptural foundations for an Islamic paradigm of women's societal role in which space, clothing and comportment were powerful factors (see GENDER; PATRIARCHY).

6. Q 33:6, *The Prophet's wives are the Mothers of the Believers*, and Q 33:53, *Muslims may not marry the Prophet's wives "after him"*

These revelations are thought to have been received at a later date than the verses of choice (Q 33:28-9) and the peerlessness and restriction verses (Q 33:30-4). Muslim qurʾānic interpretation has recognized a connection between the honorific title of "Mothers of the Believers" in Q 33:6 and the injunction against marriage with the Prophet's wives (or widows) in Q 33:53, because, according to Q 4:23, marriage with the mother is forbidden. Even though Q 33:6 and Q 33:53 are not consecutive in the established qurʾānic text, they are generally considered to belong together. Qurʾān interpreters point out that the injunction against marriage with the Prophet's wives or widows was divinely enjoined in order to glorify the Prophet, alive or dead. In fact, none of the Prophet's established wives are known to have been divorced by him and none of his widows remarried after he had died.

7. Q 66:1-5, *Release of the Prophet from certain restrictions, expiation of oaths, a wife who betrayed the secret, warning to two women who conspired against the Prophet, threat of divorce and enumeration of wifely virtues*
This group of verses has been dated to the period of, or right after, a major crisis in the Prophet's household that culminated in the Prophet's month-long seclusion from his household. The revelation relieves the Prophet from some unspecified, apparently self-imposed, restriction. Mentioned then is the duty to expiate oaths (q.v.). A matter of confidence was disclosed by the Prophet to one of his wives but she divulged it. Two women are called to repent, are sternly reprimanded, and are warned not to conspire against the Prophet. Thereafter the wives are threatened with the possibility that if the Prophet divorces them, God in exchange will give him "better wives than you, Muslims, believers, devout, penitent, obedient in worship, observant of worship and contemplation, both formerly married and virgins."

Clearly these verses also refer to a major crisis in the Prophet's household, which ḥadīth and exegetical literature again attribute to shortcomings (insubordination, greed, jealousy) on the part of the women. There is a great deal of overlap in the details of the quoted *asbāb al-nuzūl* (occasions of revelation of qur'ānic verses) materials, and some sources even collapse the occasions of revelation of Q 33:28-9 and Q 66:1-5.

8. Q 33:50, *Classes of women lawful for marriage with the Prophet,* Q 33:51, *Special privileges for the Prophet within his polygamous household,* Q 33:52, *Injunction against additional marriages?*
These verses have been dated to the late Medinan period. Q 33:50, specifying the categories of women from which the Prophet was empowered to choose his wives and concubines, was discussed at the beginning of this article. Q 33:51, most probably revealed on the same occasion as Q 33:50, grants the Prophet greater freedom in choosing — or dealing with — his wives, by permitting him to "defer" or to "take in" whom of the women he willed; the verse continues with the words "and if you desire one whom you have sent away, it is no sin for you (see SIN, MAJOR AND MINOR). This is more appropriate that their eyes be gladdened and that they should not be sad (see JOY AND MISERY), and all be satisfied with what you have given them. God knows what is in your hearts." One school of exegesis links Q 33:51 with Q 33:50 in order to read Q 33:51 as divine permission for the Prophet to enter into new marriage arrangements and terminate old ones. Another strand of interpretation stipulates that Q 33:51 applies only to the Prophet's relations with his existing spouses, whence it means a release from the rigid pattern of marital equity that Muḥammad had practiced in the past. Q 33:52 (which appears to contradict Q 33:50 and Q 33:51) instructs the Prophet that henceforth (additional) women are not lawful for him (for marriage) nor in (ex)change for (established) wives, with the exception of his slaves. According to some commentators, this revelation put an end to further marriages by the Prophet. Others interpreted the verse as limitation on the groups, or classes, or categories, from which the Prophet was empowered to choose new marriage partners. A third point of view maintained that Q 33:52 was abrogated by Q 33:51 (see ABROGATION); the stipulation of abrogation eliminated the apparent contradiction between Q 33:52 and Q 33:51 and also served to confirm the Prophet's complete freedom with regard to his marital arrangements.

The qur'ānic legislation directed at the

Prophet's wives is entirely of Medinan provenance and belongs to the last six or seven years of the Prophet's life. Considered in chronological sequence of date of revelation, the duty of seclusion behind a partition in the presence of non-relatives was the first rule imposed on the Prophet's wives. It was accompanied, or soon followed, by stringent codes of modest comportment in private and public that emphasized the women's duty to maintain seclusion in their houses, in addition to piety (q.v.), charity (see ALMSGIVING), and obedience to God and his Prophet. Added thereto were strongly worded warnings against domestic disobedience (q.v.) in the form of plots or conspiracies. While the Prophet was granted unequalled rights concerning the number and type of marriages he might wish to conclude, remarriage of his wives "after him" was forbidden.

The chronological sequence of revelations was clearly an important concern of early Muslim ḥadīth, *tafsīr,* and *fiqh* (Islamic jurisprudence), made all the more urgent by the doctrine of *naskh,* "abrogation" of an earlier revelation by a later one, that had theological as well as legal import. While in chronological terms the qurʾānic legislation on the Prophet's domestic affairs progressed toward granting him increasing control over his women, the time frame also suggests a trend toward greater restraint, not increasing "liberation," of the Prophet's women. The Qurʾān itself provides the *ratio legis* for this trend in its repeated statements of concern for the collective wellbeing, indeed the perfection, of the Prophet's household. The Prophet's polygamous household here becomes a prime example of qurʾānic reasoning in favor of righteous institutions over individual aspirations. At the same time, the qurʾānic legislation also signifies the principle of ethical individualism in its linkage between individual elect status and individual virtue (q.v.; see also ELECTION). As posited in the "verses of choice" of Q 33:28-9, double shares of divine reward are compensation for the Prophet's wives' choice to accept obligations more stringent than those which the Qurʾān imposes upon Muslim women in general. According to *sunnat Allāh,* God's "law" for the world, human virtue bears rewards both individual and communal, when virtuous institutions are maintained by the individual virtue of their members. That is to say that the Qurʾān's promise of everlasting elite status for the Prophet's consorts hinges on their acceptance of greater and graver obligations, since for their group the conditions of "obedience to God and obedience to his Prophet" are cast in more exacting terms.

The Prophet's wives in the classical ḥadīth

In a complex mixture of history and paradigm, the Prophet's wives appear in the classical ḥadīth in at least three distinct sets of personae: as models for the righteous, as elect consorts touched by the miracles (q.v.) that marked the Prophet's career, and as embodiments of female emotionalism, irrationality, greed, and rebelliousness (see REBELLION). The first of these three symbolic images of the Prophet's wives is most pervasive in the authenticated, or "sound," ḥadīth collections that bear the imprint of development of the terms of Islamic law. Second, the hagiographic material in the ḥadīth is largely linked with the legacy of the *quṣṣāṣ,* popular tellers of pious lore. Third, the image of the Prophet's wives as "ordinary women" who display all the frailties and foibles of their sex (see SEX AND SEXUALITY) is mainly found in ḥadīth works compiled for biographical purposes, such as Ibn Saʿd's (d. 230/845) *Kitāb al-Ṭabaqāt al-kubrā,* of which the eighth volume deals with the ḥadīth by and about the women of early Islam. Ibn Saʿd's collection includes items pertaining to all of the normative, hagiographic and anecdotal ḥadīth on Muḥammad's wives, and much of the material that he assembled can later be encountered in the classical *tafsīr* literature.

The Prophet's wives as models to be followed

Their Qurʾān-established rank, role as the Prophet's helpmates and supporters in his mission to preach and implement the true religion (q.v.; see also TEACHING AND PREACHING THE QURʾĀN; INVITATION), and their intimate involvement with the righteous Prophet in all of the minutiae of daily life elevated the Prophet's wives even during their lifetime to a level of prestige well above the community's other females. This special status grew loftier with the progression of time, when Muslim piety came to view the women of the Prophet's household as models for emulation. Eventually, the Prophet's wives' behavior was recognized as *sunna,* an "impeccable model," that furnished many of the criteria of what was lawful or forbidden for Muslims, especially Muslim women. These criteria were then codified qua examples in the works of early Islamic jurisprudence *(fiqh).*

The interplay between the principle of the women's righteousness and their function as categorical norm-setters is especially clear in the traditions that deal with modesty, veiling and seclusion, where the Prophet's wives are depicted as both models and enforcers of the then newly imposed qurʾānic norms. Their invisibility went beyond the restrictions placed upon Muslim women in general at that time. In addition to obligatory seclusion in their houses, the Prophet's wives were shrouded in multiple garments when abroad, such as during prayer and the pilgrimage, and they traveled in camel (q.v.) litters so unrevealing and undistinguishable that even the Prophet mistook one wife's litter for that of another. In some sources, the fact that the Prophet on his return from Khaybar wrapped his war captive Ṣafiyya in his own cloak from the top of her head to the bottom of her feet was taken as proof that Ṣafiyya was no longer a concubine but had become a wife. ʿĀʾisha is said to have hidden behind the *ḥijāb* of her house even in the presence of a blind man and to have replaced her niece's flimsy *khimār* with a thick cloth, reminding her of the revelation of Q 24:31.

At the Farewell Pilgrimage (q.v.), the Prophet is said to have enjoined his wives to stay home at all times (and even forego the pilgrimage in the future), and after he had died, several of his widows did opt for complete confinement. The most notable exception to such righteous immobility on the part of the Mothers of the Believers was ʿĀʾisha's well-established active involvement in public affairs after the Prophet's death which culminated in the Battle of the Camel. ʿĀʾisha's behavior was clearly outside of the norms reportedly observed by the Prophet's other widows. The ḥadīth overall deals with the event not by way of reports of censure that others cast against her but emphasizes the fact that ʿĀʾisha herself regretted her involvement most bitterly and passed her final days in self-recrimination.

The Prophet's wives coexisted with one another in mutual love (q.v.) and compassion and thus embodied the ideal spirit of a harmonious polygamous household. They called each other "sister" (q.v.) and praised each other's uprightness, devotion, and charity. When Zaynab bt. Jaḥsh fell ill, it was the Prophet's other widows who nursed her and, when she died, it was they who washed, embalmed and shrouded her body (see DEATH AND THE DEAD; BURIAL). They also lived lives of voluntary poverty (see POVERTY AND THE POOR) and denied themselves even lawful pleasures. Of

ʿĀʾisha, for instance, it is said that she fasted continuously (see FASTING) and freely gave alms at the expense of her own already meager food supply and that she wore threadbare clothes which she mended with her own hands. Of Maymūna it is reported that she picked up a pomegranate seed from the ground to keep it from going to waste. Zaynab bt. Jaḥsh, nicknamed "the refuge of the poor," gave away all her wealth, including the large yearly pension that she received during the caliphate of ʿUmar b. al-Khaṭṭāb (see CALIPH), since she regarded wealth as *fitna,* "temptation," and ʿĀʾisha donated in charity the five camel loads of gold (q.v.) that the Umayyad caliph had sent her for the sale of her house located near the Medinan mosque (see MOSQUE OF DISSENSION). The Prophet's wives were also profoundly knowledgeable about matters of the faith (q.v.) and they were scrupulously honest in transmitting traditions. ʿĀʾisha's knowledge was such that very old men who had been Companions of the Prophet (q.v.) came to seek her counsel and instruction. Based on the criteria provided by the medieval ḥadīth, the main components of the exemplary precedent set by the Prophet's wives are: segregation and quiet domesticity, modest comportment, invisibility through full veiling when outside of the house, ascetic frugality (see ASCETICISM), profound knowledge of the faith and devout obedience to God and his Prophet. Since the Prophet was also the husband of these women, special emphasis is placed on wifely obedience as an important dimension of female righteousness.

The Prophet's wives in early ḥadīth hagiography

The ḥadīth collections contain reports of miraculous events that embellished the lives of the Prophet's consorts. These occurrences always involve the Prophet, and it is in their relationship with him that the women were granted miraculous experiences and abilities. Before her marriage to the Prophet and the coming of Islam, Muḥammad's first wife Khadīja bt. Khuwaylid was participating in a popular, annual, pagan celebration for the women of Mecca (see PRE-ISLAMIC ARABIA AND THE QURʾĀN; SOUTH ARABIA, RELIGIONS IN PRE-ISLAMIC) that centered around an idol in the shape of a man, when the idol began to speak, predicting the coming of a prophet named Aḥmad (see NAMES OF THE PROPHET), and advising those who could among the women of Mecca to marry him. While the other women pelted the idol with stones, Khadīja paid attention to its words. Later, after she had hired Muḥammad to trade on her behalf in Syria (q.v.), she heard about the miraculous events that had occurred on this journey, and it was because of this information that she asked him to marry her (Ibn Isḥāq-Guillaume, 82-3). Most of the Prophet's other wives experienced dream visions (q.v.) prior to their marriages with him (see also DREAMS AND SLEEP). While Sawda was still married to her previous husband, she dreamt that Muḥammad approached her and placed his foot on her neck, and also saw a moon that hurled itself upon her while she lay prostrated. When Umm Ḥabība and her husband lived as temporary refugees in Abyssinia, she had a dream in which she saw her husband disfigured. On the following morning she learned that he had apostatized (see APOSTASY) and when she rebuked him, he took to drink and died soon afterwards. Then she heard a dream voice that addressed her as Mother of the Believers, and on the following morning the ruler of Abyssinia informed her that the Prophet had written a letter asking for her hand in marriage. Ṣafiyya, the woman of Jewish descent from Khaybar, saw herself in a dream standing by Muḥammad's side while an angel's wing covered the two of them. Later she dreamt that a moon had drawn close from the direction of Medina and had fallen into her lap. Her husband hit her in the face when she told him of this vision, and the mark was still visible when the Prophet married her after the conquest of Khaybar. In ʿĀʾisha's case, it was not she but the Prophet who was favored with a sign, as it is reported that Muḥammad only asked Abū Bakr for her hand in marriage after the angel Gabriel (q.v.) had shown him her picture as his future wife. Later it was only ʿĀʾisha in whose company Muḥammad is said to have received revelations (see REVELATION AND INSPIRATION); some traditions report that ʿĀʾisha could even see the angel on these occasions and exchanged salutations with him, while others say that she could not see him but that she and the angel greeted each other through the Prophet. Zaynab bt. Jaḥsh was miraculously blessed by God when the meager food that the Prophet's servant Anas b. Malik had prepared for her wedding feast multiplied until it sufficed to feed a large crowd.

The ḥadīth collections establish that all of the Prophet's terrestrial wives will be his consorts in paradise (q.v.). The angel commanded the Prophet to take Ḥafṣa bt. ʿUmar back after he had divorced her, saying that she was a righteous woman and would be his wife in heaven. Sawda implored the Prophet not to divorce her because she yearned to be his consort in heaven. The angel showed the dying Prophet ʿĀʾisha's image in paradise to make his death easier with the promise of their reunion in the hereafter. The first of the wives to join the Prophet in heaven was Zaynab bt. Jaḥsh. He had predicted this when he said that the wife who had "the longest arm" would arrive there soon after him; later the women comprehended that what he had meant was "charity," because the first to die after him was the charitable Zaynab bt. Jaḥsh. Traditions of this genre, then, are of inspirational character. They depict the Prophet's wives as divinely favored individuals, ranked above ordinary womankind and surrounded by God's grace, because they are his Prophet's chosen consorts.

The Prophet's wives as "ordinary women"

Many of the accounts of life in the Prophet's household contain detailed descriptions of the jealousies and domestic quarrels of the Mothers of the Believers. These reports present the Prophet's wives as a petty, greedy, backbiting and power-hungry lot. The unseemliness of their behavior is more glaringly highlighted by the many traditions about the Prophet's impartiality towards his wives. He is said to have been scrupulous in treating them equitably, visiting each of them once a day. After a wedding night spent with a new wife, he wished his other wives well and asked to receive their good wishes. Each wife had her turn of a fixed period of companionship and sexual contact with the Prophet, a prerogative that she zealously guarded as her right and could give to a rival if she chose. If a new bride opted for a longer period of privacy and intimacy with the Prophet after the wedding, then the other wives were entitled to the same. On travels and military expeditions, he determined by lot which two of his wives would accompany him. This equitable system was upset time and time again when a wife would think of some trick or another to detain the Prophet in her house during his daily visit. An oft-quoted story tells that Ḥafṣa bt. ʿUmar (or maybe Umm Salama) who knew of Muḥammad's love for sweets detained him by offering a honey drink, until the ruse was discovered and thwarted by a counter-ruse of ʿĀʾisha, Sawda and Ṣafiyya (or maybe it was ʿĀʾisha and Ḥafṣa).

Many traditions state that the women were dissatisfied with the manner in which food and other presents were distributed among them. But most of the jealousy narratives have a sexual and emotional theme. New arrivals in the Prophet's household are said to have evoked intense jealousies among the established wives who feared that a new rival might replace them in the Prophet's affection. Such jealousies could make a new wife appear more imposing and beautiful than perhaps she really was. ʿĀʾisha, for example, is said to have been most fearful when the Prophet had married the Meccan Makhzūmī aristocrat Umm Salama, or brought home the beautiful Arab war captive Juwayriyya, or the young Jewish war captive Ṣafiyya. Umm Salama was especially prone to jealousy and had warned the Prophet about this fact before accepting his marriage proposal. Some of the Prophet's wives reviled each other and each other's fathers and did so even in his presence; such backbiting and bragging matches are reported between Zaynab bt. Jaḥsh and ʿĀʾisha, Umm Salama and Ṣafiyya, and ʿĀʾisha and Ṣafiyya, while Zaynab bt. Jaḥsh is also said to have refused to lend one of her camels to Ṣafiyya whose mount had become defective. All of the wives were intensely jealous of the Prophet's concubine Māriya the Copt, especially after she had given birth to Ibrāhīm, the Prophet's only child after the sons and daughters whom Khadīja had borne him; their jealousy of Māriya was so intense that the Prophet had to assign her a dwelling in a loft he owned that was at some distance from his established wives' living quarters. The women also boasted among themselves (see BOAST) about who had played a special role in an "occasion of revelation," or held a special rank with the Prophet. Some traditions assert that the wives disliked Zaynab bt. Jaḥsh's reminders that her marriage to the Prophet had occurred by divine dispensation, and that the *ḥijāb* verse had been revealed on the occasion of her wedding. ʿĀʾisha, in turn, reminded the wives that she had been the only virgin bride among all of them and that the Prophet often called her his favorite wife. Some of the traditions on the Prophet's wives' mutual jealousies may very well have carried some underlying political meaning during the period of their first formulation, since the Prophet's wives hailed from different clans and even tribes of whom many were, or later turned out to be, affiliated with opposing factions in early Islamic history (see POLITICS AND THE QURʾĀN; HISTORY AND THE QURʾĀN). The Jewish background of two of Muḥammad's consorts, Ṣafiyya and Rayḥāna, and the Christian faith of his concubine, Māriya the Copt, may also at some level have influenced the shape and import of the jealousy narratives. In any case, the almost formulaic early ḥadīth image of the Prophet's wives as jealous, competitive, petty and backbiting, while perhaps in part historically correct, was retained and even highlighted in medieval Islamic scholarship because it supported *ʿulamāʾ* opinion of women's irrational nature. In part, the ongoing popularity of traditions depicting the Prophet's wives as "ordinary women" was surely due to the need and desire of the pious to collect background information on the qurʾānic verses of rebuke and censure revealed on their behalf. But this preference was also grounded in the generally low opinion of women's nature as expressed in medieval legal-theological literature as a whole, where information on the flaws of the first female elite of Islam served to reinforce an emerging blueprint of gender discrimination (see FEMINISM AND THE QUR'ĀN).

The Prophet's wives in modern Muslim interpretation

It is symptomatic of the new age and debates on women's questions that the modern and contemporary literature on the Prophet's consorts has largely excised the "anecdotal" materials so copious in Ibn Saʿd and other medieval sources. The same is largely true for the hagiographic dimension. With the exception of works of popular piety (that often have a Ṣūfī bent; see ṢŪFISM AND THE QUR'ĀN) and some traditionalist inspirational writings, contemporary Muslim literature now deemphasizes the miraculous experiences of the Prophet's wives, just as it also deemphasizes their all-too-human frailties. It is as fighters for the establishment of Islamic values — and there mainly by way of impeccable morality and manner of life — that the wives of the Prophet are now depicted. As such, they embody the model behavior that the contemporary Muslim woman can recognize and which she must strive to follow.

Modern Muslim literature on the Prophet's life and domestic affairs often includes long passages on gender issues in general. Dignity, honor, and rights both spiritual and material provided for the women in Islam are contrasted with women's chattel status in the Arabian *jāhiliyya* and other past and present godless societies, especially of the West. Criticism of the West focuses on pre-modern legal inequities and also the ongoing exploitation of the Western woman in the workplace and as a sexual object in the entertainment and advertising industries (Haykal, *Life of Muḥammad,* 318f.; al-ʿAqqād, *ʿAbqariyyat Muḥammad,* 99f.; Bint al-Shāṭi', *Tarājim,* 206f., 257; Gharīb, *Nisā',* 114f., 122f.). While women's exploitation in Western societies undermines self-serving Western claims to being "advanced," women's rights in Islam verify the collective dignity of all Muslims, indeed of the whole Islamic system, that the West (missionaries and Orientalists) had set out to defame. History itself proves the Prophet's superior nature in that Muḥammad not only founded a legal society in which women were at long last recognized, but he himself also treated women, including his own wives, better than did any other man at any time in human history before or after his lifetime (Haykal, *Life of Muḥammad,* 298; al-ʿAqqād, *ʿAbqariyyat Muḥammad,* 102f.; Bint al-Shāṭi', *Tarājim,* 208f.; Gharīb, *Nisā',* 121f.). In some of the modern literature, the medieval ḥadīth is omitted or used very sparingly (Haykal, *Life of Muḥammad;* al-ʿAqqād, *ʿAbqariyyat Muḥammad*), while in other works the old texts are read in new ways (Bint al-Shāṭi', *Tarājim*). In both approaches, the old hagiographic traditions are eliminated. Instead the Prophet's wives are depicted as helpmates and participants in the Prophet's mission, and their "jealousy," that is, their competitive love for him, is frequently attributed to piety, commitment to the cause, and their own attractive and lively natures. The Prophet's harmonious household supports the argument in favor of polygamy when its main features are legality, equity, honor, practicability, and necessity. The large size of the Prophet's harem is now interpreted as a sign of his perfected humanity (see IMPECCABILITY). That the Prophet married his many wives for reasons involving some sexual interest is indication of his sound original nature (al-ʿAqqād, *ʿAbqariyyat Muḥammad,* 110-11; Bint al-Shāṭi', *Tarājim,* 204; Gharīb, *Nisā',* 122f.). That he then had the power to fulfill the demands of his mission and also his wives' demands is proof of his superiority as a human. But mere pleasure-seeking was never a motive in his choice of any of his wives, before or after his call, in youth or old age. Muḥammad was a man of seriousness and equanimity who could have lived like a king but chose to live like a pauper. He chose frugality even though this went against the wishes of his wives who craved the means to beautify themselves for him. Clearest proof that the Prophet was free from base instincts such as lust (as claimed by the Orientalists) are the historical facts of his celibacy until his twenty-fifth year and then his monogamous marriage with a woman fifteen years his senior, to whom he was completely devoted until she died and he was more than fifty years old. In Khadīja, his first follower and supporter, he also found a substitute mother (Bint al-Shāṭi', *Tarājim,* 223; Gharīb, *Nisā',* 119). The many other marriages that the Prophet concluded after her death were either means to cement political alliances with friends and foes alike, or they were concluded in order to provide a safe haven of refuge as well as rank and honor for noble women whom the Islamic struggle had left unprotected or even destitute. Even the marriage with 'Ā'isha came about at first because the Prophet wished to strengthen his relationship with her father, Abū Bakr; it was only later that she emerged as his most beloved wife, but even then she could not take Khadīja's place in his heart (Bint al-Shāṭi', *Tarājim,* 233f., 240-1, 254, 272f.). The marriages with Ḥafṣa bt. 'Umar, Umm Ḥabība bt. Abī Sufyān, Juwayriyya of the Banū Musṭaliq and others were likewise primarily political unions but the compassion motif was never absent (al-'Aqqād, *'Abqariyyat Muḥammad,* 115-17; Bint al-Shāṭi', *Tarājim,* 242f., 304f., 319f., 355f., 377f., 382f., 387f.).

Modern Muslim biographers do not exclude the jealousy theme from their descriptions of the Prophet's domestic relations, but their use of the theme differs from the medieval ḥadīth in both mood and purpose. In many instances, jealousy is equated with the power of love and also other attractive human traits that distinguish full-blooded and lively women such as the Prophet's wives (Bint al-Shāṭi', *Tarājim,* 278f., 293). The Prophet himself permitted his wives to fill his private world with warmth, emotion, and excitement, and barring a few instances when they went out of bounds and he had to deal with them sternly, he did not mind spending his free hours observing their small battles that were kindled by their love and jealousy for him. Since the Prophet was the perfect husband, all of his wives found honor and happiness with him such as no monogamous marriage to another man could have entailed (Bint al-Shāṭi', *Tarājim,* 204f.).

The large-scale replacement of the medieval jealousy theme with the attractive modern image of the lively and loving spouse signifies the end of the classical construct of female weakness, including female powerlessness. As the Prophet's wives once again emerge as ideal women in the modern literature, the qualities now emphasized differ from the past. Prominently featured are the women's participation in the Prophet's struggle for the cause, that is especially constituted by their active role as helpmates on the home front. Here, the domesticity theme involves the glorification of the female in her God-given roles of wife and mother. The fact that of Muḥammad's actual wives only Khadīja bore him children may explain why it is she who now emerges in the debate on the wives of the Prophet as the most prominent figure, unlike the medieval ḥadīth which placed far greater emphasis on 'Ā'isha. Modern sources celebrate Khadīja as both wife and mother while she was also the Prophet's most important supporter and his fellow-struggler in his great jihād that she waged as his deputy from the moment of their first meeting until the day of her death (Bint al-Shāṭiʾ, *Tarājim,* 233-5; al-ʿAqqād, *ʿAbqariyyat Muḥammad,* 113-15, 118; Gharīb, *Nisāʾ,* 118f.; Razwy, *Khadīja,* 146-7). The interrelationship of domestic support and shared struggle for the cause is also pursued in the examples of the Prophet's later wives. Bint al-Shāṭiʾ defined the virtues of the wives of the Prophet as follows: constancy in worship, charity, devotion to the husband, raising her children by herself in order to free him for a greater purpose, self-control, dignity, pride (q.v.), courageous defense of Islam against unbelievers (see COURAGE) even if these be blood relatives (see BLOOD AND BLOODCLOT), knowledge of the doctrines and laws of Islam, and wise counsel in religious matters (*Tarājim,* 271, 297, 311-12, 317-18, 322-3, 352, 364-8, 387-8).

A perhaps more activist modern approach to the legacy of the Prophet's wives insists that Muḥammad's consorts were dynamic, influential, and enterprising, and that they were full and active members of the community. They were the Prophet's intellectual partners and they accompanied him on his raids and military campaigns and shared in his strategic concerns. He listened to their advice which was sometimes the deciding factor in thorny negotiations (e.g. Mernissi, *The veil,* 104, 113-14). The wives of the Prophet were activists who in Medina worked to secure equal status for women with men regarding economic (see ECONOMICS) and sociopolitical rights, mainly in the areas of inheritance (q.v.), participation in warfare and booty, and marital relations (Mernissi, *The veil,* 118f., 129f.). Even ʿĀʾisha's involvement in political affairs (the Battle of the Camel) after the Prophet's death, an occurrence much criticized in ḥadīth and most later religious literature, here counts as proof that the Prophet's widows had the power to be political actors in their own right (Mernissi, *The veil,* 49-61). Changed in essence but not always in form, the ḥadīth materials on the wives of the Prophet continue to play an important role as a framework of religious self-understanding, a normative mirror-image of contemporary Muslim societal realities and plans for the future.

Barbara Freyer Stowasser

Bibliography

Primary: Abū ʿUbayda, *Tasmiyat azwāj al-nabī wa-awlādihi,* ed. K.Y. al-Ḥūt, Beirut 1985; Bayḍāwī, *Anwār;* Ibn Isḥāq-Guillaume; Ibn Kathīr, *Tafsīr;* Ibn Saʿd, *Ṭabaqāt,* ed. Sachau; Ṭabarī, *Tafsīr,* Beirut 1972; Zamakhsharī, *Kashshāf,* Cairo 1953.
Secondary: N. Abbott, *Aishah — The beloved of Mohammad,* Chicago 1942; London 1985²; L. Ahmed, *Women and gender in Islam,* New Haven 1992; ʿA.M. al-ʿAqqād, *ʿAbqariyyat Muḥammad,* Beirut 1974; Bint al-Shāṭiʾ, ʿĀʾisha bt. ʿAbd al-Raḥmān, *Tarājim sayyidāt bayt al-nubuwwa,* Beirut 1984; M. Gharīb, *Nisāʾ fī ḥayāt al-anbiyāʾ,* Cairo 1977; M.Ḥ. Haykal, *The life of Muḥammad,* trans. I.R. al-Farūqī, Indianapolis 1976; M.H. Kabbani and L. Bakhtiar, *Encyclopedia of Muhammad's women companions and the traditions they related,* Chicago 1998; J. Knappert, *Islamic legends* [i], Leiden 1985; M. Lings, *Muhammad,* Cambridge 1995; F. Mernissi, *The veil and the male elite,* trans. M.J. Lakeland, Reading 1991; Nöldeke, *GQ;* Paret, *Kommentar;* id., *Koran;* S.A.A. Razwy, *Khadija-tul-kubrā,* Elmhurst 1990; Ch.D. Smith, *Islam and the search for social order in modern Egypt. A biography of Muhammad Husayn Haykal,* Albany 1983; D.A. Spellberg, *Politics, gender and the Islamic past. The legacy of ʿĀʾisha bint Abī Bakr,* New York 1994; G.H. Stern, *Marriage in early Islam,* London 1939; B. Freyer Stowasser, *Women in the Qurʾan, traditions and interpretation,* New York 1994; W. Montgomery Watt, *Muhammad at Medina,* Oxford 1962; A. Wessels, *A modern Arabic biography of Muhammad. A critical study of Muhammad Huseyn Heykal's Hayat Muhammad,* Leiden 1972.

Wolf see ANIMAL LIFE

Womb

The female reproductive organ, the uterus, by extension, the importance of kinship and blood relationships. The root of the Arabic term for "womb" (*raḥim, riḥm,* pl. *arḥām*), *r-ḥ-m,* is also the base of *raḥma,* "compassion," and the divine names *al-raḥmān* and *al-raḥīm,* the merciful and compassionate, each of which signals the feminine associations of the divine quality of mercy (q.v.; see also GOD AND HIS ATTRIBUTES; ARABIC LANGUAGE; GENDER). The use of the term "womb" in the Qurʾān most often refers either to the generative function of the female reproductive organ (Q 2:228; 3:6; 13:8; 22:5; 31:34; see BIOLOGY AS THE CREATION AND STAGES OF LIFE) or to the importance of the bonds of kinship (q.v.; *ṣilat al-raḥim;* e.g. Q 47:22, 60:3; cf. 4:1, 8:75, 33:6).

Some of the verses mention the womb in the context of the legal implications associated with conception and birth (see LAW AND THE QURʾĀN); for example women about to be divorced should not "hide what God has created in their wombs" (Q 2:228; see MARRIAGE AND DIVORCE; WOMEN AND THE QURʾĀN), and the closeness of kinship should be taken into account in settling inheritance (q.v.; e.g. Q 8:75; 33:6). In the case of these latter two verses the classical commentators (see EXEGESIS OF THE QURʾĀN: CLASSICAL AND MEDIEVAL) interpret the statement, "those related by 'the womb' are nearer to one another in the book [q.v.; God's decree]," to refer to their primary claims to inheritance based on proximity of kinship. The implication in this case was that the "brotherhood relationship" initially established between the emigrants from Mecca (q.v.) and the Medinan "helpers" (see MEDINA) should no longer affect inheritance rights (see BROTHER AND BROTHERHOOD; EMIGRANTS AND HELPERS; FAMILY). In the case of Shīʿī *tafsīr* (see SHĪʿISM AND THE QURʾĀN), the primacy of those related by the womb is interpreted as indicating the superior rights of the Prophet's descendants in authority (q.v.), sovereignty (q.v.) and faith (q.v.; Majlisī, *Biḥār,* xxiii, 257-8; see FAMILY OF THE PROPHET).

The reference to the womb's shrinking and swelling, or to its gestation periods (Q 13:8), conveys but one aspect of a complex qurʾānic embryology, including the mention of a "sperm-drop" (*nuṭfa,* Q 23:13), "a hanging element" (*ʿalaq,* Q 23:14) and a "chewed lump" (*muḍgha,* Q 23:14) during the early phases of conception. Such verses have inspired a particular genre of modern Islamic apologetic that understands these phrases as anticipating current scientific findings about the stages of pregnancy (see EXEGESIS OF THE QURʾĀN: EARLY MODERN AND CONTEMPORARY; SCIENCE AND THE QURʾĀN). In the Qurʾān the "ties of the womb," i.e. kinship bonds, are so strong that reverence for them is paired with the fear (q.v.) of God *(taqwā)* in the opening verse of Q 4 ("The Women," Sūrat al-Nisāʾ) and breaking these ties is an aberration paired with "sowing corruption (q.v.) in the land" in Q 47:22. On the last day (see LAST JUDGMENT; APOCALYPSE), however, these ties will not offer a person any relief (Q 60:3; see INTERCESSION). The idea of upholding relationships, first those based on blood ties (see BLOOD AND BLOOD CLOT) and then more remote ones, is a basic moral teaching affirmed in the Qurʾān:

> Worship (q.v.) God and join not any partners with him (see POLYTHEISM AND ATHEISM); and do good (see GOOD DEEDS; VIRTUES AND VICES, COMMANDING AND FORBIDDING) — to parents (q.v.), kinfolk, orphans (q.v.), those in need (see POVERTY AND THE POOR), neighbors who are near,

neighbors who are strangers, the companion by your side, the wayfarer [you meet; see TRIPS AND VOYAGES; JOURNEY]... (Q 4:36; see also HOSPITALITY AND COURTESY; ETHICS AND THE QURʾĀN; STRANGERS AND FOREIGNERS).

Many ḥadīths (see ḤADĪTH AND THE QURʾĀN) also refer to the ties of the womb (kinship), for example, "Worship God and do not associate anything with him, establish regular prayer (q.v.), pay *zakāt* (see ALMSGIVING), and uphold the ties of kinship" (Bukhārī, *Ṣaḥīḥ,* bk. 73 *[K. al-Adab],* no. 12).

Later philosophical (see PHILOSOPHY AND THE QURʾĀN) and Ṣūfī interpretations (see ṢŪFISM AND THE QURʾĀN) connect the womb with broader concepts of the creative process in nature.

Marcia Hermansen

Bibliography
Primary: Bukhārī, *Ṣaḥīḥ;* Majlisī, Muḥammad Bāqir, *Biḥār al-anwār,* 110 vols., Tehran 1956-.
Secondary: K. Moore et al., *Human development as described in the Quran and Sunnah,* Mecca 1992;
S. Murata, *The tao of Islam,* Albany 1992.

Women and the Qurʾān

Only one woman is actually named in the Qurʾān, but a large number of verses refer to women. A long chapter of the Qurʾān is titled "The Women" (Q 4, Sūrat al-Nisāʾ) and contains a great deal of material relating to gender (q.v.), but numerous verses (q.v.) in other chapters (see SŪRA) are also gender-related. These include exhortations (q.v.) addressed to the believing men and the believing women, revelations specific to women or to relations between men and women, and laws pertinent to marriage (see MARRIAGE AND DIVORCE), illicit sexual relations (see SEX AND SEXUALITY; ADULTERY AND FORNICATION), divorce, inheritance (q.v.), etc. Female characters appear in qurʾānic narratives about pre-Islamic figures and some verses have been ascribed to various women who lived in proximity to the prophet Muḥammad (see WIVES OF THE PROPHET). According to Islamic tradition, a number of women among the early believers had a role in the transmission of the text of the Qurʾān (see COLLECTION OF THE QURʾĀN; CODICES OF THE QURʾĀN; MUṢḤAF; TEXTUAL HISTORY OF THE QURʾĀN), and through the centuries, women learned the qurʾānic text (see READERS OF THE QURʾĀN; RECITATION OF THE QURʾĀN). Female and feminist exegetes, however, appear to be an innovation of the twentieth century (see EXEGESIS OF THE QURʾĀN: EARLY MODERN AND CONTEMPORARY; FEMINISM AND THE QURʾĀN).

Spiritual equality, symbolic weakness and social reality

In the spiritual realm, women and men are regarded in the Qurʾān for the most part as equal in the eyes of God and as having similar religious duties (see RITUAL AND THE QURʾĀN). A large number of verses are addressed to the believing men and the believing women (see BELIEF AND UNBELIEF) or, conversely, the hypocritical men and the hypocritical women (see HYPOCRITES AND HYPOCRISY) as well as the idolatrous men and idolatrous women (Q 9:67, 68, 71, 72; 24:12; 33:35, 36, 58, 73; 48:5-6, 25; 52:12, 13; 71:28; 85:10; see IDOLATRY AND IDOLATERS; GRATITUDE AND INGRATITUDE; POLYTHEISM AND ATHEISM). The most commonly quoted of these is Q 33:35: "Lo! Men who surrender unto God, and women who surrender, and men who believe and women who believe, and men who obey and women who obey (see OBEDIENCE; DISOBEDIENCE), and men who speak the truth (q.v.) and women who speak the truth, and men who persevere [in righteousness] and women who persevere (see GOOD AND EVIL; VIRTUES AND VICES, COMMANDING AND FORBIDDING), and men who are humble and women who are humble (see ARROGANCE), and men who give alms and women who give alms (see ALMSGIVING; CHARITY), and men who fast and women who fast (see FASTING), and men who guard their modesty (q.v.) and women who guard (their modesty), and men who remember God much and women who remember (see REMEMBRANCE; MEMORY) — God has prepared for them forgiveness (q.v.) and a vast reward" (see REWARD AND PUNISHMENT).

Humans as well as other creatures were created in pairs, male and female (Q 4:1; 7:189; 35:11; 49:13; 51:49; 53:45; 76:39; 78:8; 92:3 and the creation [q.v.] story below). Both are admonished to believe in God and do good works (Q 16:97; 40:40; cf. 4:124; see GOOD DEEDS; EVIL DEEDS) in order to enter paradise (q.v.). The giving of alms is specifically required of both women and men (cited above and again in Q 57:18). Moreover, the women's oath of allegiance to the Prophet is described (Q 60:12; see CONTRACTS AND ALLIANCES). Like men, believing and righteous women will go to heaven while the wrong-doers will suffer in hell (see GARDENS; HELL AND HELLFIRE), but women's fate in the afterlife is associated with that of their husbands (Q 36:55-6; 37:22; 43:70). Most problematic are a number of verses that promise believers in paradise modest, beautiful woman who are sometimes explicitly described as virgins (Q 37:48; 38:52; 52:20; 55:56, 72, 74; 56:22, 36; 78:33; see HOURIS).

Symbolically, the concept of woman in the Qurʾān is undoubtedly that of a being who is considered to be weak, flawed or passive. Menstruation (q.v.), a prime signifier of the female, is an illness or an impurity (Q 2:222; 4:43; see CLEANLINESS AND ABLUTION; ILLNESS AND HEALTH). Not surprisingly, the earth is female and humans consider themselves her masters (e.g. Q 39:69). Thus, the much-quoted verse "Your women are a tilth for you, so go to your tilth as you will" (Q 2:223) may be understood as the obverse of the earth-woman metaphor (q.v.; see also LITERARY STRUCTURES OF THE QURʾĀN). Women's subaltern status is reflected in verses that position them among orphans (q.v.), children (q.v.) and men who are too weak to fight (Q 4:2-3, 75, 98, 127; see FIGHTING; EXPEDITIONS AND BATTLES; WAR). Women's dependency is expressed not only in the fact that they are not named (except for Mary [q.v.] discussed below) but also that they are almost always ascribed to men as mother of, wife of, "women of," and so on, all forms of linkage to men (see FAMILY; KINSHIP).

In social matters, women's position is depicted ambivalently in the Qurʾān. There are a number of instances of matrilineal ascription (see PATRIARCHY): Moses (q.v.) is described by Aaron (q.v.) as "son of my mother" (Q 7:150; 20:94) and Jesus (q.v.) is referred to as the son of Mary (as will be seen below). Preference for the birth of a son over that of a daughter is one of the sins of the pagans (Q 16:58-9), for female or male offspring (or barrenness) are in the hands of God (Q 42:49-50; see POWER AND IMPOTENCE; GRACE; BLESSING). The burying alive of a girl-child is specifically mentioned as an unnatural, evil act (Q 81:8-9; see INFANTICIDE).

Gender relations are most succinctly expressed in a phrase that has been widely quoted throughout the centuries to support the superiority of men over women: "Men are the sustainers of women as God has preferred some of them over others, and because they sustain them from their wealth..." (Q 4:34). Some classical exegetes interpreted this verse in the narrow sense as a reflection of men's duty to provide material support for women (see WORK; MAINTENANCE AND UPKEEP). Others expanded the phrase to refer to men's superiority in a number of religious, political and intellectual fields (see SCHOLAR; TRADITIONAL DISCIPLINES OF QURʾĀNIC STUDY). In the twentieth century, the meaning of the verse has been subject to alternative translations and interpretations (see below). Women's status compared to that of men is expressed in a variety of contexts. Women have rights but the rights of men are a degree above them (Q 2:228). Women are ranked separately after the free man and the slave (see SLAVES AND SLAVERY) regarding the issue of retaliation (q.v.) for murder (q.v.; Q 2:178; see also BLOODSHED; BLOOD MONEY), but they are punished equally for stealing (Q 5:38; see THEFT; BOUNDARIES AND PRECEPTS; LAW AND THE QURʾĀN; CHASTISEMENT AND PUNISHMENT).

Women's testimony is another ambivalent issue in the Qurʾān (see WITNESSING AND TESTIFYING). When two male witnesses are required but no men are available, the testimony of one man and two women is specified. The reason for this inequality is clearly stated in the relevant verse (Q 2:282), "so that if one of them errs, the other can remind her." In other words, women are reliable enough to provide legal testimony but their memory is not as accurate as that of men. When making a will, however, only two male witnesses are stipulated (Q 5:106).

The seclusion of virtuous Muslim women and their separation from men who are not their kin are rooted in the interpretation of a number of rather obscure qurʾānic verses. The wives of the Prophet are ordered to "stay in your houses" (Q 33:33) and subsequently most legists explicated rules which prohibited women from traveling more than three days walking distance without the permission of their male guardians and, even then, only when accompanied by a chaperon (see JOURNEY). Another reading of the same phrase would have the wives of the Prophet be honorable or quiet in their homes (*qirna* as opposed to *qarna;* see WHISPER). Another exegetical question is whether the instruction refers only to the Prophet's wives or to other Muslim women as well. The continuation of the verse commands the women to dress modestly (see CLOTHING), pray regularly (see PRAYER), give to the poor and obey God and his messenger (q.v.), and these are surely not requirements restricted to the wives of the Prophet. Thus, one could deduce that the order to stay in your houses (or alternately to be honorable or quiet) may be extrapolated to apply to all Muslim women.

Conversely, the verse ordering the believers to speak to the wives of the Prophet from behind a curtain also prohibits them from marrying the Prophet's widows after his death (Q 33:53; see VEIL; WIDOW), a limitation unique to the Prophet's wives. In this case, separating women from male visitors by a curtain, a *ḥijāb,* would logically apply only to the Prophet's wives. Nevertheless, Muslims endeavored to seclude women within the house (see HOUSE, DOMESTIC AND DIVINE; SUNNA), whether by a curtain in a modest dwelling such as that of the Prophet or by the demarcation of more elaborate domestic quarters similar to the ancient Greek gynaeceum. The context of this verse of the *ḥijāb* is crucial to understanding its meaning (see OCCASIONS OF REVELATION; SĪRA AND THE QURʾĀN). A simple reading of the verse implies that some of the early Muslims entered the Prophet's house at all times of the day and night, without asking permission, and stayed around talking. The

Prophet was too shy to ask them to leave but God revealed an injunction against this improper behavior. In qur'ānic exegesis (see EXEGESIS OF THE QUR'ĀN: CLASSICAL AND MEDIEVAL), the circumstances upon which the verse was revealed *(asbāb al-nuzūl)* indicated that some visitors bothered the Prophet's wives to the point of sexual harassment. These accretions would dictate a more stringent approach to the separation of the women of the household from men who are not their kin, both for the Prophet's wives and, by extension, for other Muslim women as well.

The term *ḥijāb* came to refer to the proper attire for modest Muslim women when they are in public, and justification for the "dress code" is anchored in the interpretation of a number of qur'ānic verses that apply to the Prophet's women as well as to believing women in general. The issue is addressed directly in two verses admonishing men and women to be modest (Q 24:30-1). While the verse addressed to men is expressed in general terms, the modesty of women is specified as in the command to show only those ornaments that are revealed and "draw their veils (*khumur*, sing. *khimār*) over their bosoms." The ornament in question *(zīna)* seems to be a type of jangling jewelry that draws attention to the woman wearing it, since in the latter part of the verse, women are told not to stamp their feet to draw attention to this hidden ornament, apparently ankle bracelets. As for the "veil," it has been interpreted as a kerchief on the head, as a scarf that the women of Mecca (q.v.) and Medina (q.v.) wore over their chests with differing degrees of modesty, and even as a face covering. Another qur'ānic verse instructs the believing women to draw their outer garments (*jalābīb*, sing. *jilbāb*) around themselves so that they will be recognized and not bothered (Q 33:59). In the third/ninth century, the time of the crystallization of Islamic law, prominent qur'ānic commentators were not certain what parts of the body a woman was supposed to cover. This imprecision and difference of opinion among major exegetes continued for centuries, although it would appear that the "ornaments" which drew attention to a woman were gradually expanded until they encompassed the whole body. The dominant opinion among the legists, however, seems to require that Muslim women conceal their entire bodies with the exception of their feet, their hands and their faces. A well-known ḥadīth (saying of the Prophet; see ḤADĪTH AND THE QUR'ĀN) advised a young man to go see his prospective bride, indicating that her face was not covered, which would preclude legislating the face-veil for Muslim women. The ambiguity of the qur'ānic text on the issue of the *ḥijāb* leaves room for a multiplicity of social, cultural, economic and geographical factors to define the precise code of behavior for Muslim women at a given time and place.

The relationship between husbands and wives is described in general terms as mutual and equal: they are raiments for each other, helpmates and pairs for themselves (Q 2:187; 30:21; 42:11; see PAIRS AND PAIRING). Elsewhere, however, wives are described as created for their mates (Q 26:166). The balance of rights and duties of a husband and wife are discussed in greater detail in the legal proscriptions regarding marriage and divorce (elaborated below).

The work of females as well as males is valued (Q 3:195) and both women and men retain what they have earned (Q 4:32). Thus, women are independent economic individuals who may generate income and possess their own property (q.v.; see also WEALTH; ECONOMICS; TRADE AND COMMERCE).

In sum, the overall image of women in the Qurʾān is ambivalent. They are autonomous in religious obligations and economic affairs but are subject to men in the social sphere. Women are also objectified, most notably as one of the rewards for men in the hereafter (see ESCHATOLOGY). Women's modesty is specified in greater detail than that of men, albeit in terms that were obscure even to the earliest legists. This implies either that women's sexuality is more threatening than men's or that women require more guidance to protect their modesty. Matrimony is regarded as the natural state of human affairs (see ABSTINENCE; CHASTITY). These principles are amplified in a mass of laws pertaining to gender and family affairs set down in the Qurʾān.

Legal material relating to women and gender

Some eighty percent of the legal material in the Qurʾān refers to women. Marriage is regarded as a formal, legal connection and referred to as a contract (*ʿuqdat al-nikāḥ*, Q 2:237). A relative who arranges the nuptials in the name of the bride is referred to in the Qurʾān (Q 2:237) although the technical term *walī* and its precise legal definition were later derived from traditions of the Prophet. Polygyny is clearly sanctioned in the Qurʾān which permits a man to take up to four wives so long as he treats them equally (Q 4:3). A later verse in the same chapter (Q 4:129) states that it is virtually impossible not to prefer one wife over the others and admonishes the husband not to neglect any of his wives. This requirement was interpreted up to the twentieth century in technical, economic terms by which a husband was required to provide equal lodgings, food, clothing, etc. for each of his wives as well as to divide his sexual attention equally among them.

In addition to the women a man weds by a marriage contract, he may conclude an agreement with a virtuous woman for sexual relations in return for a fee and this is not considered illicit (Q 4:24). These "pleasure," or *mutʿa,* marriages, contracted for a limited time between a man and an unmarried woman, were subsequently the subject of debate among legists (see TEMPORARY MARRIAGE). Shīʿīs (see SHĪʿISM AND THE QURʾĀN) recognize them as legal to this day, while Sunnī scholars maintain that the qurʾānic reference to *mutʿa* was cancelled by several subsequent verses (Q 4:3; 23:5-6; 65:4). In addition, Sunnī authorities argue that the Prophet recommended the existing custom to his soldiers only because of exigencies specific to his time when men were separated from their wives for long periods while they went off to war. Moreover, the second caliph (q.v.) ʿUmar interpreted the Prophet's intent and banned the practice. The dispute about the legitimacy of *mutʿa* has been a major bone of contention between Sunnīs and Shīʿīs and is rooted in contradictory interpretations of the Qurʾān as well as differing approaches to religious and political authority (q.v.; Haeri, *Law of desire,* 61-4; see also POLITICS AND THE QURʾĀN; IMĀM).

Concubines (q.v.), or literally "those whom your right hand possesses" or "women whom you have purchased," are frequently mentioned in the Qurʾān alongside wives (Q 4:3, 24-5; 23:6; 33:50; 70:30) and there is no limitation on the number of concubines a man may acquire. The legal and spiritual status of slaves is regulated in the Qurʾān, including specific rules relating to sexual relations that are permitted or forbidden to them (see LAWFUL AND UNLAWFUL). Thus, a master may not prostitute his slave (Q 24:33) and he has a moral obligation to marry her off to either a free man or slave (cf. Brunschvig, ʿAbd, esp. p. 25). The status of a female slave who bears her master a child, an *umm al-walad,* is not defined in the Qurʾān; her unique rights developed during the codification of Islamic law in about the third/ninth century.

Illicit sexual relations are referred to as *zinā* (often translated as fornication or adultery) and are strictly forbidden (Q 17:32; cf. 6:151: *al-fawāḥish*). Two separate verses stipulate the punishment for such infractions: one mentions only women and specifies that they should be incarcerated in their homes for a period of time which may be until their death (Q 4:15); the other refers to a male and a female offender, both of whom are to be punished by one hundred lashes (Q 24:2; see FLOGGING). *Zinā*, however, is extremely difficult to prove because the verses referring to "the affair of the falsehood, or slander" (*al-ifk,* Q 24:4-26; see LIE; GOSSIP), require four witnesses to the act and prescribe dire punishment, eighty lashes, for a false accuser. The punishment of stoning (q.v.) for *zinā* is not in the Qurʾān but is based on the traditions of the Prophet.

Homosexuality (q.v.) and sodomy are discussed in the Qurʾān in the many references to Lot (q.v.) and his family, who were the only ones of their people who repented their lewd acts and were spared by God. Those who did not change their ways are severely condemned and both parties to a homosexual relationship are to be strictly punished (Q 4:16; 7:81). Lesbianism *(siḥāq)* is not cited in the Qurʾān; it is forbidden by ḥadīth sayings of the Prophet, as is transvestitism.

Divorce is discussed extensively in the Qurʾān: a chapter is titled "Divorce" (Q 65, Sūrat al-Ṭalāq), a long section is devoted to the subject in Q 2, and several verses appear in Q 4 (Sūrat al-Nisāʾ, "Women"). Divorce is the prerogative of the husband and he may divorce his wife in the presence of two witnesses without any formal ceremony (Q 65:2). The divorce is not final until the wife has completed three menstrual cycles (Q 2:228; see WAITING PERIOD); during that period she remains in her husband's home and he must support her (Q 65:6). The purpose, of course, is to ascertain if she is pregnant as well as to give the husband an opportunity to withdraw the divorce. The latter explanation dovetails with the preference for reconciliation between an estranged couple rather than divorce, which appears in several places in the Qurʾān (Q 2:229, 4:35). If the wife turns out to be pregnant, the divorce does not take effect until after she gives birth (Q 65:6; see LACTATION). A husband may divorce his wife and change his mind only twice; after the third divorce, she is not lawful to him until after she has married another man (Q 2:229-30).

A clause in the Qurʾān states that "it is no sin for either of them if the woman ransom herself" (Q 2:229); this is the basis for a type of divorce that is designated *khulʿ* (divestiture) in Islamic law. When a woman wishes a divorce, she may, with the permission of her husband, return to him the bridewealth *(mahr)* and any gifts she had received from him. Even in a divorce initiated by the wife, it is the husband who retains the right of divorce. Moreover, this type of divorce is economically unfavorable for the wife. A marriage contract, like any other contract, may also be annulled by a court for violation of inherent elements of the pact (see BREAKING TRUSTS AND CONTRACTS). Thus, for example, a woman whose husband is incapable of carrying out sexual relations for a long period of time could obtain an annulment. The dissolution of a marriage contract at the discretion of a court is a rather extreme measure, but could be claimed by either spouse for a variety of reasons that have differed over time and place.

The laws of inheritance are specified precisely and in great detail, leaving little room for interpretation (Q 4:7-20, 175). These regulations are extremely complex and were regarded as an area of expertise apart from the general field of law. From a gender point of view, a number of basic principles may be summarized. Women inherit, but their portion is usually half of the share of a man of the same degree of kinship. Daughters, for example, inherit half as much as sons, sisters half of the brothers' portions, and mothers half the inheritance of fathers. Women inherit from their husbands and husbands from their wives, again according to the rule of half a share. Inheritance, therefore, is an area in which women's status as legal persons, as well as the right of a woman to own her own property, is firmly anchored. Moreover, the right of married women to make wills is clearly stipulated in the Qurʾān (Q 4:12), although this privilege is more symbolic than practical because of general limitations on wills. The inheritance of maternal brothers and sisters is also alluded to (Q 4:12), reflecting ongoing semi-matrilineal ties in what was fundamentally a patrilineal society.

In addition to inheritance, women receive bridewealth (q.v.) upon marriage (termed *ajr* in the Qurʾān rather than *mahr,* the designation which became prevalent later). A woman may, however, remit part of her bridewealth to her husband of her own free will (Q 4:4). Husbands' duty to provide material support for their wives is implied in the quintessential qurʾānic verse defining gender relations (Q 4:34). A man may not withhold divorce from a woman in order to take her property, nor may he divorce her with false accusations of lewdness so that he may get part of her property (Q 4:19-20).

The unusually liberal property rights of women anchored in the Qurʾān have been the subject of much speculation. Classical Muslim scholars explained that, since the inheritance rules follow a section dealing with care for orphans, they reflect concern for the kin of Muslims who died in battles for the sake of Islam. In view of the fact that these relatives of fallen Muslim heroes would revert to the care of their families who most likely were anti-Muslim, it was deemed important to provide for them economically. Some modern scholars of early Islam (such as Goitein and Stern) have suggested that, in the mercantile city of Mecca before the advent of Islam, women had certain rights of inheritance, citing the vast property of the widow Khadīja (q.v.) and a number of other women. Thus, the social reality at the time and place of the Qurʾān's revelation could have influenced the economic provisions regarding women. The association made between women, orphans and children in the Qurʾān suggests that women were regarded as weaker social entities and therefore providing for their welfare was viewed as an ethical act (see ETHICS AND THE QURʾĀN). Women's inheritance of half the portion of a man logically follows from men's double financial responsibility to support their wives. Some have argued that women were generally not as economically incumbered as men were and therefore required fewer financial resources. In any case, the qurʾānic inheritance rules, while providing women with a crucial source of income, are also a concrete reflection of their subordinate status.

Female characters in qurʾānic narratives

Some narratives (q.v.) in the Qurʾān are about pre-Islamic figures such as Adam and Eve (q.v.), Joseph and ʿAzīz's wife, the wife of Pharaoh (q.v.) who was Moses' step-mother, Solomon (q.v.) and the Queen of Sheba (q.v.; see also BILQĪS), and Mary, mother of Jesus. They project a variety of roles and images of women, and have been the subject of various interpretations and amplifications. Some of these could change the dominant precedent or role model that emerges from the holy text.

Adam's wife (though nameless) is mentioned in the Qur'ān in three passages (Q 2:30-7; 20:115-23; 7:11-25) and is referred to in several isolated verses (Q 4:1; 7:189; 39:6), while elsewhere the creation of humanity and stories of the first man refer only to Adam. Some narratives of the creation do not mention the first man's partner, but other verses state that God created man and his mate from a single soul (q.v.). Adam alone is granted an exceptional position among the angels (q.v.) and the creatures, but this appears to be an indication of his status as a prophet (see PROPHETS AND PROPHETHOOD) rather than as a male. Both Adam and his wife, however, are instructed to dwell in the garden and both are warned not to eat of the tree of immortality (see TREES; ETERNITY; FALL OF MAN). Most importantly, in the qur'ānic version, both Adam and his wife are tempted by Satan (see DEVIL), both eat of the tree and both are expelled. (Only in one verse, Q 20:120, is Adam alone tempted.) Moreover, for the most part, Adam repents his disobedience and is forgiven and given guidance by his lord (q.v.; see also ASTRAY; ERROR). Only in one verse, do Adam and his wife admit their guilt and beg for forgiveness (Q 7:23). In short, the qur'ānic text describes the creation of the first woman (when it is referred to at all) as contemporaneous and similar to that of the first man. She is not responsible for tempting him, and if there is any unequal guilt, it is Adam who bears a greater degree of culpability. Moreover, the gender issue in the story of Adam and his wife may be viewed as marginal to the main qur'ānic message of the covenant (q.v.) between God and humanity, and his forgiving of the folly of both male and female believers (Q 7:172-3; 33:72-3).

From the earliest periods of qur'ānic exegesis, as well as in ḥadīth traditions of the Prophet, Islamic world histories and popular stories of the prophets, however, the image of Eve (Ar. Ḥawwā') is portrayed in negative terms. She is held responsible for Adam's temptation and fall, and is usually depicted as deliberately deceiving him. Only Adam's repentance is mentioned (see REPENTANCE AND PENANCE), while the participation of Ḥawwā' in a joint admission of guilt is ignored. Highlighting the transgressions of Ḥawwā' and suppressing her repentance allowed qur'ānic exegetes to multiply the punishments said to be borne by Eve (and by extension all women). These include the pain of childbirth (see BIRTH; BIOLOGY AS THE CREATION AND STAGES OF LIFE), menstruation and women's duties such as weaving, spinning, preparing dough and baking bread. Even upon his death, Adam accuses her of being responsible for his transgression and punishment. Thus, in contrast to the qur'ānic text, classical Islamic scholars portrayed the first woman as a threat to her husband and by extension to all humankind.

The seduction of Joseph (Ar. Yūsuf) by the wife of the Egyptian al-ʿAzīz is narrated as one trial in a series of ordeals that the hero must overcome in order to demonstrate his greatness. In a chapter of the Qur'ān named for the protagonist (Q 12), Joseph is thrown into a pit by his brothers (see BROTHER AND BROTHERHOOD) and sold into slavery to al-ʿAzīz, who brings him home and treats him like a son. After Joseph achieves maturity (q.v.), al-ʿAzīz's wife attempts to seduce him but he rejects her. He was actually tempted and desired her, but his faith in God as well as his fine qualities enable him to overcome evil and licentiousness. The two race for the door, the wife tears Joseph's robe from the back and at the entrance they encounter the husband. At this point, Joseph is exonerated of the wife's allegation of immoral conduct. Her husband rebukes her and all women, saying: "This is of the guile *(kayd)* of you women. Your guile is great" (Q 12:28). The wiles of women and their unbridled passion are further illustrated in a tale in which Joseph is objectified. When women in the city began to gossip about the infatuation of al-ʿAzīz's wife for the young slave, she invited them to a banquet and gave each a knife. When she ordered Joseph to appear before them, the women were so confounded by his beauty, which they likened to that of an angel, that they cut their hands with their knives. Having proven her point, al-ʿAzīz's wife threatens Joseph that if he does not obey her orders, he will be imprisoned (Q 12:30-2). Joseph appeals to the lord to fend off the women's wiles for he fears that he will capitulate to them and prefers incarceration. God answers his prayer and he is sent to prison (Q 12:33-5).

Joseph is fully and finally vindicated on the occasion of his release from prison when he appeals to the king to investigate the deceitful women who cut their hands, and the king investigates those women who had tried to seduce him (Q 12:51). The women absolve Joseph, and al-ʿAzīz's wife confesses and affirms his honesty and virtue. But Joseph admits that he was inclined to evil and thanks the lord for helping him to overcome his human instincts (Q 12:53). Joseph is taken into the king's service, becomes custodian of the storehouses, takes revenge on his brothers and performs a miracle (see MIRACLES; MARVELS; DREAMS AND SLEEP).

The story of Joseph and Zulaykha (as al-ʿAzīz's wife came to be known in Islamic literature) has provided rich material not only for commentaries on the Qurʾān, ḥadīth traditions, popular stories of the prophets and world histories, but also for mystical love poetry and visual art (see ART AND ARCHITECTURE AND THE QURʾĀN; ṢŪFISM AND THE QURʾĀN). It is frequently referred to in other genres and may have been integrated with ancient Egyptian, pre-Islamic Iranian or Indian morality tales about the guile of women as well as with the analogous narrative in the Hebrew Bible and Jewish interpretations of the Bible (see SCRIPTURE AND THE QURʾĀN; JEWS AND JUDAISM; TORAH).

In the exegesis of the Qurʾān, the focus of the story of Joseph and Zulaykha was often shifted from a tale about a prophet overcoming adversity to an account of the dangers of female sexuality and of women's cunning as embodied in the term *kayd* which appears no less than seven times in the narrative (Q 12:28, 33, 34, 50, 52). The unbridled sexuality and guile of woman is amplified in Islamic histories and stories of the prophets, and these are genres that tended toward embellishment and were not restricted by the rules of the Islamic sciences (see TRADITIONAL DISCIPLINES OF QURʾĀNIC STUDY). In these narratives, Zulaykha is punished for her transgressions, redeemed and becomes Joseph's wife and mother of his children. Thus, the dangerous sexual woman becomes an ideal spouse, in the process fulfilling her love for Joseph.

The theme of passion and love (q.v.) was particularly developed in mystical literature. Esoteric mystical commentary identified the woman Zulaykha as the lower world of matter and sensuality in contrast to Joseph who is the heart (q.v.) on a spiritual quest for gnosis (Stowasser, *Women*, 54; see INTELLECT; KNOWLEDGE AND LEARNING). While some mystical authors censured Zulaykha's attempt to subvert Joseph's innocence, others extolled her unreserved love for him. The earthly love, however, was also interpreted as a metaphor for the love of God and was expressed in clearly sexual terms. Thus, Zulaykha, the lover, desires union with the divine symbolized by Joseph's exceptional beauty (q.v.; Merguerian and Najmabadi, Zulaykha and Joseph, 497-500). Mystical poets viewed the female soul as inciting to evil (based on Q 12:53, where the feminine *nafs* is used) but may be purified through inner struggle and suffering (Schimmel, *My soul*, 68). The Ṣūfī writers of these works were men, and both their identification with Joseph, the man who overcomes his base instincts, as well as the desire to unite with Joseph the epitome of divine, even feminine, beauty, have interesting transsexual ramifications. The dramatic and concise qurʾānic story of Joseph and al-ʿAzīz's wife, we are told, is meant as a lesson and a guide for the righteous (Q 12:102, 111). It has been woven into a variety of images of women which captured the imaginations of Muslims for centuries.

Among the women related to Moses in the Qurʾān, Pharaoh's wife attained the most prominence as an example to believers because of her having convinced Pharaoh not to kill the infant Moses. She was a righteous woman who prayed to God to build her a house in paradise and save her from Pharaoh's wrongdoing and from evil people (Q 28:9; 66:11). Āsiya, as Pharaoh's wife is called in the commentaries and stories of the prophets, was one of the four most outstanding women of the world and also of the four "ladies of heaven" (along with Mary, mother of Jesus, Khadīja, Muḥammad's wife, and Fāṭima [q.v.], his daughter). Miraculous events surrounded her birth and early life, and her marriage to Pharaoh was a sacrifice she made for her people but it was never consummated. Āsiya saved and protected the infant Moses on many occasions. She suffered torture and death at the command of the wicked infidel Pharaoh, but the angel Gabriel (q.v.) succored her and neutralized her pain. Āsiya and the three other most hallowed women in Islamic tradition represent paragons of virtue. They are revered primarily for their commitment to God and obedience to his command, but as women they are variously characterized by virginity, purity and motherhood, and in Āsiya's case by her act of adoption.

The Queen of Sheba appears in the Qurʾān as a sovereign ruler who engaged in political negotiations with the wise and knowledgeable Solomon (see KINGS AND RULERS); eventually they submit to God together. Solomon is mentioned frequently in the Qurʾān where he is cited for his wisdom (q.v.), justice (see JUSTICE AND INJUSTICE) and God-given esoteric knowledge and miraculous powers. The story of the Queen of Sheba is narrated in a single chapter (Q 27:22-44). Solomon learns that there is a pagan woman ruler and sends a letter to Sheba asking its inhabitants to submit to him (or to become Muslims). The queen first turns to her advisers, claiming she has never decided a matter alone, but they defer to her command. She wishes to avoid the suffering of war and opts instead for diplomacy. Solomon tests her by disguising her throne. Upon entering his palace, she uncovers her legs thinking that she is in deep water. But Solomon reveals to her that in fact the palace was paved with glass. She responds that she has "wronged herself" and that she submits together with Solomon to God. Clearly, the story as a whole is an affirmation for Solomon, for the Queen of Sheba and for Muslims in general that God is the one and only god to whom they must submit (see GOD AND HIS ATTRIBUTES). The Queen of Sheba seems at first to be hesitant about making a decision on her own, but the qurʾānic text leaves no doubt that she is capable of independent reasoning in affairs of state and that her decisions have legitimacy. Her acumen seems equal to Solomon's when she passes the test of the throne that he has prepared for her. In the anecdote about the glass floor that appears as water, however, he clearly bests her by ruse and humiliates her as well. Nevertheless, it is intriguing that at the end of the qurʾānic story, the two submit together to God.

In exegesis of the Qurʾān, Islamic history and popular tales of the prophets and Islamic legends relating to the Queen of Sheba (or Bilqīs, as she came to be known), a major issue was the manner in which she came to be a ruler, her competence in this role and the potential precedent for Islamic society. A great beauty, she tricked the king who wanted to marry her on their wedding night, cut off his head and convinced his ministers to declare their loyalty to her. Thus, one could conclude that she attained the throne by proximity to a male ruler and by exploiting her feminine attraction and cunning. As queen and in her stand-off with Solomon, however, she proves her intelligence and good judgment, and these are qualities generally attributed to men. Interestingly, classical Islamic authors rarely address the question of whether this astute and legitimate qurʾānic queen could serve as a precedent for women's role in their own society. Among the gifts that the Queen of Sheba sent to Solomon to test his moral fiber were not only gold (q.v.) and silver but one hundred young slave boys dressed as girls and one hundred young slave girls in boys' clothing. Solomon, for his part, miraculously moved the queen's throne to his court, a slight but perhaps symbolic embellishment on the qurʾānic narrative. Solomon's cunning test of the glass floor provided a base for interpretive explanations of precisely what the queen's legs or feet would reveal about her. The vivid picture of Bilqīs standing in the water before Solomon revealing her hairy legs (or whether she had donkey's feet), surely undermines her image as a capable, independent ruler.

Maryam, or Mary, is frequently named in the Qurʾān to designate the matrilineal ascription of Jesus (ʿĪsā b. Maryam) since according to Islamic belief Jesus had no human father (e.g. Q 2:253; 4:156, 171; 5:17, 46, 75, 78, 110, 112, 114, 116; 9:31; 19:34; 23:50; 33:7; 43:57; 57:27; 61:6, 14). Both Jesus son of Mary and his mother are regarded as signs (q.v.) of God's powers and humanity's need to believe and worship (q.v.) him (Q 23:50). Mary's story is depicted in two chapters of the Qurʾān (Q 3:35-47; 19:16-34), one of which, Q 19, is named for her. The virgin birth is mentioned several times (Q 19:20; 66:12, for example) and Mary is considered to be chosen among all the women of the world (Q 3:42). The idea that both Jesus and his mother are deities is directly refuted (e.g. Q 5:75, 116), although the verses that rebut Mary's divinity raise questions about the origin of this belief. Western scholars have naturally focused on a comparison between the qurʾānic story of Mary and Jesus and the Gospels and other Christian texts and folklore (see CHRISTIANS AND CHRISTIANITY; GOSPEL; PRE-ISLAMIC ARABIA AND THE QURʾĀN). In the Qurʾān, Mary is divinely succored during childbirth with water (q.v.) from a brook and dates from a palm-tree (Q 19:23-6; see DATE PALM; SPRINGS AND FOUNTAINS).

Muslim commentators have discussed Mary's religious status, often comparing her with Fāṭima, daughter of the prophet Muḥammad, who is not explicitly mentioned in the Qurʾān. While the miraculous events surrounding her were augmented, a debate evolved about whether she was a prophet and about her ranking among the women of this world and the next. Some Muslim theologians argued that Mary (as well as Sara, the mother of Isaac [q.v.], the mother of Moses, and Pharaoh's wife Āsiya) should be considered prophets because they received the word of God from angels or by divine inspiration (see REVELATION AND INSPIRATION). But even these scholars differentiated between the prophethood *(nubuwwa)* which some women attained and the message *(risāla)* which was restricted to men. The consensus of Sunnī thinkers, however, has been to reject the notion of Mary's prophethood as heretical because as a menstruating woman she could not attain purity (see RITUAL PURITY). Despite the fact that in the Qur'ān Mary is specifically purified by God (Q 3:42), ḥadīth traditions and scholarly opinions have been marshaled to prove that Mary's purity meant that she was free of menstruation or, conversely, that she menstruated like all other women but was ethically pure. A more practical problem was God's command to Mary to bow down in prayer with the praying men (Q 3:43; see BOWING AND PROSTRATION). Classical commentators interpreted this to mean that Mary prayed with the congregation of men, contributing to the debate on whether women should pray in the mosque (q.v.) or in the privacy of the home. Another subject of debate was Mary's ranking among the chosen women of the Qur'ān: alternately including Āsiya, the Prophet's wives Khadīja and ʿĀ'isha and his daughter Fāṭima. For the most part, qur'ānic exegesis and stories of the prophets tend to exclude ʿĀ'isha from the foursome of the most excellent women of the world and the paramount females in heaven. In Sunnī as well as Shīʿī tradition, Mary and Fāṭima have been conflated as both were visited by angels, were miraculously assisted during childbirth and were free of menstruation and post-partum bleeding. Both are noted for their sorrows and suffering. Most Shīʿīs rank Fāṭima above Mary and she is sometimes referred to as Mary the Greater (*Maryam al-kubrā;* McAuliffe, Chosen of all women, 27-8; Stowasser, *Women,* 79-80). Both Muslims and Christians have focused on the image of Mary, particularly in popular piety, as underpinning a commonality between the two faiths. Similarities between the two religious traditions have been underscored for ecumenical or for missionary purposes. For many centuries, however, Mary has also been central to polemical controversies between Christians and Muslims and to the expression of mutual suspicion and misunderstanding (see POLEMIC AND POLEMICAL LANGUAGE).

The wives of Noah (q.v.), Lot and Abraham (q.v.), as well as other women in the life of Moses, are mentioned less prominently in the Qur'ān, but present a variety of female images. In addition, classical Muslim biographers and commentators tried to identify some of the numerous, seemingly anonymous women referred to in the Qur'ān through the stories connected to the revelation of the verses in which they appear. Among the well-known stories explicating a qur'ānic verse that refers anonymously to a woman is that of Zaynab, daughter of Jaḥsh, the divorced wife of Muḥammad's adopted son Zayd, whose marriage to the Prophet was expressly permitted in a revelation and served as a precedent for the legality of such unions (Q 33:37). At least three women are connected to another obscure verse that permits the Prophet to marry his paternal and maternal cousins who emigrated with him (see PROHIBITED DEGREES; EMIGRANTS AND HELPERS) and to "a believing woman if she gives herself to the Prophet" (Q 33:50). Perhaps the most famous story elucidating a qurʾānic passage is that of the slander (*al-ifk;* cited above) against ʿĀʾisha, the Prophet's wife (see ʿĀʾISHA BINT ABĪ BAKR), which explains the stringent rules for proving adultery and the harsh penalty for unsubstantiated allegations against a woman (Q 24:4-26). Shīʿīs point out that, since ʿĀʾisha is not actually mentioned in the Qurʾān, she was never exonerated of the accusation of adultery. The qurʾānic chapter "She Who Disputes" (Q 58, Sūrat al-Mujādila) opens with verses about a woman who complained to the Prophet that her husband had divorced her using the formula "be to me as the back of my mother," a custom Muḥammad had apparently abolished. Classical Muslim scholars have speculated about who the woman in question was. The chapter title "She Who is to Be Examined" (Q 60, Sūrat al-Muntaḥana) was identified as a reference to Umm Kulthūm, daughter of ʿUtba, because of its verses that sanctioned refuge from her pagan family for her and other Muslim female refugees. A female simile for breaking oaths — "a woman who breaks into untwisted strands the yarn which she has spun, after it has become strong" (Q 16:92) — led Muslim classical scholars to an obscure Abyssinian woman (see ABYSSINIA; OATHS; MAGIC; PRE-ISLAMIC ARABIA AND THE QURʾĀN).

In the Qurʾān, Muḥammad's wives, the "mothers of the believers," are quite frequently addressed and they are held up as paragons for Muslims but are also subject to obligations that are more stringent. None of these women, however, are identified by name, so it was left to classical exegesis to attempt to link revelations to wives of the Prophet, particularly by fleshing out stories about the "occasions of revelation" or *asbāb al-nuzūl.* These commentaries and ḥadīth traditions of the words and deeds of the Prophet have served as the basis for numerous anecdotes about the jealousy, covetousness and scheming of the women of his household. While a polygynous family undoubtedly provides fertile ground for petty intrigues, it would seem that the classical male Muslim scholars relished interpretations that highlighted harem politics.

The rich narratives in the Qurʾān include a variety of female characters and the images of these women were often changed in classical commentary and popular literature composed in patriarchal societies, as we have seen. Modern and feminist interpretations of the Qurʾān retrieved the original images from the holy text, provided their own role models and attempted to read these stories as women would have done.

Women's scholarship and feminist readings of the Qurʾān

A number of women among the early believers had a role in the transmission of the text of the Qurʾān. ʿĀʾisha, the Prophet's favorite wife, heard passages of the Qurʾān from the Prophet himself, ordered a full written copy to be prepared and corrected the scribe. Ḥafṣa (q.v.), daughter of the caliph ʿUmar and widow of the Prophet, gave the caliph ʿUthmān (q.v.) written pages of the Qurʾān that she had received from her father. ʿUthmān had the pages gathered into a book and declared this text to be the official version of the holy book. Ḥafṣa also corrected a scribe who was writing a qurʾānic text. During the first three or four centuries of Islam, ʿUthmān's text was only one of various versions of the Qurʾān that were ascribed to Companions of the Prophet (q.v.), the caliphs ʿUmar and ʿAlī (see ʿALĪ B. ABI ṬĀLIB), and widows of the Prophet — ʿĀʾisha, Umm Salama and Ḥafṣa. One of the Prophet's female Companions, Umm Waraqa, collected and recited the Qurʾān and may have assisted ʿUmar in assembling the text.

Throughout the centuries, girls as well as boys have learned the Qur'ān (generally by rote) in primary schools *(kuttāb, maktab)* in gender-defined spaces, occupying separate areas of the classrooms, separate rooms, classrooms or informal venues (for classical examples, see FIGS. I and II; for a contemporary female Qur'ān study group, see FIG. III). There have been attestations of this in Islamic painting, biographies, government statistics and autobiographies. Women as well as men were required to obtain the minimal knowledge needed to be good Muslims and this included gender-specific principles and laws. The Islamic religion did not serve as a barrier to this learning since traditions of the Prophet encourage the education of girls. Moreover, segregation of the genders did not preclude prepubescent girls and boys attending qur'ānic schools together (see TEACHING AND PREACHING THE QUR'ĀN). Nevertheless, to the best of our knowledge, no woman was among the classical exegetes of the Qur'ān.

Proponents of Islamic reform movements, like those of other scriptural religions, quite naturally returned to the original text of the Qur'ān to reinterpret what they regarded as incorrect readings of the divine word by classical exegetes (see CONTEMPORARY CRITICAL PRACTICES AND THE QUR'ĀN). Some of the earliest proponents of the liberation of Muslim women anchored their arguments in their rereading of the Qur'ān. The Indian Mumtaz ʿAli in his *Women's laws* (1898) promoted the explanation of Q 4:34 as meaning that women have precedence over men who work for them. He refuted the belief that Adam had precedence in creation and a privileged position over Eve as being contrary to the Qur'ān. As for the disparity between male and female witnesses, he argued that the relevant verse refers to business transactions, something with which male Arab merchants were more familiar than women. For matters of personal law, a woman would be as qualified to testify as a man. On the question of polygyny, Mumtaz ʿAli held that the condition not to treat one wife better than others effectively cancels the possibility of a man marrying more than one woman since it is humanly impossible to love several women equally. As for purdah or *pardah,* the Urdu word for the Arabic *ḥijāb,* Mumtaz ʿAli argued that only one verse of the Qur'ān refers specifically to this. Other verses recommend modesty in general terms and purdah as it developed in Muslim India was a recent, indigenous phenomenon.

The modern Syrian commentator Muḥammad Jamāl al-Dīn al-Qāsimī concluded that a woman could lead the prayer as imām based on a verse referring to Mary, but then neutralized this potential empowerment of women by falling back on a classical view that a unique woman like Mary is like a man in the eyes of God. Moreover, even if a woman might serve as a religious leader for other women, she could not participate in the communal prayer, not only because of her impurity, but also because of her physical weakness and the shame involved in mixing with men (Smith and Haddad, The Virgin Mary, 163-4, 173).

Calls for the liberation of Muslim women in the Arab world emerged from and were influenced by the *salafiyya* movement which aspired to return to the true, early untainted Islam. The Egyptian Shaykh Muḥammad ʿAbduh (1849-1905) and his follower Muḥammad Rashīd Riḍā (1865-1935) composed a new exegesis of the Qur'ān that initially appeared in their journal *al-Manār* to address contemporary problems. ʿAbduh emphasized women's humanity and their equality before God. Adam together with his wife represent humankind which is tested (see TRIAL;

[I] Late ninth/fifteenth century depiction of a mixed-gender study group, most likely for the instruction of the Qurʾān, entitled "Laylā and Majnūn at school" (ca. 895/1490, on a folio from the *Dīwān* of Ḥāfiẓ). Note the muezzin in the upper left hand corner. Courtesy of the Arthur M. Sackler Gallery, Smithsonian Institution, Washington, DC (S1986.289).

[II] Folio from the *Khamsa* of Niẓāmī depicting mixed-gender education in the classical Islamic world (Laylā and Majnūn at school). Courtesy of the John Rylands Library, Manchester, UK (fol. 107 v. of MS Pers. 36).

[III] Female Qur'ān study circle in contemporary Indonesia. Photograph courtesy of Nelly van Doorn-Harder.

TRUST AND PATIENCE), goes astray, repents and is forgiven. Mary's physical, spiritual and behavioral purity, however, granted her a distinctive status and should not be regarded as a precedent for all women. ʿAbduh is credited with the determination that the qurʾānic verse which appears to permit a man to marry up to four wives actually indicates that monogamous marriages should be the norm, by a logic similar to that of Mumtaz ʿAli. On the question of the *ḥijāb*, however, ʿAbduh refused to take a stand. By a similar methodology, Riḍā interpreted a fragment of a verse on divorce (Q 2:228) to define the relationship between man and wife as equal and reciprocal, but defers to the view of classical exegetes that a husband has sexual rights over his wife as a concomitant to her rights to material support from him. Alongside the hesitant efforts of Muslim reformists, commentaries on the Qurʾān that relied on the methods and contents of classical exegesis with regard to women's issues and female characters continued to appear.

An important innovation of this period was the utilization of qurʾānic interpretation to bolster views on the status of women, not only by recognized Islamic scholars like Shaykh ʿAbduh (who had been chief mufti of Egypt) but also by Muslim writers who did not have formal, systematic religious training. One of the most prominent, albeit misogynist, works of this kind was *Woman in the Qurʾān (al-Marʾa fī l-Qurʾān)*, by the Egyptian writer Maḥmūd ʿAbbās al-ʿAqqād. Works of this type paved the way for Muslim lay thinkers, both men and women, to engage in qurʾānic commentary.

The first Muslim woman to undertake qurʾānic exegesis was Dr. ʿĀʾisha ʿAbd al-Raḥmān (1913-96), known by her pen-name, Bint al-Shāṭiʾ. She studied Qurʾān commentary with her professor, mentor and husband, Amīn al-Khūlī, who was considered one of the outstanding modern experts in the field. Some scholars regard ʿAbd al-Raḥmān's exegesis as a reflection of al-Khūlī's theory, and in fact, in the preface to the first volume of her qurʾānic exegesis, she writes of her "attempt" to apply al-Khūlī's method to a few short chapters and compares the usual method of Qurʾān interpretation to "our new way." As the first woman engaged in what had for centuries been an all-male endeavor, it is not surprising that she and some scholars would present her ground-breaking, ambitious work as a mere extension of the theoretical framework of her male mentor. Actually, ʿAbd al-Raḥman published her first of two volumes of qurʾānic exegesis in 1962, several years before the death of her husband. Moreover, the choice of difficult, theological qurʾānic verses with no social implications whatsoever seems to be the strategy of an ambitious woman carefully invading a traditionally male domain. It is also no accident that this innovation emerged from Cairo University's Department of Arabic Language and Literature rather than from a woman studying at al-Azhar. ʿAbd al-Raḥmān's qurʾānic exegesis was published by one of the largest publishing houses in Cairo in a series devoted to literary studies of Arab poetry and other genres as well as non-Arabic literature, perhaps an additional strategy to avoid conflict with the religious establishment. Her qurʾānic commentary brought her prominence in Egypt and the Arab world but its content could not be considered feminist nor was it meant to be.

The qurʾānic underpinnings of the Islamist movements originate with the efforts of Sayyid Abū l-ʿAlā l-Mawdūdī (1903-1979), an Indian Muslim whose ideas on the seclusion of women were written in Urdu in the 1930s, translated into Arabic and subsequently in English. Of his six-volume exegesis of the Qur᾿ān, the only selection translated into Arabic was devoted to a chapter dealing with female sexuality (Q 24; cf. Swanson, Commentary on Surat al-Nur, 187). Mawdūdī interpreted some rather vague verses on visiting other homes (Q 24:27-9) in gender terms to the extent that a man must announce his arrival before entering a house even to the women in his own household. On the issue of modesty (Q 24:30-1), he regards virtually everything connected with a woman as seductive and therefore requires the most extreme forms of concealing dress, including a thick face-veil and gloves. Even a woman's perfume or voice are sexual and should be restricted. Marriage is the proper outlet for human sexuality and Mawdūdī regards the Islamic state as responsible for providing financial support for a man who is precluded from marrying because of the expense.

The Egyptian Sayyid Quṭb (d. 1966) followed Mawdūdī's lead in many respects but appears to have had a more intensive dialogue with western notions of gender and with contemporary technologies. In his exegesis on the story of Eve, he emphasizes the equal responsibility of women and men to battle Satan and their equal rewards for their struggle in the path of God (see PATH OR WAY; JIHĀD). He stresses that the Queen of Sheba was intelligent and independent. Mary, however, serves as a role model for the gender segregation for Muslim women. Quṭb's stand on women's seclusion is no less extreme than that of Mawdūdī but he responds to Freud's theories in his own coin by warning of psychological disorders that can arise if sexuality is not restrained. Thus, a man must warn even his female relatives that he will be entering the house by telephoning to ask permission. Marriage is the natural state of affairs but, despite what many commentators have stated, the husband's exclusive right of divorce is specific to dissolving a marriage and does not imply superiority over his wife.

In the 1990s, Muslim women began to read the Qur᾿ān with a feminist agenda in mind. Feminism in the Muslim world (even when it was termed secular) had frequently drawn from Islamic sources and employed Islamic discourse from its onset in the nineteenth century. The innovative aspect of Islamic feminism has been that Muslim women, who usually did not have formal religious training, have rejected the commentaries on the Qur᾿ān by generations of male exegetes who had functioned in patriarchal societies and independently interpreted the text of the divine word. In order to enhance the legitimacy of these daring projects, they often used neo-classical methods such as *ijtihād* or independent reasoning. This phenomenon has emerged in various parts of the Muslim world, has usually been spearheaded by academic women and activists, and has been disseminated by new media and networking (see MEDIA AND THE QUR᾿ĀN).

One of the earliest efforts by Islamic feminists to read the Qur᾿ān was undertaken by a non-hierarchical study group of women who met in 1990 under the auspices of Women Living Under Muslim Laws, a network founded in 1984. The proceedings were subsequently distributed in English and French, two common languages for millions of Muslims throughout the world. The participants, who remained anonymous, were from Algeria, Bangladesh, Egypt, India, Indonesia, Malaysia, Pakistan, Sri Lanka, Sudan and the United States. Six resource persons (who were also not identified) opened the sessions with presentations but they were questioned and even challenged in the ensuing discussions. The aim was to interpret the Qur᾿ān only from the Qurʾān itself and therefore great emphasis was placed on philological exegesis and classical Arabic dictionaries were employed (see GRAMMAR AND THE QURʾĀN). Nevertheless, classical Islamic sources were occasionally referred to, as well as liberal and conservative modern Muslim thinkers such as Mumtaz ʿAli and Sayyid Quṭb. The issue of skewed translations of the Qurʾān (q.v.) was raised, since translation inevitably involves a degree of interpretation (and is theologically questionable) and also since the majority of Muslims do not know Arabic well enough to understand the qurʾānic text (see ARABIC LANGUAGE; INIMITABILITY; LANGUAGE AND STYLE OF THE QURʾĀN). In view of the rich and variegated academic backgrounds of the women who studied the Qurʾān, it is not surprising that they employed universal scientific methods alongside classical Islamic ones such as psychology, sociology, literary theory, linguistics, etc. (see LITERATURE AND THE QURʾĀN; SOCIAL SCIENCES AND THE QURʾĀN).

The point of departure for Women Reading the Qurʾān was a discussion of "foundational myths" that ostensibly support the notion that men are superior to women. The first of these relate to the story of the creation of Adam and Eve, her role in the fall and the purpose of woman's creation. The women argue that the Qurʾān explicitly states that woman and man were created equal and the creation of Ḥawwāʾ from a male rib is a product of biblical and Christian influences, inaccurate translations of the original Arabic, qurʾānic exegesis, and most seriously, ḥadīth traditions of the Prophet (see ḤADĪTH AND THE QURʾĀN), many of which are not genuine. These supplements to the holy text supported the view held by most Muslims that woman is secondary, derivative and subordinate. Similarly, Eve's culpability, which raises questions about the trustworthiness of all women, is not found in the Qurʾān but is the product of subsequent patriarchal readings.

Debunking the belief that woman was created for man is tied to a lengthy discussion of the qurʾānic verse which embodies gender relations, Q 4:34, rendered by Pickthall as follows: "Men are in charge *(qawwāmūna)* of women, because Allah hath made the one of them to excel the other, and because they spend of their property (for the support of women). So good women are obedient, guarding in secret that which Allah hath guarded. As for those from whom ye fear rebellion, admonish them and banish them to beds apart, and scourge them. Then if they obey you, seek not a way against them. Lo! Allah is ever High, Exalted, Great." The women use the translation of the modernist Muslim commentator M. Yusuf Ali who interprets the phrase "Men are the protectors and maintainers of women," and emphasizes that men may only beat women lightly and as a last resort. The women focus on reinterpretation of crucial words in the verse such as *qawwāmūn*. This term had previously been taken a step further than M. Yusuf Ali to mean the basic idea of moral guidance and caring by the feminist Aziza al-Hibri (Study of Islamic herstory). One resource person at the workshop suggested that *qawwāmūna* means breadwinners and, philosophically, men ought to be breadwinners although not all men fulfill this function. Thus, the comparison is not between men and women but between men in terms of their ability to be breadwinners. A second resource person understood *qawwāmūna* as standing upright or men's upholding the rights, protection, well-being and material support of women. In other words, in Islamic society men have a psychological, social, spiritual and financial responsibility to women. Participants challenged these and other explications by the resources persons. A similar methodology was applied to the words excel *(faḍḍala)*, obedient *(qānitāt)* and rebellion (q.v.; *nushūz*).

From the fundamental principles of gender, the Women Reading the Qur'ān move on to Islamic family law and women in society. The issues of Muslim jurisprudence discussed are: divorce, post-divorce maintenance, polygamy and age of marriage, inheritance, adoption and marriage to non-Muslims. Under the rubric of women in society, the related subjects of *zinā*, evidence and punishment are addressed. Menstruation and the image of "your wives as a tilth" (Q 2:223) are discussed. Finally, the *ḥūr* (sing. *ḥawrā'*) who are promised to the righteous Muslims in paradise are considered. These have been defined in patriarchal terms as fair white virgins with large eyes but, in the interpretation of women reading the Qur'ān, all believers, male and female, will be paired with soul companions.

Amina Wadud-Muhsin produced a feminist exegesis of the Qur'ān as a whole in 1992. Perhaps because Arabic is not her native language, she came up with the radical but controversial idea that verses of the Qur'ān relating to women are an artifact of Arabic as a gendered language. As a result, many verses which appear to refer to men and women should actually be understood in more gender-neutral language. Her book has become very popular and even Arabic-speaking feminists have endorsed her methodology.

Another important forum for women to interpret the Qur'ān in accordance with their own needs has been the Persian women's magazine *Zanān* published in Tehran. *Zanān* was founded in 1992 and by 1994 had become a major voice for reform of the status of women. The magazine's editor, Shahla Sherkat, and other women well-versed in the Qur'ān have championed the right of women to use *ijtihād* or independent reasoning, thereby challenging the primacy of the clergy in the realm of interpretation. Similarly, the Iranian expatriate Nayereh Tohidi has promoted feminist *ijtihād* in Persian-language writings and lectures and promoted reinterpreting the Qur'ān. In the mid-1990s, some proponents of Islamic feminism argued that endeavors like those of *Zanan* opened a dialogue between religious and secular feminists in the heady debate carried on in the Islamic Republic of Iran and the Iranian diaspora.

Feminist exegesis of the Qur'ān by women outside the Muslim scholarly establishment has not been without its critics and it is yet to be seen what its long-term influence will be. One problem is undoubtedly the language barrier between Muslims in different parts of the world and in particular among those who do not read or write Arabic or, conversely, read neither English nor French. Translation of seminal works in this field into Arabic has greatly enhanced their prestige as well as their impact in the Arab world. Trans-global media have also facilitated the dissemination of new readings of the Qur'ān. A second generation of Islamic feminists have begun to cite the pioneering exegesis of women who have reinterpreted the Qur'ān and no longer have to analyze the holy text themselves. Nevertheless, women and men will continue to seek varying views on gender as well as specific rules relating to women and discrete female role models in the Qur'ān.

Ruth Roded

Bibliography

Primary: Bukhārī, *Ṣaḥīḥ;* Ibn Sa'd, *Ṭabaqāt;* Kisā'ī, *Qiṣaṣ*, trans. W.M. Thackston Jr., *The Tales*

of the Prophets of al-Kisāʾī, Boston 1978; Ṭabarī, *Taʾrīkh;* Thaʿlabī, *Qiṣaṣ*.
Secondary: A. Ahmad, *Islamic modernism in India and Pakistan, 1857-1964*, London 1967; M. Badran, Islamic feminism. What's in a name, in *al-Ahram online* (17-23 January 2002), 1-6; E. Baer, Muslim teaching institutions and their visual reflections. The Kuttab, in *Der Islam* 78 (2001), 73-102; J.E. Brockopp, *Early Mālikī law. Ibn ʿAbd al-Ḥakam and his major compendium of jurisprudence*, Leiden 2000; R. Brunschvig, ʿAbd, in *EI*², i, 24-40; N. Geaga, *Mary of the Koran*, trans. Lawrence T. Fares, New York 1984; A. Geissinger, The exegetical traditions of ʿĀʾisha. Notes on their impact and significance, in *Journal of qur'anic studies* 6 (2004), 1-20; S. Haeri, *Law of desire. Temporary marriage in Iran*, London 1989; A. al-Hibri, A study of Islamic herstory, in *Women's Studies international forum* 5 (1982), 217; J.J.G. Jansen, *The interpretation of the Koran in modern Egypt*, Leiden 1974; M.H. Kamali, Divorce and women's rights. Some Muslim interpretations of S. 2:228, in *MW* 74 (1984), 85-99; M. Katz, *Body of text. The emergence of the Sunni law of ritual purity*, Albany 2002; J. Knappert, *Islamic legends*, Leiden 1985; J. Lassner, *Demonizing the Queen of Sheba*, Chicago 1993; I. Mattson, *A believing slave is better than an unbeliever*, PhD diss., U. Chicago 1999; A. Mawdūdī, *al-Ḥijāb. Purdah and the status of woman in Islam*, trans. al-Ashʿarī, Delhi 1974; J.D. McAuliffe, Chosen of all women. Mary and Fāṭimah in qurʾānic exegesis, in *Islamochristiana* 7 (1981), 19-28; G.K. Merguerian and A. Najmabadi, Zulaykha and Yusuf. Whose "best story"? in *IJMES* 29 (1997), 485-508; V.M. Moghadam, Islamic feminism and its discontents. Toward a resolution of the debate, in *Signs: Journal of women in culture and society* 27 (2002), 1135-71; R. Roded, *Women in Islamic biographical collections from Ibn Saʿd to Who's Who*, Boulder, CO 1994; A. Schimmel, *My soul is a woman. The feminine in Islam*, trans. S.H. Ray, New York 2003; M.H. Sherif, What is *ḥijāb?* in *MW* 77 (1987), 151-63; J.I. Smith and Y.Y. Haddad, Eve. Islamic image of woman, in *Women's Studies international forum* 5 (1982), 135-44; ids., The virgin Mary in Islamic tradition and commentary, in *MW* 79 (1989), 161-87; G. Stern, *Marriage in early Islam*, London 1939; B. Stowasser, *Women in the Quran, tradition and interpretation*, New York 1994; M.N. Swanson, A study of twentieth-century commentary on Sūrat al-Nūr (24):27-33, in *MW* 74 (1984), 187-203; A. Wadud-Muhsin, *Qurʾān and woman*, Kuala Lumpur 1992; Women Living Under Muslim Laws, *For ourselves. Women reading the Quran*, Grabels 1997.

Wonders

see MARVELS

Wood

see TREES

Wool

see HIDES AND FLEECE

Word

see SPEECH; OATHS

Word of God

Divine verbal utterance that bridges the gap between God's transcendence and the created world. That God addresses himself to the world by means of speaking is one of the most influential concepts in the whole monotheistic tradition and is also a central issue for the Qurʾān (see REVELATION AND INSPIRATION; ORALITY; SCRIPTURE AND THE QURʾĀN; SOUTH ARABIA, RELIGIONS IN PRE-ISLAMIC). There, several verbs describe God as speaking, e.g. *nādā*, "to call" (ten times), *qaṣṣa*, "to relate" (thirteen times), or *nabbaʾa*, "to tell" (twenty-one times); but the most important verbs are *qāla*, "to say" (around 120 occurrences), and *kallama*, "to speak to" (seven times). Stemming from the same roots as the two last-named verbs, *q-w-l* and *k-l-m*, the nouns *qawl* (about twenty-two times), *kalām* (four times), *kalima* (sixteen times) and its plural form *kalimāt* (twelve times) are also attributed to God. In most of their occurrences these nouns can be rendered literally in English as "word(s)," as in *qawl rabbinā*, "our lord's word" (Q 37:31), *kalām Allāh*, "God's word" (Q 2:75), *kalimatuhu*, "his word" (Q 4:171), or *min rabbihi kalimātin*, "words from his lord" (Q 2:37). Nevertheless, they cover a broad range of meanings and, according to their different contexts, can be translated as "verbal address," "revelation," "decree," and "creative command" (see also SPEECH).

The mystery of monotheism

There are two distinct concepts that underlie biblical monotheism: On the one hand — because of the historical situation of competition with other deities — God's exclusive oneness is emphasized (see GOD AND HIS ATTRIBUTES). Characterized ontologically as the creator of the universe and cause of being (see COSMOLOGY; CREATION), and ethically as the supreme lawgiver and final judge for humankind (see JUSTICE AND INJUSTICE; LAST JUDGMENT; JUDGMENT; LAW AND THE QURʾĀN; ETHICS AND THE QURʾĀN), God is conceived of as the sole true, yet personal, agent in a monopolar world order. On the other hand, and in order to glorify God's majesty, stress is laid on his transcendent uniqueness. Although he is, at times, described in anthropomorphic terms, God, in his essence, is thought to transcend the realm of the created world (see ANTHROPOMORPHISM): He dwells not only beyond the reach of human disposal, but he also exceeds human intellectual capacities (see INTELLECT; KNOWLEDGE AND LEARNING). When, however, these two notions are combined with each other — as is the case in biblical monotheism — a clear tension appears between them. While the first concept suggests direct contact between God and the world, the second implies their definite separation. So, the question arises of how to understand the relationship between God and his creation, i.e. how to reconcile the opposing notions of transcendence and immanence.

Deeply rooted in the religious thinking of the ancient Near East, Islam — like Judaism and Christianity before it (see JEWS AND JUDAISM; CHRISTIANS AND CHRISTIANITY; PEOPLE OF THE BOOK) — proposed the "word of God" as one of the most important answers to this question. God created the universe by means of his word, and it is his word that he revealed to humankind. Nevertheless, this idea raises further questions. First, does "word of God" mean the same thing in respect to creation as in reference to revelation, or are these two entirely different concepts that only share the same terms, i.e. the creative command as opposed to the speech of God? Secondly, the notion of God's creative command as the sole causation for entities coming into being directly calls for an inquiry into the underlying assumptions concerning the relationship between language and existence. Thirdly, the idea of the "word of God" carries with it considerable difficulties in respect to the nature of revelation. Not only is the physical means of God's act of communication to be questioned; even more important is how to conceive of the nature of his speech. In order to be understandable, God has to address humankind in human language. But does that mean that the very language of revelation is part of God's essence — thus presenting a common link between God and his creation that comes close to a manifest anthropomorphism — or is revelation rather a kind of translation of God's true speech that exceeds the human capacity of understanding? And if the latter is so, how can this translation be understood? It is in the context of these questions that the qurʾānic use of the "word of God" must be considered.

Word and creation

Eight qurʾānic verses unambiguously state that God creates by means of the imperative "Be." The most prominent formula of this is "When he decrees *(qaḍā)* a thing *(amr),* he but says to it 'Be' *(kun),* and it is" (Q 2:117; 3:47; 19:35; 40:68; cf. 3:59; 6:73; 16:40; 36:82; and see below). As an expression of faith (q.v.) , this passage emphasizes God's omnipotence (see POWER AND IMPOTENCE) and suggests that, by virtue of his command, God's decree is tantamount to its realization. As a dogmatic statement, however, the exact wording by which this idea is expressed deserves closer examination. Though the single words that occur in this passage are quite common in the qurʾānic vocabulary, here they acquire meanings that are rather exceptional. The verb *qaḍā,* to begin with, is generally translated as "to decide" or "to carry out," and the noun *amr* usually denotes something like "command," "plan," "action" or "affair," thus being an appropriate complement for *qaḍā*. Indeed, there are several instances where both words appear together, as in the recurrent formulation *quḍiya l-amru* — approximately "the affair was decided" (Q 2:210; 6:8, 58; 11:44; 12:41; 14:22; 19:39). In the verse cited above, however, *amr* is described as something being spoken to; therefore the word in this context has to be understood as a kind of personalized entity. This observation is corroborated by the parallel passages Q 16:40 and 36:82 (see below), where the proper word for "thing" *(shayʾ)* is used instead. And since a thing, strictly speaking, cannot be decided or carried out — and the verb *qaḍā* thus takes on a meaning that is not entirely clear — again, the parallels Q 16:40 and 36:82 replace it by forms of the verb "to want" *(arāda)*. In addition, with the possible exceptions of Q 2:280, 193 and 8:39, this passage exhibits the only qurʾānic occurrence where forms of the verb "to be" *(kāna)* are not used as copulas or as determiners of tense, but in an absolute mode meaning "to exist." Based on these observations, the obvious implication of this passage is that there are two realms of existence, one hidden (*al-ghayb;* see HIDDEN AND THE HIDDEN) and the other manifest *(al-shahāda);* and that in the *ghayb,* there are entities conceived of as personalized beings with the ability to obey God's command (see OBEDIENCE) and to enter the realm of manifest existence. Thus, the process of creation consists of an interplay between command and obedience, and does not rest upon any alleged magical power of words. This understanding of the operational mode of the word of God goes back to the time of Hellenistic Judaism. At that time, although the idea of the creation with the word in Genesis 1 was labeled as a *creatio ex nihilo* (2 *Macc* 7:28), it was also frequently combined with the motif that God exerts his authority (q.v.) over the universe, just as a military commander does over his subordinates (*Jer* 44:26; 48:13; *Ps* 33:9; *Matt* 7:9). While rather precluding any speculations about the origins of primeval chaos, the resulting concept of creation by direct address (*Syrian Apocalypse of Baruch,* 21:4; 48:8; as cited in Schlier, *Römerbrief,* 132; also *Rom* 4:17; *Heb* 11:3; 2 *Clem* 1:8) together with the concomitant notion of the pre-existence of non-being (Philo, De migratione Abrahami 9; *Babylonian Talmud,* Nesikin, ch. Sanhedrin 91a; as cited in Schlier, *Römerbrief,* 132) causes both philosophical and theological problems: It raises the question of the ontological status of the pre-existent, and it seems to limit the divine omnipotence, by suggesting that the pre-existent possesses a certain independence from God. Nevertheless, in spite of these difficulties, this concept became successful because it helps to explain not only the primeval creation of the universe, but also the way God controls his creation and effects the phenomena of human birth (q.v.) and resurrection (q.v.; see also CREATEDNESS OF THE QURʾĀN; THEOLOGY AND THE QURʾĀN; PHILOSOPHY AND THE QURʾĀN).

The creation of the heavens and the earth is a recurrent motif that appears more than fifty-five times in the Qurʾān. The verb that is most frequently attributed to God in this respect is "to create" *(khalaqa)*. While this verb leaves the manner of creation open, other, far less frequently employed verbs suggest a similarity to handicraft activities, like "to level" (*sawwā,* e.g. Q 2:29), "to make" (*jaʿala,*

Q 6:1; 13:3), "to cover" (*aghshā,* e.g. Q 7:54; 13:3), "to raise up" (*rafaʿa,* Q 13:2), "to stretch out" (*madda,* Q 13:3) and "to rip open" (*fataqa,* e.g. Q 21:30). There is, however, one single instance where God clearly appears to be speaking in connection with the creation of the cosmos:

Then he lifted himself to heaven (see HEAVEN AND SKY) when it was smoke (q.v.), and said *(qāla)* to it and to the earth (q.v.), "Come willingly, or unwillingly!" They both said, "We come willingly." So he determined *(qaḍā)* them as seven heavens in two days, and revealed *(awḥā)* its commandment in every heaven (Q 41:11-12).

This passage exposes further peculiarities of the concept of creation by direct address. On the one hand, it illustrates what has already been said about the implications of the *kun* formula: The preexistence of heaven — amorphous as "smoke" — and earth is taken for granted (cf. Q 21:30); and both heaven and earth appear as personified and obeying God's command. On the other hand, there are also elements that enlarge the creation concept: God's command, "Come" instead of "Be," refers here only to a preparatory stage of creation, while the actual creative work is indicated by the verbs "to determine" and "to reveal." The latter verb denotes at least a kind of mental activity through which God conveys his orders to living beings (cf. Q 16:68; see below), and seems to fit in by and large with the "Be" concept. In the case of the other verb, "to determine," however, it is not clear whether the molding of the seven spheres out of the primeval smoke comes to pass by creative command, also, or is brought about in some other way (cf. Q 2:29, where "to level" replaces "to determine"). These divergences arise because the passage (Q 41:9-12) — not unlike Genesis 1 — tries to combine two different, disharmonious concepts of creation: the notion of a creative command that effects the immediate realization of its objects, on the one hand, and the idea of creation as a demiurgic process, lasting several days and passing through successive stages, on the other.

In several instances the creation of the universe with the word is referred to by the term *ḥaqq*. This term occurs 247 times in the Qurʾān, and predominantly means "reality, truth (q.v.), right." In eleven passages, however, where it says — mostly in connection with the announcement of resurrection — that God "created the heavens and the earth with the *ḥaqq*" (e.g. Q 14:19; 30:8; 45:22), it seems to mean the "wisdom" (q.v.) or "wise plan" inherent in creation. In addition, Q 6:73 shows that *ḥaqq* can encompass the creative command "Be" as well:

It is he who created the heavens and the earth with the *ḥaqq*. On the day when he utters "Be" and it is, his utterance is the *ḥaqq*. His is the sovereignty (q.v.) on the day when the trumpet is blown. He knows the unseen and the seen. He is the all-wise, the all-aware (cf. Q 19:34, where *qawla l-ḥaqq,* "the word of the truth," probably refers to the creation of Jesus [q.v.]; see below).

The origins of the extensions of meaning that *ḥaqq* undergoes in the Qurʾān — from "reality" to "wisdom" to "word of creation" — can be traced back to late Hellenistic times. "Truth" was then identified with God's precepts (*Ps* 119:86; *Dan* 9:13), and "wisdom" was understood as the originator of creation (*Wis* 7:12), so that ultimately "truth," too, could refer to the creative command (James 1:18). Against this background, Q 21:18 ("We hurl forth the *ḥaqq* upon the *bāṭil* [lit. "vain, invalid"] and it [the *ḥaqq*] overcomes it and look! the *bāṭil* is disappearing"; cf. Q 34:48-9) can be understood as another attempt to articulate the effect that the creative command "Be" exerts on the pre-existent (cf. Joseph and Asenath, 8:9; as cited in Schlier, *Römerbrief,* 132).

God's relationship to nature after creation is also described in different ways. First, there are processes that seem to function on their own, following God's initial command, like the movements of the sun (q.v.) and the moon (q.v.; cf. Q 13:2; 14:33; 31:29; 35:13). Then there is an assortment of ongoing divine activities attributed to God, especially in respect to life (q.v.) and death (see DEATH AND THE DEAD), rain and provision (see SUSTENANCE). These are indicated by such verbs as *aḥyā,* "to give life," *amāta,* "to cause to die," *anzala,* "to send down" (of rain), or *razaqa,* "to sustain" (e.g. Q 3:156; 10:59; 16:65; 30:40). Additionally, some passages express the idea that God continues to act upon nature and history in the same way he did in respect to primeval creation, i.e. by means of his command (see NATURE AS SIGNS; HISTORY AND THE QURʾĀN). This is evident in Q 21:69, which relates how God rescued Abraham (q.v.) from his people: "We said, 'O fire (q.v.), be coolness and safety for Abraham!'" In the same manner the metamorphosis of the Sabbath-breakers is effected (Q 2:65; 7:166; see SABBATH). And just as in Q 4:47 the word *amr* (command) refers to this punishment, it is likely that *amr* indicates the divine command in respect to other punishment stories and the eschatological cataclysm, as well (e.g. Q 11:40; 19:39; 46:25; cf. 2:243; see ESCHATOLOGY; APOCALYPSE; REWARD AND PUNISHMENT). It is characteristic of this *amr* not only that it happens in "the twinkling of an eye" (Q 54:50), but also that it is sometimes accompanied by, or even becomes audible as, "the cry" (*al-ṣayḥa,* e.g. Q 11:67; 15:73; 36:29; 54:31).

God's command, however, is particularly linked with the origin of life, both in this world and the hereafter. This is especially clear in the eight qurʾānic "Be" passages that justify either the message of bodily resurrection, or the denial that Jesus is the son of God. There, the idea that at the end of days the dead will be resuscitated by means of divine command is explained by referring to God's previous creative activity:

> ... He says, "Who shall quicken the bones when they are decayed?" Say: He shall quicken them, who originated them the first time.... Is not he, who created the heavens and the earth, able to create the like of them? Yes indeed; he is the all-creator, the all-knowing; his command, when he desires a thing, is to say to it 'Be,' and it is (Q 36:78-9, 81-2).

The underlying assumption of this comparison is that the unborn, like the dead, have a hidden existence until God calls them to life (see Q 2:28; 30:25; cf. 7:172). In Q 3:59, Jesus is compared to Adam (see ADAM AND EVE), in that both were created by "Be." The *tertium comparationis,* however, is not that only these two came to life in this way — this holds true for everyone (cf. the annunciation stories of Isaac [q.v.; Isḥāq] and John the Baptist [q.v.; Yaḥyā]; Q 3:38-40; 11:71-3; 19:7-9) — but rather that in their case, the activity of the creative command is particularly evident, since both have no natural father. Besides, in three much-disputed verses Jesus is called "a word from God/him" (*kalimatin mina llāh/minhu,* Q 3:39, 45) or "his word" (*kalimatuhu,* Q 4:171). And although this naming has often been explained as a reference to the creative imperative (because Jesus was created by the word "Be," he was called "word of God"), considering what has been mentioned above, it is more probable that here, as elsewhere in the Qurʾān, *kalima* has simply the connotation of a "promise" made by God (see below; see COVENANT).

Word and revelation

The idea that God speaks to humankind is central to the Qurʾān; in numerous verses, various terms characterize him as speaking (see above). Yet Q 42:51 shows that in respect to revelation, the very expression "God speaks" can be understood in different ways or modes: "It belongs not to any mortal that God should speak to him *(yukallimahu),* except (1) by inspiration *(waḥy),* or (2) from behind a veil (q.v.), or (3) that [God] should send a messenger (q.v.) and he inspires *(fa-yūḥiya)* whatsoever he will, by his leave; surely he is all-high, all-wise." Three modes of revelation, each of which is understood as a kind of speaking, are presented here in a probably hierarchical ranking. As to "inspiration" *(waḥy),* it is evident from the episode of the dumb Zechariah (q.v.; Zakariyyā) coming out from the sanctuary and signaling *(fa-awḥā)* to his people "Give you glory (q.v.) at dawn (q.v.) and evening" (q.v.; Q 19:11; cf. 3:41; see GLORIFICATION OF GOD), that it denotes a nonverbal and inaudible form of communication. It nevertheless imparts precise contents, like hidden knowledge (e.g. Q 12:15; 14:13; 17:39; see KNOWLEDGE AND LEARNING; HIDDEN AND THE HIDDEN), or orders to behave in a certain way (e.g. Q 7:117; 10:87; 20:77; 23:27), and can be conveyed either directly (mode 1) or indirectly (mode 3). (Phenomenologically, however, it seems that the latter mode is nothing but the personalization of the God-given prophetic state of mind; see in this respect the oscillating term *rūḥ* in Q 42:52.) And although *waḥy* as a mode of revelation comes close to pseudo-prophecy or dream-inspiration (cf. Q 6:93, 112, 121 and 12:44; 21:5; 52:32; see DREAMS AND SLEEP), it still represents the normal method of divine communication to former prophets and messengers as well as to the qurʾānic prophet (Q 4:163 f.; 12:109; 16:43; 42:3; etc.). Thus, in order to deliver the divine message to their audience, it is the prophet's task to translate the *waḥy*-revelation into human language.

The second mode of speaking, "from behind a veil," is contrasted to *waḥy*. This motif goes back to the idea in Hellenistic Judaism that God is hidden by a veil that surrounds his throne (see THRONE OF GOD), even when he speaks to the angels (see ANGEL). The only human being to whom he spoke "from mouth to mouth" and "from face to face," i.e. without a veil, was Moses (q.v.; cf. *Num* 12:8; *Exod* 33:11; *Deut* 34:10; see THEOPHANY). Now, while the Qurʾān concedes to Moses, and only to Moses expressly (and tacitly to the Children of Israel [q.v.] gathered at the foot of the mountain; cf. Q 2:63, 93; 4:154), that on Mount Sinai (q.v.) God "really spoke" to him (*kallama llāhu Mūsā taklīman,* Q 4:164; cf. 7:143; 2:253), it nevertheless denies him the privilege of a vision of God (Q 7:143; cf. *Exod* 33:18 f.; see FACE OF GOD). Thus, as the concept of *waḥy* is nowhere connected with the Mount Sinai revelation, the speaking "from behind a veil" can probably be understood as an indirect reference to this event, admitting that Moses heard God's true speech but explicitly denying that he saw him (see SEEING AND HEARING). This attitude towards the Mosaic revelation is in line with the general qurʾānic tendency to play down the paramount significance of the Mount Sinai events in Judaism. And so, although God "really spoke" only on Mount Sinai, there is no indication in the Qurʾān of which language he used. The Qurʾān seems to avoid the question of any concrete *lingua sacra,* but rather considers language, as such, as a God-given, effective means of communication (cf. the passages on "names" and "naming" and "clear Arabic speech," Q 2:31-3; 7:71; 16:103; 26:195, etc.; see LANGUAGE, CONCEPT OF; ARABIC LANGUAGE; LANGUAGE AND STYLE OF THE QUR'ĀN; NARRATIVES). This would imply that from the qur'ānic point of view, the word of God, his speaking, is not defined by any linguistic idiom — to put revelation in words is the task of the prophets — but only by its divine origin and content.

As mentioned above, the two most important consonantal roots from which the verbs and nouns referring to the word of God are derived are *q-w-l* and *k-l-m*. The verb *qāla*, "to say," is most often used to characterize God as speaking. Approximately half of all its occurrences appear in the context of the events in the garden (q.v.) of Eden (thirty-two times), or on the day of judgment (twenty-eight times); the rest are distributed over the course of history, frequently in connection with Moses (sixteen times). *Qāla* is nearly always followed by direct discourse, which often contains orders (e.g. Q 2:131; 7:13; 29:55; see COMMANDMENTS; EXHORTATIONS), but also announcements (e.g. Q 3:55; 38:84-5), rhetorical questions (e.g. Q 5:116; 27:84; see RHETORIC AND THE QUR'ĀN) and other kinds of statements (e.g. Q 2:33; 7:143; 10:89; see LITERARY STRUCTURES OF THE QUR'ĀN). When the corresponding noun *qawl*, "saying, word," is attributed to God, its meaning sometimes comes close to "utterance" (Q 36:58) or "message" (Q 14:27; 28:51; 39:18; 73:5). In other instances, it is used in connection with divine decisions and unchangeable decrees, such as the creative command (Q 3:59; 6:73; 16:40; 40:68, etc.). Especially when combined with the verb *ḥaqqa*, "to be realized," *qawl* stands for God's firm intention to punish the sinners, and it is not entirely clear whether this implies divine predestination (see FREEDOM AND PREDESTINATION): "If we had so willed, we could have given every soul its guidance (see ERROR; ASTRAY); but now my word *(qawl)* is realized *(ḥaqqa)*: 'Assuredly I shall fill Gehenna (see HELL AND HELLFIRE) with jinn (q.v.) and people all together'" (Q 32:13; cf. 17:16; 28:63; 37:31; 41:25; 46:18).

As to *k-l-m* and its derivations, when the verb *kallama*, "to speak to," is attributed to God, it implies that, for the addressee, being addressed by God is a special privilege. This is clear since God spoke to Moses (Q 4:164; 7:143; cf. 2:253; 42:51), the ignorant demand from him that he speak to them (Q 2:118; see IGNORANCE), and in the hereafter he will not speak to the sinners (Q 2:174; 3:77; see SIN, MAJOR AND MINOR). In Q 7:144, the noun *kalām*, "speaking, speech," also has the connotation of an "honoring address." In Q 2:75 and Q 9:6, however, *kalām Allāh* obviously refers to the whole of the revelations delivered by the qur'ānic Prophet; and in Q 48:15, it is — like *qawl* — synonymous with "God's decision" (cf. Q 3:59; 7:162). The noun *kalima*, "word, statement," signifies the divine decision not to put an end to strife about religion in this world, and to postpone punishment to the hereafter (e.g. Q 10:19; 11:110; 20:129; see CORRUPTION; RELIGIOUS PLURALISM AND THE QUR'ĀN). Just like *qawl*, it implies the intention to punish (e.g. Q 10:96; 11:119; 39:19; 40:6); but other than *qawl*, it sometimes also stands for promises (Q 7:137; 37:171; 6:115). In its singular form, it nowhere refers expressly to the creative command, and thus it is more probable that in respect to Jesus, too, it means "promise" (see above). Yet, in its plural form, *kalimāt*, it is not easy to decide whether the expression in Q 8:7, 10:82 and 42:24 *(yuḥiqqu l-ḥaqqa bi-kalimātihi)* must be translated by "He realizes the truth with his words" or "in his words." In any case, *kalimāt* mostly refers to former revelations, and bears the connotation of promises, as well (Q 2:37, 124; 6:34; 7:158; 10:64; 18:27; 66:12). The single exception to this is the simile in Q 18:109 and Q 31:27 (see SIMILES), which is of rabbinic origins and praises God's omniscience and omnipotence.

Matthias Radscheit

Bibliography
G.C. Anawati, ʿĪsā, in *EI²*, iv, 81-6; R. Arnaldez, Ḥayāt, in *EI²*, iii, 302-3; id., Khalḳ, in *EI²*, iv, 980-8; J.M.S. Baljon, The 'amr of God' in the Koran, in *AO* 23 (1959), 7-18; R. Bultmann, *Alêtheia*, in G. Kittel (ed.), *Theologisches Wörterbuch zum Neuen Testament*, 10 vols. in 11, Stuttgart 1932-79 (repr. 1966), i, 233-48; R. Casper, Parole de Dieu et langage humaine en Christianisme et en Islam, in *Islamochristiana* 6 (1980), 33-60; W. Foerster, *Ktízô*. C. Die Lehre von der Schöpfung im Spätjudentum, in G. Kittel (ed.), *Theologisches Wörterbuch zum Neuen Testament*, 10 vols. in 11, Stuttgart 1932-79 (repr. 1950), iii, 1015-22; K. Haacker, Creatio ex auditu. Zum Verständnis von Hbr 11, 3, in *Zeitschrift für die neutestamentliche Wissenschaft* 60 (1969), 279-81; O. Hofius, *Der Vorhang vor dem Thron Gottes*, Tübingen 1972; Izutsu, *God*, 151-93; D.B. MacDonald/E.E. Calverly, Ḥaḳḳ, in *EI²*, iii, 82-3; D.B. MacDonald/L. Gardet, al-Ghayb, in *EI²*, ii, 1025-6; J. Obermann, Koran and Agada. The events at Mount Sinai, in *The American journal of Semitic languages and literatures* 58 (1941), 23-48; K.-H. Ohlig, *Weltreligion Islam*, Mainz 2000, 96-100; Th. O'Shaughnessy, Creation from nothing and the teaching of the Qurʾān, in *ZDMG* 120 (1970), 274-80; id., Creation with wisdom and with the word in the Qurʾān, in *JAOS* 91 (1971), 208-21; id., *The development of the meaning of spirit in the Koran*, Rome 1953; id., God's purpose in creating according to the Qurʾān, in *JSS* 20 (1975), 193-209; id., *Word of God in the Qurʾān*. Second, completely revised edition of *The Koranic concept of the word of God*, Rome 1984; M. Radscheit, *Die koranische Herausforderung. Die* taḥaddī-*Verse im Rahmen der Polemikpassagen des Korans*, Berlin 1996, 44-6, 90-4; H. Räisänen, *Das koranische Jesusbild*, Helsinki 1971, 23-37; H. Ringgren, *Word and wisdom*, Lund 1947; A.A. Roest Crollius, *Thus were they hearing. The word in the experience of revelation in Qurʾān and Hindu scriptures*, Rome 1974; H. Schlier, *Der Römerbrief. Kommentar*, Freiburg 1977; S. Schreiner, Der Dekalog in der jüdischen Tradition und im Koran, in *Kairos* 23/1 (1981), 17-30; U. Wilckens, *Der Brief an die Römer*, Zürich 1997³, 274-5; H. Zirker, *Der Koran. Zugänge und Lesarten*, Darmstadt 1999, 51-102.

Work

The activities engaged in to earn a living; occupation. Words associated with the root *ʿ-m-l* are used over one hundred times in the Qurʾān to signify "actions" or "deeds" in the broad sense; only a few times (Q 18:79; 34:12, 13) do they signify "work" in particular. *Sh-gh-l* twice signifies "occupation," both in the sense of livelihood and what keeps one busy (Q 36:55 and 48:11). The Qurʾān's repeated emphasis on "good works" (*al-ṣāliḥāt;* see GOOD DEEDS) while reflecting little interest in the occupations of believers, indicates that shaping a proper moral outlook, rather than structuring a particular kind of socioeconomic order, is a primary goal of the revelation (see REVELATION AND INSPIRATION; ETHICS AND THE QURʾĀN).

Qurʾānic references to specific occupations may provide some indication of the social context of the revelation, although caution should be exercised in this respect since the Qurʾān uses selected metaphors (see METAPHOR), parables (see PARABLE) and images (see SYMBOLIC IMAGERY) to achieve its didactic and liturgical function (see LITERARY STRUCTURES OF THE QURʾĀN). Among references to occupations, the cultivation of crops, especially grapes, dates, other fruits and grains are plentiful (see AGRICULTURE AND VEGETATION). Domestic cattle *(anʿām)* are mentioned almost thirty times in the Qurʾān, often as a corollary to the cultivation of crops (see ANIMAL LIFE). In contrast, shepherding and pasturing animals are referred to only in the story of Moses (q.v.; Q 28:23) and in a negative light in connection with the

Bedouin (q.v.; Q 48:11). Hunting and fishing (q.v.) are indicated as activities (Q 5:4, 94-5), if not occupations. Trade *(tijāra)* and its constituent activities including weighing, measuring, buying and selling (see TRADE AND COMMERCE; WEIGHTS AND MEASURES; MEASUREMENT; MONEY; MARKETS; CARAVAN), are the most frequently cited activities in which the believers engage to earn a living *(kasb)*. There are few references to manual labor (q.v.). Aside from the references to Noah's (q.v.) ark-building (see ARK), building *(ṣ-n-ʿ)* and construction *(kh-l-q)* are generally noted negatively in connection with oppressive rulers (e.g. Q 7:137; 26:129; 89:6-12; see KINGS AND RULERS; OPPRESSION; OPPRESSED ON EARTH, THE). Forced prostitution is condemned (Q 24:33; see SEX AND SEXUALITY; ADULTERY AND FORNICATION; SLAVES AND SLAVERY). The description of servants in paradise (q.v.) as being ageless and beyond fatigue (Q 56:17; 76:19) is understood by some scholars as recognition of the tiresome nature of such work in this life (Ṭabarī, *Tafsīr,* ad loc.; see SERVANT). The Qurʾān gives some guidelines for the employment of wet-nurses (Q 2:233; see WET-NURSING), an occupation that provided an opportunity for the mother of Moses to have her infant returned to her (Q 28:12-13).

Scholars discuss the issue of the lawfulness of a believer working for an enemy or an immoral person in reference to the story of the mother of Moses and also in reference to the prophet Joseph (q.v.) working for the "king" of Egypt (q.v.; Q 12:54-6; see also ENEMIES; PHARAOH). Al-Qurṭubī (d. 671/1272; *Jāmiʿ,* ad Q 28:12-13) says that Moses' mother accepted a daily wage from Pharaoh not for nursing her son but as spoils of war (see BOOTY; LACTATION; MAINTENANCE AND UPKEEP). Scholars disagreed on the rulings that could be derived from the example of Joseph. Most scholars were concerned with the way in which authority (q.v.) was passed from the employer to the employee. If the employee derived the authority to do his job directly from an immoral person or unlawful ruler, the employment could be unlawful. If the employee was performing a divinely ordained task, like the distribution of *zakāt* (see ALMSGIVING), this may be permissible, despite the corruption of his employer (see LAW AND THE QURʾĀN; LAWFUL AND UNLAWFUL; FORBIDDEN).

A fuller picture of work in seventh-century Arabia (see PRE-ISLAMIC ARABIA AND THE QURʾĀN) has been drawn by scholars who rely mostly, but not exclusively, on textual sources. It should be noted that nomads (q.v.), although an important segment of the Arabian population, were present in much smaller numbers than sedentary people, whose professions reflected the diversity of their environments (Donner, *Early Islamic conquests,* 11-20; see CITY; ARABS). In the fertile lands of southern Arabia, agriculture and shepherding were significant occupations, as was the case in desert oases like Yathrib (see MEDINA) and Yamāma. Across Arabia, the manufacture of items from the skin and hair of animals was a major activity (see HIDES AND FLEECE). Tanning and weaving were occupations shared by nomadic and sedentary people. Leather was made into containers to store oils and other liquids and used for many other purposes (see CUPS AND VESSELS). Goat-hair and wool from camels and sheep were processed and woven for many purposes — in particular, to make carpets and Bedouin tents. Wool was the most readily available material for clothes, but a desire for more comfortable fabrics allowed a number of Meccans to make a living importing cotton, linen and silk (q.v.), all of which were produced to a limited extent in southern Arabia (see CLOTHING). A number of prominent Meccans are said to have been cloth merchants or tailors. Residents of Mecca and other towns also worked as blacksmiths, arrow-makers, saddle-makers, carpenters, butchers and builders, among other things. In Medina, some Jewish tribes are said to have specialized as goldsmiths and in trading in precious jewels (see METALS AND MINERALS; GOLD).

In seventh-century Arabia, women, like men, worked in a wide variety of occupations, including trading, manufacturing and agriculture (see WOMEN AND THE QURʾĀN; GENDER; PATRIARCHY). Specialty occupations for women included wet-nurse, beautician, singer and prostitute. There were male and female musicians, magicians and servants (see MAGIC; SOOTHSAYER). The Prophet's wife, Khadīja (q.v.), is portrayed as a successful business-woman who first met Muḥammad when she employed him to trade for her. One assumes that domestic chores like child-rearing, cooking and cleaning occupied much of the average woman's day (see CHILDREN; FAMILY; MAINTENANCE AND UPKEEP). Grinding grain and making bread appear to be two of the most tiresome daily chores most women had to perform. Ḥadīth reports show some female Companions of the Prophet (q.v.) expressing a desire for servants or slaves to help them with their work; in some cases the women were given help, in other cases, they were advised that the more pious path was to do the work themselves (see PIETY; ḤADĪTH AND THE QURʾĀN). These ḥadīth arise in scholarly discussions about the dignity or dishonor of labor. The Prophet's wives (see WIVES OF THE PROPHET; WIDOW) are said to have occupied themselves with useful tasks after his death, despite receiving large annual state allowances. ʿĀʾisha taught children (see ʿĀʾISHA BINT ABĪ BAKR), Ḥafṣa (q.v.) administered her father's agricultural estate and Zaynab bt. Jaḥsh manufactured items she gave to the poor.

Due to the nature of the sources, few definitive statements about attitudes towards work at the rise of Islam are possible. There are, however, a number of indications that a shift in the status of certain occupations occurred with the rise of Mecca (q.v.) and other towns to greater prominence. According to the martial norms of the Bedouin, most work other than fighting was done by slaves and women, while sedentary people labored to produce the food and goods Bedouin acquired through force, trade and negotiation (see WAR; FIGHTING; CONTRACTS AND ALLIANCES). Despite the lingering prejudice of Bedouin culture, there are a number of indications that before the Islamic conquests, an individual's occupation was generally not a significant marker of social status for townsmen. After the conquests (see CONQUEST), cities in the central Islamic lands exhibited more complex, varied and often hierarchical work environments than were present in seventh-century Arabia. Two centuries into the Islamic era, the Iraqi scholar Ibn Qutayba (d. 276/889; *Maʿārif*, 575-7) finds it notable that at the rise of Islam, so many of the "nobles" *(ashrāf)* among the Quraysh (q.v.) worked in professions considered base or menial in his time. These occupations include: butcher, carpenter, veterinarian, blacksmith, arrow-maker, slave trader and leather merchant. Although the Qurʾān does not associate honor or dishonor with certain occupations, or even work itself, this is widely discussed in early Islamic literature.

The Qurʾān does indicate that it is obviously preferable to be a master than a slave (Q 16:71). There are many possible reasons why a slave may have been employed instead of a free person for any given task.

Slaves were not confined to menial labor but were employed in virtually all occupations. The absolute dependence of slaves on their owners clearly gave them some advantages as employees but simple availability may have been the most critical advantage. The relationship between slavery and labor shortages in this period needs further study.

Ingrid Mattson

Bibliography
Primary: Ibn al-Athīr, ʿIzz al-Dīn ʿAlī, *Usd al-ghāba fī maʿrifat al-ṣaḥāba,* Cairo 1970-3; Ibn Qutayba, Abū Muḥammad ʿAbdallāh b. Muslim, *Kitāb al-Maʿārif,* Cairo 1969; Ibn Saʿd, *Ṭabaqāt;* Muslim, *Ṣaḥīḥ;* Qurṭubī, *Jāmiʿ;* al-Shaybānī, Abū ʿAbdallāh Muḥammad b. al-Ḥasan, *Kitāb al-Kasb,* Aleppo 1997; Ṭabarī, *Tafsīr.*
Secondary: F.M. Donner, *The early Islamic conquests,* Princeton 1981; L. Marlow, *Hierarchy and egalitarianism in Islamic thought,* Cambridge 1997; I. Mattson, *A believing slave is better than an unbeliever. Status and community in early Islamic law and society,* PhD diss., U. Chicago 1999; W. Samad, *al-Ṣina wa-l-ḥiraf ʿinda l-ʿArab fī l-ʿaṣr al-jāhilī,* Beirut 1981; M. Shatzmiller, *Labour in the medieval Islamic world,* Leiden 1994; ʿA. b. I. al-ʿUmarī, *al-Ḥiraf wa-l-ṣina fī l-Ḥijāz fī ʿaṣr al-rasūl,* Cairo 1985.

World

In English, "world" denotes mainly the entire cosmic system whether created by God, by chance, or simply having existed throughout eternity (q.v.). In its more limited sense the world means the earth (q.v.), all its inhabitants and specifically humankind characterized by certain institutions — social, religious and so on. World also conveys the sense of a special time (q.v.), as in "this world" meaning "lifetime" as opposed to "the world to come" (see ESCHATOLOGY). Some of these meanings appear in the Qurʾān but are expressed by particular words as explained as follows.

ʿĀlam

The word *ʿālam* occurs seventy-four times in the Qurʾān in the oblique plural *(ʿālamīn).* It is a loan word from either Hebrew or Aramaic/Syriac sources (see JEWS AND JUDAISM; CHRISTIANS AND CHRISTIANITY; SCRIPTURE AND THE QURʾĀN; FOREIGN VOCABULARY), although it is also found in Nabatean and Palmyran inscriptions. In biblical Hebrew it means any duration of time (q.v.; see also SPATIAL RELATIONS) and in Rabbinic usage, as in Aramaic, it denotes "age": this world *(ha-ʿōlam ha-zeh),* as contrasted with the next world *(ha-ʿōlam ha-bā).* The common qurʾānic phrase *rabb al-ʿālamīn* is equivalent to *ribbon ha-ʿōlamim,* "the master of all people," in the Jewish liturgy (see LORD).

As a rule, Muslim exegetes (see COSMOLOGY AND THE QURʾĀN) understand *ʿālamīn* in most verses and particularly in the second verse of Q 1 "Praise (q.v.) be to God, the lord of all created beings" *(rabb al-ʿālamīn)* as denoting all creatures (see CREATION): human beings, angels, devils, animals and so on (see ANGEL; DEVIL). Some exegetes exclude animals (see ANIMAL LIFE), claiming that the term applies only to rational beings (see INTELLECT). In a tradition ascribed to Ibn ʿAbbās (d. 68/687), *ʿālamīn* has the meaning of the whole creation: the heavens (see HEAVEN AND SKY) and the earth and what is in them and between them (Ibn Kathīr, *Tafsīr,* i, 43). According to al-Zajjāj (d. 311/923), *al-ʿālam* (in the singular) is whatsoever God created in this world and in the world to come (ibid., i, 44). Elsewhere, however, *ʿālamīn* can only be understood as human beings, as in "O Children of Israel (q.v.), remember my favor which I bestowed on you, and that I preferred you to all human beings" (Q 2:47; see ELECTION; GRACE; BLESSING), and "God chose Adam (see ADAM AND EVE) and Noah (q.v.) and the house of Abraham (q.v.) and the house of ʿImrān (q.v.) above all human beings" (Q 3:33; see also Q 3:96, 108, 7:80, 26:165).

In al-Ṭabarī's (d. 310/923) view (*Tafsīr*, i, 48f.), *ʿālamūn* (the nominative form) is the plural of a collective noun *(ism jamʿ)*, namely *ʿālam*, which has no singular form, like *jaysh*, army, or *rahṭ*, a group of human beings. Each nation is an *ʿālam* and each nation in a certain generation is also called *ʿālam*. Likewise, each genus of creation is an *ʿālam*. Thus *ʿālamūn* includes all things except God (cf. Qurṭubī, *Jāmiʿ*, i, 138). Al-Qurṭubī (d. 671/1272; *Jāmiʿ*, i, 139) adds another interpretation of *ʿālam* which he derives from *ʿalam* or *ʿalāma* meaning a "sign" (see SIGNS), for *ʿālam* demonstrates its producer *(yadullu ʿalā mūjidihi)*, that is, serves as a sign for the existence of its creator (cf. Rāzī, *Tafsīr*, i, 229).

Dunyā

Al-dunyā, the feminine of the elative adjective (literally, "lower, lowest," "nearer, nearest") means "this world." *Al-dunyā* is found in one hundred and fifteen places in the Qurʾān and denotes both the place and time spent in this world. Q 2:201 reads: "And others among them say: 'Our lord, give to us in this world *(al-dunyā)* good (see GOOD AND EVIL), and good in the world to come (*al-ākhira;* see REWARD AND PUNISHMENT), and guard us against the chastisement of the fire'" (q.v.; see also Q 5:33; 7:156; 9:69; 16:30; 27:29; see also HELL AND HELLFIRE). The aspect of time is clearly indicated when the word "life" *(ḥayāt)* is juxtaposed to *al-dunyā* as a combination of a noun with an adjective. It is not, however, only lifetime which is meant by *al-ḥayāt al-dunyā;* this term is also colored by moral traits (see ETHICS AND THE QURʾĀN). Lifetime is replete with temptations and evils which human beings should avoid (see TRIAL; SIN, MAJOR AND MINOR). As Q 3:185 says,

> Life in this world *(al-ḥayāt al-dunyā)* is nothing but pastime and amusement (see LAUGHTER); surely, the next world (*al-dār al-ākhira*, literally, "the last abode") is better for those who are God-fearing (see FEAR; PIETY). Do you, thus, not understand (see KNOWLEDGE AND LEARNING)?

Although the present life is nothing but the joy of delusion (Q 3:185), some people desire it, although others do not (Q 3:152). Human beings enjoy real life, states the Qurʾān, only in the next world (Q 29:64). These and other similar verses served the Ṣūfīs (see ṢŪFISM AND THE QURʾĀN; ABSTINENCE) in their censuring of this world. In his *Iḥyāʾ ʿulūm al-dīn*, al-Ghazālī (d. 505/1111) devoted a whole book to disparaging this world (Bk. 26, *Kitāb Dhamm al-dunyā*, iii, 174-99; many traditions of which are taken from Ibn Abī l-Dunyā's [d. 281/814] book by the same name).

Ākhira

Like *al-dunyā*, *al-ākhira*, the feminine of *ākhir* (the last), appears one hundred and fifteen times. This term signifies "the next world" as opposed to *al-dunyā*, "this world," or to the latter's equivalent, "the first" *(al-ūlā)*. For example, Q 93:4 reads: "And the next world is better for you than this world" (literally, "the first world"). Similar to *al-dunyā*, *al-ākhira* connotes both place and time. When it occurs with *dār* either in a construct state *(dār al-ākhira)* or as a combination of a noun and an adjective *(al-dār al-ākhira)*, it means "paradise" (q.v.), that is, the world prepared for the God-fearing, as stated in Q 7:169 "...and the last abode is better for those who fear God..." (see also Q 6:32; 16:30; 29:64; 33:29; see also HOUSE, DOMESTIC AND DIVINE). In contrast to *al-dunyā*, the connotations of *al-ākhira* are in general positive; however, the Qurʾān explicitly states that the punishment in the last abode is stronger and more enduring than that of this world (Q 13:34; see CHASTISEMENT AND PUNISHMENT). Belief in the next world is an important part of one's religion (q.v.). Just as a man gives alms (see ALMSGIVING), he should believe in the coming of this period (Q 27:3; 41:7).

al-Samāwāt wa-l-arḍ

In the Qurʾān there is no single specific word that designates the whole physical world or cosmos (see COSMOLOGY). *Al-samāwāt wa-l-arḍ* (literally, "the heavens and the earth") comes near to such a designation, namely, the entire physical entity that was created by God. "Praise be to God, who created the heavens and the earth..." (Q 6:1; see also LAUDATION; GLORIFICATION OF GOD). It also seems that the phrase *malakūt al-samāwāt wa-l-arḍ,* "the kingdom of the heavens and the earth" (Q 6:75; 7:185; see SOVEREIGNTY; KINGS AND RULERS) has the same meaning. In two instances the phrase "the heaven (in the singular) and the earth" *(al-samāʾ wa-l-arḍ)* accompanies a reference to creation (Q 38:27; cf. 30:25). Two verses (Q 26:23-4) show that *rabb al-ʿālamīn,* "the lord of the world" (literally, "worlds") is equivalent to *rabb al-samāwāt wa-l-arḍ:* "Pharaoh (q.v.) said: 'And what is the lord of the world?' [Moses (q.v.)] said: 'The lord of the heavens and earth....'" A more inclusive phrase is "the heavens and the earth and what is between them" (see e.g. Q 25:59; 32:4; 50:38).

Arḍ

Arḍ, literally, "earth," can be interpreted to mean all humanity, that is, all inhabitants of the earth. Q 2:251 reads: "If God had not repelled some people by others, all the inhabitants of the earth *(al-arḍ)* would have been corrupted (see CORRUPTION). But God is gracious to all human beings" *(al-ʿālamīn;* Rāzī, *Tafsīr,* vi, 192). In certain cases *al-arḍ* means *al-dunyā,* that is, "this world," as it is said in Q 23:112: "How long have you stayed in this world?..." *(fī l-arḍ,* lit. "in the earth"). *Al-arḍ* also contrasts with *al-dār al-ākhira,* "the last abode," which further demonstrates its meaning as "this world." Q 28:83 states: "That is the last abode; we make it for those who desire neither haughtiness (see ARROGANCE; PRIDE) nor corruption in this world *(fī l-arḍ).*"

God and the world

God created the world (the heavens and the earth and what is between them) in six days (Q 25:59). He is not only the creator of the world but also the owner of whatsoever is in it (Q 2:284; 3:129) and the knower of all that exists (Q 3:29; see POSSESSION; HIDDEN AND THE HIDDEN; POWER AND IMPOTENCE). Later Muslim scholars tried to find the notion of creation *ex nihilo* in the qurʾānic text by deducing this notion from Q 16:40: "When we desire a thing, the only word we say to it is 'Be,' and it is." Thus things were brought into existence after their nonexistence by the imperative "be" (see also Q 19:9). The world was created purposefully (Q 23:115; 44:38), so that people will worship (q.v.) God (Q 51:56). Most of the phenomena observed in the world were designed by God for the benefit of humankind (see also NATURE AS SIGNS):

Verily it is God who splits the grain of corn and the date-stone (see AGRICULTURE AND VEGETATION). He brings forth the living from the dead, and the dead from the living (see LIFE; DEATH AND THE DEAD)... He splits the dawn (q.v.), and has established the night as a time of rest (see SLEEP; DAY AND NIGHT), and the sun (q.v.) and the moon (q.v.) as a reckoning (of the festivals; see CALENDAR)... It is he who has established for you the stars to guide you in the darkness (q.v.) of the land and sea (see

WATER; PLANETS AND STARS)... And it is he who has brought down water from the heaven, and thereby we have produced shoots of every kind... In that there are signs for people who believe (Q 6:95-9; see BELIEF AND UNBELIEF).

The world is full of signs (q.v.) which might lead one to believe in God. On the basis of these verses and others of the same kind, Muslim theologians have elaborated the argument from design, according to which the design in the universe proves God's existence, unity, wisdom, rule and providence (see GOD AND HIS ATTRIBUTES).

The notion of the last abode *(al-ākhira)* presupposes the end of this world. Although the termination of *al-dunyā* is not stated explicitly in the Qur'ān, it is alluded to in the following verses: "It is he who created you of clay (q.v.), then decreed an appointed time of death *(ajal)*..." (Q 6:2), "...the affair is finished..." (Q 2:210) and "all [that dwells] on [the earth] will perish, and only the face of your lord will remain" (Q 55:26-7; see FACE OF GOD; FREEDOM AND PREDESTINATION). Rationalist theologians interpreted God's face to mean his essence. Adding to this interpretation the phrase "he is the first and the last" (Q 57:3), they concluded that just as God was alone before creation, he will be alone after the termination of the world.

In contrast to the finality of the present world, most of the traditionalist theologians claim that the world to come, which is divided into paradise and hell, will exist forever. "And as for those who believe and do righteous deeds (see GOOD DEEDS), we shall make them enter gardens (q.v.) underneath which rivers flow, to dwell therein forever..." (Q 4:57). The two Ḥanbalī theologians Ibn Taymiyya (d. 728/1328) and his distinguished disciple Ibn Qayyim al-Jawziyya (d. 751/1350) held the view that hell will finally come to an end. Their textual basis is Q 78:21-3: "Behold, Jehenna has become an ambush, for the insolent a resort, therein to tarry for ages." Since it is impossible to measure eternity by periods of time ("ages"), says Ibn al-Qayyim, the duration of hell is finite.

Whether God has already created the world to come, that is, paradise and hell, or whether he will create it after the judgment (see LAST JUDGMENT), is another question dealt with by the theologians. Most traditionalist theologians held the view that paradise and hell have already been created by God. Q 3:133 reads: "And vie with one another, hastening to forgiveness (q.v.) from your lord, and to paradise *(janna)* whose breadth is as the heavens and the earth, prepared for the God-fearing *(uʿiddat lil-muttaqīn)*." "Prepared," which also referred to hell (Q 3:131), was interpreted to mean "was already created." Rationalist theologians, however, argued that God always acts for the benefit of humankind. Since as places of reward and punishment, paradise and hell will be needed only after the day of judgment, it follows that they have not yet been created.

Binyamin Abrahamov

Bibliography
Primary: al-Ghazālī, Abū Ḥāmid Muḥammad b. Muḥammad, *Iḥyāʾ ʿulūm al-dīn,* Cairo 1933 (repr. of Būlāq 1872); Ibn Abī l-Dunyā, *Kitāb Dhamm al-dunyā,* ed. A. Almagor, Jerusalem 1984; Ibn Kathīr, *Tafsīr,* Beirut 1966, repr. 1970; *Jalālayn;* Qurṭubī, *Jāmiʿ,* Beirut 1952; Rāzī, *Tafsīr;* Ṭabarī, *Tafsīr,* Cairo 1905-11, repr. Beirut 1986-7.
Secondary: B. Abrahamov, The creation and duration of paradise and hell in Islamic theology, in *Der Islam* 79 (2002), 87-102; id. (ed.), *al-Qāsim b. Ibrāhīm on the proof of God's existence, Kitāb al-dalīl al-kabīr,* Leiden 1990; Arberry; J. Horovitz, *Jewish proper names and derivatives in the Koran,* Ohio 1925, repr. Hildesheim 1964, 55f., 71; Jeffery, *For. vocab.,* 208f.; Nöldeke, *GQ,* i, 112; Paret, *Kommentar;* Pickthall, *Koran;* G. Widengren, *Muḥammad, the apostle of God and his ascension,* Uppsala and Wiesbaden 1955, 8f.

Worship

The veneration of God (or any other being or object regarded as worthy of worship), by the performance of acts and/or the utterance of words that signify attitudes such as adoration, submission, gratitude (see GRATITUDE AND INGRATITUDE), love (q.v.) or fear (q.v.). Arabic does not have a direct semantic parallel to the English word but derivatives of the root *ʿ-b-d*, conveying ideas of obedience (q.v.), dependence (see also CLIENTS AND CLIENTAGE) and service (see SLAVES AND SLAVERY; SERVANTS), are often rendered in English translations of the Qurʾān by "worship." In a broad sense the worship of God involves fulfilling his law (see LAW AND THE QURʾĀN; VIRTUES AND VICES, COMMANDING AND FORBIDDING) and submission *(islām)* to him and in that sense it may be said that the fundamental message of the Qurʾān is the need for humankind to worship God alone (see IDOLATRY AND IDOLATERS; POLYTHEISM AND ATHEISM). In commentary (see EXEGESIS OF THE QURʾĀN: CLASSICAL AND MEDIEVAL), the Qurʾān's recurrent prohibitions against "associating others with God" *(shirk)* are often amplified to explain that we must not worship or serve *(ʿabada)* anything other than him.

In Islam acts that express obedience and submission to God, especially those duties required in fulfilment of the "five pillars of Islam" (see RITUAL AND THE QURʾĀN), are commonly referred to as the *ʿibādāt* (sing. *ʿibāda*), and it is clear that they are regarded as the most important ways in which humankind should worship God. The fundamental reason for performing those acts of service is that they are required by God. In fulfilling his requirements his servants *(ʿibād)* demonstrate their submission to his commands (see also COMMANDMENTS). Of those duties it is the five-times-daily performance of the ritual prayer (q.v.; *ṣalāt*) that is the most frequent and fundamental expression of their service or worship. Some scholars writing in English, such as E.E. Calverley, prefer to translate *ṣalāt* by "worship" rather than "prayer."

In a number of qurʾānic passages serving God is clearly linked to the performance of acts of worship. Q 7:206 refers to the way in which the angels (see ANGEL) serve God by constantly praising (see LAUDATION) and prostrating before him (see BOWING AND PROSTRATION). At Q 20:14 God is reported as saying to Moses (q.v.) from the burning bush, "There is no god but me so serve me *(fa-ʿbudnī)* and establish prayer in remembrance (q.v.) of me *(wa-aqimi l-ṣalāta li-dhikrī)*." At Q 29:16-17 Abraham (q.v.) is described as calling on his people to abandon the idols that they serve instead of God (see IDOLS AND IMAGES), to serve God and fear him *(uʿbudū llāha wa-ttaqūhu),* to seek provision (*rizq;* see SUSTENANCE) from him, to serve him and give thanks to him. Q 53:62 commands us to make prostration to God and serve him *(fa-sjudū lillāhi wa-ʿbudū)*. Clearly in all of these passages and many others and in Muslim discourse in general, the idea of serving God (or other beings) is largely coterminous with worship. According to Q 51:56, God's sole purpose in creating humankind and the jinn (q.v.; see also CREATION) was that they should serve/worship him *(illā li-yaʿbudūnī)*.

Apart from the names of the "five pillars," common words in the Qurʾān connected with the performance of ritual acts of worship relate to prostration and bowing *(s-j-d, r-k-ʿ)*, circumambulation *(ṭ-w-f)*, the offering and slaughter (q.v.) of animals (*h-d-y, n-ḥ-r, dh-b-ḥ, n-s-k;* see also CONSECRATION OF ANIMALS), remaining in a holy place (*ʿ-k-f;* see SACRED PRECINCTS), offering praise (q.v.) to God (*s-b-ḥ, ḥ-m-d;* see also GLORIFICATION OF GOD), and calling God to mind *(dh-k-r)* by repetition of his name or names (see MEMORY; GOD AND HIS ATTRIBUTES). Such acts should be carried out in an attitude of submission or obedience (*q-n-t;* e.g. Q 2:238; 3:17). Among terms that appear in the Qurʾān and are commonly used in connection with Islamic worship are *qibla* (q.v.; the direction of prayer), *masjid* (place of prostration, mosque [q.v.]), *bayt* (house, sanctuary; see HOUSE, DOMESTIC AND DIVINE; SACRED AND PROFANE), *ʿumra* (the minor pilgrimage; see PILGRIMAGE) and *ṣadaqa* (alms, charity; see ALMSGIVING).

The Qurʾān is relatively rarely concerned, however, with the details of the correct forms of such acts of worship. Frequently it merely alludes to them and seems to assume that they are normal ingredients of religious life, the forms of which are already known (see RELIGION). Even when there are passages that refer to aspects of performance (such as Q 2:183-7, concerned with fasting [q.v.] in Ramaḍān [q.v.]), they are not so full that they would allow us to reconstruct all the details of the performance simply from the Qurʾān alone. For that we would need to refer to texts outside the Qurʾān. There is clearly the possibility that we assume too readily that the Qurʾān is referring to institutions of worship existing in exactly the same forms as they are known from other Islamic texts or from observation.

The references to the ritual prayer are especially allusive and often consist of no more than calls for the "establishment" *(iqāma)* of the *ṣalāt,* sometimes linked with the command to bring the *zakāt.* There is a reference (Q 5:58) to making a call to prayer *(idhā nādaytum ilā l-ṣalāt),* but no clear and unambiguous qurʾānic text that indicates it should be performed five times daily, nor any precise details as to its timing (see DAY, TIMES OF), the sequence of bodily postures and words to be followed, the number of "cycles" *(rukūʿ)* to be performed for the different times of prayer, etc. One passage (Q 17:78-9) orders "*ṣalāt* at the setting of the sun until the darkness (q.v.) of night (*li-dulūki l-shamsi ilā ghasaqi l-layl;* see EVENING) and the *qurʾān* of the dawn (q.v.; *al-fajr*)" and also prayer (not specifically *ṣalāt*) at night (*wa-mina l-layli fa-tahajjad bihi nāfilatan laka;* see DAY AND NIGHT); another (Q 2:238) refers to the "middle" prayer (*al-ṣalāt al-wusṭā;* see NOON; RECITATION OF THE QURʾĀN).

Nevertheless, qurʾānic verses (q.v.), when suitable ones exist, are usually cited in commentaries and law books as evidence of the legal obligation regarding a particular *ʿibāda.* The obligation of *ḥajj* (and, according to some, *ʿumra* also) is related to Q 2:196 ("complete the *ḥajj* and the *ʿumra* for God") and more especially Q 3:97 ("*ḥajj* of the house is a duty upon men towards God, those who are able to find a way"; see KAʿBA). The revelation of Q 2:144-5 ("…turn your face towards *al-masjid al-ḥarām*") is taken to have imposed the duty of facing towards the Kaʿba (instead of Jerusalem [q.v.]) in prayer *(qibla).* The fast of Ramaḍān (replacing the fast of ʿĀshūrāʾ) is regarded as instituted by the revelation of Q 2:183-7, "fasting is prescribed for you … the month of Ramaḍān in which the Qurʾān was revealed …" (see REVELATION AND INSPIRATION; OCCASIONS OF REVELATION). Discussions of *zakāt* in the law-books (for whom it is intended and on what goods it is to be paid) refer to a large number of different verses, especially Q 9:60 (which actually refers to alms as *ṣadaqāt* rather than *zakāt*). When the details of Muslim practice concerning the *ʿibādāt* cannot be related to qurʾānic texts, they tend instead to be ascribed to the *sunna* (q.v.). A notable example concerns the number and times each day of the *ṣalāt,* reported as having been indicated to the Prophet in extra-qurʾānic revelations that are recorded in ḥadīths and accounts of his life (see HADĪTH AND THE QURʾĀN; SĪRA AND THE QURʾĀN).

As an alternative to the traditional view that the forms of Islamic worship are derived from such revelations, it may be theorized that they developed as a result of evolving community practices (adapting forms of rituals already in existence in the milieu from which Islam emerged) and that the textual "sources" are a result of scholars making links between the already existing practices and available texts. Making such links would sometimes involve creative interpretation of the texts (see TRADITIONAL DISCIPLINES OF QURʾĀNIC STUDY).

Muslim acts of worship frequently include the recitation of parts of the Qurʾān, and reciting the whole or extended parts of it is regarded as an act of worship in itself. Al-Ghazālī (d. 505/1111) refers to recitation *(tilāwa)* of the Qurʾān as the most important form of *ʿibāda* with the tongue, and he sets out (*Iḥyāʾ*, book 8) the conditions (such as being in a state of ritual purity [q.v.]) necessary for the ritual. The daily *ṣalāt* ritual involves saying the opening chapter (Sūrat al-Fātiḥa; see FĀTIḤA; PRAYER FORMULAS) and other short chapters or verses chosen as appropriate for the time of day or the nature of the festival (see FESTIVALS AND COMMEMORATIVE DAYS), and commonly longer passages are recited following the conclusion of the *ṣalāt*. Informal prayer ceremonies such as the *dhikr* frequently begin with and include passages of the scripture. In Ramaḍān it is customary for the whole of the Qurʾān to be recited in the mosque in thirty sections, one for each day of the month. During the ceremonies of the *ḥajj* there are many occasions when the pilgrim recites or hears parts of the Qurʾān (see ORALITY), but it is notable that some scholars disapproved of its recitation during the circumambulation *(ṭawāf)* of the Kaʿba. Although al-Shāfiʿī (d. 204/820), for example, held that the *ṭawāf* was the place of *dhikr* and the most important form of *dhikr* was reciting the Qurʾān, other scholars disapproved of qurʾānic recitation during the act of circumambulation (Muḥibb al-Ṭabarī, *Qirā*, 311). It is not clear why that should be so since in general the Qurʾān lies at the heart of Islamic worship (see also EVERYDAY LIFE, THE QURʾĀN IN; POPULAR AND TALISMANIC USES OF THE QURʾĀN).

G.R. Hawting

Bibliography

Primary: E.E. Calverly, *Worship in Islam. Being a translation with commentary and introduction of al-Ghazzālī's Book of the* Iḥyāʾ *on the worship*, London 1925; London 1957²; al-Ghazālī, Abū Ḥāmid Muḥammad b. Muḥammad, *Iḥyāʾ ʿulūm al-dīn*, 4 vols., Cairo 1933 (repr. of Būlāq 1872), esp. i, 129-87 (bk. 4, *K. Asrār al-ṣalāt;* vol. i contains bks. 1-10, on the *ʿibādāt*, including bks. 1 and 2, *K. al-ʿIlm* and *K. Qawāʿid al-ʿaqāʾid)*; Muḥibb al-Dīn al-Ṭabarī, *al-Qirā li-qāṣid Umm al-Qurā*, Cairo 1970, 311; al-Murtaḍā al-Zabīdī, Abū l-Fayḍ Muḥammad b. Muḥammad, *Itḥāf al-sāda l-muttaqīn (bi-sharḥ Iḥyāʾ ʿulūm al-dīn)*, Cairo 1331/1913; Ṭabarī, *Tafsīr*.

Secondary: M. Abul Quassem, *The recitation and interpretation of the Qurʾān. Al-Ghazali's theory*, London 1982; J. ʿAlī, *Taʾrīkh al-ṣalāt*, Baghdad n.d. (ca. 1968); G.-H. Bousquet, *Les grandes pratiques rituelles de l'Islam*, Paris 1949; S.D. Goitein, *Studies on Islamic history and institutions*, Leiden 1966 (contains studies on the early development of the *ṣalāt*, Friday worship, and Ramaḍān); W.A. Graham, *Beyond the written word. Oral aspects of literature in the history of religion*, Cambridge 1987, 102-9; M. Holland, *Inner dimensions of Islamic worship*, Leicester 1983; C.E. Padwick, *Muslim devotions. A study of prayer manuals in common use*, London 1961, repr. Oxford 1996; U. Rubin, Morning and evening prayers in early Islam, in *JSAI* 10 (1987), 40-64.

Wound

see ILLNESS AND HEALTH; SUFFERING

Wrath

see ANGER

Wretched see JOY AND MISERY; OPPRESSED ON EARTH, THE

Writing and Writing Materials

Inscribing characters, letters or words for others to read; the instruments (q.v.) used in such inscription. The Qurʾān attests to written materials and the process of writing with a variety of lexemes — both metaphorical and concrete (see METAPHOR) — supplying evidence that supplements epigraphic traces of the development of writing in seventh-century Arabia (see ORALITY AND WRITING IN ARABIA; ARABIC SCRIPT). Among the most prominent qurʾānic terms for materials used in the writing process are: ink (*midād*, Q 18:109), parchment (*qirṭās*, pl. *qirāṭīs*, Q 6:7, 91), pen (*qalam*, pl. *aqlām*; cf. Q 31:27; 68:1; 96:4). The act of writing itself — and the written product, the book (q.v.) — is most commonly denoted by derivatives of the Arabic root letters *k-t-b*, a root frequently used in the context of scripture and revelation (see REVELATION AND INSPIRATION). Other Arabic roots, such as *s-ṭ-r*, *kh-ṭ-ṭ* and *r-q-m* are also employed to convey "inscription" (cf. *yasṭurna*, Q 68:1; *masṭūr*, Q 17:58; 33:6; 52:2; *mustaṭar*, Q 54:53; *khaṭṭa*, e.g. Q 29:48; *marqūm*, Q 83:9, 20; see also SCROLLS; HEAVENLY BOOK; SCRIPTURE AND THE QURʾĀN; ORALITY).

Verses from the Qurʾān have been written on a variety of materials, from pottery shards, bones and mosaic to woodwork, metal wares and buildings (see EPIGRAPHY AND THE QURʾĀN; MATERIAL CULTURE AND THE QURʾĀN), but the most frequent form used to copy the full text of the revelation is the codex (see CODICES OF THE QURʾĀN). Traditionally written with a reed pen *(qalam)*, manuscripts of the Qurʾān (q.v.) nevertheless vary enormously in materials, format, aspect, and function.

The earliest manuscripts were copied in brown, tannin-based ink on parchment. The sources mention the skin of goat, calf, donkey, and even gazelle, but the most common animal used was sheep. The skin was cured, scraped to remove any fat or flesh remaining on the inside, sanded, stretched taut and then dried. Occasionally it was also dyed, as in the famous, now-dispersed "Blue Qurʾān." The calligrapher penned the text freehand in various styles of angular script often now known as Kūfic (see CALLIGRAPHY), on the individual folios, which were then gathered in quires and bound in leather. Most were produced in the horizontal ("landscape") format, perhaps to differentiate them from other non-qurʾānic and even non-Arabic codices.

We do not know how early these parchment manuscripts were produced, for there is, as yet, no convincing method to date any manuscript of the Qurʾān before the third/ninth century. Scholars have tried different methods, from paleography and codicology to radiocarbon analysis, in order to assign dates to the mass of undated parchment folios and fragments but no manuscript contains an authentic colophon with a date or the authentic signature of a known calligrapher. So far the only secure evidence is an endowment notice *(waqfiyya)*, such as the one in a manuscript endowed by the ʿAbbāsid governor of Damascus, Amajur, to a mosque in Tyre in 262/875-6 (dispersed; many pages in Istanbul, Türk ve Islam Eserleri Müzesi). Parchment manuscripts were certainly made before this date but as yet we do not know which ones.

From the late fourth/tenth century Qurʾān manuscripts written in brown, tannin-based ink on parchment were increasingly replaced by copies written in black, carbon-based ink on paper. The first surviving example (dispersed, e.g. Chester Beatty Library 1434 and Istanbul Uni-

[I] Examples of South Arabian cursive on inscribed stripped palm stalks, a writing material constantly mentioned in early Islamic texts (published on p. 78 of J. Ryckmans, W. Muller and Y.M. Abdallah, *Textes du Yemen antique. Inscrits sur bois*, Leuven 1994). Reproduced with the kind permission of Peeters Press, Leuven, Belgium.

[II] Brass pen box, inlaid with copper, silver and black organic material (seventh/thirteenth century Iran). Reproduced with the kind permission of the Freer Gallery of Art, Smithsonian Institution, Washington, DC (Purchase, F1936.7).

versity A6758) was transcribed by ʿAlī b. Shādhān al-Rāzī l-Bayyiʿ (sic) in 361/972. These materials had already been used to transcribe other Arabic manuscripts for at least 150 years, and their slow adoption for copying the Qurʾān was undoubtedly due to the reverence accorded the divine revelation. In comparison to earlier parchment manuscripts, the paper codices were smaller, cheaper and more portable and were usually made in vertical ("portrait") format. They were also more readily readable, as they came to be written typically in the rounded hand known as *naskh*. They often recorded variant readings (see READINGS OF THE QURʾĀN) and catered to a more diverse audience. Some manuscripts, such as the well-known copy penned by Ibn al-Bawwāb at Baghdād in 391/1000-1 (Dublin, Chester Beatty Library), were apparently made for a specifically Shīʿī clientele.

Once accepted, paper became the most common material used for Qurʾān manuscripts, adopted regularly in the eastern Islamic lands from the fifth/eleventh century and in the Maghrib from the seventh/thirteenth. It came in many sizes, from pocket-book to the large "Baghdād" sheet (approximately 100 × 70 cm), used for stupendous thirty-volume manuscripts commissioned by the Ilkhānids and Mamlūks. Transcribed in a bold *muḥaqqaq* script, sometimes in black outlined in gold and decorated in glowing colors (see ORNAMENTATION AND ILLUMINATION), these extraordinary manuscripts, which contained as many as two thousand sheets and took as long as six or seven years to transcribe and decorate, are some of the finest manuscripts produced anywhere in the world. See also SHEETS.

Sheila S. Blair

Bibliography

F. Déroche, *Le livre manuscrit arabe. Prélude à une histoire*, Paris 2004, 11-35 (on the Qurʾān);
A. Gacek, *The Arabic manuscript tradition. A glossary of technical terms and bibliography*, Leiden 2001.

Wrong

see SIN, MAJOR AND MINOR

Y

Yaghūth see IDOLS AND IMAGES

Yaḥyā see JOHN THE BAPTIST

Yaʾjūj see GOG AND MAGOG

Yaʿqūb see JACOB

Yathrib see MEDINA

Yaʿūq see IDOLS AND IMAGES

Year

The time required for the earth to complete a revolution around the sun. *ʿĀm* and *sana*, the qurʾānic Arabic words for "year," raise questions of both meaning and chronology. Q 29:14, "1000 years *(alf sanatin)* save 50 *(khamsīn ʿāman),*" contains both words and implies their equivalence. Al-Zamakhsharī (d. 538/1144; see EXEGESIS OF THE QURʾĀN: CLASSICAL AND MEDIEVAL) explains in the *Kashshāf* that the repetition of the same word should be avoided and that writing "950 years" would require more words. The Qurʾān's phrasing, as opposed to "1000," also conveyed precision. Q 22:47, "a day with God is as 1000 years" (see DAYS OF GOD), though, has been understood metaphorically (see METAPHOR; LITERARY STRUCTURES OF THE QURʾĀN), because of the particle *ka-*, "as."

ʿĀm and *sana* are not always synonymous in the Qurʾān. Al-Rāghib al-Iṣfahānī (fl. early fifth/eleventh cent.) in his *Mufradāt,* cites Q 12:49, "a year when the people have plenteous crops (see AGRICULTURE AND VEGETATION; GRACE; BLESSING)," to argue that *sana* could denote a year of barrenness, and *ʿām* a year of plenty. According to *Lisān al-ʿArab,* an *ʿām* could be a winter and a summer (see SEASONS) and therefore shorter than a *sana,* which was either a solar year or twelve lunations (see SUN; MOON). A passage from al-ʿAjjāj (d. 97/715), *min* [or, *wa-*] *marr aʿwāmi l-sinnīna l-ʿuwwami* ("from the passage of the years' lengthy summers and winters"; cf. *Tāj al-ʿarūs,* xxxii, 157, for the reading with *"wa-"*), supports such a distinction, a distinction difficult to discern from the Qurʾān.

In Q 10:5, the Qurʾān states that the moon is a way to measure the passage of time: "He it is who appointed the sun a splendor and the moon a light (q.v.; see also LAMP), and measured for it stages, that you might know the number of years and the reckoning." The stages *(manāzil)* are asterisms that track the moon's monthly path. The heliacal (just before sunrise) risings and acronychal (soon after sunset) settings of certain asterisms were called *anwāʾ* and were how the pre-Islamic Arabs (q.v.) marked time (q.v.), including festivals (see FESTIVALS AND COMMEMORATIVE DAYS), before the development of a calendar (q.v.) in the late pre-Islamic period (see PRE-ISLAMIC ARABIA AND THE QURʾĀN).

The pre-Islamic lunar calendar used the names of the months (see MONTH) that are known from the Muslim calendar, though sometimes *Ṣafar* 1, then followed by *Ṣafar* 2, took the place of *al-Muḥarram*. The length of a year of twelve lunar months, 354 days, is tied implicitly to the length of a solar year. So by 420 C.E., the pre-Islamic Arabs had adopted, probably from the Jews (see JEWS AND JUDAISM), the practice of adding an intercalary month in order to have the lunar year keep pace with the solar. Like the Jewish year, the new year would occur in the autumn. While the Jews at the time probably intercalated a month every seven of nineteen lunar years, Ginzel (*Handbuch*, 245) accepted al-Bīrūnī's (d. ca. 442/1050) report that the Arabs intercalated a month every nine of twenty-four years.

The Qurʾān banned intercalary months, on the occasion of Muḥammad's Farewell Pilgrimage (q.v.; see also PILGRIMAGE), in Q 9:37: "Postponement is only an excess of disbelief (see BELIEF AND UNBELIEF)... [so that] they allow that which God has forbidden (q.v.)." Fakhr al-Dīn al-Rāzī (d. 606/1210) comments in his *Tafsīr* (ad loc.) that adding intercalary months would be privileging *dunyā* over *dīn* (see RELIGION; WORLD). The problem remains that a precise lunar year is eight hours, 48 minutes, and 36 seconds longer than 354 days; eleven times in a thirty-year cycle, *Dhū l-Ḥijja* contains a thirtieth day.

Robert G. Morrison

Bibliography
Primary: al-Bīrūnī, Abū l-Rayḥān Muḥammad b. Aḥmad, *al-Āthār al-bāqiya ʿan al-qurūn al-khāliya*, ed. E. Sachau, Leipzig 1878 (repr. 1923); *Lisān al-ʿArab;* al-Rāghib al-Iṣfahānī, *Mufradāt;* Rāzī, *Tafsīr*, ed. ʿAbd al-Ḥamīd et al., Cairo 1933-62; *Tāj al-ʿarūs*, Kuwait 1965-2001; Zamakhsharī, *Kashshāf.*
Secondary: F.K. Ginzel, *Handbuch der mathematischen und technischen Chronologie. Das Zeitrechnungswesen der Völker*, 3 vols., Leipzig 1906; W. Hartner, Zamān, in *EI*[1], iv, 1207-12; A. Moberg, An-Nasīʾ *in der islāmischen Tradition*, Lund 1931; D.M. Varisco, The origin of the *anwāʾ* in Arab tradition, in *SI* 76 (1991), 5-28.

Yellow see COLORS

Yemen

Name derived from the Arabic *al-yaman*, which indicates the south of the Arabian peninsula. Etymologically, *al-yaman* means "the south" and is the opposite of *al-shām*, "the north" (see SYRIA). These two words are themselves derived from Arabic terms for right and left. Before Islam there is no evidence of the proper name Yaman in the sources, whether they are internal (the inscriptions of south Arabia) or external, to indicate the country. They refer to the Ḥimyarīs, the tribe which ruled south Arabia from the end of the third century C.E. In the list of titles of the fourth, fifth and sixth century Ḥimyarī kings, however, south Arabian inscriptions mention a region called *Ymnt* (apparently the Ḥaḍramawt south), a name which certainly derives from the ḥimyarite substantive *ymnt*, "south" (as opposed to *s²ʾmt* "north"; for the precise location of place names and ethnic groups, see Robin and Brunner, *Map of ancient Yemen*).

The geographical extent of the historical Yemen varies according to the historical period and point of view. For the Yemeni al-Ḥasan b. Aḥmad al-Hamdānī (d. bef. 360/971), Yemen includes all the territories south of a line which starts at Qaṭar and reaches the Red Sea midway between Mecca (q.v.) and Najrān (q.v.; Hamdānī, *Ṣifat jazīrat al-ʿArab,* 51). On the other hand, al-Masʿūdī (d. 345/956) assigns to Yemen borders which are very close to those of the current nation (*Murūj,* 1034).

The religious history of Yemen in the centuries preceding Islam is distinguished principally by the rejection of polytheism during the 380s (see POLYTHEISM AND ATHEISM; PRE-ISLAMIC ARABIA AND THE QURʾĀN; SOUTH ARABIA, RELIGIONS IN PRE-ISLAMIC), that is nearly 240 years before the *hijra* (see EMIGRATION), and by a very favorable disposition towards Judaism until the period of rule by the (Christian) Aksumites, who were followed by the (Zoroastrian) Persian Sasanians (see JEWS AND JUDAISM; CHRISTIANS AND CHRISTIANITY; MAGIANS; ABYSSINIA).

The sources

The Ḥimyarī inscriptions after the rejection of polytheism, about one hundred in number (plus around twenty fragments), are the most reliable source because they are contemporaneous and still in their original form (without the danger of alteration and manipulation of manuscript transmission). But they only shed light upon a tiny part of society and are far from objective, since their authors are concerned with themselves, whether to celebrate their glorious feats and commemorate their good works, or to establish rights of custom and property. These inscriptions, sometimes drawn up by the sovereign (eighteen, plus several doubtful instances), but most often by private individuals, are of three kinds: commemorations of buildings and various public works (for example, the building of a sanctuary portico, establishment of a cemetery, repair of the Maʾrib dam, etc.); commemorations of buildings for personal use (palaces); commemorations of the glorious deeds of the sovereign or aristocrats. These documents provide us with indirect information on the religious attitude of the ruling classes, thanks to the religious invocations they contain (and sometimes by their silence; see also EPIGRAPHY AND THE QURʾĀN). As far as archaeological remains are concerned, they are of little significance (see ART AND ARCHAEOLOGY AND THE QURʾĀN): there are some column capitals from the great church of Ṣanʿāʾ reused in the grand mosque (q.v.), some artifacts from daily life, and finally a building in Qānīʾ which could have been a synagogue (Finster, Arabien in der Spätantike). The last source consists of the Arabic traditions which were collected from the early days of Islam but have been passed on to us through works, the oldest of which have been composed at a relatively late date, more than 150 years after the *hijra.*

The rejection of polytheism

Before the unification of south Arabia by the Ḥimyarī kings Yāsir^{um} Yuhanʿim (who annexed the kingdom of Sabaʾ around 275; see SHEBA) and Shammar Yuharʿish (who conquered the kingdom of Ḥaḍramawt several years before 300), all the inscriptions, both those drawn up by the sovereign and those by private individuals, are polytheistic. Nevertheless, certain third century texts present an innovation vis-a-vis those of earlier periods: the final invocations of the dedication of the most important Sabaean temple, consecrated to Almaqah, mention this single god, whereas previously they would list all the divinities of the Sabaean pantheon and, frequently, the (personal and tribal) divinities of the authors of the text. Certain scholars have concluded from this that Almaqah must have become a kind of supreme god.

In January 384 (*ḏ-dʾw*^{n} 493 of the Ḥimyarī era), the ruling kings, Malkīkarib Yuhaʾmin and his sons Abīkarib Asʿad and Dharaʾʾamar Ayman, celebrated the construction of two new palaces, called Shawḥaṭān and *Kln*^{m}, in two inscriptions (*RES* 3383 and Garb Bayt al-Ashwal 2) coming from Ẓafār, the Ḥimyarī capital. In the final invocation, where the pagan divinities are normally mentioned, they call upon "the support of their lord (q.v.), the Lord of the Heaven" *(b-mqm mrʾ-hmw Mrʾ S*^{1}*my*^{n}*)*. These documents clearly show a new religious orientation by the Ḥimyarī authorities. The formula, which is somewhat laconic, does not, however, allow us to determine the exact nature of the new religion. A little earlier (around 380?), the same king Malkīkarib, co-ruling with just one of his sons (perhaps Abīkarib Asʿad), had a building constructed at Maʾrib described as *mkrb* (Ja 856); unknown from more ancient inscriptions, *mkrb* seems to be the Ḥimyarite term for a synagogue.

These three inscriptions reveal radical and definitive religious change since later documents are all monotheistic. Only one small text, dating from 402-3 C.E. (512 Ḥimyarite), which mentions a temple of the pagan god Taʾlab in passing, may be an exception. This religious change clearly demonstrates the success of a unification which had been initially political (with the annexation of Sabaʾ and Ḥaḍramawt) and linguistic (with the disappearance of the Ḥaḍramawtian language and, much earlier, of Madhabite and Qatabānian; see also ARABIC LANGUAGE; ARABIC SCRIPT) and subsequently affected the calendar (q.v.).

The religious position of Ḥimyarīs during the transitional period, between 300 and 380, is more hypothetical. It is probable that polytheism was dominant. The temples remained in use and all the inscriptions drawn up by private individuals (except YM 1950 which will be discussed further and two unpublished inscriptions, discovered in 2003) are polytheistic. But no royal inscriptions (with the exception of two insignificant fragments, which make no mention of religion) have yet been found, so that the personal stance of the sovereigns is not known.

The first indication of progress towards monotheism is the inscription YM 1950, dated *ḏ-ḫrf*^{n} [..]3, which bears an invocation to king Thaʾrān Yuhanʿim, co-ruling with a son whose name has disappeared, in all likelihood Malkīkarib Yuhaʾmin; from this fact, the date can be reconstructed as *ḏ-ḫrf*^{n} [47]3 or [48]3 Ḥimyarī, or August [36]3 or [37]3 C.E. The authors of YM 1950 are powerful lords *(qayls)* of an important tribe with territory bordering Ṣanʿāʾ to the north west; in this text they are apparently commemorating the construction of a sanctuary in honor of "[their lor]d the Master of Heaven" (... *mr](ʾ)-hmw Bʿl-S*^{1}*my*^{n}; see HEAVEN AND SKY). The name of the divinity appears again on line 4 in the expression *w-l-ys*^{1}*mʿn Bʿl-S*^{1}*[my*^{n}*...]*, "and which is granted by the Master of He[aven...]". No other deity is mentioned or invoked. The text seems monotheistic but its brevity prevents us from deciding whether this monotheism is pagan, Christian or Jewish. The two unpublished texts date from ca. 355 C.E. for the latest, and from the preceding decades for the earliest (see also GOD AND HIS ATTRIBUTES).

An external source, corresponding to roughly the same period, casts further light upon this. Apparently, between 339 and 344, a Byzantine embassy (see BYZANTINES), sent by Constantius II (r. 337-61) under the leadership of Theophilus the Indian, had gone to the Ḥimyarīs with the intention of converting the sovereign and obtaining "the building of a church (q.v.) for the Romans who came there and for any locals who might be disposed towards religion." The results were encouraging:

The sovereign of the people with pure-hearted judgment, was disposed towards religion and built three churches, rather than just one, throughout the country, and he did this not with the imperial funds brought by the ambassadors, but with what he eagerly contributed from his own wealth.

It seems, however, that we cannot really speak of the conversion of the Ḥimyarīs: the report of Theophilus does not mention the baptism of the sovereign or the creation of a church hierarchy. Regarding the religious practices of the Ḥimyarīs, Theophilus indicates that the people are still polytheists, even if Judaism, of which this is the first datable mention in Arabia, is particularly influential in the king's circle (Philostorgius, *Kirchengeschichte*).

During the period 300-380, it would therefore appear that Yemen was still polytheistic. From the inscriptions, the abandonment of polytheism by certain individuals dates from the reign of Thaʾrān Yuhanʿim (ca. 324-ca. 375). If Jewish and Christian monotheism did indeed gain support, the inscriptions do not yet give any indication of this. As regards the personal attitude of the sovereign, this is unknown. The official rejection of polytheism occurred in the following reign, the reign of Malkīkarib Yuhaʾmin (ca. 375-ca. 400), co-ruling with two sons, Abīkarib Asʿad and Dharaʾʾamar Ayman.

"Judaizing" monotheism, from the 380s to 525-530

For nearly 140 years, from the reign of Malkīkarib Yuhaʾmin (ca. 375-ca. 400) to that of Yūsuf Asʾar Yathʾar (522-between 525 and 530), Ḥimyarī epigraphy displays the same characteristics. Their rulers use only vague expressions and brief formulas when they refer to religion (fifteen inscriptions in total). As far as individuals are concerned, while they often do the same as their rulers (more than thirty inscriptions), they do sometimes explicitly demonstrate their sympathy towards Judaism (seven inscriptions could be described as "judaizing"). This sympathy is shown by the use of the ritual exclamations "amen" *(ʾmn)* and "shalôm" *(s*^{1}*lwm)*, or by bequests in favor of Jews (as in Ḥaṣī 1, which establishes a cemetery set aside for Jews). There are few indisputably Jewish inscriptions. The most significant (Garb Bayt al-Ashwal 1), which comes from the beginning of the fifth century, is written by one Yahūdaʾ Yakkuf *(Yhwdʾ Ykf)*, apparently a proselyte, who counts upon "the help and grace of his lord, who gave him his being, the lord of the living and the dead (see LIFE; DEATH AND THE DEAD), the lord of heaven and earth, who created all things, and on the prayers of his people Israel" (*b-rdʾ w-b-zkt mrʾ-hw ḏ-brʾ nfs*^{1}*-hw mrʾ ḥyn w-mwtn mrʾ s*^{1}*|my*^{n} *w-ʾrḍ*^{n} *ḏ-brʾ kl*^{m} *w-b-ṣlt s*^{2}*ʿb-hw Ys*^{3}*rʾl*; see CHILDREN OF ISRAEL). An addition in Hebrew is carved in the central monogram. The text contains several terms borrowed from Aramaic, notably *zkt* (Arabic *zakāt;* see ALMSGIVING) and *ṣlt* (Arabic *ṣalāt*; see PRAYER), words which are again found in the Qurʾān (see FOREIGN VOCABULARY).

Two other documents could be Jewish. There is both the inscription *CIH* 543 (date uncertain), in which is found the name Israel (q.v.; Ys^{3}rʾ), and the divine epithet "Lord of the Jews" *(Rb-yhd)*, as well as the fragment Garb, Framm. no. 7 (ca. 400-20) which mentions Israel *(Ys*^{3}*rʾl)*.

A final document, DJE 23 (also of uncertain date), may also be added to this small corpus. Written in the Hebrew language and alphabet, it sets out part of the list of twenty-four priestly classes, already detailed in the Book of Chronicles (I, 24:7-18), adding the name of the village in Palestine where each class originates. The reign of the famous king Joseph, in

Sabaean, Yūsuf Asʾar Yathʾar *(Yws*^{1}*f ʾs*^{1}*ʾr Yṯʾr* in Ja 1028/1; *Ys*^{1}*f ʾs*^{1}*ʾr* in Ry 508/2), deserves particular examination. This king does not have a south Arabian, but a foreign name, one which occurs in the Bible (Arabic Yūsuf, in Hebrew Yosef), followed by two south Arabian names. In Syriac hagiography, he has the surname Masrūq, in Greek hagiography Dounaas and in the Arabic tradition Zurʿa dhū Nuwās. The external sources (Syriac, Greek and Arabic) all depict him as a Jewish radical, who persecuted Christians, especially in the Najrān oasis. Three large inscriptions (Ry 508, Ja 1028 and Ry 507), dated *ḏ-qyẓ*^{n} and *ḏ-mḏr*^{ʾn} 633 Ḥim., as well as a handful of small engravings beside them, refer to his reign. Their author is an army commander called Sharaḥʾīl Yaqbul, who had undertaken the siege of the Najrān oasis, in the months before the persecution, which took place in November 523 according to Syriac hagiography. This dating allows us to date Ry 508, Ja 1028 and Ry 507 to June and July 523 C.E. and to place the beginning of the Ḥimyarī calendar in April 110 B.C.E. Although these documents were produced at the height of a religious war — they speak also of the destruction of churches at Ẓafār and Makhawān (in Arabic al-Makhāʾ, or Mokha, the Red Sea port) — they scarcely mention doctrinal matters. Although there are several implicit references to Judaism, the Bible is not quoted and they are not accompanied by Jewish symbols, such as the *menorah* or the *shofar* (there is not a single ancient example in Yemen). The nature of this judaizing monotheism has not yet been decisively resolved. Although very close to Judaism, it seems to have been distinct. It brings to mind instead the powerful religious currents of paganism, which imitated Judaism in the eastern part of the Roman world until the fourth century (Mitchell, Cult of Theos Hypsistos).

Some important documents contain no mention of religion. These include the two inscriptions that the kings Abīkarib Asʿad and Ḥaśśān Yuhaʾmin in the first instance (Ry 509, dated around 440) and Maʿdīkarib Yaʿfur in the second case (Ry 510, dated June 521), had engraved in central Arabia, probably at the time of operations to strengthen the Ḥujrid principality. Similarly we might also mention BR-Yanbuq 47 (April 515). This silence probably indicates a situation of instability or conflict. Finally, there is no evidence of Christianity throughout this entire period.

Christian Yemen (525/530-beginning of the 570s)

The persecution by Yūsuf provoked the intervention of the Christian Aksumite king, Kaleb. He conquered Yemen (between 525 and 530) and placed on the throne a Ḥimyarī Christian, Sumūyafaʿ Ashwaʿ (we have only one inscription, Ist 7608 bis + Wellcome A 103664), who is called Esimiphaios by Procopius. According to the Syriac and Greek hagiographies, Kaleb installed a bishop and founded a large number of churches.

A short time later, Abraha (q.v.; an Aksumite army leader) overthrew Sumūyafaʿ and seized power. He built a magnificent church at Ṣanʿāʾ, which is described by al-Azraqī (d. 250/865). From this time onwards, Ṣanʿāʾ supplanted Ẓafār as the seat of power of Yemen. Abraha tried to retain control of the tribes of the Arabian desert, previously under Ḥimyarī rule. In 552 (662 Ḥim.), he launched an important expedition to central Arabia, which reached Ḥulubān (300 km southwest of Riyadh) and Turabān (130 km east of al-Ṭāʾif; Ry 506). He would subsequently undertake the expedition which, according to Arabic Islamic traditions, was to halt before Mecca, to which the Qurʾān alludes in sūra 105 with the expression "the men with the elephants" (*aṣḥāb al-fīl;* Kister,

Campaign of Ḥulubān; Simon, L'inscription Ry 506; see PEOPLE OF THE ELEPHANT).

Although they had never been so previously, all the inscriptions henceforth are explicitly Christian, no longer making any direct or indirect reference to Judaism: Christianity has become the official religion. The Sumūyafaʿ inscription ends with the invocation: "in the name of Raḥmānān and of his son, the conquering Christ" (1st 7608 bis/16, *b-s¹m Rḥmnⁿ w-bn-hw Krs³ts³ Ġlbⁿ .[...]*). Abraha's inscriptions contain equally clear formulas. The most significant is CIH 541, which begins "With the power, help and mercy of Raḥmānān, of his Messiah and of his Holy Spirit" (q.v.; *b-ḫyl w-[r]dʾ w-rḥmt Rḥmnⁿ w-Ms¹ḥ-hw w-Rḥ [q]ds¹*), and recounts a Christian celebration: "... they came back to the town of Marib and celebrated a mass at the church in Marib, because there was a priest there, the abbot of its monastery" (ll. 65-67: ... *ʿdyw hgrⁿ Mrb w-qds¹w bt Mrb k-b-hw qs¹s¹ᵐ ʾb-ms¹tl-h*). Despite this, the Christian symbol of the cross appears only rarely: it may be noted once at the start of Ry 506, twice in the margin of Ja 544-547 and on several artifacts. It is equally noteworthy that the inscriptions never mention church authorities or make use of any biblical quotations (in contrast to contemporary Aksumite inscriptions, where there are numerous such references). All these Christian documents come from characters linked to the Aksumite regime, no doubt reflecting his political and religious inclinations, which were also those of the Egyptian church (opposed to the decisions of the Council of Chalcedon of 451 C.E.). Other Christian movements would certainly have had followers in Yemen, in particular the Nestorians, but they have left no trace. Yemen, decimated by the Aksumite conquest, then by the plague, sank into crisis: the last datable inscription (CIH 325) refers to 559-560 (669 Ḥim.). Two sons of Abraha, Aksūm (described as "the son of the king" in CIH 541/82) and Masrūq (known only through the Arabic Islamic traditions) briefly occupied the throne at the end of the 560s or the beginning of the 570s. The Aksumite dynasty, which then collapsed, was replaced by Persian Sasanian rule, which lasted for some sixty years.

The name of God and the name of the sanctuary

In the Ḥimyarī monotheistic inscriptions, God is addressed in many ways, as if his complex nature could not be expressed by a single name. In the first period (until around the 430s), he is described with a simple circumlocution, "Master of Heaven" *(Bʿl-S¹myⁿ)*, "Lord of Heaven" *(Mrʾ S¹myⁿ)* or "Lord of Heaven and Earth" *(Mrʾ S¹myⁿ w-ʾrḍⁿ)*. Next, even before the end of the reign of Abīkarib Asʿad, God begins to be given a proper name. Sometimes it is Raḥmānān *(Rḥmnⁿ)*, a name of Aramaic origin, elsewhere he is called by the title "the god, God" (Īlāhān and variants: Īl, Īlān and A'luhān, *ʾlhⁿ*, *ʾl*, *ʾlⁿ* and *ʾʾlhⁿ*) used as a proper name. Although it is not used exclusively, Raḥmānān predominates from 462 (Garb Sh .Y., *ḏ-ʾlⁿ* 572 Ḥim.) in inscriptions of all kinds, royal or private, explicitly judaizing or not, whatever their source. It was clearly successful, since it was adopted by the majority of Arab monotheistic movements, in particular the Christian Ḥimyarīs (for the first person of the Trinity [q.v.]). Sometimes the name Raḥmānān is qualified, "Raḥmānān the merciful" (Fa 74/3, *Rḥmnⁿ mtrḥmⁿ*) or "Raḥmānān the most high" (Ja 1028/11, *Rḥmnⁿ ʿlyⁿ;* see GOD AND HIS ATTRIBUTES). In three inscriptions (CIH 543, Ja 1028 and Ry 515), God is not only called "Raḥmānān," but also "Lord of the Jews"

(*Rb-yhd, Rb-hd* and *Rb-hwd*). This syntagma consists of the substantive *rb,* unknown in Sabaean (except perhaps in onomastica) in the sense of "lord (q.v.), master," and of the term *(Y)h(w)d,* which means "Jews." The most significant text, but also the most difficult to interpret, is CIH 543 of which only the opening blessing has survived: *[b]rk w-tbrk s*^{1}*m Rḥmn*^{n} *ḏ-b-S*^{1}*my*^{n} *w-Ys*^{3}*r'l w-* | *'lh-hmw Rb-yhd ḏ-hrd' ʿbd-hmw S*^{2}*hr*^{m} *w-* | *'m-hw Bd*^{m} *w-ḥs*^{2}*kt-hw S*^{2}*ms*^{m} *w-'l* | *wd-hmy Ḍmm w-'bs*^{2}*ʿr w-Mṣr* |^{m} *w-kl bhṯ-h[...],* "May they bless and be blessed the name of Raḥmānān who is in heaven, Israel and its God, the Lord of the Jews, who helped their servant Shahr^{um}, his mother *Bd*^{m}, his wife Shams^{um}, their children (of them both) ...*Ḍmm,* Abīshaʿar and Miṣr^{um}, and all their close rela[tives....]." Strangely, this document seems to indicate two divine beings, "Raḥmānān who is in heaven" and "the God (of Israel), the Lord of the Jews," plus perhaps a third, Israel, mentioned with them. Finally in Ja 1028, already quoted, we find a double exclamation at the end *Rb-hd b-Mḥmd,* "Lord of the Jews, with *Mḥmd*" (l. 12). *Mḥmd,* probably pronounced Maḥmūd or Muḥammad, meaning "deserving of praise," is definitely a divine name: for it to be considered as a human name, there would need to be a family name and an indication of the rank of *Mḥmd* in the social hierarchy (see also NAMES OF THE PROPHET).

The most remarkable piece of information is that God has the same name, Raḥmānān, in the inscriptions of the Christians and those whom we have called monotheistic "judaizers." On the other hand, the same term is not used to indicate the sanctuary (see SACRED PRECINCTS). The Jews and "judaizers" used the term *mikrāb (mkrb),* while the Christians used *qalīs* (*qls*^{1}*,* from the Greek *ekklesia*) and *bīʿat* (*bʿt,* which comes from a Syriac word meaning "egg, dome"). On one occasion we discover *ms*^{1}*gd* (Arabic *masjid*) and *kns*^{1}*t* (Arabic *kanīsa*) but the context is unclear (see MOSQUE).

An outstanding personality, king Abīkarib Asʿad

According to the Arabic Islamic traditions, Yemen became Jewish after king "Tubān Abū Karib b. Malkī Karib," also called Asʿad the Perfect (Asʿad al-Kāmil), had brought back with him two Yathrib rabbis (see MEDINA; TUBBAʿ). This conversion is often considered doubtful for two reasons. This same Abū Karib is the hero of an epic cycle, consisting of far-flung military expeditions in Asia. Besides, the figure of the king has been reconstructed by Islamic apologetics, which recognizes in Abū Karib the originator of the practical rituals at the Kaʿba (q.v.) at Mecca and one of those who believed in Muḥammad before his coming. The inscriptions allow us to see this more clearly. The Ḥimyarī royal family completely and definitively rejected polytheism during the reign of Malkīkarib Yuha'min, a sovereign who, most likely because of his advanced age at accession, is first seen co-ruling with one son (probably Abīkarib Asʿad), then with two (Abīkarib Asʿad and Dhara''amar Ayman). The relation between religious reform and the person of Abīkarib established by tradition is thus quite precise. The neglect of Malkīkarib probably stems from the particularly outstanding reign of Abīkarib, who ruled for over 50 years (at least 493-543 Ḥim.) and imposed Ḥimyarī rule on the tribes of central Arabia as shown by the inscription Ry 509 (250 km west of Riyadh) and the lengthening of the royal list of titles. The nature of Abīkarib's religious reforms is harder to determine. If the renunciation of polytheism is general, emphasizing the strength of central authority, only a number of private individuals demonstrate a particularly firm commitment to Judaism. The rulers and the majority of those responsible for inscriptions seem satisfied to refer to their commitment to monotheism, without being more specific. Similarly, there is the complete absence of the Jewish symbols so common in the Roman world during the same period. The religious reform which occurred in the reign of Abīkarib Asad was therefore not really a conversion to Judaism. It was rather a commitment of principle, giving rabbis a privileged status (Beeston, Martyrdom of Azqir), without new "followers" undertaking to follow all the very restrictive practices of Mosaic law. This in no way precludes the conversion of individuals and small groups, who thus broke with their original background. In this hypothesis, the crisis, which began after the disappearance of Abīkarib and reached its peak in the reign of Yūsuf, had as its cause not only the advance of Christianity supported by Byzantium and Aksum, but also the pressure of the central authority in favor of total conversion to Judaism: thus both Christian hagiographies and Islamic traditions also stress the appeals of king Joseph to choose between conversion to Judaism and death. The incomplete nature of the conversion to Judaism is further emphasized by the fact that neither the language, the script, the calendar nor the dating system underwent any change, whereas one would have expected a more important role for Hebrew or the adoption of the Jewish liturgical calendar.

Christian Julien Robin

Bibliography and abbreviations

Primary: al-Hamdānī, Abū Muḥammad al-Ḥasan b. Aḥmad b. Yaʿqūb, *Ṣifat jazīrat al-ʿArab,* 2 vols., ed. D.H. Müller, *al-Hamdānī's Geographie der arabischen Halbinsel,* Leiden 1884-91, repr. Leiden 1968; Masʿūdī, *Murūj;* Philostorgius, *Kirchengeschichte,* ed. J. Bidez, Berlin 1972[2].

Secondary: Y.M. Abdallah, The inscription CIH 543. A new reading based on the newly-found original, in Ch. Robin and M. Bāfaqīh (eds.), *Ṣayhadica, Research on the inscriptions of pre-Islamic Arabia offered to Professor A.F.L. Beeston by his colleagues,* Ṣanʿāʾ 1987, 3-9; M. Bāfaqīh and Ch. Robin, Inscriptions inédites de Yanbuq (Yémen démocratique), in *Raydān* 2 (1979), 15-76 (summary in Arabic: 25-7 of the Arabic section); J. Beaucamp, F. Briquel-Chatonnet and Ch. Robin, La persécution des chrétiens de Nagrān et la chronologie ḥimyarite, in *Aram* 11-12 (1999-2000), 15-83; A.F.L. Beeston, Himyarite monotheism, in A. Abdalla, S. al-Sakkar and R. Mortel (eds.), *Studies in the history of Arabia.* ii. *Pre-Islamic Arabia,* Riyadh 1404/1984, 149-54; id., Judaism and Christianity in pre-Islamic Yemen, in J. Chelhod (ed.), *L'Arabie du sud, histoire et civilisation.* i. *Le peuple yéménite et ses racines,* Paris 1984, 271-8; id., The martyrdom of Azqir, in *Proceedings of the Seminar for Arabian Studies* 15 (1985), 5-10; id., The south Arabian collection of the Wellcome Museum in London, in *Raydān* 3 (1980), 11-16; R. Degen, Die hebräische Inschrift DJE 23 aus dem Jemen, in *Neue Ephemeris für Semitische Epigraphik* 2 (1974), 111-16; B. Finster, Arabien in der Spätantike. Ein Überblick über die kuturelle Situation der Halbinsel in der Zeit von Muhammad, in *Archäologischer Anzeiger* (1996), 287-319; id. and J. Schmidt, Die Kirche des Abraha in Ṣanʿāʾ, in N. Nebes (ed.), *Arabia Felix. Beiträge zur Sprache und Kultur des vorislamischen Arabien, Festschrift Walter W. Müller zum 60. Geburtstag,* Wiesbaden 1994, 67-86; S.A. Frantsouzoff, Judaism in Ḥaḍramawt on the eve of Islam, in E. Isaac and Y. Tobi (eds.), *Judaeo-Yemenite studies. Proceedings of the Second International Congress,* Princeton 1999, 27-32; I. Gajda, *Ḥimyar gagné par le monothéisme (IVe-VIe siècle de l'ère chrétienne). Ambitions et ruine d'un royaume de l'Arabie méridionale antique,* unpublished PhD diss., Université de Provence 1997; id., A new inscription of an unknown Ḥimyarite king, Marṯadʾilān Yunʿim, in *Proceedings of the Seminar for Arabian Studies* 28 (1998), 81-8; id., Remark on the chronological terminology in the catalogue of the Yemen exhibition in Paris, in *Archäologische Berichte aus dem Yemen,* forthcoming (publication of YM 1950); G. Garbini, Frammenti epigrafici sabei, in *Annali dell'Istituto Orientale di Napoli* 33 [N.S. 23] (1973), 590 and pl. I d.; id., Una bilingue sabeo-ebraica da Ẓafar, in *Annali dell'Istituto Orientale di Napoli* 30 [N.S. 20] (1970), 153-65 and pl. I-II; id., Una nuova iscrizione di Šaraḥbiʾil Yaʿfur, in *Annali dell'Istituto Orientale di Napoli* 29 [NS 19] (1969), 559-66 and pl. II-IV; Ja.B. Gruntfest, Nadpisʾ "dvadcati četyreh čeredov" iz Beit Ḥāḍira, in *Drevnaja Aravija (materialy i soobščenija)* (Pisʾmennye pamjatniki i

problemy istorii i kul'tury Narodov Vostoka, IX godičnaja naučnaja sessija LO IV AN SSSR), Leningrad (Izdatel'stvo "Nauka") 1973, 71-81; A. Jamme, Inscriptions des alentours de Mareb (Yémen), in *Cahiers de Byrsa* 5 (1955), 265-81 and pl. I-II; id., The late Sabaean inscription Ja 856, in *Bibliotheca orientalis* 17 (1960), 3-5 and pl. I.; id., *Sabaean and Ḥasaean inscriptions from Saudi Arabia*, Rome 1966; M.J. Kister, The campaign of Ḥulubān. A new light on the expedition of Abraha, in *Muséon* 78 (1965), 425-36; K.A. Kitchen, *Bibliographical catalogue of texts. Documentation for ancient Arabia*, Part II, Liverpool 2000; S. Mitchell, The cult of Theos Hypsistos between pagans, Jews and Christians, in P. Athanassiadi and M. Frede (eds.), *Pagan monotheism in late antiquity*, Oxford 1999, 81-148; W.W. Müller, CIH 325: Die jüngste datierte sabäische Inschrift, in *Études sudarabes. Recueil offert à Jacques Ryckmans*, Louvain-la-Neuve 1991, 117-31; id., Ein hebräisch-sabäische Bilinguis aus Bait al-Ašwāl, in *Neue Ephemeris für semitische Epigraphik* 2 (1974), 117-23 and fig. 32-34, pl. IX-X; id., Religion und Kult im antiken Südarabien, in M. Krebernik and J. van Oorschot (eds.), *Polytheismus und Monotheismus in den Religionen des Vorderen Orients*, Münster 2002, 175-94; Ch.J. Robin, Les inscriptions de Ḥaṣī, in *Raydān* 7 (2001), 179-223 (including a contribution by Serge Frantsouzoff); id., Le judaïsme de Ḥimyar, in *Arabia* 1 (2003), 97-172; id, Sheba. II. Dans les inscriptions d'Arabie du sud, in *Supplément au dictionnaire de la Bible*, Paris 1996, fasc. 70 [Sexualité — Sichem], col. 1047-1254 (Sheba. I. Dans la Bible, by J. Briend, col. 1043-6); id. and U. Brunner, *Map of ancient Yemen — Carte du Yémen antique, 1:1 000 000*, München 1997 (archaeological map, 70 x 100 cm, in three colors, with index); G. Ryckmans, Inscriptions sud-arabes. Dixième série, in *Muséon* 66 (1953), 267-317 and pl. I-VI; J. Ryckmans, Le christianisme en Arabie du sud préislamique, in *Atti del Convegno internazionale sul tema : L'Oriente cristiano nella storia della Civiltà (Roma 31 marzo-3 aprile 1963; Firenze 4 aprile 1963)*, Rome 1964, 413-54; id., L'inscription sabéenne chrétienne Istanbul 7608 bis, in *JRAS* [n.s.] (1976), 96-9 and pl. I; R.B. Serjeant and R. Lewcock, The church (al-Qalīs) of Ṣanʿāʾ and Ghumdān Castle, in R.B. Serjeant and R. Lewcock (eds.), *Ṣanʿāʾ, an Arabian Islamic city*, London 1983, 44-8; R. Simon, L'inscription Ry 506 et la préhistoire de la Mecque, in *Acta Orientalia Academiae Scientiarum Hungaricae* 20 (1967), 325-37.
Sigla (n.b. for a complete bibliography of south Arabian inscriptions, see K.A. Kitchen, *Bibliographical catalogue of texts. Documentation for ancient Arabia*, Part II, Liverpool 2000): BR Yanbuq 47: Bāfaqīh-Robin, 1979, pp. 49-57 and pl. 5; *CIH: Corpus Inscriptionum Semiticarum*. Pars quarta. *Inscriptiones Ḥimyariticas et Sabaeas continens*, tomes I-III, Paris 1899-1930; *CIH* 325: Müller 1991; *CIH* 543: Abdallah 1987; DJE 23: Degen 1974; Garb Bayt al-Ashwal 1: Müller 1974; Garb Bayt al-Ashwal 2: Garbini 1970; Garb, Framm. no. 7: Garbini 1973; Garb Sh.Y.: Garbini 1969; Ḥaṣī 1: Robin 2001, pp. 182-91 and fig. 2-14 (pp. 207-15); Ist 7608 bis + Wellcome A 103664: Ryckmans J. 1976 and Beeston 1980; Ja 544-547: Jamme 1955, pp. 275-9 and pl. II; Ja 856: Jamme 1960, pp. 3-5 and pl. I; Ja 1028: Jamme 1966, pp. 39-55, fig. 13-15 and pl. X-XIII; *RES: Répertoire d'épigraphie sémitique; RES* 3383: Garbini 1970; Ry 506, 507, 508, 509, 510 and 515: G. Ryckmans 1953; YM 1950: Gajda (forthcoming).

Yesterday see TIME

Yoke see LOAD OR BURDEN

Youth and Old Age

The early and last stages of the normal [human] lifespan. The Qurʾān portrays youth and old age in two main contexts: to demonstrate God's power (see POWER AND IMPOTENCE) and to illustrate the proper relations between generations (q.v.). The "ages of man" occur in recitals of divine signs (q.v.): "There have come to me clear signs *(bayyināt)* from my lord (q.v.).... He it is who has created you from earth (q.v.; *turāb*), then from a drop of sperm, then from a clot (see BLOOD AND BLOOD CLOT); then he brings you forth as an infant *(ṭifl)*, then to reach your full strength, then to be old *(shuyūkh)*, though some among you die before that, and [in any case] to fulfill an appointed term: perhaps you will attain wisdom" (q.v.; Q 40:66-7; cf. 22:5; 30:54; 35:11; see BIOLOGY AS THE CREATION AND STAGES OF LIFE). Q 80:18-22 culminates the sequence: after God creates the embryo, smoothes its way, and causes it to die, he resurrects it (see CREATION; DEATH AND THE DEAD; RESURRECTION).

Relations between young and old, and the psychological and physical characteristics that deserve special treatment, are usually set in family (q.v.) contexts. Muslims must not regard children (q.v.) simply as possessions (Q 8:28; 63:9; see PROPERTY). Unlike pre-Islamic society (Q 6:137, 140, 151; 81:8-9; see PRE-ISLAMIC ARABIA AND THE QURʾĀN), Muslim society assumes responsibility for children's weakness (see MAINTENANCE AND UPKEEP; GUARDIANSHIP; MATURITY). Children are among the oppressed whom Muslims must fight to protect (Q 4:75; see FIGHTING; PATH OR WAY; OPPRESSED ON EARTH, THE). Orphans (q.v.) require special kindness and protection of any property they may have inherited (Q 4:2, 6-10; see INHERITANCE) but this does not include legal adoption (Q 33:4f.). At least five passages concern the proper nursing of babies (e.g. Q 2:233; 28:7-13; see LACTATION; FOSTERAGE; WET-NURSING). Wet-nurses may be hired in the absence of the mother (cf. Q 65:6). Children are born knowing nothing (Q 16:78; see KNOWLEDGE AND LEARNING; IGNORANCE); sexual innocence gives them freedom of the house (Q 24:31) but puberty restricts it (Q 24:58f.; see SEX AND SEXUALITY). Outside the family, beauty and purity are personified in the companions of paradise (q.v.; Q 52:24; 76:19), though female companions will be "of equal age" (Q 56:37; 78:33; see also HOURIS).

Aged wisdom instructs youth. Luqmān (q.v.; Q 31:13-19) first enjoins monotheism on his son, then care and gratitude to parents (q.v.); but a child is not to obey if unbelievers (see BELIEF AND UNBELIEF) try to make him worship other gods (Q 31:14f.; cf. 19:41f.; see OBEDIENCE; POLYTHEISM AND ATHEISM; IDOLATRY AND IDOLATERS). Aged parents are not to be reprimanded but addressed honorably and kindly: "My lord, have mercy on them as they raised me in childhood" (Q 17:23-4). It is duty to their old father that exposes two Midianite women to strange men (see MIDIAN), until Moses (q.v.) helps them water their flocks (Q 28:23). By contrast, Joseph's (q.v.) brothers (see BROTHER AND BROTHERHOOD) cruelly remind their father of his mental decline; Jacob's (q.v.) forgiveness (Q 12:98) is thus all the more astounding. Old age *(kibar)* strikes like a whirlwind and weak children are part of the doom that is a sign of God (Q 2:266; see REWARD AND PUNISHMENT; CHASTISEMENT AND PUNISHMENT).

Reversal of age-related characteristics is also a sign of God. John's wisdom as a youth (Q 19:12f.; see JOHN THE BAPTIST), Jesus' (q.v.) speech (q.v.) in the cradle (Q 19:29f.) and the child's hair that turns gray on the day of judgment (Q 73:17; see LAST JUDGMENT) are all unnatural to youth. Abraham's (q.v.) wife asks incredulously, "Woe is me! Shall I bear a child when I am an old woman *(ʿajūz)* and this husband of mine an old man *(shaykh)*?" (Q 11:72). Finally, Zechariah (q.v.; Zakariyyāʾ), successfully praying for an heir, describes his age in unforgettable imagery: "O lord, my bones are weak, and my head has burst into gray flame!" (Q 19:4).

R. Gwynne

Bibliography
M.F. Ansari, *The qurʾānic foundations and structure of Muslim society,* vol. 2, Karachi 1973; A. Giladi, *Infants, parents and wet nurses,* Leiden 1999; Th. J. O'Shaughnessy, The qurʾānic view of youth and old age, in *ZDMG* 141 (1991), 33-5, repr. A. Rippin, (ed.), *The Qurʾān. Style and contents,* Ashgate 2000, 177-95 (unique and fundamental).

Yūnus see JONAH

Yūsuf see JOSEPH

Z

Zabūr see PSALMS; SCRIPTURE AND THE QUR'ĀN

Zakāt see ALMSGIVING

Zaqqūm

The tree of Zaqqūm, or the cursed tree mentioned four times in the Qur'ān, with three explicit references (Q 37:62; 44:43; 56:52) and one implicit (Q 17:60). Unlike the beautiful trees with clustered fruits in paradise (q.v.; Q 69:23), the good tree of "the good word" (Q 14:24) and the heavenly tree of eternity (q.v.) from which Adam and Eve (q.v.) were prohibited to eat (Q 20:120), the tree of Zaqqūm stands out as the ugliest and the most terrifying tree described in the Qur'ān (see TREES; AGRICULTURE AND VEGETATION). It grows at the bottom of hellfire (see HELL AND HELLFIRE), its blossom *(ṭal'uhā)* like "devils' heads" (Q 37:64-5), is "bitter in taste, burning in touch, rotten in smell (q.v.), black in appearance. Whoever eats from it cannot tolerate its [revolting] taste and therefore is forced to swallow it" (Rāzī, *Tafsīr,* xxix, 174; see FOOD AND DRINK).

The one possible implicit reference to Zaqqūm is very brief and speaks of *al-shajarata l-mal'ūnata fī l-Qur'ān,* "the tree cursed in the Qur'ān" (Q 17:60) being a "trial (q.v.) for men." The majority of the commentators (see EXEGESIS OF THE QUR'ĀN: CLASSICAL AND MEDIEVAL), and the translators following suit (see TRANSLATIONS OF THE QUR'ĀN), take for granted that *al-shajarata al-mal'ūnata* is the tree of Zaqqūm (Ṭabarī, *Tafsīr,* xv, 113-15). In explanation of its description as a trial (*fitna,* Q 17:60; 37:63), the commentators often relate the story that, when the tree of Zaqqūm was mentioned for the first time in the Qur'ān, the unbelievers (see BELIEF AND UNBELIEF) were skeptical about a tree growing "at the bottom of hellfire" (Q 37:64; see UNCERTAINTY), and said: "One day Muḥammad claims that hellfire burns stones (see STONE), and the next day that it grows trees!" Thus, according to the commentators, it is indeed a trial for men: on the one hand, the believers will accept that God is capable of creating a tree that does not burn in the blazing flames of hellfire and that it will be one of many punishments for the unbelievers (see REWARD AND PUNISHMENT) and, on the other hand, the unbelievers will not believe in it and will reject (see LIE) and mock (see MOCKERY) the Qurʾān as they in fact did (Zamakhsharī, *Kashshāf,* ii, 675).

The name of the tree is derived from "deadly food," "ingestion," or "excessive drinking." The lexicographers as well as the commentators are uncertain about the origin of the word Zaqqūm. In addition to the meanings suggested above, all of which are based on speculation about what the root *z-q-m* might mean, they relate a story suggesting that it is the name of a tree which grows in the desert or an African word for *ʿajwa,* dates mashed with butter (*Lisān al-ʿArab,* iii, 1845 and Fīrūzābādī, *al-Qāmūs,* 1118). It is curious to note, however, that the same stories are repeated almost identically and always without examples of usage from any other text than the Qurʾān. The subtlest explanation is that of al-Rāghib al-Iṣfahānī (fl. early fifth/eleventh cent.), who ignores all the stories and suggests that the qurʾānic use came first and "thereafter the root was 'borrowed' for ingestion of distasteful food" (*Mufradāt,* 380).

The three explicit references occur in a typical punishment/reward qurʾānic discourse (see FORM AND STRUCTURE OF THE QURʾĀN; LANGUAGE AND STYLE OF THE QURʾĀN). All three describe the tree as one of the hellfire horrors which the unbelievers will be forced to experience. Together they provide us with a very powerful image detailing the physical description of the ugly tree and its effect on those who will be forced to eat it, i.e. the sinful (see SIN, MAJOR AND MINOR) and the unbelievers (Q 44:44; 56:51). It will "boil in their insides like molten brass *(al-muhl),* like the boiling of scalding water" (Q 44:45-6). The image is taken at its literal meaning by mainstream Sunnī commentators but is understood by rationalists as a metaphorical objectification of the mental and emotional torture awaiting the unbelievers (see METAPHOR; SYMBOLIC IMAGERY; THEOLOGY AND THE QURʾĀN).

Salwa M.S. El-Awa

Bibliography
Primary: al-Fīrūzābādī, Majd al-Dīn Muḥammad b. Yaʿqūb, *al-Qāmūs al-muḥīṭ,* Beirut 1998; *Lisān al-ʿArab;* al-Rāghib al-Iṣfahānī, *Mufradāt,* Damascus 1992; Rāzī, *Tafsīr;* Ṭabarī, *Tafsīr,* ed. Shākir; Zamakhsharī, *Kashshāf,* Cairo 1987.
Secondary: M. Asad, *The message of the Qurʾān,* Pakistan 1992; A. Geiger, *Was hat Mohammed aus dem Judenthume aufgenommen?* Leipzig 1902[2] (Bonn 1833[1]), 66; Ch. Genequand, Metaphysics, in S.H. Nasser and O. Leman (eds.), *History of Islamic philosophy,* Routledge 2001 (1996[1]), 783-801; M. Wolff (ed.), *Muhammedanische Eschatologie [*ʿAbd al-Raḥīm b. Aḥmad al-Qāḍī, *Kitāb aḥwāl al-qiyāma], nach der Leipziger und der Dresdner Handschrift zum ersten Male arabisch und deutsch mit Anmerkungen,* Leipzig 1875, 170-1 (in the Ger. trans.; this work is also known under the title *"Daqāʾiq al-akhbār fī dhikr al-janna wa-l-nār"*).

Zayd b. Ḥāritha see FAMILY OF THE PROPHET

Zayd b. Thābit see COMPANIONS OF THE PROPHET

Zaydīs see SHĪʿISM AND THE QURʾĀN

Zaynab bt. Jaḥsh see WIVES OF THE PROPHET

Zealotry

Religious and/or political fanaticism. The main qurʾānic stand on zealotry is expressed in Q 2:143 where the Muslim community is described as a "community of the middle," a community that is "in the middle between any two extremes," thereby assigning to its members the responsibility of maintaining a community that is just and moderate in all its beliefs and practices (Quṭb, *Ẓilāl,* 130-2; see

MODERATION). This characteristic is, according to the exegetes (see EXEGESIS OF THE QUR'ĀN: CLASSICAL AND MEDIEVAL), what makes the Muslim community the "best community" applauded in Q 3:110, "because the middle is the best" (Zamakhsharī, *Kashshāf,* i, 198; Rāzī, *Tafsīr,* iv, 108-12). The implication of Q 2:143, then, is that in its endeavor to be the best community, the Muslim community should not be extreme in its practice or understanding of its own religion (q.v.). Various prophetic ḥadīths support this view (see ḤADĪTH AND THE QUR'ĀN), such as "Beware of zealotry!" (*iyyākum wa-l-ghuluww fī l-dīn;* Albānī, *Ṣaḥīḥ,* no. 2680, i, 522) and "Death be to zealots!" (*halaka l-mutanaṭṭiʿūn;* ibid., no. 7039, i, 1183). Nevertheless, there appears to be no explicit, general condemnation of zealotry or religious fanaticism in the Qur'ān, although many of its characteristics are denounced in various contexts. It is worth noting, however, that words like *taṭarruf* (extremism) and *uṣūliyya* (fundamentalism) are modern translations of foreign words and hence are not used to express these meanings in the Qur'ān and classical Arabic texts. A recurrent theme of the qur'ānic discussions of how different people practice their religion is that of taking the law (see LAW AND THE QUR'ĀN) into human hands (e.g. by forbidding [see FORBIDDEN] what God has made lawful [see LAWFUL AND UNLAWFUL], an all too familiar attitude encountered among modern day zealots). The theme occurs in six different verses (Q 5:87; 6:116, 140; 7:32; 10:59; 66:1), all condemning this attitude, sometimes in a very harsh tone (e.g. Q 6:116; 10:59).

Though not mentioned in many discussions about the qur'ānic criticism of Christianity (see CHRISTIANS AND CHRISTIANITY; POLEMIC AND POLEMICAL LANGUAGE), the verb *taghlū,* "to be overzealous, to exceed the bounds," is used in two qur'ānic verses that warn the Christians against *ghuluww* as represented in their notion of Jesus' (q.v.) "sonship" to God (see POLYTHEISM AND ATHEISM; IDOLATRY AND IDOLATERS; GOD AND HIS ATTRIBUTES). It is hard to see, however, how holding to the doctrine of the Trinity (q.v.), to which these verses object, makes Christians zealots. A possible explanation for the use of *ghuluww* here can be understood to imply the literal interpretation of the text, a characteristic often associated with zealotry, in which case the Christians are being blamed for their literal interpretation of the biblical use of the word "Father" in phrases like "the cup of my Father," "to do the will of my Father," and "I must be about my Father's business" (see Cragg, *Jesus,* 31, whose argument approximates this interpretation; see also CORRUPTION; FORGERY; SCRIPTURE AND THE QUR'ĀN).

Many other qur'ānic passages can be seen as either encouraging or discouraging forms of zealotry, depending on which parts of the context one chooses to emphasize (see CHRONOLOGY AND THE QUR'ĀN; OCCASIONS OF REVELATION). Among them is religious intolerance, which the Qur'ān discourages very strongly in numerous verses (see TOLERANCE AND COMPULSION; RELIGIOUS PLURALISM AND THE QUR'ĀN). The most widely cited verse in this context is Q 109:6, which some commentators argue has been abrogated (see ABROGATION). Other exegetes deny this, especially in the light of verses such as Q 2:113, 256; 22:56, 69, all of which stress the fact that judgment (q.v.) between persons is not to be made by persons in this life but by God on judgment day (see LAST JUDGMENT). Similarly, there is no unequivocal qur'ānic judgment with regard to controversial matters such as exclusivism (see PARTIES AND FACTIONS) and the use of violence (q.v.) to achieve political aims (see

POLITICS AND THE QUR'ĀN). Islamic philosophers (see PHILOSOPHY AND THE QUR'ĀN), exegetes and jurists have argued opposing views, always on the basis of qur'ānic verses (q.v.). In sum, in its discussions of various forms of zealotry, the Qur'ān expresses firm objections to some practices and allows room for dispute about many others.

Salwa M.S. El-Awa

Bibliography
Primary: Ibn Taymiyya, Taqī l-Dīn Aḥmad b. ʿAbd al-Ḥalīm, *Majmūʿ al-fatāwā,* Cairo 1978; *Lisān al-ʿArab;* Quṭb, *Ẓilāl;* Rāzī, *Tafsīr;* Zamakhsharī, *Kashshāf,* Cairo 1987.
Secondary: N. al-Albānī, *Ṣaḥīḥ al-jāmiʿ al-ṣaghīr,* Beirut 1986[2]; K. Cragg, *Jesus and the Muslim. An exploration,* Oxford 1999; R. Firestone, *Jihad. The origin of holy war in Islam,* Oxford 1999; Kh. Jilbī, Jadaliyyat al-tafkīr wa-l-takfīr fī l-mujtamaʿ al-Muslim, in *al-Wasaṭiyya,* i, Riyadh 2002; S.A. Mawdudi, *Towards understanding the Qur'ān,* trans. Z.I. Ansari, Leicester 1988; M. Muqri', *Ḥukm qatl al-madaniyyīn,* London 1998; M. Shams al-Dīn, *Fiqh al-ʿunf al-musallaḥ fī l-islām,* Beirut 2001.

Zechariah

The father of John the Baptist (q.v.) in both the Bible and Qur'ān. Zechariah (Zakariyyā) is mentioned in four qur'ānic passages (Q 3:37-44; 6:85 [a passing reference]; 19:2-15; 21:89-90). He is not directly named as a prophet *(nabī)* but by implication is included in the collective references to prophets at Q 19:58 and prophethood *(nubuwwa)* at Q 6:89 (see PROPHETS AND PROPHETHOOD). The qur'ānic story (see NARRATIVES) of Zechariah and John is always linked to that of Mary (q.v.) and Jesus (q.v.).

The fullest account of Zechariah occurs at Q 19:2-15. There he is portrayed as a pious old servant of God who prays in secret for a successor (Q 19:3-6). When an unnamed speaker (God? angels?: see below) responds with "good tidings of a boy whose name is John" (Q 19:7; see GOOD NEWS), Zechariah asks how this can be, in view of his old age and his wife's barrenness (Q 19:8), thus prompting a simple affirmation of God's power to create effortlessly out of nothing (Q 19:9; see COSMOLOGY; CREATION). Zechariah then asks for a sign and his request is granted: he will not speak for three days (Q 19:10; see SIGNS). The passage then shifts its focus to John (Q 19:12-15). This Meccan narrative (see CHRONOLOGY AND THE QUR'ĀN) about Zechariah is set within a sequence of stories (Q 19:2-58) in which a common theme is God's bestowal of mercy (q.v.) on his faithful servants (q.v.) as they endure various trials (childlessness for Zechariah, allegations of immorality for Mary, Q 19:16-33, a hostile pagan father for Abraham [q.v.], Q 19:41-50). Note that the word "mercy" *(raḥma)* is emphasized in the opening words of the Zechariah story (Q 19:2; cf. 19:50, 53; also 19:21 in a slightly different sense). In this Meccan context the significance of Zechariah to Muḥammad and his followers thus appears to be that his story is one of many which speak encouragingly to believers of the mercy that God will show them in the midst of their difficulties (see TRIAL; TRUST AND PATIENCE). The same interpretation holds for the much briefer Meccan narrative at Q 21:89-90, which simply portrays Zechariah crying out to God and God responding with the gift of John. Stress is also laid on the humble, godfearing piety (q.v.) of Zechariah and his wife. The wider context is a sequence of stories describing God's deliverance of his faithful servants from adversity (e.g. Q 21:68-71, 74, 76-7, 83-4, 87-8). Again, Zechariah is an encouraging example of how the believer should persevere through difficulties, trusting in God.

The one Medinan passage about Zechariah (Q 3:37-44) has distinctive narrative features. In contrast to Q 19, where the story of Zechariah precedes that of Mary and Jesus, here the story of the birth of Mary (Q 3:35-6) leads into an account of the role of Zechariah as her guardian. Whenever he enters the sanctuary, Zechariah finds that she is mysteriously supplied with food by God (Q 3:37; Zechariah's guardianship of Mary is also mentioned at Q 3:44). At this point Zechariah prays for "goodly offspring" (Q 3:38) and in Q 3:39-41 the story then unfolds much as at Q 19:2-15, except that Q 3:39 mentions angels as responding to Zechariah's prayer (see ANGEL). This Medinan passage about Zechariah and John, although telling broadly the same story as in the Meccan versions, needs to be understood within the changed context of the tense relationship between Muḥammad and the Jews of Medina (q.v.) that is apparent throughout the third sūra (see JEWS AND JUDAISM). The longer narrative sequence (Q 3:33-58) is essentially a history-lesson warning the Jews that, however much they might oppose Muḥammad, God will vindicate him, just as he did other faithful servants in the past (see HISTORY AND THE QURʾĀN). This lesson is most explicit in the culminating story of Jesus, rejected by Jewish unbelievers but vindicated by God (Q 3:45-57), but it is natural to assume that the same lesson underlies the whole narrative sequence. That suggests that the brief reference to Zechariah and John might assume knowledge of the fate of John as one of the prophets killed by ungodly Jews (such prophets are mentioned often in Q 3; see Q 3:21, 112, 181, 183; see BELIEF AND UNBELIEF; POLEMIC AND POLEMICAL LANGUAGE). The inclusion of the story of Zechariah and John here would then be serving as part of an extended reminder that if Muḥammad was rejected by unbelieving Jews, that had been the experience of prophets before him; nevertheless, the prophets are all honored in the sight of God (see the affirmations bestowed upon John at Q 3:39) and the scheming of the unbelievers is ultimately frustrated. (This analysis is more fully argued in Marshall, Christianity, 12-14.)

This survey shows that while there is a constant narrative core to the qurʾānic passages about Zechariah, his significance varies with the changing wider context of the challenges faced by Muḥammad and his followers, first in Mecca (q.v.) and then in Medina. Commentators have addressed a number of issues raised by these passages. For example, many take the view that it was the sight of God's miraculous provision for Mary that emboldened Zechariah to pray for the miracle of a son (see MIRACLES). They also fill out the brief reference in Q 3:44 to give a fuller account of how Zechariah becomes Mary's guardian through a process of casting lots (see DIVINATION). They discuss the apparent problem that Zechariah's request for a sign suggests that he, a prophet, has doubted God's message (see UNCERTAINTY; IMPECCABILITY). They also address the related question as to whether Zechariah's silence for three days should be seen as a punishment (see CHASTISEMENT AND PUNISHMENT; for a range of comments on these and other points, see Ayoub, *Qurʾān*, 99-122; see also SCRIPTURE AND THE QURʾĀN). Finally, it should be noted that the exegetical tradition contains reports linking Dhū l-Kifl (q.v.) to Zechariah (and also Elijah [q.v.]; cf. Thaʿlabī, *Qiṣaṣ*, trans. Brinner, 438).

David Marshall

Bibliography

Primary (for later elaborations of the story): Abū ʿUmāra b. Wathīma al-Fārisī, *Kitāb Badʾ al-ḫalq wa-qiṣaṣ al-anbiyāʾ*, ed. in R.G. Khoury, *Les légendes prophétiques dans l'islam*, Wiesbaden 1978, 298-340 (on Zechariah, John the Baptist and Mary);

Ṭabarī, *Taʾrīkh*, ed. de Goeje, i, 733-9; al-Ṭarafī, Muḥammad b. Aḥmad b. Muṭarrif, *Storie dei profeti*, ed. and It. trans. R. Tottoli, Genova 1997, 297-304 and passim; Eng. trans. *The stories of the prophets by Ibn Muṭarrif al-Ṭarafī*, ed. R. Tottoli, Berlin 2003, 161-6; Thaʿlabī, *Qiṣaṣ*, Cairo n.d., 333-42; Eng. trans. W. Brinner, *ʿArāʾis al-majālis fī qiṣaṣ al-anbiyāʾ, or, Lives of the prophets*, Leiden 2002, 438, 621-30, 637-8.
Secondary: M. Ayoub, *The Qurʾān and its interpreters. ii. The house of ʿImrān*, Albany 1992, 99-122; Horovitz, *KU*, 113; D. Marshall, Christianity in the Qurʾān, in L. Ridgeon (ed.), *Islamic interpretations of Christianity*, Richmond 2001, 3-29; G. Parrinder, *Jesus in the Qurʾān*, London 1965 (ch. 5 discusses biblical and apocryphal parallels to the qurʾānic material on Zechariah); B.M. Wheeler, *Prophets in the Quran. An introduction to the Quran and Muslim exegesis*, London 2002, 292 (partial Eng. trans. of some classical accounts).

Zodiac

see ANIMAL LIFE; PLANETS AND STARS

Zoroastrians

see PEOPLE OF THE BOOK